The Papers of Robert Morris

JOHN CATANZARITI AND
E. JAMES FERGUSON, EDITORS

ELIZABETH M. NUXOLL AND
NELSON S. DEARMONT, ASSOCIATE EDITORS
HERBERT LEVENTHAL AND
MARY A. GALLAGHER, ASSISTANT EDITORS
ARTHUR E. SCHERR, RESEARCH ASSISTANT
CLARENCE L. VER STEEG, EDITORIAL ADVISOR

UNIVERSITY OF PITTSBURGH PRESS ∽ 1984

The Papers of

ROBERT MORRIS
1781–1784

VOLUME 6: JULY 22–OCTOBER 31, 1782

LIBRARY OF CONGRESS CATALOGING
IN PUBLICATION DATA

(Revised for volume 6)

Morris, Robert, 1734–1806.
  The papers of Robert Morris, 1781–1784.

  Vol. edited by John Catanzariti and E. James
Ferguson.
  Includes bibliographical references.
  CONTENTS: v. 1. February 7–July 31, 1781.—v. 2.
August–September 1781.—[etc.]—v. 6. July 22–October
31, 1782.
  1. Morris, Robert, 1734–1806. 2. United States—
History—Revolution, 1775–1783—Finance—Sources.
I. Ferguson, E. James (Elmer James), 1917–
II. Catanzariti, John, 1942—   . III. Title.
E302.M82   1973   973.3′092′4   72-91107
ISBN 0-8229-3485-X) (v. 6)

Published by the University of Pittsburgh Press, Pittsburgh, Pa., 15260
Copyright © 1984, University of Pittsburgh Press
All rights reserved
Feffer and Simons, Inc., London
Manufactured in the United States of America

Title-page portrait of Robert Morris by Charles Willson Peale, ca. 1782
Courtesy of Independence National Historical Park, Philadelphia

SPONSORS

Major funding for THE PAPERS OF ROBERT MORRIS has been generously furnished by the Program for Editions of the National Endowment for the Humanities, the National Historical Publications and Records Commission, and Queens College of The City University of New York. The edition is sponsored by Queens College and endorsed by the National Historical Publications and Records Commission.

The editing of this volume was made possible by grants from
Donaldson, Lufkin & Jenrette, Inc.
Dow Jones & Company, Inc.
First Pennsylvania Bank, N.A.
Philip M. McKenna Foundation, Inc.
National Endowment for the Humanities
National Historical Publications and Records Commission
Ellis L. Phillips Foundation
PSC-CUNY Research Award Program of The City University of New York
Queens College of The City University of New York
R.M. Smythe & Co., Inc.
Dorothy Ann Ver Steeg

Publication of this volume by the University of Pittsburgh Press was assisted by grants from
National Historical Publications and Records Commission
National Endowment for the Humanities
R.M. Smythe & Co., Inc.

CONTENTS

ILLUSTRATIONS

INTRODUCTION

The search for public credit and revenue dominates this sixth volume of *The Papers of Robert Morris*. Covering just over three months, the volume is crowded with a sequence of critical events. The documents portray the Superintendent of Finance struggling to sustain the American war effort until independence was officially won and, at the same time, taking measures to ensure that independence, once achieved, would rest on a stronger national government and a flourishing national economy. The means Morris adopted to restore confidence in the United States—the motif behind his efforts to reduce expenditures, tighten Continental administration, free the economy from interference by the states, and redress the scales of the Confederation by obtaining permanent revenues for Congress—was his single-minded quest to reestablish public credit without destroying his own.

The volume opens on July 22, the day Congress appointed a grand committee to consider the best means of supporting the nation's public credit. A week later Morris submitted to Congress a pathbreaking report on public credit calling for land, poll, and excise taxes, in addition to the impost of 1781 awaiting ratification by the states, to fund the national debt. On the following day, July 30, in a budget message from the Office of Finance, the Superintendent forwarded to Congress the estimates of Continental expenditures for 1783 amounting to $11 million, together with proposals for financing them through domestic revenues and foreign loans. The remainder of the volume offers a detailed documentary record of Morris's activities in the Finance and Marine Offices during the ensuing three months as Congress deliberated his proposals for revenue and public credit.

In the introductory pages that follow, the editors will trace four principal themes which weave intersecting paths through the documents in the volume. First, they will consider the Superintendent's tireless efforts to overcome obstacles to revenue collection in the states and to promote national over local interests. Secondly, they will emphasize Morris's fragile dependence on foreign loans. Thirdly, they will measure the impact of insufficient public credit and revenue on Morris's contract system and outline the financial expedients to which the Financier resorted to keep the army in the field. Finally, they will show how integral the Continental navy was to Morris's financial goals.

I

With the Yorktown campaign won and the virtual cessation of active warfare by the British on the American mainland, the Nationalist momentum that had led to Morris's appointment as Superintendent of Finance was already beginning to ebb. As sectional rivalries intensified, the states began to reassert their sovereignty, and congressional delegates attuned to local and state interests were replacing the national-minded congressmen who had welcomed Morris. Moreover, republican ideology, with its fears of centralized economic and political power and of corrupt influences emanating from the Treasury Department, was resurfacing with renewed vigor, rekindling latent antagonism to professional armies, bureaucrats, pensioners, and placemen, and reviving traditional hostility to a funded national debt with its train of speculators and stockjobbers. Spearheaded by Arthur Lee, a quintessential republican ideologue and archenemy of Morris and Benjamin Franklin, congressional localists began to focus their enmity on Morris and the Office of Finance, unappeased by the work of congressional oversight committees or by Morris's steps toward greater openness and accountability in public finance. Republican "jealousy" thus began to combine with localism to frustrate many of Morris's policies and to deny him revenues to execute them.[1]

The economic base for Morris's policies was also eroding. Though Britain had virtually ceased military action on land, its naval operations along the North American coast intensified. The British blocked American trade and disrupted wartime markets, causing the specie needed to pay taxes, always scarce, to become virtually nonexistent. The economic dislocation depleted the wealth of the American mercantile community on which the Financier depended for credit and support. The contest, as Morris himself recognized, had become a "War of Finance," in which Britain's chief weapons were its public credit and its navy. Britain capitalized on the American preference for English manufactures by encouraging a flourishing illicit trade,

---

1. See notes to Diary, June 12, July 13, and August 22 and 29; headnote to RM to the President of Congress, July 29; RM to Benjamin Franklin, September 28, 1782, and notes, and the headnote to the undated Draft Ordinance for the Impost of 1781 printed in Appendix I. RM's reputation for blending private and public business also contributed to suspicion of his measures, despite his heated denials of such charges. See Diary, August 20, and RM to Daniel Clark, May 30 and October 22, 1782.

mainly with New York, as a means of draining away American specie, and disseminated propaganda aimed at undermining American currency and credit.[2] At the same time, with a major naval campaign in the West Indies anticipated and its resources stretched to the limit, the French government was moving inexorably toward a financial crisis. The court, therefore, sought to wean the American republic from its excessive dependence on French funds, and to prod it toward greater financial self-reliance, dashing Morris's expectations for French loans or subsidies on the scale obtained in 1781.[3]

Indeed, none of the revenues on which Morris relied to meet commitments he had made earlier in the year fully materialized. American officials abroad had largely expended the foreign loans on which he had primarily depended; what remained could not easily be tapped because of British depredations on American trade. Tax revenues from Congress's $8 million specie requisition on the states for 1782, the first installment of which had been due on April 1, with the second expected in July, dribbled in. By June 30 the Financier had received only $29,925.43 from three states, and by September 30 only an additional $91,056.66 had reached the Continental Treasury.[4] None of the states had an efficient system for collecting taxes on schedule. With popular enthusiasm for the war abating and the specie shortage making it genuinely difficult for taxpayers to obtain cash, state officials delayed enforcement of tax collection and frequently postponed the due date of taxes. What taxes were collected were sometimes allocated exclusively to state purposes.

The Financier struggled to reverse these tendencies. Morris exhorted his receivers of Continental taxes to goad the state legislatures to action. He dispatched blunt missives to the state governors decrying the selfishness, localism, and pettiness of many state policies and reminding each state of its responsibilities to the nation.[5] The states responded with anger, excuses, or empty promises—but rarely with money.

Morris had little choice but to develop alternate modes of inducing

---

2. See State of American Commerce and Plan for Protecting It, May 10, 1782, and notes; RM to Alexander Hamilton, July 2; notes to Gouverneur Morris to Thomas Willing, June 18; RM to the Governor of Connecticut, July 31, Hamilton to RM, August 13, and the Quartermaster General to RM, August 24, 1782.

3. See the headnotes and notes to RM's letters to the president of Congress of July 29 and 30; and Diary, September 30, and notes.

4. [Robert Morris], *A Statement of the Accounts of the United States of America, During the Administration of the Superintendant of Finance, Commencing with his Appointment, on the 20th Day of February, 1781, and Ending with his Resignation, on the 1st Day of November 1784* (Philadelphia, 1785).

5. See RM's circulars to the governors of July 29, 30, October 5 and 21, and to the receivers of September 12 and October 5, and RM to the Governor of Maryland, July 29, to the Governor of Connecticut, July 31 and September 3, and to Hamilton, September 17 and October 28.

state action. By insisting on the publication of tax receipts in each state, even when none had been paid, the Financier sought to embarrass delinquent states into contributing. This "monthly lash," as James Madison called it, was effective in some states, but not in all, including Madison's Virginia. The Superintendent also tried to obtain information on political and economic conditions in the states, including the attitudes and reliability of prominent state office-holders. He used such information not only as a guide to policy formulation but also to assure that offices at his disposal would be occupied by capable men sympathetic to Continental measures or distributed so as to win men of influence to his policies.[6]

Morris's most important strategy for obtaining revenue and checking the drift toward localism was to link the interests of as many people as possible directly to the national government. During the months covered by this volume, Morris's strategy manifested itself in responses to public creditors who approached him for payment. Morris repeatedly advised that they could only be compensated when the states provided the revenue and urged them to exert their influence in their home states in favor of Continental taxes. With few exceptions the Superintendent also refused to allow "partial payments." Unless every public claimant in a particular category could be paid—whether army and naval officers, suppliers of public goods and services, or holders of debt certificates—none would be paid.[7] Striving to maintain uniform rules and centralized disbursements applicable to all the states, the Financier argued against the separate provision of pay by the states to their own lines of the Continental army and in favor of equal provision for all lines through specie taxes collected and disbursed by Congress. Similarly, he opposed state payment of depreciation allowances to Continental naval officers because the procedure kept up "Ideas of Disunion."[8] The Superintendent's policies were designed not only to create pressure groups lobbying within the states to strengthen Congress's hand in its calls for revenue, but also to prevent states from providing for the needs of their own citizens while abandoning their neighbors.

---

6. On the receivers' publications, see, for example, RM to William Churchill Houston, October 29, and notes; and Madison to Edmund Randolph, November 26, 1782, in William T. Hutchinson, Robert A. Rutland *et al.*, eds., *The Papers of James Madison* (Chicago, 1962–), V, 328. On appointments, see Hamilton to RM, August 13, and notes, and September 7, and RM to George Olney, August 13, and to Hamilton, August 28.

7. See Diary, July 26, RM to Charles Young and Bertles Shee, August 16, to Nathanael Greene and George Washington, October 5, to Joseph Watson, October 9, to Washington, October 15, to Hamilton, October 16, and to Olney, October 16 and 24.

8. See RM's reports to Congress of September 27 and October 4, and notes.

Morris tested this strategy when, in September, he persuaded Congress to suspend interest payments on loan office certificates in bills of exchange on France. The suspension of interest payments placed all public creditors on an equal footing, thereby making it possible for Morris to unite the holders of loan office certificates with other creditors into a powerful lobby mobilized behind the ratification of the impost of 1781 and other taxes under congressional rather than state control. Such a maneuver would, if successful, overcome state opposition, give Congress a secure revenue independent of state control, and provide the security for further loans, thereby reducing the amount of taxation needed for the current expenses of the war. Moreover, it would attach the public creditors to the national government and help offset the centrifugal tendencies that Morris feared would shatter the union once the threat of a British victory was eliminated.

In the Financier's view, public credit could only be established in the long run by providing for the payment of interest on all forms of the Continental debt out of domestic tax revenues committed exclusively to that purpose. To this end, on July 29 Morris submitted to Congress a report on public credit designed to provide funding of all Continental debts through additional taxes such as land, poll, and excise levies. This report, the single most important state paper of his administration, not only embraced the political strategy aimed at tipping the scales of the Confederation in Congress's favor, but provided a theoretical formulation of Morris's positions on taxation and borrowing based on his understanding of the nature of the American economy and his expectations about its future development.[9]

To help restore public confidence and overcome opposition to the payment of taxes, the Financier sought to wipe out reminders of past financial abuses and violations of public faith. Not long after submitting his report on public credit, Morris began to implement his earlier plans for settling state, individual, and departmental accounts of the Revolution. The first commissioners Congress had authorized the Superintendent to nominate took up their duties in July. Morris and his Treasury officials developed instructions the commissioners were to follow and the form of the final settlement certificates they were to issue to all persons to whom sums were found due upon settlement of their accounts. By converting the mass of certificates issued by military officials for goods and services purchased or seized for the army into national debt securities, the commissioners of accounts thus played an important role in Morris's plans to restore "dead" paper to productive use. In this way Morris

---

9. See the headnote to RM to the President of Congress, July 29; and RM to George Webb, October 28.

began the liquidation of much of the public debt which by funding he hoped to restore to value.[10]

Morris also planned to employ the commissioners to eliminate another form of "dead" paper. Since Congress's last efforts to create a nondepreciating Continental paper currency had proved unavailing, the Superintendent argued that all paper money had to be absorbed by taxation and destroyed as quickly as possible. "For so long as there be any in Existence," the Financier asserted, "the Holder will view it as a monument of national Perfidy." Consequently, in September Morris recommended that the commissioners for settling state accounts receive and destroy all the old money, that the amounts redeemed be credited against state currency quotas under the act of March 18, 1780, and that states sinking excess currency be given credit at the rate of 40 to 1 of specie on accounts prior to 1782. Congress, however, agreed to accept old currency only up to the amount of each state's quota and remained stalemated over Morris's other recommendations until the end of the Confederation.[11]

II

However strongly the Superintendent exhorted the states to pay Continental taxes, he had decided that for the present he must place his chief reliance on additional foreign loans to pay current expenditures. Morris devoted a substantial portion of his July 29 report on public credit to refuting arguments against such loans. But he did not wish to become totally dependent on foreign loans, nor did he believe they could be obtained unless secured by tax revenues mortgaged to the payment of the interest on the public debt, a view shared by French officials.

Nevertheless, he welcomed the news in September of the successful opening of a Dutch loan by John Adams. Although aware of Adams's warnings against drawing too heavily on the loan, since it was uncertain how rapidly and completely the subscription would fill, Morris in his instructions for the application of the funds spoke as if the entire sum had been obtained. His opponents were even more optimistic, both about completing the subscription and the prospects for additional loans. They cited the Adams loan as evidence for their belief that no funding plan was needed to attract new loans, and hence the impost and the other taxes sought by

---

10. See RM to Jonathan Burrall, August 19, and notes, RM's circulars of September 7 and 19 to the commissioners of accounts, and the instructions to the commissioners from the Comptroller of the Treasury and other papers relating to the settlement of accounts printed under October 14 and 18.

11. See RM's report to Congress of September 7, and notes. The quotation is from RM to the President of Congress, July 29.

Morris were unnecessary as well as unjust. Moreover, as had been the case with earlier loans, the announcement of the Dutch loan intensified state reluctance to make additional contributions to the war effort. In its budget plans for 1783 Congress drastically reduced the amount to be called for in taxes from the states, while approving the request for the $4 million foreign loan the Financier had suggested. Executing the wishes of Congress, in October Morris dispatched letters designed to elicit the funds from the French, or failing that, from the Dutch.[12]

Besides making every effort to obtain additional loans abroad and provide for their effective use in sustaining the war effort, the Superintendent was also preparing to meet interest payments on outstanding foreign loans, conserve American funds in Europe, and settle American accounts abroad. The French, not only seeking to deter further loan applications, also wished to ensure that they would receive some return on their previous loans to the United States. For this obligation the Financier would eventually have to make provision. In September he authorized payment of the interest on the French-backed Dutch loan of 1781 and began seeking commodities for exportation to meet interest payments which would come due in 1783 on the Adams loan. Morris also took steps to ensure that whatever foreign funds did become available would not be applied without his approval to the payment of American expenditures and debts in Europe, a problem which had previously led him to overestimate available foreign resources. Finally, in order to end the confusion in foreign accounts and come to terms with the long-standing charges about financial abuses abroad, the Financier urged Congress to provide for the final settlement of American accounts abroad.[13]

III

If the lack of public credit and a reliable system of taxation threatened Morris's operations at every turn, it was nowhere more apparent than in the problems of Morris's contract system, which reached a crisis in the period covered by this volume. Not long after taking

12. See the headnote and notes to RM to the President of Congress, July 30; Diary, September 11, and notes, September 13, and notes, and September 30, and notes, and RM to John Adams, September 27, to Benjamin Franklin, September 27 (first letter) and September 28, to the Willinks, van Staphorsts, and de la Lande and Fynje, September 24 and 28 (2 letters), to La Luzerne, October 2, and to Joshua Barney, October 7 (first letter).

13. See Franklin to RM, August 12, September 26, and October 14, and notes, RM to John Morin Scott, August 15, to a Committee of Congress, August 26, to the President of Congress, September 19, and notes, and to Daniel Clark, September 23, and notes, RM's Circular to Franklin, Adams, and John Jay, September 25, Diary, September 30, and notes, and RM to Franklin, and to Ferdinand Grand, both September 30.

office in June 1781, the Superintendent had introduced competitive bidding for contracts to supply Continental army posts in Pennsylvania, with the intention of expanding the system "as fast and as far as any reasonable Prospects of Revenue would warrant." Morris had financed the Pennsylvania contracts from funds advanced to him to fulfill the state's quota of Congress's specific supply requisitions. But he intended to underwrite later contracts—for West Point, the Moving Army, the Northern Department, New Jersey, and the small posts in Massachusetts, Maryland, and Virginia—on the basis of Congress's specie requisition for 1782.[14]

The largest contract, that for the Moving Army, now encamped in New York, Morris negotiated in April 1782 with a consortium of contractors headed by Comfort Sands and Company, holder of the West Point contract. In the following months, the Moving Army contractors, with Morris's and Washington's consent, absorbed the New Jersey agreement and combined their enlarged contract with that for West Point. Administered by the firm of Sands, Livingston and Company, the West Point and Moving Army contract collapsed in October under the weight of internal and external pressures.

At the heart of the problem was the continuing national shortage of specie. The Moving Army contract required the Superintendent to pay the contractors in coin on a monthly basis as their accounts were settled at the Treasury. Though their contract was with the United States, the contractors emphasized that they had entered into the agreement primarily on the strength of Morris's personal credit. With the smaller contracts of 1781 Morris seemed to have little difficulty in meeting his commitments to the contractors, but by June of 1782 he found it difficult to raise the larger sums required for the West Point and Moving Army contractors because of the failure of the states to provide the expected Continental revenues on the requisition for 1782.

Under these circumstances, Morris resorted to a variety of expedients to pay the contractors. He began to rely heavily on his own notes, bank notes, and other paper. "From one End of this Continent to the other," Morris had boasted, "I can obtain Whatever is wanted for the public Service, by a *Scrip* of the Pen."[15] Though aimed at the British in New York, this assertion was not an idle boast. As a preliminary to an anticipated reliance on notes of the Bank of North America, the Financier had, since the Yorktown campaign, been paying for numerous current expenditures with his own bearer notes, familiarly known as "Mr. Morris's notes." When the contractors tried to obtain cash for Morris's notes and bank notes from the nearest Continental receivers,

14. RM to Nathanael Greene, December 19, 1781.
15. RM to Gouverneur Morris, April 3, 1782.

they found that the receivers' meager balances were simultaneously being drained by notes Morris had supplied to the Quartermaster Department of the army and bills of exchange Morris had used to finance naval expenditures. The contractors' difficulties in securing payment not only disclosed Morris's increasing reliance on expedients he wished to avoid, but they underlined the importance of his personal credit in sustaining the Confederation.

Although Morris intended his paper anticipations as temporary expedients until public credit could be restored, his efforts to wean the government from dependence on his personal credit largely failed. With the Bank of North America weakened by the stagnation of American trade and his credit with the bank damaged by his inability to repay its loans to the government promptly, Morris was unable to phase out his own notes and rely solely on bank notes as a stable medium of exchange and device for anticipating taxes. In fact, although he carefully regulated the number and timing of his own notes so as to limit their depreciation, and occasionally suspended their use, during the period covered by this volume the Financier substantially increased the amount of such anticipations. He did, however, discontinue his original bearer notes and replace them with timed notes bearing his own signature but specifying that they were drawn on account of the United States. His reliance on such notes—their public nature was now more manifest but they nevertheless still incorporated a degree of personal liability—continued well into 1783. It was but one means by which Morris continued to substitute his personal credit "for that which the Country had lost."[16]

When his notes proved insufficient, Morris fell back on other stopgap measures to pay the contractors and provide subsistence to the army. He borrowed money or credit from business associates on public account, backing the loans by pledging his personal credit; expressed willingness to receive promissory notes issued to army officers by Paymaster General John Pierce for his private as well as public account; and personally supported the contractors' requests for discounts at the bank. As with Morris's notes, all these approaches involved placing his private credit and influence behind public ventures.[17]

Morris also manipulated the sale of bills of exchange drawn against foreign funds in Europe. The credit crisis of mid-1782 and the economic uncertainties associated with the onset of peace talks in Paris made it increasingly difficult to market bills of exchange in Philadelphia. Morris, therefore, adopted the contemporary practice of selling his bills of exchange on credit, taking notes from the

16. See RM's Circular to the Receivers of Continental Taxes, August 29, and notes. The quotation is from RM to the Governor of Virginia, January 15, 1782.

17. See RM to William Duer, June 12, and notes, and July 23, to William Smallwood, July 29, and Diary, July 10, August 20, and notes, and August 30, 1782.

purchasers, and discounting them at the bank. The failure of some purchasers to pay off their notes promptly jeopardized Morris's plans to use their money to redeem Pierce's promissory notes falling due on August 1. When one bill purchaser proved unable to make payment, the Financier agreed to take over his ship, the *Duc de Lauzun*. Similarly, to avoid competitive sales with the French, the Superintendent agreed with John Chaloner, agent for French army contractors Jeremiah Wadsworth and John Carter, to divide a sale of bills. Morris then discounted at the bank all the notes received for both their shares, turning money over to Chaloner only as the payments came due on the notes.[18]

When these manipulations in the Philadelphia bill market proved inadequate to tap foreign revenues, Morris turned to other sources. He sent some bills of exchange to Boston for sale there through his Continental receiver for Massachusetts. He dispatched a secret emissary to British-held New York City to raise cash for his contracts by selling bills of exchange there—with disappointing results. Rather than take substantial losses in the weak Philadelphia bill market and risk bidding down the prices of all the bills of exchange used to support the war effort (the French ones as well as his own), the Financier launched a plan late in October to sell his bills for a profit in Havana.[19]

Morris's expedients kept his operations in motion, but they were not sufficient to continue the Moving Army contract on its uncertain footing. Finally, on September 9, pledging his continuing efforts to keep the army supplied but confessing that "at present I really know not which way to turn myself," the Superintendent released to Washington two letters he had withheld that disclosed his precarious financial situation. "Repeated Warnings" to the states, the exasperated Morris told Washington, were "like preaching to the Dead." Two days later, while these letters were in transit to headquarters, the contractors sent Morris a letter announcing that they would stop issuing rations on October 1 unless he paid past due balances and provided future remittances in cash.[20]

Morris responded by negotiating a new contract for West Point and the Moving Army for the remainder of 1782 with Wadsworth and Carter. The new contractors exacted a significantly higher price per ration in return for an extension of credit to the government. After concluding the agreement, Morris spelled out the consequences in a circular to the states citing the higher cost of the new

---

18. See Diary, August 20, and notes to Diary, September 2.
19. See RM to Washington, August 13, and notes, to James Lovell, September 7, and to Le Couteulx and Company, September 24, and notes.
20. See the headnote to Comfort Sands, Walter Livingston, William Duer, and Daniel Parker to RM, September 11, and notes.

contract as the inevitable result of their failure to raise revenues for Congress and the concomitant lack of public credit.[21]

Not all the problems with the contracts were external in nature. Experience showed that the early contracts were not drawn with the rigor required for their effective enforcement, and Morris was unable to oversee their execution adequately from Philadelphia. Moreover, the procedures for issuing rations and keeping accounts worked out by the Finance and War Offices were unacceptable to the contractors. Issuing regulations had to be modified more than once before satisfactory methods were devised, but not before some low bidders, who found their profit margins squeezed, had enraged the army by issuing inferior rations in insufficient quantities and at inconvenient locations. Comfort Sands, a man with fewer military ties than most of the other contractors, drove Washington to distraction by his methods of maximizing profits at the army's expense, notably by his tardiness in establishing standing magazines and his unwillingness to cooperate flexibly to meet other needs of the army. Morris finally succeeded in obtaining an acceptable inspector of contracts in September 1782. Issuing and accounting procedures were reformed in November for the 1783 contracts. The system worked better thereafter, but the American contractors were never tested during an active campaign.[22]

IV

As Agent of Marine, Morris envisioned a rebuilt Continental navy as a maritime force that would both serve his broader goals of revenue collection and public credit and counter the shift of British strategy after Yorktown from land to naval warfare. A revitalized Continental navy, by protecting American commerce and safeguarding the export of American agricultural products, would contribute to the economic prosperity on which the nation's economic growth and political consolidation depended. On July 30 the Financier recommended to Congress that the tattered remnants of the American navy be rebuilt at the rate of six ships per year and wrote in the budget $1.8 million for the construction of the first six warships in his proposed Continental budget for 1783. In light of its meager resources and of the arrival in August of news of the opening of peace negotiations, however, Congress scuttled Morris's plans to

---

21. See the headnote to RM's Contract with Wadsworth and Carter, October 12; also RM to the President of Congress, and his Circular to the Governors of the States, both October 21.

22. See Washington to RM, May 17–25, and notes, and October 31, RM to the President of Congress, April 20, and notes, and RM's Commission to Ezekiel Cornell, September 19, 1782, and notes.

rebuild the navy and in October eliminated all such appropriations from his proposed budget.[23]

Even before this development, Morris appears to have realized that his dream for a strong navy was unattainable for the foreseeable future. For the short term, the Superintendent sought to acquire ships without having to finance their construction. He leased the *General Washington* from Pennsylvania in May and purchased her during the summer. Mindful of the expense involved in completing the *America* at Portsmouth, New Hampshire, and, in any case, without the means to man her, Congress, on Morris's recommendation, bestowed the unfinished 74-gun ship on the French ambassador as a gift to the king of France to replace the *Magnifique,* which had run onto a rock in Boston harbor. This gesture to America's ally, intended no doubt in part to encourage further French loans to the United States, may also have stimulated Chevalier de La Luzerne's interest in exploring the feasibility of constructing French naval vessels in America. Morris encouraged La Luzerne's inquiries with a brief primer and estimates of shipbuilding costs, but nothing came of the idea.[24] Morris's acquisition of the *Duc de Lauzun* in payment of an otherwise irrecoverable debt to the United States partly offset the loss of the *America,* and there was still some hope for the completion of the *Bourbon.*

Meanwhile, Morris directed the few ships at his command to respond to the British threat to American commerce and to meet his immediate need for money. Since the British blockade of the American coast had taken a significant toll on American commerce and seamen during the spring and summer of 1782, Morris's summer cruising orders to Captains John Barry and John Manley instructed them to annoy and attack enemy shipping. Morris expected the capture of British vessels to net prisoners who could be exchanged for the numerous American merchant seamen held in New York and for those recently released from British prisons under an exchange agreement reached by Benjamin Franklin. Although it was far short of the maritime assistance requested by Morris, the arrival in August of some of the French West Indian fleet under the Marquis de Vaudreuil for refitting at Boston alleviated temporarily the obstacles to American trade.[25]

Morris also used naval ships as dispatch vessels and armed transports to import the specie he so desperately needed. In May he had dispatched the swift-sailing *General Washington* under Captain Joshua

---

23. See the headnote to RM to the President of Congress, July 30.
24. See John Paul Jones to Gouverneur Morris, September 2, and notes, and RM to La Luzerne, October 4, and notes.
25. See Diary, July 29, August 3 and 13, and notes, and RM to John Barry, July 12 (two letters), and to John Manley, August 8, 1782.

Barney to the West Indies to solicit naval assistance from the French
and Spanish fleets there and to ferry safely private remittances of
specie to American merchants from Havana. However, the Financier
had to abandon temporarily other plans to sell his bills of exchange
on France in Havana and have Barney or Captain John Barry of the
Alliance return with the proceeds. Barney's arrival on July 17 with
$60,000 in privately owned specie alleviated somewhat the cash
shortage in Philadelphia that had posed a threat to the Bank of
North America. Early in October, Morris had assigned the *General
Washington* to packet service and sent it under Barney to France with
dispatches directing Franklin to negotiate a French loan for 1783
and to put as much of the money as possible on the *Washington* for
its return trip.[26] Later in the month the Superintendent began to
outfit the newly acquired *Duc de Lauzun* for a voyage to Havana to
sell provisions and bills of exchange on public account in hopes of
obtaining funds to pay the increasingly restless American army.[27]

V

As November approached, Morris continued to serve a Congress
which had departed significantly from his guidance on fiscal policy.
Much to his disappointment, Congress had decided to seek from the
states less than a quarter of the revenues Morris had requested to
meet current expenditures for 1783, relying primarily on foreign
loans to close the gap without first providing secure funds for their
repayment. Moreover, despite mounting pressure from public creditors in Philadelphia and elsewhere who were angered by the suspension of interest payments on their public securities, Congress had
bypassed Morris's long-term funding proposals, adopting instead
only a small funding requisition on the states to pay the current
interest on the public debt, while calling on recalcitrant Rhode
Island for a definitive response to the as yet unratified impost of
1781. Powerless to swell the trickle of tax revenues from the states
and left in suspense about the fate of Congress's appeal for another
French loan, a harried Morris continued to juggle his financial expedients while mapping out new initiatives for obtaining specie and
credit abroad.

---

26. See RM to Le Couteulx and Company, September 24, and notes, to Franklin,
September 27 (first letter), and notes, and to Joshua Barney, October 7 (first letter).
27. On the restlessness of the army and the Superintendent's response, see Washington to RM, October 2, and notes, and RM to Washington, October 15 and 16.

EDITORIAL METHOD

Arrangement

This series will present the official Diary, correspondence, and other documents of Robert Morris during his administration as Superintendent of Finance and Agent of Marine, 1781–1784. The Diary, a daily record of transactions in the Office of Finance, provides the organizational basis of the series. Arranged in chronological sequence, Diary entries have been given a standardized form, each date appearing as a centered caption above the text of the entry. If the date of an entry is doubtful, it appears in square brackets.

The documents following each day's Diary entry are arranged in a sequence introduced in volume 5. First in this sequence are letters and papers of key importance presented in regular type with appropriate footnotes, the letters from the Office of Finance and the Marine Office preceding letters sent to Morris. The sequence concludes with routine documents of that day presented in the same order in reduced type, a format explained under the next heading. As in previous volumes, when a letter received is answered the same day, it precedes the reply. Although this series is restricted to Morris's official papers, the editors may occasionally reproduce selections from his as well as Gouverneur Morris's private and business correspondence which throw light on the management of the Office of Finance. Record entries for documents not found will be given only in the few cases where extracts are available in autograph dealers' catalogues or are quoted in other texts. Enclosures other than letters to and from Morris are reproduced at the discretion of the editors.

Documents in Reduced Type

Documents the editors regard as routine and of secondary significance are reproduced in reduced type without salutation, complimentary close, signature, and inside address. The salutation, complimentary close, and signature are retained, however, if in the editors' judgment they are important to an understanding of the letter; the complimentary close is also kept if it forms part of the last sentence. Addresses and endorsements are omitted, but any light they shed on authorship and date will be discussed in footnotes. The textual principles outlined below apply to documents in reduced as well as regular type.

Dating

The editors have placed the dateline at the head of each document, regardless of its place in the manuscript, and have supplied dates for documents in which they are partially or wholly missing. Such documents are placed according to the following rules:

1. When no day within a month can be assigned, the document is placed after all others in that month.

2. When no month can be conjectured, the document is placed at the end of the year.

3. When the year is missing and a probable one can be supplied, it is inserted in square brackets with a question mark and the document placed at the end of that year.

4. When a single year cannot be assigned, inclusive dates are conjectured within square brackets, and the document is placed following all others at the end of the first year.

5. Documents for which no date can be conjectured will be arranged under the heading "n.d." in the final volume of the series.

Punctuation

The editors have been guided by the following rules in rendering manuscript punctuation:

1. A period is placed at the end of every sentence. When the ending is uncertain, the original punctuation is retained.

2. When a precise mark of punctuation cannot be determined, modern usage is observed.

3. Passages made obscure or unintelligible by casual or incorrect punctuation are silently corrected. Where more than one meaning may be derived from such a passage, its original punctuation is retained and an explanatory note attached.

4. Passages lacking punctuation are supplied with minimum punctuation.

5. When used in place of periods, commas, semicolons, or question marks, dashes are replaced by the appropriate mark of punctuation. Dashes and commas randomly distributed in the manuscripts are silently removed.

Spelling

The original spelling in the manuscripts has been preserved, subject to the following exceptions:

1. Proper names are always left unchanged in the text of a document but are presented correctly in all editorial material.

2. When the misspelling of a proper name is so unclear as to be misleading, the correct spelling is placed in square brackets immediately following it or in a footnote. In all other cases the correct spelling is placed in the text and a note is subjoined.

3. Slips of the pen and typographical errors are silently corrected, but in doubtful cases the editors provide an explanatory note.

Capitalization

Manuscript capitalization is retained with the following exceptions:

1. The first word of every sentence is capitalized.

2. Names of persons, their titles, geographical places, and days of the week and names of the month are capitalized regardless of the usage in the manuscript.

3. In doubtful cases, modern usage is followed.

Abbreviations and Contractions

Abbreviations and contractions are normally expanded. The following textual marks deserve special note:

1. The ampersand is expanded to "and," but is retained in the forms "&c." and "&ca.," in the names of business firms, and in financial accounts.

2. The thorn is expanded to "th."

3. The tilde is replaced by the letter(s) it represents. Example: "recv̄d" is expanded to "received."

4. The ℗ sign is expanded to the appropriate letters it depicts (e.g., per, pre, and pro) in correspondence and Diary entries, but is retained in tabular financial accounts.

5. Marks indicating repetition are replaced by "ditto," "do.," or the word(s) they represent.

In the following cases abbreviations and contractions are presented as they occur in the manuscript:

1. In the names of persons and titles, places, and days of the week and names of the months. If the abbreviated form of a proper noun is obscure, the expansion is entered in square brackets immediately following it.

2. In units of weight and measure, and monetary designations.

3. In words in which the apostrophe is used to indicate missing letters. Examples: "pray'd," "cou'd," and "tho'."

4. In any other abbreviations and contractions that remain in modern usage.

In all cases, superscript letters are brought down to the line.

Indecipherable Passages

In every case the editors have attempted to conjecture letters, words, and digits which are missing, illegible, or mutilated. Their procedure is as follows:

1. Where the conjectural material amounts to no more than four letters, it is inserted silently if there is no question what the word is.

2. Where such material amounts to more than four letters, and the letters are conjecturable, it is inserted in the text in square brackets. Example: "[Penns]ylvania." If the editors' conjecture is uncertain, it is followed by a question mark enclosed within the brackets. Material supplied by the editors from a text other than the one printed is also inserted in square brackets.

3. Passages which are not conjecturable are indicated by the editorial insertion of an italicized explanatory phrase in square brackets, such as [*illegible*] or [*torn*].

4. Missing or illegible digits are indicated by suspension points, their number corresponding to the estimated number of such digits, as in "£[..]0.10.2."

5. A blank left in the manuscript by the author is so depicted and the fact mentioned in a footnote.

Revisions in Manuscripts*

1. Interlineations in the text and brief additions in the margin are usually incorporated silently in the text in the place indicated by the writer. Substantial marginal additions are also placed in the text at the appropriate point, either with the editorial insertion [*in the margin*] before and after them or with editorial comment suitable to the passage.

2. An effort is made to decipher scored-out passages. When a legible excision is deemed significant, the deleted passage is either placed in the text in angle brackets ⟨⟩ before the words substituted or is presented in a footnote.

3. When their importance warrants it, variant readings derived from the collation of several texts of a document with the basic or master text are entered in footnotes.

Reproduction of Italicized Material

Proper names, nouns, and passages italicized in printed documents, as was the eighteenth-century fashion, are reproduced in

---

*This section has been revised.

roman type. This rule does not apply to words or passages which, in the judgment of the editors, the writer wished to emphasize by using italics.

Ciphers and Translations

Ciphers, which Morris sometimes employed in correspondence with American representatives abroad and on rare occasions in domestic communications, are discussed in editorial notes to the documents written in that medium. Translations have been supplied for documents written in foreign languages. Annotation is keyed both to foreign-language texts and translations.

A Note on the Text of the Diary

The text of the Diary kept in the Office of Finance by Morris and, on occasion, by Gouverneur Morris consists of three manuscript volumes in the writing of clerks. The Diary is characterized by the extensive use of "ditto," "do.," and appropriate marks to represent these abbreviations. For the sake of readability the editors have in many instances substituted for such abbreviations the words they were intended to replace. In doubtful cases, either the manuscript usage is retained or a note is subjoined.

EDITORIAL APPARATUS

Classification of Manuscripts

When a document is represented by two or more manuscripts, the editors have selected the most authoritative for publication and listed each in the order of descending authority in the source identification note which, with the exception of Diary entries, follows each document.

Descriptive Symbols for Manuscripts

AD	Autograph Document
ADS	Autograph Document Signed
ADft	Autograph Draft
ADftS	Autograph Draft Signed
AL	Autograph Letter
ALS	Autograph Letter Signed
AM LbC	Agent of Marine Letterbook Copy
D	Document
DS	Document Signed
Dft	Draft
DftS	Draft Signed
Diary	Diary in the Office of Finance, Robert Morris Papers, Library of Congress
LS	Letter Signed
LbC	Letterbook Copy
MS, MSS	Manuscript, Manuscripts
Ofcl LbC	Offical Letterbook Copy of the Office of Finance, Robert Morris Papers, Library of Congress
[S]	Signature removed

Other Abbreviations

PCC	Papers of the Continental Congress, 1774–1789, Record Group 360, National Archives
RG	Record Group
WDC	War Department Collection of Revolutionary War Records, Record Group 93, National Archives

Location Symbols

These symbols, used in the National Union Catalog of the Library of Congress, and derived from a list published by the Library, denote institutions in which manuscripts described in this volume have been found. Each volume of this series will contain a revised table.

CSmH	Henry E. Huntington Library, San Marino, California
Ct	Connecticut State Library, Hartford
CtHWa	Wadsworth Atheneum, Hartford, Connecticut
CtHi	Connecticut Historical Society, Hartford
CtMyMHi	Mystic Seaport, Inc., Mystic, Connecticut
CtY	Yale University Library, New Haven, Connecticut
DLC	Library of Congress, Washington, D. C.
DN	United States Department of the Navy, Department Library, Washington, D. C.
DNA	National Archives, Washington, D. C.
De-Ar	Delaware Public Archives Commission, Dover
M-Ar	Massachusetts Archives, Office of the Secretary of State, Boston
MB	Boston Public Library
MH	Harvard University Library, Cambridge, Massachusetts
MHi	Massachusetts Historical Society, Boston
MdAA	Maryland Hall of Records, Annapolis
MdAN	United States Naval Academy Museum, Annapolis
MdHi	Maryland Historical Society, Baltimore
MiU-C	William L. Clements Library, University of Michigan, Ann Arbor
NCooHi	New York State Historical Association, Cooperstown
NHi	New-York Historical Society, New York City
NN	New York Public Library, New York City
NNC	Columbia University Library, New York City
NNPM	Pierpont Morgan Library, New York City
NSyU	Syracuse University Library, Syracuse, New York
Nc-Ar	North Carolina Department of Archives and History, Raleigh
NcU	University of North Carolina Library, Chapel Hill
Nh-Ar	New Hampshire Division of Records Management and Archives, Concord
NhHi	New Hampshire Historical Society, Concord
Nj	New Jersey State Library, Trenton
NjP	Princeton University Library, Princeton, New Jersey
OClWHi	Western Reserve Historical Society, Cleveland
PHC	Haverford College Library, Haverford, Pennsylvania

PHarH	Pennsylvania Historical and Museum Commission, Harrisburg
PHi	Historical Society of Pennsylvania, Philadelphia
PPAmP	American Philosophical Society, Philadelphia
PPIn	Independence National Historical Park, Philadelphia
R-Ar	Rhode Island State Archives, Providence
Vi	Virginia State Library, Richmond

The following symbols represent repositories located outside of the United States:

AGI	Archivo General de Indias, Seville
AMAE	Archives du Ministère des Affaires Étrangères, Paris
PRO	Public Record Office, London

Annotation

While the editors believe that no purpose would be served by an extended discussion here of the nature and extent of this form of editorial contribution, they wish to comment on four procedures followed in this series:

1. Annotation is restricted to subjects essentially related to Morris's conduct of the Office of Finance. Routine transactions are disregarded, unless for some reason they are significant, obscure individuals are identified sparingly or not at all, and an effort is made to keep the number of cross-references to a minimum.

2. Whenever the date of a resolution, order, ordinance, report, or other action of Congress is stated in the text of a footnote, the editors have not supplied a citation to the *Journals of the Continental Congress*, which is cited fully in the table of Short Titles below.

3. In cross-references to dates of other documents published in this series, the year is omitted when those documents appear in the same volume and belong in the same year.

4. Documents printed in reduced type (see above under Editorial Method) in general will receive minimal annotation. This will consist of: whatever textual notes may be necessary; the title, date, location, and substance of documents mentioned in the text, or if not found, a note to that effect; occasional cross-references; and the identification of correspondents. Correspondents who have not been previously identified will be identified as usual; those who have will be briefly reidentified.

Short Titles

This list of frequently cited titles will be revised as future volumes in the series appear.

Acts and Laws of Massachusetts
   Acts and Laws of the Commonwealth of Massachusetts [1780–1805]
   (Boston, 1890–1898)
Alden, *Charles Lee*
   John R. Alden, *General Charles Lee: Traitor or Patriot?* (Baton
   Rouge, La., 1951)
American State Papers
   Walter Lowrie, Matthew St. Clair Clark *et al.*, comps., *American
   State Papers: Documents, Legislative and Executive, of the Congress of
   the United States* (Washington, 1832–1861)
Balch, *French in America*
   Thomas Balch, *The French in America during the War of Indepen-
   dence of the United States, 1777–1783,* trans. Thomas Willing
   Balch, Edwin Swift Balch, and Elise Willing Balch (Philadelphia,
   1891–1895)
Biog. Dir. Cong.
   Biographical Directory of the American Congress, 1774–1961 (Wash-
   ington, 1961)
Boatner, *Encyclopedia of the American Revolution*
   Mark M. Boatner III, *Encyclopedia of the American Revolution*
   (New York, 1966)
Boyd, ed., *Jefferson Papers*
   Julian P. Boyd *et al.*, eds., *The Papers of Thomas Jefferson* (Prince-
   ton, 1950–)
Brunhouse, *Counter-Revolution in Pennsylvania*
   Robert L. Brunhouse, *The Counter-Revolution in Pennsylvania,
   1776–1790* (Harrisburg, 1942)
Burnett, ed., *Letters*
   Edmund Cody Burnett, ed., *Letters of Members of the Continental
   Congress* (Washington, 1921–1936)
Burson, *Don Esteban Miró*
   Caroline M. Burson, *The Stewardship of Don Esteban Miró, 1782–
   1792* (New Orleans, 1940)
Butterfield, ed., *Adams Diary and Autobiography*
   Lyman H. Butterfield *et al.*, eds., *Diary and Autobiography of John
   Adams* (Cambridge, Mass., 1961)
Butterfield, ed., *Rush Letters*
   Lyman H. Butterfield, ed., *Letters of Benjamin Rush* (Princeton,
   1951)
Calendar of Maryland State Papers
   Calendar of Maryland State Papers (Annapolis, 1943–1958)
Campbell, *Sons of St. Patrick*
   John H. Campbell, *History of the Friendly Sons of St. Patrick and of
   the Hibernian Society for the Relief of Emigrants from Ireland* (Phila-
   delphia, 1892)

Carey, ed., *Debates*
> Mathew Carey, ed., *Debates and Proceedings of the General Assembly of Pennsylvania, on the Memorials Praying a Repeal or Suspension of the Law Annulling the Charter of the Bank* (Philadelphia, 1786)

Chastellux, *Travels*
> Marquis de Chastellux, *Travels in North America in the Years 1780, 1781 and 1782*, trans. and ed. Howard C. Rice, Jr. (Chapel Hill, N. C., 1963)

Clark, *Gallant John Barry*
> William Bell Clark, *Gallant John Barry, 1745–1803: The Story of a Naval Hero of Two Wars* (New York, 1938)

Clark and Morgan, eds., *Naval Documents*
> William Bell Clark and William James Morgan, eds., *Naval Documents of the American Revolution* (Washington, 1964–)

Colonial Records of Pennsylvania
> *Colonial Records of Pennsylvania, 1683–1790* (Harrisburg, 1851–1853)

Contenson, *Société des Cincinnati*
> Ludovic de Contenson, *La Société des Cincinnati de France et la guerre d'Amerique, 1778–1783* (Paris, 1934)

DAB
> Allen Johnson, Dumas Malone *et al.*, eds., *Dictionary of American Biography* (New York, 1928–1958)

Davies, ed., *Documents of the American Revolution*
> K. G. Davies, ed., *Documents of the American Revolution, 1770–1783 (Colonial Office Series)* (Shannon, Ireland, 1972–1978)

Dict. Amer. Naval Ships
> *Dictionary of American Naval Fighting Ships* (Washington, 1959–1981)

DNB
> Leslie Stephen, Sidney Lee *et al.*, eds., *The Dictionary of National Biography* (London, 1885–1959)

East, *Business Enterprise*
> Robert A. East, *Business Enterprise in the American Revolutionary Era* (New York, 1938)

Ferguson, *Power of the Purse*
> E. James Ferguson, *The Power of the Purse: A History of American Public Finance, 1776–1790* (Chapel Hill, N. C., 1961)

Fitzpatrick, ed., *Writings of Washington*
> John C. Fitzpatrick, ed., *The Writings of George Washington from the Original Manuscript Sources, 1745–1799* (Washington, 1931–1944)

Fowler, *Rebels Under Sail*
> William M. Fowler, Jr., *Rebels Under Sail: The American Navy during the Revolution* (New York, 1976)

Gawalt, ed., *John Paul Jones' Memoir*
    Gerard W. Gawalt, trans. and ed., *John Paul Jones' Memoir of the American Revolution Presented to King Louis XVI of France* (Washington, 1979)
Hastings and Holden, eds., *Clinton Papers*
    Hugh Hastings and J. A. Holden, eds., *Public Papers of George Clinton, First Governor of New York, 1775–1795, 1801–1804* (New York and Albany, 1899–1914)
Hays, comp., *Calendar of Franklin Papers*
    I. Minis Hays, comp., *Calendar of the Papers of Benjamin Franklin in the Library of the American Philosophical Society* (Philadelphia, 1908)
Hedges, *The Browns: Colonial Years*
    James B. Hedges, *The Browns of Providence Plantations: Colonial Years* (Cambridge, Mass., 1952)
Heitman, *Register*
    Francis B. Heitman, *Historical Register of Officers of the Continental Army during the War of the Revolution, April, 1775, to December, 1783,* new ed. (Washington, 1914)
Henderson, *Party Politics in the Continental Congress*
    H. James Henderson, *Party Politics in the Continental Congress* (New York, 1974)
Hoadly and Labaree, eds., *Public Records of Connecticut*
    C. J. Hoadly and Leonard W. Labaree, eds., *The Public Records of the State of Connecticut* (Hartford, 1894–)
Hutchinson and Rutland, eds., *Madison Papers*
    William T. Hutchinson, Robert A. Rutland *et al.,* eds., *The Papers of James Madison* (Chicago, 1962–)
James, *Oliver Pollock*
    James Alton James, *Oliver Pollock: The Life and Times of an Unknown Patriot* (New York, 1937)
JCC; Journals
    Worthington C. Ford *et al.,* eds., *Journals of the Continental Congress, 1774–1789* (Washington, 1904–1937)
Kinnaird, ed., *Spain in the Mississippi Valley*
    Lawrence Kinnaird, ed., *Spain in the Mississippi Valley, 1765–1794: Translations of the Materials from the Spanish Archives in the Bancroft Library (Annual Report of the American Historical Association for the Year 1945* [Washington, 1946–1949])
Labaree and Willcox, eds., *Franklin Papers*
    Leonard W. Labaree, William B. Willcox *et al.,* eds., *The Papers of Benjamin Franklin* (New Haven, 1959–)
Laws of New York
    Laws of the State of New York (Albany, 1886–1887)

Lee Papers
> The Lee Papers (New-York Historical Society, *Collections*, Pub.
> Fund Ser., IV–VII [New York, 1872–1875])

Lincoln, comp., *Calendar of Jones Manuscripts*
> Charles Henry Lincoln, comp., *A Calendar of John Paul Jones*
> *Manuscripts in the Library of Congress* (Washington, 1903)

McCrady, *South Carolina in the Revolution*
> Edward McCrady, *The History of South Carolina in the Revolution,*
> *1780–1783* (New York, 1902)

McDonald, *E Pluribus Unum*
> Forrest McDonald, *E Pluribus Unum: The Formation of the Ameri-*
> *can Republic, 1776–1790* (Boston, 1965)

McIlwaine, ed., *Journals of the Council of Virginia*
> H. R. McIlwaine *et al.*, eds., *Journals of the Council of the State of*
> *Virginia* (Richmond, 1931–1967)

McIlwaine, ed., *Official Letters*
> H. R. McIlwaine, ed., *Official Letters of the Governors of the State of*
> *Virginia* (Richmond, 1926–1929)

Maclay, *History of American Privateers*
> Edgar Stanton Maclay, *A History of American Privateers* (New
> York, 1899)

Main, *Antifederalists*
> Jackson Turner Main, *The Antifederalists: Critics of the Constitution,*
> *1781–1788* (Chapel Hill, N. C., 1961)

Main, *Political Parties*
> Jackson Turner Main, *Political Parties before the Constitution* (Cha-
> pel Hill, N. C., 1973)

Maryland Archives
> W. H. Browne *et al.*, eds., *Archives of Maryland* (Baltimore, 1883–
> 1956)

Mitchell and Flanders, eds., *Statutes of Pennsylvania*
> James T. Mitchell and Henry Flanders, eds., *The Statutes at Large*
> *of Pennsylvania from 1682 to 1801* (Harrisburg, 1896–1911)

Morison, *John Paul Jones*
> Samuel Eliot Morison, *John Paul Jones: A Sailor's Biography* (Bos-
> ton, 1959)

Morris, *Peacemakers*
> Richard B. Morris, *The Peacemakers: The Great Powers and Ameri-*
> *can Independence* (New York, 1965)

Morris, ed., *John Jay: Winning of the Peace*
> Richard B. Morris *et al.*, eds., *John Jay, The Winning of the Peace:*
> *Unpublished Papers, 1780–1784* (New York, 1980)

[Morris], *Statement of Accounts*
> [Robert Morris], *A Statement of the Accounts of the United States of*

America, During the Administration of the Superintendant of Finance, Commencing with his Appointment, on the 20th Day of February, 1781, and Ending with his Resignation, on the 1st Day of November, 1784 (Philadelphia, 1785)

Nuxoll, "Congress and the Munitions Merchants"
Elizabeth M. Nuxoll, "Congress and the Munitions Merchants: The Secret Committee of Trade during the American Revolution, 1775–1777" (Ph.D. diss., City University of New York, 1979)

N.-Y. Hist. Soc., *Colls.*
New-York Historical Society, *Collections*

O'Donnell, *Chevalier de La Luzerne*
William Emmett O'Donnell, *The Chevalier de La Luzerne, French Minister to the United States, 1779–1784* (Bruges, 1938)

OED
The Oxford English Dictionary (Oxford, 1933)

Palmer, ed., *Calendar of Virginia State Papers*
William P. Palmer *et al.*, eds., *Calendar of Virginia State Papers and Other Manuscripts Preserved . . . at Richmond* (Richmond, 1875–1893)

Papenfuse, *In Pursuit of Profit*
Edward C. Papenfuse, *In Pursuit of Profit: The Annapolis Merchants in the Era of the American Revolution, 1763–1805* (Baltimore, 1975)

Paullin, *Navy of the American Revolution*
Charles Oscar Paullin, *The Navy of the American Revolution: Its Administration, Its Policy, and Its Achievements* (Chicago, 1906)

Pennsylvania Archives
Samuel Hazard *et al.*, eds., *Pennsylvania Archives: Selected and Arranged from Original Documents in the Office of the Secretary of the Commonwealth* (Philadelphia and Harrisburg, 1852–1935)

PMHB
Pennsylvania Magazine of History and Biography

Polishook, *Rhode Island and the Union*
Irwin H. Polishook, *Rhode Island and the Union, 1774–1795* (Evanston, Ill., 1969)

Powers, "Decline and Extinction of American Naval Power"
Stephen T. Powers, "The Decline and Extinction of American Naval Power, 1781–1787" (Ph.D. diss., University of Notre Dame, 1965)

Price, *France and the Chesapeake*
Jacob M. Price, *France and the Chesapeake: A History of the French Tobacco Monopoly, 1674–1791, and of Its Relationship to the British and American Tobacco Trades* (Ann Arbor, Mich., 1973)

Prince, *Federalists and Civil Service*
> Carl E. Prince, *The Federalists and the Origins of the United States Civil Service* (New York, 1977)

Report on American Manuscripts in the Royal Institution
> Historical Manuscripts Commission, *Report on American Manuscripts in the Royal Institution of Great Britain* (London, 1904–1909)

Saunders and Clark, eds., *State Records of North Carolina*
> William L. Saunders and Walter L. Clark, eds., *The State Records of North Carolina* (Raleigh, Winston, and Goldsboro, 1886–1906)

SCHGM
> *South Carolina Historical and Genealogical Magazine*

Showman, ed., *Greene Papers*
> Richard K. Showman *et al.*, eds., *The Papers of General Nathanael Greene* (Chapel Hill, N. C., 1976–)

Staples, *Rhode Island in the Continental Congress*
> William R. Staples, *Rhode Island in the Continental Congress, with the Journal of the Convention That Adopted the Constitution, 1765–1790* (Providence, 1870)

Sumner, *Financier*
> William Graham Sumner, *The Financier and the Finances of the American Revolution* (New York, 1891)

Syrett and Cooke, eds., *Hamilton Papers*
> Harold C. Syrett, Jacob E. Cooke *et al.*, eds., *The Papers of Alexander Hamilton* (New York, 1961–)

van Winter, *American Finance and Dutch Investment*
> Pieter J. van Winter, *American Finance and Dutch Investment, 1780–1805, with an Epilogue to 1840*, rev. and trans. ed. with the assistance of James C. Riley (New York, 1977)

Ver Steeg, *Morris*
> Clarence L. Ver Steeg, *Robert Morris, Revolutionary Financier, with an Analysis of his Earlier Career* (Philadelphia, 1954)

Wharton, ed., *Rev. Dipl. Corr.*
> Francis Wharton, ed., *The Revolutionary Diplomatic Correspondence of the United States* (Washington, 1889)

Wilson, comp., *Acts of New Jersey*
> Peter Wilson, comp., *Acts of the Council and General Assembly of the State of New Jersey from the Establishment of the present Government, and Declaration of Independence to the End of the First Sitting of the Eighth Session on the 14th Day of December, 1783* (Trenton, 1784)

WMQ
> *William and Mary Quarterly*

EDITORS' ACKNOWLEDGMENTS

Without the assistance from a great many institutions and individuals this volume would not have been possible in its present form. This is materially true of the National Endowment for the Humanities and the National Historical Publications and Records Commission, the Federal agencies which have generously sustained the Morris edition over the years. George F. Farr, Jr., and Kathy Fuller of the Endowment's Division of Research Grants and Frank G. Burke, Roger A. Bruns, and George L. Vogt of the Commission's staff have been sources of valued advice and encouragement.

The editors also wish to express their gratitude to the following organizations and individuals for their generous grants: First Pennsylvania Bank, N.A., and J. Bartow McCall, Executive Vice President, who has been a warm advocate for the project; The Philip M. McKenna Foundation, Inc., especially Alex G. and Donald C. McKenna, Directors; Donaldson, Lufkin & Jenrette, Inc., and Richard H. Jenrette, Chairman and Chief Executive Officer; the Ellis L. Phillips Foundation, its President, Ellis L. Phillips, Jr., and its Executive Director, Patricia Cate; Dow Jones & Company, Inc., and Warren H. Phillips, Chairman and Chief Executive Officer; and Dorothy Ann Ver Steeg.

In addition, the editors wish to thank the following organizations and individuals for helping the project in other ways: Dr. Malcolm C. McKenna of the American Museum of Natural History; the national headquarters staff of the Robert Morris Associates in Philadelphia, particularly former President Douglas W. Dodge, Clarence R. Reed, Executive Vice President, Theodore C. McDaniels, Administrative Vice President and Secretary-Treasurer, and Luis W. Morales, John M. Murphy, Charlotte Weisman, and Maxine Elkin; Dr. Michael A. MacDowell, President of the Joint Council on Economic Education in New York City; Professor Arthur M. Schlesinger, Jr., Albert Schweitzer Chair in the Humanities at the Graduate School of The City University of New York; John J. Ford, Jr., of Rockville Centre, New York, for his valuable advice on matters numismatic; John E. Herzog and Diana E. Herzog, President and Vice President of R. M. Smythe & Co., Inc., of New York City, for generously sharing their collection of early American debt certificates; and the late Richard M. Hexter, formerly of Donaldson, Lufkin & Jenrette, Inc., and Ardshiel Associates, Inc., of New York City, for the continuing interest he took in the edition from its formative stages.

For the increasingly important supplemental aid and institutional support received from Queens College of The City University of New York the editors wish to thank President Saul B. Cohen, whose enthusiasm and good will have placed them under special obligation. The editors are also pleased to acknowledge the effective cooperation of Provost William Hamovitch, Vice President Donald J. Meyer, Professor Helen S. Cairns, Dean of Graduate Studies and Research, Professors James N. Jordan, Dean of the Social Sciences, and Keith Eubank, Chairman of the History Department, Hannah Petzenbaum, Director of the Office of Grants and Contracts, and Ronald C. Cannava of the Office of Public Relations. Other individuals at the College have also put the editors in their debt. In the Office of Grants and Contracts, Hannah Petzenbaum and her staff (Edward M. Leight III, Guatama M. Prasad, Margaret J. Hesher, Mildred Davison, and Frances J. Richard) have stood ready at all times to assist the editors with their grant-related chores. At the Paul Klapper Library, Chief Librarian Matthew J. Simon, Raymond R. Wile, Shoshana Kaufmann, Mollie Mervis, Lenora Nusbaum, Mimi B. Penchansky, Izabella Taler, and Ruth Hollander have always helped to make the Library's resources conveniently available to the project.

The index to this volume was compiled with the assistance of computer facilities at Queens College and the University Computer Center of The City University of New York. It could not have been accomplished without the sustained encouragement and guidance of the following individuals: Dr. Charles T. Cullen, Editor of The Papers of Thomas Jefferson at Princeton University, who gave generously of his time and breadth of experience with computer-assisted indexing and text processing; Professor Robert L. Oakman of the Department of English at the University of South Carolina, whose prodigious knowledge of computer applications in the humanities was important to the editors at an early stage; and Professor David R. Chesnutt, Editor of The Papers of Henry Laurens at the University of South Carolina, who was always ready to answer the editors' questions. At Queens College the editors are indebted to Professor Seymour Goodman, whose encouragement and technical advice early on was crucial to the endeavor, and to Dr. Richard E. White and his staff at the Queens College Computer Center, particularly Alan J. Boord and Edward Z. Hu, for their indispensable support.

In the Morris Papers editorial office, Kathleen Haslbauer, our secretary, was helpful in the preparation of this volume and resourceful in executing tasks that would have otherwise distracted the editors. For translating the French document in this volume the editors again find themselves happily in debt to Professor Robert W. Hartle of the Department of Romance Languages, Queens College.

Finally, the editors' warm thanks are extended to the following individuals in various libraries and manuscript repositories.

The National Archives: Mary Giunta, Sara Dunlap Jackson, Richard F. Cox, Jr., Anne H. Henry, and David Pfeiffer, Archivists of the National Historical Publications and Records Commission, and James Harwood and Clarence F. Lyons, Jr., of the National Archives staff; New York Public Library (Astor, Lenox, and Tilden Foundations): John Miller, Leon Weidman, and Jerome Stoker of the recently disbanded American History Division, Lawrence P. Murphy, Francis Mattson, and Daniel Traister of the Rare Book Room, Paul Rugen, Jean McNiece, and John D. Stinson of the Manuscript Division, Gunther E. Pohl, Timothy Beard, and Barbara Hillman of the Local History and Genealogy Division, and Faye Simkin and Walter Zervas of the Administration Office; Graduate School Library of the City University of New York: Jane Moore, Clair D. Bowie, Carol B. Fitzgerald, Priscilla M. Pereira, Helga Feder; Library of Congress: Fred Coker, Charles Kelley, Gary Kohn, and Marianne Roos of the Manuscript Division; Smithsonian Institution, National Museum of American History: L. W. Vosloh, Specialist in American Numismatics; Historical Society of Pennsylvania: James E. Mooney, Director, Peter J. Parker, Chief of Manuscripts, and Linda Stanley and Loretta Zwolak in the Manuscript Room; Princeton University Library: Jean F. Preston, Curator of Manuscripts; Massachusetts Historical Society: John D. Cushing, Librarian, and Malcolm Freiberg, Editor of Publications; Massachusetts Archives: Leo and Helen Flaherty, Dennis Means, and Toby Pearlstein; American Antiquarian Society: Kathleen A. Major, Keeper of Manuscripts, and Nancy Burkett, Head of Readers' Services; Maryland Hall of Records: Edward C. Papenfuse, Lois Anne Hess, and Phebe R. Jacobsen; New-York Historical Society: Thomas J. Dunnings, Jr.; Pennsylvania Historical and Museum Commission: Henry E. Bown, Louis M. Waddell, and Roland M. Baumann; American Philosophical Society: Whitfield J. Bell, Jr., James E. McClellan, and Stephen Catlett; Houghton Library, Harvard University: Rodney G. Dennis; Yale University Library: Judith A. Schiff; Connecticut Historical Society: Ruth M. Blair; Connecticut State Library: Wilda Van Dusen of The Papers of Jonathan Trumbull, and Robert Claus and Eunice Gillman DiBella; Rhode Island Archives: Phyllis Silva; Columbia University Library: Kenneth A. Lohf; New York State Historical Association: Amy Barnum and Marion Brophy; Syracuse University Library: Metod M. Milac; Maryland Historical Society: Richard J. Cox and Drew Gruenburg; Henry E. Huntington Library: Harriet McLoone; William L.

Clements Library: Barbara Mitchell and Arlene P. Shy; Naval History Division, Department of the Navy: William J. Morgan; The Papers of Benjamin Franklin, Yale University: William B. Willcox; The Papers of Nathanael Greene, Rhode Island Historical Society: Richard K. Showman and Robert McCarthy; The Papers of Thomas Jefferson, Princeton University: Charles T. Cullen and Robert R. Crout; Fordham University: Elaine F. Crane; Archivo General de Indias, Seville: Rosario Parra; Archives du Ministère des Affairs Étrangères, Paris: Martial de La Fourniere, P. Enjalran, and Jean Favier; and Lion G. Miles of West Stockbridge, Massachusetts. The editors also wish to thank Ronald von Klaussen of New York City for generously sharing a small but important cache of manuscripts from his private collection.

The Papers of Robert Morris

VOLUME 6: JULY 22–OCTOBER 31, 1782

Diary: July 22, 1782

I returned this Morning at Nine OClock.[1]

The Honble Mr. Duane Chairman of a Committee for enquiring into the Management of this Office had written me a Note on Saturday appointing this Day to Commence their enquiry, and he came to the Office in expectation that I should be ready but not having received the Note until my return I was not ready and further as there is much business to be done this Week which will require the whole of my Attention I proposed to suspend this enquiry until next Week to which Mr. Duane agreed.[2]

Jos. Nourse Esqr. applied to have the Accounts of Expenditures returned to him in order that he might make additions &c. which was done.

Capt. Js. Nicholson reminded me that he is waiting my Orders to return to the Bourbon Frigate and I am only waiting until I can command a Sufficient Sum of Money.[3]

Haym Solomon several times with me respecting Exchange &c.

The Hon. Mr Lee called also expecting to proceed in the enquiry &c.[4]

Wm. Turnbull Esqr called and pressed much for Money for William Duer Esqr.[5]

Mr. Bellamy Crawford came.[6] I examined into his Case and find it totally out of my Power to releive him which I am very sorry for having a strong desire to give Assistance to a distressed Family.

James Milligan Esqr. respecting sundry Arrangements in settling Accounts. Mr. Hodgdon for Money.

Docr. Campbell for Money in part of his Balance but on examining his Account I find he Charges for Services rendered after he was deranged.[7] Upon enquiring into the reason it appears that there was no Surgeons to Releive him. I therefore sent for Mr Milligan, desired him to seperate the Accounts and send me Copies of the Vouchers for extra Service.

Lewis R. Morris Esqr. applied for the Bills of Exchange to pay the Quarters Salary of the foreign Ministers &c.[8] I told him my time will not permit their being got ready so soon as he seemed to wish.

Colo. Nichs. Rogers called and I delivered him the Letter to Wm. [i.e., Mr.?] Donaldson Yates which had been promised.[9]

Lieut. Colo. Brockholst Living[s]ton called requesting a payment of part of the balance due to him and which he claims particularly as no depreciation has ever been made good to him.[10]

Geo. Eddy called and I shewed him the Letters I had received respecting his flag Ships.[11]

His Excellency Genl. Washington called and had a Conference on several matters relative to the public Affairs.

Wrote a Letter to Alexr Hamilton Esqr.

Wrote a Letter to Hezekiah Merrill Esqr.[12]

Wrote a Letter to Geo. Olney.

Wrote a Letter to James Lovell.

Wrote a Letter to Wm. C. Houston.

Issued a Warrant on Mr Swanwick in favor of Saml. Hodgson [Hodgdon] £112.10.0.

1. RM had taken a weekend "excursion into the Country." See Diary, July 19, 1782.

2. On the congressional committee to investigate the Office of Finance, see Diary, June 12, 1782, and notes. James Duane's letter is dated July 19.

3. See Diary, February 14, 1782, and notes.

4. Arthur Lee was on the committee mentioned in note 2 above.

5. See RM to Duer, July 23, and notes.

6. On Crawford's case, see Diary, July 19, 1782, and notes.

7. On Campbell's application, see Diary, May 8, 1782, and notes.

8. Lewis R. Morris was an undersecretary in the office of the Secretary for Foreign Affairs. For the new way of paying foreign ministers, see RM to the President of Congress, May 8, 1782, and notes.

9. On this matter, which pertained to settling accounts for transport services during the Yorktown campaign, see Diary, July 19, and notes, and RM to Donaldson Yeates, July 23, 1782.

10. Henry Brockholst Livingston had recently returned from Spain where he served as John Jay's private secretary while on leave of absence from the army. His claim was for military pay and depreciation. See Matthew Ridley to RM, April 20, and notes, and Diary, July 24, 25, and 26, 1782.

11. On George Eddy, the Yorktown merchants capitulant, and the ships *Fame* and *New York*, see RM's Agreement with Eddy, printed under March 13, and notes, and RM to Daniel Clark, July 15, 1782, and notes. The letters, not found, may have been from Clark. See RM to Clark, July 23.

12. Letter not found.

To James Lovell

Office of Finance 22. July 1782

Sir,

I have received your Letters dated at Boston on the fourth and fifth of this Instant.[1] I entirely approve your refusing the Certificates you mention. The Proposition (whatever it is) on which the

Interrogatories respecting them was founded ought to be discouraged, as Credit cannot be given on Account of the Taxes for any Paper but Bank Notes and my Drafts on Mr: Swanwick.[2] I wrote you on the second Instant authorizing the Sale of as many Bills as would enable you to pay all the Drafts I had made upon you and on the tenth Instant directing the Sales of all you have so that Nothing be added on that Subject. I am Sir your most obedient and humble Servant

RM

 MS: Ofcl LbC, DLC.
    1. Letters not found. Lovell was the receiver of Continental taxes for Massachusetts.
    2. Although not mentioned here, RM had already agreed to accept in taxes the promissory notes issued as pay to army officers earlier in the year by Paymaster General John Pierce. See RM to the Governor of Maryland, July 16, 1782; and on the notes, RM to George Washington, January 26, 1782 (first letter), and notes.

From Jonathan Burrall

Philadelphia 22d July 1782

Sir,

Colo. Trumbull will present to you my adjustment of the late Commissary General Joseph Trumbull's account and certificate for the balance;[1] but as a doubt arises in my Mind whether it ought to be considered as of Specie Value (altho' the whole business was transacted before depreciation is allowed to take place)[2] I must beg your Attention to a Report of a Committee, and Resolution of Congress of March 31st. 1779. The Report is long and concludes thus "That your Committee have been shewn a state of the Commissary Generals cash account of money received and issued from which it appears that little, if any, Public Monies have been taken to his private use and that a Compensation for Services done by the Said Commissary Genl. still remains to be made at a time too when the Value of our Currency is greatly altered from what it was when the Services were performed: Whereupon your Committee report the following resolution" &c.[3] The Resolve which follows allows him a Commission of ½ per Cent on the gross Sum expended in the departments and a further Commission of 2½ per Cent on his own particular Purchases, and directs that the Amount be immediately paid to the administrator of his Estate, but as it could not then be ascertained the money has never been paid. The Commissions amount to 62,230⁶⁵⁄₉₀ Dollars and upon an adjustment of the whole account there is a balance due to him of 40,237⁷⁷⁄₉₀ Dollars as you will see by the Enclosed State of his account. I must request your directions whether this balance be considered as hard Money as the Value was when the business was transacted or be Estimated at the Value money was when the resolution passed being the 31st. March 1779.[4] I have the Honor to be, with the Highest respect your very humble Servant

                                                                    J Burrall

The Honble. Robert Morris

ENDORSED: Letter of 23 July 1782/Superint finance/24./Referred to Mr Clymer/Mr Jackson/Mr Telfair.
MS: Copy, PCC, DNA.
    1. The accounts of the deceased Commissary General Joseph Trumbull had been settled by his brother, Jonathan Trumbull, Jr., and recently reviewed by Jonathan Burrall, commissioner of accounts for the Commissary Department. Burrall's "adjustment," with accompanying certification, is calendared under July 18, 1782. See RM to the President of Congress, April 18, and Diary, February 19, and notes, July 19, and notes, and July 23 and 24, 1782. For the final settlement certificates devised as a result of the settlement of these accounts, see RM to Burrall, August 19, and notes.
    2. September 1, 1777, according to the Continental scale of depreciation adopted by Congress on June 28, 1780. See note 4 below.
    3. The foregoing quotation differs in nonessential details from the manuscript report in PCC, no. 20, I, 255–256, which in turn is not strictly reproduced in JCC, XIII, 396. The closing quotation mark has been supplied by the editors.
    4. This letter raised serious issues as to the settlement of Congress's accounts in old Continental currency. The accounts of Joseph Trumbull, generally regarded as an honest and scrupulous procurement officer, related to an early period of the war before Continental currency depreciated or when it was just beginning to depreciate. The state of the currency at that time was misrepresented by the official Continental scale of depreciation adopted in 1780, which underestimated depreciation and fixed its starting point at September 1, 1777. The market exchange in 1777 was about $3 currency to $1 specie.
    After Trumbull's death, his heirs asked Congress to determine the amount of and pay the commissions due him for his services. Congress in 1779 still refused to acknowledge depreciation and was supporting tender laws. In establishing his commissions by an act of March 31, when currency was verging on 16 to 1 of specie, Congress had no other way of compensating Trumbull's heirs for the low value of the currency they would receive than by setting his commissions high. Because his accounts were not settled, however, no payments were made to his heirs at this time.
    The matter came up again when Burrall, examining Trumbull's accounts, became uncertain whether the amount of the commissions should be considered as specie (a reasonable alternative since most of the transactions took place before September 1, 1777), or whether the commission should be stated in terms of Continental currency at its specie value as of March 31, 1779, the date of Congress's resolutions. In the first instance, the amount (as calculated in Burrall's statement of the accounts) would have been $62,230, which RM thought high, and in the second (at 11 to 1), $5,653, which he considered low. RM referred the matter to Congress in a noncommittal letter of July 23, 1782. The committee reporting on it declared on August 13 that, notwithstanding the Continental scale of depreciation, paper money had depreciated before September 1, 1777, as indicated by the very figures in Trumbull's accounts, and that to pay him specie commissions on inflated currency transactions before that date would be unjust, particularly because the commissions set by the act of 1779 were too high. Since the committee regarded both methods of settlement as inequitable, it put forth the startling idea of bypassing the Continental scale of depreciation and using a commodity standard—the price of some common article which could be taken as registering the progressive decline of the currency.
    Congress returned this proposition to the committee with instructions to confer with the Financier. RM's pragmatic advice was to report the amount of Trumbull's commissions without explaining how the figure was arrived at, and this strategy the committee tried on October 1, proposing to Congress an allowance of $29,505. But Congress refused to evade the issue and, in instructing another committee to report the amount of the commissions, directed also that the basis of computing them be

explained. Ultimately, the committee came up with the figure of $21,992 old Continental currency which Trumbull had retained and his heirs would be allowed to keep, plus $12,000 in specie, although the committee avoided any real explanation of how it arrived at these figures. Immobilized by the dilemmas born of past policies, Congress took no action, but on January 23, 1783, Alexander Hamilton of New York, seconded by Oliver Ellsworth of Connecticut, resolved the issue by simply reasserting and confirming official policy, even though it might cost Congress more money. Their proposal, which Congress adopted, instructed the commissioner settling commissary accounts to state Trumbull's accounts in terms of the specie value of Continental currency at the end of each month (the procedure implied use of the Continental scale of depreciation) and to compute his commissions in specie on the basis of the rates set by the act of March 31, 1779. See RM to the President of Congress, July 23, and Diary, September 2; *JCC*, XVII, 566–569, XXII, 415n., XXIII, 464–465n., 631 and n., 691–692n., XXIV, 64; and Ferguson, *Power of the Purse*, 32, 68–69.

From Alexander Hamilton

Poughkepsie [New York] July 22d. 1782

Sir

Agreeable to my letter to you from Albany[1] I came to this place and had an interview with a Committee of the Legislature in which I urged the several matters contained in your instructions.[2] I strongly represented the necessity of solid arrangements of Finance, and, by way of argument, pointed out all the defects of the present system. I found every man convinced that something was wrong, but few that were willing to recognise the mischief when defined and consent to the proper remedy. The quantum of taxes already imposed is so great as to make it useless to impose any others to a considerable amount. A bill has however passed both houses payable in specie, bank notes or your notes for Eighteen thousand pounds. It is at present appropriated to ⟨Congress⟩ your order, but I doubt whether some subsequent arrangement will not take place for a different ⟨application⟩ appropriation. The Commander in Chief has applied for a quantity of forage, which the legislature ⟨has employed in⟩ is devising the means of furnishing, and I ⟨imagine⟩ fear it will finish by diverting the ⟨present⟩ Eighteen thousand pounds to that purpose.[3] I have hitherto been able to prevent this, but as it is of indispensable importance to me to leave this place immediately[4] to prepare for an examination for which I have pledged myself the ensuing term which is at hand;[5] it is possible after I have left it, contrary ideas will prevail. ⟨violent⟩ Efforts have been made to introduce a species of negotiable certificates which I have strenuously opposed ⟨[and so far with?] success. There is the same danger when I am gone with respect to this as with respect to the former matter⟩. It has not yet taken place; but I ⟨will not answer⟩ am not clear how the matter will terminate.

Should the bill for the Eighteen thousand pounds go out in its present form I cannot hope that it will produce in the treasury above half the sum; such are the vices of our present mode of collection.

A bill has also passed ⟨both houses⟩ the Assembly for collecting arrearages of taxes, payable in specie, bank notes, your notes, old Continental emissions at One hundred and twenty eight for one and a species of certificates issued by the state for the purchase of horses. This is now before the Senate.[6] The arrearages are very large.

Both houses have unanimously passed a set of resolutions to be transmitted to Congress and the several states ⟨declarative⟩ proposing a Convention of the states to enlarge the powers of Congress and vest them ⟨with them⟩ with funds.[7] I think this a very eligible step though I doubt of the concurrence of the other states; but I am certain without it, ⟨you⟩ they never will be brought to cooperate in any reasonable or effectual ⟨manner⟩ plan. Urge reforms or exertions and the answer constantly is what avails it for one state to ⟨do⟩ make them without the concert of the others? It is in vain to expose the futility of this reasoning; it is founded on all those passions which have the strongest influence on the human mind.

The Legislature have also appointed at my instance a Committee to devise in its recess a more effectual system of taxation and to communicate with me on this subject.[8] A good deal will depend on the success of this attempt. Convinced of the absurdity of multiplying taxes in the present mode, where in effect the payment is voluntary, and the money received exhausted in the collection, I have laboured chiefly to instil the necessity of a change in the plan, and though not so rapidly as the exigency of public affairs requires, truth seems to be making some progress.

There is no other appropriation to the use of Congress than of the Eighteen Thousand pounds.[9]

I shall as soon as possible give you a full and just view of the situation and temper of this state.[10] This cannot be 'till after my intended examination; that over I shall lay myself out in every way that can promote your views and the public good.

I am informed you have an appointment to make of a Commissioner of accounts for this state. Permit me to suggest the expediency of choosing a citizen of the state,[11] a man who to the qualifications requisite for the execution of this office adds an influence in its affairs. I need not particularise the reasons of this suggestion; in my next I will also take the liberty to mention some characters.[12]

I omitted mentioning that The ⟨Legislature⟩ two houses have also passed a bill authorising Congress to adjust the quotas of the states on equitable principles agreeable to your recommendation.[13] I have the honor to be with sincere attachment and respect Sir Your most Obedient Servant

I enclose you the bond executed jointly with General Schuyler.[14]

MSS: ADft, Hamilton Papers, DLC; transcript, Francis Baylies Papers, DLC.

1. Hamilton was the receiver of Continental taxes for New York. The editors have restored some of the legible excisions in his ADft.

2. Hamilton's letter from Albany was dated July 13. Regarding his meeting with committees of the New York Senate and Assembly, see Hamilton to Governor George Clinton of New York, July 16, 1782, Syrett and Cooke, eds., *Hamilton Papers*, III, 109 and n. For the instructions to which Hamilton probably alludes, see RM to the Receivers of Continental Taxes, April 13; also RM to Hamilton, July 2, 1782.

3. Although the New York legislature had recently pleaded inability to render support to Congress, except to take up Continental certificates already issued, it enacted on July 22 a tax of £18,000 for which only gold or silver, Morris's notes, and notes of the Bank of North America were receivable. The state treasurer was directed to pay the money to the Continental loan officer or other person designated by the Superintendent of Finance. Another act of July 22 empowered the governor to borrow up to £10,000 and remit this money to the same Continental officers as part of the state's quota of the requisition for 1782. When George Washington made a special appeal for forage, the legislature, instead of raiding the Continental tax as Hamilton feared, responded with an act of July 24 which allocated funds from various state taxes to forage procurement. There was, however, a condition attached: either the Quartermaster General had to have "covenanted" with the state agent, Udny Hay, to pay for the forage in specie or Morris's notes issued before February 1, 1783, or RM had to have signified to the governor that the state was to get credit for the forage on the current specie requisition instead of on old specific supply requisitions. Although RM had already reluctantly acceded to the latter alternative, choosing to pay in warrants receivable for the specie requisition (a concession which Quartermaster General Timothy Pickering pointed out he had not granted to any other state), the deal fell through when the Superintendent learned that Hay's prices for forage and pasturage were too high. *Laws of New York*, I, 472–476, 505–508, 520; Washington to Clinton, July 11, 1782, Fitzpatrick, ed., *Writings of Washington*, XXIV, 428–429; Pickering to Hugh Hughes, and to Henry E. Lutterloh, both July 17, 1782, WDC, no. 85, pp. 88–93; and the Quartermaster General to RM, August 3, and notes.

4. Hamilton interlined the next 18 words to the semicolon.

5. Hamilton refers to his examination for admission to the bar in New York. See Syrett and Cooke, eds. *Hamilton Papers*, III, 122, 189.

6. This bill, "An Act to compel the payment of the arrearages of taxes," passed on July 24, 1782. *Laws of New York*, I, 513–519.

7. For these resolves and congressional action on them, see Resolution of the New York Legislature Calling for a Convention of the States to Revise and Amend the Articles of Confederation, [July 20, 1782], Syrett and Cooke, eds., *Hamilton Papers*, III, 110–113.

8. For the establishment of this joint committee, see *ibid.*, 116n.; also Hamilton to RM, September 14. The committee apparently failed to accomplish anything; Governor Clinton reminded the legislature at the opening of the next session in January 1783 that the tax laws had not yet been revised. See *Votes and Proceedings of the [New York] Assembly, &c. At the second Meeting of the Sixth Session* [Poughkeepsie, 1783], 98.

9. Hamilton evidently ignored the clause in the other act of July 22 which authorized the governor to pay the proceeds of a £10,000 loan to a Continental official designated by RM, but discussed it in later correspondence which has not been found. See note 3 above; and RM to Hamilton, August 28.

10. See Hamilton to RM, August 13.

11. RM's policy was never to appoint a citizen of a state to settle the accounts of that state.

12. Hamilton's next letter to RM, dated July 27, was acknowledged in RM's reply of August 28 but has not been found.

13. "An Act to authorize the United States in congress assembled, to adjust the proportions of this State towards the expences of the war, in a mode different from that prescribed by the articles of confederation," passed on July 22, 1782, *Laws of New*

York, I, 504–505. Since New York was crippled by enemy occupation throughout the war, the state had a vested interest in introducing the principle of equity into the procedure by which each state's share of the common charges was determined. See Ferguson, *Power of the Purse,* 210; and notes to William Churchill Houston to RM, June 29, 1782.

14. Enclosure not found. See RM to Hamilton, July 2, 1782.

To Alexander Hamilton

Office of Finance July 22nd. 1782

I have received your letter dated at Albany the 13th Instant. As I can have no doubt but that your Efforts will be applyed to promote the Public Interests, I hope the Journey you propose to Poughkepsie may prove every way agreable to your Wishes.[1]

MSS: LS, Hamilton Papers, DLC; Ofcl LbC, DLC; transcript, Francis Baylies Papers, DLC.

1. According to Hamilton's notation on this letter, he replied to RM on August 3, but that communication has not been found.

To George Olney

Office of Finance 22d July 1782[1]

I have received your Letters dated at Providence on the sixth and eighth of this Instant with the half part of the Notes by Mr. Brown and other Enclosures referred to. My Letters to you dated the twenty third of June and second of July contain such Instructions as were thought necessary respecting the Certificates that had been paid to you on account of Taxes. I also wrote on the thirteenth Instant in Answer to the Letter written by you on the twenty seventh Ultimo: and which contained the application made to you by sundry merchants of Providence on the Subject of exchanging Bank Notes. I expect these Communications will teach you in Season and prove satisfactory for your Government in the several Matters they refer to.

MS: Ofcl LbC, DLC.

1. Olney was the receiver of Continental taxes for Rhode Island. None of his letters and enclosures mentioned in this reply from RM have been found.

To William Churchill Houston

Office of Finance
22nd: July 1782[1]

I am favored with your's dated at Trenton on the 20th: Instant. I receive with pleasure the Assurances you give of such Assistance as may be in your power on the subject of my Circular Letter of the 12th: Instant. Altho' your Enquiries may not be attended with all the Success you wish, yet much may be expected from them.

Your Observations respecting the Money paid by Mr: Wilkins into the United States Treasury are just. I approve your solicitude to preserve regularity and system in the Public business under your Care, and will take such Order that Collectors shall in future be accommadated without introducing any Intricacies into your transactions.

MS: LS, Houston Collection, NjP.

1. Houston was the receiver of Continental taxes for New Jersey. He endorsed this letter as having been received on July 25.

Diary: July 23, 1782

Colo. Trumbull called this Morning relative to the Settlement of his late Brothers Account as reported by Mr. Burrall, but being engaged I could not enter into any discussion with him and therefore told him my intention of reporting thereon to Congress for their Decission.[1]

Mr. John Clingman brought me a Letter from Colo. Cook Contractor for Wyoming[2] desiring me to pay thirty pounds to Mr. Clingman and I granted a Warrant for that Sum.

Capt. James Nicholson to remind me that he waits for orders. I say he waits for money only.

Lewis R. Morris Esqr. for the Bills for our Ministers abroad. I desired longer time to get them ready being extremely hurried.

Mr Wm. Dunwoodie a Messenger from Wm. Duer Esqr.[3] tells me he cannot get the Balance of Subsistence money from the Paymaster General and therefore applies to me for the same. I desired him to call in the Morning.

Colo. Pickering in great Distress for Money to make good engagements already entered into and to carry on the Business of his Department with reputation urges the execution of his plan for Issuing Notes redeemable in Taxes. I promise to Consider well of this plan which is rather dangerous to execute altho at first View it appears feasible.[4]

Messrs. Hazelwood & Co[5] apply for Money and their Moderation in making Demands altho much is due to them induces me to accomodate them as much as consistantly can be done.

Mr Alexr. Stewart applied for a Flag to be granted to Mr. Musco Livingston to enable him to bring from Jamaica his family and Effects and supposing that Congress had referred this Business to me to take order I desired Mr. Stewart to procure from the War Office or from Mr Thompsons the form of a Flag. Upon his Application to the latter Mr. Thompson informed me that I was expected to make report to Congress on this Subject which shall be done.[6]

Mr. Van Wagener [Van Wagenen] applied again for part of the Money on his Account but I told him the impossibility of complying with his Wishes and ordered his Debt upon Interest.

His Excellency General Washington called, and we had a farther Conference on several matters of public Business.

Mr. Hodgdon Commissary of Military Stores for Money.

Mr. Edwd. Williams on behalf of Doctr Bond[7] for money &c.

Mr. Ephm. Blaine and Mr Wm. Wilson called for Money on Account of the Contractors at Fort Pitt.[8] I desired them to call again.

Mr. Geo. Eddy called and I shewed him the Letters I had written

to Mr. Daniel Clarke respecting the Flag Ships informing him that
he must be guided by Mr Eddy's orders &c.[9]

Genl. Lincoln had a Conference on several matters respecting his
and my Departments.

Doctor T. Bond junior for Money. I told him he must rub through
another Month. The many Demands for Money, the engagements I
am under to pay Mr. Pierces Notes[10] and other matters together with
the price the several French Agents were selling their bills at, being
under 6/ induced me to strike for some Sums at 6/ but as I am
informed the French Agents have sold most of their Bills I determined this Day to demand 6/3d and accordingly asked that price of
Mr. Alexr. Robertson who called to make a purchase. He declines
giving that price but I think it best to continue the Demand.

Wrote a Letter to Donaldson Yeates Esqr.

Wrote a Letter to Geo Webb Esqr.

Wrote a Letter to the Hon. Thoms. Jenifer.

Wrote a Letter to William Duer Esqr.

Wrote a Letter to Daniel Clarke.

Wrote a Letter to His Excellency the President of Congress.

Issued a Warrant on Mr. Swanwick in favor of Jos: Pennell
£127.10.0.

1. Concerning the settlement of Joseph Trumbull's accounts, see Jonathan Burrall to RM, July 22, and notes.

2. Letter not found.

3. William Duer was the contractor for the posts north of Poughkeepsie in New
York.

4. For Timothy Pickering's scheme to issue quartermaster certificates grounded
on the collection of state taxes levied in compliance with the requisition for 1782, see
Hints on Tax Notes from the Quartermaster General, July 24.

5. John Hazelwood and Peter Summers were the contractors for the post at
Philadelphia.

6. See RM's Report to Congress on the Case of Musco Livingston, July 25, and
notes.

7. Dr. Thomas Bond, Jr., purveyor of the Continental Hospital Department.

8. The contractors were David Duncan and Michael Huffnagle. See William Irvine to RM, July 5, 1782, and notes.

9. See RM to Clark, July 23; RM's most recent letters to Clark were dated July 9,
15, and 16.

10. Over $140,000 worth of promissory notes issued by Paymaster General John
Pierce to officers for pay were to fall due on August 1, 1782. See RM to George
Washington, January 26, 1782 (second letter), and notes.

To the President of Congress
(John Hanson)

Office of Finance 23d. July 1782

Sir

I enclose the Copy of a Letter from Mr. Burrall the commissioner
for settling the Commissary's Accounts.[1] On examining the matter

referred to in that Letter I find that the Report of the Committee points Evidently at a depreciated State of the Continental Money. It is however to be remembered that Expectations were then cherished of being able to restore the pristine Value. Should the Commission in question be valued by the Table of depreciation at the Time of passing the Resolution which was $\frac{6541}{72,000}$, or a little more than Eleven for one the Compensation will appear low, and on the Contrary if taken as Specie it might be thought high. Under these Circumstances it becomes necessary to have recourse to the decision of Congress. I am Sir, with great Respect Your Excellency's most obedient and humble Servant

Robt Morris

The President of Congress

ENDORSED: Letter from the Supt. of Finance/23d July 1782/With a letter from J. Burral on/the allowance made to J Trumbull/by act of 31 March 1779. Whether it/is to be valued by table of depreciation/or taken as specie.
MSS: LS, PCC, DNA; Ofcl LbC, DLC.
 1. For the enclosed letter concerning the accounts of the late Joseph Trumbull and a discussion of the question put to Congress in the present letter, see Jonathan Burrall to RM, July 22, and notes.

To William Duer

Office of Finance 23. July 1782

Sir,

I duly received yours of the third Instant.[1] I have altho the Accounts are not yet finally adjusted advanced to Mr Turnbull five thousand Dollars and I have obtained of the Bank the Credit you desired. I hope you may meet with all possible Ease and Satisfaction in the Execution of your Business. As to the Designs of the Enemy I am convinced that they can be nothing more than to harass and Alarm for as to any serious Impression by a considerable Body of Men I am perswaded that they are not in a Capacity to make it and dear Experience has already shewn the Folly of the Attempt. I am Sir your most obedient and humble Servant

RM

MS: Ofcl LbC, DLC.
 1. Duer was the contractor for the Northern Department. His letter had been delivered by William Turnbull, his Philadelphia agent, on July 10 (see Diary of that date) but has not been found.

To Daniel of St. Thomas Jenifer

Office of Finance 23d. July 1782[1]

Sir,

Your Favor of the eighteenth Instant with its Enclosures has been duly received. I shall be not a little disappointed if the extent of your present Supplies be only adequate to transport[2] the Cloathing. I expect and my Necessities require much larger Sums as you cannot but be convinced of. I shall communicate your Proposal respecting the Tobacco to those I think likely to become Purchasers and will most willingly afford you every Assistance in my Power. Your advertisement has been sent to the Printers and will appear in the News papers to Morrow.[3] I am Sir your most obedient Servant

RM

MSS: Ofcl LbC, DLC; LbC, Intendant's Letterbook, MdAA.
   1. Jenifer was Maryland's intendant of the revenue.
   2. This word is underlined in Jenifer's letterbook copy.
   3. See notes to Jenifer to RM, July 18, 1782.

To George Webb

Office of Finance 23. July 1782

Sir

Your Favor dated at Richmond the twelfth Instant with the Enclosures has been duly received.[1] The Picture you present me of your State has a very unpleasing Aspect and I am much grieved to find that the Legislature of Virginia should exhibit a Conduct so very different from what might have been expected; the Necessity of seasonable Supplies must be so obvious to all that the Procrastination used in your State can hardly be ascribed to supineness alone. I hope the Experience which they will acquire by Conviction may not be purchased at too high a Price. You may expect to be furnished with a Newspaper from hence agreeable to your Request. I am Sir your most obedient Servant

RM

MS: Ofcl LbC, DLC.
   1. Letter and enclosures not found. Webb was the receiver of Continental taxes for Virginia.

From Matthew Ridley

Robert Morris Esq.   Amsterdam. July 23d. 1782[1]
Sir

I shall ⟨now⟩[2] certainly leave here in a few days, only waiting for Mr Barclay, who has been here 7 or 8 Months about dispatching the Goods. It is impossible to describe the trouble and difficulties he has in this business and I am afraid he will at last be obliged to leave a part unshipped. The freight is always paid down here. S. Myers has taken some, the freight payable in America to accomodate Mr Barclay but I do not know another that will. *Dr. F.* refuses to let Mr Barclay draw any more on him, from necessity I suppose, but the consequence will most probably be that a part[3] of the Goods must be left. Mr Gillon seems generally blamed about this business.[4]

Peace is Vanishd I think for the present Mr Fox has done himself great honor by his conduct and I have not the least doubt Ld. Shelburne will fully confirm his suspicions of him. Beware of all insiduous offers.

The Loan here goes on slowly though I do not find there is any doubt of its being compleated.[5] *Le Couteulx*[6] *have hinted* ⟨*to me?*⟩[7] *a Wish that this Money might go* through[8] *their hands*—their principal Motive I believe is that it may not[9] appear to the world that only an occasional use was made of them in the last transaction.[10]

The Boys are hearty. I beg my kind respects to Mrs. Morris and all Friends and am respectfully Sir Your most Obedient servant.

The Congress is arrived at L'Orient.

MS: LbC in Ridley's hand, part encoded, Ridley Letterbook, box 5, Ridley Papers, MHi.
1. A Baltimore merchant and friend of RM's, Ridley had gone to Europe in 1781 to purchase supplies and obtain loans for the state of Maryland, taking with him RM's two eldest sons, Robert, Jr., and Thomas, and overseeing their education on the Continent. Since Ridley used ciphers in this manuscript, the editors have italicized passages which he crossed out with diagonal slashes upon substituting the appropriate ciphers interlinearly. Presumably these passages were enciphered in the recipient's copy, which has since disappeared.
Under the dateline Ridley added the following record:
  "1st: per the Recovery Capt Spooner via Baltr.
  2 per the Tammenick Capt Sellers via Phila."
2. Ridley crossed out this word with diagonal slashes, possibly intending to encipher it, but did not substitute the appropriate cipher.
3. Here Ridley scored out what appears to be "must" or "most."
4. On Thomas Barclay's efforts to ship supplies left behind by Alexander Gillon, see Benjamin Franklin to RM, March 4, and notes, and June 25, and notes, and RM to the President of Congress, September 19, 1782, and notes.
5. On the American loan negotiated in Holland, see notes to RM to the President of Congress, July 29.
6. What may be an ampersand here in manuscript was struck out by Ridley but not encoded.
7. Ridley scored out this material.
8. Ridley may have intended to encode this word. He crossed it out with diagonal slashes but did not substitute a cipher.
9. Ridley inserted this word interlinearly.
10. On RM's use of Le Couteulx and Company, see Ridley to RM, June 22, and notes, and RM to Le Couteulx and Company, September 24, 1782, and notes.

To Daniel Clark

Office of Finance 23d. July 1782

Your Letter dated at Richmond the 10th. Instant and one of the 13th. with the Enclosure came duly to hand.[1] Your offers of Service to Mr. Eddy are founded on motives of Politeness which merit my Acknowlegement.

I cannot give you any Advice respecting the prosecution of your Purchases after the Contract with Mr. Coffin is completed. You must be wholly governed therein by the Orders of Mr. Eddy who being acquainted with all

the Circumstances will no doubt pursue every proper measure to enable you
to Complete that Business. Your Drafts on me for the amount of such
Purchases will be duly honored. The feeling Manner in which you describe
the Situation of your Friend Mr. Pollock while it evinces your Zeal for his
Welfare gives me very great Pain. I sincerely wish him Success in all his just
Pursuits.

MS: Ofcl LbC, DLC.
    1. Letters and enclosure not found. Clark was purchasing tobacco in Virginia to
fulfill the terms of RM's contract with George Eddy on behalf of Ebenezer Coffin. See
the Agreement with Eddy, printed under March 13, 1782, and notes.

To Donaldson Yeates

Office of Finance 23 July 1782
    I have received your Letter dated at Elk the seventeenth Instant and am
surprized that any Difficulties should remain respecting the Hire of the
Vessels therein referred to.[1] I expected that those Accounts were all settled
as my Letter to you of the tenth of April last (Copy whereof I now enclose)
expressed my Determination to fulfill the Contracts entered into by Messrs.
Ridley and Pringle on account of the Transport Service. I therefore request
you will finish this Business as soon as possible and shall be Glad to receive
the Estimates you promise me.

MS: Ofcl LbC, DLC.
    1. Letter not found. Yeates was the deputy quartermaster general for Maryland
and Delaware; RM had entrusted him with the task of settling the accounts for
transports employed during the Yorktown campaign.

Diary: July 24, 1782

This Morning His Excellency Genl. Washington called to take
leave being on his Departure for Camp.
    Colo. Trumbull called also respecting an Act of Congress fixing
his Salary whilst settling his late Brothers Accounts.[1] I desired his
Account under that Act may be exhibited to Mr. Milligan.
    The Hon: Colo. Lee called expecting a Committee of Congress
was here but that Committee is to meet next Week. Had some Conversation with this Gentleman respecting Affairs in Virginia when he
communicated part of a Letter from the Governor of that State
mentioning that 1200 Militia are called out to Garrison York and
Gloucester and a Contract made for their Support &c. This intelligence astonished me and I determined instantly to apply to the Secy
at War and have an enquiry made into the necessity or propriety of
such a measure.[2]
    Mr. Hodgdon Commissary of Military Stores producing a Letter
from the Hon. Secretary at War desiring supplies of Money to be
given him to enable the purchase of materials necessary for the
Laboratory at Burlington &c.[3] I granted a Warrant for 160 Dollars.

Commodore Hazelwood again for the money he Solicited. I granted him one thousand Dollars.

Colo Dyer brought me a Letter from Colo. Trumbull relating to the Balance of his late Brothers Accounts. I told him that I should this Day report to Congress and he being a member would have an Opportunity of taking care that Justice is done.[4]

Mr. Vanwagener [Van Wagenen] had the Order for putting his Money on Interest.

Doctr. Campbells Certificates were returned by Mr Milligan with Copies of the Vouchers for Extra Services, and I ordered the Balance of his pay &c on Interest, granting a Warrant for his Extra Services.

I sent for Mr. Hilligas desiring him to produce some Drafts of Genl. Lincoln on the Presidt. of Congress the property of Mr. Izzard[5] which had been deposited with Mr. Hilligas until I could order a Settlement of them. This Gentleman said he had left them with me, but this was not the Case and I insist on his finding them.

Lieut Colo. B. Livingston. I promised to consider his Case, speak to Mr. Milligan and give an Answer.

Mr. Sands[6] applies for Money on Account of the Contractors for the moving Army.

Mr. Pierce Paymaster Genl. for Money to pay Baron Steubens Allowances but on looking into the Acts of Congress relative to the Barons Department of Inspector General Mr Pierce discovered that those which had been referred to in Genl. Lincolns Letter to me are repealed and that in fact there are not any allowances provided for the Inspector Genl. This I represented to the Secretary at War and advised that Baron Steuben being here should make application to Congress.[7]

Mr. Ths. Lloyd Clerk of Mr Hilligas applied to be employed as a Rider his health requiring it. I thought of employing him in the business of the Hessians at Reading[8] and asked if Mr. Hilligas would be his Security, but the latter declined.

1. On May 5, 1779, Congress had appointed Jonathan Trumbull, Jr., to settle the accounts of his deceased brother, Commissary General Joseph Trumbull. See below in this Diary at note 4.

2. Arthur Lee, a Virginia delegate to Congress, was a member of the committee investigating the Office of Finance, but evidently had not learned of the postponement of its sessions (see Diary, July 22). The information he conveyed was from a letter Governor Benjamin Harrison of Virginia had sent to the state's delegates in Congress informing them that, in response to Comte de Rochambeau's request, seconded by George Washington, the state had garrisoned York and Gloucester with about 520 militia. (RM apparently computed the force at 1,200 men by including a reserve of 600 militia held in readiness to reinforce the garrison.) Virginia, Harrison stated, preferred to contract for their supply instead of pursuing "the extravagant mode of feeding them with specific articles furnish'd by the Country." The ration was the same as that for the Continental army but cost the state 10 pence Virginia currency, about 25 percent more than RM's contract for the Moving Army. "This perhaps may be thought high with You but we look on it as moderate," the governor

informed the delegates. "If the Financier does not approve it He may take it on Himself after december at which time the Contract will end."

The object of Harrison's letter was to instruct the Virginia delegates to secure credit for the expense on the Continental specie requisition for 1782. Congress on July 24 assigned the letter to a committee consisting of Ezekiel Cornell of Rhode Island, Joseph Montgomery of Pennsylvania, and Thomas McKean of Delaware, but a meeting with RM planned for the next day failed to materialize. The Superintendent eventually met with Cornell and Montgomery on August 22, at which time he was shown a letter from Secretary at War Benjamin Lincoln saying that both Washington and Rochambeau had told him Yorktown would be evacuated and that in consequence he had ordered the Continental stores there removed; Lincoln said he knew of no compelling reason for maintaining the militia at the garrison. RM told the committee that the expense of the garrison was unnecessary and that he wanted the accounts sent to him as soon as possible so Congress could determine what if any part of the expenses were chargeable to the United States. The committee reported the substance of RM's views to Congress, which adopted them on August 27, and the Financier promptly forwarded Congress's resolutions to Harrison. Harrison to the Virginia Delegates, July 11, and the Virginia Delegates to Harrison, July 23, 1782, Hutchinson and Rutland, eds., *Madison Papers*, IV, 405–406n., 430, 431n.; Lincoln to Cornell, August 22, 1782, PCC, no. 20, II, 283–284; Diary, July 25 and August 22, RM to Cornell and Montgomery, August 22, and to the Governor of Virginia, August 30, and the Governor of Virginia to RM, September 23.

3. Lincoln's letter to Samuel Hodgdon has not been found (see Hodgdon to RM, July 24, and notes). A laboratory was a place where combustible material was manufactured. Burlington, New Jersey, was a center of munitions production.

4. The letter from Lieutenant Colonel Jonathan Trumbull, Jr., has not been found. Eliphalet Dyer (1721–1807) was a Connecticut delegate to Congress, 1774–1779 and 1780–1783. *Biog. Dir. Cong.*

5. The reference is probably to drafts issued by Major General Benjamin Lincoln during the siege of Charleston in 1780 (see Diary, July 25, 1781, and notes). Ralph Izard was a delegate to Congress from South Carolina.

6. Richardson Sands.

7. The absence of any authorization for travel and other expenses of the inspector general of the Continental army, Baron von Steuben, was the result of an oversight by Congress. On January 10, 1782, Congress had passed an act reorganizing the office of the inspector general and repealing all previous legislation related to his department. Although this act provided for the pay of his subordinates, it failed to provide any pay for the inspector general himself. Secretary at War Benjamin Lincoln reported this omission to Congress on July 25, and the following day Congress authorized Steuben to draw $80 per month in expenses in addition to his regular pay as a major general. The letter from Secretary Lincoln to RM on this subject has not been found. For a previous request for money for Steuben, see George Washington to RM, March 4, 1782, and notes.

8. On this business, see the Instructions of RM and Benjamin Lincoln on the Liberation of German Prisoners, July 11, 1782, and notes.

Hints on Tax Notes from the Quartermaster General (Timothy Pickering)

[Philadelphia, July 24, 1782]

To the Honble. R. Morris Esqr. Superintt. of Finance, the following hints relative to an emission of *tax-notes*, were presented July 24th 1782, at Philadelphia.[1]

It is the universal cry—That the people have not cash to pay their taxes: But That they have the produce of the soil in abundance, and would cheerfully part with it in discharge of their taxes.

If these positions are true, and I believe they are, may there not be an emission of bills of a tenour like the following, with great advantage to the public?

This Bill shall be accepted at the treasury of the United States, and by any receiver of the Continental taxes, as an equivalent for ten specie dollars, in payment of the tax of eight millions of dollars demanded by Congress, by their act of the   day of 1781.[2]

Notes of the above tenour would be received by the people as Cash, at least to the amount of their several quotas of the tax.

Being grounded on the present tax, they could not fail of redemption by the payment of it: of consequence a depreciation is scarcely to be apprehended: especially as

One tenth part of the tax issued in such notes might answer the wished for purpose, that of relieving the public from its present embarrassments for want of cash: Or

Should cash afterwards remain scarce, either the same notes, or another set in the like form, might be emitted.

Such notes, I have no doubt, would readily be taken by most of the people to whom I am under engagements, in the states where the Continental tax is assessed. I think that Colo. Hatch might with such notes discharge the heavy debt lying against him for the hire of the ox-teams provided in Massachusetts for the last campaign, to the satisfaction of the parties.[3] Mr. Pomeroy in Connecticut paid the hire of the teams he procured, with pay-table notes, dollar for dollar; altho' such quantities had been emitted as to equal or exceed (as he informed me) the amount of the tax for calling them in; which finally occasioned a depreciation of a hundred per cent.

To prevent any loss to the public, every person intrusted with the disposal of such notes, might be made answerable that he paid them away only at cash prices. If any of the present creditors refused to accept them at that rate, such could only remain, as they now do, unpaid; and if any persons, whose services, goods or produce shall be wanted by the public, refuse to furnish either on such payment— still we shall, in such cases, be in no worse condition than we now are: On the other hand, if the collectors are importunate, multitudes will very gladly receive as cash what will answer as well in payment of their taxes; and thus we may obtain considerable supplies. On this ground the assembly of New-York might be induced to assess the tax which they have hitherto neglected, because, they say, they are unable to pay it.

MS: LbC, WDC, DNA.
1. See Diary, July 23, for an expression of RM's doubts about Pickering's plan. There is no evidence that RM approved it; but see RM's Circular to the Receivers of Continental Taxes, August 29, and notes.

2. Spaces left blank in manuscript. On the specie requisition for 1782, adopted on October 30 and apportioned among the states on November 2, 1781, see RM to the President of Congress, November 5, 1781, and notes.
    3. See the Quartermaster General to RM, October 17, and notes.

From Samuel Hodgdon

Philada. July 24 1782[1]

Inclosed you have an estimate for the articles mentioned in the last Indent from Burlington which are those particularly refer'd to by Colo Lamb in his Letter to the Secretary at War.[2] The estimate handed you to day is a previous one which remains to be furnish'd and is of equal importance.[3]

MS: LbC, WDC, DNA.
    1. Hodgdon was the commissary general of military stores.
    2. A copy of the "Estimate for sundry Articles wanted for the use of the Artificers and Laboratory at Burlington," totaling £59.8.8, dated Philadelphia, July 24, 1782, addressed to the Superintendent of Finance and notated as "delivered the 24th July and paid the same day," is in WDC, no. 148, p. 42. The articles were requested in a letter of John Lamb, colonel of the 2d Continental Artillery Regiment stationed at Burlington, New Jersey, to Secretary at War Benjamin Lincoln, July 19, 1782, Lamb Letterbook, NHi. See Diary, July 24.
    3. This estimate has not been identified.

From Samuel Nicholson

Extract of a Letter from Samuel Nicholson Esquire dated Boston July 24. 1782[1]

I beg leave to represent to you my ordering Lieut. Knies under an Arrest for neglect of Duty in contemptiously treating Lieutenant Benja. Page the Deans first Lieutenant and myself both his Superior Officers. Some time last Month I was going on Board the Deane in one of the Ship's Boats and was seen by Mr. Knies who was then commanding Officer on Board and sitting close to one of the Cabin Ports smoking his Pipe. He did look out of the Port and we saw each other. I came along side and entered the Ship without any one to give me a Rope, man the Side, or take the least Notice of me. I cannot say but I was much hurt, as I never experienced such Treatment before but passed it over. Soon after Mr. Page 1st. Lieutenant of the Ship received the same Treatment of the same Officer and on his informing me of it, I thought it my Duty to put him under an Arrest as he had some Time before requested.

MS: AM LbC, MdAN.
    1. This communication from Captain Nicholson, commander of the Continental frigate *Deane*, recently renamed the *Hague*, was annexed to RM's Warrant Appointing a Court-Martial for the Trial of Michael Knies, August 14. For earlier charges brought by Knies, see RM's Warrant Appointing a Court of Inquiry on Samuel Nicholson, June 26, 1782.

Diary: July 25, 1782

Mr Geo Eddy came to shew me a Letter from Daniel Clarke Esqr. and told me that he doubted being able to pay his note given to me for the Cost of Tobacco on the Day it may become due and desired me to procure him another discount in which I am ready to assist him but desired him to apply to the Directors himself.[1]

Mr. Jacob Bright applied respecting some Claims he has upon Colo. Blaine.[2] I told him that Colo. Blaine must settle his own Affairs.

Mr. Nichs. Low[3] applied about Bills of Exchange and I referred him to Haym Solomon the Broker being myself too much engaged.

Mr. R. Sands presses me very much for Money alledging that Colo. Lowrey is here and must have upwards of 2,000 Dollars to pay for Transportation &c. I sent for Mr. Lowrey and gave him a Draft on Mr. Swanwick for 1500 Dollars and a Warrant for 700 Dollars.[4]

This Morning agreeable to the request of the Hon: Mr Cornell I went to the State House at nine OClock to meet a Committee of which he is Chairman on the Virginia Militia Business.[5] I met Mr Cornell and the Secy at War and staid there until ten OClock and the other Members of the Committee not appearing, I declared in presence of several Members of Congress that I could not spend my time in waiting there and that if Gentlemen will not keep their Appointments they must excuse me and with this declaration I came away. Soon after my return to the Office the Honorable Mr. McKeane came there and told me that he was one of the Members of that Committee and that he had been detained by Calls to transact business as Chief Justice of this State. Mr McKean left with me the Acts of the several Legislatures for granting an Impost of 5 per Cent and the Draft of an Ordinance for carrying the Same into Execution requesting me to consider the Same.[6] We had conversation on other matters of public Business.

Majr. Jackson called and requested me to return him the papers he had a few days delivered to me respecting Commodore Gillon which I did on his promise to replace them with me immediately.[7]

Tench Francis Esqr. came after money for Thos. Lowrey Esqr. which I settled as already mentioned. I consulted Mr. Francis respecting farther advances to be made to me by the Bank.[8]

Mr. Dessaussure called for his Commission. &c.[9]

Colo. Livingston called again respecting his Claim on which I sent for Mr. Milligan who shews me that this Gentleman is referred to the State to which he belongs for Depriciation.

Wrote a Letter to Eleazer McComb Esqr.
Wrote a Letter to the Hon. Secy. at War.
Wrote a Letter to Alexr. Stewart Esqr.[10]
Wrote a Letter to Capt. Vanheer [von Heer].
Wrote a Letter to the Revd. Doctr Wm Gordon.
Wrote a Letter to John Moylan Esqr.
Wrote an Estimate of Expences of Office of Finance for 1783.[11]
Wrote a Letter to Willm. C. Houston Esqr.

Wrote a Report to Congress concerning Musco Livingstons Family.

1. On the note given to RM by George Eddy and discounted at the Bank of North America, see Diary, July 10, 1782, and notes. The letter from Daniel Clark, who was purchasing tobacco for RM in Virginia, has not been found.

2. Jacob Bright (1729–1802) of Philadelphia, holder of a number of civil and military offices in the city, including inspector of flour for Philadelphia city and county, was described as a "biscuit baker" in the Philadelphia directory of 1785. W. A. Newman Dorland, "The Second Troop Philadelphia City Cavalry," *PMHB*, LIV (1930), 184–185; Francis White, comp., *The Philadelphia Directory* . . . (Philadelphia, 1785).

3. Nicholas Low (1739–1826) was a prominent Whig merchant of New York; he held one share in the Bank of North America. Low later became a director and the largest investor in the Bank of New York and a director of the first Bank of the United States. *DAB;* East, *Business Enterprise,* 183, 293, 294, 298; Lawrence Lewis, Jr., *A History of the Bank of North America, the First Bank Chartered in the United States* (Philadelphia, 1882), 134.

4. Richardson Sands and Thomas Lowrey were two of the contractors for the Moving Army. Concerning the draft on John Swanwick, see RM to William Churchill Houston, July 25, and notes.

5. On this committee and its work, see Diary, July 24, and notes.

6. The draft ordinance for collecting the impost is printed in appendix I to this volume; see the notes thereto for Thomas McKean's involvement and the current standing of the impost in the states.

7. See Diary, June 19, 1782, and notes.

8. Tench Francis, another contractor for the Moving Army, was also cashier of the Bank of North America.

9. Daniel De Saussure had been appointed commissioner for settling the accounts of Maryland.

10. Letter not found. On Stewart, see Diary, July 23, and notes.

11. This document, signed by James McCall, RM's secretary in the Office of Finance, is printed as an enclosure to RM to the President of Congress, July 30.

Report to Congress on the Case of Musco Livingston

[Office of Finance, July 25, 1782][1]

The Agent of Marine to whom was referred the Report of the Secretary at War on the Memorial of Musco Livingston begs Leave to report.[2]

That the United States have taken sundry measures to cut off all commercial Intercourse with Great Britain.

That there is Reason to believe that this has been attended with the salutary Effect of influencing in their Favor the Opinions of commercial Powers.

That it might therefore be imprudent to countenance by any means the Importation of British goods.

That Property can at all Times be changed and carried from one Country to another by the means of Bills of Exchange altho' not perhaps with so great Advantage as by the safe Transportation of Produce.

That such superior Advantage from the safe Transportation of british Produce would naturally raise disagreeable Emotions in those who encounter great Risque in carrying on their lawful Commerce.

The following Resolution therefore is submitted.

That the Agent of Marine be directed to grant Letters of Passport and safe Conduct to such Vessel as may be employed by Musco Livingston to sail from some Port of the United States in Ballast to the Island of Jamaica, and to bring from thence the Family and Effects of the said Musco Livingston Provided that Nothing in such Passport contained, shall authorize the Importation into these United States, or any of them, of any Goods, Wares, or Merchandizes ⟨the Growth, Produce or Manufacture of any Place under the Dominion of the King or Kingdom of Great Britain⟩ excepting money, plate, Household furniture and wearing apparel for the use of his family.[3]

Robt Morris

ENDORSED: 204/report of the Supr. of/Finance as Agent of/Marine on the case of/ Musco Livingston
MSS: DS, PCC, DNA; Ofcl LbC, DLC.

1. The DS is undated; the date has been supplied from the Ofcl LbC.

2. Musco Livingston, who appears to have been a relative of Governor William Livingston of New Jersey, had left Jamaica in 1776 to support the American cause, and served as a naval lieutenant aboard the Continental frigate *Boston* under a commission granted to him in 1778 by Benjamin Franklin. Congress, however, refused him a permanent commission. In August 1781 Livingston asked Congress for a passport to bring his family from Jamaica; on August 23 Congress authorized the Board of War to issue the passports on whatever terms it deemed appropriate. This evidently was not done, however, for the request was renewed the following year in a memorial on Livingston's behalf by the Philadelphia business firm of Stewart and Totten. Congress referred the memorial, which has not been found, to Secretary at War Benjamin Lincoln; his report of July 11, 1782, recommended that the Agent of Marine was the one who should grant the passports. A resolution apparently was also introduced authorizing the Agent of Marine to issue the passports for Livingston to bring "his family and effects" to the United States and to require Livingston to post bond that he would not engage in illicit trade with the enemy, which Congress at this time was endeavoring to suppress. Congress referred Lincoln's report to RM as Agent of Marine on July 11, but the following day reconsidered the resolution. Perhaps mindful of Congress's concern with clandestine commerce and the abuse of passports, RM in the present report recommended that Livingston be prohibited from bringing any goods of the British Empire into the United States. Adopting the report on July 25, Congress authorized the Agent of Marine to issue the passports but allowed Livingston to bring in specified personal effects without regard to country of origin (see the following note); Livingston, however, was required to "give bond with sufficient sureties, to be lodged in the office of finance, in such a sum as the Superintendant of Finance shall think proper, not to contravene in any respect the true intent and meaning of this resolution." *JCC*, XIV, 1008, XV, 1075, XX, 727, 755–756, 769–770, XXI, 893, 906; Paullin, *Navy of the American Revolution*, 119; Edwin Brockholst Livingston, *The Livingstons of Livingston Manor* (New York, 1910), 537–538; Musco Livingston to the President of Congress, August 22, 1781, PCC, no. 78, XIV, 485–488; and Diary, July 23, August 7 and 8. On Congress's efforts to suppress illicit trade, see notes to Gouverneur Morris to Thomas Willing, July 18, 1782.

3. The passage in angle brackets was crossed out and the 14 words that follow it were substituted by an unidentified hand while RM's report was under consideration by Congress (see the preceding note). In the Ofcl LbC the excised passage remains intact as the concluding words of the report.

To the Clothier General (John Moylan)

Office of Finance 25th. July 1782

Your several Letters requesting money to enable a punctual complyance with Engagements made on behalf of the Public I have received.[1] The Contents are painfull to me because I cannot gratify your's and my own Wishes by Compliance. My Inclination will induce me to releive you as soon as it is in my Power and I must request that you do not enter into any other Contracts or Engagements without first obtaining my Consent.

MS: Ofcl LbC, DLC.
1. Letters not found.

To William Gordon

Philada. 25. July 1782

In Consequence of your Letter of the nineteenth June[1] I sent for Mr. Dudley, told him the Information you had so kindly given to me and assured him of my Desire to make him easy and happy. The Business in which he is intended to be employed is like many other important matters retarded by the tediousness of the States in supplying the Continental Treasury.

The Honble. Secretary at War has commenced a Correspondence with General Gates at my Request which I think will produce what he wishes. Be assured that I take particular Pleasure in promoting the Interest and Happiness of worthy Men and that I am with great Esteem Sir Your most obedient and humble Servant

MSS: Ofcl LbC, DLC; Bancroft transcript, NN; transcript, Robert Morris Collection, CSmH.
1. Letter not found. Gordon, a congregational minister of Roxbury, Massachusetts, had previously befriended Benjamin Dudley, a metallurgist who was involved in RM's preparations to establish a mint; Gordon had long been a friend of Major General Horatio Gates, whose correspondence with Secretary at War Benjamin Lincoln is discussed in the notes to RM to Gates, May 31, 1782.

To Bartholomew von Heer

Office of Finance 25. July 1782

I have received yours of the tenth and twenty fourth Instant[1] and I have directed the Payment of forty Pounds to enable you to march to Camp. This however I could not do without distressing other Parts of the Public service. Such is my Situation. I must therefore postpone for the present a Compliance with the other Estimates for your Corps.

MS: Ofcl LbC, DLC.
1. Letters not found. Captain von Heer was the commander of the provost or *maréchaussée* corps of light dragoons.

To William Churchill Houston

Office of Finance Phila: July 25th. 1782[1]

These Lines are to inform you I have this day drawn a Bill of Exchange at Twenty days sight on Mr. John Swanwick for Fifteen Hundred Dollars in favor of Thomas Lowrey Esquire or Order. He will indorse the same to you, and I beg you will advance the Money for it transmitting afterwards this Bill to the Continental Treasurer who will receive the Money from Mr. Swanwick for it and credit you accordingly.

MSS: LS, Houston Collection, NjP; Ofcl LbC, DLC.
    1. Houston was the receiver of Continental taxes for New Jersey. According to his endorsement on the LS, Houston received it on July 26; he replied on July 27.

To Eleazer McComb

Office of Finance 25 July 1782
    I have received your Letter dated at Dover on the fifth Instant.[1] A Commissioner has already been appointed to Settle the Accounts of the State of Maryland with the United States who will shortly repair thither for that Purpose. The Commissioners for settling the Accounts of the several States must expect to go into each County of the State they are appointed to, as Circumstances may require for expediting the Business. Those also who may be appointed to adjust the Accounts of the several Departments of Quarter Master, Commissary and Clothier General with those of the Hospital and Marine must likewise expect to Travel into each State where Business has been Transacted relative to their respective Departments. If under this Discription you are willing to Accept any of the Appointments that are yet open I will with pleasure put you in the nomination. Your Character for Abilities and Integrity being such as to Justifie my Expectations that the Public will be benefited by your Services.

MS: Ofcl LbC, DLC.
    1. Letter not found. McComb, Delaware state auditor of accounts, was seeking appointment as a commissioner for settling Continental accounts. See RM to McComb, June 15, 1782, and notes.

To the Secretary at War
(Benjamin Lincoln)

Office of Finance 25th. July 1782
    I enclose you the Copies of two Certificates filed in the Treasury Office as also of a Certificate from the Comptroller of three hundred and sixty Dollars in Favor of Doctor Campbell for extra Services.[1] By the Director's Certificate[2] it appears that it was not *convenient or practicable* to releive Doctr. Campbell by any of the Surgeons who on the Arrangement of the first of Feby. were retained in Service.[3] The Inconvenience is not a very good Reason why the Public should unnecessarily be put to Expence but the Impracticability if it existed is convincing. I have not however heard either that the Army was very sickly at that Period or the Surgeons of it *on Duty* at distant Posts. It becomes therefore my Duty Sir to lay these Things officially before you.

MS: Ofcl LbC, DLC.
    1. Enclosures not found. On Dr. George W. Campbell's claims, see Diary, May 8, 1782, and notes.
    2. Presumably that of Dr. John Cochran, director general of military hospitals.
    3. The reduction in the Hospital Department that took effect on February 1, 1782, had been ordered by Congress in an act of January 3, 1782.

Diary: July 26, 1782

Haym Solomon respecting Exchange. My Anxiety to provide for the regular discharge of the Paymaster General's Notes which fall due the first of August[1] occasions very frequent Consultations on this Subject because I wish to preserve the Exchange tho I am in great want of the Money. On the same Subject I have many Consultations with Mr Swanwick and indeed my time is principally Consumed in forming Contrivances to pay some Debts and to parry the payment of what I cannot accomplish.

Mr Abner Nash and Mr. Wm. Wayne present me for Acceptance Drafts of Genl. Greene which must be paid if possible but which I am afraid to Accept.[2]

Lieut. Jno. Brown who had the care of the Prison Ship at Boston applied to know how his Arrearages are to be paid to him.[3] I replyed that he could not reasonably expect payment from the United States whilst the State of Massachusetts to which he belongs witholds both Revennue and Taxation. He asked for a Continuance in his Employment and I referred him to the Secretary at War.

The Reverend Mr. Keith late Chaplain to the Frigate Confederacy applied for the Settlements of his Accounts and for Pay. I told him that a Commissioner will soon be appointed to Settle all the Accounts of the Navy[4] and as to pay he and others must preach Taxation into practice before payment can be made.

Mr. Nichs. White[5] for Money for the Quarter Masters Department which I cannot grant.

Colo. Blaine and Mr. Wm. Wilson for Money for the Contractors at Fort Pitt. I granted them a Warrant for £800.

Mr. Jesse Browne for orders.[6] I directed him to be ready the beginning of the Week.

I sent for Doctor Binney[7] respecting his engagements for money borrowed to the Use of the Hospital and promised him releif in a short time.

Honble. and Revd. Doctr Witherspoon called to inform me of a Committee appointed to Consider respecting the Interest of Loan Office Certificates. I desired the Committee might not proceed until I report on that Subject, Mr. G. Morris being now employed in drawing that Report.[8]

Majr. Butler called for the Money due on Mr. Mumfords Bill accepted by Mr. Pennell.[9] Mr. Pennell is out of Town and Mr Butler disatisfied that the money shall be paid on Monday next.

Doctor Brownson respecting Estimates for the Southern Army. I did not see him but sent him word those Estimates were not come from the War Office and when they did come I have not money to execute them.[10]

Monsr. La Caze applied for some of the Canon at the Head of Elk on behalf of his Friends at Baltimore but not knowing how many or which they wanted he deposited with Mr. Swanwick his Draft on the Bank for 2,500 Dollars and I gave him an Order to Donaldson Yates Esqr. for Cannon to that Amount.[11]

Colo. Pickering for Money which he cannot have.[12]

Colo. Livingston for his Depreciation for which I referred him to his State.

Mr. Jno. Mease with Account of Contingent Expences of the Lottery &c.

Wrote a Letter to Donaldson Yeates Esqr.

Wrote a Letter to Joseph Nourse Esqr.[13]

1. The notes of Paymaster General John Pierce had been issued to Continental army officers for two months' pay. See RM to George Washington, January 26, 1782 (second letter), and notes.

2. See Nathanael Greene to RM, January 27, 1782. Abner Nash (ca. 1740–1786), governor of North Carolina in 1780–1781, was elected as a delegate to Congress on May 13, 1782, but did not attend sessions until November (*DAB;* Burnett, ed., *Letters,* VI, xlix). Wayne cannot be identified with certainty, but he may have been a Philadelphia Quaker and at some time a member of the Pennsylvania Society for the Abolition of Slavery. See the references in PCC, no. 53, p. 85; and *PMHB,* LXVIII (1944), 290.

3. John Brown was a lieutenant in the Continental navy (Paullin, *Navy of the American Revolution,* 508). For the prison ship at Boston, see Diary, April 19, 1782, and notes.

4. The appointment of Joseph Pennell to settle the accounts of the Marine Department was not made until June 1783. See notes to RM to the President of Congress, February 18, 1782.

5. Nicholas White was a clerk to Samuel Miles, deputy quartermaster general for Pennsylvania.

6. Brown was an express rider to the northern states for the Office of Finance.

7. Barnabas Binney (ca. 1751–1787) of Massachusetts, who had served in the Continental Hospital Department since 1776, chiefly in the Middle Department, had been elected hospital physician and surgeon by Congress on October 7, 1780. Heitman, *Register;* Philip Cash, *Medical Men at the Siege of Boston, April, 1775–April, 1776: Problems of the Massachusetts and Continental Armies* (Philadelphia, 1973), 160.

8. John Witherspoon, a New Jersey delegate to Congress, had previously served on a committee appointed to consider the question of stopping the payment of interest on loan office certificates in bills of exchange. For this committee's report and the Superintendent's response, see notes to RM's Report to Congress on the Continental Loan Offices, June 13, 1782. The committee alluded to by Witherspoon was very likely the grand committee Congress appointed on July 22 "to take into consideration and report the most effectual means of supporting the credit of the United States." For the report being drafted by Gouverneur Morris and a discussion of its authorship, see the headnote and notes to RM to the President of Congress, July 29.

9. Joseph Pennell was paymaster of the Marine Department. Thomas Mumford had been furnishing supplies for the *Alliance.* For his draft on Pierce Butler (1744–1822), a prominent legislator, planter, and militia officer of South Carolina, see RM to Mumford, July 12, 1782; on Butler, see *DAB,* and Heitman, *Register.*

10. Nathan Brownson, former governor of Georgia, was the deputy purveyor of military hospitals in the Southern Department. See Diary, July 29.

11. On the purchase of surplus cannon by Lacaze and Mallet, see RM to Donaldson Yeates, July 26, and notes, Diary, August 14 and 28; and on the sale of cannon, RM to Yeates, March 4, 1782.

12. See the Quartermaster General to RM, July 26, and notes.

13. This letter was written by James McCall.

To Bartholomew Booth

Philadelphia July 26th 1782[1]

I take the liberty to introduce to your Acquaintance and Civilities John Vaughan Esqr the Son of a Friend of mine in London. You will find him an agreable and Worthy young Gentleman. He will call upon you in consequence of my having informed him that you wish to sell some Lands. As his Father has commissioned him with my approbation to make some purchases, at present he goes to look about him and when he makes his Choice I shall assist him in making the bargain and the payment.

I heard from my two Boys in May last. They are detained in France on Account of the troubles in Geneva and I am Rather fearfull that they may loose some Valuable time. They always will retain an Affection for you and your Family, and that Circumstance with others, has fixed in me the most respectfull attachment and esteem.

MS: Copy, Robert Morris Papers, NN.

1. This letter was addressed to the Reverend Booth at the "Forest of Needwood" in Frederick County, Maryland, where the Episcopal clergyman operated a school previously attended by RM's two eldest sons, Robert, Jr., and Thomas, who had gone to Europe late in 1781 with Matthew Ridley. On the subject of this and the following three letters, see RM to Charles Lee, July 26, and notes.

To William Byrd

Philadelphia July 26th 1782[1]

My attention is perpetually called to Objects of a Public Nature, which does not permit me to regard those private Concerns that relate[2] even to my own Interest. General Lee asked my assistence when I had not the means of complying with his Wishes altho the inclination was good. A Gentleman is gone to View his Estate and if he becomes a purchaser the General will be enabled to pay any money he owes immediately.

MS: Copy, Levis Collection, PHi.

1. This letter is addressed to "Wm. Bird Esqr" and was in reply to one received by RM but not found. Which of the William Byrds was a creditor of Charles Lee, however, cannot be said with certainty. See Alden, *Charles Lee*, 294, 296; and RM to Lee, July 26, and notes.

2. Here RM struck out the word "regard" and added in his own hand the words "relate" and "to."

To Horatio Gates

Philada. July 26th. 1782[1]

You will receive this from John Vaughan Esqr. a Young Gentleman recommended to my attention by his Father Saml. Vaughan Esqr of London an old Friend and Correspondant before the Revolution and likely to become so again. Mr. Vaughan is Commissioned by His Father to purchase Lands with my approbation. I have advised him to Visit Genl Lee's Estate, examine into its Value, situation &c and if he approves it is probable the purchase will be made as I think Lee is disposed to sell reasonably.

I remember you expressed a wish to sell your place, if so, shew it to Mr Vaughan, let him see its good and bad properties, name a moderate price and it may suit him to buy both. He is not yet ready to make payment but soon will be and whatever engagements he makes with my approbation I will engage for. Assist him also in respect to Genl Lee's Estate or any other he may see or hear of.

Genl. Lincoln promised me that he would open a Correspondance with you in Order to extricate you from the disagreable part of your Situation as an officer. He is a Worthy Man and I depend on his promise. My Compliments to Mrs. Gates and believe me Dear Sir Your Sincere Friend and Obedient Servant

MSS: ALS, Gates Papers, NHi; copy, Levis Collection, PHi.
1. For the background to this letter to Major General Gates of Berkeley County, Virginia, see notes to RM to Charles Lee, July 26; and RM to Gates, May 31, 1782, and notes.

To Charles Lee

Philada July 26th 1782[1]

You have drawn on me for money when I had none and called on me to make remittances for you when it was out of my Power and altho it was necessary to tell you so, I could not spare time to do it.

I contrived however to pay the bills you drew, but the remittance[2] to Mr Bird is not made yet, he has written to me but I have not replyed.[3] I am fond of serving my acquaintances and Friends when in my power but my Money is already gone into other hands and I cannot command it. Perhaps however I may now serve you effectually. This letter will be delivered to you by Mr John Vaughan a young Gentleman from England Son of Saml. Vaughan Esqr. of London, a very deserving young man to whom I pray your attention and Civilities. His Father has Commissioned him to purchase some Land with my approbation, I recommend to buy yours, he goes down to see it and to enquire into its value, pray shew him every thing good and bad. You are a Man of Honor and will not deceive him. If he like the purchase I think you had best come up with him. He is not yet Possessed of the means of making payment, but soon will be. On this point he will explain himself and in the mean time I may probably find the ways and means of advancing or procuring what may be absolutely necessary for you to Receive, But you must think of a moderate price. I am bound by *Confidence* to assist him and at the same time I desire to serve you being Dear Sir Your Obedient humble Servant

MS: Copy, Levis Collection, PHi.
1. This and the preceding three letters derive from RM's involvement as an intermediary in the sale of former Major General Lee's Prato Rio estate in Berkeley County, Virginia (for the background, see Benjamin Franklin to RM, January 19, and notes, and RM to William and Mary Katherine Goddard, March 4, 1782, and notes). Lee had written to RM on July 20.
2. The copyist originally made this word plural; he then tried to erase the *s* but did so imperfectly.
3. William Byrd's letter has not been found; RM's reply is dated July 26.

James McCall to the Register of the Treasury
(Joseph Nourse)

Office of Finance 26. July 1782[1]

Inclosed are Returns for the Months of May and June last from Joseph Borden Esqr. Commr. L[oan] O[ffice] for the State of New Jersey of Interest paid in Bills of Exchange on France, also on Account of the ⅟₁₀ of Money Emitted pursuant to Act of Congress of the 18th. March 1780. Likewise the Emission of Money made pursuant to Act of Congress of the same Date as before mentioned ⁹⁄₁₀ whereof to the Account of the State and ⅟₁₀ for the use of the United States, issuable at the Rate of one for twenty of the Old Emissions when brought in to be destroyed.

MS: Ofcl LbC, DLC.
1. McCall was RM's secretary in the Office of Finance. None of the enclosures to this letter have been found.

To Donaldson Yeates

Office of Finance 26th July 1782[1]

I am to request that you will deliver to the Order of Messrs Lacaze and Mallet any number of Cannon which were landed at the Head of Elk by General Knox not exceeding in Value[2] the Sum of two thousand five hundred Dollars agreeable to the Prices published, that amount being already deposited, and transmit me the Receipt of the Person or Persons who may make Choice of them.[3]

MSS: LS, Manuscript File, WDC, DNA; Ofcl LbC, DLC.
1. Yeates was the deputy quartermaster general for Maryland and Delaware stationed at the Head of Elk.
2. RM inserted the preceding two words interlinearly in his own hand.
3. The LS is filed with a letter from Lacaze and Mallet to Yeates, dated Philadelphia, July 26, 1782, directing him "to deliver the Cannon, agreeable to the annex'd order of Robt. Morris Esqr., to the Order of Messrs. Zollickoffer and Messonier of Baltimore"; a letter from Zollickoffer and Messonnier to Yeates, dated Head of Elk, Maryland, August 7, 1782, directing Yeates "to deliver to Captn. James Simpson of the Head of Elk Packett Two Cannon Six Pounders on Account of Messrs. Lacase and Mallets order within mentioned"; and Simpson's receipt to Yeates of August 10, 1782. See Manuscript File, no. 26952, WDC; and Diary, July 26.

From the Quartermaster General
(Timothy Pickering)

[Philadelphia] July 26. 1782

I have received from the Secy. at War the inclosed estimate (transmitted to him from Lancaster by Genl. Hazen) of the expence of fitting up a public stable at Lancaster to cover the guard over the prisoners which are there confined. The estimate was sent me in a letter from the Secretary at War, of which the inclosed is an extract. I shall wait on you for your answer on this subject.[1]

MS: LbC, WDC, DNA.
1. For a copy of "An Estimate of the expence of repairing and fitting up of a public stable at Lancaster, to cover the guard over the prisoners there," prepared by "John Moore bricklayer" and totalling £289.12.6, see WDC, no. 103, p. 126. According to a note Pickering wrote at the bottom of the copy, "Genl. Hazen thought the estimate very

extravagant, and that half the sum would do, if it could be now advanced." The covering letter Pickering received from Secretary at War Benjamin Lincoln has not been found. RM evidently rejected Pickering's request; see Diary, July 26.

Diary: July 27, 1782

Mr. Jesse Brown, I desired him to be ready for departure the beginning of next week.

This Day I proposed to Major Clarkson and Colo. Smith that they should go, one to Reading and the other to Frederick Town to Transact the Business of the Hessian Prisoners which they declined.[1]

I then Sent Colo. James Read[2] to Reading on that business after Consulting the Hon: Secy at War on the Subject and desiring him to order in all Prisoners. I also Consulted Tench Francis Esqr. on this business as I want the Bank to make me advances on this Fund.[3]

Issued a Warrant on Mr Swanwick in favor of Jos. Pennell £507.11.11.

1. On the desire of Matthew Clarkson and William Stephens Smith to seek "Glory at the Post of Danger," see Diary, July 3, 1782, and notes.
2. Read was RM's secretary in the Marine Office.
3. On the recall of prisoners who had been allowed to work out and the effort to recruit and indenture German prisoners, see Diary, May 1, and notes, and Instructions of RM and Benjamin Lincoln on the Liberation of German Prisoners, July 11, 1782, and notes. By consulting with Francis, the cashier of the Bank of North America, RM evidently was trying to borrow money on the security of funds to be raised from the fee of $80 required for the "liberation" of each German prisoner.

From William Churchill Houston

Trenton [New Jersey] 27 July 1782[1]

By Post I have yours of 19 instant, circular; and that of 22; and Yesterday that of 25 was handed me by Mr Lowrey, who also presented your Bill on Mr Swanwick of the same Date for fifteen Hundred Dollars, payable at twenty Days. I ventured to pay the whole Sum instantly, for two reasons. One, that I have still a few Hundred Dollars in Hand for an Exigency or to answer Persons calling with Notes; the other, that Mr Lowrey tells me a great Part of this money is due to Waggoners and others on the Communication to the Army, who want Cash to pay their Taxes. It will therefore probably return to us shortly.

1782 Dr   The receipt of Continental Taxes for the State of New-Jersey
          from July 20 to 27 inclusive
          To Cash received from the State Treasurer seven Hundred
          Dollars   Dlls 700

MS: ADft with subjoined ADftS return, Houston Collection, NjP.
1. Houston was the receiver of Continental taxes for New Jersey.

Diary: July 29, 1782

Capt. McPherson called to offer his Service as a Broker.[1] I told him I had already engaged with one who hithertoo has served me well. He proceeded to give me some Anecdotes against Solomon[2] but being in haste I begged to be excused, observing that if Solomon misbehaved he would loose his employers and those who Conduct well will get them.

Haym Solomon came and proposed a Sale of Bills to the Providore of the French Hospital alledging that he has frequently sold him Bills on Credit and that his engagements have allways been punctually complied with, and after Consulting with Mr. G. Morris I agreed to supply him with the Bills wanted.[3]

Genl. Lincoln having granted a Warrant on the Paymaster General to Baron Steuben and the latter not being able to proceed on his Duty without Money I granted the Paymaster General a Warrant for 500 Dollars. Also a Warrant for 150 Dollars to Mr. Jesse Brown who cannot perform his Journey without it.

Mr. Ebenezer Cowell and others who have worked for the Commissary Genl. of Military [Stores] apply most pressingly for money. I told them it is not in my power to supply Mr. Hodgdon at present but that it shall be done soon as possible, desired to have a List of their Names and the Sums due to them which was sent me by Mr Hodgdon.[4]

Doctr. Brownson for money for the use of the Hospital in the Southern Department. I told him the impossibility of supplying it. He asked when he might expect it. My Answer was that I do not know, that having been so much deceived myself I will not deceive others with expectations but will supply him when in my power.

Henry Hill Esquire called at my request respecting the Money due upon Bills of Exchange.[5] I find he has not yet received it and he seems very unwilling to give me his Note altho I pressed very much for it to lodge in the Bank. He said he will call again within 24 hours.

Mr. D. C. Claypole[6] for Money of which I promised the payment shall not be long delayed.

Mr. Geo. Eddy, I shewed him Mr Clarkes Letters respecting the Tobacco, informed him that the Bills come fast on me for the Money. He says he is disappointed of Money and wishes to be permitted to go into New York for it.[7]

Mr. Thoms. Bradford brought me the papers of a Flag of Truce from Bermuda. I desired him to manage the business as heretofore until the Appointment of a Commissary of Prisoners can take place.[8]

This Day Capt. Lyons[9] called and informed me of the arrival of Monsr. Vadreuil with thirteen Sail of the Line and three Frigates on this Coast.[10]

Wrote a Letter to the Governors of the Different States.

Wrote a Letter to shew the Effects of yearly Loan of 10 pounds at 6 per Cent.[11]

Wrote a Letter to Genl. Smallwood.

Wrote a Letter to Jos. Nourse Esqr.[12]

Wrote a Letter to His Excelly. the Govr. of Maryland.

Wrote a Letter to John Lyon Esqr.

Wrote a Letter to Geo. Olney.

Issued a Warrant on Mr Swanwick in favor of Jos. Pennell £524.15.0.

1. The caller was probably Captain John Macpherson (1726–1792), a wealthy and eccentric privateersman of the French and Indian War. In 1776 he claimed that he had been promised command of the American navy (which he envisaged as a fleet of row galleys) by a committee of Congress. Thereafter he continually sought a naval command or concocted plans to outfit vessels to engage the enemy at his own expense, and as late as 1781 unsuccessfully applied for the position of a commissioner of the Navy Board of the Middle Department. Among his varied activities, he acted as a bill, merchandise, and real estate broker, gave lectures on science and moral philosophy, and published the first city directory in the United States, for Philadelphia, in 1785. See Macpherson's memorials to Congress of March 12, 29, and May 31, 1776, March 19, 1778, June 15 and July 25, 1779, and January 6, 1781, in PCC, no. 78, XV, 23–26, 29–32, 53–56, 321–324, no. 42, V, 150–157, no. 41, VI, 207–210; *JCC*, III, 296, V, 544–545, XIV, 859, XXXII, 382, XXXIV, 188n.; William Macpherson Hornor, ed., "Extracts from Letters of John Macpherson, Jr., to Samuel Patterson, 1766–1773," *PMHB*, XXIII (1899), 51; Thompson Westcott, *Historic Mansions and Buildings of Philadelphia* (Philadelphia, 1877), 218; Dorothea N. Spear, comp., *Bibliography of American Directories Through 1860* (Worcester, Mass., 1961), 273.

2. Concerning Haym Salomon's status as bill broker to the Office of Finance, see Diary, July 12, 1782, and notes.

3. The bills of exchange presumably were sold to Brassine, an agent of de Mars, the director of hospitals in Rochambeau's army. RM later described the agent as a malefactor named Fontaine who had fled from France to America, assumed the name of de Brassine, and was knowingly employed in the hospital department by de Mars, in whose public and private business he shared. RM and Salomon later became involved in a protracted dispute with them over bills of exchange that ended in litigation. See RM to de Mars, February 24 and 28 (first letter), to Benoît Joseph de Tarlé, March 13, and to Benjamin Franklin, May 27, and Franklin to RM, July 27, 1783.

4. See Samuel Hodgdon to RM, July 29, and notes, and for RM's eventual payment of these men, Diary, September 4. Cowell had been a gunsmith in Allentown, Pennsylvania, before removing to Philadelphia in 1779. See Hutchinson and Rutland, eds., *Madison Papers*, III, 87n.

5. On Hill's negotiation of bills of exchange for RM, see Diary, April 17, 1782, and notes.

6. David Chambers Claypoole, publisher of the *Pennsylvania Packet*, was official printer to Congress.

7. The letters of Daniel Clark, RM's agent for buying tobacco in Virginia, have not been found. On the Yorktown tobacco, see RM's Agreement with George Eddy, printed under March 13, 1782, and notes. Instead of New York, Eddy went to Elizabeth, New Jersey, opposite Staten Island. A meeting place of the American and British lines, the town was a place of communication between the contending forces (e.g., Gouverneur Morris to RM, March 22, 1782, and notes), a listening post for British spies, a center of illicit trade with British-held New York, and a way station for persons traveling under flags of truce. See Diary, August 2 and 14; and Leonard Lundin, *Cockpit of the Revolution: The War for Independence in New Jersey* (London and Princeton, 1940), 377–378.

8. The flag of truce from Bermuda has not been further identified. Thomas Bradford (1745–1838) a Philadelphia printer who succeeded his father as publisher of the *Pennsylvania Journal* in 1778, had been appointed deputy commissary general of prisoners in January of that year. Although said to have left office in 1780 (Heitman, *Register*), he evidently continued in it at Philadelphia until the reorganization of prisoner administration in August 1782. *DAB;* Fitzpatrick, ed., *Writings of Washington*, X, 310, XXI, 144n.–145n., XXII, 150; and Diary, August 14, and notes.

9. Probably Captain Archibald Lyons, an officer on the privateer *Revenge*, Captain Gustavus Conyngham, which the British captured in 1779. Lyons eventually escaped from Forton prison in England and returned to the United States with the assistance of Benjamin Franklin. See Lyons to Franklin, March 17, and Franklin to Lyons, March 24, 1781, Hays, comp., *Calendar of Franklin Papers*, II, 362, III, 527; and Robert W. Neeser, ed., *Letters and Papers Relating to the Cruises of Gustavus Conyngham, a Captain of the Continental Navy, 1777–1779* (New York, 1915), xlvii–1.

10. After the defeat of the combined French and Spanish forces at the Battle of the Saints in the West Indies, part of the French fleet under Marquis de Vaudreuil headed toward Boston for repairs. See the headnote to RM's State of American Commerce and Plan for Protecting It, May 10, 1782, and notes.

11. See RM to the President of Congress, July 29.

12. This letter was written by James McCall.

Circular to the Governors of the States

(Circular)   Office of Finance 29th. July 1782[1]
Sir

Finding that several States are still in the Habit of making partial payments to their Troops as well as of expending Monies for the Purchase of Cloathing, It becomes my Duty to inform you that the Requisitions for the Service of the Current Year included both the Pay and Cloathing of the Continental Army. Any Payments which the several States may think proper to make or any expenditures for Cloathing or the like cannot be admitted in deduction from the Quota assigned them.[2] It becomes necessary for many reasons which I will not trouble your Excellency with the Enumeration of that Nothing be received from the States but money;[3] this alone can prevent those intricate Accounts which hitherto have involved every Thing in a Labarinth of Confusion. Had the States complied with the Requisitions made on them for the Current Service in any Degree proportionate either to the Magnitude or Urgency of the Occasion We should e'er this have had the Pleasure of knowing that our Army enjoyed all the Emoluments they have a right to ask for. I take the Liberty to add that it would be proper to cause Accounts to be transmitted to the Pay Master General as speedily as possible of what has been advanced for Pay that he may at least prevent a Double Credit for the same sums. With Respect to the Pay which may have become due anteriorly to the first day of January 1782, it will become a Part of that Debt from the United States for the Funding of which Revenues will be required from the several States so soon as Congress shall have digested their Resolutions on that Subject.[4] I have on many Occasions delivered the Sentiments contained above to several of the States as Circumstances called or Occasion required but it appears necessary to make the formal Communication to all and therefore I must pray your Excellency to excuse any Repetitions which may have happened.

Before I close this Letter I must observe Sir that of four Millions payable according to the Requisitions of Congress by the first Instant, I did not receive forty thousand Dollars.[5] Judge then of the Anticipations which were necessary to bring us where we are. Judge of the Situation in which we are placed and be not Surprized at any Consequences which may follow from that Universal Neglect which is alike unaccountable and inexcusable. I have the Honor to be with very great Respect Sir, your Excellency's most Obedient and humble Servant.

Robt Morris

His Excellency The Governor of Delaware

MSS: LS, to the President of Delaware, Executive Papers, De-Ar; LS, to the President of New Hampshire, Meshech Weare Papers, Nh-Ar; LS, to the Governor of Massachusetts, M-Ar; LS, to the Governor of Rhode Island, R-Ar; LS, to the Governor of Connecticut, Jonathan Trumbull Papers, Ct; LS, to the Governor of New Jersey, Nj; LS, to the Governor of Virginia, Continental Congress Papers, Vi; Ofcl LbC, DLC, LbC, Letterbook of Governor Alexander Martin of North Carolina, 1782–1785, Nc-Ar; Force transcript, to the President of New Hampshire, DLC; Sparks transcript, to the Governor of New Jersey, MH.

1. According to their endorsements, the texts sent to Connecticut and Massachusetts were received, respectively, on August 7 and 14. The letter to Maryland was enclosed in RM to the Governor of Maryland, July 29.

2. In extreme destitution, Congress on April 10, 1780, had invited the states to compensate their lines in the Continental army for losses from currency depreciation and to take over their current pay. For these contributions to the general welfare the states were to get credit in their accounts with the United States. How far into the future the states were to continue to provide military pay remained a question, and many of them advanced money to their troops in 1781 and 1782. This decentralized system was antithetical to RM's efforts to strengthen Congress. Intent upon centralizing disbursements, he asserts in the present letter a position not yet sanctioned by Congress: that the states would receive no credit for payments to troops on the current requisition for 1782. For previous statements of this position, see RM to Daniel of St. Thomas Jenifer, March 12, to George Olney, June 23, and to the Governor of Rhode Island, June 26, 1782. An even stiffer proposal, backed by Congress but ultimately unenforceable, that the states be given no credit on account and that any payments to the troops be considered "a free Gift," was made in RM's Report to Congress on the Representation of the New Jersey Legislature, September 27, and notes.

3. By virtue of RM's opposition Congress had ruled out the acceptance of specific supplies and quartermaster and commissary certificates under the requisition for 1782 (see RM to the President of Congress, November 5, 1781, and notes). Except under special circumstances and on terms dictated by his own necessities, RM's policy was to "allow no Article in Account on the requisitions of Congress except Cash to my receiver" (to Daniel of St. Thomas Jenifer, June 23, 1782). "Cash," however, included certain paper instruments, including Morris's notes, notes of the Bank of North America, and notes issued under RM's auspices by Paymaster General John Pierce. See RM to Nathanael Greene, and to the Governor of North Carolina, both October 17; for exceptions, see the Quartermaster General to RM, August 3, and notes, and RM to Daniel Clark, September 23, and notes.

4. Having interdicted state payments to the army after 1781, RM here announces a policy already put into execution without formal authorization by Congress: debts due to the army prior to 1782 were to be assumed by Congress, merged with the public debt, and funded by federal taxes (see RM to Daniel of St. Thomas Jenifer, March 12, 1782, and notes). In his letter to the President of Congress, July 29, RM recommended, as he had before, federal taxes on land and polls, as well as excise taxes, in addition to the impost already requested from the states.

5. The requisition for 1782 of $8 million was to be paid quarterly in equal proportions, with half the total falling due on July 1, 1782.

To the President of Congress (John Hanson)

This report on public credit—the keynote document in this edition—is the chief exposition of Robert Morris's plan to erect a funding system. Accurately described by Clarence L. Ver Steeg as "the most important single [American] state paper on public credit ever written prior to Hamilton's First Report on Public Credit,"[1] the Superintendent of Finance's report presaged in many of its recommendations the funding program Hamilton proposed in 1790.

The document is significant on several levels. First, Morris presented the funding plan as the cornerstone of his financial program for restoring public confidence, promoting economic growth, and strengthening the national government to ensure the viability of American independence. As such, the report represents the fullest expression of Morris's political economy, tailored, however, to an audience that was primarily influenced by republican attitudes steeped in an agrarian, localist tradition. Second, drawing from a variety of sources, the report stands as the first systematic effort to introduce to America the financial revolution that had taken place in Britain during the eighteenth century. Finally, Congress's failure to adopt Morris's plan, despite substantial pressure from public creditors, set the stage for a political crisis during the winter and spring of 1783.

I

Morris submitted his report on public credit with the intention of reviving public confidence in Congress and establishing the national government as a stronger political and economic force within the balance of power between the states and the Confederation. As the Financier and his assistant, Gouverneur Morris, reflected on the evolution of the war from the vantage point of the Office of Finance, they became convinced that Congress had squandered the public confidence so essential to nourishing national credit.[2] The war, they agreed, had begun as a crusade in defense of the right of self-taxation. Capitalizing on the *rage militaire* which gripped Americans, Congress in 1775 had adopted the widespread colonial monetary practice of issuing paper bills of credit in anticipation of taxes and was able to finance the early stages of the war by currency emissions which held the confidence of the people. But Congress, the Morrises thought, all too soon fell under the influence of "projectors"—men of little experience in government who ignored the wisdom of history and established nations—and issued more currency than could command the confidence of the public. Without adequately providing for its redemption and lacking the power to levy taxes, Congress could not withdraw its paper from circulation. The value of the unsecured currency eroded in the late 1770s, a process accelerated, Robert and Gouverneur believed, by laws making paper currency legal tender. Currency depreciation in turn led to legislation regulating the prices of commodities and sanctioning the impressment of private property. As a result, commerce, agriculture, and manufacturing were ruined.

On March 18, 1780, Congress virtually repudiated its currency by issuing a new emission in its place at 40 to 1. Whatever the justice of Congress's action, which Robert Morris at the time thought constructive, the new emission, tied to the old paper, soon depreciated. Meanwhile, Congress turned to laying requisitions in specific supplies, but by this time, according to the Morrises, the people's confidence was undermined and Congress's credit destroyed. Hovering on the edge of financial collapse, Congress early in 1781 replaced its ineffective committees with executive departments, the most important of which was the Office of Finance. By this time, the Morrises concluded, "the convulsive Labors of Enthusiasm" propelling the Revolution had nearly spent themselves. Political freedom had already been secured by the state constitutions. Now the nation needed to address itself to the more sober tasks of bringing the noble but costly military conflict to a victorious close and consolidating independence. "Nothing remained but Vigor, Organization and Promptitude to render this a considerable Empire," Gouverneur Morris observed. What was left of the Revolutionary contest, Robert Morris wrote in the same vein, was only a "War of Finance,"[3] one, at least in his view, that needed to be won before America could become truly independent.

The strategy adopted by Robert Morris and other like-minded Nationalists to win this financial struggle was to acquire for Congress independent revenues to fund the public debt. Early in 1781 Congress itself asked the states to vest it with power to levy an impost—a duty on imports committed to discharge the war debt. After assuming office in June 1781, Morris vigorously pursued a series of measures of which the funding proposal was the capstone. He urged that the impost amendment to the Articles of Confederation be a key first step toward funding the public debt and pressed the states to repeal legal tender and price control legislation. Even before this he had succeeded in obtaining Congress's approval to establish a national bank that would create a stable paper currency and promote commerce on a national scale. Again with Congress's sanction in July, the Superintendent introduced contracts for supplying the army, by this means assigning army procurement to private business interests and eliminating much of the cumbersome and expensive military bureaucracy. During the winter of 1781–1782 Morris persuaded Congress to lay requisitions on the states in specie rather than paper money, commodities, or certificates, and he also set in motion his plans for a mint and national coinage.

Finally, at Morris's urging, Congress in February 1782 enacted ordinances for the settlement of the accounts of the Revolution. It then remained to be determined how the national debt, so ascertained, would be funded. Article VIII of the Confederation stipulated that the expenses of the war were to be paid out of the common treasury supplied by the states on congressional requisitions apportioned according to the value of their lands and improvements. Reflecting the Superintendent's distrust of this ineffective requisition system as a source of revenue for debt funding, the report on public credit embodied revenue proposals which bypassed article VIII and claimed primary congressional responsibility for the debt, thus bringing nearer to maturity Morris's policies for altering the political balance of the Confederation.

As an exposition of the Superintendent's political economy, the report remained faithful to Morris's conceptions of justice, economic liberty, and the nature of the American economy. The public debt, defined as "a Species of Property" in the report, represented for Morris a moral obligation that the United States was bound in justice to honor. Adopting a contractual view of morality, the Financier for the past year had lectured the states that justice required "a Payment of Debts and a Performance of Promises," and that, in this matter, governments were subject to the same tests as individuals. Indeed, Morris asserted, the determination to fulfill moral commitments defined national character. Public faith consequently must be kept sacred and free from the fraud that "would stamp our national Character with indelible Marks of Infamy, and render us the Reproach and Contempt of all Mankind."[4] It was essential, contended Morris, that the inchoate American union be given "a proper Political Form and Consistency" founded on "the Solid Base of Justice." This could only be accomplished, the Superintendent declared, "by being just to Individuals, to each other, to the Union, to all; by generous grants of solid Revenue, and by adopting energetic measures to collect that Revenue." It was by this means alone, Morris exhorted shortly after taking office, that the moral obligation of the debt would be discharged, that public confidence in Congress would be restored, and "that these States must expect to establish their Independence and rise into Power, Consequence, and Grandeur."[5]

Morris's view that the war for independence was as much a struggle for economic as for political liberty was embedded in the report on public credit. As early as 1777 he had articulated the view that commerce should be as "free as air." In his mind there was no inherent conflict between the interests of merchants and those of society—they naturally went "hand in hand" and needed "no other prompter or tutor."[6] Vigorously defending these views during the disputes and disturbances which raged over economic policy in Congress and Philadelphia in 1778–1779, Morris carried them into office as Superintendent of Finance. As Superintendent he wished to impress upon "the Minds of all persons in power"—in Congress and the state governments—the axiom "that Commerce shou'd be perfectly free, and property Sacredly secure to the Owner."[7] Once tender laws, price-fixing regulations, and other restraints on property that had taken hold in the states during the war were swept away, Morris predicted, Americans would "enjoy and possess that freedom for which they contend."[8]

As Superintendent, Morris rejected as undesirable and ineffective the notion of using force to compel men to abandon their self-interest. He relied instead upon "the Strong Principle of Self-Love, and the immediate Sense of private Interest," the prescription of David Hume, to channel men's actions toward the public good.[9] Through incentives, Morris hoped to ensure the reciprocity of public and private interest. Thus the report on public credit incorporated forceful laissez-faire attitudes, particularly in its arguments against government interference with speculation, and in its assertion of "every man being able to judge better of his own business and situation than the government can do for him." At the same time, the primary mode of argument in the report focused on directing national economic development through the manipulation of public credit, including tax policy and other inducements.

Morris's report also made implicit assumptions regarding the nature of the American economy which originated in what he had described as "the intimate Connection between the Commerce, the Agriculture and the Finances of a Country."[10] Agriculture and commerce frequently symbolized for contemporaries opposing configurations of values for defining and directing the course of national political, social, and economic development, as recent studies of republican attitudes have suggested.[11] Silas Deane illustrated the force of this dichotomy when, in one of his allegedly intercepted letters, he advised the Financier early in 1781 what he sensed Morris knew only too well from experience: that most members of Congress and the state legislatures were hostile to commerce and that some even believed American attention "should be turned to agriculture, and the manufacturing of articles of the first necessity." Their views were so narrow, Deane lamented, "that they never have seen that agriculture and commerce mutually depend on, and support each other." This indigenous hostility to commerce led Deane to doubt "whether our commerce would not suffer as greatly from internal checks and embarrassments, as from external ones," and whether independence would prove to be a blessing.[12] Although Morris rejected the implications of Deane's assertions for American independence, for him, as for Deane, there was no inherent conflict between virtue and commerce on the one hand or between landed and trading interests on the other. Indeed, Morris was prepared to make the interdependence of agriculture and commerce a focal point of his political and economic energies during the 1780s.[13]

Throughout the decade Morris emphasized that agricultural and commercial expansion had to go hand in hand. Long a major exporter of agricultural commodities, especially flour and tobacco, Morris argued forcefully that the development of commercialized farming for export production was a prerequisite to American economic independence. "The produce of the Country," he had observed in 1781, was " ... the only Source of national Wealth." Given the nature of the American economy, Morris could only have meant agricultural produce.[14] Americans, he maintained, would work prodigiously once convinced that they could possess their property securely. "That labour lays the foundation for Commerce," Morris continued. "Unrestrained liberty in this, will find vent for our own Superfluities and bring us in return whatever we stand in need of from other Countries." Once Americans were led to produce surpluses in excess of subsistence or strictly domestic consumption, commerce would flourish in a balanced national economy characterized by universal plenty.[15]

As a brief for public loans "to lighten the Weight of present Burthens," the report on public credit assumed the inevitability of American economic and population growth. Against the common view of the public debt as a national burden that would weigh heavily on posterity, Morris maintained that the debt would be easily borne later by the more numerous and more affluent Americans who would reap the benefits from the freedom that the Revolutionary generation had purchased with its blood and treasure. Moreover, according to a key argument Morris addressed to critics of public loans, the current return on capital investment in the United States was double the cost of borrowing. It followed that loans resulted in the creation of new wealth equal to the interest paid on them. Applying this idea to the national government, Morris held that it was more advantageous under present circumstances for the United States to borrow than to tax in order to meet the heavy burden of current expenditures required by the war effort. Citizens would thus be left free to employ productively funds they would otherwise have had to pay in taxes.

Morris envisioned government borrowing in both the American and European credit markets. Domestic loans offered the advantages of lending stability to the Confederation government "by combining together the Interests of moneyed Men for it's Support," reducing the tax burden on the poor, and giving a salutary check to speculation. But the Financier recognized that domestic borrowing would divert money from private investment in land and trade and drive up the already high general rate of interest. For the present, therefore, the Superintendent believed foreign loans obtained on the basis of sound public credit were the best means for Congress to pursue.

Since public loans presumed the ability to borrow and confidence in the borrower, Morris contended that Congress could regain its public credit only by providing for its past debts through a funding system established securely on the basis of domestic revenue sources. Such revenues, Morris maintained, could not be obtained without a reliable system of taxation. Although the Superintendent believed that taxation which "intrench[ed] on the Subsistence of the People" was "burthensome and oppressive," he argued that under an enlightened administration like his own, in a country with abundant natural resources, moderate taxation would serve to stimulate national wealth by creating a need for money. The obligation to "keep Money in Readiness for the Tax Gatherer" would counter people's natural disposition to "Indolence and Profusion" and habitualize taxpayers to thrift. For the same reason Morris was quite prepared to establish a level of taxation beyond what was actually needed to support government and defend the state in order to spend the surplus "in works of public utility, such as the Opening of Roads and Navigations."

In order to fund the national debt Morris strongly advised Congress to seek a balanced slate of taxes which would equitably accommodate the wide-ranging variety of economic conditions and interests in the states. He had made the 5 percent duty on imported goods adopted by Congress in 1781 the first building block of his revenue system, but since the impost alone would not be adequate to fund the debt, Morris additionally recommended land and poll taxes and an excise on spirits in his report on public credit. None of Morris's tax proposals were entirely new, and, if each measure had its earlier advocates, each also had its staunch opponents.[16]

Morris's report singled out land, the progenitor of wealth, as "foremost for the Object of Taxation" and most suitable "to be burthened with those Debts which have been incurred by defending the Freedom of its Inhabitants." Because "the free Husbandman is the natural Guardian of his Country's Freedom," Morris asserted, the land tax was especially appropriate to the American republic. He admitted that this argument might at first sight seem astonishing to a nation of farmers, but insisted that logic was on his side against ingrained and unthinking "Delusion . . . kept up by the Artifice of others." Beneficial effects would arise, moreover, from the impact of the tax upon large, undeveloped land holdings. Proprietors of these tracts, Morris maintained, kept much of it from the "industrious Cultivator," and by "keeping the Price higher by Monopoly than otherwise it would be, they impede the Settlement and Culture of the Country." A tax on every 100 acres would not significantly burden small and middling owners, Morris insisted, and by dispersing concentrated holdings, it would have "the salutary Operation of an Agrarian Law, without the Iniquity." Although such arguments clearly were intended to persuade a Congress largely dominated by agrarian interests, Morris believed the per-acre land tax best met his criteria for debt-funding revenues that were easily identifiable, certain as to yield, convenient and inexpensive to collect, and broadly reflective of the nation's natural and expanding wealth. Unlike Hamilton, Morris eschewed for the present the popular expedient of selling western lands as one foundation for debt funding, and devoted the last section of his report to a rebuttal of reasons advanced for that mechanism.

Once specific domestic tax revenues adopted by Congress and the states were pledged to debt funding, Morris intended to open national loans. Under his plan, loan office certificates and other Continental debt paper were to be accepted in the subscriptions at face value without discrimination in favor of original holders. Moreover, the surpluses which Morris planned to raise from Continental taxes would be assigned to a sinking fund that would instill confidence in investors and serve as a further source of new loans. Although Morris was viscerally opposed to consolidating the debt at a lower rate of interest, as Hamilton would do in 1790,[17] he later held out to Congress the possibility that if Continental revenues assigned to debt funding were "clear, certain, permanent and increasing," future national loans might be obtained at 4 percent and perhaps even at 3 percent, or that old loans could be renegotiated once securities rose to par. If, on the other hand, revenues were precarious, borrowing might have to be undertaken at rates as high as 8 percent or "perhaps not at all."[18] With public credit restored on Morris's principles, however, the United States would be well positioned to borrow for current expenditures both at home and abroad while the nation grew and acquired wealth from the commercial energies unleashed by debt funding.

Commerce would be the principal beneficiary of the capital that would be called into life from the "dead" paper lying unused and unproductive. Since the return on invested capital in the United States was greater than the interest on the debt, funding would place new wealth into the hands of propertied, monied men "who could render it most productive." If invested wisely, and Morris evidently expected the capital to be invested rather than spent on consumption, the capital created by funding would produce a clear gain in national income from which all Americans presumably would benefit. Moreover, funding the debt would encourage foreign investment and promote American commerce. The interest paid to foreign investors, Morris argued, far from being a drain on the balance of trade, was less than the return foreign capital would bring if invested in the American market. The net inflow "would Supply the Want of Credit to the mercantile Part of Society."[19] Funding would thus render justice to the public creditors, shore up public confidence in Congress, and unite propertied and entrepreneurial interests in support of the Confederation.

The fulfillment of Morris's vision of economic nationalism, founded on the twin pillars of agriculture and commerce, depended to a large extent on the availability of credit. The report carried the implication that the new capital created by funding would provide a source for the capitalization of banks and a foundation for note issues essential to economic growth in a nation chronically short of coin and a sound paper currency. The Bank of North America, a standing model for such banks, had been conceived by the Superintendent as an institution that would "supply the Necessities of the Husbandman as well as the Merchant."[20] In the report on public credit, and again in the bank debates of 1786 in Pennsylvania, Morris argued that those who worked the land were linked to the great chain of credit which extended from Europe to the American backwoods. Merchants in the coastal seaports gave credit to the country shopkeepers and urban employers, who in turn made it available to farmers and mechanics. As an indispensable nexus in the chain, the bank would provide credit to underwrite mercantile ventures and the landed improvements essential to the production of agricultural surpluses. The marketing of those surpluses by the mercantile community would draw specie from abroad and increase the amount of money and credit available in America. "Let the landed and commercial interest shake hands," Morris exhorted in 1786, "for they do and must promote each others advantage."[21]

The report on public credit above all was a prescription for the new nation's rise to preeminence through maritime commerce founded on the widespread cultivation of agricultural exports. There can be little doubt that Morris would have agreed with Gouverneur Morris, his assistant in the Office of Finance, that Americans were peculiarly suited by history, geography, and temperament to take advantage of their unique potential. "Highly Commercial, being as it were the first born Children of extended Commerce in modern Times, we must be maritime," Gouverneur wrote at the time Congress received the report on public credit.[22] The dual role of commerce as both catalyst and beneficiary of debt funding formed the core of Robert Morris's plan for establishing public credit and propelling the nation along the path of prosperity and economic growth. From maritime commerce would come the wealth that would be tapped by Continental taxes in the states for debt funding. Tax revenues would provide the surpluses for internal improvements which Robert Morris believed were essential to the creation of a national market, and, after the war, rebuilding the United States navy for the protection of American overseas trade.[23] Both needs were appropriate to the agriculturally based, maritime and commercial empire envisioned by Robert Morris.

II

What were the sources of Robert Morris's ideas on taxation and borrowing as expressed in the report on public credit? Precise answers are difficult to define, but three unmistakable influences can be identified: the financial revolution that had taken place in Great Britain earlier in the century; the writings of British and French political economists; and the wartime debate over republican political economy in America which linked financial and political policies and focused on the proper distribution of power between the states and the Confederation.

The historical antecedents of Morris's funding proposal lay in eighteenth-century developments in Britain. At the core of Britain's economic and political strength was its funded debt. The British funding system permanently pledged or mortgaged revenue from specific taxes to regular payment of the interest on the public debt. Systematic repayment of the principal was abandoned after the sinking fund established to retire the debt was diverted on a regular basis to other purposes or used to form the basis for new loans. Britain's funded debt financed the recurrent wars with France and its allies and promoted the economic growth that led to the industrial revolution. The paper generated by tax-free debt holdings served as a general medium of exchange, a source of business capital, the foundation of banking institutions, and a profitable investment for otherwise idle funds. Administered mainly through large corporations, including the Bank of England, the South Sea Company, and the East India Company, the funding system was credited with securing political stability by generating loyalty to the government through the economic interest of public creditors.[24]

The British experience was well known but not imitated in colonial America. In the colonies government expenditures had been met chiefly by emissions of paper currency in anticipation of taxes. If the notes depreciated, taxes merely absorbed them at lower value. Public debts were, therefore, extinguished cheaply and seldom with interest payment on the part of the government. The notes did not attract investment and promote the development of business enterprise. Appropriate to an agrarian economy which lacked banks, this mode of public finance was associated in the colonies with minimal government and the low taxes and relatively rapid retirement of debt which Americans had come to regard as economic counterparts of their political liberties.

In casting aside these expedients, Morris's funding proposal in large measure attempted to recapitulate British experience. Like many other Whigs, Morris decried the overweening British ambition that would reduce Americans to slavery,[25] but there is little in his writings to indicate fear of the pervasive, liberty-threatening corruption that many other Americans attributed to British society and political institutions arising from the commercialization of the economy and the harnessing of the national debt. Indeed, Morris unashamedly admired the almost limitless credit England could command either from foreign loans or "from the Bowels of domestic Credit and Confidence." "Admiring we should endeavour to imitate," the Superintendent enjoined the state governors early in his administration. Once debt servicing was assured by permanent revenues, Morris predicted, the American "funds" would be as secure as Britain's and the nation would possess "the inestimable Jewel of Public Credit."[26]

Undoubtedly Robert Morris's ideas on public credit owed more to his extensive experience as a merchant, public official, and keen observer of the marketplace than they did to particular treatises on political economy of the previous half century. Yet, although Morris did not consider himself a person of intellectual attainments or as one who was well read,[27] he was not indifferent to works on subjects of immediate and practical interest. Moreover, his assistant, Gouverneur Morris, had for some time studied and written on political economy, and to him the Superintendent generally seems to have delegated the task of deriving theoretical formulations and defenses of his policies.

Both Robert and Gouverneur Morris were familiar with recent Scottish and English economic writings, including those arguing the merits of the British national debt and funding system. The Superintendent is known to have possessed Adam Smith's *Wealth of Nations* and at least

one volume by the English political economist Thomas Mortimer.[28]
Moreover, material on coinage which Gouverneur prepared for the
Office of Finance included information derived from Sir James Steuart's *Inquiry into the Principles of Political Oeconomy* of 1767.[29] Gouverneur's earlier financial writings also indicate a familiarity with the
ideas of David Hume and Richard Price.[30] Whether these and other
treatises influenced their ideas and policies, or whether they were
simply sources of respectable arguments for preconceived views, cannot be finally determined.

Certainly the Morrises drew selectively and eclectically from these
sources. The report on public credit, as well as Robert Morris's important supplementary letter to Congress of March 8, 1783, show the
influence of Smith's discussions of the merits of the land tax, the ratio
between interest rates and profits, and the need for specific tax rates
rather than valuations based on the discretion of tax collectors or
assessors. Like Smith, the Superintendent and his assistant rejected
bullionist notions of wealth, including the belief that the exportation
of specie necessarily constituted a national loss. Mortimer's work
would have provided an extended foundation or substantial reinforcement for Robert Morris's conception of the interdependence of agriculture and commerce. Moreover, in both Smith and Mortimer the
Morrises certainly found kindred antiregulatory and free trade attitudes more to their liking than the broader latitude for government
management of the economy that Steuart sanctioned.

Robert and Gouverneur, nevertheless, rejected most of the criticisms of the British national debt and funding system advanced by
Smith, Hume, Price, and others. Instead, in emphasizing the blessings
to be derived from national public credit, they drew heavily on Steuart
and Mortimer, who regarded the British national debt as a useful tool
of public finance, particularly during wartime, and believed in the
beneficence of the debt for economic growth. Whether the Morrises
favored a perpetual national debt, or merely one that would continue
only until national political and economic stability had been achieved,
is less certain.

Robert Morris was also developing a familiarity with French economic writings. The *Memoirs* of the duc de Sully, the great French
mercantilist and finance minister under Henry IV, were in Morris's
possession when he was elected Superintendent of Finance.[31] As some
of the arguments in support of the land tax in Morris's report reveal,
he was also acquainted with French physiocratic doctrine. Of all the
French works that had come to his attention, however, the most significant was the *Compte Rendu* published in 1781 by the Swiss-born,
Protestant financier Jacques Necker, which Morris had arranged to be
translated for his personal use.[32] Besides sharing Morris's admiration
for the public credit engendered by the British funding system,
Necker's book expressed other views that would have appealed to
Morris, particularly the general emphasis on orderly and rational financial and credit procedures, and the insistence on greater openness
and public accountability in the management of national finances.
Necker also favored a discount bank along lines similar to the Bank of
North America and condemned unsecured paper money emissions.
Moreover, Necker served Morris as a model for emulation, particu-
larly for his reputed integrity and disinterestedness as financier and
for his espousal of economy in government even in the face of power-

ful vested interests. Necker's image may have influenced Morris as
much as his writings, for it embodied both the personal qualities and
financial policies for which Morris expressed admiration and hoped to
adapt to American conditions.

Of perhaps greater importance in providing the context for the
report on public credit was the ongoing American debate over the
development of a republican political economy which drew on a century of Anglo-American experience. Spurred by independence, this
public dialogue on an American economy had been given an urgent
edge during the period from 1779 to 1781 because of the general
collapse of Continental and state paper currencies and the need to
devise alternate forms of public finance to sustain the war effort.
Although the discussion was nationwide in scope as writers and
statesmen introduced and considered proposals ranging over issues
of taxation, borrowing, debt, and the desirability and consequences
of economic growth, it was perhaps carried on with keenest interest
in Philadelphia, where Thomas Paine, Pelatiah Webster, William Barton, and Gouverneur Morris were among the major contributors.
The following paragraphs are intended only to suggest the range
and complexity of the debate.

Thomas Paine and Robert Morris had been on opposite sides in the
Deane-Lee affair of 1777–1778 and had tangled in the bitter controversy over price regulation in Philadelphia in 1779. Nevertheless,
Paine's democratic republicanism was tinged with hard money attitudes, influenced by the detrimental effects of currency depreciation
on his artisan followers and colored by a cosmopolitan appreciation of
the progressive role of free commerce in stimulating economic growth
for the new American empire. Paine also understood the usefulness of
economic tools such as banks and a national debt in forging the central
government he had advocated from the first. During the dark days of
October 1780 he penned "The Crisis Extraordinary," calling for an
invigorated commitment to keep the army in the field and maintain
national solvency. Paine proposed raising £2 million annually by equal
portions of taxation and borrowing. Half the taxes were to be raised
by duties on imports and prizes "ascertained and regulated by Congress, and ingrafted in that form into the law of each state." He proposed to obtain the remainder by a tax on land and houses "or such
other means as each state may devise." Paine's belief that America had
to encourage the propertied to commit themselves fully to independence and national government eventually led to his rapprochement
with Robert and Gouverneur Morris in September 1781. Thereafter
Paine became a spokesman for the Office of Finance policies. In the
months following the report on public credit he would write on behalf
of the impost of 1781 and other Continental taxes. Later in the decade
Paine would join with the Morrises to answer attacks on the Bank of
North America.[33]

Representing a different strain of thinking, less closely associated
with Robert Morris but sharing some ideas in common, were the political economists Pelatiah Webster and William Barton. Webster, a Con-
necticut-born, Philadelphia merchant, wrote a series of essays "on Free
Trade and Finance," the first of which were published anonymously in
the Philadelphia press in 1779 and 1780. Like the Morrises, Webster
defended unfettered commerce as the means by which money would
return to circulation, goods would become available, and taxes could be

paid. Unlike them, he opposed a national debt, arguing against reliance on domestic and foreign loans (or even subsidies), and objecting particularly to the payment of interest to foreigners. Anxious to stabilize the amount and value of the currency, he opposed anything that would increase the effective money supply beyond what was actually needed by the economy as a medium of exchange. Certificates of public debt, he feared, would merely increase the money supply and hasten depreciation. Webster, therefore, called for the imposition of taxes equal to the amount needed for current expenditures. Levied at specie value, the taxes were to be payable at the option of the taxpayer either in specie or in paper money at its real market value at the time the taxes were paid. Such a system, he argued, while providing for current expenses, would fix the value of the currency by creating a demand for it and limiting the amount in circulation. Asserting that inflation was actually more burdensome to the poor than taxation, he opposed the exactions forced by currency depreciation as well as those imposed by impressment. Instead, he called for payment of a tax or a series of taxes, estimated at the equivalent of four dollars per person but apportioned according to an individual's ability to pay.[34]

William Barton, an obscure political economist from Lancaster, Pennsylvania, also favored continued reliance on Continental paper money, with its value stabilized and supported by appropriate Continental and state tax policies rather than by tender laws. In 1781 he advocated payment of interest in specie on new emission currency issued under the act of Congress of March 18, 1780, with redemption to be completed within six years, the opening of a land office in Pennsylvania to sell state lands for paper money or specie, and a requirement that a sixth of all taxes be payable in specie, with nonjurors to the Pennsylvania constitution of 1776 being required to pay a third in specie. Barton also proposed the establishment of a national bank whose currency would gradually replace the paper money issued by the government. For Barton, the preservation of public credit lay in the support of a revitalized paper currency, not in the payment of interest on loan office certificates or other debts; consequently, he advocated appropriation of the income from the impost to the redemption of Congress's four-tenths share of the new emission, while the states would levy taxes for the redemption of the other six-tenths over a six-year period. Barton also proposed to vest attributes of sovereign authority in the Continental government, including the sole right to issue paper money and strike coinage and the ability to support its credit by import duties and a general land tax. Such *ad valorem* levies, he argued, would be productive of income in the states in proportion to their wealth and therefore preserve a just equilibrium between the interests of all.[35]

Also well known to Robert Morris were Alexander Hamilton's ideas for reestablishing public credit. Hamilton was closely associated with Philip Schuyler, his father-in-law, and James Duane, both of whom, as New York congressmen, had long worked in association with Robert and Gouverneur Morris in grappling with financial issues. The young Hamilton had written the newly elected Financier a long letter in April of 1781 expounding his ideas on commerce and credit and outlining his plan for a national bank. "Finding many points of it to Coincide with my own Opinions on the Subject," the Superintendent had praised Hamilton for his "performance." Soon afterward, Hamilton

began a more ambitious year-long series of essays under the rubric of
"Continentalist." Writing in the *New-York Packet, and American Adver-
tiser*, he advocated the necessity of increasing the powers of Congress
and providing it with an independent revenue from the sale of western lands and the proceeds of various taxes, including levies on lands
and polls and a duty on imports. Permanent funds from such sources,
Hamilton maintained, would permit Congress in future to borrow
abroad on its own credit, thus lightening the load of taxation.[36]

More than any other set of American writings, however, the report
on public credit embodied most fully ideas on finance which Gouverneur Morris had developed in reports as a delegate to Congress in
1778 and 1779 and in a series of essays published under the *nom de
plume* of "An American" in the *Pennsylvania Packet* early in 1780.[37] Like
most writings of the period, the essays dealt initially with the question
of paper money, then under consideration by Congress prior to the
adoption of the act of March 18, 1780, and the inefficacy of economic
regulation. In the essay published in the *Packet* on March 11, 1780,
Gouverneur expounded arguments in favor of foreign loans, a view
he had earlier espoused as a member of Congress.[38] His articles in the
same newspaper of April 11 and 15 examined the necessity of reestablishing public credit. The ideas expressed in these essays most closely
parallel those in the Financier's report on public credit. The April 15
article advocated land and poll taxes and a sinking fund to discharge
the public debts and retire Continental currency; some of the arguments advanced in support of the land tax are repeated in the Superintendent's report. Gouverneur's proposals in the April 15 essay for a
tax on exports and ship tonnage to support the navy and for taxes on
cattle, horses, and windows were not included in the Financier's report. Despite the similarity of themes, the report on public credit does
not always use the same examples from Gouverneur's earlier writings,
and there is little direct borrowing of text.[39]

It is not surprising that the Superintendent assigned the task of
drafting the report on public credit to his young assistant.[40] Despite his
youth and irrepressible whimsy, Gouverneur was widely acknowledged to possess genius,[41] and other state papers he prepared in cooperation with the Financier confirmed the "first rate abilities" Robert
Morris had earlier found in the younger man.[42] Although Gouverneur
thus played an important collaborative role in drafting the report, it is
nonetheless clear, as Ver Steeg concluded, that "all the evidence indicates that the finished document contained the sentiments and the
imprint of the Superintendent of Finance."[43]

III

The immediate objective of the report on public credit was to tie the
payment of interest on the public debt to domestic revenue sources
assigned to Congress, thereby strengthening the Confederation government and limiting American dependence on France. Its timing was
determined in large part by a series of events involving continuing
agitation by public creditors.

In October 1781 the Superintendent had begun preparations to
calculate the national debt for Congress's inspection. He directed the
Continental loan officers to prepare a list of all certificates that had
been issued and ordered them not to issue any additional certificates

Interest-bearing loan office certificates, the "war bonds" of the Revolution, held the status of a "preferred" debt. First authorized by Congress on October 3, 1776, at 4 percent interest, the certificates were continued in several issues thereafter. The specimen shown here is from the first 6-percent issue of February 22, 1777. The interest on the face value of this certificate, issued before March 1, 1778, would have been paid in bills of exchange on France (see the example following p. 53); those issued after that date drew interest in paper money that rapidly depreciated. A third variety, known as "specie" loan office certificates, was authorized by Congress in 1781. They were supposed to have been purchased in hard money, but the small amount issued was used instead to pay outstanding debts. Disgruntled by Congress's cessation of interest payments in September 1782, holders of the early certificates like the one shown here were the most vocal of the public creditors. (For an estimate of the loan office debt in 1782, see enclosure 2 to Morris to the President of Congress, July 29, 1782; for a discussion of loan office certificates and their significance in the financial history of the Revolution, see Ferguson, Power of the Purse, *35–40, 43, 53–55, 68–69, 149, 151, 184.)*

The certificates were printed on watermarked paper, the borders varying in color with denominations which ranged from $200 to over $10,000. The indented $500 specimen illustrated here, signed by Samuel Hillegas, son of Michael Hillegas, Treasurer of the United States, and countersigned by Nathaniel Appleton, commissioner of the Continental loan office of Massachusetts, is printed in black with red borders on paper watermarked with a pattern and the words "[CONTIN]ENTAL LOAN OFFICE ." Appleton endorsed the back of the certificate at one end as follows: "One Years Interest paid/Second Years Interest paid/Third years Interest paid/Fourth Years Interest paid." At the other end is the following endorsement signed by the Register of the Treasury: "Treasury Department/Registers Office 29 May 1818/This Certificate is genuine/agreeing with the Records/in this Office of out-/standing Certificates/Joseph Nourse/Regr." The certificate was cancelled when the holder submitted it during the liquidation of the Revolutionary war debt authorized by Congress in 1818. The certificate is filed in Account 37231 of the 1818 settlement, Miscellaneous Treasury Accounts, First Auditor of the Treasury Department, Segregated Series, Records of the United States General Accounting Office, RG 217, National Archives, Washington, D.C. Courtesy of the National Archives and Records Service.

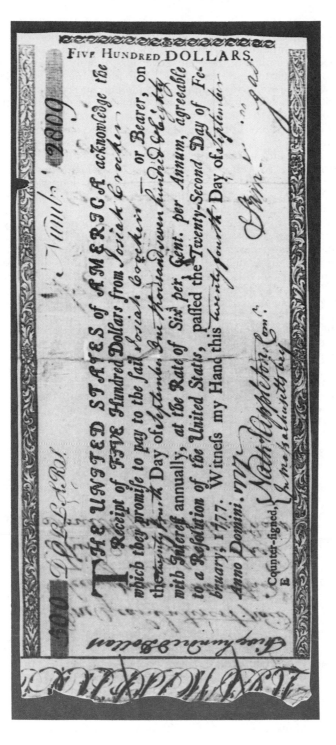

Loan office certificate dated September 24, 1777. 9¹³⁄₁₆" × 4¹⁄₄"

for the payment of interest, a practice which had developed to placate
creditors who had not received scheduled interest payments in paper
money.[44] Such "little timid Artifices," the Superintendent explained in
his October 19 circular to the state governors, merely increased the
number of certificates and depreciated their value; the accumulation
of debts without revenue to fund them would only succeed in destroying public credit without relieving the public creditors. Unless the
states provided the necessary revenues, Morris asserted, neither the
principal nor the interest of the public debt could be paid.

Although Morris cautioned the governors against continued reliance on foreign aid, he nevertheless still expected France at least to
continue to make interest payments on the early loan office certificates, then a major part of the acknowledged public debt. Moreover,
in November, he emphasized to Benjamin Franklin that providing
domestic revenues to fund the public debt "must not . . . be urged with
too much Rapidity" to the French court because the impost was not yet
ratified and other measures remained to be taken. "In the mean
Time," the Financier observed to Franklin, "there is a well grounded
Expectation that the Clamors of our Creditors will induce the several
Legislatures to comply with the Requisitions of Congress upon that
Subject."[45] By January of 1782 Morris was reporting that his order
prohibiting the payment of interest in loan office certificates had produced considerable unrest among the public creditors, that more dis-
quiet could be expected, and that he intended to direct the blame for
inaction at the states.[46] Meanwhile, the Financier repeatedly urged the
public creditors to support his policies in the states, assuring them at
the same time of the ultimate soundness of the debt. Not all the
creditors were appeased. "If you are so thouroughly convinced . . . of
the solidity of payment of the funded debt of America!" the contentious Pierre Landais exclaimed sarcastically, "you will oblige me to buy,
and I'll sell you very cheap two loan office notes I am incumbered
with."[47]

Morris submitted his first formal proposal to fund the debt in a
letter to Congress of February 27, 1782, calling for the adoption of
land, poll, and excise taxes.[48] Congress had not yet responded to the
letter when matters came to a head in May after La Luzerne publicly
announced that France would no longer be responsible for the payment of the interest on the early loan office certificates. If Congress
drew any bills of exchange for interest, it would have to lodge funds
abroad to pay them or deduct the cost from whatever remained of the
loans and subsidies already pledged by France for continuation of the
war effort. With taxes on the requisition for 1782 coming in so slowly,
Morris could ill afford such a deduction, and in any case he continued
to believe it was necessary to use domestic sources to fund the public
debt while applying whatever French funds existed toward current
expenditures. Furthermore, with the ratification of the impost stalled,
credit at the bank strained, and consideration of his February tax
proposals suspended in Congress, the Superintendent's options were
limited. Consequently, in June, Morris proposed to Congress that interest payments in bills of exchange on France be suspended and that
future interest be paid from revenues from the pending impost.[49]
These recommendations alarmed certificate holders in Philadelphia
and inspired a remonstrance and petition to Congress from a committee of these public creditors led by Blair McClenachan and Charles

Pettit (printed in Appendix II). Read in Congress and referred to the
Financier on July 8, this document provided the perfect catapult for
launching the Financier's report on public credit.

Morris submitted the report to Congress against the backdrop of a
general credit crisis which was severely constricting American commercial enterprise. The slump was brought on by the continuing
shortage of money in the states. By the beginning of 1782 paper
currency had been virtually destroyed by depreciation, and Pennsylvania, under Morris's leadership, as well as other states, had repealed
laws making it a legal tender. What specie existed was either being
hoarded or drained to pay for the rising flood of British manufactures
reaching the American market illicitly through British-held territory.
The coastal blockade the British navy had aggressively imposed after
Yorktown, in addition to causing heavy ship losses, choked off the
exportation of American produce and the importation of specie. By
the summer of 1782 market uncertainties arising from expectations of
peace were intensifying the trade doldrums. With money a scarce
commodity, private loans became difficult to obtain even at increasingly higher interest rates and discounting by the bank was curtailed
or suspended altogether.[50]

The credit slump was particularly acute in Philadelphia. Pennsylvania's usury laws, which limited interest rates to 6 percent per annum,
had ceased to be effective in capping interest rates charged by private money lenders. De facto interest rates in Philadelphia sometimes
climbed to 5, 10, 12 percent *per month* and even higher.[51] The causes
and date of origin of usurious money lending in Philadelphia were
matters of dispute.[52] Whatever their origin, the Superintendent was
consistently recording interest rates of 5 percent per month prevailing in Philadelphia's private money markets when he submitted the
report on public credit.[53]

By this time the Superintendent was already deeply involved in the
activities of the public creditors, many of whom were now experiencing financial difficulties. His discussions with them began on June 26,
when Colonel Walter Stewart, McClenachan's son-in-law and a major
holder of loan office certificates in his own right, arrived at the
Office of Finance to protest the proposed stoppage of interest payments. When Stewart threatened to hold a public meeting of certificate holders, Morris suggested a committee first be formed of "Sensible cool Men" who might inform themselves of the necessities under
which Congress acted. A group of creditors held such a meeting and
elected a committee consisting of McClenachan, Charles Pettit, John
Shee, John Ewing, and Jonathan Dickinson Sergeant. Of these, all
except Shee were identified in varying degrees with the constitutionalist party in Pennsylvania politics, rather than with Morris's Republican party. The committee, Sargeant excepted, met with Morris by
appointment on June 28 and was informed that no funds existed to
pay interest and that the passage of the impost and certain other
Continental taxes was necessary to fund the public debt. Such taxes,
Morris asserted, were obstructed by a few members of Congress and,
particularly, by members of the state legislatures whose approval was
necessary for ratification of new tax measures under the terms of the
Articles of Confederation. Morris advised the public creditors to
unite and use their influence to secure the necessary legislation, and
to "turn out" delegates influenced by "local and Popular Views."

Thus, Morris opened a campaign to mobilize public creditors in support of his funding program.[54]

The McClenachan committee moved promptly to rally public creditors in Philadelphia. On July 2 it addressed a letter to Congress expressing concern that the impending suspension of interest payments in bills of exchange would destroy public credit and bring on "the absolute ruin of many of the earliest and best Whigs in America."[55] The committee requested Congress to postpone action until the views of public creditors in Philadelphia could be ascertained at a meeting planned for July 5.[56] At the meeting, held at the Pennsylvania State House, McClenachan was chosen chairman and Benjamin Rush secretary. Many creditors believed, or affected to believe, that funds were available in Europe but were allocated to other purposes. After a reportedly heated discussion, resolutions were passed to appoint a committee to address Congress on the subject and request that interest be paid on loan office certificates issued after March 1, 1778, as well as on the earlier certificates whose interest was now to be suspended.[57] The committee was also instructed to open correspondence with public creditors in other states. A more bipartisan group, composed of McClenachan, Pettit, Ewing, Rush, and Thomas Fitzsimons, was elected as the committee.[58]

On July 9, the day after the committee's remonstrance to Congress was referred to Morris for a report, the Superintendent promised the petitioners "a full and ample Report in favor of Establishing Revenue sufficient to pay the Interest of the whole public Debts." He advised the committee members to make "one common Cause" with public creditors everywhere to influence the state legislatures and to throw "their whole Support" behind a funding system when Congress adopted it. Cautioning the committee to "avoid the language of Threats which has already been Complained of in their proceeding," the Financier promised his assistance to "reasonable Measures Conducted with propriety." The conversation took a more negative turn upon Morris's "Happening to mention" he would inform Congress that no interest could be paid in 1782. To this the committee expressed "great Dissatisfaction," and McClenachan threatened to have nothing more to do with the committee if the interest of 1782 were not paid. Although McClenachan did remain on the committee, he and other creditors were unwilling at times to follow Morris's advice on the strategy to pursue in order to obtain payment of interest on the debts of the Confederation.[59]

The Office of Finance, nevertheless, appears to have influenced creditor attitudes expressed in the Philadelphia press. On July 10 an essay appeared in the *Pennsylvania Gazette* under the pseudonym "Leonidas," one of a series of letters on the French alliance, public credit, and the need for a strong Continental navy that Benjamin Rush had already begun writing at the behest of Chevalier de La Luzerne, the French minister. Entitled "On Public Credit as the Means of obtaining a Navy," the essay incorporated several themes Morris had urged upon the creditors, arguing for the need to reestablish public credit by a faithful discharge of interest, characterizing loan office certificates as a bond of union, and supporting the impost and other Continental taxes. Later installments, following similar lines, suggest that Rush's "Leonidas" letters were influenced by his discussions with Morris as a member of the creditors' committee.[60]

Although Morris had announced to the creditors' committee his intention to report on public credit, as late as July 16 the drafting of the report apparently had not yet begun. On that day he told a member of Congress it was "not practicable for us to report for some time having directed a State of the public Debt to be made out, as a foundation for what I have to say on the Subject." Once the Superintendent received the statement of the debt on July 18 work could commence and a week later he recorded that Gouverneur Morris was "being now employed in drawing that report."[61] Delivered to Congress on July 29, the report was not taken up until August 5, when it was referred to a grand committee composed of one member from each state which had been appointed on July 22 "to take into consideration and report the most effectual means of supporting the credit of the United States."[62]

Meanwhile, the Philadelphia creditors turned to Pennsylvania and other states for support. Their committee asked the Pennsylvania Assembly on August 19 to memorialize Congress. A week later it published a broadside addressed "To the Citizens of America, who are the Creditors of the United States," narrating its activities and negotiations with Morris and Congress and announcing that it would again petition the Pennsylvania Assembly. The committee, following Morris's suggestion, also proposed to correspond with public creditors elsewhere. Defending Continental taxes as important not only to the interests of security holders but to the public welfare as well, the committee urged creditors everywhere to compel their state legislatures to levy the taxes recommended by Congress.[63]

A second appeal from the creditors to the Pennsylvania Assembly bore fruit in a memorial of the assembly to Congress of August 28. The memorial declared that Pennsylvanians had subscribed so heavily to loan office certificates that many were now partially or totally dependent upon the payment of interest for a "decent Subsistence." It further argued that "for a considerable time past" no interest had been paid on certificates issued after March 1, 1778, and that the continuation of interest payments on those issued before that date had kept alive the hope that means would be found of discharging interest on the later subscriptions. If Congress now suspended interest on the earlier certificates, the creditors would suffer, in addition, an "enormous depreciation in the Value of the Principal." Pennsylvania had always deemed loan office certificates a Continental obligation, the memorial contended, with the expectation that Congress would find a way of "paying or funding" them under a "general Plan" in common with other debts the United States owed to Pennsylvanians for services and supplies. The state had given generously to Congress without stipulating preferential reimbursement for its citizens; now, however, the assembly wished to give them priority, but in a way that would conform to Congress's plans. Accordingly, the memorial requested Congress to "devise and recommend such general Plan" as would settle and ascertain "the unliquidated Debts of the United States," pay all or part of them, and provide for the regular payment of interest on the entire debt until the principal could be discharged. Congress committed the memorial on August 30.[64]

While the Pennsylvania memorial was under consideration, the grand committee on September 4 returned with a report, written by John Rutledge of South Carolina, which covered a wide field. Because several northern and smaller states were underrepresented and could not cast votes, Congress dismissed for the present the committee's statement "that the western lands if ceded to the U.S. might contribute towards a fund for paying the debts of these States."[65] For the same reason Congress rejected the committee's recommendation that the states be asked to levy land, poll, and excise taxes at specified rates and appropriate the income to funding the debts.[66] Instead, Congress adopted the committee's proposal for a special requisition of $1.2 million specie to be apportioned on the states "as absolutely and immediately necessary for payment of the interest of the public debt," the sum to be raised by the states by "such taxes as shall appear to them most proper and effectual."[67]

In accord with the tenor of the Pennsylvania Assembly's memorial, Congress's resolution allowed the income from the requisition to be applied to the interest, not only of loan office certificates—all of them, including later as well as the earlier issues—but on all "liquidated debts of the United States." Although the definition of what constituted federal obligations was thus enlarged, another part of Congress's resolution surrendered ground Morris had been defending by authorizing the states to use the proceeds of the requisition to pay the interest directly to their own citizens who were creditors of the United States before remitting any surplus to the Continental treasury.[68] The requisition thus distributed the debt to the states. Congress referred the requisition to the grand committee to apportion and report the state quotas and the following day, September 5, directed Morris to send the requisition to the states with an extract from his report and estimate of the public debt. Five days later Congress approved the state quotas and on September 18 voted to credit payments on the requisition "to the accounts of the several states on interest."

Congress's action on the requisition drew qualified praise from congressmen who were committed to managing the debt within a strict construction of the Articles of Confederation. While it was under discussion, Congressman David Howell of Rhode Island, where the impost was snagged, depicted the requisition as "constitutional and in my opinion much better than the Impost." Not long after, as part of a broad condemnation of the latent evils embedded in the impost, the Rhode Island delegates elaborated on their argument that debt funding along the lines proposed by Morris did not accord with the Confederation. Congress's preconfederation commitment to the public creditors, the delegates asserted, was limited to providing the interest by annual requisition, and article VIII of the Confederation made no additional guarantee of debt security. The public creditors would be paid, the Rhode Islanders contended, but only "to the extent of their Just demands and that in a Continental way, and no other." Should the impost be adopted instead, the horde of customs officials, "the Tribes of half-pay Officers, Pensioners, and public creditors . . . would enlarge, extend and increase their power, and soon induce *the necessity* of pursuing the remaining parts of the Plan, by adopting the Land Tax, the Poll Tax, and the Excise. After which, the bond of Union, to use the phrase of the Advocates of these Measures, would be complete. And," the delegates concluded, "we will add the Yoke of Tyranny fixed on all the states, and the Chains Rivotted."[69]

Of the taxes recommended by Morris, the land tax was the most controversial because of its implications for article VIII. The Financier was later advised that the greatest objection to the tax in Congress was its "Inequality."[70] Most of the opposition came from the southern states, whose delegates viewed the tax as a means by which northern, more highly developed, states would thrust the cost of the war on them "by the hundred Acres without regarding the quality or buildings." Despite the "Many pretty reasons" the Superintendent offered in support of the land tax, one North Carolina delegate remarked, his plan was unacceptable because it would saddle the state "with near double the quota of public Debt that should in Justice fall to our share."[71] Although the Confederation Congress would not sanction even a modified land tax, Morris remained committed to the idea, and during the debates in the United States Senate on Hamilton's financial program in 1790 he proposed it again as the best revenue source for debt funding.[72]

Morris was plainly dissatisfied with the requisition of September 4. He duly sent the requisition to the state governors on September 12 with the request that it be "considered according to its Magnitude," and dispatched copies to the Continental receivers, along with his letters to Congress of July 29 and 30, instructing them to "obviate Misrepresentation, and inculcate at proper Opportunities those Principles of national Integrity which are essential to our Safety."[73] But since past experience had proved to him that the states could not be relied on to pay their quotas, Morris scorned the "constitutional" debt-funding views championed by the Rhode Island delegates and other localists as inadequate for a funding system which would establish the Confederation's public credit.[74] The "substituting a mere temporary Expedient is dangerous," the Superintendent wrote to Alexander Hamilton, receiver for New York, on October 16. "Happy to find that the public Creditors are organizing themselves," Morris believed "their Numbers and Influence joined to the Justness of their Cause must prevail if they persevere."

Beyond the requisition, Congress for the present could agree to nothing more than Morris's earlier proposal for stopping interest due after March 1, 1782, on loan office certificates payable in bills of exchange on Europe. Congress adopted the prohibition on September 9 and the Superintendent rushed the directive to the loan offices by express.[75] The suspension of interest payments provoked an immediate outcry from public creditors in Philadelphia and its environs. According to Chevalier de La Luzerne, a tumultuous group assembled at the Exchange, where confusion reigned for over an hour as some creditors declaimed against Congress and France for refusing to continue interest payments. Only after an unidentified merchant and certificate holder addressed the crowd, attributing the suspension to the destitution of Congress and the inexplicable obstinacy of Rhode Island in refusing to ratify the impost, was the throng somewhat mollified. Nevertheless, many creditors continued to complain bitterly that Congress had not provided sufficient notice of suspension of interest on loan office certificates or at least timely payment for the current year.[76]

Since payment of the $1.2 million specie requisition by the states would be difficult to collect, and Pennsylvania's quota of $180,000 was not equal to the interest on federal debts owed in the state, protests continued. Acting on behalf of the state's public creditors, Pennsylvania Congressman Joseph Montgomery introduced resolutions to provide for speedier and more certain payment of interest. On September 17 he proposed the appropriation of $500,000 out of the Dutch loan,

Drawn on American funds in France by Congress's Treasurer of Loans (an office subsequently discontinued), this indented bill of exchange was issued to pay the holder the interest on the face value of one or more loan office certificates issued before March 1, 1778. More than other kinds of bills of exchange, they could be sold on the commercial market for close to their face value in specie. It was these bills that the Superintendent of Finance persuaded Congress to stop issuing on September 9, 1782, the day before the next interest payment was due, thus eliciting sustained protests by public creditors in Philadelphia and other cities (see the headnote and notes to Morris to the President of Congress, July 29, 1782).

One caustic reaction to the suspension was expressed in the form of an "Epitaph" for a loan office certificate published in the Philadelphia Freeman's Journal of September 25, 1782. In this piece, quoted here in full, the Philadelphia public creditors' committee appears in the guise of "five skilful physicians" who published a "prescription" in broadside form addressed "To the Citizens of America, who are the Creditors of the United States," while the bitter reference to "a false professing friend" probably refers either to France in the person of its minister in Philadelphia, Chevalier de La Luzerne, or to Morris: "Sacred to the memory of/No. 37,/A Loan Office Certificate,/which departed this life, Sept. 9, 1782./aged five years and eight months./Stop reader,—and contemplate the fate of all/mortal things./This promising child was honourably descended,/being got by Public Credit on Public Spirit,/Jan. 2, anno Dom. 1776./Though born in a dark and gloomy hour,/and of apparent weakly constitution,/it once bid fair long to live,/an honour to its parents, and useful to mankind./Young as it was, America will not disdain/to own uncommon obligations/to this child,/and its numerous brethren and sisters./All of whom, though born at different times,/expired at the same instant,/and are buried in the same grave./The tears of widows and orphans,/of helpless age and feeble infancy,/have plentifully flowed on this sad occasion./Having long stood/the open assaults of its enemies, and these not a few,/it fell untimely by poison/secretly administered/by the hand of a false professing friend./Vain were the attempts/of five skilful physicians even to protract its fate;/while they were prescribing—alas! the patient died./For the benefit of a posterity which will never be born,/and to preserve from a like untimely death/those who will never live,/they have published their prescription./Reader! if thou canst restrain thy indignation,/do not curse/the authors of this sad catastrophe;/but admire the bounty of providence,/which has bestowed such large portions of/patience and resignation/on the whigs of America,/that they can starve without repining,/and kiss the hand that dashes from their lips,/the cup of earthly comforts."

The fourth bill of exchange illustrated here, printed in brown and black, is watermarked "UNITED STATES 4." The back is endorsed: "Pay the Contents to Mr Thomas Patterson/or Order Value Received." For numismatic details and illustrations of bills of exchange Congress drew on its European funds for other purposes, see William G. Anderson, The Price of Liberty: The Public Debt of the American Revolution (Charlottesville, Va., 1983), 87–90. The bill of exchange is from the National Numismatics Collection, no. 2458. National Museum of American History, courtesy of the Smithsonian Institution, Washington, D.C., photo no. 83–5637.

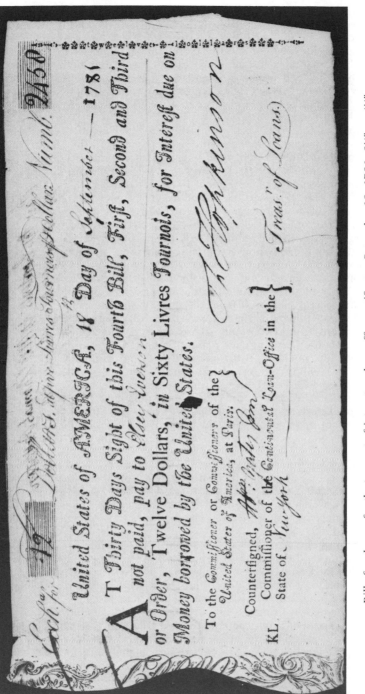

Bill of exchange for the payment of interest on loan office certificates, September 18, 1781. 8½″ × 4¼″

but the measure was dropped after an unfavorable report by a committee which had conferred with the Financier.[77] Following the recommendation of the grand committee, Congress on October 10 also
rejected as inexpedient another motion by Montgomery that a requisition be made on each state to provide for payment of both the interest
on the liquidated public debt and the half-pay pensions due retired
army officers.[78] However, Congress did resolve to demand from
Rhode Island and Georgia "an immediate definite answer" on the
impost ratification.

None of Congress's actions satisfied the Philadelphia public creditors. At a second formal meeting on September 26 they had created
an enlarged committee of nine, more balanced in terms of state politics, to continue efforts toward uniting creditors throughout the
nation in support of revenues to fund the debt. This committee
petitioned the Pennsylvania Assembly on October 31 for support of
measures likely to obtain funds for the regular and punctual payment of the interest on the public debt until the principal was discharged. Read on November 1, the petition was referred the following day to the assembly's committee on ways and means. A draft
memorial to Congress prepared by the committee was debated paragraph by paragraph and approved in final form by the assembly on
November 11 for transmittal to the state's congressional delegation.[79]

This second memorial from the Pennsylvania Assembly, signed by
the speaker under the date of November 12, pointedly inquired as to
what steps Congress would advise the state to take. According to
James Madison, its language plainly "imported a disposition" to divert
to debt repayment revenues assigned to Congress under current requisitions. Congress referred the Pennsylvania memorial to the same
committee which had been given the August 28 memorial.[80] In its
November 20 report on the two Pennsylvania memorials, the committee could do little more than allude to measures already adopted but
dependent upon action still to be taken by the states: ratification of the
impost; compliance with the special requisition for $1.2 million; and
emulation of New York's recent cession of its western claims to Congress—a step toward constituting western lands as a fund to discharge
federal debt.[81] In answer to Pennsylvania's complaint that there were
large unsettled claims against Congress in the state for services and
supplies, Congress ordered the Superintendent of Finance to report
on the delay in settling civilian claims under the ordinance of February 20, 1782.[82]

Nothing envisaged by Congress held much promise for an immediate solution to Pennsylvania's problems. On December 4 the Pennsylvania delegates announced to Congress that their assembly was drafting
legislation to provide for direct state payment of interest on the federal
debt and intended to finish it that evening. The assembly, they added,
was offended by Congress's failure to reply to the memorials and saw
little chance of obtaining general funds through any action of Congress.
One of the delegates remarked privately that diversion of revenues to
debt payment by the state would not impair the war effort since Congress had ample funds in Europe. Belief in foreign resources was one
which both Congress and the Financier were anxious to dispel, particularly since it was being propagated by foes of the impost, notably the
delegate from Rhode Island, David Howell, with the implication that
Congress had no real need for the impost or other federal taxes.

Congress reacted quickly, appointing a committee composed of Alexander Hamilton, Madison, and Rutledge to confer at once with a committee from the Pennsylvania Assembly in order to correct any misunderstanding as to the availability of funds from abroad. The congressmen explained to the Pennsylvania committee that French loans were already committed, that the Dutch loan had yielded only 1.5 million guilders and was presently inactive, and that the requisition of $2 million for 1783 was less than what was needed for current expenditures. If Pennsylvania and other states formally violated the right of appropriation given to Congress by the Articles of Confederation, the Union would collapse. Assumption of the national debt by the states, the committee argued, "was not only a breach of the federal system but of the faith pledged to the public Creditors; since payment was mutually guaranteed to each & all of the Creditors by each & all of the States." The committee also appealed to Pennsylvania's self-interest when it noted that, by assuming the debt to its citizens, the state might end up paying more than its proportional share of the debt than if it were apportioned equitably among the states. Impressed by these arguments, the Pennsylvania Assembly subsequently agreed to defer the matter until its next session.[83]

Under the shadow of Pennsylvania's impending action, Congress on December 6 instructed Morris "to represent to the several States the mischeifs which such [separate] appropriations would produce." It coupled this resolution with one sending a special mission to Rhode Island to persuade the assembly to ratify the impost. After official confirmation of Rhode Island's rejection arrived on December 11, Congress on December 16 adopted a committee report drafted by Alexander Hamilton to rebut the state's arguments against the impost, and appended two resolutions designed to obviate fears the state had raised about the indeterminate amount and duration of the debt and Congress's lack of accountability to the states for the funding revenues. The first resolution provided an implicit commentary on Morris's plan for a sinking fund that could be used as security for future loans. Pledging discharge of the principal of the debt "within a reasonable period, by which a nation may avoid the evils of an excessive accumulation of debt," the resolution stipulated that surplus revenues were to "form a sinking fund, to be inviolably appropriated to the payment of the principal of the said [war] debt, and shall on no account be diverted to any other purpose." By the second resolution Congress promised, as soon as the public debt could be liquidated, to furnish each state with annual statements of the debt, interest on the debt, and the proceeds and disposition of the funds provided for its redemption. Armed with the December 16 report and resolves, and having conferred at the direction of Congress with Morris and other department heads, the congressional deputation set out on December 22 to reverse the Assembly's decision. It turned back, however, after learning that Virginia had repealed her ratification of the impost.[84]

IV

National debt funding on the British model now seemed doomed. The impost of 1781, Congress's own recommendation, which Morris had supported unremittingly, was to all appearances dead. Morris had been unable to convince Congress to adopt the proposals he had submitted in his report on public credit for securing and assigning additional Continental taxes to debt funding. The funding requisition of September 4 he seems to have regarded as a temporary and unproductive expedient. In addition, revenues for current expenditures from the states on the requisitions for 1782 and 1783 were sparse; tax collection proved difficult and some states postponed the levies because of the shortage of specie. One result had been the collapse and renegotiation of the West Point and Moving Army contract in October 1782.[85] The Superintendent's expectations of meeting his engagements, present and future, lay in obtaining further loans, foreign or domestic. This, he believed, would be impossible unless the public debt was funded by established Continental revenues.

A new strategy presented itself on December 31 when the Superintendent was approached by a deputation of army officers from headquarters at Newburgh seeking payment of their claims. If Morris could unite the army, to whom large sums were owed or promised, with the other public creditors, Congress might be persuaded to ask the states for, and overcome their resistance to, taxes coextensive with the public debt. In January 1783 Morris hastily devised a plan to provide the troops with a part of their current pay, but he deferred the army's larger claims to back pay and pensions pending a general settlement. Nor would the Financier advise additional congressional applications for foreign loans until the success of earlier requests was known or adequate domestic revenues for debt funding were obtained.[86] What the states needed, Morris appears to have decided during this period, was an ultimatum. With little warning the Superintendent provided it on January 24, 1783, when he announced to a stunned Congress his intention to resign in May unless permanent domestic revenues were obtained to fund the debt. Morris's action, igniting a political crisis that lasted the spring, thrust his financial policies to the center of national debate and tested the cohesion of the Confederation.

Office of Finance July 29th. 1782[87]

Sir

The Reference which Congress were pleased to make, of a Remonstrance and Petition from Blair McClenaghan and others,[88] has induced me to pray their Indulgence while I go somewhat at large into the Subject of that Remonstrance. The Propriety and Utility of public Loans, have been Subjects of much Controversy. Those who find themselves saddled with the Debts of a preceding Generation, naturally exclaim against Loans; and it must be confessed that when such Debts are accumulated by Negligence, Folly or Profusion, the Complaint is well founded. But it would be equally so against Taxes, when wasted in the same Way. The Difference is, that the Weight of Taxes being more sensible, the Waste occasions greater Clamor, and is therefore more speedily remedied; but it will appear that the eventual Evils which Posterity must Sustain from heavy Taxes, are greater than from Loans. Hence may be deduced this Conclusion, that in Governments liable to a vicious Administration it would be better to raise the current Expence by Taxes, but where an honest and wise Appropriation of Money prevails, it is highly advantageous to take the Benefit of Loans. Taxation to a certain Point is not only proper but useful, because by stimulating the Industry of Individuals, it increases the Wealth of the Community. But when Taxes go so far as to intrench on the Subsistence of the People, they become burthensome and oppressive. The Expenditure of Money ought in such Case to be (if possible) avoided; and if unavoidable, it will be most wise to have Recourse to Loans.

Loans may be of two Kinds, either domestic or foreign. The relative Advantages and Disadvantages of each, as well as those which are common to both, will deserve Attention. Reasonings of this Kind, (as they depend on Rules of Arithmetic), are best understood by numerical Positions. For the Purposes of Elucidation, therefore, it may be supposed, that the annual Tax of any particular Husbandman were fifteen Pounds, during a ten Year's War, and that his net Revenue were but fifteen Pounds, so that (the whole being regularly consumed in Payment of Taxes) he would be no richer at the End of the War, than he was at the Beginning. It is at the same Time notorious that the Profits made by Husbandmen, on Funds which they borrowed, were very considerable. In many Instances their Plantations, as well as the Cattle and farming Utensils, have been purchased on Credit, and the Bonds given for both have shortly been paid by Sales of Produce. It is therefore no Exageration to state the Profits at twelve per Cent. The enormous Usury which People in Trade have been induced to pay, and which will presently be noticed,[89] demonstrates that the Profits made by other Professions are equal to those of the Husbandman. The Instance therefore taken from that, which is the most numerous Class of Citizens, will form no improper Standard for the whole. Let it then be farther supposed in the Case already stated, that the Party should annually borrow the Sum of ten Pounds,[90] to pay Part of his Tax of fifteen Pounds, at six per Cent. On this Sum then he would make a Profit of twenty four Shillings, and have to pay an Interest of twelve shillings. The enclosed Calculation[91] will shew that in ten years he would be indebted one hundred Pounds, but his additional Improvements would be worth: near[92] one hundred and fifty, and his net Revenue be increased near twelve after deducting the Interest of his Debt; whereas if he had not borrowed, his Revenue would have continued the same, as has already been observed. This Mode of Reasoning might be pursued farther, but what has been said is sufficient to shew that he would have made a considerable Advantage from the yearly Loan. If it be supposed that every Person in the Community made such [a] Loan, a similar Advantage would arise to the Community. And lastly if it be supposed that the Government were to make

a Loan, and ask so much less in Taxes, the same Advantage would
be derived. Hence also may be deduced this Position, that in a Society where the Average Profits of Stock are double to the Interest at
which Money can be obtained, every public Loan, for necessary Expenditures, provides a Fund in the Agregate of national Wealth
equal to the Discharge of it's own Interest. Were it possible that a
Society should exist in which every Member would, of his own accord, industriously pursue the Increase of national Property, without Waste or extravagance, the public Wealth would be impaired by
every species of Taxation. But there never was, and unless human
Nature should change, there never will be such a Society. In any
given Number of men there will always be some who are Idle, and
some who are extravagant. In every Society also, there must be some
Taxes, because the Necessity of Supporting Government and defending the State always exist. To do these on the cheapest Terms is
wise. And when it is considered how much Men are disposed to
Indolence and Profusion, It will appear that (even if these Demands
did not require the whole of what could be raised) still it would be
wise to carry Taxation to a certain Amount, and expend what should
remain after providing for the Support of Government and the
national Defence, in works of public utility, such as the Opening of
Roads and Navigations. For Taxes Operate two Ways towards the
increase of national Wealth. First they Stimulate Industry to provide
the Means of Payment. Secondly, they encourage Oeconomy so far
as to avoid the Purchase of unnecessary Things, and keep Money in
Readiness for the Tax Gatherer. Experience Shews that those Exertions of Industry and Oeconomy grow by Degrees into Habit. But in
Order that Taxation may have these good Effects, the Sum which
every Man is to pay, and the Period of Payment, should be certain
and unavoidable.

This Digression opens the way to a comparison between foreign
and domestic Loans. If the Loan be domestic, Money must be diverted from those Channels in which it would otherwise have
flowed, and therefore, either the Public must give better Terms than
Individuals, or there must be Money enough to supply the Wants of
both. In the latter Case, if the Public did not borrow, the Quantity of
Money would exceed the Demand, and the Interest would be
lowered; borrowing by the Public, therefore, would keep up the
Rate of Interest, which brings the latter Case within the Reason of
the former. If the Public outbid Individuals, those Individuals are
deprived of the Means of extending their Industry. So that no Case
of a domestic Loan can well be supposed, where some public Loss
will not arise to counterballance the public Gain; except when the
Creditor spares from his Consumption to lend to the Government,
which Operates a national Oeconomy. It is however an Advantage

peculiar to domestic Loans, that they give Stability to Government, by combining together the Interests of moneyed Men for it's Support; and consequently, in this Country, a domestic Debt would greatly contribute to that Union, which seems not to have been sufficiently attended to, or provided for, in forming the national Compact. Domestic Loans are also useful from the farther Consideration that as Taxes fall heavy on the lower Orders of a Community, the Releif obtained for them by such Loans, more than counterballances the Loss sustained by those who would have borrowed Money to extend their Commerce or Tillage. Neither is it a refinement to observe, that since a Plenty of Money and consequent Ease of obtaining it, induce Men to engage in Speculations which are often unprofitable, the Check which these receive is not injurious, while the Releif obtained for the Poor is highly beneficial.

By making foreign Loans, the Community (as such) receive the same extensive Benefits which one Individual does in borrowing of another. This Country was always in the Practice of making such Loans. The Merchants in Europe trusted those of America. The American Merchants trusted the Country Storekeepers; and they the People at large. This advance of Credit may be Stated at not less than twenty Million of Dollars. And the Want of that Credit is one principle Reason of those Usurious Contracts mentioned above. These have been checked by the Institution of the Bank, but the Funds of that Corporation, not permitting those extensive Advances which the Views of different People require, the Price given for particular Accommodations of Money continues to be enormous; and that again Shews, that to make domestic Loans would be difficult if not impracticable. The Merchants not having now that extensive Credit in Europe which they formerly had, the obtaining such Credit by the Government, becomes in some Sort necessary. But there remains an Objection with many against foreign Loans, which (tho it arises from a superficial View of the Subject) has no little Influence. This is, that the Interest will form a Balance of Trade against us, and drain the Country of Specie; which is only saying in other Words, that it would be more convenient to receive Money as a Present, than as a Loan. For the Advantages derived by the Loan exist, notwithstanding the Payment of Interest. To shew this more clearly, a Case may be Stated which in this City is very familiar. An Island in the Delaware overflowed at high Water has, for a given Sum, suppose a thousand Pounds, been banked in, drained and made to produce by the Hay sold from it at Philadelphia a considerable Sum annually, for Instance two hundred Pounds. If the owner of such an Island had borrowed (in Philadelphia) the thousand Pounds to improve it, and given six per Cent Interest, he would have gained a net Revenue of one hundred and forty Pounds.

This certainly would not be a Balance of Trade against his Island, nor the draining it of Specie. He would gain considerably, and the City of Philadelphia also would gain, by bringing to Market an increased Quantity of a necessary Article. In like manner, Money lent by the City of Amsterdam to clear the Forests of America, would be beneficial to both. Draining Marshes and bringing Forests under Culture are beneficial to the whole human Race, but most so to the Proprietor. But at any Rate, in a Country and in a situation like ours, to lighten the Weight of present Burthens (by Loans) must be good Policy. For as the Governments acquire more Stability, and the People more wealth, the former will be able to raise, and the latter to pay much greater Sums than can at present be expected.

What has been said on the general nature and Benefit of public Loans, as well as their particular Utility to this Country, contains more of Detail than is necessary for the United States in Congress, tho perhaps not enough for many of those to whose consideration this Subject must be Submitted. It may seem Superfluous to add that Credit is necessary to the obtaining of Loans. But among the many extraordinary Conceptions which have been produced, during the Present Revolution, it is neither the least prevalent, nor the least pernicious, that Foreigners will trust us with Millions, while our own Citizens will not trust us with a Shilling. Such an opinion must be unfounded and will appear to be false at the first Glance; Yet Men are (on some Occasions) so willing to deceive themselves, that the most flattering Expectations will be formed from the Acknowledgement of American Independance by the States General.[93] But surely no reasonable Hope can be raised on that Circumstance, unless something more be done by ourselves. The Loans made to us hitherto, have either been by the Court of France, or on their Credit. The Government of the United Netherlands are so far from being able to lend, that they must borrow for themselves. The most therefore which can be asked from them, is to become Security for America to their own Subjects, but it cannot be expected that they will do this, untill they are assured, and convinced, that we will punctually pay. This follows necessarily from the Nature of their Government, and must be clearly seen by the Several States, as well as by Congress, if they only consider what Conduct they would pursue on a similar Occasion. Certainly Congress would not put themselves in a situation which might oblige them to call on the several States for Money to pay the Debts of a foreign Power. Since then no Aid is to be looked for from the Dutch Government, without giving them Sufficient Evidence of a Disposition and Ability to pay both the Principal and Interest of what we borrow; and since the same Evidence which would convince the Government, must convince the Individuals who compose it; Asking the Aid of Government must either be unnecessary or ineffectual. Ineffectual before the Measures taken to establish our Credit, and unnecessary afterwards.

We are therefore brought back to the Necessity of establishing public Credit. And this must be done at Home, before it can be extended abroad. The only Question which can remain, is with Respect to the Means. And here it must be remembered that a free Government whose natural offspring is public Credit, cannot have sustained a Loss of that Credit unless from particular Causes; and therefore those Causes must be investigated and removed, before the Effects will cease. When the continental Money was issued, a greater Confidence was shewn by America, than any other People ever exhibited. The general Promise of a Body not formed into, nor claiming to be a Government, was accepted as current coin, and it was not until long after an Excess of quantity had forced on Depreciation, that the Validity of these Promises was questioned. Even then the public Credit still existed in a Degree, nor was it finally lost untill March 1780,[94] when an Idea was intertained that Government had committed Injustice. It is useless to enter into the Reasons for and against the Resolutions of that Period. They were adopted, and are now to be considered only in Relation to their Effects. These will not be altered by saying that the Resolutions were misunderstood; for in those Things which depend on public Opinion it is no matter (so far as consequences are concerned) how that opinion is influenced. Under present circumstances therefore, it may be considered as an uncontrovertible Proposition, that all paper Money ought to be absorped by Taxation (or otherwise) and destroyed before we can Expect our public Credit to be fully reestablished. For so long as there be any in Existence, the Holder will view it as a monument of national Perfidy.

But this alone would be taking only a Small Step in the important Business of establishing national Credit. There are a great Number of Individuals in the United States, who trusted the Public in the Hour of Distress, and who are impoverished, and even ruined by the Confidence they reposed. There are others, whose Property has been wrested from them by Force to Support the War, and to whom Certificates have been given in lieu of it which are entirely useless.[95] It needed not Inspiration to shew, that Justice establisheth a Nation,[96] neither are the Principles of Religion necessary to evince, that political Injustice will receive political Chastizement. Religious Men will cherish these Maxims in proportion to the additional Force they derive from divine Revelation. But our own Experience will Shew, that from a Defect of Justice this Nation is not established; and that her Want of Honesty is severely punished by the Want of Credit. To this Want of Credit must be attributed the Weight of Taxation for Support of the War, and the Continuance of that Weight by Continuance of the War.

It is therefore with the greatest Propriety your Petitioners already mentioned have stated in their Memorial, that both Policy and Justice require a solid Provision for funding the public Debts. It is with Pleasure Sir that I see this numerous, meritorious and oppressed Body of Men, who are Creditors of the public, begining to exert themselves for the obtaining of Justice. I hope they may succeed, not only because I wish well to a righteous Pursuit,[97] but because this Success will be the great Ground work of a Credit which will carry us safely thro the present just, important and necessary War, which will combine us closely together on the Conclusion of a Peace, which will always give to the Supreme Representative of America a Means of acting for the general Defence on Sudden Emergencies, and which will, of consequence, procure the Third of those great Objects for which we contend, *Peace, Liberty, and Safety.*

Such Sir are the cogent Principles by which we are called on to provide solid Funds for the national Debt. Already Congress have adopted a Plan for liquidating all past Accounts;[98] and if the States shall make the necesssary Grants of Revenue, what remains will be a simple executive Operation which will presently be explained. But however powerful the Reasons in favor of such Grants, over and above those Principles of moral Justice which none, however exalted, can part from with Impunity, still there are Men who (influenced by penurious selfishness) will grumble at the Expence, and who will assert the impossibility of sustaining it. On this Occasion the Sensations with Respect to borrowing are reversed. All would be content to relieve themselves, by Loan, from the Weight of Taxes, but many are unwilling to take up, as they ought, the Weight of Debt. Yet this must be done, before the other can happen, and it is not so great but that we Should find immediate Releif by assuming it, *even if it were a foreign Debt.* I say if it were a *foreign* Debt, because I shall attempt to shew, first that being *a domestic Debt,* to fund it will cost the Community Nothing and secondly that it will produce (on the Contrary) a considerable Advantage. And as to the first Point, one Observation will Suffice. The Expenditure has been made, and *a Part* of the Community have sustained it. If the Debt were to be paid, by a single Effort of Taxation; it could only create a Transfer of Property from one Individual to another, and the agregate Wealth of the Whole Community would be precisely the same. But since Nothing more is attempted than merely to fund the Debt by providing for the Interest (at six per Cent) The Question of Ability is resolved to this single Point, whether it is easier for *a Part of the people* to pay one hundred Dollars, than for the *whole People* to pay six Dollars. It is equally clear, tho' not equally evident, that a considerable Advantage would be produced, by funding our Debts, over and above what has been already mentioned, as the Consequence of National Credit.

This Advantage is threefold. First, many Persons by being Creditors of the Public, are deprived of those Funds which are necessary to the full Exercise of their Skill and Industry. Consequently the Community are deprived of the Benefits which would result from that Exercise, whereas if these Debts which are in a manner dead, were brought back to existence, monied men would purchase them up (tho perhaps at a considerable Discount) and thereby restore to the Public many useful Members who are now entirely lost; and extend the Operations of many more to considerable Advantage. For altho not one additional Shilling would be, by this Means, brought in; yet by distributing Property into those Hands which could render it most productive, the Revenue would be increased, while the original Stock continued the Same. Secondly, many Foreigners who make Speculations to this Country would, instead of ordering back Remittances, direct much of the Proceeds of their Cargoes to be invested in our public Funds; which, according to Principles already established, would produce a clear Advantage, with this Addition (from peculiar Circumstances) that it would Supply the Want of Credit to the mercantile Part of Society. The last, but not least, Advantage is, that in restoring Ease, Harmony and Confidence, not only the Government (being more respectable) would be more respected, and consequently better obeyed; but the mutual Dealings among Men, on private Credit, would be facilitated. The Horrors which agitate People's Minds, from an Apprehension of depreciating Paper, would be done away. The secret Hoards would be unlocked. In the same Moment, the Necessity of Money would be lessened, and the Quantity increased. By these Means the Collection of Taxes would be facilitated, and thus, instead of being Obliged to give valuable Produce for useless Minerals, that Produce would purchase the Things we stand in need of, and we should obtain a sufficient circulating Medium, by giving the People what they have always a Right to Demand, solid Assurance in the Integrity of their Rulers.

The next Consideration which Offers, is the Amount of the public Debt, and every good American must lament that Confusion in public Affairs, which renders an accurate State of it unattainable. But it must continue to be so, until all accounts both at Home and abroad be finally adjusted. The enclosed is an Estimate furnished by the Comptroller of the Treasury,[99] from which it appears that there is already an acknowledged Debt, bearing Interest, to the Amount of more than twelve Million of Dollars. On Part of this also there is a large arrearage of Interest, and there is a very considerable Debt unsetled, the Evidence whereof exists in various Certificates given for Property applied to the public Service. This[100] (including Pay due to the army previous to the present Year) cannot be estimated at less than between seven and eight Millions.[101] Our Debt to his most

Christian Majesty is above five Millions.[102] The nearest Guess therefore, which can be made at the Sum total, is from twenty five to
twenty seven million of Dollars, and if to this we add what it may be
necessary to borrow for the Year 1783 the Amount will be (with
Interest) by the Time proper Revenues are obtained, considerably
above thirty Millions. Of course the Interest will be between eighteen
hundred Thousand and two Million Dollars. And here, previous to
the Consideration of proper Revenues for that Amount, it may not
be amiss to make a few general Observations. The first of which is,
that it would be injurious to the United States to obtain Money on
Loan without providing before hand the necessary Funds. For if
those who are now so deeply engaged to Support the War, will not
grant such Funds to procure immediate Relief, certainly those who
come[103] after them will not do it, to pay a former Debt. Remote
Objects, dependent on abstract Reasoning, never influence the Mind
like immediate Sensibility. It is therefore the Province of Wisdom to
direct towards proper Objects that Sensibility which is the only Motive to Action among the Mass of Mankind. Should we be able to get
Money from the Dutch, without first providing Funds, which is
more than doubtful; and should the several States neglect, afterwards, making Provision to perform the Engagements of Congress,
which is more than probable; the Credit of the United States,
abroad, would be ruined for ever. Very Serious Discussions also
might be raised among foreign Powers,[104] our Creditors might have
Recourse to arms, and we might dishonorably be compelled to do,
what dishonestly we had left undone. Secondly, the Idea which
many entertain of soliciting Loans abroad to pay the Interest of
⟨our⟩ domestic Debts, is a Measure pregnant with it's own Destruction. If the States were to grant Revenues sufficient only to pay the
Interest of present Debts, we might perhaps obtain new Credit,
upon a general Opinion of our Justice, tho' that is far from certain.
But when we omit paying, by Taxes, the Interest of Debts already
contracted, and ask to borrow for the Purpose, making the same
Promises to obtain the new Loans which had been already made to
obtain the Old, we shall surely be disappointed. Thirdly, it will be
necessary, not only that Revenues be granted, but that those Revenues be amply sufficient for the Purpose, because (as will presently
appear) a Deficiency would be highly pernicious, while an Excess
would be not only unprejudicial but very advantageous. To perceive
this with all necessary Clearness, it must be remembered that the
Revenues asked for on this Occasion must be appropriated to the
Purposes for which they are asked, and in like Manner the Sums
required for current Expenditure, must be appropriated to the current Service. If then the former be deficient, the latter cannot be
brought in to Supply the Deficiencys and, of course, the public

Credit would be impaired; but should there be an Excess of Revenue, it could be applied in Payment of a Part of the Debt immediately, and in such Case if the Credits should have depreciated, they would be raised to Par, and if already at Par, the Offer of Payment would induce Creditors to lower the Interest. Thus in either Case, the Means of making new Loans on good Terms would be extended, and the Necessity of asking more Revenues obviated. Lastly, these Revenues ought to be of such a Nature as naturally and necessarily to increase; for Creditors will have a greater Confidence when they have a clear Prospect of being repaid, and the People will always be desirious to see a like Prospect of Releif from the Taxes. Besides which, it will be necessary to incur some considerable Expence after the War in making necessary Establishments for a permanent naval Force,[105] and it will always be least objectionable to borrow, for that Purpose, on Funds already established.

The Requisition of a five per Cent Impost, made on the third Day of February 1781, has not yet been complied with by the State of Rhode Island; but as there is Reason to beleive that their Compliance is not far off, this Revenue may be considered as being already granted.[106] It will however be very inadequate to the Purposes intended. If Goods be imported and Prizes introduced to the Amount of twelve Millions annually, the five per Cent would be six hundred thousand, from which at least one sixth must be deducted, as well for the Cost of Collection, as for the various Defalcations which will necessarily happen, and which it is unnecessary to enumerate. It is not safe therefore to estimate this Revenue at more than half a Million of Dollars, for tho it may produce more, yet probably it will not produce so much. It was in Consequence of this that, on the twenty seventh Day of February last, I took the Liberty to Submit the Propriety of asking the States for a Land Tax of one Dollar for every hundred Acres of Land, a Poll Tax of one Dollar on all freemen, and all male Slaves between sixteen and sixty (excepting such as are in the federal Army, and such as are by Wounds or otherwise rendered unfit for Service) and an Excise of one eighth of [a] Dollar, per Gallon, on all distilled Spirituous Liquors. Each of these may be estimated at half a Million, and should the Product be equal to the estimation, the Sum total of Revenues for funding the public Debts, would be equal to two Millions. What has been the Fate of these Propositions I know not,[107] but I will beg leave, on this Occasion, not only to renew them but also to state some Reasons in their favor, and answer some Objections against them.

And first, as to a Land Tax. The Advantages of it are, that it can be reduced to a Certainty as to the Amount and Time. That no extraordinary Means are necessary to ascertain it. And that Land, being the ultimate Object of human Avarice, and that particular

Species of permanent Property which so peculiarly belongs to a
Country as neither to be removed nor concealed, it stands foremost
for the Object of Taxation; and ought most particularly to be burthened with those Debts which have been incurred by defending the
Freedom of its Inhabitants. But besides these general Reasons, there
are some which are in a Manner peculiar to this Country. The Land
of America may, as to the Proprietors, be divided into two Kinds,
that which belongs to the great Landholders and that which is
owned and occupied by the industrious Cultivator. This latter Class
of Citizens is, generally speaking, the most numerous and most valuable part of a Community. The Artisan may, under any Government
minister to the Luxuries of the Rich, and the Rich may, under any
Government, obtain the Luxuries they covet. But the free Husbandman is the natural Guardian of his Country's Freedom. A Land Tax
will probably, at the first mention, startle this Order of Men, but it
can only be from the Want of Reflection, or the Delusion must be
kept up by the Artifice of others. To him who cultivates from one to
five hundred Acres, a Dollar per hundred is a trifling Object; but to
him who owns an hundred Thousand it is important. Yet a large
Proportion of America is the Property of great Landholders, they
monopolize it without Cultivation; they are (for the most Part) at no
Expence either of Money or personal Service to defend it; and,
keeping the Price higher by Monopoly than otherwise it would be,
they impede the Settlement and Culture of the Country. A Land
Tax, therefore, would have the salutary Operation of an Agrarian
Law, without the Iniquity. It would relieve the Indigent, and ag-
grandize the State, by bringing Property into the Hands of those
who would use it for the Benefit of Society. The Objections against
such a Tax are twofold, first that it is unequal, and secondly that it is
too high. To obviate the Inequality, some have proposed an Estimate
of the Value of different Kinds of Lands. But this would be improper, because first it would be attended with great Delay, Expence
and Inconvenience. Secondly it would be uncertain, and therefore
Improper, particularly when considered as a Fund for public Debts.
Thirdly, there is no reason to beleive that any Estimate would be
just; and even if it were, it must be annually varied or else come
within the Force of the Objection as strongly as ever; the former
would cost more than the Tax, and the latter would not afford the
Remedy asked for. Lastly, such Valuations would operate as a Tax
upon Industry, and promote that Land Monopoly which every wise
Government will study to repress. But further, the true Remedy for
any Inequality will be obtained in the Apportioning other Taxes, of
which there will always be enough to equalize this. Besides, the Tax
being permanent and fixed, it is considered in the Price of Land on
every Transfer of Property, and that produces a Degree of Equality

which no Valuation could possibly arrive at. In a word, if exact numerical Proportion be sought after in Taxes, there would be no End to the Search. Not only might a Poll Tax be objected to as too heavy on the Poor and too light on the rich, but when that Objection was obviated, the phisical Differences in the human Frame would alone be as endless a Source of Contention, as the different Qualities of Land. The second Objection that the Tax is too high, is equally futile with the former. Land which is so little worth that the Owner will not pay annually one Penny per Acre for the Defence of it, ought to belong to the Society by whom the Expence of defending it is defrayed. But the Truth is that this Objection arises from, and is enforced by, those Men who can very well bear the Expence, but who wish to shift it from themselves to others. I shall close this Subject by adding, that as such a Tax would, besides the Benefits to be derived from the Object of it, have the farther Advantage of encouraging Settlements and Population, This would redound, not only to the national Good, but even to the particular Good of the Land holders themselves.

With Respect to the Poll-Tax there are many Objections against it, but in some of the States a more considerable Poll Tax already exists, without Inconvenience. The Objections are principally drawn from Europe, by Men who do not consider that a Difference of Circumstances makes a very material Difference in the Nature of political Operations. In some Parts of Europe, where nine tenths of the People are exhausted by continual Labor to procure bad cloathing and worse Food, this Tax would be extremely oppressive. But in America, where three Days of labor produce Sustenance for a week, it is not unreasonable to ask two Days out of a year as a Contribution to the Payment of public Debts. Such a Tax will, on the Rich, be next to Nothing, on the midling Ranks it will be of little consequence, and it cannot affect the Poor, because such of them as are unable to labor will fall within the Exception proposed. In fact, the Situation of America differs so widely from that of Europe, as to the matter now under Consideration, that hardly any Maxim which applies to one will be alike applicable to the other. Labor is in such Demand among us, that the Tax will fall on the Consumer. An able bodied Man who demands one hundred Dollars Bounty to go into military Service, for three Years, cannot be oppressed by the annual Payment of one Dollar, while not in that Service. This Tax also will have the good Effect of placing before the Eyes of Congress the Number of Men in the Several States; an Information always important to Government.

The Excise proposed is liable to no other Objection than what may be made against the Mode of Collection; but it is conceived that this may be such as can produce no ill Consequences. Excise Laws exist, and have long existed, in the several States. Of all Taxes those on

the Consumption of Articles are most agreable; because, being mingled with the price, they are less sensible to the People. And without
entering into a Discussion with which Speculative Men have amused
themselves, on the Advantages and Disadvantages of this Species of
Taxation, it may be boldly affirmed that no Inconvenience can arise
from laying a heavy Tax on the Use of ardent Spirits. These have
always been equally prejudicial to the Constitutions and Morals of
the People. The Tax will be a Means of compelling Vice to support
the Cause of Virtue; and, like the Poll Tax, will draw from the Idle
and Dissolute that Contribution to the public Service, which they will
not otherwise make.

Having said thus much on the Propriety of these Taxes, I shall pray
leave to assure you of my ready Acquiescence in the Choice of any
others which may be more agreable to the United States in Congress;
praying them nevertheless to consider, that as the Situation of the
respective States is widely different, it will be wise to adopt a Variety
of Taxes, because by that Means the Consent of all will be more
readily obtained, than if such are chosen as will fall heavy only on
particular States. The next Object is the Collection, which for the
most obvious Reasons ought to be by Authority derived from the
United States. The collecting of a Land Tax, as has been observed
above, will be very simple. That of the Poll Tax may be equally so,
because Certificates of the Payment may annually be issued to the
Collectors, and they be bound to return the Certificates or the Money,
and empowered to compell a Payment by every Man not possessed of
a Certificate. If, in addition to this, those who travel from one State to
another be obliged to take out and pay for a new Certificate in each
State, that would operate an useful Regulation of Police;[108] and a
slight Distinction between those and the common Certificates, would
still preserve their Utility in numbering the People. It is not necessary
to dwell on the Mode of collectng these Branches of Revenue, because
(in Reason) a Determin[ation] on the Propriety of the Taxes should
precede it. I will only take the Liberty to drop one Idea with Respect
to the Impost already required. It is conceived that Laws should be so
formed, as to leave little, or nothing, to the Discretion of those by
whom they are executed. That Revenue Laws in particular should be
guarded in this Respect from odium, being (as they are) sufficiently
odious in themselves. And, therefore, that it would have been well to
have stipulated the precise Sum payable on different Species of Commodities. The Objection is, that the List (to be accurate) must be
numerous. But this accuracy is unnecessary, the Description ought to
be very Short and General, so as to comprize many Commodities
under one Head; and the Duty ought to be fixed according to their
average Value. The Objection against this Regulation is, that the Tax
on fine Commodities would be trivial, and on coarse Commodities

great. This indeed is true, but it is desirable for two Reasons. First, that coarse and bulky Commodities *could* not be smuggled to evade the *heavy* Duty; and that fine Commodities *would* not be smuggled to evade the *light* Duty. Secondly, that coarse Commodities (generally speaking) minister to the Demands of Necessity or Convenience, and fine Commodities to those of Luxury. The heavy Duty on the former would operate an Encouragement to produce them at Home, and by that Means a Stoppage of our Commerce in Time of War would be most felt by the Wealthy, who have always the most abundant Means of procuring Relief.

I shall now Sir take the Liberty to Suppose, that the Revenues I have mentioned, or some others to the Amount of at least two Millions net annual Produce, were asked for and obtained, as a Pledge to the public Creditors; to continue untill the Principal and Interest of the Debts contracted, or to be contracted, should be finally paid. This Supposition is made that I may have an Opportunity (thus early) to express my Sentiments on the Mode of Appropriation. It would be as follows. Any one of the Revenues, being estimated, a Loan should be opened on the Credit of it, by Subscription, to a certain Amount and public Debts of a particular Description (or Specie) be received in Payment of the Subscriptions. This funded Debt should be transferable, under particular Forms, calculated for the Prevention of fraudulent, and facilitating of honest Negotiations. In like Manner on each of these Revenues should Subscriptions be opened, proceeding by Degrees so as to prevent any sudden Revolutions in Money Matters; such Revolutions being always more or less injurious. I should farther propose, that the Surplus of each of these Revenues (and Care should be taken that there would be a Surplus) should be carried to a Sinking Fund, on the Credit of which, and of the general Promises of Government new Loans should be opened, when necessary. The Interest should be paid half yearly; which would be convenient to the Creditors and to the Government, as well as useful to the People at large: because by this Means, if four different Loans were opened at different Times, the Interest would be payable eight Times in the Year, and thus the Money would be paid out of the Treasury as fast as it came in, which would require fewer Officers to manage the Business, keep them in more constant and regular Employment, dispense the Interest so as to command the Confidence and facilitate the Views of the Creditors, and return speedily the Wealth obtained by Taxes into the Common Stock. I know it will be objected, that such a Mode of Administration would enable Speculators to perform their Operations. A general Answer to this would be, that any other Mode would be more favorable to them. But farther, I conceive, first, that it is much beneath the Dignity of Government to intermeddle in such Considerations. Secondly, that Speculators always do least Mischief where they are left most at Liberty. Thirdly, that it is not in human Prudence to counteract their Operations by Laws; whereas when left alone they invariably counteract each other. And fourthly, that even if it were possible to prevent Speculation, it is precisely the Thing which ought not to be prevented; because he who wants Money to commence, pursue or extend his Business, is more benefited by selling Stock of any Kind (even at a considerable Discount) than he could be by the Rise of it at a future Period; Every Man being able to judge better of his own Business and Situation, than the Government can for him. So much would not, perhaps, have been said on the Head of this Objection, if it did not naturally lead to a Position which has been ruinous and might prove fatal. There are many Men (and some of them honest Men) whose Zeal against Speculation leads them to be sometimes unmindful, not only of sound Policy, but even of Moral Justice. It is not uncommon to hear, that those who have bought the public Debts for small Sums, ought only to be paid their purchase Money. The Reasons given are, that they have taken Advantage of the distressed Creditor, and shewn a Diffidence in the public Faith. As to the first, it must be remembered that in giving the Creditor Money for his Debt, they have at least afforded him some Relief, which he could not obtain elsewhere; and if they are deprived of the expected Benefit, they never will afford such Relief again. As to the Second, those who buy up the public Debts shew at least as much Confidence, in the public faith, as those who sell them; but allowing (for Argument's sake) that they have exhibited the Diffidence complained of, it would certainly be wiser to remove than to Justify it. The one Mode tends to create, establish and secure public Credit; and the other to sap, overturn and destroy it. Policy is therefore on this (as I believe it to be on every other occasion) upon the same Side of the Question with Honesty. Honesty tells us, that the Duty of the Public to pay is like the same Duty in an Individual. Having benefited by the Advances, they are bound to replace them to the Party, or to his Representatives. The Debt is a Species of Property, and whether disposed of for the whole nominal Value, or the half, for something or for Nothing, is totally immaterial. The Right of receiving, and the Duty of paying, must always continue the same. In a word, that Government which can (thro' the Intervention of its Courts) compel Payment of private Debts, and Performance of private Contracts, on Principles of distributive Justice, but refuse to be guided by those Principles, as to their own Contracts and Debts, merely because they are not amenable to human Laws, shews a flagitious Contempt of moral Obligations, which must necessarily weaken, as it ought to do, their Authority over the People.

Before I conclude this long Letter, it would be unpardonable not to mention a Fund which has long since been suggested, and dwells still in the Minds of many. You Doubtless Sir anticipate my naming of what are called the back Lands. The question as to the Property of those Lands, I confess myself utterly incompetent to decide, and shall not, for that Reason, presume to enter on it. But it is my Duty to mention, that the offer of a Pledge the Right to which is contested, would have ill Consequences, and could have no Good ones. It could not strengthen our Credit because no one would rely on such a Pledge, and the Recurrence to it would give unfavorable Impressions of our political Sagacity. But admitting that the Right of Congress is clear, we must remember also, that it is disputed by some considerable Members of the Confederacy. Dissentions might arise from hasty Decissions on this Subject, and a Government torne by intestine Commotions, is not likely to acquire or maintain Credit, at Home or abroad. I am not however the less clear in my Opinion, that it would be alike useful to the whole Nation, and to those very constituent Parts of it, that the entire Disposition of these Lands should be in Congress. Without entering therefore into the litigated Points, I am induced to beleive, and for that Reason to suggest the proposing this Matter to the States as an amicable Arrangement. I hope to be pardoned when I add, that considering the Situation of South Carolina and Georgia, it might be proper to ask their Consent to Matters of the clearest Right. But that, supposing the Right to be doubtful, urging a Decision in the present Moment might have a harsh and ungenerous Appearance. But if we suppose this matter to be arranged, either in the one Mode or in the Other, so that the Right of Congress be rendered indisputable (for that is a previous Point of indispensible Necessity) the remaining Question will be as to the Appropriation of that Fund. And I confess it does not appear to me, that the Benefits resulting from it are such as many are led to beleive. When the Imagination is heated in Pursuit of an Object, it is generally overrated. If these Lands were now in the Hands of Congress, and they were willing to mortgage them to their present Creditors, unless this were accompanied with a due Provision for the Interest, it would bring no Relief. If these Lands were to be sold for the public Debts, they would go off for almost nothing. Those who want Money could not afford to buy Land. Their Certificates would be bought up for a Trifle. Very few moneyed Men would become possessed of them, because very little money would be invested in so remote a Speculation. The small Number of Purchasers would easily and readily combine. Of Consequence they would acquire the Lands for almost Nothing, and effectually defeat the Intentions of Government, leaving it still under the Necessity of making farther Provision; after having needlessly squandered an immense Property. This Reasoning is not new. It has been advanced on similar Occasions before, and the Experience which all America has had of the Sales of confiscated Estates, and the like, will now shew that it was well founded. The back Lands, then, will not answer our Purpose without the necessary Revenues. But those Revenues will alone produce the desired effect. The back Lands may afterwards be formed into a Fund, for opening new Loans in Europe on a low Interest, redeemable within a future Period (for Instance twenty Years) with a right reserved to the Creditors of taking Portions of those Lands, on the Non Payment of their Debts, at the Expiration of that Term. Two Modes would offer for Liquidation of those Debts. First to tender Payment during the Term, to those who would not consent to alter the Nature of the Debt; which (if our Credit be well established) would place it on the general Footing of national Faith. And Secondly, to sell Portions of the Land (during the Term) sufficient to discharge the Mortgage. I perswade myself that the Consent of the reluctant States might be obtained, and that this Fund might hereafter be converted to useful Purposes. But I hope that, in a Moment when the Joint Effort of all is indispensible, no Causes of Altercation may be mingled, unnecessarily, in a question of such infinite Magnitude as the Restoration of public Credit. Let me add, Sir, that unless the Money of Foreigners be brought in for the Purpose, Sales of public Land would only absorp that Surplus Wealth, which might have been exhaled by Taxes, so that in Fact no new Resource is produced. And that, while (as at present) the Demand for Money is so great as to raise Interest to five per Cent per Month, public Lands must sell extremely low were the Title ever so clear; what then can be expected when the Validity of that Title, is one Object of the War? I have the Honor to be with great Respect your Excellency's most obedient Servant[109]

Robt Morris

His Excellency The President of Congress

[ENCLOSURE 1]
Calculation

[Office of Finance, July 29, 1782]

CALCULATION to show the Effects of a Yearly Loan of £10 for ten Years on the Supposition that the Interest of Money be £6 and Profits £12 ℔ Ct.

Dr.			Cr.
First Year borrowed	£10.	First Year borrowed	£10.
	£10.		£10.
Second Year Interest at 6 ℔ Cent	.6	Second Year Profits at 12 ℔ Ct.	1.2
	£10.6		£11.2
paid Interest	.6	paid	.6
	£10.		£10.6
borrowed	10.	borrowed	10.
	£20.		£20.6

Third Year Interest	1.2	Third Year Profits	2.472
	£21.2		23.072
paid Interest	1.2	paid	1.2
	20.		21.872
borrowed	10.	borrowed	10.
	30.		31.872
Fourth Year Interest	1.8	Fourth Year Profits	3.824
	31.8		35.696
paid Interest	1.8	paid	1.8
	30.		33.896
borrowed	10.	borrowed	10.
	40.		43.896
Fifth Year Interest	2.4	Fifth Year Profits	5.267
	42.4		49.163
paid Interest	2.4	paid	2.4
	40.		46.763
borrowed	10.	borrowed	10.
	50.		56.763
Sixth Year Interest	3.	Sixth Year Profits	6.811
	53.		63.574
paid Interest	3.	paid	3.
	50.		60.574
borrowed	10.	borrowed	10.
	60.		70.574
Seventh Year Interest	3.6	Seventh Year Profits	8.468
	63.6		79.042
paid Interest	3.6	paid	3.6
	60.		75.442
borrowed	10.	borrowed	10.
	70.		85.442
Eighth Year Interest	4.2	Eighth Year Profits	10.253
	74.2		95.695
paid Interest	4.2	paid	4.2
	70.		91.495
borrowed	10.	borrowed	10.
	80.		101.495
Ninth Year Interest	4.8	Ninth Year Profits	12.178
	84.8		113.673
paid Interest	4.8	paid	4.8
	80.		108.873
borrowed	10.	borrowed	10.
	90.		118.873
Tenth Year Interest	5.4	Tenth Year Profits	14.264
	95.4		133.137
paid Interest	5.4	paid	5.4
	90.		127.737
borrowed	10.	borrowed	10.
	100.		137.737
End of tenth Year Interest ..	6.	End of tenth Year Profits ...	16.528
	106.		154.265
paid Interest	6.	paid	6.
	100.		148.265
Yearly Interest ...	6.	Yearly Profits	17.791
		deduct Interest ..	6.
		Net Profit	11.791

[ENCLOSURE 2]

Estimate of the Public Debt by Joseph Nourse

[Register's Office, Treasury Department, July 16, 1782]

An Estimate of Monies loaned to the United States at certain Periods and reduced to Specie Value by Tables of Depreciation, also of the Debts on the Funded Books and certain Credits to Individuals ordered by Congress on Interest to be passed in the Treasury Books, with a Calculation of Interest for one Year on the whole Debt.

	Nominal Dollars	Amount bearing Interest on France	Value in Specie	Amount of One Years Interest
LOAN OFFICE				
Loaned from the opening of the several Offices until the 1 September 1777	3,778,900.		3,778,900.	226,734.
.... from the 1st September 1777 to the 1st March 1778	3,426,600.		2,515,134.56	150,908. 9
.... from ..... ditto .... to .. ditto .... Suppositious Sums in the State of Georgia	32,600.	7,238,100.	23,436.43	1,406.17
.... from the 1st March 1778 to the 1st April 1780	41,429,612.		4,521,186.21	271,271.15
.... from .... to .. ditto .... Suppositious Sums in the States of North				
Carolina, South Carolina & Georgia	3,435,800.		259,916. 5	15,394.86
.... from the 1st April 1780 to the dates of the last Returns	11,248,500.		281,212.45	16,872.67
.... from .... to .. ditto .... Suppositious Sums in the States above mentioned	2,305,000.		57,625.	3,457.45
Certificates of Specie Value Issued pursuant to Orders of Congress for Depreciation on Pay &c to Hazens, Armands, Van Heers, their respective Corps, & in discharge of other Debts due by the United States			153,728.23	9,923.62
LOTTERY Certificates Issued in the first Class for Prizes drawing Interest from the 27th May 1778	46,000.		17,780.82	1,066.76
.... ditto ..... in the second do. for Prizes drawing Interest from the 29th June 1779	60,500.		4,123.20	247.35
.... ditto ...... in the third do. for Prizes drawing do. from the 29th April 1780	176,500.		4,412.45	264.68
.... 4th Class Mr. Joseph Bullock one of the Managers of the Lottery estimates $2/5$ of the Prizes drawn in the 4th Class to be the Property of Individuals				
.... the Prizes drawn amount to 5,000,000 and of the said $2/5$ths there may be Issuable in Certificates to the Amount of the Residue payable in Cash for Prizes of 50 Dollars each	1,480,000.		37,000.	2,220.
	520,000.		13,000.	780.
BILLS drawn by Major General Lincoln and accepted by the Board of Treasury pursuant to Orders of Congress and their Value in Specie ascertained by the late Auditor General pursuant to an Act of Congress of the 23rd July 1780 remaining unpaid	3,065,838.60		60,275.72	3,616.49

FUNDED DEBT, there have been Funded and passed to the Credit of Individuals pursuant to Warrants from the Superintendent of Finance .... 266,872.54 ..... 16,012.32

The following Sums are passed to the Credit of Individuals in the Treasury Books pursuant to the Orders of Congress

    Amt. ordered to his Cr. 1st. 507,641 Livr. Martinico at 8 1/4 dollr. 61,532.22

William Bingham do. .... ditto ....2d. 110,324 ...... do 13,372.60

          74.94.82

      deduct the Amt. of his Debt .... Amount to his Cr. 43,904.82

      31,000.

Amt. ordered to his Credit £19,445.11.11 Sterlg.

John Ross To his Debit in Bills of Exchange 9,531.10.9 .... Amount to his Cr. 44,062.53

Stephen Ceronio 6,745.45

Oliver Pollock 59,255.78

Moses Hazen 13,386. 2

Arthur Lee 7,150.54

Major Genl Sullivan .... 1,500. .... 176,005.44 ..... 12,170,609.60 ..... 10,560.29

    63,767,750.60   7,238,100.   12,170,609.60   730,236.50

     7,238,100 amt. bearing Int. on France.

  71,005,850.60 Total amt. of Nominal Dollars.

The above Estimate of Monies loaned on Certificates issued from the several Loan Offices is formed from the Returns and other Papers render'd to the Treasury by the ascertaining the amount of Continental Money loaned in each Month and reducing the same to Specie on the 15th by the averaged Depreciation. If the Loan Officers that have transmitted their Registers have been accurate with regard to the daily Issues of Certificates, and the Time from which they respectively draw Interest the Loan Office Debt of those States may be ascertained with some degree of precision, but this being a work of Time the above mode has been adopted as the most accurate and expeditious to answer the present purpose. The Registers Certificates Issued in the States of New York, Delaware, Virginia, North Carolina, South Carolina and Georgia have not yet been transmitted. Certificates have in so many Instances been antidated by the Loan Officer by virtue of sundry Acts of Congress authorizing their drawing Interest from the Time Monies were deposited or Debts contracted that a careful examination of the Checks and Accounts made out therefrom and calculation of the Value of every daily Loan appear the only mode to arrive at absolute certainty. I beg leave to remark that the foregoing Observation is made on a View of the Registers already transmitted. The suppositious Sums estimated to have been loaned in the States of North Carolina, South Carolina and Georgia are made on the whole amount of Certificates sent, and partial Accounts of their Issues, no regular Returns ever having been received from those States. The Loan by Lottery is more accurate as tve Certificates Issued for the Prizes drawn in the first, second and third Classes are dated and draw Interest from fixed Periods. The Funded Debt and Credits to Individuals are taken from the Books.

          Registers Office 16th July 1782

    (Signed)   Joseph Nourse Rr.

James Milligan Esqr.
Comptroller of the Treasury

ENDORSED: 80/Letter 29 July 1782/Superintendt of finance/Aug 5/Referred to the grand committee/On the nature and benefit of public/loans. Necessity of establishing credit/to obtain them. Means of establishing/Credit. Revenues and taxes proposed/and the mode of Application pointed out
MSS: LS and enclosures, PCC, DNA; Ofcl LbC, DLC; copy, Meshech Weare Papers, Nh-Ar; copy, M-Ar; copy, R-Ar; copy, Jonathan Trumbull Papers, Ct; copy, Continental Congress Papers, Vi; copy, William Churchill Houston Collection, NjP; copy lacking last manuscript page, Abraham Yates, Jr., Papers, NN; LbC, M-Ar; LbC, Letterbook of Alexander Martin, 1782–1785, Nc-Ar; copy, Shelburne Papers, MiU-C; copy, Colonial Office, Class 5/Volume 108, fols. 109–125, PRO; copy, Lowell Collection, MHi; Force transcript, DLC.

1. Ver Steeg, *Morris*, 124. According to Ver Steeg (*ibid.*, 128), this report together with RM's letter to the President of Congress of August 28, 1781, on the settlement of state accounts with the Union, which was not sent to Congress until November 5 of that year, "constitute the Superintendent of Finance's Reports on Public Credit; these Reports reflect a penetration, a boldness in design, and a breadth in scope perhaps not equaled among the Financier's contemporaries."

2. What follows in this and the succeeding paragraph represents a composite view drawn from RM's draft letter to Jacques Necker, June 15, 1781, RM to Benjamin Franklin, November 27, 1781 (first letter), and Gouverneur Morris to Francisco Rendón, March 5, 1782, and to Matthew Ridley, August 6, 1782. Similar views were expressed in Gouverneur Morris's "An American" essay in the *Pennsylvania Packet* of March 23, 1780 (see headnote at note 37). See also RM's Circular to the Governors of the States, February 9, 1782.

3. The phrase is from RM to Alexander Hamilton, July 2, 1782.

4. By this standard, RM could extol Pennsylvania's ratification of the impost not only as a model for other states to emulate but as lasting evidence of its "regard for the sacred Principles of moral Justice and adherence to the exalted Dictates of national Obligation" (to the Speaker of the Pennsylvania Assembly, February 13, 1782). In discussing the reluctance of the states to grant revenues for debt funding not long after taking office, the Superintendent wrote that "in matters of Public Credit long delay is equivalent to direct Refusal." By July 1782, as the report on public credit was being contemplated, Morris was privately characterizing the states' neglect as "deeply criminal." See RM's Circular to Rhode Island, New York, Delaware, Maryland, and North Carolina, July 27, 1781, and to Richard Butler, July 18, 1782.

5. The sources for this paragraph, in order of quotation, are RM to the Governors of North Carolina, South Carolina, and Georgia, December 19, and to the Governor of Massachusetts, September 15, 1781, to Moses Hazen, January 15, 1782, to Silas Deane, June 7, 1781, and RM's circulars to the governors of July 25 and 27, 1781, and March 9, 1782. For the significance of contractual justice in the contemporary defense of commerce as a civilizing force, see Drew R. McCoy, *The Elusive Republic: Political Economy in Jeffersonian America* (Chapel Hill, N. C., 1980), 36.

6. RM to [William Hooper], January 18, 1777, quoted in Ver Steeg, *Morris*, 38. This letter, which cannot be located in the manuscript collection at PHi in which Ver Steeg found it, contains Morris's reaction to a proposal for a Chamber of Commerce then being considered by Congress.

7. RM to George Washington, July 2, 1781. The source of the quotation has not been identified.

8. RM to the Public, May 28, 1781. See also RM to John Jay, July 13, and to the Governors of North Carolina, South Carolina, and Georgia, December 19, 1781.

9. See RM to Jay, July 13, 1781.

10. See RM to José de Solano, May 16, 1782. See also RM to the Commissioners of Accounts, September 4, 1783.

11. See, for example, J. G. A. Pocock, "Virtue and Commerce in the Eighteenth Century," *Journal of Interdisciplinary History*, III (1972), 119–134, esp. 128–134. For recent literature suggesting a greater appreciation of the role of commerce in the Jeffersonian schematic for American social development, see McCoy, *Elusive Republic*, 76–104; and Joyce Appleby, "Commercial Farming and the 'Agrarian Myth' in the Early Republic," *Journal of American History*, LXVIII (1982), 833–849, and "What is

Still American in the Political Philosophy of Thomas Jefferson?" *WMQ*, 3d ser., XXXIX (1982), 287–309.

12. Deane to RM, June 10, 1781.

13. Although RM has long been recognized as a spokesman for American commercial development and, more recently, as a representative of "Court" thinking, his commitment to a balanced national economy in which commercialized agriculture played a fundamental role has not been fully appreciated. RM's views, shared by a range of opinion within the Republican party in Pennsylvania, served as a broadly based political appeal of considerable strength in the Republicans' electoral victories of the early and late 1780s against the supporters of the constitution of 1776 and the critics of the bank. For the development of this theme, see Douglas M. Arnold, "Political Ideology and the Internal Revolution in Pennsylvania, 1776–1790" (Ph.D. diss., Princeton University, 1976), 195–207, 225–232. Recognition of the importance of commercial agriculture to the Philadelphia mercantile community is recorded, for example, in notes to RM's Report to Congress on a Memorial of the Merchants of Philadelphia, May 4, 1782. For earlier appreciations of RM's emphasis on economic development, see Ferguson, *Power of the Purse*, 120–124; Ferguson, "The Nationalists of 1781–1783 and the Economic Interpretation of the Constitution," *JAH*, LVI (1969), 241–261; and Stuart W. Bruchey, *The Roots of American Economic Growth, 1607–1861: An Essay in Social Causation* (New York, 1965), 102–107. For assessments of RM as a representative of "Court" thinking, see Lance Banning, *The Jeffersonian Persuasion: Evolution of a Party Ideology* (Ithaca, N. Y., 1978), 127–140, esp. 135–136; and James H. Hutson, "Country, Court, and Constitution: Antifederalism and the Historians," *WMQ*, 3d ser., XXXVIII (1981), 361–362.

14. Manufacturing is specifically mentioned in the report on public credit only with reference to production for the home market as a means to avoid dangerous dependence on foreign sources for the necessities of life, particularly in wartime.

15. RM to Washington, July 2, and to the Governor of New York, December 11, 1781.

16. For the debate in the states over the incidence of various kinds of taxes, see Robert A. Becker, *Revolution, Reform, and the Politics of American Taxation, 1763–1783* (Baton Rouge, La., 1980).

17. As a United States Senator from Pennsylvania in 1790, RM remained hostile to scaling down the debt and evidently was prepared to vote against the assumption of state debts if the full 6 percent interest was not paid. Under the compromise reached, 6 percent interest was paid on the principal and 3 percent on the interest of the funded debt. See Edgar S. Maclay, ed., *The Journal of William Maclay, United States Senator from Pennsylvania, 1789–1791*, introd. Charles A. Beard (New York, 1927), 288, 314–315, 318, 321, 324; Kenneth R. Bowling, "Politics in the First Congress, 1789–1791" (Ph.D. diss., University of Wisconsin, 1968), 224–225; and Jacob E. Cooke, "The Compromise of 1790," *WMQ*, 3d ser., XXVII (1970), 541.

18. See RM to the President of Congress, March 8, 1783.

19. For RM's later defense of foreign investment in the Bank of North America, see Carey, ed., *Debates*, 54–56.

20. See RM's Circular to the Governors of the States, September 4, 1781.

21. See Carey, ed., *Debates*, 35–36, 38, 43–44, 55, 83, 89, 94, 96–97; and Ferguson, "Nationalists," 248–251.

22. Gouverneur Morris to Matthew Ridley, August 6.

23. For RM's plans to rebuild the Continental navy, submitted simultaneously with the report on public credit, see the headnote to RM to the President of Congress, July 30.

24. This and the following paragraph are based on E. James Ferguson, "Political Economy, Public Liberty, and the Formation of the Constitution," *WMQ*, 3d ser., XL (1983), 389–412, and sources cited there.

25. See Diary, November 3, 1781.

26. See RM to the President of Congress, February 11, 1782, his Circular to the Governors of Massachusetts, Rhode Island, New York, Delaware, Maryland, and North Carolina, July 27, 1781, RM to the Governor of Rhode Island, December 29, 1781, and to Pierre Landais, January 16, 1782.

27. See Carey, ed., *Debates*, 41.

28. See Diary, December 27, 1781. The Mortimer volume probably was *The Elements of Commerce, Politics and Finances, in Three Treatises* . . . (London, 1772), the most extended development of his ideas. RM could also have been familiar with similar themes as developed in Mortimer's *Every Man his own broker* . . . (London, 1761), an antistockjobbing tract that had gone through nine editions by 1782; *A New and Complete Dictionary of Trade and Commerce* . . . (London, 1766–1767) in two volumes; and *The National Debt no National Grievance* . . . *By a Financier* (London, 1768), which Mortimer published anonymously but acknowledged as his own in the *Elements*.

29. See RM to the President of Congress, January 15, 1782 (first letter), and notes, and Gouverneur Morris to Thomas Willing, June 18, 1782.

30. See notes 37–38 below.

31. See John Swanwick to RM, [ca. February 20, 1781]. RM had also sent for two French economic treatises on public account during his first year in office; see RM to Benjamin Franklin, September 14, 1781, and notes.

32. See RM to Necker, June 15 and December 3, 1781, and to de Mars, June 12, 1782, and notes.

33. Philip S. Foner, ed., *The Complete Writings of Thomas Paine* (New York, 1945), I, 171–188; the delineation of Paine's thought in Eric Foner, *Tom Paine and Revolutionary America* (New York, 1976), 98–182; and Diary, September 18, 1782, and notes.

34. The essays are conveniently reprinted in Webster's *Political Essays on the Nature and Operation of Money, Public Finances, and Other Subjects* . . . (Philadelphia, 1791), 9–182. Although it was Webster who had called for the creation of the office of Superintendent of Finance, he broke with RM later in the decade by endorsing the idea of discriminating in favor of original holders in funding the public debt.

35. [William Barton], *Observations on the Nature and Use of Paper-Credit; and the Peculiar Advantages to be derived from it, in North-America: from which are inferred the Means of Establishing and Supporting it, including Proposals for Founding a National Bank* (Philadelphia, 1781). The pamphlet was addressed to Congress and the Pennsylvania Assembly. Presented with a copy, Nathanael Greene attributed its ideas almost wholly to the influence of Charles Pettit, a leader of the public creditors in Philadelphia and later RM's chief rival as financial statesman in Pennsylvania. "Whoever might be the writer, I am confident you was the dictator," Greene wrote to Pettit on August 29, 1782. "There was not a single feature in it but that I knew the moment I beheld it to have originated with you, as the matter perfectly corresponded with the substance of our frequent conversations on those subjects." William B. Reed, *Life and Correspondence of Joseph Reed* (Philadelphia, 1847), II, 386.

36. See Hamilton to RM, April 30, and RM to Hamilton, May 26, 1781. For the six "Continentalist" essays, July 12, 1781–July 4, 1782, see Syrett and Cooke, eds., *Hamilton Papers*, II, 649–652, 654–657, 660–665, 669–674, III, 75–82, 99–106. For an extended letter of 1779 on American finances that may have been addressed to RM, see *ibid.*, II, 234–251.

37. The essays appeared in the issues of February 17, 24, 29, March 4, 11, 23, and April 11 and 15, 1780. Autograph drafts of the first five essays are in the Gouverneur Morris Papers, NNC.

38. See, for example, the undated autograph drafts docketed as "Some Thoughts on the Finances of America intended for Congress but not completed . . . " and "Observations on Finances: Foreign Trade and Loans," nos. 818 and 814 in the Gouverneur Morris Papers, NNC. For discussions of Gouverneur's earlier financial proposals in Congress, see Mary-Jo Kline, "Gouverneur Morris and the New Nation, 1775–1789" (Ph.D. diss., Columbia University, 1970), 109–112, 117–123, 125–126, 129–130, 165–168, 174, 211–212; and Max M. Mintz, *Gouverneur Morris and the American Revolution* (Norman, Okla., 1970), 129–133.

39. For one indication of borrowing, see text at note 96 below.

40. See Diary, June 28 and July 26, 1782.

41. Though, it should be said, some doubted his judgment. Reporting the rumor that RM had been slain in a duel by Alexander Gillon (see notes to Diary, September 19), Major General Nathanael Greene reflected to Charles Pettit that "Governeur Morris is in the order of promotion; but the confidence of the people is wanting. His

abilities are great; but I fear he has more of genius than judgment." See Greene to Pettit, December 21, 1782, Joseph Reed Papers, NHi.

42. RM to Richard Peters, January 25, 1778, quoted in Kline, "Gouverneur Morris," 100–101.

43. Ver Steeg, *Morris,* 128.

44. See RM's Circulars to the Continental Loan Officers, October 13, and notes, and to the Governors of the States, October 19, 1781.

45. See RM to Benjamin Franklin, November 27, 1781 (first letter).

46. See RM's Circular to the Governors of Massachusetts, Rhode Island, and Maryland, January 3, 1782.

47. See Landais to RM, January 22, 1782.

48. RM had first mentioned these taxes toward the end of his letter to the president of Congress of August 28, 1781, on the settlement of state accounts with the United States.

49. See RM's Report to Congress on the Continental Loan Offices, June 13, and notes, and RM's Report to Congress on the Interest of Loan Office Certificates, June 27, 1782, and notes.

50. See the headnote to the State of American Commerce and Plan for Protecting It, May 10, notes to Gouverneur Morris to Thomas Willing, June 18, 1782; and Merrill Jensen, "The American Revolution and American Agriculture," *Agricultural History,* XLIII (1969), 119.

51. In the colonies, usury laws generally had limited annual interest rates to 6 percent during the eighteenth century, a ceiling that remained in effect throughout the Revolution. Given the great demand for money and high inflation during the war, however, the maximum rate became the customary rate in public transactions, and Congress soon had to abandon its efforts to float domestic loans at rates lower than 6 percent. For the debate in 1777 over raising the interest rate on loan office certificates from 4 to 6 percent, in which RM played a prominent role in securing the higher rate, see Paul H. Smith *et al.,* eds., *Letters of Delegates to Congress, 1774–1789* (Washington, D. C., 1976–), VI, 117, 146, 193, 245, 259, 260–262, 274–277, 282, 295, 346, 368, 372–373, 379, 383, 386, 400–401, 403–404, 420–421. Exceedingly little work has been done on American interest rates during this period, but see Sidney Homer, *A History of Interest Rates* (New Brunswick, N. J., 1963), 274–279; and E. A. J. Johnson, *The Foundations of American Economic Freedom: Government and Enterprise in the Age of Washington* (Minneapolis, 1973), 178–181.

52. Gouverneur Morris and RM evidently disagreed on this point. Gouverneur subsequently dated the practice to the era of the British occupation. In contrast, RM who later had to defend the Bank of North America against the charge of having caused usury by forcing its borrowers into the hands of money lenders so that they could preserve their punctuality in payments to the bank, insisted in 1786 that "Usury sprung up on the decease of the continental money" and that the bank helped hold down interest rates by increasing the availability of credit. See Gouverneur Morris to Alexander Hamilton, January 27, 1784, Syrett and Cooke, eds., *Hamilton Papers,* III, 501, 502; Carey, ed., *Debates,* 24–25, 44, 115; and McDonald, *E Pluribus Unum,* 36, 41, 44, 46, 49.

53. For the question of interest rates as they arise in RM's papers, see RM to Richard Butler, August 26, and Diary, August 28, 1782, and RM to Thomas Jefferson, April 8, 1784.

54. See Diary, June 26, 28, and RM to Pettit, June 28. For the financial difficulties being faced by some leaders of the public creditors' group, see RM to Blair McClenachan, April 22, Diary, June 10, Francis Hopkinson to RM, December 19, and (for Pettit) Nathanael Greene to RM, December 20, 1782. Both McClenachan and Hopkinson had to sell their stock in the Bank of North America in 1782; for the McClenachan sale, see the Discount (January–June 1782) and Stock Transfer (July 1782–March 1789) Book, Bank of North America Papers, PHi. For the political affiliations of the leaders of the Philadelphia public creditors, see the sometimes conflicting identifications in Brunhouse, *Counter-Revolution in Pennsylvania,* 55, 72, 86, 90, 170–171; Main, *Political Parties,* 435; and Arnold, "Political Ideology," 187, 211.

55. On this point, see John Witherspoon's speeches in Congress, [August 5? and September 9, 1782], Burnett, ed., *Letters,* VI, 416, 464, 465.

56. McClenachan *et al* to the President of Congress, July 2, 1782, in PCC, no. 78, XVI, 303–306.

57. No record of an official suspension of interest on loan office certificates issued after March 1778 has been found. However, the proposed payment in Continental currency appears to have been largely terminated in 1780 when the discontinuation of further currency emissions dried up the source of funds that the loan officers used to pay the interest. For a time the loan officers refused to return their blank unsold certificates and issued them instead to some certificate holders in payment of interest, but RM forbade this practice in October 1781. See his Circular to the Continental Loan Officers, October 13, 1781, and notes.

58. See the reports in the *Pennsylvania Packet*, July 6, and *Pennsylvania Gazette*, July 10, 1782; Burnett, ed., *Letters*, VI, 380–381, 382; Hutchinson and Rutland, eds., *Madison Papers*, IV, 387; and Chevalier de La Luzerne to Vergennes, July 9, 1782, Correspondance politique, Etats-Unis, XXI, 396–401, AMAE.

59. See Diary, July 9, 1782. Although the Financier may have attempted to manipulate the public creditors to keep their activities channeled in support of his measures, it should be emphasized that they were never under his control.

60. On the "Leonidas" essays, see the headnote and notes to RM to the President of Congress, July 30. Whether Rush or other newspaper writers had access to the arguments as expounded in the report on public credit is uncertain, but RM showed the letter to at least two leaders among the public creditors, William Bingham and Thomas Fitzsimons. See Diary, August 22 and September 24.

61. See Diary, July 16, 18, and 26, 1782.

62. The grand committee was also given RM's letter to Congress of July 30 with the estimates for 1783 as well as committee reports on his letter to Congress of February 27 relative to land, poll, and excise taxes and his report of June 13 on the suspension of interest payments.

63. This address, signed by McClenachan, Pettit, Ewing, Rush, and Fitzsimons, was dated August 26, 1782. It was circulated as a broadside (Portfolio 146, no. 12, Broadside Collection, DLC) and (with the committee's remonstrance to Congress of July 8 and its petition to the Pennsylvania Assembly of August 19, 1782) as the postscript to the *Pennsylvania Packet* of September 5, 1782. See also "A Hint to the Public Creditors of New Jersey, Pennsylvania, Delaware, and Maryland," by "Mentor," published in the *Pennsylvania Gazette* and the *Freeman's Journal* of October 16, 1782. Although the full extent to which the Philadelphia creditors succeeded in mobilizing public creditors elsewhere has not been ascertained, a meeting of creditors was soon held in New Jersey, Connecticut's public creditors petitioned Congress in December, and a group of public creditors in New Hampshire led by John Langdon contemplated a meeting early in 1783. Under the leadership of Philip Schuyler and his son-in-law, Alexander Hamilton, creditors in New York convened in September at Albany where they proposed a convention of state creditors and appointed a committee to correspond with creditors elsewhere with a view to holding a national convention, although no such convention was held.

On the creditors' movement in New York, see Hamilton to RM, September 28, and notes, and October 9, and RM to Hamilton, October 16, 1782, and notes; Syrett and Cooke, eds., *Hamilton Papers*, III, 171–177; and Ferguson, *Power of the Purse*, 151–152. For the New Jersey creditors, see Richard P. McCormick, *Experiment in Independence: New Jersey in the Critical Period, 1781–1789* (New Brunswick, N. J., 1950), 171–179. For the petition of the Connecticut creditors of December 18, 1782, see PCC, no. 42, II, 164–167; and *JCC*, XXIV, 37n. For the New Hampshire group, see the notice in the *New Hampshire Gazette*, January 18 and February 1 and 8, 1783.

64. The memorial, signed by Speaker Frederick A. Muhlenberg (PCC, no. 69, II, 413–416), was read in Congress on August 30 and referred on to the grand committee. Its report, which has not been found, was on November 1 assigned to another committee which received a second memorial from Pennsylvania. See *JCC*, XXIII, 539–540n.

65. The fiscal crisis which brought RM to office had created general sentiment for using "back" or western lands as a source of revenue for funding public debts. But, apart from the uncertainty as to which western boundaries and territorial claims

would ultimately be recognized in a peace treaty with Britain, title to the western lands (as RM noted in his report) was rendered doubtful by continuing disputes over the cession of state land claims to the Confederation. Several states had not yet ceded their titles to Congress, and the terms of the three states which had offered cessions (New York, Connecticut, and Virginia) had not yet been accepted. In particular, the Virginia cession of 1781, which occasioned the final ratification of the Articles of Confederation, was mired in controversy because of its restrictive provisions, notably one voiding the claims of companies of land speculators to parts of the ceded territory (see notes to RM to Daniel Clark, May 30, 1782). Opposition to the terms of the Virginia cession remained strong among congressional delegates from "landless" middle states (those without western lands), such as New Jersey, Maryland, Pennsylvania, and Delaware, many of whose leading constituents were members of various land companies. Moreover, Rhode Island, urging reliance on western lands for debt funding, insisted that it should not have to violate its commercial interests by ratifying the impost while various states refused to cede their western lands to Congress or the interest of the land companies blocked acceptance of the cessions made (see David Howell's letters in Burnett, ed., *Letters*, VI, 399–404, 412, 502–503, 506, 530, 542–543; the comments of New York delegate Ezra L'Hommedieu in *ibid.*, 501, 531; and "Caractacus," in *Freeman's Journal*, June 19, 1782).

Despite RM's disclaimer of the short-term usefulness of western lands as a security for public loans, Congress clung to the idea. The status of western lands as revenue source nevertheless remained unresolved until Congress, under financial pressures and the necessity of fulfilling promises of land bounties made during the war to Continental troops, accepted Virginia's cession of the "Old Northwest" on March 1, 1784, thus creating the national domain. Under the Ordinance of 1785, a plan was devised for surveying the land and, after tracts allotted for bounties had been set aside, allowing each state a quota of what remained, to be sold for public securities through the loan offices in each state. Implementation of this plan went slowly and it was replaced in 1787 by a system of large-scale grants. This plan failed to raise revenue quickly enough to relieve the Confederation Congress of its financial problems. Land sales brought in only $760,000 to the Continental Treasury through 1788 (see Ferguson, *Power of the Purse*, 238–239). In general, see Merrill Jensen, "The Cession of the Old Northwest," and "The Creation of the National Domain, 1781–1784," *Mississippi Valley Historical Review*, XXIII (1936), 27–48, XXVI (1939), 323–342; Thomas P. Abernethy, *Western Lands and the American Revolution* (New York, 1937), 270–273; Boyd, ed., *Jefferson Papers*, VI, 571n.–575n.; and Henderson, *Party Politics in the Continental Congress*, 305–306.

66. The committee followed the rates suggested by Morris for the land and excise taxes, but for the poll tax it recommended $1 for free males between 21 and 60 and half that for males between 18 and 21, whether free or slave. The committee did not specify whether the states or (as RM insisted in his letter to Congress of February 27, 1782) Congress should collect the levies.

67. The requisition was probably intended to discharge the interest for 1782 (see Burnett, ed., *Letters*, VI, 511). It should be noted that Congress set no time limit for state action.

68. Congress substituted this measure for a proposal in the grand committee's report that would have allowed the Superintendent to draw on the state treasurers for the amounts of their respective quotas. For other proposals from this period, see *JCC*, XXIII, 546 and n.

There appears to have been some sentiment in Congress at this time for assigning every Tuesday and Thursday "for the consideration of the finances of the United States and for devising means for the restoration of publick credit until Congress come to some determination thereon" (*ibid.*). The arrival of news of the Dutch loan (see notes to Diary, September 11), however, probably contributed to the postponement of consideration of other measures and turned Congress's attention toward efforts to secure other foreign loans. On the Dutch loan, see note 93 below; for the efforts to obtain other foreign loans at this time, see the headnote to RM to the President of Congress, July 30.

69. David Howell to Welcome Arnold, August 23, and the Rhode Island Dele-

gates to Governor William Greene, October 15, 1782, Burnett, ed., *Letters*, VI, 454, 505.

70. See RM to the President of Congress, March 8, 1783.

71. Hugh Williamson to Governor Alexander Martin of North Carolina, September 2, 1782, Burnett, ed., *Letters*, VI, 462–463.

72. Maclay, ed., *Journal of William Maclay*, 280.

73. See RM's circulars to the state governors and the receivers of Continental taxes of September 12.

74. Not long before his retirement from office in 1784 with the debt still unfunded, RM contemptuously scolded Rhode Island for failing to comply with "what some among them are pleased to call the *constitutional* Requisition. Which if the Term means any thing ought constitutionally to have been complied with near two Years ago. I am weary of this Sort of mock or mimick Government." RM to George Olney, July 19, 1784.

75. The next interest payment was due on September 10. See notes to RM's Report to Congress on the Continental Loan Offices, June 13, 1782.

76. For a report of this meeting, see La Luzerne to Vergennes, September 10, 1782, Correspondance politique, Etats-Unis, XXII, 215–220, AMAE, where La Luzerne indicates he had met with the unidentified speaker the day before. For a caustic epitaph for a loan office certificate "which departed this life" at the hands of Congress on September 9, see the *Freeman's Journal*, September 25, 1782.

77. See Diary, September 18, and notes.

78. Precisely how this proposal differed from Congress's $1.2 million requisition of September 4 is unclear. Perhaps no quota was intended; Montgomery may have presumed that the states would assume payment for all interest due to their citizens— as Pennsylvania eventually did.

79. *Minutes of the First Session, of the Seventh General Assembly, of the Commonwealth of Pennsylvania* . . . [October 28–December 4, 1782] (Philadelphia, [1782]), 717, 720, 733–734. The editors have been unable to find an English text of the October 31 memorial, but for a French translation see Correspondance politique, Etats-Unis, XXII, 445–449, AMAE. The members of the creditors' committee of nine were Blair McClenachan, Benjamin Rush, Peter Wikoff, John Ewing, William Bingham, Charles Pettit, Frederick Kuhl, Thomas Fitzsimons, and John Bayard. For the bipartisan character of the public creditors' movement in Pennsylvania, see Owen S. Ireland, "The Ratification of the Federal Constitution in Pennsylvania" (Ph.D. diss., University of Pittsburgh, 1966), 144, 148–150; and Roland M. Baumann, "The Democratic-Republicans of Philadelphia: The Origins, 1776–1797" (Ph.D. diss., Pennsylvania State University, 1970), 44–45.

80. See the memorial in PCC, no. 69, II, 417–420; *JCC*, XXIII, 723n.; Diary, November 16, 1782; and Hutchinson and Rutland, eds., *Madison Papers*, V, 293.

81. The November 20 report has not been found, but the substance of it is described in Madison's "Notes of Debates" for November 20 (Hutchinson and Rutland, eds., *Madison Papers*, V, 293–295). It was referred in turn to another committee which issued a more elaborate report that was read and accepted by Congress on January 30, 1783 (*JCC*, XXIII, 745n.). The report blamed the states for Congress's inability to perform its engagements with public creditors and reiterated its objections to "private and partial provision" by individual states. Stressing Congress's efforts to settle public accounts, the report nevertheless argued that any attempt to pay past debts would be an insupportable burden on revenues for current expenses and that provision could be made only for the payment of interest. After documenting the continuing gap between income and expenditure, Congress pledged to persevere in its effort "to procure the establishment of revenues equal to the purpose of funding *all* the debts of the United States," and in this connection called upon Pennsylvania to cede its western lands to the United States. Effectively Congress's reply to the Pennsylvania legislature, the report was reprinted in several newspapers. See, for example, the *Independent Gazetteer* (Philadelphia), February 25, 1783; and the *Connecticut Journal* (Hartford), March 11, 1783.

During the next session, the Pennsylvania Assembly made separate provision for its Continental creditors by giving them certificates of interest receivable in taxes and by levying a tax payable half in certificates and half in hard money. To RM's chagrin, Pennsylvania's lead was eventually followed by many of the other states. See Diary, May 21, 1783; Ferguson, *Power of the Purse*, 220–250; E. James Ferguson, "State Assumption of the Federal Debt During the Confederation," *MVHR*, XXXVIII (1951), 403–424; and Forrest McDonald, *Alexander Hamilton: A Biography* (New York, 1979), 80–82, 86–90.

82. *JCC*, XXIII, 745, 757. For his report, see RM to the President of Congress, December 3, 1782 (second letter).

83. Hutchinson and Rutland, eds., *Madison Papers*, V, 362–364, 365n.–367n.; and *JCC*, XXIII, 761.

84. The quotation is Madison's description of Congress's instruction to RM. See Hutchinson and Rutland, eds., *Madison Papers*, V, 373–374, 374n.–377n., 414–415, 416n.–417n., 442, 445n., 449, 472–473. See also notes to RM to the Governor of Rhode Island, August 2, and Diary, December 7, 1782.

85. See RM's Circular to the Governors of the States, and RM to the President of Congress, both October 21.

86. See Diary, December 31, 1782, January 9, 13, 16, 17, 1783, Franklin to RM, December 23, 1782, RM to Franklin, January 11 and 13, 1783, to Ferdinand Grand, and to La Luzerne, both January 13, and La Luzerne to RM, January 18, 1783.

87. The top of the first manuscript page of the MHi copy is endorsed in an unidentified hand: "Transmitted by Tench Coxe from the treasury Department May 12 1781 [i.e., 1791]," when Coxe was assistant secretary of the treasury. For the provenance of the PRO text, see notes to RM to the President of Congress, July 30. RM enclosed a copy of the report in his circulars to the governors of the states and the receivers of Continental taxes of September 12, 1782.

88. See the headnote following note 49 above.

89. On interest rates in Philadelphia during the war, see the headnote at note 51 above.

90. The words "at six percent" are inserted here in all other texts.

91. See enclosure 1.

92. This word and the same word repeated later in the sentence are in Gouverneur Morris's hand. The last word at the bottom of each manuscript page and a few additions of minor import were also inserted in his hand.

93. Although RM did not believe further foreign loans were likely without the previous passage of tax measures to repay them, others remained considerably more optimistic about the prospects for foreign loans, particularly after news arrived in June that the States General of the United Provinces had recognized the independence of the United States on April 19. Proposals were soon made in Congress that John Adams, the American minister at The Hague, be instructed to ask the Dutch government for a loan or loan guarantee. A committee report of July 5 on the subject had been referred to RM on July 9 (PCC, no. 186, pp. 40, 41). Not until September did RM and Congress learn that Adams had in fact succeeded in negotiating a loan for 5 million guilders from a consortium of Dutch bankers (see Diary, September 11, and notes). The loan, the first obtained solely on the credit of the United States, was a private subscription, not backed in any way by the Dutch or French governments, and filled up slowly. Nevertheless, it became a major source of revenue for RM in 1783 and 1784.

94. The reference is to Congress's act of March 18, 1780, which repudiated $^{39}/_{40}$ths of the value of Continental currency.

95. On impressment and the certificate debt arising from it, see Ferguson, *Power of the Purse*, 57–65, 67–68; for RM's views on the certificate debt, see his letters to the president of Congress of August 28 and November 5, 1781, and notes.

96. This was a phrase Gouverneur Morris had used to caption an undated draft essay, "To the general Assembly of the State of Pensilvania," which he wrote under the pen name of "A Citizen," [ca. 1780–1781], Gouverneur Morris Papers, no. 817, NNC. The phrase was probably derived from Prov. 14:34 ("Righteousness exalteth a nation") or Prov. 16:12 ("the throne is established by righteousness").

97. In all other texts the phrase reads "to so righteous a pursuit."

98. RM refers to the acts of February 20 and 27, 1782; see notes to RM to the

President of Congress, December 10, 1781, and notes, and February 18, 1782, and notes. For the process of settling the accounts, see RM's circulars to the commissioners of accounts for the states and departments of September 7 and 19, 1782, respectively, and notes.

99. See enclosure 2. The estimate was delivered to RM on July 18. See Diary of that date.

100. The word "service" is inserted here in the Ofcl LbC.

101. The commissioners of accounts for individual claims ultimately issued certificates worth over $3.7 million. Debts owed the army prior to April 1780 had been absorbed by the states, but the final settlement of army accounts added another $11 million in final settlement certificates to the national debt. See notes to RM to Jonathan Burrall, August 19; and Ferguson, *Power of the Purse*, 179–180.

102. On the American debt to France, see RM to the President of Congress, May 8, and notes, Benjamin Franklin to RM, June 25, and RM to Franklin, July 5, 1782.

103. MS: "came."

104. This word is retained in some of the texts, but not in others.

105. For RM's current proposals for rebuilding the navy, see the headnote to RM to the President of Congress, July 30.

106. RM was far too optimistic, for Rhode Island rejected the impost in November. See the headnote above and notes to RM to the Governor of Rhode Island, August 2.

107. See notes to RM to the President of Congress, February 27, 1782.

108. The preceding two words were inserted interlinearly by Gouverneur Morris.

109. This complimentary close and the addressee's name below are in the writing of Gouverneur Morris.

To the Governor of Maryland
(Thomas Sim Lee)

Office of Finance 29. July 1782

Sir,

I have now before me your Excellency's two Favors of twelfth Instant. You will find my Answers as well in a former Letter as in the enclosed Circular.[1] For what remains I must only declare to you my Regret at finding your Prospects so Gloomy. The Idea that Taxes cannot be raised because of the Want of Specie is very general indeed it is almost universal and yet nothing can be more ill founded. If the People be put in the Necessity of procuring Specie they will procure it. They can, if they will. Tobacco may not sell at one moment, Grain at another or Cattle at a third. But there are some Articles such as Horses which will sell at all Times and every Article will sell at some Times. The Mischief is that when a Purchaser offers, the Party not being under a necessity of selling insists on a higher Price than the other can afford to give. Thus the Commerce is turned away to another Quarter. Nothing but the necessity of getting Money will bring Men in general to lower their Prices. When this is done Purchasers will offer in Abundance and thus it will be found that the Tax instead of lessening will encrease the quantity of Specie. But so long as the Want of it can be pleaded successfully against Payment of Taxes: so long that Want will continue. And then all which remains to consider is whether the Army can be maintained by such a Plea. The States Sir must give Money or the Army must disband. I have the Honor to be Sir your Excellency's Most obedient Servant

RM

MS: Ofcl LbC, DLC.
1. See RM to the Governor of Maryland, July 16, and his Circular to the Governors of the States, July 29, 1782.

From William Whipple

Portsmouth New Hampr 29th July 1782[1]

Sir

Since my last which was under the 30th June nothing new has taken place, not a farthing of the present Year's Tax has yet come in to the Treasury. I had commenced the Monthly publications previous to the receipt of Your favor of the 29th June and shall continue them agreeable to Your order; I some time ago desired the Publisher of the New Hampshire Gazette[2] to send his paper weekly to the Office of Finance which he tells me he has done regularly, but its probable they may be stoped by the way, as the post master tells me is very often the case with papers coming this way by which means it's a rare thing to see a Philadelphia paper here. I think a free circulation of newspapers might be of public Utility. I have the Honour to be &c

Honble Robt Morris Esq &c

MS: LbC, William Whipple Letterbook, John Langdon Papers, PHi.
1. Whipple was the receiver of Continental taxes for New Hampshire.
2. The *New Hampshire Gazette* (Portsmouth) was published by Daniel Fowle (1715–1787). *DAB.*

To John Lyon

Office of Finance 29. July 1782

I have received the Letter which you did me the Honor to write on the seventeenth Instant. I now return enclosed your Certificates.[1] Accept I pray you my hearty Wishes that your work may alike redound to your own Benefit and that of Society. I am perswaded from the Certificates you sent that its own Merit will have more Influence than my Patronage but any Aid which I can afford to an useful Treatise of the Kind shall not be wanting.

MS: Ofcl LbC, DLC.
1. The letter and certificates have not been found. Lyon was the author of *The Touchstone: A Philosophical Controversy, Interspersed with Satire and Raillery; Wherein a New and Elegant Improvement of the Theory of the Earth and Moon's Motion is Asserted and Proved Beyond Contradiction* (Annapolis, 1781), which attacked the findings of astronomer Andrew Ellicott, a teacher at the Baltimore Academy. The work for which Lyon sought RM's endorsement apparently was a treatise on arithmetic for schools; in 1782

Lyon asked the Maryland House of Delegates to protect it from infringement, but there is no evidence that the treatise was ever published. See Harrison Williams, "John Lyon, Mathematician," *Maryland Historical Magazine*, XLI (1946), 254–255.

To George Olney

Office of Finance 29. July 1782[1]

I have received your Favor of the fifteenth Instant.[2] The Monies sent by Mr. Brown he will bring you the proper Discharge for. I approve of your Conduct with respect to the Certificates and I hope you will not be burthened with any more of them but as these Matters must be taken up and considered you may keep what you have until some Determination can be taken with Relation to them.

MS: Ofcl LbC, DLC.
1. Olney was the receiver of Continental taxes for Rhode Island. On the certificates mentioned in this letter, see RM to Olney, July 2, and notes, and August 13 and 22, 1782.
2. Letter not found.

To William Smallwood

Office of Finance 29th. July 1782

I have received the Letter which you did me the Honor to write on the twenty sixth Instant with its Enclosure.[1] I take this earliest Opportunity to inform you in Reply and thro you all others whom it may concern that I will receive either for the Public or on my own private Account the Paymaster's General's notes as Cash.

MS: Ofcl LbC, DLC.
1. The letter and enclosure from Major General William Smallwood of Maryland have not been found. On the notes issued by Paymaster General John Pierce, mentioned below in the present letter, see RM to George Washington, January 26, 1782 (second letter), and notes.

James McCall to the Register of the Treasury (Joseph Nourse)

Office of Finance 29th. July 1782[1]

Inclosed are two Returns, or rather Accounts Current from Abraham Yates Junr. C[ontinental] L[oan] O[fficer] at Albany in the State of New York both for the month of June last. One of them is a State of the Specie Certificates the other the Emissions of Money made pursuant to Act of Congress of the 18th of March 1780.

MS: Ofcl LbC, DLC.
1. McCall was RM's secretary in the Office of Finance. The enclosures to this letter have not been found.

From Samuel Hodgdon

Philada. July 29. 1782

Agreeable to your request signified to me by some of the Armourers to whom the public are indebted, I inclose a duplicate of an estimate given in on the 31st of May last, which determines the sums due them respectively to that period.[1]

MS: LbC, WDC, DNA.

1. Hodgdon was the commissary general of military stores. For the estimate, see Diary, June 1, and notes, and July 29, 1782.

Diary: July 30, 1782

The Hon. James Duane, Arthur Lee, Mr. Osgood and Clarke a Committee of Congress appointed for the purpose of examining into the Execution and Management of the Duties of the Superintendant and Subordinate Branches of the Office of Finance came by appointment to Commence their Enquiries, and first they examined into the State of the public Debt of which I gave them every information in my power. They then adjourned until Thursday next when they are to meet again and proceed in their enquiries.[1]

Colo. Miles writes for about £44 due to Waggoners which if paid they will take up the Goods for the Southern Army &c.[2] I granted a Warrant for the Same.

Henry Hill Esquire called again respecting the money due to me for Bills which he cannot yet obtain and is unwilling to pass his Note to be discounted at the Bank—so that I am likely to be disappointed of upwards of 22,000 Dollars part of the provision I had made for the Payment of the Paymaster Generals Notes on the first of August.[3]

The [Hon.] William [i.e., Samuel] Wharton called to ask me sundry Questions relative to Monies appropriated in Europe to the purposes mentioned in the Letter of Estimate which I sometime since laid before Congress, all which I answered to his Satisfaction.[4] I took this occasion to observe to Mr Wharton that as a Committee were now going thro the examination of the Office of Finance, it would be best not to begin the Examination of the Marine Office until the other be finished to which he assented and promised to inform the Committee appointed on that Business of which he is Chairman.[5]

Colo. Ephm. Blaine called for £100 to be paid him on Account of the Contract at Fort Pitt which was before promised, is due, and therefore I granted a Warrant for the Same.

Colo. Patton and Colo. Gurney Commissioners for conducting the Defence of Delaware Bay &c. brought the Accounts for the Voyage of the Ship Genl. Washington to the Cape &c. to which I objected alledging that by agreement the United States were only to pay any actual Expence incurred by the Voyage, and as this Ship has fortunately taken Prizes the half of which will defray the Expences of the Voyage, I am of Opinion that according to the Spirit of the Agreement and the nature of the Service in which the Ship was employed

The United States ought not to be called on for any money but that the 4,000 Dollars already advanced ought to be returned.[6] However as the Commissioners were of a different opinion I proposed leaving the matter to Arbitration they to choose one person who no doubt will be a Citizen of Pensylvania, I to name another not a Citizen of that State, these two to be part of the Arbitrators, that in like manner we shall name two others whose Names being put into a Hat, one of the Names should be drawn and the person whose Name should happen to be drawn out with the two first named to be the Arbitrators and their decision final between the State of Pensylvania and the United States.[7] This being agreed to, The Commissioners named Charles Pettit Esqr., I named the Hon. Jno. Lowell Esqr. of Massachusetts, they named John Maxwell Nesbitt Esqr. and I named the Hon. Jno. Rutledge Esqr. of South Carolina whose names being wrote on two pieces of papers and folded, The Secy. of my Office Mr. McCall was called up and desired to draw one of those papers which he did and it proved to have Govr. Rutledg's name. I sent immediately to these Gentlemen requesting them to appoint a time for meeting and they fixed tomorrow at ten OClock.

Wm. Turnbull Esqr. wrote me that he had accepted a Bill for 1,000 Dollars payable in five Days on Account of Wm. Duer Esqr. Contractors for Albany &c. requesting me to supply the Money to pay it, more than that Sum being due, Mr. Turnbull followed his Note[8] and after some Conversation I promised to supply the Money when due if Convenient.

James Milligan Esqr. came to the Office respecting several matters on which I gave my Opinion, and advice. I told him the Committee would Call to examine his Office &c. with which he is well pleased.[9]

Thos. Bradford Esqr. the Commissary of Prisoners came to know my Opinion whether the Flag Vessels now getting ready for Carolina[10] should be stopped in their proceedings on Account of a French fleet being on the Coast[11] but as I do not see any reason at present why that should be done, I gave my opinion not to impede them until some Cause for so doing shall appear.

Mr. Francis applies for Money on Account of the Contractors for York and Carlisle.

Wrote a Letter to Genl. Parsons.
Wrote a Letter to Jno. Hopkins Esqr.
Wrote a Letter to Colo. Pickering.
Wrote a Letter to the Governors of the different States.
Wrote a Letter to His Excellency the President of Congress.
Wrote a Letter to Jos. Nourse Esqr.[12]
Wrote a Letter to Jno. Bradford.
Wrote a Letter to James Lovell.
Wrote a Letter to Donaldson Yates.

Issued a Warrant on Mr. Swanwick in favor of Jos. Pennell £90.0.0.

1. For the committee to investigate the Department of Finance, see Diary, June 12, and notes, Minutes of the Committee of Congress on the Department of Finance, July 30, 1782, and below in this Diary at note 9.

2. Samuel Miles was the deputy quartermaster general for Pennsylvania. For the wagons, see Diary, July 12, 1782.

3. On this subject, see Diary, July 26, and notes, and July 29, and notes.

4. Concerning this inquiry into the disposal of American funds in Europe, see RM to the President of Congress, May 24, 1782, and notes. Wharton, a Delaware delegate to Congress, was a member of the congressional committee considering the matter.

5. On the oversight committee for the Marine Department, see Diary, July 13, 1782, and notes.

6. On RM's use of the *General Washington*, see Diary, May 15, 1782, and notes.

7. It was a common mercantile practice to settle disputes by arbitration, a procedure which was accorded legal standing. See Richard B. Morris, *Studies in the History of American Law, with Special Reference to the Seventeenth and Eighteenth Centuries* (New York, 1930), 60–61.

8. Turnbull's note has not been found.

9. The committee inquiring into the Department of Finance (see note 1 above) was also directed to examine "the several branches of the same," including the office of Comptroller of the Treasury James Milligan.

10. After Charleston, South Carolina, was captured in May 1780, British officers, violating the articles of capitulation, sent many captured civilians, among them a number of state officials, to St. Augustine in East Florida. Although their families, including women, children, and servants, were at first permitted to remain in the captured city, they were subsequently banished by the British. In July 1781, arrangements having been made for the exchange of the St. Augustine exiles, they and their separated families, together with refugees from Georgia, converged on Philadelphia. Congress on July 23 solicited private donations and opened a loan of $30,000 for their support, with repayment pledged by South Carolina and Georgia. The commissioners appointed by Congress on July 24 to receive the donations and administer the loan were William Bingham, John Bayard, George Meade, Jacob Barge, and James Hutchinson. They sent out appeals to state executives, but only in Massachusetts and Pennsylvania was any money raised.

Following reconstitution of the South Carolina government during the winter of 1781–1782, the legislature instructed its delegates in Congress to initiate a request that the British return the refugees to their homes, particularly the women and children, and bear the expense of the journey. Congress on April 3, 1782, referred the resolution to Washington, who on May 21 took up the question with Sir Guy Carleton, the British commander in New York. Carleton immediately agreed to furnish three flag vessels to convey the refugees to any port Washington named, all at British expense. Congress on June 14 directed Secretary at War Benjamin Lincoln to supply Washington with a list of the persons referred to by the resolution of the South Carolina Assembly and the ports to which they chose to be conveyed. After Washington sent it to Carleton on July 4, the British commander dispatched the truce vessels to Philadelphia with instructions to their commanders to supply rations to the passengers during the voyage. The refugees who chose to embark were ultimately transported to Georgetown, South Carolina, and Edenton, North Carolina. Carleton's unquestioning compliance with American demands, coming amid British efforts to conclude a separate peace with the United States and secure favorable prisoner exchanges, aroused Washington's distrustful apprehensions of Britain's pursuit of "*conciliatory War*." After conciliatory overtures failed, Washington's requests for the transport of additional refugees in the fall of 1782 were ignored by Carleton. See RM to the President of Congress, July 20, 1781, and notes; notes to Diary, August 29, 1781; and RM to John Cruden, August 5, 1782; McCrady, *South Carolina in the Revolution*, 371–380; *JCC*, XX, 748–749, XXI, 852; Fitzpatrick, ed., *Writings of Washington*,

XXIV, 270, 273–274, 296, 326–327, 400, XXV, 114; and *Report on American Manuscripts in the Royal Institution*, III, 7–8, 15, 17, 96, 104.
   11. See Diary, July 29, and notes.
   12. Letter not found.

Circular to the Governors of the States

(Circular)   Office of Finance 30th July 1782
Sir,

   I do myself the Honor to enclose the Extract of a Letter received from a confidential Correspondant in one of the United States.[1] The Evil there mentioned is of so dangerous a Nature, that should it prevail in any Degree the Consequences may be fatal. I know that the selfish Spirit there complained of is but too prevalent, and it is very long since I bore my Testimony against it, from a just apprehension, that the safety of our Country might be thereby endangered. If it is of Consequence that a war which has cost already so much Blood and Treasure be safely and honorably concluded, it must be vigorously prosecuted. If it is to be vigorously prosecuted, the means must be granted. If the means are to be granted, The several States must contribute speedily and effectually. If one has a Right to prefer local to general Interests, others have the same Right. If one exercise that Privilege, so may all. And if all do, there is an End of our Efforts. Congress had foreseen the Danger, and called on the States to provide for collecting the continental, seperate from the State Taxes.[2] Since this has not been done perhaps the reasons of the Refusal may account for the Facts stated in the Extract. I must pray of your Excellency to provide such Remedy, to any Thing of this sort which may exist in your State, as shall be within your power, and that you will urge the Legislature to make that Solid provision, which can alone prevent it in future. I have the Honor to be Sir Your Excellency's Most Obedient and humble Servant[3]

                                                              Robt Morris

His Excellency The Governor of Massachusetts

ENDORSED: Robert Morris Esqr./Received Augst. 14th: 1782
MSS: LS, to the Governor of Massachusetts, M-Ar; LS, to the President of New Hampshire, Meshech Weare Papers, Nh-Ar; LS, to the Governor of Rhode Island, R-Ar; LS, to the Governor of Connecticut, Jonathan Trumbull Papers, Ct; LS, to the Governor of New Jersey, Nj; LS, to the President of Delaware, Executive Papers, De-Ar; LS, to the Governor of Maryland, Vertical Files, Miscellaneous Manuscripts, MdHi; LS, to the Governor of Virginia, Continental Congress Papers, Vi; Ofcl LbC, DLC; LbC, Letterbook of Governor Alexander Martin of North Carolina, 1782–1785, Nc-Ar; Force transcript, to the President of New Hampshire, DLC; Sparks transcript, to the Governor of New Jersey, MH.
   1. For the extract, enclosed here as an anonymous communication, see Samuel

Holden Parsons to RM, July 18, 1782. A copy of the present circular was enclosed in RM to Parsons, July 30.

2. For the act of November 2, 1781, see notes to RM to the President of Congress, November 5, 1781.

3. According to its endorsement, the text sent to Connecticut was received on August 7.

To the President of Congress
(John Hanson)

The estimates submitted in this letter formed the proposed Continental budget for 1783 and were meant to be considered in conjunction with Morris's recommendations for federal taxes to fund the interest on the national debt contained in his July 29 report to Congress on public credit. In addition to recommending a foreign loan, the letter also presented Morris's farsighted proposal to reconstruct the depleted Continental navy. Together with the July 29 communication and other documents, the letter and its enclosures were read in Congress on August 5 and referred to the grand committee appointed on July 22 "to take into consideration and report the most effectual means of supporting the credit of the United States."[1]

Immersed in consideration of interest payments on loan office certificates, the grand committee did not take up Morris's proposal for a $4 million foreign loan for 1783 until after September 9 when the Superintendent urged Congress to act promptly before the onset of winter hindered communication with Europe. His request was read the following day and referred to a committee composed of James Duane of New York, Joseph Montgomery of Pennsylvania, and James Madison of Virginia, whose report of September 14 recommended a $5 million loan. A motion made by John Rutledge of South Carolina, seconded by Hugh Williamson of North Carolina, proposed that $5 million, including the loan in Holland now in progress,[2] be borrowed in Europe and applied to expenses incurred in 1782 for carrying on the war. Duane, seconded by Madison, advanced an amendment excluding the Holland loan from the sum requested, but it was defeated in a roll call vote in which three New England states and New Jersey cast negatives, New Hampshire and Delaware were balanced on opposing sides but unable to cast votes for lack of sufficient representation, and Georgia was divided. Acting on a compromise motion of Rutledge's, seconded by Duane, Congress on September 14 finally approved a loan of $4 million exclusive of the Dutch loan, ordered Morris and Secretary for Foreign Affairs Robert R. Livingston to begin negotiations in France and Holland, and instructed Benjamin Franklin to bring the loan to the attention of the French court and cooperate in obtaining it. Although advice was soon received from Franklin that anything beyond the 6 million livres already granted by France for 1782 was virtually out of the question, Congress on September 23 directed him to persevere.[3]

The grand committee then took up the budget for 1783. In its report, which Congress considered on October 16, the committee revised the estimates downward. The estimate prepared by Benjamin Lincoln and submitted by Morris appears to have been based on an army of 30,000 men, but the committee evidently expected at least a third less.[4] Accordingly, although the committee added $304,447 for the "Civil and military staff," it reduced the figures for pay by about 30 percent and for rations by 33 percent, with corresponding deductions of 25 percent each in the Hospital, Quartermaster, and Military Stores Departments. The committee also slashed projected expenditures in the Clothing Department by some 85 percent to a mere $200,000, and eliminated an appropriation for one year's half-pay pensions for retired officers by postponing action on the subject. The greatest single reduction, however, was in Morris's budget for the Marine Department, which was cut by 88 percent, from $2.5 million to $300,000. The appropriation for the civil list remained unchanged; only the allotment for contingencies was raised, by some 19 percent. Having emerged at the conclusion of its labors with a figure of $6 million instead of the $9 million requested by the Financier, the committee proposed to raise $2.8 million (instead of $5 million) by requisition and if possible borrow the remainder.

In adopting the committee's report on October 16, Congress reduced the amount of the requisition still further to $2 million, far less than Morris had wanted, and suspended further action pending results of the applications for foreign loans. Two days later Congress apportioned the requisition among the states in four equal quarterly payments, the first of which was due on April 1, 1783. As in the requisition for 1782, Congress asked the states to levy taxes for the United States separately from those for their own use, to instruct their collectors to pay the money directly to persons appointed by the Superintendent (instead of to the state treasurers), and to authorize Morris's appointees to "recover" the money from collectors in the same manner as state treasurers recovered state taxes. The receivers, as before, were to be subject only to the orders of Congress or the Superintendent of Finance. Every delegate voted in favor of these provisions except the two from Rhode Island and one from New Jersey.[5]

In view of the cuts in the naval budget, it might be concluded that sentiment for rebuilding the American navy was not strong. However, one delegate to Congress reported soon after Morris's proposal reached the floor, that a revitalized navy was "very much the conversation out of doors, and appears to be popular."[6] Numerous newspaper articles discussing the topic in the spring and summer of 1782 attest to widespread interest in the idea. British depredations had evoked enthusiastic support for a navy among merchants who stood to gain from the protection it would afford to commerce. Others expressed hope that a seaborne force could check the mounting illicit trade with the enemy, decrease American dependence on France, reopen opportunites for young Americans to achieve glory, and inject life into what was widely perceived as an evaporated American "virtue."[7] Benjamin Rush, over the signatures of "Retaliation" and "Leonidas," argued that a revived navy and a sound public credit were reciprocal prerequisites for securing American independence,[8] but few Americans would have agreed with his nationalistic wish, privately expressed to Nathanael Greene, that peace with Britain "be deferred till the naval war has given us as many fleets and admirals as a land war has given us armies and generals."[9] Nor were all commentators on the subject sanguine about building a substantial fleet. Besides the financial obstacles, writers noted the difficulty of manning large ships while so many

American seamen were still in British hands. Moreover, few publicists put the same stress that Morris and Rush did on a Continental navy as opposed to state fleets.

The Rush articles, and probably others, were encouraged by Chevalier de La Luzerne, the French minister. Like Morris, La Luzerne was seeking to channel American resources in ways suited to the current naval thrust of British and French strategies.[10] In a letter of August 9, La Luzerne reported to his court that the publications appeared to him to have been well received, adding that he had also raised the subject in private conversations with several congressional delegates, and that they were now talking about constructing a respectable navy. Men of ardent imagination, La Luzerne related, spoke of no less than ten ships of the line, while more moderate persons thought that with French assistance the United States could put five or six ships of the line to sea next year. Since the plan would require French support, La Luzerne requested the advice of his superiors. However, even before learning from Foreign Minister Vergennes that the court approved his actions but could not make French resources available to implement such a scheme, La Luzerne had already qualified his support as peace approached, for fear that such a navy could eventually threaten French interests in the Newfoundland fisheries.[11]

Long experience in maritime matters, both as an overseas shipping merchant and as a respected naval administrator in Congress during the early years of the war, had molded Morris into an unqualified advocate of American naval power. When Congress devolved the duties of Agent of Marine on the Superintendent of Finance in September 1781, however, the Continental navy created in 1775 had been so severely crushed that only the 36-gun frigate *Alliance* and the 34-gun frigate *Deane* (renamed the *Hague* in 1782) remained in service.[12]

Morris's efforts to strengthen the navy during his first eleven months as Agent of Marine had proved disappointing. Construction of the *America*, a 74-gun ship of the line being built in Portsmouth, New Hampshire, and of the 28-gun frigate *Bourbon*, on the stocks at Chatham, Connecticut, was stalled because an empty treasury prevented him from advancing adequate funds for their completion.[13] Although Morris rented the 24-gun warship *General Washington* from Pennsylvania in May 1782 for a voyage to Havana in quest of specie,[14] he declined to acquire the frigate *South Carolina*, until recently commanded by Commodore Alexander Gillon of the South Carolina navy, because of the unfavorable terms offered.[15]

The urgent call in this letter for reconstructing the Continental navy developed at length a position Morris expressed to Congress in letters of April 15 and 24, 1782, a time when the British blockade of the American coast began seriously to impair his financial operations. Believing that the United States was by no means helpless in confronting British might, Morris considered it within even Congress's limited resources to build the relatively few vessels needed to equalize British naval superiority on the American coast. Meanwhile, until ships could be built, his naval strategy had been to seek an immediate assignment of French and Spanish warships to the American coast, an approach essayed in the State of American Commerce he submitted to Congress on May 10, 1782. After the defeat of the allied naval forces in the West Indies during the Battle of the Saints, however, the need for an

American fleet became more urgent. The Marine Department estimate enclosed in the present letter therefore projected completion of
the *America* and the *Bourbon* and construction each year of six ships of
the *South Carolina* class.

Mindful of its slender resources and encouraged by the ongoing
peace negotiations, Congress (as noted above) dashed the Superintendent's hopes for a rapid buildup of the Continental navy. Rush was
also disappointed. "I expected to have bequeathed at least a naval war
to my children," he was soon to report to Greene, "but Mr. [Charles
James] Fox, the British nation, the States of Holland, nay more, all
Europe say we *must have peace*."[16] Thus, the approach of peace dissipated Morris's dream of a respectable Continental navy that would
protect American commerce, thereby producing revenues that could
be tapped by Continental taxes; and with it died whatever hopes Morris had of using support for the navy to restore public credit through
funding of the national debt.

Although Morris was to remain an advocate of a strong navy,[17] the
continuing shortage of funds made him the administrator of its re-
trenchment as peace approached.[18] He acquired the *General Washington* and the *Duc de Lauzun* later in the year,[19] but by the time he left
office in November 1784 only the *Alliance* remained. The Board of
Treasury that succeeded the Superintendent sold the frigate in 1785,[20]
and the American navy would not be revived until 1794.

Office of Finance, 30th. July 1782

Sir

I do myself the Honor to enclose for the Inspection of Congress
Estimates for the Service of the Year 1783 amounting in the whole
to eleven Millions.[21] I should be strictly justified in Praying a Requisition of the United States for that Sum, but I conceive that the Demands made should be the lowest which our Circumstances will
possibly admit of. I am persuaded that if the United States in Congress will adopt those Means of Oeconomy which are in their
Power[22] We may save two Millions, and therefore on a Presumption
that those Means will be adopted I shall ask only Nine Millions.
Congress will observe that the Estimates for the Marine Department
amount to two Millions and an half, whereas there was no Estimate
made for that Service in the last year any more than for the civil List.
There can be no doubt that the Enemy have changed their Mode of
Warfare, and will make their principal Exertions in the naval Line.[23]
It becomes us therefore to make like Exertions and that for the
plainest Reasons. Experience has shewn that the Efforts to obtain a
large Army have for many Years proved utterly fruitless.[24] The only
Effect of those Efforts has been to enhance the Price of such Men as
were obtained and thereby to disable the States who exerted themselves to raise Recruits from pouring Supplies into the public Treasury. Thus we have not only been unable to get more men, but also
to pay and support those which we had gotten. Admitting however
that the required Number were obtained and properly supported as

an Army These things are clear, first that without Naval Aid, we
could not make an Impression on the Enemy's Posts. Secondly, that
they would be able to harrass and distress us in every Quarter, by
predatory Incursions. Thirdly that they would prevent us from receiving those Supplies which are necessary alike to the operation and
Existence of our Army. And fourthly that their Inroads on our
Commerce would produce such distress to the Country as to render
our Revenues utterly unproductive and finally bring our Affairs to
Destruction. An Army therefore without a Navy would be burthensome without being able to give essential Aid supposing the Enemy
to have changed their System of carrying on the War, But if we had
a Navy we should be able, first to prevent the Enemy from making
predatory Incursions. Secondly we should at least keep their Ships
on our Coast, together, which would prevent them from injuring
our Commerce or Obstructing our Supplies. Thirdly if they kept in
this Country an equal, or superior force we should by that means
have made a powerful Diversion in favor of our Allies and contributed to give them a Naval Superiority elsewhere. Fourthly if our
Enemy did not keep an equal, or superior force in this Country we
should be able by Cruizing to protect our own Commerce, annoy
theirs, and cut off the supplies directed to their Posts so as to distress
their Finances, and releive our own. Fifthly, by oeconomizing our
Funds, and constructing Six Ships annually we should advance so
rapidly to Maritime importance, that our Enemy would be convinced
not only of the Impossibility of subduing us, but also of the Certainty that his forces in this Country must eventually be lost without
being able to produce him any possible Advantage. And sixthly, we
should in this Mode recover the full Possession of our Country without the Expence of Blood, or treasure which must attend any other
Mode of Operations, and while we are pursuing those Steps which
lead to the Possession of our Natural Strength and Defence I trust
Sir that the Influence of these Considerations will not only lead the
Counsels of America, to adopt the measures necessary for, establishing a Navy, but that by oeconomizing as much as possible we may be
able (from the Sums now to be asked for) to do more in that Line
than is contained in the Estimate, but as this must depend on Circumstances, which we cannot command, so it is not prudent, or
proper to rely on it. Having already stated the lowest necessary Sum,
at Nine Millions I proceed Sir, to propose that four Millions be
borrowed, which will reduce the quota's to five Millions. I make this
Proposition under the Idea, that the Plans contained in my Letter of
yesterdays date be adopted. The quota's then being five millions and
the Revenues for funding our Debts which are proposed in that
Letter being two Millions, the Sum total of what will be taken from
the People will amount only to Seven Millions, and of that full twelve

hundred thousand will be paid back, as the interest of our Domestic
Debt, so as not to be in fact any Burthen on the whole People, tho' a
necessary Releif to a Considerable part of them. On this plain State I
shall make no Comment. I shall only pray that as much Expedition
may attend the Deliberations on these Objects as the Importance of
them will permit so that the States may be in a Situation to make
speedy Decisions. And this is the more necessary as the Negociations
for a Loan must be opened in Europe early next Winter. I have the
Honor to be, with great Respect Sir Your Excellency's most obedient
and humble Servant.[25]

Robt Morris

His Excellency The President of Congress

[ENCLOSURE]

General Estimates for 1783[26]

[Philadelphia, June 23–July 30, 1782]

General Estimate for the Year 1783[27]

	Dollars.
War Department by Estimate from the Minister	8,106,648.10
Marine Department	2,500,000.
Civil List	181,214.38
Contingencies	212,137.42
	Dollars 11,000,000.

Estimate of the Pay and Expence of the Army for the Year 1783[28]

Pay of the Army, &c	℔ Estimate No. 1	3,741,385.
Hospital Department	do. No. 2	137,570.60
Quarter Master Generals department	do. No. 3	958,011.22
Clothier Generals department	do. No. 4	1,281,400.
Commissary General Military		
Stores department	do. No. 5	66,521.20
Cost of Rations	do. No. 6	1,921,760.
		8,106,648.10

War Office July 13th. 1782
Approved
(Signed) B: Lincoln Secy. at War

Hon: Robt. Morris Esqr.
Superintendant of the Finances
of the United States of America

[War Department Estimate No. 6]
Estimate of the Number and Cost of Rations wanted for the Year 1783[29]

	Rations
1,666 Officers are entitled to	4,601 ℔ day
29,978 NonCommissioned Officers	
and Privates	29,978
1,000 Women	1,000

7,000 Prisoners of War	6,000	
1,000 Fatigue Rations	500	
500 Waggoners, Labourers, &c in the different departments	750	
	42,829	
	365	
	214,145	
	256,974	
	128,487	
	15,632,585	
Add for Rations in the several Departments, Waste, Contingencies, &c . . . 10 ₩ Cent	1,563,258	

Dollars.

17,295,843 at 10d. 1,921,760.

[Marine Department Estimate for 1783][30]

Estimate of the Expence of compleating the Ship America and of equipping, Vitualling and manning her.

Ship wrights Bill including the Launching &ca &ca	16,000		
Coppering the Bottom	10,000	26,000	
Smiths Bill	7,000		
Joyners Bill	2,000		
Plummers Bill	1,000		
Painters Bill	1,000		
Block makers Bill	3,500		
Carvers Bill	500		
Riggors Bill	2,000		
Boatbuilders Bill	500		
Hearth Copper and bricklayers Bill	500	18,000	
Anchors	4,500		
Masts and Yards	4,500		
Two Suits of Sails at 15,000 each	30,000		
Rigging Cables and Stores	40,000		
Ship Chandlery	15,000		
Water Cask	4,500		
Ballast	6,000	104,500	
Cannon	20,000		
Carriages	1,500		
Ordnance Stores	25,000	46,500	
Surgeons Stores		1,500	196,500
Recruiting 700 men at 15 Dollars each	10,500		
Pay at 8 dollars ₩ month	67,200		
Vitualling	67,200	144,900	
Contingencies		3,600	148,500
			345,000

Estimate of the Expence of compleating, Equipping, Victualling and
    Manning the Bourbon Frigate.

To compleat the Hull and for Masts, Spars, Joyners work, Iron Work, Carvers work, Blocks, Painting and Coopers Work and to bring the Ship to New London		34,000	
Riggers, Bricklayers and Boat Builders Bill		1,500	
Anchors	2,000		
Two Suits of Sails at 5,000 each	10,000		
Rigging Cables and Stores	15,000		
Ship Chandlery	5,000		
Water Cask	2,000		
Ballast	2,000	36,000	
Cannon	5,000		
Carriages	500		
Ordnance Stores	5,000	10,500	
Surgeons Stores		500	82,500
Recruiting 250 men at 15 dollars each	3,750		
Pay at 8 dollars ℔ month	24,000		
Vitualling	24,000	51,750	
Contingencies		750	52,500
			135,000

Estimate for the 12 Months Expences of the Frigates Alliance and   [31] at
    250 men each is 500 men.

Recruiting 500 men at 15 dollars each	7,500
Pay at 8 dollors ℔ Month	48,000
Vitualling	48,000
Contingent Expences	16,500
	120,000

Estimate of the Expence of Building, Equipping, Vitualling and Manning
    Six Ships of the Dimensions of the South Carolina.[32]

Ship wrights Bill including Launching &ca &ca	52,000	
Coppering the Bottom	8,000	60,000
Smiths Bill	18,000	
Joyners Bill	4,000	
Plummers Bill	1,000	
Painters Bill	1,000	
Block makers Bill	3,000	
Carvers Bill	500	
Riggors Bill	2,000	
Boat builders Bill	500	
Hearth Copper and Brick layers Bill	500	30,500

Anchors	4,000		
Masts and Yards	4,000		
Two Suits of Sails at 10,000 each	20,000		
Rigging Cables and Stores	20,000		
Ship Chandlery	10,000		
Water Cask	4,000		
Ballast	4,000	66,000	
Cannon	16,000		
Carriages	1,000		
Ordnance Stores	20,000	37,000	
Surgeons Stores		1,000	194,500
Recruiting 500 men at 15 Dollars each	7,500		
Pay at 8 dollars ℔ month	48,000		
Victualling	48,000	103,500	
Contingencies		2,000	105,500
			300,000
	Multiply by	6	
			1,800,000
The America	345,000		
The Bourbon	135,000		
The Alliance			
	120,000	600,000	
The [33]			
Contingencies		100,000	
			2,500,000

Civil List[34]

		Dollars.
Presidents Household suppose		12,000.
Secretary's Office	No. 1	8,300.
Office of Finance	2	14,282.78
Treasury Department	3	65,558.60
Office of Foreign Affairs	4	68,018.50
War Office	5	9,055.30
Marine Office	6	4,000.
	Dollars	181,214.38

[Civil List Estimate No. 2]

Estimate of the Expence of the Office of Finance for the Year 1783[35]

			Dollars.90ths.
Salaries to the Superintendant			
" Assistant			
" Secretary			12,150.
" Six Clerks, &c			
" Waiter			
Office Rent, of two Houses			933.30

		Dollars.	
Wood 40 Cords hickory, Sawing, Carting & Wharfage @ 8 Dollrs:		320.	
Sweeping Chimneys, 10 Drs., Hearth & Sweeping Brushes 5 Drs:		15.	335.

Stationary, &

		Dollars.	
15 Reams Quarto Post Paper	@ 35/	70.	
6 Quire blotting do.	1/3	1.	
6 Blank Books	60/	48.	
1500 Quills	17/6	35.	
4 Gallons black Ink	30/	16.	
½ Gallon red do.		3.	
1 doz: Boxes small Wafers		1.18	
1500 large do.	@ 7/6	15.	
4 lb. Sealing Wax	35/	9.30	
6 Pieces pink Tape, for tying up Papers		3.	
		201.48	

News Papers of five Printers 16 pr: Week	48.		
Printers Bills for different Kinds			
of Warrants, Advertisements, &c	200.	248.	449.48

	Dollars.	
Candles, 1 Box Spermaceti	30.	
" 3 Boxes Tallow	45.	75.

Carpenters Bills, &c for sundry Jobbs say about 20 dollrs. ⅌ month		100.	
Incidental Expences		240.	340.

J. McCall, Secry.   Dollars 14,282.78

[Civil List Estimate No. 6]
Estimate of the Expence of the Marine Office for the Year 1783[36]

Deputy Agent	1,000
Paymaster	1,000
Commissary of Prisoners	1,200
Stationary, Wood, Rent, Printing & other Contingencies	800
	4,000

ENDORSED: 81/July 30. 1782/Estimates for service of 1783/9 mill[ions] asked for. Necessity of/attending to and encreasing navy/81/Letter 30 July 1782/Superintd. finance/ Aug 5/Referred to the grand/Committee
MSS: LS, PCC, DNA; Ofcl LbC, DLC; copy, Meshech Weare Papers, Nh-Ar; copy, M-Ar; copy, R-Ar; copy, Jonathan Trumbull Papers, Ct; copy, Continental Congress Papers, Vi; copy, William Churchill Houston Collection, NjP; copy, Morris-Harwood Papers, MdHi; copy, Benjamin Franklin Papers, PPAmP; copy, Benjamin Franklin Papers, CtY; copy, Ferdinand J. Dreer Collection, PHi; copy, PPIn; LbC, Letterbook of Alexander Martin, 1782–1785, Nc-Ar; copy, Shelburne Papers, MiU-C; copy, Colonial Office, Class 5/Volume 108, fols. 125–127, PRO; Force transcript, DLC.
1. See Charles Thomson's Notes of Debates, August 5, 1782, Burnett, ed., *Letters*, VI, 421–422.
2. See notes to Diary, September 11.
3. On the proposed loan, see RM to the President of Congress, September 9, and 18, and notes, Diary, September 10, RM to Franklin, September 27 (two letters), and notes, Franklin to RM, June 25; and Franklin to Livingston, June 25, 1782, Wharton, ed., *Rev. Dipl. Corr.*, V, 510–511.
4. Although troop quotas in 1783 totaled over 33,000, enlistments were actually about 13,500 (see notes to RM and Richard Peters to George Washington, August 13, 1781). Apparently an army of that size was not only not available but was, in the opinion of French minister La Luzerne, not needed given the present military inactivity (see La Luzerne to Vergennes, August 9, 1782, Correspondance politique, Etats-Unis, XXII, 19–27, AMAE). Lincoln's estimate was formulated before plans for consolidating the army were adopted by Congress on August 7, 1782. See note 22 below for Congress's ongoing effort to reduce military expenditures.
5. For an explanation of the Rhode Island vote, see notes to William Churchill Houston to RM, August 10.
6. See Thomas McKean to Samuel Adams, August 6, 1782, Burnett, ed., *Letters*, VI, 430; also Adams to McKean, September 19, 1781, Harry Alonzo Cushing, ed., *The Writings of Samuel Adams* (New York, 1904–1908), IV, 262–263.
7. On sentiment regarding the navy, see for example, "Pylades," "Orestes," "A.B.," and "Candid," in the *Freeman's Journal*, April 17 and 24, May 29, and August 28, 1782, and the articles cited in note 8 below. "Pylades" and "Orestes" have been attributed to Philip Freneau (see Lewis Leary, *That Rascal Freneau: A Study in Literary Failure* [New Brunswick, N. J., 1941], 428; and the works cited in notes to Diary, August 22). On the perceived decline of American virtue, see Charles Royster, *A Revolutionary People at War: The Continental Army and American Character, 1775–1783* (Chapel Hill, N. C., 1979), 284–287; and Royster's " 'The Nature of Treason': Revolutionary Virtue and American Reactions to Benedict Arnold," *WMQ*, 3d ser., XXXVI (1979), 163–193.
8. Rush's "Retaliation" and "Leonidas" articles on the French alliance, public credit, and the navy are in the *Pennsylvania Journal*, May 15, 22, 29, June 19, July 4, 10, 17, 31, and August 14, 1782. The last five pieces were also printed in the *Pennsylvania Gazette*, July 3, 10, 17, 31, and August 14, 1782; the July 4 piece is published in Butterfield, ed., *Rush Letters*, I, 273–277. For a discussion, see David Freeman Hawke, *Benjamin Rush: Revolutionary Gadfly* (Indianapolis and New York, 1971), 255–259, 437n.
9. See Rush to Greene, April 15, 1782, in Butterfield, ed., *Rush Letters*, I, 268.
10. On the shift to naval warfare, see the headnote to RM's State of American Commerce and Plan for Protecting It, May 10, 1782, and notes.

11. See La Luzerne to Vergennes, August 9 and December 27, and Vergennes to La Luzerne, October 14, 1782, Correspondance politique, Etats-Unis, XXII, 19–27, 368–373, 592–603, AMAE. See also William C. Stinchcombe, *The American Revolution and the French Alliance* (Syracuse, N. Y., 1969), 191–192; and O'Donnell, *Chevalier de La Luzerne*, 207n.

12. See the headnote to RM to the President of Congress, September 8, 1781, and notes.

13. See notes to John Langdon to RM, April 20, 1781, and to Diary, February 14, 1782.

14. See Diary, May 15, 1782, and notes.

15. See Diary, May 3, 1782, and notes; also below in this headnote and note 32.

16. Benjamin Rush to Nathanael Greene, September 16, 1782, Butterfield, ed., *Rush Letters*, I, 285.

17. See RM to Alexander Hamilton, April 16, to the President of Congress, May 3, July 10, 1783, and March 19, 1784, and his reports to Congress of July 22 and 31, 1783.

18. See Paullin, *Navy of the American Revolution*, 244–251; Powers, "Decline and Extinction of American Naval Power," 162–187; and Fowler, *Rebels Under Sail*, 70, 84–86.

19. On the acquisition of the *Duc de Lauzun*, see notes to Diary, September 2. On the *General Washington*, see note 14 above.

20. RM subsequently acquired it. See Powers, "Decline and Extinction of American Naval Power," 185–186n.

21. RM had solicited the estimates in his Circular to the Secretary at War, the Secretary for Foreign Affairs, and the Secretary of Congress, June 20, 1782.

22. RM evidently alludes to economies already contemplated by the very active committee appointed "to consider the most just and practical means of reducing the expenditures of the United States in the several departments." This committee, consisting of Ezekiel Cornell of Rhode Island, Samuel Osgood of Massachusetts, Ralph Izard of South Carolina, Theodorick Bland, Jr., of Virginia, and James Duane of New York, was appointed on June 25, 1782, and assumed the tasks of three previous committees, including one appointed on June 11 also referred to by the same title (PCC, no. 186, pp. 34, 38). Its greatest accomplishment was to report resolutions, adopted by Congress on August 7, which consolidated undermanned regiments and retired excess officers (of whom it was thought there were twice too many for the men actually in service) as of January 1, 1783. This measure alone, one congressman calculated, would have saved $700,000 annually if the retired officers had not been eligible for half-pay pensions. During the summer and fall of 1782, Congress adopted several other proposals by this committee to revise the organization and pay schedules of various departments of the army. *JCC*, XXII, 336n., 349–351n., 353n., 378–379, 380–382, 413–415, 425–427, XXIII, 540–541, 651n., 682–686, 693, 721–722, 732–733; Abraham Clark to Elias Dayton, July 29, John Taylor Gilman to President Meshech Weare of New Hampshire, August 5, September 17, and to Josiah Bartlett, August 5, and Charles Thomson's Notes of Debates, August 7, 1782, Burnett, ed., *Letters*, VI, 395–396, 413, 474, 414, 432; and notes to Diary, April 27, July 1, and October 28, 1782.

23. See note 10 above.

24. Successive army reorganizations attested to this problem. For the reorganizations of 1780 and 1782, see RM and Richard Peters to George Washington, August 13, 1781, and notes; and note 4 above. Regarding Congress's troop requisition for 1782, see RM to Washington, January 26, 1782 (first letter), and notes.

25. Copies of this letter were enclosed in RM's Circulars to the Governors of the States and the Receivers of Continental Taxes, both September 12, and RM to Benjamin Franklin, September 27 (first letter). Sir Guy Carleton in New York eventually obtained copies of this letter as well as the letter to Congress of July 29 and forwarded them to London with comments about RM's difficulties. See Carleton to Thomas Townshend, January 18, 1783, calendared in Davies, ed., *Documents of the American Revolution*, XIX, 366–367 (no. 2159, enclosure xi).

26. Caption from PCC, no. 144, p. 8. Reproduced here are the general estimate, the War Department estimate with subestimate 6 for the cost of rations, the Marine Department estimate prepared by RM, and civil list estimate with subestimates 2 and 6

produced by RM as Superintendent of Finance and Agent of Marine. The contingency estimate, which has not been found, and other subestimates have not been reproduced.

27. MS: D, PCC, no. 141, I, 11–12.

28. MS: Copy, PCC, no. 144, pp. 9–12. Lincoln's estimate was presented to RM on July 13, 1782 (see Diary of that date). For subestimate 6, of interest with regard to RM's contract system, see text at note 29 below. War Department subestimates 1–5 are in PCC, no. 144, pp. 19–26, 13–16, 27–34.

29. MS: D, PCC, no. 141, I, 57–58.

30. MS: D, PCC, no. 144, pp. 36–39.

31. Space left blank in manuscript. The ship was the frigate *Deane*, soon to be renamed the *Hague*.

32. The *South Carolina* was originally *L'Indien*, a frigate built in Amsterdam in 1777 for the American commissioners to France. A vessel of 1,430 tons, *L'Indien* was 170 feet in length, $43^{1}/_{4}$ feet in the beam and 144 feet in the keel, had a hold $16^{1}/_{2}$ feet deep, and required a complement of 550. Acquired for the South Carolina navy in 1780 by Commodore Alexander Gillon, who renamed her, the *South Carolina* at various times sported between 40 and 44 guns, though Gillon described her dimensions as those of a 74-gun ship. After giving up the idea of obtaining her for the Continental navy (see Diary, May 3, 1782, and notes), RM later appears to have visited the *South Carolina* at Philadelphia in connection with his developing plans to use her design as a model for future American warships (see Gillon to RM, June 1782). The *South Carolina*'s sleek lines were much admired and inspired the design of the first frigates of the United States Navy authorized by Congress in 1794. *Dict. Amer. Naval Ships*, III, 437, s.v. *"Indien"*; Powers, "Decline and Extinction of American Naval Power," 99n.; Gillon to John Laurens, March 22, 1781, in D. E. Huger Smith, ed., "The Mission of Col. John Laurens to Europe in 1781," *SCHGM*, I (1900), 28–32; Smith, "Commodore Alexander Gillon and the Frigate South Carolina," *ibid.*, IX (1908), 211, 216; and Morison, *John Paul Jones*, 331.

33. Space left blank in manuscript. See note 31 above.

34. MS: D, PCC, no. 144, pp. 41–42. For civil list subestimates 2 and 6, for the Office of Finance and the Marine Office, respectively, see text at notes 35 and 36. Civil list subestimates 1 and 3–5 are in PCC, no. 144, pp. 17–17A, 45–48, 51, 49–50, 52–53.

35. MS: D signed by James McCall, PCC, no. 144, pp. 43–44. This estimate is registered in the Diary of July 25.

36. MS: D, PCC, no. 144, p. 35.

To Samuel Holden Parsons

Office of Finance 30 July 1782[1]

Sir,

I received your Favor of the eighteenth Instant for which I pray you to accept my sincere Thanks. I do myself the Honor to enclose the circular Letter which I have written in Consequence[2] and by which you will perceive that I have complied with your wish in not making Use of your name. I shall be at all Times happy to be favored with such Information tending to promote the public Service as you may find it convenient to convey. I pray you to beleive me with great Esteem Sir your most obedient and humble Servant

RM

MSS: Ofcl LbC, DLC.

1. Major General Parsons of Connecticut had recently retired from the Continental army.

2. See the Circular to the Governors of the States, July 30.

To the Quartermaster General
(Timothy Pickering)

Office of Finance 30th: July 1782

Sir,

It is now several Days since I received your Letter of the nineteenth Instant.[1] It is very true that I have kept you long in this City, with the Weekly Hope of receiving Money, that I have assured you of my Disposition, to support the Credit of your Department, And that I encouraged you to expect Money for Forage, and other Objects which you have engaged for. The shameful and cruel Neglect of those who ought long since to have provided me with the Means, puts it out of my Power.

I find the most extreme Difficulty in performing my own Engagements, and live in hourly Apprehension of the most fatal Consequences. I think it my Duty to acknowledge the Attention you have at once paid to your own Department, and to my Situation. I wish it were in my Power to make you a better Reward, than Thanks.

Whenever the State of my Funds will permit I will relieve you, and in the Interim, you must obtain the Forbearance of Creditors, and incur no new Expence.

If any Evils arise those must be answerable, by whose Negligence they have been occasioned. I am Sir, Your most Obedient Servant[2]

Robt Morris

Col. Pickering
Qr: Mr: Genl:

ENDORSED: Honble. Robt. Morris Esqr. S. F./July 30. 1782. received 30th/in answer to mine of the 19th respecting/the cause of my detention in Philaa, and his encouragements of furnishing me/with money.
MSS: LS, Manuscript File, WDC, DNA; Ofcl LbC, DLC; LbC, WDC, DNA.

1. The only text of this letter found by the editors, Pickering's LbC, is dated July 17 and is printed under that date. However, RM's acknowledgment and Pickering's endorsement on the present letter (see above) indicate that the text received by RM very likely was dated July 19.

2. RM delivered this letter to Pickering on July 31 (see Diary of that date). After returning to army headquarters at Verplanck's Point, New York, Pickering wrote a letter to Andrew Dunscomb, an assistant quartermaster, explaining why so little payment could be made to creditors of the Quartermaster Department. In a postscript Pickering added that he was enclosing RM's letter, "which with the candid, will justify him as well as myself for the failures of payment referred to in this letter [to Dunscomb]. As tis the original, you will carefully preserve it." A paragraph in a second letter to Dunscomb of the same date from Pickering instructed him to "read or shew" the first one "to such of the people on whom you think it may make a good impression. I wish them to reflect that they and I have but one common interest in every public measure, and that they form a part of that public whose servant I am." Pickering to Dunscomb, September 5, 1782, WDC, no. 84, pp. 84–86, no. 85, pp. 179–181; the quotations are on pp. 86 and 180.

Minutes of the Committee of Congress
on the Department of Finance

[Office of Finance, July 30, 1782][1]
Minutes of Committee
on Department of Finance
Finance Office 30th July 1782
Present Mr Duane, Mr Osgood, Mr Clarke, Mr Lee.[2]
Agreed to meet for the dispatch of this Commission
Tuesdays, Thursdays, and Saturdays, at 9 oCl A.M.

Enterd on the first Object of the Enquiry—vizt.
I. The Publick Debts.
a. Examind Account of Debts due on Loan office Certificates[3] and
    debts due on Subsequent Certificates called Funded Debts[4] vide
    Accounts.
b. The Mode of settling those Accounts and giving the Certificates
    explaind.
c. Clause of a Report read intended to be presented by the Finan-
    cier to Congress respecting European debts &c. This Report will
    be accompanied by the Account [*illegible letter or symbol*].[5]
d. The Financier observes that the Accounts with the several States
    and departments in the staff are not yet enterd upon from the
    difficulty of getting Commissioners. Commissioners only ap-
    pointed for Connecticut, New Jersey, Virginia. Maryland[6]

Adjournd to Thursday Morning 9 oCl

ENDORSED: Minutes of Committee/on Department of Finance
MS: D in the writing of James Duane, PCC, DNA.
    1. The committee to investigate the "department of Finance, including the several
branches of the same," chaired by James Duane of New York, the author of the
minutes printed here, was one of five committees appointed on July 2, 1782, to
oversee the operations of the executive departments created by Congress in 1781.
Duane had established the agenda for this first meeting in a letter to RM of July 19;
for RM's account of the meeting, see Diary, July 30. For a general discussion of the
finance committee and its work, see notes to Diary, June 12, 1782.
    2. Thomas McKean of Delaware was the only committee member not present at
this first meeting.
    3. On the loan office debt, see RM's Report to Congress on the Continental Loan
Offices, June 13, 1782, and notes.
    4. This category of the public debt is described in an estimate RM submitted to
Congress as debts that "have been Funded and passed to the Credit of Individuals
pursuant to Warrants from the Superintendant of Finance" (see enclosure 2 to RM to
the President of Congress, July 29). Although RM accepted office with the understanding that he would not be responsible for debts incurred prior to his administration, he requested in his letter to Congress of May 14, 1781, that the settlement of
such debts "be compleated by the Modes already Adopted" and that "whatever remains unpaid may become a Funded Debt and that it may in that Form be Committed
to me to provide for the yearly interest and for the *eventual* discharge of the Princi-

pal." These debts, after being settled at the Treasury, accumulated 6 percent interest annually until paid. Separate account books, referred to as "Auxiliary Books for funded debts," were evidently opened in November 1781 to record these transactions, which primarily consisted of back pay, subsistence, or depreciation payments to various army officers, staff department officials, and other Continental employees. On RM's warrant, certificates transferable only at the Treasury office were issued and signed by Register of the Treasury Joseph Nourse to certify the balances due; the Superintendent from time to time referred to these balances as the "funded debt." The "funded debt" remained a distinct category of the national debt, separate from loan office certificates and from the various final settlement certificates issued by the commissioners of accounts. However, various individuals holding loan office certificates, final settlement certificates, and other forms of debt cancelled them at the Treasury, registered the sums owed, and received in exchange Nourse's certificates. These sums were thereby incorporated into the accounts for the "funded debt," also referred to as the "registered debt." Removed from the category of the funded debt as of 1784 were sums owed to foreign officers, for whom a special category of debt was established under an act of February 3, 1784, for which the interest was to be paid annually by Ferdinand Grand, banker for the United States in France. Of course, strictly speaking, since no revenue was available, the debt was not actually funded until the enactment of the Hamiltonian funding program in 1790. See Diary, October 27 and 29, November 9, 1781, February 4, 5, and 19, 1782, RM to Francis Wade, December 28, 1781, to Nourse, January 15, February 5 (first letter), and April 11, 1782, to Bodo Otto, April 8, 1782, to Benjamin Franklin, June 26, 1782, to the President of Congress, July 29, 1782, and March 10, 1783 (second letter), and enclosures, and RM's report to Congress of July 31, 1783; *JCC*, XXIV, 276 and n., 487–488 and n., XXVI, 235–236, XXVIII, 446–448; accounts of the liquidated debt in 1785 and in 1787 in PCC, no. 141, I, 87–89, 361; "Abstract of the Liquidated and Loan-Office Debt of the United States, on the 3d March, 1789," in Syrett and Cooke, eds., *Hamilton Papers*, VI, 114–115; and the entries in Treasury Waste Books C, D, and E (e.g., Waste Book C, pp. 31, 32, 33, 34) in Records of the United States General Accounting Office, RG 217, DNA; and Ferguson, *Power of the Purse*, 255–256, on the transfer of the debt.

5. The editors have not found a report to Congress from the Financier in 1782 on the foreign debt, but he did enclose an estimate of the foreign debt in a letter to Congress of March 10, 1783.

6. This word was added by an unidentified hand. RM's progress report on the settlement of accounts, contained in a letter to the president of Congress of December 3, 1782, disclosed that the appointment of commissioners for settling individual and state debts remained stalled. For the background, see RM to the President of Congress, December 10, 1781, and notes, and February 18, 1782, and notes; for the procedures to be followed in making a final settlement of accounts, see Diary, July 18, 1782, and notes, and the ensuing formal instructions of the Comptroller of the Treasury printed under October 14, 1782.

From George Washington

Head Quarters Newburgh [New York]
July 30. 1782

⟨Dear⟩ Sir

Since my arrival here General Heath has put into my hands, the Letter from Messrs. Sands & Co (of which the enclosed is a Copy) in answer to one from the Genl to the Contractors, on the subject of repeated deficiency in the supply of provisions, during my absence,[1] and the great distress of the Troops consequent thereof.[2]

As the Representation contained in this Letter differs materially from the *idea* of the state of facts, which I had conceived from my conversation with you—I thought it essential to transmit it, in order that my mistake might be remedied, in case I had misunderstood your Meaning.

I know, Sir, full well the innumerable embarrassements with which you are surrounded on all sides; and therefore if there is unavoidably a deficiency in complying with the Contract on the part of the public, I would wish not to push the Contractors ⟨in an unreasonable manner⟩, but on the other hand to make every thing as easy with the Army as possible: Altho it is *certain* the service is much impeded, desertion vastly encreased, and the disposition of the Troops extremely soured, by their frequent want of Provisions[3] and being sometimes 2 or three days too without and some Corps a whole Month without a drop of spirits either to Officers or Men. But if the failure has happened through the fault of the Contractors, when they were actually furnished with the Means of effecting the necessary purchases, their Conduct is infamous beyond discription or parallel, and deserves the severest reprehension and punishment.

Sincerely disposed to interpose all my influence in promoting your Momentous Plans, I entreat you will give me an answer by the bearer and believe that I am with the most perfect esteem and regard Sir Your Most Obedient Servant[4]

The Honble Robert Morris Esqr
Superintendt of Finance

ENDORSED: Head Quarters 30th July 1782/to/Hono Robert Morris Esqr/Complaint of Messrs Sands & Co/for Want of Money—Quere?
MSS: Dft in the writing of David Humphreys with revisions in Washington's hand, Washington Papers, DLC; Varick transcript, Washington Papers, DLC.

1. The remainder of this paragraph is in Washington's hand
2. On July 28, the day after Washington returned to camp from Philadelphia, Major General William Heath, commander during his absence, sent him a letter he had received from Sands, Livingston, and Company, contractors for West Point and the Moving Army, in reply to complaints relayed to them about the quality of beef issued in the rations. The contractors laid the blame for shortages and poor quality on RM's delinquency in payment. "We have been so often and so repeatedly disappointed in getting our Money from the Public that we are obliged to buy from day to day wherever a little Credit is to be had. We have from time to time informed Mr. Morris of the necessity of being paid regular; and told him, that unless we were, it would be impossible to supply the Troops. We have now due a large Balance for last month's supplies and another month almost out. Mr. Livingston sets out immediately to get [our?] Money if possible—if he gets it to hand your supplies will be regular—till that is the case you must not expect it. Every thing on our part shall be done that is possible." See Sands, Livingston, and Company to Heath, and Heath to Washington, both July 28, 1782, Washington Papers, DLC; also Heath to Comfort Sands and Company, July 27, 1782, Heath Papers, MIIi. For RM's response to Livingston's mission, see Diary, August 2. On the disputes between the army and the contractors and the eventual dissolution of the contract, see Washington to RM, May 17–25, and notes, and Comfort Sands, Walter Livingston, William Duer, and Daniel Parker to RM, September 11, 1782, and notes.
3. Washington inserted the remainder of this sentence in his own hand.
4. RM received this letter from Washington during the evening of August 2 and replied on August 5.

To John Bradford

Office of Finance 30 July 1782

I have received your Favor of the twenty eighth of June from Boston.[1] I am sorry the Act of Congress I transmitted was not equal to the Object. As to the Demand of the State of Connecticut there can be no Difficulty; neither indeed is it material how their Account stands with the United States for if they will bring in a Charge for the Articles delivered you the Commissioner will naturally pass such Charge admitting it to be proper in other Respects. If it shall appear on the final Adjustment that Connecticut is indebted to the United States or vice versa both Cases are provided for in the Ordinance for settling Accounts.

MS: Ofcl LbC, DLC.
1. The letter from Bradford, former Continental prize agent at Boston, has not been found. On the subject in question, see Bradford to RM, April 24, and notes, and RM to Bradford, May 7, and notes, to Bradford, and to the Governor of Connecticut, both August 26, and to Samuel Eliot, Jr., September 27, 1782.

To John Hopkins, Jr.

Office of Finance 30 July 1782

I have received your Favor of the third Instant with it's Enclosures. The State of the Paper Money will I beleive soon be brought on in Congress and then I will take Care to forward their Decissions.[1]

MS: Ofcl LbC, DLC.
1. Hopkins was the Continental loan officer of Virginia. His letter has not been found, but one of the enclosures may have been a resolution of the Virginia House of Delegates of July 2, 1782, pertaining to the disposal of old Continental currency under the act of Congress of March 18, 1780. See RM's report to Congress of September 7, and notes.

To James Lovell

Office of Finance 30th. July 1782

I received your Favor of the eighth Instant with the Enclosures.[1] I wish the Efforts of your Assembly may have the desired Effect. As to the Exchange I am sorry to find it is so low with you. It is rising here and I this Day sold 120,000# at 6/6 for five Livres.[2]

MS: Ofcl LbC, DLC.
1. Letter and enclosures not found. Lovell was the receiver of Continental taxes for Massachusetts.
2. This was close to par.

John Brown to William Morris

Marine Office 30 July 1782[1]

Your Letter of the 29 June last from New London enclosing your Warrant as Lieutenant of Marines and expressing your desire to resign it has been received at this Office[2] and I am directed by the honble. Mr. Morris Agent of Marine to inform you that he has accepted of your resignation altho he is sorry to see, (what he conceives you to be) a worthy Officer depart from the Service. He wishes you much happiness in private Life as does also Sir your very humble Servant.

by Order John Brown

MS: AM LbC, MdAN.
1. Brown was an assistant to RM in the Marine Office. Lieutenant Morris of the Continental marines had been assigned to the frigate *Alliance* now refitting at New London.
2. Letter not found. Lieutenant Morris had left a letter of the same date at New London for Captain John Barry explaining the personal reasons behind his decision to retire, but upon his return from Philadelphia Barry listed him as a deserter. See William Morris to Barry, June 29, 1782, Barry Letterbook, Naval History Society Collection, NHi; and Barry to RM, August 2.

To Donaldson Yeates

Office of Finance 30th. July 1782[1]

I am to request that you will deliver to the Order of Mr. George Henry one pair of nine Pounders being part of the Ordnance brought from York Town Virginia and landed at the Head of Elk by General Knox. The said Gentleman having paid to the Treasurer of the United States the Price offered by an Advertizement of the 25th. February last from this Office.[2]

MS: Ofcl LbC, DLC.
1. Yeates was the deputy quartermaster general for Maryland and Delaware stationed at the Head of Elk.
2. The advertisement is dated February 26, 1782.

Diary: July 31, 1782

This Morning the Commissioners for defending Delaware &c. Called upon the business of the Ship Washington, when the Arbitrators Govr. Rutledge, Mr. Lowell and Mr Pettit being also met we stated the Case to the Satisfaction of both parties and left them to determine the Principles on which this Account is to be settled agreeable to what they shall think equitable and just.[1]

Wm. Denning Esqr. called in Consequence of the Letters which have passed between us[2] and after some Conversation I agreed to Nominate him Commissioner for Settling the Accounts of the Quarter Master Department and wrote a Letter to the President of Congress accordingly.

The Hon. Major Genl. Gates called on a Visit, but had some Conversation on his Situation as an Officer &c.[3]

Mr. Jesse Brown was this day dispatched with a number of Letters for the Eastern States from this Office but not the whole I wished him to Carry as they could not be got ready.

Capt. Wm. Hardy applied to me on behalf of his Son[4] when I convinced him nothing could in his present Situation be done for him. He then preferred sundry matters calculated for his own benefit, which I was obliged to pass by, being out of that line of propriety I choose to move in.

Capt. Jeremiah Freeman who had written me two Letters on the Subject of his Wants and Claims came to the Office by my Appointment when I explained the reasons which put it out of my power to releive him.[5]

Colo. Tench Tilghman called on a Visit and as I am perfectly acquainted with this Gentleman's Virtue, Integrity and Abilities I shewed him the Act of Congress Authorizing me to Appoint an Inspector of the Contracts &c. and offered him the Commission which he has under Consideration.[6]

I sent to Mr. Nourse for the Accounts of public Expenditures since my being in Office which he has Sent to me.[7]

Colo. Pickering with Sundry Claims for Money all of which I put off and delivered him my Letter of this Date.[8]

I sent for the Paymaster General and desired his returns of notes Issued to Officers on Account of their Pay.[9]

Colo. Blaine for Money.[10]

I sent for Haym Solomon the Broker and ordered his Accounts of Monies due for Bills &c. in order to provide Mr. Pierce with the means of paying his Notes.

Mr Pierce sent me the returns of his notes which Amount to 140, 266^{28}/$_{90}$ Dollars being paid to the Officers of the whole Army on Account of their Pay for 1782.[11]

Wrote a Letter to His Excellency Govr. Trumbull.

Wrote a Letter to His Excellency the Presdt. of Congress.

1. See Diary, July 30, and notes.
2. See RM to William Denning, April 20 and June 5 and 29, 1782.
3. See RM to Horatio Gates, May 31, 1782, and notes.
4. See Diary, October 30, 1781, and notes.
5. Freeman had been captain lieutenant in Roman's Pennsylvania Independent Artillery Company, which was to have become part of the 4th Battalion of Continental Artillery in 1778; the company had become defunct by the time Freeman retired on January 1, 1781. His letters to RM have not been found. Heitman, *Register;* John B. B. Trussell, Jr., *The Pennsylvania Line: Regimental Organization and Operations, 1776–1783* (Harrisburg, Pa., 1977), 193–194.
6. Tilghman, an aide to George Washington, declined the offer (see Diary, August 5). For the act of Congress mentioned by RM and the eventual appointment of Ezekiel Cornell, see notes to RM to the President of Congress, April 20, 1782.
7. The actual accounts sent by Joseph Nourse, Register of the Treasury, have not been found. On the publication in November of the Superintendent's accounts for 1781, see notes to Diary, June 12, 1782.
8. See RM to the Quartermaster General, July 30.
9. For the promissory notes issued to army officers by John Pierce, see RM to George Washington, January 26, 1782 (second letter), and notes.
10. Ephraim Blaine was calling on behalf of the contractors for Fort Pitt. See Diary, July 23, and notes.
11. Pierce's returns have not been found; for a summary, see Diary, August 1.

To the Governor of Connecticut
(Jonathan Trumbull)

Philadelphia 31 July 1782

Sir

I had the Honor of your Letter dated at Lebanon the eleventh Instant by Mr Brown, and beg Leave now to make my Acknowlegements of it and the Enclosures.[1] I am happy that your Legislature have so early adopted the Recommendation of Congress on the Subject of settling Accounts, but I regret the Proviso contained in their Act, as I am much afraid that on a full Consideration of the Question, it will appear to be impracticable for Congress to confine themselves to any one precise Mode of ascertaining the Quotas which could now be suggested.[2] It will be in their Wisdom to adopt the Mode on a View of all Circumstances which cannot be obtained by any particular State. Your Excellency will perceive that if each Legislature were to mark out it's own Mode, no Determination could take Place unless the Mode prescribed by each should be the same, which is next to impossible. On such general Questions the better Way seems to be that Congress should be vested with Authority, and possessed of Information, and that each State should take Care of it's own Interests, by appointing the best Representatives in Congress, a Precaution which will I presume be taken for many other Reasons.

I expect that Congress will soon make some very pointed Decisions on the Subject of Paper Money[3] and I shall forward them as soon as they are adopted. In the Interim I cannot take upon me to give any directions.

I am happy to learn that your State has made greater Exertions for the public Service than I had been informed of, but on this Occasion I must take the Liberty to suggest that as well for the Credit of your State as the Interest of the United States, every thing you have furnished to the Contractors and Quarter Masters cannot too soon be converted into Cash Accounts. Thus for Instance I would not hesitate a Moment to advance in Notes the Sum necessary to pay for the Articles you have furnished, which Notes being paid over to Mr. Merrill would in his Accounts be carried to the Credit of your State[4] but I am not less dunned for Money by Reason of the Supplies which the States may make, nor indeed have I any Right to expect it for if the Contractors purchase on Credit it is their own Benefit, and they will have the Money due them from me, and pay their Debts out of it.

With respect to the Engagements of the State to their Officers and

Soldiers I shall say nothing here, as my Sentiments are contained fully in a Circular Letter written a few days since,[5] which your Excellency will have received. If States or Individuals make Advances to Officers or Soldiers they must be repaid by those Officers and Soldiers. But the Individual must not plead his Advance in discharge of his Tax, nor the State in discharge of its Quota. As to the Complaint made by the People of a Want of Money to pay their Taxes it is nothing new to me, nor indeed to any body. The Complaint is I beleive quite as old as Taxation and will last as long. That Times are hard, that Money is scarce, that Taxes are heavy, and the like are Constant themes of Declamation in all Countries and will be so. But the very Generality of the Complaint shews it to be ill founded. The Fact is that Men will always find Use for all the Money they can get hold of,[6] and more. A Tax Gatherer therefore will always be an unwelcome Guest because his Demand must necessarily interfere with some pleasurable, or profitable Pursuit. Hundreds who cannot find Money to pay Taxes, can find it to purchase useless Gew Gaws, and expend much more in the Gratification of Vanity, Luxury, Drunkenness, and Debauchery than is necessary to establish the Freedom of their Country. To say they cannot sell their Cattle is only saying in other Words, they will not sell them for any Man can sell who will accommodate the Purchase to the Price. In proportion as Prices lower, all will flock to buy, and thus Money will be brought in, if as is said it be really scarce.

I cannot undertake to decide on the Propriety of that kind of Commerce with the Enemy which your Excellency mentions. Congress have thought proper to prohibit it for many wise Reasons influencing them and their Decisions on the Subject are coincident with the Sentiments of the warmest[7] Whigs among us.[8] Perhaps if a Commerce were at all to be permitted it should be by letting them have Articles, which they could get elsewhere and such as are useless, or pernicious, but we may well doubt of the Propriety of selling them live Stock which they cannot bring from abroad. I shall not however, go into an Examination of the Question for which I hope your Excellency's Excuse, as the Determination of the United States in Congress[9] is with me conclusive. I have the Honor to be, with great Respect Sir Your Excellency's Most obedient and humble Servant

Robt Morris

His Excellency Govr. Trumbull
Lebanon

ENDORSED: Office of Finance/31st July 1782/de sundry/received 21st Augt. seq.
MSS: LS, Trumbull Papers, Ct; Ofcl LbC, DLC.
   1. Letter and enclosures not found. One of the enclosures probably was the Connecticut act mentioned in the next note.

2. Regarding Congress's request for authorization to apportion the expenses of the war among the states without being bound by the eighth Article of Confederation, see notes to William Churchill Houston to RM, June 29, 1782. Connecticut responded with "An Act providing for the settlement of the Accounts between this State and the United States," but a proviso required that each state's quota be calculated according to the value of land and improvements as specified in the eighth Article of Confederation or "in proportion to the number of Inhabitants of every Age and Sex in each State, including Negroe and Molattoe Servants or such Proportion of them as the United States in Congress Assembled shall Judge equitable." The proviso also stipulated that any deductions made from state quotas on account of enemy depredations were to be "averaged to all the States in proportion to the Sums that shall remain after such Deduction." Connecticut also complied with Congress's request, contained in the ordinances of February 20 and 27, 1782, for settling public accounts, that the states authorize the commissioners of accounts to summon witnesses and question them under oath. In a second act it also acceded to Congress's request in the February 27 act that the United States be empowered to bring suit in state courts for the recovery of debts due to the United States. These acts, passed during the session of May 9–June 15, 1782, are in Hoadly and Labaree, eds., *Public Records of Connecticut*, IV, 163–164, 168–171. For the response of other states to Congress's appeals for enabling legislation on the settlement of accounts, see notes to RM to Francis Wade, August 9.

3. For congressional action on state compliance in withdrawing old Continental currency under the terms of the act of March 18, 1780, see RM's report to Congress of September 7, and notes.

4. RM also proposed similar arrangements to other states for converting specific supplies into cash or notes that could be applied to the specie requisition for 1782 (see notes to Walter Livingston to RM, July 29, and to William Whipple to RM, August 5). For the case with regard to Connecticut, see Ebenezer Barnard, Jr., to RM, November 4, 1782.

5. RM's Circular to the Governors of the States, July 29.

6. In LS and Ofcl LbC: "off."

7. The word "firmest" is used in the Ofcl LbC.

8. For recent congressional action against trade with the enemy, see notes to Gouverneur Morris to Thomas Willing, June 18, 1782. Criticism of Connecticut's illicit trade with New York in connection with its ability to pay taxes is made in the Quartermaster General to RM, August 24.

9. The preceding two words are omitted from the Ofcl LbC.

Objections to the Impost in Rhode Island from David Howell

[Philadelphia, ca. July 31–August 2, 1782]

Some objections against passing an Impost Law, in the State of Rhode Island and Providence Plantations, briefly stated at the request of the Superintendent of Finance, by his humble servant, D. Howell.[1]

It is assumed that the usual mode of taxation draweth supplies from the people, proportionate to what they possess, and have defended by the public, and is therefore founded on the most obvious principles of justice. But the measure proposed would either draw a disproportionate supply from the merchant, as such, or from the consumers in general; if from the merchant, according to what he imports; if from the consumer, according to what he consumes. In either case, it would bear hard on the citizens of Rhode Island and Providence Plantations, who both import and consume of important articles, a greater proportion than any other state. As the State of Rhode Island and Providence Plantations is subjected from its maritime situations to greater losses and risks in war, without any claim of reimbursement, therefore, in virtue of any compact or stipulation on the Federal Union; if any revenue can be raised from trade in the way proposed, or any other, the State is entitled to the exclusive benefit thereof, and that the amount annually passed to their credit, and be collected by officers of their own appointment, in common justice recognized in confederation. Should a duty be laid on imported goods the prices of such country produce as may be substituted in their room will be raised, (should said duty be superadded to the former prices of imported goods,) and preserve nearly their usual proportion thereto. These being drawn from neighboring states, will eventually come charged with a similar duty, and thus the neighboring states in particular, and the Union at large, will draw a substantial revenue out of the earnings and industry of the citizens of Rhode Island and Providence Plantations. Duties imposed directly on country produce, or inland embargoes by neighboring states, may in future put the inhabitants of Rhode Island and Providence Plantations on the necessity of subsisting themselves more, if not altogether, on imported goods, and increase the burdensome operations of the impost proposed. But while trade remains free to all the world and unfettered with duties, the State, though small, still remains independent.

So far from creating ways and means, or lightening our taxes, the measure proposed would incur the enormous additional charge of taking off from arts and industry a numerous train of men for the collection and after management of this revenue; and supporting them in comparative idleness only to shift the mode of raising supplies, and to throwing taxation into another channel to the lasting injury of certain descriptions of citizens.

After all this additional charge incurred, the revenue proposed would not be productive. It would be the interest of the merchant to avoid paying it, and the interest of the State to countenance him. Profanations of oaths and corruption in various forms would follow. No definite plan for the execution of the impost law has yet been promulgated. Whether penalties are to be recoverable or prosecutions commenced in the common or maritime courts, is not declared; and the operation of the law may be rendered more grievous by the mode of enforcing it.[2] The State wishes to preserve inviolate, Article 8th of the Confederation;[3] and whenever their quota of continental requisitions shall be made agreeably thereto, to be permitted to raise it in their own way.

N. B. The State is largely interested in Loan Office Certificates,[4] and desirous of discharging interest and principal with honor.

PRINTED: Staples, *Rhode Island in the Continental Congress*, 391–392.

1. David Howell of Rhode Island, the author of these "objections," had been elected a delegate to Congress on May 1, 1782, partly on the strength of his unremitting opposition to the impost amendment, expressed forcefully in a series of articles written under the pseudonym of "A Farmer" in the *Providence Gazette* during the spring of 1782. Upon arriving in Philadelphia early in June and finding "that all the members of Congress, as well as the inhabitants, were universally in favor of the impost, and concluding that my single voice would be unavailing against the general current," Howell recalled not long after, "I cautiously avoided entering unnecessarily into the discussion of the subject." That Howell indeed kept his own counsel is suggested by his first recorded visit to the Office of Finance on July 2 in company with Ezekiel Cornell, the other Rhode Island delegate in attendance, who supported the impost. RM noted in his Diary of that date that both men "seem to think that the Impost Law will at Length be passed in that State."

Howell first revealed his views toward the end of July when he and Cornell appeared before a committee of Congress appointed on July 22 to "enquire into the obstacles which have retarded a compliance" with the impost and "to report the proper means for obtaining the full effect of the said requisition" (PCC, no. 186, p. 44). At the committee's invitation RM attended the hearing and heard Howell explain the reasons why Rhode Island had not yet ratified the impost. Howell cogently recapitulated his arguments at length in a letter to Governor William Greene of July 30–31, commenting in a postscript to this missive that "Mr. Morris has this moment sent me a note, requesting the reasons, in writing, why our State has not complied with the recommendation for five per cent., as he is about to write to the State on that subject." RM's note has not been found, but the context of Howell's comment would suggest that he received it on July 31 and set to work at once. The editors therefore have tentatively assigned his undated "objections" to July 31. A manuscript text has not been found, however, and the editors have been compelled to reproduce here a nineteenth-century transcript. RM enclosed a copy of the "objections" and endeavored to rebut them in his letter to the Governor of Rhode Island of August 2. Howell's statement to RM was less elaborate than the letter to Governor Greene, which also touched upon Rhode Island's insistence upon the surrender of western land claims by other states and emphasized more forcefully the political dangers of surrendering elements of state sovereignty to Congress. The letter to Governor Greene is printed in full in Staples, *Rhode Island in the Continental Congress*, 381–387 (quotations at 382 and 387), and in part in Burnett, ed., *Letters*, VI, 399–404. For a discussion of Howell's "A Farmer" articles and his election to Congress, see Polishook, *Rhode Island and the Union*, 69–73.

2. RM had recently received the draft of an ordinance for executing the impost (see Diary, July 25); it is printed in Appendix I to this volume. For the enforcement provisions, see sections 11–14.

3. This article designated the value of land and its improvements as the basis for determining each state's share of the general expenses of the Union. For a discussion of Congress's effort not to be bound thereby, see notes to William Churchill Houston to RM, June 29; and RM to the Governor of Connecticut, July 31, 1782, and notes. For Howell's argument that annual requisitions were the "constitutional" mode of debt funding, see the headnote and notes to RM to the President of Congress, July 29.

4. Rhode Island as a whole was not heavily interested in loan office certificates at this time, only about 6 percent of the total amount having been originally issued in the state. It would appear that transfers of loan office certificates took place mainly after interest payments were discontinued in 1781 and 1782. An analysis of public security holdings in Rhode Island in 1790, as far as they can be determined, including loan office certificates and other forms of federal securities, is in Ferguson, *Power of the Purse*, 280–282. For accounts of Rhode Island's economic interest in opposing the impost, see Hedges, *The Browns: Colonial Years*, 323–325; Main, *Antifederalists*, 88–90; Polishook, *Rhode Island and the Union*, 53–80; and McDonald, *E Pluribus Unum*, 20–22.

To the President of Congress
(John Hanson)

Office of Finance, 31st: July 1782

I do myself the Honor to report to Congress the name of William Denning Esq: whom I have appointed to be the Commissioner for settling the Accounts of the Quarter Masters Department, according to the Act of the twenty Seventh of February last. Should Congress disapprove of this appointment I hope to be favored with their Order's. Mr. Denning is so well known, that it is unnecessary for me to say any thing of his character or Abilities, particularly to Congress as he has already had the Honor of Serving the United States as a Commissioner of the late Board of Treasury.[1]

MSS: LS, PCC, DNA; Ofcl LbC, DLC.
    1. This letter was read in Congress on August 1. On the settlement of staff department accounts, see RM to the President of Congress, February 18, 1782, and notes.

List of Documents Relating to Alexander Gillon
Sent to a Committee of Congress

[Office of Finance, July–September? 1782][1]

A List of Sundry Letters and papers relating to Commodore Gillon's Transactions in Holland

(Colo Bland is required to return this List along with the papers)

1st. Three Letters from Messrs. John de Neufville & Son to Congress, dated Augt 28th, Sept 14th, 18th, 1781[2]
   2. A Letter from Doctor Franklin to Congress dated Nov. 5. 1781.[3]
   3. A Letter from Major Jackson to J.[4] de Neufville & Son Augt: 7. 1781[5]
   4. Three Letters from Lewis de Neufville to Major Jackson, Augt. 16th, 25th; Sept 18th. 1781[6]
   5. A Letter from Commodore Gillon to Messrs John de Neufville & Son (without date)[7]
   6. A Letter from L. de Neufville to Commod. Gillon 16th Augt. 1781.[8]
   7. A Copy of Colo Lauren's Agreement with Commodore Gillon[9]
   8. An Invoice of the Goods Shipped on board the South Carolina.[10]

MS: D, PCC, DNA.
    1. This undated list, written in an unidentified hand, was later endorsed by another hand as follows: "Papers Sent to the Committee by Rt. Morris Esqr Supt. of Finance. Those not here are referrd to in the Report of the Committee and lodged with the Secy. of Congress." RM's autograph initials appear below the endorsement. The committee in question, chaired by Theodorick Bland, Jr., had been appointed on July 12 to investigate the transactions made on Congress's account in Europe by John Laurens, William Jackson, and Commodore Alexander Gillon of the South Carolina navy (see notes to Diary, September 19). Since RM noted in the Diary of September 19 that he had previously supplied the committee with papers, the list presumably can be assigned to the months of July, August, or September. RM had probably procured the documents on the list from Congress (JCC, XXII, 141) and Jackson (Diary, July 25). Copies of some of them may have been enclosed in James McCall to the South Carolina Delegates in Congress, May 31, 1782.
    2. Only the letter of September 14, 1781, has been found. See Miscellaneous Papers of the Continental Congress, 1774–1789 (Microcopy 332, roll 4, f. 596), RG 360, DNA.
    3. Printed in Wharton, ed., Rev. Dipl. Corr., IV, 825–828.
    4. The copyist originally wrote "L" then reworked it to "J."

5. See Miscellaneous PCC, roll 4, f. 616.

6. The letters, from Leendert (or Leonard) de Neufville to Jackson, are in Miscellaneous PCC, roll 4, f. 612, 523, 526.

7. Letter not found.

8. In Miscellaneous PCC, roll 4, f. 515.

9. A memorandum of this agreement, dated Paris, April 28, 1781, is in D. E. Huger Smith, ed., "The Mission of Col. John Laurens to Europe in 1781," *SCHGM*, I (1900), 141–144.

10. Invoice not found.

Diary: August 1, 1782

This day many People expected that my engagements to supply the Paymaster Genl. with money to discharge the Notes which he under that engagement had issued to the Officers of the Army on Account of their pay, would be broke, and consequently that my public Credit would be lost and a Train of Evils easy to be conceived, ensue to the United States, but having warranted Mr. Pierce the Paymaster Genl. to give his Notes in February last to all the Officers of our Army Viz: to all Subalterns for the Amount of three Months pay that is for Jany., Feby. and March 1782, and to the Captains and higher Grades for two Months viz: Jany. and Febr. 1782 I have for some time past been providing for the performance of this engagement and to accomplish it, have been distressed in a variety of Channells. When this engagement was taken it was at the pressing instance of the Commander in Chief and to enable the Officers to Cloath themselves which they could not have done without that Seasonable Aid.[1] At the time this engagement was made I had a right to expect that four millions of Dollars would be paid into the Treasury of the United States as agreeable to the requisitions of Congress two millions were to be paid on the first day of April and two millions on the first day of July.[2] Instead of receiving those Sums I have not to this Hour received 50,000 Dollars on Account thereof and have therefore been Compelled to raise this Money by selling Bills of Exchange on France. Upon sending for Mr. Pierce's return of the Notes Issued I find they Amount to Dolls.　　　$140,266^{28}\!/_{90}$
of which Mr Sands is possessed of[3]　　　　　　　　39,000

Which he has delivered up on my paying part [of]
the Amount now and part to be paid a short time　　$101,266^{28}\!/_{90}$
hence which leaves to be provided for

There is due to me by Mr. Hill[4]　　　£ 8,750

　　　　　Wallace & Co.　　　　2,600

　　　　　Whiteside & Co.　　　5,125

　　　　　Constable　　　　　　600

　　　　　Solomon　　　　　15,000

　　　　　La Caze　　　　　　155 is about[5] $85,946^{28}\!/_{90}$

And as these Debts will be punctually paid they leave only an unprovided Balance of 15,320 Dolls. which I think will be ready before payment is demanded. So that the hopes and expectations of the Malicious and Disaffected will in this instance be disappointed.

I sent for Mr. Swanwick and directed him to Collect the several Debts above mentioned and to provide Mr. Pierce with Money to pay his Notes as fast as demanded if possible, I then drew a Warrant on the Treasurer of the United States in favor of the Pay Master Genl. for the whole amount of his notes, Mr Swanwick will pay Mr. Pierce the Money for it and finally pay the Warrant to Mr. Hilligas the Treasurer instead of so much Money on account of the Bills and I directed Solomon the Broker to Sell more Bills to provide for the Balance as well as for other purposes.

Monsr. Tetard Interpreter in the Office of the Secy of Foreign Affairs brought a large Packett Containing Dispatches from Mr Jay to be decyphered by my Cypher in which they are written[6] and Mr. G. Morris spent this day in decyphering the same.

The Hon. Mr. Duane, Mr. Osgood, Mr Lee and Mr Clarke came this Morning on the enquiry into the business of this Office and after examining into the Expenditures since my Acceptance they adjourned until Saturday next at 9 OClock.[7]

Genl. Cornell called to communicate to me some advices from Rhode Island respecting the proceedings of their Government &c.

Mr. R. Sands applied for money on Account of the moving [army] Contract but on account of the payment of Mr. Pierces Notes agreed to wait till to Morrow.

The Hon. Secy. of Foreign Affairs came about his Dispatches and after Mr. Morris had finished the decyphering he read them to us. They are long, Accurate and interesting.[8]

Capt. De Bert of Armands Corps brought me Letters from Colo Armand praying for releif from his Distresses for want of Horses &c.[9]

I granted a Warrant on the application of Mr Francis to the Contractors for York and Carlisle to pay a Bill they have drawn.

Wrote a Letter to the Hon: Messrs. Tellfair, Jones and Few Delegates for the State of S Carolina.[10]

1. On pay issued to army officers in promissory notes of John Pierce, see RM to George Washington, January 26, 1782 (second letter), and notes.
2. RM refers to the requisition for 1782 which Congress authorized on October 30 and apportioned among the states on November 2, 1781.
3. Richardson Sands of Comfort Sands and Company, army contractors who had agreed to accept the notes.
4. Henry Hill and the other individuals and firms listed here had been purchasing bills of exchange from RM on credit, some for resale in Philadelphia and elsewhere. On Hill's transactions, see Diary, April 17, 1782, and notes.
5. The total of this column, £32,230 Pennsylvania currency, RM has here converted to dollars.

6. For Office of Finance Cipher no. 1, employed in correspondence with John Jay, American minister to Spain, see RM to Jay, July 7, 1781, and notes. Most important among the dispatches was Jay's lengthy missive to Secretary for Foreign Affairs Robert R. Livingston of April 28, 1782, from Madrid, which summarized his activities since his previous dispatch of October 3, 1781, and included copies of numerous letters Jay exchanged with others (Wharton, ed., *Rev. Dipl. Corr.*, V, 336–377). This letter and Jay's letters to RM of April 25 and 28 and his missing letter to Gouverneur Morris of April 28, 1782, were delivered by Major David Salisbury Franks. For the effect of Jay's dispatch in Congress, see Livingston to Jay, [August 8, 1782], Morris, ed., *John Jay: Winning of the Peace*, 312–315n. See also Livingston to Jay, September 12, 1782, Wharton, ed., *Rev. Dipl. Corr.*, V, 721; and Gouverneur Morris to Jay, August 6.

7. See Diary, August 3. For the congressional investigation of the Office of Finance, see Diary, June 12, 1782, and notes.

8. See note 6 above.

9. The letters from Charles Armand-Tuffin, Marquis de La Rouërie, commander of a legion of dragoons, have not been found. Captain Claudius de Bert de Majan, a Frenchman, was the paymaster of Armand's corps; Congress commissioned him brevet major on February 6, 1784. Contenson, *Société des Cincinnati*, 219.

10. Edward Telfair, Noble Wimberly Jones, and William Few were actually delegates to Congress from Georgia.

From the Comptroller of the Treasury (James Milligan)

[Philadelphia] Comptroller's Office August 1st 1782

Sir

The Contractors for victualing the moving Army, as also those for victualing the Garrison of West Point and its Dependencies, have rendered their accounts for the Months of May and June. They inform me that the Contract of Francis and Slough for supplying the Posts in New Jersey, having with your Consent been dissolved on the first of May, these Posts have been since that Time, supplied by the Contractors for the moving Army,[1] but besides this, I find the last mentioned Contractors charge for supplying the Posts of Peekskill and the Connecticut Hutts on the North River, which were before reckoned a Part of the Dependencies of West Point, and victualed under that Contract at half a ninetieth part of a Dollar per Ration, less than is allowed to the Contractors for the moving Army. As this Difference of Price will amount to something considerable on the whole, and as the West Point Contract still subsists, I conceive it to be necessary that I should be informed by what Authority or Agreement the Alteration took place; If it has been done by the Orders of his Excellency the Commander in Chief, I request that I may be furnished with an Official Copy of such Orders, that the Officers of this Treasury may be justified in admitting the Charge.[2] The Contractors for West Point give credit in these Accounts for a quantity of provisions received of Colo. Charles Stewart, the late Commissary General of Issues to which they have affixed certain Prices, but as there are no Kind of Vouchers whatever to ascertain either the

Quantities received, or the Prices Stipulated (excepting the word of the Contractors which we are not authorized to admit as sufficient Evidence on such Occasions) I am doubtful whether a final Settlement can be made until the necessary Documents are obtained.

I mention these Matters to you that if you think proper you may give such Directions as will tend to remove the Difficulties. I am with the greatest Respect Sir Your most obedient humble Servant[3]

James Milligan

Honorable The Superintendant of Finance

MS: Copy, Washington Papers, DLC.
    1. See notes to George Washington to RM, March 28, 1782.
    2. For a discussion of the merger of the West Point and Moving Army contracts, see Diary, May 13, 1782, and notes. Regarding the issues under the two contracts, see Washington to RM, August 11, and notes, and Proposals from Comfort Sands and Company, printed under September 2, and notes.
    3. This letter from Milligan was enclosed in RM to Washington, August 5.

To Edward Telfair, Noble Wimberly Jones, and William Few

Office of Finance Augt. 1. 1782

I am honored with your Letter of the thirtieth of July,[1] and wish it was in my Power to inform you in reply that a Commissioner for settling the Accounts of your State had been nominated: But this is not the Case. The Salaries allowed to such Commissioners are objected to as insufficient by many Men of suitable Character and Abilities who have on this Account refused to engage in the service. Some however have accepted and I conceive it to be my Duty to carry the Act of Congress into Execution on the Terms prescribed if possible. My Endeavors to this End shall be continued and when a suitable Person is named for Georgia you shall be informed of it.

MS: Ofcl LbC, DLC.
    1. Letter not found. Telfair, Jones, and Few were delegates to Congress from Georgia. Concerning the act of Congress of February 20, 1782, mentioned in the present letter, see notes to RM to the President of Congress, December 10, 1781.

Diary: August 2, 1782

I sent this morning for Wm. [i.e., Mr.] Alexr. Robertson and proposed paying him a Draft on New York for the Amount of Mr. Pierces Notes in his hands which he declined but promised to keep those Notes until the end of next Week.[1]

Mr. Whiteside applied to me for Bills for Lrs 100,000 for which he offered 6/6 for five Livres payable in Sixty Days and as Mr Eddy had returned a Bill drawn in his favor in May last No. 88 for that Sum which had been delivered to him on a Condition to pay that price in 60 Days or return it I sold the same to Mr. Whiteside as above being threepence more than the Current price for Cash.[2]

Had a good deal of Conversation with Haym Solomon respecting Exchange &c.

Lieut. Miller of the second Virginia Regiment applyed for his pay for January, February and March last alledging that he had not received Mr. Pierces Notes.[3] I referred him to the Secy at War being in his Department and not in mine.

Mr. Ths. Edison applied to me as he said by the Direction of the Honble Mr. Clarke. I asked this Gentleman why he had not attended Mr Tetard the Interpreter upon the business which I had allotted for him and which by his acquiescence he left me to beleive he meant to perform. I observed that if he had any objections they ought to have been made to me at the time, or he should have written to inform me of them but leaving me in the beleif that he was performing a public Service, which he totally Neglected, was doing a public injury, and on the whole I desired since he does not like the employment I have provided for him, to know what he proposes for himself therefore he can take time to consider of it and inform me when he pleases.[4]

Walter Livingston Esquire one of the Contractors for the moving Army came down for Money and stating to me that the Army are without Beef and in want of Bread &c. I answered that the Contractors if that be the Case deserve punishment, for that tho' my payments to them may not have always been full up to the Contracts[5] terms yet there has been no deficiency's that will justify them in suffering any Wants to the Army &c. I told him I will if it becomes necessary publish to the World the exact State of this Affair &c.

Mr. R. Sands was with him and to him I appealed whether I had not ever evinced the strongest desire to Supply money when asked for &c.

Wm. Denning Esqr. called to inform me that he is taking Extracts from the public Book in order to Commence his Operations as a Commissioner for Settling the Accounts of the Quarter Masters Department. He asked for his Commission and the Instructions which cannot be got ready before he goes out of Town but which I promised to send after him.[6]

Mr Bullock one of the Managers of the Lottery applied for Money to pay off the Accounts for expence of drawing it. I promised to supply the same next Week.[7]

Colo. Pickering for Money, I gave none. He wanted to buy some Goods for Waggoners on Credit I told him of better bargains. He wanted to pay for some Forage I desired him to obtain a months Credit.

Mr. Geo. Eddy applied for Assistance in gaining Govr. Livingstons passport to and from Elizabeth Town to get money.[8] I referred [him] to Charles Thompson Esqr.

Wrote a Letter to His Excellency the President of Congress.

Wrote a Letter to His Excellency the Govr of Rhode Island.

1. See Diary, July 16, 1782.
2. The caller was Peter Whiteside, a Philadelphia merchant and business associate of RM's. For George Eddy's connection with the Superintendent, see RM's Agreement with Eddy, printed under March 13, 1782, and notes.
3. For the pay of the army in notes issued by Paymaster General John Pierce, see RM to George Washington, January 26, 1782 (second letter), and notes.
4. For RM's difficulties with Thomas Edison, see notes to Diary, June 28, 1782.
5. The copyist originally wrote this word in the singular; the *s* was subsequently added.
6. See RM to the Commissioners for Settling the Accounts of the Departments, September 19, and the Instructions of the Comptroller of the Treasury to the Commissioners for Settling the Accounts of the Departments, October 14. Denning's commission has not been found.
7. See Diary, August 14 and 21.
8. See Diary, July 29.

To the President of Congress
(John Hanson)

Office of Finance 2d. August 1782

Sir,

It is some Time since the fourth Class of the United States Lottery was drawn, and I now do myself the Honor to enclose for Congress a List of the fortunate Numbers.[1] I have already been applied to, to know how the Prizes are to be paid, but the Lottery is among those Things, which on my entering into Office I stipulated that I should have nothing to do with.[2] It is true that in some Instances I have been prevailed on by the Necessity of the Case to waive the Benefits of this Stipulation but on the present Occasion I must beg Leave, not only to submit the Matter entirely to Congress but to avoid giving any Opinion about it. I shall not trouble you with other Reasons for this Request, than the Multiplicity of my Business, which will so accumulate, as to be involved in Confusion unless I can pay an undissipated Attention to such Parts as are necessary to be done. I have the Honor to be, with great Respect Sir, Your most obedient and humble Servant

Robt Morris

His Excellency The President of Congress

ENDORSED: 83/Letter 2 Aug 1782/Superintendt Finance/Aug. 5. 1782/Referred to Mr McKean/Mr Ramsay/Mr Huntington/Mr Jackson/Mr Telfair/On the subject of the lottery
MSS: LS, PCC, DNA; Ofcl LbC, DLC.
1. Enclosure not found. According to a notation of John Mease, one of the managers of the lottery, the drawing of the 4th and last class closed on April 16, 1782 (PCC, no. 137, I, 729). For a discussion of the lottery and Congress's response to the present letter from RM, see notes to RM to the Managers of the United States Lottery, December 12, 1781.
2. RM's refusal to be responsible for debts incurred before his administration is stipulated in his letter to the President of Congress of May 14, 1781.

To the Governor of Rhode Island
(William Greene)

Office of Finance August 2d 1782

Sir

I presume you have been before this informed that all the States except Rhode Island have acceded to the Impost Law.[1] A Committee of Congress, lately appointed on this Subject, did me the Honor to request my Attendance with that of your Delegates, to hear the Objections from them, and know from me the Circumstances attending the Requisition.[2] After a long Conversation, the Committee were about to confer on a Report, which at my Request they were pleased to Suspend, that I might have this last Opportunity of praying your attention to the Subject. And I was induced to make that Request, as well for the avoiding those disagreable Discussions which cannot exist between the Union and an Individual State without inducing pernicious Consequences, as because it appeared to me that the Reasons urged against passing the Impost are not so conclusive as some have thought them to be.

The honorable Mr. Howell was so kind as to promise that he would State his Objections in writing, this he has done, and a Copy of them is enclosed.[3] They are:

1st. That the Impost would draw a disproportionate Supply from either the Merchant or Consumer. (2nd) That Rhode Island imports and consumes more of foreign Articles (in Proportion) than any other State (3rd) That from her maratime Situation she is exposed to great Losses. (4th:) That the exclusive Benefit of the Impost should be carried to account of the State. (5th:) That the Impost will raise Prices, and therefore Manufactures brought from the neighbouring States, will draw a Revenue from Rhode Island. (6th:) That Duties imposed by the neighbouring States, may compell Rhode Island to subsist by foreign Articles. (7th:) That many men will be employed in the Collection. (8th:) That it would be evaded by Smuggling. And (9th:) That the Collection may be objectionable. To each of these I will reply in their Order.

1st:) To determine whether the Impost will act proportionately or not, we must consider in what Respect the Proportion is to be taken. If it be a Proportion between two of the States, that will be considered under the second Head. If it be a Proportion among the People of the same State, it is only recurring to the question, whether Taxes on Consumption are useful; for so long as no Man pays the Tax, but he who chuses to purchase the Article, the Disproportion (if any) is of his own creating. The Necessity of a Revenue, to a certain Amount, must be admitted. Is it then wise to raise a Part of it from the Consumption of foreign Articles? I say *the Consumption* because the Tax undoubtedly falls on the Consumer and not on the Importer. If this be not a wise Tax, what shall be substituted? Articles of primary and immediate Necessity are made in the State of Rhode Island. Both Food and Raiment can be had, without crossing the Atlantic in Search of them. Every man therefore, is at Liberty to use foreign Articles or not. If he does use them, the Tax is voluntary, and therefore cannot be considered as disproportionate, any more than for one Man to wear Silk, while another wears Wool.

(2nd) That Rhode Island consumes more foreign Commodities in Proportion than any other State in the Union, cannot be admitted. Rhode Island certainly makes many Commodities, but the more Southern States are in the Habit of importing every thing.

(3rd:) That Rhode Island is from its Situation liable to the unhappy accidents of War, is true. But this incidental Evil, arising from an advantageous Position cannot be adduced as a Plea for Exemption from public Burthens. New York has suffered at least as much, and as long.

(4th:) That the exclusive Benefits of an Impost should be carried to the State where it is collected, is a Position unjust in itself, and which would for ever prevent laying any Duties, wherefore it would cut off not only one of the most productive, but one of the most useful Branches of Revenue. Rhode Island, Pennsylvania, and some other States carry on the Commerce of their Neighbours, as well as their own, from which they derive great Riches. The Duties are always (like the Risques and the Expences) paid by the Consumer; for unless this be so no tolerable Reason can be assigned why foreign Commodities should be dearer in War than in Peace. If then, a considerable Duty were laid by the commercial State, it would fall on its uncommercial Neighbour. That Neighbour therefore would immediately take Measures to carry on its own Commerce, and prohibit the bringing of Articles from the commercial State. These[4] Measures would produce a Repeal of the Duty. I take no Notice *here* of the Altercations which would arise; it is sufficient to shew, that the private View of Revenue for the State would be defeated.

(5th, and 6th:) These Objections do not appear to me to apply, because in the first Place I can hardly suppose the neighbouring States will ever think of laying Duties on their own Produce; for if any of them should, her Citizens would be the Sufferers. Secondly, if the Article of Produce be left uncontrolled by the Government, every Individual will be a Check on the Avidity of his Neighbour, and if by this Means a Piece of American Goods can be vended cheaper in Rhode Island than a Piece of foreign Goods, the Consumer in Rhode Island will by the Purchase of it, save Money to himself, and therefore to the Country. And as the Duty is collected only on foreign Goods, he will not Pay the Duty, and of course the Duty on his State, will be so much the less.

(7th:) The seventh Objection will apply more strongly to almost any other Kind of Tax, because this may be collected by a very small number of Men.

(8th:) The eighth Objection I cannot admit, because forming my Opinion of that State, from what I conceive to be the Character of the Gentleman who makes the Objection, I cannot beleive it to be valid. Smuggling was formerly not disreputable, because it was the evading of Laws which were not made by proper Authority, and therefore not obligatory. But nothing can be more infamous than to defraud our own Government of so small a Pittance, and I trust, that if any Individual were inclined to do so, he would be detected by the first Person who saw him, and would be as much exposed to the Resentment and Contempt of his fellow Citizens, as an Informer would have been in the Times above alluded to.

(9th:) The last Objection ought not to be made, because there is no Reason to suppose that Congress would devise Means to oppress their fellow Citizens.[5] But it is one of our greatest Misfortunes that Men are apt to Reason from one Thing to another, which is very dissimilar. The Parliament of England cared nothing about the Consequences of Laws made for us, because they were not affected by them. This is always the Case, under such Circumstances, and forms one of the most powerful Arguments in Favor of free Governments. But how can it be supposed that a Member of Congress who is liable to be recalled at a Moment's warning, would join in Measures which are oppressive to the People, and which he must necessarily himself feel the Weight of, without deriving any Advantage from them. For it is not here, as in England, that there is a King to buy Votes for bad Purposes. If the Members of Congress be seduced, it must be by the Congress, which is absurd. If indeed the Congress were either an hereditary Body, self existent, or if they were self elected, there might be Room for apprehension, but as they are, there can be none.

Now Sir the State of things is shortly this. The United States are deeply indebted to the People of America. They have called for Revenues to pay their Debts in a Course of Years, being the only Means of reviving Credit, and lightening present Burthens. All the States consent but Rhode Island, to whose Citizens a very considerable Part of this Debt is due, of Consequence the whole is suspended. The Reasons assigned are purely local and I verily beleive are founded on mistaken Principles. The Revenue, however, if granted is insufficient. More must be demanded, and consequently, as all Taxes are unpleasant, some State will be found to oppose any which can be devised, on quite as good Ground as the present Opposition. What then is the Consequence? I am Sir Your Excellency's Most obedient and most humble Servant[6]

Robt Morris

His Excellency the Governor of Rhode Island

MSS: LS, R-Ar; Ofcl LbC, DLC.

1. Rhode Island had procrastinated on the question of the impost, refusing to act and withstanding even the persuasions of the congressional delegation which had visited the northern states to urge compliance with the requisition for 1782 (see notes to RM to the President of Congress, May 17, 1782; and Polishook, *Rhode Island and the Union,* 75–76). Georgia also had not ratified the impost, a point often ignored by both supporters and opponents of the measure, and of uncertain import because Congress in 1781 had declared that the approval of states occupied by the enemy was not necessary for the impost to go into effect. See the headnote to RM's Circular to the Governors of Massachusetts, Rhode Island, New York, Delaware, Maryland, and North Carolina, July 27, 1781, and notes, Circular to the Governors of South Carolina and Georgia, December 6, 1781, and notes, and Circular to the Governors of Massachusetts, Rhode Island, and Maryland, January 3, 1782, and notes.

2. For this committee and a partial account of its meeting with the Rhode Island and Georgia delegates, see notes to David Howell's Objections to the Impost in Rhode Island, printed under July 31; and Howell to Governor Greene, July 30–31, 1782, in Staples, *Rhode Island in the Continental Congress,* 382–385.

3. See the document cited in the preceding note.

4. "Those" in Ofcl LbC.

5. For procedures under consideration for collecting the impost, see the draft ordinance for collecting the impost printed in the appendix to this volume.

6. This letter and subsequent letters on the impost from RM evidently remained unanswered by Rhode Island (see RM to the Governor of Rhode Island, September 3 and October 24, and RM's Circular to the Governors of Rhode Island and Georgia, October 17). After Congress on October 10 demanded "an immediate definitive answer" on the impost, the Rhode Island Assembly unanimously rejected it on November 1. The letter advising of the vote, dated November 30, was read in Congress on December 12, six days after Congress decided to send a deputation to Rhode Island. Later in the month, Congress received news that Virginia had revoked its ratification. Polishook, *Rhode Island and the Union,* 79–80, 85–88; for the suggestion that too much stress has been put on Rhode Island's rejection and that "it is quite probable that Virginia would have repealed her act even had Rhode Island given in," see Main, *Antifederalists,* 74n.

From William Duer

Albany [New York] Augt. 2d. 1782

My dear Freind

Though I am just recovered from a severe Attack of the Rheumatism and Fever, I have been obliged to Write you a long Letter in your Official Capacity.[1] The Situation I am in has obliged me to be Explicit, for I can with Truth assure you that by the long Detention of the Messenger and his Returning with only 5000 Drs. of the 7,900 Drs. I Expected to Receive[2] my Credit has been on the Brink of Ruin, and the Subsistance of the Troops under this Contract put in the most Critical Situation. When I Embarked in the Line of Contractorship, it was not on the Common Principle of gaining by it as much Money as I could make, though I make no Pretensions of having Engaged in it without a View of Intrest. A thorough Conviction of the Wisdom of the System you had adopted for restoring Order to the Shattered State of our public Finances, an Anxious Wish to Support my Freind in the Execution, of a most Critical Department, and a hope that I might gain some Reputation, and Experience which might promote my own Intrest and that of the Public in future in a more Extensive Line, these were the Strongest Motives that Induced me to offer myself a Candidate for the Contracts, and to take the present one on such low Terms.

Soon after the Contract was Signed I received a Letter from you by which I plainly discovered your Anxiety about the Performance of the Contract, from the strong Wishes you Exprest for Mr. Livingston's taking a Share in it.[3] I was then sensible, and have since been Confirmed in this opinion that great Pa[i]ns had been taken to Instill into your Mind an Opinion of my Want of Capacity or of Perseverance to fulfill, what I would boldly Venture to Undertake. Notwithstanding Mr. Livingston had not acted with me the most ingenuous Part, and had refused to Sign the Contract though he told me he would do it, if he meant to take a Share in it, yet as it was your Wish that he Should be admitted I sufferd him to make his own Terms (a Task he is very Capable of).[4] I determined however by my Conduct to Convince you and others that the Prejudices suggested against me were ill founded, by a fit Determination to sacrifice all private Ease, and persuits to the Discharge of the Trust I had Imposed on myself. Whatever other Defects I may have, I trust my Freind you (who have been a Witness of the Zeal and Perseverance which I Ever manifested in Discharging my public Duties) will not readily suppose I could be gu[i]lty of Inattention in a Matter, where the Consequence might be ruinous to the Public, and destructive of my own Character. I have not; on the Contrary I can venture to affirm that notwithstanding the low Price of the Contract, and Unforeseen Embarassments which have attended the Execution, no Troops have been more Uniformly Supplied, with better Provisions, or more to the Satisfaction of the Officer and Soldier than the Troops under this Contract. The Readiness with which the Warrants for the Monies due in May and June had been granted contributed not a little to the Satisfaction I gave in Executing the Contract. I have said in my Official Letter that the Contract has been hithe[r]to a losing one; it has so, from the Causes I have there mentioned: it now begins to make up for former Losses; but this must absolutely depend on the Expedition with which the money due is transmitted, and on the whole Sum being punctually paid. Your change of Conduct in not granting a Warrant for the monies due on the June Issues (as you did for those of April, and May,) has induced me to imagine that you may have been suspected of Partiality in granting a

Warrant for the Sum due this Contract with more Readiness than it was granted to others. I know you have many Malicious Observers, who would Insinuate that the Warmth of your Attachments leads you to Preferences Incompatible with your Public Character. On this Account I have judged it adviseable to support my Claim to the Monies being punctually paid me at the Expiration of Every Month; I have submitted the Contract to the Opinion of Several Persons Eminent in the Law, and to two Merchants of Reputation, they are Unanimously of Opinion that my Claim is well founded. I should not be thus Strenuous in Insisting on this Point could I, my Freind, Execute the Contract without it, but I seriously pledge to you my honor, that from the Lowness of the Contract, the great Distances of the Different Posts, the Diffidence of persons in trusting Contractors Since the Publication of your Letter to Mr. Merril and of the Receipts of Taxes,[5] and from other Circumstances which Relate to my own private Affairs, it will be out of my Power to Continue the Supply unless the whole of the Monies due on the last, and present Month, are Instantly Supplied. Let me therefore my dear Freind Entreat you not to Suffer a Person to be Sacraficed, by the Inattention or Delays of those who are appointed to Examine the Contractors Accounts,[6] whose utmost Exertions are daily used to support the public Interest, and to Evince the Wisdom of the measures you have adopted. I am sensible of the Difficulties you labor under in your public Station, and of the Cruel Disappointments you have met in your Expectations from the different States, but I take the Liberty of Submitting it to your Consideration, whether, if the Means of defraying the Subsistance of the Army depend on the Exertions of the different States, and you have not a Well grounded Assurance that the Monies for this Purpose will be punctually paid, it will not be Ultimately for the public Good, both for yourself and the Contractors to declare their Inability to Subsist the Army any longer. Such a Declaration may rouse a Stupid, Unthinking People (scarcely deserving the Object they are Contending for) from their present Lethargy. Whereas if either you or the Contractors from a Zeal to supply by private Exertions what is defective in public ones, give Expectations, which it is afterwards found Impracticable to Satisfy, both your and their public Utility will be altogether lost, when the States recovered from their present Delirium, and Impressed with the Wisdom of your Measures shall Establish permanent, and distinct Funds for defraying the Expences of the War; for let the Measure be Ever so long deferred *it must be done*. Forgive, my Freind, the Freedom of this Observation, it proceeds from a Heart zealous for your Reputation and Ease, as well as the Interest of the States. For my Part, I have decided what Part it is best for me to act. And Unless the Public can from this day forward punctually perform their Engagements to me, without my being Subjected to the Delays and Evasions of the

Clerks in Office, I will Instantly quit the Execution of the Contract, whilst I can do it with a Credit, and Reputation hitherto Unsullied. I write to you in haste, with an Anxious Mind, and trembling hand. I dont know whether you will be able to Expound my Letter. It is a Duty I owe you, and myself, to be Explicit, and I therefore trust you will not be offended with me. I would not if possible feel your Disapprobation (if well founded) for a Moment. Nothing but the Critical Situation I am in could have drawn from me the Letters I now write to you. Lady Kitty[7] joins me in Affectionate Remembrance to yourself and Mrs. Morris: we Sincerely wish your domestic happiness may in some Measure alleviate the Anxiety you must feel from the Arduous Task you are Engaged in. I am with Unfe[i]gned Attachment Your Obliged and Affectionate Humble Servant[8]

Wm. Duer

Robert Morris Eqr.

ENDORSED: Albany 2d Augst. 1782/Wm Duer Esqr.
MS: ALS, Robert Morris Papers, DLC.
   1. Duer held the contract for the Northern Department. His "Official" letter was probably one of August 6, which has not been found; it was accompanied by two private letters, the one printed here and another (also not found) which was undated but was referred to by Duer as one of August 3. By his account, James Geary, Duer's messenger, delivered the official letter to the Office of Finance on August 12 and returned the following day with the private letters. See RM to Duer, August 29, and Diary, August 12 and 13; and Geary to Duer, August 15, 1782, Duer Papers, NHi.
   2. RM had supplied Duer with $5,000 and obtained credit for him at the Bank of North America. See RM to Duer, July 23.
   3. See RM to Duer, February 7, 1782 (second letter).
   4. On Walter Livingston's role as a silent partner in the Northern Department contract, see notes to Livingston to RM, January 19, 1782.
   5. The reference is to RM's letter of June 14, 1782, to Hezekiah Merrill, receiver of Continental taxes for Connecticut, justifying his reasons for ordering the publication of tax receipts, or the absence of them, by the receivers.
   6. Duer's messenger, James Geary, subsequently complained of the incredible slowness, incompetence, and protracted quibbling of the Treasury officials who examined the accounts, which had to be cleared before RM made payment. See Geary to Duer, August 15, 1782, Duer Papers, NHi; for the Superintendent's comments on the contractors' accounts, see RM to George Washington, August 5.
   7. Catherine Alexander Duer, Duer's wife.
   8. Following delivery of this letter, RM promised Duer's messenger "the Whole of the Monies due on the Accounts Current for June and July" and gave him warrants totalling $3,500 as well as permission to draw upon William Turnbull, Duer's Philadelphia agent and a business associate of RM's, for $1,500 in advance of what was owed to Duer on the accounts. See James Geary to Duer, August 15, 1782, Duer Papers, NHi; and Diary, August 13 and 26.

The Governor of New York (George Clinton) to Gouverneur Morris

Pokeepsie, 2d Augt. 1782[1]

Dear Sir,

   I was favored with your Letter of the 11th June[2] a few Days before the late Meeting of the Legislature. While they were together I had not a Moment's Leisure to acknowledge the Receipt of it & I have since been prevented by a visit I made immediately on their rising to the Frontiers of Ulster County. I enclose you a copy of the Titles of the Laws of the Session[3] by which you will perceive that some Efforts are made to aid the public Treasury. The Tax to be levied is payable in Cash only & to be collected immediately.[4]

I have ever been fully sensible of the Weight of the Objections ag't a Tax in specified Articles. It was not, however, an easy Task to convince the bulk of the People of the Impropriety of the Measure. Congress first introduced it by substituting Supplies for the Army in Specific Articles to be furnished by the different States instead of so much cash.[5] This was held out as a matter of Ease & convenience to the People & they were led to conclude it be so from the Opinion they entertained of the Wisdom of that respectable Body without giving themselves the Trouble of thinking on the Subject & determining for themselves. When specific Supplies was abolished & Cash demanded in Lieu of them the People murmured & complained of their want of Money. This introduced the receiving of Wheat at a certain Price pr. Bushel in Payment of Taxes & tho an expensive & bad expedient, it was perhaps the only one that could then have been adopted without increasing the Discontent which was too generally prevalent. It was the most natural & easy Transition & the State well knew that Wheat could easily be converted into money, & in the Mean Time it was believed that the People being gratified would begin to reflect & abandon so Troublesome & unprofitable a system, & this I am persuaded is already pretty generally the Case, so that I expect in future it will have but few Advocates.

Congress in fixing the Quotas of the different states I am sensible must be embarrassed by the extraordinary Merit each State ascribes to itself from its Exertions,[6] but of these they are the proper Judges, and if there be any who have exhausted their Resources from extraordinary Zeal, Sense of immediate Danger or whatever else may have been the motive, the public Burthens ought now to be apportioned accordingly, for it is idle to ask more of any State than it is able to contribute as, whenever this is the Case, & I am certain it was in the last Quota demanded of us, instead of promoting, it is most likely to discourage & prevent all kind of Exertion.

You are certainly much deceived when you suppose we could have no other Mart for our Wheat than the Contractor. The current Price of Flour was sixteen shillings per lb.[7] when the Contractor commenced purchasing—it continued so until lately & they might have had all that belonged to the State at that moderate Price. About two months ago it began to rise & though there was a Prospect of its still rising higher, as it actually did, being now from 18s to 20s for common Flour, yet the State Agent[8] had Orders & did sell his to the

Contractors at the then current Price.* I sincerely wish the people would be persuaded to forego the use of Luxuries & even of Articles which habit has in some measure made the Necessaries of Life & apply the monies they expend in that way to the support of the War, but I fear it will require more than human Rhetoric to persuade them—the force of Example is very strong & if it could be began at the Seat of the American Gov't. I should have hopes of its prevailing.

In a Line which I recd. by Mr. Wm. Paulding,[9] you mention a Desire of being inform'd of the objections of the Council of Revision ag't the Bill for suspend'g suits ag't public Officers. I now enclose you a Copy of them.[10] There was another Objection which you will allow had Weight (tho' it could not be included with those of the Council) vizt. that of their being exempted from Suits only until September, after which you will readily agree they would have rushed in upon them like a Torrent & this Temporary Exemption proved their Rescue.

I am &c &c

G. Clinton

Govr. Morris, Esqr.

---

*Our great Missfortune is, that our Country is so much wasted & destroyed by the Inroads of the Enemy that we have comparatively but little to spare beyond what is sufficient to Barter for Salt and other Articles and * * necessary.

PRINTED: Hastings and Holden, eds., *Clinton Papers*, VIII, 21–23.

1. Since the manuscript of this letter was almost entirely destroyed by the Albany fire of 1911, the editors have had to reprint the text from the published edition of Clinton's papers cited above, where the addressee is incorrectly identified as RM.

2. Letter not found.

3. Document not found.

4. For the tax act, see notes to Alexander Hamilton to RM, July 22.

5. For congressional requisitions in specific supplies starting in late 1779, see notes to John Morin Scott to RM, May 30, 1781; and Ferguson, *Power of the Purse*, 48–50.

6. On the question of state contributions to the general welfare and credits to them in the settlement of accounts with the Union, see notes to RM's Circular to the Governors of the States, July 25; and RM to the President of Congress, August 28, 1781, and notes.

7. That is, per barrel. See Walter Livingston to RM, June 29, 1782, and notes.

8. Udny Hay.

9. Letter not found.

10. "An Act to stay suits against public officers for a limited time" had been passed by the legislature in response to a recommendation of Congress of March 19, 1782 (see notes to the Quartermaster General to RM, March 8, 1782). However, as Philip Schuyler, a member of the legislature, had informed RM on June 28, the Senate had not repassed the bill over the veto of the Council of Revision because of the "cogent" objections the council (Governor Clinton, Chief Justice Richard Morris, and Justice Robert Yates) had adopted on April 13 as follows:

"This Council, without seeing the necessity of a declaratory clause in the said bill, that officers and servants of this or the United States are liable to pay the debts by them contracted on behalf of the public, convinced should the question at any time be raised, the courts of justice can decide it upon the laws already extant, object against the enacting clause in the said bill as inconsistent with the public good.

"Because the suspension of one of the most essential rights of the subjects, that of appealing to the courts of justice for the recovery of a just demand, is an exercise of legislative power which may be drawn into a dangerous precedent, and tend to destroy the confidence of the people and afford the subject, upon the same grounds, a pretext for a denial of paying the public taxes or debts due to each other."

After Quartermaster General Timothy Pickering made another appeal to Congress and the New York government, the state legislature on March 21, 1783, passed "An Act for staying Execution in suits against public officers, on Contracts and Acts by them made and done in behalf of the United States, and this state." The act did not, as requested by Congress, stay suits against public officers, but only suspended executions of judgments against them for actions certified by the judge as undertaken on behalf of the United States or the state of New York. The legislation was renewed annually until 1785. For the council's objections, see Alfred B. Street, *The Council of Revision of the State of New York; Its History, A History of the Courts with which Its Members were Connected; Biographical Sketches of Its Members; and Its Vetoes* (Albany, 1859), 244; for the manuscript, see the Council of Revision Minutes, 1778–1783, NHi. See also *Laws of New York*, I, 559–560, 683; *Votes and Proceedings of the [New York] Senate, &c.* [October 1, 1781–March 28, 1783] [Poughkeepsie, 1782–1783?], 67, 68, 133, 147, 153; President John Hanson to Clinton, March 21, 1782, enclosing the act of March 19, PCC, no. 16, p. 146; RM's Circular to the Governors of the States, August 17, 1782, and the Quartermaster General to RM, August 5, 1782, and January 20, 1783. For an assessment of the Council of Revision, see Alexander Hamilton to RM, August 13, and notes.

To the Paymaster General
(John Pierce)

[Philadelphia, August 2, 1782][1]

Mr Morris presents his Compliments to Mr Pierce and desires to know whether Jos. Clay Esqr. Deputy Pay Masr in the Southern Army is in that Station at present, whether he has any unsettled accounts with the United States and what is his Character as an Officer in that Station.

Friday Morning

MS: AL, Manuscript File, WDC, DNA.

1. This letter of inquiry about Joseph Clay of Georgia is endorsed in Pierce's hand as having been received from RM on August 2, 1782. RM may have been considering Clay for appointment as a commissioner to settle the accounts of North or South Carolina. A written reply from Pierce has not been found. On Clay's status, see Nathanael Greene to RM, September 1.

From John Barry

On board the Frigate Alliance
New London harbour [Connecticut] Augt. 2nd. 1782

Inclos'd you have a Letter from Doctr. Linn to me with my answer to him.[1] I can assure you his private business was not the Inducement which actuated me to give him leave. He is naturally of a Weak Constitution, add to that he was Very disagreeable to the Officers in the Ward Room, and as my desire is, to Keep a Quiet Ship, I thought it best on the whole to get Clear of him, especially as his place Could be well fill'd by Doctr. Geagan, an old Surgeon of the Navy and which I hope will meet your Approbation. Since my arrival here the Chief Carpenter has Run away without Accounting for the Stores he had on board, or what he has receiv'd since our arrival. I have wrote Mr Russell to have him apprehended and put in Goal in Boston.[2] I am Certain he is gone that way. I am sorry the Laws of the States are not more severe against

Deserters from the Navy—in short the Sherriff of Boston will not Keep any of them in Goal without positive orders from the Governor. I could wish if you think it Consistent, there were something done respecting the harbouring and Confinement of Deserters from the Navy—untill that is the Case, we Cannot expect to Keep Men on board Continental Ships. While I was absent Mr William Morris a Lieut. of Marines left the Ship without Leave, or without Accounting for the Money he had received to Defray his Expences to and from Philadelphia. His Conduct in so doing is so notorious, that I have re-turn'd him as a Deserter from the Ship and which I hope will meet your Approbation. I have not appointed any one in his Room for I think there is too many Marine Officers on board already.

I have the pleasure to acquaint you that I sail to morrow with a Good Ships Company, and I hope ere Long you will hear from me.[3] A Return of the Ships Crew I shall send Mr John Brown.

MS: LbC, John Barry Letterbook, Naval History Society Collection, NHi.

1. The letters exchanged by Barry, captain of the *Alliance*, and John Linn, surgeon on the same vessel, dated July 22, 1782, are in Barry's letterbook.

2. See Barry to Thomas Russell, deputy agent of marine for New England, July 31, 1782, in Barry's letterbook.

3. The *Alliance* sailed from New London on August 4 (Clark, *Gallant John Barry*, 271). He gave an account of his cruise in a letter to RM of October 18.

Diary: August 3, 1782

The Honble. Mr Duane, Mr. Osgood, Mr Clarke and Mr Lee the Committee of Congress met agreeable to appointment and enquired into the public Expenditures, public Revenues and plans for improv-ing the Revenue &c. after which they adjourned to Tuesday next at 9 OClock in the Morning.[1]

I sent for Mr. Milligan and desired him to make out and send me a State of the Contractors Accounts for West Point and the moving Army.[2]

Colo. Pickering the Quarter Master Genl. brought Sundry papers respecting Forage to be supplied the Army by the State Agent of New York. I took the determination not to accept the Terms on which that Forage is offered being too high and therefore proposed giving to Colo. Pickering my Drafts on Mr. Swanwick to the amount of 45,000 Dollars to enable him to take up Money from the Re-ceivers of Taxes in the Eastern States by giving those Drafts in Ex-change for Money and by this Means the Quarter Master Genl. may be enabled to execute the Duties of his Department.[3]

Wm. Denning Esqr. called for his Commission and to take leave.[4]

The Hon. Mr. Lowell of Boston being on the point of returning home called and had a long Conference on the present Measures and Systems for Conducting the public Business. He seemed well pleased and promised his Support in Massachusetts and I cannot but regret that this worthy Gentleman is about to leave Congress.

His Excellency the Minister of France called to Communicate a

Letter he has received from the Marquis De Vadreuill[5] in Consequence of which I sent Mr Brown[6] to the Coffee House to inform the Merchants that they should now dispatch their Ships with all possible expedition as the french Fleet must now be at the mouth of Delaware.[7]

Mr. Turnbull for money on Account of William Duer Esqr. but he agreed to wait longer.[8]

1. See notes to Diary, June 12, 1782, for a discussion of this committee's work.

2. The accounts prepared by Comptroller of the Treasury James Milligan were enclosed in RM to George Washington, August 5.

3. For further discussion, see the Quartermaster General to RM, August 3, and notes. For the drafts on Swanwick sent to Connecticut, see the Quartermaster General to RM, August 24, and notes.

4. See Diary, August 2, and notes.

5. The letter from Marquis de Vaudreuil, commander of the French fleet in American waters, to Chevalier de La Luzerne, French minister at Philadelphia, has not been found.

6. John Brown, RM's assistant in the Marine Office.

7. For the movements of the French fleet, see Diary, July 29, and notes.

8. See notes to Duer to RM, August 2.

From the Quartermaster General
(Timothy Pickering)

Philadelphia August 3rd. 1782

Sir,

As soon as I had your consent to receive forage of the state of New York, thro' their Agent, on Account of the taxes demanded of them by Congress, I wrote letters to Colo. Hughes, my deputy there, and to Colo. Lutterloh, commissary of forage, desiring them to enter into a contract with the State Agent, for the necessary supplies, provided he would furnish them on as reasonable rates as any private contractor for Cash in hand. But before my letters arrived, the distresses of the army had induced the Commander in Cheif to write to Governor Clinton, requesting the aid of the legislature, then sitting. In consequence thereof an act passed the 24 Ultimo directing the Sum of Six thousand pounds to be paid to the State Agent Colo. Udney Hay, out of certain taxes unappropriated (but not yet collected) for the purpose of purchasing forage: provided I previously covenantd with Colo. Hay to pay for the Same by a certain day, or that you consented to credit the State with the amount of Such forage.[1]

My letters, directing a contract to be made with the State Agent, afterwards arriving, Colo. Hay, (dropping, as it appears, the character of Agent) was induced to make his proposals for Supplying forage on contract; but on condition that your draughts on the treasurer of the State were previously put into his hands.

Without making any observations, I beg leave to lay before you those papers on the Subject which have been transmitted to me by Colo. Lutterloh and Colo. Hughes, and which appear necessary for your information, together with an extract of my letter to Colo. Lutterloh, authorizing him and Colo. Hughes to make a contract with the State Agent, as before mentioned.

I request I may be honoured with your answer in writing as speedily as possible.[2] I am, Sir, very respectfully, your most Obedient Servant

Tim. Pickering Q.M.G.

Papers inclosed[3]

No. 1. Colo. Hays letter dated July 26. 1782 to T. Pickering Q.M.G.
2. The act of the legislature of N. York passed 24th. July 1782.
3. Another act passed July 22nd. 1782.
4. Extract of a letter dated July 17th. 1782 from T. Pickering to Colo. Lutterloh Commissy. of Forage.
5. Letter from Colo's. Lutterloh and Hughes dated July 29th. 1782 to Tim. Pickering Q.M.G.
6. Colo. Hay's proposals for Supplying forage dated July 29th. 1782.
7. Extract of an Act passed April 14th. 1782.

MS: LbC, WDC, DNA.
1. On these arrangements, see notes to Alexander Hamilton to RM, July 22.
2. Having received this letter and its enclosures from Pickering, RM decided that Hay's prices were unacceptably high, rejected the proposed arrangements, and gave Pickering $45,000 in his notes to be exchanged for funds presumably harbored by the Continental tax receivers in states "eastward of Pennsylvania." On August 24, however, Pickering reported that an express sent to Hartford bearing notes had returned without a shilling. It appears, nonetheless, that Pickering's deputies were able to buy forage with Morris's notes and bills until September 1782, when agents of the French army were purchasing on better terms than Pickering could offer. Even so, Pickering thought he could get forage in Connecticut if provided with $17,500 to $20,500 in the notes of small denominations suitable for paying taxes which the Financier had begun to issue (on this type of Morris's note, see RM's Circular to the Receivers of Continental Taxes, August 29, and notes). Already overextended in note issues, RM had to decline the proposal. See Diary, August 5, RM to the Quartermaster General, August 5 and September 26, the Quartermaster General to RM, August 24 and September 19; and Pickering to Udny Hay, to Hugh Hughes, to William Churchill Houston, and to Henry E. Lutterloh, all August 5, 1782, WDC, no. 85, pp. 126–129, 131–133. On the general problem of forage procurement, see notes to RM to the Secretary at War, June 29, 1782.
3. Of the enclosed papers, nos. 1, 5, and 6 have not been found and nos. 2–4 are cited in notes to Alexander Hamilton to RM, July 22. No. 7, "An Act for the payment of certain contingent expences of this State," was a general bill to pay debts due to a wide range of public officials, private citizens, militia, and in case of default, state troops on the frontier, in money and commodities. See *Laws of New York*, I, 491–498.

Diary: August 5, 1782

Mr. Henry Dering called for Money on Account of his Contract for Lancaster but agreed to wait longer.

Mr. T. Tilghman this Day told me that his Stay with the Army will be so short, that he thinks his Acceptance of the Appointment of

Inspector of Contracts &c. which I offered to him last week[1] would not be of use to the Public as he cannot remain long enough to render essential Service. I am very sorry that it does not suit him and told him so, adding that I think this Office of great importance and that it shall remain Vacant unless I can meet with [a] Person in whom I can safely repose the greatest Confidence. I requested him to mention this to the General as well as the Affairs of the Contractors for the moving Army which I laid before him.

Mr. Geo. Henry[2] called to inform me of Ships going to France on Thursday next.

Comr. Hazelwood[3] for Money. I granted a Warrant for 1,000 Dollars.

Capt Hodge of the Navy who lately Commanded the Packett Active returned from Captivity and reported his being Captured by a British Frigate the Proserpine Capt. Taylor and sent into Jamaica.[4]

Jno. Pierce Esqr. Paymaster General called respecting the notes for their pay which they returned to him last Spring, and now want them back.[5] I desired him to keep them and that I will Confer with the Secy. at War respecting their Pay.

Colo. Pickering called for an Answer respecting the Forage, desiring to have it in writing I agreed, see my Letter to him of this Date. I desired him to Call on Mr Swanwick for the Drafts Amounting to 45,000 Dollars and informed him that he might take up 2,000 Dollars thereon from Mr. Houston at Trenton.[6] Colo. Pickering delivered me the Copy of my Draft on Mr. Swanwick dated the 6th July in his favor for 400 Dollars which is taken in the mail into New York. I desired him to lodge the Account with Mr. Swanwick to prevent payment thereof. He desired to have a Duplicate Bill which I decline but will give him another of this Date.

Consulted Solomon the Broker about raising the price of Bills of Exchange which I think is practicable but my great want of money will not permit me to stop.

Major Franks called to relate his Affairs or Transactions in Europe in Consequence of his mission thither but being hurried I proposed some other Time when leizure will permit.[7]

Wm. Perkins applies for money for Cartouch Boxes delivered to the Commissary General of Military Stores having upwards of £120 due to him. I agreed to pay 100 Dollars upon application of Mr. Hodgdon.

Mr. Thos. Bradford[8] called to inform of a Flag of Truce being arrived from Antigua.

Don Francisco Rendon to make enquiry's on which to found intelligence to Havannah.[9]

Edwd. Keran respecting his Accounts[10] which I desired might be sent to Mr. Milligan.

Israel Brodeaux commenced this day a Clerk in this Office.

The Hon. Mr Lowell to take leave.

The Hon Arthur Lee Esqr. for explanation of an article in the State of European Accounts which I gave to his Satisfaction.[11]

Wrote a Letter to His Excellency General Washington.

Wrote a Letter to Colo. T. Pickering.

1. See Diary, July 31, and notes.

2. George Henry of Philadelphia, who in December 1778 was appointed Pennsylvania's commissary of naval stores and also put in charge of selling vessels and naval stores belonging to the state as well as tools and stock of the state gun factory. See the references to him in *Colonial Records of Pennsylvania*, XI, 641, 644, 649, 765; and *Pennsylvania Archives*, 1st ser., V, 355, VII, 139–140, 190, 239, 333, 365.

3. John Hazelwood, a contractor for the Continental post at Philadelphia.

4. On Captain John Hodge and the *Active*, see notes to the Navy Board of the Eastern Department to RM, September 12, and to Diary, November 29, 1781.

5. The antecedents to this entry are unclear, but the reference is probably to the advance of pay to Continental army officers in Pierce's promissory notes, on which see notes to RM to George Washington, January 26, 1782 (second letter). The officers were not obliged to accept these notes, and some had apparently refused them.

6. See Timothy Pickering to William Churchill Houston, receiver of Continental taxes for New Jersey, August 5, 1782, WDC, no. 85, p. 131.

7. For the services of Major David Salisbury Franks as a diplomatic courier, see notes to RM to the President of Congress, July 9, 1781; and John Jay to RM, April 28, 1782.

8. Bradford was deputy commissary general of prisoners.

9. Rendón was Spain's unofficial representative in the United States; his letters to Juan Manuel de Cagigal of August 10 and 22, 1782, are in Papeles Procedentes de Cuba, legajo 1319, AGI.

10. Edward Keran had been clerk to the commissary general of military stores. Congress had referred his petition to RM on July 25.

11. Lee may have called upon RM as a member of a committee of Congress appointed on July 25 to examine and report on American funds in France; he was also a member of the oversight committee on the Office of Finance. See notes to RM to the President of Congress, May 24, and to Diary, June 12, 1782.

To John Cruden

Philada. August 5th. 1782

Sir

I have been honoured with the receipt of your letter of the 8th Ultimo enclosing one from my old Friend and Correspondant Mr Bean.[1] There was a Time when I took particular pleasure in shewing attention to every thing which cam[e] from that Gentleman. Our present situations do not admit of any other intercourse than ⟨that of⟩ the exchange [of] good wishes for personal happiness ⟨and Success⟩. Whenever Public affairs are so Circumstanced as that Consistently with the Duties we owe to our respective Countries, We can extend that intercourse so as to promote the honor and interest of each other, I shall on my part be most ready to assist you and Mr Bean in the execution of your Commercial plans. There will be openings for such transactions as will benefit[2] the Public as well as the individuals immediately Concerned, but as I do not mean to avail myself or Friends of such occasions untill it can be done with the entire approbation of America I think it unnecessary to exchange Cyphers for that circumstance might give rise to ⟨unworthy⟩ injurious Suspicions.

I have applied to the Gentlemen that have distributed amongst the distressed Carolinians the Sums Subscribed by the Citizens of this place for their releif, and have received from them a List of all that are now in this City.[3] The aid[4] you propose to send will be very acceptable and is very necessary to several of them. Shoud any expressions in the Notes added to this List be offensive your good sense will point out, that they do not come from the Parties in distress but from the Gentleman who on their behalf made it out and whose feelings I suppose hav[e] dictated upon the occasion. I am bound to send it forward as handed to me and will only add that to facilitate your desire of relieving the distressed will afford me great pleasure and you may freely command my assistance to that purpose. I am very respectfully Sir Your most obedient and most humble Servant

RM

J. Cruden Esqr.
New York[5]

ENDORSED: Draft of a Letter Philadelphia/August 5th. 1782 to/J: Cruden Esqr N. York
MS: ADftS, Robert Morris Papers, NN.
1. Cruden, a loyalist, was in New York City preparing to resign as British commissioner of sequestered property in South Carolina. His letter of July 8 from New York has not been found; the enclosure was a letter from Samuel Bean to RM of May 26, 1782, proposing that RM join him in engrossing the American tobacco market. Although in the present letter RM declined to become involved, he reversed himself and expressed interest in the proposal a few days after receiving word that peace negotiations had begun in Paris. There is no evidence, however, that the plan advanced any further. See RM to Cruden, August 13, Cruden to RM, August 15, and Diary, August 8 and 13.
2. Here RM began to write "our Countr[ies?]," but then lined out the words.
3. On the South Carolina refugees, see notes to Diary, July 30. The list has not been found.
4. RM settled on this word after having first written and then excised the words "relief" and "assist[ance]."
5. On August 8 RM asked Washington to forward this letter to Cruden in New York.

To the Quartermaster General
(Timothy Pickering)

Office of Finance 5th. August 1782[1]

Sir

I have received this Morning yours of the third Instant, and considered it with the various Enclosures. I find the Prices of the Articles which the State Agent of New York offers to deliver are much too high, and indeed he himself apologizes for it by the Circumstance *that Payment is to be made from a Tax which will not be collected in a considerable Time.* Thus then the State is to be credited more than the Article is worth because purchased on Credit from its own Citizens. And this Credit is to be given on a Requisition for Monies long since due. I, Sir, Act on the Part of the United States. I will make for them no such Bargain, but shall adhere to the Demand for Money, and Money only. Having already agreed to put some Cash into your Hands, I can only add my sincere Desire to support you, and my Assurance that I will do so to the utmost of my Power. I am Sir Your most obedient Servant

Robt Morris

Coll. Timothy Pickering
Quarter Master General

ENDORSED: Honble. R. Morris Esqr. S. F./Augt. 5. 1782/received s[ame] d[ay]/rejects the modes of supplying forage/proposed by the law and state agent of N. York/acted upon s[ame] d[ay].
MSS: LS, Manuscript File, WDC, DNA; Ofcl LbC, DLC.
    1. This letter, which rejected New York's proposals for forage procurement, was clearly meant to serve as a rebuke to the state and its agent Udny Hay. Pickering enclosed copies to Hay as well as to his own deputies in letters of August 5 (see notes to Quartermaster General to RM, August 3). RM enclosed a copy in his letter of August 28 to Alexander Hamilton, the receiver of Continental taxes for New York.

To George Washington

Office of Finance 5 Augst. 1782[1]

Dear Sir,

    I received your Letter of the thirtieth of July late in the Evening of Friday the second Instant. The Ideas which in Conversation with you I endeavoured to impress were, that I should at all Events fulfill my Part of the Contracts entered into for feeding your Army, That I had constantly attended to the Claims of the Contractors. That I should continue to do so, and that I beleived I had in many Instances been in Advance to them. On Saturday Morning I desired the Comptroller to make out a State of these Accounts, which State I have received this Morning and now enclose Copies.[2] Your Excellency will perceive from the State Number one, of the Accounts of the Contractors for West Point, that I have for a Considerable Part of the Time been Considerably in Advance to them, instead of their being one Month in Advance to me. Besides which it is to be observed, that the Amount stated for Provisions, they received out of the public Stores is entirely as they themselves have Stated it,[3] and that the Accounts not being as yet settled I ought not to have paid perhaps so much as I have done, because certainly there is no Way to secure the public Interest, but by with holding Money until Accounts be adjusted.[4] And this Sir leads me to an Observation, which applies fully to the whole of this Business. When I contracted to pay monthly it was well understood, that I should pay what appeared to be due for the preceding Month. Now until the Account be settled at the Treasury, there is in Fact nothing due which I can take Notice of as such. Supposing the Accounts and Vouchers to be all kept and delivered with that Accuracy and Simplicity which they ought, it is probable that they would get settled in the Course of a Week. Supposing then the greatest Dispatch which can reasonably be expected in transmitting and settling the Accounts, paying and remitting the Money, &ca. the Contractors could not have expected any Thing else than to have been two Months in Advance. And if they do not keep and transmit their Accounts and Vouchers with due Regularity they ought to have expected a still longer detention, especially if I were disposed to comply only with the Letter of my Agreements, But tho' I neither have done, nor will do any Thing, which could be construed into taking an undue Advantage, I think myself not only justifiable, but I think and will contend, that it is my duty to take Care, that there be always such an Arrearage, as will make the Public perfectly Safe. I do not examine Accounts, and therefore if I would take the meer Assertion of any Man, or Set of Men, the Consequences might be most pernicious. With respect to the Contractors for the Moving Army whose account is contained in the Enclosure number two, I confess that I was deficient, one Hundred Dollars, in the Payments for April and May, but when it is recollected, that the Advances Stipulated for were under the Idea then[5] entertained, that the whole Army would take the Field on the first day of May, and expend (at the rate of only eighteen Thousand Rations per Day) sixty thousand Dollars Monthly, and when it is further recollected, that nothing like this has happened, it will then appear, that I have more than complied with what they had any Right to expect, and that if they had prepared as they ought to have done, Funds equal to the Supply of between two and three months Pay,[6] nay, if they had prepared Funds equal to the expected Supply of only one Month, they have never yet been in a Situation when the Deficiencies of the Public (had the Public been defective) could have injured the Army. And now Sir, if you examine the Account number two, you will see, that they have received quite as much, as they had any Right to expect previous to a Settlement of their Accounts. And indeed you will see by the enclosed note from Mr. Swanwick,[7] that they have received even more than is stated in that account. But as these various Contractors have as I am informed lately joined Stocks and Contracts,[8] I have made a short State in the Paper Number three,[9] of the Issues according to their Accounts, and of the Payments made from which it will appear, that there are not four thousand Dollars due for the Month of June, and that if a Credit is given for Provisions, purchased of the State of Connecticut, the Public are at least four thousand Dollars in Advance. They say that there are forty thousand Dollars due for the Issues in July, but the Accounts are not yet *even presented,* notwithstanding which, I shall pay them a considerable Sum this Week.

I should not however do Justice, were I not to Observe that the Contractors for West Point have made considerable Advances for the Purpose of Cloathing the Officers, which Cloathing they were paid for in Notes of the Pay Master General due on the first of August.[10] I owe them yet on those Notes between nineteen and twenty thousand Dollars. If I had asked Indulgence in the Situation to which the Demand for those Notes, and the Delays of the States had reduced me, I might, I think, have expected it, but I have asked none, and I am thoroughly perswaded, that the Contractors were intimidated by the Apprehension, that those Notes would break me, and thereby prevented from applying as they ought to have done, their own Money and Credit. I do myself the Honor to enclose Sir, the Copy of a Letter to me from the Comptroller,[11] to which I will pray that your Excellency will enable me to make the proper Answer.[12] With sincere Friendship and Esteem I am my Dear Sir Your most obedient and humble Servant[13]

Robt Morris

His Excellency General Washington

[ENCLOSURE 3]

Statement of Issues and Payments for the West Point and Moving Army Contracts

[Philadelphia, August 5, 1782]

Issues for the Moving Army and West Point according to the Accounts from the Treasury but as many of these are not yet settled it is to be presumed that if there be Errors they are in Favor of the Public.

1782

West Point.	January	$28,448.^{53}/_{90}$
	February	25,549.46
	March	23,776.15
	April	23,535.63
	May	16,677.62
	June	17,182. 8
		135,169.67

Deduct for defective Vouchers
in Accounts of Janry: and Febry: 1,003.62   134,166. $^{5}/_{90}$

    Moving Army—May   21,901.$^{63}/_{90}$
           June   23,960. $^{7}/_{90}$ 45,861.$^{70}/_{90}$

                                                    180,027.75

Paid Contractors for West Point
  at sundry Times   131,118.23
Paid Contractors for Moving
  Army   45,088.30   176,206.53

    Due to the Contractors   3,821.22

They have received from the State of Connecticut for Account of the Public 800 Bbls. Provisions which may be estimated at 15 Dlls. per Bll., but say only 10 Dlls., this will make the Public in Advance above 4,000 Dolls. There is due to the Contractors for their Issues in July they say 40,000 Dolls. but their Accounts are not yet come down.

ENDORSED: Office of Finance 5th Augt 1782/from/Hono Robert Morris Esqr/inclosing account of Monies advanced to/Contractors &c with Copy of/Letter from Comptroller/Answered 11th.
MSS: LS, Washington Papers, DLC; Ofcl LbC, DLC; copy, Robert Morris Collection, CSmH.
    1. This "mildly reassuring" letter was the first of several that RM wrote to Washington during the summer and fall of 1782 about his increasing difficulties in paying the army contractors. What the Financier failed to emphasize in this letter as a principal source of the contractors' discontent was that the bulk of his payments to them had been made in bank notes and his own notes and not in the specie required by the contracts (see Ver Steeg, *Morris*, 148). See RM to Washington, August 13, 20, 29 (two letters), and 30, September 9 (two letters) and 25, and October 15 and 16. For the eventual dissolution of the West Point and Moving Army contract, see notes to Comfort Sands, Walter Livingston, William Duer, and Daniel Parker to RM, September 11.
    2. See Diary, August 3. Enclosure no. 1, entitled "Messrs. Comfort Sands and Co Contractors for West Point and it's Dependencies, their account current with the United States," and enclosure no. 2, entitled "Messrs Tench Francis, Comfort Sands and Co, Thomas Lowry, Oliver Phelps, Timothy Edwards, and Walter Livingston, Contractors for Supplying the Moving Army, their Account Current on a Contract Commencing the 1st. May 1782 with the United States," both prepared by Joseph Nourse and dated at the Register's Office, August 3, 1782, are in the Washington Papers, DLC.
    3. This was disclosed in the Comptroller of the Treasury to RM, August 1.
    4. For a contractor's observations on the examination of accounts, see William Duer to RM, August 2, and notes.
    5. "Men" in Ofcl LbC.
    6. This word is missing from the other texts.
    7. The text of this enclosure, an ADS in the writing of John Swanwick, cashier of the Office of Finance (Washington Papers, DLC), is as follows: "These are to Certify whom it may Concern that on the 25th. day of July 1782 I delivered to Thos. Lowrey Esqr. on behalf of the Contractors for the Moving Army a draft on myself for fifteen hundred Dollars Specie for which the Said Lowrey was paid by W. C. Houston Esqr Receiver of Continental Taxes for the State of New Jersey. Witness my hand Augt. 6th 1782."
    8. See Diary, May 13, 1782, and notes.
    9. This enclosure is printed at the end of the letter.

10. For a discussion, see RM to Washington, January 26, 1782 (second letter), and notes.
11. See note 3 above.
12. The foregoing sentence was omitted from the CSmH copy.
13. Washington replied on August 11.

From George Washington

Head Quarters [Newburgh, New York] 5th Augst 1782

Sir

On my Return from Phila. I found many Complaints against Mr Sands[1] for frequent want of provisions—as well as Badness of Quality in what he did furnish. Both these Greivances have subsisted till the present time and the Troops have been without their Rations for several Days at various Times. In Casting about for a Remedy, I find, none is provided in the Contracts, but what is to be applied by the Superintendant who is to be appointed by you.[2] I have therefore to request most earnestly, that you will appoint this person without Delay, and that he may repair to the Army as soon as possible. Mr. Sands's Disposition is such that I have not the least hope of Relief from him—so long as he can impose upon the Army and thereby serve his own Interest, with Impunity I am perswaded he will continue to do it. I am Dear Sir &c.[3]

Superintendt of Finance

ENDORSED: Head Quarters 5th Augst 1782/to/Superintendt of Finance/to appoint Superintendt for/the Army
MSS: Dft in the writing of Jonathan Trumbull, Jr., Washington Papers, DLC; Varick transcript, Washington Papers, DLC.
1. Comfort Sands and Company held the contract for West Point and was a principal partner in the Moving Army contract. The contracts were merged as of July 1. See the preceding letter and notes.
2. On the appointment of an inspector of contracts for the main army, see RM to the President of Congress, April 20, 1782, and notes.
3. RM replied to Washington on August 9.

From William Whipple

Portsmouth [New Hampshire] 5th August 1782[1]

Sir

I am Honoured with yours of the 16, last month also Your Circular Letter of the 12th inclosing a Copy of Your letter to the several States of the 25 July 1781. I shall immediately take measures to procure the information you require. Since my last respects to you the Executive of this State have employed an agent to dispose of a Quantity of Beef Cattle to the Contractors. If he succeeds its probable there will be some receipts in my next publication as the proceeds are order'd into my hands; this is the only prospect I have at present and what the Amount will be is altogether uncertain.[2] With the Greatest Respect I have the Honor to be &c.

Honle Robert Morris Esq

MS: LbC, William Whipple Letterbook, John Langdon Papers, PHi.
1. Whipple was the receiver of Continental taxes for New Hampshire. Preceding the present letter in Whipple's letterbook is one of August 4 to RM which is crossed out and marked in the margin as "not sent." The text of that letter reads as follows: "I have Just heard from Mr. Langdon that an Express is immediately going for Philadelphia. I embrace the opportunity to acknowledge the receipt of Your favor of the 16th last month also Your Circular letter of 12 inclosing the Copy of Your Letter to the several States of 25th July 1781. I shall immediately take measures to obtain the information you require which shall transmit so soon as possible."
2. New Hampshire's sale of cattle to the beef subcontractors for the Moving Army brought in receipts of $3,000 in Morris's notes from Timothy Edwards. The sum was eventually credited to the state's account of specie taxes paid on the requisition for 1782, but proved to be the only payment made by New Hampshire during RM's term of office. See William Whipple to RM, September 23 and October 27, 1782, and April 8, 1783, Joseph Whipple to RM, December 21, 1782, and January 25, 1783, and RM to William Whipple, August 28 and October 9, 1782, December 1, 1783, and January 6 and 16, 1784, and to Joseph Whipple, January 21, 1783; and tax receipts listed in PCC, no. 137, III, 345. For RM's plan to obtain taxes from New Hampshire in connection with the sale of cattle, see Diary, September 4, and notes.

From William Churchill Houston

Trenton [New Jersey] 5 August 1782

I regret that unusual Avocations, some of which have called me to a Distance from Home, have prevented me from attending to your Commands as soon as I should otherwise have done.[1] Believe it will be out of my Power to collect any Thing on the Subject of specifick Supplies; few, or no Accounts being yet rendered by those who had the Conducting of that Business. Upon the other Matters have procured some Information. The return which ought to have been made by Post, is now sent; having been then abroad.

1782 Dr   The Receipt of Continental Taxes in the State of New Jersey
              from 27 July to 3 August inclusive
          To Cash received from the State Treasurer four Hundred
              Dollars   Dlls 400

ENDORSED: Copy of Letter to Robert/Morris Eqr 5 August/1782 with return/from 27 July to 3 Augst/400 Dlls
MS: ADftS with subjoined ADft return, Houston Collection, NjP.
1. Houston was the receiver of Continental taxes for New Jersey. The "Commands" he mentions probably refer to RM's Circular to the Receivers of Continental Taxes, July 12, 1782.

From the Quartermaster General
(Timothy Pickering)

Philadelphia Augt. 5. 1782

I have just received from Colo. Hughes D[eputy] Q[uarter] M[aster] a letter dated the 31st ultimo relative to the suits threatened to be brought against me and the officers of the department, by our creditors in the state of New-York. What relates to the subject is contained in the extract inclosed,[1] which it appeared proper that I should lay before you.

MS: LbC, WDC, DNA.
    1. Enclosure not found.

Diary: August 6, 1782

This morning the Hon: Mr. Duane came to the Office whilst I was at Breakfast, went away again leaving Word for the Committee to meet at his Lodgings after which he sent me word they were adjourned.[1]

The Hon. Genl. Cornell called to Converse respecting the old Continental Currency and sundry other public matters.[2] I read him my Letter to the Governor of Rhode Island respecting the Impost Law which he approved.[3]

Mr. Geo Eddy respecting the Affair of Tobacco in Virginia. I shewed him Mr Clarkes Letters.[4]

Colo. Tench Tilghman called to take leave and for my Dispatches to General Washington.[5]

Capt. James Nicholson to know what he shall write &c. I wish to send this Gentleman to the Ship but have not money yet.[6]

Lewis R. Morris Esquire for Bills for the foreign Ministers &c. their second Quarters Salary. I gave orders to have them made out.[7]

Received and wrote Sundry Letters &c. &c.

Wrote a Letter to Monsr. Grand.

Wrote a Letter to Doctor Brownson.[8]

Issued a Warrant on Mr Swanwick in favor of
Francis and Slough   £149.9.8
Issued a Warrant on Mr Swanwick in favor the
President, Directors &c the Bank   12.9.9

    1. James Duane of New York was chairman of the congressional committee investigating the Office of Finance. See notes to Diary, June 12, 1782.
    2. Ezekiel Cornell was a Rhode Island delegate to Congress. On the question of old Continental currency, see RM's report to Congress of September 7, and notes.
    3. The letter is dated August 2.
    4. The letters from Daniel Clark have not been found.
    5. Tilghman, Washington's aide, had brought the general's July 30 letter to RM and presumably carried the Superintendent's answer of August 5.
    6. See Diary, July 22, and notes.
    7. On the salaries of foreign ministers, see RM to the President of Congress, May 8, 1782, and notes.
    8. For the possible subject of this letter, which has not been found, see Diary, August 12, and notes.

Gouverneur Morris to John Jay

Philadelphia August 6th. 1782

Dear Jay

I received your Letter of the twenty eighth of April by Major Franks.[1] It came too late for I had already applied the copy of a certain Correspondence in the Manner you intended when you sent it.[2] I decyphered and read your Letter to the Minister of Foreign Affairs.[3] If I were with you or had Time to use my Cypher, I would say somewhat on it. I think that Congress will not be silent. Should you have done nothing I advise you to the maxim festina lente.[4] You will know the Reasons when this reaches you or soon after, Wind and Weather permitting, for both must you know be consulted before Instructions can be ascertained to an ultramarine Agent.

I am surprized that you have not had [any?] of my Letters since last Autumn but that Circumstance proves the Position I have just advanced. A question. Are you acquainted with the Organization of the Office for Foreign Affairs? Letters from the Minister are submitted to Congress *in Toto*. I learn you are going to Versailles; if the Account be true, and it came from yourself, this will find you there. I do not however expect any Thing like Peace at present because I do not expect Peace. This may not be so intelligible to every Body else as it is to you. Sed festina lente I repeat again. Your Friends here are well. Your Brother James has I am told, gone to England. If so his political Race like a New Market Course has run round in a Circle and brought him back to where he started. I am sorry for him or rather I reciprocate your Feelings on the Occasion. It is somewhat extraordinary, Doctor Franklin's Son, your Brother and Mr. Laurence's Self[5] are in England. Mr. Adams I suppose has no Connection there, tho by the bye situated as he is he should be cautious not to connect himself with those who have. You will see by our News Papers that the States resolve away at an enormous Rate not to make Peace nor Truce nor any Thing else with Britain: nimium ne crede Colori.[6] Look at the other Side of the Question and you will find that, to use a vulgar Expression they pay Taxes like nothing at all. I use this Expression almost literally for the only Difference is that they pay Nothing, instead of paying like nothing. With this Hint however you must combine one Consideration which is that nobody will be thankful for any Peace but a very good one. This *they* should have thought on who made War with a Republic. I am among the Number who would be extremely ungrateful for the Grant of a bad Peace. My public and private Situation will both concur to render the Sentiment as coming from me unsuspected. Judge then of others. Judge of the many headed fool whose Sense can feel no more than his own wringing. I am not extravagant in my Demands nor impressed with the Quixotism of destroying either a Giant or an Enchanter because I fear not the Force of one nor Charms of the other but I wish that while the War lasts it may be real War, and that when Peace comes it may be real Peace.[7] Adieu yours[8]

Gouv Morris

ENDORSED: G. Morris 6 Augt/1782/Received Sep.
MSS: LS, John Jay Papers, NNC; Bancroft transcript, NN.
1. Letter not found. Gouverneur Morris was RM's assistant in the Office of Finance. Jay was the American minister to Spain and one of the commissioners for negotiating peace with Great Britain. He had left Madrid on May 21 and arrived in Paris on June 23.
2. The correspondence had been enclosed in Jay to Gouverneur Morris, November 10, 1781 (ADftS in Jay Papers, NNC), and concerned Lewis Littlepage (1762–1802), a young Virginian whom Jay had taken into his home in Madrid. After their relationship became strained, Jay sent the papers to Gouverneur for use in counteracting any misrepresentation Littlepage might make in America. See Richard B. Morris et al., eds., John Jay, the Making of a Revolutionary: Unpublished Papers, 1745–1780 (New York, 1975), 770n.; and Morris, ed., John Jay: Winning of the Peace, 218–219, 284n.
3. The letter was Jay to Robert R. Livingston, April 28, 1782; see Diary, August 1, and notes.
4. "Make haste slowly," a maxim of Augustus as recorded in Suetonius's Life.
5. Respectively, William Franklin (1731–1813), the illegitimate son of Benjamin Franklin and last royal governor of New Jersey, who had been a loyalist active in New York City before returning to England in August 1782 (DAB); Sir James Jay, who had arranged his own capture by the British (see notes to RM to John Jay, June 5, 1781; and Morris, ed., John Jay: Winning of the Peace, 250–253, 498–499; and Henry Laurens, who had been released on parole from the Tower of London in December 1781 and was eventually exchanged for Lord Cornwallis. Laurens remained for a time in England, but finally joined the Paris talks on November 29, 1782, the day before the signing of the preliminary articles of peace. Morris, Peacemakers, 264–268, 376–377.
6. "Trust not too much to your bloom," from Vergil's Eclogues. On the state resolutions against British peace overtures, see notes to RM to Daniel of St. Thomas Jenifer, June 11, 1782.
7. For the Morrises' views on peace, see Gouverneur Morris to Matthew Ridley, August 6, RM to John Vaughan, August 25, to Vicomte de Noailles, September 25, to Ridley, October 6, to Benjamin Franklin, September 30 and October 7 (second letter), to George Washington, October 16, and RM's Circular to the Governors of the States, October 21.
8. This word is in Gouveneur Morris's hand.

Gouverneur Morris to Matthew Ridley

Philadelphia 6 August 1782[1]

Dear Ridley

I received by the Non Such a Copy of your Letter from Paris of the twentieth of April. Accept my sincere Thanks for it. I repeat for form's Sake that the Bill in favor of Mr. Pringle was paid as I suppose he has advised you. It is a long Time since I have heard from Carmichael. Colo. Livingston was taken and his Letters previously destroyed. Major Franks brought none to me from him. I am not surprized at that as he was to my knowlege very much occupied about that Time.

I am well convinced of two Things. One that a Peace will not easily be made and another that it is not much for the Interest of America that it should be made at present.[2] Whoever will take a retrospective View of our Affairs will find amid all their Changes (and God knows they have been sufficiently variable) that we have made a silent but rapid and constant Progress towards Strength and Greatness. Our Position, our Numbers, our Resources and our probable Increase are all important. Our Knowlege is not unimportant. Highly Commercial, being as it were the first born Children of extended Commerce in modern Times, we must be maritime. Freedom was secured by the several Constitutions; Freedom in the extreme. Nothing remained but Vigor, Organization and Promptitude to render this a considerable Empire. These can only be acquired by a Continuance of the War which will convince People of the necessity of obedience to common Counsels for general Purposes. War is indeed a rude, rough Nurse to infant States and the Consequence of being committed to her Care is that they either die young or grow up vigorous. We have at least lived thro the Cradle and are familiarized to her Looks of Horror. The Power of Congress is like a young Tree which when first planted is much endangered but when the Roots once begin to shoot it acquires Strength e'en "in the Visitation of the Winds which take the Mountain[3] Billows by the Top." A Tree so visited seldom overgrows. Such a Tree becomes if not large at least solid and tho not showy is surely strong. Metaphors are not Reasons, neither are Assertions Proofs, unless indeed they be taken as the Evidences of Opinion. The Confederation has not given to Congress sufficient authority. This becomes daily sensible and that Sense will remedy the Evil. But if the War cease the Conviction of our Weakness will also cease untill shewn by another War and then perhaps it may be too late.

I have long since given to Carmichael my Sentiments on a War between the Russians, Imperialists and Turks. The Part which the King of Prussia would take was pointed out by his Wisdom and his Situation. I rather doubt whether such a War will take Place just now. We have no remarkable Events here, other than what the Gazettes will anounce. Savannah evacuated certainly, Charlestown probably. Sir Guy Carleton very polite. The several assemblies passing hightoned Resolutions.[4] All these Things however are of little Consequence but the Solidity which our Governments are daily acquiring is of great Consequence. There are always some small Matters which influence much and are frequently overlooked. During the Ferment of the Revolution like as in other Ferments the Dregs were uppermost. The Liquor is daily refining. In other Words Men of Sense and Property are getting into the Places which such Men ought to fill. The People are begining to be convinced that those Men are alone fit to govern and in a very little Time the Rulers of America will be well obeyed if they pursue the Paths of Honesty which I hope they will do. Adieu believe me truly your Friend[5]

Gouv Morris

ENDORSED: Received. Septr. 29./Answered Oct: 10th. 1782
MSS: ALS, Ridley Papers, MHi; LS, MB.

1. Ridley, who was supervising the education of RM's eldest sons on the Continent, was Maryland's agent in Europe. He had left Paris for Holland in mid-May and returned at the end of August.
2. For the Morrises' views on peace, see the preceding letter and notes.
3. Gouverneur struck out this word in the LS and substituted "ruffian."
4. For the peace overtures of Sir Guy Carleton, the commander of British forces in North America, and the states' responses, see notes to RM to Daniel of St. Thomas Jenifer, June 11, 1782.
5. Ridley received the LS on September 27 and the ALS two days later; he replied from Paris on October 10.

To Ferdinand Grand

Office of Finance 6th. August 1782[1]

My last Letters to you were of the third, fifth and sixth Ultimo the first and last of which enclosed Lists of sundry Bills of Exchange drawn by me as Superintendant of Finance on you in favor of sundry Persons from No. 146 to 179 inclusive making thirty four Setts, amounting to 368,916 Livres 4 Sous Tournois. Also an Abstract of the whole Sum drawn to the third day of July last which was to serve for your Government.

I now enclose you a further List of Bills of Exchange of this date drawn by me as Superintendant of Finance at thirty and sixty days sight on you in favor of sundry Persons as therein mentioned numbered 180 to 250 inclusive making seventy one Setts and amounting to four hundred and seventy one thousand nine hundred and eighty nine Livres twelve sous and ten Deniers Tournois. The amount of each Bill is extended opposite to its Number in the List.[2]

You will be pleased to honor and Pay these Bills punctually on Account of the United States of North America.

MS: Ofcl LbC, DLC.
1. Grand was banker to the United States in Paris.
2. List not found.

From the Secretary at War
(Benjamin Lincoln)

[Philadelphia, August 6, 1782][1]

General Knox Requests in the most pointed terms that the above Articles may be supplied. I therefore approve the Estimate and Second his wishes.

MS: LbC, WDC, DNA.
1. Lincoln's note is subjoined to an "Estimate of the Sum necessary to procure the following Stores wanted for the Laboratories at West Point and in the Field," dated Philadelphia, August 6, 1782, and totaling £639.19.8, in WDC, no. 148, pp. 43–45. The estimate and letter were probably enclosed in Samuel Hodgdon to RM, August 7.

Diary: August 7, 1782

Mr John Scott one of the Stewards of the Hospital applied for pay &c. Referred him to the Purveyor Doctor Bond.

Haym Solomon Broker respecting Bills, Money &c. I authorized him to sell Bills for Cash at 6/3d and on Credit at 6/6.

Capt. Js. Nicholson brought me an Estimate of the Money which he thinks will be wanted immediately to carry on the Bourbon Frigate.[1]

Mr. Saml. Murdoch and Mrs. Sweers to pray for leave that he [Cornelius Sweers] may go for the West Indies and they decline giving the Security I proposed for the Debt he owes the United States.[2] I promised an Answer in a few Days.

Walter Livingston Esqr. one of the Contractors for the moving Army being in this City called and I shewed him the State of their Accounts to the end of June and the Copy of the Letter written a few days since to General Washington respecting it[3] when he Confessed that he had expected from the information given him by Mr. Sands that there was much more Money due to the Contractors than these Accounts shew. I promised to pay him a Sum on Account of the Supplies for July in a day or two.

Mr. Robt Adam of Alexandria[4] brought a draft of Jno. Sansum for 100 Dollars for which I granted a Warrant.

Doctr. Ths. Bond Junr. for Money. Referred him to next Week.

Miss Mary Linn praying for money on a Certificate of the Quarter Master General and to releive her Brother a Prisoner &c.

Colo. Pickering for money for various purposes all which my poverty Contrary to any inclination obliged me to refuse.

Capt. De Bert of Armands Legion respecting the Affairs on which Colo. Armand has written to me.[5] I told him that I shall confirm the Contract made with Colo. Lewis for supplying Provisions[6] and Authorize further Contracts for the same purpose. I desired him to get Colo. Armands Accounts settled at the Comptrollers Office and as to Horses the Legion not being called to active Service those Horses cannot at present be provided.

Mr. Alexr. Stewart applied for a Passport for Mr. Musco Livingston which I promised should be ready to Morrow and Mr Morris has drafted the Same.[7]

The Hon. Secy. at War called with Capt. De Bert of Armands Legion and approved of what passed. He desired one hundred Dollars for Contingent Charges of the War Office which were granted.

Wrote a Letter to Samuel Foreman Esqr.[8]

1. The estimate has not been found.
2. On the claim against Cornelius Sweers, see Diary, June 5, 1782, and notes.
3. See RM to Washington, August 5, and notes.
4. Adam (1731–1789), principal of Robert Adam and Company, was a Scots-born wheat and tobacco merchant. Robert A. Rutland, ed., *The Papers of George Mason, 1725–1792* (Chapel Hill, N. C., 1970), I, xxix–xxx.
5. See Diary, August 1, and notes; on the supply of Armand's corps, see RM to Edward Carrington, June 11, 1782, and notes.

6. The contract has not been found. The contractor, evidently Samuel Lewis of Augusta County, Virginia, had previously supplied Continental troops. See the references to him in McIlwaine, ed., *Journals of the Council of Virginia*, II, 255, 377, III, 87, 558–559; Boyd, ed., *Jefferson Papers*, III, 501, 527, 528, 537, 562; and Diary, January 8 and 10, 1783.

7. See RM's Report to Congress on the Case of Musco Livingston, July 25, and notes. The passport prepared by Gouverneur Morris has not been found.

8. Letter not found.

From Samuel Hodgdon

Philadela. Augt. 7: 1782

By special direction of the honorable Secy at War I enclose an Estimate for certain Supplies wanted immediately by the Army.[1] For want of the Money due on the Estimates already rendered, I am in great distress and wholly unable to proceed in procuring the supplies essentially Necessary for the Army in the Field. The people no longer confiding in my promises, are determined to address you to obtain Relief. If possible I most earnestly request to be furnish'd with a sum sufficient to discharge the estimates you have on hand, without which every branch of business must Stop.

MS: LbC, WDC, DNA.

1. Hodgdon was the commissary general of military stores. The enclosed estimate was probably the one subjoined to the Secretary at War to RM, August 6.

George Washington to Gouverneur Morris

Head Qrs. Newburgh [New York] Augst 7 1782

I asserted pretty roundly to you, but not more confidently than it was asserted to me, that General Dalrymple had Sailed for England.

Since my return to this place I have seen a letter from him to Genl. Knox,[1] which, at the same time that it contradicts both assertions, announces his speedy departure for the Albion Shore. If he should remain in New York after this, charge it to his account—not mine—and give me credit for the ingenuity of my recantation.

Present me respectfully to Mrs. Morris and Kitty Livingston—to Mr. Morris also. It is unnecessary to assure you, how much I am Yours

MSS: ALS, Washington Papers, DLC; Varick transcript, Washington Papers, DLC.

1. The letter from William Dalrymple, dated July 17, 1782, is in the Henry Knox Papers, IX, 42, MHi.

Diary: August 8, 1782

The Honble. Mr. Clarke called as one of the Committee of enquiry but the Chairman and other Members not being come he told me they had in Contemplation to establish some more regular mode of enquiry before they came again.[1] We had some Conversation respecting the Appointment of a Commissioner for settling the Accounts of the Hospital Department &c.[2]

The Hon. Mr. Wharton then came in to enquire into some Articles of the Accounts rendered by the Compte De Vergennes, Doctr.

Franklin and Chevr Luzerne respecting which I gave him every information in my power.[3]

Walter Livingston Esqr. one of the Contractors for the moving Army came to the Office but being very Busy I could not see him and sent word by a Clerk that I would send for him when I was ready to finish his business.

The Hon: Mr Roote called about some accounts which had been settled by Jnoa. Trumbull junr. as Commissioner for Settling the Accounts of his Brother the late Commissary General. I desired him to leave these Accounts untill I can converse with Mr. Milligan the Comptroller on the Subject.[4]

Mr. Stewart called respecting the Flag for Musco Livingston and Mr. G: Morris instructed him in what is further to be done in that business.[5]

Mrs. Sweers wrote me a note praying for Liberty for Mr. Sweers to go for the West Indies.[6] I sent for Jared Ingersol Esqr. one of the Council employed in that Cause and desired him to proceed therein so as to recover from Sweers the Money due to the U: States. See my Letter of this Date to him and Mr. Sergeant.

Henry Hill Esqr. called to inform me of the Steps he is taking to pay the money due.

Mr: Geo. Eddy the same as above.

I sent for Haym Solomon in my Distress to raise money for me which he will try to Effect.

Thos. Willing Esqr. President of the Bank called to inform me that the Directors agreed to renew the Discount for 100,000 Dollars due the 5th Instant but cannot extend another Discount for a like Sum as their Funds are not equal to bear such an advance wherefore I proposed to Mortgage to them an Order of the President and Council of Pennsylvania on their Treasurer to which he agreed.[7]

The Hon. Secy. at War came to the Office and proposed that I should Authorize Mr. Pierce the Paymaster Genl. to Issue his Notes payable in four Months hence to such Officers as have not already received them in Consequence of the former Order. I desired him to send the Paymaster General to me in the morning, and that I will adjust the matter with him.[8]

The Hon. R. R. Livingston Esqr. came and announced to us that a negotiation is opened at Paris for a General Peace.[9]

Wrote a Letter to James Lovell Esqr.

Wrote a Letter to Jona. Serjeant and Jared Ingersoll Esqrs.

Wrote a Letter to the Hon. Daniel Carrol Esqr.

1. For the committee of Congress investigating the Office of Finance, of which Abraham Clark of New Jersey was a member, see notes to Diary, June 12, 1782.

2. For this appointment, see notes to RM to the President of Congress, February 18, 1782.

3. On Congressman Samual Wharton's business, see Diary, July 30, and notes.

4. Jesse Root was a delegate to Congress from Connecticut. On the settlement of the accounts of the deceased Commissary General Joseph Trumbull by his brother, Jonathan Trumbull, Jr., see Diary, February 19, and notes, and Jonathan Burrall to RM, July 22, 1782, and notes. The question at hand concerned the final settlement certificates to be issued for the balances due individuals in those accounts; see Diary, August 16, 19, 20, and RM to Burrall, August 19 and 22.

5. See RM's Report to Congress on the Case of Musco Livingston, July 25, and notes.

6. Note not found.

7. The $100,000 due was the second loan to the United States from the Bank of North America (see RM to the Register of the Treasury, February 5, 1782, and notes). The order in question was the warrant for £32,500 RM had received from Pennsylvania in his capacity as agent of the state for purchasing specific supplies owed on former requisitions. See the headnote to RM to the President of Pennsylvania, June 26, 1781, and notes, RM to the President of Pennsylvania, May 8, 1782, and notes, and Diary, May 10 and August 9, 1782.

8. RM at first agreed to allow Pierce to issue more of his promissory notes to army officers who had not previously been paid, but then decided instead to give him his own notes on Swanwick for that purpose. See Diary, August 9 and 12; for the background, see RM to George Washington, January 26, 1782 (second letter), and notes.

9. Unofficial news of the opening of general peace negotiations in Paris had been slowly accumulating in Philadelphia during the preceding week from sources in New York and Europe. Franklin's dispatches of June 25 and 28 from Paris had not yet arrived, however, and the first official hint that negotiations were in progress was laid before Congress on August 2 in a brief letter of May 14 to Livingston from John Jay relating that Franklin had called him to Paris and that he would leave Madrid in a few days. The exact source of Livingston's information has not been determined, but it may have been derived from Rivington's *New York Royal Gazette*, which on August 3 reported passage of the Enabling Act by the House of Commons and the appointment of Thomas Grenville to negotiate peace in France, and on August 6 printed a letter to Washington of August 2 from Sir Guy Carleton and Rear Admiral Robert Digby, the British peace commissioners at New York, announcing the beginning of the Paris talks. Extracts of these articles appeared in the *Pennsylvania Packet* of August 8 and 10 respectively. Washington himself had enclosed the Carleton-Digby letter in one of August 5 to the president of Congress; precisely when these letters arrived in Philadelphia has not been ascertained, but they were not officially received and read in Congress until August 9. Although suspicions about British motives remained high in Congress, most American commentators agreed that negotiations were indeed underway. For the letters mentioned above, see Wharton, ed., *Rev. Dipl. Corr.*, V, 417, 510–513, 525–526; Fitzpatrick, ed., *Writings of Washington*, XXIV, 466; and for Carleton and Digby's letter, PCC, no. 152, X, 669–671. For Congress's response to their letter, see Charles Thomson's Notes of Debates, August 9, 1782, Burnett, ed., *Letters*, VI, 438 and n.; and notes to Diary, June 18, 1782. See also Hutchinson and Rutland, eds., *Madison Papers*, V, 20–21, 22n., 27, 38–41, 45–48n., 49.

To Daniel Carroll

Office of Finance 8th August 1782[1]

Sir,

In Conversation with Mr Cadwallader[2] he dropt the Hint that probably you might be induced to accept the Office of Receiver of Continental Taxes for the State of Maryland. I readily seized the Idea because the Office is of such Importance that I heartily wish it to be in the Hands of a very respectable Character. Should you therefore think proper to take it you will apply to Mr. Zephania[h]

Turner who has all the Papers[3] and by that Means every proper Arrangement can be immediately taken. But if you should not I am to request that you will confer with Mr. Jenifer[4] on the Subject and between you fix on some proper Person. I need not describe the Qualifications as the various Instructions will shew that at least Calmness of Temper with good Sense and Intergrity are necessary. I shall object only to Mr. Harwood the Loan Officer whom I should certainly have appointed had he not held that Office. But there are Reasons applicable to some of the States which would not permit my Compliance with applications in Favor of Loan Officers and therefore to avoid all unnecessary Discussions I made the Rule general not to appoint any of them previous to the Final Settlement of their Accounts. I pray you to beleive me with real Esteem your most obedient and humble Servant.[5]

RM

MS: Ofcl LbC, DLC.
   1. Carroll was a delegate to Congress from Maryland.
   2. John Cadwalader (1742–1786), former brigadier general of the Pennsylvania militia, had resettled in Maryland and was currently a member of the House of Delegates. *DAB*.
   3. RM had sent the papers to Turner in a letter of May 24, 1782. A Marylander, Turner had recently been appointed commissioner for settling Virginia's accounts with the United States.
   4. Daniel of St. Thomas Jenifer, Maryland's intendant of the revenue.
   5. Carroll evidently did not accept the appointment as receiver for Maryland, but instead recommended George Lee for the post; RM, however, appointed Benjamin Harwood, brother of Thomas Harwood the Continental loan officer. See Diary, August 31, and RM to Benjamin Harwood, September 13 and October 1.

To John Manley

Marine Office 8 August 1782

To John Manly Esqr. Captain in the Navy of the United States the Hague[1]

Sir,

You will as soon as possible proceed on a Cruize and as to the Places where you Cruize and to which you are to send the Prizes you will be governed entirely by your own Discretion in which I have Confidence. Your Objects are annoy the Enemies of the United States and facilitate the Exchange of our Seamen Prisoners with them.[2] You will continue your Cruize as Long as Circumstances will permit and make such Port on your Return as you shall think most proper. Inform me from Time to Time of what may have passed worthy of Attention and communicate such Intelligence as you may gain.

Having left you to pursue intirely the Dictates of your own Judgment; I hope that the promptitude of your Genius will now be evidenced. I must however recommend to you the Establishment and support of the most rigid and exact Discipline on Board of your Ship. This is so essential both in Officers and Men that I am determined never to overlook any Instances of the Want of it which may fall within my Observation.

Annexed is a List of the Names of Persons to whom you are to Address your Prizes.[3] I sincerely wish you Health and a pleasant and successful Cruize, and am Sir, your most obedient Servant

RM

MS: AM LbC, MdAN.

1. The Continental frigate *Hague* (formerly the *Deane*) was being refitted in Boston after returning from a cruise under Captain Samuel Nicholson, whose conduct was currently the subject of a court of inquiry. RM enclosed these instructions in his letter to Thomas Russell of August 8, evidently with the name of the recipient left blank. Since Nicholson's status was uncertain, Russell, following RM's orders, apparently assigned the command to Manley, who had only recently been exchanged. To RM's dismay, Manley did not set sail until after September 11. He cruised in the West Indies until his return to Boston in May 1783, making several captures, including the *Baille,* the last valuable prize taken during the Revolution. Upon his return Manley was arrested and court-martialed on charges made by one of his officers. The court, which sat intermittently at Boston between September 16 and December 3, 1783, found Manley guilty, and RM confirmed the court's sentence that his commission be revoked. See Stephen T. Powers, "Robert Morris and the Courts-Martial of Captains Samuel Nicholson and John Manley of the Continental Navy," *Military Affairs,* XLIV (1980), 13–17; and RM's Circular to John Barry and Manley, August 13, RM to Thomas Russell, September 17, and Diary, October 18.

2. On the importance of the second objective, see notes to Diary, June 18, 1782.

3. The enclosed list has not been found but the names probably were identical to the ones RM sent to John Barry in letters of July 12 and 17, 1782.

To Thomas Russell

Marine Office 8 Augu[s]t 1782

Sir,

I have been duly favored with your Letters of the fifth and seventeenth Instant.[1] I pray you to accept my Thanks not only for the Pains you have taken and the Exertions you have made but for the generous Offer of Advances which your Conduct has so well supported.

I am very sorry that I cannot at present apply to Congress in favor of Captain Samuel Smith.[2] I wish much to have such Men as you describe him to be in the public Service and I hope the Time is not far off when there will be openings for their Admission but at present there are so many supernumerary Lieutenants in the Navy that it would be unjust.

I presume that Mr Lovell[3] has obviated entirely the Necessity of making you Remittances as I learn from him that he has made you a considerable Payment in Bills and as I hope and expect that whatever Ballance may remain will be paid soon from the Produce of your Taxes. It is I am sure unnecessary for me to say that I shall be glad of the Accounts whenever they can be transmitted.

The Dissentions between Capt Nicholson and his Officers are certainly disagreable but I am not sorry that they have broken out afresh because otherwise I perceive from your Letter that I should have been under the Necessity of disagreing to the Compromise. While I know nothing of their Animosities and Charges they with Respect to me have no Existence; but when once a Charge of criminal Nature is made the public Interest is concerned in prosecuting the accused and it shall always be done notwithstanding any after Reconciliations between Parties and Witnesses.[4]

I enclose Instructions with a Blank for the Name.[5] You will put in that of Samuel Nicholson unless the Court of Enquiry should be of Opinion that he ought to be tried by a Court Martial in which Case you will insert the Name of the eldest Captain with you.

I enclose the Copy of an Act of Congress of the 10 July 1782 relating to the Distribution of Prizes[6] which you will please to take Notice of and communicate to those whom it may concern, particularly to the Officers and Men of this Frigate which you will observe from the Instructions is now called the Hague.[7] I am Sir your most obedient and humble Servant.

RM

MS: AM LbC, MdAN.
1. The letters, presumably of the preceding month, have not been found. Russell was the deputy agent of marine for New England.
2. See RM to Russell, October 15.
3. James Lovell, receiver of Continental taxes for Massachusetts.
4. See notes to RM's Determination on the Court of Inquiry on Samuel Nicholson, October 17.
5. These were probably the instructions to John Manley of August 8.
6. On this act, see notes to RM to the President of Congress, June 20, 1782.
7. For the renaming of the *Deane,* see the Secretary of Congress to RM, June 4, 1782.

To George Washington

Philada. August 8th. 1782

Dear Sir

Having occasion to Answer a letter lately received from a Mr. Cruden in New York, I beg leave to trouble you with the care of sending it in by such opportunity as may first occur.[1]

I am preparing Money for the Contractors. Their demands so immediately on the back of the Pay Master Generals Notes due the 1st Instant press me closely.[2] I am most truely Dear Sir Your affectionate humble Servant[3]

R Morris

His Excy Genl Washington

ENDORSED: Philada. 8th. Augt. 1782/from/Honble. Mr. Morris/requesting to forward a letter/only/acknowledged 23d.

MS: ALS, Andre deCoppet Collection, NjP.

1. See RM to John Cruden, August 5, and notes.

2. For a discussion of RM's difficulties in paying the contractors, see notes to Comfort Sands, Walter Livingston, William Duer, and Daniel Parker to RM, September 11.

3. This letter to Washington was delivered by Richard Wells. See Washington to RM, August 23.

To James Lovell

Office of Finance 8th. Augt. 1782

I received your several Favors of the twelfth and twentieth of last month,[1] the Contents of which I approve of. The Money you lent to Major Franks he promises to repay here and when he does it will be credited to you as a Remittance for the Sales of Bills of Exchange.

MS: Ofcl LbC, DLC.

1. Letters not found. Lovell was the receiver of Continental taxes for Massachusetts.

To Jonathan Dickinson Sergeant and Jared Ingersoll

Office of Finance 8. August 1782[1]

I do myself the Honor to enclose you certain Papers relating to the Cause between the United States and Cornelius Sweers in which you are Counsel for the United States.[2] I am to request that you will take the proper Measures for securing their Interest.

MS: Ofcl LbC, DLC.

1. Sergeant (1746–1793) was a lawyer who had been a New Jersey delegate to Congress in 1776 and 1777 before removing to Pennsylvania to serve as attorney general, 1777–1780. Ingersoll (1749–1822) was an English-trained, Philadelphia lawyer who had been a delegate to Congress from Pennsylvania in 1780 and 1781. DAB; Biog. Dir. Cong.

2. The enclosed papers have not been found. On the Sweers case, see Diary, June 5, 1782, and notes.

Diary: August 9, 1782

I sent for Mr. Jno. Chaloner and urged to him the necessity and propriety of supporting the Exchange having been told that he was on the point of selling a large Sum very low. He agreed that such offers had been made to him as I suggested and I proposed a plan by which that Sum might be disposed of more agreeably to which he assented.[1]

Having agreed to deposite the last Order given to me by the Supreme Executive Council of Pensylvania on their Treasurer at the Bank in Security for the advances made by them on the Public Account I directed Mr Swanwick to deposite the same and take up Mr Sands and other notes now there.[2]

I sent for the Paymaster General and agreed to authorize him to Issue new notes to such Officers as had no[t] received of the former.[3]

Lieut. Stevens of the 3d Virginia Regiment[4] applied for some of Mr Pierces notes and I promised that Mr Pierce will be authorized to Issue them.

Mr John Hall applied for Money due to him by the Commissary Genl. of Military Stores Depart[ment].[5] I told him as I did Jno. Conway and several other poor Men who have pay due from that Department that Mr Hodgdon should be furnished with means to pay as soon as possible.

Capt. Allibone and Colo. Patton called to inform me they have thoughts of selling the Ship General Washington when she comes up again. They informed me of this because I had last Voyage expressed a desire to buy her.[6]

Walter Livingston Esqr. and Mr. Edwards two of the Contractors for the moving Army called when I complained very much of their having suffered the Army to want Provisions, asserted that I have complied with my part of the Contract, but that they have not fullfilled the Expectations they gave me when that Contract was made nor aided or assisted me agreeable to promise. Mr. Edwards urged many Causes which had Conspired to disable them from doing these things and amongst other Reasons he urged that the Eastern States not paying their Taxes made the People afraid to trust them with Cattle &c. &c.[7]

Mr. Jos. Wilson[8] came and proposed to purchase Bills for 200,000 Livres deliverable the 15th. December next and to pay on Account thereof £6,000 the 15th. of this month, £2,000 the 15th Septr., £2,000 the 15th October and the balance on the 15th November and as I had Consulted with Mr. Chaloner on this Subject and we had agreed that it is adviseable to Accept 6/1½d per five Livres, I agreed with Mr Wilson on these terms, Mr Chaloner being[9] to supply half the Bills and receive half the payments and I am to supply the other half.[10]

Lewis R. Morris Esquire called to inform me of a mistake made in the Bills given for the first Quarters Salary of the foreign Ministers &c. which I agreed to rectify by giving a Bill for the Deficiency.[11]

Wrote a Letter to Francis Wade Esqr.

Wrote a Letter to His Excellency Genl Washington.

Issued a warrant on Mr. Swanwick in favor of Doctor Bond £60.0.0.

1. John Chaloner, the Philadelphia agent of Jeremiah Wadsworth and John Carter, contractors for the French army, had recently been asked by François de Barbé-Marbois, the French consul general, to raise the price of bills of exchange but had replied that previous attempts to raise the price to 6 shillings 6 pence for 5 livres

had failed. When on August 6 or 7 Chaloner was asked by potential purchasers to sell bills for up to 250,000 livres, with £7,000 to be paid immediately and £2,000 per month until paid, the bills to be delivered when payment was completed in November, he offered to sell at 6 shillings instead of the 5 shillings 6 pence preferred by the purchasers. According to Chaloner's description of his meeting this day with the Superintendent, the same parties applied to RM. "Their intention was evidently to take up finally with the lowest offer and therefore kept plying between us. He wished to have the Sale and yet offerd not to interfere if I would stick at and demand 6/–. I then proposed that at whatever price the sale might be negotiated or by whom each of us should supply half the bills and receive half of each payment to this Mr. Morris chearfully acceded and as I by agreement with him peremptorily asks 6/3 we suppose they will take 6/1½. The talk of Peace perhaps may influence them all that has appeared in publick on this subject you have inclosed; the credibility of which say (unconditional Independence) is greatly lessend by the report of sundry Captains librated on Parole and who arived this day, they say all the Capts is sent out and previous thereto a couple from each state was brought before Admiral Digby who informed them that America had got the Independence they so long fought for and that if Congress did not accept of it and make Peace thereon He hoped the People would choose another Congress. A doubt of its acceptance announced in this formal manner raises a suspicion that it is Conditional. . . . Mr Morris declares he fully beleives it to be unconditional." See Chaloner to Wadsworth and Carter, August 6, 8, and 9, 1782, Chaloner and White Letterbook, PHi; see also below in this Diary at note 8, and Diary, August 20, and notes. On the news of peace talks, see Diary, August 8, and notes.

2. See Diary, August 8, and notes.

3. However, see Diary, August 12.

4. First Lieutenant William Stevens (d. 1825) had been taken prisoner during the siege of Charleston in 1780 and was now on parole. Heitman, *Register.*

5. On the money owed to Hall, see the estimate cited in notes to Diary, June 1, 1782.

6. For RM's purchase of the *General Washington,* see notes to Diary, May 15, 1782.

7. For a discussion of the eventual dissolution of the West Point and Moving Army contract, see notes to Comfort Sands, Walter Livingston, William Duer, and Daniel Parker to RM, September 11.

8. Joseph Wilson (d. 1809), an Irish merchant residing in Philadelphia; he later returned to Ireland. Campbell, *Sons of St. Patrick,* 140.

9. The copyist evidently omitted one or more words here.

10. See note 1 above.

11. On the payment of salaries to American ministers abroad, see notes to RM to the President of Congress, May 8, 1782.

To Francis Wade

Office of Finance 9. Augt. 1782

Sir,

I have been duly honored with your Letter of the eighth Instant[1] and have now the Honor to enclose a Copy of the Act of Congress recommending a Stay of Suits against public Officers.[2] The Act which I had put into the Hands of Lawyers is still there. The Object of it is to enable the Commissioners employed by the United States to recover the Public Property which Individuals may be possessed of, Debts due to the United States &ca.[3] I heartily wish the State of the public Treasury admitted of paying all Debts due by the United States but this [is] not the Case. You will always have with you my best Wishes and heartiest Support in prosecuting and bringing to

Trial and Punishment all Defaulters and all who are guilty of any Fraud to the Detriment of the Public. In so doing you will certainly merit the Aid and Thanks of all good Men. I am Sir your most obedient Servant

RM

MS: Ofcl LbC, DLC.

1. Letter not found. Wade, a deputy quartermaster in Delaware, was being sued by creditors of the United States; he had also brought suit on behalf of the United States to recover a debt. See Diary, March 23, and notes, April 10, and notes, and August 15, 1782, and notes.

2. On this act, see notes to the Quartermaster General to RM, March 8, 1782.

3. Congress on February 3, 1778, directed the Committee of Commerce to recommend persons to enter legal prosecution in state courts for recovery of "all commercial debts" due to the United States and to claim Congress's share of prize captures. This resolution was followed on February 9 by a request that the states pass laws to facilitate the recovery of debts due the United States. Congress, however, was reluctant to stipulate a format for such laws and neglected to furnish any guidelines to the states (*JCC*, XV, 1310). When the Department of Finance was created on February 7, 1781, the Superintendent was given the duty "to compel the payment of all moneys due to the United States, and in this official character, or in such manner as the laws of the respective states shall direct, to prosecute on behalf of the United States, for all delinquencies respecting the public revenue and expenditures," and on April 27 following was authorized to appoint persons to defend or engage in legal prosecutions in his behalf. Later, when the ordinances of February 20 and 27, 1782, for settling public accounts were adopted, Congress again rejected the idea of instructing the states as to the terms desired in an act for recovering debts due to the United States and merely requested that they pass enabling legislation. Nevertheless, at RM's direction Richard Peters and James Wilson were drafting a model act (see Diary, April 10, 1782). It was probably this proposed law that RM asked the Philadelphia lawyer William Lewis to review in July. After Lewis objected to several parts of the act, RM accepted his offer to draft another (see Diary, July 16, 1782). But as this letter to Wade indicates, the model act was not yet completed.

Of all the states, Pennsylvania made the fullest, if not the earliest, compliance with Congress's requests. On August 24 the assembly appointed a committee to prepare and bring in a bill conformable to Congress's February 20 ordinance on state accounts. Following prolonged consideration of the committee's bill in the assembly and opinions from the judges of the state supreme court and Attorney General William Bradford, Jr., a revised bill was enacted on March 20, 1783, as "An Act for the Settlement of the Public Accounts of the United States of America." When on January 28, 1783, Lewis brought to RM his draft act to recover debts owed the United States (see Diary of that date), the Financier indicated his intention to transmit it to the Pennsylvania Assembly, but whether or not Lewis's formulation had an impact on the bill's gestation has not been ascertained. In its final form, however, the act represented the state's response to all aspects of the enabling legislation Congress requested in its ordinances of February 20 and 27, 1782, on the settlement of state and departmental accounts, including the recovery of debts owed to the United States. RM enclosed a copy of the Pennsylvania act in a circular to the state governors of May 20, 1783. While not actually recommending passage of the same act by other states, the Superintendent observed that the states would have to give assistance to the commissioners of accounts if they were to carry out their duties. Nevertheless, not all states passed enabling legislation during RM's term of office. On the Pennsylvania act, see *Minutes of the First[-Third] Session, of the Sixth General Assembly, of the Commonwealth of Pennsylvania* . . . [October 20, 1781–September 21, 1782] (Philadelphia, 1781[–1782]), 673; *Minutes of the First Session, of the Seventh General Assembly, of the Commonwealth of Pennsylvania* . . . [October 28–December 4, 1782] (Philadelphia, [1782]), 723, 803, 806, 818, 825, 860, 870, 875; and Mitchell and Flanders, eds., *Statutes of Pennsylvania*, XI, 71–80. See also RM to the Governor of Connecticut, July 31, 1782, and notes, to

William Denning, February 12, and to John Avery, June 23, 1783, Joseph Pennell to RM, May 25, 1784, RM's Circular to the Governors of the States, May 26, and the Governor of Virginia to RM, June 11, 1784. For other examples of state enabling legislation, all passed previous to the Pennsylvania act, see William Waller Hening, ed., *The Statutes at Large; Being a Collection of All the Laws of Virginia, from the First Session of the Legislature, in the Year 1619* (Richmond, etc., 1810–1823), XI, 32–33; Wilson, comp., *Acts of New Jersey*, 269–270; Hoadly and Labaree, eds. *Public Records of Connecticut*, IV, 163–164, 168–171; and *Acts and Laws of Massachusetts*, 1782–1783, pp. 135–136. See also *At the General Assembly of the Governor and Company of Rhode-Island and Providence Plantations . . .* [October 1783 session] [Providence, 1783], 31–32; and for an act passed in 1785 after RM's retirement from office, Thomas Cooper and David J. McCord, eds., *Statutes at Large of South Carolina* (Columbia, 1836–1873), IV, 667–668. On the congressional acts of February 20 and 27, 1782, for the settlement of state and departmental accounts, see notes to RM to the President of Congress, December 10, 1781, and February 18, 1782.

To George Washington

Office of Finance, 9th. Augst. 1782

Sir,

I had the Honor to receive your Excellency's Favor of the Fifth Instant, last Evening. I beg Leave to refer, for a State of Matters between the public and the Contractors, to mine of the Fifth Instant. I should long since have appointed the Officer you mention, could I have got a proper Person. I had applied to General Cornell, and he had (in a manner) undertaken, but afterwards declined. Colo. Tilgman will give your Excellency an Account of some Conversation with him on the Subject.[1] I wait to hear from you or him, or both, before I go into an Appointment. I pray you Sir, to beleive that I am with the greatest Esteem and Respect Your Excellency's most obedient and humble Servant[2]

Robt Morris

His Excellency General Washington

ENDORSED: Philada: 9th. Augt. 1782/from/Honble. Mr. Morris/Affairs of the Contract/ Acknowledged 23d.
MSS: LS, Washington Papers, DLC; Ofcl LbC, DLC.
1. See Diary, August 5, and notes.
2. This letter was delivered by Richard Wells. See Washington to RM, August 23.

Diary: August 10, 1782

Mr. Robt. Hazelhurst[1] applied to know the price of Bills of Exchange as he desired to give me the preference of his money. I asked 6/3d for five Livres and he said he would return if he could not supply himself cheaper.

Mr. Parr applied for money for the Contractors at Lancaster.

Letters from Mr. Sands and from Mr. Perkins for money &c.[2]

Letter and report of a Committee from Genl Scott for my Consideration and remarks.[3]

Colo. Humpton brought a Letter from Frederick Town to shew me respecting the enlistment of Germans &c.[4]

Mr. Pierce made application for money and several arrangements taken with Mr Swanwick to provide Money &c.

Wrote a Letter to Monsr Grand.

Wrote a Letter to the Comptroller.

Issued a Warrant on Mr. Swanwick in favor of Jos.
Pennell   £ 70.5.0

Issued a Warrant on Mr. Swanwick in favor of the
Bank for Interest   147.3.0

1. Robert Hazlehurst, brother of Isaac Hazlehurst, was "a Young Gentleman bred in the Mercantile Line" who moved to Charleston, South Carolina, early in 1783 and established a business firm under his own name. See RM to Nathanael Greene, February 8, 1782; RM to Tench Tilghman, June 28, 1784, NNPM; *Journals of the House of Representatives of the Commonwealth of Pennsylvania. Beginning the twenty-eighth Day of November, 1776, and Ending the Second Day of October, 1781. With the Proceedings of the several Committees and Conventions, Before and at the Commencement of the American Revolution. Vol. I* (Philadelphia, 1782), 691–692; and [Robert Morris], *In the Account of Property* ([Philadelphia], n.d.), 28.

2. Letters not found.

3. The letter from John Morin Scott, a New York delegate to Congress, has not been found, but the report undoubtedly was the one he wrote as chairman of a committee appointed on July 29 to prepare instructions for a commissioner to settle the accounts of American agents in Europe. For a discussion of his report and RM's response, see notes to RM to the President of Congress, May 8, 1782.

4. Letter not found. For Humpton's previous involvement in the recruitment of German prisoners, see Diary, July 18, 1782, and notes.

To the Comptroller of the Treasury
(James Milligan)

Office of Finance 10 Augt. 1782

Sir,

It is some time since I received Mr. Grands Accounts. Shortly after I directed a Translation. This is just now brought to me and I enclose it with the Original.[1] I do not expect that you can go into a Settlement of it at present but I wish you to make a very careful Perusal and Examination, to compare it with such Accounts as you have which are connected with it, and to send me such Observations on the whole as may arise from it. I am Sir your most obedient and humble Servant.

RM

MS: Ofcl LbC, DLC.

1. Upon deciding, at Benjamin Franklin's request, to retain Grand as banker to the United States in Paris, RM directed him in a letter of December 3, 1781, to close and transmit his old accounts and open new accounts for subsequent transactions. Grand apparently submitted his old accounts in one of the missing letters RM acknowledged in his replies of July 5 and September 28, 1782, but neither the original nor the

translated accounts have been found. Grand evidently did not fully understand RM's directions as to the separate accounts he was to open for the Superintendent's transactions, and the Financier elaborated them at length in the September 28 letter.

From William Churchill Houston

Trenton [New Jersey] 10 August 1782[1]

Sir

I am advised by Mr Clarke one of our Delegates in Congress that 'an Enquiry is making how many of the States have recognised the Appointments of Receivers of Continental Taxes pursuant to the recommendation of Congress of 2 November 1781.'[2] As Resort will probably be made, if not made already, to the Office of Finance for Information on this Subject, the last Tax-Act published in one of the Newspapers lately sent, shows the Attention of our Legislature to that requisition, and I believe in every necessary Respect a Receiver of Continental Taxes is amply recognised here.[3] I am, Sir &c

WCH

Robt Morris Esqr, Superintendt &c.

1782 Receipt of Continental Taxes in the State of New Jersey from August 3 to August 10 inclusive
To Cash received from the State-Treasurer one Thousand eight Hundred and sixty Dollars   Dlls 1860

ENDORSED: Letter to Mr Morris Su/perintendent of Finance/10 Aug 1782 with re/turn of 1860 Dlls
MS: ADftS with subjoined ADft return, Houston Collection, NjP.
    1. Houston was the receiver of Continental taxes for New Jersey.
    2. On this act, see notes to RM to the President of Congress, November 5, 1781. Abraham Clark of New Jersey had been chairman of a committee which recently reported on the receivers' publications. See notes to RM to William Whipple, June 4, 1782.
    3. New Jersey and Massachusetts explicitly recognized the office of receiver of Continental taxes by title in state tax levies to fulfill the Continental requisition for 1782. Only New Jersey complied substantially with the request of Congress that state tax collectors pay over receipts on Continental account directly to the Continental receivers rather than to the state treasuries. Rhode Island had initially agreed to, then quickly rescinded, such a measure. Massachusetts empowered its state treasurer to pay the taxes levied for the requisition to receiver James Lovell. Without specifically recognizing the office of receiver, by August 1782 Rhode Island, Connecticut, and New York had facilitated the receivers' operations by authorizing their treasurers to pay Continental revenues for 1782 to the order of the Superintendent of Finance or the person appointed by him.
    Other states adopted procedures that bypassed the receivers altogether or took no action. Pennsylvania required that RM draw on the state treasurer for the funds. Maryland's treasurer was authorized to remit the revenue directly to the Continental treasury or pay it to the order of Congress. South Carolina skirted the issue by levying taxes only in specific supplies handled by state appointees. New Hampshire, Virginia, and Delaware had not yet specified any mode by which their taxes would be turned over to the Continental authorities. However, on December 28, 1782, Virginia authorized its treasurer to turn over a portion of the state's quota to the Continental receiver, while Delaware's legislation, not enacted until 1783, empowered its treasurer to make

payment to the order of Congress or the Superintendent of Finance. North Carolina and Georgia had as yet taken no action at all to fulfill the requisition for 1782.

A clause in Congress's requisition for 1783 renewed the earlier request to the states regarding the mode of payment to the receivers (see the headnote to RM to the President of Congress, July 30). Coming just a week after Congress had demanded a conclusive answer from Rhode Island on the impost of 1781, the recommendation drew a pointed response from the Rhode Island delegates that defined the constitutional import of the issue. Attacking the clause, principally because it put the receiver beyond state control and would "in its operation and tendency be repugnant to the Letter and Spirit of the Confederation," the delegates urged the state assembly to "check the oblique and covert, as well as the direct and open approaches of Despotism" (see Burnett, ed., *Letters*, VI, 513). On the constitutional significance of the receivers and RM's insistence on Congress's right to collect Continental taxes, see notes to RM to the President of Congress, November 5, 1781; RM to the Governor of Rhode Island, October 24, 1782; the headnote to the Draft Ordinance for the Impost of 1781 in Appendix I of this volume; and RM to the President of Congress, March 8, 1783.

For state tax legislation in 1782 as it concerns the receivers, see notes to the following documents: William Whipple to RM, May 20 and June 30 (New Hampshire), RM to James Lovell, May 14 (Massachusetts), to George Olney, June 23 and September 17 (Rhode Island), to Hezekiah Merrill, May 14 (Connecticut), Alexander Hamilton to RM, July 22 (New York), Houston to RM, May 25 and June 15 (New Jersey), RM to the Speaker of the Pennsylvania Assembly, February 13 (Pennsylvania), Daniel of St. Thomas Jenifer to RM, June 14 (Maryland), the Governor of North Carolina to RM, June 22 (North Carolina), RM to George Abbott Hall, June 10, and Nathanael Greene to RM, March 9, 1782 (South Carolina). On Virginia, see RM to George Webb, June 11, 1782; and Hutchinson and Rutland, eds., *Madison Papers*,V, 457–458. On Delaware, see *Laws of the State of Delaware* ... [October 14, 1700–August 18, 1797] (New Castle, Del., 1797), II, 751–762; and *Votes and Proceedings of the House of Assembly of the Delaware State* (Wilmington, 1783), 57–58.

To Fizeaux, Grand and Company

Office of Finance 10 Augt. 1782[1]

This serves to advise of my having drawn on you as Superintendant of Finance of the United States of America the undermentioned four Setts of Bills of Exchange No. 1 a 4 inclusive amounting to 9929 Livrs. 10 S. Tourn.

Viz: No. 1. July   16, 1782, in favor of Haym Solomon   4776. 5
       2. "   17   do.   do.   734.15
       3. "   29   do.   do.   1538.10
       4. Augt: 10   do.   do.   2880.
                                          ————— 9929.10

These Bills you will please to Honor and punctually Pay on Account of the United States of North America.

P.S. I take it for granted that Mons. Grand Banker in Paris has prepared you to pay these drafts and you are to reimburse yourselves on him.

MS: Ofcl LbC, DLC.

1. Fizeaux, Grand and Company was a banking firm in Amsterdam with close ties to Ferdinand Grand, banker to the United States in Paris.

To Ferdinand Grand

Office of Finance 10. Augt. 1782[1]

My last Letter to you was of the sixth Instant with a List of Bills of Exchange of that date drawn by me as Superintendant of Finance at thirty and sixty days sight on you in favor of different Persons as therein mentioned numbered 180 to 250 inclusive making seventy one Setts and amounting to four hundred and seventy one thousand nine hundred and eighty nine Livres 12S. 10D. Tournois.

Herewith you will receive another List of Bills drawn by me as Superintendant of Finance at thirty and sixty days Sight on you in favor of sundry Persons as there specified numbered 251 to 298 inclusive making forty eight Setts and amounting to two hundred and thirty nine thousand seven hundred and forty two Livres 13S. 4D. Tournois.

These, as well as my former Bills you will be pleased to honor, and pay punctually on Account of the United States of North America.

P.S. I have also drawn four Bills on Messrs. Fizeau Grand and Co. of Amsterdam amounting to Lrs. 9929.10S. for which they are to reimburse on you.[2]

MS: Ofcl LbC, DLC.
1. Grand was banker to the United States in Paris.
2. See the preceding letter.

From the Quartermaster General (Timothy Pickering)

Philaa. Augt. 14 [i.e. 10]. 1782[1]

Some unexpected business occurring, I was prevented getting in town to-day in time to see you. And as I intend to set out next Monday morning for the army, I shall not have that pleasure, unless you have any commands which require my coming again to town.

Permit me to renew my application for £148 to pay Van Heer according to my promise, and for £13.18.1½ to pay Jacob Baker for thread furnished for making knapsacks, which was by agreement payable in three months from the 27th of April last. These sums Colo. Miles will receive when you order them to be paid. He will also wait your determination on the several estimates laying before you which have been presented by me.

I forgot to mention that in about a month Colo. Miles will call on you for money to pay for the making the waggoners shirts, to the amount of about £25—unless you previously direct another mode of payment.

MS: LbC, WDC, DNA.
1. This misdated letter almost certainly belongs to Saturday, August 10. It is filed in Pickering's letterbook (WDC, no. 85, p. 158) between a letter of August 9 and his second letter to RM of August 10. Both letters to RM were acknowledged in the Diary of Monday, August 12, presumably the day Pickering left his rented farm at the Falls of the Schuylkill about five miles outside of Philadelphia for the journey to headquarters. He was at Morristown, New Jersey, by August 14 and at camp in New Windsor, New York, by August 17 (WDC, no. 85, p. 164, no. 84, p. 47). Perhaps the most important reason for Pickering's absence from headquarters is explained in the Quartermaster General to RM, July 17, and RM's reply of July 30, 1782. For other, more personal, reasons, see the explanation offered in Gerard H. Clarfield, *Timothy Pickering and the American Republic* (Pittsburgh, 1980), 75–77.

From the Quartermaster General (Timothy Pickering)

Philaa. Augt. 10. 1782

Mr. Wister will present you an order drawn by me in favour of William Wister for £332.10.8 for sixty eight pieces of linens[x] purchased by my direction, to make shirts for waggoners and artificers. These shirts will be charged at their full cost to the receivers of them, on account of their pay, and to their amount save an immediate advance of money. I have directed a few woolens for jackets and over-alls to be purchased on the same princi- ples. I could have saved you from the trouble of this application, by inclos- ing some of the bills you lately gave me, but then I should have thought it proper to advise you of it, as they would be presented to Mr. Swanwick for payment. That course in this case which you prefer I shall pursue.[1]

[x N.B. To be paid in three months.][2]

MS: LbC, WDC, DNA.
    1. Receipt of this letter was noted in the Diary of August 12.
    2. Brackets thus in manuscript.

From George Washington

Head Quarters [Newburgh, New York]. 11th Augst. 1782

Sir

I have received by Colo Tilghman your Letter of the 5th instant, with a particular State of your Accounts with the Contractors for Money advanced them.

I am much obliged by this Communication, as it will enable me to combat the Constant Assertions which are made by Mr Sands,[1] that the Contract is not fulfilled on your part.

I am very glad to find that Mr Edwards, one of the Beef Contrac- tors, is gone on to Phila. for the purpose of investigating with cer- tainty the true Causes of the failure which they experience in the Article of Money. Your free Conversation with that Gentleman will I hope bring on Explanations that may prove very usefull in the fu- ture conducting the Contracts.[2]

For the Satisfaction of the Comptroller I have the Honor to in- close you Copy of my General Orders respecting Issues to be made under the two Contracts.[3] I have the Honor to be &c.

GW

Hono Robt Morris

ENDORSED: Head Quarters. 11th Augst 1782/to/Hono Robt Morris
MSS: Dft in the writing of Jonathan Trumbull, Jr., Washington Papers, DLC; Varick transcript, Washington Papers, DLC.
    1. Comfort Sands, one of the principals in the combined West Point and Moving Army contract.
    2. For RM's discussions with Timothy Edwards, a beef subcontractor for the Mov- ing Army, see Diary, August 9.
    3. The question of issues under the combined West Point and Moving Army con- tract had been raised in a letter of August 1 from the Comptroller of the Treasury which RM had sent to Washington. The general orders Washington enclosed were probably those of April 29, 1782, which set the bounds of the two contracts. See also Proposals from Comfort Sands and Company, printed under September 2, and notes. See Fitzpatrick, ed., *Writings of Washington*, XXIV, 183.

From Abraham Yates, Jr.

Albany [New York] 11th Augt. 1782[1]

Sir,

As I have not yet been favoured with an Answer to my letter of the 4th of May last, I apprehend I shall meet with Some Embarrassment in the Execution of the Duties of my Office unless I receive Instructions for my Conduct.

You will undoubtedly have observed from my Returns that the Bills of Exchange in my possession are very Inadequate to the payment of the Demands which will soon become due for Interest. Convinced that a partial payment will be attended with bad Consequences and Conceiving myself not authorized to keep back such Payment while I have any Bills in my possession, I must again beg your attention to the Subject-Matters of my former Letter and again take the Liberty to repeat that my necessities require an immediate Supply of Mony.[2]

Inclosed I do myself the pleasure to Transmit you returns for the Month of July last.[3] I am Sir your most Obedient Servant[4]

A. Y. Junr. C.L.O.

The Honble. Robt. Morris Esqr. Supdt. of Finance

MS: LbC, Continental Loan Office Letterbook, Yates Papers, NN.

1. Yates was the Continental loan officer of New York. He had originally written the date of the "10th" then struck it out.

2. Yates had already written to the New York delegates in Congress on August 9 asking them to find out whether interest on loan office certificates in bills of exchange was to be paid, and, if so, advising them of his immediate need for $47,700 in bills of exchange (letter in Continental Loan Office Letterbook, Yates Papers, NN). On the stoppage of interest payments, which was proposed by RM and eventually adopted by Congress, see RM's Report to Congress on the Continental Loan Offices, June 13, 1782, and notes.

3. Returns not found.

4. RM replied to Yates on August 22.

Diary: August 12, 1782

Mr Pierce applied respecting a further Issue of his Notes[1] which I declined and told him that I will draw orders in his favor on Mr. Swanwick.

Mr. Jos. Traversie applied for his Money ordered by Act of Congress[2] and I signed a Warrant for 100 Dollars.

Two Letters from Colo. Pickering advising of his Drafts &c.[3]

Major Franks came respecting his Accounts which I desired might be made out and laid before me. Had a good deal of Conversation with him respecting his Voyage.[4]

Mr. Jos. [James] Geary Clerk to William Duer Esqr. with Letters from him as Contractor complaining loudly for want of Money &c.[5]

Genl. Gates called respecting his Affairs.

Mr. Willm. Turnbull called for 1500 Dollars on Account of the Contract for Albany &c. I signed a Warrant for the Same.

The Hon. Secy. at War called to shew me a Letter from Genl Washington ordering Colo. Armands Legion to March to the Southward and desiring Money to enable them to Move &c.[6] I desired an Estimate.

Benjm. Town for Money which I promised to morrow.[7]

Doctr. Brownson applies for two months pay promised by the Secy at War and as he did not receive for January and February last I signed a Warrant for 240 Dollars.[8]

Sundry Soldiers of the German Regiment applied with a Petition for their pay &c. I told them it is not possible for me to pay them, having no Money.[9]

Mr White of New York State applied for Employment.

Colo. Miles applies for Money but in vain. I have it not.

I sent for Colo. Wood of Winchester and proposed his undertaking the Business of liberating the German Prisoners of War on the Terms fixed by Congress &c. to which he agreed and I am to prepare his Instructions.[10]

Lieut Beaulieu applied for the Balance of his Account being permitted by Congress to return to France &c. I desired time to Consider on the Subject.[11]

Mr. Geo. Eddy agreed to Set off to morrow for the Jersey and to pay a Sum of money not less than 2,000 Guineas to Mr. Henry Ramson [Remsen] at Morris Town for the Use of Sands Livingston and Co. Contractors for the moving Army for which I am to Account with him.[12]

This morning Mr Oliver Pollock of New Orleans called on me and took up all the morning in conversing on his Affairs.[13]

1. Concerning this request by Paymaster General John Pierce, see Diary, August 8, and notes.

2. Joseph Traversie, a Canadian, had been appointed a captain by General Richard Montgomery during the Canadian campaign, though he had no commission from Congress; he was later "employed on secret service to the Northward." On August 8, 1782, Congress directed RM to pay him $100 in full for "services and support" since November 15, 1780, the point to which his accounts had been settled, and granted him a monthly allowance of $10 until further order.

3. The letters are dated August 10.

4. See Diary, August 5, and notes.

5. These letters are identified in notes to Duer to RM, August 2.

6. For the letter directing Charles Armand's corps to join Nathanael Greene's southern army, see Washington to Secretary at War Benjamin Lincoln, August 6, 1782, Fitzpatrick, ed., Writings of Washington, XXIV, 469–470.

7. Benjamin Towne (d. 1793), printer of the Pennsylvania Evening Post, 1775–1784, evidently was owed money for printing inspection returns, muster rolls, and

other forms for the War Department. See *DAB;* Dwight L. Teeter, "Benjamin Towne: The Precarious Career of a Persistent Printer," *PMHB*, LXXXIX (1965), 316–330; Treasury Waste Book C, p. 516, Records of the United States General Accounting Office, RG 217, DNA; and Diary, August 14.

8. For the two months' pay given to army officers, see RM to George Washington, January 26, 1782 (second letter), and notes.

9. On the pay of the disbanded German Battalion, see Diary, October 26, 1781, and notes, and January 2 and 4, 1782. The petition has not been found.

10. See RM to James Wood, August 14, and notes.

11. On Louis Joseph de Beaulieu, see Diary, July 17, 1782, and notes, and for his eventual payment, Diary, August 14, 19, and 21.

12. This attempt to pay the contractors failed, apparently because Eddy was unable to obtain the money he was to give to Remsen. See Diary, August 14, 20, 27, 30, and RM to Remsen, August 21, and to Walter Livingston, August 25, and notes; for RM's role in the eventual dissolution of the combined West Point and Moving Army contract, see notes to Comfort Sands, Walter Livingston, William Duer, and Daniel Parker to RM, September 11.

13. It is possible that this last entry refers to the morning of August 13 and was meant to be included in the Diary of that date. On the settlement of Pollock's accounts as Congress's commercial agent at New Orleans, see Diary, September 10, and notes, and RM's Report to Congress of a Letter to Bernardo de Gálvez, November 21, 1781, and notes. For his current efforts to obtain commodities from the United States on account of money owed him, see Diary, August 21, 24, 30, and September 2, 25, and 27.

From Benjamin Franklin

Honble R Morris Esqr.   Passy August 12th 1782

Sir

I have received, many of them at the same time, your sundry letters of March 23, April 8 and 17, May 17, 18,[1] two 23 two and 29. It would be a Satisfaction to me if you would likewise mention from time to time the Dates of those you receive from me.

Most of your Letters pressing my obtaining more money for the Present year. The late Losses suffer'd in the W. Indies,[2] and the unforseen necessary expences the Reparation there and here must occasion render it more difficult, and I am told impossible. Tho' the good Disposition of the Court towards us continues perfect. All I can say on the Head of money more than I have said in preceeding Letters, is, that I confide you will be careful not to Bankrupt your Banker by your Drafts, and I will do my utmost that those you draw shall be duly honored.

The Plan you intimate for discharging the Bills in favor of Beaumarchais, tho' well imagined was impracticable.[3] I had accepted them, and he had discounted them, or paid them away, or divided them among his Creditors. They were therefore in different hands with whom I could not manage the Transactions proposed. Besides, I had paid them punctually when they became due, which was before the Receipt of your Letter on that subject.

That he was furnish'd with his Funds by the Government here is a Supposition of which no foundation appears.[4] He says it was by a

Company he had formed: and when he sollicited me to give up a Cargo in part of Payment, he urg'd with Tears in his Eyes the Distress himself and associates were reduc'd to by our Delay of Remittances. I am glad to see that it is intended to appoint a Commissioner to settle all our public Accounts in Europe.[5] I hope he will have better success with M. Beaumarchais than I have had. He has often promised solemnly to render me an Account in two or three Days. Years have since elaps'd and he has not yet done it. Indeed I doubt whether his Books have been so well kept as to make it possible.

You direct me in yours of May 17th. "to pay over into the Hands of Mr Grand on your account such monies belonging to the United States as may be in Europe distinct from those to be advanced for the current year."[6] I would do it with Pleasure if there were any such. There may be indeed some in Holland rais'd by the new Loan,[7] but that is not in my Disposition tho I have no Doubt that Mr Adams will on occasion apply it, in support of your Credit. All the Aids given by the Crown, all the Sums borrow'd of it, and all the Dutch Loans of ten Millions,[8] tho' the Orders to receive have been given to me, the Payments from the *Tresor Royal*, have all been made on my orders in favor of Mr. Grand, and the Money again paid away by him on my Drafts for Public Services and Expences, as you will see by his accounts, so that I never saw or touched a Livre of it, except what I received from him in Discharge of my Salary and some Disbursments. He has even received the whole Six Millions of the Current Year,[9] so that I have nothing in any Shape to pay over to him. On occasion of my lately desiring to know the State of our Funds that I might judge whether I could undertake to Pay what you were directed to Pay Mr. William Lee by Vote[10] of Congress "as soon as the State of Public Finances would admit" Mr Grand wrote me a note with a Short Sketch of their then supposed situation which I enclose.[11] You will Probably have from him as soon as possible a more perfect Account[12] but this will serve to show that I could not prudently comply with your wish in making that Payment to Mr Lee, and I have accordingly declin'd it; the Less unwillingly as he is intitled by the Vote to Interest.

I send herewith the Accounts of the supplies we have received in Goods which I promised in my last. The sum of their Value is included in Settlement made with this Court mentioned in a former Letter.[13] Herewith I also send a Copy of the Contract which has been long in hand, and but lately compleated.[14] The Term of the first yearly payment we are to make, was readily changed at my request from the first to the third year after the Peace; the other marks of the Kings bounty towards us will be seen in the Instrument. The interest already due, and forgiven, amount to more than a Million and half; what might become due before the Peace is uncertain. The Charges, of Exchange, Commissions, Brokerage &ca. &ca. of the Dutch Loan, amount to more than 500,000 Livres, which is also given, so that we have the whole sum net; and are to Pay for it but 4 per cent. This Liquidation of our accounts with the Court was compleated before the Vote of Congress directing it came to hand. Mr Grand examined all the Particulars, and I have no doubt of its being approved.

Mr Grand to whom I have communicated your letter of April 17th. will soon write to you fully.[15] We shall observe the general Rule you give respecting 5th, 6th, 7th and 8th Bills.[16] The attention, care and pains, necessary to prevent by exact accounts of those accepted, and Examination of those offered, Impositions which are often attempted, by presenting at a distant time the 2nd, 3rd, &ca is much greater than I could have imagined. Much has been saved by that attention, of which of late we keep an Account; But the Hazard of Loss by such attempts might be diminished together with the Trouble of examination, by making fewer small Bills.

Your Conduct, Activity and address as Financier and Provider for the Exigencies of the State is much admired and praised here, its good Consequences being so evident, particularly with regard to the rising Credit of our Country, and the Value of Bills. No one but yourself can enjoy your growing Reputation more than I do.

Mr Grand has undertaken to Pay any Ballance that may be found due to Messrs. le Couteulx, out of the Money in his hands.[17] Applying for so small a Sum as 5000 Livres would be giving Trouble for a Trifle as all application for money must be considered in Council.

Mr Grand having already received the whole six Millions, either in money or accepted Bills payable at different Periods, I expect he will deliver up to me the Bills for that Sum which you have drawn upon me; the rather as they express Value received by you. I never heard any mention here of intended Monthly Payments, or that the money could not be obtained but by your drafts. I enclose a Letter by which the Payment was ordered of the last three millions.[18]

I observe what you mention of the Order that ministers salaries are to be hereafter paid in America.[19] I hereby impower and desire you to receive and remit mine. I do not doubt your doing it regularly and timely; for a minister without money I perceive makes a ridiculous Figure here, tho' secure from arrests. I have taken a quarters advance of Salary, from the 4th of last month, supposing it not intended to *muzzle* immediately *the mouth of the ox that treadeth out the Corn*. With great Esteem, I am, Sir, Yours &ca. &ca.

(signed) B. Franklin

Your Boys are well Mr Ridley and Mr Barclay still in Holland.[20]

mss: Copy, PCC, no. 82, DNA; copy, PCC, no. 100, DNA; extract, PCC, no. 110, DNA; extracts in the writing of Arthur Lee, Records of Boundary and Claims Commissions and Arbitrations, RG 76, DNA; extract, George Washington Papers, DLC; extract, James Monroe Papers, NN.

1. The copy in PCC, no. 100, gives the remainder of the sentence as "two of 23rd. and 29th." The text printed here, however, appears to acknowledge RM's two letters of May 18, two letters of May 23, and one letter of May 29.

2. The reference is to the defeat of de Grasse and the French fleet in the Battle of the Saints in April. See the headnote and notes to RM's State of American Commerce and Plan for Protecting It, May 10, 1782, and notes.

3. See RM to Franklin, May 29, 1782.

4. For discussion of Beaumarchais's claims, see notes to Beaumarchais to RM, June 3, 1782.

5. On the settlement of the accounts of American agents in Europe, see notes to RM to the President of Congress, May 8, 1782.

6. The opening quotation marks have been supplied from the copy in PCC, no. 100; the quotation is approximate. Ferdinand Grand was banker to the United States in Paris.

7. On the Dutch loan of June 1782, negotiated by John Adams, see notes to RM to Franklin, August 28, 1781, and to Willink and Company, September 24, 1782.

8. For the French-guaranteed loan of 1781 in Holland, see Franklin to RM, September 12, 1781, and notes.

9. For the French loan of 6 million livres for 1782, see Franklin to RM, March 4, 1782, and notes.

10. MS: "Note." The quotation which follows from the congressional act of September 12, 1781, ordering payment to William Lee differs slightly from the resolution; a copy of the act was enclosed in RM to Franklin, November 27, 1781 (first letter), and notes. For a discussion of the eventual payment, see RM's Report to Congress on a Letter from William Lee, June 6, 1782, and notes.

11. The enclosure has not been found but may possibly have been the note from Grand to Franklin of July 20, 1782, enclosing a statement of RM's accounts projected to the end of the year in which all the available funds were anticipated and a deficit of 2 million livres was indicated. The letter, in the Franklin Papers, PPAmP, is calendared in Hays, comp., Calendar of Franklin Papers, II, 489.

12. Few of Grand's letters to RM have been found. The "more perfect" account referred to was probably dispatched in Grand's letters of August 19 or October 14, which RM acknowledged as having received in letters to Grand of January 2 and 13, 1783. RM was then seriously alarmed by a shortage of funds he had not anticipated. See RM to Franklin, and to La Luzerne, both January 13, 1783.

13. Franklin's last letter was dated June 25, 1782. The enclosed account, which has not been found, was for supplies furnished in lieu of those lost aboard the Lafayette. The "Settlement" of accounts referred to was probably that stated in Franklin's letter to RM of March 4, 1782.

14. Congress on May 28, 1782, had authorized Franklin to settle accounts of the United States with France. On the contract, which set the terms for payment of the American debt to France, see RM to the President of Congress, May 8, and notes, and Franklin to RM, June 25, 1782, and notes.

15. See note 12 above.

16. On additional sets of bills of exchange, see RM to Franklin, March 23, 1782, and notes.

17. See RM to Grand, May 18, 1782 (second letter).

18. Enclosure not found. For the information that the French loan for 1782 was to be paid to the United States in equal monthly installments, see notes to Franklin to RM, March 4; and RM to Franklin, May 17, 1782.

19. See RM to Franklin, May 17, 1782.

20. In December 1782 this and other letters from Franklin to RM became involved in the aftermath of Congress's censure of David Howell, a Rhode Island delegate, for disclosing information about the status of American credit and the availability of foreign loans that was contained in dispatches Congress had received from Europe.

The texts of this letter and that of April 8, 1782, filed together in PCC were endorsed as follows by Secretary of Congress Charles Thomson (PCC, no. 82, II, 159): "Copy of letters of 8 April and 12 August 1782 from Doct Franklin to the Superintendt of finance, which were received and Read in Congress 27 Decr. 1782." On January 2, 1783, Thomson subjoined the following signed notation: "Pursuant to the order of Congress of this day I delivered this copy into the hands of Mr Howell, but to my surprise after Congress adjourned found it left on the table." See *JCC*, XXIII, 837, XXIV, 3, 32–36; and Diary, December 28, 1782.

From Pierre Eugène Du Simitière

[Philadelphia] Arch Street Augst. 12th. 82

I have to request the favour of you to inform me when I could (with conveniency to your Self) have half an hour Private audience which will much oblige him that has the honour to be with great respect Sir[1]

MS: LbC, Du Simitière Papers, DLC.
  1. Du Simitière was the Swiss-born artist and naturalist of Philadelphia.

From William Whipple

Portsmouth [New Hampshire] 12th Augt. 1782

I have received Your Circular Letter of the 19th last month[1] and shall pay due attention to Your orders respecting the Bills Drawn on Mr: Swanwick. I have lately waited on the Executive of this State to obtain the information required in Your Circular Letter to the States of the 25 July 1781[2] and find much greater difficulty in answering Your views than I at first apprehended however have taken such measures as I flatter myself will enable me to answer some of Your most material Questions in the Course of a few weeks.

MS: LbC, William Whipple Letterbook, John Langdon Papers, PHi.
  1. To the receivers of Continental taxes. Whipple was the receiver for New Hampshire.
  2. A copy of which RM had enclosed in his circular to the receivers of July 12, 1782.

George Plater to Gouverneur Morris

[Sotterley, near Leonardtown, Maryland, August 12, 1782]

I thank you for your Letter of News of 29th ultimo.[1] The Behaviour of the Dutch at this Time, amidst the Temptations of the british, is noble and does em the greatest Honor. I was much afraid the english wou'd have succeeded and patched up a separate Peace, but I see the french have out done them in Policy in this Instance as in many others—a commercial Intercourse with Holland, and her Fleets combating those of our Enemy, cannot but be productive of great Advantages to America. I suppose it is a Certainty that thirteen french Lines of Battle Ships are arrived—tis said they were joined off Chesapeak by twenty seven more but this is not confirmed—what is expected from them; is N York the Object? by the french Army marching northward our Politicians so give it out. I have long apprehended that De Grasse was used ill in the late Action by some of his Captains, if so I hope they will merit Punishment equal to their Demerit. We have nothing from the South late, except that the british are about to evacuate, or have evacuated Charles Town, which I do not believe. Mrs. P wrote to you by last

Post—she writes to you again by this. My best Wishes attend you, remember me to Doctr. Jones and all inquiring Friends—particulary to Clarkson, who I think ought to have saved the Life of Galvan, as he was mad, and might in a short Time have returned to his Senses, and continued a useful Officer.[2]

Sotterley Aug: 12th 1782

MS: ALS, Gouverneur Morris Papers, NNC.
    1. Letter not found. Plater, a former member of Congress, was president of the Maryland Senate. His letters to Gouverneur Morris, RM's assistant in the Office of Finance, were a diverting mixture of private and public topics.
    2. The reference is to William Galvan, a Frenchman or French West Indian who arrived in Charleston, South Carolina, in 1776 and ultimately obtained a major's commission from Congress in January 1780 while Plater was a delegate; he served in the Inspectors Department and led light infantry at the Battle of Green Spring in July 1781. Leaving a farewell letter to three American friends, one of whom was Matthew Clarkson, former assistant secretary at war, Galvan took his own life at a Philadelphia inn on July 24, 1782, after a Mrs. Allen, a "beautiful and accomplished widow of the first distinction in the country," rejected his amorous overtures. See *JCC*, XIII, 417–418, XV, 1419–1421, XVI, 44; Boatner, *Encyclopedia of the American Revolution*, 410; Chastellux, *Travels*, I, 103, 276n.–277n., II, 379; Morris, ed., *John Jay: Winning of the Peace*, 458, 460n.; and the diary of Elizabeth Drinker (PHi), who reported that Galvan was "disappointed in Love, and Money matters" (entry for July 26, 1782, quoted from transcript made available to the editors by Professor Elaine F. Crane of Fordham University). This sketch supersedes the brief note at Diary, December 15, 1781.

Diary: August 13, 1782

This morning[1] Capt. John Greene arrived in a Flag Ship from Plymouth in England and called at my Office to give such information as he knew.[2]

Mr Parr[3] applied for Money, I promised in a Day or two.

Mr Whitesides respecting a Bill of David Ross and Co. which I told him must be paid.

Mr. Jas. Geary Clerk of Wm. Duer Esqr. I promised him 2000 Dollars this Day and Dispatch in the Course of a Week.[4]

Mr Swanwick brought me the State or rough Estimates of several accounts and money Affairs which have but a melancholy Aspect.

The Hon. Secy of Foreign Affairs came after Capt Green and the news he brought.[5]

His Excellency Governor Dickinson called to recommend a Receiver of the Impost for the State of Delaware. I told him that I never recommend any Person to an Office of which I have not the Appointment and that when I have the appointment the only recommendations I admit of is good Character and Abilities suited to the Duties of the Station but in this Instance I have not the Appointment.[6]

I had sent Yesterday for the Clothier General. He came this Day when I communicated to him Colo. Walter Stewart's report (as Inspector of the Army) respecting Shoes of infamous Quality being served to the army. I desired him to take an Extract of that part of the report and to return the Original. I desired that he should immediately make enquiry into this Business and inform me the particulars as he alledged that the Shoes Complained of are not the Contract Shoes, but that they are the remains of the Old Stock received for Hides, Debts &c.[7]

I sent for Henry Hill Esqr. and pressed him to take measures for Obtaining the money which he is to pay me for Bills of Exchange and which I am in great Want of.[8] This Gentleman has always shewed a great desire to assist the public Service. He went away and returned again informing me that he was determined to pursue my advice and had engaged a proper Person to go after that money and that it afforded him the Opportunity of trying for more from the same Source wherefore I agreed to supply him with two Bills of Lrs. 100,000 each at thirty Days Sight to be paid for at 6/3d for five Livres in a Short time or to be returned and to facilitate this business I gave his Agent a Letter to His Excellency General Washington of this Date.

Wrote a Letter to James Lovell Esqr.

Wrote a Letter to Wm C. Houston.

Wrote a Letter to Gco. Olney.

Wrote a Letter to Wm. Whipple.

Wrote a Letter to Daniel Clarke.

Wrote a Letter to Hezekiah Merrill.

Wrote a Letter to John Warren.

Wrote a Letter to Mr Daniel Hale.

1. For a possible prior entry of this date, see the last paragraph of the Diary of August 12.

2. While commanding a merchantman on leave as a captain in the Continental navy, Green had been captured by the British and confined in Mill Prison (for his activities there and RM's efforts to secure his release, see Green to RM, November 20, 1781, and notes). In accordance with an agreement concluded between the Shelburne ministry and Benjamin Franklin in May 1782, Green and other American marine prisoners held in England were sent to America to be exchanged for an equivalent number of British prisoners of war (see notes to Diary, June 18, 1782). The first of the flag-of-truce ships, the *Symmetry*, captain Francis Maxwell, reached the Delaware on August 12 with 216 prisoners, and the *Tyger*, captain George Harrison, carrying 132, 11 of whom had died en route, arrived a few days later. Since a contagion still raged aboard the *Tyger*, it was sent to the "Pest House." Three other ships, transporting about 700 prisoners, reached Boston later in the month.

With Green's assistance RM set in motion the exchange of prisoners. He arranged for Maxwell and Harrison to communicate with Sir Guy Carleton, the British commander at New York, and, after receiving assurances from Carleton that signed statements by the two captains regarding the number of British marine prisoners turned over to them would be accepted in the final settlement of prisoner accounts, arranged for the delivery to the flag ships of 150 naval prisoners held in Philadelphia and the surrounding area. He also promised the delivery of all other marine prisoners to convenient British-held posts but, in accordance with congressional policy, refused to deliver over British soldiers.

Meanwhile, more immediate problems remained to be solved. In response to a "memorial and petition" from the prisoners, Congress on August 15 ordered Secre-

tary at War Benjamin Lincoln to secure permission from the Supreme Executive
Council of Pennsylvania to lodge the prisoners in the Philadelphia barracks and
directed the Agent of Marine to "take order for their being supplied with rations."
RM also had to respond to questions posed by the British captains. Their request for
funds to pay charges incurred while their vessels were lying in port the Financier met
by personally countersigning notes on a New York City merchant, although he carefully noted in the Diary that it was at the public risk. Another issue, raised by the
captain of the *Symmetry*, was payment for food he had provided to the American
prisoners under the threat of force over and above what the British government had
authorized. RM recommended to Congress on August 23 that the United States pay
for it, but after debate on August 28 a favorable committee report was recommitted
and apparently allowed to die. See Diary, August 14, 15, 16, 17, 19, 20, 21, 22, 23,
September 2, 10, 12, 14, 16, 18, RM's Orders to the Guard for the Ship *Symmetry*,
August 15, to Carleton, August 20 and September 16, to Washington, August 22, and
to the President of Congress, August 23, and notes, and Carleton to RM, September
2; Hutchinson and Rutland, ed., *Madison Papers*, V, 67n.; Charles Thomson's Notes of
Debates, August 28, 1782, Burnett, ed., *Letters*, VI, 459–460; Commissioners for Sick
and Hurt to Harrison, May 22, and to Maxwell, May 24, Maxwell to Carleton, August
16, Michael Humble (master of *Lady's Adventure* in Boston) to Carleton, August 19,
William Brown (master of *Hope* in Boston) to Carleton, and Harrison to Carleton,
both August 20, Thomas Cartell (master of *Adamant* in Boston) to Carleton, August
25, 1782, and lists of English prisoners submitted by Maxwell and Harrison in September, all in British Headquarters Papers, NN (photocopies), and calendared in
Report on American Manuscripts in the Royal Institution, II, 494, 496, III, 74, 78, 79, 80,
91, 117, 145; and Davies, ed., *Documents of the American Revolution*, XIX, 335. For
information undoubtedly obtained from Green, see RM's Circular to John Barry and
John Manley, August 13; and note 5 below. For attacks on Franklin for his role in this
exchange, see La Luzerne to Vergennes, August 15, 1782, Correspondance politique,
Etats-Unis, XXII, 85, AMAE.
    3. William Parr, a contractor for the Continental post at Lancaster, Pennsylvania.
    4. For Geary's mission, see notes to Duer to RM, August 2.
    5. According to French Minister Chevalier de La Luzerne and the Philadelphia
merchant John Chaloner, Green brought information of peace prospects from members of the British cabinet. See La Luzerne to Vergennes, August 15, 1782, Correspondance politique, Etats-Unis, XXII, 87–89, AMAE; and Chaloner to Jeremiah
Wadsworth, August 13, 1782, Chaloner and White Letterbook, PHi.
    6. Concerning the appointment of collectors of the 5 percent impost under consid-
eration by the states, see RM to Nathaniel Appleton, May 28, 1782, and notes; and
Appendix I to this volume.
    7. The report by Stewart, inspector for the northern army, has not been found,
but Washington reported that Clothier General John Moylan "thinks himself ag-
grieved thereby and has solicited that an inspection of the shoes now in store may take
place." Washington ordered the inspection and report on August 26, but the results
have not been ascertained. See Moylan to Stewart, August 19, Stewart to Moylan,
August 22, Stewart to Washington, August 22, with enclosed complaints, and August
26, Washington Papers, DLC; and Fitzpatrick, ed., *Writings of Washington*, XXV, 66.
    8. For Henry Hill's assistance to RM in negotiating bills of exchange through New
York, see Diary, April 17, 1782, and notes.

Circular to John Barry and John Manley

Circular   Marine Office 13 August 1782[1]
Sir

    By a flag which is just arrived here with Prisoners from Plymouth
in old England in a passage of seven weeks[2] I am informed that a
fleet of two hundred Sail of Transports under Convoy of a forty
Gun ship and two Frigates were on the point of Sailing to America

part of which was bound for Charles Town, part for New York and part for Quebeck. I hope this Information may prove usefull and am Sir your most obedient and humble Servant

RM

MS: AM LbC, MdAN.

1. Barry and Manley were captains, respectively, of the Continental frigates *Alliance* and *Hague*. For their missions, see RM to Barry, July 12 (two letters), and notes, and to Manley, August 8, 1782, and notes.

2. See Diary, August 13, and notes.

To Daniel Clark

Office of Finance 13. Augt. 1782

Sir,

I have received your Letter dated at Richmond the 24th. with two dated at Petersburg the 26 of July, also that dated at Williamsburg on the third Instant.[1] The several drafts you mention therein have come to hand and all have been accepted, but those in favor of Daniel Tyson and John Field will remain unpaid until you inform me of having received the Value. You must be particular in advising me of such Bills as you draw for account of Mr. Eddy and they will meet with due honor. I shall speak to him on the Subject of sending Cash to you, altho I think you may raise it fast enough by drafts. I shall be pleased to find that the Tobacco I was to furnish on behalf of the Public has all been delivered and shall expect Mr. Coffin's Receipts therefor as you have promised me.

I have no knowlege of the Governors Reason's for detaining the Flags. I can therefore say nothing thereon until I receive Information which I expect from you by the next Post. I will then write you particularly on the Subject,[2] and remain Sir your obedient Servant

RM

MS: Ofcl LbC, DLC.

1. Letter not found. Clark was purchasing tobacco in Virginia to fulfill RM's Agreement with George Eddy, which is printed under the date of March 13, 1782.

2. On July 29, 1782, Governor Benjamin Harrison of Virginia temporarily ordered all flag-of-truce vessels detained, evidently to prevent the British from receiving intelligence of the French evacuation of matériel by ship from Yorktown. The order was revoked on August 19, and RM did not find it necessary to write Clark on the matter. See McIlwaine, ed., *Journals of the Council of Virginia*, III, 129; and McIlwaine, ed., *Official Letters*, III, 282, 283–284, 298.

To John Cruden

⟨Mr Wells⟩[1]   Philada August 13th. 1782

Sir

Circumstances have so materially altered since the 5th Instant when my former letter to you is dated, that I think there woud not be any impropriety in ⟨Our prosecuting⟩ laying the Foundation for a plan to be executed upon the Conclusion of Peace and if you will fix a time when you can be at Elizabeth Town I will send a person to ⟨Converse with you⟩ Meet you for that purpose.[2] I am Sir Your Obedient Servant

RM

To Jno Cruden Esqr.

ENDORSED: Philada. Augt 13th 1782/Jno Cruden
MS: ADftS, Robert Morris Papers, NN.
    1. Richard Wells, an emissary of Henry Hill's to New York City (see RM to George Washington, August 13), may originally have been the intended bearer of this missive to Cruden, a North Carolina loyalist now in the city.
    2. For the plan to engross the American tobacco market, see Samuel Bean to RM, May 26, and notes, and RM to Cruden, August 5, 1782, and notes. The altered circumstances cited by RM undoubtedly were the reliable reports he had received announcing the opening of negotiations for a general peace in Paris. See Diary, August 8, and notes, and August 13, and notes.

To John Paul Jones

Marine Office 13 August 1782

Sir,

I have received your several Letters of the 14 and 20 March, 2 and 8 April, 3 and 20 May, 17 and 24 June, 1 and 29th. July and 3d. Instant.[1] That of the 29th. of July was brought me the day before Yesterday by the Post and that of the third Instant came to hand last Evening. My reason for not answering your several Letters was that I had the weekly Expectation of being able to make solid Arrangements for launching the America but as I met with new Disappointments every Week Procrastination from Time to Time has led us on to this Period. I now send by Mr. Storer Notes to the Amount of twenty thousand Dollars which will I think enable Mr Langdon speedily to put that Ship in the Water.[2] If you were acquainted with half my Embarrassments you would not be surprized to find that the Delays have happened which you feel so sensibly. I can with great Truth assure you that I have felt with and for you and that if my Wishes could have afforded any releif you would have been releived entirely. As it is I have done all in my Power and now add the Assurance that you may rely on my utmost Exertions and may be assured of my friendship and Esteem. I am Sir your most obedient and humble Servant

RM

PS. The present Prospect of public Affairs seems to be such as will probably preclude you from the Opportunity of gathering fresh Laurels but you have already gained a Reputation which will render your Retirement honorable till new Wars shall call forth your Talents to new Exertions.

MS: AM LbC, MdAN.

1. Letters not found. Captain Jones of the Continental navy was in Portsmouth where his command, the *America*, was awaiting completion.

2. See RM to John Langdon, August 13, and Diary, August 15.

To John Langdon

Marine Office 13 August 1782

Sir,

I have received your Letters of the 6 May, 3 and 10 June, 8 July and 3 August,[1] which are yet unanswered. That of the 3d. of August was brought to me last Evening by Mr Storer. My Reason for delaying to answer your Letters was the Expectation I have constantly entertained of being able to make you a Remittance which would put you entirely at Ease. Circumstances of various kinds had brought down my Notes to a very considerable Discount in the Eastern States.[2] It was therefore improper to send on any more because the sending them was a clear Loss to the Public. In this Situation not having Money, the States neglecting to raise Taxes and heavy Demands pouring in on me from every Quarter I had daily to encounter Difficulties which I hourly expected to sink under. I might indeed have gained a temporary Releif by some Expedients but this would have brought on inevitable Ruin and therefore it was better to bear the pressure of present Evils than to adopt Remedies which must prove fatal. At Length we begin to see Day light before us. The Collection of the Taxes in the Eastern States and other Measures which have been taken to the same Effect will have brought Paper into Demand before this reaches you and I have in that Conviction sent you twenty thousand dollars in Notes which any of the Receivers will give the Cash for and therefore as there is now Money in the Chest at Boston and more will be speedily brought thither I expect you can realize them as fast as you please.[3] From the Representations which have been made to me by the Chevalier Jones[4] I expect that this Sum will enable you to put the America in the Water and secure her thro the ensuing Winter. At any Rate you will now be able to launch her and I hope that no delay may intervene which can possibly be avoided.[5] I have the utmost reliance on your Exertions and I expect that those of your State will soon step in to my releif. I am Sir with great Respect your most obedient and humble Servant

RM

MS: AM LbC, MdAN.

1. Letters not found. Langdon was supervising the construction of the *America* at Portsmouth, New Hampshire.

2. Regarding the depreciation of Morris's notes in New England, see Ver Steeg, *Morris,* 117–119.

3. William Whipple, the receiver of Continental taxes for New Hampshire, however, was unable to convert the notes into cash. See RM to Whipple, August 13, and Whipple to RM, August 31.

4. See the preceding letter.

5. For the launching of the *America,* see notes to Langdon to RM, April 20, 1781.

To James Lovell

Office of Finance 13. Augt. 1782

Sir,

I have received your Letter of the thirty first of July[1] and am glad to find that Monies are at length begining to come into your hands from the Taxes of Massachusetts. I am in Hopes that the Stream of Revenue will now flow plentifully God knows we stand sufficiently in need of it. I wish you would close the Sales of the Bills of Exchange and transmit me the Accounts charging therein your ⅛ per Cent so that the whole may be properly entered and as to any Balance in Hand you will remit it in the usual Way. I mentioned in my last that the Money you had advanced to Major Franks would be repaid by him here on your Account wherefore you ought to charge it as so much remitted by him and then the whole will stand properly together. I am Sir your most obedient and humble Servant

RM

MS: Ofcl LbC, DLC.

1. Letter not found. Lovell was the receiver of Continental taxes for Massachusetts.

To Hezekiah Merrill

Office of Finance 13 Augt. 1782

Sir

I have received your Letter of the fifth Instant.[1] It is a matter of no Consequence whether the Collectors or others pay you Cash or Notes for the one is as good as the other; but it is of Consequence, that the public money be not left in the Hands of Collectors. I hope therefore you will not cease to stimulate the Treasurer[2] or others whose Business it may be to urge the Payments. I am Sir your most obedient Servant

RM

MS: Ofcl LbC, DLC.

1. The letter from Merrill, the receiver of Continental taxes for Connecticut, has not been found. His first payment, of the same date, for $1,797⁷⁵⁄₉₀ is listed in PCC, no. 137, III, 357.

2. John Lawrence was treasurer of Connecticut from 1769 to 1789. James Kirby Martin, *Men in Rebellion: Higher Governmental Leaders and the Coming of the American Revolution* (New Brunswick, N. J., 1973), 207.

To George Olney

Office of Finance 13. Augt. 1782

Sir,

I have received yours of the twenty second and twenty ninth of July.[1] I have transmitted to the Postmaster General the Extract from yours of the twenty ninth of what relates to that Subject enclosed in the following Note: "Mr. Morris presents his Compliments to the Postmaster General and prays his Attention to the enclosed Extract of a Letter from the Receiver of Taxes for Rhode Island to him."[2]

I am happy to hear that the Treasurer has agreed to retain the Certificates for Blankets &ca.[3] You appear to have mistaken a little the Kind of Men whose Characters I wish to be made acquainted with. It will be useful to know leading Persons of whatever Disposition they may be because Reliance may be made on the Good and it is well to beware of the Evil.[4]

There has not been any mail taken coming from the Eastward so that you need not be apprehensive of the Loss of Letters hitherto. There was one taken on it's Way from hence, and one coming from the Southward. I am Sir, your most obedient and humble Servant

RM

MS: Ofcl LbC, DLC.
    1. Letters not found. Olney was the receiver of Continental taxes for Rhode Island.
    2. The recipient's copy of this note to Postmaster General Ebenezer Hazard has not been found.
    3. Concerning the certificates, see RM to Olney, July 29, and notes. Joseph Clarke, Continental loan officer of Rhode Island, was also the state treasurer.
    4. RM's request for information on "the Characters and Dispositions of public Men" was made in his letter to the receivers of April 13, 1782.

To George Washington

Office of Finance 13th August 1782

Sir

The urgent Demands on me for Money oblige me to use a Thousand different Expedients. The bearer of this letter Mr. Richd Wells[1] is on his way to New York. He goes for the purpose of receiving a very considerable Sum of Money and will if Successful pay it to your Excellency to be held at my orders. I am therefore to request that he may have every Facility in going to New York and bringing the Money from thence.[2] I will by another Opportunity mention to your Excellency the Disposition of a Part, and the Remainder at a future Period. The Sum being uncertain I cannot give such pointed Directions as I could wish. I am to pray that your Excellency will receive whatever he may bring and sign Receipts therefor as for so much on Account of the United States to be held at my order. I am Sir with great Respect your Excellency's most obedient and humble Servant

Robt Morris

His Excellency General Washington

ENDORSED: Philada. 13th. Augt. 1782/from/Honble. Mr. Morris/by Mr. Wells/acknowl-edged 23d
MS: LS, Washington Papers, DLC.
1. The preceding two words are in RM's hand. Richard Wells (d. 1801), who also carried RM's letters to Washington of August 8 and 9, was an English-born, Quaker merchant from Burlington, New Jersey, and brother-in-law of Henry Hill (see the following note). He had long since moved to Philadelphia, where he served in the Pennsylvania Assembly, was secretary of the American Philosophical Society, and a director of the Library Company. Labaree and Willcox, eds., *Franklin Papers,* XX, 15n.; William Wade Hinshaw and Thomas Worth Marshall, *Encyclopedia of American Quaker Genealogy* (Ann Arbor, Mich., 1936–1950), II, 549; and John Jay Smith, ed., *Letters of Doctor Richard Hill and His Children* (Philadelphia, 1854), xii, xviii.
2. His operations effectively stymied by the intensive British blockade of the American coast (see the headnote to RM's State of American Commerce and Plan for Protecting It, May 10, 1782, and notes), the Superintendent sought to obtain specie by selling bills of exchange in New York City through the auspices of Henry Hill, a political ally in state politics and a director of the Bank of North America (see Diary, April 17, 1782, and notes). The remittances, however, were slow in coming, and Hill, "In prosecuting ways and means to serve the worthy Mr. Morris," agreed to send an emissary to New York to bring out the specie. Dispatching Wells to headquarters, Hill offered Washington the following cryptic explanation in a letter of August 16 (Washington Papers, DLC): "The Event may not answer our wishes and is one of those that depend much on experiment, guarded however by many precautions, particularly in respect to my chief agent the Bearer, whose tried address and intimate connection with me justify the Choice of him. There can interfere no matters thro-out his trans-action that may render my credit questionable with you, for this deposite I shall preserve most inviolably." RM expected to receive at least $17,000, $12,000 of which he needed to meet his specie payments to the contractors for West Point and the Moving Army, but the effort was largely a failure. The small amount obtained evi-dently was paid in the light gold the British found it profitable to export to the states (on this point, see Gouverneur Morris to Thomas Willing, June 18, 1782, and notes). See Diary, August 13, 15, and September 9, RM to Washington, August 17 and 20, and to Walter Livingston, August 29, and notes, Washington to RM, September 2 and 4 (first letter); and Fitzpatrick, ed., *Writings of Washington,* XXV, 51.

To William Whipple

Office of Finance 13. August 1782[1]

Sir,

I received by the Post your favor of the twenty ninth of July. I am very sorry to learn that there is so great Backwardness in paying the Taxes. How shameful is it that Money must be remitted to New Hampshire to finish a single Ship on the Stocks at Portsmouth. But it is in vain to dwell on this disagreable Subject. I rely on your making every proper Representation as Opportunities shall offer.

I wish that in future you would enclose the news Paper in your Letters to me as I apprehend that Tricks are frequently played at the Post Office by curious Persons and that is the best means of avoiding them.

I send by this Opportunity Notes to Mr. Langdon to the Amount of twenty thousand Dollars and I would fain Hope that you will be in a Situation to take up the greater Part if not the whole of them.[2] I am Sir with great Respect your most obedient Servant

RM

ms: Ofcl LbC, DLC.
1. Whipple was the receiver of Continental taxes for New Hampshire.
2. See RM to John Langdon, August 13, and notes.

From Nathanael Greene

Headquarters [Ashley Hill, South Carolina]
August 13th 1782

Sir

Some little time past I saw a letter of yours to Lt Co Carrington on the subject of clothing that gave me some pain.[1] You Express a surprise at the complaints of a want of clothing in this Army after the large drafts which have been made for money to provide this Article. And at the same time you seem to hint as if the evil must originate in a great measure in the negligence of the Troops in not taking proper care of the clothing provided. Was this the case the Army would deserve censure and the troops to suffer. But to convince you that that is not the case I do my self the honor to enclose you a return of all the clothing forwarded from Philadelphia from May 1781 to July 82 that has ever arrivd at the Army.[2] The supply is so triffling compard to our wants that it has served little other purpose than to mock our distress, a few being clothed the other appeared the more wretched. Some cloth and clothing was provided at York in Virginia but very triffling and even that never came to hand until it was too late to make use of the woolen ⟨clothing⟩ and I have stored it or at least the greater part of it for fall issues. Had our supplies been ever so ample for a well regulated Army they would have been deficient for ours from its peculiar composition. Virginia and North Carolinia have sent men into the field for such short terms that by the time they could be clothed they had a right to claim their discharge. North Carolina has had few other Soldiers than non jurors and disaffected and those for different terms of service. And all both from Virginia and North Carolina join the Army generally in a most rag[g]ed wretched condition. With an Army of this composition, in a campaign of uncommon Activity with frequent defeats you must naturally suppose greater supplies of clothing would be necessary. I made use of every precaution to preserve the little clothing we had; but I could not strip the troops who had served out their time when they were discharged nor could I refuse them their proportion of clothing while in service. I discharged the whole Virginia line last Winter who carried off great part of the best clothing we had. And when I came down in to this lower Country in December last the Army was in a deplorable condition with out blankets, shoes, shirts or overalls. In this condition they continued all Winter except some partial supplies which the Governor of this State was good enough to get by stealth out of Charles Town for our relief. For notwithstanding our distress I would not engage in this business my self; for fear of unjust imputations. As no supplies arrivd in the course of the Winter our condition notwithstanding the few things got by the Governor began to be wretched beyound description. Murmuring and discontent prevailed among the Soldiers to a great degree and finally it discovered itself in a very serious way. In this critical situation I urged the Governor to try to get us a more ample supply. He engaged a merchant who brought out goods sufficient to afford to the greater part of the Army one pair of overalls, one shirt and a linnen Cotee. But for upwards of two months before we got these things more than one third of our Men were entirely naked with nothing about them but a bre[e]ch[3] clout and never came out of their Tents; and the rest were as ragged as wolves. Indeed Sir I think you can have no idea of our distress. While we were thus situated for clothing our condition was little better in the Article of provision. Our beef was perfect carrion and even bad as it was we were frequently without any. I foresaw the difficulty of getting good beef in this Country early in the Spring unless it was stall fed. I wrote early in the winter both to Virginia and North Carolinia to put up a large number of Cattle to stall feed to be driven to the Army in the Spring;[4] but neither of the States sent us a single head. Nor has North Carolinia sent us any during the campaign altho frequently applied to. Virginia being so remote I did not urge our demand on that State. An Army thus clothed and thus fed without spirits may be considered in a desperate situation. However we have struggled through it. Our supplies of provision are better but even now they are scanty and uncertain. Some clothing is arrivd from the Northward which added to what the Governor provided renders the troops pretty comfortable and the Army very contented and easy especially as we have it in our power to issue rum eight times a month and this is what I propose to continue during the hot season as I think it essential to the health of the Troops to have rum twice a week. Indeed I would give them rum every day was I not apprehensive my drafts would exceed your abilities to pay as I find few of the States have paid any part of their taxes. You will consider in a climate like this there is no possibility of subsisting the

Troops to the same advantage as you can more Northwardly and do justice to the rights of humanity.

I also saw a letter of yours to Mr Hall which gave me some uneasiness.[5] You seem to think the scale of expence which Halls estimate amounted to ought to admit of an issue of 12,000 Rations. Our actual issues is about Six. Inclosed I send you an estimate[6] the greater part taken from the books of issues, And also an estimate of the issues of forage. But as these articles are furnished by the State they will not distress you. Our issues are large for our operating force but the Staff and Militia swells them greatly.[7] Our Ration is 1¼ pounds of beef and 1¼ pounds of rice. This is rather more than the ration to the Northward but the lesser parts of the ration cannot be had here which you issue by Contract and an additional quantity of beef is allowed in lieu thereof. We have contracted all our Posts except such as are essential to our communication and put the Army on as oeconomical plan as possible all things considered. In North Carolina where they had formerly twenty Posts we have only one. We have also broke up that pernicious practice of having Continental Stores seized as they were passing through a State for the use of it. This practice was attended with every evil, it multiplied our expences four fold, and always left the Army without supplies. But it was with difficulty we could check it. The Quarter Master Department I hope will make but small drafts on you, as all his Waggoners and most of his officers are from the line. Indeed the Army furnishes most or all the Men for the Ordnance, commissaries and Quarter Masters department. It lessens our force but it also contracts the public expence.

I see by your letter to Hall this State is to be allowed for the Articles they furnish the prices allowed by Congress for specifick supplies. Those are very high much more so than they could be got for cash. But it may be just enough to this State and Georgia who have sufferd such ravages. But was I at liberty or had I the means to pay I could contract for the subsistence of the Army at the same rate as your contracts are to the Northward.[8] However there appears to be a great change taking place in this Country which will give you more time and a better opportunity to regulate your business of finance in these States. The Enemy are making every preparation for the evacuation of Charles Town and I think it will take place in less than a fortnight.[9] Most of the army will march to the Northward the moment the enemy evacuate.

I hope you'l excuse this long letter in which I have been perhaps more particular than you may wish; but I am anxious that you should have a proper idea of our real situation and that nothing is left unessayed to aid the distressed situation of our finances; which I

am confident you will be convinced of when you take into consideration the extensive scale the war has been upon in this Country and
the numerous disaffected in [it]. I am with great esteem and regard
Your most Obedient humble Servant

N Greene

The honble Robert Morris

MSS: ADftS, Greene Papers, CSmH; George Washington Greene transcript, CSmH;
extract, Samuel Osgood Papers, NHi.
    1. Major General Greene was commander of the southern army, which was en-
camped about 12 miles outside of Charleston (see McCrady, *South Carolina in the
Revolution*, 669–670). The letter he refers to was RM to Edward Carrington, deputy
quartermaster general for the southern army, June 6, 1782. Concerning clothing for
Greene's army, see notes to RM to Greene, June 10, 1782.
    2. Enclosure not found.
    3. Transcript: "buck."
    4. See Greene to Governor Benjamin Harrison of Virginia, December 27, 1781,
PCC, no. 71, II, 349–351. Harrison enclosed Greene's missive in a letter to the
President of Congress of January 21, 1782, with the comment that "Congress alone
are capable of affording him such Assistance as will be adequate to his Demands."
That letter and Harrison's reply to Greene of the same date are in McIlwaine, ed.,
Official Letters, III, 131–133. Greene's correspondence with the governor of North
Carolina has not been found.
    5. See RM to George Abbott Hall, June 10, 1782.
    6. Estimate not found.
    7. The Osgood extract consists of the preceding six sentences subjoined to the first
four sentences of the succeeding paragraph.
    8. For RM's contrasting views on the extension of contracts to the southern army,
see notes to Diary, May 22, 1782.
    9. Although preparations for the evacuation of Charleston began on August 7 and
British vessels arrived early in September, the evacuation was not completed until
December 14, 1782. See McCrady, *South Carolina in the Revolution*, 670.

From Alexander Hamilton

Albany [New York] Augt. 13th. 1782[1]

Sir,

    I promised you in former letters to give you a full view of the
situation and temper of this state: I now sit down to execute that
task.[2]

    You have already in your possession a pretty just picture of the 1st
drawn by the Legislature in   [3] perhaps too highly coloured in
some places, but in the main true. It is the opinion of the most
sensible men, with whom I converse, who are best acquainted with
the circumstances of the state, and who are not disposed to exagger-
ate its distresses as an excuse for inactivity, that its faculties for
revenue are diminished at least two thirds.

    It will not be difficult to conceive this, when we consider, that five
out of the fourteen counties of which the state was composed, including the capital, are in the hands of the enemy—that two and
part of a third have revolted—two others have been desolated, the

greater part, by the ravages of the enemy and of our own troops—and the remaining four have more or less suffered partial injuries from the same causes. Adding the fragments of some to repair the losses of others, the efficient property, strength and force of the state will consist in little more than four counties.

In the distribution of taxes before the war the city of New York used to be rated at one third of the whole; but this was too high, owing probably to the prevalency of the country interest; its proper proportion I should judge to have been about one fourth; which serves further to illustrate the probable decrease of the state.

Our population indeed is not diminished in the same degree, as many of the inhabitants of the dismembered and ruined counties, who have left their habitations, are dispersed through those which remain; and it would seem that the labor of the additional hands ought to increase the culture and value of these; but there are many deductions to be made from this apparent advantage—the numbers that have recruited the British army—those that have been furnished to ours—the emigrations to Vermont and to the neighbouring states, less harrassed by the war, and affording better encouragements to industry; both which have been considerable. Besides these circumstances, many of the fugitive families are a burthen for their subsistence upon the state. The fact is labor is much dearer than before the war.

This state has certainly made in the course of the war great exertions, and upon many occasions of the most exhausting kind. This has sometimes happened from want of judgment, at others from necessity. When the army, as has too often been the case, has been threatened with some fatal calamity, for want of provisions, forage, the means of transportation &c, in consequence of pressing applications from the Commander in Chief, the Legislature has been obliged to have recourse to extraordinary expedients to answer the present emergency, which have both distressed and disgusted the people. There is no doubt that with a prudent and systematic administration the state might have rendered more benefit to the common cause, with less inconvenience to itself, than by all its forced efforts; but here as every where else we have wanted experience and knowlege. And indeed had this not been the case, every thing every where has been so radically wrong, that it was difficult, if not impossible, for any one state to be right.

The exposed situation of the frontier and the frequent calls upon the inhabitants for personal service on each extremity, by interfering with industry, have contributed to impoverish the state and fatigue the people.

Deprived of foreign trade, our internal traffic is carried on upon the most disadvantageous terms. It divides itself into three branches;

with the city of New York, with Jersey and Pensylvania, and with New England.[4]

That with New York consists chiefly of luxuries on one part and returns of specie on the other. I imagine we have taken goods from that place to the annual amount of near £30,000. The Legislature have passed a severe law to prevent this intercourse; but what will laws avail against the ingenuity and intrepidity of avarice?[5]

From Jersey and Pensylvania we take about thirty thousand pounds more and we pay almost intirely in cash.

From Massachusetts and other parts of New England we purchase to the amount of about £50,000, principally in tea and salt. We sell to these states to the value of about £30,000. The articles of tea and salt alone cost this state the annual sum of sixty thousand pounds.[6]

The immense land transportation of which the chief part is carried on by the subjects of other states is a vast incumbrance upon our trade.

The principal article we have to throw in the opposite scale is the expenditures of the army. Mr. Sands informs me that the contractors for the main army and West point lay out in this state at the rate of about 60,000 dollars a year: Mr. Duer, for these northern posts about Thirty thousand:[7] If the Quarter Master general expends as much more in his department, the whole will amount to about 180,000 dolls. I speak of what is paid for in specie or such paper as answers the purposes of specie.

These calculations cannot ⟨necessarily⟩ absolutely be relied on because the data are necessarily uncertain; but they are the result of the best information I can obtain; and if near the truth, prove that the general ballance of trade is against us; a plain symptom of which is an *extreme* and *universal* scarcity of money.

The situation of the state, with respect to its internal government is not more pleasing. Here we find the general disease which infects all our constitutions, an excess of popularity. There is no *order* that has a will of its own. The inquiry constantly is what will *please* not what will *benefit* the people. In such a government there can be nothing but temporary expedient, fickleness and folly.

But the point of view in which this subject will be interesting to you is that which relates to our finances. I gave you in a former letter a sketch of our plan of taxation;[8] but I will now be more particular.

The general principle of it is an assessment, according to *circumstances and abilities collectively considered.*

The ostensible reason for adopting this vague basis was a desire of equality: It was pretended, that this could not be obtained so well by any fixed tariff of taxable property, as by leaving it to the discretion of persons chosen by the people themselves, to determine the ability of each citizen. But perhaps the true reason was a desire to discriminate between the *whigs* and *tories*. This chimerical attempt at perfect equality has resulted in total inequality; or rather this narrow disposition to overburthen a particular class of citizens (living under the protection of the government) has been retorted upon the contrivers or their friends, wherever that class has been numerous enough to preponderate in the election of the officers who were to execute the law. The exterior figure a man makes, the decency or meaness of his manner of living, the personal friendships, or dislikes of the assessors have much more share in determining what individuals shall pay, than the proportion of property.

The Legislature first *assesses,* or quotas the several counties. Here the evil begins. The members cabal and intrigue to throw the burthen off their respective constituents. Address and influence, more than considerations of real ability prevail. A great deal of time is lost and a great deal of expence incurred before the juggle is ended and the necessary compromises made.

The Supervisors, of whom there are upon an average sixteen in each county, meet at the notification of the County-clerk, and assign their proportions to the sub-divisions of the county; and in the distribution play over the same game, which was played in the Legislature.

The Assessors assembled on a like notification, according to their fancies, determine the proportion of each individual; a list of which being made out and signed by the Supervisors is a warrant to the collectors. There are near an hundred upon average in each County.

The allowance to these officers has been various; it is now six shillings a day besides expences: in some cases they have been limited to a particular time for executing the business; but in general it is left to their discretion, and the greater part of them are not in a hurry to complete it, as they have a compensation for their trouble, and live better at the public charge than they are accustomed to do at their own. The consequence is not only delay but a heavy expence.

It now remains for the collectors to collect the tax, and it is the duty of the supervisors to see that they do it. Both these offices, as well as that of the assessors, are elective; and of course there is little disposition to risk the displeasure of those who elect. They have no motive of interest to stimulate them to their duty, equivalent to the inconvenience of performing it. The collector in intitled to the trifling compensation of sometimes four—sometimes six pence out of each pound he collects, and is liable to the trifling penalty of twenty or five and twenty pounds for neglect of duty. The supervisors have no interest at all in the collection; and it will on this account appear not extraordinary, that with continual delinquencies in the collector[s] there has never been a single prosecution.

As I observed on a former occasion, if the collector happens to be a zealous man and lives in a zealous neighbourhood the taxes are collected; if either of these requisites is wanting the collection languishes or intirely fails.

When the taxes are collected, they are paid to the County treasurer; an officer chosen by the Supervisors. The collectors are responsible to him also; but as he is allowed only one fourth or one half per Cent, he has no sufficient inducement to incur the odium of compelling them to do their duty.

The County Treasurer pays what he receives into the state Treasurer who has an annual salary of £300; and has nothing to do but to receive and pay out according to the appropriations of the legislature.

Notwithstanding the obvious defects of this system, notwithstanding experience has shown it to be iniquitous and ineffectual and that all attempts to amend it without totally changing it are fruitless, notwithstanding there is a pretty general discontent from the inequality of the taxes, still ancient habits, ignorance, the spirit of the times, the opportunity afforded to some popular characters of skreening themselves by intriguing with the assessors, have hitherto proved an over-match for common sense and common justice as well as the manifest advantage of the State and of the United States.

The temper of the state, which I shall now describe, may be considered under two heads, that of the rulers and that of the people.

The rulers are generally zealous in the common cause, though their zeal is often misdirected. They are jealous of their own power; but yet as this state is the immediate theatre of the war their apprehensions of danger and an opinion that they are obliged to do more than their neighbours make them very willing to part with power in favour of the Fœderal Government. This last opinion and an idea added to it, that they have no credit for their past exertions has put them out of humour and indisposed many of them for future exertions. I have heard several assert, that in the present situation of this state, nothing more ought to be expected, than that it maintain its own government, and keep up its quota of troops. This sentiment however is as yet confined to a few, but it is too palatable not to make proselytes.

There is no man in the government who has a decided influence in it. The present governor[9] has declined in popularity, partly from a defect of qualifications for his station and partly from causes that do him honor—the vigorous execution of some necessary laws that bore hard upon the people, and severity of discipline among the militia. He is, I believe, a man of integrity and passes with his particular friends for a statesman; it is certain that without being destitute of understanding, his passions are much warmer, than his judgment is enlightened. The preservation of his place is an object to his private fortune as well as to his ambition; and we are not to be surprised, if instead of taking a lead in measures that contradict a prevailing prejudice, however he may be convinced of their utility, he either flatters it or temporises; especially when a new election approaches.

The next character of a most uniform influence is General Schuyler.[10] He has more weight in the Legislature than the Governor; but not so much as not to be exposed to the mortification of seeing important measures patronised by him frequently miscarry. Your knowlege of him and my connection prevent my enlarging. I shall only add that he hazards his popularity in support of what you wish and what the public safety demands.

I omitted speaking of the Lt Governor[11] in his place; I shall only say he is an honest man, without pretensions. I shall be silent on the subject of the Chancellor and of Mr. Duane;[12] because I could not give you any additional light into their characters.

Mr. Scot[13] you also know. He has his little objects and his little party. Nature gave him genius; but *habit* has impaired it. He never had judgment; he now has scarcely plausibility; his influence is just extensive enough to embarrass measures he does not like; and his only aim seems to be by violent professions of popular principles to acquire a popularity which has hitherto coyly eluded his persuit. His views as a statesman are warped; his principles as a man are said to be not the purest.

In the senate Judge Platt, Judge Paine and Mr. Yates[14] have each their share of influence.

The first is a man of plain sense, thoroughly acquainted with agriculture. He intends to do well whenever he can hit upon what is right.

The second is a man of strong natural parts and as strong prejudices; his zeal is fiery, his obstinacy unconquerable. He is as primitive in his notions, as in his appearance. Without education, he wants more knowlege, or more tractableness.

The third is a man whose ignorance and perverseness are only surpassed by his pertinacity and conceit. He hates all high-flyers, which is the appellation he gives to men of genius. He has the merit of being always the first man at the Legislature. The people have been a long time in the *habit* of choosing him in different offices; and to the title of prescription, he adds that of being a preacher to their taste. He *assures* them, they are too poor to pay taxes. He is a staunch whig, that deserves to be pensioned by the British Ministry. He is commissioner of the loan office in this state.

In the assembly the leading members are, Mr. Malcolm,[15] Mr Laurance, Mr. Lansing, Judge Tredwell and Mr. Humphreys.[16]

Malcolm has a variety of abilities: he is industrious and expert in business; he wants not resource and is pretty right on the subjects of the day; but he is too fond of popularity and too apt to think every scheme bad, that is not his own. He is closely linked with Scot, because he can govern him: A man of warm passions, he can controul all but his vanity, which often stands in the way of his interest. He is accused of duplicity and insincerity. He has it in his power to support or perplex measures, as he may incline, and it will be politic to make it his interest to incline to what is right. It was on this principle I proposed him for a certain office.

Laurence is a man of good sense and good intentions—has just views of public affairs—is active and accurate in business. He is from conviction an advocate for strengthening the Fœderal government and for reforming the vices of our interior administration.

Lansing is a good young fellow and a good practitioner of the law; but his friends mistook his talents when they made him a statesman. He thinks two pence an ounce upon plate a *monstrous tax.* The county of Albany is not of my opinion concerning him.

Treaddle [i.e., Tredwell] is esteemed a sensible and an honest man.

Mr. Humphreys has his admirers, because he is pretty remarkable for *blunder* and vociferation. He said the last session in the assembly that it was very inconvenient for the country members to be detained at that season, that for his own part no motive would induce him to stay, but *to sacrifice* the interest of his country.

In the council of revision,[17] which is composed of the Governor, Chancellor and the three Judges;[18] Mr. Morris the chief Justice is a well meaning man. Judge Yates is upright and respectable in his profession. Hobart is solemn and sententious. He thinks rightly in the main as to the imperfections of our present system, both general and particular and the proper remedy; but he has a prodigious propensity to a *convulsion;* and he augurs many fine things from a second *bankruptcy* and a total derangement of our affairs. "Then (says he) and not 'till then *Order* will rise out of confusion."

I have now touched upon the principal *public* characters among us; there are others who have their little circles of influence; some of whom deserve more others much less. I have contented myself with outlines, because Mr. G Morris will be able to give you much more satisfactory portraits. What I have done is only in compliance with your request.

The rulers of this state are attached to the alliance, as are the whigs generally.

They have also great confidence in you personally; but pretty general exception has been taken to a certain letter of yours written I believe in the winter or spring.[19] The idea imbibed is, that it contains a reflection upon them for their past exertions. I have on every account combatted this impression, which could not fail to have an ill effect, and I mention it to you with freedom, because it is essential you should know the temper of the states respecting yourself.

As to the people, in the early periods of the war, near one half of them were avowedly more attached to Great Britain than to their liberty; but the energy of the government has subdued all opposition. The state by different means has been purged of a large part of its malcontents; but there still remains I dare say a third whose secret wishes are on the side of the enemy; the remainder sigh for peace, murmur at taxes, clamour at their rulers, change one incapable man for another more incapable; and I fear if left to themselves would, too many of them, be willing to purchase peace at any price, not from inclination to great Britain, or disaffection to independence, but from mere supineness and avarice.[20] The speculation of evils from the claims of Great Britain gives way to the pressure of inconveniences actually felt; and we required the event which has lately happened, the recognition of our independence by the Dutch[21] to give a new spring to the public hopes and the public passions. This has had a good effect. And if the Legislature can be brought to adopt a wise plan for its finances, we may put the people in better humour, and[22] give a more regular and durable movement to the machine. The people of this state as far as my observation goes, have as much firmness in their make[23] and as much submissiveness to government as those of any part of the Union.

It remains for me to give you an explicit opinion of what it is practicable for this state to do.[24] Even with a judicious plan of taxation I do not think the state can afford or the people will bear to pay more than seventy, or eighty thousand pounds a year.[25] In its intire and flourishing state according to my mode of calculating it could not have exceeded two hundred and thirty or forty thousand pounds; and reduced as it is with the wheels of circulation so exceedingly clogged for want of commerce and a sufficient medium more than I have said cannot be expected.[26] Passed experience will not authorise a more flattering conclusion.

Out of this is to be deducted the expence of the interior administration and the money necessary for the levies of men. The first amounts to about £15,000[27]—as you will perceive by the inclosed state; but I suppose the Legislature would choose to retain ⟨£15,000⟩ £20,000.[28] The money hitherto yearly expended in recruits has amounted to between twenty and thirty thousand pounds; but on a proper plan ten thousand might suffice. There would then remain forty thousand pounds for your department.

But this is on the supposition of a change of system; for with the present I doubt there being paid into the Continental treasury one ⟨half⟩ third[29] of that sum.[30] I am endeavouring to collect materials for greater certainty upon this subject. But the business of supplies has been so diversified, lodged in such a variety of independent hands and so carelessly transacted that it is hardly possible to get any tolerable idea of the gross and nett product.

With the help of these materials I shall strive to convince the Committee[31] when they meet that a change of measures is essential; if they enter cordially into right views we may succeed; but I confess I fear more than I hope.

I have taken every step in my power to procure the information you have desired in your letter of July 81.[32] The most material part of it, an account of the supplies furnished since March 80 has been committed to Col Hay. I have written to him in pressing terms to accelerate the preparation.[33]

You will perceive Sir, I have neither flattered the state nor encouraged high[34] expectations. I thought it my duty to exhibit things as they are not as they ought to be. I shall be sorry, if it give an ill-opinion of the state for want of equal candor in the representations of others; for however disagreeable the reflection, I have too much reason to believe that the true picture of other states would be in proportion to their circumstances equally unpromising. All my inquiries and all that appears induces this opinion. I intend this letter *in confidence to yourself* and therefore I indorse it *private*.

Before I conclude I will say a word on a point that possibly you could wish to be informed about. The contract up this way is executed generously to the satisfaction of the officers and soldiers, which is the more meritorious in the Contractor[35] as in all probability it will be to him a losing undertaking.

I have the honor to be with sentiments of unfeigned esteem Sir Your most Obedient and humble servant[36]

A Hamilton

The Honble The Superintendant of Finance

[ENCLOSURE][37]

Expences of our internal Government

To the Governor ...... for salary	£1500[38]
To the Chancellor ...... do	400
To the Secretary of State & Clerks about	300
To the Attorney General....by estimation	100[39]
[To the] Chief Justice ...... salary	400
Puisne Justices each 350 £ do	700
for travelling expences by estimation 40 days in the year at 12/ per day each	100[40]
Auditor	300
Aide De Camp to the Governor Lt. Col Pay & rations .	360
Occasional do. at the same rate	

Delegates to Congress 34/ pr day while attending and 6 days going and coming abt	1500
Treasurer........Salary	300
Members of Legislature 8/ pr. day, upon an average [*torn*] members for 88[41] days (including coming & going)	1936
two Clerks of do. each 20/ a day for 72 days .... time actually together	144
two Door Keepers each 10/ pr day....do	72
Printer for printing laws &c. about	300
	8412

Incidental expences

To the poor annually about	500	
To the Indians do	000[42]	6588
Charges of Militia expresses occasional officers & other occasional demands allowd	6088[43]	⟨3500⟩
		⟨11884⟩

Reg   say   ⟨£12000⟩

⟨£15000⟩

Transmitted a copy of the above to Mr. Morris
Aug.   1782

ENDORSED: Albany 13 August 1782/Alexr Hamilton Esqr/Receiver of Contl Taxes/ &c/Characters
MSS: ALS, Hamilton Papers, DLC; ADft fragment, Hamilton Papers, DLC; incomplete transcript, Hamilton Papers, DLC.

1. This penetrating expository letter on the economy and politics of New York State from Hamilton's pen—he was not yet thirty—was a response to the fifth section of RM's private instructions to the receivers of April 13, 1782, and RM's circular to the receivers of July 12, 1782, in which they were asked to obtain answers to questions RM had previously posed to the state governors in a circular of July 25, 1781. Hamilton had promised the report in his letter to RM of July 22, 1782. His analysis drew RM's praise for its "accurate, clear and comprehensive Descriptions of general and particular Characters, Sentiments and Opinions" which "do equal Justice to your Talents both for Observation and Description" (to Hamilton, August 28). To RM's disappointment, however, Hamilton had previously announced his intention to resign as receiver for New York, an office the Superintendent had only recently persuaded him to accept.

The ALS published here is the recipient's copy endorsed in RM's hand. It had originally been part of the corpus of RM's papers inherited by his younger daughter, Maria Morris Nixon, who in the mid-nineteenth century could find "but one letter from Genl Hamilton"—the present one—among RM's surviving manuscripts. "[A] distinct recollection of the high estimation in which my Father held Genl Hamilton, and of the great regard and unreserved confidence which subsisted between them," Mrs. Nixon lamented, "adds much to the sorrow and regret I have long felt for the loss and destruction of my Father's papers." Mrs. Nixon made a transcript (listed in the manuscript identification note above) available for John C. Hamilton's edition of Hamilton's writings but withheld the portion characterizing New York politicians. The ALS eventually left the possession of RM's family and circulated among private collectors before being sold in 1917, apparently to Hamilton's grandson, and coming to rest alongside the fragmentary ADft (see note 20 below) in the Library of Congress. The letter was not published in its entirety until 1916. See *The Magazine of History*, XXIII (1916), 158–170; and Syrett and Cooke, eds., *Hamilton Papers*, III, 132n. For a discussion of RM's papers, see volume I of this series, xxvii–xxxii.

2. For Hamilton's efforts to obtain information for this letter, which continued even after it had been dispatched to RM, see Syrett and Cooke, eds., *Hamilton Papers*, III, 123–124, 126–127, 130–132, 147–148, 163–164. See also notes 7 and 33 below.

3. Space left blank in manuscript. Hamilton refers to a long letter from Governor George Clinton of New York to the President of Congress of February 5, 1781 (PCC, no. 67, II, 344–361), recounting New York's role in the war effort, describing the exhausted condition of the state, and asking Congress to furnish the state with money. The letter was enclosed in Clinton to the New York Delegates in Congress, February 5, 1781, Hastings and Holden, eds., *Clinton Papers*, VI, 634–635.

4. The account of New York's commerce and balance of external payments which follows is in substantial agreement with that of a recent historian in emphasizing the state's financial dependence upon military purchases of agricultural commodities by Congress, by the state governments of New York and New England, and to a lesser degree by the French and British forces. These purchases paid for necessary imports. It appears, however, that Hamilton exaggerated New York's adverse balance of trade with other regions and the outward flow of specie in order to minimize expectation that the state would be able to comply with congressional requisitions. See Bernard Mason, "Entrepreneurial Activity in New York During the American Revolution," *Business History Review*, XL (1966), 190–212, esp. 193–196, 211–212. See also note 7 below.

5. Under a New York act passed on April 13, 1782, goods brought into the state from enemy possessions in the United States would be liable to confiscation. A later act, passed on July 22, 1782, defined as contraband all British property and goods produced in Britain, its colonies and dependencies, or in ports of the United States under British power, brought "into this or any of the other United States in vessels the property of the subjects of the king of Great Britain or in any other way from places within the power of the enemy." *Laws of New York*, I, 479–482, 509–513. For a discussion of the illicit trade with New York City and congressional attempts to interdict it, see notes to Gouverneur Morris to Thomas Willing, June 18, 1782.

6. Hamilton wrote this sentence in the margin.

7. For Hamilton's correspondence with Comfort Sands and Company and William Duer, see Syrett and Cooke, eds., *Hamilton Papers*, III, 95–96, 106, 146. See also note 4 above.

8. Dated July 22.

9. George Clinton was governor of New York, 1777–1795 and 1801–1804.

10. Former Major General Philip Schuyler, Hamilton's father-in-law, was a New York Senator.

11. Pierre Van Cortlandt (1721–1814) served as lieutenant governor of New York from 1777 to 1795. *DAB*.

12. The Chancellor of New York, Robert R. Livingston, was also serving as Secretary for Foreign Affairs under Congress; James Duane was a delegate to Congress and a leader of the conservatives in New York State.

13. John Morin Scott, a delegate to Congress from New York.

14. Respectively, Zephaniah Platt (1735–1807), a lawyer who served in the New York Senate from 1777 to 1783 and as a delegate to Congress in 1785 and 1786 (*Biog. Dir. Cong.*; Burnett, ed., *Letters*, VII, lxxii, VIII, xci); Ephraim Paine (1730–1785), a Dutchess County physician who was a member of the state senate from 1780 to 1784 and served in Congress in 1784 (*Biog. Dir. Cong.*; Burnett, ed., *Letters*, VII, lxxii); and Abraham Yates, Jr., of Albany, Continental loan officer of New York, 1779–1786, and state senator, 1778–1790, whose expectations of being appointed receiver of Continental taxes for New York were disappointed by RM (see Yates to RM, November 4, 1782, and notes).

15. William Malcom (d. 1792), colonel of the New York levies, whom Hamilton had evidently recommended as commissioner of accounts for New York or possibly to succeed himself as receiver. RM instead directed Hamilton to offer the post of com-

missioner of accounts for either New Hampshire or Rhode Island, but Malcom declined. In 1784 the West Point and Moving Army contractors selected him as an arbitrator in their claims against the United States. Heitman, *Register;* RM to Hamilton, August 28 and October 16, 1782, and Memorandum of Agreement with Sands, Livingston and Company, September 1, 1784.

16. Respectively, John Laurance of New York City, judge advocate general of the Continental army, 1777–1782; John Lansing, Jr. (1754–1829), Albany lawyer who served in the state assembly from 1780 to 1788 except when he attended Congress as a delegate in 1785 and subsequently opposed the ratification of the United States Constitution (*DAB;* Burnett, ed., *Letters,* VIII, xci); Thomas Tredwell (1743–1831), a Suffolk County lawyer and assemblyman from 1777 to 1783 (*Biog. Dir. Cong.*); and Cornelius Humphrey of Dutchess County, a member of the assembly from 1781 to 1786 (Syrett and Cooke, eds., *Hamilton Papers,* III, 139n.).

17. The state constitution of 1777 provided for a Council of Revision, consisting of the governor, the chancellor, and the judges of the supreme court, or any two of them in conjunction with the governor, to assemble during sessions of the legislature. If the Council, or a majority of it, deemed any act passed by the legislature unconstitutional, it was authorized to state its reasons to the legislative house in which the act originated. The act then had to be passed by a two-thirds vote of both houses. An act automatically became law, however, if the Council did not take action within ten days, unless the legislature adjourned before then, in which case its objections were to be submitted on the first day of the next session.

18. The three judges of the New York Supreme Court mentioned by Hamilton were: Chief Justice Richard Morris (1730–1810), a half brother of Gouverneur Morris; Robert Yates (1731–1801), the future opponent of the United States Constitution; and John Sloss Hobart (1738–1805), who was currently acting as an arbitrator in the disputes between the army and the contractor for West Point. *DAB;* and on Hobart as arbitrator, notes to George Washington to RM, June 8, 1782.

19. The letter was RM to the Governor of New York, December 11, 1781. For his comment on this matter, see RM to Hamilton, August 28.

20. Hamilton's fragmentary ADft begins here and continues to the end of the letter. Only the most significant variations from the ALS have been noted below.

21. The United Provinces recognized American independence on April 19, 1782. See notes to RM to the President of Congress, July 29.

22. In the ADft the remainder of the sentence had read "put the [machine?] in motion."

23. Hamilton had substituted this word for "temper" in the ADft.

24. Here in the ADft Hamilton had written then crossed out the words "and what may be expected."

25. In the ADft Hamilton had originally written "sixty or seventy thousand pounds annually."

26. Hamilton had written then lined out the following passage in the ADft: "I take it to be a true principle that the quantity of taxes a people can pay is in a compound ratio to the quantity of property and the quickness of the circulation of that property. From information I have collected." See note 36 below.

27. Hamilton originally wrote a different figure, possibly "£12,000." In the ADft the figure appears to be "£12,000," possibly reworked from "£15,000."

28. In the ADft Hamilton had apparently first written "£20,000," then reworked it to "£15,000."

29. In the ADft Hamilton had first written "fourth," then substituted "third."

30. At this point in the top margin of the ADft Hamilton had written, then excised, the following words: "Rents of all the land in England £14000000 Stg at 20 years."

31. For the joint committee on taxation, see Hamilton to RM, July 22, and notes.

32. See notes 1 and 2 above.

33. See Hamilton to Udny Hay, August 3 and September 7, 1782, Syrett and Cooke, eds., *Hamilton Papers,* III, 124–125, 160–161. Hay was the supply agent of New York State.

34. In the ADft Hamilton had substituted this word for "your."

35. In the ADft Hamilton had substituted this word for "Mr. Duer." William Duer

was contractor for the posts north of Poughkeepsie in New York, including Albany, where Hamilton wrote the present letter.

36. Hamilton turned the last page of his draft upside down and wrote in the top margin: "The ability of a people to pay taxes is in a compound ratio to the q[uantity?] of the property in a state and to the quickness of the circulation of property."

37. ms: ADft, Hamilton Papers, DLC. endorsed: No 10/Expences of the Internal Government/of this State/1782/Copied.

38. Hamilton appears to have originally written "1000" before reworking the number.

39. Hamilton reworked this figure from "200."

40. Hamilton substituted this number for "72."

41. Hamilton reworked this number from one he had originally written.

42. Hamilton reworked these zeroes over another number which is now unreadable.

43. Hamilton appears to have originally written "2000" or "3000" before reworking the number.

From Walter Livingston

Philadel: Augt. 13. 1782

Sir

Yesterday I received a letter of the 8th. Instant from Mr. Comfort Sands which is of a nature too Serious to justify any delaying its communication.[1]

He in substance informs me that upon mature deliberation he and his Brother have determined to give up their part of the Contract unless the Ballances due from the Public are paid, and that they will accordingly quit it as soon as I return.[2]

It may be observed that besides former ballances 35,000 dollars and upwards are due upon the Supplies of last month. The daily expense accruing since may be estimated at 1,500 dollars.

It is my duty not to deceive you and no inducement whatever would tempt me to hazard the welfare of the Army. I therefore take the earliest opportunity to declare that if Messrs. Sands relinquish the Contract I cannot be responsible for its execution being neither able to advance money for the Supplies, nor to procure them on Credit beyond the express terms of the Contract: at the same time that my want of health disqualified me from undergoing the fatigue of the active branch of the Business which was originally by compact assigned to Messrs. Sands. Far from wishing to shrink from my Engagements even if I was sure they would be attended with a loss, I am willing and even desireous to perform them with the utmost strictness, if any Gentlemen capable of Sustaining the necessary advances of money will assume the share held and the service which were to have been performed by Messrs. Sands.

The perplexity in which this business is involved gives me an anxiety from which I have reason from your known Benevolence to expect all the releif in your power.

I beg leave on this occasion to observe that if the army should be put into motion an advance agreably to the contract will be required for the expensive article of transportation as I am fully persuaded that the Service will otherwise be rendered impracticable.

Permit me to add that it is become necessary that a person should as soon as possible be appointed by you to decide disputes between the army and the Contractors as the Contract directs.[3] I am Sir &c

The Honle. Robert Morris Eqr.
Superintendant of Finance

 MS: Copy in Livingston's writing, George Washington Papers, DLC.
   1. Sands's letter has not been found. Livingston and Comfort Sands and Company were the principal partners in the contract for West Point and the Moving Army.
   2. For the eventual collapse of the contract, see Comfort Sands, Walter Livingston, William Duer, and Daniel Parker to RM, September 11, and notes.
   3. Livingston enclosed this text in a letter to Washington of August 31, 1782 (Washington Papers, DLC); on this letter, see notes to RM to Livingston, August 29. For RM's response, see Diary, August 14, and notes. Concerning the selection of Ezekiel Cornell as inspector of contracts for the main army, see notes to RM to the President of Congress, April 20, 1782.

To Daniel Hale

Office of Finance 13. Augt. 1782
   I have received your Letter dated at Albany the third Instant.[1] I think you must be mistaken in saying that you left in my Possession the Contract made by Messrs. Duer and Co. with General Schuyler for I do not find it amongst the Papers of this Office. The Counterpart which was transmitted to me by his Excellency General Washington,[2] shall be transcribed and sent by Mr. Geary to William Duer Esqr. which may prevent any Inconvenience to him by the Loss of the Original.

MS: Ofcl LbC, DLC.
   1. Letter not found. Hale was an agent for William Duer, contractor for the Northern Department.
   2. See the contract enclosed in Washington to RM, May 15, 1782.

To William Churchill Houston

Office of Finance 13th August 1782[1]
   I have received your favor of the tenth Instant and shall pay the proper attention to it when Necessary.

MSS: LS, Houston Papers, NjP; Ofcl LbC, DLC.
   1. Houston was the receiver of Continental taxes for New Jersey. According to Houston's endorsement, he received the letter on August 16.

To John Warren

Office of Finance 13th Augt. 1782
   I have received your Letter of the twenty fifth of July last[1] and shall direct the Comptroller of the Treasury to make the proper Examinations of the Resolutions of Congress and adjust the Accounts accordingly.[2] Mr. Osgood shall know the Result and will be able to transmit it to you.

MS: Ofcl LbC, DLC.

1. On the subject of this letter from Dr. John Warren of Boston, which has not been found, see Diary, December 26, 1781, and notes. The recipient's copy of RM's reply was evidently misaddressed to James Warren of Plymouth, Massachusetts (see RM to James Warren, September 30). The two men were unrelated.

2. See RM to the Comptroller of the Treasury, August 14.

Diary: August 14, 1782

Mr. Geo. Eddy called to inform me [he] is just going for New Jersey when he expects to pay Mr Ramson [Remsen] about eight thousand or ten thousand Dollars on my Account to be by him paid over to the Contractors.[1]

Mr Jos. Bullock called for money to pay the Contingent Charges of drawing the Lottery, promised the same next Week.[2]

Mr Willm. Wister for Money on Account of Colo. Miles—could not supply him.

Mr. Thos. Bradford respecting Prisoners &c. As the Department to which he belongs is now broke up[3] I told this Gentleman that in future Mr Brown Secy to the Marine Office might transact that Business without creating any additional Expence, Consequently that his Mr. Bradfords Services would no longer be wanted.

Mr Pierce Paymaster General applied for money but I cannot give him any this Day.

Capt. Allibone Called to offer me the Ship General Washington for Sale. I told him that I cannot make the purchase unless my receipt for the Amount of the Purchase money as so much paid by the State of Pennsylvania to the United States on account of Specific Supplies would do for payment. He said that would not do and we parted.[4]

I sent for Capt. Jno. Green to [inquire?] where the Cartel Ship is and the Terms on which she comes out.[5]

The Hon. Mr. Clarke called and told me he had been desired to forward a Letter from me to a Mr. Forman[6] and supposing I meant him some public Employment he called to give me his Character &c. but as I had no such thing in View this precaution was not necessary altho it is always usefull to know Characters.

Mr. B. Town for Money due by the Secy at War for which I signed a Warrant.

The Hon. Secy at War called and had a Conference on sundry matters of Public Concern.

Mrs. Sweers called respecting her Husband. I referred her to Mr. Ingersol the Council in this Cause.

Walter Livingston Esqr. wrote me a Letter last night very serious in its nature and Contents and he met this Day with Mr. Milligan at my Office agreeable to my desire, when I signed a warrant for 4,000

Dollars in his favor on Account of the Contractors for the moving Army, told him what other payments I expect to make[7] and then laid before him the remarks of the Clerks and auditors on the accounts rendered by Messrs. Sands and Co. and desired Mr. Milligan to State fully all his Complaints against the Contractors. Mr. Livingston desired to have the whole in Writing which was promised him.[8]

Capt. De Bert of Colo. Armands Legion called and told me Mr. Milligan objected to settle the Accounts he had brought from Colo. Armand for Cloathing his Corps because he had not the Accounts for recruiting &c. I took the Accounts and promised to speak to Mr Milligan on the Subject. He desired payment of Subsistence money due to the Corps. I said it Should be paid before he leaves the City. He asked for the Horses wanting to mount the Legion amounting to ninety. I told him it is impossible; he pressed this point much and my answer was allways it is impossible.

Lieut. Beaulieu for Money; desired him to Call next Week.

Mr. Dudley with a Letter &c.[9] I desired him to call next Week.

Doctr. Bodo Otto for Money which is impracticable.[10]

Mr. Mallet called to inform me that they had taken but one pair of Guns and the Money deposited over and above their Cost must be returned.[11]

Mr Wm. Scott for a Certificate for the Balance due on his Account as settled by Mr. Burrall.[12] I told him these cannot be Issued until we have proper Forms &c.

Mr. Carrell for money; referred him to the Commissary Genl. of Military Stores &c.

Mr. Parr for money for the Contractors for Lancaster; granted 1,000 Dollars.

Mr Weed the Goaler informs me there are 71 Naval Prisoners in his Custody. I propose sending them away directly.[13]

Isaac Howell and Peter Thompson late Inspectors of the Press for money—put them off for the present.

Had a long Conference with Mr. Milligan, received many other Applications for money—and many Letters &c, &c.

Wrote a Letter to David Ross Esqr.

Wrote a Letter to Jos. Nourse.[14]

Wrote a Letter to James Milligan.

Wrote a Letter to Jos Borden.

Wrote a Letter to James Wood.

1. See Diary, August 12, and notes.
2. See Diary, August 2.
3. Thomas Bradford had been a deputy commissary of prisoners before Congress on July 24, 1782, repealed all previous "resolutions and appointments respecting the department of commissary general of prisoners" and vested the responsibility for negotiating the exchange of marine prisoners in the Agent of Marine. See Diary, June 18, 1782.

4. For RM's eventual purchase of the *General Washington,* see notes to Diary, May 15, 1782.

5. See Diary, August 13, and notes.

6. The reference is probably to Aaron Forman, assistant deputy quartermaster general at Morristown. Abraham Clark was a New Jersey delegate to Congress.

7. Livingston later reported that in response to his August 13 letter the Financier "verbally gave me every assurance of assistance" (to Washington, August 31, 1782, Washington Papers, DLC; see notes to Livingston to RM, August 29). Among the other expected payments was one to be made in New Jersey through the auspices of George Eddy (see above in this Diary) and another of $12,000 to be obtained from New York City (see RM to Washington, August 13, and notes), but these efforts were largely ineffectual. See also Diary, August 20, and notes.

8. This material cannot be identified with certainty, although it may have included "some observations made by the Auditors and Comtroller on the Contractors last account for the issues of July," which Secretary at War Benjamin Lincoln enclosed in a letter to Washington of August 19, 1782 (Washington Papers, DLC), but which have not been found. Less likely is an undated paper, entitled "Observations made by the Clerks of Accounts on the account of Comfort Sands and Company extracted from their States of those Accounts," which comments on the contractors' accounts for April, May, and June and is filed under August 1, 1782, in the Washington Papers, DLC. For Milligan's earlier criticisms of the contractors' accounts, see his letter to RM of August 1, and notes. See also Diary, August 15.

9. Benjamin Dudley was assisting RM with the establishment of a mint. The letter has not been identified.

10. Otto had formerly been a physician and surgeon in the Continental army.

11. See Diary, July 26, and notes.

12. William Scott had served as Pennsylvania's commissioner of purchases for York County. Jonathan Burrall was the commissioner for settling Commissary Department accounts.

13. See notes to Diary, August 13.

14. Letter not found.

To James Wood

Office of Finance 14. Augt. 1782

Sir,

You will receive herewith the Instructions from the Minister of War and myself of the eleventh of July for liberation of the German Prisoners at Frederick Town in Maryland and Winchester in Virginia.[1] You will perceive by these Instructions that you are to Account for the Monies you receive in such Manner as the Superintendant of Finance shall direct. You will receive discharges from General Lincoln which you will Acknowlege and Account for by returning them or the Sum of eighty Dollars each in Lieu of them. You will pay to the Officer whom General Lincoln may appoint for making Enlistments such Monies as he may direct and take the Officers Receipt as for so much Money received from the Minister at War which Receipt you will transmit to this Office and thereupon the proper Discharge shall be made out for you. You will likewise purchase up such Bank Notes or Orders drawn by me on Mr. Swanwick as you may meet with in Order that they may be remitted which will save the Risque and Expence of Transporting the Money. I am Sir your most obedient Servant

RM

MS: Ofcl LbC, DLC.
1. Colonel Wood of the Virginia line had recently agreed to undertake this business (see Diary, August 12). On the liberation of German prisoners, see notes to Diary, May 1, and to the instructions of July 11, 1782.

To Joseph Borden, Jr.

Office of Finance 14. Augt 1782

I received your Favor dated the twelfth Instant[1] and in Compliance with your Request write a Line to inform you, that at present you cannot receive the money you desire, which I am very sorry for.

MS: Ofcl LbC, DLC.
1. Letter not found. Borden was Continental loan officer of New Jersey.

To David Ross

Office of Finance 14. Augt. 1782

I am favored with your Letter dated at Petersburg on the 3d. Instant.[1] The draft you therein advise in favor of Messrs. Whitesides and Co. for 5500 dollars shall be paid altho it occasions considerable Inconvenience at the present moment. And I expect you will be able to recover the Money from Mr: Braxton and others for payment of their Bonds given for the Amount of Goods they bought it being impossible for me to spare what is sufficient for that Purpose, and to discharge the numerous Demands against the Public which are dayly exhibited to me.

MS: Ofcl LbC, DLC.
1. Letter not found. Ross had formerly been the commercial agent of Virginia. For his involvement in purchases made under the Yorktown capitulation agreement, the subject of this letter from RM, see notes to George Washington to RM, November 19, 1781.

To Thomas Russell

Marine Office 14. August 1782

I have received your Letter of the 29 July.[1] Inclosed is a Warrant ordering a Court martial for the Trial of Lieut. Michael Knies of the frigate Hague on charges made against him by Capt. Samuel Nicholson which you will please to have brought on.[2] From the Articles enclosed in your Letter it would seem that the Act of Congress of the tenth of July last has not reached you. You will certainly receive it before this arrives and you will find it necessary to make correspondent Alterations.

I approve of your advancing two Months pay to some of the Officers and men belonging to the frigate Alliance for the Support of their Families which you will charge to that Frigate and in due Time furnish the Accounts.

MS: AM LbC, MdAN.
1. Letter not found. Russell was the deputy agent of marine for New England stationed at Boston.
2. See Nicholson to RM, July 24; the enclosed warrant is dated August 14.

To the Comptroller of the Treasury
(James Milligan)

Office of Finance 14. Augt. 1782

Enclosed is Copy of a Letter I have received from Mr. Warren at Boston whereby you will see that he apprehends there has been some Error in settling the account relative to the Education of his late Brothers Children.[1] I request you will make the necessary Examination into that account and if any Errors appear that you will inform me of the Result of your Enquiries.

MS: Ofcl LbC, DLC.

1. Dr. John Warren's letter of July 25 has not been found. See RM to Warren, August 13, and notes.

Warrant Appointing a Court-Martial for the
Trial of Michael Knies

Marine Office, August 14, 1782.[1] This document is addressed to "Abram Whipple, Hoysted Hacker, Samuel Tucker, Daniel Waters and Silas Talbot Esqrs Captains and John Brown and Peter Develle Esqrs. Lieuts. in the Navy of the United States of America." Except for their appointment here as a court-martial "for the Trial of Michael Knies a Lieutenant on board the frigate Hague," this text is identical in wording to RM's Warrant Appointing a Court-Martial for the Trial of Arthur Dillaway, June 26, 1782.

MS: AM LbC, MdAN.

1. This warrant, enclosed in RM to Thomas W. Russell, August 14, was annexed to an extract from Samuel Nicholson to RM, July 24. Knies (d. 1783) had served as 3d lieutenant on the *Hague* (formerly the *Deane*) since May 1, 1781. *Massachusetts Soldiers and Sailors of the Revolutionary War* (Boston, 1896–1908), IX, 341.

Diary: August 15, 1782

Mr. Parr applied for more money on Account of the Lancaster Contract and I must if possible supply him this Week.

Mr. Swanwick with various Communications respecting money matters.

Colo. Francis Wade having written me many Letters respecting Law Suits brought against him and Suits which he has Commenced against others[1] I sent for him and told him that I perceived he thought me obliged by Duty to do something for his releif but that he must defend himself against all Actions that are brought against him even as a publick Officer, that Congress had passed a recommendation to the several Legislatures for making Laws to Stay Executions in all Cases where the Transaction was actually on Account of the United States. That I had furnished him with a Copy of that recommendation[2] and that I hoped it would have the desired Effect in the State of Delaware where he is sued but that I would also speak with Governor Dickinson on the Subject and in regard to a Suit which he Colo. Wade had brought on behalf of the United States against a Mr. Harvey, that I will speak to the Hon: Mr. McKean[3] to support it.

This Morning I dispatched Capt. Storer who came Express from Mr Langdon and supplied him with 100 Dollars to pay Expences which is charged to Mr. Langdons Account.[4]

Mr. Alexr. Robertson applied to me for Drafts on New York for which he proposed to pay Mr. Pierces Notes to the Amount of 2400 Dollars. I applied to Mr Hill who furnished me with Richard Wells Drafts on Jos. Stansbury for that Sum and I delivered them in Exchange for the notes. These notes of Mr Pierces together with a note of Mr. Hills for 1600 Dollars I delivered to Mr. Swanwick with orders for him to pay the whole 4,000 Dollars to Mr. Pierce who is to Discount Mr Hills note at the Bank.[5]

The Honble. Mr. Howell called to see the last Letters written to the State of Rhode Island respecting the Impost Law and we had some Conversation with him respecting Land Tax, Poll Tax and Excise &c.[6]

The Hon. Mr. Duane and Mr Clarke came to the Office but after some Conversation together postponed the meeting of the Committee until Tuesday next.[7]

Capt Greene brought to the Office Capt Maxwell master of the Cartel Ship Symmetry. He shewed me his Instructions and Pass Port.[8] From the first I discover that after landing the Prisoners in America he is to obey such Orders as he may receive from the British Commander in Chief. I therefore desired him to write his Letters, send them to this Office and I will dispatch them for New York with Letters of my own informing that I propose sending by this Ship seventy one naval Prisoners now in this Goal.[9]

Honble. Secy at War came here at my request when I desired him to give a general Order to the Contractors at this Post and to the Contractors of the moving Army to Issue Rations upon the orders of Mr. John Brown Secy. of the Marine Department which he did. I mentioned to him my Apprehensions that the Issuing of Rations to the Prisoners in Goal here is not Conducted with regularity and desired him to examine into the matter. I told him my intention to exchange the naval Prisoners with which he was well pleased. I desired him to name the Person who is to receive money for recruiting Germans. He said he will receive it himself and deliver it over to the proper Officers.[10] I laid before the honble. Secy at War the remarks of the Auditors on the Contractors Accounts[11] and proposed to him for Consideration that they should settle the monthly Issues to each Corps so as that one Voucher signed by the Commanding Officer might Serve.

Doctr. Ths. Bond junr. applied for money for the use of his Department and I signed a Warrant for 500 Dollars.

Richd. Philips Steward of His Excellency the President of Congress applied for an Order on Mr Swanwick to pay the Presidents Warrant of 300 Dollars on Mr Hilligas but I directed Mr. Swanwick to pay Mr. Hilligas money.

Wrote a Letter to James Milligan Esqr.[12]

Wrote a Letter to the Honble Wm. [i.e., John Morin] Scott, and His Excelly. the Govr of Delaware.

Issued a Warrant on Mr Swanwick in favor of Jos Pennell	£ 22.18.4
Issued a Warrant on Mr Swanwick in favor of the Bank for Discounts	9. 2.1
Issued a Warrant on Mr Swanwick in favor of Samuel Storer	37.10.0
Issued a Warrant on Mr Swanwick in favor of T. Francis	907.16.4

1. The letters from Wade, a deputy quartermaster in Delaware, have not been found.
2. See RM to Wade, August 9, and notes.
3. Thomas McKean, a delegate to Congress from Delaware.
4. See RM to John Langdon, August 13.
5. Henry Hill, a Philadelphia merchant, owed the Financier money on the sale of bills of exchange (see Diary, July 29, 30, and August 13, and notes). On Robertson's role, see Diary, July 16, 1782, and notes.
6. RM's last letter to Rhode Island on the impost was dated August 2; for an earlier letter, see RM's Circular to the Governors of Massachusetts, Rhode Island, and Maryland, January 3, 1782. The Superintendent's latest recommendation of land, poll, and excise taxes, made in his letter to the president of Congress of July 29, had been referred on August 5 to the grand committee considering "the most effectual means of supporting the credit of the United States." David Howell, a Rhode Island delegate to Congress, was a member of that committee.
7. James Duane of New York and Abraham Clark of New Jersey were members of a congressional committee investigating the Office of Finance. See notes to Diary, June 12, 1782.
8. The instructions to Francis Maxwell from the Commissioners for the Sick and Hurt, dated May 24, 1782, are cited in notes to Diary, August 13. His passport has not been found.
9. See Diary, August 16.
10. On the recruitment of German prisoners, see notes to Diary, May 1, 1782.
11. See Diary, August 14, and notes.
12. Letter not found.

To John Morin Scott

Office of Finance 15. Augt. 1782

Sir,

I do myself the Honor to return the Draft which you transmitted to me on Saturday last. I had not until this Day sufficient Leizure for an attentive Perusal of it. I am sorry to add that I cannot approve of the Plan. With perfect Respect I have the honor to be Sir your most obedient and humble Servant[1]

RM

[ENCLOSURE]²

Draft Report of a Committee of Congress on the Settlement of Accounts in Europe

[Philadelphia, ca. August 10, 1782]

The Committee to whom was referred on Reconsideration the Resolution of the 28th. May 1782 for appointing a Commissioner to liquidate and finally settle the Accounts of all the Servants of the United States who have been intrusted with the Expenditure of public Monies in Europe having conferred with the Superintdt. of Finance report it as their Opinion that the Liquidation and final Settlement of the said Accounts ought to be made only at the Treasury of these United States.

That nevertheless it is absolutely necessary for the purpose of doing full Justice to these United States and the Accountants on the most satisfactory Grounds that some person should be authorized in Europe to receive of the Accountants all the said Accounts attended with a production to and inspection by him of the original Vouchers duly attested and proved and with Authenticated Copies of the same and of the Affidavits or other proofs to verify the original Vouchers, to be by such person transmitted without delay to the Office of the Superintendent of Finance that thereby the proof may be exactly identified. That instead of sending a Commissioner expressly for that purpose, a measure that would be attended with delay and extraordinary Expence and be exposed to Hazard and disappointment, the Committee recommend that the Consul General of these United States resident in France be ⟨appointed⟩³ authorized for that purpose.⁴

They further report that in their Opinion those Accounts ought to be so framed as to consist of a particular detail of all the Sums of Money which have from Time to Time come to the Hands of the Accountants respectively with their respective dates of Receipt and the Gifts, Aids, Loans, Subsidies and funds of whatever Nature or Kind on which they may have been respectively received and the Public Officers and other Persons from whom respectively with all which the Accountants respectively ought distinctly, fairly and accurately to debit themselves in Account with These United States.

That as the Burthen of the proof of the several Expenditures must necessarily lie on the Accountants; they ought respectively to attend their Credits in Account with the United States with clear, minute and satisfactory Proofs not only of the actual Expenditures and of the Times when and persons to whom and uses for which; but also of the Ground of Authority on which the same were respectively made.

And for the better carrying of this Report into Execution should the same be approved of by Congress the Committee beg Leave to report the following form of a special Commission to the said Consul General and Instructions thereon to wit

"The *United States of America in Congress assembled* to all to whom these presents shall come send Greeting. Know Ye That reposing special Trust and Confidence in the Abilities, Integrity and diligence of   [5] Esqr. Consul General for these United States Resident in the Kingdom of France these United States in Congress assembled have specially authorized, assigned and appointed and by these presents *Do* specially authorize, assign and appoint the said   [6] Esqr. to demand, have, receive and take of and from all and every person and persons who has or have at any Time or Times before the day of the date of these presents, been authorized and empowered by these United States in Congress assembled or any person or persons acting under their Authority, to receive or has or have received on Account and for the Use of these United States in Europe any Sum or Sums of Money whether in the Nature of a Gift, Aid, Loan, Subsidy or from any other fund of any Nature, Kind or Quality whatsoever, a just, full, true and particular Account or Accounts of all and every such Sum and Sums of Money so received and of the Expenditure of the same respectively or of so much thereof as shall have been expended and to have and demand of and from any and every such Accountant such proofs of his Accounts as the said [7] shall deem just and reasonable. And the same Accounts and each and every of them together with the several Vouchers, Evidences and Proofs concerning the same respectively to transmit without Delay, certified under the Seal and Signature of his aforesaid Office of Consul General to the Office of Superintendant of the Finances of these United States wheresoever the same may be, And also in all things to observe, perform and fulfil the Instructions herewith sent bearing equal date with these presents. In Testimony &ca."

The Form of Instructions to attend the Commission:

"Instructions attending a special Commission bearing even date with these presents to   [8] Consul General of the United States of America resident in France to demand, have, receive and take of and from all and every person and persons who has or have received for the Use of these United States any Sums of Money in Europe and expended the same or any part thereof the Accounts and Vouchers of such Receipts and Expenditures to wit

1. You are without delay to call on every such Account of whom You shall have Knowledge, by a written application requesting him to render to You without delay particular, clear, full and perfect Accounts of all such Monies as have come to his hands on Account of these United States by Receipts in Europe from any public of-

ficers or other persons specifying therein the respective Amounts and dates of such Receipts the persons from whom, and the Gifts, Loans, Subsidies or other funds from which the same respectively arose for all which The Accountant is to debit himself in Account with these United States. And You are to take every Means in your power to discover whether the United States are credited in such Account with all the Monies received by the Accountant to their use.[9]

2dly. As the burden of the proof as to the Expenditure of the Monies will lie on the Accountant Every Article of Credit which he shall give himself in his Account with these United States, must be particularly, distinctly and clearly stated expressing if for Monies the persons to whom paid and the Uses to which, if for Goods not only the particular Bales, Chests, Trunks and Packages but also[10] the particular Invoices of each, the Vessels wherein shipped or the person or persons to whom delivered for Transportation.

3dly. You are to require the production of Vouchers for every Article with which the US shall be charged tracing every such Article up to the person or persons who originally furnished the same[11] and You are carefully to examine into the Authenticity, Veracity and Fairness of every Voucher [which] shall be produced to You, whether it be Shop Note, Bill of parcels, Invoice, Receipt, or Bill of Lading; and you are to Cause notarial Copies of the same to be made and attested by the Oaths of the persons respectively who shall have given the originals, and on refusal to give such Oath You are to attend the Copy with proof of such refusal; and in every Case to take due Care so to circumstantiate the Voucher or Vouchers in point of Evidence as that a proper Judgment may be formed here what Credit ought to be given to the same and how far the same may tend to support the Article or Articles of Charge in the Accounts to which the same shall relate.

4thly. You are to transmit the said Accounts and Vouchers either together or from Time [to time] in different Parcels as they may concern different Accounts and persons certified by You under your hand and Seal of Office, to the Office of Superintendent of Finance of these United States wheresoever the same shall be Doing in all Things in and concerning the premisses as by your Commission and these Instructions You are required. In Testimony, &ca."

MS: Ofcl LbC, DLC.

1. Scott, a New York delegate to Congress, was chairman of a committee assigned on July 29 to reconsider the appointment of a commissioner to settle the accounts of American agents in Europe, define his powers, and prepare his instructions in consultation with RM. The committee's draft report enclosed here was returned to RM on August 20 (see Diary of that date). The Superintendent responded in detail in his letter to the committee of August 26. For a discussion, see notes to RM to the President of Congress, May 8, 1782.

2. MS: Dft in the writing of John Morin Scott, PCC, no. 26, pp. 385–396, DNA.

ENDORSED: "Draft of Report of Committee on Reconsideration of Resolution 28th. May 1782 respecting the public Accountants in Europe."

    3. It should be noted that Congress had not yet appointed a consul general in France. Thomas Barclay, the American consul there now—whom Congress ultimately appointed commissioner to settle European accounts on November 18, 1782—was not appointed consul general until January 2, 1783.

    4. Scott wrote this paragraph in the margin.

    5. Space left blank in manuscript.

    6. Space left blank in manuscript.

    7. Space left blank in manuscript.

    8. Space left blank in manuscript.

    9. Scott wrote this sentence in the margin.

    10. Scott wrote the preceding four words in the margin.

    11. Scott wrote the preceding 15 words in the margin.

From John Cruden

New York 15 August 1782

Sir

    I did myself the Honor of writing to you soon after my arrival here, inclosing a letter from Mr. Bean which I fear has not reached you[1] haveing fortunately met here the Bearer My friend Mr Winslow of No Carolina I cheerfully Embrace the Opportunity of addressing you and of inclosing duplicates of Mr Beans. I came here if possible to Relinquish my Office in Carolina, which I hope now to accomplish very Speedily. The Pacifick disposition of my Country toward yours, and an Earnest wish to See a Reunion on terms the most honorable to America (which under these Circumstances shall be my Country) has induced me to propose the Restitution of the property Seized by me in Carolina, to its former Owners in the hope and firm belief that it will produce a Similar Effect on them by Exerting them to Restore the Property of the British Subject. One thing I am convinced of, that the measure of Sequestration has been Eventually most fortunate for the Gentlemen of So Carolina whose Estates were Seized by me, for if the measure had not been adopted, many Estates now Entire and in higher Cultivation than when I took them into my Charge, would have been torn to pieces by needy Creditors; to the injury of my health, and the great Embarrasment of my private Affairs, have I preserved the property, and given Relief to those who were dependant upon the property Seized, for Support. What I trust will operate on the minds of the people in Carolina as a Spur to them in makeing Restitution to the British Subjects, many of whom do not hesitate to Say that had it not been for me, they would have Received Payment of the Debts from the Estates of Absentees whilst the Country was in possesion of the British Army, the fact is undeniable but when the Gentlemen of Carolina Consider that if the property had been Sold under these Circumstances, their Estates must have gone at one fifth of their Value, they will I trust speedily Convince the British Subjects that [they] will not be losers by My Attention to their property.[2]

The Moment sir is perhaps the Most important the World Ever beheld and if the Congress at Paris is broken up, and that Peace is not the Consequence of their Meeting, *The Wars* in all appearance will be Removed by G. Britain from this Country and carried on against France and Spain, and in that case Tobbacco will still Continue to be Valuable, and by following up the plan digested by Mr Bean and myself we should have the Article at Command.

The following Mode strikes me as the most Eligible for prosecuting the great Scheme. In the first place I have to propose to you *Carte Blanche,* and to be the grand Mover in America (altho invisible), in Virginia D. Ross[3] I think may be Secured, in The Carolinas and Georgia I am Master of the Field, and you are the best judge of Men for being Ostensible in Pensylvania and Maryland, when the business is once fairly set on foot I will strain Evry Nerve to have it brought Safely to the British Market. I am about Establishing a House at St Thomas and St Croix to be Composed of two Gentlemen of great Commercial knowledge and Strickt Honor and intigrity, and perhaps, by that Channel in Neutral Bottoms to Europe much may be done.

If Sir this plan meets with your approbation I shall Expect soon to hear from you under Cover to my worthy friend Mr Jos. Taylor late of Boston[4] for whom I have from an intimate knowledge of his Merit, the most Sincere Regard, and who I mean should transact the business here. As the Success of this Grand Scheme must depend on two things Equally important, Namely Secrecy and information, for both of which I trust neither my friend Taylor nor Myself are deficient, perhaps in the first I may be Equal if not Superior to any Commercial Man in the British interest in America.

I need not Mention to you the Necessity of making the business Appear as Diffusive and in as many hands as possible, that the Scheme May not Create jealousy in the Minds of Commercial Men in both Countries.

I shall I hope return Speedily to Carolina to put an End to my Office, and if from publick business I can have an interview with you it would be a Most desirable Circumstance As I am persuaded, I could lay before you a Variety of Matters that would give you Satisfaction and that Might prove highly beneficial to you as an individual and to your family for Ever.

If I should apply for Leave to go to Philada. it will be through the Channell of the Members of Congress for So Carolina, if you wish to meet me, I need not point out to you what should be done, as you will doubtless by your freinds procure leave for me to Visit you without appearing in the Request.

I hope you will forgive me for the free manner in which I address you if what I have proposed is not agreable to you I know you have too much regard for your freind Bean to take what we have proposed in bad part, what I give you my Sacred Honor is Meant to Serve you. I have inclosed my Cypher   And I have the Honor to be with due Respect Sir Your Most Obedient and Most Humble Servant

J. Cruden

Robert Morris Esqr.

MS: ALS, Lovering-Taylor Family Papers, DLC.
    1. Cruden was the British commissioner for sequestered estates in South Carolina. His letter to RM of July 8 has not been found, but the enclosed letter from Samuel Bean, which contained a proposal to engross the American tobacco market, is dated May 26, 1782. The present letter evidently was written before Cruden received RM's letter of August 5 and a subsequent missive of August 13. Whether Cruden actually sent the present letter is uncertain; no reply from RM has been found.
    2. For assessments of Cruden's work as commissioner for sequestered estates in South Carolina, see R. Arthur Bowler, *Logistics and the Failure of the British Army in America* (Princeton, 1975), 89–91; and Jeffrey J. Crow, "What Price Loyalism? The Case of John Cruden, Commissioner of Sequestered Estates," *North Carolina Historical Review*, LVIII (1981), 215–233.
    3. David Ross, the former commercial agent of Virginia.
    4. Joseph Taylor, a loyalist merchant who was involved with George Eddy in RM's agreement to export Yorktown tobacco to New York.

From Charles Lee

[Berkeley County, Virginia] August the 15th 1782[1]

My Dear Sir

Your Freind Mr Vaughan has been with me; He seems a sensible and well-bred young Man, and upon my word (according to the vulgar saying) He seems to have all his eye teeth about him. You as our common Friend enjoind me to be moderate in the price I shoud set on my estate. I really think I have been very moderate. When the bargain I had made with Dorsey[2] was talkd of in the Country all those who pretend to be connoiseurs said that I had given it away— and those I have reason to think my freinds, and who do not talk for talking sake, and who are at the same time esteemd competent judges of the value of lands, have seriously remonstrated with me for my folly. They all agree that taking all its circumstances together, its command of water, it's excellence and abundance of pasture, in short if I may use the expression its managiability, at a small ex-pence, as a grazing farm, renders it preferable to almost any estate in Virginia at least of an equal extent. Some assert it is worth ⟨three⟩ two half Joes an acre, others more—perhaps these valuations are wild and extravagant, I myself think honestly they are, but as Mr Goddard wrote me word that you yourself flatterd me, that there was a probability of obtaining at least three guineas and a half an acre,[3] I conclude you will not think I have transgressing[4] the bounds of modesty in proposing to Mr Vaughan two guineas and a half. Mr Vaughan argues very ingeniously and arithmetically on the value of Money on these times,[5] that He knows means of laying out money to greater advantage than the purchase of lands. All this may [be] very true, but as I have not the secret, and the generality of the Land holders are no wiser than myself, He will find it difficult (if He is seriously determind to buy land) to make so advantageous and easy a purchase as I have offerd—but however My Dear Freind, such is my uneasiness at my present debts, that if you think I ought in duty to myself to make any farther abatement I am ready to do it—as to the means, mode and time of payment I rely entirely on you, but it is necessary that I shoud be furnishd with a certain sum immediately for the payment of my debts, and less than eight hundred pounds sterling will not suffice. I know not what is the cause, My Dear Freind, but of late I find myself much affected in my health—perhaps it is my state of rustication, perhaps the embarrassment of my private affairs, and perhaps in great measure the disagreeable aspect of public affairs—for, with submission, the prospect is not only disagreeable but hideous, at least to a Man of my feelings and sanguine expectation. I have ever from the first time I read Plutarch, been an Enthusiastick for liberty, and (to my cost I now find) for liberty in a republican garb—indeed it is a natural to a young Person whose chief companions are the Greek and Roman Historians and Orators to be dazzled with the splendid picture—but alas, I now find, this perfect kind of liberty coud be only supported by qualities not possessd by the Individuals of the modern world—a public and patriotick spirit reigning in the breast of evry individual superseding all private considerations—it was this spirit alone that carried sevral of the Græcian States and the Roman Republic triumphantly through so many ages—for as to the formal literal construction of their Governments, They were defective to absurdity—it was virtue alone that supported em. All writers agree that virtue must be the basis of republics and most of all of federate republics—have the Americans this necessary virtue? On the contrary are they not on their setting out more corrupted than the oldest People in Europe—and it is no wonder, They are corrupted by the laws themselves, which Mr Montesquieu says is a corruption incurable, because the evil is in the remedy itself—but to shorten my sermon, the Empire of G Britain is overturnd, and the situation of America neither promises happiness, security nor glory, the House of Bourbon alone can cry out Io triumphe.[6] This you will say I ought to have seen before, I confess it, and the sense of my want of foresight perhaps concurrs strongly to the uneasy situation of my mind, and of course so sensibly affects my health and spirits. I shoud make you a thousand apologies for having so improperly drawn upon you but it was entirely owing to my not reading with sufficient attention one of Goddards letters, which if I had done I shoud have submitted to evry distress rather [than] have so imposd myself on your freindship—but as it is done I can only in the style of a naughty boy cry out, pray, Dear Sir, forgive me this time, and I will never do so no more. I wish you and your family most sincerely health, prosperity and spirits, and entreat you to continue your freindship for yours

C Lee

P.S.

I have since agreed to reduce my price to fifty shillings per acre— if you think this reasonable.

ADDRESSED: Robert Morris Esq'r/Philadelphia   ENDORSED: Berkley County/Virginia 15 August/1782 Genl Lee
MS: ALS, Robert Morris Papers, CSmH.
1. This letter from former Major General Lee is endorsed in RM's hand. It was written in answer to a communication from RM of July 26, which had been delivered by John Vaughan, a prospective purchaser of Lee's Prato Rio estate.
2. For the previous agreement between Lee and Edward and Ezekiel John Dorsey, see notes to RM to William and Mary Katherine Goddard, March 4, 1782.
3. Goddard's letter has not been found.
4. Passage thus in manuscript.
5. Thus in manuscript.
6. Thus in manuscript.

To the President of Delaware
(John Dickinson)

Office of Finance, August 15, 1782. This letter nominating William Winder, Jr., of Maryland as commissioner for settling Delaware's accounts with the United States is identical in substance to RM's letter to the governor of Maryland of May 7, 1782.[1]

MSS: LS, Executive Papers, De-Ar; Ofcl LbC, DLC.
1. The Delaware legislature approved Winder's appointment on October 31. See RM to Winder, November 15, 1782.

Orders to the Guard for the *Symmetry*

[Marine Office, August 15, 1782][1]
You are to repair with your Guard on Board the said Ship Symmetry. You will permit Francis Maxwell the Commander of the said Ship to pass and repass from the Ship to the Shore at his pleasure. You are not to permit any other Person or Persons to come on Board or go on Shore from the Ship but such of the Crew as the said Commander shall send for Refreshments. Nor are you to suffer any Goods to be sent from the said Ship or put on Board without special Orders. Given at the Marine Office 15 Augt. 1782.

MS: AM LbC, MdAN.
1. This document is entitled: "Orders to the Guard for the Ship Symmetry Francis Maxwell Commander now in the Port of Philadelphia." For the background, see notes to Diary, August 13.

From Samuel Hodgdon

Philada. Augt: 15. 1782[1]

The importunity of the poor men to whom the public are indebted for services performed in the Laboratory must be my apology for troubling you again on the subject of the estimates laid before you.[2] Convinc'd of your desire to provide payment I have only to lament that you are not furnished with the means; the distresses of the persons mentioned in the estimates have determined them to address you personally but knowing such applications must be disagreeable surrounded as you are with business I have requested them to wait untill I could obtain a line from you on the subject. This I have now to request, and shall be infinitely oblidg'd by a compliance.[3]

MS: LbC, WDC, DNA.
1. Hodgdon was the commissary general of military stores.
2. Punctuation supplied by the editors. The reference may be to the estimates mentioned in Hodgdon to RM, August 7, or in Hodgdon to RM, July 29.
3. For RM's immediate response, see Diary, August 16.

From Samuel and Moses Myers

Amsterdam Augt 15th. 1782[1]

At the request of his Excellency John Adams Esqr: we take the liberty to Cover and forward by this Conveyance sundry News papers, and Pamphlets, which his Excellency gave us last Saturday at the Hague. We wish them safe to hand; and we are with tenders of our best services, Your Honor's Most Obedient and very Humble Servants.[2]

MS: LS, PCC, DNA.
1. Samuel (1755–1836) and Moses Myers (ca. 1752–1835) and their partner, Isaac Moses (on whom see notes to Diary, August 27, 1781), were members of a trading house of New York and Amsterdam. Involved in many aspects of wartime commerce, the firm was shipping for Thomas Barclay some of the supplies left in Holland by Alexander Gillon. In 1784 Isaac Moses unsuccessfully applied for the appointment of Moses Myers as American consul at Amsterdam. However, the following year the firm became insolvent and dissolved, precipitating the bankruptcy of Isaac Moses as well in 1786. The Myerses later resettled in Virginia and regained their positions as prominent merchants, Moses in Norfolk and Samuel ultimately in Richmond. Joseph R. Rosenbloom, *A Biographical Dictionary of Early American Jews: Colonial Times Through 1800* (Lexington, Ky., 1960), 128, 129; Syrett and Cooke, eds., *Hamilton Papers*, III, 26n., 600 and n., 601–602; *JCC*, XXVI, 179 and n.; Samuel and Moses Myers to Benjamin Franklin, July 22, 1782, Hays, comp., *Calendar of Franklin Papers*, II, 489; and Matthew Ridley to RM, July 23, 1782.
2. The enclosures have not been identified. Similar letters were received by President of Congress John Hanson and Secretary for Foreign Affairs Robert R. Livingston. See PCC, no. 78, XVI, 311, 319.

From John de Neufville and Company

[Amsterdam] 15 Augt. [1782]

We have of Late so often intruded our letters upon you, and have not for a long time been hono'd with a line from you[1] that 'tis with reluctance we trouble you so often, but our old worthy friend Come. Jones desires us to inclose our answer to his Letters[2] under your Cover and as it offers us an opportunity of reitterating our respects we Cannot but avail ourselves of it with pleasure being Sincerely

MS: LbC, John de Neufville Papers, NHi.

1. De Neufville and Company was a Dutch merchant house active in the American market. Its most recent private letters to RM were dated April 15 and June 10, 1782. RM's last private letter to the firm evidently was dated June 5, 1781 (Summary of Letters Received, p. 94, de Neufville Papers, NHi). He had written the firm in his official capacity on March 9, 1782.

2. The letters have not been found. For Jones's connections with de Neufville, see the references listed in Lincoln, comp., *Calendar of Jones Manuscripts*, 277–278.

Diary: August 16, 1782

John Swanwick came with several Estimates and Accounts respecting money, notes &c.

Mr. Jos. Watkins lately employed in the Department of Military Stores brought some Papers respecting the Estate of Cornelius Sweers and told me that Mr Ingersol who is of Counsel for the United States sent him to know whether I am willing to enter into a Compromise with Mr. Lewis Attorney for Mr. Sweers.[1] I answered that I had written Mr. Ingersol to perform his Duty and recover the Monies due to the United States and that I must abide by those Orders having none others to give.

Capt. Greene and Capt. Maxwell brought me the Latters letter to Sir Guy Carleton and a Certificate relative to the Prisoners brought in the Ship Symmetry.[2] Capt. Maxwell told me that the Prisoner[s] had forced him to Issue more Provisions than by his Orders he was authorized to allow them, and he asks what is to be done or how the Surplus quantity is to be paid for. I desired that the Facts may be all ascertained and given to me in writing that I may Consider them and then he shall have my Answer.

I sent for Mr Hodgdon and requested that he do not permit the Persons employed in his Department to come after me any more for Money as I shall when in my power enable him to supply them without any solicitation whatever.

I sent for Mr Pierce and desired him to give me a List of the names of those Officers who have applied since the first of August for his notes to Amount of their pay for January and February last &c. which he did and I gave him Drafts on Mr Swanwick for the Amount being 1740 Dollars payable at four months.[3]

The Hon: Mr. Root called again respecting Certificates for the Balance of an account settled by Mr Burral on behalf of Mr Trumbull but as I had not Consulted Mr. Milligan on this matter yet I deferred giving an answer.[4]

Mr Bellamy Crawford again respecting his Accounts, Rations &c. I took his papers and gave them to the Hon Secretary at War who says he will explain to Mr Crawford what he is entitled to.

Mr Parr for Money for Lancaster Contract; informed him that Mr. Swanwick would give him Notes to Discount.

I sent for Haym Solomon and delivered him a Waggoner receipt for twenty dry Hides sent by Geo. Abbot Hall Esqr. from South Carolina and desired him to sell the same to the best advantage of the United States.[5] I also desired Solomon to call on Colo Miles for a few Casks of Pott Ash or Pearl Ashes which I am informed are in his Stores being the property of the United States and to sell the same to the best Advantage.

Mr B. Dudley applied for money for his Expences. I promised him a Supply by Mr. Swanwick.

Mr Wm. Spragus came with Mr. Dudley and proposes a method of curing Beef and other Animal Flesh without Salt &c.

Colo. Lomoigne[6] applied for his Subsistence Money. I desired his Accounts may be laid before me by the Paymaster General &c.

Wrote a Letter to Messrs. Young and Shee.

1. For the suit against Sweers, see notes to Diary, June 5, 1782. His attorney was probably William Lewis.
2. The letter of Francis Maxwell, dated August 16, 1782, is cited in the notes to Diary, August 13. The certificate has not been found.
3. See Diary, August 8, and notes.
4. On this question, see Diary, August 19, and notes.
5. For this origins of this matter, see RM to George Abbott Hall, January 18, 1782 (first letter).
6 The reference is to Colonel Jean Baptiste Joseph, Chevalier de Laumoy, of the engineer corps in the Continental army.

To Charles Young and Bertles Shee

Office of Finance August 16th 1782

Gentlemen,

The Applications that are made at this Office for the Transaction of Public Business are numerous, and many of them lately have been of so pressing a Nature, as to leave me scarce a Moment's Recess, to which you must attribute my not having sooner acknowledged the Receipt of your several Favors of the 24th and 26th of last Month.[1]

I have no Doubt that you are Creditors of the Public in the Manner and to the Amount you mention; and there is scarce a Day passes on which my Feelings are not pained by similar Declarations. I sincerely wish it were in my Power to administer Relief; but that cannot be until the several States grant Revenues for the Purpose, to obtain which my Solicitations are unceasing. To accept in Payment of Debts due to the United States any Certificates which may have been given to Public Creditors for former Demands, would be an Innovation on the Systems which have been adopted to alleviate the general Distresses, and would produce well grounded Complaints of Partiality. I am very sorry that the Circumstances attending your Voyage have been so unfavourable,[2] and sincerely wish it had been otherwise, being led both by Habit and Reflection to wish well to the Commerce of my Country. With great Respect I am, Gentlemen, Your most obedient Servant.

Robt Morris

Messrs. Young and Shee, Merchants

MSS: LS, OClWHi; Ofcl LbC, DLC.
1. Letters not found. Young and Shee were merchants of Philadelphia.
2. Probably a reference to the matter mentioned in their letter to Congress of September 30, 1782. See notes to RM's report to Congress of October 3, 1782.

Diary: August 17, 1782

This morning I sent for Tench Francis Esqr. and pointed out to him a better way of stating his Account than that in which he had drawn it, so that every Article might be clearly understood, he took it back for that purpose and at the same time applied to me for money on Account of the Contract at York and Carlisle.

The Hon: Secy at War called to introduce a Lieut. Marsden of the Navy. This Gentleman has a Claim on the United States for balance of Wages due to him, but on Conversing with [him] I find he had been entered on the Books of the Alliance Frigate as having *run* therefore I told him he had best to get that Matter cleared up, and at any rate that he cannot now have pay.

The Hon. Doctor Witherspoon[1] called respecting bills of Exchange which he wants to buy and I told him 6/3d for five Livres is the lowest price he to pay in a month.

This Day I sent for Capt. Jno. Green and asked if he would go to New York respecting the business of the Flag Ship in which he came from England and respecting Prisoners. He answered that he is ready to perform any public Service in which I desire to employ him.[2]

Mr. Swanwick came with Estimates of money wanted &c &c. I sent to him a Letter from Mr Sands requesting money.[3]

Colo. James Wood brought a Letter from the Hon: Secy. at War[4] requesting me to pay the Balance of his Account for the Waggon Hire and to advance him about 170 Dollars on that Account as it will be of great public advantage &c. wherefore I complied therewith.

Several Persons after money but I put them off.

Wrote a Letter to His Excellency the President of the State of Pennsylvania.

Wrote a Circular to the States.

Issued a Warrant on Mr. Swanwick in favor of
Sands, Livingston and Co.   £ 628. 2.6

Issued a Warrant on Mr. Swanwick in favor of
Parr and Derring   1527.15.0

Issued a Warrant on Mr. Swanwick in favor of the
Bank for Discounts   13. 6.0
Issued a Warrant on Mr. Swanwick in favor of
Colo. James Wood   63.15.0

1. John Witherspoon, a New Jersey delegate to Congress.
2. See Diary, August 13, and notes.
3. This may be the letter mentioned in the Diary of August 10.
4. The letter from Benjamin Lincoln has not been found.

Circular to the Governors of the States

(Circular)   Office of Finance 17th August 1782[1]
Sir

Having some Reason to believe that the enclosed Resolution has
not hitherto been transmitted to all the States I do myself the
Honor to forward it to your Excellency from this Office and pray
that it may meet with the due Attention.[2] With great Respect I have
the Honor to be Sir Your Excellency's most obedient and humble
Servant

Robt Morris

His Excellency the Governor of Massachusetts Bay

ENDORSED: Robert Morris Esqr./Received Septemr. 5th: 1782/Suits against Quarter
Masters &c.
MSS: LS, to the Governor of Massachusetts, M-Ar; LS, to the President of New Hampshire, Meshech Weare Papers, Nh-Ar; LS, to the Governor of Connecticut, Jonathan
Trumbull Papers, Ct; to the President of Delaware, Executive Papers, De-Ar; to the
Governor of Virginia, Continental Congress Papers, Vi; Ofcl LbC, DLC; LbC, Letterbook of Governor Alexander Martin of North Carolina, 1782–1785, Nc-Ar.
   1. The endorsement on the Connecticut text indicates that it was received on
September 2.
   2. The enclosure was an act of Congress of March 19, 1782, asking the states to stay
existing and prevent future suits against public officials for debts contracted while
providing supplies and services to the United States (see the Quartermaster General to
RM, March 8, 1782, and notes). Only Pennsylvania, New Jersey, and New York seem to
have taken action on this issue. The New Jersey act, passed June 24, 1782, and renewed
at least once, on June 19, 1783, empowered the court in which action was taken against
a public officer for debt to direct a stay of proceedings if the debt was due from the
state or from the United States for the supply of the army. Pennsylvania's act, passed
November 29, 1782, authorized state courts to stay proceedings against public officers
if the defendants did not have enough public money in their hands to pay the debt. The
act was to remain in force for 18 months and then until the end of the next assembly
sitting. Public officials may also have benefited from a later act, passed March 31, 1783,
preventing "vexatious prosecutions" and suits against either civil or military officers for
actions undertaken in obedience to orders of Congress, the assemblies, or other public
bodies. For the New York legislation, see Governor of New York to Gouverneur Morris, August 2, and notes. For New Jersey, see Wilson, comp., Acts of New Jersey, 300, 340;
and Timothy Pickering to John Lawrence, January 30, 1783, WDC, no. 87, p. 53. For
Pennsylvania, see Mitchell and Flanders, eds., Statutes of Pennsylvania, XI, 11–14, 98–
99. Concerning New Hampshire, see Diary, and RM to the President of New Hampshire, December 24, 1782; and for the response in Virginia, Hutchinson and Rachal,
eds., Madison Papers, IV, 92n.

To the President of Pennsylvania
(William Moore)

Office of Finance 17. Augt. 1782

Sir,

Agreably to the Instructions of the United States in Congress I do myself the Honor to enclose to your Excellency the Copy of a Memorial of John Mitchell and of a Paper enclosed therein that such Provision may [be] made therein agreably to the Requisition of the nineteenth of March last as in the Wisdom of your State shall seem meet.[1] I am with Respect &ca.

RM

ms: Ofcl LbC, DLC.

1. Neither the letter to Congress of August 14, 1782, from John Mitchell, former deputy quartermaster general at Philadelphia, "complaining that a suit has been brought against him for articles purchased for the use of the army," nor the "Paper enclosed therein," have been found. Congress referred the letter to Pennsylvania ca. August 15. On the act of Congress of March 19, 1782, see the notes to the preceding document.

To George Washington

Office of Finance 17 Augt 1782[1]

Sir

I found it necessary, in order to get money for alleviating my distresses,[2] to sell bills which I knew were to be negotiated thro New York. The remittances coming in too slowly, induced my assent to a plan for bringing out the specie. This is[3] the money which I lately wrote to you about.[4] I am respectfully your Excellency's most obedient and humble Servant

Robt Morris

His Excellency Gen. Washington

ENDORSED: Office of Finance 17th Augst 1782/from/Hono. Robert Morris Esqr/Money expected from N York a/rises from Sale of Bills/Answered 2d Sepr.

mss: LS, part in cipher, Washington Papers, DLC; encoded Dft in the writing of Gouverneur Morris, Robert Morris Papers, CSmH; deciphered copy in Washington's writing, Washington Papers, DLC.

1. This LS, except for the signature, is in Gouverneur Morris's hand. All but the dateline, salutation, complimentary close, signature, and addressee's name is written in the Office of Finance cipher employed by RM and Washington. See notes to RM to Washington, August 22, 1781.

2. Washington deciphered this word as "distress."

3. Washington deciphered this word as "was."

4. See RM to Washington, August 13, and notes.

From William Churchill Houston

Trenton [New Jersey] 17 August 1782[1]

Governour Livingston has transmitted you the Acts of the Sitting of our Legislature in the Months of May and June last.[2] They will inform you of several Measures by them taken to further the publick Service at this Time. I have paid Bills on Mr Swanwick in Favour of Col Pickering Q[uarter] M[aster] G[eneral] to the Amount of two Thousand Dollars; and am now paying another left in the Hands of Col John Neilson, D[eputy] Q[uarter] M[aster] for this State to the Amount of fifteen Hundred Dollars more.

1782 Dr   The Receipt of Continental Taxes in the State of New-Jersey
          from August 10 to 17 inclusive
          To Cash received of the State Treasurer, seven Hundred and
          fifty Dollars   Dlls 750

MS: ADftS with subjoined ADftS return, Houston Collection, NjP.
1. Houston was the receiver of Continental taxes for New Jersey.
2. The letter of August 13 from Governor William Livingston of New Jersey has not been found. RM's reply is dated September 10.

George Washington to Gouverneur Morris

Head Quarters New Burg [New York] 18th: Augt. 1782

Dear Sir

Congress having again directed me to propose to the British Commanders in Chief at New York the appointment of Commissioners to settle forthwith a General Cartel for the exchange of prisoners, taking care that the Liquidation of accounts and settlement of the Balance due for the maintenance of prisoners be provided for therein. I have this Day communicated their resolution to Sir Guy Carleton and Admiral Digby.[1]

If the meeting now proposed should be acceded to, the principal parts of the business which was agitated and discussed at the former[2] will be involved in it, and therefore the Gentlemen who were before appointed by me would be more proper than any others, as being more fully acquainted with the several points in controversy, to manage the conference upon our parts. For this reason it would be highly agreeable to me to reappoint you in conjunction with Major Genl. Knox and perhaps a third should it be deemed necessary[3] could you make it convenient to attend.

I shall be glad of your answer as soon as possible that I may be prepared to meet that of the British General and Admiral who I make no doubt will accede to our offer. I am with great Esteem Dear Sir

Gouverneur Morris Esq:

ENDORSED: Newburg 18th. Augt. 1782/to/Gouverneur Morris Esqr.
MSS: Dft in the writing of Tench Tilghman, Washington Papers, DLC; Varick transcript, Washington Papers, DLC.
    1. Washington's letter to Sir Guy Carleton is in Fitzpatrick, ed., *Writings of Washington*, XXV, 38. For a discussion of the congressional resolution of August 12 and the context in which the present letter was written, see notes to Diary, June 18, 1782.
    2. For the previous conference on prisoners held at Elizabeth, New Jersey, see Gouverneur Morris to RM, March 22, 1782, and notes.
    3. Tilghman interlined the preceding 9 words.

Diary: August 19, 1782

Doctr. Brownson wrote me a note enclosing Copies of two Letters which he had received from Doctor Thoms Bond junr. Purveyor of the Hospitals referring him to me for Supplies of Money &c.[1] I desired Mr. Brownson to Call again at two Clock. He did so and after informing him that I cannot spare him money I proposed giving him Drafts on Mr. Swanwick payable in January next for 500 Dollars for which he might obtain Money as he passes thro Maryland or Virginia and so carry it on to the use of the Hospitals in the Southern Department.

Colo. Charles Stewart[2] Called and wants money to pay off the late Issuing Commissaries alledging that he has borrowed £600 towards that business which he wants to repay and to get as much more as will enable him to put all the said Issuers on a similar footing agreeable to a promise which he alledges I made to him last Winter. I told him that the Money cannot now be spared. He said he would call again.

Mr. Sharp Delany came to Consult me relative to the best means of supplying the Treasury of Pennsylvania with the money which they now want.[3]

Capt. Jno. Green came here with Capt. Harrison of the Cartel Ship just arrived. I desired him to go thro the Offices as with the other Ship, that is to report his Ship and shew his Passport at the Naval Office and at the Secy. Office.[4] He happened to mention the Sick People on board and I desired they might call on the health Officer. This they did and the Doctors finding a Contagious fever on Board ordered the Ship down to the Pest House.[5]

Jno. Pierce Esqr. Paymaster Genl. for money.

Colo. Lomoigne [Laumoy] called respecting the Balance of his Subsistence. I sent him word that I shall give the necessary Orders to the Paymaster.

Lieut. Boilleau [Beaulieu], desired him to call on Wednesday.

Revd. Doctr. Witherspoon for a Bill of Exchange which I sold to him at 6/3d for five Livres to take his Note payable in thirty days for the Amount.

Colo. James Smith came in Consequence of the referrence of Congress on his Accounts.[6] I told him that Mr. Burral should settle the Accounts and give him Certificates of the Balance due which is all that can be done until revennue is granted to pay the Interest &c.

Honble Mr. Jesse Root applied respecting Accounts settled by Mr. Trumbull to which I promised an Answer to morrow and immediately sent for Mr. Milligan to consult him on the Subject.

Mr Swanwick with various Orders, Drafts &c.

Mr. Josiah Hewes having brought a bill drawn by Mr   [7] Hudson brother of Jono. Hudson for £50 for Service performed by him &c. I told him it cannot be paid.

Messrs. Hazelwood and Blackiston write for Money which they must have.[8]

James Milligan Esqr. came with several Papers, Drafts of Orders &c.[9] We agreed that the Commissioners for settling Accounts shall Issue the Certificates for Balances due and drew up the Form. See my Letter of this Date to Jona. Burrall Esqr.

Wrote a Letter to Jona. Burrall Esqr.

1. The letters have not been found.
2. Stewart was the former commissary general of issues.
3. Delany was a member of the Pennsylvania Assembly. Pennsylvania eventually borrowed £5,000 from the Bank of North America. See Diary, March 19, and notes, and September 7, 1782, and notes.
4. See notes to Diary, August 13.
5. The pest house established by Pennsylvania for the quarantine of those entering the port of Philadelphia with infectious diseases was located on Province, now State, Island near the mouth of the Schuylkill River. J. Thomas Scharf and Thompson Westcott, *History of Philadelphia, 1609–1884* (Philadelphia, 1884), I, 210, 267, 480, 1664–1666.
6. Smith, a former assistant commissary of purchases, had recently memorialized Congress, "complaining of sundry suits being brought against him for purchases made for the use of the United States, and praying for monies to enable him to discharge his debts &c." Congress ca. August 15 referred the matter of the lawsuits to Pennsylvania and his accounts to RM. On the accounts, see RM to Smith, September 26, 1781, and notes; on the question of lawsuits, see RM's Circular to the Governors of the States, August 17, and notes.
7. Space left blank in manuscript.
8. Letter not found. John Hazelwood and Presley Blackistone, together with Peter Summers, held the Philadelphia contract for 1782.
9. The papers brought by Comptroller of the Treasury James Milligan cannot be identified, but they may have included draft instructions to the commissioners of accounts. See Diary, August 30, and notes.

To Jonathan Burrall

Office of Finance 19th. August 1782[1]

Sir

I enclose you two Papers. Number one is the Form of a Certificate to be given to the Persons to whom Monies shall appear to be due by the United States. The Date will be on the Day of delivery and the Day at which the Ballance became due will be the Period from which

Interest is payable. Number two is the form of a Receipt to be given by the Party. The Numbers and Dates of these Receipts should correspond with those of the Certificates. The Receipts must be taken in a Book kept for that Purpose. I had intended to have printed Blanks for the Certificates but I find this would have been but a small saving of Time and there will be less Danger of Counterfeits if they be all written by one Person which I would recommend. I am Sir your most Obedient and Humble Servant

RM

This Letter sent to all the Commr. of Accounts.[2]

[ENCLOSURES]

No.   State of   178 [3]

On the final Settlement of an Account between the United States and   there appeared to be due to (him, her or them as the Case may be) the Sum of

Dollars.

I do therefore Certify that the said Sum is payable with Interest at six per Cent from the   Day of   17   To the said

or Bearer
A. B.
Commissioner

No.   State of   178

Received from   Commissioner &c. the full Amount of a Ballance due to me by the United States in a Certificate from the said Commissioner bearing even Date herewith for

Dollars payable with Interest

at six per Cent from the   Day of   17   to me or Bearer.

MSS: Copy, PCC, DNA; Ofcl LbC, DLC.

1. This letter to Burrall, commissioner for settling the accounts of the Commissary Department, prescribed the form of final settlement certificates subsequently issued by the commissioners for settling public accounts. Drawn in the first instance in response to the settlement of the accounts of former Commissary General Joseph Trumbull (see Burrall to RM, July 22, and notes, and Diary, August 8, 16, 19, and 20), the letter was sent seriatim to all the commissioners of accounts as Gouverneur Morris indicated on the PCC text printed here (see note 3 below), which was enclosed in RM to the President of Congress, August 26, 1783. Regulations for issuing the certificates were laid down, and the paper and watermarks used were described, in a circular to the commissioners from Comptroller of the Treasury James Milligan on October 18, 1782. The detailed instructions Milligan issued to the commissioners with RM's approval are printed under October 14, 1782.

The process of settling the public debt which began in 1782 had been initiated by RM's letters to the president of Congress of December 10, 1781, and February 18, 1782, and was carried out under congressional ordinances of February 20 and 27, 1782. Prior to this period the domestic debt officially claimed by Congress consisted of $11 million in loan office certificates. By the time the commissioners of accounts liquidated the outstanding domestic debt in the 1790s, they had issued about $17 million in final settlement certificates, including $11 million in Pierce's notes, final settlement certificates issued by John Pierce, commissioner of army accounts, for the army debt which Congress assumed in 1783. For a discussion of the settlement of individual and staff department accounts, see Ferguson, *Power of the Purse*, 179–202, 251–253; on the army debt, see notes to RM to Daniel of St. Thomas Jenifer, March 12, 1782.

2. This line, in Gouverneur Morris's hand, does not appear in the Ofcl LbC.

3. The spaces on this and the following lines in both forms were left blank in manuscript.

From Charles Lee

[Berkeley County, Virginia] August ye 19th, 1782[1]

My Dr Sir,

Since I clos'd my long letter (which I wish you may have patience to read)[2] in order to be secure against any suspicion of being thought unreasonable in the price in[3] I have put on my lands I have consulted every gentleman I have met with respect to its real value—it is true I have only met with two, Dr. Bull and Mr. Cook Nourse's Son in law—the former is of opinion I ought by no means to part with it for less than two guineas and a half p'r acre—the latter thinks that three Pounds Virginia Currency that is two pounds eight shillings sterling would be sufficient—in short I have not heard of a single man (Messrs. Nourse and old Wormley excepted) who have thought of a lower valuation—the first is proverbial for making bad bargains for he some time ago sold the best part of his estate for about the fourth part of its value—and when he has said that such a thing is only worth so much it is highest Treason to his infallibility to differ—no Welshman mounted on a mule is half so obstinate—the second Mr. Wormley (tho' a very honest man) is as remarkable for stamping a very high value on what belongs to himself and depreciating what belongs to other People All his own Geese are Swans all his pewter silver and all his drayhorses are mountain Arabs. He himself lately sold a tract of land which is certainly not worth the third part of mine for five thousand pounds sterling—but in short the lowest valuation put on mine by fair Judges (that of Mr Cook) is two pounds eight shillings sterling per acre, but upon my honour (from all I can learn) your friend Mr Vaughan will have a very good purchase if you decide (for I leave the difference to you) that the sum should be fifty shillings—if the contract is assented to I suppose it will be necessary that I should go to Philadelphia and if this is necessary Mr Vaughan or somebody must furnish me with a necessary sum for the journey—for I have not a farthing in the world. Adieu God bless you My Dr sir

Charles Lee

PRINTED: *Lee Papers*, IV, 27–28.

1. The editors have been unable to find a manuscript text of this communication from former Major General Lee—evidently his last extant letter to RM before his death in Philadelphia on October 2. See Diary, October 3 and 4.

2. See Lee to RM, August 15.

3. Thus in printed text.

Diary: August 20, 1782

Mr. Elizh. Weed Keeper of the new Goal came respecting the Commitment of a negro Seaman considered as a Prisoner of War. I referred him to Genl. Lincoln.

Mr. John Chaloner called to speak with me this morning but as I was very busy I requested he would call again and accordingly he came in the Afternoon when he told me he is in want of the twenty thousand Dollars lent by him on my private Obligation to the use of the United States. This money was lent in May last to be repaid in a few Days but as he had not occasion for it sooner he did not Call. I told him that at present the payment will be very inconvenient, but that it must if possible be effected, as the money has been so long in the Service of the Public I agreed to pay Interest for the use of it, this being barely just as he might have obtained a great deal more from Individuals. I informed Mr Chaloner of the bargain concluded with Mr. Jos. Wilson, shewed him the time when the Bills are to be delivered and the times of payment and as it was our Agreement that each shou'd Supply half of those Bills and receive half the Money, I now proposed that if agreeable to him I would supply the whole of the Bills sold to Mr Wilson and receive all the payments, but Mr Chaloner said no, he chose to stand to the original Agreement, by which means the Public fall £3,000 or 8,000 Dollars more in his debt as I have received 16,000 Dollars from Mr Wilson together with Sundry notes for the remainder the whole of which I have ordered to be discounted at the Bank and consequently shall have to provide the payments for Mr. Chaloner as they fall due.[1]

Mr. Swanwick with sundry Claims for money fallen due upon Acceptances &c.

Sharp Delany Esqr. to Consult me farther as to the ways and means of raising money for the Government of Pennsylvania.

The Hon: Arthur Lee Esqr. came this morning as a member of a Committee of Enquiry, staid one hour and no other Member of that Committee appearing he then retired and I complained of loosing my time so uselessly.[2]

Genl. Cornell called to shew me some intelligence respecting payment of Taxes in Rhode Island &c. On Conversing with this worthy Gentleman about the Office of Inspector of Contracts he said if I could wait until the end of this year he would accept the Appointment.[3]

The Hon. Speaker of the Assembly of Pennsylvania[4] very kindly communicated some Letters and Papers from Washington County whereby it appears that a Mr. Pentecoste and a Mr. Canon one a member of the Council and the other of the Assembly from that County, had to favor their own base views, insinuated that my agreeing to receive Flour at Fort Pitt in payment of the Taxes for that County, was founded in a view to Ship the flour to New Orleans and pockett the Profit myself that would arise upon the Sale of it. (See my Letters in March last to General Irwin and Mr Canon on this Subject.)[5] It is true that if the County delivered more flour than should be necessary for the Garrison of Fort Pitt, I determined to sell the Surplus either on the Spot at Fort Pitt or at Orleans and whatever the flour produced at either place was to be applied to the public Service. I returned these Papers to the Speaker of the House with a note[6] thanking him for the Communication lamenting that thro folly and malignity these men should pursue practices tending to injure the State, but as to their insinuations against me they are so totally unfounded and Contemptible that I do not think it worth while to trouble the House or myself about them.

Mr. Sands writes me a Letter for 4,000 Dollars on account of the Balance due to him on Mr Pierces Notes.[7] I am to pay this 4,000 Dollars in Drafts on Mr. Swanwick and ordered them to be made out.

Colo. Miles, Genl. Gates, Capt DeBert &c. Called when I was engaged and could not see them.

Colo. Bland Called and requested me to Supply the Virginia Delegates with about £30 or 100 Dollars for the use of Prisoners just returned from England in the Cartels who are Subjects of their State. This I agreed to and took their Draft on the Treasury of Virginia for the Same.[8]

The Honble. Mr. Root applying again, I informed him that after Consulting with Mr. Milligan it was agreed that the Commissioners for the respective Departments are to grant Certificates for the Balance due and that Mr Bural is to grant those for Settlements made by Mr Trumbull.[9]

Mr. Dominique L'Eclise called to settle his Account, but I desired him to call tomorrow.[10]

Colo. Chs. Stewart applied for Money to compleat the Payment of one months Salary to the Deputys and Clerks employed in his late Department, Claiming this upon a Promise made him last Winter and in order to fullfill it I gave him one Order on Mr Swanwick for 500 Dollars and one other for 3,500 Dollars.[11]

Como. Hazelwood for Money which I must if possible Supply.

Capt. Jno. Green with Capt Maxwell of the Cartel. I desired the former to get Capt. Harrison of the last Cartel to write his Letters to Sir Guy Carleton[12] and the latter brought his Accounts to shew the Quantity of Provisions which the Prisoners have compelled him to Issue on the Passage beyond what the Orders he received permitted and for which he desires payment.[13] I promised to Consider of this Matter.

Walter Livingston Esqr. and Charles Stewart on behalf of the Contractors for the moving Army Claim payment of 47,000 Dollars Amount of Issues for the month of July at West Point and to the moving Army. I stated that I have already paid 10,000 Dollars, 4,000 Dolls:, 1750 Dollars.[14] I agreed to pay Mr. Francis 5,000 Dollars on their Account, that they should receive from Mr Eddy at Morris Town 10,000 Dollars[15] and from Genl. Washington out of the Money to be paid by Mr. Hill 12,000 Dollars[16] and to pay Mr Whiteside for Rum they bought of him 4,000 Doll with which they are Satisfied and in addition to this I agreed to give them drafts on Mr Swanwick for 20,000 Dollars more to enable them to take up Monies from the Receivers of the several States so as to keep the Public rather in advance for the Contractors &c.

Colo. Stevens of the 2d. Regt. of Artillery for Balance of Subsistence Money and as the Corps are going to march from Burlington, I granted a Warrant for the Same.[17]

Honble. General Scott, Mr. Lee, and Mr Rutledge as a Committee of Congress on the Plan of settling the Accounts of those Persons in Europe who have been entrusted with money of the United States. The Committee desired to hear my reasons against their intended report. Mr G. Morris and myself both gave our reasons and finally they left the report that we might further Consider it, and put our reasons in Writing or prepare a report more to our Mind.[18]

Wrote a Letter to His Excellency General Washington.

1. As this Diary entry indicates, John Chaloner of Philadelphia, agent for Jeremiah Wadsworth and John Carter, contractors for the French army, had previously advanced $20,000 on RM's personal credit. The debt was still outstanding later in August when Wadsworth and Carter needed the money to enable Rochambeau to pay the French army (see Diary, May 23 and August 28, 1782). RM had also incurred an additional debt to Chaloner; in an effort to prevent competition in selling bills of exchange on France from lowering exchange rates, he and Chaloner agreed on August 9 to share in a sale of 200,000 livres in bills to the Philadelphia merchant Joseph Wilson (see Diary, August 9, and notes). Each was to provide half the bills, deliverable on December 15, and to divide the several payments of money Wilson was to make before that date. As RM here discloses, however, he had already appropriated Wilson's first payment and discounted Wilson's notes for the balance at the bank; hence he was liable to Chaloner for his share as the installments fell due, as well as for the 6 percent annual interest arising on the original $20,000 loan. RM was also in Chaloner's debt for notes and acceptances held by Chaloner which had fallen due.

The Financier was hard pressed to make the various payments as they fell due and sought to borrow the money and credit of business associates such as William Bingham, John Ross, and John Holker. As an inducement, he promised Bingham and Ross that he would direct immediate payment in bills of exchange of the balances due them for their previous services as Continental agents abroad, but Bingham lent only $12,000 of the $20,000 requested. Holker lent his note for $10,000 to be discounted at the bank, but RM resolved not to use it unless absolutely necessary and appears not to have done so (see Diary, August 24, 27, 28, 30, 31, September 3, and October 23). Subsequently, in exchange for repayment of the entire debt due them, Ross and Bingham lent their credit at the Bank of North America to facilitate the Superintendent's repayment of one of the goverment's bank loans (see Diary, December 17, 19, 30, 31, 1782, and March 28 and April 8, 1783). The Financier's attempt on August 31 to repay Chaloner's original $20,000 loan, however, was not immediately successful, but repayment appears to have been substantially completed by September 25. Later payments had to be made for the interest, the bills of exchange sold to Joseph Wilson, and the Morris paper held by Chaloner (see List of Monies Owed to John Chaloner, September 7, and Diary, September 21, 25, and 28).

The cash shortage faced by Wadsworth and Carter also formed an obstacle to RM's plan for the firm to assume the combined West Point and Moving Army contract for 1782. By September the contract was on the verge of collapse because of the Superintendent's failure to pay the contractors and the competitive purchasing of supplies for the French army and navy by Wadsworth and Carter's agents (see Comfort Sands, Walter Livingston, William Duer, and Daniel Parker to RM, September 11, and notes). Under the terms of the new contract signed with Wadsworth and Carter in October, the Financier did not have to make any advances to the contractors; instead he received three months' credit in return for a one-third increase in the price of the ration. Since Wadsworth and Carter would not have the resources to provide the credit unless RM repaid his debts to Chaloner, however, the Superintendent unofficially promised to pay all the sums as they came due. After signing the contract, the firm forwarded to Chaloner RM's note for £12,500 Pennsylvania currency which fell due on November 4, urging payment. Although RM made occasional payments, he did not completely repay Wadsworth and Carter until March 1783. Even then Carter reported RM's final payment to have been made "much against the grain" (Carter to Wadsworth, March 19, 1783, Jeremiah Wadsworth Papers, CtHi). Concerning the contract with Wadsworth and Carter, see Diary, September 18 and 23, and Wadsworth to RM, October 5, and Carter to RM, October 9. For documentation of the payments, see [Morris], *Statement of Accounts, passim;* and Waste Book C, p. 486, and Waste Book D, pp. 23, 99, 178, 320, Records of the United States General Accounting Office, RG 217, DNA. See also Chaloner to Wadsworth and Carter, August 8, 9, 17, 20 (second letter), November 4, 7, and to Carter, December 12, 1782, Chaloner and White Letterbook, PHi; John Swanwick's receipt to Chaloner, December 14, 1782, Chaloner and White Papers, PHi; Wadsworth and Carter to Chaloner, August 13, 16, and August 1782, Carter to Chaloner, October 9, November 23, and December 10, 1782, Wadsworth and Carter Letterbook 3, Wadsworth Papers, CtHi; Carter to Wadsworth, June 5, September 23, 25, 29, October 2, 1782, and March 19, 1783, Chaloner to Wadsworth and Carter, September 9 and 12, 1782, and Carter to Chaloner, June 5, August 13, October 29, and December 10, 1782, Wadsworth Papers, CtHi.

2. For the congressional committee investigating the Office of Finance, see notes to Diary, June 12.

3. Ezekiel Cornell, a Rhode Island delegate to Congress, accepted the appointment in September (see notes to RM to the President of Congress, April 20, 1782). His commission is dated September 19.

4. The papers delivered by Speaker Frederick Augustus Conrad Muhlenberg have not been identified, but probably included two depositions concerning Dorsey Pentecost's participation in separatist disturbances in Washington County (in *Pennsylvania Archives*, 1st ser., IX, 572–573). One of the depositions reported that at a meeting of people in May, Pentecost had given the following reply to a question about the county's quota and how it was to be paid: "He answered the Tax was very large and only to be paid in Gold or silver, wch the people were not able to do; a Gentleman present answered He had seen Financier Genl Morris's Letter signifying his desire for the good of the Inhabitants of this County to accept Flour in Lieu of Specie for the Amount of Taxes, to wch Mr. Penticoast replied that the people might pay their Taxes in Flour, but that Bob. Morris knew his own Ends by so doing and meant only to serve himself, that He would receive the Flour at his own price and after supplying the Troops here, He would send the remainder to Orleans, sell it to the best advantage & put the proffits in his own pockett. That the people were in such circumstances, that it would be so difficult, expensive, & troublesome, in sending wheat to different Mills, and adjusting every particular person's Quota of Tax, that it would be impossible for the people to comply therewith, and that they had three choices, two of wch He had already recited, to which he spoke largely, or thirdly to pay none at all, as that was their only refuge, and as part of the people might by law be exempted, the remainder could not be punished by law should they stand out against paying altogether, and that He, the said Mr. Pentecoast, seemed to give it as his opinion and advice that the last mentioned manner of proceeding seemed the most Eligible for them in their present Situation."

5. See RM to John Cannon, and to William Irvine, both April 4, 1782.

6. Note not found.

7. Letter not found. For Pierce's promissory notes held by Sands and Company, see Diary, August 1, and notes.

8. Theodorick Bland, Jr., writing for the Virginia delegates in Congress, subsequently told Governor Benjamin Harrison that about 40 of the American marine prisoners who had recently arrived in Philadelphia on British cartel ships were Virginians. See Hutchinson and Rutland, ed., *Madison Papers*, V, 67; and notes to Diary, August 13.

9. See RM to Jonathan Burrall, August 19, and notes.

10. Dominique L'Eglize (L'Eglise) (b. ca. 1719) was a French-born Canadian merchant who served as an American spy in Canada for Major General Philip Schuyler in 1777. In October 1778 Congress awarded him a monthly allowance for pay and subsistence in return for residing in the Northern Department and making his services available and in 1779 directed that he receive the pay and subsistence of a captain, but his stipend was discontinued when he became a supernumerary officer under a resolution of December 31, 1781. Responding to his petition of July 15, 1782 (PCC, no. 41, V, 285–288), Congress on August 8 resolved that his accounts be settled, instructed RM to pay as much of the balance as L'Eglize stood in immediate need of, and directed that he be allowed $10 per month in the future. In the years after the war L'Eglize petitioned unsuccessfully for full payment of the balance; however, he collected his pension until at least 1794. *JCC*, XII, 992, 1056–1057, 1099, 1124, XV, 1103, 1104n., 1149, 1184, 1341, XXII, 404, 406–407n., XXVIII, 58–59, 433, XXIX, 531, 663n., 839n., 848; Syrett and Cooke, eds., *Hamilton Papers*, XVII, 516; and Diary, August 21.

11. See Diary, August 19, and William Churchill Houston to RM, August 31.

12. Captain George Harrison's letter to Carleton of August 20 is cited in the notes to Diary, August 13.

13. See RM to the President of Congress, August 23, and notes.

14. On the payments recorded here, compare to the enumeration given in RM to George Washington, August 20.

15. See Diary, August 12, and notes.

16. See notes to RM to Washington, August 13, and the documents cited there.

17. By September the 2d Continental Artillery had moved to West Point and its dependencies. Ebenezer Stevens (d. 1823) of Rhode Island was lieutenant colonel of the regiment. Charles H. Lesser, ed., *The Sinews of Independence: Monthly Strength Reports of the Continental Army* (Chicago, 1976), 232, 233n., 234; Heitman, *Register*.

18. For the committee's intended report, see the enclosure to RM to John Morin Scott, August 15; RM's reply to the committee is dated August 26. For a discussion, see notes to RM to the President of Congress, May 8, 1782.

To Guy Carleton

Office of Finance 20. Augt. 1782

Sir,

I do myself the Honor to enclose to your Excellency Letters from the Masters of two flag Ships which have arrived in this Port with american Prisoners.[1] I have sent them in by Mr. John Green one of the Persons that came in the Symetry who will bring such Orders as your Excellency may think proper to transmit to those Gentlmen. I have further to mention Sir that I intend delivering to one of them such british marine Prisoners as may be in this Place or it's vicinity when they depart provided their Receipt shall be deemed a proper Evidence of the Delivery on a Settlement of the Account hereafter. On this point I shall be happy to learn your Sentiments. It might perhaps have been more proper to have addressed myself to Admiral Digby especially as Mr Greene carries the Duplicate of a former

Letter to him. But as the King's Servants in England have placed the Masters of these Flags under your Excellency's Directions I was led to conclude that if the concurrence of the Admiral should be necessary you would take the Trouble of obtaining it. I have the Honor to be with perfect Respect Sir your Excellency's most obedient and humble Servant

RM

MSS: Ofcl LbC, DLC; copy, Colonial Office, Class 5/Volume 107, fol. 207, PRO.

1. The enclosed letters to Carleton, commander in chief of the British forces in North America, were those from Captains Francis Maxwell, August 16, and George Harrison, August 20, 1782 (see notes to Diary, August 13; also Diary, August 16 and 20). Carleton enclosed copies of this missive from RM and its enclosures in a letter to the Secretary of State for the Southern Department, October 6, 1782. See Davies, ed., *Documents of the American Revolution*, XIX, 333, 335, 336 (no. 2005, enclosure xxviii).

To George Washington

Office of Finance 20th. August 1782

Sir,

The Contractor's Accounts both for West Point and the moving Army for the Month of July amount by their State to the Sum of Forty seven Thousand Dollars; of this I have already paid about Twenty five Thousand.[1] I have taken Arrangements for Payment of Ten thousand at Morristown, and I am to request that from the Monies payable to your Excellency in the Manner I mentioned in a former Letter[2] you would pay them Twelve thousand Dollars. These several Sums will amount to the whole of what is due to them, but I have not stopped here: I gave them in the Middle of July Twenty Thousand Dollars in Orders on Mr. Swanwick. In the Begining of August Ten thousand more, and now Twenty thousand more, making in the whole Fifty thousand Dollars. The Money for these Notes I doubt not they will readily obtain, and of Course I must be considered from that Time as so much in Advance for them. I hope therefore that we shall have no Complaints from that Quarter again. These Notes form an Anticipation of the Taxes, and it is not by any Means a considerable One, for with the Exception of some small Sums not worth mentioning, it consists of Forty five Thousand to the Quarter Master General,[3] Twenty Thousand to Mr. Langdon for the Ship America,[4] and the Fifty Thousand just mentioned. I expect the Payment of them from New York and the States Eastward of it; and I[5] hope that the greater part of this Money must be already collected from the People. I have given Colonel Charles Stewart Orders to the Amount of Three thousand five hundred Dollars, and I am to request that your Excellency would transmit to Mr. Duer the Sum of Five thousand Dollars, and to [me][6] his Receipt for them. Whatever may remain in your Hands after paying the two Sums of Five and Twelve thousand Dollars, you will be so kind as to invest in the Purchase of my Orders on Mr. Swanwick from such of the Persons already mentioned as you may think it most useful to possess of the Specie in that Way. I have the Honor to be Your Excellency's most obedient and most humble Servant.

Robt Morris

His Excellency General Washington

ENDORSED: Office of Finance 20th Augst 1782/from/Hono Mr Morris/Cash to be paid to Contractors/Acknowledged 2d. Sepr.
MSS: LS, Washington Papers, DLC; Ofcl LbC, DLC.
    1. The enumeration of payments in this letter should be compared to the list in the Diary of August 20.
    2. Dated August 13.
    3. See Diary, August 3.
    4. See RM to John Langdon, August 13.
    5. The word "would" is added here in the Ofcl LbC.
    6. This word is supplied from the Ofcl LbC. LS: "use."

From the Governor of North Carolina (Alexander Martin)

[North Carolina] August 20th. 1782

Sir

I have had the Honor to recieve your Letter of the 9th. of July[1] with a Copy of an act of assembly of New Jersey enclosed; as also yours of the 25th. of July respecting the accounts and revenue of this State, being under cover addressed to the Reciever of Continental Taxes,[2] an officer who hath not yet existance among us, as the Legislature made no provision for him, concieving themselves unable to do anything on that business for the present.[3] I did myself the honor to write to you the 22d. of June, in short, their reasons; for whom I mean not further to apologize, but shall urge on them the complyance with the Resolutions of Congress on this important subject, at their earliest meeting on the first of November next at Hillsborough, when I shall again lay before them those Resolves and all your Letters respecting the same.

I shall endeavor to give you every information respecting our paper emissions and internal revenue as soon as I am furnished with the necessary documents; Your Zeal in supporting the Continental revenue the main sinew of the foederal war hath my highest approbation; and I am only sorry this State concieved herself unable to furnish her proportional Aid, at this Time.

You have enclosed a Copy of the acts of our General Assembly passed last session, and those of the preceeding agreeably to your request.[4] I am with esteem yours &c

The Honble. R. Morris esquire, Superint. of Finance

MS: LbC, Letterbook of Alexander Martin, 1782–1785, Nc-Ar.
1. RM's Circular to the Governors of the States.
2. On July 12, 1782, RM had sent a circular to the receivers of Continental taxes asking them to answer the questions previously posed in his circular to the governors of July 25, 1781.
3. On the appointment of a receiver for North Carolina, see notes to RM to the Governors of North Carolina, South Carolina, and Georgia, December 19, 1781.
4. The copies RM received have not been found. RM replied to Governor Martin's letter on September 11; see also RM's letter to him of October 17.

Diary: August 21, 1782

Capt De Bert of Colo. Armands Legion brought the Comptrollers Certificates for the Balances due to the Officers and Men of those Corps, also a Certificate of a Balance due to Colo. Armand for Transportation of and making up Cloathing for the Soldiers for which he was assured of Payment at the War Office. He brought Mr. Milligans Letter respecting his Amount of Expences since here attending these Settlements[1] and he produced Loan Office Certificates formerly received for pay and Depriciation requesting a Payment of the Interest.[2] He requests payment of one fifth part of the Officers Balances as they belong to no State and of Course had not been paid any thing for depreciation on their pay. I agreed to put the Balances due to the Corps on Interest, to give him Drafts on Mr Swanwick such as will be received in the Taxes of Virginia for Colo. Armands Balance so that he may receive the Money there. I refused to pay the Interest on the Loan Office Certificates alledging that altho I had paid Hazens Regiment their Interests yet it was in Virtue of special Resolves of Congress. But that I will Consider the Claim of one fifth for depreciation in which they seem to have right on their Side. He claimed all a Balance due for Subsistence which I promised should be paid.

Mr. Oliver Pollock called at the Office and requested to see Don Galveys [Gálvez's] Letter to Congress respecting his Debt and the answer returned thereto all which I shewed him.[3]

Mr. Jos. Bullock applied for money to pay Contingent Charges for drawing the Lottery. I signed a Warrant for the same.

Lieut. DeBeaulieu applied again for his Money. I therefore signed a Warrant for it but directed Mr Swanwick to pay him half in Money and half in a Bill.

Mr Swanwick on Sundry Arrangements for payments &c.

Colo. Miles applied for Money. I told him it is impossible and that I will inform him when able to do any thing for his releif.

Walter Livingston Esqr. with whom I took such arrangements as satisfied him for the present as to money matters see my Letter to Genl. Washington on the Subject and he sets out this Day for Morris Town where he is to receive ten thousand Dollars but if disappointed is to send back to me for it.[4] I desired him to propose a Contract for supplying the Quarter Master General with Forage and to Converse with Colo. Pickering on the Subject.[5]

Capt. Geo. Harrison of the Ship Tyger Cartel Ship brought me his Letter for Sir Guy Carleton and a Return of the Prisoners which came over in his Ship.[6]

I sent for Colo. Eleazer Oswald and gave him an Order on Mr Hilligas for a quantity of Paper in order to Print inland Orders for the Use of this Office. See the Warrant.[7]

Mr Saml Wheeler who made the Rollers for the Mint applies for money. I had a good deal of Conversation with this ingenious Gentleman.[8]

Dominique L'Eglise applied for his Money. I paid him part, put the rest upon Interest and pointed out the Mode by which he may receive Quarterly the Sum allowed him by Congress.[9]

The Hon. Mr Duane came to speak in favor of several public Officers who are threatened with Law Suits and ruin in the State of New York on Account of their Transactions for the United States.[10] Mr Duane thinks a speedy appointment of a Commissioner to settle Accounts will releive them. I assured him that I am ready to make the Appointment whenever a proper Person offers or can be found to accept it.[11]

Wrote a Letter to Henry Remson Esqr.

1. Letter not found.
2. On the depreciation allowance to Armand's legion, see RM to the Comptroller of the Treasury, November 20, 1781, and notes.
3. For the letters in question, see RM's Report to Congress of a Letter to Bernardo de Gálvez, November 21, 1781, and notes.
4. On this payment, which was not made, see RM to Henry Remsen, August 21, and notes, and to Walter Livingston, August 29, and notes. RM's letter to Washington is dated August 20.
5. On forage contracts, see notes to RM to the Secretary at War, June 29, 1782.
6. See RM to Carleton, August 20, and notes.
7. Oswald was a Philadelphia printer who had previously done work for the Office of Finance. The "inland Orders" were probably the domestic bills of exchange drawn by RM on John Swanwick, cashier of the Office of Finance. See OED, s.v. "Inland"; and RM's Circular to the Receivers of Continental Taxes, August 29, and notes.
8. On the proposed mint, see the headnote to RM to the President of Congress, January 15, 1782 (first letter), and notes.
9. See Diary, August 20, and notes.
10. For a discussion of this problem, see the Quartermaster General to RM, March 8, 1782, and notes.
11. See RM to the Governor of New York, November 21, 1782.

To Henry Remsen

Office of Finance 21. Augt. 1782[1]

Mr. George Eddy was under Engagement to pay you a considerable Sum of Money for Sands Livingston and Company Contractors for the moving

Army on my Account as Superintendant of Finance which I suppose he has done. Walter Livingston Esqr. one of those Gentlemen is the Bearer of this Letter and will take the money from you. He will give you his Receipt which can be cancelled when you get back your own to Mr. Eddy and that will be shortly after Mr Eddy has brought it hither.

MS: Ofcl LbC, DLC.

1. Remsen was a New York City merchant living in Morristown, New Jersey. On the transactions discussed in this letter, see Diary, August 12, and notes, and August 20.

Diary: August 22, 1782

This Morning Major General Horatio Gates called and shewed me a Copy of his Letter to General Washington,[1] and assured me that he knew nothing of a Publication in last Wednesdays Freemans Journal[2] until told of it yesterday by Colo. Walton[3] after dining with Mr Presidt. Hanson and disapproves much of that Part of said Publication which alludes to him. He asked how he should repay me the Money which I had lent him. I answered that I must by and by place it against his Pay and that I have occasion to do the same with others to whom I have advanced money rather than make partial Payments.

Wm. Bingham Esquire came to the Office this Morning by Appointment when I shewed him the Letters written to Congress for revenue and with the Estimates for 1783.[4] He expressed great Satisfaction and approbation, observed that the public Creditors were bound to support those Measures and he did not doubt but they will do it. Mr. Bingham after much Conversation on public Affairs introduced his own and asked whether a farther payment could not be made to him. I answered not at this time, but that I hope in the Year 1783 he may receive his whole balance. He mentioned that part of his Account which took place thro Mr Wereat and I repeated my Sentiments on that matter in the same way that I had given them to the Comptroller of Accounts.[5]

Mr. Swanwick came to take Arrangements for the payments of sundry Claims &c.

The Hon. Arthur Lee came on the Committee of the Enquiry but none of the other members appearing after some Political Conversation he departed again.[6]

James Wilson Esqr. informed me that he had been applied to by Commodore Gillon to retain him as Counsell in Case the United States should sue him on a Contract made in Holland &c.[7] I told Mr Wilson I expect his Assistance to the United States agreeable to a former Conversation when I first came into Office, then telling him I should look to him for assistance in all matters that required an able Lawyer here.

Capt De Bert sent up his Account of Expences and I have since delivered it to Genl. Lincoln who says he will do the needfull.

The Honble Colo. Atlee came to know what measures have been adopted for settling the accounts of Individuals in this State with the United States, I told him that one Commissioner Mr Burral is appointed for the Commissary Department and another Mr Denning for the Quarter[master]s Department and that I am looking out for a proper Commissioner for the State Accounts &c.[8]

Capt. Jno. Green came to the Office and I gave him the Papers which had been delivered to me by Capt Maxwell of the Symmetry to establish his Claim for Provisions supplied the Prisoners beyond the Allowance and instructed Capt Greene what is farther necessary.[9]

The Honble. Mr Montgomery and General Cornell Committee of Congress brought a Letter from the Governor of Virginia of the 11th July and one from the Secy. at War of this Date and desired my opinion on the Subject of said Letters.[10] I soon gave the same at large but as they desired it in writing, I contracted the reasoning and gave them the Substance in my Letter to them of this Date.

Many Claims for Money that I cannot Satisfy.

Wrote a Letter to Geo Olney Esquire.

Wrote a Letter to James Lovell.

Wrote a Letter to Wm. C. Houston.

Wrote a Letter to James Lovell.

Wrote a Letter to the Hon. Genl. Cornell and Mr. Montgomery.

Wrote a Letter to Jonathan Burral Esqr.

Issued a Warrant on Mr Swanwick in favor of the Contractors for the moving Army £1,015.16.10.

1. After his defeat at the battle of Camden in 1780 and his removal from command, Gates had retired to his plantation in Virginia, complaining periodically to RM and others about his mistreatment by Washington and Congress and demanding a court of inquiry. In May 1781 Congress opened the way for Gates to report to headquarters for reassignment, but despite repeated encouragement from RM he was persuaded to accept only after Secretary at War Benjamin Lincoln in July 1782 tendered an invitation to rejoin the army and Congress on August 14, 1782, rescinded its earlier resolution that a court of inquiry be held on Gates's conduct and ordered that he be given such command in the main army as Washington directed. Once in Philadelphia, Gates advised Washington in a letter of August 17 (Washington Papers, DLC) that, after returning briefly to Virginia to settle his affairs, he would accept a command, as he was "exceedingly anxious to be present at the Great concluding Stroke of this War," and pledged his "inviolable attachment." In reply, Washington instructed Gates on August 27 to report to the army on the Hudson. See Gates to RM, September 4, 1781, and notes, RM to Gates, May 31, 1782, and notes, and Gates to RM, September 12, 1782; and Fitzpatrick, ed., Writings of Washington, XXV, 68.

2. The reference is to a letter of "Virginius" (allegedly Arthur Lee), dated Philadelphia, August 14, 1782, published in the Freeman's Journal of August 21. It was the second of two "Virginius" letters (the first had appeared on August 7) in reply to recent articles by Benjamin Rush under the signature of "Leonidas" arguing for reestablishment of the American navy. "Leonidas" in his August 14 essay had asserted that American virtue in 1782 was greater than that in 1775–1776 because the half-hearted and Tories had now fallen away; the Whigs of 1782 were purer and more

disinterested and hence could be relied on to advance the money, by subscription, to build a navy. Although "Virginius" also claimed to be a supporter of a strong navy, he was irked by Rush's invidious comparison of the patriots of 1775–1776 with current leaders and insisted that public virtue had indeed declined since the early years of the Revolution, largely because so many former Tories had entered public life in Pennsylvania in 1781 and 1782 in the interest of material gain. It was in this context that "Virginius" alluded to Gates's earlier demand for a court of inquiry: "Britain, even Britain, lost as she is to every sense of justice and humanity, allowed the captive general of Saratoga an enquiry. Does his conqueror deserve less in a land of freedom. The reflection fires the bosom of sympathy, whilst the mind revolts with abhorrence at the accumulation of his wrongs." Whether or not Lee penned the "Virginius" essays, they triggered ferocious invective against him in the Philadelphia press. For a contemporary identification of Lee as "Virginius," see Benjamin Rush to Nathanael Greene, September 16, 1782, Butterfield, ed., *Rush Letters*, I, 286, 287n.; see also James Madison to Edmund Randolph, October 8, 1782, Hutchinson and Rutland, eds., *Madison Papers*, V, 187–188, 190n.–191n. However, in the *Freeman's Journal* of November 6, 1782, editor Francis Bailey denied that Lee had ever written a line for his newspaper. For the assertion that the "Virginius" essays may have been written by the poet, polemicist, and future Jeffersonian Philip Freneau (1752–1832), assistant editor of the *Freeman's Journal,* see Philip Marsh, *Freneau's Published Prose: A Bibliography* (Metuchen, N. J., 1970), 35, 36; and Marsh's *Philip Freneau: Poet and Journalist* (Minneapolis, 1967), 88 and n., 91. For the debate on the navy, see the headnote to RM to the President of Congress, July 30, and notes.

3. George Walton, a former delegate to Congress from Georgia.

4. RM refers to his letters to the president of Congress of July 29 and 30.

5. On these accounts, see Diary, June 21, 1782.

6. On the committee of Congress investigating the Office of Finance, see notes to Diary, June 12, 1782.

7. For the investigation of Alexander Gillon's conduct in Holland, see Diary, September 19, and notes.

8. Samuel John Atlee was a Pennsylvania delegate to Congress. For the nomination of Benjamin Stelle as the commissioner for settling accounts in that state, see RM to the President of Pennsylvania, November 23, 1782.

9. For the papers given to Green, see notes to RM to the President of Congress, August 23.

10. For a discussion of these letters, see notes to Diary, July 24.

To Ezekiel Cornell and Joseph Montgomery

Office of Finance
22nd. August 1782[1]

Gentlemen

Having considered the Letter written by His Excellency the Governor of Virginia on the 11th. July last to the Honorable Delegates in Congress from that State, and also the Letter of the Honorable Secretary at War of this date to General Cornell, and duly attended to such other Information as I have received on this Subject, I cannot but lament that so unnecessary an Expence has been incurred let it fall where it may. I supply'd the Secretary at War when requested with the Sum which he estimated as necessary to defray the Expence of removing the public Stores from York to the Head of the Bay, and I observe that He is of Opinion a Garrison at that Place is unnecessary. That being the Case I cannot hesitate to declare the impropriety of continuing a needless Expence at a Time when those parts of the public Service which are indispensible are daily suffering for Want of Money.

With respect to the Expence already incurred I could wish to have a full State of all Circumstances together with the Accounts and Vouchers transmitted as soon as possible to this Office in order that Congress may be enabled to determine whether the whole or any part of it is to be paid by the United States. I have the Honor to be Gentlemen, Your obedient humble Servant

Robt Morris

To The Honble. General Cornell and Mr. Montgomery

ENDORSED: Letter from the/Superintendant/of Finance to the/Committee
MSS: LS, PCC, DNA; Ofcl LbC, DLC.
1. Cornell was chairman and Montgomery was a member of a committee Congress had appointed on July 24 to consider the question of maintaining garrisons at York and Gloucester, Virginia. For a discussion of the documents and subjects mentioned in this letter, see Diary, July 24, and notes.

From William Irvine

Fort Pitt Augt: 22d 1782[1]

Sir

Mr: Wilson returned without an answer to my letter of the 5th July. I presume it may not be unnecessary to inform you that Messrs. Hoofnagle and Duncan seem undetermined whether they will enter into a contract for the ensuing year or not, Mr: Hoofnagle rather positively told me he would not. ⟨As the time is now short⟩

There is not the smallest prospect of Provision being got in for Taxes.[2] The County ⟨Lieuten⟩ Commissrs. or assessors have not done any thing towards laying a Tax. I am sorry to give you so much trouble in this business, but think it highly proper you should be Apprized of it. I have the honor to be &c

Honble. Robt: Morris Esqr

MS: ADft, Irvine Family Papers, PHi.
1. Brigadier General Irvine was the commander at Fort Pitt.
2. RM had agreed to accept flour in lieu of specie taxes from the inhabitants of Washington County. See Diary, August 20, and notes.

To Jonathan Burrall

Office of Finance 22d Augt. 1782

Mr. William Scott delivered your Letter of the thirteenth Instant enclosing a Copy of his Account and your Certificate thereon.[1] I told him you would be furnished with the Form of such a Certificate as must necessarily be delivered to each of the public Creditors when their respective Accounts are settled.[2] He therefore left the Account and I now return it, this Gentleman will at a future Day call on you for the Certificate of the Balance due to him.

In answer to yours of the twenty first Instant[3] I am to observe that the

Certificates of Accounts settled by Mr. Trumbull ought in my Opinion to contain the Name of the Person by whom the Settlement was made.

MS: Ofcl LbC, DLC.
1. Letter and enclosures not found. Burrall was the commissioner for settling the accounts of the Commissary Department.
2. See RM to Burrall, August 19.
3. Letter not found.

To William Churchill Houston

Office of Finance August 22d. 1782

I have received your favor dated at Trenton on the 17th. Instant with the State of your Receipt for the Week preceding, and noticed your Payment of my Drafts on Mr. Swanwick.[1]

MSS: LS, Houston Collection, NjP; Ofcl LbC, DLC.
1. Houston, the receiver of Continental taxes for New Jersey, endorsed this letter from RM as having been received on August 29.

To James Lovell

Office of Finance 22. Augt. 1782

I have received your favor dated at Boston on the eighth Instant with the Enclosures and approve the Returns.[1] Now that the Stream of Revenue has got in Motion in your State, I hope it will continue to flow Plentifully.

It would be well in stating the several Articles of Remittance, to mention also the hard Cash remaining on hand the Knowlege of this might be useful.

MS: Ofcl LbC, DLC.
1. The letter from Lovell, receiver of Continental taxes for Massachusetts, has not been found but it very likely contained his first two returns of $15,000 and $3,696^{23}/$_{90}$. The remittances are recorded in PCC, no. 137, III, 349.

To James Lovell

Office of Finance 22. Augt. 1782

The purport of these Lines is meerly to advise you that I have this day drawn a Bill on you at twenty Days Sight in favor of Mr. Joseph Jacobs for 4,000 dolls. which I beg you will punctually Pay charging the same to the United States.

MS: Ofcl LbC, DLC.

To George Olney

Office of Finance 22 Augt. 1782

I am favored with your Letter dated at Providence on the fifth Instant with its Enclosures.[1] As it was not necessary that the Certificates should be mentioned in your Publication I approve of your Silence respecting them and think your Reasons for it solid.

MS: Ofcl LbC, DLC.
1. The letters and enclosures sent by Olney, receiver of Continental taxes for Rhode Island, have not been found, but the enclosures may have included his seventh

return with receipts of £2,597.7.6, or (at 6 shillings to the dollar) approximately $8,658 for the month of July and the first five days of August. His first six returns, from May 9 to June 22, 1782, contained receipts of approximately $9,502. See PCC, no. 137, III, 353.

To George Washington

Office of Finance 22d August 1782

I have directed Capt. John Green who is the Bearer of this Letter to carry in some Letters from the Captains of two flag Ships which have arrived from England (on board one of which he was a Passenger) enclosed in a Letter from me to Sir Guy Carleton.[1] I am to request your Excellency would facilitate his going in and that he be permitted to stay untill he obtain the Answer which those Ships are now waiting for in this Port.[2]

MSS: LS, Washington Papers, DLC; Ofcl LbC, DLC.
1. RM's letter to Carleton is dated August 20.
2. The endorsement on the LS notes that the request for the passport was "granted." For Green's journey, see Diary, September 2.

To Abraham Yates, Jr.

Office of Finance 22. Augt. 1782[1]

I have received your Favor dated the eleventh Instant with the Enclosures. Congress have now under their Consideration the Interest of the Public Debts. I cannot do any thing relative thereto until they have decided, you shall then be furnished with the necessary Information.

MS: Ofcl LbC, DLC.
1. Yates was the Continental loan officer of New York.

Diary: August 23, 1782

Mr. Philip Marstellar applied to know when the Accounts of the Quarter Masters Department will be Settled he having acted as Deputy Qr Master for Lancaster County in Pennsylvania. I told him that a Commissioner is appointed for that purpose and now in the execution of his Duty.[1] He asked for money now due to him from Colo. Miles, referred him to Colo. Miles for Payment.

This Morning Capt John Greene brought me the Papers of Capt. George Harrison respecting his Claim for extra Provisions &c.[2] I then delivered my Dispatches to Capt. Green for Sir Guy Carleton respecting these Transports[3] and signed an Order to the D[eputy] Q[uarter] Mr Gl: for a Horse, but he had none belonging to the Public as Capt Green informs me, therefore I desired him to hire one.

Colo. Charles Stewart applying for the money I had promised him on account of his Deputies &c. I ordered him a Payment of 3,000 Dollars in a Draft on Mr Swanwick and had a long Conversation with him respecting the Contract &c.[4]

Mr. Geary Clerk of Wm. Duer Esqr. and Co. having obtained a

Settlement of their accounts calls for a balance of upwards of 6,000 Dollars. I told him that I have desired Genl. Washington to send Mr Duer 5,000 Dollars out of some money which I expect he will receive and that I will pay him the rest here soon as possible.[5]

Lieut. Peck of the New Jersey Regiment[6] called as he said by direction of the Paymaster General for the Subsistence money due to the Jersey Brigade. I told him that the Paymaster Genl. ought to do his own Business and make the application himself, that if I had money this Subsistence would have been paid without application, that as I have it not I cannot pay it at present but that it shall be done soon as possible.

The Honble Mr Bland and the Secy at War called at the Office to Confer on the Contract of Mr. Robsaumen with the United States for making Salt petre, when after going thro the Papers it was agreed that the Contract ought to end and Mr Robsaumen make out his Account and transmit the Same with Vouchers to this Office for Settlement, The Secy at War to report to Congress.[7]

Mr Wm. Nourse sent in a Petition and Account.[8]

I sent for Mr Pierce the Paymaster General and complained of his sending Lieut. Peck and others to me to ask their Subsistence and other Claims which he ought to answer and told him that unless he does his own business, I shall think it incumbent on me to exercise the Authorities with which I am entrusted. He justified himself by observing that many Gentlemen had at different times obtained money by Personal Applications after being refused by him; if this was so I told him it was at the particular recommendation of the Secy. at War and shall be avoided in future and I desire that all such applications may come from him.

Capt. Joshua Barney came to Complain that two naval Prisoners of War are now parading at the Coffee House, altho the practice of the Enemy is to confine our People when Captured &c. I told him that all Prisoners are in the keeping of the Secy at War and desired that he would go to the War Office and inform General Lincoln of this matter.

Wrote a Letter to His Excellency the President of Congress. Abm. Yeates Junr.[9]

1. For the selection of William Denning as commissioner to settle Quartermaster Department accounts, see notes to RM to the President of Congress, February 18, 1782.

2. These papers have not been found, but similar papers submitted by Captain Francis Maxwell were enclosed in RM to the President of Congress, August 23.

3. See RM to Carleton, August 20, and notes.

4. Charles Stewart, the former commissary general of issues, was currently the issuing contractor for West Point and the Moving Army.

5. See RM to Washington, August 20, and to William Duer, August 29.

6. First Lieutenant John Peck, paymaster of the 2d New Jersey Regiment.

7. On the motion of Theodorick Bland, Jr., a Virginia delegate to Congress, Con-

gress on May 30, 1782, had ordered RM and Secretary at War Benjamin Lincoln to "enquire into a contract made by Congress or a committee of Congress [in 1775], with Mr. Jacob Rubsamen, for the purpose of instructing the people of Virginia in the mode of making salt-petre, &c. and report the wages due to him on that account, and whether his further services are necessary, together with the mode to be adopted for paying him." Their report, dated August 26, was adopted by Congress the same day. Rubsamen's accounts remained unsettled, but in 1786 he withdrew his claim after Congress declared that he had been in actual service only until the end of 1776, for which period he had already been paid (for the background, see *JCC*, XXX, 397, 435–437). Rubsamen, of Manchester, Virginia, was the manager of saltpeter works on the James and Appomattox Rivers and of lead mines in Montgomery County; he was Bland's brother-in-law. See *WMQ*, 1st ser., V (1897), 157n.; Charles Campbell, ed., *The Bland Papers: Being a Selection from the Manuscripts of Colonel Theodorick Bland, Jr.* . . . (Petersburg, Va., 1840–1843), I, 149; Palmer, ed., *Calendar of Virginia State Papers*, III, 426, VIII, 90.

8. The documents received from William Nourse, evidently a son of James and a brother of Joseph Nourse, Register of the Treasury, have not been found, but may have related to his pay as midshipman on the Continental frigate *Confederacy*. Nourse subsequently served as clerk to his father while the latter was commissioner of accounts in Maryland and later was a clerk in various Treasury Department offices. See PCC, no. 141, I, 94, 120, 121, 155, 248, 293, II, 78, 315; and *Calendar of Maryland State Papers*, no. 4, pt. 2, The Red Books, 278.

9. This letter is dated August 22.

To the President of Congress
(John Hanson)

Office of Finance August 23d. 1782

Sir

Mr Francis Maxwell Master of the Symetry Transport, one of the Flag Ships lately arrived at this Port from England with American Prisoners, has demanded Payment for Provisions furnished to the said Prisoners on the Passage hither. His Instructions were to issue to the Prisoners the same allowance that British Soldiers have whilst on Board Transports at Sea, but not satisfied therewith, they in a Body (two hundred and sixteen in Number) demanded from him an addition to that Allowance informing him at the same Time that if he did not comply with their Demand they would take the Provision by Force, thereupon he ordered such additional Quantity to be issued as satisfied them. This additional Allowance constitutes the Charge which he now requires Payment of from the United States. Were I to express my private Sentiments, they would be, that the Dignity of the United States might be improperly committed by refusing the Payment. But as no Act of theirs exists by which I am authorized to determine, I request your Excellency will do me the Honor to lay this State of the Transaction before Congress, and pray their Decission.[1] I have the Honor to be Sir your Excellency's most obedient and most humble Servant.

Robt Morris

His Excellency The President of Congress

ENDORSED: 84/Letter 23 Aug 1782/R Morris Agent of Marine/Read 26 Aug./referred to Mr. Duane/Mr. Howell/Mr Izard/claim of F Maxwell Mr. of/a flag ship with prisoners for/payment for provisions beyond/the stated allowance extorted by the said prisoners

MSS: LS, PCC, DNA; Ofcl LbC, DLC.

1. Filed with this letter in PCC, no. 137, I, 733–735, were Maxwell's deposition, dated August 23 and certified by John Green, and an undated account of additional provisions Maxwell issued to the prisoners between July 2 and August 14. For Congress's response to this letter from RM, see notes to Diary, August 13.

From William Irvine

Fort Pitt Augt: 23d 1782[1]

Sir

This will be handed to you by Mr: Thomas Parkison together with his Accounts and Vouchers for Rations furnished the Militia of Washington County under my orders, and also a Copy of ⟨the⟩ his agreement with me.[2]

The nature of the Service the Militia are employed on, particularly being so far detached and in such small parties, renders it all together impracticable to obtain either Returns or Certificates, so accurate as I could wish, and alluded to in the Contract, yet I am persuaded, from many concuring circumstances the Number of Rations he charges have been fairly Issued—Viz five thousand two hundred and Sixty one. I am certain more men have been out on duty than he has charged Rations for, many of whom have been fed by frontier Inhabitants at whose Houses they were Quartered.

Every possible step has been taken to prevent fraud in this business, and I am of opinion the endeavours have been successfull.

I hope I shall not be under a necessity of keeping any Militia out longer than the first of October, the whole expence will be small when compared with that of former years, and I flatter myself not less real service has been performed. I have the honor to be Sir your most Obedient Humble Servant

The Honble. Robt. Morris Esqr.

Copy

[ENCLOSURE][3]

Agreement between William Irvine and Thomas Parkison

[Fort Pitt, May 3, 1782]

Articles of Agreement Indented and Concluded on at Fort Pitt this 3d day of May 1782. Between William Irvine Esqr. Brigr Genl. (by authority invested in him by the Hble Robert Morris Esqr. Superintendt. of Finance) of the one part, and Captn. Thos. Parkison of Washington County State Pena, of the other part

Witnesseth

that said Parkison for the Consideration here in after mentioned doth hereby for himself his Exrs. &[c?] and administrators promise and agree to and with Genl. Irvine, to furnish and Issue Rations to the Militia of the County afore said Called out into actual service by order of Genl. Irvine, and Stationed at the following places Viz—at Montorin Bottom, Yellow Creek, Mingo Bottom and Wheeling or Grave Creek—the Ration to consist of one pound of Flower, and one pound of Fresh Beef or pork or three quarters pound of Salt meat. Two Quarts of salt is to be issued to every hundred Rations of fresh meat. And General Irvine agrees on his part to allow said Parkison Eleven-pence half-peny for every such Ration Issued by him, and is to use his best endeavours with the Superintendant of Finance to procure money for the payment of the same at the end of two months from the Commencement of the Issues, which is to be the tenth Instant. Said Parkisons Vouchers for Rations Issued is to be returns signed twice Every week by Commissioned officers Commanding the Compys or parties—the provisions and weekly returns to be examined and compared by a Field officer on duty having charge of the Militia then in service—whose certificates and also that of the county Lieutenant or Sub Lieutenant that so many Militia of said County were in actual Service at that time by the Generals orders—for the Number of days of what ever months—the Returns and Certificates to be dated and Clear, which Certificates and Returns or duplicates must be ⟨left with⟩ Lodged with General Irvine.

For the true performance of the above agreement said Capt. Thos. Parkison doth bind himself his Execurs. and administrators (in Case of Failure) in the penal sum of three hundred pounds specie to be paid ⟨in⟩ unto the Hble Robt. Morris Esqr. Superintendant of Finance in behalf the United States.

In witness whereof we have hereunto set our hands and affixed our seals this 3d. day of May 1782

Signed ⟨and⟩ Seal'd and
Delivered in the presence of
   John Rose

                                 Thomas Parkison
                                 Wm: Irvine

MS: Copy in Irvine's writing, Irvine Family Papers, PHi.
    1. Brigadier General Irvine was the commander at Fort Pitt.
    2. The accounts and vouchers have not been found. For the origins of the Parkison contract, see RM to Irvine, March 6, 1782 (first letter), and notes.
    3. MS: DS, Irvine Papers, PHi. The signatures are accompanied by seals.

From George Washington

Head Quarters [Newburgh, New York] 23d Augst 1782
Dear Sir

Mr Wells, who handed me your several Favors of the 8th, 9th and 13th, arrived here on the 21st and was immediately furnished with passports from me to proceed to the Enemys outposts.[1]

If he succeeds in his purposes and brings out any thing to my Care, I shall most cheerfully comply with your Request in receiving and disposing of it.[2]

Colo. Tilghman communicated to me your Ideas respecting the appointment of an Inspector to the Army.[3] I agree with you that as the Office will be of the highest importance and trust, the Officer should be a Man not only of Ability, but of ⟨respectability⟩ the most established character in as much as very much would depend upon his decisions, especially between the Contractors and the Army. I am of opinion that if a civil Character could be found, he would answer better than a military one, as the Contractors would perhaps think a military Man prejudiced in favor of the Army. A Civil Character well acquainted with business would on many accounts answer better than a military, for instance where purchases are to be made to make up the deficiencies of the Contracters or to lay up Magazines should the Army have reason to march suddenly and secretly out of the limits of the Contractors for the moving Army. This you will observe is given as mere matter of opinion, and not with a wish to influence your choice. Could I recommend a proper person I would chearfully do it, but as I have no such at present in my view I shall be fully satisfied with any Gentleman whom you may think qualified.

Hono Robert Morris

ENDORSED: Head Quarters 23d Augst 1782/to/Hono Robert Morris/Mr Wells gone to N York/Inspector to the Army submit/ted to his Choice
MSS: Dft in the writing of Jonathan Trumbull, Jr., and Tench Tilghman, Washington Papers, DLC; Varick transcript, Washington Papers, DLC.
    1. On the mission of Richard Wells to New York City, see the notes to the letter of August 13.
    2. To this point the letter is in Trumbull's writing; the remainder is in Tilghman's hand.
    3. That is, an inspector of contracts for the main army. See Diary, August 5, and notes.

Diary: August 24, 1782

Received a Letter from James Nourse Esqr. declining to Act as a Commissioner of any State.[1]

Mr. O: Pollock makes Application for some public Flour to be delivered to him on Account of his Claim on the United States. I sent to Mr: Hollingsworth and Mr Blaine who have the flour for a Return of the Quality, Quantity &c. before I give any Reply.[2]

Mr Oster[3] applies to me to give up the House he now lives in which I had rented with this office. I agreed to do so.

John Carter Esqr. applied to inform me that he must now call on me for 20,000 Dollars lent me in May last by Mr Chaloner and for 8,000 Dollars their part of the Money paid by Mr Jos: Wilson on account of Bills of Exchange sold him.[4]

Capt. Allibone called and got away all the Papers that had been lodged with me respecting the Ship General Washington.[5]

The Honble Secy at War called when we had a long Conference respecting the Army, their rations, Subsistence Pay &c.

Lieut. Peck called again respecting the Subsistence of the Jersey

Brigade. I referred him to the Paymaster General by a message per Mr McCall.[6]

Sundry other Persons called respecting Money but having none for them I did not see them.

Issued a Warrant on Mr Swanwick in favor the
Contractors for York and Carlisle   £1161.18.11
Issued a Warrant on Mr Swanwick in favor the
Bank for Discounts   2. 3. 4
Issued a Warrant on Mr Swanwick in favor of T:
Francis for Discounts   2. 4. 5

1. The letter from Nourse, a Virginia planter and politician, has not been found. RM's offer to appoint him a commissioner of accounts is not recorded but may have been conveyed through his son Joseph, Register of the Treasury. Nourse eventually changed his mind, and RM nominated him as commissioner to settle accounts in Maryland in a letter to the governor of February 27, 1783.
2. See Diary, August 12, and notes.
3. Martin Oster, the French vice-consul in Philadelphia.
4. See Diary, August 20, and notes.
5. For RM's involvement with the *General Washington*, which he now wanted to purchase for the United States, see Diary, May 15, 1782, and notes.
6. See Diary, August 23.

From the Quartermaster General (Timothy Pickering)

New Windsor [New York] August 24th: 1782 Evening

Sir

My express to Hartford for money in exchange for your bills has just returned without a shilling.[1] Having the utmost confidence of receiving a small supply, in notes at least, if there were no Cash, I ventured to promise the farmers payment for the forage they should now bring in on the delivery of it: expecting a reinforcement from Massachusetts before his first supply should be expended. If there also I am unsuccessful, I shall indeed be wretched. I had determined to make no more such promises, however encouraging the prospect of fulfilling them: but impelled by the wants of the army to attempt every means of obtaining the necessary supplys, I forgot my resolutions. But—if I make another, without the money in hand—I shall deserve a jail.

Mr. Pomeroy, my deputy at Hartford has given me a detail, with which it seems proper that you should be acquainted. If your receiver has already given you similar information, I shall beg your pardon for troubling you with this. It is contained in the inclosed extract of a letter from Mr: Pomeroy dated the 22nd: instant.[2] It appears they are waiting for the circulation of notes, with which to pay their taxes—what cash they procure will be necessary for continuing their infamous traffick with New York.[3] I can only wish there existed a Power competent to punish, with double taxes, a State so little disturbed by the enemy, so little incumbered with debt, and yet so unpardonably negligent of its duty to the confederacy.

Permit me also to inclose the advertisement of the Treasurer of that State, for the purpose of *inforcing the collection of taxes.*[4] The collectors must possess uncommon sensibility if that gentle admonition should stimulate them to the smallest exertions: it is rather an opiate to lay them a sleep. But I beg your pardon for these unnecessary observations it is not always easy to suppress our resentments. I am Sir with great respect your most Obedient Servant

Tim. Pickering
Q.M.G.

MS: LbC, WDC, DNA.

1. For the bills of exchange on John Swanwick given to Pickering, see Diary, August 3. Pickering had sent three bills of $1,500 each to Ralph Pomeroy, the deputy quartermaster general for Connecticut. Pomeroy acknowledged and discussed them in the letter to Pickering cited in the following note.

2. Pomeroy's letter, dated at Hartford, is in the Manuscript File, no. 25437, WDC. The extract actually received by RM has not been found, but it probably contained the following paragraphs bracketed in manuscript: "According to your directions I have made application to the Receiver of this State, who has not received any Money or Bank Notes except the trifling Sum of twenty five pounds in one note. I am also by him informed that a Number of Bills Similar to those now sent have been negotiated with some of the Collectors which are already lodged with him instead of Mr. Morris's Notes which the Collectors received of me (those Bills being payable at Sight). The receiver gives me not the least encouragement of being able to exchange any sum in any given time.

"I know of no way whereby money can be raised with them in this Quarter. I have been most assiduosly engaged for three or four Months past to exchange the Notes you was kind enough to Send me last Spring for the purchase of oxteams have not yet compleated the payments to about a Sixth part.

"There is very little money raised here in Taxes. In this Town perhaps as able as any, only twenty Dollars has been collected in Money. There are many people who have demands unsetled which in fact not only delays the payment of their own Rates but also of their Neighbours.

"In almost every Town in this State Contractors for the Army have bought or published their designs of Buying Provisions to pay in Money or Mr. Morris Notes, which the People wait for in many places."

Pickering apparently did not include Pomeroy's next paragraph commenting on RM's bills of exchange (see note 1 above): "I believe there is nothing to be done with these Bills of Exchange without cutting them up. I dont mean cutting them for the purposes of Circulation but for the accomodation of Individuals to pay rates and negociated with the Collectors by orders from the Treasury Office or some Mode Similar, and in this way no money can be raised."

3. For a general discussion of the illegal trade with New York City, see notes to Gouverneur Morris to Thomas Willing, June 18, 1782.

4. The advertisement dated "State of Connecticut, Treasury-Office, Hartford, July 22, 1782," and addressed "To the several Collectors of State Taxes," was as follows: "It is a disagreeable circumstance, that the payment of Taxes is so much delayed: What can be the cause, but misinformation? Many of you have this idea, that execution is not to issue; so far is this from the case, that no longer than in May last the General Assembly passed the following resolve. 'Resolved by this Assembly, That the Treasurer take effectual care to enforce the collection of taxes according to law.' As

the subscriber hath hitherto endeavoured to comply with Acts of Assembly, especially those relating to his office, nothing, but the most vigorous exertions, can prevent him from complying with the above resolve. That the taxes may so be paid in for the future, there may be no expence to the Collectors, is the wish and desire of gentlemen, Your most obedient humble servant, John Lawrence, Treasurer." The notice appeared in the *Connecticut Courant and Weekly Intelligencer* of July 30 and August 6 and 13, 1782.

From William Churchill Houston

Trenton [New Jersey] 24 August 1782[1]
The two weeks past very little Money has been paid me by the Treasurer; but as several of the Collectours have not yet come in, hope I shall be enabled to furnish better returns soon.

1782 Dr   The Receipt of Continental Taxes for the State of New-Jersey
           To Cash received from the State Treasurer from 17 August to 24
               inclusive two Hundred Dollars   Dlls 200

MS: ADft with subjoined ADftS return, Houston Collection, NjP.
   1. Houston was the receiver of Continental taxes for New Jersey.

To John Vaughan

Philadelphia August 25th 1782
Dear Sir
Your letter of the 19th Instant[1] was delivered to me on Friday Evening and I could not spare time for a Reply untill this morning, (Sunday), in consequence of what you say respecting your letters at the Post Office, I thought it necessary for me to open two which had arrived since your departure from hence, by a Flagg ship with Prisoners from England, one of them proves to be from your Brother,[2] who observes that your Father "has nothing more to add to his former letters,"[3] and then he says "I can however inform you that letters have been written to Williams, Barton and Harrison, each, Respectively, to ship uninsured on each Bottom Armed two hundred Pounds untill the amount of two thousand Pounds be laid out in Goods, Saleable, Guarding against the danger of Hurricane Months in the Islands."[4] From these parts of your Brothers letter I conclude, first, that your Father continues determined to make a purchase, and Secondly that each of the Houses above named are to Ship Goods to the Amount of two thousand Pounds Sterling, so as that the whole Amount of the Shipments will be Six thousand Pounds Sterling. Thirdly that he depends on these Shipments to enable you to make payment. Hence it naturally follows that if you agree with General Lee, He must wait for his Money untill it Suits you to Pay, as your ability will depend on the arrival of the Goods for I do not observe any alternative, there being no authority for you to draw in case of the Goods being captured or lost, Neither do

I find that you are authorized to exceed the Sum of Six thousand
Pounds Sterling in the Purchase of Two places or Tracts of Land. It
follows then that, if Genl. Lee refuses your offer of Six thousand
Pounds Sterling you cannot make the purchase, if he accepts it, the
Land is capable of being divided to Suit your Fathers design, consequently the whole sum being laid out in one such Tract can be no
objection. General Lee writes me that he must have at least Eight
hundred Pounds Sterling immediately to Pay his Debts,[5] I think this
point may be accomplished scarce as money is, or indeed if necessary
I think you may Venture to draw for this Sum promising your
Father to remit him the same amount from the Sale of the Goods
after paying the rest of the Purchase, and it must be observed that if
any of the Goods are taken or lost you must still have recourse to[6]
your Father to make up the deficiency. You will have seen by the
Public Prints that a Treaty for a General Peace is on foot, whether
this desireable object will be accomplished or not is uncertain, but I
think the appearances are favorable, under this Idea you will expect
the Land to become Valuable, but under this Idea your Goods must
be much less Valuable than if the War continues,[7] however danger
of Capture and loss will also be lessen'd, If the War continues Exchange will remain at a moderate price, upon a Peace it will rise, all
these circumstances I mention as points for your consideration, and
upon the whole. my opinion formed upon the information's frequently repeated to me of the Value of General Lee's Estate, is, that
at Six thousand Pounds Sterling you will not Pay too dear for it; I
think you cannot with propriety go farther, Eight hundred Pounds
Sterling to be paid down; for the remainder he must take your
Bonds bearing Interest at Six percent per annum untill paid But as
he does not know you sufficiently, the Deeds may be lodged in the
hands of a Friend under a Proper obligation for the delivery
thereof, upon payment of the Money, in short this Point may be
readily Settled when the General and you are here because I will do
in that respect what may be necessary therefore if he agree's to take
the Six thousand Pounds and to wait for five thousand Pounds or
Five thousand two hundred Pounds at your Convenience, I think
you had best fix the time for meeting here, or come up together.
Should General Lee refuse your Offer, you will have time to look
farther and you have seen that there is plenty of Good Land in
America. I cannot help observing that with your mother I fear that
the very Sanguine expectations formed by your Father of the enjoyments which this Country is to afford him, will in some degree be
disappointed For altho our Liberties are established so that every
man does almost what he pleases, individually and has his full share
in Government[8] yet a mind formed and trained so long as Mr
Vaughans hath been under Monarchical Government cannot at once

relish the manners and customs of Republicans,[9] these Considerations however do not militate against this Purchase because whether your father visits America or not, or whether he approves of the Estate or not it will I beleive always be worth the Money you give for it. I shall expect the pleasure of seeing you soon and remain Dear Sir Your most Obedient humble Servant

Robt Morris

PS. The letters from your Mother and Brother are enclosed.

Mr. John Vaughan
Berkley County Virginia

ENDORSED: R. Morris Received 1 Sepr.
MSS: LS, Madeira-Vaughan Collection, PPAmP; ADftS, Robert Morris Papers, NN.
    1. Letter not found. Vaughan, a young Englishman, had recently come to the United States to obtain land for his father, who was planning to emigrate. This reply from RM concerns the prospective purchase of Charles Lee's estate in Virginia. See also RM to Lee, August 25.
    2. For the arrival of the cartel ships from England with American marine prisoners, see notes to Diary, August 13. The letters from Vaughan's mother and his brother Benjamin (see postscript) have not been found.
    3. The quotation marks surrounding this passage have been supplied from the ADftS. Except for the variations noted here and below and the rearrangement of some passages, the ADftS is virtually identical in substance to the LS.
    4. This quotation mark has been supplied by the editors.
    5. See Charles Lee to RM, August 15.
    6. Here in the ADftS, RM excised the words "drafts bills."
    7. On this point, see the headnote to RM's State of American Commerce and Plan for Protecting It, May 10, 1782, and notes; on land values, see also RM to Richard Butler, August 26.
    8. RM interlined the preceding eight words in the ADftS.
    9. RM continued to develop this subject in the ADftS for the next eight lines, but then made a number of revisions before excising those lines altogether. In the following tentative reconstruction of what RM intended to say the editors have inserted in angle brackets those words which he appears to have deleted while revising the passage: "He will find also less ⟨of that there is more?⟩ of that Stern Virtue ⟨which⟩ and ⟨those plain⟩ simplicity of manners which strike his admiration ⟨exist in the immagination⟩ than he expects. Luxury and dissipation have gained a considerable footing ⟨amongst us⟩ and when people from all parts of Europe come to ruin amongst us I believe the Americans will but too soon [*estimated two lines torn away*]."

To the President of Delaware
(John Dickinson)

Office of Finance 25th, August 1782

I do myself the Honor to enclose to your Excellency a Petition of Francis Wade, according to the Direction of Congress upon that Subject.[1] The Resolution of the nineteenth of March has already been transmitted,[2] and therefore I shall not trouble your Excellency with a second Copy.

MSS: LS, Executive Papers, De-Ar; Ofcl LbC, DLC.
    1. Wade's petition has not been found; for Congress's action on it, see *JCC*, XXII, 449, XXIII, 530. See also Diary, August 15, and notes.
    2. In RM's Circular to the Governors of the States, August 17.

To Charles Lee

Philada. August 25th. 1782

Mr Vaughans Servant delivered me your letters of the 15th and 19th Instant and one of the latter date from His Master,[1] by which I find he has made you an offer of £6000 Stg for your Estate, this Sum being the extent of what His Father has authorized him to Invest in Land. The Question which is first to be solved remains solely with you, for if you refuse that Sum I conceive that the bargain is at an end and that he must look out elsewhere. Shou'd you agree to accept that offer I conceive every thing else may be made easy. He may be able to pay down the £800 Sterlg you want and His Bonds for the remainder bearing Interest untill discharged will be good but to Secure them beyond a doubt The Deeds of Conveyance may be deposited so as to revert to you if he does not perform or to be delivered to him on payment of The Money. His Father has ordered Goods to be shipped out here to enable him to make the payments and I suppose he will be ready to give you the money sooner than you will want it. Mr Goddard must have mistaken when he said I fixed any Value to your Land, for I did not know sufficiently, to pronounce an opinion. He told me you had sold to Mr Dorsey at much less than the Value and unless you could repay the Money received of that Gentleman you would suffer exceedingly. I told him that must not be and that to prevent it I would supply the sums which he said were necessary. I recollect very well my desiring him to inform you that if you continued in the mind of selling not to do it without letting me know, for I then recollected that another Gentleman had on a former occasion, said he meant to purchase. I have told Mr Vaughan that from every information I have received your Estate is well Worth the Money he has offered for it and that it will always be worth the Money if his Father should not like it or chooses to sell again. It may be worth more for ought I know but I cannot advise him to exceed his limits as he may have choice of Lands for his Money. If you agree I suppose you will come up together or fix a time for meeting here and I shall do every thing that can be reasonably expected on my part to make your dealings mutually Convenient and agreable. Shoud Mr Vaughan encline to purchase the whole or any part of your Stock you had best have an Inventory and appraisment or agreement of the Value made out before you come up. As your Politics and mine are totally different I choose to decline that Subject, indeed my time is too much employed to permit me to write any but letters of business. I Wish however for your Sake that your Sentiments and Conduct were different from what they appear to be, for I am Dear Sir Your Friend and obedient humble Servant

MS: ADftS, Robert Morris Papers, NN.

1. John Vaughan's letter has not been found. RM replied to Vaughan on August 25.

From Alexander Hamilton

Albany [New York] Aug. 25. 82

This letter serves only to transmit the two last papers:[1] I wish the measures I have taken to satisfy you on the points you desire to be informed of, had been attended with so much success as to enable me now to transmit the result. But I find a singular confusion in the accounts kept by the public officers from whom I must necessarily derive my information, and a singular dilatoriness in complying with my applications, partly from indolence and partly from jealousy of the office.[2]

I hope by the next post to transmit you information on some particulars.[3]

MSS: ALS, Hamilton Papers, DLC; transcript, Francis Baylies Papers, DLC.

1. Hamilton refers to newspapers that he, as receiver of Continental taxes for New York, was expected to send RM on a regular basis.

2. For Hamilton's efforts to obtain the information requested in RM's circular to the receivers of July 12, 1782, see Syrett and Cooke, eds., *Hamilton Papers*, III, 123–125, 126–127, 130–132, 147–148, 163–164.

3. See Hamilton to RM, August 31, and notes.

Diary: August 26, 1782

Mr. Peter Whiteside Called to inform me that he has some Soldiers Shirts, Linnens fit for Soldiers and other Articles which the Clothier General wished to purchase, but he wanted to know the mode of payment. He said he would take Cash or Bills of Exchange. I agreed to pay the latter if the purchase is made.

Capt. De Bert of Colo. Armands Corps for the Officers Certificates.[1] I promised to determine the Point this Day.

Colo. F. Nicholls applies for money on account of the Contract for Frederick Town and Winchester. I told him that I have not Money to Spare but am willing to advance the amount in bills of Exchange.

The Honble. Jno. Rutledge, Revd. Mr. Montgomery and John [i.e., Samuel] Osgood Esqrs. came as a Committee of Congress for the Establishment of Pacquet Boats to and from Europe. I told them that the business would be easy if we had money but in our present Circumstances impossible.[2]

Haym Solomon informs me that there is no Sale for Bills of Exchange nor can he raise any money for me.

Major Franks requested me to Certify a part of my instructions to him when going with Dispatches for Madrid which I did adding that he received no pay for going to Europe with Dispatches other than his Expences and his pay as an Officer.[3] I desired the Major to Exhibit his Account of Expences to the Comptroller for Settlement. Promised to Serve him when suitable Opportunity Offered but advised him against any Expectations of Employment in the Diplomatic Line which he seemed to have formed.

Mr Dudley called and pressed very much to be set to Work.[4]

Mr. Jos. Wilson applied to have it inserted in my Obligation to him for Bills of Exchange that the Bills shall be of my own drawing or endorsing. I said this unnecessary but as he seems anxious I will draw the Bills now and let them remain until the 15th December ready to be delivered to him on that Day.[5]

Capt. Josh. Barney Called to inform me that Mr. Standley intended to purchase the Ship General Washington unless I want her and in that Case he will refrain. I desired him to call to morrow.[6]

Mr Geary Clerk to William Duer Esqr. applying I signed a Warrant for 2,000 Dolls. and desired him to wait in Town himself a few Days. I promised also some notes.[7]

Mr. R. Sands applying for money I desired to see him and on enquiring respecting the Drafts which I gave him in July on Mr. Swanwick[8] I find that he had negotiated of those 3,000 Dollars which was the Amount of the Money he asks for and my Poverty obldged me to decline paying any more at present altho inclined to assist him farther soon as possible.

Wrote a Letter to the Hon: Mr Scott, Mr Rutledge and Mr. Lee.

Wrote a Letter to His Excellency Genl. Washington.[9]

Wrote a Letter to His Excellency the Governor of Connecticutt.

Wrote a Letter to James Nourse Esqr.[10]

Wrote a Letter to John Bradford.

1. See Diary, August 21.

2. Rutledge's committee had been directed to confer with the Superintendent. After being advised of RM's plans to purchase the *General Washington* (see Diary, August 29), the committee reported the same day that the ship, "a swift sailing vessel," was available "on reasonable and advantageous terms," and Congress promptly ordered RM to acquire the vessel as a packet. For a discussion, see Diary, May 15, 1782, and notes.

3. The certificate, dated August 26, was signed by RM on August 31 (see Diary of that date). Franks enclosed it in a memorial to Congress seeking reinstatement in the Continental army, from which he had been inadvertently deranged while in Europe. Congress on October 22 voted to allow Franks the rank and pay of a major until January 1, 1783, when he was to be retired from service under a new army reorganization. See *JCC*, XXIII, 574 and n.; Franks's undated memorial to the President of Congress, in PCC, no. 41, III, 268–271; and on some aspects of his mission, John Jay to RM, April 28, 1782.

4. Benjamin Dudley was assisting RM in establishing a mint. See the headnote to RM to the President of Congress, January 15, 1782 (first letter), and notes.

5. See Diary, August 9 and 20, and notes.

6. See above in this Diary at note 2.

7. See Duer to RM, August 2, and notes.

8. Probably those promised in the Diary of July 17. Richardson Sands was a contractor for West Point and the Moving Army.

9. This entry refers to Gouverneur Morris's letter to Washington of this day.

10. Letter not found.

To Richard Butler

Philada. August 26th. 1782[1]

Dear Sir

Mortifying as it is to write what follows yet the total impracticability of borrowing Money in this place renders it necessary. The advantages which daily offer to Men who have the command of Money, determine those few that have it, (for indeed they are very few), not to part with it. You will be able to form some Idea of these advantages when I tell you, that the Jew Brokers and others have informed me in the course of my inquiries that *Sub Rosa* they frequently get 5 per Cent per month from good Substantial men for the use of Money with pledges lodged for the repayment. They add that before the establishment of the Bank they frequently got ten per Cent and upwards. This my Dear Sir is the fruits of Depreciated Money, Broken faiths &c. I am so much shocked at Sums like this that I have quitted the pursuit, lamenting that your application had not been made sooner, for it is not a great while since I helped a Friend of yours and mine to a Sum of money which I paid, to this person who lent it to him and you might then have come in for a part, but it is gone and untill Credit and Confidence are better restored I dont believe much Money can be borrowed in America. This very Circumstance will for a considerable time prevent any rise in the Value of Lands as there will be even after Peace is Concluded more sellers than buyers,[2] so that should you loose the Tract you now had in View I am perswaded you will have other and perhaps more favourable opportunities of making a purchase. I have proposed to Congress to make requisitions of such Revennues from the several states as if obtained will enable them to do justice to the Public Creditors in the Number of which the army are included and it gives me pleasure to add that by all I can learn Congress are much disposed to enter into the measure.[3] Shoud they make the Demand the rest will depend on the several Legislatures and I hope the necessity of doing Justice will have its due Weight with the whole. With Sincere esteem and respect I am Dear Sir Your obedient humble Servant

RM

To Colo Richd Butler
Carlisle

ENDORSED: Philada. 26 August 1782/Colo Richd Butler/ Copy of a letter to him
MS: ADftS, Robert Morris Papers, NN.
    1. Butler, a colonel in the Pennsylvania line of the Continental army, had previously sought a loan from RM in order to purchase land (see Butler to RM, June 1 and July 11, and RM to Butler, July 18, 1782). The present letter probably was written in response to a letter from Butler of August 13 (ALS sold by Stan. V. Henkels on January 16, 1917, lot 224) which has not been found.
    2. For another comment on land values, see RM to John Vaughan, August 25.
    3. See RM to the President of Congress, July 29.

To a Committee of Congress (John Morin Scott, Arthur Lee, and John Rutledge)

Office of Finance, 26th. August 1782

Gentlemen

I have re-examined the Report on Settlement of our public Accounts in Europe[1] with great Attention; it proceeds on the two following Assumptions, first that such Settlement should be *only* at the Treasury here, and secondly (which is indeed a Consequence of the first) that some Person be authorized to receive the Accounts &c. in Europe and transmit them hither.

I shall not take the Liberty to make any very particular Observations on the various Parts of this Report, the Point of most consequence (in my Idea) was to discover what particular Authorities were to be conferred on the Commissioner, as to the Establishing of Charges against the United States. I find that by the Commission he is to have and demand from every Accountant such Proof of his Accounts as he (the Commissioner) shall *deem just and reasonable.* I find also that by the third Article of the Instructions, he is ordered to require *Vouchers* for every *Charge* against the United States, that he is carefully to examine into the *Authenticity, Veracity* and *Fairness* of every *Voucher* produced to him, And that he is to take due Care so to *circumstantiate* the Vouchers *in Point of Evidence* as that a *proper* Judgement may be formed here what *Credit* ought to be given to them, and *how far they support the Charges.* I find also that, by the last Article of his Instructions, he is ordered *in all Things concerning the Premisses* to do as by his Commission and Instructions he is directed. I will not pretend to determine what Latitude of Interpretation the Commissioner would think himself authorized to give to his Commission and Instructions, but as the Commission is in its nature open and public, it would seem that the Accountant would have Notice to produce such Proof of his Account as the Commissioner should *deem just and reasonable.* The Commissioner would be bound, I suppose, by his Instructions to call for *Vouchers* to support every *Charge,* and *Evidence* to convince him that those Vouchers are *Authentic, fair and true.* It would then appear to be the Duty of the Commissioner to *circumstantiate* that Evidence. But it is reserved to the Officers of the Treasury Department here *to form a proper Judgement what Credit is to be given to these Vouchers, and how far they support the Charges,* and therefore it is theirs to determine, finally, what Proof of an Account shall be *deemed just and reasonable.* If their Decission differ from that of the Commissioner, either the account must be rejected or the Accountant must be called on to produce further Evidence. The former would be unjust; the latter would be very expensive and subject the Accountant to Hardships which he might properly complain of. But it appears to be very unlikely that the Officers of the Treasury here would differ from the Commissioner; for they must take up every Thing on his Representation, and as to the Credibility of Witnesses, and many other Things equally important, he must be the more competent Judge. If then it be the Idea of the Report that the Commissioner is to decide on the Voucher (and this I confess appears to me the Idea) then he is substantially, tho' not formally, empowered to settle the Account, and the Expence will be increased because much Time will be spent here in going thro' the Accounts a second Time for the sake of Form, when they have been adjusted by him in Matters of Substance. A Consideration which may attract the

Notice of the Committee is this, that in going thro' Accounts many
Articles of Credit must be admitted in one Account before they can
form a Debit in another. Thus, for Instance, when Money has been
paid by one Man to another for the Purpose of purchasing Arms or
Cloathing, it must be credited to him by whom it was paid, before it
can be charged to the Receiver. Supposing therefore the public accounts abroad to be ever so clear, the Commissioner even in calling
for them at the Hands of one, must necessarily admit them to be just
as exhibited by the other. Thus, in the Case already put, he may
either demand the Money or the Goods, but he cannot demand
both. Lastly, among many other Considerations (for I would avoid as
much as possible going into Detail) it cannot have escaped the Committee, that however the public Servants of the United States may be
amenable in such Mode as Congress shall appoint, the Subjects of
foreign Powers will account only in that Way which is usual among
them, and Recourse must be had to the Laws of the Country against
them. It is true that the Accounts have in the first Instance originated with Servants of Congress, but when in any Case Congress
have ordered that to be done which would oblige their Servants to
employ other Persons for the accomplishment of it, those Servants
can only be responsible for the Characters of those whom they employed. It is not perhaps unworthy of Attention also, that whoever
may have the Settlement of the Accounts in Question, he should be
authorized to prosecute such Suits as may be necessary. For altho'
such Suits may, and perhaps ought to be in the name of the public
Servant by whom the Party was employed, yet in many Instances the
Expence must be borne by the Public; not to mention that the Servant may be dead, absent, or out of their Service.

I must now therefore Gentlemen with great Submission take the
Liberty to examine the first Assumption in the Report, and which
is indeed the Ground work of the whole, vizt, that the Settlement
of these *Accounts should be only at the Treasury here.* It appears exceedingly doubtful whether they could be justly settled at the Treasury at all, and it is exceedingly clear that *any* Account can be
better Settled on the Spot where the Business it relates to has been
transacted than any where else. But *public* Accounts ought above all
others to be so settled. The Magnitude and Extent of such Accounts, added to the Disadvantages which the public Always labors
under in being obliged to transact its Business by Means of others:
These are Circumstances which open a wide Door to Frauds and
Impositions, if Things are to be judged of at the Distance of a
thousand Leagues. Even as to Accounts in America, Congress have
thought it expedient to appoint Commissioners, and every Reason
in Favor of that Measure must operate with additional Force as to
Accounts in Europe. The only Question which can arise is this,

Whether the Commissioner abroad will possess equal Integrity and Judgement with the Officers in the Treasury Department. Now as to his Integrity, it is alike assailable whether he be appointed to settle the Accounts himself or to collect the Evidence for others, and if he should be corrupted, the consequences must be alike pernicious. But it is admitted by the Report, and is indeed clear in itself, that a Commissioner must be appointed for the one Purpose or for the other. The only Doubt therefore must be as to his Judgement and this at least is clear that he will have a better opportunity of Judging, and better Materials to direct his Opinions. If the Accounts are settled here, the Judgment of the Comptroller must in the last Resort *decide*. If therefore a commissioner can be chosen who is an honest Man, and who has equal Ability with the Comptroller, He will be able to serve the United States more effectually than the Comptroller could do. This would be a considerable Saving of Expence, and if with a View to farther saving Congress shall appoint their Consul to do this Duty I can have no Objection.

What I would propose therefore is:[2] That a Commissioner be appointed by Congress with full Power and Authority to liquidate and finally to Settle the Accounts of all the Servants of the United States who have been entrusted with the Expenditure of public Monies in Europe, and all other Accounts of the United States in Europe, and to commence and prosecute such Suits, Causes and Actions as may be necessary for that Purpose, or for the Recovery of any Property of the said states in the Hands of any Person or Persons whatsoever.[3]

That in the various Branches of his Duty he shall in such Matters of Form as regard meerly the stating of Accounts proceed agreeably to Rules to be prescribed to him by the Comptroller of the Treasury.[4]

That two Clerks to the said Commissioner be appointed in like Manner[5] and that it shall be their Duty to examine all the said Accounts when exhibited, to correct all Errors, and to note in writing what may appear exceptionable, either as to the Propriety of the Charges or the Validity of the Vouchers.

That after such Examination the Commissioner shall hear the Party and the Clerk, and shall finally decide thereon, and for the greater Security against the Danger of Enemies and of the Seas, shall lodge the original Accounts and Vouchers with the Remarks made thereon by the Clerks and the final Adjustment in the Office of the Consul General of the United States in France, and shall send quadruplicate Copies thereof to the Superintendant of Finance, that one of the said Copies may be lodged in the Treasury, and the Account be entered of Record by the Register, of which Notice shall be given to the said Consul General that the originals may be thereafter transmitted to the Superintendant.[6] And

That the said Commissioner and Clerks respectively take an Oath before some Person duly authorized to administer an Oath faithfully to execute the Trust reposed in them respectively.[7]

With Respect to any particular Instructions to be given to such Commissioner, the Committee (should they agree with me in Opinion on the general Plan) will submit such as they may think proper to Congress.[8] On a former Occasion I put the Accounts transmitted by Mr. Deane into the Hands of the Comptroller,[9] that he might from an Examination of them be more capable of drawing any Instructions which should become necessary on this Subject. If the Committee chuse to see Mr. Milligan, I will desire him to wait on them at such Time and Place as they may appoint.

With perfect Respect I have the Honor to be Gentlemen Your most obedient and humble Servant

Robt Morris

The Honorable Mr. Scott
                Mr: Rutledge
                    and
                Mr: Lee

ENDORSED: 86/Letter, Augt. 26th. 1782/Robt Morris/To the Committee on the subject/ of appointing a commissioner/to settle the Accounts in Europe/see Report of Committee/Sept. 3d. 1782/acted on Novr. 8th. 1782
MSS: LS, PCC, DNA; Ofcl LbC, DLC.

1. The report in question, a draft submitted to him by John Morin Scott, is printed as the enclosure to RM to Scott, August 15. It was returned to RM and Gouverneur Morris on August 20 with the request that they reconsider it and commit their objections to writing (see Diary, August 20). This letter was the result. Although two of the Morrises' suggested resolutions were rejected and two others were emended by the committee, as noted below, their key proposal—that the commissioner be given full and final authority to settle American accounts in Europe—became part of the report which the committee, with James Madison in place of Scott, delivered on September 3 and which Congress adopted on November 18, 1782. For a general discussion, see notes to RM to the President of Congress, May 8, 1782.

2. The resolution that follows was incorporated almost verbatim into the committee's report and adopted by Congress on November 18.

3. Written by an unidentified hand on the last manuscript page of the LS below RM's signature, and marked for insertion here, are the words: "and that the Sup. of Finance be directed to report forthwith the necessary Instructions for the said Commissioner agreable to the resolve of ——." The committee ultimately included a resolution of similar import in its report, and RM was so ordered on November 18. RM had originally been directed to draft the commissioner's instructions by a resolution of May 29, 1782. For the instructions, see RM to Thomas Barclay, December 5, 1782.

4. This paragraph was crossed out by an unidentified hand and was not included in the committee's report.

5. The unidentified hand noted above struck out the preceding three words, substituted "by him," and crossed out the remainder of the paragraph. As submitted by the committee and adopted by Congress on November 18 the resolution authorized the commissioner "to appoint one or more clarks, with such allowance as he may think reasonable."

6. This paragraph was also struck out by the unidentified hand noted above and was not included in the committee's report to Congress.

7. This paragraph was reproduced verbatim in the committee's report and adopted by Congress on November 18.

8. See, however, note 3 above.

9. See Diary, June 24, 1782.

To the Governor of Connecticut (Jonathan Trumbull)

Office of Finance 26th August 1782

Sir,

Mr. John Bradford of Boston has written to me sundry Letters on the Subject of certain Goods which he purchased from the State of Connecticut for the Use of the United States.[1] Mr. Bradford was desirous that the Money due for these Goods should be credited to Connecticut on the Requisitions of 1782, but this I could by no Means permit. I have however no Objection to passing it to their Credit on former Requisitions, and when it is considered that this was really a Payment by Connecticut to the Use of the United States it would seem extremely hard to urge the Officer to advance now his own Monies, and leave him to recover them from the United States hereafter, especially if it should appear that the State is really indebted to the United States. How that Account stands can only be determined on the general Settlement, but under present Circumstances I must conceive it would be more proper that the State should acquit Mr. Bradford and charge the Union with the Amount. Any Arrangements for this Purpose I shall readily concur in, provided always that it be not deducted from the Quota for the Service of the Current Year. This Letter will go open to Mr. Bradford who will probably write to your Excellency more fully on the Subject of it. I am, Sir, With perfect Respect and Esteem Your Excellency's most obedient and humble Servant

Robt Morris

His Excellency The Governor of Connecticut

ENDORSED: 26th Augt 1782/Office of Finance/de Jno Bradford Esqr./received 16th Septr. seq. enclosed
MSS: LS, Trumbull Papers, Ct; Ofcl LbC, DLC; copy with RM's signature written in Gouverneur Morris's hand, Trumbull Papers, Ct.

1. The only extant letter from Bradford on this subject is dated April 24, 1782. See notes to RM to Bradford, July 30.

Gouverneur Morris to George Washington

Philadelphia 26th Augst. 1782[1]

Sir

I received your Excellency's Favor of the eighteenth Instant last Evening. I pray you to accept my most grateful Acknowledgements for this mark of Approbation and Confidence. As the Enemy appears to be desirous of doing Justice the Meeting about to take Place will I trust be under better Auspices than the former. It may perhaps be successful. Nothing would give me greater Pleasure than to comply with your Excellency's Wishes, but the Situation of things here will not permit of it. I must therefore pray your Excuse. I am Sir with perfect Esteem and Respect Your Excellency's most obedient and humble Servant

Gouv Morris

His Excellency General Washington

MSS: LS, Washington Papers, DLC; Ofcl LbC, DLC.
    1. Gouverneur Morris was RM's assistant in the Office of Finance. In this letter he declined to serve as a commissioner to negotiate with the British outstanding disputes pertaining to prisoners.

To John Bradford

Office of Finance 26. Augt. 1782

I have received your Letter of the seventh Instant[1] and am very desirous to facilitate the Adjustment of your Affair with the State of Connecticut but as I have already informed you I cannot permit any Deduction from the State Quota to the Year 1782. I have however written a Letter to Governor Trumbull on the Subject which is left open for your Perusal,[2] and that you may yourself address him in such Manner as you think proper.

MS: Ofcl LbC, DLC.
    1. Letter not found. Bradford was the former Continental prize agent for Massachusetts.
    2. This letter is dated August 26.

Report of Robert Morris and Benjamin Lincoln to the President of Congress (John Hanson)

War Office—August 26. 1782[1]

The Superintendant of Finance and the Secretary at War to whom was referred the application of Mr. Rubsaman, employed by the United States in making saltpetre—beg leave to report.

That, in their opinion, his services, as an instructor in making saltpetre, are no longer needed, and that he present his accounts against the United States for settlement.

MS: D signed by Lincoln, PCC, DNA.
    1. On this report, endorsed as having been "passed Augt 26th 1782," see Diary, August 23, and notes. The complimentary close, signature, and addressee's name are in Lincoln's hand.

Certification of Instructions to David S. Franks

[Philadelphia, August 26, 1782][1]

Extract from the orders of The Honble. Robert Morris to Major David S. Franks on his embarking for Europe in July 1781.[2]

"For the rest you retain your Commission and the pay annexed to it, and I will obtain an extension of your Furlough from the Commander in Chief."

I do certify that the above is a true Copy, and that the Major has [not] received, nor is to receive, any other emolument for his Service in carrying dispatches to and from Europe.

Philada. 26th. Augst. 1782

MS: DS, PCC, DNA.

1. On this certificate, which RM signed on August 31, see Diary, August 26, and notes.

2. RM's instructions to Franks were dated July 13, 1781. Their complete text has not been found.

Diary: August 27, 1782

This morning I received a Letter from Mr Patterson Loan Officer of Delaware State[1] with a Bundle of Loan Office Certificates all of which with the Invoice I sent to Michael Hilligas Esqr. Treasurer of the United States.

Capt DeBert Called for his Papers but they not being Compleated ordered that they shall be finished speedily as possible.[2]

The Hon: Mr. Duane came on the Committee of Enquiry but not one of the other Members of the Committee attending he did not proceed to Business.[3]

Mr. Geary Clerk to Mr Duer for some Notes on Mr Swanwick but they are not ready.

Mr. Bullock for two Accounts brought hither by him or Mr. Mease as Managers of the Lottery in order to obtain Money to pay the Same. I returned them as they are their Vouchers.

Mr Chaloner called but I did not see him.

Mr. Alexr. Robertson requesting a Bill on New York for 3,200 Dollars for which he will give his Note payable in thirty Days. I sent to Henry Hill Esqr. and obtained from him the Drafts for which he gave his Note and I must get it discounted.[4]

Capt James Montgomery[5] and Capt: [6] naval Prisoners on Parole applied to me as Agent of Marine with Letters from David Sproat Esqr. Commissary General of Prisoners at New York remonstrating against the Detention of British Prisoners in our Goal and against Prisoners on Parole entering into Public Service in violation of their respective Paroles.[7] I told these Gentlemen that with respect to the British Prisoners in the New Goal I had sent last Saturday Capt John Greene to New York on that Business having determined last Week to send them away by the Cartel Ships now here.[8] I gave these Gentlemen my opinion that they ought to Contradict Mr. Sproats Assertions respecting Prisoners on Parole as they know the same are not founded in Truth.

Jno. Moylan Esquire applies for money but I have none. He asked if Genl Lincoln had Communicated a Letter from General Washington respecting Shirts for the army.[9] I told him that he had not. He asked about purchasing Linnens, and I said the present State of the Treasury will not warrant any Purchases and that my prospects respecting money do not brighten.

This Afternoon an Express arrived from Walter Livingston Esqr. informing me that Mr George Eddy being disappointed he had not paid any Money to Mr Remson at Morris Town for the Use of the Contractors[10] and therefore he desires me to send up ten thousand Dollars immediately, which will be a hard Task at present. I sent to some Friends for assistance but every Body seems to be in want of money instead of being able to assist me.

I sent for Solomon and desired him to try every Way he could devise to raise Money and then went in quest of it myself.

Wrote a Letter to the Hon. Secy at War.

Wrote a Letter to Colo. Armand Marquis de Rourie.

Wrote a Letter to the Hon. Intendant of Maryland.

Wrote a Letter to Richd. James.

Issued a Warrant on Mr. Swanwick in favor of Benjm. Dudley £7.15.0.

1. Samuel Patterson's letter has not been found.
2. See Diary, August 26, and notes.
3. James Duane was chairman of the congressional oversight committee for the Office of Finance. See notes to Diary, June 12, 1782.
4. For a similar transaction, see Diary, August 15.
5. Montgomery (d. ca. 1810), a privateer captain, had formerly served in the Pennsylvania navy. Campbell, *Sons of St. Patrick,* 464; Paullin, *Navy of the American Revolution,* 390–391.
6. Space left blank in manuscript.
7. Sproat's letters have not been found.
8. See notes to Diary, August 13, for a discussion.
9. The reference is to a letter to Moylan, the clothier general, of August 3, 1782, in which Washington, noting that the troops "in general are possessed of but one Shirt each," urged that "every Exertion be used, and every Resource be tried, for procuring such a Supply of Shirts as that two may be issued to every Soldier at the next Delivery, which must be as early as possible." Despite the admitted lack of money, Washington wrote, "great Uneasiness" and "very pernicious Effects" could be expected if the army found that the states had linen and no effort had been made to obtain it, and this he directed Moylan to represent "to those who are competent to have the Business put in a Train of Negotiation, if they should judge proper." Fitzpatrick, ed., *Writings of Washington,* XXIV, 457–458.
10. See Diary, August 12, and notes.

To Charles Armand

Office of Finance 27. Augt. 1782

Sir,

I received your Letter of the twentieth of last Month by Capt. Deberdt[1] who appears to be a very sensible, attentive and industrious

Man. He has pursued his Business closely and tho long detained here it has not been his Fault.

With respect to any Pay to your Men that Thing is impossible. Whenever any one Soldier receives his Pay every other Soldier shall receive it. I will give no Preference to one over another neither will I permit it to be given by the States if I can prevent it.[2] I have not Money to pay the whole Army and therefore I will not pay any Part of it because I will not do any thing which is partial or unjust.

I would be very glad to provide for you the Horses you want but really the Circumstances of the Treasury are such that I dare not attempt it and certainly cannot accomplish it. Whenever I am in Capacity to do it I will. In the mean Time I have paid General Lincoln nineteen hundred and seventy Dollars to enable you to march to the Southward according to the Orders from General Washington.[3]

I approve the Contract you have made for Subsistence of your Legion and will support it. I hope you may have extended it on the same Terms for the Time you continue there in which Case I will take Care to make the Payments.[4]

The Accounts of your Legion to the first of January last are adjusted and the Balances due to the Officers are put on Interest, the remaining fifth is paid, as is also the Subsistence Money which is due to them.[5]

Your Account of the Cloathing is also settled and this Balance paid. All these Payments which I have mentioned are in Orders drawn by me on Mr. Swanwick payable at sixty days from the Date and as these Orders are receivable in Taxes and payable to the Bearer I have no Doubt that you can readily negotiate them for Specie and in Payments without any Discount. This not only saves the Expence of transporting Silver but enables me to extend my means of Payment and to anticipate the Taxes.

Captain Deberdt's account for his Expences has also been adjusted and the Payment has been made to him in Cash. I wish you sir all possible Health, Success and Glory and I pray you to beleive me most sincerely disposed to contribute to your Ease or Pleasure. With Esteem and Respect I am &ca.

RM

MS: Ofcl LbC, DLC.

1. Letter not found. Colonel Charles Armand-Tuffin, Marquis de La Rouërie, commanded a legion of cavalry which had recently been stationed in Charlottesville and Staunton in western Virginia. Captain Claudius de Bert was paymaster of the corps.

2. Concerning RM's opposition to partial payments to the army and payments by the states to their Continental lines, see Diary, March 4, 1782, and notes.

3. Washington, through Secretary at War Benjamin Lincoln, had on August 6 ordered Armand's legion to join the southern army under Major General Nathanael Greene, but these orders were changed, evidently at Lincoln's suggestion, and the

legion instead marched northward to Winchester, Virginia. See Fitzpatrick, ed., *Writings of Washington*, XXIV, 469–470, XXV, 100; RM to the Secretary at War, August 30, and Diary, August 31. For the purchase of horses at a later date, see Diary, February 10, 1783.
    4. See Diary, August 7, and notes.
    5. See Diary, August 21.

To Richard James

Office of Finance 27th. Augt. 1782

Sir,

The Post before the last brought me your Letter dated on the seventh Instant at Cumberland Old Court House with an Account of your Issues at that Post.[1] I transmitted the Account with the Vouchers to the Comptrollers Office where it has gone through the necessary Forms of Examination and is found to be right except in a Charge of one Bushel of Oats issued beyond the Quantity prescribed (amount thirty eight pence) and which being deducted leaves the Balance in your Favor on that Account nineteen hundred and fifty three Dollars and thirty one ninetieths of a Dollar as appears by the Comptrollers Certificate transmitted to me on the twenty first Instant.

I have sent you by this Conveyance two thousand Dollars in my Drafts on Mr John Swanwick of this City payable at sixty days from the date[2] which I expect you will find to be a very ready Currency either for the Purposes of Commerce or in the payment of Taxes. If presented through the channel of Commerce they will meet with due Honor, and they are made receivable for Taxes[3] on which Account I would prefer their being returned as a Remittance for so much of the States Quota by my Receiver.

I desire you will continue to forward your Accounts and vouchers in future as you have begun, and when they are examined and Certified by the Comptroller you will find me regular in my Payments. I am Sir your most obedient Servant

RM

MS: Ofcl LbC, DLC.
    1. Letter not found. Richard James, a prominent planter, businessman, and office-holder of Cumberland County, Virginia, held the contract for supplying the post at Cumberland Old Court House, an assembly point for recruits of the Virginia line. James had been awarded the contract by Lieutenant Colonel Edward Carrington, deputy quartermaster general for the southern army, whom RM had authorized to make contracts in Virginia (see RM to Carrington, June 6, 1782, and notes). See the references to James in Boyd, ed., *Jefferson Papers*, IV, 455–456, XVI, 87–88; Palmer, ed., *Calendar of Virginia State Papers*, I, 264, 434, 464, II, 95, 231, 261, III, 468, IV, 331, 435, VIII, 81; *Virginia Magazine of History and Biography*, XVII (1909), 379n., XVIII (1910), 26–27, XXVII (1919), 62; and *WMQ*, 1st ser., V (1896), 103.
    2. On these drafts, see RM's Circular to the Receivers of Continental Taxes, August 29, and notes.
    3. On this point, see RM to Edward Carrington, June 11, 1782, and notes.

To Daniel of St. Thomas Jenifer

Office of Finance, 27th. Augst: 1782[1]

Sir

I have lived in constant Expectation of hearing good Tidings from you, and never was I in a Situation which rendered it more necessary. A Month had elapsed on the 18th Instant since you wrote to me and raised the Expectation of speedy Releif. I shall not detain you unnecessarily by reading a long Letter. All I have to say is comprized in a very short Compass. Unless I receive considerable Sums from the States very speedily I must stop Payment, and then those consequences will be severely felt which I have in vain attempted to describe. I am Sir very respectfully, your most obedient and very humble Servant

Robt Morris

Honorable Intendant of Maryland

ENDORSED: Letter 27th. August 1782/received 30 same Month/from Honl. R. Morris Esqr./Recorded
MSS: LS, Adjutant General's Papers, MdAA; Ofcl LbC, DLC; LbC, Intendant's Letterbook, MdAA.
    1. Jenifer was Maryland's intendant of the revenue.

To the Secretary at War
(Benjamin Lincoln)

Office of Finance 27. Augt. 1782

I have received your Letter of the nineteenth of August[1] and would have answered it more speedily could I have answered it satisfactorily. I must now inform you that I cannot undertake to pay the Sums you mention for the purchase of Shells without diverting money from Services which are indispensible—many such services are now suffering.

MSS: Ofcl LbC, DLC; copy, Henry Knox Papers, MHi.
    1. Letter not found.

Diary: August 28, 1782

Mr. Jno. Chaloner called this Morning and told me that he must be repaid the twenty thousand Dollars lent to me in May last, as the Connections of his Employers Messrs. Wadsworth and Carter with the French Army were such as obliged them to supply Count Rochambeau with Money to pay his Troops and that they must have this Sum on Saturday wherefore I promised that at all Events the money should be Ready.[1] After casting about to find the Ways and means of satisfying this Demand and that of the Contractors for the moving Army as well as others that are daily made on me, I sent for the Broker Haym Solomon, for William Bingham Esqr. and for Mr. John Ross being informed that the two last named Gentlemen have money by them.

Mr. Deshler[2] applied with two Orders of Mr Moylan Clothier General which are become due but which I cannot now pay.

Received a Letter from Mr. Geo. Eddy[3] and wrote him in Reply.

Colo. Miles wrote to me for pay to some Waggons just Returned from the Southern Army. I sent for him and proposed to pay them with Drafts on Mr Swanwick at Sixty Days Sight, to which he is to give Answer.

John Pierce Esqr. Paymaster General called to Consult me on several Points. 1st. He shewed me several Certificates of Quarter masters and Commissaries for monies due from the United States to a Mr Reed formerly employed in his Department in which he misbehaved and in Consequence thereof is now in Burlington Goal.[4] Mr. Pierce obtained these Certificates from him and holds them in his Hands as a Security for the Balance due from Reed to the United States until the whole affair can be Settled.

2d. He asked Subsistence money for Genl. Howe. I replyed that having no Money, I could furnish him with Drafts on Mr Swanwick at Sixty Days Sight for that purpose.

3ly. He asked whether he should transmit Certificates to Officers of the Balances due to them in Order that they may have their Accounts Settled by their respective States. I answered that my opinion is that the States should transmit to him Certificates of the payments they have made to Officers in order that their Accounts may be finally settled at his Office.[5]

Mr. Carter Called and confirmed what Mr. Chaloner had said respecting the payment of 20,000 Dollars lent me in May and 8,000 Dollars received of Mr Wilson.

I sent for Capt. Joshua Barney and after enquiring of him the State and Condition of the Ship General Washington of which he is the Commander and which is this day to be sold, I told him that She is wanted for a Packett, desired him to attend the Sale and bid as high as 20,000 Dollars for her, this Sum being in my opinion as much as she can be deemed Worth, under present Circumstances and if a Peace takes place, it is vastly more than her Value, if War Continues considerably less. I desired him also to inform Mr Standley that he was bidding for the Public as Mr Standley had said he would buy this Ship if I did not Want her.[6]

I consulted Mr. Maddison, Mr Charles Thompson and Doctor Witherspoon as to the purchase of the Ship Genl. Washington and told them my Design therein before my Orders were given to Capt. Barney and they all approved the purchase.

Received a Note from Mr. Mallet and directed Mr. Swanwick to settle the Affair of the Guns and his Deposite.[7]

Mr. Bingham came to the Office agreeable to my Desire. I told him that having learnt of his having a Considerable Sum of Money by him, my necessities had induced me to form a design of getting it of him for some time. I told him the urgent Demand made on me, that being bound by every tie of Honor, punctuality and integrity to pay Mr. Chaloner and not knowing where else it is practicable for me under the present Circumstances of things to obtain the Money. He must not refuse me. He answered that he had taken Arrangements for the employment of his money, that I must be Sensible of the advantages it will now produce to him &c. all which being very true, I told him I would not offer him an Interest of 5 per Cent per Month &c. as is now the practice, but hoped he would exert his Patriotism. He observed that he was much disabled in this respect by the large Sum detained from him by Congress on account of his Engagements made in their behalf at Martinico.[8] This Gentleman had urged me exceedingly some time past to order the payment of another hundred thousand Livres to his Banker in Paris on account of that Debt, and as my opinion is that the Honor of Congress is pledged to discharge the Debts due to their Agents abroad to enable them to pay those who trusted them with Supplies for America, I now proposed that if Mr. Bingham will Supply me with twenty thousand Dollars on Saturday next, I will repay the Same as soon as possible and in return for the favor of Service to the Public I will order the payment of 100,000 Livres to his Banker in part of the Debt due to him from the United States. He urged that the Sum now required is more than he is possessed of and that he fears not being able to raise that part which he is now deficient besides that parting with what he has will totally derange his Affairs &c. Finally he promised to Consider and give me an answer and in the Evening I received his Letter of this Date agreeing to the proposal.[9]

Mr Jno. Ross also came agreeable to request and after making the Same Proposition to him that I had done to Mr Bingham their Situation as to their Claims on the United States being the Same, He declared his apprehension that it will not be in his power to raise the Money, but said he would try and let me know. I have not yet heard from him.[10]

Mr. Geary, Mr. Duers Clerk called to tell me that he must return to Albany and to ask for a Pass, which I signed and desired him to tell Mr Duer that he shall soon hear from me.

Solomon the Broker came and I urged him to leave no Stone unturned to find out Money and the Means by which I can obtain it.

The Hon Secy at War sent Mr Hodgdon with an Estimate of the

expence of Transporting Cannon and other Stores from York in Virginia to the Head of Elk.[11] I told Mr. Hodgdon that having no money I would pay him in Drafts on Mr Swanwick to which he agreed.

The Hon: Doctor Witherspoon called to know whether the Contractors to the northward wanted Cattle and how they can pay for them; on these points I satisfied him. Had some Conversation respecting Virginia Militia, Revenue, Loans &c.

Capt Barney came and informed me that John Wright Stanley Esqr. had bought the Ship at £50 more than my limits but that if I wish it he will let me have her. I desired Capt. Barney to request Mr. Stanley to call on me, and accordingly Mr Stanley came and told me that Capt Barney had neglected to inform him that I intended to purchase the Ship. That he in conjunction with several other Gentlemen had bought her for a Cruizer, but that for his own Part he is ready to relinquish the purchase in my favor and if I desire it he will Consult the other Gentlemen concerned with him to know if they will do the same. I requested him to do this and inform me the Result.

Wrote a Letter to James Lovell Esqr.
Wrote a Letter to William Whipple.
Wrote a Letter to William C. Houston.
Wrote a Letter to Geo. Olney Esqr.
Wrote a Letter to John Hopkins.
Wrote a Letter to George Eddy.

1. See Diary, August 20, and notes.
2. Probably David Deshler (d. 1792), a German-born merchant of Philadelphia and friend of Benjamin Franklin. See Labaree and Willcox, eds., *Franklin Papers,* XII, 328–330; *PMHB,* VI (1882), 141–145, IX (1885), 196n., LVI (1932), 151; and *JCC,* XIV, 685.
3. Letter not found.
4. The details relating to the case of Thomas Reed, a former deputy paymaster general, have not been ascertained. See, however, Diary, February 28, 1782; and Reed to [Pierce], April 12, 1782, Manuscript File, no. 22342, WDC.
5. This response was in accordance with RM's view that the army debt was Congress's responsibility. See notes to RM to Daniel of St. Thomas Jenifer, March 12, 1782.
6. On this subject, see below in this Diary, and Diary, August 26, and notes.
7. See Diary, August 14, and notes. The letter from Michael Mallet has not been found.
8. Concerning William Bingham's accounts as American agent at Martinique, see James Lovell to RM, July 5, and notes, Bingham to RM, August 7, and RM to Lovell, September 7, 1781.
9. Letter not found.
10. For the context of the Bingham and Ross negotiations, see notes to Diary, August 20. On Ross's claims against the United States, see notes to Diary, June 23, 1781.
11. Estimate not found.

To George Eddy

Office of Finance 28th. Augt. 1782

Sir,

I this Moment received your Letter of the twenty third Instant[1] and was not a little surprized at it. You must remember to have seen Mr Clark's Letters to me on this Subject.[2] You cannot have forgotten that these Vessels have been seized for carrying on a Contraband Trade. And that altho one of them was acquitted the other will in all human Probability be most justly condemned.[3] It must also be fresh in your Memory that contrary to my Opinion, contrary to your own, contrary to Mr. Clarke's Advice and Solicitations the Tobacco was laden by Mr. Coffin on Board of both Vessels instead of compleating the Cargoe of one. In Addition to all this I must request your Recollection that I have paid and am daily paying for this Tobacco. I must therefore be repaid. I am Sir your most obedient Servant

RM

P.S. One of the Delegates of Virginia informs me that the Ship Fame is condemned.

MS: Ofcl LbC, DLC.
   1. Letter not found. Eddy, the agent for Ebenezer Coffin, a merchant capitulant, was exporting tobacco from Virginia to New York City pursuant to an agreement with RM printed under March 13, 1782.
   2. The letters of Daniel Clark, RM's agent for purchasing tobacco for Eddy in Virginia, have not been found.
   3. On the *New York*, see notes to RM to Clark, July 15, 1782. As RM notes in the postscript, the second ship, the *Fame*, was condemned; however, the vessel was eventually released and reached New York City with its cargo of tobacco.

To Alexander Hamilton

Office of Finance 28th August 1782

Sir,

I have duly received your several Favors of the twenty second and twenty Seventh of July and tenth and thirteenth of August.[1] My not answering them is owing to Causes which you will easily conceive; because you will easily conceive the Multiplicity of Objects to which I must turn my Attention. I am very sorry to learn that you can no longer continue in the Office of Receiver.[2] It would have given me great Pleasure that you should have done so, because I am sure that you would have rendered very signal Services to the public Cause: This you will now do in another Line more important, as it is more extensive; and the Justness of your Sentiments on public Affairs induce my warm Wish that you may find a Place in Congress so agreable as that you may be induced to continue in it.

I should readily have complied with your Wish as to a Successor, but there are many Reasons which have called my Attention to and fixed my Choice upon Doctor Tillotson.[3] We will converse on this Subject when we meet. I am however very far from being unmindful of your Recommendations; and altho I cannot name the Citizen of any State to settle the Accounts of that particular State consistently with the general Line of Conduct I have laid down for myself; yet I shall do in other Respects what is in my Power. I have not hitherto been able to fix on a proper Commissioner for the State of New York.[4] The Office is vacant for New Hampshire and Rhode Island. I enclose you a Copy of the Ordinance on the Subject,[5] that you may know the Powers, Duties and Emoluments; and I have to request that you offer these Places to Colol. Malcolm and Mr Lawrence.[6] You will make the first offer including the Choice as your own Judgement may direct. Should the Gentlemen, or either of them accept, you will be so Kind as to give me early Notice. I will then immediately recommend them to the States respectively and on receiving their Approbation, the proper Instructions &c can be expedited.

I am sorry to learn that any Letter of mine should have given Offence, but I conclude that this Effect must follow from many Parts of my Writings and Conduct, because the steady Pursuit of what appears to be the true Line of Duty will necessarily cross the various oblique Views of Interest and Opinion. To offend is sometimes a Fault, always a Misfortune. The Letter in Question is, I suppose, under the date of the Eleventh of December, of which I enclose you a Copy.[7] Let me at the same Time assure you that in all your excellent Letter of the thirteenth Instant, I must[8] esteem the Clause now in question, because it contains that useful Information which is least common. I will make no apologies for the Letter to any One, because Apologies are rarely useful, and where the Intention has been good, they are to candid Minds unnecessary. Possessed of the Facts, you can guard against Misrepresentation; and I have ever found that to be the most hostile Weapon which either my personal or political Enemies have been able to wield against me.

I have not *even yet* seen the Resolutions of your Legislature relative to an Extension of the Powers of Congress.[9] I had supposed the same Reason for them which you have expressed. Indeed Power is generally such a darling Object with weak Minds that they must feel extreme Reluctance to bid it farewell; neither do I believe that any Thing will induce a general Consent to part with it, but a perfect Sense of absolute Necessity. This may arise from two Sources, the one of Reason, and the other of Feeling; the former more safe and more uncertain; the latter always severe and often dangerous. It is, my dear Sir, in Circumstances like this, that a patriot Mind seeking the great good of the Whole on enlightened Principles, can best be distinguished from those vulgar Souls whose narrow Opticks can see but the little Circle of selfish Concerns. Unhappily such Souls are but too common, and but too often fill the Seats of Dignity and Authority. A firm, wise, manly System of federal Government is what I once wished, what I now hope, what I dare not expect, but what I will not despair of.

Your Description of the Mode of collecting Taxes,[10] contains an Epitome of the Follies which prevail from one End of the Continent to the Other. There is no End to the Absurdity of human Nature. Mankind seem to delight in Contrast and Paradox; for surely Nothing else could sanctify (during a Contest on the precise Point of being Taxed by our own Consent) the arbitrary Police which on this Subject almost universally prevails. God grant you Success in your Views to amend it. Your Ideas on the Subject are perfectly correspondent to my own. As to your Doubt on the Mode of collecting it, I would wish to obviate it by the Observation, that the farther off we can remove the Appointment of Collectors from popular Influence, the more effectual will be their Operations, and the more they conform to the Views of Congress, the more effectually will they enable that Body to provide for general Defence. In political Life, the Creature will generally pay some Deference to [the Creator. The][11] having a double Set of Officers is indeed an Evil, but a good Thing is not always to be rejected because of the necessary Portion of Evil which in the Course of Things must be attached to it. Neither is this a necessary Evil, for with a proper federal Government, Army, Navy and Revenue, the civil Administration might well be provided for by a Stamp Act, Roads by Turnpikes, and Navigations by Tolls.

The Account you give of the State is by no Means flattering, and the more true it appears, the more Concern it gives me. The Loan I hope will be compleated; and I wish the *whole* Amount of the Tax may be collected. The forage Plan I have disagreed to, and enclose for your Information the Copy of my Letter on that Subject to the Quarter Master General.[12] I believe your State is exhausted, but perhaps even you consider it as being more so than it is. The Certificates which now form an useless Load will (if the United States adopt, and the several States agree to a Plan now before Congress)[13] become valuable Property: This will afford great Relief. The Scarcity of Money also may be immediately relieved, if the Love of popular Favour would so far give Way to the Love of public Good as to enforce plentiful Taxation. The Necessity of having Money will always produce Money. The Desire of having it produces, you see, so much as is necessary to gratify the Desire of enjoying foreign Luxuries. Turn the Stream which now flows in the Channels of Commerce to those of Revenue, and the Business is compleated. Unfortunately for us this is an Operation which requires Fortitude, Perseverance, Virtue, and which cannot be effected by the weak or wicked Minds, who have only partial, private or interested Views.

When I consider the Exertions which the Country you possess has already made under striking Disadvantages, and with astonishing Prodigality of national Wealth by pernicious Modes of applying it, I persuade myself that regular consistent Efforts would produce [much more than you] suppose.

For your accurate, clear and comprehensive Descriptions of general and particular Characters, Sentiments and Opinions, accept my sincere Thanks and warm Approbation. They do equal Justice to your Talents both for Observation and Description.

Mr. Duer's Attention to the Business of his Contract is very pleasing to me and honorable to himself. I am sorry that he should loose by it, but to avoid this as much [as possible I am determined to support him by liberal Advances so soon as it shall be in my Power to do it. I pray you to believe me very sincerely your Friend and Servant.

RM]

mss: L[S], Hamilton Papers, DLC; Ofcl LbC, DLC; transcript, Francis Baylies Papers, DLC.

1. The letters of July 27 and August 10 have not been found.

2. It was evidently in the letters of July 27 or August 10 that Hamilton announced his intention of resigning as receiver for New York because of his appointment as a delegate to Congress on July 22 (Syrett and Cooke, eds., *Hamilton Papers*, III, 117). His resignation was required under article V of the Confederation, which prohibited delegates to Congress from "holding any office under the united states, for which he, or another for his benefit receives any salary, fees or emolument of any kind" (*JCC*, XIX, 215). Since the effective date of Hamilton's term in Congress was November 4, it has been suggested that he agreed to remain as receiver only until October 31; however, he continued to issue receipts as receiver as late as November 9, the day before he turned over the papers of the office to his successor. See Syrett and Cooke, eds., *Hamilton Papers*, III, 194–198.

3. Thomas Tillotson, a hospital physician and surgeon in the Northern Department, was offered the post by RM early in September and accepted. See RM to Tillotson, September 5 and November 18, 1782. Hamilton may have recommended William Malcom (see Hamilton to RM, August 13) or John Laurance.

4. See Hamilton's comments on this office in his letter to RM of July 22.

5. On the congressional ordinance of February 20, 1782, see notes to RM to the President of Congress, December 10, 1781.

6. Both men declined. See Hamilton to RM, September 28.

7. The letter was RM to the Governor of New York.

8. The Ofcl LbC renders this word as "most."

9. See Hamilton to RM, July 22, and notes.

10. In Hamilton to RM, August 13.

11. The words in brackets here and below have been supplied from the Ofcl LbC.

12. Dated August 5. On the loan, tax, and forage plan, see notes to Hamilton to RM, July 22.

13. See RM to the President of Congress, July 29.

To George Olney

Office of Finance 28th. Augt. 1782

Sir

I am favored with your Letter dated at Providence on the twelfth Instant.[1] The Bills I have drawn on Mr. Swanwick are to be paid when presented tho before they become due; My Views in issuing them at so long sight are to prevent their returning unexpectedly and that they may be absorped from Circulation for the Purpose of Remittances by the public Servants in your Line.[2] I am Sir Your most obedient Servant

RM

MS: Ofcl LbC, DLC.

1. The letter from Olney, receiver of Continental taxes for Rhode Island, has not been found, but may have covered his eighth return of £285.15.9¾, or (at 6 shillings per dollar) approximately $953. See the list of his returns in PCC, no. 137, III, 353.

2. On these bills of exchange, see RM's Circular to the Receivers of Continental Taxes, July 19, 1782, and notes.

To John Hopkins, Jr.

Office of Finance 28th. Augt. 1782

I have been favored with your Letters dated at Richmond on the fifteenth and Sixteenth Instant with your Return for the last Month Enclosed in the former.[1] No new Loan Office Certificates have been issued for old ones Lost, or on any other Account. On Occasions like the present it is unnecessary for those who have lost their Certificates will be equally secure while in Possession of the proper Proofs of such Loss as if new Certificates were granted them. Their Demands being thereby fully ascertained they will obtain the same Place with others as Part of the Public Debt, when Funds for the Payment of Interest are established.

MS: Ofcl LbC, DLC.

1. Letters and return not found. Hopkins was the Continental loan officer of Virginia.

To William Churchill Houston

Office of Finance 28th August 1782[1]

I have received your Favour dated at Trenton on the 24th Instant. The Mode in which you transact the Business mentioned in it has my Approbation. I hope for more effectual Supplies, which you may be assured are very necessary.

MSS: LS, Houston Collection, NjP; Ofcl LbC, DLC.

1. Houston's endorsement indicates that he received this letter on August 30 and answered it the following day.

To James Lovell

Office of Finance 28th. Augt. 1782

I have received your Favor dated at Boston on the fourteenth Instant with your weekly Return of the same date.[1] I am Sorry to say that it is short of the Expectations I had formed. I hope for more plentiful Supplies.

MS: Ofcl LbC, DLC.

1. The letter and return sent by Lovell, receiver of Continental taxes for Massachusetts, have not been found, but the return, his third, was for $3,638⁶⁹⁄₉₀. See the list of his returns in PCC, no. 137, III, 349.

To Thomas Russell

Marine Office 28. August 1782

I am favored with yours of the seventh Instant[1] by which I find that you had a good Prospect of speedily manning the Hague which I hope has not changed as I shall be much pleased to hear of that frigate being gone to Sea.

Inclosed is a Book of Resolutions of Congress relating to the Navy[2] which will answer your Purposes for the present until I can send you a complete set of the Journals of Congress which I shall do by the first convenient Opportunity.

MS: AM LbC, MdAN.

1. Letter not found. Russell was the deputy agent of marine for New England.
2. Book not found.

To William Whipple

Office of Finance 28 Augt. 1782[1]

I have received your Favors dated at Portsmouth on the fifth and twelfth Instant. I hope you will receive a considerable Payment from the Sales of the Beef you have mentioned.

I have full Reliance on your Exertions in every Instance to promote the public Good, and I hope your Endeavors to gain Information may be Successful.

MS: Ofcl LbC, DLC.

1. Whipple was the receiver of Continental taxes for New Hampshire.

Gouverneur Morris to Richard Morris

[Philadelphia, August 28, 1782][1]

Dear Brother

I enclose you an excellent Pamphlet written by Payne.[2] I think you will like it. Lewis is well. Remember me I pray to my Sister affectionately and to your Children. Believe me yours

Philadelphia 28 August 1782

MS: ALS, Morris-Popham Papers, DLC.

1. This letter was addressed in manuscript to "Honorable Chief Justice of New York." Richard Morris (1730–1810), Gouverneur Morris's half brother, succeeded John Jay as chief justice of the New York Supreme Court in 1779. *DAB*.
2. For this pamphlet, see Thomas Paine to RM, September 6, and notes.

Diary: August 29, 1782

The Honble: Mr. Duane, Arthur Lee, Abram Clarke and Samuel Osgood Esqrs. Committee of Enquiry came this Morning and proceeded in their business.[1] They desired me to make out an Account of all the money's that have come into my hands and those which I have paid, they desire the reasons for employing Mr Swanwick may be Stated[2] and they proceeded in other parts of their enquiry until the Hour for going to Congress arrived. They enquired into the reasons for appointing Receivers of Continental Taxes in each State and Mr. Clarke expressed doubts of my Authority to make those Appointments, I therefore produced the Act of Congress of the 3d. November 1781[3] which satisfied him on that point. I informed the Committee that my reasons for making new appointments in preference to employing the Loan Officers were first, the Loan Officers have not settled their Accounts with the United States and some of them have long Accounts depending. Secondly altho some of them may be fit, all are not. Thirdly, had the money paid by the States for the current Expences of the Year been put into the Hands of the Loan Officers the People entitled to Interest on Loan Office Certificates Issued by these Gentlemen would have been very clamorous for payment. They would not have entered into or admitted the Distinction of monies Granted for Revenue or for current Expences of the Year. Discontents would have prevailed and Tumults or Revolts have ensued &c.[4]

Capt. De Berdt of Armands Corps, after finishing all other Business wrote me a Letter respecting Horses for that Corps.[5] I told him that I had already given my Answer on that Point[6] but if General Lincoln had anything farther to say to me on that Subject I was ready to Confer with him. He told this to the General; who came to the Office and we agreed that it cannot be done at present.

I sent for Mr Haym Solomon several times this Day to assist me in raising money.

Mr. Pierce wrote me that he wants Money to pay an Order of General Howe, but that the Secry. at War refuses a Warrant for that Money. I sent a verbal Answer that it cannot be paid without a Warrant.

Mr. Archd. Stewart called by desire of Mr. J. Geary to carry money or notes for Mr. Duer. The Notes are sent by him.[7]

Mr. John Laehy sent by Walter Livingston Esqr. for Money received 10,000 Dollars this Day to carry to said Mr Livingston for the Contractors.[8]

Capt Barney came and informed me that altho Mr Stanley who bought the Ship General Washington is willing to give her up to me

Yet several other Gentlemen are interested in that purchase who will not relinquish their right in her. I had this Morning mentioned to the Committee my Intention of buying this Ship and asked their Advice, in Consequence whereof they proposed the Question in Congress as Mr. Secretary Thompson informs me and that they agreed I should make this Purchase.[9]

Wrote a Letter to Walter Livingston Esqr.

Wrote a Letter to General Washington.

Wrote a Letter to William Duer.

1. For the work of this committee, see notes to Diary, June 12, 1782.

2. A statement of this kind has not been found. The issue of John Swanwick's employment as cashier of the Office of Finance arose primarily because his position was not on the congressional civil list. Arthur Lee, RM's most persistent critic in Congress, had complained privately on this point to one of his New England allies: "All the Monies of the U.S. ought to go into the Treasury and be issued from thence," Lee avowed, "the Treasurer being a chosen and sworn Officer and giving security for his fidelity. Mr. Morris has began to deviate from this line by putting half the Monies of the Public into the hands of his quondam Clerk, where he may not only have a more certain use of them for his private purposes, but be covered in every thing he does. Should this manouvre pass muster, the whole will soon go into the same channel, and the Institution and checks of a treasury be rendered entirely useless. I am apprehensive that it will not only pass uncorrected, but receive the collateral approbation of an allowance to this Swanwick for his services. The accumulation of Offices in this man, the number of valuable appointments in his gift, the absolute controul given him over all the Revenue officers, his money, and his art; render him a most dangerous man to the Liberty of this Country, as his excessive avarice does to the Treasure of the public so much in his power" (to Samuel Adams, August 6, 1782, Burnett, ed., *Letters,* VI, 429). Swanwick in fact was not listed as cashier in the enumeration of Treasury Department employees RM enclosed in a letter to the president of Congress of March 10, 1783; for his duties as cashier, see Diary, June 8, 1781, and July 17, 1783, and RM to the Comptroller of the Treasury, July 23, 1783. Swanwick was also receiver of Continental taxes for Pennsylvania and was currently overseeing RM's private business affairs.

3. RM was referring to the act of November 2, 1781, which apportioned the $8 million requisition for 1782 among the states and authorized the Superintendent of Finance to appoint receivers in each state (see notes to RM to the President of Congress, November 5, 1781). On November 3 Congress instructed RM to forward the act to the states.

4. RM repeated similar reasons in his letter to the president of Congress of April 29, 1784. Implicit in the present discussion was the political unreliability of some of the loan officers; see notes to RM to the President of Congress, November 5, 1781.

5. The letter from Claudius de Bert, paymaster of Charles Armand's Partisan Corps, has not been found.

6. See RM to Armand, August 27.

7. See RM to William Duer, August 29.

8. See RM to Walter Livingston, August 29.

9. For the committee in question, see Diary, August 26, and notes.

Circular to the Receivers of Continental Taxes

Circular   Office of Finance 29th August 1782
Sir,

I have for certain Reasons thought it expedient to issue no more Orders on Mr. Swanwick *payable at Sight,* but to destroy them as they

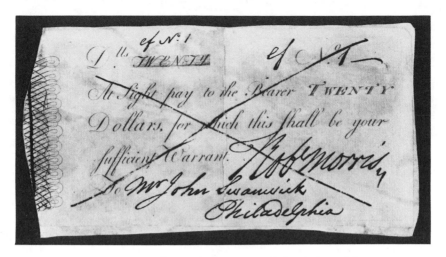

Morris's note: $20 sight draft (cancelled). 6⁵⁄₁₆″ × 3³⁄₈″

Morris floated these bearer demand notes as personal obligations drawn for public purposes on John Swanwick, his cashier in the Office of Finance. Issued in denominations of $20, $50, and $80 beginning in July 1781, the notes circulated at or near par where Morris's mercantile reputation was well established. Toward the end of August 1782 Morris announced his intention to withdraw them and substitute timed notes on account of the United States which were to be made out to a specific individual or bearer rather than simply to the bearer. Cancelled specimens of the $20 denomination were intended for enclosure in Morris's circular to the receivers of Continental taxes of November 8, 1782, but the indented note shown here, one of only three extant sight drafts known to the editors, was sent to William Churchill Houston, receiver for New Jersey, in a letter of November 9. For a discussion of the origins and functions of this and other forms of Morris paper, see Morris's Circular to the Receivers of Continental Taxes, August 29, 1782, and notes. The other cancelled specimens of the $20 sight drafts are in the Morris-Harwood Papers at the Maryland Historical Society in Baltimore and the Lowell Collection at the Massachusetts Historical Society in Boston. The note illustrated here is from the William Churchill Houston Collection, courtesy of Princeton University Library, Princeton, New Jersey.

are brought in;[1] and as the larger Bills of Exchange mentioned in my Letter of the Nineteenth of July last, tho an excellent Mode of general Remittance, will not by Reason of the Greatness of the Sums answer the Ends intended by the States in making my Notes receivable in Taxes,[2] I have thought it alike useful to the Public and convenient to the People to issue Notes in the following Form: "At Sixty Days from the Date pay on Account of the United States   Dollars to   [3] or Bearer." These Notes are signed by me, directed to Mr. Swanwick, and are for Sums of One Hundred, Fifty, Thirty and Twenty Dollars. Each of them has in the Body of the Bill in Water Marks UNITED STATES, and the Bills of One hundred Dollars have a Water Mark 1, those of Fifty 2, those of Thirty 3, and those of Twenty 4.[4] You will receive them as Cash, and when you have Cash you will give it for them in like Manner as for Bank Notes, and that without any Regard whether they have any Time still to run or whether the Sixty Days are expired.[5] I am, Sir, Your most obedient Servant,

Robt Morris

To the several Receivers for the different States
Wm C. Houston Esqr.[6]

ENDORSED: Letter circular from Robert/Morris, Esqr Superintendent/29 August 1782/Received 5 Sept 1782/Answered 7
MSS: LS, to William Churchill Houston of New Jersey, Houston Collection, NjP; Ofcl LbC, DLC.
1. RM's sight drafts drawn on John Swanwick, cashier of the Office of Finance, were issued in denominations of $20, $50, and $80 and were payable to the bearer upon presentation. Printed by copper plate without watermark or other distinguishing characteristics, the notes, as RM later explained, were "numbered, lettered, signed and directed in my own hand writing," but contained no indication that they were drawn on account of the United States. The notes were first issued on August 28, 1781, and most of the original supply was in circulation by early 1782. In April 1782 the Financier instructed the receivers of Continental taxes to receive them "as money" and asked the governors of Virginia and North Carolina to have their tax collectors receive them "as Specie." As with all of RM's notes, however, the sight drafts were not a legal-tender issue.
RM had originally intended to issue his sight notes "only as a prelude to [notes of the Bank of North America] by way of opening the Public Eye to their Utility as well as to apply my personal Credit to the Public service." The Financier abandoned this limited purpose as he continued to rely on his own notes in anticipation of tax revenues, even though he was apprehensive that they would compete for acceptance with bank notes (also copperplate issues payable at sight). Moreover, because it was impossible to calculate when and in what amounts his sight notes would be presented for redemption in Philadelphia, the Financier, as early as June, had planned to discontinue issuing them in favor of timed notes. His intentions were finally realized in the present letter. This action coincided with the dismissal of the copperplate printer to the United States (see RM to the President of Congress, June 11, 1782, and notes) and may have been triggered by the potential threat of counterfeiting. When bogus $20 sight notes actually appeared later in the year, the Superintendent recalled all the remaining sight notes in circulation. See Diary, July 27, and notes, August 28, and December 26, 1781, and January 9, 1782, RM to Ridley and Pringle, November 13, 1781, to John Langdon, February 19, 1782, to Donaldson Yeates, April 10, RM's

Circular to the Receivers of Continental Taxes, April 15, RM to the Governors of Virginia and North Carolina, April 30, to James Lovell, May 14, and notes, and to Thomas Russell, June 18, and William Whipple to RM, June 30, 1782, and notes. For the recall of the sight notes, see RM's circular to the receivers of November 8, 1782, enclosing canceled specimens of the $20 notes.

2. For a discussion of the bills of exchange RM drew on Swanwick, which anticipated the 60-day notes described in note 4 below, see RM's Circular to the Receivers of Continental Taxes, July 19, 1782, and notes. Additional data may be gleaned from RM to Hezekiah Merrill, July 12, and to Daniel Clark, September 23 and October 22 (first letter), Diary, August 21, and notes, William Churchill Houston to RM, November 2, RM to George Olney, November 5, and to George Webb, November 19, and Joseph Whipple to RM, December 21, 1782.

3. This and the preceding space were left blank in manuscript.

4. These new 60-day notes signed and drawn by RM on Swanwick were payable to a particular individual or bearer rather than just the bearer. Although RM employed watermarked paper to inhibit counterfeiting, it is not known whether he used printed blanks or had the notes drawn by hand for his signature (see RM to George Webb, August 30, and to Richard James, November 29, 1782). Unlike the bearer notes, the 60-day notes provided for payment "on Account of the United States." No specimens have been found.

Although advised to issue the notes in smaller denominations to facilitate the collection of taxes, the Superintendent held to the opinion that small notes in circulation among farmers and common people who lacked confidence in the government were prone to depreciation and counterfeiting, and preferred that notes of large denominations circulate as a medium of exchange among merchants and other people of means who were capable of evaluating the security behind them (see Alexander Hamilton to RM, September 21, RM to Hamilton, October 5, and the Quartermaster General to RM, November 5, 1782). RM's straitened resources eventually compelled him to issue timed notes on Swanwick at longer sights, generally of 4, 6, or even 12 months (see John Swanwick to the Paymaster General, January 29, the Quartermaster General to RM, June 20, William Churchill Houston to RM, July 19, 1783; and Pickering to Richard Claiborne, July 22 and August 16, 1783, WDC, no. 87, pp. 80, 92). The most significant emission of this kind was the six-month notes which the Financier issued in June 1783 to provide three months' pay to the Continental army before it disbanded. For a recapitulation of these notes, see RM to the President of Congress, July 18, 1783.

5. Tradition has it that Morris's notes were in popular parlance "called 'Long Bobs' and 'Short Bobs,' according to the periods of their maturity" (Sumner, *Financier,* II, 151). The editors, however, have not found a single contemporary use of these terms. Although it is possible this terminology referred to the 60-day and sight notes respectively (as argued by Eric P. Newman, "The Official United States Circulating Currency of Robert Morris: A New Find in American Numismatics," *The Numismatist,* XC [1977], 2229–2235), it could also refer to the difference between the 60-day notes and those of six months' or longer duration, or, alternatively, between notes which when received had a short or long time left to run before being redeemable in Philadelphia. But, as RM explained, "The length of the Sight is never considered when the Paper is brought in on the Taxes" (to John Read, February 22, 1783).

The uses to which RM put his own notes varied over time. In 1781 and early 1782 the sight drafts were used rather widely, though with some depreciation, by officials in the Quartermaster Department, but also occasionally for army subsistence and other military and naval expenditures. However, when Continental taxes failed to come forth from the states on schedule in mid-1782, the receivers and state tax collectors were hard pressed to exchange RM's drafts for cash, a situation exacerbated by competition between quartermaster officials and the contractors whom RM began to pay in notes rather than in specie. By the summer of 1782 RM began to rely heavily on the large bills of exchange he drew on Swanwick (see note 2 above), which did not circulate widely but gave first call to certain contractors and government agents on tax revenues collected in the states.

The dollar amount of 60-day notes RM introduced in the present letter has not been determined, but it is clear that he became progressively more cautious about circulating notes bearing his signature because of the difficulties in redeeming his paper and the personal liability he believed himself to incur from such emissions. In the fall of 1782 RM temporarily refused to issue more notes to quartermaster officials (see Diary, September 23, RM to Ralph Pomeroy, September 25, and to the Quartermaster General, September 26), and with the collapse of the West Point and Moving Army contract in October, the Superintendent ceased paying the major contractors in his notes and instead began making advances and payments in bills of exchange on France, giving himself a chance to redeem his earlier notes and bills (see the headnote to Comfort Sands, Walter Livingston, William Duer, and Daniel Parker to RM, September 11, and notes, and Diary, November 12, 1782). It is significant that subsistence notes paid to army officers in 1783 were signed by Treasurer Michael Hillegas rather than by RM (see the plan of November 20, 1782, devised by RM and Secretary at War Benjamin Lincoln). Aside from the 60-day notes given to the Quartermaster Department, RM appears to have used those notes in 1783 primarily for the one month's pay advanced to commissioned army officers early in the year (see RM to the Paymaster General, January 20, 1783).

The extent to which RM's notes were a personal liability has never been satisfactorily resolved. He had introduced his notes in large measure "to apply my personal Credit to the Public service," and he regarded himself as personally responsible for their payment, at least until they were ultimately redeemed by the government. Such responsibility is clearest for his sight drafts, which contained no indication of government obligation. His 60-day notes and six-month notes, however, embodied public accountability in their texts and watermarks, possibly because of RM's increasing concern with the slow rate at which Continental revenues were being received from the states. When confronted with the necessity of providing three months' pay to the disbanding army in the form of six-month notes bearing his signature, he reluctantly agreed to continue as Superintendent, if adequately backed by Congress and the states, in order to issue and redeem them on the strength of his personal credit. (For an explicit statement revealing RM's apprehensions at making himself liable for payment after leaving office when he would be at the mercy of his successors, see his letter to a committee of Congress of April 14, 1783; also RM to Benjamin Franklin, May 26, 1783.) Congress, it should be stated, never formally authorized the Superintendent to issue notes on the public credit. Prodded by Arthur Lee of Virginia, however, Congress in September 1783 asked RM for an accounting. The Superintendent responded with a letter to the president of Congress of November 10, 1783, enclosing a record of all the notes he had issued "on the Credit of the United States." Upon leaving office RM pledged himself personally for payment to the holders of any of his notes remaining in circulation, and a special fund was set up under Swanwick for their redemption. It is consonant with the available evidence to conclude that during his term of office RM in effect served as security for the government by issuing his own notes, for public credit was never sufficient to permit him to rely on currency that was not founded to a large degree on his personal credit. For documentation bearing on this question, see RM's advertisement of October 11, 1784; the statement of Joseph Nourse, [post 1784], in *American State Papers*, class 9, Claims, I, 728; Sumner, *Financier*, II, 150–151, 157–161, which should be used with care; Ver Steeg, *Morris*, 117–120, 169; and the article by Newman cited above arguing their official status.

6. This line is in RM's writing.

To William Duer

Office of Finance 29th. August 1782

Sir

I have received your Letter of the sixth Instant in which you refer to one I received by Mr. Geary without Date as of the third.[1] Your Complaints are I beleive in some Measure well founded but your

Vivacity gives them more Weight than I could have wished in your own mind. You will I am sure very read[il]y acknowlege that a Settlement of the Account ought generally speaking to precede the Payment of Monies. You will see clearly that this Rule is more forcible in public than in private Transactions. And you cannot but admit that where the Delay is to be attributed to the Claimant he must suffer the Consequences. On the other Hand I shall agree that where Delays in the Settlement of Accounts proceed either from the Fault of the public Officers or unavoidable Circumstances the Individual ought not to suffer. The Officers in the Treasury Department have generally as far as my Knowlege extends done their Duty well. In the particular Case you allude to the Mistake might easily happen because the Advance was taken from the face of the Books without any necessary Recurrence to the Contract All Monies being paid on Warrants from my Office and being immediately entered from those Warrants.

I acknowlege that your Contract is on moderate Terms, I am perswaded of your Assiduity, and as I hear no Complaints I am convinced that Justice is done to the Army. For these Reasons I am sincerely desirous to give you every possible Support but I must be confined within the Bounds of Possibility. My Task has been and continues to be very arduous. In Order to stimulate the States I was to shew the necessity of Exertion and this admitted only the Choice of two great Evils Either to let them continue in their Supineness or by declaring my Wants to injure my Credit and weaken thereby my own Operations. The latter was a partial and temporary Evil, the former was permanent and fatal.

In Order to releive the immediate Wants of the Officers I authorized the issuing of Notes last Winter which were payable the first of this Month.[2] These amounted to upwards of one hundred and forty thousand Dollars. The amount of Taxes you and all the World are acquainted with. To have passed safely thro so many Difficulties will tend to establish Credit more firmly and I think you will yourself by this Time feel more Confidence in yourself and in the Public than you did.

Mr. Geary states your Account to me in a Note of the twenty seventh thus.[3] Due by the Comptrollers Certificate seven thousand six hundred and eighty nine Dollars. Officers Accounts seven hundred and seven and an half from which Sums deducting two thousand there will remain six thousand three hundred ninety seven and an half. He desires that this Money may be sent by Mr. Archibald Stewart[4] the bearer of his Note. I have estimated that your Expenditures during this Month will together with the above Balance make between twelve and thirteen thousand Dollars. I provide for the whole as follows. First I had already directed General Washington out of a Fund which I had taken Measures to place in his Hands to pay you five thousand Dollars.[5] I hope that Sum may have reached you before this comes to hand. I now give Mr. Stewart notes to the amount of five thousand dollars[6] and I deliver to him a Letter for General Washington desiring that three thousand Dollars more in Specie may be forwarded.[7] Should my Expectations in that Quarter be defeated I will send you eight thousand Dollars from Hence by Express.[8] I will also (in Consideration of the Lowness of your Contract and the Inconveniences you have already labored under) send you during the Course of next Week five thou[sand Doll]ars more in Notes which will place you in Advance of the World. I have no Doubt that these Notes will properly Managed be in your Hands equally valuable with Cash. They will pay Taxes every where, and all the Receivers are bound to exchange them for such Cash as they may have. Now Sir I have to request that you will take Care and have your Accounts drawn as regularly as possible and when I see what is the amount I will endeavor to make you similar Payments in Notes so as to keep you in Advance. Thus I shall procure you a greater Benefit than you expected by your Discount at the Bank and free both you and me from the Pain of making Application to them. I hope these Arrangements will prove equally convenient and useful to you. Believe me I pray you Your most obedient and humble Servant

Robt Morris

William Duer Esquire Contractor for the Northern Army

ENDORSED: Letter from Honble/Robt: Morris Esqr: dated/Phila: 29th: Augt:—received/Sept 7th:—1782

MSS: LS, Duer Papers, NHi; Ofcl LbC, DLC.

1. These letters have not been found, but see Duer's private letter to RM of August 2, and notes. Duer was the contractor for the posts north of Poughkeepsie in New York.
2. See Diary, August 1, and notes.
3. Note not found.
4. On Stewart, a clerk of Duer's, see East, *Business Enterprise*, 117.
5. See RM to Washington, August 20. This payment, from monies to be obtained in New York City, was never actually made.
6. RM sent another $5,000 in notes by Stewart on August 30. See RM to Duer of that date.
7. See RM to Washington, August 29 (second letter).
8. Upon learning of the failure to supply Duer through Washington, RM sent $7,000 to him, of which $2,000 was in his own sight drafts (see RM to Duer, September 13). For the interim, see Duer to RM, September 6 and notes.

To Walter Livingston

Office of Finance 29 Augt. 1782

Sir,

I have received your Letter of the twenty fifth Instant and am exceedingly distressed at the Intelligence it contains.[1] However I must perform my Promise to you and have in Consequence thereof just now signed a Warrant for ten thousand Dollars in favor of the Contractors for the moving Army. The Manner in which these Contracts are blended prevents me from making the Discriminations I would wish and therefore you must settle the Matter among yourselves. I am Sir your most obedient Servant

RM

MS: Ofcl LbC, DLC.
    1. This letter has not been found (see below). A partner in Sands, Livingston and Company, the firm which held the recently combined West Point and Moving Army contract, Livingston had arrived in Morristown, New Jersey, on August 24 to collect $10,000 RM had promised to pay him there (see Diary, August 12, and notes). Livingston had intended to proceed to headquarters to obtain an additional $12,000 RM had arranged to put into Washington's hands (see RM to Washington, August 13, and notes), but "Being disappointed in not receiving the first Sum," he later advised the general, "I went to New-Ark and made application to the Gentleman who was to have furnished it but in vain. I raised but $800 dolls. which enabled me to discharge a few debts here before the Troops left this." On August 25 Livingston dispatched an express to RM with a letter (not found) that "informed him of my Situation and that Mr. Sands had no money." Livingston also informed Washington that Comfort Sands had arrived at Morristown on August 27 "and is gone forward to Mr. Morris resolved to surrender the Contract unless the Ballance of the July account being 22,000 dollars is immediately paid. I am apprehensive that Mr. Sands will not succeed and that he will quit the Contract." The quotations are from Livingston to Washington, dated Morristown, August 31, 1782, Washington Papers, DLC; see also Diary, August 14, and notes. For RM's ensuing meetings with Sands, see Diary, August 31 and September 2.

To George Washington

Office of Finance 29 Augt. 1782

Sir,

I have now to address your Excellency on a Subject which cannot be more painful to you than it is to me.[1] I am determined to Act justly and therefore when I find that I shall be unable to pay the Contractors I will give them due Notice that they may retire in Season. This Period is fast approaching and without the States make infinitely greater Exertions than they have hitherto done it must soon arrive. To comprize this Matter in a short Compass. Your Army is fed at a Dollar for nine Rations or three Dollars and a third per Month to feed a Soldier. Twenty four Thousand Rations per Day would therefore Amount to eighty thousand Dollars Monthly, which is more than had been paid by all the States on the first Instant. The Object of this Letter Sir is to request that your Excellency will consider how your Army is to be subsisted or kept together if I am obliged to disolve the Contracts. I pray that Heaven may direct your Mind to some Mode by which we may be yet saved. I have done all that I could and given repeated Warnings of the Consequences but it is like preaching to the Dead. Every Exertion I am capable of shall be continued whilst there is the least glimmering of Hope. I have the Honor to be with great Respect Sir your Excellency's most obedient and humble Servant

RM

MSS: Ofcl LbC, DLC; copy, PCC, DNA; copy, Benjamin Franklin Papers, PPAmP.

1. RM withheld this letter, as well as his confidential explanatory covering letter to Washington of August 30, for more than a week in hopes that he might still obtain revenues to prevent the impending collapse of the West Point and Moving Army contract. When this proved impossible, the Superintendent sent both missives in another letter to the general of September 9 explaining his "extreme Reluctance to wound your Mind with the Anxieties which distress my own," but he probably retained that letter several more days, for Washington did not receive it until September 21 (see Washington's first letter to RM of September 22). By this time, pending negotiations with the contractors, RM could only leave it to the reluctant Washington to decide whether to submit the August 29 letter to the states as originally intended. Washington chose not to, but RM himself addressed the governors on October 21 after a new contract had been negotiated (see Washington to RM, September 22, RM to Washington, September 25, and, on the collapse of the contract, notes to Comfort Sands, Walter Livingston, William Duer, and Daniel Parker to RM, September 11).

The text of the present letter received by Washington has not been found. The PCC texts of both this and the August 30 letter to Washington were enclosed in RM to the President of Congress, October 21; the PPAmP texts were sent to Benjamin Franklin in a letter of January 11, 1783.

To George Washington

Office of Finance 29th. August 1782

Sir

I am to request your Excellency that out of the sums which may come to your Hands in the Manner already mentioned, You will endeavour after making the Payments of which I informed you in a former Letter, to transmit three thousand Dollars more to Mr. Duer at Albany.[1] I am Sir with great Respect Your Excellency's Most Obedient and Humble Servant

Robt Morris

His Excellency General Washington

ENDORSED: Office of Finance. 29th Augst 1782/from/Hono Robert Morris Eqr/to pay Mr Duer 3,000 Dollars/not to be done—no Money
MSS: LS, Washington Papers, DLC; Ofcl LbC, DLC.

1. See RM to Washington, August 20, and to William Duer, August 29.

Diary: August 30, 1782

Mr Geo. Eddy this Day returned from New Jersey and informed me that he had been disappointed in his Expectations of receiving Money there and requested that I would take up his note in the Bank.[1] I told him that it is impossible as I had in Consequence of his not paying Mr. Livingston at Morristown the Sum he promised been obliged to send that Money by Express and consequently cannot releive him.[2] He complains of the detention of the Flag Ships in

Virginia to which I answer that the Captains had caused that the[3] Detention by improper Conduct &c.[4]

Mr Wm. Hawes for the Balance due to the Contractors at Springfield.[5] I desired him to wait until Monday when I promised him half in Specie and half in notes to which he agreed.

This day I proposed to the Consideration of the Honble: Mr Geo. Clymer the Acceptance of some of the public Employments as soon as his time in Congress shall expire.[6] This Gentleman's Abilities, Integrity and worthy Character entitle him to anything he will undertake.

Mr. Oliver Pollock Called respecting the Provisions in Store at this place. I referred him to Colo. Blaine and Mr. Hollingsworth to enquire the Quality and Value.[7]

The Honble: Mr. Holker called and I requested him to lend me his Credit by giving me a Note payable in thirty Days for ten thousand Dollars in order to have it Discounted at the Bank, promising to pay it myself at the end of that time and then return it to him. This he most readily agreed to and gave me his Note, but I do not intend to use it unless compelled by absolute Necessity.[8]

Colo. Miller Contractor for York and Carlisle called for his Balance. I gave him notes for £200 and promised to pay the rest to Mr Francis and I sent Colo. Blaine's Account Sale of the Flour to Mr Francis and requested him to Call for that Money on Mr Blaine to be applied to the use of those Contractors.[9]

Capt. Josh. Barney Called to tell me that Mr. Stanley says I may now have the Ship General Washington as all the Gentlemen except one or two agree to give her up. I desired him to ask the Commissioners Messrs. Gurney, Allibone and Patton to call here on that Business.[10]

Capt. DeBerdt called for the Money for his Expences. I signed the Warrant and told him Genl Lincoln and myself had agreed that it is improper to grant the Horses at this time wanted by Colo. Armands Corps.[11]

Mr. Milligan brought Drafts of Instructions to the several Commissioners appointed and to be appointed for settling Accounts.[12]

Mrs. Mathews Lady of Governor Mathews of Carolina wrote me requesting me to Supply her with a £100[13] and as General Greene wants Money I supplied that Sum and remit her Drafts on the Governor to the General.

Colo. Guerny [Gurney] one of the Commissioners for the Ship General Washington came respecting that Ship but some fresh Difficulties occurring we agreed to postpone the Settlement until Monday 12 OClock.[14]

This Evening Mr: Jesse Brown arrived very much to my Releif altho' he brings but small Remittances.[15]

Wrote a Letter to William Duer Esqr.

Wrote a Letter to his Excellency the Minister at War.
Wrote a Letter to Geo. Webb Esqr.
Wrote a Letter to James Lovell Esqr.

Issued a Warrant on Mr Swanwick in favor of Nichols and Rawlins	£750. 0.0
Issued a Warrant on Mr Swanwick in favor of Mrs. Mathews	100. 0.0
Issued a Warrant on Mr Swanwick in favor of Jos: Pennell	7,500. 0.0
Issued a Warrant on Mr Swanwick in favor of Jos: Pennell	1,875. 0.0
Issued a Warrant on Mr Swanwick in favor of John Langdon	7,500. 0.0
Issued a Warrant on Mr Swanwick in favor the Contractors the moving Army	562.10.0
Issued a Warrant on Mr Swanwick in favor John Pierce	682.10.0

1. On the intended transaction at Morristown, see Diary, August 12, and notes. Concerning Eddy's note at the Bank of North America, see Diary, July 10, August 31, and September 17 and 20, 1782.

2. See RM to Walter Livingston, August 29.

3. Words thus in manuscript.

4. See RM to George Eddy, August 28, and notes.

5. The contractors at Springfield, Massachusetts, were William Smith and Charles Sheldon.

6. George Clymer, a political ally of RM's in state politics, was not reelected to Congress when Pennsylvania chose a new delegation on November 12, 1782. See Burnett, ed., *Letters*, VI, 1.

7. See Diary, August 12, and notes.

8. RM's request was grounded in an acute shortage of revenues. See notes to Diary, August 20.

9. Tench Francis was a contractor of record for York and Carlisle, Pennsylvania. Miller was a subcontractor. Concerning Ephraim Blaine's flour sales, see Diary, September 21.

10. See notes to Diary, May 15, 1782.

11. See RM to Charles Armand, August 27; and notes.

12. This is a reference to the instructions being prepared for the commissioners of accounts for the states (see Diary, July 18, 1782, and notes, for previous references) and the departments. The final instructions issued by Comptroller of the Treasury James Milligan are printed under October 14.

13. Letter not found.

14. See Diary, September 2.

15. Brown was the Office of Finance express rider to the northern states.

To William Duer and Company

Office of Finance. 30. Augt. 1782[1]

Sir,

Mr. Stewart having tarried a Day longer than was expected, has given me the Opportunity of remitting you by him five thousand Dollars more in my Drafts on Mr. Swanwick payable Sixty days after the Date. I expect these drafts will answer every Purpose of Money to you as they are receivable in the Taxes of every State and negotiable in private Business. You are charged for them as for Money and if you do not use the whole Credit will be given for what may be returned. I am Sir with respect and Esteem your most obedient and humble Servant

                                                                    RM

MS: Ofcl LbC, DLC.
    1. Duer was the contractor for the Northern Department. For the antecedents to this letter, see RM to Duer, August 29.

To George Washington

Office of Finance 30. Aug: 1782[1]

Sir,

My Letter of the twenty ninth which is enclosed I have written for two Reasons one that you may be informed and I may stand justified in every Respect should the Event take Place; the other which is the principal one that you may found a warm Application on it to the States. You will I hope keep *this* entirely to yourself. You will see that I have not entrusted a View of it to my Secretary or to any of the Clerks. The Effect of your Application must depend on raising a very general Alarm. I have the Honor to be with great Esteem and Respect your Excellency's most obedient and humble Servant

                                                                    RM

MSS: Ofcl LbC, DLC; copy, PCC, DNA; copy, Benjamin Franklin Papers, PPAmP.
    1. The text received by Washington has not been found, but RM's remarks would suggest that it was written entirely in his hand or was prepared for his signature by his trusted assistant, Gouverneur Morris. For the circumstances surrounding the letter, see notes to RM to Washington, August 29 (first letter).

To George Webb

Office of Finance 30 Aug: 1782

Sir,

I have received your Letter of the sixteenth Instant.[1] With Respect to Bank Notes any private and particular Marks are Known only to the Directors and their immediate Officers I am myself ignorant of them. The Paper issued by myself is first Notes struck with a Copper Plate which you have seen and which I am now destroying as they come in. Secondly Bills of Exchange in the usual Form and thirdly Notes of which I gave you Information and a Discription in my Letter of Yesterday.[2] I have principally trusted to my Signature and in the last Case to the additional Security of Water Marks in the paper against Counterfeits. I am Sir your most obedient Servant

                                                                    RM

MS: Ofcl LbC, DLC.
1. Letter not found. Webb was the receiver of Continental taxes for Virginia.
2. For descriptions of the Morris paper issued to date, see RM's Circular to the Receivers of Continental Taxes, August 29, and notes.

To James Lovell

Office of Finance 30. Aug. 1782[1]

The Intent of these few Lines is meerly to advise that I have this day drawn a Bill on you in favor of Captain Fearis or Order for the Sum of one thousand five hundred Dollars being in full for a like Sum advanced by him here. I beg you will punctually pay this Bill charging the same to account of the United States.

MS: Ofcl LbC, DLC.
1. Lovell was the receiver of Continental taxes for Massachusetts.

To the Governor of Virginia
(Benjamin Harrison)

Office of Finance 30th. August 1782

I do myself the Honor to enclose an act of the United States of the twenty seventh Instant to which I am to pray your Excellency's attention.[1] I shall be happy to receive such Details as it may be thought proper to transmit on this Subject, that I may lay them before Congress for their Decision.

MSS: LS, Continental Congress Papers, Vi; Ofcl LbC, DLC.
1. For a discussion of this act, which concerned the status of the garrisons at York and Gloucester, see notes to Diary, July 24. Three texts of the act, two of them signed by Secretary of Congress Charles Thomson, are filed with this letter in the Continental Congress Papers, Vi.

To the Secretary at War
(Benjamin Lincoln)

Office of Finance 30 Augt. 1782

I have this Instant received your Letter of this Day's date and must entirely approve of your Idea with Respect to Armands Legion which I wish to have executed as soon as may be.[1]

MS: Ofcl LbC, DLC.
1. Lincoln's letter has not been found, but it probably proposed to change standing orders for the legion to join the southern army and instead have the corps march from its current base in western Virginia to Winchester in the northern part of the state. See notes to RM to Charles Armand, August 27; and Diary, August 31.

Diary: August 31, 1782

The Honble. Daniel Carrol Esqr. recommended Mr Geo. Lee of Blackensburg for Receiver of Taxes for that State.[1]

I sent for Mr. Hilligas and directed him to carry the half Bank

Notes which he has received[2] to the Bank and take Credit for them in order that he may be ready to pay Mr. Chaloner.[3]

I sent for Mr Swanwick and desired him to Collect all the Money that he possibly can in order to compleat the Payment of 20,000 Dollars to Mr: Chaloner.

Mr. Geo: Eddy came and told me he can take up the greater part of his note at the Bank but requests my Assistance in Case of need which I promised.[4]

Mr. Sherbel Breed who came Express from Thoms. Mumford Esqr. applies for remittances to that Gentleman but I told him he must stay a while.[5]

The Honble. Mr. Lee and Mr Osgood came expecting to meet the Committee of enquiry but the Chairman had given me Notice that the Committee are not to meet this Day.[6]

Messrs Comfort and Richardson Sands called at the Office, we had a long Conversation respecting the Complaints of the Army against the Contractors and the Complaints of the Contractors for Want of Money and finally they delivered me a Paper containing some Propositions to which I promised an Answer on Monday.[7]

Mr. Jno. Chaloner Called for his 20,000 Dollars and I sent Mr Swanwick to Muster if possible the Money for him.

Majr. Franks presented a Certificate for me to Sign importing that I had employed him on public Business, and that his reasonable Expences were to be paid. I Signed the same.[8]

Major Jackson brought back the Drafts which I had given to Genl Lincoln on Mr. Swanwick for 1970 Dollars to enable the movement of Colo Armands Corps to the Southward. I desired him to deliver them to Mr Swanwick and take his receipt for them. Major Jackson also brought a new Estimate of the Expence of moving that Corps to Winchester Amounting to 730 Dollars and I ordered Notes on Mr. Swanwick to be made out to that Amount.[9]

Capt. Barney called to know if I had purchased the Ship General Washington. I told him the Commissioners were to meet me on Monday at 10 OClock on that Subject.[10]

Mr Fitzsimmons with a Message from the Bank informing me of their Wants &c &c. I must if possible repay some of their Monies &c.[11]

Issued a Warrant on Mr. Swanwick in favor Sands Livingston & Co.	£7,500. 0.0
Issued a Warrant on Mr. Swanwick in favor Sands Livingston & Co. to Dr Brownson	187.10.0
Issued a Warrant on Mr. Swanwick in favor Colo. Charles Stewart	187.10.0
Issued a Warrant on Mr. Swanwick in favor Colo. Charles Stewart	1125. 0.0

Issued a Warrant on Mr. Swanwick in favor Col
James Wood   41. 5.0
Issued a Warrant on Mr. Swanwick in favor John
Pierce   180. 0.0

1. The nominee was probably George Lee (1736–1807), a merchant and planter, evidently of Blandensburg, in Prince George's County. Half uncle of Governor Thomas Sim Lee, he had served in Maryland provincial conventions early in the war and held a number of local offices, including lengthy service as a justice in Prince George's and Charles Counties, before, during, and after the war. RM, however, chose Benjamin Harwood as the receiver for Maryland (see RM to Harwood, September 13). This sketch is based primarily on data generously furnished to the editors by Edward C. Papenfuse and Lois Anne Hess of the Legislative History Project at MdAA. See also Edward C. Papenfuse et al., Directory of Maryland Legislators, 1635–1789 ([Annapolis], 1974), 43; Edward C. Mead, ed., Genealogical History of the Lee Family of Virginia and Maryland (New York, 1871), 111; and Gaius M. Brumbaugh and Margaret R. Hodges, Revolutionary Records of Maryland (Washington, 1924), 25–34 passim.
2. RM's circular to the receivers of Continental taxes east of the Hudson River of May 15, 1782, directed them to cut bank notes in half and transmit the halves separately to the Treasurer of the United States.
3. For the money owed to John Chaloner, see Diary, August 20, and notes.
4. See Diary, August 30, and notes.
5. See Diary, September 2 and 3.
6. For the committee of inquiry into the Office of Finance, which was chaired by James Duane of New York, see notes to Diary, June 12, 1782.
7. The document delivered by the Sands brothers, two of the contractors for West Point and the Moving Army, has not been found. For their next meeting, see Diary, September 2.
8. The certification is dated August 26.
9. For the change in destination of Armand's corps, see RM to the Secretary at War, August 30. William Jackson was the assistant secretary at war.
10. See Diary, September 2.
11. See Diary, September 3.

From William Whipple

Portsmouth [New Hampshire] 31st: Augt: 1782[1]

Sir

Your favor of the 13th instant I received yesterday by the post, I suppose it was intended to be sent by Mr Langdons express who arrived here a week ago.[2] That Gentleman applied to me for money for the Bills, but to my great mortification I had none to give him, not having received a farthing[3] he therefore immediately set out for Boston, where I hope he will be more successful. This I wish the more ardently as I am confident if he has not an immediate supply the ship will not be got in the water this year, and I am very apprehensive a total loss will be the consequence of her remaining on the stocks another Winter.[4]

It is very painful to me[5] that there is a necessaty of remitting money to New Hampshire for the Use of the Ship Building here, but hope I shall be able to give you a more favorable account of Receipts in the Course of next month. I shall make such Representations to the General Court at their next Session (which commences the 10th Sept:) as I shall find best calculated to produce greater exertions in Collecting Taxes. I have the Honour to be &c

Honble Robt Morris Esqr

MS: LbC, William Whipple Letterbook, John Langdon Papers, PHi.
1. Whipple was the receiver of Continental taxes for New Hampshire.
2. See RM to John Langdon, August 13. Langdon was overseeing the construction of the Continental ship of the line *America* in Portsmouth.
3. Whipple interlined the preceding five words after the comma.
4. For Whipple's more detailed comments on the *America,* see notes to John Paul Jones to Gouverneur Morris, September 2.
5. Whipple originally began this paragraph with the following words but then expunged them: "Painful as it is I shall be under the necessaty of Publishing to [the] world that ⟨I have received not received any⟩ no part of the Quota of New Hampshire for carrying on the war has been received."

From Alexander Hamilton

[Albany, New York, August 31, 1782][1]
I send you herewith all the acts of the Legislature of this state since the Government has been organized; on the margin of which I have numbered all the acts relative to the matters you mention in your letter of July 81 to the states agreeable to the within list.[2] I inclose you the papers of the last week.

The indolence of some and the repugnancy of others make every trifle lag so much in the execution that I am not able at this time to give you any further information. I wish to hear from you on the subjects of my former letters previous to the meeting of the Committee the 15th. of the ensuing month.[3]

Albany Aug. 31st 1782

MSS: ADftS, Hamilton Papers, DLC; transcript, Francis Baylies Papers, DLC.
1. Hamilton was the receiver of Continental taxes for New York.
2. Hamilton refers to RM's Circular to the Governors of the States, July 25, 1781, a copy of which RM had enclosed in his circular to the receivers of July 12, 1782. For a description of the enclosure Hamilton may have sent in the present letter, see Syrett and Cooke, eds., *Hamilton Papers,* III, 157n.
3. See Hamilton to RM, July 22, and notes, for the committee in question.

From William Churchill Houston

Trenton [New Jersey], 31 August 1782[1]
I have been favoured with both yours of 22 and 28 instant.[2] Mr Charles Stewart called Day before Yesterday with your Bills on Mr Swanwick to the Amount of 3500 Dollars; the five Hundred Dollars which he says are immediately requisite on the Line to the Army, I shall endeavour to pay, though rather more at a loss than I have hither to been.

The small receipt for the week is enclosed.

Dr   The Receipt of Continental Taxes for the State of New-Jersey
1782   To Cash received from the State-Treasurer from 24 August to 31
           inclusive three Hundred Dollars   Dlls 300

MS: ADftS with subjoined ADftS return, Houston Collection, NjP.
1. Houston was the receiver of Continental taxes for New Jersey.
2. Here Houston wrote then crossed out the words "and a."

From Nathanael Greene

Head Quarters [South Carolina]
Sept 1st 1782[1]

Sir

Some time ago when appearances indicated further serious operations in this Country, I wrote to the State of North Carolinia and Maryland to furnish for the use of the Legion a number of good dragoon horses.[2] At present the necessity does not seem so great as at the time the requisition was made altho our number of Cavalry is dayly declining and near one third of our men dismounted. If you think therefore it will be better for the general welfare of the United States to discontinue the purchases which may be making in consequence of my requisition in Maryland you will please to give order accordingly. In North Carolinia I have already put a stop to them unless the horses can be had on good terms. In that case to purchase the number required.

I am happy to inform you that the Army still continues in pretty good temper. If the officers could get their subsistence money it would be a great relief to us; and I should be in hopes to gain time several months longer without oppressing you for pay. At the same time I would observe both Men and Officers think [it] hard that they have not received some. An Army is a critical machine, it is convulsed in an hour and thrown into the greatest disorder. You will therefore take such measures as you think the public service requires and I shall promote them all in my power.

I find the State of North Carolinia want to furnish specifick supplies at the old rates,[3] when the articles can be had by contract at least 60 or 100 per centum lower. I have written the Governor on the subject and told him we would take such of the specifick articles as we wanted; but I shou'd expect them at the cash price and if he did not choose to fix that I would direct the public agents to receipt for the Articles and leave you and the State to settle the value.[4] Will you please to write them and me your opinion upon this subject. It will become more and more interesting. If the States can pay their tax in specifick articles at an advance price they will never collect a money tax; but if the specifick articles are fixed at the cash price they will gain little by the measure. Col Carrington will write you more fully on the matter.[5]

I find by a letter from Mr Milligan to Col Dart that the Auditor of the Army is discontinued.[6] Please to have another person appointed to settle accounts of contingent expences. Some person will be absolutely necessary. It is immaterial what he is called if he acts by authority and I find by the resolutions of Congress this power is vested in you.[7]

Mr. Clay the paymaster to the Southern department has resigned. Is there any mode for him to account for the Money and bills he has had for the public service? Please to point it out if there is and direct me what orders to give thereon before I finally accept his resignation.[8] I am Sir Your Most Obedient humble Servant

N Greene

The honble Robert Morris Esqr

ENDORSED: to Mr. R. Morris/Sept. 1. 1782/Army still in/good Temper/subsistence Money/much called for
MS: ADftS, Greene Papers, CSmH.
    1. Major General Greene was the commander of the southern army.
    2. A draft of Greene's letter to Governor Thomas Burke of North Carolina, dated April 28, 1782, is in the Greene Papers, MiU-C; for the reply, see Governor Alexander Martin to Greene, May 24, 1782, Saunders and Clark, eds., *State Records of North Carolina*, XVI, 687; and for the assembly's action, *ibid.*, XIX, 120–121. For the request to Maryland, see the Governor of Maryland to RM, July 12, 1782 (second letter), and notes.
    3. Greene is referring to the rates established by the specific supply requisitions of 1780.
    4. Greene probably refers to his letter to Governor Alexander Martin, August 29, 1782, Saunders and Clark, eds., *State Records of North Carolina*, XVI, 403–404.
    5. For RM's response to North Carolina's position, see RM to Edward Carrington, to Greene, and to the Governor of North Carolina, all October 17.
    6. The letter from Comptroller of the Treasury James Milligan to John Sandford Dart, auditor of accounts for the southern army, has not been found.
    7. See, however, RM to Greene, October 17.
    8. Joseph Clay, deputy paymaster general for the southern army, had resigned on April 24, 1782, to enter the Georgia Assembly. See Allen D. Candler, ed., *The Revolutionary Records of the State of Georgia* (Atlanta, 1908), III, 94; RM to the Paymaster General, August 2, and notes, to Greene, October 17, Greene to RM, December 3, 1782, February 9 and March 17, 1783, RM to Clay, and to Greene, both May 17, and to Clay, October 22, 1783.

Diary: September 2, 1782

Mr Ths. Lowry called on Me with a Bill of the Contractors for the Moving Army in his favor.[1] I declined accepting but told him it shall be paid and desired him to present the same to Mr. Swanwick that he may take record of it.

Messr Comfort and Richardson Sands[2] called agreeable to appointment but as I was very Busy I requested them to call again at Six OClock this Evening.

Seeing Colo. Matlack[3] in the Street passing this Office I sent for him and told him I had formed the design of making Personal application to the Council respecting the slow Collection of Taxes by which Means I am extremely embarrassed and the public Service suffers for want of money. He is of Opinion that Council cannot do any thing to Effect in this Matter as they have already urged and recommended to the Commissioners and Collectors repeatedly to exert themselves and Support me by Speedy Collections and Payments and he is of Opinion that was Council to fine the delinquent Collectors or to proceed to harsh Measures more harm than Good will result therefrom—however he promised to Consult Council on this Subject or some of them.

The Honble Ralph Izard Esqr. brought one of Genl Greenes Drafts for 250 Guineas now due. I could not pay but promised payment soon as possible.

Mr Shubel Breed urged to be dispatched back to Mr. Mumford. I desired him to draw upon me in favor of those Mr. Mumford had ordered him to pay Money to and that I will make up Notes for the remainder and dispatch him to Morrow. Mr: Breed accordingly drew in favor of Mr. Bridges, Mr. Marshall and Mr. Swanwick. I directed the latter to take Note of said Drafts for Payment in turn.[4]

The Honble: Mr. Telfair and Mr Clymer as a Committee of Congress respecting the Account of the late Mr Commissary Genl. Trumbull the report they made on my Letter having been recommitted. I advised them to apply to Mr. Jona. Burral the Commissioner of that Department and to let him State the Account of Commissions agreeable to the Principles in the Report and then Report the Sum it amounted to as the Sum to be allowed, which they approved.[5]

Colo. Dyer called on the same Subject and was also Satisfied.

The Hon: Mr. Howell called to recommend Colo. Silas Talbot to Command the Ship Washington.[6] He also recommended a Mr. Still to be employed as a Commissioner for Settling Accounts.[7]

Mr. Jos. Wilson called and proposed that I should give him Bills at long Sight instead of his waiting until December for them.[8]

Oliver Pollock Esqr. called to remind me of his memorial which I had not yet read.[9]

John Pierce Esqr. for Money to satisfy the Demands on him, and with his returns I cannot give him Money.

Monsr Baulney Treasurer of the French Army called upon me first to Visit and then to inform me that Mr. David Ross had not paid Mr. Pleasants Bills on him remitted by me thro the Minister of France.[10]

Colo. Gurney, Colo. Patton and Capt. Allibone Commissioners for the Ship General Washington came to the Office this Day at twelve OClock agreeable to Appointment and after some Conversation I agreed on behalf of the United States to purchase that Ship at the Price she was struck off at public Vendue to Jno. Wright Stanley Esqr. he agreeing to relinquish the bargain in favor of the Public altho some of the Gentlemen concerned with him in that purchase are averse thereto. It is agreed between these Commissioners and myself that this Ship shall be paid for in Nine Months. I am to give them a Draft on David Rittenhouse Esqr. Treasurer of Pennsylvania for the Amount but if not paid by him within that period the Balance which may remain due upon that order is to be paid by the Superintendent of Finance at the end of nine Months aforesaid. I agreed also to take the Iron and lead Ballast together with Provisions that did belong to this Ship but which were not Sold with her and to pay for them in the same manner.[11] I also requested these Gentlemen (having observed their[12] great care and attention in executing the Trust committed to them) to fit out this Ship for Sea with all possible expedition keeping regular and exact Accounts of their expenditures. I told them that Capt. Barney is to have the Command and desired she may be fitted with all things necessary but with all possible frugality and Occonomy.[13]

I sent for Mr Claudius P. Raguet who has not paid his Obligation given for Bills of Exchange sold him, said Obligation being discounted at the Bank on application of Mr Hilligas, and required Security.[14] This Gentleman declares he has Property for more than sufficient to all his engagements requesting a further indulgence of time, or offers to deliver Goods suitable for the public Service as cheap as can any where be had. I desired him to call on the Clothier General to see the Goods, the prices &c. and if he made a purchase on Good Terms for the public I shou'd be Content.

Messrs. Comfort and Richardson Sands came in this Evening when a long Conversation took place on their Affairs in which various Difficulties seemed to be removed and I assured them of my entire Disposition to supply Money to them as fast as is possible, and if at any time it is detained longer than it ought I begged they would exert themselves and support instead of plagueing and Distressing me with importunity.[15]

This Evening Capt. Jno. Green returned from his Embassy to New York and informs me that he went down the North River with a Flag granted by His Excellency Genl Washington[16] but was stopped by the Guard Ships at Kingsbridge, that Capt Coates the Senior on that Command took his Letters and sent them in to Sir Guy Carlton, that he waited on Board the Ship two Days expecting Liberty to go in to the City or to receive Answers but at last was told he could not be allowed to go in, but must return, and accordingly he is come back without any reply to my Letters respecting Prisoners &c.[17]

1. Thomas Lowrey of New Jersey, holder of a one-sixteenth share in the Moving Army contract, had withdrawn from the contract in June 1782 shortly after it merged with the West Point contract, his private affairs no longer permitting him to give the necessary attention to the business. He had nevertheless continued to provision the troops in New Jersey until the end of June, and agreed to continue to purchase flour

for the contractors on a commission basis and to sell whiskey he had already ordered to the other contractors "at first cost." Lowrey stipulated, however, that he was to be repaid for all advances at the end of each month or as soon as he furnished his invoices and vouchers. See Lowrey to Charles Stewart, June 4, Robert Blair to Stewart, June 6, Aron Dunham to Stewart, June 14, Comfort Sands and Company and Walter Livingston to Stewart, June 17, and Lowrey's agreement to purchase flour, June 22, 1782, all in the Stewart Papers, NCooHi.

2. Two of the contractors for West Point and the Moving Army.

3. Timothy Matlack, secretary of the Supreme Executive Council of Pennsylvania.

4. See RM to Thomas Mumford, September 2.

5. On this subject, which RM had broached to Congress in a letter of July 23, and the report in question, see Jonathan Burrall to RM, July 22, and notes.

6. Talbot, a captain in the Continental navy from Rhode Island, had commanded the *General Washington* as a privateer in 1780 but lost it soon after to the British. The vessel was retaken in 1782, but Talbot did not get the command. Maclay, *History of American Privateers*, 110–111; and notes to Diary, February 21 and May 15, 1782.

7. The reference is to Benjamin Stelle of Rhode Island, who served as an adjutant in the state forces from 1775 to 1777 and in Continental service as assistant and deputy paymaster in the Eastern Department from April 1778 to April 1781. RM subsequently nominated him as commissioner to settle Pennsylvania's accounts with the United States, an office he held until 1787. Heitman, *Register; JCC*, XXXII, 246–247; and RM to the President of Pennsylvania, November 23, and to Stelle, December 17, 1782.

8. See Diary, August 9, and notes.

9. Pollock's memorial has not been found.

10. See RM to Chevalier de La Luzerne, January 12, 1782 (second letter).

11. The state ultimately failed to make payment on RM's draft on Rittenhouse. See Diary, November 19, 1782, and June 6, 1783; and Waste Book D, pp. 181, 538–540, and Waste Book E, p. 81, Records of the United States General Accounting Office, RG 217, DNA.

12. MS: "there."

13. See RM to Gurney, Patton, and Allibone, September 4; for the background, see notes to Diary, May 15, 1782.

14. Claudius Paul Raguet (also known as Claudin Paul Raguet and Charles P. Raguet), a French-born Philadelphia businessman, had bought the bills of exchange from the Office of Finance with a note for about £2,900. His note was discounted at the Bank of North America, but Raguet was unable to pay when it fell due. As recorded in this Diary entry, RM agreed to take goods from his store, but Raguet did not have what the army needed. Raguet then tendered a ship he had under construction, later named *Duc de Lauzun*. RM at first refused this offer, but changed his mind early in October when approached, first by Francisco Rendón, and then by Thomas Randall and Thomas Truxtun, all creditors of Raguet, who suggested that RM go in with them in recovering their debts by taking the ship. The Superintendent agreed, and the four acquired the vessel, RM in his official capacity. Shortly afterward the Financier bought out the other partners, giving them bills of exchange, thus converting the ship into a Continental naval vessel. It was outfitted by Thomas Fitzsimons and sent to Havana in November under Captain John Green with a cargo and bills of exchange to sell for specie.

The account of the *Duc de Lauzun* in *Dict. Amer. Naval Ships*, II, 302, is unreliable on the vessel's provenance. The ship was named after Armand Louis de Gontaut Biron, Duc de Lauzun (1747–1793), commander of a legion of foreign volunteers in the French army who had served brilliantly in the Yorktown campaign and, with Comte des Deux-Ponts, was chosen to carry the news of the Yorktown victory to France. He returned to Philadelphia in September 1782 aboard the *Aigle* and *Gloire* (see notes to Diary, September 16), rejoined the French army in New York later in the month, and ultimately returned to France in March 1783 (see Balch, *French in America*, I, 224, II, 160–163; Chastellux, *Travels*, I, 255–256; and Evelyn M. Acomb, trans. and ed., *The Revolutionary Journal of Baron Ludwig von Closen, 1780–1783* [Chapel Hill, N. C., 1958], 354).

For references to Raguet and the ship among RM's papers, see Diary, September 3, 5, October 7, 15, 17, 18, 22, 26 (where the ship is first described by name), and

November 8, RM to Raguet, September 11 and 19, to Thomas Randall and Company, October 17, 1782, and for the Superintendent's defense of his conduct with respect to the ship, RM to Theodorick Bland, Jr., April 16, 1783 (first letter); on the voyage to Havana, see notes to RM to Le Couteulx and Company, September 24, 1782. On Raguet, whose son Condy Raguet (1784–1842) became a notable merchant and economist, see Morris U. Schappes, ed., "Excerpts from Robert Morris' 'Diaries in the Office of Finance, 1781–1784,' Referring to Haym Salomon and Other Jews," *American Jewish Historical Quarterly*, LXVII (1977), 49n.; *PMHB*, LV (1931), 327, 328, 329, 330, 331; and *DAB*, s.v. "Raguet, Condy."

15. According to Walter Livingston, Comfort Sands had come to Philadelphia with the intention of resigning the West Point and Moving Army contract if RM did not immediately pay the contractors' balance for July (see notes to RM to Livingston, August 29). For a probable outgrowth of the meeting recorded in this Diary entry, see Proposals from Sands and Company, printed under September 2, and notes.

16. See RM to Washington, August 22.

17. For the reply, see Guy Carleton to RM, September 2.

To Thomas Mumford

Marine Office [2] Septem: 1782[1]

Sir,

I have received your Letter of the sixteenth of August by Mr. Breed.[2] The Account cannot be adjusted for want of the original Vouchers. It will be best that you keep exact Copies and transmit the originals by a safe Conveyance. When they arrive the whole shall be adjusted and proper Measures be taken for Payment of the Balance should any remain due. You will observe Sir that I had expected the Payment of these Monies out of the Quota of your State and had not therefore made Provision for the Purpose here. Governor Trumbull writes me on the twenty third of August[3] "Care is taken that the two Taxes granted for Payment of our Quota to the United States be kept distinct from any other Taxes, the first amounts to £18000 payable 1 of April last, the other amounts to £72,000 payable 1st of July last.[4] Warrants are out and the Collectors busy and in earnest collecting the same." He also writes[5] "that seventy Barrels of Beef, and one hundred and twenty Barrels of Pork, were supplied you for the ship Alliance." These will I perceive by your Accounts amount to near three thousand Dollars. He also writes me[6] "that the Time is expired for Payment of about five hundred Barrels of Beef and Pork sold you." This Article may I suppose amount to upwards of seven thousand Dollars. Finally he writes in the same Letter certain Expectations of selling the remainder of their salted Provisions and that my Notes are in full Credit equal to the precious Metals. You are doubtless informed that the Proceeds of all these salted Provisions are appropriated to the continental Use and of Consequence they may be paid for by my Notes or if they should have been already paid for in Specie there will be a fund for the Redemption of those Notes. Under these Circumstances I had determined to make you Payment by a Remittance of them but as Mr Breed mentioned certain Sums which you have directed him to pay here I have agreed to Pay his Drafts in favor of Robert Bridges for nine hundred and eleven Dollars and one Quarter and in favor of Messrs. Christopher junr. and Charles Marshall for six hundred and two Dollars and thirty three ninetieths and in favor of Mr John Swanwick for thirty three Dollars and $^{15}/_{24}$, and as you expressed a Wish to receive some smaller Notes I send you in such Notes three thousand dollars more. I cannot doubt but that these Notes will be Cash to you immediately and will enable the state to make me a considerable remittance. In order to facilitate the Matter more I shall enclose a Copy of this letter to the Governor.[7] I am Sir with respect your most obedient humble Servant

RM

MSS: AM LbC, MdAN; copy, Jonathan Trumbull Papers, Ct.

1. The AM LbC is misdated September 12, although located among letters preceding September 3.

2. The letter, which has not been found, was delivered to RM on August 31 (see Diary of that date). Mumford, a merchant of Groton, Connecticut, had been supplying the *Alliance* at New London.

3. The complete text of this letter has not been found.

4. On the taxes raised by Connecticut for the requisition for 1782, see notes to RM to Hezekiah Merrill, May 14, 1782.

5. The quotation mark that follows has been supplied by the editors.

6. The quotation mark that follows has been supplied from the Ct text.

7. See RM to the Governor of Connecticut, September 3.

From Guy Carleton

[New York, September 2, 1782][1]

Sir

I am to acknowledge the Receipt of your Letter dated the 20th. of Augt. inclosing Letters from the Masters of two Flag Ships from England.

You say sir that you intend delivering to one of those Masters such Brittish marine Prisoners as may be in Philadelphia or its vicinity when they depart provided their Receipt shall be deemed a proper Evidence of the Delivery on a settlement of the account hereafter,[2] in answer to which I am to acquaint you that the Receipt of either of the masters of the above mentioned ships will be considered as a sufficient proof of the Delivery of all such prisoners as shall be placed on board them.

I am to hope Sir that you will as much as possible enlarge the circle from which the Brittish are to be collected in order that those to be delivered may bear a proportion in number to those transmitted from England[3] and I have just been informed by the Naval Commissary here that there are numbers at present confined in Jersey. I am Sir

MSS: Undated Dft, Carleton Papers, PRO; copy, Carleton Papers, PRO.

1. Carleton was the commander of British forces in North America. The date of his letter has been supplied from the copy listed above.

2. The remainder of the paragraph was substituted in the margin for the following crossed-out passage: "This cannot well be otherwise the⟨ir⟩ Receipt [of] either of the masters of the above will undoubtedly be such evidence but I cannot help wishing Sir that you had made some Intimation of the number so to be returned. You do indeed say that they shall be sent in one of the Transports and one of the masters estimates their number to be about 70 but as the number delivered at Philadelphia exceed 300."

3. For a discussion of this point, see notes to Diary, June 18, 1782.

Proposals from Comfort Sands and Company

[Philadelphia, ca. September 2, 1782?][1]

Proposals made to Mr Morris by Comfort Sands & Co

That at the request of the Commander in chief, both Contracts for West Point and the Moving Army, from the first day of July last have been considered as one by the different Contractors, and the Accounts all brought in against the Public in one General Account. The Auditors and Comptrolers object to the settlement of them in that way unless they have the directions of the Superintendant of Finance. The Contractors will either agree to the mode proposed by Mr. G. Morris, that is, for the Commander in chief to determine the Number, West Point Garrison should be considered, and for that Number deduct a half penny per Ration, or will from the Number of Rations issued in those Posts, which will appear by the return, abate the half penny per Ration.

MS: Copy, Washington Papers, DLC.

1. These undated proposals were the outgrowth of the decision to merge the West Point and Moving Army contracts (see Diary, May 13, 1782, and notes). The text printed here, subjoined to a copy of RM's letter to the Comptroller of the Treasury of September 3, was sent to Washington by Comfort Sands in a letter of March 4, 178[3] (Washington Papers), during a dispute over the settlement of the contractors' accounts. In his covering letter Sands recalled that the proposals had been made in or about September 1782, and that in consequence of the ensuing agreement RM had written his September 3 letter to the Comptroller. This circumstance and RM's conference with the Sands brothers of September 2 (see Diary of that date) suggest the date conjectured by the editors. For the antecedents, see the Comptroller of the Treasury to RM, August 1, and notes, and the documents cited there.

From George Washington

Head Quarters Verplanks Point [New York] 2d
Septemr 1782

Dear Sir

I have had the honor of receiving your Cypher of the 17th. and letter of the 20th: ultimo. Should the money alluded to in the first be paid into my hands, it shall be applied as you direct.

I should have had hopes from yours of the 20th. that all difficulties between you and the Contractors had been settled, had I not received a letter from Mr. Walter Livingston dated at Morristown the 31st. of last Month and in which he[1] informs me that Mr. Sands had gone forward to Philada. with fresh Complaints, and that he was very apprehensive of the consequences. I can only hope his fears are ill grounded.

Mr. Gouverneur Morris having signified to me that it will be inconvenient to him to attend as one of the Commissioners at the proposed meeting,[2] I shall be under the necessity of appointing some Gentleman of the Army in his stead. As the matter relating to accounts will probably be the first entered upon, I shall be glad to know whether those depending upon us are in any more forwardness than they were before, and whether Mr. Skinner[3] is possessed of them. If he is not, he, or some person who has been conversant in them, should be prepared to attend the Commissioners. Skinner would be preferable to any other, because he will be at the same time perfectly acquainted with all transactions in the department of Commy of Prisoners. I imagine he is at this time in Philada.[4]

If you have any fresh matter which you would wish inserted in the instructions which I am to draw for the new Commissioners, be pleased to furnish me with it as soon as possible. I only wait an answer to some points which I have proposed to Congress, to enable me to fix the time and place of meeting.[5] I have the Honor to be &c

Hono Robert Morris

ENDORSED: Verplanks. 2d ⟨Augst.⟩ Sepr 1782/to/Hono Robert Morris Esqr/Letter from Mr Walter Livingston/Accounts for Commissioners on Settlement/for Prisoners &c
MSS: Dft in the writing of Tench Tilghman, Washington Papers, DLC; Varick transcript, Washington Papers, DLC.
    1. Here Tilghman wrote and then crossed out the words "encloses the Copy of one he had written to you after the." This refers to Livingston to RM of August 13, which Livingston enclosed in a letter to Washington of August 31, 1782. For a discussion of the August 31 letter, see notes to RM to Livingston, August 29.
    2. See Gouverneur Morris to Washington, August 26.
    3. Abraham Skinner, the commissary general of prisoners.
    4. RM sent James Mullins, a clerk who was familiar with the prisoner accounts. See RM to Washington, September 12.
    5. See Washington to the President of Congress, August 28, 1782, Fitzpatrick, ed., *Writings of Washington*, XXV, 71–72; and for Congress's response, *JCC*, XXIII, 544n., 551, 555–559n., 581–582. On the meeting of the commissioners, which was held at Tappan, New York, see notes to Diary, June 18, 1782.

From Anthony Wayne

Drayton Hall 12 Miles from
Charlestown [South Carolina] 2nd[–29] Sepr 1782[1]

Dear Sir

I took the liberty of addressing several letters to you during the last Campaign without being favored with a single line in return,[2] which I must attribute to that constant succession of business in which you are necessarily engaged, or to the miscarriage of letters, that but too frequently find the way into Charlestown, where they are opened without ceremony, but the contents never communicated, except thro' the chanel of news papers, and that only when the subject matter militates against us;[3] so much by way of Apology ⟨for neglect on your part⟩ in your favor, and now for a few Queries on which I wish your Opinion—were the overtures of peace and an offer of Independance to America by the British Ministry anticedient, or subsequent to the receipt of the particulars of the Advantages gained over the Count De Grasse?[4] if Subsequent, may not the War be procastrinated? 2nd[5] as the withdrawal of the British troops from America ⟨seems?⟩ appears to be a determined *Manoeouvre,* will not that event have a tendency to lull the United States into security, in that case, have we nothing to apprehend from a second visit ⟨from the British⟩ should the British be successful in[6] the West Indias?

These may be Ideal apprehensions, but I candidly confess to you, that I feel them very forceably; nor has the resolve of Congress of the 7th Ultimo alleviated those apprehensions;[7] however good man time can alone determine whether I am right or wrong.

It's with inexpressible pain and anxiety that I see our little army mouldering away to a handful by the baneful effects of short inlistments, and the fatal fevers natural to this inhospitable climate, ⟨which has already distroyed us more men than we should have lost in the severest action.⟩

29th Sepr.

My pen was wrested from me by a sudden and Dangerous fever before I[8] could finish my letter of the 2nd Instant and it is not more than twenty four hours since I have been able to resume it. I fondly flatter myself, that I am ⟨now⟩ nearly clear of that ⟨fever⟩ disorder which I realy dread ten thousand times more, than I do a Musket or a Cannon ball,[9] our Worthy General is also just recovering from a very violent attack of that same Caitiff fever which has already ⟨carried off⟩ more than Decimated this army;[10] as this will be delivered by an Officer, I have ventured to Inclose a return[11] of the Pennsa. line, the Scale fit for action will show you[12] better than words can paint, our real situation.

⟨Inclosed is the Charlestown paper of this day it?⟩[13] If we are to give credit to the speeches of Lord Shelburn, Mr Fox, and the King in July American Independance has not yet been agreed to but to be made a Question the next session of Parliament; should they meet with some disasters previously, it will be acknowledged—if they are fortunate it will not; for despondency under Misfortune, and Arrogance in prosperity is the true Caracteristic of the British Nation[14] may she prove the ofspring of fortunes eldest Daughter is the sincere wish of your most Obedient and very Humble Servant

AW

ENDORSED: 2nd Sepr. 1782/to/Robt. Morris Esqr.
MS: ADftS, Wayne Papers, PHi.

1. Following an expedition into Georgia, during which he took possession of Savannah in July, Brigadier General Wayne and his forces had recently rejoined the southern army outside Charleston. See Kenneth Coleman, *The American Revolution in Georgia, 1763–1789* (Athens, 1958), 141–145.

Wayne's punctuation marks in the ADftS printed here are highly idiosyncratic; where they are not distinguishable, the editors have resorted to modern usage. Another text of this letter, evidently derived from a lost manuscript—possibly the one received by RM—has been printed in "Letters to Robert Morris, 1775–1782," N.-Y. Hist. Soc., *Colls.*, Pub. Fund Ser., XI (1878), 481–482. It differs markedly in punctuation from Wayne's draft and contains a substantially modified concluding paragraph. The most significant differences between the two texts have been collated in the notes that follow.

2. Wayne's unanswered letters to RM include those of September 14, October 26, and November 6, 1781, none of which RM received. A long time elapsed before RM received the present letter. See RM to Wayne, February 4, 1783.

3. In the N.-Y. Hist. Soc. text the letters "find their way into the hands of the enemy who open them [without] ceremony, but never communicate the contents except thro' the channel of newspapers and that only, when the subject matter militates *against us.*"

4. Wayne refers to de Grasse's defeat by the British in the Battle of the Saints. See the headnote and notes to RM's State of American Commerce and Plan for Protecting It, May 10, 1782.

5. This number is not in the N.-Y. Hist. Soc. text.

6. The remaining words of the sentence in the N.-Y. Hist. Soc. text are "other Quarters?"

7. Congress on August 7 had reorganized and consolidated the Continental army and provided for the retirement of excess officers (for a partial discussion, see notes to Diary, July 1, 1782). The remainder of the paragraph in the N.-Y. Hist. Soc. text is "however good man time will determine."

8. In the N.-Y. Hist. Soc. text the remainder of the sentence is given as "had finished my letter of the 2d, & I only now snatch a short interval to reassume it."

9. For the preceding 13 words the printed N.-Y. Hist. Soc. text gives "much more than I do the D——l, a musket or a cannon ball."

10. Wayne interlined the remainder of the paragraph.

11. The N.-Y. Hist. Soc. text gives "weekly return."

12. Remainder of sentence in the N.-Y. Hist. Soc. text: "our real situation much better than words can paint it."

13. In the N.-Y. Hist. Soc. text this paragraph is as follows: "Whilst I am writing, several persons this morning from Charlestown, announce the arrival of the transports from New York to take off the Garrison &c. the Evacuation of the place will certainly take place in the course of three weeks; but if we are to give any credit to London papers of the 13th July in which are the speeches of Mr Fox. Lord Shelburn & the King, they have not yet given up America; should they meet with a disaster, Independence will be acknowledged—if they are fortunate, it will not: may Britain therefore prove the offering of fortune's *eldest daughter* is the sincere wish of your Friend and hum. Servt."

14. Wayne appears to have written "Nature" before reworking it into "Nation."

John Paul Jones to Gouverneur Morris

Portsmouth, New Hampshire Septr. 2d. 1782

Your kind Letter, my dear Morris, of the 13th. Ultimo and the public one of the same date[1] are as welcome favors and as necessary to me as fresh Air and the saving hand of Freindship to a drowning Man. I know your ability, and am convinced your freindship for our

Country will manifest itself so effectually that we may avail of the loss of the Magnifique at Boston—I know it has been proposed by some *wise Heads* to offer the "America" as a present to replace that ship.[2] Are we in a condition to make presents? If we were, I should be against offering to give a friend *an empty Eggshell*. You know me I find since "you are sure I will rejoice at the present appearances of Peace"—An honorable Peace is and always was my first wish! I can take no delight in the effusion of human Blood; but, if this War should continue I wish to have the most active part in it. With the highest sense of your kind attentions and good Opinion, and with the most earnest desire to deserve, by my conduct the delicate praises of a Freind of your high worth and public Spirit, I am, sincerely and affectionately your most Obliged

Paul Jones

The Honble. Governeur Morris Esqr. Assistant Minister of Finance &c. &c.

MS: ALS, MdAN.

1. The private letter from Gouverneur Morris has not been found; the public letter was RM to Jones, August 13. Jones was the commander of the *America*, a 74-gun Continental ship of the line under construction at Portsmouth.

2. On August 10, 1782, while entering Boston Harbor with the aid of a heedless local pilot, the 74-gun French ship *Magnifique* of Marquis de Vaudreuil's squadron struck a rock and was wrecked. James Lovell and William Whipple, the receivers of Continental taxes for Massachusetts and New Hampshire, whose disappointing tax receipts were of little assistance to RM to completing the *America*, both recommended that it be presented to France in place of the *Magnifique*. Lovell made the suggestion in a letter to RM which has not been found, but Whipple, who on August 19 "had some thoughts of writing Mr: M. on this subject but did not know but he or some body else might think me too forward," instead urged John Taylor Gilman, a New Hampshire delegate to Congress, to represent the matter to the Financier at once, "being fully convinced she will not be made useful under the American flagg for if every other obstacle was removed, the difficulty of maning her would be unsurmountable." Gilman undoubtedly conveyed these views when he called at the Office of Finance on September 3, and for reasons laid out in the Diary of that date RM immediately concurred. Acting at his behest, Congress that same day unanimously instructed the Agent of Marine to present the ship to Chevalier de La Luzerne, the French minister at Philadelphia, which RM did on September 4. After an abortive effort on October 23, the *America* was successfully launched on November 5 and ceremoniously presented by Jones to the former commander of the *Magnifique*. Its career in the French navy was less than glorious, however, for she was condemned in 1786 on account of dry rot from the green timber used in her construction. See Whipple to Gilman, August 19, 1782, Whipple Letterbook, John Langdon Papers, PHi; Motion Concerning the "America," [September 3], and Madison to Edmund Randolph, September 10, 1782, Hutchinson and Rutland, eds. *Madison Papers*, V, 99–100, 115; Vaudreuil to La Luzerne, September 20, 1782, Wharton, ed., *Rev. Dipl. Corr.*, V, 747; Gawalt, ed., *John Paul Jones' Memoir*, 62–63; Morison, *John Paul Jones*, 326–330; notes to RM to Langdon, April 20, 1781; Diary, September 3 and 4, Whipple to RM, August 31, RM to the President of Congress, September 3, to La Luzerne, and to Thomas Russell, both September 4, to Langdon, September 4 and 5, and to Lovell, September 10, Jones to RM, September 22, and RM to Jones, October 9. For the suggestion that with the gift of the *America* "Morris seems to have tried to put La Luzerne and the King in a favorable state of mind" before requesting a loan for 1783, see O'Donnell, *Chevalier de La Luzerne*, 192n.–193n.

George Plater to Gouverneur Morris

[Sotterley, near Leonardtown, Maryland, September 2, 1782]

Your Favors of 8th and 19th Aug:[1] are come to hand for which I thank you—in the former by Mr. Stone you seem to think that those who flatter themselves with the Hope of Peace may be deceived. Tis possible they may, but I think there are stronger Appearances than I have yet seen. Independence in the first Instance I did not expect would be admitted. I do not and never did think that the Enemy were so weakened by the War as to be despised, but I believe they, as well as we, are tired of this War, and I pray Night and Morn that we may soon have a good Peace. Pray has the Affair of Lipincut [Lippincott] blown over; I hear nothing of it. We are honored by the Company of Mr. and Mrs. Richd. Lloyd. I am called off to play Piquet[2] with the fair Lady, therefore must conclude with assuring you that I am Yours most sincerely

Sotterley, Sept. 2d 1782

MS: ALS, Gouverneur Morris Papers, NNC.
1. Letters not found. Plater was president of the Maryland Senate.
2. A card game. *OED*.

Diary: September 3, 1782

Alexr. Fowler Esqr[1] applying with the Comptrollers Certificate of a Balance due to him and being a civil List Officer I paid part in Drafts on Mr Swanwick and the rest registered on Interest.

Mr. Shubal Breed was this Day dispatched to Thos. Mumford Esqr. with a remittance in Notes &c. See my Letters to him.[2]

I sent for Mr. Geo. Eddy and shewed him Mr. Clarkes last Letters wherein he says he cannot get either Money or Tobacco for Drafts on this Place.[3]

The Honble. Mr: Gilman called to shew me Letters from New Hampshire respecting the Ship America and respecting the Sale of Beef Cattle &c.[4]

This day dispatched Mr John Brown for Boston &c.

This day I requested a Committee of Congress for a Conference.[5] The Hon: Mr Rutledge, Mr Osgood and Mr Maddison were appointed and I proposed to them the presenting the 74 Gun Ship America to his most Christian Majesty, who has lately lost the Le Magnifique a 74 in the Harbor of Boston. The Committee were unanimously of Opinion with me that this unfortunate incident afforded Congress an Opportunity of shewing one proper mark of the Sincerity of their Attachment to their Ally by enabling his Minister to continue the force of his Fleet at a time when it could not otherwise be done. Besides the propriety which there is in shewing this Mark of attachment and Gratitude to His most Christian Majesty, I have several other strong and pointed reasons which induced me to propose and will always support this Measure. The want of Money in our Treasury to Fit, Equip, and Man this Ship is amongst the Number and is perhaps sufficient to insert here.[6]

Mr. B: Dudley applied for a Passage for his Friend Mr. Sprague per the Washington to France and for Mrs. Dudley back &c.

The Honble: Mr. Holker applied most pressingly for a payment of Ten thousand Dollars on Account of Cloathing sold me for the Army last Winter.[7] I was obliged to promise the Money in a short time.

Jno. Moylan Esqr. Clothier General came respecting Shirts &c. for the Army. I desired him to go to the Store of Mr Raguet and see what Articles he has suitable for the United States.[8] I advised that he should purchase there such things as will suit the public Service provided he will Sell them on the same Terms as if he went with the Money in hand to pay for them as I deem this the most effectual Mode of securing the public Debt. I desired the Clothier General to enquire the Quantity of Shirts and Linnens he could buy and the prices and Terms of Payment and to return me a list of the Persons from whom he can purchase &c.

The Hon: Mr Clarke and Mr Lee of the Committee of enquiry called but the other Members not appearing they went away again.[9]

This morning Mr. McPherson (Broker) called at my House and shewed me an Advertizement he was directed by a Mr. Black to publish offering for Sale one of the Clothier Genls. Drafts accepted by Mr Swanwick per my order which fell due the first of August and is not yet paid.[10] This Bill is for 160 £ and he offers it for £100. On seeing this I did suppose the design malicious and therefore told Mr McPherson if he or his Employer chose to publish that Advertizement they might do it, but they will please to consider it is against the Public at large and not against me, If I had been supplied with money I should have paid to a day, that I use every exertion to preserve punctuality but cannot do impossibilities. He said he beleived this was dictated by the Distress of the Party and I desired to see him. He accordingly brought the Gentleman to the Office and as it proved to be realy from Necessity I promised him releif in a very short time.

The Hon: Secretary at War came to Consult respecting Prisoners at Boston but being very much engaged I desired he would postpone the Matter awhile and promised to call upon him at the War Office.

Mr Wheeler applied for Money which I promised in a short time.

Capt. Truxen [Truxtun] for an Order to the Flag Ship[11] to remove out of his Way which I desired Mr Brown to comply with.

Mr. Henry Dering Contractor at Lancaster for money.

Messrs. William Bingham, Jno. M. Nesbit and Thos. Fitzsimmons came as a Deputation from the Directors of the Bank to request me to make them some payments as the State of the Bank requires it. I acknowleged the propriety of their application as I have been obliged to trespass on the Bank and therefore promised to replace some of the Monies soon as possible.

Wrote a Letter to the Comptroller of the Treasury.

Wrote a Letter to his Excellency the Governor of Rhode Island.

Wrote a Letter to the Post Master General.

Wrote a Letter to James Cumberland Esqr.[12]

Wrote a Letter to his Excellency the Govr. of Connecticut.

Wrote a Letter to Danl. Clarke.

Wrote a Letter to Bernard Dougherty.

Wrote a Letter to Hezh. Merril.

Issued a Warrant on Mr Swanwick in favor John Pierce	£ 759.1.3
Issued a Warrant on Mr Swanwick in favor Jos: Pennell	3375.0.0
Issued a Warrant on Mr Swanwick in favor the Contractors for York and Carlisle	315.0.0
Issued a Warrant on Mr Swanwick in favor Sands Livingston & Co.	1125.0.0

1. Alexander Fowler had been elected an auditor of the army by Congress in 1779 and served at Fort Pitt in the Western Department, where he later supplied the garrison from his store. See *JCC*, XIII, 217, 392, XV, 1242, 1252, XX, 571–572; and Diary, July 28, 1783, July 28, 30, and August 2, 1784, Joseph Marbury to RM, July 12, and RM to Fowler, July 28 and August 18, 1784.

2. See RM to Thomas Mumford, September 2, and Joseph Pennell to Mumford, September 3.

3. RM refers to two letters from Daniel Clark of August 23, which have not been found. See RM to Clark, September 3.

4. Only one of the letters communicated by John Taylor Gilman, a New Hampshire delegate to Congress, has been identified, that of August 19 from William Whipple recommending that the *America* be given to France (see notes to John Paul Jones to Gouverneur Morris, September 2). On the question of beef cattle, see Whipple to RM, August 5, and Diary, September 4, and notes, and September 5.

5. See RM to the President of Congress, September 3.

6. For a discussion, see notes to John Paul Jones to Gouverneur Morris, September 2.

7. See RM's Agreement with John Holker, November 2, 1781, and notes.

8. See Diary, September 2, and notes.

9. For this committee, see notes to Diary, June 12, 1782.

10. On April 16, 1782, RM had agreed to accept drafts drawn on him by Clothier General John Moylan in payment for goods purchased for the army. Unable to make payment on these acceptances as they fell due, the Superintendent ordered Moylan not to draw further without his concurrence. See Diary, April 16, May 18 and 27, and June 14, and RM to the Clothier General, May 17, 1782.

11. One of the British flagships which had recently brought American prisoners to Philadelphia. See notes to Diary, August 13.

12. Letter not found.

To the President of Congress
(John Hanson)

Marine Office 3 Sepr. 1782[1]

Sir

There is a Matter which I wish to submit to the Consideration of Congress but it is of such a Nature that I would avoid writing. I therefore pray to confer with such Committee as it may be thought proper to appoint for the Purpose of conferring with the Superintendant of Finance as Agent of Marine. Should it not be inconvenient I could wish the Conference to take Place very speedily. With Perfect Respect I have the Honor to be Sir your Excellency's most obedient and humble Servant

Robt Morris

His Excellency the President of Congress

ENDORSED: This the Origin of the/Gift of the America to/his Most Christ. Maj./The Motion was made by/Mr Osgood/Mr Rutledge/Mr Madison/1782
MSS: LS, City Collection, PPIn; AM LbC, MdAN.
1. This letter dealt with the gift of the *America* to France (see Diary, September 3, and notes to John Paul Jones to Gouverneur Morris, September 2). Except for RM's signature, the text is entirely in Gouverneur Morris's hand.

To the Governor of Connecticut
(Jonathan Trumbull)

Office of Finance 3d September 1782

Sir,

I have received your Excellency's Letter of the Twenty third of August.[1] I hope we shall soon feel some Benefits from the Taxes of your State, more especially as One of them has been due so long since as the first of April last. I do assure you, Sir, the Affairs of America are brought into a most critical Situation by the Delays and Neglects which have happened in Taxation: so much so, that the boldest Man would not answer for the Consequences. That Circumstances of the most alarming Nature have not already happened must be considered as a Kind of Miracle.

I enclose for your Perusal the Copy of a Letter to Mr Mumford.[2] You will perceive that I have provided him the Means of paying for the Provisions bought of the State. I am, Sir, respectfully Your Excellency's most obedient and humble Servant.

Robt Morris

His Excellency Governor Trumbull

MSS: LS, Trumbull Papers, Ct; Ofcl LbC, DLC.

1. This letter has not been found, but extracts are quoted in RM to Thomas Mumford, September 2.

2. See the preceding note.

To Hezekiah Merrill

Office of Finance 3. Septr. 1782

Sir,

I have received your Letter of the twenty sixth of August.[1] I am very sorry to hear that you receive so little. By the Governor's Letters[2] I am taught to expect much; it would be very distressing to be disappointed as I place great Reliance on his Assurances. I am sorry too that you did not send on what little you had received. In future I must request that if it be but twenty Dollars you would send them. It will be unnecessary to exchange one Species of Notes for another and as it may involve Intricacies and create Observation I could wish it were avoided. I am Sir very respectfully your most obedient Servant

RM

MS: Ofcl LbC, DLC.

1. Letter not found. Merrill was the receiver of Continental taxes for Connecticut; for his first payment, see notes to RM to Merrill, August 13.

2. See, for example, Governor Jonathan Trumbull as quoted in RM to Thomas Mumford, September 2.

To the Governor of Rhode Island (William Greene)

Office of Finance September 3d. 1782

Sir

I learnt Yesterday by Accident that the several Restrictions in the Impost Laws of the different States have been forwarded to your Legislature and that they have been informed that Georgia has not acceeded to the Recommendation.[1] I write this short Letter to observe that it was not expected the States of South Carolina and Georgia would pass the necessary Laws because of their distracted Situation, but yet South Carolina has passed it, and Georgia has probably followed her Example by this Time.[2] As to the Restrictions[3] depend on it that no Law will be considered as a Compliance with the Requisition which contains Clauses contrary to the Spirit of it. Such Clauses have already been in one Instance objected to on the Part of Congress not without Success.[4] I am Sir respectfully your Excellency's most obedient and most humble Servant

Robt Morris

His Excellency The Governor of Rhode Island

MSS: LS, R-Ar; Ofcl LbC, DLC.

1. This information was conveyed in a letter from David Howell, a Rhode Island delegate, to Governor Greene of July 30, 1782 (Staples, *Rhode Island in the Continental Congress*, 381–382). RM may have learned this from Howell himself on September 2, but the Diary entry for that date recording his visit does not mention the impost.

2. In a letter of August 2 RM had told Governor Greene that all the states but Rhode Island had ratified the impost. Contrary to RM's prediction about Georgia, however, that state did not approve the impost of 1781. For the two southernmost states, from which RM had requested compliance, see RM's Circular to the Governors of South Carolina and Georgia, December 6, 1781, and notes.

3. This word is singular in the Ofcl LbC.

4. RM probably refers to Connecticut, whose original act of ratification limited the duration of the impost to three years after the war. Following a request by Congress that the law be revised, Connecticut again ratified the impost during the session of May–June 1782, omitting the objectionable restriction. See the headnote to RM's Circular to the Governors of Massachusetts, Rhode Island, New York, Delaware, Maryland, and North Carolina, July 27, 1781; Main, *Antifederalists*, 90; Hoadly and Labaree, eds., *Public Records of Connecticut*, IV, 153–154.

To the Comptroller of the Treasury (James Milligan)

Office of Finance 3. Septr. 1782

Sir

I have entered into an Agreement with Mr. Sands in Consequence of which I am to request that the Accounts both for West Point and the Moving Army may be settled at ten pence per Ration subject to a Deduction of one half penny per Ration for all such as shall appear to have been delivered at West point and its Dependencies, excepting those to the Hospitals.[1] I am Sir your most obedient Servant

RM

MSS: Ofcl LbC, DLC; copy, Washington Papers, DLC.

1. For the antecedents to this letter, see the Proposals from Comfort Sands and Company, printed under September 2, and notes.

To Daniel Clark

Office of Finance 3 Sepr. 1782

Your Letters of the twenty third Ultimo have been received[1] and in your next I expect the receipt for the Tobacco. I suppose the Ship New York is sailed and expect soon to hear of her arrival. Mr. Eddy will write you the needful respecting the Fame. He has seen your Letters[2] and wishes to have her detained until he sends further Instructions.

MS: Ofcl LbC, DLC.

1. The letters have not been found. Clark was RM's agent for purchasing tobacco in Virginia.

2. See Diary, September 3.

To Bernard Dougherty

Office of Finance 3. Sept. 1782[1]

I have received your two several Letters[2] and am to request that you will apply on the Subject of them to the Secretary at War. If he thinks it proper that Issues of Provisions should be made by you in future he will give the proper Instructions and such as may be delivered agreably to those Instructions shall be paid for.

The Accounts for Supplies furnished attended with proper Vouchers must be sent to the Office of the Comptroller of the Treasury. Should he find any monies due to you by the United States he will Certify it to me and I will make Provision for the Payment.

MS: Ofcl LbC, DLC.

1. Dougherty was a Republican member of the Pennsylvania Assembly from Bedford County who had previously been authorized to supply state forces operating on the frontier there. In September 1782 he was directed to furnish rations to militia ordered to Fort Pitt from York and Cumberland counties in connection with a proposed expedition into the Indian country (see Diary, September 7, and notes). This letter to Dougherty suggests that he also provided provisions for Continental troops in the western part of the state. See Brunhouse, *Counter-Revolution in Pennsylvania*, 54, 59, 106; *Colonial Records of Pennsylvania*, X, 531–532, 593, XIII, 101, 128–129, 374, 446, 594, XIV, 181, 200, 507.

2. Dougherty's letters have not been found.

To Richard James

Office of Finance 3 Septr. 1782

I have received your Letter dated on the twenty second of last Month.[1] Your Draft on me in favor of Mr. William Renald [Ronald] for two hundred and fifty Dollars shall be paid. I wrote you on the twenty seventh Ultimo and sent therewith two thousand Dollars in my Drafts on Mr. John Swanwick payable sixty days from the Date, which was something more than the Amount of your issues to the last of July. I must beg leave to refer you to that Letter for Particulars. I desire you will continue to be Regular in your Supplies and in forwarding Accounts thereof hither with the proper Vouchers, and you will find due Attention will be paid to that Part of the Public Business.

MS: Ofcl LbC, DLC.

1. Letter not found. James held the contract for supplying Continental troops at Cumberland Old Court House, Virginia. Instructions for the delivery of this letter to him are in RM to the Postmaster General, September 3.

Joseph Pennell to Thomas Mumford

Marine Office
Philada: 3rd. Sept. 1782

Inclosed you have Mr Shuball Breeds Receipt for Nine thousand Dollars which I have paid him this Day on your Account by order of the Honble Robert Morris Esquire Agent of Marine which Sum agreeable to his Receipt he is to deliver to you and I have in conformity charged you therewith.[1]

MS: ALS, Miscellaneous Manuscripts, CtHi.

1. Pennell was the paymaster of the Marine Department. This letter to Mumford, a Connecticut merchant, was addressed "Thomas Mumford Esqr./per Favour Mr Breed} Norwich." According to the endorsement, presumably in Mumford's hand, the $9,000 was paid "in Mr. Morriss notes."

To the Postmaster General
(Ebenezer Hazard)

Office of Finance 3 Septem: 1782

I request you will be pleased to recommend the Letter directed for Mr. Richard James,[1] to the particular Care of the Post Master at Richmond and desire him to forward it immediately; and in Case no safe Conveyance offers that he will forward it by Express.

MS: Ofcl LbC, DLC.
    1. Dated September 3.

To Silas Talbot

Marine Office 3d September 1782

I have received enclosed from Mr. Russell your Letter of the Eleventh of August.[1] You shall hear from me more fully on the Subject of it.[2] At present I recommend it to you to keep the Contents of your Letter to me secret for Reasons which you will easily comprehend.

MSS: LS, CtMyMHi; AM LbC, MdAN.
    1. Neither the letter of Talbot, a captain in the Continental navy, nor the letter from Thomas Russell, the deputy agent of marine for New England, have been found. Whether the subject of Talbot's communication was a desire for an active command—see the Diary of September 2 for David Howell's recommendation on his behalf—or was related to the investigation of Captain Samuel Nicholson's conduct, one of several naval courts now underway in Boston, can only be conjectured.
    2. A further reply from RM has not been found. The present brief letter was addressed to Talbot at Boston.

Diary: September 4, 1782

Mr. John Darragh applying with a Letter from Colo. Ephram Blaine late Commissary General.[1] I desired him to go for Colo. Blaine which he did and they jointly represent that this Gentleman Mr Darragh has on hand a Quantity of Flour belonging to the United States, that his Account is for Cost of Wheat, of Grinding, Storage, Halling &c. I desired he may bring up the Flour directly and I will order payment of his balance when the flour is received.[2]

Mr. Dering Contractor at Lancaster for Money. I promise him Money to morrow 1,000 Dollars at least.

Mr. Wheeler for Money. I desired him to leave his Claim with Mr McCall Secretary in this Office and I will enable the discharge of his notes in the Bank when due.

Mr Geo. Henry for Money lent me. I desired Mr Swanwick to repay it.

I sent to the Honble. Mr Gilman and told him I should send a Person to purchase Beef Cattle in New Hampshire with my Notes[3] and requested that he will write to the Governor desiring every aid and facility may be given to his operations which Mr Gilman promised to do.[4]

Colo. Nichs. Lutz Contractor for Reading. I promised him 800 Dollars to morrow.

Messrs. Wadsworth and Carter called at the Office by appointment. They inform me of their desire to promote the Service of the United States in the transaction of their business as Agents to the French Army and indecd I have already experienced some assistance from them. I proposed that they shall send a Person to New Hampshire to bring Beef Cattle for the French Army and that the purchase be made with my Notes on Mr Swanwick so as to enable me to recover the Taxes of that State. To this they agreed and I gave them Drafts on Mr. Swanwick to the Amount of 12,000 Dollars for which they are to pay me Money as fast as they use them and if not used to return the Notes—see their receipt &c.[5]

This Day I wrote to his Excellency the Minister of France enclosing the Act of Congress respecting the Ship America and afterwards waited on him to inform that I should order the Ship to be launched and delivered to his Order at Portsmouth.[6] His Excellency seemed much pleased at this Mark of Attention to his King but said he would not by his acknowlegements anticipate the King's Declarations on this Subject.

Mr. Ebr. Cowell wrote me a Letter on behalf of himself and others[7] to whom Mr. Hodgdon Commy. of Military Stores is indebted and as I see these Peoples necessities are too urgent to permit their Waiting for money I sent for Mr. Hodgdon and proposed paying him one fourth of their Demands monthly in orders on Mr Swanwick until finally paid—to which he agreed.

Wrote a Letter to James Lovel Esqr.

Wrote to his Excelly. the Minister of France.

Issued a Warrant on Mr Swanwick in favor John
Pierce   £168.15.0

Issued a Warrant on Mr Swanwick in favor John
Pierce   37.10.0

Issued a Warrant on Mr Swanwick in favor Nichs
Lutz   64.16.4½

1. Blaine's letter has not been found.

2. See Diary, September 18.

3. For the background to this plan, see Diary, September 3, and notes. For RM's effort to execute it, see below in this Diary at note 5.

4. A letter on this subject from Gilman to President Meshech Weare of New Hampshire has not been found.

5. The receipt has not been found. After Wadsworth and Carter learned that the cattle previously delivered to the Moving Army contractors was of poor quality, they declined to purchase from the state and returned the $12,000 in notes RM had given them. See RM to William Whipple, October 9, and Diary, November 16, 1782.

6. See notes to John Paul Jones to Gouverneur Morris, September 2.

7. Letter not found. For an earlier request, see Diary, July 29, and notes.

To Francis Gurney, John Patton, and William Allibone

Marine Office 4. Septem: 1782

Gentlemen

The honorable and confidential Appointment you hold under the State of Pennsylvania induces me to desire you will fitt out the Ship Washington which I lately purchased from you.[1] This Vessel is intended for the Present as a Packet to Europe.[2] She is therefore to carry eight Guns and forty Men Officers included,[3] four Guns more may be put in the hold to be used in a Case of Emergency, and she is to have six Months Provisions. Any particular Directions in a Business you are so well acquainted with would be more than superfluous. It is not from any Doubts in my mind but a general Compliance with my Duty that I recommend as rigid Occonomy as may consist with the good of the Service. I am Gentlemen very respectfully your most obedient Servant

RM

MS: AM LbC, MdAN.

1. The recipients were the Pennsylvania commissioners for the defense of the River Delaware. For the purchase of the *General Washington*, see Diary, September 2, and notes.

2. See Diary, August 26, and notes.

3. RM modified his orders with regard to the crew in a letter to the commissioners of September 12.

To John Paul Jones

Marine Office 4. Septem: 1782

Dear Sir

The enclosed Resolution will shew you the Destination of the Ship America.[1] Nothing could be more pleasing to me than this Disposition excepting so far as you are affected by it. I know you so well as to be convinced that it must give you great Pain and I sincerely sympathize with you. But altho you will undergo much Concern at being deprived of this Opportunity to reap Laurels on your favorite Field yet your regard for France will in some Measure alleviate it and to this your good Sense will naturally add the Delays which must have happened in fitting this Ship for Sea and the Improbability of getting her manned even after she was fitted. I must entreat of you to continue your Inspection until she is launched and to urge forward the Business. When that is done if you will come hither I will explain to you the Reasons which led to this Measure and my Views for employing you in the Service of your Country. You will on your

Route have an Opportunity of conferring with the General on the Plan you mentioned to me in one of your Letters.[2] I pray you to beleive me with the most sincere Esteem and respect your affectionate Friend and obedient Servant

RM

MSS: AM LbC, MdAN; copy from "Extrait du Journal des mes Campagnes," Jones Papers, DLC.

1. The reference is to the resolution of Congress of September 3 making a gift of the *America* to France. For a discussion, see notes to Jones to Gouverneur Morris, September 2.

2. The letter in question has not been found. Whether it related to a plan—later said by Jones to have originated with RM and Chevalier de La Luzerne, the French minister—to acquire the *South Carolina* (formerly the *Indien*) from Alexander Gillon of the South Carolina navy for Jones to command at the head of an expeditionary force against Bermuda, can only be conjectured. Although the plan derives a degree of plausibility from the Superintendent's initial interest in purchasing the *South Carolina* (see Diary, May 3, 1782, and notes), and from Washington's comments about the same time on the advantages to be gained by a Bermuda expedition (Memorandum, May 1, 1782, Fitzpatrick, ed., *Writings of Washington*, XXIV, 203–204, 215), there is not a single reference to it in RM's papers. John Brown, RM's assistant in the Marine Office, later advised Jones that his good standing in RM's opinion might yet secure him "command of A Capital Ship yet this fall—however when more certain I shall be more explicit." Nothing further has been ascertained on this subject, but it is conceivable that RM may have been planning to give Jones the command of one of the large naval ships modeled on the *South Carolina* he had recently sought authorization from Congress to construct (see RM to the President of Congress, July 30, and notes). See Gawalt, ed., *John Paul Jones' Memoir*, 63–64; Morison, *John Paul Jones*, 330–331; John Brown to Jones, October 1, 1782, Jones Papers, DLC (summarized in Lincoln, comp., *Calendar of Jones Manuscripts*, 183). For RM's relations with Gillon, see Diary. September 19, and notes.

To Chevalier de La Luzerne

Marine Office
Septr. 4th. 1782

Sir

In conformity to the enclosed Act, of the 3d Instant, I have the honour to present to you the America, a Seventy Four Gun Ship, in the name of the United States for the Service of His most Christian Majesty.[1] On their part, I pray your Excellency's acceptance of that Ship. Let me at the same time indulge myself in assuring you of the pleasure I feel at being rendered an Instrument to express the gratefull affection of my Sovereign to their Royal Ally. With perfect Esteem and Respect I have the Honor to be Sir Your Excellency's most obedient and humble Servant

Robt Morris

His Excellency The Minister of France

MSS: ALS, Correspondance politique, supplément, Etats-Unis, AMAE; AM LbC, MdAN.

1. See Diary, September 4, and notes.

To John Langdon

Marine Office 4. Septemr. 1782

Sir,

By the Act of Congress of which I enclose a Copy the America is given to the King of France.[1] I am therefore to desire that not a moment may be Lost in putting her into the Water. You will then deliver to such Person as Monsr. de Vaudreuille shall appoint. I mean that she should be launched at the Expence of the United States and I hope Matters may be in such Train that many Days will not have elapsed before that Event takes Place. I am Sir with great Respect your most obedient Servant

RM

ms: AM LbC, MdAN.

1. See notes to John Paul Jones to Gouverneur Morris, September 2. Langdon was overseeing the construction of the *America* at Portsmouth, New Hampshire.

To Thomas Russell

Marine Office 4. Septem: 1782

Sir,

I have received your Letter of the 19th. of the last Month with the Proceedings of a Court Martial held for the Trial of Lieut. Delleway[1] the Sentence of which Court I have confirmed as you will find by the inclosed Paper[2] which you will please to communicate to whom it may Concern. I shall be well satisfied if the Court sitting on Capt: Nicholson's Case conclude that Matter speedily.[3]

I thank you for what you have communicated respecting the French seventy four Gun ship and am very sorry for that Accident. Congress have determined to repair that Loss to his most Christian Majesty in some Degree by presenting the America now on the Stocks at Portsmouth.[4] I am Sir your most obedient Servant

RM

ms: AM LbC, MdAN.

1. The letter and enclosed "Proceedings" have not been found. Russell was the deputy agent of marine for New England at Boston.

2. Dated September 4.

3. On this case, see Samuel Nicholson to RM, July 24, and notes.

4. For the wreck of the *Magnifique* and the gift of the *America* to France, see notes to John Paul Jones to Gouverneur Morris, September 2.

From George Washington

Head Quarters Verplanks Point [New York] 4th: Sept. 1782

Dear Sir

Previous to the meeting of our Commissioners, who will be Majors General Heath and Knox, I am under the necessity of applying to you to provide the means of their support while they are upon the Commission. I shall propose Orange town as the place of meeting.[1] I should suppose five hundred Dollars, and that in Specie (as they will be in a part of the Country where paper will not be negotiable) will be as little as can be calculated upon, as they can derive no assistance from public Stores. The time of meeting will be in ten days from hence at farthest. I shall therefore be much obliged to you for furnishing the above sum before that period— indeed it will be indispensable, as our Gentlemen cannot possibly proceed without it.

I have the honor to be with very great Respect and Esteem Dear Sir Your most obedient and humble Servant

P.S.[2] I forward a packet by Mr. Wells which I received from Mr. Lovell.[3]

The sum of Money brought out by Mr. Wells is so short of your expectation, and that in Gold, that I have thought it most advisable to send it forward by him. It would not answer the payments you directed and I did not look upon myself at liberty to average them.[4]

Honble. Mr. Morris
Superintendant of Finance

ENDORSED: 4th: September 1782/to/Honble. Mr. Morris/to supply Commissioners with/Money
MSS: Dft in the writing of Tench Tilghman, Washington Papers, DLC; Varick transcript, Washington Papers, DLC.
    1. On the meeting of the American and British negotiators at Orange Town (also known as Tappan), New York, to resolve differences with respect to the exchange of prisoners, see notes to Diary, June 18, 1782.
    2. The postscript originally written here by Tilghman, but then crossed out, is as follows: "I have received a packet from Mr. Lovell to you, said to contain Remittances in paper. I shall send it forward by the first Express or good private opportunity not chusing to trust it by the post."
    3. See Fitzpatrick, ed., *Writings of Washington*, XXV, 123n.
    4. For the effort to have Richard Wells obtain specie in New York City, see RM to Washington, August 13, and notes.

From George Washington

Head Quarters 4th: September 1782

Dear Sir

I am under the necessity of enclosing you the Copy of a letter I have this day received from Mr. Walter Livingston, with that of one from him to Mr. Richardson Sands.[1] From these you will perceive to how precarious a situation we are reduced in regard to the Article of Flour. The Quantity for which Mr. Livingston calls upon Mr. Richardson Sands is so very trifling, that it is scarcely worth attention, and I clearly foresee, that if some of the Gentlemen, concerned in the Contract besides the Mr. Sands's, do not interfere, the Army will shortly be out of Bread. In my opinion, except you are convinced that some of the Contractors besides the Sands's, will undertake to procure the Flour, you had best direct the purchase yourself.

The Contractors seem long since to have dropt the Idea of issuing Rum or any kind of Spirit. You will see by Mr. Livingstons letter that he had purchased 53 Teirces of French Rum, but that there were no other prospects. The Army are now going upon a very heavy fatigue—that of cutting six thousand Cords of Wood for the Winter firing of West Point. The Soldiers already complain of the stoppage of their Rum when only upon common duties. With how much more reason will they do it, when it will become really essential to carry them thro the hard service upon which they will be put.

It gives me pain to be so often under the necessity of applying to you upon matters with which in reality you ought never to be troubled, but as I can scarcely ever lay my Eyes upon any of the acting Contractors, I am obliged to make our distresses known in time, that you, having the staff in your hands, may apply the remedy and make the stoppages accordingly. I would beg your attention to the Article of Rum as well as Flour. Vinegar, an almost equally essential Article, is hardly ever issued, or if it be, it is of so vile a quality, that it is not much better than sour Water.[2] In short, I must say, that Mr Sands's whole conduct too plainly indicates an intention to make every thing to himself at the expence of the Army and the public. I am with every Sentiment of Regard Dear Sir Your most obedient and humble Servant[3]

ENDORSED: 4th: September 1782/to Honble. Mr. Morris/Account of the precarious state/of supplies/by Express—McClintock.
MSS: Dft in the writing of Tench Tilghman, Washington Papers, DLC; Varick transcript, Washington Papers, DLC.

1. Livingston's communication to Sands (see below in this note) has not been found, but his letter to Washington of September 3 (Washington Papers, DLC) was a reply to the general's request for information as to the contractors' magazines. After enumerating the foodstuffs already stored and those soon to arrive at Kings Ferry, Livingston assured Washington that more beef was readily available, but that only a twelve-day supply of flour had been laid in, and, further, that little flour was to be had in New York and none in New Jersey. The only possible source was Philadelphia, and Livingston asked Washington to forward by express his letter directing Richardson Sands to buy 500 barrels, six days' supply, there and send it to Morristown, New Jersey. "If Mr. Morris will furnish him with Money or Credit it can be done," Livingston explained, "otherwise it will be out of his power." Meanwhile, Livingston continued, the contractors would buy what flour they could in New York "in full Confidence of receiving a Supply of Cash from Mr. Morris."

2. For the medical ideas underlying the belief in the need to provide vinegar and rum to the army, see Benjamin Rush's "To the Officers in the Army of the United States: Directions for Preserving the Health of Soldiers," April 22, 1777, in Butterfield, ed., *Rush Letters*, I, 142–143; and Nathanael Greene to Washington, May 25, 1777, in Showman, ed., *Greene Papers*, II, 92–93n. See also Washington to RM, October 31, RM to Washington, and Greene to RM, both December 19, 1782, and RM to Greene, January 20, 1783.

3. RM received this letter on the evening of September 8. See RM to Washington, September 9 (first letter).

Confirmation of Court-Martial Proceedings for the Trial of Arthur Dillaway

[Marine Office, September 4, 1782][1]

The Agent of Marine of the United States of America, having read and duly considered the Proceedings of a Court martial for the Trial of Lieut. Arthur Delleway begun and held on Board the Continental frigate Deane in the harbor of Boston on the eighth day of August Anno Domini 1782 does hereby approve and confirm their Sentence whereby Lieutenant Delleway is acquitted with the highest honor.

Given at the Marine Office in Philadelphia the fourth day of September 1782.

MS: AM LbC, MdAN.
1. This document was enclosed in RM to Thomas Russell, September 4. The warrant for Dillaway's trial is printed under June 26, 1782.

To James Lovell

Office of Finance 4. Septr. 1782[1]

These serves to advise of my having drawn on you this day a Sett of Bills of Exchange in favor of Mr. William Chace or Order at twenty days sight for fifteen hundred Dollars being for a like Sum deposited in my Hands by him which I request may be duly honored.

MS: Ofcl LbC, DLC.
1. Lovell was the receiver of Continental taxes for Massachusetts.

Diary: September 5, 1782

I sent for Mr Haym Solomon to consult respecting the sale of Bills and find the French Agents continue to undersell me therefore must wait.

Signed a Warrant for 100 Dollars for Mr Dering. Also one for 800 Dollars for Mr Lutz.[1]

Mr Wadsworth and Mr Carter called, I pressed them to send immediately to New Hampshire after Cattle[2]—and to keep up Exchange.

Received a Letter from Mr Raguet[3] and appointed half after six to meet him.

Major Jackson called by desire of the Secretary at War to shew me two Letters from General Hazen at Lancaster proposing to hire out the German Prisoners to Work and give my Opinion in favor of the Proposition.[4]

Mr. Fitzsimmons came from the Bank with a State of the Cash and to urge me to make them some payments which I promised soon as possible.[5]

Mr. Cumberland Dugan[6] wanted a Bill on Boston, I offered at twenty Days sight, he insisted on Ten and we parted.

Mr. Claudius P Raguet came this Evening and proposed to me the taking of a Ship which is now on the Stocks near ready to Launch at

Kensington, for a Packet in the public Service or for any other Purpose so that he may be enabled to discharge his Note. I told him that such a Ship is not wanted for the public Service that I know of. He pressed me much to assist him and seems very desirous to pay his Debt. We are to meet again to Morrow Evening.[7]

Wrote a Letter to Brigr. General Irvine.

Wrote a Letter to Thomas Tillotson Esqr.

Wrote a Letter to Colo. Pickering.

Wrote a Letter to Peter Whiteside Esqr.

Wrote a Letter to His Excellency the Governor of North Carolina.

1. Dering and Lutz were contractors for Lancaster and Reading, Pennsylvania, respectively.

2. See Diary, September 4.

3. Letter not found.

4. The letters of Brigadier General Moses Hazen, who commanded the troops guarding the prisoners at Lancaster, York, and Reading, Pennsylvania, have not been found. For a discussion of the treatment of German prisoners, see notes to Diary, May 1, 1782.

5. See Diary, September 3.

6. Dugan was an Irish-born merchant who had moved from Boston to Baltimore in 1771. J. Thomas Scharf, *The Chronicles of Baltimore* (Baltimore, 1874), 70, 267, 294.

7. See notes to Diary, September 2.

To William Irvine

Office of Finance 5th September 1782

Sir,

I have received your several Letters of the Fifth of July and twenty second and twenty third of August.[1] I had intended answering the first by Mr Wilson, who brought it, but I was about the Time of his setting off incapacitated from doing it. I am very sorry to find the State of the Country you are in to be such as you represent it; but I am convinced that your Representations are just, and require the serious Attention of Government. Mr. Parkinson's Accounts are in the Hands of the proper Officers, and will be duly attended to.[2] I am very much obliged by your Attention to the public Business and Interests. I am persuaded that it has been very great and useful. I know not as yet what Determinations will be taken with Respect to the Savages in your Quarter; but I hope that no more Militia will be found necessary, for they create a very great Expence, answer very little Purpose, and what agravates the Matter still more, is the Consideration that after all, many of the Inhabitants of that Country, as we are lately informed, only wait a favourable Moment to disown the Government they now sue to for Protection.[3]

With real Esteem I am, Sir, Your Most obedient and humble Servant

Robt Morris

General Irvine
Fort Pitt

MSS: LS, Irvine Papers, PHi; Ofcl LbC, DLC.
1. The August 22 letter from Brigadier General Irvine, commander at Fort Pitt, has not been found.
2. See Diary, September 6.
3. On the proposed expedition against the Indians in western Pennsylvania, see Diary, September 7, and notes.

To John Langdon

Marine Office 5 Septem: 1782[1]

Sir,

I wrote to you Yesterday on the late disposition of the Ship America but being then hurried I only desired in general Terms that she might be launched and delivered to the Officer appointed to receive her. I am now to acknowlege your Letter of the 19 of August.[2] I presume that Mr. Storer has before this Time got forward with the Notes in your favor. I make no Doubt but that these Notes will answer every necessary Purpose for putting this Ship in the Water complete. You will observe Sir that it is the Design of Congress she should replace that lately lost in Boston Harbor. Mr. De Vaudreul will I presume make every Effort in his Power to fit her for Sea and as the Materials can I suppose be easily collected and carried round from the King's Stores at Boston I should hope that this Vessel might be ready for sea in a very short space of Time. I am sure that you will exert yourself on the present Occasion which it is my Duty most earnestly to recommend to you. Mr. Russell and Mr. Lovell at Boston will facilitate you as far as lies in their Power and so will Mr. Whipple. I wish you every possible Success and am Sir your most obedient and humble Servant

RM

MS: AM LbC, MdAN.
1. Langdon was overseeing the completion of the Continental ship *America* at Portsmouth, New Hampshire.
2. Letter not found.

To the Governor of North Carolina (Alexander Martin)

Office of Finance 5 Sepr. 1782

Sir,

I have been duly honored with your Excellency's Favor of the third of July last; I should have answered it sooner but no proper Conveyance offered speedily and the Delay at first placed it among Papers which I had not Time afterwards to take up. I am very happy to find your Excellency so thoroughly impressed with the honest Solicitude of doing what is right with the old continental Paper and with Relation to the public Debts. I have much Reliance on the public Spirit of your State and hope that in Proportion as the Rays of Prosperity beam forth it may shine more brightly. As to the several Certificates for Things taken to the Use of the United States your Excellency will have observed that Congress have made Provisions for adjusting them in the general Plan for Settlement of Accounts.[1] I have to add that the Revenues for funding those Debts when ascertained are now under Consideration.[2] Should the Plans proposed be recommended and adopted I have little Doubt but that all those would at a small Expence to the People be converted into a very valuable Property.

It is now a considerable Time since Mr Parker of South Carolina carried forward a number of Notes issued for the Purpose of collecting more easily the Taxes of your State. These were accompanied with a Letter to Mr. Burke as Governor requesting him to appoint a Receiver of Taxes for the State in my Name[3] I have heard Nothing on the Subject since and shall be extremely Glad of any Information your Excellency may be able to obtain and think proper to transmit. If no Steps have been taken to carry the Plan proposed into Execution hitherto I should presume that under present Circumstances it will be unnecessary. With perfect Respect I have the Honor to be Sir Your Excellency's most obedient Servant

RM

MSS: Ofcl LbC, DLC; LbC, Letterbook of Alexander Martin, 1782–1785, Nc-Ar.
1. Commissioners appointed under the act of February 20, 1782, to settle individual and state accounts with the United States were authorized to liquidate certificates given by the Quartermaster and Commissary Departments for supplies furnished to the army and issue final settlement certificates therefor. See RM to the President of Congress, December 10, 1781, and notes.
2. See RM to the President of Congress, July 29, and notes.
3. See RM to the Governor of North Carolina, April 26, 1782, and notes.

To the Quartermaster General (Timothy Pickering)

Office of Finance 5th September 1782

Sir

I have received your Letter of the twenty fourth of August and lament the Distresses which excited those feelings under which it was written. I am much obliged by the Information you have given me and shall always be glad to receive it. Every State in the Union is far too lax and languid Connecticut is exemplarily so, Yet they have like all others no Sort of Objection to boast of their own Exertions. I am Sir, very respectfully your most obedient Servant

Robt Morris

Colo. Pickering Qr Mr General

ENDORSED: Robert Morris Esqr. S. F./Septr. 5. 1782./received 15th—in answer to/mine of the 24th of August/Connecticut exemplarily/Languid in her collection of/Taxes.
MSS: LS, Manuscript File, WDC, DNA; Ofcl LbC, DLC.

To Thomas Tillotson

Office of Finance 5 Sepr. 1782
Colo. Hamilton having resigned the Office of Receiver for your State I take the Liberty to make you an Offer of it.[1] Colo. Hamilton will be able and willing to give you every necessary Information as to the Duties and Emoluments of that Office. I shall be happy to hear from you as soon as may be convenient and am Sir your most obedient and humble Servant

MS: Ofcl LbC, DLC.
1. See RM to Alexander Hamilton, August 28, and notes.

To Peter Whiteside

Office of Finance 5 Septr. 1782[1]
I request that you will Order from Baltimore to this Place nine Casks of french Indigo which arrived from Cape Francois in your Ship Audacious Capt. Robertson on Account of the United States. They were shipped by Monsr La Vaud and are wanted here at this Time, therefore the sooner they arrive the better.

MS: Ofcl LbC, DLC.
1. Whiteside was a Philadelphia merchant and a partner of RM's in the firm of Peter Whiteside and Company.

From Matthew Ridley

Paris Septemr. 5th: 1782[1]
This will I hope be delivered you by Mr. Wright son of Mrs. Wright of whom you have no doubt heard much. I seize with pleasure this opportunity of Mr. Wright as he has frequently seen the children and will be able to give you a good account of them. He tells me he has taken the Boys Profiles for Mrs. Morris: that they are but roughly done as he was hurried but are good likenesses. They are both hearty.

I write you in great haste and for news must refer you to Mr Wright and the Couriers de L'Europe which I have desired him to take from the Person I sent them by to Nantes and to deliver them to you.

I am without any Letters from you which rather surprizes me.[2] I cannot but think you have written and that they have miscarried. It is unlucky I am anxious about my Children and wish much for your Advice respecting them.

Mr. and Mrs. Jay are here both in health as is their little Girl. Pray let Miss Livingston know this. Present my kind respects to her and Mrs. Morris and my several Friends of your Circle. I write no one but you by this Conveyance.

Dr. F[ranklin] is ill but we hope nothing serious will happen from it. He has had a touch of the stone and since being better of that has the flying Gout. Accept my most sincere wishes for your and Mrs. Morris's good health and believe me respectfully Sir Your most Obedient and Obliged Servant

MSS: ALS, Robert Morris Papers, NN; LbC, Ridley Papers, MHi.
1. Ridley, an agent of Maryland for obtaining supplies and loans in Europe, was acting as the guardian of RM's two eldest sons, Robert, Jr., and Thomas, who were being educated on the Continent.
2. RM's last two letters to Ridley were dated July 4 and 8, 1782.

Diary: September 6, 1782

Mr. Fitzsimmons and Mr Cumberland Dugan called to purchase a Bill for 3,000 Dollars on Boston and accordingly I sold to the latter my Draft on Mr. Lovell for that Sum.[1]

Genl. St. Clair called to request a supply of money on some principle or other, but I told him I cannot on any Account go into the practice of partial payments, neither have I any Money that can be spared for pay to the Army &c. &c.

Colo. Lutz[2] bringing a Certificate of the Balance due to him I signed a Warrant for the same and ordered it to be paid in Notes, recommending him to urge the Collection of Taxes.

Mr. Henry Dering[3] applied also but says the Clerks cannot get thro' the examination of his Accounts in time wherefore I ordered a payment of 4,000 Dollars to him in Notes.

Colo. Wm Cook[4] called for his money but agreed to wait.

Lieut. Gamble[5] applied respecting two Prisoners on Parole but I told him nothing can be done in that matter until I hear from Sir Guy Carlton.[6]

Mr. Leper desired to know if I will receive of Mr Pierces Notes in discharge of his Obligation. I replied yes.

Lieut. Beaulieu applied with orders for the Subsistence due to two Officers and prayed payment because he is to receive the same for Debts the said Officers owe him. I refused this request being convinced it will if agreed to introduce evil practices in assigning such Warrants.

Mr. Parkinson for his Money[7] and finding that Nothing but Money could do for him I ordered payment.

Colo. Miles for Money. I cannot give him Money but supplied Notes for £195 to pay Waggon hire.

Mr. James Mullin applied for money for his Account. I desired to know if he is well acquainted with the Accounts between the Enemy and us for support of Prisoners of War &c:[8] he says he is and I sent him for Mr. Milligan in order to Consult him on this head but Mr. Milligan unluckily is Sick.

Capt. Philips Kollock applied to know about an Exchange of Prisoners &c.[9]

Wrote a Letter to Geo. Olney Esqr.

Wrote a Letter to Alexr. Hamilton.

Wrote a Letter to Jos. Borden.

Wrote a Letter to Nat: Appleton.
Wrote a Letter to Jno. Hopkins.
Wrote a Letter to Jno. Brown.
Wrote a Letter to Jno. Clerk [i.e., Clark].
Wrote a Letter to James Lovell.

1. See RM to James Lovell, September 6.
2. Nicholas Lutz, the contractor for Reading, Pennsylvania.
3. Dering was a contractor for Lancaster, Pennsylvania.
4. William Cooke, the contractor for Wyoming, Pennsylvania.
5. Probably James Gamble (d. 1795) of the 4th Pennsylvania Regiment. Heitman, *Register*.
6. See Carleton to RM, September 2, and notes.
7. See RM to William Irvine, September 5.
8. James Mullins formerly was a clerk in the department of the commissary general of issues. For his role in the forthcoming prisoner negotiations, see notes to Diary, June 18, 1782.
9. Phillip Kollock was one of a group of Philadelphia ship captains who petitioned Congress on June 13, 1782, to take speedy action for the exchange of American marine prisoners in New York City or for granting them relief. The petition is filed in PCC, no. 142, VI, 272–273; on the subject in general, see notes to Diary, June 18, 1782.

To George Olney

Office of Finance 6. Septr. 1782

Sir,

I have received your Letters dated at Providence on the sixteenth and nineteenth of last Month with the several Enclosures.[1] The proper official Discharge has been sent by Mr. Brown[2] for the Money he brought from you. The Plan proposed in yours of the nineteenth has my Approbation. The Legislature will be thereby informed how delinquent the State is in the Payment of its Quota and Knowing that more ample Supplies are Indispensible will I hope be induced to aid the Collection with all their Power and Influence. I am Sir your most obedient and humble Servant

RM

MS: Ofcl LbC, DLC.
1. Letters and enclosures not found. Olney was the receiver of Continental taxes for Rhode Island.
2. Jesse Brown, express rider for the Office of Finance to the northern states.

To John Wendell

Office of Finance 6. Sepr. 1782

Sir,

I am honored with your Letter dated on the twenty second of July at Portsmouth.[1] Be pleased to accept my Thanks for your good wishes and the favorable Opinion you have expressed of my Attempts to promote the public Interests in Prosecution whereof I shall always be happy to feel the Assistance of Gentlemen of Abilities and Influence.

The Ship America has lately been presented by Congress to his most Christian Majesty.[2] The Notes you mention will find their Way to New Hampshire if Credit is given to them but that Credit must be equal to Specie; If a greater Price should be demanded when payment is to be made in Notes than would be taken in Silver, they have not full Credit and consequently will continue to circulate where they are considered as of equal value with solid Coin which is the Case in most of the States. If the People with you would sell their Beef and other Produce at moderate Prices Money would soon be introduced among them for Purchasers will always Resort to the cheapest Market.

The Bank being a private Corporation has no other dependence on Government than for Repayment of Monies lent. You may be assured its Solidity is such as will support all its Operations, these become dayly more extensive and useful their Notes having acquired the fullest Confidence. I am Sir very respectfully Your most obedient Servant

RM

ms: Ofcl LbC, DLC.
    1. Letter not found. Wendell was a merchant of Portsmouth, New Hampshire, who had previously corresponded with RM.
    2. See notes to John Paul Jones to Gouverneur Morris, September 2.

From William Duer

Albany [New York] Septemr. 6th. 1782

Sir,

I do myself the honor of transmitting our accounts for the month of August; they have been ready since the first Instant but detained in order to obviate any well founded Objections which might have arisen on the Settlement of the former Accounts.[1]

The Arrival of Mr: Geary on the 5th: with only two thousand Dollars of the money due, which amounted after a final Settlement of the Accounts for four months to 8397⁴⁵⁄₉₀ Dollars has thrown me into the most Cruel perplexity.[2] Since the Commencement of the Contract the last day of each month has been fixed on for making payment on the Contract engagement. Many people were waiting in this City from different Quarters in full expectation of receiving the Amount of their Demands which I had given them full assurance of receiving in Consequence of the promises you had given Mr: Geary and which he informed me of in a Letter from Phila.[3] All of these I have been obliged to put off, and to keep the Small Sum sent to enable me to keep the Troops Supplied for the present month. The consequence is my Credit is impaired and the Confidence in public assurances which had begun to revive is again destroyed. I shall not dwell longer on a Subject painfull both to you and myself, being Confident that nothing but an Inability to perform your Public engagements, has put you to the disagreeable necessity of failing in the payments of the Months of June and July. I am no longer master of the price of any article, and scarcely in a Situation to furnish the Supplies from day to day. I am therefore bound in Justice to myself to declare that I consider myself totally freed from the Contract, which I can no longer execute on the present terms without ruin to the Concern. My anxiety for the Public Interest will Induce me to Continue my exertions to keep the Troops under the Contract from disbanding for Want of Provisions, provided I receive your Assurances on the following points. Vizt:

1st: That this Contract the most difficult in execution of any which has been made shall on a final Settlement of Accounts, be placed on as good a footing as any other Contract for the Supply of the Troops.

2d: That the monies due on the future monthly accounts shall be punctually advanced on producing the Account Current, and that I shall not be subject to the Cruel and expensive procrastination in Settlement of Accounts which I already have been.

If Sir, you think it proper to give me these assurances and transmit with the Utmost dispatch the Messenger I now Send with the monies due, which exceed Eight thousand Dollars, I will Continue as I have done my exertions to supply the Troops to their Satisfaction. And in order to accommodate you by every means in my power I will consent to receive five thousand Dollars only in Specie, provided you will advance four thousand five hundred of your own notes, with which I shall not be Chargeable 'till they are returned for payment at your office. This will make only an advance of 1400 Dollars in your notes beyond the Sum Actually due. But it is necessary I should explain myself clearly, that unless this Sum is Instantly transmitted I expect the Whole Ballance in Specie.

Such is my present Situation that I shall find the Utmost difficulty to maintain the Troops to the end of September, and if the messenger I now send does not return before that day I shall be constrained to stop the Supplies of the Troops on the first day of October. I have wrote to General Washington informing him of my Situation and of the resolution I am obliged to enter into.[4]

The only prospect I have for the support of myself and my Family is to engage in a Commercial Line in this State at the Close of the War. And if I suffer my Credit to receive the Shocks it has done from my Public engagements, it will be extremely difficult for me to retrieve it.

The Considerations I have mentioned will I doubt not Justify me in your Opinion for the determination I have been obliged to make.

The long detention of Mr: Geary has thrown my accounts so far back that it is impossible for me to send him down again; and I have no person capable of managing the business at the Auditors Office but himself; as therefore the whole Account to the end of July have been adjusted and reported on, I trust no Objection will be made in advancing the money on the Account Current agreeably to the practice in the first months of the Contract.

I shall wait with impatience the return of the Messenger, which I cannot help flattering myself will afford as much Satisfaction, as I have experienced distress for these two months past. I am Sir, with great respect &c &c[5]

Honble Robt: Morris Esqr:
Phila:

ENDORSED: Copy of a Letter to Robt Morris,/Esqr: Super Intendt: of Finances
MS: Copy, George Washington Papers, DLC.

1. The accounts enclosed by Duer, contractor for the posts north of Poughkeepsie in New York, have not been found. For the dispute between RM and the contractors over the settlement of their monthly accounts, see Comfort Sands, Walter Livingston, William Duer, and Daniel Parker to RM, September 11, and notes.

2. James Geary had spent much of August in Philadelphia attempting to obtain payment for Duer. Although he departed on August 28 with only $2,000, the next day RM sent Duer an additional $5,000 in his own notes, but his efforts to provide Washington with specie to send Duer failed. See Diary, August 12, 13, and 28, and RM to Duer, August 29, and notes.

3. This was probably Geary to Duer of August 15, 1782. See notes to Duer to RM, August 2.

4. Duer's letter to Washington of September 13 (Washington Papers, DLC), enclosing the letter to RM printed here, explained that he had since received RM's letter of August 29 indicating that Washington would provide him with $8,000 in specie beyond the $10,000 in Morris's notes remitted to him by Archibald Stewart, that he had been informed by Stewart that Washington had not yet received the promised money, and that RM's drafts "(though Useful to Anticipate ⟨Demands⟩ Supplies) will not Answer to satisfy past Engagements." Since "The Want of Exertion in the States in collecting Taxes has put it out of Mr. Morris Power to fulfill his Engagements with that Punctuality which is essential to the Execution of Contracts, Especially one at so low a Rate as the Northern Contract," Duer asked Washington to appoint someone to supply the troops beginning October 1 in case he should not receive the money and assurances to enable him to continue "without utter Ruin to myself." "I have the Satisfaction of knowing that hitherto I have been able to Execute a difficult and disadvantageous Contract, with some Degree of Reputation to myself," Duer concluded, "and if I am reduced to the Necessity of Surrendering the Contract, I can without the least Apprehension of Censure submit it to be determined by a proper Tribunal, whether the public or myself are the Defaulters." Washington found Duer's letter "really alarming." See Washington to Duer, September 18, 1782, Fitzpatrick, ed., *Writings of Washington*, XXV, 175. For the money which Washington was to have provided, see RM to Washington, August 13, and notes.

5. RM replied to Duer on October 2. For the interim, see RM to Duer, September 13, and notes.

From Daniel of St. Thomas Jenifer

Intendants Office September 6th. 1782[1]

Sir,

I have received the Letter which you did me the honor to write the 27th. Ultimo.

Your not hearing from me was neither owing to neglect of Duty or want of inclination, but from its not being in my power to afford you any agreeable information. I very sensibly feel the force of your observations and I can assure you that nothing in my power shall be wanting to prevent the fatal Consequences you apprehend.

Altho' you have not received Money immediately from the Maryland Treasury, yet very considerable Sums have been advanced by this State on Continental Account since the 1st. of January last to the 3d. of September—to wit—£45,497.19.2 Specie, $\overset{Ct}{816.2.17}$ Flour, £105,500 lbs Tobacco,[2] and 76,162 Rations allowing 1 lb pork and 1¼ lb flour to each ration—the daily Issues now are between 5 and 600. There is in the Treasury Six thousand pounds Specie Subject to your Order, and I have about One thousand pounds for the purpose of Transporting Cloathing from the Head of Elk to the Southern Army,[3] which also waits your Orders. I expect that further Sums will be daily coming in.

By a Letter I received from Capt. Middleton he desires me to lay in Forage at this place for 20 Horses purchased by this State for Colo. Lees Legion, to prepare them under his own Eye for the Journey to the Southern Army.[4] I have no directions as to this business by Law of this State or Resolution of Congress. If they are Collected to this post it is probable they will remain at it some time. The Law directs that they should be sent as soon as Collected to the Southern Army, and I wish not to be troubled with them. I am with the highest respect Sir, Your obedient humble Servant

Dan of St. Thos: Jenifer Intendt.

MS: LbC, Intendant's Letterbook, MdAA.

1. Jenifer was Maryland's intendant of the revenue.
2. Thus in manuscript. Although prefaced by a pound sign, the figure given for tobacco was probably meant to denote weight. See RM to Jenifer, September 30.
3. See Jenifer to RM, July 18, 1782, and notes.
4. John Middleton's letter has not been found. Concerning the horses, see notes to the Governor of Maryland to RM, July 12, 1782 (second letter).

From Thomas Paine

Borden Town [New Jersey], Sepr. 6th. 1782

Sir

I am enjoying the Company of my friends Col. Kirkbride[1] and Mr. Borden[2] at this place, where I purpose, (as is my yearly custom) of spending two or three weeks, unless any thing in the political world should occasion my return sooner.

As one of my principal designs in getting out my last piece[3] was to give it the chance of an European publication, which I suppose it will obtain both in France and England, I desire you to accept of 50 Copies to send to any part of Europe or the West Indies.[4] I am Sir Your Obedient Humble Servant

Thos: Paine

Honble Robt. Morris Esqr.

ADDRESSED: Honble. Robt. Morris Esquire/Philadelphia   ENDORSED: Borden Town/6 Septr 1782/Thos Paine Esqr/with 50 Copies of his/reply to Abbe Raynal
MS: ALS, Robert Morris Papers, CSmH.
1. Colonel Joseph Kirkbride III (1731–1803), originally of Bucks County, Pennsylvania. He had served in the state assembly from 1776 to 1778, his friendship with Paine apparently dating from this time. After the British burned his home in 1778, Kirkbride evidently resettled at Bordentown, New Jersey. See PMHB, II (1878), 292n.–293n., III (1879), 446.
2. Probably Joseph Borden, Jr., the Continental loan officer of New Jersey.
3. This was Paine's Letter Addressed to the Abbe Raynal on the Affairs of North-America: in which the Mistakes in the Abbe's Account of the Revolution of America are Corrected and Cleared Up (Philadelphia, 1782). See Paine to RM, November 26, 1781, and notes; and David Freeman Hawke, Paine (New York, 1974), 128–131. Gouverneur Morris had already distributed copies; see Gouverneur Morris to Richard Morris, August 28, and Daniel of St. Thomas Jenifer to Gouverneur Morris, September 6.
4. Paine also distributed 50 copies each to George Washington and Secretary for Foreign Affairs Robert R. Livingston, and made 13 dozen available to Secretary of Congress Charles Thomson. Livingston sent copies to American ministers in Europe (Wharton, ed., Rev. Dipl. Corr., V, 726, VI , 5, 114); several French editions appeared. See Hawke, Paine, 130.

To Nathaniel Appleton

Office of Finance 6. Sepr. 1782
In consequence of the Application contained in your Letter of the twenty second of last Month[1] Orders have been given to Mr. Hillegas to transmit Bills to replace those which were Lost. I hope they will get to hand in Season.[2]

MS: Ofcl LbC, DLC.
1. Letter not found. Appleton was the Continental loan officer of Massachusetts.
2. On this transaction, see Michael Hillegas to Appleton, October 21, 1782, transmitting replacement bills of exchange for John Shattuck, in Records of the Office of the Comptroller General, General Correspondence, box 1, RG 4, PHarH.

To Joseph Borden, Jr.

Office of Finance 6. Sepr. 1782
I have received your Favor of the twenty seventh of August.[1] Before the Bills can be extended Mr. Wikcoff must make Proof of the Loss and exact Copies of the Bills lost must be transmitted.

MS: Ofcl LbC, DLC.
1. Letter not found. Borden was the Continental loan officer of New Jersey. For the subject discussed in this letter to him, see Diary, September 27.

To John Brown

Office of Finance 6. Septem. 1782[1]

I enclose you a Copy of the Clerks State and Auditors Report on a certain Account of the late navy Board of Boston exhibited by you[2] to the End that you may inform the Gentlemen who were of that Board and give them an Opportunity to supply the defective Vouchers.

MS: Ofcl LbC, DLC.
1. Brown, RM's assistant in the Marine Office, had been dispatched to Boston on September 3. See Diary of that date.
2. Enclosures not found. For Brown's contentious relationship with the Navy Board of the Eastern Department, see RM to Brown, March 25, 1782, and notes.

To John Clark

Office of Finance 6. Septem. 1782

I have received your Letter of the thirtieth of August[1] and would chearfully have made the Application you desire could I consistently have done it. Enclosed you have Copy of the Clerks Observations, Auditors Report and Comptrollers Certificate on your Claim.[2] Had I transmitted your Petition[3] I must at the same Time have transmitted this Paper and that would have injured your Affairs. I therefore returned your Petition to Mr. Nicholson to dispose of according to your Directions.

MS: Ofcl LbC, DLC.
1. Letter not found.
2. These documents, all dated June 22, 1782, rejected Clark's claim for depreciation of pay as a former auditor of accounts for the main army on the grounds that it was precluded by congressional resolutions of April 10 and November 15, 1780. They and other papers relating to Clark's claim, which remained unsettled at his death, are filed in Petitions and Memorials, Resolutions of State Legislatures, and Related Documents (15A-G1), Records of the United States Senate, RG 46, DNA. See also RM to Clark, and to the Comptroller of the Treasury, both June 13, 1782; and Syrett and Cooke, eds., *Hamilton Papers*, XXVI, 731.
3. Clark's petition has not been found.

To Alexander Hamilton

Office of Finance 6th. September 1782[1]

I have received your Favor dated at Albany on the 25th of last Month, with the Enclosures. I am much obliged by your attention in the Business you allude to, and knowing that your abilities and Zeal to promote the public Good are equal to the most arduous Undertakings I have no doubt but your Endeavours will be successful.

MSS: LS, Hamilton Papers, DLC; Ofcl LbC, DLC; transcript, Francis Baylies Papers, DLC.
1. Hamilton was the receiver of Continental taxes for New York. This letter was addressed to him at Albany.

To John Hopkins, Jr.

Office of Finance 6. Septr. 1782

I have received your Favor dated at Richmond on the twenty third of last Month.[1] The Continental Money which you are possessed of must remain with you, when any further Determinations are made respecting it you shall be duly Informed thereof. I know nothing of the State Money you Mention and therefore cannot give any Advice concerning it.

MS: Ofcl LbC, DLC.
1. The letter from Hopkins, Continental loan officer of Virginia, has not been found. Concerning the Continental money mentioned in this letter to him, see RM's report to Congress of September 7, and notes.

To James Lovell

Office of Finance 6. Sep: 1782[1]

These serves to advise of my having drawn on you this Day a Sett of Bills of Exchange in favor of Mr. Cumberland Dugan or Order at twenty Days sight for three thousand Dollars being for a like sum deposited in my hands by him which I request may meet due honor.

MS: Ofcl LbC, DLC.
1. Lovell was the receiver of Continental taxes for Massachusetts. On the subject of this letter, see Diary, September 5 and 6.

To the Secretary at War
(Benjamin Lincoln)

Office of Finance 6. Septr. 1782

I do myself the honor to enclose the Extract of a Report made on Settling the Accounts of Messrs. Francis and Slough.[1] The Matters there mentioned appear deserving of attention.

MS: Ofcl LbC, DLC.
1. The enclosed Treasury report has not been found. Whether it concerned their accounts as contractors for the posts in New Jersey, which had been subsumed under the Moving Army contract in May, or as contractors for York and Carlisle, Pennsylvania, has not been determined.

Daniel of St. Thomas Jenifer to Gouverneur Morris

Annaps. [Maryland] Septr. 6th. 1782[1]

Dear Morris,

I thank you for Common Sense's Letter to the Abbe Raynal,[2] it is well wrote, and will be of Service to any person, that may hereafter Publish a History of the American War.

Your letter to Coll Plater was immediately forwarded to him.[3]

My Nephew is greatly indebted to you for the polite notice you have taken of him in your information given to a person with whom he is so intimately connected. I am with great truth your affectionate friend

Present my compliments to Mrs. Morris and Miss Livingston

MS: ALS, Gouverneur Morris Papers, NNC.
1. Jenifer was Maryland's intendant of the revenue.
2. On this work, see Thomas Paine to RM, September 6, and notes.
3. This letter was probably one of August 8 or 19, neither of which has been found. See George Plater to Gouverneur Morris, September 2.

Diary: September 7, 1782

Colo. Ephram Blaine called to inform me of the Quarrels which have arisen between Mr. Duncan and Mr. Hoofnagel respecting the execution of their Contract and adds that he is disposed to undertake the execution of it himself to which I have no objection, all I ask is that it shall be done agreeable to the Contract.[1]

Mr. James Mullin called respecting the Accounts of the Prisoners but as I wish to Consult Mr Milligan on these Accounts I referred Mr. Mullin for the present to Mr. Governeur Morris who has knowledge on the Subject obtained last Winter when a Commissioner for Prisoners &c.[2]

This Morning the Hon: General Potter Vice President of Pennsylvania and the Hon: John Bayard Esqr.[3] a Committee of the Council and Messrs. Dougherty, Montgomery, Clay, McGaw and   a Committee of the Assembly of Pennsylvania[4] waited on me respecting an Expedition or Expeditions intended to be undertaken in the Western Country against the Indians for the Protection of the Frontier Inhabitants. They brought me an Estimate of the expence which did not Amount to £5,000 Pennsylvania Currency. They desired to know whether I can answer that Expenditure and how it must be Conducted. I told them that the State of the Continental Treasury will not admit of any Expenditure whatever and that if the Expedition is undertaken Pennsylvania must in the first Instance find the Money, but if the Expedition be undertaken as Continental that State must have Credit in Account with the United States for the Amount of their Advances and in that Case that we will either employ Commissaries or Contract for the Provisions necessary and finally that I will Consult with the Secy at War on this Subject and let them know the result.[5]

John Pierce Esqr. made Application for four Months Notes for Officers and desired at a leisure time a Conference.

James Milligan Esqr. having got the better of the Fever which lately attacked him called at this Office but Mr. Mullin being gone I deferred engageing Mr. Milligan in any Business until Monday.

The President of the Bank wrote to me for 200,000 Dollars now due to that Corporation or to renew the Securities &c.[6]

Mr: Jno. Sansum Express, returned from General Greens Head Quarters in So. Carolina.

Wrote a Letter to the Commissioners for Settling Accounts.

Wrote a Letter to John Wendell.[7]

Wrote a Letter to James Lovell.

Wrote a Letter to Francis Gurney and Wm. Alibone.

1. The contract for Fort Pitt.

2. For Gouverneur Morris's service as a commissioner for prisoners, see notes to Gouverneur Morris to RM, March 22, 1782. On the question of the accounts, see George Washington to RM, September 2, and notes.

3. John Bubenheim Bayard (1738–1807), a member of the Supreme Executive Council from Philadelphia, where he was a merchant, had previously served as speaker of the state assembly. Like vice-president James Potter, he was an active constitutionalist. He supported the creation of a second bank in Pennsylvania in 1784 and was a member of Congress in 1785 and 1786. *DAB;* Brunhouse, *Counter-Revolution in Pennsylvania,* 105–107, 118–119, 150; and Burnett, ed., *Letters,* VIII, xciv.

4. The members of the assembly committee were Bernard Dougherty of Bedford County; William Montgomery of Northumberland County, a gristmill and sawmill owner; William Maclay (1734–1804) of Northumberland County; Robert Magaw (d. 1790) of Cumberland County, who had been a colonel in the Continental army; and an unidentified member for whom a space was left blank in the manuscript of the Diary. Montgomery was a constitutionalist, and Dougherty and Maclay were associated with the Republicans; Magaw's political affiliation has not been ascertained. All but Maclay (see *DAB*) and Magaw (Heitman, *Register*) have been previously identified. For the committeemen's orientation in state politics, see Brunhouse, *Counter-Revolution in Pennsylvania,* 59, 106, on Dougherty and Maclay; and Main, *Political Parties,* 435, 438, on Maclay and Montgomery.

5. The proposed expeditions against the Indians at Sandusky, Ohio, and the Genessee towns were a reaction to the renewal of brutal Tory and Indian attacks on the frontier precipitated largely by the massacre of peaceful Moravian Indians by American militiamen in March 1782 (for the gruesome details of this renewed border warfare, see Boatner, *Encyclopedia of the American Revolution,* 82, 305–308, 434, 439, 1194). Some Pennsylvania leaders, however, advocated the expeditions as a means to head off separatist movements by western settlers against Pennsylvania and the United States. On August 23 the Pennsylvania Assembly appointed a committee to meet with committees of the Supreme Executive Council and Congress on the critical state of affairs on the frontier. On the basis of a report by its committee, Congress on September 5 gave Washington discretionary authority to reassign Pennsylvania troops of the Continental line to march with the state's militia on a western campaign. Meanwhile, Potter and Magaw, representing the council and assembly respectively, discussed the expeditions with Washington. Although he did not truly favor the campaign, Washington agreed, subject to Congress's approval, to dispatch Hazen's Regiment and the current Pennsylvania recruits for the Continental army, provided other troops could relieve Hazen's men from guarding prisoners at Lancaster. But he advised Secretary at War Benjamin Lincoln that he foresaw "an insurmountable difficulty to putting the expeditions in motion, which is, a want of Money, provided it is to come out of the Continental treasury, and which I plainly perceive is their expectation ultimately if not immediately" (to Lincoln, and to President William Moore, both September 2, 1782, Fitzpatrick, ed., *Writings of Washington,* XXV, 105–107, 110–111).

As this Diary entry indicates, RM was unprepared to allocate current revenues to the expeditions, though he agreed to credit the state on account and make provisioning arrangements if the expeditions were deemed a Continental responsibility. After finding that Washington's letters had left the ultimate decision to Congress, RM recommended that Pennsylvania apply to Congress (see Diary, September 9 and 10). Having received Washington's letter, Lincoln on September 11 asked Congress whether he should order the Pennsylvania recruits to march with state troops on the frontier expeditions (see PCC, no. 149, I, 679–680). The committee reporting on Lincoln's letter suggested such an order be made contingent upon Pennsylvania's providing money; however, Congress's resolution of September 13 avoided the stipulation and merely directed Lincoln to employ the recruits or other Continental troops in the western campaign as Washington directed.

With the situation clarified by the act of Congress, RM agreed on September 16 to pay the cost of supplying the Continental troops but asked Pennsylvania to provision them along with the state forces and accept reimbursement later. The Financier also promised to provide blankets for the Continental contingents (see Diary, September 16 and 17, RM to Moore, September 19, and Moore to RM, September 20). At the last minute, however, Washington halted the expeditions before they were launched. In a letter of September 23 to President Moore, Washington disclosed that he had received a communication from Sir Guy Carleton, the British commander at New York, indicating that no further Indian assaults were contemplated. Since the frontier was now quiet and the Indians could be left "to the Direction of their British Managers, who at present seem disposed to keep them in a State of Quiet and Tranquility," Washington thought it best to suspend operations, lest "instead of giving security to the Inhabitants on the Frontiers, we should again rouse, their savage Neighbors to acts of self Defence and Revenge, in which, it is more than probable the English not considering themselves as Parties will not attempt to restrain their Rage and Fury" (Fitzpatrick, ed., *Writings of Washington*, XXV, 198–199).

Pennsylvania intended to finance the expedition out of a £5,000 loan for frontier defense obtained from the Bank of North America in September (see Diary, April 12, 1782, and notes). The state had originally sought a loan of £30,000 from the bank for this purpose in April. In the notes to Diary, March 19, 1782, the editors attributed the state's difficulty in obtaining the loan to political differences between the largely Republican bank directors and the constitutionalist-dominated Supreme Executive Council. However, more significant factors were also at work. Pennsylvania was experiencing a severe credit crisis in mid-1782, and the bank's own financial difficulties were such as to force a temporary suspension of discounting (on the bank's liquidity problems, see the headnote to RM's State of American Commerce and Plan for Protecting It, May 10, and notes, and Gouverneur Morris to Thomas Willing, June 18, 1782, and notes). Moreover, the bank's directors had several reasons to fear further public loans: RM was proving unable to repay sums borrowed from the bank on Continental account; the state had failed to make adequate payments on a treasury warrant given to RM and discounted by him at the bank; and the revenues pledged by the state for repayment of the loan originally requested were not considered adequate security either by the bank or by private lenders, given the current lax enforcement of tax collection in the state. (It is worth noting that the bank also rejected Maryland's request for a loan at this time; see RM to Daniel of St. Thomas Jenifer, July 12, 1782.) Not until September was the assembly's Ways and Means Committee able to negotiate a short-term defense loan at the bank for the reduced figure of £5,000 on the security of the state loan office revenues, which were evidently considered more certain than tax revenues. The loan, though comparatively small, was paid in specie rather than in the bank notes that RM had suggested be used in April.

Since some of the specie from the bank loan had already been delivered to Fort Pitt to finance the western campaign, now canceled, RM secured permission from Pennsylvania to apply it to Continental expenditures in that area, pledging to replace the money at Philadelphia. When the state called for repayment and the Superintendent sought to use the money instead to offset sums the state owed on Continental requisitions, the state insisted that the bank loan could be used only for frontier defense. While the exact terms of the final settlement are obscure, RM's accounts indicate that he repaid the money to the state by June 30, 1783. Competition between the state and Continental governments for scarce funds was breaking down the closely intertwined financial relationships which the Superintendent had developed with his home state, and eventually produced conflicts with Pennsylvania's fiscal officers, who were generally connected with the rival constitutionalist party.

See, in general, Brunhouse, *Counter-Revolution in Pennsylvania*, 113–115; also *Colonial Records of Pennsylvania*, XIII, 348–350, 352–357, 359; *Pennsylvania Archives*, 1st ser., IX, 629, 630, 635; and Burnett, ed., *Letters*, VI, 472. On the frontier defense loan, see Diary, October 5, 1782, and May 7 and 17, 1783, RM to Irvine, October 7, 1782, and John Nicholson to RM, March 24 and May 13, 1783; James Wilson, *Considerations on the Bank of North-America* (Philadelphia, 1785), reprinted in Robert Green McClosky, ed., *The Works of James Wilson* (Cambridge, Mass., 1967), II, 847; *Colonial Records of Pennsylvania*, XIII, 363, 370, 372; Mitchell and Flanders, eds., *Statutes at Large of Pennsylvania*, X, 533–534; Treasury Waste Book D, pp. 283–284 (March 18, 1783), Waste Book E, p. 32 (May 21, 1783), Records of the United States General

Accounting Office, RG 217, DNA; and Mathew Carey, ed., *Debates,* 105–106. For the Superintendent's financial agency for Pennsylvania, see the headnote to RM to the Speaker of the Pennsylvania Assembly, June 26, 1781; notes to Diary, July 19, 1781; and RM to the President of Pennsylvania, November 9, 1782.

6. The letter from Thomas Willing has not been found. See, on this subject, Diary, September 3 and 5.

7. This letter is dated September 6.

To the Commissioners of Accounts for the States

Office of Finance 7. Sep. 1782[1]

Sir

The Comptroller of the Treasury having given you his Instructions as to the Form of settling Accounts[2] there are two Particulars to which I will call your Attention. It has constantly been kept in View by Congress that Interest should be allowed to the States for any disproportion of Advances and this Idea is still pursued in the Ordinance under which you act. You must therefore on every Advance made by the State after fixing the value precisely allow an Interest at six per Cent until the first Day of this Year and charge a like Interest on Advances to them.[3]

In settling the Accounts with Individuals you will consider that artful Men have frequently taken Advantage of the Public and that in many Instances public Officers have taken advantage of the weak and unprotected. You will therefore always remember that it is your Duty to do Justice. In the Prosecution of this Duty you will take Care also to discover, bring to light, pursue and punish Fraud and Peculations of every Kind wherever you may meet with them. I wish you Success and am Sir your most obedient and humble Servant

RM

MSS: Ofcl LbC, DLC; copy, marked "Circular," PCC, DNA; copy in the writing of William Barber, commissioner for New York, Philip Schuyler Papers, NN; copy, Abraham Yates, Jr., Papers, NN; copy, Continental Congress Papers, Vi.

1. This was RM's first letter to the commissioners appointed to settle the accounts of the states and their citizens with the United States under the congressional ordinance of February 20, 1782 (see RM to the President of Congress, December 10, 1781, and notes). By this date the Financier had nominated commissioners only for Maryland, New Jersey, Virginia, Connecticut, and Delaware; only the first four had received the required state confirmation (see RM to William Winder, Jr., November 15, and to the President of Congress, December 3, 1782). The present letter therefore was very likely sent out seriatim as appointments were made but probably not before the detailed instructions from the Comptroller of the Treasury (see note 2 below) and queries and answers on particular points, printed under the date of October 14, had been put into final form (see RM to Lewis Pintard, November 20, 1782). Other documents made available to the commissioners as they were appointed included RM's letter to Jonathan Burrall of August 19 and the Comptroller's letter to the commissioners of October 18 prescribing the form of final settlement certificates they were to issue. (Except for Milligan's letter of October 18, RM enclosed copies of these documents, including the PCC copy of the present letter, to the president of Congress on August 26, 1783.) The commissioners were also sent copies of the journals of Congress for 1782 and received later instructions from RM under May 8 and September 4, 1783, and June 2, 1784.

From time to time Congress and the Financier enlarged the responsibilities of the commissioners of accounts for the states. On July 12, 1782, Congress had authorized them to settle the accounts of the Continental loan officers in their respective states, and on September 18 it directed them to receive and destroy the old Continental currency and send accounts of that money to the Office of Finance (see RM's reports to Congress of June 13, and notes, and September 7, 1782, and notes). With a view toward systematizing government finance, the Superintendent himself in his letter of September 4, 1783, directed the commissioners to report on the geographical, moral, political, and commercial conditions in their respective states.

The commissioners' work proved to be arduous and beset with difficulties (see, for example, RM to the President of Congress, August 12, and the documents referred to in that letter, Zephaniah Turner to RM, October 22, RM's report to Congress of November 5, and RM to Stephen Gorham, December 15, 1783). Recruiting the commissioners proved no easy task for the Superintendent, and there were several resignations. Although the settlement of individual accounts was virtually complete by 1787 (Ferguson, *Power of the Purse*, 179–186), the settlement of the Confederation's accounts with the states continued until 1793 under the Federal government (*ibid.*, 203–219, 322–324, 332–333; and Benjamin Walker to Alexander Hamilton, September 15, 1789, Syrett and Cooke, eds., *Hamilton Papers*, V, 373–376). For a companion to the present letter, see RM's Circular to the Commissioners of Accounts for the Departments, September 19.

2. Although given preliminary formulation with RM's assistance in July, James Milligan's instructions to the commissioners of accounts for the states are actually dated October 14 and are printed under that date.

3. On the question of interest paid on the Confederation's debts, see RM to the President of Congress, August 28, 1781, and notes.

Report to Congress on the Resolve of the Virginia House of Delegates Respecting Old Continental Money

[Office of Finance, September 7, 1782]

The Superintendant of Finance, to whom was referred the Resolve of the House of Delegates of Virginia of the Second of July last,[1] begs Leave to Report
The following Resolution.

That the Commissioners appointed to settle the Accounts of the several States agreably to the Act of the Twentieth of February 1782, be, and they are hereby directed to receive so much of the old Continental Money as may be in the *respective Treasuries* and to count, examine, and destroy the same. That they transmit to the Superintendant of Finance, Accounts of the Monies so destroyed. *That such Monies* shall be credited to the said States on their several Quotas fixed by the Resolutions of the eighteenth of March 1780, and where the Amount shall exceed such Quotas shall be credited to the States respectively as hard Money at the Rate of Forty for One on the Accounts previous to the first Day of January 1782.

All which is humbly submitted.[2]

Robt Morris

Office of Finance
[7] Sepr. 1782[3]

Congress began to issue Continental bills of credit in a variety of denomina-
tions in June 1775 and by the end of 1777 had issued currency in such
quantities as to lead to rapid depreciation. On March 18, 1780, Congress
officially revalued its currency at the rate of $40 paper to $1 of specie and
asked the states to withdraw these non-interest-bearing notes through taxation
at a rate of $15 million per month and replace them with new emission
currency. (Concerning the origins and decline of Continental currency, see
Ferguson, Power of the Purse, *25–33, 44–47, 51–52, 65–67; for the*
problems in liquidating it, see Morris's Report to Congress on Old Continen-
tal Currency, September 7, 1782, and notes.)

    The design of the bill shown here is typical of Continental currency issues.
On the face is an emblem containing a Latin inscription ("the outcome is in
doubt") surrounding an eagle fighting with a heron. The back of the bill
shows a nature print of elm and maple fruit in skeletonized form derived
from designs developed by Benjamin Franklin for Pennsylvania colonial
currency. A detailed, illustrated discussion of Continental currency issues
from a numismatic standpoint may be found in Eric P. Newman, The
Early Paper Money of America, *Bicentennial ed. (Racine, Wis., 1976),*
33–57. The specimen reproduced here is from the National Numismatics
Collection, no. 56830, National Museum of American History, courtesy of
the Smithsonian Institution, Washington, D.C., photo nos. 83–5633,
5634.

Continental currency: $3 bill of the emission of February 17, 1776. 3¾″ × 2⅖″

Bills of new emission currency were issued in various denominations by most of the states in accordance with the act of Congress of March 18, 1780. Each state could emit no more than one-twentieth of the amount of old Continental currency it withdrew and was required to reserve four-tenths of the new bills for the use of Congress, for which it was to receive credit in account with the Confederation. The bills were to bear 5 percent interest payable in specie or in sterling bills of exchange drawn by Congress on American funds in Europe and were to be redeemed in specie, one-sixth of the bills each year, the whole within six years (i.e., by December 31, 1786). Congress guaranteed payment of the bills if state funds proved insufficient.

Combining new engravings with border cuts and emblems from the January 14, 1779, issue of Continental currency, the design on the face of the bills is printed in black and the back in red and black. The bills were struck by the firm of Hall and Sellers of Philadelphia on paper watermarked either "UNITED STATES" or "CONFEDERATION" (in two lines) and sent to the Continental loan offices in each state. The face of each denomination varied somewhat from state to state, since each indicated the state and the date of state legislation authorizing the emission, was hand numbered, and was signed by state appointees. The back of each denomination varied only in the signatures of the congressionally appointed commissioners signing the guarantee on behalf of the United States in each state.

The Massachusetts bill depicted here was numbered by Nathaniel Appleton, Continental loan officer for the state, signed on its face for the state by Richard Cranch and Loammi Baldwin, and signed on the back for the United States by Peter Boyer. The bill is surcharged in red with the words "INTEREST PAID ONE YEAR" and watermarked "UNITED STATES." Appleton described his procedures for issuing the new emission currency in Massachusetts in a memorial to Congress of February 21, 1787, in Papers of the Continental Congress, no. 41, I, 101, Record Group 360, National Archives, Washington, D.C. For an illustrated numismatic discussion of the Massachusetts new emission bills and those issued by other states, see Eric P. Newman, The Early Paper Money of America, *Bicentennial ed. (Racine, Wis., 1976), 137, 171, 198, 216, 243, 309, 349, 398. For Morris's views on the act of March 18, 1780, see his letters to the president of Congress of August 28 and December 10, 1781, and July 29, 1782, and his report to Congress of September 7, 1782. The bill pictured here is from the National Numismatics Collection, no. 7034, National Museum of American History, courtesy of the Smithsonian Institution, Washington, D.C., photo nos. 83–5635, 5636.*

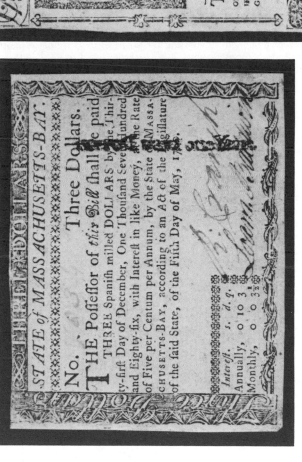

New emission currency of Massachusetts: $3 bill of May 5, 1780. 3⅗″ × 2¼″

ENDORSED: 87/Sepr. 7th 1782/Report of the Super: Finance/on a resolution of the/Assembly of Virginia/Delivered Sept 9. 1782/Read. Entered/respecting receiving, counting/and destroying old continental money/and crediting the state for extra [quantity?]
MSS: DS, PCC, DNA; Ofcl LbC, DLC.

1. The resolution of the Virginia House of Delegates (copy, PCC, no. 75, pp. 371–372), which Congress had referred to RM on August 29, concerned the procedure to be followed in destroying old Continental currency withdrawn by the state under the act of Congress of March 18, 1780 (see, on this act, notes to John Morin Scott to RM, May 30, 1781). The prescribed procedure was for the states to deliver the old money in their hands to the Continental loan officers, who were to deface the bills by stamping a hole through them and to give the states a corresponding credit on account. The money was then remitted to the Continental Treasury, where commissioners appointed by Congress supervised the burning of it (*JCC*, XVII, 800, XVIII, 1106, XX, 720). In order to save the expense of carting the money to Philadelphia, and perhaps to discourage the issue of new emission currency exchanged for it at the rate of 40 to 1, the Virginia resolution ordered the state treasurer to punch through the old currency then on hand and to be received thereafter and retain it until Congress gave directions to have it forwarded or destroyed; the resolution also directed Governor Benjamin Harrison to ask Congress to appoint a committee in the state to supervise destruction of the currency (see Harrison to the Virginia Delegates, August 16, 1782, Hutchinson and Rutland, eds., *Madison Papers*, V, 57–58n.).

The Superintendent's report printed here, besides recommending that the old currency be received and destroyed by the commissioners RM was nominating to settle state and individual accounts under the ordinance of February 20, 1782, interjected a controversial element far beyond the scope of the Virginia resolution. In the last sentence RM also proposed that states which delivered more than their quotas of the old money be credited for the excess at the rate of 40 to 1 of specie on accounts up to January 1, 1782. Since most of the old money redeemed by the states had been taken in by them at much lower rates, the Financier's recommendation appeared to have an arbitrary quality: it rewarded states which had had the will and the opportunity to comply with the act of March 18, 1780, particularly Massachusetts, which by this time had already collected more than its quota.

By fixing the scale of depreciation at 40 to 1, however, RM's proposal also threatened to create a precedent for assigning the currency a high value. The nonpossessing states would then face the prospect of being charged for unredeemed currency at high rates in the settlement of their accounts with the Union—"they must make good their Quota by one Silver Dollar instead of 40 such Paper Dollars," as the North Carolina delegates put it—or if they could not take up the money by levying taxes, of having to buy currency at artificial values from the possessor states or from private speculators. The nonpossessing states also argued that incidents of war had prevented their withdrawal of the old money, and that more fortunate states should not be allowed to redeem more than their quotas—the delinquent states would then have access to their portion of it (see Elias Boudinot to the Governor of New Jersey, October 23, and the North Carolina Delegates to Governor Alexander Martin, October 25, 1782, Burnett, ed., *Letters*, VI, 525, 526). RM, however, had long taken the position that the decisions of Congress, once made, should be executed whenever possible, and he was determined to enforce the 40 to 1 ratio set by the act of March 18, 1780 (see RM to the President of Congress, August 28, 1781, and notes, Diary, April 22, 1782, and notes, and RM's Circular to the Governors of the States, May 9, 1782).

Congress received and read RM's report on September 9 and took it under consideration on September 18. Abraham Clark of New Jersey, seconded by John Rutledge of South Carolina, moved that the commissioners to settle state and individual accounts be directed to "examine, receive, and destroy" old Continental currency in the hands of the states and transmit to the Superintendent accounts of the money destroyed, with the proviso, however, that the destruction be limited to the amount of state quotas under the act of March 18, 1780. This proposal preserved the physical existence of the surplus currency and left unexpressed the rate at which it would be evaluated. The two Massachusetts delegates, Samuel Osgood and Jonathan Jackson, moved and seconded a motion to destroy all the old money sunk by the states, not merely the amount of their quotas, but they got no support from the other delegates, and the motion passed as originally stated.

Although the thrust of RM's report was rejected, the issue was revived in November when a memorial of the Massachusetts legislature was received in Congress (see PCC, no. 65, II, 201–214; and *JCC*, XXIII, 754n.). The memorial complained that enormous quantities of Continental currency had flowed into the state in its last days and died there, causing losses to the people which Massachusetts attributed to the failure of other states to preserve the value of the currency by redeeming their quotas of it. The legislature warned, in consequence, that it might be difficult to comply with current requisitions. On November 25 Congress referred the memorial to the grand committee which was considering "the most effectual means of supporting the credit of the United States" (see the headnote to RM to the President of Congress, July 29, and notes), along with another September 18 motion of Osgood's proposing that old Continental currency sunk in excess of quotas be credited to the possessing states "according to the current value thereof compared with Gold and Silver at the time when such State had delivered over its proportion to the loan Officer." The grand committee was in unanimous agreement that states which had sunk surpluses should in justice receive an allowance to be apportioned among the debtor states, and ultimately all but one member of the committee supported a plan of Congressman Thomas Fitzsimons of Pennsylvania under which outstanding old emissions would be taken up by the commissioners of accounts and exchanged for final settlement certificates. Consensus collapsed, however, when the committee and later Congress could not agree on the value to be assigned to the old money. The question was postponed, and although periodically revived, was never settled during the Confederation. The subject can be traced in Madison's Notes on Debates, November 26 and December 7 and 24, 1782, Hutchinson and Rutland, eds., *Madison Papers*, V, 321–324n., 377–381n., 442–443, 446n.; and *JCC*, XXIII, 831–832, XXIV, 39–42, XXVII, 395–397.

Official figures on state deliveries of the old Continental currency are inconsistent. On the information available to RM at this time, see his Circular to the Governors of the States, May 9, 1782, and the enclosures printed there. An account of the currency destroyed under the act of September 18, 1782 (*JCC*, XXX, 25), shows that, except for a small amount in New Hampshire, none of the commissioners of accounts reported gathering in any currency from the states up to January 1786, when of over $241 million issued, some $130 million was still unaccounted for. For a later statement, see *American State Papers*, class 3, Finance, I, 58–59.

2. This line is in Gouverneur Morris's writing.

3. The foregoing two lines, both torn at the left margin, are in Gouverneur Morris's writing.

To Francis Gurney and William Allibone

Office of Finance 7th. Septem: 1782

Gentlemen,

It would afford me much Pleasure to comply with your wishes; but it is not in my Power to make the Payment requested in your Note of this date.[1] Neither did I expect the Demand would have been made in such haste, as the Ship by her Success in the Voyage provided a Fund sufficient for the Expenditure. You may depend that I will discharge the Balance as soon as with Propriety it can be done. I have the honor to be very respectfully Gentlemen your most obedient and humble Servant

RM

MS: Ofcl LbC, DLC.

1. The note from Gurney and Allibone, commissioners of Pennsylvania for defense of the River Delaware, has not been found but concerned payment for the *General Washington,* which RM had recently purchased. See Diary, September 2, and notes.

From Alexander Hamilton

Albany [New York] Septmr. 7. 1782[1]

Sir,

I have had the inclosed ready for some time; but in hopes of receiving the returns of the certificates mentioned in memorandum B I delayed sending the present sketch.[2] Having even received no answers from some of the parties who live at a distance from me,[3] I suspect they have done their business in so disorderly a manner (to say nothing worse of it) that they are at a loss how to render the accounts; and I have therefore concluded not to detain any longer what I had procured.

I do not take the step mentioned in ⟨Letter⟩ memorandum A because I doubted its propriety: It might raise expectations about the old money which possibly it may not enter into your plans to raise; and besides this by knowing what has been called in in each state (which from the sketch I send you will appear as to this) you can determine the ballance of emissions remaining out, except what may have worn out and been accidentally destroyed. If you desire this step to be taken I will obey your commands.

I have said nothing of the rates of depreciation because I imagine your letter written in July 80[4] had referrence to the rates at which the money was then actually circulating; and the circulation has now totally ceased. The laws I sent you by the last post[5] will inform you of the rates fixed at different periods by the legislature: forty; seventy five and lastly one hundred and twenty eight.

I am obliged to infer there is a studied backwardness in the officers of the state who ought to give me the information you require respecting the supplies of different kinds which have been furnished to the use of The United States. Indeed I find on inquiry that their joint information will not be so full as to satisfy your intentions; and that this cannot be done, 'till you have appointed a commissioner of accounts authorised to enter into all the details aided by some legislative arrangement, which may be obtained the next session. I have the honor to be With the greatest respect and esteem Sir Your most Obedient Servant

AH

ENDORSED: To Robert Morris Esqr/⟨Aug.⟩ Septembr 7. 1782
MSS: ADftS, Hamilton Papers, DLC; transcript, Francis Baylies Papers, DLC.

1. Hamilton was the receiver of Continental taxes for New York.

2. Neither the enclosure nor memorandums A and B mentioned by Hamilton have been found.

3. On August 3 Hamilton had asked Udny Hay, New York State agent, for "an account of all the money, provisions, transportation, &c., furnished by this state to the United States, since the 18th. of March 1780," and for "the amount of any certificates or paper money in any shape, which, through your office, have passed into circulation, distinguishing the different species." Having received no reply, Hamilton addressed Hay again on September 7. See Syrett and Cooke, eds., *Hamilton Papers*, III, 124–125, 160–161; for similar letters sent to Robert Benson, clerk of the New York Senate, on August 18 and September 7, see *ibid.*, 147–148, 159–160.

4. This was RM's Circular to the States, July 25, 1781, which requested information about money and supplies furnished to the United States as well as the kind, extent, and depreciation of paper currencies circulating in the respective states. RM had enclosed the letter in his circular to the receivers of July 12, 1782.

5. See Hamilton to RM, August 31, and notes.

To James Lovell

Office of Finance 7. Septemr. 1782[1]

Enclosed you have the (first, second, third and fourth, fifth, sixth, seventh and eighth) Bills of Exchange drawn by me on Mons. Grand in eleven Setts all of this Date and amounting as by the enclosed List to one hundred thousand Livres Tournois being numbered from 326 to 336 inclusive.[2] The price of Bills here is six shillings and three pence of this Money for five Livres Tournois. Below that Price you are not to sell but if they can be disposed of at or above that Price you will make Sale of them. All these as well as the former Bills are accounted for by Mr Swanwick who has charged them to you. To him therefore you will render the Accounts Sales and settle with him finally for the Proceeds, on Account of which by Credits for my Drafts on you. Your Receipts of Taxes will be settled with Mr. Hillegas and the Remittances made to him.

MS: Ofcl LbC, DLC.

1. Lovell was the receiver of Continental taxes for Massachusetts.

2. Two of the bills of exchange from set 331 are extant. The sixth bill is illustrated in this volume. The seventh is in PHC.

From William Churchill Houston

Trenton [New Jersey] 7 Septr 1782[1]

I am favoured with yours of 29 ultimo circular, the Contents of which shall be duly observed.

My Return for the past week is enclosed.

Receipt of Continental Taxes in the State of New-Jersey
1782   From Septr. 1 to 7 inclusive received from the Treasurer of the State
         five Hundred Dollars   Dlls 500

MS: ADftS with subjoined ADftS return, Houston Collection, NjP.

1. Houston was the receiver of Continental taxes for New Jersey.

List of Monies Owed to John Chaloner

[Philadelphia, September 7, 1782][1]

John Moylans Certificate due 3 August   564
J Swanwicks acceptance of Dl. Clarkes Bills
   due 23 Augt   2666.⁶%₉₀

The bill of exchange was the eighteenth-century equivalent of a check. Selling a bill of exchange usually involved four parties. First was the person purchasing a bill (the payer), who needed to remit funds to a distant place. He would buy a bill from an individual (the drawer) who had money to his credit in an account with a merchant or banker in that place. The drawer for his part wrote out an order directing his correspondent (the drawee) to pay a specific amount to whomever the payer might specify (the payee). The drawer turned over the bill of exchange to the buyer in a set of four copies to avoid any complications through loss in transit. The buyer in turn sent each of the bills in the set by different conveyances to someone to whom he owed money or with whom he wished to lodge funds on account. The payee would present the first bill to arrive to the drawee for payment of the required sum within the time stipulated. Acceptance of one bill upon arrival automatically cancelled the other bills in the set. Nonacceptance or nonpayment of the bill by the drawee would cause it to be returned to the buyer or payer by the payee with a "protest." Mercantile custom defined the "usance" of the bill, i.e., the period after "sight" following which the bill had to be paid after being presented to the drawee. Bills were "discounted" when the payee chose not to wait until this period elapsed and sold the bill to a third party at less than the face value of the bill, in effect paying an interest charge. In practice, this procedure could become more complicated, since bills were transferred, often several times in succession, from one party to another, by endorsement, before finally being presented for payment.

The mechanics for the bill of exchange illustrated here varied to some extent from the standard arrangements. The bill was drawn by Morris (the drawer) on Ferdinand Grand, banker to the United States in Paris (the drawee), presumably against funds derived from the French loan of 1782 for 6 million livres. Rather than being sold directly to a buyer, it was, like many of the Superintendent's overseas bills, made out to a broker or agent, in this instance, James Lovell, receiver of Continental taxes for Massachusetts, but more commonly to Haym Salomon, broker to the Office of Finance. The broker, upon sale to a buyer, transferred it to him by endorsement. In this case, Lovell's signed endorsement on the back, "Please to pay the within Contents to Mr Duncan Ingraham Junr or his Order," indicates the buyer to whom he sold the bill, a member of Ingraham and Bromfield, a Boston firm with a branch in Amsterdam. Drawn at 60 days' sight for 4,000 livres tournois (about $740), this bill was the sixth in a set of eight, Morris having expanded the number because of the increased risks of wartime shipping. Because of Morris's difficulties in selling bills of exchange in Philadelphia, he enclosed it to Lovell in a letter of September 7 instructing him to sell, at prices not lower than those stipulated, this and accompanying sets of bills to persons in Boston and vicinity who needed to make remittances to Europe. Lovell was to use the proceeds from the sale to pay inland or domestic drafts Morris had drawn on him (for the background, see Morris to Lovell, May 4, 1782, and notes).

Save for the signature and title in Morris's hand, the blanks in this pre-printed bill were filled in by John Swanwick, Morris's unofficial cashier in the

Bill of exchange drawn by Robert Morris on Ferdinand Grand, September 7, 1782.
9³⁄₁₆″ × 3⁵⁄₈″

Office of Finance. While most of Morris's overseas bills of exchange were prepared on several kinds of preprinted forms, evidently kept in books, some were entirely handwritten. These bills of exchange drawn on public account should be distinguished from those Morris drew on his private account as a merchant. This discussion is based on the learned and lucid treatment of the history and mechanics of bills of exchange, including both domestic and overseas drafts and the factors influencing the rate of exchange for bills, in John J. McCusker, Money and Exchange in Europe and America, 1600–1775: A Handbook *(Chapel Hill, N. C., 1978), esp. 18–23. The bill of exchange illustrated here is from the Etting Papers, Members of Congress, II, 102, courtesy of the Historical Society of Pennsylvania, Philadelphia.*

J Pierces Notes	580	
Notes by R Morris in favour of the Contractors		
for Moveing Army Due 15 Sepr.	3000	6810.60
	—	
Balance due on Note of hand	4591	
Amount received of J Willsons first Payment	8000	
Amount due Do 2d. Do	2666.60	15267.60
	—	—
	Dollars	22,078.30

MSS: D, Jeremiah Wadsworth Papers, CtHi; LbC, Chaloner and White Letterbook, PHi.

1. This list is subjoined to John Chaloner to Wadsworth and Carter, September 9, 1782 (Wadsworth Papers, CtHi), in which Chaloner reported "at foot you have a list of Monies due from Mr Morris on or before the 15th Instant, a Copy of which I gave him Saturday Night, and I find him by no means prepared to pay it particularly the four first Articles amounting to 6810 Dlls for which he is desirous I should take bills at 6/3." On these debts, see Diary, August 20, and notes.

Diary: September 9, 1782

This Morning Mr. McCall produced a number of Letters recommending Mr. Edwd. Wright for his diligence, Capacity &c. As I know several of the Gentlemen who wrote those Letters would only grant them [if they?][1] were merited, I agreed that Mr. Wright be employed as a Clerk in this Office in room of Mr. Crawford who lately left us.[2]

Colo. Ephram Blaine came with Mr McClay to introduce and recommend him to me, and Mr. McClay offered his Services to supply Provisions to the Troops in Case of an Expedition being undertaken against the Indians upon Susquehannah &c.[3]

Thomas Smith Esqr. Loan Officer of this State applied with the return from his Office and asked my advice as to what he is to do to Morrow in regard to Issuing Bills of Exchange in payment of Interest on Loan Office Certificates.[4] I told him that I expect Congress will decide on that matter this day, but if they do not, I cannot give advice; he will in cither Case know his Duty. He asked for Money and I told him expressly I will not give any until his Accounts are Settled, and informed him what is done in that respect.[5]

Mr. Swanwick brought sundry Warrants and papers respecting Money matters which were Signed.

Major Franks called below Stairs but I was too much engaged to see him.

Henry Hill Esquire called to inform me of the return of his Agent from head quarters.[6]

The Honble. Mr. Clarke, Mr. Gilman, Mr. Montgomery and Colo. Dyer came a Committee to enquire respecting Interest Bills &c.[7] They asked if there were no Funds provided in France to pay such Bills. I repeated to them the Intelligence communicated to Congress on this Subject in my letter of the 27th May last. They asked me if the distant Loan Officers are possessed of Bills. I informed them that many of them are but that I beleive those Bills had been remitted to them for the purpose of paying last years Interest, but that I beleive the practice at these Offices is to Issue the Bills to the first appliers, so that if Persons apply first for the Interest of the present Year they will get the Bills whilst there is any in the Office. I informed them I shall not order any more Bills to the several Offices unless directed by Congress to do it, as I cannot see how they are to be paid, on the Contrary I would long since have ordered all the Bills from them but I did not conceive myself justifiable to do so whilst Congress held this Affair under Consideration.[8]

This Day Tench Francis Esqr. returned me his Accounts of the Money brought from Boston, the Expences on it &c.[9]

Colo. Miles applied for Notes to pay Waggoners returning from General Greens Army which I complied with.

Major Jackson for Money, promised him to morrow.

Mr. Henry Wynkoop applied for a Credit on Rhode Island and I gave him Notes for 3,000 Dollars in Exchange for his Notes for the like Sum to be negotiated at the Bank.[10]

The Honble: Secretary of Congress sent me the Act of this Date for stopping the payment of Interest by Bills on France, in Consequence whereof I dispatched one Express for Portsmouth New Hampshire, with Letters to the Loan Officer at that place, at Boston, Rhode Island and Connecticut. I sent another for Mr. Borden at Bordentown, and another to Delaware, Maryland and Virginia, and to morrow shall dispatch another for Albany who is also to carry money to the Contractors agreeable to my promise.[11]

The Honble. Secretary at War brought Letters of Messrs. Phelps and Edwards in their Justification as Contractors &c.[12]

Capt. Barney called and I informed him that he is to take two passengers at the request of the Minister of France, that he is to lay in their Stores &c. or rather that Stores will be laid in for him and them.[13]

James Milligan Esqr. called but I could not see him.

I sent for Mr. Nourse and desired him to make a State of the Bills now in the Hands of the Loan Officers.[14]

Wrote a Letter to His Excellency the President of Congress.

Wrote a Letter to the Continental Loan Officers.

Wrote a Letter to His Excelly Genl. Washington.

Wrote a Letter to Mr Jenifer.

Wrote a Letter to Geo: Olney Esqr.

Issued a Warrant on Mr Swanwick in favor John Pierce   £168.15.0

Issued a Warrant on Mr Swanwick in favor Colo. Saml. Miles   54. 7.6

1. Editors' conjecture for an estimated two or more words inadvertently omitted from the manuscript at this point.

2. The oath of office sworn by Edward Wright, Jr., is in PCC, no. 195. His letters of recommendation have not been found.

3. William Maclay represented Northumberland County in the Pennsylvania Assembly and served on the committee which had conferred with RM about the proposed expedition against the Indians (see Diary, September 7, and notes). The supply agent selected by the assembly was Bernard Dougherty.

4. On this question, see below in this Diary at notes 7 and 8.

5. On the settlement of the accounts of the Continental loan officers, see RM's Report to Congress on the Continental Loan Offices, June 13, 1782, and notes.

6. The agent was Richard Wells. See RM to George Washington, August 13, and notes.

7. This committee, composed of Joseph Montgomery of Pennsylvania, Abraham Clark of New Jersey, and Eliphalet Dyer of Connecticut, was appointed on September 9 to confer with RM and report immediately (PCC, no. 186, p. 53). Although the fourth congressman in attendance, John Taylor Gilman of New Hampshire, was not a member of the committee, his interest in this subject may have derived from the fact that his father, Nicholas Gilman, was the Continental loan officer of New Hampshire.

8. The committee's report (in *JCC*, XXIII, 553–555) is briefly summarized in the notes to RM's Report to Congress on the Continental Loan Offices, June 13, 1782; for the result, see below in this Diary at note 11.

9. See Francis to RM, September 9, and notes.

10. See RM to George Olney, September 9, and notes. Wynkoop was a Pennsylvania delegate to Congress.

11. See note 8 above and RM's Circular to the Continental Loan Officers, September 9, and notes.

12. Oliver Phelps and Timothy Edwards, two of the contractors of record for the Moving Army, were currently supplying beef to the Moving Army under a subcontract. Their letters have not been found.

13. Lieutenant Joshua Barney was captain of the *General Washington*, which RM had recently purchased on behalf of the United States for service as a packet between the United States and Europe. For the passengers he took at the request of Chevalier de La Luzerne, see Diary, October 7, and notes.

14. This document has not been found.

Circular to the Continental Loan Officers

Office of Finance 9th September 1782

Sir,

In Obedience to an Order of Congress just now passed, I am to require that you issue no Bills of Exchange for Interest on Loan Office Certificates due subsequent to the first Day of March last.[1] You will be pleased to transmit me all the Bills of Exchange now in your Office.[2] I am, Sir, Your most obedient Servant,

Robt Morris

Nathaniel Appleton Esquire

ENDORSED: [*torn*] Robt Morris Esqr/Septemr 9th. 1782/prohibiting Bill Exchange to be/issued for Interest after March/1st 1782
MSS: LS, to Nathaniel Appleton of Massachusetts, Feinstone Collection, PPAmP; LS, to Abraham Yates, Jr., of New York, Yates Papers, NN; LS, to Thomas Harwood of Maryland, MdHi; Ofcl LbC, DLC.

1. The resolution under which RM acted was passed on September 9 (see Diary, September 9, and notes). For the background to this measure, see notes to RM's Report to Congress on the Continental Loan Offices, June 13; and the headnote to RM to the President of Congress, July 29, 1782.

2. The endorsement on the letter to Abraham Yates indicates that it was "received 20 Septr. 1782 per Post." Responses to this letter may be assayed in Diary, September 11 (which records a message from Joseph Borden of New Jersey), Yates to RM, September 21 and October 4, and RM to John Hopkins, Jr., to William Imlay, and to Samuel Patterson, all October 3.

To the President of Congress
(John Hanson)

Office of Finance 9th September 1782

Sir

I did myself the Honor to propose in my Letter of the thirtieth of July last the borrowing of four million Dollars for the Service of the ensuing Year. It always gives me Pain to repeat any Applications to Congress because it is my Duty to suppose they pay every proper Attention to those Things which are submitted to their Consideration. But I must take the Liberty on this Occasion to observe that the many Engagements I have been compelled to make for the Purpose of supporting the public Service to the present Moment will all fall due between this and the first of the next Year.

My Prospects of Relief from the Revenues of America are slender indeed. As a safe Opportunity for Europe will offer in a few days[1] Congress will be pleased to consider that the Moments are very precious. They will consider that I cannot Act in this Business without their Authority, and that it will take some Days to prepare the necessary Dispatches even after that authority is given. I hope Sir I shall not be understood as desiring to precipitate any Acts or Resolutions. We are fast approaching to the Winter. If every Thing could be ready by the fifteenth of this Month we could not reckon on the arrival of Dispatches at Paris before the Beginning of November. A Month is but a short Period to transact this important Business and this would not leave another Month for the Winters Passage back.[2] With perfect Respect I have the Honor to be Sir Your most obedient and humble Servant

Robt Morris

His Excellency The President of Congress

ENDORSED: [88]/Letter Sept 9. 1782/Super finance/Read 10/Referred to Mr Duane/Mr Montgomery/Mr Madison/Pressing a determination on/his proposal to borrow 4 Mill[ion]/dollars in Europe
MSS: LS, PCC, DNA; Ofcl LbC, DLC.

1. See the following letter.

2. For Congress's response to this letter, see the headnote to RM to the President of Congress, July 30, 1782.

To the President of Congress
(John Hanson)

Marine Office 9th September 1782

Sir

I do myself the Honor to inform your Excellency that Agreably to the Order of Congress of the twenty ninth of last month I have purchased the Ship Washington.[1] She is now fitting out as a Packet under the Command of Lieutenant Barney and will be ready for Sea in a few days. I shall order her to make the first convenient Port in France unless Congress shall think Proper to point out some other Destination.[2] With perfect Respect I have the Honor to be Sir Your most Obedient and humble Servant

Robt Morris

His Excellency The President of Congress

ENDORSED: 89/Letter Sept 9. 1782/Agent of Marine/Read Sept. 10./That he has purchased/the ship Washington
MSS: LS, PCC, DNA; AM LbC, MdAN.
   1. See Diary, August 29, and notes.
   2. Congress took no action on this letter. For the sailing instructions issued for the voyage, see RM to Joshua Barney, October 7 (first letter).

To George Washington

Office of Finance 9th September 1782

Sir,

I received your Excellency's Letter of the fourth last Evening.[1] I this Morning sent for Mr. Francis, one of the Contractors, and directed him to purchase five hundred Barrels, for which I will pay the Cash, and five hundred more on Credit; and forward it on as fast as procured.[2] I am, Sir, with great Respect Your Excellency's most obedient and humble Servant,

Robt Morris

His Excellency General Washington

ENDORSED: Office of Finance 9 Sepr 1782/from/Hono Robert Morris/1000 bbs flour will be sent/on./Reply to mine. 4th.
MSS: LS, Washington Papers, DLC; Ofcl LbC, DLC.
   1. RM refers to Washington's second letter of September 4.
   2. Francis was one of the partners in Sands, Livingston and Company, the contractor for West Point and the Moving Army. Both RM and the contractors authorized additional purchases by Francis on September 11 (see Diary of that date; and for purchases by Richardson Sands, Diary, September 18). For the contractors' appraisal of the situation, see Comfort Sands, Walter Livingston, William Duer, and Daniel Parker to RM, September 11, and notes.

To George Washington

Office of Finance
Septr. 9th. 1782

Dear Sir

The dates of the enclosed Letters will shew you my extreme Reluctance to wound your Mind with the Anxieties which distress my own.[1]

At the time they were written I was sore pressed on every quarter, but a gleam of Hope broke in upon me and induced me to bear up still longer against the Torrent of demands which was rushing upon me.[2] These would long since have overwhelmed me had I been supported *only* by the Revennues drawn [from][3] the States. At length however my other resources which are nearly exhausted have become useless by the total Stagnation of Trade, owing to the expectations of Peace.[4] There is therefore no other dependance left but the Taxes, and unless these become immediately productive of Funds sufficient to feed our Troops, I need not describe the Consequences. Already I am in Arrear Spite of all my Efforts. I am determined however to continue those Efforts to the last Moment, but at present I really know not which way to turn myself.[5] With the most sincere esteem I am My Dear Sir your most obedient and most humble Servant[6]

Robt Morris

His Excellency Genl Washington

ENDORSED: From/The Honble. R. Morris/9th. Sepr. 1782
MSS: ALS, Simon Gratz Collection, PHi; Ofcl LbC, DLC; copy, PCC, DNA; copy, Benjamin Franklin Papers, PPAmP.

1. The enclosures were RM to Washington, August 29 (first letter) and August 30, in which RM warned that he might be forced to notify the contractors that he could no longer pay them. For the delay in delivering the present letter and its enclosures, see notes to the August 29 letter.

2. The "gleam of Hope" RM recalled may have derived from his conversation with contractors Comfort and Richardson Sands on September 2 "in which various Difficulties seemed to be removed" (see Diary of that date and notes). RM at that time also could still hold out hope that Richard Wells would return from New York City with specie. See RM to Washington, August 13, and notes; and note 4 below.

3. This word is in all other texts.

4. RM evidently refers to his inability to sell bills of exchange on France. Earlier in the year his sales had been impaired by the British blockade of the American coast (see the headnote to RM's State of American Commerce and Plan for Protecting It, May 10, 1782, and notes). Besides the current uncertainty owing to the opening of general peace negotiations in Paris (see Diary, August 8, and notes), RM's sales were undermined by the continuing problem of competition with French agents (see Diary, August 9, and notes, and September 5 and 12). The timing of the present letter to Washington, however, also coincided with the return of Richard Wells from New York City without the specie anticipated by RM (see Diary, September 9) and, probably, with the arrival of Washington's first letter of September 4 disclosing the failure of Wells's mission.

5. As Clarence L. Ver Steeg has noted (*Morris,* 149), RM was driven to this statement "for the first time in his administration, and really for the first time in his career." Later in the month RM responded to this crisis by vacating his contract for West Point and the Moving Army and negotiating a new one at greater expense but with three months' credit provided by the new contractors. See notes to Comfort Sands, Walter Livingston, William Duer, and Daniel Parker to RM, September 11, and to Diary, September 22.

6. The PCC text was enclosed in RM to the President of Congress, October 21, the PPAmP copy in RM to Benjamin Franklin, January 11, 1783.

From Tench Francis

Philadelphia 9th: Septem: 1782[1]

Sir

In consequence of your Orders I set off for Boston with Major Nicholas where I arrived in nine days. I found the Treasure had been delivered to Govr. Hancock by the Captain of the Frigate who had taken the Govrs. Receipt for it. On which I applied for Permission to remove it to a convenient place to count or weigh and pack it agreeable to your directions but the Governor absolutely refused to let it be removed from his Cellar and insisted the Business should be done in his House. He said it was safest to do it there as the Guards were provided and would attend until I put it into my Waggons. With all the Care and dispatch possible we counted and Weighed the whole, when we found a deficiency of 449 Crowns. This we flattered ourselves might be a Mistake, as we were obliged to go through a great part of the Business in a dark Cellar the Casks were almost all filled with bilge Water which rotted the Bags to a pulp, and therefore they could not be compared with the Invoice. We could not think of opening all our Boxes and go through a second Counting to rectify our Mistake, but concluded it best to give a Receipt for the Whole Sum. We were both of opinion that the Expence of our Oxen which were all bought and in pasture with the Wages and Expences of the Teemsters who were all provided would greatly over balance any advantages of a second Counting, besides we were daily in dread of the rainy season which would injure the Roads. Add to this our Escort was on March to Boston. On counting the Money into the Bank I find the Deficiency only 366 Crowns,[2] which I shall think very hard if I am made Answerable for. Inclosed you have my Account.[3] I am with the greatest Respect Your most Obedient[4]

(signed) Tench Francis

Hon'ble: R Morris Esqr.

ms: Copy, PCC, DNA.

1. This letter concerns the settlement of Francis's account for conducting the shipment of French specie overland from Boston to Philadelphia in the fall of 1781. Of the approximately $463,000 delivered for the use of the United States, RM subscribed $254,000 to capitalize the Bank of North America. See RM to Francis, September 11,

1781 (first letter), and notes, and the headnote to RM's Plan for Establishing a National Bank, with Observations, May 1, 1781.

2. Approximately $406. For the rate of exchange, see PCC, no. 142, II, 31.

3. Account not found.

4. After a long inadvertent delay RM enclosed Francis's letter to the president of Congress on January 21, 1784. For the sequel, see *JCC*, XXVI, 246; and RM's report to Congress of October 1, 1784.

To Daniel of St. Thomas Jenifer

Office of Finance 9. Septr. 1782

I received your Letter of the sixth Instant this Morning. I shall send to you an Express for whatever Monies you may have on hand in a Day or two and by him I shall write you particularly.[1]

MSS: Ofcl LbC, DLC; LbC, Intendant's Letterbook, MdAA.

1. Jenifer was Maryland's intendant of the revenue. His letter of September 6 has not been found, but evidently advised RM that he had £7,000 on hand and expected more soon. See RM to Jenifer, September 13 (two letters).

To George Olney

Office of Finance 9. Sept. 1782[1]

The Bearer of this Letter Mr. Henry Wynkoop has three Bills payable at thirty days from the Date to himself or Order drawn by me on Mr. John Swanwick. I wish you may have it in your Power to advance him the Cash for all or any of these Bills as he may chuse in such Case you will be so Kind as to do it immediately. This Gentleman intends making a Purchase at Rhode Island and therefore should you not be in Cash it will probably suit both him and the Seller to deposit the Bills and take your Engagement for paying out of the first Monies you receive.

MS: Ofcl LbC, DLC.

1. Olney was the receiver of Continental taxes for Rhode Island. On the subject of this letter, see Diary, September 9, and notes.

Diary: September 10, 1782

This Day Mr Edward Wright junr. was entered as a Clerk in this Office.

The Honble. Mr. Duane came to consult Mr G: Morris respecting a report on the Subject of Exchangeing Prisoners &c.[1]

Messrs. Hazelwood and Co. apply for Money and ought to be Supplied.[2]

I sent for Capt Maxwell and Capt. Harrison of the Cartel Ships and delivered to them Sir Guy Carletons Letters which they opened and read after which they shewed the same to me. I desired them to get ready to receive the Prisoners as I intend to send the whole by them.[3]

Messrs. Wm. Montgomery and Mr McClay members of the Assembly of Pennsylvania came to the Office this morning respecting the intended Expeditions against the Indians.[4] I promised to send for

General Lincoln and Consult him on that Subject. I did so. Genl. Lincoln came and upon my asking him whether these Expeditions are Authorized to be undertaken at the Continental expence, he rather thought not. I requested to see the Letters of Genl Washington on the Subject, they were brought and I perceived clearly that he had not directed such Expedition[5] wherefore I proposed that Genl. Potter and Mr. Bayard Members of the Executive Council of Pennsylvania should be sent for. They came and the above members of the Assembly returning I mentioned the necessity of applying to Congress and informed these Gentlemen that without the approbation of Congress I could not act in the Business. They agreed to apply.

The Honble. Jno. Rutledge Esqr. applied on behalf of Doctor Jones of Georgia for Money allowed to him by Act of Congress,[6] that Gentleman or one of his Colleagues having alledged that I had refused this Money to him. I told the Governor such assertion is not true that these Gentlemen had not applied to me that they had applied to Mr Swanwick, who very truly told them he had no money, but finally I agreed to advance the Money to Doctor Jones.

Mr. Henry Hill made a payment of 11,000 Dollars which I delivered to Mr. Swanwick in Bank Notes.[7]

I sent for Capt. James Nicholson and proposed his returning to Connecticut with 4,000 or 5,000 Dollars in Notes as I cannot get Money for him; to this he agreed and is to set out the begining of the next Week.[8]

The Hon: Secy at War and myself had a long Conference on several matters of public Business.

Colo. Moylan Clothier General applied respecting the Purchase of Linnens for Soldiers Shirts. I desired him to call on me tomorrow on this Subject.

The Hon: Mr Duane, Mr. Madison and Mr Montgomery Committee of Congress came on the Business of a foreign Loan being appointed in Consequence of my Letter on that Subject.[9] The Hon. Secry. of Foreign Affairs also attended and after a Conference on the Subject it was agreed that we prepare the Draft of a resolution and lay it before the Committee.[10]

Wrote a Letter to Geo. Olney Esqr.

Wrote a Letter to James Lovell.

Wrote a Letter to His Excellency Govr. Livingston.

Wrote a Letter to Hezk. Merrill.

Issued a Warrant on Mr. Swanwick in favor John Pierce £90.0.0.

1. James Duane of New York was a member of a committee to which Congress on September 3 had referred a letter from Washington to the President of Congress of August 28 requesting instructions for negotiating a general cartel for the exchange of

prisoners of war (PCC, no. 186, p. 52; Fitzpatrick, ed., *Writings of Washington*, XXV, 71–72). Congress took up the committee's report on September 5 and again on September 9, when it was approved with emendations and ordered to serve as Washington's instructions (for a brief summary of the report and the issues at stake, see notes to Diary, June 18, 1782). Gouverneur Morris had been one of the commissioners for the American side at the last unsuccessful conference held at Elizabeth, New Jersey, earlier in the year.

2. John Hazelwood was a contractor for the post at Philadelphia.

3. For the British cartel ships, see notes to Diary, August 13. Carleton's letters to the captains have not been found.

4. On the subject of this entry, see Diary, September 7, and notes.

5. The reference is to Washington's letters of September 2 to Secretary at War Benjamin Lincoln and President William Moore of Pennsylvania. See notes to Diary, September 7.

6. For the salary payments Congress authorized for the delegates from the three southernmost states, see Diary, July 11, 1781, and notes.

7. For Hill's arrangements with RM, see notes to Diary, April 17, 1782.

8. Nicholson had been overseeing completion of the Continental frigate *Bourbon* at Chatham, Connecticut.

9. See RM to the President of Congress, September 9, and notes.

10. The draft resolution has not been found.

To James Lovell

Office of Finance 10. Septr. 1782

Sir

I have received your several Letters of the twelfth, sixteenth and twenty ninth of last Month.[1] I have paid Attention to what you say on the Resolution of your House of Representatives of the nineteenth of June concurred in by the Senate on the twentieth.[2] It would give me great Pleasure that I could agree to Place this Matter on the Footing which they wish but this cannot be. I have applied to General Lincoln to know from him whether he had given Messrs. Tuckerman and Jenkins any Encouragement to expect that the Amount of their Demand should be paid out of the Revenues of 1782. He declares in pointed Terms that he did not and as to any Representation which he can be supposed to have made of the public necessities when he was [in] Boston that certainly ought not to influence because it must be remembered that he was in Virginia when the flour was lent. This Declaration is the more authoritative as he at the same Time expresses a due Sense of their Zeal and gives them the full Merit of their Exertions. He reminds me also that those Gentlemen made Application thro him to me for an Allowance of this very Demand. The Answer which I gave to the Individuals must form my Answer to the State.[3] *The quotas required by Congress for the Service of 1782, can not be applied in Payment of former Debts.* If the State are content to pay this Debt and charge it to the United States on the old Accounts I have not the least Objection. But it is not a Matter in which I can hesitate whether it shall be deducted from the

Quota for the present Year. And I am thoroughly perswaded that if the State of Massachusetts knew as well as I do the Consequences of establishing such a Precedent they would remonstrate against instead of supporting it. I shall communicate this Matter to the Delegates of Massachusetts and doubt not they will write to the Governor on the Subject.[4]

You will find that Congress have pursued the Idea which you suggested as to the Mode of œconomizing reputably by given away the Ship America[5] But I do not think that Œconomy would alone have been a sufficient Reason for this valuable Present because certainly it ought to be a constant Object with every true American to establish a respectable Marine. I am however well pleased with what is done because I think it a seasonable Tribute of Gratitude to a Prince whose Exertions in our Favor have been both generous and Great.

I am very sorry to find that your weekly Receipts are so small[6] for I had hoped that when once your State got in Motion the Collections would have been rapid and the Amount very considerable. Indeed I have relied on this and should I be disappointed very pernicious and perhaps fatal Consequences may ensue.

I think it best that you do not reissue any Notes after you have once received them tho I think it will be at the same time prudent always to keep a small Reserve of Cash for Paying small Notes. You will see that I have issued such[7] and I perswade myself that they will meet with a very general Credit and Circulation now that the Taxes are collecting.

As to the Purchase of Bills on this Place I do not think it advisable for you to do it because I can always find Means to draw the Money out of your Hands quite as fast as you can possess yourself of it. I am Sir with Esteem your most obedient and humble Servant

RM

MS: Ofcl LbC, DLC.

1. Letters not found. Lovell was the receiver of Continental taxes for Massachusetts.

2. The resolve, dated June 21, 1782, directed that Edward Tuckerman and John Jenkins be paid £717 from the state treasury for 240 barrels of flour they had loaned to the Continent, the money "to be charged to the United States, and deducted out of the first moiety of the Continental tax." Acts and Laws of Massachusetts, 1782–1783, p. 216.

3. No previous reference to this matter has been found among RM's papers.

4. No letter on this subject has been found.

5. See notes to John Paul Jones to Gouverneur Morris, September 4.

6. RM probably refers to Lovell's fourth and fifth returns of August 21 and 28 for $1,924⁶⁹⁄₉₀ and $2,351³²⁄₉₀ respectively. See the list of Lovell's returns in PCC, no. 137, III, 349.

7. No doubt a reference to RM's Circular to the Receivers of Continental Taxes, August 29, in which RM introduced his new 60-day notes in denominations as low as $20.

To Hezekiah Merrill

Office of Finance 10. Sepr. 1782

I have received your Favor dated at Hartford on the second Instant.[1] In my Letter to you written on the third Instant I have expressed my Sentiments on the Subject of small Notes. I shall not therefore now trouble you with the Repitition.

MS: Ofcl LbC, DLC.

   1. Letter not found. Merrill was the receiver of Continental taxes for Connecticut.

To the Governor of New Jersey
(William Livingston)

Office of Finance 10 Septr. 1782

I have received your Favor of the thirteenth of August enclosing the Acts passed at the last setting of your Legislature[1] for which I pray you to accept my Thanks.

MSS: LS, Livingston Papers, NN; Ofcl LbC, DLC.

   1. Letter and enclosure not found.

To George Olney

Office of Finance 10. Sepr. 1782

I have been favored with your Letter dated at Providence on the twenty sixth of last Month.[1] I hope you may not be disappointed in your Expectations, and that I shall shortly receive from you ample Supplies.

MS: Ofcl LbC, DLC.

   1. Letter not found. Olney was the receiver of Continental taxes for Rhode Island.

Diary: September 11, 1782

Last Night arrived the Ship Heer Adams Capt. Smedley from Amsterdam with Cloathing &c. for the Army.[1]

The Hon: Mr: Telfair and Noble Wimberly Jones Esqrs applied (under the Act of Congress directing me to supply certain Sums to the Delegates of the Southern States) for a Supply of money as Delegates of the State of Georgia. I agreed to Supply Mr Telfair with 350 Dollars and Doctor Jones with 1,000 Dollars—after which I complained that these Gentlemen or one of them had said that I had refused this money, which I deny for this is the first application made to me for it. Mr Telfair said they had applied to Mr Swanwick who did not pay it. To this I urged that he assigned the reason; viz: that he had no Money.

I also complained to Doctor Jones that he had not stated exactly or Candidly what passed sometime since between him and me relative to Mr. Edison[2] and after some Conversation on this Subject it rather appears as if there had been something mistaken and something misapprehended in the matter.

Lewis Morris Esqr. came from the Hon. Secy. of Foreign Affairs and communicated the Letters from Mr Adams &c.[3]

Colo. Moylan Clothier General came and I laid before him the Invoice of Goods by the Ship Adams Capt Smedley[4] telling him that we need not purchase Shirts &c. He said the Officers of the Army had been enquiring about these Goods. I told him that Part of them which is fit for Officers must be sold and they supplied with money to buy for themselves.

Colo. Cook[5] applied for Money referred him until tomorrow.

Mr. Lloyd the Express returned from Bordentown and said he had delivered the Letter to Mr. Borden who had however delivered a few Bills of Exchange first but said no more shou'd go out.[6]

Majr. Storey Aid to Lord Sterling called requesting a Settlement of his Accounts for the time he acted in the Quarter Masters Department.[7] I told him that Mr Dunning is to settle those Accounts and to him he must apply.

Mr. Jno. Barclay[8] Called to settle the Freight which shall be paid for the public Goods by the Ship Heer Adams Capt. Smedley, and after some Conversation we agreed that Mr. Jno. M. Nesbit and Mr Thos. Fitzsimmons with one other Gentleman to be chosen by them shall fix the Freight and that the Invoices of the Goods both Public and Private shall be laid before them, that so they may be enabled to judge properly.[9]

Thos. Hayward Esqr. applied for Money for a Draft to be paid to Genl. Greene to which I agreed.[10]

At my request the Hon: Mr. Paca came here when I consulted him respecting a proper Person residing at Annapolis to be made Receiver of that State but he could not name one with Satisfaction to himself.[11]

Tench Francis Esqr. shewed me a Letter from Charles Stewart requesting him to purchase 3,000 Bbls. Flour for the Contractors.[12] I joined in requesting Mr. Francis to buy all he could and that I will Support him with money if possible.[13]

Wrote a Letter to Geo. A Hall Esqr.

Wrote a Letter to P. Raguet.

Wrote a Letter to the Honble. Genl. Greene.

Issued a Warrant on Mr Swanwick in favor John
Pierce   £123.15.0

Issued a Warrant on Mr Swanwick in favor the
Bank of No. America   3.13.1

Issued a Warrant on Mr Swanwick in favor the
Bank of No. America   194. 5.9

Issued a Warrant on Mr Swanwick in favor the
Contractors for the moving Army   750. 0.0
Issued a Warrant on Mr Swanwick in favor Thos.
Hayward   300. 0.0

1. See text at notes 4 and 8 below, and RM to the President of Congress, September 13, and notes.

2. Concerning Noble Wimberly Jones's involvement in the case of Thomas Edison, see notes to Diary, June 28, 1782.

3. On September 11, Robert R. Livingston received and forwarded to Congress a group of dispatches carried by the *Heer Adams*, Captain Samuel Smedley. They included letters from John Adams dated April 19 through July 5, 1782, covering Adams's diplomatic reception in Holland and his negotiation of a treaty of commerce and a Dutch loan. Also arriving were letters from Henry Laurens, C. W. F. Dumas, Francis Dana, and Thomas Barclay, together with the accounts of Silas Deane (PCC, no. 184, III, 41, and no. 79, II, 291). Which of these were shown to RM cannot be determined with certainty, but the dispatch the Office of Foreign Affairs was most anxious to communicate to RM was no doubt Adams's letter of July 5 announcing the opening of a subscription for a loan of 5 million guilders to the United States by a consortium of Dutch bankers. The letter was accompanied by one to Livingston of July 11 from the Dutch bankers, Wilhem and Jan Willink, Nicolaas and Jacob van Staphorst, Jacobus de la Lande, and Hendrik Fynje, and the five contracts for the loan Adams had made with them on June 11. Congress on September 11 referred Adams's letter and accompanying papers to a committee composed of Jonathan Jackson of Massachusetts, Thomas McKean of Delaware, and John Rutledge of South Carolina with the injunction that the documents were "to be kept secret till further orders" (PCC, no. 186, p. 54). According to this committee book entry, RM and Livingston were to be "notified" of the injunction, but it evidently was lifted on September 12. The committee met with RM on the related matter of managing American funds in Europe (see Diary, September 13, and notes), though its report did not address that subject. Adopting the committee's report on September 14, Congress approved Adams's contracts for the loan and ordered Livingston to transmit the ratification to Holland. Earlier that same day, in response to RM's letter of September 9, Congress had resolved to borrow $4 million in Europe over and above the Holland loan (see notes to RM to the President of Congress, July 30). Adams's letters are in PCC, no. 84, IV, 95, 113 (printed in Wharton, ed., *Rev. Dipl. Corr.*, V, 594-595, 595-597); copies of the contracts are in PCC, no. 84, IV, 97, and no. 104, IV, 110; the Dutch bankers' letter is in PCC, no. 145, pp. 173-174. The Dutch loan was the first obtained by the United States solely on its own credit. In his July 5 letter Adams had advised that the subscription would fill up slowly and had asked Congress not to draw until it knew how much it could count on, but then to draw immediately. RM, however, promptly took steps to draw against the Dutch loan through Havana. See RM to Le Couteulx and Company, September 24, and notes.

4. Invoice not found.

5. William Cooke, the contractor for Wyoming, Pennsylvania.

6. Joseph Borden, Jr., was the Continental loan officer for New Jersey. The letter was RM's Circular to the Continental Loan Officers, September 9, directing them to cease issuing bills of exchange on France in payment of interest on loan office certificates and to return bills in their possession.

7. See notes to Diary, August 14, 1781; and Diary, and RM to William Alexander, Lord Stirling, both September 18, 1782.

8. John Barclay (d. 1816), born in Ireland, moved to Philadelphia not long before 1779 and became a shipper and later president of the Bank of Pennsylvania, mayor of Philadelphia, and state senator. His relationship, if any, to Thomas Barclay, who shipped the public goods on the *Heer Adams*, has not been ascertained. See Campbell, *Sons of St. Patrick*, 95.

9. See Diary, September 13, 1782, and March 10, 1783.

10. See RM to Nathanael Greene, September 18. The applicant was probably Thomas Heyward, a former delegate to Congress from South Carolina.

11. William Paca was a judge of the Court of Appeals in Cases of Capture who resigned later in the year after being elected governor of Maryland; he was a distant relation of RM's by marriage (William White Bronson, *Account of the Meeting of the Descendants of Colonel Thomas White, of Maryland* . . . [Philadelphia, 1879], 161, 172). Paca later suggested Benjamin Harwood as receiver of Continental taxes for Maryland. See RM to Harwood, September 13.

12. Letter not found.

13. See RM to George Washington, September 9 (first letter), and notes.

To Nathanael Greene

Office of Finance 11th September 1782[1]

Sir,

I have received your Letters of the Tenth of July and thirteenth of August. I sincerely thank you for your Sympathy in those Distresses which are inflicted on my Office: Be assured that they are as great as you can imagine. Your kind Assurances of Aid in carrying my Plans into Execution, give me great Pleasure, and the more so as your Conduct has constantly demonstrated that these are solid Principles of Action, and not Empty Professions. I have been, and I am most thoroughly convinced of your Attention to that Oeconomy which you know to be necessary for our political Salvation.

When I wrote to Col. Carrington on the Subject of Cloathing, I had not the most distant Idea of insinuating any Waste, Negligence or Inattention on your Part. But I wrote to the *Quarter Master,*[2] whose Business I conceived it to forward Supplies, expressing my Astonishment that so much had been forwarded to so little Effect. This would naturally stimulate Enquiry and Exertion, so as at least to bring what few Resources we have into Action, and produce a proper Application of them.

In like Manner my Letter to Mr. Hall proceeded on the Estimates which he had handed to me; and he now, in Answer, informs me that these Estimates were too large, so that you will perceive my Ideas were well founded.[3] I did agree to the Prices for the Provisions which you mention, but this was under the Assurances that they could not be purchased cheaper for Cash, nor indeed so cheap. I confess that I was surprized, and have expressed my Opinions that they were extravagant.[4] I shall be much obliged to you, even now if you will adjust this Matter on proper Terms, and I shall direct Mr Hall to apply to you for your Advice on the Subject.[5]

Nothing can be more agreable to me than to be favored fully with your Sentiments on the Objects of my Department, and indeed on every Other. Mr. Hall will have informed you that it was my Intention to have procured both Rum and Salt for your Army,[6] and I am happy to find that you had already made the Provision of those Articles on such advantageous Terms as to the Times of Payment.

When the Evacuation of Charlestown shall have taken place, and the Force which may be continued in that Quarter be determined on, I will take such Arrangements for their Subsistence as a View of the State of our Finances shall admit of. At present I must wait for Information, which I hope soon to receive. I am, Sir, with sincere Esteem Your most obedient and humble Servant

Robt Morris

Major General Greene

ENDORSED: From Mr Morris/Sepr. 11th. 1782.
MSS: LS, Robert Morris Papers, CSmH; Ofcl LbC, DLC; Bancroft transcript, Revolutionary Papers, NN; extract, Samuel Osgood Papers, NHi.
    1. Major General Greene was the commander of the southern army.
    2. RM was alluding to his letter of June 6, 1782, to Edward Carrington, deputy quartermaster general for the southern army. On the effort to supply clothing to the southern army, see RM to Greene, June 10, 1782, and notes.
    3. RM's letter to George Abbott Hall, the receiver of Continental taxes for South Carolina, is dated June 10, 1782. Hall's reply, possibly that of August 14, has not been found.
    4. The NHi extract comprises the preceding portion of this paragraph.
    5. See RM to Hall, September 11.
    6. See RM to Hall, July 12, 1782.

To George Abbott Hall

Office of Finance 11. Sepr. 1782

Sir,

I have received your Letter of the fourteenth of August.[1] I am informed that the Prices fixed for the Supplies in your State are higher than the Cash Prices. I thought them high and only consented to them on the Assurances made me that they could not be purchased even so cheap. By Letter of this date I have requested General Greene to adjust this matter on proper Terms and am now to desire that you apply to him for his Advice on the subject. I am perswaded that no Gentleman in your State can wish the Continent to be charged more than the Thing is worth and therefore I attribute any over Charge to Misinformation which will I am sure be readily corrected on further Consideration. I am Sir your most obedient Servant

RM

MSS: Qfcl LbC, DLC; copy, Samuel Osgood Papers, NHi; Bancroft transcript, Revolutionary Papers, NN.
    1. Letter not found. Hall was the receiver of Continental taxes for South Carolina.

From Comfort Sands, Walter Livingston, William Duer, and Daniel Parker

The ultimatum contained in this letter from four of the West Point and Moving Army contractors was the result of a meeting held at Rhinebeck to discuss the "Critical State of the Army with Respect to Supplies."[1] It set the stage for the dissolution of the combined contract held by Sands, Livingston and Company and for the Financier's negotiation of a new contract for the remainder of 1782 with the firm of Wadsworth and Carter.

Although Morris contended that he was observing the substance of the existing contract, by May and June he survived only by thrusting notes upon the contractors, his own or those of the Bank of North America. This paper frequently could not be converted into specie upon demand by the receivers of Continental taxes, and if the contractors offered it in buying supplies, they had to accept a discount of 5 to 10 percent. If they bought on credit, they had to pay higher prices.[2] It did not help matters that, at Morris's direction, the states' delinquency in paying requisitions was publicized every month by the receivers of Continental taxes.[3] Even in the form of notes, Morris's payments were usually late, at least in terms of the contractors' interpretation of the agreement, which stipulated the first of the month for what was due for the preceding month. Morris insisted that vouchers had to be passed by the Treasury before payment could be made, and, in view of the inevitable bureaucratic delay, thought the contractors should expect to be two months in advance to the government. The contractors repudiated this idea and complained bitterly of nit-picking Treasury officials.[4]

Not all of the contractors' difficulties were of the Financier's making. In the general credit squeeze induced by the British blockade followed by rumors of peace, the contractors had difficulty at times in getting discounts from the Bank of North America.[5] When they tried to save money by skimping in the issue of rations, they aroused the intense resentment of Washington and the army.[6] Their greatest problem, however, was French competition. As the French army and navy moved northward from Virginia and Maryland, purchasing agents of the French army contractors, Wadsworth and Carter, drew on the same supplies that provisioned the American army. Competition was most intense in flour purchases. Those who had flour to sell preferred French purchasers because they had cash in hand and were nearly indifferent as to price. The supply of flour became scarce in New York as a late summer drought shut down mills and forced the Moving Army contractors to buy in New Jersey and Philadelphia, increasing their transportation costs. Some of the consequences of the French troop movements had been foreseen, and the contractors had predicted their own ruin if they had to compete with the French. Morris, however, led them to believe they would stand a good chance of becoming suppliers for the French as well as the American army, whereupon competition would be eliminated and their chances of profit greatly enhanced.[7]

The Superintendent's financial situation worsened during the summer. His resources were critically strained by having on August 1 to redeem over $140,000 in Pierce's promissory notes which had been issued the previous winter to pay officers' salaries.[8] Short of money for every purpose, with the Bank of North America reducing discounts, his access to funds in Europe curtailed by the difficulty and expense of selling bills of exchange, and having no easy way to import a substantial amount of specie,[9] Morris, as he later explained to Congress, found himself "incapable to supply the Monies required."[10] He advised General Washington to prepare to feed the army by impressments.[11] Successive warnings came from the contractors,[12] and finally the ultimatum in the September 11 letter published below.

The Financier was rescued by Jeremiah Wadsworth and John Carter, the contractors for the French army, who approached Morris about bidding on the American army contract for 1783. On September 18, the day after Morris received the September 11 letter,[13] he discussed the situation with John Carter, then in Philadelphia, and encouraged the firm to take up a contract sooner than expected. Morris broke off existing agreements, and a new contract was completed at army headquarters on October 12 by Ezekiel Cornell, inspector of contracts for the main army, in consultation with Washington.[14] Wadsworth and Carter undertook to supply West Point and the Moving Army from October 16 to December 31, 1782, but the new arrangements did not affect Morris's smaller contract with William Duer, who continued as before to supply the Northern Department.

In making the changes in the main contracts, Morris was guided by a number of considerations, which he outlined to the president of Congress in a letter of October 21. Chief among them was his securing three months' credit—he would not have to pay anything to Wadsworth and Carter until February 1783. Unmentioned by Morris in his official explanation were his financial relations with Wadsworth and Carter, and the fact that supply of the French and American main forces were now conveniently unified, although under the French army suppliers rather than the former American contractors.[15]

During his negotiation with Wadsworth and Carter, which he vainly tried to keep secret, Morris continued to deal with Sands, Livingston and Company. Walter Livingston was reluctant to give up supplying the army, and on October 1 privately suggested to Gouverneur Morris that if a wealthy backer could be found, he, Livingston, combined with Duer and Daniel Parker, might continue, even though Sands and Company withdrew. No wealthy backer materialized, but the Superintendent received an offer on October 9 from Livingston, Duer, and Parker. By this time his only interest in the original contractors was to ensure that the army would be supplied until Wadsworth and Carter took over, and in this he succeeded; Sands, Livingston and Company agreed to provide rations through October 15 if given the money to buy and transport flour. Morris initially agreed to advance $8,000 in specie and $5,000 in notes. Less easily resolved were their claims for indemnity for losses arising from the dereliction of government; the ensuing legal controversy long outlasted Morris's administration, extending into the next century.[16]

[Rhinebeck, New York, September 11, 1782]

Sir

The present critical Situation of the Army with respect to Supplies, especially in the Article of Flour, is of too alarming a Nature to Justify on our Part a longer Silence. Were we reduced to this Dilemma by our own Negligence we should not presume to write to you on the Subject; but when we can make it evidently appear, that the want of a seasonable and ample Supply arises from a Delay in the Payment of the Monies due to us from the Public, and from what we actually received falling short of what was due, we owe it to you and ourselves to open with Candor the present State of Supplies, to point out to what Causes the Army is reduced to the present Crisis, and to unfold explicitly what are our Prospects as to a future Provision, and what our Expectations from you as Superintendant of the Finances of the United States.

With respect to the present State of Supply, altho the Army is at present in no Want of Beef, such is our Contract with the Gentlemen who furnish it,[17] and their Disposition, that unless we can punctually pay them in Specie, for the Supplies of August at the Time it becomes due from us, which is on the 15th of September (and of this from your Declaration we have at present no Expectation) they have it in their Power either to cease the Supply, or in Case they consent to receive over your Notes, in Order to continue their Purchases they will endeavor to make the Contractors liable to all Damages which may accrue from the Difference in Purchase betwixt Specie and your Notes. We have Reason to believe they will not cease to purchase Beef, but we have no Doubt they will (if not prevented in Season) make us liable to all Damages which may arise from the Circumstance last mentioned:[18] Of this we shall have Occasion to Speak more at large. With Respect to the Supply of Flour, there is not at present more than ten Days on Hand, and from the present Scarcity of that Article in this State, the high Price to the Eastward, the Approach of the french Army, whose Purchasers are begining to traverse the Country, added to the exhausted State of the Streams and the Season of the Year, which are Obstacles to the Threshing and Manufacture of Wheat, little or no Dependence can be placed on procuring any Supply of Flour in this State till the latter End of October. This Want of Flour is actually to be imputed to the Want of seasonable Payments, as will appear by the following State of Facts:

On the 20th April 16,000 Dollars were due: This Sum was paid on the 22d. with which we were satisfied.

On the 15th.[19] May 14,000 Dollars more were due: On the 29th. 6,900 Dollars (being near the Balance of that Payment) was sent forward in Bank Notes: these we were obliged to return in Order to Convert into Specie, which was not effected till the 15th June. Had this Money come on by the 20th May, at which Time we had a Right to expect it, we had it in our Power to secure a Quantity of Flour at two Dollars, and even under that Price. On the first of July was due to the Contractors

A Balance of   15,861 Dollars
On the 4th July received   1,000 Dollars
On the 18th ditto   5,000
On the 27th ditto   700   6,700
                                                      9,161 Dollars
                                                      Balance

So that the Sum of 5,000 Dollars due on the first was not paid till the 18th; and the Balance of 9,161 Dollars we did not receive during the Course of that Month; these two Sums last mentioned added to the Sum due on the fourteenth of May (had they been punctually paid) would have effectually secured a sufficient Magazine of Flour for the dry Season at no higher Price than two Dollars per Hundred Weight. For the Periods of Money due and received, we refer to the Contractors Account in the Register's Office; and the other Points we can support by the most incontestable Evidence. This was the critical Period of Failure.

In the middle of June the Contractors foreseeing the Necessity of laying up an Ample and Seasonable Supply of Flour wrote to you that if they could depend on the Balance due on the 1st of July vizt 15,861 Dollars, it would be in their Power to secure a large Quantity of Flour. Your Answer on this Occasion, a Copy of which you transmitted to His Excellency General Washington, was to require of the Contractors to fulfill the Stipulations which they had entered into.[20] Tho the first perusal of this Letter gave us Pain, least we might unintentionally have given Offence, we derived a Consolation from this Consideration that the earnest Manner in which you called upon us to perform our Engagements proceeded from a full Conviction of your own Ability to fulfill those you had entered into on the Part of the Public. We were therefore in daily Expectation of this Money coming on, in order to strike for the Purchase of Flour we had in View, when the Contractors for the Fleet lately arrived at Boston purchased and exported out of this State 2700 barrels at one time, and almost the whole of the Remainder was bought up, and sent out by Individuals. Thus the Opportunity of laying a Magazine of Flour in this State was irretrievably lost.

We come now to the Month of July. The Issues in that Month, West Point included, were 47,000 Dollars. On the 2d of August was received 5,000, on the 9th 10,000 Dollars: But it is to be observed, that these two Sums only over paid the June Issues 6,000.

Paid on the July Issues   6,000 Dollars
On or about the 14th August was
    received   4,000
On the 20th paid Mess. Francis and
    Whitesides   9,000

Received by Mr Livingston in Jersey   800
On, or about 29th August   10,000 29,800 Dollars.

So that the whole receipt for July is   29,800
Which deducted from Amount of Issues   47,000 leaves a
Balance due this Day of   17,200 Dollars.
Twelve thousand Dollars of this Sum we expected to have received
from His Excellency General Washington, but to our great Regret
and Disadvantage, were baffled in our Expectations.

The Amount of Issues for the Month of August, West Point included, will amount to   48,000 Dollars
which added to the Balance due for July—being 17,200 Dollars
makes the present Advance   65,200 Dollars

We beg Leave now to consider our future Prospects with Respect
to Supplies. Tho' we cannot but place full Dependence on your
forwarding instantly the 12,000 Dollars that we were disappointed in
receiving from General Washington, you have declared explicitly to
Mr Sands that we are to expect no Payment in Specie for the August
Issues. We are extremely alarmed at this Declaration. The Army has
taken the Field; a Junction is formed by the French, whose Credit
and Mode of Pay is Superior to our own: This will of Course enhance Prices and the Difficulty of procuring Credit. Should the Operations of the Troops be impeded for Want of a Supply, we shall be
held up and considered as the Persons responsible for all the Consequences flowing from this Disappointment.

Our real Situation with Respect to the Payments we have received
cannot be explained without wounding *your Credit*[21] and weakening
still further our own Operations, which are founded principally on
that Basis. It becomes therefore *our* Duty to open our Situation with
Candor to yourself and His Excellency the General, to whom we
have transmitted a Copy of this Letter.[22]

It is true that you have advanced to us 50,000 Dollars in your own
Drafts, not less than twenty thousand Dollars of which are not payable till the 15th of January and February next. However useful
these Bills, with proper Caution, might be made to anticipate a future Supply, they will not answer to discharge Payments already due,
and which were contracted to be paid for in Specie. Amongst these
Engagements the most capital is that for Beef, which amounts to one
half the Cost of the Ration: To discharge this is our principal Difficulty. The Gentlemen who furnish that Article constantly press for
the whole Payment in Specie the Moment it becomes due, whether
we received it from the Public or not. We cannot place Dependence
on making an Agreement with them to take Drafts, and should we—
Contrary to our Expectation—effect it, we have Grounds to apprehend that they would expect an Augmentation of the Price; for they

have declared that they expect a strict Fulfillment of the Contract, and Compensation for the Damage they alledge that they have already sustained. Under such Circumstances it would be criminal in us to hold up the Expectation of a Supply which we do not foresee means of executing. It is true that the Drafts that we have received, are receivable in Taxes in the different States and that the Receivers are bound to exchange them for Cash when they have it on Hand; but the slow Collection of Taxes in this and most of the States, notwithstanding your Efforts to stimulate to them, affords too much Reason to apprehend that Monies will not flow into the different Treasuries in Proportion to the Demand made on them. Were these Drafts confined to the Contractors and the Taxes appropriated in the first Instance to the Payment of the Provision Contracts, some Dependence might be placed on them as a future Resource, but the Fact is, that not only a Number of them have been placed in the Hands of the Quarter Master and Clothier General, but a considerable Sum has been remitted to Mr Russell, Mr Langdon and Mr. Mumford. Those placed in the Hands of the Officers in the public Departments will of Course be distributed to their respective Assistants, who, from the great demands made on them and the Want of proper Management, will pass them for Services and Articles of Supply at a higher Rate than if they paid for them in Specie. This begets a Depreciation injurious to your Credit and ruinous to us. The other Gentlemen from their Profession as Merchants will of Course manage them with more Prudence, if they do negotiate them. But we know that Mr. Langdon and Mr Russell have made Demands upon Mr Lovell for the Amount of their Drafts, and have actually prevented our obtaining those Sums which might Otherwise have been Secured. When we made this Contract we can with Truth assure you that we placed more Dependence on your personal than on your Official Character: We were anxious to second the views of your Administration, and we had every Reason to suppose from your own Declaration, that you had Resources adequate at least to the Subsistance of the Army—without placing so great a Dependence on the Exertions of the different States. We are far from supposing that you had the most distant Intention of leading us into an Error—At the Time you supposed yourself adequate to these Demands you certainly had Grounds for the Opinion—We presume you have been deceived. We have still the utmost Confidence in your Determination to support us, by every Means in your Power, and are anxious to make every Exertion to afford an ample Supply to the Army: But we are constrained to declare explicitly that we can no longer be answerable for the Supply of the Troops on Terms agreed upon in the Contract. If, Sir, it is not in your Power to pay us in future in Specie and at regular monthly Payments agreeably to the

Terms of our Contract we trust to your Candor and Justice that you will give us Assurances of Indemnification at the Close of the Contract for all Damages sustained from the Public Inability to perform their Engagements, and that you will (if you can go no further) advance on producing our monthly Account Current, at least one Half of the Amount of the Ration in Specie, and supply us from Time to Time with such a Number of your Drafts as shall be found adequate to the Object of Supplying. This must of Course be very considerable, not less than a whole Month's Advance Supply: That is to say if the monthly Amount of Rations is 45,000 Dollars, we shall at all Events receive on producing our Accounts and Vouchers, 22,500 Dollars in Specie and 67,000 in your own Drafts. These must necessarily be deposited in the Hands of different Commissioners of Taxes, in order to redeem the Money that may come into their Hands, and in Cases of Emergency we may be obliged to lodge them as a Deposit for Monies borrowed till such Time as we shall be able to repay it, for it will be better both for yours and our own Credit to pay in critical Situations a Premium for Money, than, by a general Circulation of the Bills, beget a Depreciation, the Bounds of which it is impossible to ascertain.[23] We flatter Ourselves, Sir, that the Peculiarity of our Situation, in which it is impossible for us to express Ourselves without giving you Pain, and not subject us hereafter to the charge of Deception, will hold us excused for troubling you with this Letter. We share fully in all your Feelings: We do not wish to shrink from the Support of the Army and of your Administration, in which we consider the Welfare of our Country to depend, but we owe it to you and Ourselves to open our real Situation. We shall continue our Exertions to supply the Army till the first Day of October, and make every possible Provision for a future Support: But if we do not receive your Assurances on the Points we have mentioned before that Period, we shall on that Day be reduced to the painful Necessity of surrendering a Trust too hazardous for us to continue in with the limited Prospects that we have in View. We have the Honor to be With great Respect and Esteem Your most obedient and most humble Servants[24]

At Rhinebeck September 11th 1782	(Signd)	Comfort Sands Walter Livingston William Duer Daniel Parker

MSS: Copy, PCC, DNA; copy, Washington Papers, DLC; copy, Benjamin Franklin Papers, PPAmP.

1. The quotation is from Sands, Livingston, Duer, and Parker to George Washington, September 11, 1782 (Washington Papers, DLC), which enclosed a copy of the present letter. "From the pain we have felt in writing," the contractors observed to the general, "we Judge what Your Feelings must be in reading, our letter to Mr Morris,

but we Owe it to the Public and Ourselves, and in a particular Manner to Your Excellency, rather to run the Hazard of giving pain, than to Expose ourselves hereafter, to the Imputation of a want of Candor, and Your Army to the fatal Consequences which might Result from it." Charles Stewart, the issuing contractor, evidently did not approve of the letter, for Walter Livingston wrote him as follows on December 16, 1782 (Walter Livingston Letterbooks, Robert R. Livingston Papers, NHi): "I differ from you in thinking our letter of the 11th. Sepr. from Rhinebeck 'hard on Mr. Morris.' I still approve of every Sentence. We acted a candid and a generous part, we asked less than we were entitled to by Contract."

According to the contractors' letter to Washington, "Most of the Gentlemen Concern'd" in the contract attended the meeting. The combined West Point and Moving Army contract was administered by Sands, Livingston and Company, of which Comfort Sands and Walter Livingston were the principal partners. Although not signatories of either of the original contracts, William Duer and Daniel Parker held interest in Livingston's share of the Moving Army contract. For the other contractors of record and interested men, see notes to Diary, May 13, 1782.

2. See, for example, RM to William Churchill Houston, May 9, to Tench Francis and Richardson Sands, May 29, to George Olney, June 12, to Washington, August 20, and notes, Comfort Sands and Company and Walter Livingston to RM, June 17, 1782, and Diary, May 28, June 11, 1782. For the contractors' comments, see Comfort Sands and Company to Washington, June 17, 1782, Washington Papers, DLC; Walter Livingston to Duer, June 7, 1782, Walter Livingston Letterbooks, Robert R. Livingston Papers, NHi; Parker to Sands, Livingston and Company, September 17, 20, October 10, 1782, Parker Letterbook, MH; Affidavit of Comfort Sands, December 24, 1819, Papers relating to the petition of Ebenezer Stevens and others, Records of the United States Senate, RG 46, DNA.

3. See notes to RM to William Whipple, June 4, 1782.

4. See Comptroller of the Treasury to RM, August 1, Duer to RM, August 2, RM to Duer, August 29, to Washington, August 5, to Comfort Sands, and to Walter Livingston, both July 12, 1782, and Diary, August 14, 1782. See also Duer to John Holker, August 2, 1782, Holker Papers, DLC; John Chaloner to Wadsworth and Carter, February 9, 1782, Chaloner and White Letterbook, PHi. An undated document described as "Governeur Morris's remarks respecting the contractors' accompts" (*American State Papers*, Class 9, Claims, I, 721) asserted that Sands, Livingston and Company's accounts for May had been delivered on July 4, 1782, "in so irregular a manner that they could not pass through the officers, nor were they ever reported on by the clerks of accounts until the 30th of January, 1783."

5. See, in general, the headnote to RM's State of American Commerce and Plan for Protecting It, May 10, 1782, and notes; also RM to William Duer, June 12, 1782.

6. See Washington to RM, May 17, 1782, and notes, and sources cited there.

7. See Walter Livingston to RM, May 26, and notes, Washington to RM, June 16 and September 4 (second letter), and notes, the Quartermaster General to RM, September 19, and Sands, Livingston and Company to RM, September 25, 1782. See also John Chaloner to Nehemiah Hubbard, April 9, 1782, Chaloner and White Letterbook, PHi; Walter Livingston to Comfort Sands, May 25, June 8, and September 28, and Duer and Livingston to Sands, September 12, 1782, Walter Livingston Letterbooks, Robert R. Livingston Papers, NHi; Charles Stewart to Livingston, March 14, Livingston to Stewart, April 28, July 28, August 4 and 9, and September 1, 1782, Stewart Papers, MH.

8. See Diary, August 1, and notes.

9. On this problem, see notes to RM to Le Couteulx and Company, September 24.

10. See RM to the President of Congress, October 21.

11. See RM to Washington, August 29 (first letter), and notes, August 30, and September 9 (second letter).

12. See Walter Livingston to RM, August 13, Diary, August 14 and 20, and RM to Livingston, August 29, and notes.

13. See RM to Ezekiel Cornell, September 20.

14. See RM to Cornell, September 20, and Diary, September 23.

15. See the headnote to RM's Contract with Wadsworth and Carter, October 12.

16. On the litigation, see Ezekiel Cornell to RM, October 5, and notes.

17. On the beef subcontract with Oliver Phelps and Timothy Edwards, see notes to the Contract for the Moving Army, April 6, 1782.

18. For the damages demanded by the subcontractors, see note 16 above.

19. DLC copy: "14th."

20. See Comfort Sands and Company and Walter Livingston to RM, June 17, and RM to Sands and Company and Livingston, and to Washington, both June 22, 1782.

21. This and the other italicized words in this paragraph are not underlined in the Washington Papers text.

22. See note 1 above.

23. RM probably rejected the contractors' request for at least a one month's advance in his notes because of the problems already resulting from the "crowding" of his notes by the contractors and from the competition between the contractors and other holders of his notes and bills to exchange them with tax collectors and receivers for specie. See, for example, Alexander Hamilton to RM, September 21 and October 9, RM to Hamilton, October 5, Ezekiel Cornell to RM, October 5, and RM to John Langdon, October 15; and Daniel Parker to Sands, Livingston and Company, September 17, 20, October 4, and 10, and to Richardson Sands, October 10, 1782, in Daniel Parker Letterbook, pp. 62, 63, 65, 66, 67, MH. On the notes and bills of exchange currently in use by RM, see his Circulars to the Receivers of Continental Taxes, July 19, and notes, and August 29, 1782, and notes.

24. RM enclosed this PCC text in his letter to the President of Congress of October 21; the PPAmP text was enclosed to Benjamin Franklin, January 11, 1783.

To the Governor of North Carolina (Alexander Martin)

Office of Finance 11. Septr. 1782

I have been favored with your Excellency's Letter of the twentieth of August enclosing a Copy of the Acts of your last Session of Assembly for which I pray you to accept my Thanks as well as for your Kind sentiments in my Favor and the assurances of your Aid in Support of the Measures adopted for promoting the public Service. I pray your Excellency to beleive that I am with Esteem and Respect your most obedient Servant

MS: Ofcl LbC, DLC.

To Claudius P. Raguet

Office of Finance 11. Septr. 1782

I have considered the Propositions contained in your Note of the tenth Instant[1] and am sorry that it is not in my Power to acquiesce therein. The Public have not occasion at this Time for such a Ship as you mention—nor do I want one for my own Account.

I must therefore as my Duty requires enjoin you to make Provision for the discharge of your Obligation with all possible Speed.

MS: Ofcl LbC, DLC.

1. Raguet's letter has not been found. For the background, see notes to Diary, September 2.

From George Washington

Head Quarters [Verplancks Point, New York] 11th. Septemr 1782

When applications, of a similar nature to the inclosed, are made to me,[1] I am under the necessity of referring them to you. I know your distress on the score of public Money and can therefore only request that you will assist Colo. Varrick in whole or in part of his present demand as soon as circumstances will admit.

MSS: Dft in the writing of Tench Tilghman, Washington Papers, DLC; Varick transcript, Washington Papers, DLC.
1. A marginal gloss in Tench Tilghman's hand indicates that the enclosure was "Colo. Varricks letter of 3d. Sepr. 1782" to Washington written from Poughkeepsie. Richard Varick was Washington's private and confidential secretary; his letter (in Washington Papers, DLC) requested $800 for back pay due three of his clerks who were copying Washington's correspondence. For the Financier's response, see RM to Washington, September 19 (third letter).

Diary: September 12, 1782

Haym Solomon brought some Notes taken for Bills and says that Bills continue unsaleable.

Colo. Wm. Cook for Money. I granted a Warrant for 600 Dollars.

Capt Barney respecting the manning of the Ship Genl. Washington and after a good deal of Conversation I continued the Determination of manning her as a Packet with 50 men.[1]

Mr. Moylan Clothier General brought a Bill drawn upon him by his Deputy Mr Brooks in favor of Messrs. Grier and Co. who had enabled him to pay the Taylors employed in making up the Soldiers Cloathing and who is exceedingly distressed for the Money. I agreed to Supply 300 Dollars in Cash and that Mr. Moylan should accept the remainder payable in thirty Days.

Thos. Willing Esqr. President of the Bank came to the Office respecting some of my Transactions with the Bank which were deranged.

Sundry Letters and applications for Money.

Capts. Harrison and Maxwell of the Flag Ships apply to be Supplied with Money. I deferred an Answer but ask whether they are ready to receive the Prisoners which they are and I shall order them on Board.[2]

Wrote a Letter to his Excellency the Govr of North Carolina.[3]

Wrote a Letter to Jona. Burrall Esqr.

Wrote a Letter to His Excelly. Genl Washington.

Wrote a Letter to the Governors of the States.

Wrote a Letter to the Receivers of Taxes.

Issued a Warrant on Mr Swanwick in favor of Joseph Pennell £375.0.0.

1. See RM to Francis Gurney, John Patton, and William Allibone, September 12.
2. See notes to Diary, August 13.
3. This letter is dated September 11.

Circular to the Governors of the States

Circular   Office of Finance 12th September 1782
Sir

I do myself the Honor to enclose to your Excellency (Number one and two) two Acts of Congress, the first is of the fourth and the second of the tenth Instant.[1] It is my particular Duty Sir to pray the attention of your State to these acts. The Subject is important and will I doubt not be considered according to its Magnitude. Number three is an Order of the fifth Instant. I have thought it most proper to send you the whole Letter referred to in that Order as also of the Letter of the thirtieth of July enclosing Estimates for the ensuing Year which has a necessary Relation to the other.[2] When Congress shall have finally determined on these Objects I shall do myself the Honor to transmit the Result. With perfect Respect I am Sir Your Excellency's most obedient and humble Servant

Robt Morris

His Excellency the Governor of Connecticutt[3]

ENDORSED: 12th Septr. 1782/Office of Finance/enclosing/No 1. 1,200,000 dollars quotaed/for payment of Interest on Debts/the money raised in each state/to be so applied/No 2 Septr 10th 1782/Quota of Connecticut 133,200 dollars/6½d on the £/No 3 Septr 5 Copies of the Estimates/of the domestic debt and Letter/to be sent to each State/received 30th instant
MSS: LS, to the Governor of Connecticut, Jonathan Trumbull Papers, Ct; LS, to the Governor of New Hampshire, Meshech Weare Papers, Nh-Ar; LS, to the Governor of Massachusetts, M-Ar; LS, to the President of Delaware, Executive Papers, De-Ar; LS, to the Governor of Virginia, Continental Congress Papers, Vi; Ofcl LbC, DLC; LbC, Letterbook of Governor Alexander Martin of North Carolina, 1782–1785, Nc-Ar.
    1. The act of September 4, 1782, levied a new $1.2 million requisition upon the states to pay the interest on the public debt; the act of September 10 apportioned the requisition among the states. For a discussion, see the headnote and notes to RM to the President of Congress, July 29.
    2. Congress's order of September 5, 1782, directed RM to send the states his estimate of the public debt and an extract from his letter to the president of Congress of July 29, 1782, in which the estimate was enclosed. RM's letter of July 30 was also addressed to the president of Congress.
    3. This line is in Gouverneur Morris's hand.

Circular to the Receivers of Continental Taxes

Circular   Office of Finance 12th September 1782
Sir,

Enclosed you will find Copies of my Letters of the 29th and 30th of July to Congress.[1] I know not what Determinations they may come to on these Subjects; but I transmit the Letters that you may be possessed of the Matter fully, obviate Misrepresentation, and inculcate at proper Opportunities those Principles of national Integrity which are essential to our Safety. I am, Sir, With Esteem, Your most obedient and humble Servant

Robt Morris

P.S. You will also find enclosed Acts of Congress of the 4th and 10th Instant.[2]

Wm Churchill Houston Esqr.
Receiver for New Jersey[3]

ENDORSED: Honble Robt Morris/12 Septr/1782
MSS: LS, to William Churchill Houston of New Jersey, Houston Collection, NjP; LS, to Benjamin Harwood of Maryland, Morris-Harwood Papers, MdHi; Ofcl LbC, DLC.
1. The letter of July 29 asked for $2 million in federal taxes to fund the public debt; the letter of July 30 presented estimates of Continental expenses for 1783 and recommended a requisition on the states for $5 million and a foreign loan of $4 million.
2. See notes to the preceding letter.
3. These two lines are in Gouverneur Morris's hand.

To Francis Gurney, John Patton, and William Allibone

Marine Office 12. Sept. 1782[1]

Gentlemen

On reconsidering my Instructions to you of the 4 Instant respecting the Packet ship General Washington, I have concluded to allow forty Seamen to be shipped for that Vessel exclusive of her Officers which are mentioned underneath. You will please therefore to proceed accordingly, and the Monies which you may Want for Disbursments will be paid to you by Joseph Pennell Esqr. Paymaster of the Navy to whom I have given Directions on that Head. I am Gentlemen your most obedient and humble Servant

RM

The Captain

Three Lieutenants	Carpenter
one Surgeon	Cook and Steward
Boatswain	
Gunner	

MS: AM LbC, MdAN.
1. Gurney, Patton, and Allibone were the commissioners of Pennsylvania for the defense of the Delaware River. The subject of this letter to them was discussed with Joshua Barney, captain of the *General Washington*, in the Diary of September 12.

To John Langdon

Marine Office 12. Septem: 1782

Sir,

I have received your Letter of the twenty fifth and am very sorry to find that you seem to despond.[1] After the Exertions you have already made I am sure you will not abandon the Business when so near to a Completion. On the contrary I perswade myself that you will redouble your Exertions in Proportion as they become more necessary. Your Letter appears to have been written under the Influence of an Opinion that my mind had received unfavorable Impressions from Misrepresentation. But reflection will certainly convince you that I have invariably reposed the fullest Confidence in your Zeal and Abilities. That you have not been more regularly supplied with Money cannot be more painful to you than it is to me. But when you compare the trifling Sums I have received with the Extent and Magnitude of the Services to be performed by them you will pity a situation the Distresses of which cannot be conceived by those who have not witnessed them. Before I close this Letter I feel myself bound to make one Observation to you. You evidently beleive that you have Enemies who wish to attribute your Conduct to mercenary Principles: Supposing this to be the Fact you must see in an Instant what Advantages they would derive from your abandoning the Vessel at the present Moment. I pray you to beleive that I am with Esteem your most obedient Servant

RM

MS: AM LbC, MdAN.
1. Letter not found. Langdon, a merchant and political figure of Portsmouth, New Hampshire, was finishing the construction of the *America.* For the recent gift of this vessel to France, see notes to John Paul Jones to Gouverneur Morris, September 2.

To George Washington

Office of Finance 12th September 1782

Sir,

I have before me your Excellency's several Letters of the 23d of August, and 2d and 4th Instant. I have now the Pleasure to inform you that General Cornell has agreed to accept the Office of Inspector of the Contracts &c. for your Army,[1] and will soon proceed on the Business of his Department. I hope you may find Relief from this Appointment, and that it may prove perfectly agreable to you. If Mr. Skinner was in Town, I did not see him, but I have thought it best to send James Mullins to attend the Commissioners with the

Accounts.[2] He can act as a Clerk for them during the Meeting. My chief Reasons for sending him, are, that he made up the Accounts of Issues, as Clerk to the Commissary General, that he affords a safe Conveyance for the five hundred Dollars mentioned in your Excellency's Letters, and that he may perhaps prove useful to the Commissioners. I am entirely persuaded of the Propriety of such Instructions as your Excellency may think proper to give as to the Accounts. With perfect Respect I have the Honor to be Your most obedient and humble Servant

Robt Morris

His Excellency General Washington

ENDORSED: Philada. 12th. Septemr./1782/from/Honble. Mr. Robt. Morris/with 480 dolls./Answered 22d
MSS: LS, Washington Papers, DLC; Ofcl LbC, DLC.
    1. For Ezekiel Cornell's acceptance of this post, see notes to RM to the President of Congress, April 20, 1782.
    2. Mullins, however, did not leave for headquarters until September 14 (see Diary of that date). For the upcoming conference on prisoners, see notes to Diary, June 18, 1782.

From Horatio Gates

Virginia 12th: September 1782

My dear Sir

Having just received Gen: Washingtons Letter of the 27th: Ultimo from His Head-Quarters,[1] I am preparing to set out on Monday morning, and as I purpose to lose no Time in Philadelphia, must beg you will order a Tent and Marqui to be ready for me as I pass through there; that, I had to the Southward, I left with General Huger,[2] when I was recalled from Thence. The Public never supplied me with more than one Other Tent, that you lay in, in 77, and by 80 it was Rotten. I received your Affectionate Letter of July last[3] upon my return Home, it was wrote with all the Sincerity, and Friendship for which I ever have, and ever shall esteem the Writer; my worthy Friend may rest assured, I will never be behind hand with him in that warmth of Affection, and Attachment, that the very best Disposition to Friendship can produce. Men in enviable Station, Soldiers, and Men of Honour, should above all Other Men pay the Greatest Regard to These professions, and never make them but when they Sacredly mean the fullfillment thereof, and such I wish and believe are the foundation of those we have so frequently made to each other. Ms: Gates[4] Joins me in wishing you all the Happyness this World can bestow. I am Dear Sir Your Affectionate Faithfull Humble Servant

Horatio Gates

MS: ALS, Preston Davie Collection, NcU.
1. See Diary, August 22, and notes, for Washington's letter and the background to this communication from Major General Gates.
2. Brigadier General Isaac Huger (1742/1743–1797) of South Carolina who had held several important commands in the southern theater. *DAB*.
3. Probably RM's letter of July 26, 1782.
4. This was Elizabeth Phillips Gates (ca. 1736–1783), whom Gates married in 1754 in Halifax, Nova Scotia. She was the daughter of a lieutenant in the British army who was related by marriage to English gentry. Paul David Nelson, *General Horatio Gates: A Biography* (Baton Rouge, La., 1976), 12, 277. This note corrects the identification given in notes to Gates to RM, June 3, 1781.

To Jonathan Burrall

Office of Finance 12 Septem. 1782

I have duly received your Letter of the fourth Instant[1] and after reflecting on it I am [of] Opinion all Circumstances considered that the Accounts of the Pay of the several Assistants may be settled on their producing a Certificate of their having settled their issuing Accounts with their Principal but these Accounts must be settled with a Reservation—viz: that the Balance is to be carried to their Credit on settling the Accounts of Issues should they appear in such Accounts to be indebted to the United States. Of Consequence they cannot at present receive negotiable Certificates in Payment of their Balances. A List of those Balances may be returned to me.

MS: Ofcl LbC, DLC.
1. Letter not found. Burrall was the commissioner for settling the accounts of the Commissary Department.

To Thomas Russell

Marine Office 12 Sepr. 1782

I have duly received your Letter of the twenty eighth of August[1] and I regret with you that the Hague should be detained by the Disputes which have arisen among her Officers. But I really see no Remedy. I hope however the Enquiry will have been terminated before this Moment. In such Case the frigate may sail immediately.

I am glad that Captain Barry's Prize has arrived and perfectly approve of your Determination with respect to her. The Accounts Sales &ca. will be forwarded of Course.

MS: AM LbC, MdAN.
1. Letter not found. Russell was the deputy agent of marine for New England.

From William Irvine

Fort Pitt Sepr: 12th 1782[1]

This will be handed to you by Mr. Perry who informed me he has some intention to Contract for supplying the Troops at this Post with provision. He has requested me to write you, more by way of introduction than a recommendation, as he says he can obtain sufficient security for any engagements he may enter into. All I know of the man, is, that he is possessed of considerable property and I believe has as much credit in this Country as any other man.

MS: Copy in Irvine's writing, Irvine Family Papers, PHi.
1. This letter from Brigadier General Irvine, the commander at Fort Pitt, was delivered to RM on September 30. See Diary of that date.

Diary: September 13, 1782

I proposed this morning to Mr. Fitzsimmons that he should go to Mr. Jenifer for Money &c. but it did not suit him.[1]

Mr. James Mullins asserting that the late Commissary Genl of Issues Charles Stewart Esqr had promised him and Mr Gartley his other Clerk that I would pay their Wages since the first of January last. I agreed that Mr Stewart should Settle and Certify their Balances and I will pay them.

Mr. Jno. Grier who possesses Mr. Brook's drafts on the Clothier General came to the Office and says he cannot possibly support his Credit with less than 400 Dollars in Money down, about 1000 Dollars in Acceptances of 30 Days and the rest in my Notes of 60 Days to which I agreed as this Gentleman has been and will again be Serviceable.

Mr. John Barclay called respecting the Ship Heer Adams and to know how the freight is to be paid. I desired the Ship may be put up at Auction and Sold, the lead belonging to the Owners equally divided, the public Goods delivered to Mr Swanwick and the Account of Ship and Freight settled together at the end of thirty Days, when I will either Pay or receive the Balance as the Case may require.[2]

Mr. Wm. Brown applied to Settle his Accounts and receive pay for Provisions supplyed by him to Colo. Wm. [i.e., Richard] Butler's Troops in an Expedition from Carlisle.[3] I desired him to Settle the Accounts with Mr. Milligan and that on his Certificate I will Pay.

Mr: Edwd. Williams for Money for the Purveyor of the Hospitals.[4] I told him that at present I have it not, but next week I hope to give them some money.

The Honble. Secy at War and Genl. Cornell came to the Office when we adjusted that General Cornell shall be Inspector of the Contracts &c. and fixed the Sundry Papers &c: to be given him.[5]

The Hon: J: Rutledge, T. McKeane, Mr. Jackson a Committee of Congress on the Subject of drawing or Importing Money from Europe. I gave them many reasons which proved to their Satisfaction that Congress had best leave that open to my management but told them what is really true that I have no objection of fixing the matter.[6]

Wrote a Letter to William Duer Esqr.

Wrote a Letter to Benjm. Harwood.

Wrote a Letter to Danl. St Thoms. Jenifer.

Wrote a Letter to Danl. St Thoms. Jenifer.

Wrote a Letter to his Excelly. the Prest. of Congress.
Wrote a Letter to Chs. Stewart.
Wrote a Letter to Wm Denning.
Issued a Warrant on Mr Swanwick in favor Geo.
Inglis   £   27. 5.10
Issued a Warrant on Mr Swanwick in favor Jno.
Wilson   81. 5.
Issued a Warrant on Mr Swanwick in favor the
Bank of No. America   94.10
Issued a Warrant on Mr Swanwick in favor Sands
Livingston & Co   1191.10. 6

1. Thomas Fitzsimons was a director of the Bank of North America; Daniel of St. Thomas Jenifer was Maryland's intendant of the revenue. See Diary, September 3, for the request that RM make payments to the bank; also RM to Jenifer, September 13 (two letters).
2. See Diary, September 11, and notes.
3. The editors' correction of the copyist's error is based on the entry in Treasury Waste Book D, p. 15, Records of the United States General Accounting Office, RG 217, DNA.
4. The purveyor was Thomas Bond, Jr.
5. Ezekiel Cornell had already agreed to the appointment as inspector of contracts for the main army (see RM to George Washington, September 12, and notes). RM's commission to Cornell is dated September 19.
6. The disposal of American funds in Europe had previously been committed to RM's management in congressional resolutions of November 27 and December 3, 1781 (see notes to RM to Benjamin Franklin, November 27, 1781 [first letter]). The committee did not address this question in its report of September 14 on the Dutch loan (see notes to Diary, September 11), but earlier that day a strong motion made by Arthur Lee and seconded by Theodorick Bland, Jr., that would have instructed the American ministers in Europe "to conform strictly" to the earlier resolutions, was defeated in a roll call vote of 5 to 3, with two states divided and three unable to vote because of inadequate representation. Congress, however, did adopt (evidently without roll call) another motion by James Madison, seconded by James Duane, that was identical in substance although perhaps milder in tone. The unaminous vote of the Pennsylvania delegation against Lee's motion suggests that it was perceived as an attack on his archenemy, Benjamin Franklin. For another assessment, see Hutchinson and Rutland, eds., *Madison Papers*, V, 124–125n.; concerning congressional action on related questions raised by Franklin's letter to RM of June 25, 1782, see RM to the President of Congress, September 18, and notes, and September 19, and notes.

To the President of Congress
(John Hanson)

Office of Finance 13th September 1782

Sir,

   The Ship Heer Adams, commanded by Capt Smedley, has brought public Goods to the Amount of Two Hundred and forty one Thousand eight Hundred and eighty eight Dutch Guilders, being about Twenty two Thousand six Hundred and seventy seven Pounds Sterling. I have the Pleasure to inform Congress that these are Part of the Goods purchased by Order of Colonel Laurens in

Holland. Mr. Barclay had shipped and was shipping the Remainder of them. I hope they will arrive.[1] Such Goods as are fit for the Army will be at the proper Times put into the Hands of the several Departments to which they belong. Some of the Cloathing being too fine for the Soldier's Use, I propose to have it sold for Account of the Public.[2] I have the Honor to be, Sir, Your Excellency's Most obedient Servant

Robt Morris

His Excellency The President of Congress

ENDORSED: 90/Letter Sept 13. 1782/Supert. Finance/Read 14./Arrival of Ship Herr Adams/with cloathing
MSS: LS, PCC, DNA; Ofcl LbC, DLC.
    1. On these goods, see Benjamin Franklin to RM, March 4, 1782, and notes. The antecedents in Holland are recounted in detail in van Winter, *American Finance and Dutch Investment*, I, 37–43.
    2. Later RM decided to sell all the clothing. See Diary, September 25.

To William Duer

Office of Finance 13. Septr. 1782

Sir,

Having Reason to apprehend that you would be disappointed in the Monies you expected to receive thro General Washington[1] I have thought it best to dispatch the Bearer Express at the public Expence with seven thousand Dollars whereof two thousand are in my old Notes.[2] I am Sir your most obedient Servant

RM

MS: Ofcl LbC, DLC.
    1. Duer was the contractor for the posts north of Poughkeepsie in New York. For the money he expected from Washington, see RM to Duer, August 29, and notes.
    2. See Diary, September 14. On changes in the form of Morris's notes, see RM's Circular to the Receivers of Continental Taxes, August 29, and notes.

To Benjamin Harwood

Office of Finance 13th September 1782[1]

Sir,

At the Recommendation of the honorable Mr. Paca,[2] I take the Liberty to offer you the Office of Receiver of Continental Taxes for the State of Maryland. Should you think proper to accept it, you will be pleased to call on Mr. Zephaniah Turner, who will deliver you the necessary Papers.[3] You can then execute the Securities, and transmit them. It was hinted to me, that your Brother would accept this Office, and I should immediately have made him the Offer: But there were Reasons which rendered it necessary to adopt a general Rule not to appoint any of the Loan Officers, and I could not consistently make him an Exception to it, which I really wished to do.[4] I am, Sir, With Esteem Your most obedient Servant,

Robt Morris

Benjamin Harwood Esqr.
Annapolis

ENDORSED: Letter/Robert Morris Esqr./13th. Septr. 1782
MSS: LS, Morris-Harwood Papers, MdHi; Ofcl LbC, DLC.
   1. Harwood, who accepted the appointment tendered in this letter, was an Annapolis merchant in partnership with his brother Thomas, the treasurer of the western shore and commissioner of the Continental loan office in Maryland. Benjamin succeeded his brother as loan officer in 1793 and apparently continued in that capacity until 1801. Edward C. Papenfuse, *In Pursuit of Profit*, 122; Prince, *Federalist and Civil Service*, 150; and RM to Harwood, October 1.
   2. See Diary, September 11, and notes.
   3. See RM to Zephaniah Turner, May 24 and June 11, 1782.
   4. RM's reasons for not appointing Continental loan officers as receivers are explained in the Diary of August 29.

To Daniel of St. Thomas Jenifer

Office of Finance 13. Sepr. 1782

Sir,
   Not having been able to meet with a proper Person to whom it would be convenient to go for the Money in your Possession[1] I deferred it until this Day. In the Interim I have advised Persons carrying Money hence to take Bank Bills which you would Exchange. I request you will do this to facilitate bringing the Money hither. As a Receiver is not yet appointed[2] I take the Liberty of subjecting you to this Trouble. I am Sir your most obedient and humble Servant

RM

MS: Ofcl LbC, DLC.
   1. See RM to Jenifer, September 9, and notes. Jenifer was Maryland's intendant of the revenue.
   2. See the preceding letter.

To Daniel of St. Thomas Jenifer

Office of Finance 13. Septem. 1782

Sir,
   The Bearer of this Letter Captain Greene will present you a Bill on Mr. Swanwick for twenty thousand Dollars payable to himself or Order at Sight.[1] As you mention the having on Hands seven thousand Pounds and that you was daily in Expectation of receiving more I have no Doubt that you will be able to pay this Bill. Should you have Bank Notes, my Notes or the Pay Masters they will be

equally acceptable with Specie. The Bill will on Payment be indorsed by Captain Green and shall be taken in Payment by the Receiver of your State when he shall be appointed for so much in Discharge of your Quota. I am Sir your most obedient and humble Servant

RM

MSS: Ofcl LbC, DLC; LbC, Intendant's Letterbook, MdAA.
1. For RM's instructions to John Green, a captain in the Continental navy, see Diary, September 14.

Gouverneur Morris to Henry Knox

Philaa: 13 Sepr 1782[1]

Dear Knox.

Our Sovereign Lords the Congress have at Length assented to (not approved of) our conduct at Elizabeth Town.[2] After the abusive Letter of Sir H. Clinton,[3] it would have seemed to be proper that an immediate approbation should have taken Place, even tho the Matter might have been somewhat questionable. As it is, they have (unwittingly) done us the highest honor. They have been compelled, to adopt our Principles; and if one could with Propriety scrutinize and criticize the Conduct of our Masters, we might think that they have only erred in imitating Sir Henry's Talents for Bilingsgate, and in going into unnecessary forms of a Great Seal &ca. &ca. The Bearer of this will bring you Copies of the Accounts against the Enemy as far as hitherto collected.[4] I think it is a Million to one that the British Genl. is not able to meet you with adequate Powers, I mean as to *Form Great Seals* &ca. &ca. Present me to Mrs. Knox. Adieu yours

Gouv Morris

P.S. Skinner[5] has sent his Accounts which are with the Treasury.

MS: ALS, Knox Papers, MHi.
1. Gouverneur Morris and Knox had served as Washington's commissioners at a conference held at Elizabeth, New Jersey, in April 1782 to negotiate a general cartel for the exchange of prisoners with the British and resolve outstanding issues pertaining thereto (see notes to Gouverneur Morris to RM, March 22, 1782). Although Gouverneur Morris had declined to serve again at a forthcoming prisoner conference to be held in Tappan, New York, Knox had agreed to attend with William Heath. See Gouverneur Morris to Washington, August 26.
2. Congress had long postponed taking any action on their reports (see notes to Diary, May 1 and June 18, 1782), but finally took up the subject in response to letters from Secretary at War Benjamin Lincoln of August 26 and Washington of August 28. Lincoln's letter informed Congress that Washington desired its determination on the proceedings of Knox and Morris so that, if approved, they could serve as the basis for further negotiations toward a general cartel which Congress had directed Washington to renew on August 12. Congress referred the letters to a committee composed of Theodorick Bland, Jr., James Duane, and Ezekiel Cornell (PCC, no. 186, pp. 59, 60). The committee's report was debated on September 5 and adopted in final form on September 9. Unlike the first draft of the report, which was largely in Duane's writing and specifically approved of the actions of Morris and Knox, the final report instead

reaffirmed the principles for which they had contended at the conference. See *JCC*, XXIII, 551, 555–559n.; Lincoln's letter is in PCC, no. 149, I, 611–612; Washington's is in Fitzpatrick, ed., *Writings of Washington*, XXV, 71–72.

3. Probably a reference to Sir Henry Clinton's letter to Washington on April 22, 1782, which Washington had forwarded to Congress on April 30 (Fitzpatrick, ed., *Writings of Washington*, XXIV, 190). Clinton's letter had accused the American commissioners of insensitivity to the plight of the prisoners and "a premeditated design of objecting to the extent of my Commissioners powers, that they might have a pretext for declaring that a general Cartel would not be agreed to." A copy of the letter is in PCC, no. 169, VIII, 396–411.

4. The bearer was probably James Mullins. See RM to Washington, September 12, and Diary, September 14.

5. Abraham Skinner, the acting commissary general of prisoners.

To Joseph Bradford

Marine Office 13. Septem: 1782

I have received your Letter of the twenty sixth of August last.[1] On examining into the Matter I find that your Accounts are among those Transactions which originated previously to my Acceptance of the Office I hold. A Commissioner will speedily be appointed to settle all the Accounts of the Marine Department and yours will then come in of Course.

MS: AM LbC, MdAN.

1. Letter not found. Bradford cannot be identified with certainty; he may have been a Philadelphia ship captain (see the references in Clark and Morgan, eds., *Naval Documents*, III, 1104–1105; and PCC, no. 196, XI, 72). The nature of his claim against the United States has not been identified.

To William Denning

Office of Finance 13. Sepr. 1782[1]

Enclosed you have Copy of an Agreement for Sale of Public Provisions to Mr. Sands.[2] In Order finally to determine the Prices of such Provisions it is agreed that you with such Person as Mr. Sands may name shall examine into and fix it or in Case that Person and you differ that you shall chuse a third.

I must request your Attention to this Business as speedily as may be.

MS: Ofcl LbC, DLC.

1. Denning, a New York merchant, was the commissioner for settling the accounts of the Quartermaster Department.

2. Agreement not found. See also the following letter.

To Charles Stewart

Office of Finance 13th. Septr. 1782

No Return having yet been made of the public stores in your Department delivered to the Contractors for West Point and it being necessary to a Settlement of their accounts I am now to require that such Return be forthwith made.[1]

MSS: LS, Stewart Papers, MH; Ofcl LbC, DLC; copy, Stewart Papers, NCooHi.

1. Stewart was the issuing contractor for the West Point and Moving Army contract, but this letter was addressed to him as commissary general of issues; the LS is endorsed as having been "received the 20th. by Mr. Mullins." For Stewart's response, see notes to Ezekiel Cornell to RM, October 5.

Diary: September 14, 1782

Jos: Nourse Esquire called respecting the Account of Provisions Issued to Prisoners under the Contract's, whether he is to add the prices to the Account of Articles. I directed that the Account of Articles only should be made out and delivered to Mr. Mullins that he may take the same to the Commissioners now appointed for Setling a general Cartel.[1]

Capt. Jno. Green called to offer his Services in Assisting to get the Prisoners out of the New Goal on Board the Flag Ships[2] but General Lincoln not being ready I engaged Capt. Greene to go to Annapolis to bring Money from the Intendant Mr. Jenifer and accordingly dispatched him with my Letters of this Date to Mr. Jenifer and Mr. Harwood[3] desiring him to hire a light Waggon and take a trusty Person with him.

Genl St Clair called on me and laid open his Distress for want of Money. I shewed him that it is not in my Power to give him Money on Account of his Pay until all the Officers of the Army receive it and that if I do Supply him it must be by Loan. This Gentleman's Distress is beyond Discription, not a Dollar in his Possession at a time when Duty calls him to Camp and a starving Family to remain behind him. I must therefore supply him someway or other, and it is exceedingly hard to Advance perpetually my own money to those whom the Public distress by non payment.

Mr. James Mullin having now got the Papers necessary for the Commissioners on Prisoners I signed a Warrant for 500 Dollars in his favor which he is to receive and carry up to the said Commissioners and bring their receipt for the Same. I granted him 100 Dollars on Account of his own Pay and Expences of which he is to render an Account and I desired him to set out immediately for Head Quarters.

Capt James Nicholson called to tell me that he will set out for the Bourbon Frigate on Wednesday but presses for Cash. I told him that he cannot have Cash that Notes on Mr. Swanwick are receivable in the Taxes of Connecticut and if he cannot carry on the Ship with those notes she must Stop for I cannot spare money. He asked whether it might not be as well to leave her on the Stocks all Winter unless we had materials, and ready to send her to Sea when Launched. I replied that he must write on this Subject when she is near ready, and I will then determine.

I had hired Mr Llyod [Lloyd] to go Express with money agreeable to my Promise to Mr Duer at Albany[4] but Accidently meeting with Major Hale he agreed to receive and take up the Money therefore I dismissed Mr Lloy'd.

Mr: John Barclay came to inform me that the naval Officer[5] declines to permit the goods of the United States to be landed from the Heer Adams until the State Duties are Secured &c.

1. See RM to George Washington, September 12.
2. See notes to Diary, August 13.
3. The letters to Benjamin Harwood and Daniel of St. Thomas Jenifer are dated September 13. For Green's return with $20,000, see Diary, September 24.
4. See RM to Duer, September 13.
5. Dr. Frederick Phile (d. 1793), naval officer of the port of Philadelphia from 1777 until his death. Butterfield, ed., *Rush Letters*, II, 721n.; Prince, *Federalists and Civil Service*, 304; and Diary, September 16 and 17.

From Alexander Hamilton

Albany [New York] Sepr. 14th 1782[1]

Sir,

I have the honor to acknowledge the Receipt of your letter of the 29th. of August; the contents of which shall be executed.[2]

I have just received by the post accounts of the specific supplies furnished by this state; copies of which I shall prepare to be transmitted to you by the next post, as I am to return the Originals, which are for the inspection of the legislature. I hope to add to these accounts of the money supplied.[3]

I have written to you a number of letters since my journey to Poughkepsie; of which as they contain some things of a confidential nature, I am not without anxiety to learn the safe arrival.[4] I should also have been happy to have received your instructions against the meeting of the Committee,[5] which is to take place to morrow. As they will have other business, if I hear from you by the next post it will not be too late. I am at a loss to know whether I ought to press the establishment of *permanent funds* or not; though unless I receive your instructions following my own apprehensions of what are probably your views, I shall dwell upon this article. I have the honor to be With perfect respect Sir Your most Obedient Servant

AH

I enclose you a copy of a letter from the Governor of the 2d instant [by] which you will see his hopes;[6] [mine] are not so good. In this [cou]nty, always delinquent, little is doing.

ENDORSED: To Robert Morris Esqr/Sep. 14 1782
MSS: ADftS, Hamilton Papers, DLC; transcript, Francis Baylies Papers, DLC.
1. Hamilton was the receiver of Continental taxes for New York. For his status at this time, see RM to Hamilton, August 28, and notes.
2. The letter of August 29 was RM's circular to the receivers of Continental taxes.
3. The accounts were probably enclosed in Robert Benson to Hamilton, September 10, 1782, Syrett and Cooke, eds., *Hamilton Papers*, III, 163–164; see also Hamilton to RM, September 21.

4. See Hamilton to RM, July 22 and, especially, August 13.
5. The joint committee on taxation, on which see Hamilton to RM, July 22, and notes.
6. Governor George Clinton had written to Hamilton on September 2 that he was "led to hope that the Taxes will be speedily collected & paid in." See Syrett and Cooke, eds., *Hamilton Papers*, III, 158.

From William Churchill Houston

Trenton [New Jersey] 14 Septr. 1782[1]

Sir

Large Demands are daily making upon me on Account of the Quarter-Master General, and the Contractours for supplying the Army. Draughts on Mr Swanwick to the Amount of three Thousand Dollars from each are now in this Town waiting for Payment. I am endeavouring to discharge them as Money comes in, but that is very slowly. If Payment to one is more necessary than to the other, I would be glad to be guided by your Directions, as both are equally pressing and importunate. The Line I have taken is to divide as equally as I can between both, in which, if not instructed to the contrary, I suppose it will be best to continue.[2]

My Return for the past Week is enclosed.

1782 Dr The Receipt of Continental Taxes in the State of New-Jersey
     To Cash received from the State-Treasurer from Septr. 7 to
        14 inclusive six Hundred Dollars   Dlls 600
                                                   W C Houston

Honble Robt Morris Esqr
Financier Genel, &c.

ENDORSED: Copy Letter to Robert/Morris Financer Genel/14 Septr 1782/With Return 600 Dlls
MS: ADft with subjoined ADftS return, Houston Collection, NjP.
    1. Houston was the receiver of Continental taxes for New Jersey.
    2. RM replied on September 17.

Diary: September 16, 1782

Genl. St Clair again applied for Money. His necessities are so urgent that I cannot resist them and desire Mr. Swanwick to supply 320 Dollars from my own Monies to be hereafter taken from the Generals Pay.

Jacob Krey Esqr. applied for Payment of sundry of Mr Moylans Bills for Shoes and offered to take Notes for the greatest part so as to receive payment from the Taxes of Lancaster County.[1]

Monsr. Cure Called to offer some ready made Soldiers Shirts but as I had reason to suppose these are a parcel for which I had agreed with Solomon I desired Monsr. Cure to call in the morning. I sent for Solomon who says these Shirts are the same and that Monsr. Brassin[2] employed him to sell them to me, and he says Monsr Balny[3] sold them to Monsr Cure whilst Solomon was treating with me for them.

Genl. Cornell called to Announce that he is ready to depart for Camp as Inspector of the Contracts &c. Our Clerks being all busily employed I told the General the necessary Papers shall be made out for him in the Course of a few Days.[4]

Capt. Maxwell and Harrison of the flag Ships applied for Money to pay their Charges here the Prisoners being on Board.[5] I told them that I have no Directions to supply them. They desired me to endorse their Drafts and they can readily get Money accordingly I endorsed their Bill on Henry White Esqr New York for 233⅓ Dollars this Date at five Days sight in my favor, endorsed to John Shields[6] who is to supply them with the Money for it. I have made this endorsement in my own name but at the Public Risque as it was absolutely necessary that the Captains should be supplied.

                                        Philadelphia 16th September 1782
Exchange for 233⅓ Dollars
Five days after Sight of this my first of Exchange Second of the same Tenor and Date unpaid, Pay to Robert Morris Esqr. or Order Two hundred thirty three and one third Dolls. for Value received which charge to the Accounts of the Ships Symetry and Tyger commanded by Sir your most humble Servants
To Henry White Esqr. New York[7]   Geo. Harrison
                                                 Francis Maxwell
                                        Philadelphia 16 September 1782
Exchange for 233⅓ Dollars
Five days after Sight of this my Second of Exchange, first of the same Tenor and date unpaid, Pay to Robert Morris Esqr. or Order, Two hundred thirty three and one third Dollars for Value received which charge to Account of the Ships Symetry and Tyger commanded by Sir your most humble Servants
To Henry White Esqr. New York   Geo Harrison
                    (Copy)   Francis Maxwell

His Excelly. The Minister of France Called to enquire respecting some Ships said to be in the River, but having no information at that time he departed. Soon after I received intelligence of the arrival at Cape Henlopen[8] of two French Frigates, that they were chased by the British Fleet and drove on shore[9] on which I sent to the Minister and offered any Assistance he wished for, but as his Excelly. had not received a knowlege of any particulars nothing could be determined on that Point.

Doctr Phile the Naval Officer came to the Office and asserts that Goods imported into the State of Pennsylvania on Account of the United States are liable to the State Duty of Impost and in order to obtain the Landing of those from the Ship Heer Adams I was obliged to give Bond for the payment of the Duties reserving the right of representing the matter to Congress &c.

Mr. McClay and Colo. McGaw as a committee of Assembly of Pennsylvania called respecting the feeding of the Continental Troops ordered on the Expedition to the Westward.[10] I told them that as Congress have ordered some Continental Troops on those Expeditions without Stipulating for any Supplies of Provisions from the State, I should supply the said Troops but it would only accumulate Expence and Charges to have two Setts of Commissaries and therefore if the State as they Conduct the Expeditions will supply these Troops I will pay the Cost of the Rations during the Time they do not draw them from the Contractors and if the Cost should be more than the Contract Price, on having that proved, I shall be ready to do Justice.[11] They mentioned Blankets for the Troops and I promised to try if I can supply them, without asking any advances from the State on that Account as they offered to lend some Money for that purpose but it must be speedily repaid.

Wrote a Letter to Colo. Richard Butler.

1. The applicant was probably Jacob Krug, a Lancaster tanner who had contracted to make shoes in November 1781. He represented Lancaster County in the Pennsylvania Assembly. I. Daniel Rupp, *History of Lancaster County . . .* (Lancaster, 1844), 396, 426; Diary, November 24, 1781.

2. On Brassine, see notes to Diary, July 29.

3. César Louis de Baulny, treasurer of the French army in America.

4. These papers for Ezekiel Cornell very likely included his commission of September 19 and RM's letter to him.

5. For the background, see notes to Diary, August 13.

6. John Shields was one of two Philadelphia merchants of that name in 1785. See *Macpherson's Directory, for the City and Suburbs of Philadelphia . . .* (Philadelphia, 1785), 121.

7. White (d. 1786), a loyalist merchant, was the resident commissary in New York for supplying British troops in the West Indies. See Lorenzo Sabine, *Biographical Sketches of Loyalists of the American Revolution, with an Historical Essay* (Boston, 1864), II, 417–418; and the references to him in *Report on American Manuscripts in the Royal Institution,* II, 430, III, 3, IV, 8, 261.

8. In Sussex County, Delaware, at the southern entrance to Delaware Bay.

9. The ships were the French frigates *Aigle* and *Gloire,* which were attacked by a British 74-gun ship. The *Aigle* ran aground and was destroyed, but the *Gloire* was able to reach Philadelphia with the *Aigle's* passengers. The 2.5 million livres carried by the French ships was saved. See notes to Benjamin Franklin to RM, June 25, 1782, and sources cited there; and RM to Vicomte de Noailles, September 25.

10. See Diary, September 7, and notes.

11. RM repeated this offer in a letter to the president of Pennsylvania of September 19.

To Guy Carleton

Marine Office Philada. 16th Septr. 1782[1]

Sir

I had the Honor to receive your Excellencys Letter of the Second. I have directed all such Marine Prisoners to be put on board the Cartels as can conveniently be collected.[2] I shall take the earliest Measures to cause all the Marine Prisoners in the United States to be sent to the most convenient of your Posts as well as to collect the Lists of those who have been liberated on Paroles &ca. so that the Account may be speedily and satisfactorily settled. I have the Honor to be Your Excellencys most Obedient and humble Servant

Robt Morris

His Excellency Sir Guy Carleton

ENDORSED: Robert Morris Esqr./to/Sir Guy Carleton/16th Sepr. 1782/Received the 29.
MSS: LS, Carleton Papers, PRO 30/55/49; LS marked "Copy," Carleton Papers, PRO 30/55/49; AM LbC, MdAN; copy, Foreign Office, Class 95/Volume 10, PRO.
  1. Carleton was the commander of British forces in North America with headquarters at New York.
  2. For the background, see notes to Diary, August 13.

From George Washington

Head Quarters [Verplancks Point, New York] 16th: Sept. 1782

Dear Sir

Partly for want of answers to my letters to you of the 2d. and 4th: instants, requesting Money for the use of our Commissioners and the accounts for the maintainance of Prisoners, and partly for want of answers to some matters proposed by me to Congress, I have been under the necessity of deferring the meeting, which was appointed on the 18th. to the 26th: of this month.

It will be extremely disagreeable to me to be obliged again to defer the proposed meeting. I therefore most earnestly request, that so much of the business as depends upon you, may be forwarded to me between this and the 26th. as much before as possible.[1]

I take the Liberty to inclose to you a Copy of the Contractors Instructions to their Issuers in West Point, and to quere, whether they are authorised by you, to take all their Receipts for their Issues, as delivered under the Contract for the moving Army?[2] I have the Honor to be &c[3]

GW

Honble. Mr. Morris

ENDORSED: Head Quarters 16th Sepr 1782/to/Hone Robert Morris Esqr/renewing Request for Money and papers/for Commissioners—whose Meeting has been/postponed for Want of them/Copy of Contractors Instructions for Issues/at West Point sent him
MSS: Dft in the writing of Tench Tilghman and Jonathan Trumbull, Jr., Washington Papers, DLC; Varick transcript, Washington Papers, DLC.

1. RM had already responded to Washington's request in a letter of September 12.

2. The enclosure, a copy of Sands, Livingston and Company to the Issuing Commissaries, July 20, 1782, instructing them to take receipts for rations issued to the army as "Received of the Contractors for the Moving Army," had been sent to Washington by Henry Knox, the commander at West Point, in a letter of September 11, 1782 (Washington Papers, DLC). At issue was the fact that rations for West Point were priced a half penny less than those for the Moving Army. See RM to Washington, September 19 (first letter); and notes to Diary, May 13, 1782.

3. This paragraph was substituted by Jonathan Trumbull, Jr., for a paragraph and complimentary close originally written by Tench Tilghman as follows: "I have received yours of the 9. I have the honor to be &c." The reference was to RM's first letter of September 9.

To Richard Butler

Office of Finance 16. Sep: 1782

I have received your Favor of the fourth Instant.[1] In Consequence thereof I have directed that Mr. Brown's Accounts be settled and will take Care that they be duly paid. I have taken Notice also of what you say as to the Execution of the Contracts for York and Carlisle and shall make such Mention of it to Messrs. Francis and Slough the Contractors as that all future Causes of Complaint may (I hope) be obviated.

MS: Ofcl LbC, DLC.

1. Letter not found. Butler was colonel of the 5th Pennsylvania Regiment stationed at Carlisle, Pennsylvania. On the accounts mentioned in this letter to him, see Diary, September 13.

To Robert Digby

Marine Office 16. Septem: 1782

I have the honor to acknowlege the receipt of your Excellency's Letter of the second Instant, enclosing the duplicate of an Answer to mine of the fifth of July also dated on the second.[1]

MS: AM LbC, MdAN.

1. Rear Admiral Digby of the British navy commanded the North American station with headquarters at New York. His letter and enclosure have not been found.

Diary: September 17, 1782

Jno. Pierce Esquire Paymaster General applied for Subsistence money for Lee's Legion at the request of Capt Carnes,[1] I told him that I have no Money but advised him to advance it from his other Funds until it can be replaced.

Jacob Kruy Esqr for his Money.[2] I desired Mr Swanwick to pay two Bills in Money and the other in Notes.

Monsr. Caure respecting Shirts. I told him that I had already been ill Used about those Shirts and will have nothing more to say to them.

Mr. Geo. Eddy returned and I desired him to repair to the Bank and Settle his notes. He informed me that the Ship New York with 570 hhds. Tobacco is arrived at New York.[3]

I sent for the Clothier General and requested him to purchase the 300 Blankets required by the Secretary at War for the Troops destined on the Pennsylvania Expeditions at as low Price and as long Credit as possible.[4]

Capt. James Nicholson came when I ordered him his notes, Letters &c to be got ready for his Journey to Connecticut.[5]

Doctor Phile the Naval Officer called and informed me that the Attorney General[6] had given it as his opinion that the Goods of the United States are not Subject to the Pennsylvania Impost and therefore he need not take any further measures on that Subject.

The Honble. Mr. Clarke called to enquire whether the Commissioner for settling the State Accounts is employed. I told him he is waiting for his Instructions, Books &c.[7] He asked if the receiver of the State of New Jersey is paid 1500 Dollars per Annum. I told him he is to have ⅛ per Cent and no more.[8]

I sent for Mr Edward Fox and I told him that it had been insinuated to me by a member of Congress that I ought to enquire what had been his political Conduct in the begining of this Contest before I nominated him to any Commission &c. and desired him to take his own time and mode of satisfying me on this Subject.[9]

Wrote a Letter to Jos Woodbridge and Capt. James Nicholson.

Wrote a Letter to James Richardson.

Wrote a Letter to James Lovell.

Wrote a Letter to Geo Olney.

Wrote a Letter to William Whipple.

Wrote a Letter to Alexr. Hamilton.

Wrote a Letter to Hezk. Merril, Wm. C: Houston.

Issued a Warrant on Mr Swanwick in favor John
Pierce   30. 0.0

Issued a Warrant on Mr Swanwick in favor Jos.
Pennell   37.10.0

1. Patrick Carnes of Virginia, captain in Lieutenant Colonel Henry Lee's legion of light dragoons. Heitman, *Register*.

2. The applicant was probably Jacob Krug. See Diary, September 16, and notes.

3. See RM's Agreement with George Eddy, printed under March 13, 1782, and notes. Concerning Eddy's notes, see Diary, August 30, and notes.

4. See Diary, September 7, and notes.

5. See RM to Nicholson, September 17, and notes.

6. William Bradford, Jr., attorney general of Pennsylvania.

7. Abraham Clark was a delegate to Congress from New Jersey. Lewis Pintard had

already been appointed commissioner to settle New Jersey's accounts with the United States, but due to confusion in forwarding his papers a considerable time elapsed before he was able to undertake his assignment (see RM to Pintard, November 20, 1782). For the instructions to the commissioners, see RM to the Commissioners for Settling the Accounts of the States, September 7, and notes.

8. The receiver of Continental taxes for New Jersey was William Churchill Houston. For the fees allowed the receivers, see RM's letter to the receivers of April 13, 1782, and notes.

9. The congressman making the charges against Fox was Abraham Clark (see RM to Fox, September 25, and Diary, September 25 and 26). For Fox's appointment as commissioner for settling Hospital Department accounts and the doubts about his loyalties, see notes to RM to the President of Congress, February 18, 1782.

To Alexander Hamilton

Office of Finance 17. Sepr. 1782[1]

Sir,

I received by the Post your Favor of the seventh Instant. I have always suspected that the disorderly manner of doing Business in many Parts of this Continent has enabled People to commit Frauds or what is the same thing as to the Public Loss covered their Ignorance, Indolence and Extravagance. It is only by probing these Matters to the Bottom that the Extent of the Evil can be discovered and I shall be very happy that the Legislature step in with their Authority to the Aid of my Efforts. The Commissioner for settling the Accounts of your State shall be appointed as soon as a proper Person offers which no one has yet done.[2] You have formed a proper Conception as to what were my Views in enquiring into the Rates of Depreciation which are now of but little Consequence indeed of none unless to know what Degree of real Taxation may be necessary to absorp the Remainder of the useless Paper Mass which has so long burthened all our Movements.

I am by no Means surprized at the Backwardness which you meet with from public Officers in rendering an Account of Supplies furnished to the Public. The several States and many of their public Officers have so long been in the Habit of boasting superior Exertions that what was at first Assumption has advanced along the Road of Beleif to perfect Conviction. And the Delusion is now kept up by the Darkness in which it is inveloped. It is not impossible that somewhat both of Interest and Importance is concerned in leading the Public Officers to keep up the Mistery. I am Sir your most obedient and humble Servant

RM

MS: Ofcl LbC, DLC.
1. Hamilton was the receiver of Continental taxes for New York.
2. See RM to the Governor of New York, November 21, 1782.

To William Churchill Houston

Office of Finance 17th September 1782[1]

Sir

I have received your favor dated on the 14th Instant at Trenton with its enclosure. I am Sorry the sums you Receive are not equal to the Demands made on you; whilst that continues to be the Case I wish rather that the Preference be in favor of the Contractors but not so as totally to neglect others. I hope your Receipts will encrease so as to remove present Embarrassments and prevent them in future. I am Sir Your most Obedient and humble Servant

Robt Morris

William C. Houston Esqr.
Receiver for New Jersey

ENDORSED: Letter Robt Morris Esqr Sup/erintendent &c 17 Septr/1782/Answered 21
MSS: LS, Houston Collection, NjP; Ofcl LbC, DLC.
  1. Houston was the receiver of Continental taxes for New Jersey.

To John Paul Jones

Marine Office 17. September 1782

Sir

I am favored with your Letter of the second September and am thankful for the Information which it contains.[1] From my late Directions to Colo. Langdon respecting the America[2] I expect that Ship will be completed and launched and delivered agreable to my Intention. I would rather that the Guard who were employed shou'd be paid by Colonel Langdon than by you as otherways it would make a Division in the Accounts which should be avoided. You will be pleased to mention this to him.

I must repeat that I shall depend much on your Attention to have the America put into the Water with proper Dispatch and when you come this way I shall be happy to salute you being with much Regard dear Sir your most obedient and humble Servant

RM

MS: AM LbC, MdAN.
  1. Captain Jones's letter has not been found, but it undoubtedly concerned the *America,* his intended command under construction at Portsmouth, New Hampshire, which Congress had recently decided to give to France. See Jones to Gouverneur Morris, September 2, and notes.
  2. See RM to John Langdon, September 4, 5, and 12.

To John Langdon

Marine Office 17. Septem: 1782

Sir,

I am favored with your Letter of the second Instant:[1] and am glad that Mr. Russell has assisted you in negotiating my Bills from which I expect that you will be able to proceed on with the Ship America so that she may be launched with every dispatch which it is my great desire should be given her. The Property of that Ship being changed I can have no doubt but your Applications to the Commander of the french Squadron for any Articles which may be required for launching her will be readily granted. I remain Sir with much respect your most obedient and humble Servant

RM

MS: AM LbC, MdAN.

1. Letter not found. Langdon was overseeing the construction of the *America* at Portsmouth, New Hampshire.

To James Lovell

Office of Finance 17. Septr 1782

Sir,

I have to acknowlege the Receipt of your Favor dated on the fourth Instant with Enclosures.[1] The pressing Occasions which the Public have for Money makes me Regret that your weekly Returns are for such small Sums, but knowing that your Exertions will not be wanting, I hope for more ample Supplies very soon. I am Sir your most obedient Servant

RM

P.S. I wish your Letters always to contain the Rate of Exchange with you.

MS: Ofcl LbC, DLC.

1. The letters and enclosures from Lovell, the receiver of Continental taxes for Massachusetts, have not been found. One of the enclosures was probably his sixth return of September 4 for $2,389⁷⁰⁄₉₀. See the list of his returns in PCC, no. 137, III, 349.

To Hezekiah Merrill

Office of Finance 17. Septem: 1782

Sir,

I have received your Letter dated on the ninth Instant at Hartford with the Enclosure and thank you for it.[1] I wish you could have informed me that considerable Sums had been paid to you on account of the Taxes.[2] I am Sir your most obedient and humble Servant

RM

MS: Ofcl LbC, DLC.
1. The letter and enclosure from Merrill, the receiver of Continental taxes for Connecticut, have not been found.
2. According to a list in PCC, no. 137, III, 357, Merrill's payments of August 30 and September 2 were for 5839^{45}/_{90}$ and $1,300 respectively.

To James Nicholson

Office of Finance 17 Sept. 1782[1]

Sir,

Enclosed you have a Letter from me to Joseph Woodbridge Esqr.[2] relative to some thirty two Pound Cannon which he saved from the British Ship Culloden. These he offered at thirty Shillings per hundred Wt. on one hundred and twenty Pound per Pair also to let the Money be considered as a Debt on Interest. From the enclosed Letters[3] you will perceive the Principles on which I make the Purchase and therefore you will in making the Terms conform to those Ideas which are held up to Mr. Woodbridge and render them as convenient to the Public as possible. As the Purchase is not sought by the Public you cannot of Course be governed by those Prices which obtain in the Sales of Guns fitted to more general use; but rather by the real Value of them even supposing a Peace to take Place. I am Sir your most obedient Servant

RM

MS: Ofcl LbC, DLC.
1. Captain Nicholson of the Continental navy was returning to Connecticut to oversee the completion of the frigate *Bourbon*.
2. Probably the letter dated September 17.
3. Probably RM to Woodbridge, November 8, 1781, and June 6, 1782; and possibly Woodbridge's letters to RM of October 15, 1781, and August 14, 1782, neither of which has been found.

To George Olney

Office of Finance 17. Sept. 1782

Sir,

I have received your Letter dated at Providence on the second Instant with the Enclosures.[1] It is with much Concern I hear that the Payment of Taxes has been postponed by your Legislature.[2] If the Consequences of that Measure had been duly considered its Impropriety must have appeared. Uncertainty in the public Revenues will necessarily render them ineffectual, it being impossible to preserve

Oeconomy in conducting the Public Business if the most solid Reliance cannot be placed on the Supplies.

I cannot admit the Appropriation you mention as any Part of the Quota required by Congress, it being my Determination that Credit shall not be given to the States for any Thing but Money.[3] If a contrary Principle were admitted the Consequences would be a general Remissness in Payment and frequent improper Applications. I am Sir Your most obedient Servant

RM

MS: Ofcl LbC, DLC.

1. The letter and enclosures from Olney, receiver of Continental taxes for Rhode Island, have not been found.

2. For the Continental taxes levied by Rhode Island in compliance with the congressional requisition for 1782, see notes to RM to Olney, June 23, 1782. Since the towns had difficulty in raising the supplies, some failing even to appoint collectors, in August the legislature postponed to October 31 payment of the £12,000 tax originally due on September 1 and deferred various penalties for delinquent taxes. *At the General Assembly of the Governor and Company of the State of Rhode-Island and Providence Plantations . . .* [August 1782 session] [Providence, 1782], 19, 20–21, 25; and RM to Olney, December 31, 1782.

3. Possibly a reference to RM's recurring dispute with Rhode Island over certificates issued for clothing and blankets for which the state wanted credit on the Continental specie requisition for 1782 (see RM to Olney, June 23 and October 23, and to the Governor of Rhode Island, June 26, 1782); or to a resolution of the Rhode Island legislature in August 1782 authorizing Benjamin Bourne, assistant deputy quartermaster general, to draw on the state treasury for £420 specie to pay the owners of ox teams hired for the Continental army in 1781. Although the sum was to be paid out of the next state tax, Rhode Island may have wanted to have that payment credited against its quota of the Continental requisition for 1782. *At the General Assembly of the Governor and Company of the State of Rhode-Island and Providence Plantations . . .* [August 1782 session] [Providence, 1782], 9–10.

To Thomas Russell

Marine Office 17. Septemr. 1782

Sir,

I am favored with your Letter of the fifth Instant:[1] The long detention of the frigate Hague is extremly mortifying but as I have already expressed the strong desire I have for her dispatch I shall not now say any more on that Subject being confident of your Exertions for that purpose. I am much obliged to you for your Assistance to Colo. Langdon in negotiating my Notes and expect you will not be troubled any more in that Way.

I am surprised at Mr. Tillinghursts interference with the Alliances prize Schooner Polly. I have now wrote to him[2] and have sent the Resolutions of Congress which were passed at the time that the Business of the Navy was put under my Direction and have informed him of your Appointment. I enclose a Draft upon him in your favor for the Proceeds of the Sales of the Prize Schooner Polly which I expect he will immediately Pay and which you will please to place to the Credit of the United States, being Sir with much Regard your most obedient and humble Servant

RM

MS: AM LbC, MdAN.
1. Letter not found. Russell was the deputy agent of marine for New England stationed at Boston.
2. See RM to Daniel Tillinghast, September 17.

To Daniel Tillinghast

Marine Office 17. September 1782

Sir,

I have received by Yesterday's Post a Letter from you dated the sixteenth of July last.[1] With respect to any Ballances due from the marine Department they will be all taken up in the Course of settling the marine Accounts by the Commissioner to be appointed for that Purpose. These debts were contracted previously to my Administration and are to be settled in like Manner with other such Debts. It would have given me Pleasure to have complied with the Request you make of continuing you in the Agency but every Thing of that sort has long been put an End to by Resolutions of Congress of which I enclose a Copy.[2] Subsequent to that Resolution I appointed Mr. Russell of Boston to be my Deputy in the marine Business for the Eastern States. He has accepted and faithfully exerted himself in this Business. I have therefore given him an Order on you for the Amount of the Continent's Share of the Prize Schooner Polly taken by the Alliance Frigate which he informs me you took Possession of and sold. I have the honor to be Sir your most obedient and humble Servant

RM

MS: AM LbC, MdAN.
1. Letter not found. Tillinghast, a merchant of Providence, Rhode Island, had participated in the building of Continental frigates in Rhode Island before being appointed Continental prize agent for that state by Congress on April 23, 1776. As Continental agent Tillinghast played an important role in receiving and forwarding prize goods and cargoes of the Secret Committee of Trade to Washington's army, but after 1776 he was occupied chiefly with supplying Continental vessels. See Nuxoll, "Congress and the Munitions Merchants," 235–237.
2. RM refers to the resolutions of September 7, 1781, which assigned the duties of the Agent of Marine to the Superintendent of Finance and directed the Continental agents and other Marine Department employees to cease their operations and deliver their records to RM. See the headnote to RM to the President of Congress, September 8, 1781, and notes.

To William Whipple

Office of Finance 17. Septr. 1782[1]

Sir,

I am favored with your Letter dated at Portsmouth on the

thirty first of last Month. The Account you give of your State respecting the Payment of Taxes is indeed an unfavorable One; But I have hopes that your zealous and well timed Exertions to forward the laying and Collection, will be attended with Success, and that I shall shortly feel the good Effects. I am Sir your most obedient Servant

RM

MS: Ofcl LbC, DLC.
   1. Whipple was the receiver of Continental taxes for New Hampshire.

To Joseph Woodbridge

Office of Finance 17. Septr. 1782

Sir,

Since writing the aforegoing Letter[1] (which has been detained by Reason of the Detention of Capt. Nicholson owing to his being indisposed and other Circumstances) I have been favored with yours of the fourteenth of August.[2] You will perceive that it was then my Intention to have purchased your Cannon. As Congress have lately made a Present of the Ship America to the King of France,[3] The Object of my intended Purchase no longer exists. But as Expectations of the Sale have been raised in your Mind by the public Servants and it is not impossible that they may still be wanted in the Course of the War I am content to take them on such Terms as Capt. Nicholson may agree to.[4] I am Sir with Respect Your most obedient Servant

RM

MS: Ofcl LbC, DLC.
   1. RM to Woodbridge, June 6, 1782. Woodbridge was a merchant of Groton, Connecticut, who had offered to sell cannon to the United States.
   2. Letter not found.
   3. See notes to John Paul Jones to Gouverneur Morris, September 2.
   4. See RM to James Nicholson, September 17. RM and Nicholson eventually decided not to purchase the cannon. See Diary, and RM to Woodbridge, January 13, 1783.

To John Cotton, Jr.

Marine Office 17. Septem: 1782

I have received your Letter of the fourteenth of June last by Capt: Nicholson.[1] I have now to inform you that Congress have some Time since determined that a Commissioner shall be appointed to settle the Accounts of the Marine Department.[2] Hitherto no proper Person for that Business has offered but so soon as this Officer shall be appointed he will proceed in the Business and take up your Accounts in their Course so that it would be adviseable that you should prepare them for Settlement as soon as may be. If you should accomplish this before the Commissioner can proceed on them it might be well to send forward a Copy to this Office.

MS: AM LbC, MdAN.
    1. Letter not found. Cotton was a Connecticut shipbuilder who was currently constructing the Continental frigate *Bourbon*.
    2. See notes to RM to the President of Congress, February 18, 1782.

To James Richardson

Office of Finance 17. Sept. 1782

I duly received your Letter of the eighth of August last which it became necessary to transmit with the enclosed Account to the Comptroller of the Treasury. A Copy of his Report to me is enclosed.[1] I also enclose a Bill drawn by me on Mr. Swanwick in your Favor for two thousand five hundred Dollars. This you will pass to the Credit of the United States on Account of your Contract. Mr. Lovell will give you the Cash for it as fast as he can. The Accounts must however be finally adjusted at the Treasury here in the manner which the Comptroller will prescribe.

MS: Ofcl LbC, DLC.
    1. The letter and account received from Richardson and the report of Comptroller of the Treasury James Milligan thereon have not been found. Richardson held the Office of Finance contract for supplying the Continental garrison at Boston; he suffered losses on the contract because bills of exchange RM remitted to him in payment were discounted. See Richardson to Charles Stewart, April 6, 1784, Stewart Papers, NCooHi.

Diary: September 18, 1782

His Excellency the Minister of France wrote to me this Morning requesting to be supplied with a quantity of french Guineas from the Bank.[1] I went to Mr Francis,[2] he to the President and Directors, and the Matter was soon and chearfully accomplished.

Mr. Elizh. [Elijah] Weed came to inform me that some more naval Prisoners had arrived and I directed that they might be sent in the flag Ships.[3]

The Honble: Mr. Duane, Mr Carrall [Carroll], Mr. Williamson, Mr Rutledge and Mr Jackson a Committee of Congress on the Subject of a motion made in Congress by Mr. Montgomery for applying Part of the Holland Loan to payment of Interest &c. I stated to them my Situation fully and truly and left them to report as their Judgement might direct after that Communication.[4]

This day dispatched Capt. James Nicholson.

Colo. Ephm Blaine and Mr John Darrah came here the latter having brought up a Quantity of Flour I ordered the payment of his Balance agreeable to a former Promise that he should be paid if he brought up that Flour.

John Carter Esqr. arriving very opportunely from Camp I told him of my Difficulties with the Contractors for the moving Army and entered into a Conversation with him that probably may be very useful in that respect.[5]

Major Storey respecting his being employed in the civil Departments, I advised him to offer his Services to Mr Denning Commissioner of Qr [Quarter] Msr. [Master] Department.

Alexr Robertson applied for a Credit on New York which after Consideration I declined giving.

Major Franks Claims one fifth part of the Balance of his Account for Depreciation[6] and I require a Certificate from the Secry at War of his being entitled thereto.

Docr Witherspoon applied to me respecting the hireing out British Prisoner to Work &c.[7]

I sent for Mr R Sands and advised him to purchase the public Flour of Colo. Blaine and that I will enable him to pay for it.[8]

Wrote a Letter to the Honble. Genl Green.

Wrote a Letter to Major Genl Lord Stirling.

Wrote a Letter to His Excellency the Prest. of Congress.

1. The letter from Chevalier de La Luzerne has not been found.

2. Tench Francis, cashier of the Bank of North America.

3. On the exchange of marine prisoners, see notes to Diary, August 13.

4. In its report of September 18 the committee asserted that "they have examined into the present state of the Treasury, the supplies for the army and the engagements and prospects of the Superintendant of the Finances; and are of opinion that the appropriation of any part of the Dutch loan for the discharge of the interest of domestic debts, or for any other purpose than the immediate support of the army, may endanger the publick safety; and that the motion referred to your Committee ought therefore to be rejected." For the context of this effort to divert part of the Dutch loan to the payment of the interest due on loan office certificates, see notes to RM's Report to Congress on the Continental Loan Offices, June 13, 1782; and *JCC*, XXIII, 585n. On the Dutch loan, see notes to Diary, September 11.

5. This was no doubt a preliminary to the dissolution of the combined West Point and Moving Army contract held by Sands, Livingston and Company and its replacement by a contract with the firm of Wadsworth and Carter. See notes to Comfort Sands, Walter Livingston, William Duer, and Daniel Parker to RM, September 11.

6. According to a resolve of December 31, 1781, all army officers below the rank of brigadier general who did not belong to a state line or independent corps were entitled to receive pay and subsistence, as well as compensation for depreciation, up to January 1, 1782.

7. On the question raised by John Witherspoon, a New Jersey delegate to Congress, see notes to Diary, May 1, 1782.

8. Richardson Sands was a partner to Comfort Sands and Company. For the urgent effort to obtain flour for the army, see RM to Washington, September 9 (first letter), and notes.

To the President of Congress (John Hanson)

Office of Finance 18th September 1782

Sir,

I have the Honor to enclose for the Inspection of Congress a Letter I received by the Eagle from Doctor Franklin dated the twenty fifth of June. I shall be glad that it be returned to this Office when it shall have been read.[1] I am Sir Your Excellency's most obedient and humble Servant

Robt Morris

His Excellency The President of Congress

ENDORSED: 91/Robt. Morris Esqr. Supr./finance/18th. Sepr 1782/read 18th.
MSS: LS, PCC, DNA; Ofcl LbC, DLC.
   1. Franklin's letter to RM of June 25, 1782, is mistakenly given in the *Journals* as one of June 15 (see *JCC*, XXIII, 591). Congress on September 18 assigned the part relating to "money matters" to a committee consisting of Arthur Lee of Virginia, Ralph Izard of South Carolina, and James Duane of New York, but the committee appears not to have delivered a report. Instead, on the motion of John Rutledge of South Carolina, seconded by Lee, Congress resolved on September 23 that Franklin be informed (his June 25 letters to RM and Secretary for Foreign Affairs Robert R. Livingston notwithstanding) "it is the direction of Congress that he use his utmost endeavours to effect the loan" of $4 million sanctioned on September 14 (see notes to RM to the President of Congress, July 30; and for the Financier's private counsel thereon, RM to Franklin, September 28).
   Franklin's complaints about Alexander Gillon were referred to a committee which had been appointed on July 12, 1782, to inquire into purchases in Holland in which Gillon was involved (concerning this committee's report of November 1, see notes to Franklin to RM, March 4, 1782; and Diary, September 19, and notes).
   For additional action on Franklin's letter, see RM to the President of Congress, September 19, and notes. On the loss of the French frigate *Aigle*, see Diary, September 16, and notes.

To Nathanael Greene

Office of Finance 18th September 1782

Sir,

By Mr Hayward who is just Setting off for South Carolina I send this Letter enclosing a Bill of Exchange on Governor Mathews in your Favor for two hundred sixty six and two thirds Dollars also a note of Mr Hayward himself for eight hundred Dollars.[1] These Sums amounting together to one thousand sixty six and two thirds Dollars you will receive as a Remittance for the use of your Department. I am Sir with respect your most obedient Servant

Robt Morris

Major Genl. Greene

PS. I have on former Occasions remitted you first and second Bills from Governor Mathews on Charles Drayton Esqr. in favor of Doctor John Witherspoon for one hundred and seventy three Dollars endorsed to you by him.[2] I shall be glad to hear what has been their Fate.[3]

ENDORSED: from Mr. Morris/Sepr. 18th. 1782
MSS: LS, Robert Morris Papers, CSmH; Ofcl LbC, DLC.
   1. See Diary, September 11, and notes. Greene was the commander of the southern army.

2. For the first occasion, see RM to Greene, September 14, 1781; Greene acknowledged receipt in a letter to RM of November 21, 1781.

3. See RM to George Abbott Hall, and to the Governor of South Carolina, both January 22, and Greene to RM, February 2, 1783.

Gouverneur Morris to Nathanael Greene

Philadelphia 18 Sepr. 1782

Dear Sir,

I did not answer your last Letter[1] because I have expected you would soon come on. The Affair of the Legion is adjusted to your Wish at least I think so.[2] The Southern Gentlemen wish you to continue where you are (ie) in Carolina. I think you should be here as speedily as possible. Remember me to Mrs Greene. I think you told me in a former Letter that she would write to me. I suppose she has forgot or neglected it. Adieu yours very truly

Gouv Morris

Major Genl. Greene

ENDORSED: Govr Morris/Sept 18th 1782
MS: ALS, Greene Papers, MiU-C.
1. Letter not found.
2. The reference may be to Charles Armand's legion. See RM to Armand, August 27, and notes.

To William Alexander, Lord Stirling

Office of Finance 18th. Septem. 1782

My Lord

Your Letter of the third Instant has been delivered to me by Major Story[1] to whom I am much inclined to render every Service that can be done consistantly with those Arrangements that are now established in the management of Public Business. He wishes for Employment in some of the civil Departments and I shall be glad if any thing offers wherein he can be useful to the Public and to himself.

I pray your Lordship to accept my Thanks for your obliging Offers of Service in the Department you are about to take the Command of. I am with very great Respect your Lordship's Most obedient Servant

MS: Ofcl LbC, DLC.
1. Letter not found. Stirling, a major general in the Continental army, had recently been given command of the troops in the Northern Department (Fitzpatrick, ed., *Writings of Washington*, XXV, 86, 89–90). For the applications for John Story, his aide, see Diary, September 11 and 18.

Diary: September 19, 1782

William Harris Esqr. applied respecting Bills of Exchange and I agreed to Sell to his House of Wm. Nichols the Sum they want provided they agree to give my Price which he is to consider of.

Mr. Bennet of Connecticut having written me a Letter[1] requesting the Commission and Instructions of Mr Melancton Smith of New York as Commissioner for the State of Connecticut[2] and having attended several Days soliciting these Papers which are not ready I requested that this Gentleman might not give himself the trouble of waiting for them as they cannot be finished in the Time he Wishes.[3]

This Day I sent for Commodore Gillon and told him agreeable to my former Intimation I should long since have proposed to enter on the Consideration of the Matters depending between the United States and him but that a Committee of Congress had been appointed to take up the Business who had called for the Papers then in my Possession and as I had waited for their Report I did not call upon him until now that fresh Complaints arrived from France when I thought my Duty obliged me to call upon him and that it seemed the more necessary as he seems to be on the point of Departure.[4] I told him that the Care of continental Property being committed to me I think myself obliged to Demand of him a Settlement or if that cannot be had before he goes Security for any Sum that may be justly due to the United States. Commodore Gillon alledged that he had done his Duty and that the States have no Claim on him. I told him truly that I only wish for Justice to take Place and am very willing to Conduct this Business to that end in the manner least disagreeable to him and myself. I desired him to Consult the Delegates of Carolina, the Committee of Congress or any other Friends and whatever shall be right and proper I will agree to.

This Day I sent for Genl. Cornell and shewed him the Letters which I have received from the Contractors.[5] I told him he must now proceed to Camp as Inspector of the Contracts &c to which he agreed. I entered into a full explanation of my Sentiments desired him to get ready and that I will immediately prepare his Commission and all necessary Papers &c.[6]

Capt Jos Barney calling on me very frequently about matters Concerning the Ship Genl Washington I was this Day obliged to refer him to Mr John Brown who can have more ready Access at times when it will not interrupt me, in matters of greater Moment.

Colo. Miles and several other Persons for Money.

The Honble. Colo. Few Delegate of Georgia for Money on Account of that State for his Support.[7] I told him my Situation but promised to provide for him.

Wrote a Letter to the Contractors &c.

Wrote a Letter to James Lovell Esqr.

Wrote a Letter to Commiss. for settling Accounts.

Wrote a Letter to C. P. Raguet.

Wrote a Letter to Richard James.

Wrote a Letter to His Excelly. Genl Washington.

H1

Wrote a Letter to His Excellency the President of Congress.
Wrote a Letter to His Excellency Genl Washington.
Wrote a Letter to Jona. Burrall.
Wrote a Letter to His Excelly. the Presidt of Pennsylvania.

1. Letter not found.
2. See RM to the Governor of Connecticut, June 4, 1782. Connecticut had approved Smith's nomination on July 3. See Hoadly and Labaree, eds., *Public Records of Connecticut*, IV, 262.
3. See RM to the Governor of Connecticut, October 28.
4. The papers relating to Alexander Gillon of the South Carolina navy were in the hands of Theodorick Bland, Jr., of Virginia, Jonathan Jackson of Massachusetts, and David Howell of Rhode Island, a committee which had been appointed on July 12 to inquire into the causes of the detention of supplies procured in Holland by special envoy John Laurens and his secretary, William Jackson, under agreements with Gillon in 1781. The "fresh Complaints" were those presented in Benjamin Franklin's letter to RM of June 25, 1782, which RM had forwarded to Congress on September 18. Congress immediately referred the letter to the Bland committee, which was more anti-Franklin than pro-Gillon. Its report, drafted by Bland and delivered on September 26 (PCC, no. 186, p. 57) but not acted on until November 1, was an indictment of Franklin's conduct. James Madison described it as "one of the most signal monuments which party zeal has produced." Of Gillon the report merely said that, although he had apparently engaged in subterfuges, there was no indication that he had committed any specific breach of his contract with Laurens sufficient to warrant suit for legal damages. Although Congress declined to adopt the committee's proposed resolution of censure against Franklin, on a motion of the South Carolina delegates it dismissed the report as it concerned Gillon and referred the relevant documents to RM who was directed to arrange with South Carolina to settle the case by arbitration if the United States was found to have suffered damages, the delegates having pledged their state to abide by the decision. That same day Gillon came to the Office of Finance and asked for RM's decision. After receiving the papers, the Financier conferred with Jackson, now assistant secretary at war, whom he had consulted earlier, and was assured "most solemnly of the injustice and impropriety of Mr. Gillon's Management and Conduct." James Wilson, acting as United States counsel, was called in, given the papers, and asked his opinion as to the legal case against Gillon, but nothing more was done immediately. South Carolina, for its part, appears to have assumed responsibility for the commodore's acts while serving as its agent. On May 11, 1784, RM advised Jacob Read, a South Carolina delegate, that he did not think the case could be decided until a report was delivered by Thomas Barclay, the commissioner for settling accounts in Europe. Nothing further seems to have occurred during RM's term of office. See Franklin to RM, March 4, and notes, RM to Franklin, September 30, 1782, the list of documents relating to Gillon printed at the end of July 1782, Diary, October 14, 21, 23, November 1, 7, 8, 25, 1782, and November 26, 1783, RM to Ferdinand Grand, May 9, 1783, and to Read, March 30 and May 11, 1784; documents relating to the committee's and RM's investigations in PCC, no. 168, I, 733–740; Henderson, *Party Politics in the Continental Congress*, 310–311; Madison to Edmund Randolph, October 15, 1782, Hutchinson and Rutland, eds. *Madison Papers*, V, 200, 201n.; and the latest account in Richard G. Stone, Jr., " 'The *South Carolina* We've Lost': The Bizarre Saga of Alexander Gillon and His Frigate," *American Neptune*, XXXIX (1979), 159–172.
    RM was also involved in other difficulties with Gillon. He demurred over the commodore's proposed use of "liberated" German prisoners to man the *South Carolina* (see Diary, October 5, and notes) and, if John Paul Jones is to be believed, attempted with Chevalier La Luzerne to wrest control of the ship from Gillon and give the command to Jones (see notes to RM to Jones, September 4). By the end of the year their relationship had evidently become strained enough to lend credence to rumors that Gillon had slain the Financier in a duel (see Nathanael Greene to Charles Pettit, December 21, 1782, Joseph Reed Papers, NHi). Gillon subsequently returned to

South Carolina where he led the opposition to RM in the legislature. See Gillon to
Arthur Lee, November 29, 1783, Lee Papers, MH.

   5. Principal among these was Comfort Sands, Walter Livingston, William Duer,
and Daniel Parker to RM, September 11.

   6. The papers for Cornell no doubt included RM's commission to him of September 19, and RM to the Contractors for the Moving Army and West Point, and to
George Washington (second letter), both September 19, and to Cornell, September
20, with the enclosed letter from Comfort Sands, Walter Livingston, William Duer,
and Daniel Parker to RM of September 11.

   7. These allowances were authorized by Congress. See Diary, July 11, 1781, and
notes.

To the Commissioners of Accounts for the Departments

Office of Finance 19. Sepr. 1782[1]

Sir,

   The Comptroller of the Treasury having given you his Instructions as to the Form of settling the Accounts[2] there is one Matter to
which I conceive it my Duty to call your particular Attention. You
cannot be ignorant that the public Officers in the several Departments have been charged with Peculation, Fraud and speculating
with the public Money. These charges are of the most serious Nature and therefore whether true or false they ought to be enquired
into. If true the severest Punishments which the Laws will permit
ought certainly to be inflicted: but if false it is a Justice due the
Individuals to establish that Falsity and rescue their Honor from
unmerited obloquy.

   To judge properly on this Subject altho a very desirable Object is
not very easily practicable. It is not however the less a Duty to
attempt it and as the best Means of attaining to it I propose that
you should in passing thro the Cash Accounts of the Officers in
your Department make a kind of Monthly Statement so as to see
what Sums they have respectively been possessed of. If it shall
appear that it has been paid to the public Use as fast as received
the Suspicion Ends unless there is Reason to apprehend that Payments are antedated. If on the contrary a considerable Balance has
constantly been in the Hands of any Person there will be some
Ground of Jealousy and of Consequence a more pointed Attention
on your Part will be requisite. If in this Case it shall further appear
that considerable Sums were due to Individuals and not paid until
long after the Suspicions will naturally be encreased. Enquiry in
such Cases will probably lead to other Corroborating Circumstances; such are great and unusual Expence of Living beyond the
Bounds either of the Public Salaries and Allowances or the private
Fortune of the Party also the sudden Acquisition of Wealth without
any visibly adequate Means to which may be added the Neglect of

public Duties connected with an Attention to other Business and the consorting with those Characters noted for being concerned in Speculations. Under such Circumstances it will be proper to make more close Investigation. The Examination of proper Witnesses who may be supposed to have been privy to the Frauds on Oath will probably give a Clue to come at Proof and at the same Time you will naturally demand of the Party why public Money was kept in his Hands and Debts left unsatisfied. You will also in such Cases charge him with the Monies received at their real Value and hold him to Account for that Value unless very good Reasons be assigned to the contrary and the contrasting of those Reasons with the Observations you have made and the Informations you have received will perhaps open up the whole Scene. I know that this Duty will be both laborious and painful but you will always remember that this is what is expected from you by the Community who have entrusted you to be the Guardians of their Property and deposited in your Hands the sacred Trust of public and private Justice. I am Sir your most obedient and humble Servant

RM

MSS: Ofcl LbC, DLC; copy, PCC, DNA.

1. This was RM's first letter to the commissioners appointed to settle the accounts of the five great staff departments under the congressional ordinance of February 27, 1782. RM had already named commissioners for the Commissary and Quartermaster Departments and in October would appoint commissioners for the Hospital and Clothing Departments (see RM to the President of Congress, February 18, 1782, and notes). The present letter very likely was sent out seriatim as appointments were made, but probably not before the Comptroller of the Treasury's instructions were formulated (see note 2). The commissioners of accounts for the departments also received a copy of RM's letter to Jonathan Burrall of August 19, RM's circular of October 3, and another letter from the Comptroller of October 18, as well as the Financier's general letters to the commissioners of May 8 and September 4, 1783. The PCC text of the present letter was enclosed in RM to the President of Congress, August 26, 1783. Work on the staff department accounts continued into the 1790s (see Ferguson, *Power of the Purse,* 189–193; and for their status at the beginning of Washington's administration, Benjamin Walker to Alexander Hamilton, September 15, 1789, Syrett and Cooke, eds. *Hamilton Papers,* V, 373–376). For a companion to the present letter, see RM to the Commissioners of Accounts for the States, September 7, and notes.

2. James Milligan's instructions are dated October 14.

To the President of Congress (John Hanson)

Office of Finance 19th. of Septr. 1782

Sir

The Acts of Congress of the twenty seventh Novr. and third Decr. last and the Act of the fourteenth Instant induce me to pray the Attention of Congress to the Instructions given on the tenth of July

1781 to their Consul General in France.[1] I am the more compelled to do this by finding from a Letter of Mr. Franklin which was yesterday submitted to Congress[2] that Mr. Barclay is making considerable Purchases. The Just Sense which Congress entertain of the Regularity to be observed in the Administration of their Servants obviates the necessity of any Reflections on my Part.[3] I have the Honor to be with perfect Respect Your Excellency's Most obedient and humble Servant

Robt Morris

His Excellency The President of Congress

ENDORSED: 92/Letter from Superintendt./of Finance/19th. Septemr. 1782./referred to/ Sept. 19th. 1782/Mr Duane/Mr Montgomery/Mr Carroll/On instructions given to/T Barclay Consul
MSS: LS, PCC, DNA; Ofcl LbC, DLC.
1. On the acts cited, all of which gave RM authority over American funds in Europe, see Diary, September 13, and notes. The instructions to Thomas Barclay, then vice consul, had given him authority "in cases of absolute necessity" to draw on American funds in Europe. They are printed in JCC, XX, 736–737; a copy signed by Secretary of Congress Charles Thomson and endorsed by RM is in PCC, no. 137, I, 769.
2. Benjamin Franklin's letter of June 25, 1782, was submitted in RM to the President of Congress, September 18.
3. Congress referred this letter on September 19 to a committee composed of James Duane of New York, Joseph Montgomery of Pennsylvania, and Daniel Carroll of Maryland, which met with RM the following day (see Diary, September 20). Approving the committee's report on September 23, Congress issued additional instructions to Barclay, directing him to pay "the strictest regard" to the arrangements previously entrusted to RM and not to draw money or buy any clothing "or effects" without the express authorization of the Financier or Congress. RM forwarded the resolutions to Barclay in a letter of September 25, and on the same day directed Franklin to discontinue purchases of European goods, saying he had decided in the future to buy them by contract in the United States. According to Matthew Ridley, Franklin had already refused to let Barclay draw any further on him to finance his operations. See Ridley to RM, July 23.

To the Contractors for West Point and the Moving Army

Office of Finance 19 Sep 1782

Gentlemen.[1]

The Bearer Ezekiel Cornell Esqr. is appointed by me to be the Inspector of the Contracts for the main army.[2] I trust that you will find in this Gentleman's Candor the amplest Resource for unavoidable Difficulties while at the same Time he gives by an unblemished Integrity the proper Security to the Public. I have desired and empowered him to settle all disputes now existing and I dare say he will do it effectually. I am Gentlemen Your most obedient and humble Servant

RM

MS: Ofcl LbC, DLC.

1. The contractors were Sands, Livingston and Company, on whom see notes to Diary, May 13, 1782.

2. See the following document.

Commission to Ezekiel Cornell

[Office of Finance, September 19, 1782][1]

To Ezekiel Cornell Esquire Greeting

Whereas the United States in Congress assembled, did on the 7th. of May last Resolve in the words following i.e. that the Superintendant of Finance be and is hereby authorized to appoint an Inspector for the main and another for the southern army to take care that the contracts for supplying rations be duly executed by the contractors: that the said Inspectors shall also be and they are hereby fully empower'd and directed to attend to the expenditures of public property in the several departments of the army, and report any fraud, neglect of duty or other misconduct by which the public property is wasted, or expence unnecessarily accumulated so that the party charged therewith may be tried by court martial on such charges exhibited against him by either of the said Inspectors, and that neither the said Inspectors nor the said Contractors or their property be liable to arrest or subject to martial law except by the express order of the Commander in Chief or commander of the army to which the Inspectors shall respectively be appointed, any Resolutions or Acts of Congress heretofore made notwithstanding. Now therefore in pursuance of authority so as aforesaid vested in me, I do hereby appoint you Ezekiel Cornell to be the Inspector for the main Army giving and granting to you the said Office with all and singular the Rights, Powers, Priviledges, and Emoluments to the same belonging or in any wise appertaining.

Given under my hand and seal in the Office of Finance this 19th. of September in the year of our Lord 1782.

Robt. Morris

ENDORSED: General Orders/Octr. 9. 1782
MSS: Copy, Manuscript File, WDC, DNA; copies, Orderly Books, WDC, no. 64, pp. 127–129, no. 67, pp. 58–62, no. 68, pp. 22–24, DNA.

1. An Office of Finance text of this commission has not been found; Washington published it as part of his General Orders of October 9, 1782, directing that Cornell "be respected and obeyed accordingly" (Fitzpatrick, ed., *Writings of Washington*, XXV, 248 and n.). See also RM to Washington, September 19 (first and second letters), and Washington to RM, September 22 (second letter) and October 3. For the creation of the post of inspector of contracts for the main army and the background to Cornell's appointment, see RM to the President of Congress, April 20, 1782, and notes. On the breakdown of the West Point and Moving Army contract held by Sands, Livingston and Company and Cornell's negotiation of a new contract with the firm of Wadsworth and Carter, see notes to Comfort Sands, Walter Livingston, William Duer, and Daniel Parker to RM, September 11.

To Richard James

Office of Finance 19. Sepr. 1782

Sir,

I have received your Letter of the seventh Instant by Mr. Morton.[1] Your Accounts have been settled. Your last Balance has been transmitted in Notes by the Post and is I suppose received before this hour.[2] I have directed the Payment of a thousand Dollars of the present in the same way. The Remainder I have at the urgent Request of Mr. Morton agreed to his receiving in Specie which from Circumstances not necessary to go into a Detail of happens just now to be extremely inconvenient to me. I presume that the Notes will procure you the Money either from the State Treasury or by enabling you to purchase and to pay with them as for Cash or else by exchanging them with Persons making Remittances hither. The two Bills you mention shall be duly honored. The Amount being five hundred and thirty six and two third Dollars will be deducted from your next Balance which will I suppose be more convenient to you than if it were done now. I am Sir your most obedient and humble Servant

RM

ms: Ofcl LbC, DLC.
1. Letter not found. James was the contractor for the Continental post at Cumberland Old Court House, Virginia.
2. See RM to James, August 27.

To the President of Pennsylvania (William Moore)

Office of Finance 19th September 1782

Sir

The Minister at War having applied to me to make Provision for sundry Continental Troops which are (in Pursuance of an Act of Congress of the thirteenth Instant) directed to be employed by the State of Pensilvania in certain Expeditions about to be undertaken by that State.[1] And having informed me farther that a Part of those Troops will march from Fort Pitt and another Part of them from Carlisle I have to propose to your Excellency that these Troops be subsisted at the Expence of your State during the Service in which you mean to employ them. That the usual Receipts be taken from the proper Officers for the Rations which may be issued and that I pay on Behalf of the United States the Contract Prices of such Rations at the Posts of Fort Pitt and Carlisle for the Troops which march from those Places respectively. This appears to me to be the simplest Mode of Settlement,[2] but if not approved of I will take arrangements for feeding the continental Troops while on the Expeditions, in which Case I must request to be favored with the Informations necessary for my Direction. With perfect Respect and Esteem I have the Honor to be, Sir Your Excellency's most obedient and humble Servant

Robt Morris

His Excellency The President of Pennsilvania

ENDORSED: From Superintendant of/Finance/Read in Council Septr. 20./1782
MSS: LS, Society Miscellaneous Collection, PHi; Ofcl LbC, DLC.
   1. For this proposed expedition, see Diary, September 7, and notes.
   2. RM had proposed this solution on September 16. See Diary of that date.

To Claudius P. Raguet

Office of Finance 19. Sep: 1782[1]

Sir,
   The Directors of the Bank call upon me for Payment of your Note and my Duty requires that I insist on your providing for the discharge of that Note without further loss of Time. To write this Letter is painful but my Duty must be performed and I hope Sir you will save me the disagreable Necessity of pursuing or repeating any disagreable Measures to obtain this Object. I am Sir Your most obedient and humble Servant

RM

MS: Ofcl LbC, DLC.
   1. For the background to this letter, see Diary, September 2, and notes.

To George Washington

Office of Finance 19th. September 1782

Sir
   I received yours of the sixteenth Instant yesterday Morning. I trust that your Excellency will have received every Thing relating to my Department in due Season for the Meeting of the Commissioners upon the eighteenth.
   I agreed with Mr Sands that the Issues should be adjusted at the Treasury as made to the moving Army, and that a half Penny per Ration should be allowed to the Public for the Issues at West Point. The Manner of determining the Amount of these Issues I shall leave to Mr. Cornell to adjust.[1] He will take your Excellency's Advice on the Subject. With perfect Respect I have the Honor to be Sir Your most obedient and humble Servant

Robt Morris

His Excellency General Washington

ENDORSED: Office of Finance 19th Sepr 1782/from/Hono. Robert Morris Esqr/agreed with Mr Sands for his Mode/of Issuing at Wes[t] Point/Answered 3d. October
MSS: LS, Washington Papers, DLC; Ofc1 LbC, DLC.
    1. See RM's commission of this date to Ezekiel Cornell, inspector of contracts for the main army.

To George Washington

Office of Finance 19th September 1782

Sir,

The Bearer of this Letter, Mr. Ezekiel Cornell is appointed to be the Inspector of the Contracts for your Army.[1] I have a perfect Reliance both on his Zeal and Integrity, and am persuaded that your Excellency may repose the utmost Confidence in him. I write this Letter to recommend him to your favorable Notice, and to pray that he may meet your Excellency's Aid in performing the Business committed to him. With perfect Respect I have the Honor to be Your Excellency's most obedient and humble Servant

Robt Morris

His Excellency General Washington

ENDORSED: Office of Finance 19 Sepr 1782/from/Hono Robert Morris Esqr/Genl Cornel appointed Intendant/and recommended/Answered 3d. Octobr.
MSS: LS, Washington Papers, DLC; Ofc1 LbC, DLC.
    1. See RM's commission of this date to Cornell.

From the Quartermaster General (Timothy Pickering)

Camp Verplanks Point [New York] Sep. 19 1782

Sir,

Before the arrival of the french army[1] I was enabled, tho' not without great difficulty to procure on a credit of two or three months, hay for the current supply of the army,[2] by shewing candidly to the people on what my assurances of payment were grounded, viz, the bills of exchange with which you supplied me.[3] Just at their arrival, I received a small supply of cash from Boston, with some notes, which as the only hope of procuring forage, enabled me to promise payment for half the Forage which should be furnished, on the delivery, and the other half in two, or at farthest in three months depending on future remittances for fulfilling the latter engagement. This would have succeeded to my utmost wishes as to hay (grain commands the cash in hand) had not the French agents at that moment been spread over the country: for they made more than prompt payment—they actually lodged money with the farmers before they took away a particle of forage, and at as high prices as I was obtaining it on partial credit. They sweep the country round. The supplies to our army are of consequence failing. Apprehensive of these effects, I wrote to Mr. Pomeroy, my deputy in Connecticut desiring him to come to the towns bordering on New York there to purchase what grain he could.[4] On his arrival at Danbury he found the French agents there before him, and that a gentleman, whom I had three weeks before requested to purchase a quantity for me, and whose promises of payment I had engaged to fulfil, had actually contracted to deliver *five thousand bushels* to the French, though he could procure *none* for the American Army. Nevertheless Mr. Pomeroy thinks he can procure a considerable quantity of grain for forage, in lieu of taxes in cash, and at as cheap rates as the french give in ⟨cash⟩ money provided he can pay the arre[a]rages due the farmers for forage and pastures furnished since the first of January last, and for present supplies, by giving them notes receivable for their hard money taxes. New notes, calculated to answer that end, Mr. Pomeroy informs me you have lately provided.[5] Until such arrearages are settled, they serve for an excuse to the people for not paying their taxes. From fifteen to eighteen thousand dollars in such *tax* notes, he says will discharge those arrears, and twenty five hundred dollars more will secure so much grain as when added to other supplies will insure the army from suffering the ensuing fall and winter. I am aware that the transportation will be considerable: but the drought is so unusually severe and the crops of corn and buckwheat so universally cutt off, there is little doubt but grain will in a few days take an extraordinary rise; whence I am led to think it adviseable instantly to engage a supply, even at thirty or forty miles distance from the Hudson. The Transportation of the greater part may be suspended till it can be effected in slays.

With this account of my situation I beg leave to submit the matter to your determination. Mr. Pomeroy will have the honour to hand this to you, and can give such farther information as you shall require.

Such notes as those before described, will be received in this state as readily almost as cash, to the amount of the farmers taxes who can supply me with forage But they must be of small denominations— for the continental tax is ⟨higher⟩ light. If I can be furnished with a couple of thousand dollars in such notes, and receive more if those succeed they may greatly relieve me. Only cash or such small notes for taxes will procure grain as without one or the other the farmers will not thresh and before the usual threshing time arrives. I have every reason to fear prices of grain of every kind will be greatly enhanced.[6] I have the honor to be &c

Tim: Pickering QMG

MS: LbC, WDC, DNA.

1. The French army moving northward from Virginia in July tarried at Baltimore until August 23, reached Philadelphia by the end of the month, and by the middle of

September was encamped at Crompond, now Yorktown Heights, in Westchester County, New York, where it was only about 10 miles away from the Americans at Verplanck's Point. The army resumed its march on October 22, reached Providence on November 10–11, departed for Boston on December 1–4, was embarked on Vaudreuil's squadron by December 7, and set sail for the West Indies on December 24. Chastellux, *Travels,* II, 473–476, 638.

2. On the procurement of forage, see notes to RM to the Secretary at War, June 29, 1782.

3. See Diary, August 3, and notes.

4. Pickering to Ralph Pomeroy, September 8, 1782, WDC, no. 85, pp. 193–194.

5. See RM's Circular to the Receivers of Continental Taxes, August 29, and notes.

6. Pomeroy handed this letter to RM at the Office of Finance on September 23. The Superintendent refused to increase his note issue until the states retired more of them, but offered to convert notes of large denomination held by Pickering into smaller amounts. See Diary, September 23, 24, 25, and RM to Pomeroy, September 25, and to the Quartermaster General, September 26.

To Jonathan Burrall

Office of Finance 19. Septem: 1782

I have received your Letter of the seventeenth Instant.[1] I cannot give you an Opinion on that Subject. You are the Judge and your Judgment ought not to be influenced by my Sentiments. At least on Occasions like the present.

MS: Ofcl LbC, DLC.

1. Letter not found. Burrall was the commissioner for settling the accounts of the Commissary Department.

To James Lovell

Philadelphia 19th. Sepr. 1782

I received yours of the fifth Instant respecting Capt Manly[1] and can tell you only in reply that your Recommendations shall on all Occasions be attended to, altho it may not always be proper to comply exactly with them and in the present Instance I had before the receipt of your said Letter given to Mr. Russell the Instructions which I thought most consistent with the Public Interest and my Duty.[2]

MS: Ofcl LbC, DLC.

1. Letter not found. Lovell was the receiver of Continental taxes for Massachusetts.

2. See RM to Thomas Russell, August 8, and notes.

To George Washington

Office of Finance 19th September 1782

I have received your Excellency's Letter of the eleventh Instant enclosing the Copy of a Letter from Colo. Varick. I enclose herein Notes to the amount of eight hundred Dollars for which I am to pray that your Excellency will take and transmit his Receipt as for so much received of Mr. Swanwick for which he Colo. Varick is to be accountable.[1]

MSS: LS, Washington Papers, DLC; Ofcl LbC, DLC.

1. According to the endorsement on the LS, the money for Varick was "sent him on 26th per Lt Dodge of 2d N York Regt." Washington answered RM's letter on October 3.

Diary: September 20, 1782

Mr. Geo Eddy applied respecting Discounts at the Bank but I referred him to the President and Directors &c.

Genl. Cornell came this Day when I delivered him his Papers,[1] paid him 300 Dollars on Account of his Salary &c.

Capt. James Nicholson having been detained called to shew me a Letter respecting the Frigate Bourbon[2] and we agreed to finish and let her remain on the Stocks.

The Honble. Mr. Montgomery, Mr. Duane and Mr Carrol Committee of Congress respecting Mr. Barclay's Powers as Consul I produced the Instructions of Congress to him and they were of Opinion that certain Parts ought to be repealed.[3]

Mr. Ths. Vanderpoole this Day engaged as a Clerk in this Office.

Mr Williams for money for the Hospital. I sent him Word he cannot be Supplied at present but I hope soon will be.

The Honble. Mr. Holker having written me a Letter respecting the payment of 9,600 Dollars in part of the large Sum now due to him[4] I sent for him, he came and on his reminding me of what had passed and telling me the Situation he is reduced to in dependance on that payment I find his Claim irresistable therefore I granted the Warrant for that Sum and went to the Bank and borrowed it of them for six Days.

Don Francisco Rendon respecting 4,000 Dollars lent him respecting which I wrote him a Note.

Mr. Milligan Called respecting the Instructions to the Commissioners &c. on which I gave my opinion &c.[5]

Wrote a Letter Ezk. Merrill [i.e., Cornell] Esqr.

Issued a Warrant on Mr Swanwick in favor Nchs Spencer	£ 50.19.1
Issued a Warrant on Mr Swanwick in favor Jno. Pierce	240. 0.0
Issued a Warrant on Mr Swanwick in favor Richd Varrick	300. 0.0
Issued a Warrant on Mr Swanwick in favor the Bank	2.13.6
Issued a Warrant on Mr Swanwick in favor Ezk. Cornell	112.10.0

1. The papers given to Ezekiel Cornell, the newly appointed inspector of contracts for the main army, are identified in the notes to the Diary of September 19.

2. Letter not found.

3. See RM to the President of Congress, September 19, and notes.

4. The letter from John Holker has not been found, but undoubtedly referred to his clothing sales to the United States. See RM's Agreement with Holker, November 2, 1781, and notes.

5. The instructions were those of the Comptroller of the Treasury to the commissioners of accounts for the states and staff departments printed under October 14.

Circular to the Governors of the States

Circular   Office of Finance 20 Sepr. 1782

Sir,

Since my Letter of the twelfth Instant Congress have been pleased on the eighteenth to pass another Act on the same Subject of which I do myself the Honor to enclose a Copy.[1] With perfect Respect I have the Honor to be Sir your Excellency's most obedient and humble Servant[2]

Robt Morris

His Excellency The Governor of New Hampshire[3]

MSS: LS, to the President of New Hampshire, Meshech Weare Papers, Nh-Ar; LS, to the Governor of Massachusetts, M-Ar; LS, to the Governor of Connecticut, Jonathan Trumbull Papers, Ct; LS, to the President of Delaware, Executive Papers, De-Ar; LS, to the Governor of Virginia, Continental Congress Papers, Vi; Ofcl LbC, DLC; LbC, Letterbook of Governor Alexander Martin of North Carolina, 1782–1785, Nc-Ar.
    1. The act of September 18 stated that the money raised by the states under the requisition of September 4 and 10, 1782, would be credited to the states upon receipt, placed on interest, and the quotas thereof subject to retroactive adjustment in accordance with the resolution of Congress of October 6, 1779. The principles for the adjustment of state quotas on Continental requisitions were laid down in the first requisition of November 22, 1777.
    2. Notations on the Massachusetts circular indicate that it was read in the State Senate on October 17 and in the House of Representatives on October 18. The endorsement on the Connecticut text indicates that it was "received from Post Master 13th Octo. seq."
    3. This line is in the writing of Gouverneur Morris.

To Ezekiel Cornell

Office of Finance 20 Septr. 1782[1]

Sir,

By the enclosed Letter[2] you will perceive that the Contractors *declare explicitly they can no longer be answerable for supplying the Troops on Terms agreed on in the Contract.* That they ask of me *Assurances of Indemnification at the Close of the Contract for all Damages sustained from the public Inability to perform their Engagements.* And that they close with the cautionary Declaration *that if they do not receive such Assurances before the first of next Month they must surrender &ca.* The Account of Things as stated in their Letter (which I received on the seventeenth Instant) is not accurate but I have not Leizure at present to shew the Mistakes. Some Cause of Complaint they have the Reasons of which it is unnecessary to enumerate. Had they on winding up the Business been able to shew 1st. That on the whole the Public had not performed it's Part of the Agreement and 2ly. That they had suffered material Injury by such non Performance Justice would have required a due Compensation for Damages sustained and no Man in the World would have been more ready than myself to acknowlege their Claim and assist in procuring the proper Redress. It might from hence be inferred that I should as readily make the Assurances required but Sir I will by no Means consent to it. My Reason is shortly this that from the Moment such Assurances are made there is no longer any Restraint on their Conduct. Negligence or Profusion may extend the Damages to any Amount and my Promise will bind the Public to abide by the pernicious Consequences. Now altho I have privately the best Opinion of the Men yet publickly I will not trust the Contractors because I ought not to do it as a faithful Servant of the Public.

From what has been said I presume it must follow that you will have to make Provision for supplying the Troops upon their Failure. This I request you to do and whatever Agreements or Engagements you may enter into on that Subject I will take Care to comply with. I am Sir your most obedient and humble Servant[3]

RM

mss: Ofcl LbC, DLC; copy, PCC, DNA; copy, Benjamin Franklin Papers, PPAmP.

1. Cornell was the newly appointed inspector of contracts for the main army; his commission is dated September 19.

2. Comfort Sands, Walter Livingston, William Duer, and Daniel Parker to RM, September 11. The notes to that letter discuss the dissolution and renegotiation of the combined West Point and Moving Army contract.

3. The PCC text of this letter was enclosed in RM to the President of Congress, October 21, the PPAmP text in RM to Benjamin Franklin, January 11, 1783.

To Francisco Rendón

Office of Finance 20 Sepr. 1782[1]

Sir

The Assurances I have received that you would repay the Sum of four thousand Dollars long since lent you I need not repeat. What I have now to say is that ⟨after such Assurances I must suppose you to be in a Capacity to perform your Obligation. I must therefore desire that you pay⟩ having reposed entire Dependence in these Assurances I have formed my Engagements accordingly and must therefore desire you to pay the above Sum during the Course of the present Week. I am Sir with perfect Respect your most obedient and humble Servant.

Monsr. Francisco Rendon

ENDORSED: draft of a letter 20 Septr 1782/to Dn Francisco Rendon
MS: Dft in the writing of Gouverneur Morris, Miscellaneous Manuscripts Robert Morris, NHi.

1. Rendón was the unofficial Spanish representative to the United States. The endorsement quoted above is in RM's hand.

From the President of Pennsylvania
(William Moore)

In Council Philada. 20th Septr. 1782

Sir,

Your letter of 19th instant having been read in Council and the propositions it contains considered,[1] I am now to inform you, that the arrangements taken by the Council are perfectly consistent with your ideas from the time of the troops marching from Fort Pitt and Northumberland respectively.

It nevertheless appears to be reasonable that in case of a loss of provisions, being destroyed by the enemy, that the United States should bear a proportion of such loss according to the number of the troops of the United States compared with the number of Militia engaged in the expedition.

ENDORSED: 1782 Septr. 20th. To/Honble Robert/Morris Esqr./Superintendant of/ Finance
MS: Dft in the writing of Timothy Matlack, Records of Pennsylvania's Revolutionary Governments, RG 27, PHarH.
1. See *Colonial Records of Pennsylvania*, XIII, 374.

From Daniel of St.Thomas Jenifer

[Annapolis, Maryland] September 20th. 1782

Capt. Green delivered me the Letter which you did me the honor to write on the 13th instant,[1] and in Consequence thereof he has received from the Treasurer Twenty thousand Dollars for your Bill on Mr. Swanwick.

MS: LbC, Intendant's Letterbook, MdAA.
1. RM's second letter to Jenifer of September 13. Jenifer was Maryland's intendant of the revenue.

Diary: September 21, 1782

I sent for Colo. Ephram Blaine and informed him that the Account Sales of Flour rendered by him appears to be at very low Prices. He alledges the Quality was bad, the Flour being both Sour and musty. I told him he ought to [have] had a Survey on it, that however when the Account is Settled he must prove the Circumstances. I then requested him to furnish me with an Estimate of the Cost of that Flour to the United States which he promised to do. Colo Blaine observed to me that the Contract for Fort Pitt is expired[1] and that he is willing to continue it thro' the Year on the same Terms. I promised to consider of this Matter and after looking into that Contract I sent him Word that I will accept the Offer.[2]

John Chaloner Esqr. called upon me in the most pressing Manner for Money due to him on my Acceptances, Drafts &c. which I promise to Supply if possible by the 25th. Instant.[3]

Commodore Hazelwood also applys for money.

John Moylan Clothier Genl. for Money and for Notes.

Colo Cook for Money which I granted.

Wrote a Letter to John Moylan Esqr.

Wrote a Letter to David Ross Esqr.

1. The expired contract had been held by David Duncan and Michael Huffnagle. See notes to William Irvine to RM, July 5, 1782.

2. For further negotiations, see Diary, September 30.

3. For RM's obligations to Chaloner, see Diary, August 20, and notes.

To David Ross

Office of Finance 21. Sepr. 1782

Sir,

I have received your Favor of the sixth Instant[1] and am glad to find the Mistake of the Paymaster is set Right. The money due by Mr. Braxton must be paid by Mr. Braxton for I have not interfered neither will I interfere in that Transaction.[2] Permit me to take this Opportunity of expressing my extreme Surprize that a Bill drawn by Mr. Pleasants on you[3] which I took at his most earnest request and which I remitted to the French Treasury has after various Delays and Pretences on your Part been finally protested for non Payment. This Sir is the Account of that Business given to me by Mr. de Baulny Treasurer of the Army of Monsr. de Rochambeau. I am with Respect your most obedient Servant

RM

ms: Ofcl LbC, DLC.

1. Letter not found. Ross was a merchant and former commercial agent of Virginia who was involved in transactions arising from the Yorktown capitulation.

2. For the bonds posted by Carter Braxton and others for goods purchased at Yorktown, see RM to Ross, August 14, and notes.

3. This bill of exchange, drawn by Thomas Pleasants, Jr., who had been an agent of Virginia acting under Ross, was probably one of those enclosed in RM to Chevalier de La Luzerne, January 12, 1782 (second letter). For disputes relating to these bills, see RM to Ross, November 29, Diary, December 13, 1782, February 3 and March 13, 1783, and RM to Benoît Joseph de Tarlé, March 13, 1783.

From Alexander Hamilton

Albany [New York] Sepr. 21st 1782

Sir,

The hurry in which I wrote to you by the last post,[1] prevented my examining particularly the papers which I informed you I had received. On a more careful inspection of them, I found them not so complete as I had hoped. There is a general state of specific supplies, but the returns referred to in that for the particulars were by some mistake omitted. I have written for them, but they have not yet arrived; when they do I shall lose no time in forwarding them.

I observe there is nothing respecting transportation; and there is a part of the supplies for the period before Col Hay came into office,[2] which is estimated on a scale of proportion too vague a method to be satisfactory. I have urged him to find me an account of the transportation and to collect as speedily as possible official returns of the supplies above mentioned.

There is a practice obtaining which appears to me to contravene your views. The Contractors I am informed have gotten into a method of carrying your bills immediately to the collectors and drawing the specie out of their hands; by which means the paper never goes into circulation at all; but passes so to speak immediately out of one hand of the public into the other. The people therefore can never be familiarized to the paper nor can it ever obtain a general currency.

If the specie were to come into the Receivers and the Contractors were left under a necessity of exerting their influence to induce the inhabitants to take your notes to be afterwards redeemed by the Receivers agreeable to your plan, this would gradually accustom the people to place confidence in the notes; and though the circulation at first should be momentary it might come to be more permanent.

I am in doubt whether on the mere speculation of an evil without your instructions I ought to take any step to prevent this practice. For should I forbid the exchange, it might possibly cause a suspicion that there was a preference of the paper to the specie which might injure its credit.[3]

I have thought of a method to prevent without forbidding it in direct terms. This was to require each collector to return the names of the persons from whom he received taxes, and in different columns specify the kind of money, whether specie, your notes or bank Notes in which the tax was paid, giving the inhabitants receipts accordingly and paying in the money in the same species in which it was received. This would cover the object.

I have tried to prevail upon the County treasurer of this place to instruct the collectors accordingly; but the great aim of all these people is to avoid trouble; and he affected to consider the matter as an Herculean labour. Nor will it be done without a legislative injunction.

A method of this kind would tend much to check fraud in the collectors, and would have many good consequences.

I thought it my duty at any rate, to apprise you of the practice, that if my apprehensions are right it may not be continued without controul. I have reason to believe it is very extensive—by no means confined to this state.

Permit me to make one more observation. Your Notes though in Credit with the Merchants by way of remittance do not enter far into ordinary circulation, and this principally on account of their size; which even makes them inconvenient for paying taxes. The taxes of very few amount to twenty dollars a single tax; and though the farmers might combine to sell their produce for the notes to pay the taxes jointly; yet this is not always convenient and will seldom be practiced. If the Notes were in considerable part of five, eight or ten dollars, their circulation would be far more general, the merchants would even in their retail operations give specie in exchange for ballances; which few of them care to do or can do with the larger notes; though they are willing to take them for their goods.[4]

ENDORSED: Albany/Sepr 21st 1782
MSS: ADft, Hamilton Papers, DLC; John C. Hamilton transcript, owned by Mrs. William H. Swan, Hampton Bays, New York, on deposit NNC; transcript, Francis Baylies Papers, DLC.
1. See Hamilton to RM, September 14. Hamilton was the receiver of Continental taxes for New York.
2. Udny Hay was appointed New York state agent to supply the Continental army on June 29, 1780. See Hastings and Holden, eds., *Clinton Papers*, V, 892, 893–894.
3. Hamilton was soon confronted with this issue. See Sands, Livingston and Company to Hamilton, September 25, 1782, Syrett and Cooke, eds., *Hamilton Papers*, III, 169; his reply has not been found (*ibid.*, 171), but see Hamilton to RM, October 9.
4. Syrett and Cooke, eds., *Hamilton Papers*, III, 168n., suggest that one or more manuscript pages may be lacking, although they note that the J. C. Hamilton transcript of this letter ends at the same point. RM replied to Hamilton on October 5.

From William Churchill Houston

Trenton [New Jersey] 21 Septr 1782[1]

Sir

I have received ⟨the Line⟩ yours of the 17 instant. Its Contents shall be attended to.

Contrary to the Expectations I had formed the Receipt of this week is little or Nothing. I look forward with better ⟨Prospects⟩ Hopes to the Time when the Tax will be payable to me imediately, and not through the Hands of the Treasurer of the State.[2]

The Assembly of this State is now sitting; which I mention as Information that if you have any Thing to transmit it may come in time. They will not sit above ten or twelve Days. I am, &c.

Receipt of Continental Taxes for the State of New-Jersey
1782 Cash received from the State-Treasurer from Septr. 14 to 21 inclusive two Hundred Dollars

Dlls 200
W C Houston

ENDORSED: Copy letter to Robert/Morris Esq Superintend/&c 21 Septr 1782/return
200 Dlls
MS: ADft with subjoined ADftS return, Houston Collection, NjP.
    1. Houston was the receiver of Continental taxes for New Jersey.
    2. Houston refers to the tax due on October 1, 1782, part of which was to be paid
directly to him. See Houston to RM, June 15, 1782, and notes.

To the Clothier General (John Moylan)

Office of Finance 21. Sepr. 1782
    I have received your Letter of this Date.[1] I mean to pay your Bills for the
Blankets with Punctuality But I will neither accept them nor any others. You
may inform the Merchants of this as a general Regulation from which I
cannot depart.

MS: Ofcl LbC, DLC.
    1. Moylan's letter has not been found, but evidently concerned the blankets for the
Pennsylvania expedition which RM had directed him to purchase. See Diary, September 17.

From Abraham Yates, Jr.

Albany [New York] 21st September, 1782
    Your favor of the 22d in answer to mine of the 11th Ultimo and yours of
the 9th Instant Respecting Bills of Exchange I have before me.[1]
    I have no more than one Bill of Exchange of 18 dolls. left in my Office
which shall be transmitted you with the Return for this present Month.

MS: Copy, Yates Papers, NN.
    1. The September 9 letter was RM's Circular to the Continental loan officers. Yates
was the loan officer for New York.

From John Paul Jones

Extract of A Letter from Captain Jones to the Agent of Marine
Dated at Portsmouth in New Hampshire 22nd. Septr. 1782.[1]

Sir
    The Letter you did me the Honor to write me the 4th. of this
Month, respecting the disposition of the America, was presented to
me the Day before yesterday by Monr. De Martegne, who is appointed by the Marquis De Vaudreuil to command that superb ship.[2]
It would certainly have Afforded me greater satisfaction to have
retained that command, after having taken so much pains for these
fifteen Months past, in the fondest hope to render it essentially
useful to our cause and Honorable to our Flag. I can say I have in
that period, experienced a greater portion of care and anxiety than
in any other equal period of the Revolution. It is my *Tenth* Command which is now broken, but it is a Sacrifice I shall make with
pleasure, to shew my gratitude to France and my invariable attach-

ment to the Common Cause. I do not consider myself as being dishonored by the *late* Act of Congress; and when I have thought, and do think my Honor affected, or overlooked by my Sovereign, I have felt, and do feel myself particularly happy, by such severe Trials, to shew the World, that my Patriotism has been superior to Ambition, and a Stranger to Self Interest. The America is caulked and graved. The lower Deck Ports are enlarged and fitted. The Riders, Pointers, and Wingers in the Hould are all finished. The Rudder and Capstern are in Hands. And the ways are far advanced. I shall with pleasure continue my inspection and advice agreeable to your Orders till the Ship is Launched, and you may be assured I will urge forward the business with my utmost energy.

MS: Extract, PCC, DNA.
    1. This extract was enclosed in RM to the President of Congress, October 7 (first letter).
    2. Jones was captain of the *America,* which Congress had recently decided to present to France upon completion (see notes to Jones to Gouverneur Morris, September 2). Marquis de Vaudreuil was commander of the French fleet, which was then at Boston. On the new captain of the *America,* Jean Baptiste de MacCarthy-Martaigue, former commander of the *Magnifique,* which had been wrecked upon entering Boston harbor earlier in the year, see Contenson, *Société des Cincinnati,* 217.

From George Washington

Head Quarters [Verplancks Point, New York] 22d. Septemr. 178[2]
Dear Sir
    I am really more alarmed at the Contents of your letters of the 29th: and 30th. of Augt. and 9th. of this month,[1] than at any occurrence which hath lately happened—and I am embarrassed with respect to one paragraph in that of the 30th. of Augt. vizt. "The other which is the principal one, that you may found a warm application on it to the states. You will I hope keep this intirely to yourself, you will see that I have not intrusted a view of it to my secretary or any of the Clerks." ⟨How⟩ On what am I to found an application to the states but upon your information of your inability to comply with your Contracts in consequence of their tardiness in paying their Taxes? Should I proceed of my own accord, as it were, they will think I am stepping out of my line, and may perhaps hint to me that this reprehension would come more properly from another quarter. Untill I hear from you, I do not think myself at liberty to make use of your name. But ought we not, my dear Sir, to consider the danger of trusting a matter of so much importance, just at this moment when perhaps the enemy are balancing upon the total evacuation of these States, to a circular letter to the Legislatures. Letters of this kind are, from their nature, as public as the prints, and seldom fail

by one means or the other to get into the hands of the enemy. I have ⟨sometimes⟩ several times found personal applications by ⟨persons⟩ Gentlemen of influence have much more effect than letters. Of this you will judge—and I think another matter ought immediately to be taken into most serious consideration. If you should be of opinion that the most strenuous exertions of the states will not enable them to pay in a sufficiency of Specie to comply with the Contracts, ought not a change of measures to be resolved on without loss of time. That if we must, thro' necessity, revert to the ruinous system of Specifics, it may be done in time to lay up Magazines before the Winter sets in.[2]

Your letters of the dates beforementioned, not coming to my hands till yesterday, will account for these sentiments being with held from you so long.[3] I am with much esteem and regard Dear Sir Your most Obedient Servant

G: Washington

ENDORSED: To/The Hon: R: Morris Esq/22d. Sep. 1782.
MSS: ADftS in the writing of Tench Tilghman and Washington, Washington Papers, DLC; Varick transcript, Washington Papers, DLC.
1. These letters discussed the approaching collapse of the West Point and Moving Army contract. For the background, see notes to RM to Washington, August 29 (first letter).
2. To this point the letter is in Tilghman's hand. The remainder of the letter, including the signature and endorsement, is in Washington's hand.
3. RM replied on September 25.

From George Washington

Head Quarters [Verplancks Point, New York] 22d. Septemr 1782
Dear Sir

I have been honored with yours of the 12th: and am exceedingly happy to find that General Cornell has accepted the office of Inspector of the Contracts &c. I wish to see him as soon as possible as his presence becomes every day more and more necessary.

Mr. Mullins delivered me 480 dollars he having taken 20 to defray his Expenses. This he says was by desire of Mr. Swanwick. I have yet received no instructions from Congress, altho' they are most essentially necessary to the Commissioners.[1] I have the honor to be &c.

Honble. Mr. Morris

ENDORSED: Head Quarters 22d Sepr 1782/to/Hono Robert Morris/acknowleges his of 12th./Mr Mullins arrived and delivered 480 Dols
MSS: Dft in the writing of Tench Tilghman, Washington Papers, DLC; Varick transcript, Washington Papers, DLC.
1. Congress had approved instructions on September 9. See notes to Diary, June 18, 1782; and Gouverneur Morris to Henry Knox, September 13, and notes.

From the Quartermaster General
(Timothy Pickering)

Camp Verplanks Point [New York]
Septr. 22d. 1782

The Bearer Mr. Sheldon, is one of the contractors who engaged to furnish the materials for building the powder magazine at Springfield. One half the money was paid last June—the other half, amounting to sixteen hundred and sixty six dollars, is now due by the terms of the contract. Colo. Hatch, my deputy, who made the contract, has drawn on me for that Sum, expecting, as Mr. Sheldon was going to Philadelphia, that it would be paid there. It is not indeed possible for me to pay it. I cannot obtain a sufficiency to provide the supplies indispensably necessary for the army. I am therefore compelled to request you to order the payment of that draught. The necessity of fulfilling this contract was discussed on the former application, which renders it unnecessary for me to add any thing more at this time.[1]

MS: LbC, WDC, DNA.
1. The previous application was Pickering's letter of June 17, 1782. Sheldon delivered the present letter to RM on September 26. See Diary of that date.

Diary: September 23, 1782

Majr Saml Nicholas applied this Morning for Pay. I told him that there is no Money to give him, but if there was I imagine he is entitled to Prompt payment under the present regulations but that his Account shall be settled and the Balance put on Interest.[1]

Mr. Carter called on me this morning respecting money which is due.[2] I promised him part in a few Days and then entered into a Conversation with him respecting the Contract for the moving Army, proposing that Mr Wadsworth and himself should take it up if the present Contractors decline &c.[3] and in Consequence of this Conversation I sent Mr. Lloyd Express to Genl. Cornell with my Letter of this Date.

Comr Hazelwood applied for money and I desired Mr Swanwick to pay him what can at present be spared.

Ralph Pomeroy Esqr. brought me Letters from Colo. Pickering proposing to grant him more Notes for the purpose of paying Debts and to purchase Forage &c.[4] I offered many Arguments against multiplying my Paper at present but finally promised to Consider of the Matter until to Morrow.

Wrote a Letter to Daniel Clarke Esqr.

Wrote a Letter to George Webb.

Issued a Warrant on Mr Swanwick in favor Nichs
Spencer   £ 36. 2.1

Issued a Warrant on Mr Swanwick in favor Nichs
Spencer   26.14.8

Issued a Warrant on Mr Swanwick in favor Hazelwood & Co.   225. 0.0

1. RM took up the question of Nicholas's pay in the broader context of the national debt in his report to Congress of October 4.

2. See Diary, August 20, and notes.

3. For the collapse of the current West Point and Moving Army contract, see notes to Comfort Sands, Walter Livingston, William Duer, and Daniel Parker, September 11.

4. Only one letter on this subject from Quartermaster General Timothy Pickering, that of September 19, has been found.

To Thomas Barclay

Office of Finance 23d. Sepr. 1782

Sir,

Your several Letters of the ninth and sixteenth March, thirtieth of April, twentieth June, tenth July and eleventh July with one of the twentieth June in Cypher have been received.[1] The Ship Heer Adams is safely arrived in this Port. Her Goods are delivered and she is sold for twenty thousand Dollars. The Freight will be settled by Gentlemen chosen for that Purpose and any Balance due by the United States will be deducted from the continental half of the Sales.[2] If the Accounts are compleated in Season I will enclose a Copy. The Brig Sukey is also safely arrived at Boston. We have no Accounts from the other Vessels but I hope they may all arrive in Safety. I am in hourly Expectation of hearing from you that all our Goods in Europe have been shipped, at least I expect that they will have been sent away before this reaches you. Congress have in Contemplation a Plan for adjusting all the Accounts of their public Servants in Europe.[3] This when compleated will provide for the Adjustment of Mr. Dean's.[4] Justice is indeed due to him in common with all other Men but his Conduct has been such as to preclude the Idea of any Thing like Favor. I am Sir your most obedient Servant[5]

RM

MS: Ofcl LbC, DLC.

1. Letters not found. Barclay was the American consul general in France.

2. See Diary, September 11, and RM to the President of Congress, September 13, and notes.

3. On the plan, and Barclay's appointment as commissioner to settle accounts in Europe, see RM to the President of Congress, May 8, and notes, and RM to a Committee of Congress, August 26, 1782, and notes.

4. Barclay had previously been empowered to settle Silas Deane's accounts. See Benjamin Franklin to RM, March 30, 1782, and notes.

5. This letter was carried by Captain Joshua Barney of the *General Washington*. See RM to Barney, October 7 (first letter).

To Daniel Clark

Office of Finance 23. Sept. 1782

Sir,

I enclose you Copy of a Letter of the thirteenth Instant from Mr Webb Receiver of Taxes for Virginia.[1] In Consequence of which I also enclose you Bills for one, two, three, four, five, six, seven, eight, nine and fifteen thousand Dollars amounting in the whole to sixty thousand Dollars. These are drawn on Mr Swanwick and made payable to you or Order at one Year from the Date. These Bills I shall direct Mr. Webb to receive as Cash from the state on Account of the Continental Taxes. If you can purchase Tobacco with them from the Government at such Price that I can in any reasonable Time sell it again without loss I wish you to do so. I am Sir your most obedient Servant

RM

MS: Ofcl LbC, DLC.

1. George Webb's letter has not been found, but apparently suggested purchase of public tobacco from Virginia with Morris's notes in order to enable the state to make payment on the congressional specie requisition for 1782. Although the arrangements described in the present letter to Daniel Clark—who was purchasing tobacco in Virginia for the Superintendent (see RM's Agreement with George Eddy, printed under March 13, 1782, and notes)—mention only resale of the tobacco on public account, probably RM's main purpose in trying to acquire tobacco from the state at this time was to ship it to Europe to pay the interest due in June 1783 on the Dutch loan negotiated by John Adams and approved by Congress on September 14 (see notes to Diary, September 11). RM supplemented these directions in his letter to Clark of September 25. Since the letters did not specify whether the tobacco purchases were to be on public or private account, Clark suspected they were at least partly private, and may have based his original overtures to Virginia authorities on that assumption, causing them to be rejected. However, RM emphasized to Clark on October 22 that the purchase was "purely on public Account."

On November 8, Governor Benjamin Harrison informed the Virginia delegates that the scarcity of cash in Virginia would make it impossible to pay the congressional specie requisition for 1782 unless the state was allowed to do so in tobacco. When the delegates presented RM with a proposal to pay tobacco at the current price in place of cash, they were surprised to hear that RM, through Clark, had made a proposal "to that very effect to the amount of 60,000 Dollars, which had been lying some time before the Executive unanswered." Harrison responded that he had rejected Clark's offer to buy tobacco from Virginia's "Agent for Commutables," in exchange for notes payable in four months, as a mere private speculation. The misunderstanding corrected, Clark then made a formal offer to the governor which was accepted, and an order was issued to deliver 800 hogsheads to the receiver of Continental taxes and take notes in payment. Additional purchases were made later. There was considerable haggling over prices, but the Superintendent issued firm instructions that Clark pay no more than the market price, despite the fact that he was paying in notes rather than cash. In 1783 RM shipped much of the tobacco procured by Clark to Holland to pay interest due on the Dutch loan and sold the rest to Lacaze and Mallet and other merchants to raise needed cash. See Diary, September 24, RM to Clark, October 17, and 22 (first letter), December 9, 17, 1782, and January 22, 1783, to Webb, September 23, October 17, 1782, and January 22, 1783, and to the Willinks, van Staphorsts, and de la Lande and Fynje, September 28, 1782 (first letter); Hutchinson and Rutland, eds., *Madison Papers*, V, 258, 324, 328, 381–382n.; McIlwaine, ed., *Official Letters*, III, 395; and *Journals of the Council of Virginia*, III, 195.

To Ezekiel Cornell

Office of Finance 23. Sepr. 1782[1]

Sir,

This Day's Post has brought me a State of Receipts for the Week. The whole Amount is short of seven thousand Dollars and of that which is received I do not touch one thousand in Specie. The rest is paid in Paper which was an Anticipation. My Engagements are very numerous and weighty and altho I have determined to incur no new Expence not even the slightest yet those already incurred are sufficient to ruin the Credit I had taken so much Pains to establish unless I can procure some Respite. I am reduced therefore to this Point that unless Means can be devised to feed the Army at a long Credit I must desire the Contractors to desist and desire the General to subsist his Troops by military Collection. I need say no more to impress you with the Necessity of making the best Agreement with Colo. Wadsworth which you can.[2] You will confer with the General on the Subject and take his Advice. You will of Course keep the Purport of this Letter secret until I shall find it proper to make it public.

This goes by Express and I shall wait his Return before any farther Steps are taken; you will therefore detain him until you can write definitively on the Subject. Perhaps it may be best to form and complete the Contract under the Inspection of the General. I am Sir your most obedient Servant

RM

MSS: Ofcl LbC, DLC; copy, PCC, DNA; copy, Benjamin Franklin Papers, PPAmP.
1. The other texts of this letter to Cornell, inspector of contracts for the main army, indicate that it was addressed to him at Washington's headquarters at Verplancks Point, New York. The PCC copy was enclosed in RM to the President of Congress, October 21, 1782, the PPAmP text in RM to Benjamin Franklin, January 11, 1783.
2. See Diary, September 23, and notes.

From the Governor of Virginia (Benjamin Harrison)

Council Chamber [Richmond] Sept. 23d. 1782

Sir

I have receiv'd your favor of the 30 Ultimo and shall forward the Accounts of the Expences attending the Garrisoning the post of York Town under the call of Gen: Washington, as soon as I can procure them.

The Regulations you have enter'd into for clothing the Continental Army, will render useless to the State a quantity of necessaries now in France furnish'd by his most Christian Majesty, as the Terms we have them on (which I have before transmit'd to you) are such as will make the payment easy to the United States, we shall be obliged to you to take them off our Hands and take the Debt so far as they go on the States. You have a copy of the Invoice enclosed[1] by which you will see that they will be useful and necessary for the Army, which will I hope induce you to oblige the State. Mr. Thos. Barclay is appointed to transact this Business with the Court of France to whom you may write to make the transfer if you like the proposal, and should have an immediate Oppertunity of getting the Goods over, and I will forward similar orders to him as soon as I am favor'd with your determination.[2] Besides the above Articles we have a large Quantity of Arms and Military Stores procured in the same Manner as the Goods, which are much wanted for the defence of the State. Can you put me in a way of getting them over with any tolerable prospect of safety?[3] If you can you will extremely oblige me. Mr. Ross has just imported from Ostend a Thousand suits of Soldiers clothing which he will offer you; if it should be in any Manner convenient I wish you to take them, and draw an order on the State for payment, which shall be made out of our November Collection. I have two reasons for my request, the one that Mr. Ross when he gave orders for their being ship'd (about two years ago) had some assurance of their being taken by the State. The other that if we had them I am confident they would forward the recruiting Service much, the cash for which is now in Hand, and if the people could see that they would[4] be well cloathed (which has not been the case hitherto) they would enlist fast.[5] I am with respect &c

B. H.

MSS: LbC, Executive Letterbooks, Vi; copy certified by James McCall on October 15, 1782, PCC, DNA.

1. An extract from the invoice is printed as the enclosure to RM to the President of Congress, October 9.

2. For previous correspondence concerning the clothing, and the act of Congress of October 22 complying with Harrison's request, see RM to the Governor of Virginia, April 27, 1782, and notes, and documents cited there; also RM to the Governor of Virginia, October 23, and to Thomas Barclay, October 27, the Governor of Virginia to RM, November 16, RM to the Governor of Virginia, and to Thomas Barclay, both November 29, to Chevalier de La Luzerne, December 31, 1782, and to Franklin, January 19, 1783.

3. For RM's reply on this point, see his letter to Harrison of October 23.

4. The word "certainly" is included here in the DNA text.

5. RM agreed to have the clothing examined and a price set for its purchase. See RM to David Ross, November 29, 1782.

From William Whipple

Portsmouth [New Hampshire] 23d September 1782[1]

Sir

On my return from Concord where the Genl: Court have had a short Session, I received Your two favors of the 28th: and 29 Augt.[2] I shall duely attend to Your instruction respecting Your draughts on Mr: Swanwick; none of them have yet appeared here. I was in great hopes I should have prevailed on the Legislature to take more effectual measures for the immediate supply of the Treasury but my endeavors have been hitherto unsuccessful. I have not the least prospect but from the sale of the Beef mention'd in a former letter[3] and that I fear will fall short of my expectations, but small Receipts are better than none. I have the Honour to be

Honble Robt: Morris Esqr

MS: LbC, Whipple Letterbook, John Langdon Papers, PHi.
1. The recipient's copy of this letter from Whipple, the receiver of Continental taxes for New Hampshire, was inadvertently dated August 23. See RM to Whipple, October 9.
2. The letter of August 29 was a circular to the receivers of Continental taxes.
3. Dated August 5.

To George Webb

Office of Finance 23. Sepr. 1782

In Consequence of the Information contained in your Letter of the thirteenth Instant I now send to Mr. Clarke sundry Bills payable to him or Order at twelve months from the Date.[1] Should he purchase any of your State Tobacco you will receive those Bills as Cash for a Payment on the Part of the State to the United States and transmit them to me.

MS: Ofcl LbC, DLC.
1. The letter from Webb, receiver of Continental taxes for Virginia, has not been found. RM's letter to Daniel Clark is dated September 23.

George Plater to Gouverneur Morris

[Sotterley, near Leonardtown, Maryland, September 23, 1782]

Your most acceptable Favor of the 9th demands my Thanks. I thank you too for the pretty little poetical Peice enclosed.[1] I never trust much to Appearances, and I agree with you that if we *cou'd* have made more Exertions after Cornwallis's Fall, they might have had an happy Effect, but I do not see how this was to have been done, without adding Wings to our Armies. The Operations before York I think brought on October 19th—the Distance the Army had then to move to any other Scene of Action, suppose to N York, wou'd inevitably have thrown them too far into the winter Season to have done any thing then effectually, especially when the french Fleet had left our Coast. It is said here, that there is another Change in the british Ministry, that Mr. Fox is out—this comes by Way of the W Indies—if true it shows great Instability in their Councils. The fairist of the fair had left us before the Receipt of yours, or I shou'd have taken much Pleasure in presenting your Compliments. Whenever I play at any Game with a fine Woman be assured I allways take Care to point properly—but enough of this, let me bid you adieu for the present, and believe me Yours most sincerely

Sotterley Sept. 23d 1782

MS: ALS, Gouverneur Morris Papers, NNC.
1. Gouverneur Morris's letter and enclosure have not been found. Plater was the president of the Maryland Senate.

Diary: September 24, 1782

Mr Geo Eddy applied to me to order a farther purchase of Tobacco to load his other flag Ship the Fame in Virginia. I did so by my Letter of this Date to Mr Clarke.[1]

Capt Jno. Green this Day from Maryland with 20,000 Dollars on Account of their Taxes for which I sent him with a light Waggon last Week.[2]

I sent for Mr Fitzsimmons and shewed him my report to Congress on the subject of providing Funds for paying the Interest of the Public Debts &c.[3]

Colo. Pomeroy came again to obtain Notes &c. which I refused and wrote him a Letter of this Date.[4]

Colo. Pettit called also on the Subject of Interest on public Debts &c.[5]

Wrote a Letter to Jno. Moylan Esqr.[6]

Wrote a Letter to Daniel Clarke.[7]

1. The letter to Daniel Clark is dated September 25.
2. See Diary, September 14, and notes.
3. Thomas Fitzsimons was a Philadelphia merchant and a director of the Bank of North America. The report shown to him was RM to the President of Congress, July 29. See the headnote and notes to that document for Fitzsimon's involvement in the actions of public creditors on this issue.
4. The letter to Ralph Pomeroy is dated September 25.
5. For Charles Pettit's involvement, see the reference cited in note 3 above.
6. This letter was written by James McCall.
7. See note 1 above.

To Ferdinand Grand

Office of Finance 24. Septem. 1782[1]

Sir,

As it is possible that my Bills on you may go to an Extent somewhat beyond the Funds in your Possession I have taken the Precaution to give you a Credit on Messrs. Wilhelm [and] Jan Willink Nicolaas and Jacob Van Staphorst De la Land and Fynje under whose Direction a Loan was opened in Holland which is I expect by this Time compleated. This is done as you will perceive by the enclosed Letter which is left open for your Perusal.[2] I am Sir your most obedient and humble Servant

RM

MS: Ofcl LbC, DLC.
1. Grand was banker to the United States in Paris. This letter to him was carried by Captain Joshua Barney of the *General Washington*. See RM to Barney, October 7 (first letter).

2. See RM to the Willinks, van Staphorsts, and de la Lande and Fynje, September 24. RM was in fact overdrawn on Grand for even more than could then be covered by the proceeds of the Dutch loan of 1782. See RM to Franklin, January 11 and 13, to Grand, and to La Luzerne, both January 13, and Grand to RM, February 15, 1783.

To Le Couteulx and Company

Office of Finance 24. Septem: 1782

Gentlemen,

Enclosed you have Letters of this Date to the House of Messrs. Le Couteulx at Cadiz and to Messrs. Wilhelm [and] Jan Willink Nicolas and Jacob Van Staphorst De la Land and Fynje at Amsterdam.[1] These two Letters which I am to request that you will forward are left open for your Perusal and will explain to you the Object which I now have in View. The United States having Monies in Holland which are very necessary for the public Service here I have deemed it best to bring them thro the Havanna for the following Reasons. First Bills of Exchange cannot be negotiated here to the necessary Amount and are even then negotiated at the Rate of thirteen per Cent Discount. Secondly as it is therefore necessary to import Money the Risque is less from the Havanna than from Europe. Thirdly it might not be agreable to the Prejudices of many to draw from Europe their circulating Coin and fourthly I expect that a considerable Gain will be made on the Negotiations. Thus for Instance to take it in its greatest Extent I am informed that Bills on Cadiz at thirty Days sell at the Havanna for an Advance of eight per Cent and that Bills on Paris sell at Cadiz for an Advance of nine per Cent and that there is also an advance on Bills drawn from Paris on Amsterdam to which may be added that a considerable Time is also gained in these various Negotiations and therefore if any Benefit can be derived to the United States from that Circumstance you will govern yourself accordingly. In this as well as in every other Circumstance relating to the Business I have on you Gentlemen the most perfect Reliance. I think it will be best for you to know immediately of the Gentlemen in Amsterdam whether they will answer your Drafts to the Amount because if they should raise any Obstacles in the Way those may be removed in Season from this Country provided an early Notice be transmitted for I expect you will receive this Letter by the Time Mr.   [2] reaches the Havanna if not before and I do not suppose that his Bills can reach Cadiz in less than two Months and of Course at one Usance[3] only (and they shall if that can be done without Loss be drawn at two Usances) they will not be payable until three Months and then if Time is necessary you will direct the House in Cadiz to draw at two Usances more which will bring the Business to between five and six Months from your Receipt of my Letters. At any Rate it will not do that Mr.   Bills be protested. I must rely on you to prevent an Accident which would be attended with such fatal Consequences and [I][4] shall take measures to put you in Capacity to answer them seasonably. With perfect Respect I am Gentlemen your most obedient and humble Servant

RM

P.S. You will observe that there is in the foregoing Letter a Blank for the Name of the Person who is to be employed in this Business. The Reason is that the Gentleman I spoke to on the Subject is prevented by the Circumstances of his Family from going to the Havanna.[5] I shall write to you farther on the Subject when I shall have taken other Arrangements.

MSS: Ofcl LbC, DLC; copy, PCC, DNA.

1. With these letters of September 24, RM launched a number of schemes to import specie from Havana (for previous efforts, see RM to the Governor of Cuba, July 17, 1781, and notes, and to Joshua Barney, May 18, 1782, and notes). The first initiative, discussed in the present letter to Le Couteulx and Company of Paris, RM's private banker in Europe, would have made some of the proceeds of the Dutch loan of 1782 available at Havana by selling for specie there bills of exchange drawn on the firm of Jacques, Louis and Laurent Le Couteulx and Company of Cadiz; this firm would be reimbursed by its Paris branch, which in turn would draw upon the Dutch banking consortium handling the Holland loan of 1782 (on the loan, see notes to Diary, September 11).

Another set of expedients was based on a loan expected from France in 1783, initially presumed by RM to be the $4 million which Congress had requested. (The French loan in actuality turned out to be only 6 million livres, little more than a fourth of the requested amount.) RM requested Benjamin Franklin to have Spain make a million dollars of it available in specie at Havana and provide a convoy for shipment to an American port, the government to be compensated by payments in Europe. (Later RM thought the French navy would be more likely to afford convoy.) More immediately, he desired Franklin to give the Paris branch of Le Couteulx and Company $500,000 to be used to buy bills of exchange on Havana at a discount expected to be at least 25 percent. After the bills had been presented and converted into specie at Havana, the proceeds were to be held at RM's disposal. Neither of these plans was executed. However, the Financier managed to get 600,000 livres (about $111,923) of the French loan for 1783 in specie directly from France; Captain Joshua Barney brought it back from Europe in the *General Washington*, which carried the preliminary articles of peace and sailed under a flag of truce (see RM to Franklin, September 27 [second letter], October 1 and 7, and to Le Couteulx and Company, September 27, 1782, and May 8, 1783).

RM also achieved limited success in importing specie along the lines of the first initiative. Late in 1782 he sent John Brown to Havana as supercargo aboard the *Duc de Lauzun*, Captain John Green, with a commercial cargo to sell and bills of exchange on Le Couteulx and Company of Cadiz. Although RM reduced the ceiling on the bills Brown was authorized to sell from an initial $500,000 to $200,000, Brown reported on March 4 that he was able to dispose of only $67,422; he indicated that sales would have been better if the bills had been based on RM's personal credit rather than the credit of the United States. Brown also managed to sell the cargo of flour and beef for $25,707 (for a slightly different statement of the voyage's proceeds as later settled at the Treasury, see [Morris], *Statement of Accounts*). After deductions for transport, duties, and other expenses, a total of $72,447 in specie was shipped on public account, plus some specie on private account, first aboard two Continental vessels, the *Lauzun* and Captain John Barry's *Alliance*, but after repeated encounters with the enemy, entirely on the speedier *Alliance*, which slipped into Newport, Rhode Island, on March 20, 1783. Since RM had intended to apply part of the proceeds to paying the army, his minimal success in the venture was a severe disappointment (for RM's disposition of the money, see RM to George Olney, March 29, 1783 [first letter]).

The Superintendent carried out the Havana scheme behind a veil of secrecy. At the inception of the plan he confided it in cipher to Washington with the caution that "the profoundest secrecy should be observed lest the enemy should prevent the execution of it." He gave only the vaguest intimation of his plans to a congressional committee, and in January he declined to reveal the specific measures to a grand committee of Congress that was considering a memorial from the army officers at Newburgh, saying, as Madison noted, "that he could not as yet disclose them without endangering their success." Called upon to explain his conduct the following April, RM sent copies of the pertinent letters, including the PCC text of the present one, in a communication to Theodorick Bland, Jr., chairman of a committee of Congress and a prominent critic of the Financier's policies, along with a resolution of July 3, 1781, which had empowered him to import money and goods on account of the United States at his discretion. See RM to Barry, October 14 and November 23, Diary, October 16, RM to George Washington, October 16, to Le Couteulx and Company, October 25, 1782, and April 12, 1783, to Jacques, Louis and Laurent Le Couteulx and Company, October 25, 1782, and May 17, 1783, to the Marquis del Real Socorro, and to John Brown, both November 23, 1782, to the Governor of Cuba, and to John Green, both November 27, 1782, to Theodorick Bland, Jr., April 16, 1783 (first letter), Barry to RM, January 22 and March 20, 1783, Brown to RM, March 4 (two letters) and March 25, 1783, Jacques, Louis and Laurent Le Couteulx and Company to RM, December 24, 1782, and February 4, 1783; Madison's Notes on Debates, January 7, 1783, Hutchinson and Rutland, eds., *Madison Papers*, VI, 18–20n.; and Clark, *Gallant John Barry*, 289–303. Unlike the Grands and other Protestant bankers employed by the Americans in France, Le Couteulx and Company of Paris was a Catholic firm. It has been characterized by one historian as "the most ancient and distinquished, in many ways, the first bank in France," one with "an almost legendary reputation," as reflected in the contemporary anecdote "that in more than three hundred years the firm had never been late in the payment of a bill of exchange." See Price, *France and the Chesapeake*, II, 746–747; for the firm's desire to be involved in the disposition of the Dutch loan, see Matthew Ridley to RM, July 23 and November 20, 1782.

2. This and another space below were left blank in manuscript. See the postscript.
3. The time period allowed by mercantile custom for bills of exchange to be paid.
4. Bracketed word supplied from the PCC text.
5. The person intended almost certainly was Thomas Fitzsimons, a Philadelphia merchant and a director of the Bank of North America (see Diary, September 28). This postscript and the one to the following letter to the Cadiz branch were very likely written on or after September 28 and possibly as late as October 7, when RM entrusted the letters to Captain Joshua Barney of the *General Washington*. See RM to Barney, October 7 (first letter).

To Jacques, Louis and Laurent Le Couteulx and Company

Office of Finance 24. Septem: 1782

Gentlemen[1]

I am about to send Mr.   [2] from this Place to the Havanna with orders to draw on you to the Amount of five hundred thousand Dollars if he shall find Vent for his Bills. Whatever he may draw for you will be pleased to honor and pay taking your Reimbursment on Messrs. Le Coulteulx and Co. at Paris to whom I have written on this Subject and who will I expect write to you. I expect you will be able to gain a considerable advance on your Bills which is one Reason for directing the Drafts on you in the first Instance. Your Commissions for doing this Business shall be regulated by Messrs. Le Couteulx and Co. who being perfectly acquainted with the customary Rules on large Money Negotiations and being Persons of great Integrity and Honor will I am perswaded do equal Justice to you and to the United States. You will be pleased Gentlemen from Time to Time when Occasions offer to transmit me your Accounts with such Information as you may find necessary. I have the Honor to be Gentlemen your most obedient and humble Servant

RM

P.S. The Gentleman whom I intended to send to Havanna on this Business being prevented from going by his family Circumstances I shall write you farther on the Subject hereafter.[3]

MSS: Ofcl LbC, DLC; copy, PCC, DNA.
1. Jacques, Louis and Laurent Le Couteulx and Company were bankers in Cadiz. This letter to them was enclosed in the preceding letter to Le Couteulx and Company of Paris and received by the Cadiz firm on December 19, 1782 (see their reply of December 24, 1782). The PCC text was enclosed in RM to Theodorick Bland, Jr., April 16, 1782 (first letter).
2. Space left blank in manuscript. See the postscript.
3. For the date of this postscript, see notes to the preceding letter.

To the Willinks, van Staphorsts, and de la Lande and Fynje

Office of Finance 24. Septr. 1782

Gentlemen,[1]

Presuming from the Letters of yourself and of the honorable Mr. Adams that the Loan opened on Account of the United States of America under your Auspices is filled[2] I do myself the Honor to enclose you sundry Acts of Congress by which you will see that the Amount is subject to my Disposal. Whatever Measures I may take you will from Time to Time receive due Notice of unless the Miscarriage of Letters by the Accidents to which they are at present subjected should prevent.

I have now in View a Money Negotiation which may or may not take Place according to Circumstances but which will probably be accomplished to the Amount of from one to two Million of Florins.[3] If it should be effected Messrs. Le Couteulx and Co. Bankers at Paris will have Occasion to draw on you. I am now therefore to desire that the Bills drawn by that House to whatever Amount be punctually honored and paid on Account of the United States. It is in a Reliance on this that I shall take my Measures and a Failure of Payment would be attended with the worst Consequences. I have the Honor to be with perfect Respect Gentlemen your most obedient and humble Servant[4]

RM

MSS: Ofcl LbC, DLC; copy, PCC, DNA.
1. Wilhem (b. 1750) and Jan (b. 1751) Willink, Nicolaas and Jacob van Staphorst, and Jacobus de la Lande and Hendrik Fynje were three Amsterdam firms which formed a consortium for raising the first Dutch loan to the United States, secured by John Adams in June 1782. The Staphorsts and de la Lande and Fynje were pro-American firms connected with the Dutch Patriot Party. The Willinks, who like the Fynje family were Mennonites, were not identified with any political faction; unlike the other two firms, however, they were a prominent, well-established company whose reputation for wealth commanded confidence. Although de la Lande and Fynje went bankrupt by 1786, the other two firms long remained active in American trade and finance, and were involved in RM's postwar private business. See van Winter, *American Finance and Dutch Investment*, I, 27–32, 61, 66n., 82–97, 117–118, 121n., 122n., 163, 277–278, 364n.–366n., 383n., II, 637–640, 953–954, 970–971, 973–975.
2. RM's presumption was incorrect; the subscription filled up slowly (see notes to RM to the President of Congress, July 29). For the letters mentioned and Congress's acceptance of the loan, see notes to Diary, September 11; concerning RM's management of it, see Diary, September 13, and notes.
3. About $400,000 to $800,000.
4. This letter was enclosed in RM to Le Couteulx and Company, September 24. The PCC text was enclosed in RM to Theodorick Bland, Jr., April 16, 1783 (first letter).

To the Willinks, van Staphorsts, and de la Lande and Fynje

Office of Finance 24. Sepr. 1782

Gentlemen

Presuming that the Loan opened under your Auspices is compleated I have to request that you answer such Bills as may be drawn on you by Mr Grand Banker of Paris.[1] These will be only in Case the funds in his Hands should be deficient in answering my Drafts on him which will not I imagine be the Case but it may possibly happen because Bills which had been drawn a great while ago by Authority of Congress at a very long sight have come upon him to an Amount which I cannot precisely ascertain and because there are Drafts on him for purchases made on Account of the United States in Europe the Sum of which it is in like Manner impossible for me to ascertain. The Credit therefore which I now give him on you is provisional in Case his Funds should be deficient. I think however that the Deficiency if any cannot be great. I am Gentlemen your most obedient and humble Servant

RM

MS: Ofcl LbC, DLC.
1. See RM to Ferdinand Grand, September 24, in which the present letter to the Dutch bankers was enclosed.

James McCall to the Clothier General (John Moylan)

Office of Finance 24. Sepr. 1782

Mr. Morris has received your Letter of Yesterday, and desired I would acquaint you that he agrees to the Purchase of Blankets from Messrs. Nesbitt and Company; and that he will furnish you with the Amount in Bills at the rate you mention.[1]

MS: Ofcl LbC, DLC.
1. Moylan's letter has not been found; the blankets may have been for the proposed Pennsylvania expedition, on which see Diary, September 7, and notes. McCall was RM's secretary in the Office of Finance.

From Samuel Hodgdon

Philadelphia 24th Sept 1782

I have the honor to inclose a Letter from Colonel John Patton;[1] on the subject of which I should be happy to receive your direction; previous to my answer which is immediately requested.

MS: LbC, WDC, DNA.
1. For the subject of Patton's letter, which has not been found, see Diary, September 25. Hodgdon was the commissary general of military stores.

Diary: September 25, 1782

I sent this morning for Solomon the Broker but he says he cannot sell any Bills of Exchange.

The Honble. Mr. Clarke called respecting the Affairs of Mr. Pollock and mentioned some Things which I think it will be proper to enquire into but he is to inform me farther respecting his Author.[1] He gave me leave to shew his Letter to Mr Fox and I enclosed it accordingly.[2]

I received from Mr Eddy his note for 10,000 Dollars and directed Mr. Swanwick to get it discounted at the Bank.

Ralph Pomeroy Esqr. applied again for Notes &c. which I declined Issuing as at first.

Mr. Chaloner applied again for his money and I am happy to pay him the greater part.[3]

Mr. Hodgdon called for an Answer to his Letter respecting the Iron Masters getting German Soldiers on Account of their Claims to which I agreed.[4]

Genl Elbert and Major Turner applied for a distribution of the Cloathing imported in the Heer Adams. I informed them the quantity is not sufficient for the whole Army and that I cannot make partial Distribution beside that the Debts of the Cloathing Department are so heavy as to render it absolutely necessary to Sell those Goods in order to pay the said Debts.[5]

Wrote a Letter to Mr Fox.
Wrote a Letter to Ralph Pomeroy Esqr.

1. Abraham Clark of New Jersey was chairman of a committee to which Congress on September 23 had referred a letter of September 18 from Oliver Pollock. See Diary, September 27, and RM to James Duane, October 11, and notes.

2. See James McCall to Edward Fox, September 25, and Diary, September 26.

3. See Diary, August 20, and notes.

4. See Samuel Hodgdon to RM, September 24, and Diary, September 26 and October 15, and notes.

5. See RM to the President of Congress, September 13, and to George Washington, October 15.

To John Adams

Philadelphia September 25th: 1782

Sir

Your letter of the 22nd April has been delivered to me by Mr. Peter Paulus[1] to whom I shall most chearfully afford such advice or countenance as he may stand in need of. But it seems this Gentlemans wants are not confined to those Points, he applies to me for a Supply of Money to set up his Trade. I have explained that your desires in his favor do not extend to the advance of Money, and I am exposed by my Station to too many such Applications. They have indeed proved extreamly inconvenient and I am compelled to resist them all in my Power. It is probable that I shall be obliged to Number this Gentleman in the list of those whose Necessities encrease my[2] advances.

I congratulate your Excellency most Sincerely on the event of the 19th April[3] from which I hope and expect that our Country will derive essential benefits. With great Respect and Esteem, I have the Honor to be Your Excellencys most obedient and humble Servant[4]

Robt Morris

His Excellency John Adams Esqr.
Minister &ca
Hague

MSS: LS, Adams Papers, MHi; LS marked "Duplicate," Adams Papers, MHi; ADftS, Robert Morris Papers, DLC.

1. Adams was the American minister to the Netherlands and one of the commissioners for negotiating peace with Great Britain. This private reply to his missing letter of introduction for Paulus was RM's first communication to Adams since entering office as Superintendent (see the circular to Benjamin Franklin, Adams, and John Jay of September 25 for RM's first official missive to him). Paulus also carried a letter from Charles Dumas to RM of July 4, 1782. He evidently became an innkeeper in Philadelphia and participated in colonizing activities in Spanish Louisiana later in the decade. See Kinnaird, ed., *Spain in the Mississippi Valley*, pt. 2, p. xxv; and Burson, *Don Esteban Miró*, 128.

2. Here in the ADftS RM began to write the word "inconv[eniences?]," but then struck it out.

3. The date the United Provinces recognized the independence of the United States. RM commented on the event in his letter to the president of Congress of July 29.

4. This letter was carried by Captain Joshua Barney of the *General Washington* (see RM's first letter to him of October 7). Adams received it on November 5 and replied on November 6 and 7 from Paris, where after a 10-day journey, he had arrived on October 26 to join the peace negotiations. See Butterfield, ed., *Adams Diary and Autobiography*, III, 37.

To Thomas Barclay

Office of Finance 25 Septr. 1782

Sir,

Enclosed is the Copy of Acts of Congress of the twenty seventh of November and third December 1781, and fourteenth and twenty third Instant by which you will perceive that you are restricted from drawing on the Funds of the United States as also from making farther Purchases on their Account.[1] I am to request that as to all Goods already purchased they may be shipped as speedily as possible. I leave to your Discretion entirely the Mode of Shipping, the Terms, and the particular Port of Destination. You will prudently consult the Interest of the United States, and act according to the Dictates of your own Judgment. As this will involve some Expence I have by the enclosed Letter given you a Credit for fifty thousand Livres on Mr. Grand of Paris.[2] You will from time to time transmit your Accounts, and if it shall appear necessary, and the Circumstances of America will permit, I will then extend this Credit. But I conceive that the abovementioned Sum will be amply sufficient for present Purposes. I am Sir your most obedient and humble Servant[3]

RM

MS: Ofcl LbC, DLC.

1. Barclay, the American consul general in France, had been unraveling problems in connection with goods purchased in Holland by John Laurens and William Jackson (see Benjamin Franklin to RM, March 4, 1782, and notes, and further on the involvement of Alexander Gillon therein, Diary, September 19, and notes). On the acts of Congress enclosed by RM, see notes to Diary, September 13, and RM to the President of Congress, September 19, and notes.

2. See RM to Ferdinand Grand, September 25.

3. This letter and its enclosures were carried by Captain Joshua Barney of the *General Washington*. See RM to Barney, October 7 (first letter).

Circular to Benjamin Franklin, John Adams, and John Jay

(Duplicate) Office of Finance 25th September 1782

Sir,

I do myself the Honor to enclose for your Perusal Acts of Congress of the twenty seventh of November and third of December 1781, and the fourteenth and twenty third Instant.[1] In Consequence I have to request that all Bills hitherto drawn by Authority of Congress be paid, and the Accounts of those Transactions closed. After this is done, and I hope and believe that while I am writing this Letter it may have been already accomplished, you will be freed from the Torment and Perplexity of attending to Money Matters. I am persuaded that this Consideration will be highly pleasing to you, as such Things must necessarily interfere with your more important Attentions.

I have long since requested the Secretary of Foreign Affairs to desire you would appoint an Agent or Attorney here to receive and remit your Salary which will be paid Quarterly: In the mean Time it is paid to him for your Use.[2] As to any contingent Expences which may arise, I shall readily make the necessary Advances upon Mr. Livingston's Application. These Arrangements will I hope be both useful and agreable to you. I am, Sir, With perfect Respect Your Excellency's most obedient and humble Servant[3]

Robt Morris

His Excellency Franklin Esqr.

ENDORSED: Office of Finance/Sept. 25. 1782/Payment of Interest Bills/Proposes my appointing an/Attorney, &c
MSS: LS, Franklin Papers, PPAmP; LS, to Franklin, Franklin Papers, CtY; LS marked "3d," to Franklin, Ferdinand J. Dreer Collection, PHi; LS, to Adams, Jay Papers, NHi; LS marked "Duplicate," to Adams, Adams Papers, MHi; LS marked "3d," to Adams, Adams Papers, MHi; LS, to Jay, Jay Papers, NHi; LS marked "3d.," to Jay, Jay Papers, NHi; LS marked "4th.," to Jay, PPIn; Ofcl LbC, DLC.
    1. On these acts, which committed American funds in Europe to RM's disposition, see Diary, September 13, and notes, and RM to the President of Congress, September 19, and notes.
    2. On this subject, see RM to the President of Congress, May 8, 1782, and notes.
    3. This letter was carried by Captain Joshua Barney of the *General Washington* (see RM's first letter to him of October 7). Jay's endorsement on the first NHi LS indicates that it was "Received 5 Novr."

To Benjamin Franklin

(Duplicate)   Office of Finance 25th September 1782
Sir,

In my Letter of the 27th November last[1] I requested your Excellency to cause Purchases to be made of certain Articles contained in an Invoice exhibited to me from the War Office. The Difficulties which have hitherto attended every Purchase and Shipment of Goods on public Account, and other Circumstances, have determined me to obtain all future Supplies by Contracts here, and therefore I am to request that no future Purchases may be made. I have directed Mr. Barclay to send out whatever may have been already purchased on public Account.[2] With perfect Respect I have the Honor to be Sir Your most obedient and humble Servant[3]

Robt Morris

His Excellency Benjamin Franklin Esquire

ENDORSED: Office of Finance/Sept. 25. 1782/No future Purchases to be/made
MSS: LS, Franklin Papers, PPAmP; LS, Franklin Papers, CtY; LS marked "Triplicate,"

Ferdinand J. Dreer Collection, PHi; LS marked "4th," PPIn; Ofcl LbC, DLC; copy in the writing of Arthur Lee, Records of Boundary and Claims Commissions and Arbitrations, RG 76, DNA.

1. The reference is to RM's first letter to Franklin of that date.
2. See RM to Thomas Barclay, September 25.
3. This letter was entrusted to Captain Joshua Barney of the *General Washington.* See RM to Barney, October 7 (first letter).

To Vicomte de Noailles

[Philadelphia, September 25, 1782]

Permit me my Dear Count to return You a thousand thanks for your kind remembrance as well as for your attention in executing the Commissions which your desire to oblige led you to undertake for Mrs Morris.[1] It is unfortunate that your Labours have been lost, and the more so as by that means we are deprived the opportunity of seeing, approving and praising your Taste in the choice of the things. ⟨as to the value it⟩ You will lament as I do exceedingly the loss of so fine a Frigate as the Eagle and particularly as it occasions so great a disapointment to the ⟨Count⟩ Chevr. Le Touche. That Brave officer is at present a Prisoner in New York but we expect him out on Parole.[2] The several Gentlemen who came Passengers with him and in the Glory Frigate are safely Landed and did me the honor to dine with me yesterday when we had the pleasure to drink your Health.[3] The only thing that can attone for your not returning to us again is the consideration of your being detained by a reward granted to your Merits by that Sovereign whom you Love and Honor to the greatest degree. I hope with you for a general Peace, but we are told the negotiations are broke of[f] and that, that desirable event is removed to a greater distance than we had reason a short time since to expect.[4] You make me very happy by the kind notice you have taken of my two little Boys.[5] I hope they will deserve such attention as it may be convenient for you to pay them and that at some future day they will express their gratitude by a respectfull attachment to your person. Mrs. Morris requests me to present You her thanks and best Wishes and I beg you will believe that with great esteem and affection[6] I have the honor to be My Dear Sir Your most obedient and humble Servant[7]

RM

Philada Septr 25th 1782
A Monsr
Monsr Le Compte de Noailles

ENDORSED: Septr. 25th 1782/Le Compte Noailles
MS: ADftS, Robert Morris Papers, NN.
1. Brother-in-law of Lafayette, Noailles was an officer in the French army who had fought at Yorktown before returning to France. He had offered to purchase items in

France for Mary Morris (see RM to Noailles, November 26, 1781), but the goods were shipped aboard the French frigate *Aigle*, commanded by Compte de La Touche-Tréville, which was wrecked off the American coast. See Diary, September 16, and notes, and RM to Matthew Ridley, October 6.

2. However, see RM to the Governor of Delaware, October 18.

3. For the French officers who came on the *Aigle* and the *Gloire*, see Balch, *French in America*, I, 224–225.

4. Numerous French and American dispatches carried aboard the *Aigle* and *Gloire* had arrived safely (see Wharton, ed., *Rev. Dipl. Corr.*, V, 743). For the information they contained regarding the status of the peace negotiations, see, for example, Hutchinson and Rutland, eds., *Madison Papers*, V, 153–154, 155, 157, 158–159; and *JCC*, XXIII, 603.

5. RM evidently conveyed a similar message with regard to his sons in a letter to Marquis de Lafayette of September 27, 1782 (ALS [i.e., ADftS?] sold by Stan. V. Henkels, January 16, 1917, lot 68); the text of that letter is not available. For the education of RM's two eldest sons in Europe, see RM to Matthew Ridley, October 14, 1781, and notes.

6. RM substituted this word for the unfinished phrase "sincere atta[chment?]."

7. The recipient's copy of this letter and RM's missive to Lafayette mentioned in note 6 above were undoubtedly carried by Captain Joshua Barney of the *General Washington*. See RM to Barney, October 7 (first letter).

To Ralph Pomeroy

Office of Finance 25 Sepr. 1782

Sir,

I have this Morning received and considered your letter of the twenty second Instant.[1] I give due weight to your Observation that the Payment of Monies due to your People by Paper receivable in the Taxes would at once facilitate the Collection and establish a Credit on which future Supplies might be obtained. A View of these Things had led me very early to extend a considerable paper Circulation which has constantly returned upon me for Payment instead of being absorbed by the Taxes.[2] A Desire of supporting the various Branches of public Service has induced me to make considerable Anticipations relying on the most pointed Assurances from the most respectable Authorities that I might expect very considerable Aid from the States and particularly from Connecticut. It is I am sure Sir unnecessary to inform you how much I have been deceived. I am therefore determined not to extend my Engagements any farther but to wait until the Taxes shall have enabled me to comply with those already made. I am at the same Time not only willing but desirous that you should pay off the Monies you owe and therefore if Colo. Pickering will appropriate to this Purpose a Part of the large Notes he has received from me I will readily exchange them for small ones. But I am very unwilling that new Debts should be contracted for the shameful and I think I might say treasonable Negligence of those (whoever they are) whose Duty it is to compel the Collection of Taxes takes away the Hope of being able to pay them and it is my Determination not to Promise where I do not see the

Prospect of Performance. It is for this Reason (founded on those Principles of Justice and Truth which alone can be relied on) that I am determined as I have already said not to Extend my Engagements before I have complied with those already made. I know well that the Service must suffer but I also know that an early Suffering is better than a late Ruin and I find myself reduced to the Necessity of chusing between these two Evils by the Negligence of the States. Whatever be the Consequence it must be theirs to answer it and I hope the People will at length distinguish between those who admonish them to their Good and those who flatter them to their Destruction. I am Sir your most obedient and humble Servant

RM

MSS: Ofcl LbC, DLC; copy, Jonathan Trumbull, Jr., Papers, CtHi; copy, Manuscript File, WDC, DNA.

1. The letter from Pomeroy, deputy quartermaster general for Connecticut, has not been found, but for its import, see Diary, September 23, and notes. RM enclosed a copy of this reply to Pomeroy in his letter to the Quartermaster General of September 26.

2. On this point, see RM to Alexander Hamilton, October 5, and notes.

To George Washington

Office of Finance 25 Sepr. 1782

Dear Sir

I have just now received your Letters of the twenty second Instant. The Doubt you are in with Respect to my Letters of the twenty ninth and thirtieth of August will be easily resolved on an Inspection of them. The Letter of the twenty ninth is of a Nature to be transmitted, if necessary, to the several States. That of the thirtieth explains my Reasons for writing the other, and the Paragraph you have extracted will be quite clear by inserting a Word thus. "You will I hope keep this (Letter) entirely to yourself" &ca.

The Necessity of your Writing to the States, as well as the Matter which you will have to mention must depend very much on the Conclusions which Genl Cornell shall come to with the Contractors or with Colo. Wadsworth. You will determine as you find best.[1]

When I found that the Supplies of Money from the States would prove so very inadequate as they have done, I determined to check all other Expence and think only of feeding the Army. This Conduct I am now rigidly pursuing, and shall endeavor to accomplish the Object and to pay the Engagements I have already made without which my Credit (which has alone supported us hitherto) must be ruined.

We have lately had an arrival here of Linnens which the Cloathier says are sufficient to make thirty thousand Shirts, but he is already so much indebted to the poor People who have worked for him and who are starving for want of their Wages,[2] that he can not procure Credit to get them made.[3] Money I have none. And even if he could run in Debt still farther, it would only increase the mischief for I see no Prospect of Payment.[4] And thus while People who live in Ease and even in Luxury avoid under various Pretexts the Payment of taxes a great Portion of the Public Expence is borne by poor Women who earn their daily Bread by their daily Labor. I am Sir your most obedient and humble Servant

Robt Morris

His Excellency General Washington

ENDORSED: Office of Finance 25th Sepr 1782/from/Hono. Robert Morris/Answered 3d. October
MSS: LS in the writing of Gouverneur Morris, Washington Papers, DLC; Dft in the writing of Gouverneur Morris, Robert Morris Papers, CSmH.
    1. Washington decided not to write the states; see notes to RM to Washington, August 29 (first letter). For Ezekiel Cornell's role, see RM's letters to him of September 20 and 23. In general, see notes to Comfort Sands, Walter Livingston, William Duer, and Daniel Parker to RM, September 11.
    2. In the Dft Gouverneur Morris first wrote the word "Money," crossed it out, apparently in favor of the word "Hire," and finally substituted "Wages."
    3. For RM's effort to pay Clothing Department debts, see Diary, September 25, and notes.
    4. In the Dft Gouverneur Morris originally wrote the remainder of the letter as follows: "It is enough to make a Man's Heart bleed when he thinks that People who live in Ease and even in Luxury avoid under various Pretexts the Payment of Taxes and by that Means force so heavy a Portion of the Expence on poor Women who live by the Work of their Fingers. But it is in Vain to represent these Things to Men who will court Popularity at the Price of public Ruin." He then reworked the passage in the Dft to its final formulation. For further reference to the needleworkers, see RM to Washington, October 15; and the complaints of "A Suffering Mother" in *Freeman's Journal*, September 25, 1782.

From Sands, Livingston and Company

Fishkill [New York] Sept. 25, 1782[1]

Sir:

We wrote you the 11th, from Rhinebeck, by Mr. R. Sands;[2] we then informed you of our situation with respect to flour, and gave him positive directions to forward on all he could get,[3] and by advice from him last post, find that article as scarce there as it is here, which alarms us much; we have not three days supply on hand, and what little scattering flour there was left in this state, the French purchasers have bought, and have advanced the price one dollar per hundred; they having the ready cash, and giving any price, will command any article from us. We are at present without cash, and have, for this some time past, expected the $12,000 you promised us; but as yet it has not come to hand.[4] We requested Mr. R. Sands to call on you for it, and also for $20,000 in bank notes; they begin to answer; the greatest part of those we received before, we have sent to the eastward to get exchanged. The mills are so dry here, that we can get no wheat ground; our whole dependence must be on Philadelphia; if that fails, the army must suffer for want. We depend that you furnish the cash for to purchase and transport the flour, for without money the teamsters will not cart a load. We have the honor to be, With great respect, Your obt. humble servants,

Sands, Livingston, & Co.

Hon. Robert Morris

PRINTED: U.S., Congress, Senate Document 62, February 25, 1820, p. 24.

1. The editors have been unable to find a manuscript text of this letter from Sands, Livingston and Company, the contractors for West Point and the Moving Army. They wish to thank Robert C. Gramberg of Hickory Hills, Illinois, for calling their attention to the text reprinted here. The letter was published with minor variations in *American State Papers*, Class 9, Claims, I, 716.

2. The letter is from Comfort Sands, Walter Livingston, William Duer, and Daniel Parker.

3. For the Superintendent's efforts to obtain flour, see RM to George Washington, September 9 (first letter), and notes.

4. See RM to Washington, August 20, and notes.

To Daniel Clark

Office of Finance 25 Sepr. 1782[1]

Money being very scarce here it is very inconvenient to Mr. Eddy to send down Money for the Purchase of Tobacco. You will therefore exert yourself to procure the Quantity necessary for lading the Fame in the same Manner with that already procured and if you should get any on public Account according to my Letter of Yesterday[2] you may apply it in that Way.

MS: Ofcl LbC, DLC.

1. Clark was RM's agent for purchasing tobacco in Virginia. For the background to this letter, see Diary, September 24.

2. RM refers to his letter to Clark of September 23.

To Edward Fox

Office of Finance 25 Sep. 1782

Mr. Morris presents his Compliments to Mr. Fox and encloses a Letter he received from the honble. Abm. Clarke Esqr. written in Consequence of Mr Fox's Letter of the twentieth Instant which Mr. Morris sent to Mr Clarke for perusal.[1]

MS: Ofcl LbC, DLC.

1. None of the letters mentioned herein have been found. For the background, see Diary, September 17, and notes.

To Ferdinand Grand

Office of Finance 25. Septem: 1782[1]

The United States in Congress having placed all their Monies under my Direction and it being probable that Thomas Barclay Esqr. their Consul

General may stand in need of some Funds to defray contingent Expences I am to request that you will answer his Drafts to the amount of fifty thousand Livres should he find it necessary to extend them so far.

MS: Ofcl LbC, DLC.
1. Grand was banker to the United States in Paris. This letter was enclosed in RM to Barclay, September 25.

Diary: September 26, 1782

Mr. Chs. Sheldon from Springfield Massachusetts came this morning with a Draft of Colo. Hatch on Colo. Pickering and a Letter from the Latter requesting me to pay it.[1] Mr. Sheldon has also brought the Account of rations Issued at that Post and some of Mr. Pierces Notes.[2] I lamented that he must be disappointed in his expectations of money, but whilst his and the other States withold the Taxes it is impossible for me to Pay punctually; finally I promised to afford him all the releif in my Power.

The Honble. Mr Clarke and Mr Conduit [Condict] brought a representation made by the Assembly of New Jersey to Congress on behalf of the Officers of their Line in the Army. This remonstrance I disapprove very much but it must be laid before Congress.[3]

Mr. Edwd Fox met Mr. Clarke at this Office and had a Conversation on the Hints which Mr Clarke had given me respecting Mr Fox which seemed to turn in Favor of the latter Gentlemans Character. He is to produce some other Testimonies to the same purport.[4]

Mr. Par[r] called to request Orders for Genl. Hazen to pay money received from the Hessians to the Contractors to which I agreed.[5]

Wrote a Letter to the Comptroller of the Treasury.
Wrote a Letter to Colo. Pickering.
Wrote a Letter to Ezekl. Cornell Esqr.

Issued a Warrant on Mr. Swanwick in favor of the Bank	£ 4. 8.6
Issued a Warrant on Mr. Swanwick in favor John Pierce	307.10.0
Issued a Warrant on Mr. Swanwick in favor Benjm. Dudley	51.18.3
Issued a Warrant on Mr. Swanwick in favor John Moylan	315. 0.0

1. See the Quartermaster General to RM, September 22, and notes.
2. The account has not been found. For the promissory notes which Paymaster General John Pierce had issued to army officers for the purchase of clothing, see Diary, August 1, and notes.
3. See RM's report to Congress of September 27, and notes.
4. See Diary, September 17, and notes.
5. See RM to Moses Hazen, September 27. William Parr was a contractor for Lancaster, Pennsylvania, where German prisoners were being guarded by Hazen's

regiment. Concerning the money received from the Hessians, see the Instructions of RM and Benjamin Lincoln on the Liberation of German Prisoners, July 11, 1782, and notes.

To Ezekiel Cornell

Office of Finance 26. Septr. 1782

Sir,

It was just now hinted to me that your Appointment would be considered as a Breach of the Confederation.[1] Did I misunderstand you or whence did I collect the Idea that you had resigned your Seat in Congress? If you have not resigned already, I must request that you loose no Time in doing it. For not to mention the Doubts which might arise on the Validity of Acts done by you, I am perswaded that as neither of us wish a Breach of the Confederation so we should be very unwilling to be suspected of, much less charged with having committed one. I am Sir Your most obedient Servant

RM

MS: Ofcl LbC, DLC.

1. On September 19 RM had commissioned Cornell inspector of contracts for the main army (see notes to RM to the President of Congress, April 20, 1782). Had Cornell continued in Congress as a member from Rhode Island he would have violated article V of the Confederation which prohibited delegates from holding any other office of profit under the United States (see notes to RM to Alexander Hamilton, July 28). No reply to this letter from RM and no formal resignation by Cornell have been found, but his last verifiable mention in the *Journals* is in a roll call vote of September 18. Cornell thus left David Howell as the sole Rhode Island delegate for three weeks until the arrival of Jonathan Arnold on October 10 (*ibid.*). Under criticism from the Rhode Island Assembly, Cornell resigned the post of inspector of contracts in November (see RM to Cornell, November 29, 1782). The published *Journals* are in error in stating that a letter was referred to a committee of which he was a member on December 10, 1782. For the actual committee, see the docketing on the letter of Baron von Steuben to the President of Congress, December 5, 1782, PCC, no. 19, V, 553–556.

To the Quartermaster General (Timothy Pickering)

Office of Finance 26th September 1782

Sir

I received your Letter of the nineteenth Instant by Mr. Pomeroy and that of the twenty second by Mr. Sheldon.[1] The Situation to which I am reduced by the Negligence of the States is such that I can not face my present Engagements, it would therefore be Madness to involve myself in new Ones. It is my Determination to occupy myself only in discharging Debts already contracted until better Prospects arise and of Consequence I shall be unable to find Money for any but indispensible Services, perhaps it will be impracticable to obtain enough even for those. The General is fully apprized of my Situation and will I am confident cooperate in every Measure for restricting Expence which is practicable. I am Sir Your most obedient and humble Servant

Robt Morris

Colo. Pickering

P.S. A Copy of my Letter to Mr. Pomeroy is inclosed.[2]

ENDORSED: Honble. Robert Morris Esqr./Septr. 26. 1782./received 30th/In answer to mine of the 19th. and 22d./Cannot face his old engagements—will therefore not involve himself/in new ones./Will only discharge old debts un/til better prospects arise—as he will/be able to furnish money only for/indispensable services, perhaps not/for them./The Genl. apprized of his situ/ation.
MSS: LS, Manuscript File, WDC, DNA; Ofcl LbC, DLC.
   1. See Diary, September 23 and 26.
   2. The letter is dated September 25.

From Benjamin Franklin

[Passy, September 26, 1782][1]

By letters from the Commissioners formerly, if you have them in your office it may appear to you that the Farmers general, soon after our arrival here, advanced us a million upon a contract for furnishing them with 5000 hhd. of tobacco which were to have been delivered by Christmas 1778. Only three cargoes, on that account have been receivd by them. I have settled with them and given my acknowlegment of the debt due to them.[2]

MS: Extract in the writing of Arthur Lee, Records of Boundary and Claim Commissions and Arbitrations, RG 76, DNA.
   1. The complete text of this letter has not been found, but Franklin was probably responding to RM's letter of July 1. RM acknowledged receving two copies of the dispatch in his letters to Franklin of January 13 and 19, 1783; in the latter he noted that the second copy had enclosed a long-awaited text of Franklin's agreement with Vergennes of July 16, 1782 (on which see notes to RM to the President of Congress, May 8, 1782). The first text to arrive was read in Congress on December 27, 1782, in connection with controversies revolving around the status of foreign loans. See PCC, no. 185, III, 50.
   2. Benjamin Franklin, Silas Deane, and Arthur Lee had been American commissioners in France, 1776–1778. Under the contract signed by Franklin and Deane on March 24, 1777, the Farmers General were to pay 2 million livres, 1 million to be advanced immediately, for 5,000 hogsheads of tobacco to be delivered within the year. The second million was never paid because little tobacco was shipped under the contract. At the end of the war the United States still owed the Farmers General 846,771 livres tournois on the advance of the first million. See Price, *France and the Chesapeake*, II, 714–715; the contract in Wharton, ed., *Rev. Dipl. Corr.*, II, 300–301; and Franklin to RM, October 14.

To the Comptroller of the Treasury
(James Milligan)

Office of Finance 26. Sepr. 1782

I have on various Occasions expressed my Desire that the several Departments should settle their Accounts quarterly at the Treasury.[1] I am now therefore to desire that you will call on all those who have received public Money to render their Accounts for Settlement, you will be pleased hereafter to inform me of the Effect of your Application that I may govern myself accordingly.

MS: Ofcl LbC, DLC.
    1. See, for example, Diary, June 14, 1782, and notes.

Diary: September 27, 1782

Mr. Caldwell[1] came to Solicit a Bill of Exchange in payment of his Blankets &c. to which I agreed.

Mr Patton door Keeper to Congress came for money to buy Wood for Congress which I promised very soon.

The Honble. Mr L'Hommedieu called to recommend Mr Abram Yates to be the Receiver of Continental Taxes in the State of New York when I informed that Doctr Tillotson is appointed.[2]

Mr David C. Claypoole for Money. Mr Pointells[3] Clerk for money. Doctor Bond also for money—but was obliged to put them off.

Mr Sheldon also for money which he must have in a day or two.

Mr. Oliver Pollock brought hither Capt. James and Mr Robt. Elliot[4] one of whom had informed the Honble. Mr Abram Clarke that Mr Pollock had obtained a great advance on the Goods he supplied to the State of Virginia and to the United States from New Orleans. Upon examining Capt. James and Mr Robert Elliot he declared that he was not in that Country at the time and that the information he has on the Subject was from Mr John Henderson Mr Pollocks Clerk when he was in this City soliciting a Settlement of Mr Pollocks Accounts[5] and the Instance particularly alluded to was a parcel of Goods sold by a Capt. Barber to the Commanding Officer of the Virginia Troops, who drew a Bill on Mr Pollock to pay for the same. Mr Pollock declares that he had no other Concern than paying part of that Bill and charging what he did actually pay to the State of Virginia.[6]

Wrote report to Congress.

Wrote a Letter to Mozes Hazen Esqr.

Wrote a Letter to Samuel Elliot.

Mr Jno. Sansum applied for a Settlement and I desired him to exhibit his Account which he did and I find some objections thereto.

Mr P. Wykoff applies for a renewal of Bills of Exchange but I sent him Word that he must apply at the Loan Office of New Jersey from whence he got the Bills Lost.[7]

    1. Probably Samuel Caldwell of the Philadelphia firm of Mease and Caldwell which dealt in clothing.
    2. For the appointment of Thomas Tillotson, see RM to Alexander Hamilton, August 28, and notes.
    3. William Poyntell (1756–1811) was a stationer, bookseller, and papermaker of Philadelphia. H. Glenn Brown and Maude O. Brown, "A Directory of the Book-Arts

and Book Trade in Philadelphia to 1820 including Painters and Engravers," *Bulletin of the New York Public Library,* LIV (1950), 33; Clifford K. Shipton and James E. Mooney, comps., *National Index of American Imprints Through 1800: The Short-Title Evans* (Worcester and Barre, Mass., 1969), II, 695; and Diary, November 1, 1782.

4. Robert Elliot had been recruited by James Willing and Oliver Pollock in 1778 (as was Captain James Elliot; see notes to Diary, March 30, 1782) and traveled down the Mississippi to New Orleans on Willing's expedition (see notes to Diary, September 10, 1781). On April 1, 1778, Pollock commissioned him captain of marines on the Continental ship *Morris,* outfitted by Pollock and commanded by William Pickles. He was later involved in the Kaskaskia expedition of George Rogers Clark. Elliot had been in Philadelphia in 1780 petitioning Congress for pay and settlement of his accounts, but was paid only for his three months' service under Willing. An undated memorial from Elliot complains about Pollock's distribution of prize money to Elliot and his men. On Elliot and the disputes which occurred between Pollock and Willing's men and which could have affected their testimony regarding him, see Charles R. Smith, *Marines in the Revolution: A History of the Continental Marines in the American Revolution, 1775–1783* (Washington, 1975), 440–441; James, *Oliver Pollock,* 146–147; Kinnaird, ed., *Spain in the Mississippi Valley,* pt. 1, pp. 282–284; and Nuxoll, "Congress and the Munitions Merchants," 495–496; *JCC,* XIX, 124, XX, 697–698, XXI, 791; and Elliot's petitions to Congress and related documents in PCC, no. 41, III, 17, 34, 61–66, and no. 19, II, 217–223.

5. On the Continental claims presented in Pollock's behalf by John Henderson (1737–1787) and later by Daniel Clark, see *JCC,* XIX, 32 and n., 41, 71, 118–119, 130, 142 and n., 312 and n., 341–342, XX, 491; Hutchinson and Rutland, eds., *Madison Papers,* III, 99n., VI, 477n.; Diary, September 10, 1781, and notes, and RM's Report to Congress of a Letter to Bernardo de Gálvez, November 21, 1781, and notes.

6. The charges mentioned in this Diary entry derived from the western campaign of George Rogers Clark, which was undertaken and financed by Virginia largely with bills of exchange drawn either on Oliver Pollock at New Orleans or the state treasury. At issue was the sale of supplies in 1780 by Captain Philip Barbour (d. 1797) to Captain Robert George (1756–1837), a kinsman of Clark's who was then commander of Virginia's troops at Fort Jefferson on the Mississippi River below the mouth of the Ohio River. Both George and Clark later reported to the governor of Virginia that Barbour had agreed to accept payment for the goods in Virginia currency, but then contrived to get the bills of exchange drawn on Pollock payable in gold or silver. Clark initially believed that Pollock and Barbour had engaged in premeditated fraud by charging transactions in depreciated paper at specie prices, but eventually withdrew the accusations and supported Pollock's claims. However, many other reports of abuses in drawing and negotiating bills of exchange had reached Virginia, and a special state commission was appointed early in 1782 to examine and settle all accounts of expenditures for the western campaign on the spot. Among its assignments was the task of checking the authority of Clark's officers for drawing bills and determining whether they were intended to be paid in specie or depreciated currency. Virginia refused to settle or make payment on Pollock's accounts until these questions were resolved. Despite RM's private letter of January 15, 1782, to him in support of Pollock, Governor Benjamin Harrison had advised the commission on January 29 that while he was "unwilling to charge [him] with any sinister practices having in general heard well of him yet I confess I have my doubts of him and wish his whole Transactions . . . to be minutely inquired into." See the correspondence in McIlwaine, ed., *Official Letters,* III, 138, 139–140; also James, *Oliver Pollock,* 139–145, 148, 156, 161, 173–174, 177–178, 181–183, 201, 212–217n., 226–227, 237, 300–305; James Alton James, *The Life of George Rogers Clark* (Chicago, 1928), 124–126, 155–157, 293–294; Clarence W. Alvord, ed., *Cahokia Records, 1778–1790 (Illinois Historical Collections,* II [1907]), 478n.–479n. Hutchinson and Rutland, eds., *Madison Papers,* III, 20–22, 98, 99n., 256, 257n., 342–344n., 345n., IV, 377–378 and n., VI, 477n.; Kinnaird, ed., *Spain in the Mississippi Valley,* pt. 1, pp. 294–295, 303–304; Diary, September 25, and RM to James Duane, October 11, and notes.

7. Possibly either Peter Wikoff (ca. 1740–1827) of Monmouth, New Jersey, formerly a captain in the New Jersey state forces, or the Philadelphia merchant and auctioneer of the same name who rejected the post of clothier general in 1779 and

who later played a prominent role in the public creditors' movement. On the first, see James Steen, *History of the Wikoff Family* (Red Bank, N. J., 1905), 4–6. On the second, see Labaree and Willcox, eds., *Franklin Papers*, IX, 35n., XII, 101; Brown and Brown, "Directory of the Book-Arts and Book Trade in Philadelphia to 1820," *Bull. N. Y. Pub. Lib.*, LIV (1950), 141; *Colonial Records of Pennsylvania*, XV, 197; Brunhouse, *Counter-Revolution in Pennsylvania*, 171; documents in PCC, no. 14, pp. 143, 145, 147, 149, no. 41, II, 156–158, VI, 269–272, 283, no. 43, pp. 275–311, no. 78, VI, 403–409, XXIV, 53–54; and headnote and notes to RM to the President of Congress, July 29. See also RM to Joseph Borden, Jr., September 6 and December 28, 1782.

To John Adams

(Duplicate)   Office of Finance 27th September 1782

Sir,

I do myself the Pleasure to congratulate you on the Success of your patriotic Labors in Holland.[1] The general Tribute paid to your Abilities on this Occasion will so well dispense with the Addition of my feeble Voice, that I shall spare your Delicacy the Pain of expressing my Sentiments.

The enclosed Resolutions and Copies of Letters will convey to you so fully the Views of Congress, and explain so clearly my Conceptions on the Subject, that very little need to be added.[2] If the Application to France should fail of Success, which I cannot permit myself to believe, you will then have a new Opportunity of shewing the Influence you have acquired over the Minds of Men in the Country where you reside, and of exerting it in the Manner most beneficial to our Country.

Before I conclude this Letter I must congratulate your Excellency on the Success of the Loan you have already opened, and which I consider as being by this Time compleated.[3] With perfect Respect I have the Honor to be, Sir, Your Excellency's most obedient and humble Servant[4]

Robt Morris

His Excellency John Adams Esquire

ENDORSED: M. Morris 27. Sep. 1782
MSS: LS, Adams Papers, MHi; LS marked "Triplicate," Feinstone Collection, PPAmP; Ofcl LbC, DLC; copy, Benjamin Franklin Papers, PPAmP; copy, Correspondance politique, Etats-Unis, AMAE.

1. As American minister to the United Provinces, Adams had won Holland's recognition of American independence in April and had secured the first loan on American credit there in June (see RM to the President of Congress, July 29, and notes, and Diary, September 11, and notes).

2. The enclosures doubtlessly were RM's first letter to Benjamin Franklin of September 27 and the documents enclosed therein.

3. RM entrusted this letter to Captain Joshua Barney of the *General Washington* (see RM's first letter to him of October 7). Adams received it on November 5 and replied the following day, stating that less than 2 million of the 5 million guilders had been obtained to date. See also Adams to RM, November 7.

4. The PPAmP copy of this letter to Adams was enclosed in RM to Franklin, September 27 (first letter). See the notes to that letter for the origin of the AMAE text.

Report to Congress on the Representation of the New Jersey Legislature

[Office of Finance, September 27, 1782]

The Superintendant of Finance, to whom was referred the Representation of the Legislature of the State of New Jersey of the twenty fourth Instant,[1] begs Leave to Report

That the Requisition of eight Millions for the Service of the current Year including the Sums necessary for paying the Army,[2] if that Requisition is complied with by the States, the *whole* Army will be regularly and compleatly paid; *and partial Payments* (always pernicious) will be avoided.

That the Situation of the Accounts between the several States and the United States, the common Assertion of each State that it has made Efforts beyond all Others (an Assertion which must be false as to Some), the baleful Effects of this Declaration in diminishing the Efforts of all, and the Confusion which must ensue and be prolonged from the Existence of such Causes demonstrate the Necessity of paying all Expences from one common Treasury and replenishing that Treasury by the common Contribution of all according to established Principles; So that in future all Accounts should be reduced to Demands for Money on one Side and Payments of it on the Other.[3]

That the Plans of an Administration on these just and simple Principles have been adopted by Congress, and by their constant Care and Attention are now carrying into Execution in such Manner as to promise beneficial Consequences.

That if these Plans are broken in upon, and every State again permitted to expend the Money of the Union according to their Pleasure, it will be impossible to conduct the Affairs of America either with Regularity or Oeconomy.

That it is therefore a Duty which Congress owe alike to the Interests of their Constituents and to their own Dignity (which cannot be wounded without wounding at the same Moment the Majesty of the People they represent) to take the most decisive Measures for preventing the further Progress of this Evil.

The following Resolution therefore is submitted:

Whereas the United States in Congress assembled have required the Sum of eight Million Dollars for the Service of the Year 1782 in which Service is included the Pay of the Army. And whereas the punctual Payment of the Quotas assigned to the several States would have prevented any just Complaints for the Want of Pay and every Obstruction to the Service in the several public Departments, so that the Evils which have arisen or which may arise are entirely to be attributed to the very great Deficiency of the States in complying with the said Requisition: And whereas Congress have been informed that several of the said States while they neglect the proper Supply of the public Treasury have made Payments to the Troops levied in such State, whereby it happens that Murmur and Complaint must arise in the Army very detrimental to the Service, because that equal Justice is not done to all which it is the earnest Desire of Congress to render: And whereas such Payments must derange and finally overturn the Systems which have been adopted for administering the public Revenue and performing the Business of the several Departments, and must involve the said Business in Confusion, and finally produce Contests, Divisions, and dangerous Animosities; for Prevention thereof

Resolved,

That any Monies paid by any of the States to the Officers and Soldiers of the american Army as Pay for the Year 1782 be considered as a free Gift: That the same be not charged to such Officers and Soldiers in their Account of Pay, and that it be not credited to the State by whom it shall have been or shall be advanced.[4]

Resolved,

That the States be required to make speedy Payment of their several Quotas into the public Treasury, that Congress may be thereby enabled to pay the Officers and Soldiers of the american Army the whole Amount of their Pay for the present year before the Expiration thereof.

All which is humbly submitted.[5]

Robt Morris

Office of Finance 27 Sepr. 1782[6]

MSS: DS, PCC, DNA; Ofcl LbC, DLC.

1. The New Jersey representation (in PCC, no. 68, pp. 599–602) was referred to RM on September 26. Earlier in the day it had been shown to RM by New Jersey delegates Abraham Clark and Silas Condict. It summarized an appeal to the legislature by the officers of the state line, who claimed that their pay was in arrears, that other states were paying their troops in the Continental army, that according to reports of the receiver of Continental taxes for New Jersey the state contributed its fair share of requisitions, yet there was still no money for the troops. Accordingly, the New Jersey legislature warned that unless Congress paid at least part of their arrears the state would be forced to do it by withholding a corresponding part of the money intended for the use of Congress "however disagreeable to the State and inconvenient to the Union such partial Provisions by particular States may by experience be found." See also Diary, September 26 and 30; and Clark to the Speaker of the New Jersey Assembly, September 26, 1782, Burnett, ed., *Letters*, VI, 494.

2. For the requisition for 1782, see RM to the President of Congress, November 5, 1781, and notes.

3. For RM's support of centralized disbursements and opposition to the partial payment of troops, see RM to Daniel of St. Thomas Jenifer, March 12, and notes. For the settlement of the states' accounts with the Confederation, see RM to the President

of Congress, December 10, 1781, and notes, and RM to the Commissioners for Settling the Accounts of the States, September 7, 1782.

4. This proposal went further than RM's previously expressed position that state
advances to the army were not to be credited to the money requisition for 1782; it
denied the states credit in their accounts with the Confederation. See notes to RM's
Circular to the Governors of the States, July 29.

5. RM's report was delivered on September 27 and referred by Congress the
following day to a committee composed of Samuel John Atlee of Pennsylvania, James
Madison of Virginia, and Elias Boudinot of New Jersey. Adopting the committee's
report on October 1, Congress passed three resolutions. The first directed that the
New Jersey legislature be informed that Congress was making every effort to pay
arrears of army pay up to January 1, 1782, that prompt payment of the requisition
for 1782 would enable Congress to make payments for the future, and that Congress
disapproved partial payments by the states. The second resolution incorporated the
substance of the first of RM's two resolutions (see text at note 4 above) but omitted the
"free Gift" formulation in favor of declaring that state payments to the army in 1782
were to "be considered as advanced in behalf of the United States, and that the same
be not credited to the State by which the advance shall have been made." The third
resolution adopted RM's second resolution verbatim save for the deletion of the last
four words. RM enclosed copies of the resolutions with appropriate commentary in
letters of October 5 to the governors of the states, the receivers of Continental taxes,
and Generals Nathanael Greene and George Washington (see also Diary, October 16,
and notes). On October 3 the Congressional report and resolutions were laid before
the New Jersey Assembly, which nevertheless authorized the appropriation of one
month's pay for its troops. The upper house concurred on October 5. The quotations
are from the resolutions as given in the *Journals;* for the report as drafted by James
Madison, see Hutchinson and Rutland, eds., *Madison Papers,* V, 173–175. For New
Jersey's action, see *Votes and Proceedings of the Sixth General Assembly of the State of
New-Jersey, at a Session begun at Trenton on the 23d Day of October, 1781, and continued by
Adjournments. Being the third Sitting* [September 18–October 5, 1782] (Trenton, 1782),
19; *A Journal of the Proceedings of the Legislative-Council of the State of New-Jersey, in
General Assembly convened at Trenton, on Tuesday the twenty-third Day of October, in the Year
of our Lord, One Thousand Seven Hundred and Eighty-One. Being the second and third
Sittings of the Sixth Session* [May 15–October 5, 1782] (Trenton, 1782), 36; and William
Churchill Houston to RM, October 5.

6. This line is in Gouverneur Morris's hand.

To Benjamin Franklin

Office of Finance 27th Septemr. 1782

Sir,

I have the Honor to enclose the Copy of Acts of Congress of the
fourteenth and twenty third Instant, together with the Copy of my
Letter of the thirtieth of July covering the Estimates for the Year
1783.[1] These Estimates are not yet finally decided on.[2] By the Act of
the fourteenth you are (as you perceive) instructed to communicate
the Resolution for borrowing four Millions of Dollars to his most
Christian Majesty, and first to assure His Majesty of the high Sense
which the United States in Congress assembled entertain of his
Friendship and generous Exertions; secondly their Reliance on a
Continuance of them; and thirdly the Necessity of applying to his
Majesty on the present Occasion. From this, and even more particularly from the Act of the twenty third; you will see that it is the wish
of Congress to obtain this Money from or by Means of the King.

After the decisive Expressions contained in those Resolutions of the Sense of our Sovereign, I am sure that it is unnecessary for me to attempt any Thing like Argument to induce your Exertions. I shall therefore rather confine myself to giving Information.

The grateful Sense of the King's Exertions which has so warmly impressed your Bosom, operates with undiminished Force upon Congress; and, what is of more Importance in a Country like ours, has the strongest Influence upon the whole Whig Interest of America. I have no Doubt but the King's Minister here[3] has given his Court regular Information on this and every other Subject of equal Importance, and therefore any general Assurances on your Part will be complimentary and in some Degree superfluous. But there is a Kind of Knowledge not easily attainable by Foreigners in any Country, particularly on such a Matter as the present. It is not amiss therefore that I should convey it to you, and your good Sense will apply it in the most proper Manner. You (of all Men in the World) are not now to learn that the sower english Prejudice against every Thing french had taken deep Root in the Minds of America. It could not have been expected that this should be obliterated in a Moment: But by Degrees almost every Trace of it has been effaced. The Conduct of Britain has weaned us from our Attachments, and those very Attachments have been transferred in a great Measure to France. Whatever Remains of monarchical Disposition exist are disposing themselves fast to a Connection with the french Monarchy: For the british Adherents begin to feel the Pangs of a deep Despair; which must generate as deep Aversion. The british Army here felt the national Haughtiness encreased by the Contempt which as Englishmen they could not but feel for those who had combined against the Freedom of their own Country. Every Part of their Conduct therefore towards the Tories while they flattered themselves with Victory shewed how much they despised their American Friends. Now that a Reverse of Fortune has brought on a little Consideration, they find a total Seperation from this Country unavoidable: They must feel for the Fate of their Country; they must therefore hate, but they must respect us too, while their own Adherents are both detested and despised. Treated thus like common Prostitutes it is not in Human Nature so much to forgive as not to feel in Return.[4] Since General Carleton's Arrival, or rather since the Change of Ministers, the British have shewn that their Intention is, if possible, to conciliate the Rulers of America, and by the Influence of a common Language and similar Laws, with the Force of ancient Habits and mutual Friendships not yet forgotten, not only to renew again the commercial Intercourse, but to substitute a new federal Connection to their ancient Sovereignty and Dominion.[5]

The Assurance therefore which Congress has directed you to

make must not be considered in the Number of those idle Compliments which are the common Currency or small Change of a Court. It is an Assurance important, because it is founded in Truth; and more important still, because it is dictated by the Affections of a whole People. If I may venture an Opinion still farther, it is principally important, because of the critical Situation of Things. The sudden change of Britain from Vengeance and War to Kindness and Conciliation, must have Effects, and those Effects, whether they be Contempt or Affection, will depend less perhaps on them than upon Others. It cannot be doubted that they will ring all the Changes upon their usual Theme of gallic Ambition. They will naturally insinuate the Idea that France will neglect us when we have served her Purposes, and it would be very strange if they did not find some Converts among that Class of People who would sacrifice to present Ease, every future Consideration. What I have said will I am confident put your Mind into the Train of Reflections which arise out of our Situation; and you will draw the proper Conclusions and make a proper Application of them.

Congress have directed you further to express to the King their Reliance on a Continuance of his Friendship and Exertions. I have no Doubt that a full Beleif of this Reliance will be easily inculcated. Indeed I rather apprehend that we shall be considered as relying too much on France, or in other Words doing too little for ourselves. There can be no sort of Doubt that a mighty good Argument may be raised on the usual Position that the Nation which will not help itself does not merit the Aid of Others, and it would be easy to tell us that we must put our own Shoulders to the Wheel before we call upon Hercules. In short if the Application be refused or evaded, Nothing can be easier than to assign very good Reasons why it is done. But you have very justly remarked in one of your Letters that it is possible to get the better in Argument, and to get Nothing else.[6] So it might be here. True Sagacity consists in making proper Distinctions, and true Wisdom in taking Determinations according to those Distinctions. Twenty Years hence when Time and Habit have settled and compleated the federal Constitution of America Congress will not think of relying on any other than that Being to whose Justice they appealed at the Commencement of their opposition. But there is a Period in the Progress of Things, a Crisis between the Ardor of Enthusiasm and the Authority of Laws, when much Skill and Management are necessary to those who are charged with administering the Affairs of a Nation. I have already taken Occasion to observe that the present Moment is rendered particularly critical by the Conduct of the Enemy, and I would add here (if I dared even in Idea to seperate Congress from those they represent) that now above all other Times Congress must rely on the Exertions of their Ally. This Sentiment would open to his Majesty's Ministers many Reflections the least of which has a material Connection with the Interests of his Kingdom; But an Argument of no little Weight is that which applies itself directly to the Bosom of a young and generous Prince, who would be greatly wounded to see that Temple, dedicated to Humanity, which he has taken so much Pains to rear, fall at once into Ruins by a Remission of the last Cares which are requisite for giving Solidity to the Structure. I think I might add that there are some Occasions on which a good Heart is the best Counsellor.

The third Topic which Congress have directed you to dwell upon is the Necessity of their present Application, and it is this which falls most particularly within my Department; for I doubt not that every Sentiment on the other Objects has been most forcibly inculcated by the Minister of Foreign Affairs. I might write Volumes on our Necessities and not convey to you so accurate an Idea as by the Relation of a single Fact which you may see in the Public News Papers. It is that the Requisitions of last October for eight Millions had produced on the first Day of this Month only one hundred and twenty five thousand Dollars. You are so perfectly a Master of every Thing which relates to Calculation that I need not state any Thing of our Expences. You know also what were our Resources beyond Taxation and therefore you have every Material for forming an accurate Idea of our Distresses. The Smallness of the Sum which has been paid will doubtless astonish you, and it is only by Conversation or a long History that you could see why it has been no greater. The People are undoubtedly able to pay, but they have easily persuaded themselves into a Conviction of their own Inability, and in a Government like ours the Beleif creates the Thing. The Modes of laying and levying Taxes are vicious in the Extreme:[7] The Faults can be demonstrated, but would it not be a new Thing under the Sun that People should obey the Voice of Reason? Experience of the Evil is always a Preliminary to Amendment, and is frequently unable to effect it. Many who see the Right-road and approve of it, continue to follow the wrong road because it leads to Popularity. The Love of Popularity is our endemial Disease and can only be checked by a Change of Seasons. When the People have had dear Experience of the Consequences of not being taxed, they will probably work the proper Amendment; but our Necessities in the Interim are not the less severe. To tell America in such a Situation that she should reform her interior Administration would be very good Advice; but to neglect affording her Aid, and thereby to lose the capital Objects of the War, would be very bad Conduct. The Necessity of the present Application for Money arises from the Necessity of drawing by Degrees the Bands of Authority together, establishing the Power of

Government over a People impatient of Control, and confirming the federal union of the several States, by correcting Defects in the general Constitution. In a Word it arises from the Necessity of doing that infinite Variety of Things which are to be done in an infant Government placed in such delicate Circumstances that the People must be woed and won to do their Duty to themselves and pursue their own Interests. This Application also becomes the more necessary in order to obviate the Efforts of that british Faction which the Enemy are now attempting to excite among us. Hitherto indeed they have been unsuccessful unless perhaps with a very few Men who are under the Influence of disappointed Ambition; but much Care will be required when their Plans are brought to greater Maturity. The savage Inroads on our Frontiers have kept up the general Horror of Britain. The great Captures made on our Coasts have also rather enraged than otherwise, tho such Captures have always the twofold Operation of making People wish for Peace as well as for Revenge. But when the Enemy shall quit our Coasts (and they have already stopped the Inroads of their savage Allies) if the People are urged at once to pay heavy unusual Taxes, it may draw forth and give weight to Arguments which the boldest Emissaries would not at present hazard the Use of.

I have already observed that Congress wish to obtain this Money either from or by Means of the King. The most cautious Prudence will justify us in confiding to the Wisdom of his Ministers the Portrait of our Situation. But it might not be very wise to explain to others those Reasons for the Application which lie so deep in the Nature of Things as easily to escape superficial Observers. I shall enclose a Copy of this Letter to Mr. Adams, and you will find herein a Copy of what I say to him on the Subject.[8] I hope the Court will take such Measures as to render any Efforts on his Part unnecessary. But you and he must decide on what is best for your Country. I must trouble you still farther on this Subject with the Mention of what you will indeed collect from a cursory reading of the Resolutions, that Congress have the strongest Reason for their Procedure when they direct your utmost Endeavors to effect this Loan, notwithstanding the Information contained in your Letters. If the War is to be carried on this Aid is indispensible, and when obtained will enable us to act powerfully in the Prosecution of it. If a Peace takes place it is still necessary, and as it is the last request which we shall then have Occasion to make I cannot think that it will be refused. In a Word, Sir, we must have it.[9] With perfect Respect I have the Honor to be, Sir, Your Excellency's most obedient and humble Servant

Robt Morris

His Excellency Benjamin Franklin Esquire

MSS: LS, Franklin Papers, PPAmP; LS marked "4th.," Sol Feinstone Collection, PPAmP; Ofcl LbC, DLC; copy, Correspondance politique, Etats-Unis, AMAE; incomplete copy, Adams Papers, MHi.

1. On the resolutions of September 14 and 23 concerning a new $4 million loan in Europe approved by Congress, see notes to RM to the President of Congress, July 30 and September 18. Secretary for Foreign Affairs Robert R. Livingston, probably enclosing Congress's special requisition on the states of September 4 and 10 (see notes to RM's Report to Congress on the Continental Loan Offices, June 13, 1782), had already advised Franklin on September 12 that "Mr. Morris, who writes from an empty treasury amidst perpetual duns, will speak more feelingly." Wharton, ed., *Rev. Dipl. Corr.*, V, 726.

2. Congress, however, did not act on the estimates until October 16, when it approved a scaled-down budget. See notes to RM to the President of Congress, July 30.

3. Chevalier de La Luzerne.

4. This sentence was omitted from previous printings of the letter in Jared Sparks, ed., *Diplomatic Correspondence of the American Revolution* (Boston, 1829–1830), XII, 262–269; a six-volume edition of the same (Washington, 1857), VI, 541–546; and Wharton, ed., *Rev. Dipl. Corr.*, V, 771–775.

5. The North ministry had fallen in March 1782; Sir Guy Carleton, the new commander in chief of British forces in North America, arrived in New York on May 5 (see notes to Gouverneur Morris to RM, March 31, 1782). As RM noted below in this letter, Carleton's conciliatory attitudes and peace overtures (see notes to the Secretary of Congress to RM, May 7, and to Diary, June 18, 1782) were offset by Britain's continuing attacks on American commerce and savage frontier warfare (see notes to Diary, September 7; on the coastal attacks, see the headnote to RM's State of American Commerce and Plan for Protecting It, May 10, 1782). For references to discussions of British proposals to give the United States a status equivalent to that of Ireland, see La Luzerne to Vergennes, September 28, 1782, Correspondance politique, Etats-Unis, XXII, 291.

6. See Franklin to RM, March 9, 1782.

7. See, for example, RM to Daniel of St. Thomas Jenifer, March 12, and for a hostile critique of the New York tax system, Alexander Hamilton to RM, July 22 and August 13, 1782.

8. See RM to John Adams, September 27; RM also enclosed a copy of this letter to Franklin in one to Chevalier de La Luzerne of October 2. See also Diary, September 30.

9. RM entrusted this letter to Captain Joshua Barney of the *General Washington* (see RM's first letter to him of October 7). After receiving it, Franklin addressed Comte de Vergennes, the French Minister of Foreign Affairs, on November 8, 1782, imploring French approval of the loan. The letter (in Correspondance politique, Etats-Unis, XXII, 433–434, AMAE) is printed in Albert Henry Smyth, ed., *The Writings of Benjamin Franklin* (New York, 1905–1907), VIII, 619–620. Besides the AMAE text of the present letter to him cited in the manuscript identification note above, Franklin's letter to Vergennes covered copies of the following documents: acts of Congress of September 14, 23 (with an explanatory note by Franklin), and October 3, extracts from letters of Secretary for Foreign Affairs Robert R. Livingston to Franklin of September 12 and 18, and RM to John Adams, September 27, and to Franklin, September 28 and October 7, 1782 (second letter), all in Correspondance politique, Etats-Unis, XXII, 233–235, 243, 275–280, 295–296, 328–329, 363, AMAE. See also Franklin to RM, December 14, 1782; for the result, see notes to RM to Le Couteulx and Company, September 24.

To Benjamin Franklin

(Duplicate)   Office of Finance 27th September 1782
Sir

By my Letter of this Date you will be informed of the Intention of Congress to provide for a principal Part of the Expenditures of the

Year 1783 by Loan. I expect that you will be able to obtain the four Millions of Dollars either from the Court of France or by their Assistance. I wish an immediate Disposition of a Part in the following manner. That the Court of Spain should give Orders for the Shipment of a Million of Dollars at the Havanna free of Duties, and to be convoyed by One or more Ships of the Line to an American Port; the Money to be paid to them during the Year in Europe.[1] I wish this Order may be so expedited as that Captain Barney in the Washington, by whom this Letter goes, may carry it out to the Havanna, and receive the Money, which will by that Means arrive here Sometime during the Winter, and of Course will, I expect, come safely as well as seasonably.[2] I wish that Half a Million Dollars may be paid to Messrs. Le Couteulx and Company as soon as possible, to enable them to execute my Orders as to a particular Negociation which I commit to them.[3] Whatever else of the Money is obtained in France, will of Course be paid to Mr. Grand, subject to my Order. If any Part of the Money be negociated in Holland, it will be, I suppose, proper to leave it in the Hands of those who negociate the Loan, subject to my farther Disposition. I am, Sir, Your most obedient and humble Servant[4]

Robt Morris

His Excellency Benjamin Franklin Esqr

ENDORSED: Office of Finance/Septr. 27. 1782/Disposition of the 4 Million/of Dollars, if obtained
MSS: LS, Franklin Papers, PPAmP; LS, Franklin Papers, CtY; LS marked "4th.," Ferdinand J. Dreer Collection, PHi; Ofcl LbC, DLC.
    1. See notes to RM to Le Couteulx and Company, September 24, for RM's efforts to obtain specie through Havana.
    2. RM modified his orders with respect to the convoy in a letter to Franklin of October 1 and in a dispatch of October 7 RM withdrew his request that the *General Washington* be sent to Havana. See also RM to Joshua Barney, October 7 (first letter).
    3. See the following letter.
    4. RM entrusted this letter to Captain Joshua Barney of the *General Washington* (see RM's first letter to Barney of October 7). A copy was enclosed in RM to Chevalier de La Luzerne, October 2.

To Le Couteulx and Company

(Duplicate)   Office of Finance 27th September 1782
Gentlemen,
    I write to Mr. Franklin under this date to place in your Hands five hundred thousand Dollars as soon as possibly he can.[1] I hope it may be effected speedily. My Object in making this Deposit, is, that you may remit to the Amount of that Sum to the Havanna, provided Bills on that Place can be purchased at a Discount of twenty five per Cent, by which I mean that seventy five Dollars in Europe should purchase One hundred Dollars in Havanna. If the Negociation can-

not be effected upon those Terms, you will retain the Money in your Hands subject to my after Direction. I suppose that those (or better) Terms can be obtained for the following Reasons. The Person who has Money in the Havanna, by selling Bills, will immediately possess himself of the Amount for which they are sold; and therefore allowing Time for the Bills to go over and be presented with the thirty days of Payment and the further Time which would be necessary to remit that Money from the Havanna to Cadiz, and he would gain from eight to twelve Months Time, which is in itself important. But in Addition to this, there is the duty of nine per Cent on exporting Cash from the Havanna, a Freight which[2] I suppose considerable, a Risque which is very great, and perhaps a farther duty on the Arrival at Cadiz; to which may be added the Advance on Bills drawn at Cadiz on the different Parts of Europe. If you can accomplish the Negociation on the Terms I have mentioned, you will then remit the Bills to a good House in the Havanna, to receive the Money and hold it subject to my Order; and you will, if you can, fix the Terms on which that House are to do the Business. Whether any Thing of this Sort takes place or not, I am to request that you will give me every Information on the Subject which you can acquire. I am, Gentlemen, Your most obedient and humble Servant

Robt Morris

Messrs. Le Couteulx & Co.
Bankers at Paris

MSS: LS, Private Collection; Ofcl LbC, DLC.
    1. See the preceding letter. Le Couteulx and Company was a Paris-based firm which RM employed from time to time on public business. This letter to them was carried by Captain Joshua Barney of the *General Washington*. See RM to Barney, October 7 (first letter).
    2. Ofcl LbC: "which is."

To Samuel Eliot, Jr.

Office of Finance 27. Septem: 1782

I have to Acknowlege the Receipt of your Favor dated at Boston on the second Instant.[1] I wrote on the twenty sixth of last Month to his Excellency the Governor of Connecticut and also to Mr. Bradford respecting the Business you Mention; I then informed them that the Amount of those Goods which had been purchased by Mr. Bradford for the Use of the United States would not be admitted as a Charge against the Quota required from Connecticut for the Service of the current Year. I also informed the Governor that I had no Objection to its being charged to the United States in settling the Accounts of former Requisitions, which Determination ought I conceive to satisfy the State, and would releive Mr. Bradford from the Hardship of advancing his own Monies. I expect therefore that it will be adopted.

MS: Ofcl LbC, DLC.
    1. Letter not found. Eliot was maritime agent in Massachusetts for the state of Connecticut.

To Moses Hazen

Office of Finance 27. Septem. 1782

I have received your Favor dated at Lancaster on the twelfth Instant.[1] The Manner in which you have applied the Money produced by discharging the German Prisoners, has my Approbation. The Secretary at War will send you more of the Discharges, and I desire you will exchange the Monies that shall arise from them for my Drafts on Mr. John Swanwick, payable sixty Days after Date, in favor of the Contractors; And remit them agreeable to my Orders.

MS: Ofcl LbC, DLC.

1. Letter not found. Brigadier General Hazen was commander of the troops guarding prisoners at Lancaster, Pennsylvania. See Diary, September 26, and notes.

Diary: September 28, 1782

Genl Gates made application for Money for back rations. I told him he must apply to the Paymaster General.

Mr. Chs. Sheldon applying again for money. I ordered Mr. Swanwick to pay him 1,000 Dollars and the rest in Notes. This he said is not sufficient and he must wait longer.

Mr. Jno. Chaloner for more money which he says is indispensible and I directed Mr Swanwick to pay him 2,666⅔ Dollars.[1]

Capt S. Nicholson arrived this Day from Boston and Mr Dublois a Gentleman of that place brought the proceedings of the Court of Enquiry &c.[2] These Gentlemen mentioned some irregularities in the Post Office at Fis[h]kill. I sent for Mr Hazard the Post Master Genl. informed him of it and desired an Enquiry, Remedy &c.

Colo. Adams of the Maryland Line[3] applied for Notes for the Pay of the Officers of that Line and after much Talk went to the War Office.

Having proposed to Mr. Thomas Fitzsimmons a Business in which I thought he might serve his Country and himself by a Voyage to the West Indies, he this Day told me that his domestic Circumstances will not permit him to Undertake it.[4]

Colo. Wm. Massey applied with a Letter from Genl Lincoln recommending me to pay a Balance due on a Gratuity made by Congress to this Gentleman and I promised a part thereof.[5]

Issued a Warrant on Mr Swanwick in favor Jos. Pennell	£354. 6.6
Issued a Warrant on Mr Swanwick in favor Jos. Pennell	363.15.0
Issued a Warrant on Mr Swanwick in favor Sands & Co.	49. 7.0

1. This was a payment on Chaloner's share of the bills of exchange sold to Joseph Wilson. See Diary, August 9, and notes, and August 20, and notes.

2. For the court of inquiry on Captain Samuel Nicholson of the Continental navy, see RM's determination under date of October 17.

3. Lieutenant Colonel Peter Adams of the 3d Maryland Regiment. Heitman, *Register*.

4. For the voyage RM had in mind, see RM to Le Couteulx and Company, September 24, and notes.

5. Lieutenant Colonel William Massey of South Carolina had served as deputy mustermaster general for the Southern Department from October 20, 1777, until the Muster Department was abolished by Congress on January 12, 1780, under an act which authorized its officers to receive an extra year's pay. Although in March 1782 Secretary at War Benjamin Lincoln had rejected a proposal that the arrears due Massey by that act be discharged (*JCC*, XXII, 207, 213), he evidently changed his position in the letter to RM mentioned in this Diary entry but not found. On October 1 RM gave Paymaster General John Pierce $140 for Massey, but apparently substituted a $400 payment on November 9; see *JCC*, XXIII, 735–736n.; Pierce to Lincoln, October 14, 1782, PCC, no. 149, II, 143–146; and [Morris], *Statement of Accounts;* and Treasury Waste Book D, p. 105, Records of the United States General Accounting Office, RG 217, DNA. On Massey, see Heitman, *Register*.

To Benjamin Franklin

1st. (By C[ipher] Nr. 4)[1]   Philadelphia 28th. Sept. 1782

Sir,

In my Letter of yesterday, I have dwelt on the resolutions of Congress, in the manner requir'd by my duty as their Servant. I will now add a few hints, as Your friend. Your Enemys industriously publish, that your age and indolence have unabled you for your station, that a Sense of obligation to France seals your lips when you should ask their aid, and that (whatever your friends may say to the contrary) both your connections and influence at Court are extremely feeble. I need not tell you that messieurs Lee and company are among the foremost who make these assertions, and many others not worthe[2] mention.[3] I should not have given you the pain of reading even these but that (as you will see from the resolution of the twenty third instant)[4] Congress have believed your grateful sensibilities might render you unwilling to apply with all that warmth which the sense of their necessities convinces them is necessary. In addition to the general reflection how envy has pursued superior merit in all ages, You will draw a farther consolation from this, that many who censure you are well disposed to cast like censure on France, and would fain describe her as acting only the part of self interest, without a wishe to render us effectual aid. You will I am sure attribute what I now say to a friendly desire of apprizing you of things useful for you to know, and you will so act, as to convince every man that your exertions are what I verily believe them to be. I am Sir, your most obedient Servant[5]

Robt Morris

His Excellency Benjm. Franklin Esqr.

ENDORSED: Mr Morris/Office of Finance/Sept. 28. 1782/on/Personal or private Affairs
MSS: LS in cipher with interlinear decipherment, Franklin Papers, PPAmP; deciphered copy, Correspondance politique, Etats-Unis, AMAE; Ofcl LbC in cipher, DLC.

1. Except for the dateline, salutation, complimentary close, signature, and inside address, the LS is written in a cipher previously employed in RM's letters to Franklin of April 8, 17, and May 29, 1782. The text reproduced by the editors is the decipherment written interlinearly on the manuscript by an unidentified amanuensis of Franklin's. The parenthetical notation, possibly in the same hand, must be an error, for Office of Finance Cipher no. 4 (Franklin Papers, DLC) does not match the word-number relationships used in the above-mentioned letters. For the ciphers that may have been used, see notes to RM to Franklin, April 8, 1782, and to RM to Franklin, July 13, 1781.

Other texts of this letter have appeared on the autograph market from time to time, the most recent example being a LS enciphered in Gouverneur Morris's hand (sold by Sotheby Parke Bernet Inc. on November 14, 1978, lot 531). Another text was published in N.-Y. Hist. Soc., *Colls.*, Pub. Fund Ser., XI (1878), 483–484, under the heading of "Copy of a Letter to Dr. Franklin in Cypher," and was described there as "In the handwriting of Gouverneur Morris—no signature." This text was reprinted with minor typographical alterations in Wharton, ed., *Rev. Dipl. Corr.*, V, 779, where it was tentatively said to be a letter from Gouverneur Morris. See also Burnett, ed., *Letters*, VI, 491n.

2. Word deciphered thus in manuscript, but possibly intended as "worth the." Rendered as "worthy the" in the AMAE text.

3. The single-minded hostility to Franklin harbored by Arthur Lee and his supporters was of long standing and reached back beyond the Deane-Lee affair to Lee's competition with Franklin for the Massachusetts agency before the war and to their representation of rival land companies. As news of the opening of peace negotiations revived the old congressional debate over the extent to which the American negotiators were bound to follow French direction, Lee in recent months had renewed his accusations of Franklin's subservience to France, charging that he had been joined to the American commission "by the absolute order of France" at a time when Congress had evidence that he was "both a dishonest and incapable man." The latter charge Lee reiterated during an ongoing congressional investigation of Alexander Gillon's transactions in Europe, which provided new opportunities for the denunciation of Franklin's supposed financial mismanagement and malfeasance (see notes to Diary, September 19). Lee depicted Franklin's handling of the Gillon affair as tantamount to "an absolute robbery," and in recent letters to his partisans linked RM and Franklin as abusers of the power of the purse on opposite sides of the Atlantic. Lee had also implied that Franklin's western land claims tainted his role in negotiating the fate of western lands as a peace commissioner.

Mindful of the interrelationship between attacks on Franklin and suspicion of France, French Minister La Luzerne was also keeping his court informed on the activities of Lee and his allies in Congress, particularly their criticism of Franklin. His reports at this time emphasized, in addition to the complaints already mentioned, criticisms of Franklin's handling of the negotiations for the exchange of marine prisoners (on which see notes to Diary, June 18, 1782) and for the exchange of Henry Laurens for General Cornwallis, as well as of Franklin's discussions with the Swedish minister to France regarding a possible treaty between Sweden and the United States.

Just whom RM regarded as Lee's cohorts is unclear, but among his supporters in and out of Congress were fellow delegates Theodorick Bland, Jr., of Virginia and Ralph Izard of South Carolina, and his brothers William (now in Europe) and Richard Henry Lee. See Henderson, *Party Politics in the Continental Congress*, 15, 192–213, 322–323; La Luzerne to Vergennes, August 12 and 15, September 18, and October 20, 1782, Correspondance politique, Etats-Unis, XXII, 59–63, 84–87, 238–239, 395–396, AMAE; Burnett, ed., *Letters*, VI, 326, 384–385, 388, 389–390, 428–430, 447–449, 452, 498–499; also notes to RM's Report to Congress on a Letter from William Lee, June 6, and to Arthur Lee to RM, October 5, 1782. On the controversies regarding western lands, see notes to RM to the President of Congress, July 29.

4. See notes to RM to the President of Congress, September 18.

5. This letter was carried by Captain Joshua Barney of the *General Washington* (see RM's first letter to him of October 7). Franklin sent a deciphered text to Vergennes on November 8 (see notes to RM's first letter to Franklin of September 27) and replied to RM in a private letter of December 23 which has not been found. See RM to Franklin, May 30, 1783.

To Ferdinand Grand

Office of Finance 28. Sept. 1782

Sir,

I have received your several Letters of the second of February, eleventh of March and sixth of May with their Enclosures.[1] I am sorry to find that your Funds are so feeble but I must rely that they will be equal to all Demands on them. I see by the Accounts you have sent me that you have not fully understood my Instruction to open a separate Account of my Transactions.[2] Instead of that you have only opened a new Account in my Name. Now what I have to request is that you charge in the Account under my Name only those Sums which are paid by my Order. Any Monies paid by Order of Mr. Franklin you will in like Manner charge in the Account kept under his Name and then whenever you wind up these Accounts you may carry the Balance of the latter into the former and if it be in your Favor place it against the Amount of Monies received since January last. By which I mean that the Loans and Subsidies till the End of the Year 1781, including therein the Amount of the Dutch Loan[3] be all placed to the Credit of Mr. Franklins Account in the Debit of which will be included Mr. de Beaumarchais Bills[4] as well as every other Money paid by Order of M: Franklin on the other Hand all the Monies which the Court may have advanced for the Year 1782, and all such Monies as may come to your Possession from the Loan opened by Mr. Adams in Holland[5] you will place to the Credit of my Account. The Effect as to yourself will be the same let these Accounts be stated how they may because there will always be one Sum total of Receipts and another of Payments. But there is a material Difference as to me because I wish that the whole of my Transactions be kept so distinct from all others as that they may be seen at a single Glance.[6]

From what I have said you will perceive that it is my Desire you should alter such of the Accounts transmitted as are in my Name so as to make them consist with the Ideas I have just now stated. I am Sir your most obedient and humble Servant

RM

MS: Ofcl LbC, DLC.
1. Letters and enclosures not found. This letter to Grand, banker to the United States in Paris, was entrusted to Captain Joshua Barney of the *General Washington*. See RM to Barney, October 7 (first letter).

2. See RM to the Comptroller of the Treasury, August 10, and notes.

3. On the French-guaranteed Dutch loan of 1781, see notes to Benjamin Franklin to RM, September 12, 1781.

4. See Caron de Beaumarchais to RM, June 3, 1782, and notes.

5. See notes to RM to the President of Congress, July 29.

6. These instructions reflected RM's understanding that his official transactions as Superintendent commenced on January 1, 1782. See RM to the President of Congress, May 14, 1781, and notes; and for a discussion of RM's accounts, notes to Diary, June 12, 1782.

To the Willinks, van Staphorsts, and de la Lande and Fynje

Office of Finance, 28. Sepr. 1782

Gentlemen,

I am to request that you will as speedily as you can inform me not only of the Amount of the Monies borrowed under your Direction and which remain at my Disposal after making all Deductions but that you would also particularize the Sums which will fall due for the Interest and the Times at which they are to be paid, that I may make the proper Provision in due Season.[1] At present I shall direct some Shipments of Tobacco to be made to your Address for this Purpose of which I shall order proper Notice to be given that you may make the Insurances. What may be the Amount of these Shipments I cannot possibly tell under our present Uncertainties as to the Continuance and Conduct of the War.[2] I am Gentlemen your most obedient and humble Servant

RM

MS: Ofcl LbC, DLC.

1. For the Dutch loan of 1782 being raised by the consortium of Dutch bankers RM addressed in this letter, see notes to RM to the President of Congress, July 29; and the following letter and notes.

2. On the tobacco shipments, see notes to RM to Daniel Clark, September 23.

To the Willinks, van Staphorsts, and de la Lande and Fynje

Office of Finance 28. Sepr. 1782

Gentlemen,

Your Letter of the eleventh of July last has been received and read in Congress and the five Contracts entered into with you have been duly satisfied.[1] I presume that before this comes to hand that Loan will have been compleated and in Consequence I have by my Letter of this date eventually disposed of a considerable Part of it in Favor of Mr. Grand and of Messrs. Le Couteulx and Co. of Paris.[2] Any ulterior Dispositions which may be made you shall be duly informed of in Season. When I find Opportunities of selling Bills I will draw upon you and therefore if such Bills arrive I am now to request that they be duly honored. With perfect Respect I have the Honor to be Gentlemen yours &c

RM

MS: Ofcl LbC, DLC.
  1. See notes to Diary, September 11.
  2. RM almost certainly refers to his letters to the Dutch bankers of September 24.

From Alexander Hamilton

[Albany, New York, September 28, 1782][1]

Sir

I have been honord this week with your letters of the 28 August, 6th, 12th and 17th instant with their inclosures.[2]

It gives me the most real pleasure to find that my past communications have meet ⟨with⟩ your approbation; and I feel a particular satisfaction in the friendly confidence which your letters manifest.

I am persuaded that substantial reasons have determined your choice in a particular instance to Doctor Tillotson; and I am flattered by the attention you have Obligingly paid to my recommendations of Col. Malcolm and Lawrence.[3] Those Gentlemen are now here: they make you the warmest acknowlegements for your offer, but decline leaving the State; which indeed is not compatible with the present prospects of either of them.

I am glad to have had an oppertunity of perusing your letter to this state[4] at which so much exception has been taken; because it has confirmed me in what I presumed, that there has been much unjustifiable ill humour upon the occasion. I will make use of the knowledge I have to combat misrepresentation.

Yours of the 29th. of July to Congress is full of principles and arguments as luminous as they are conclusive. Tis to be lamented that they have not had more weight than we are to infer from the momentary expedient adopted by the resolutions of the 4 and 10th: which will alone not be satisfactory to the public Creditors; and I fear will only tend to embarrass your present opperations without answering the end in view. The more I see the more I find reason for those who love this country to weep over its blindness.

The committee on the Subject of Taxation are met;[5] some have their plans and they must protect their own children however mishapen; others have none but are determined to find fault with all. I expect little, but I shall promote any thing though imperfect that will mend our situation. With sentiments of the greatest respect and esteem I have the honour to be Sir Your most obedient and humble servant

A Hamilton

The public creditors in this quarter have had a meeting and appointed a Committee to devise measures; the Committee will report petitions to Congress and the Legislature and an address to the public creditors in other parts of the State to appoint persons to meet in convention to unite in some Common Measure. I believe they will also propose a general convention of all the creditors in the different States.[6]

ENDORSED: Copy Septr 28th/to Mr. Morris/(1782)
MSS: ADftS, Hamilton Papers, DLC; transcript, Francis Baylies Papers, DLC.

1. The date has been supplied from the endorsement. The recipient's copy, which has not been found, was also undated. See RM to Hamilton, October 16.

2. The letter of September 12 was a circular to the receivers of Continental taxes covering RM's letter to the president of Congress of July 29 and the resolutions of September 4 and 10 referred to in this reply from Hamilton. Hamilton was continuing as receiver for New York until his successor, Thomas Tillotson, took office.

3. See RM to Hamilton, August 28, and notes.

4. The reference is RM to the Governor of New York, December 11, 1781. See RM to Hamilton, August 28, and notes.

5. For the joint committee of the New York legislature on taxation, see Hamilton to RM, July 22, and notes.

6. Concerning the public creditor movement in New York and elsewhere, see the headnote to RM to the President of Congress, July 29, and notes. For the address mentioned by Hamilton, see "To the Public Creditors of the State of New York," [September 30, 1782], Syrett and Cooke, eds., *Hamilton Papers*, III, 171–177.

From William Churchill Houston

Trenton [New Jersey] 28 Septr 1782[1]

I am favoured with yours, circular, of the 12 instant with it's several interesting Enclosures. Their Importance will call my Attention to make the requisite Use of them.

The Receipt of the present week has been principally in Bills drawn on Mr Swanwick; and though it has put little Cash into my Hands, the general Effect cannot be the less.

1782

Dr The Receipt of Continental Taxes for the State of New Jersey from
        Septr. 21 to 28 inclusive

To Cash received from The Treasurer of the State two Thousand four Hundred and seventy five Dollars	Dlls 2475
To do received from John Wilkins, Esqr Collectour of the County of Gloucester in Part of the first Payment of the Tax ⟨payable⟩ laid by the Act of 22 June last two Thousand Seven Hundred and sixty five Dollars	2765
Total five Thousand two Hundred and fourty Dollars	Dlls 5240

5240 Dlls

MS: ADft with subjoined ADftS return, Houston Collection, NjP.

1. Houston was the receiver of Continental taxes for New Jersey.

From William Whipple

Portsmouth [New Hampshire] 28th Sepr: 1782

Having accepted the appointment of a Commissioner for settleing the dispute between Pensylvania and Connecticut I purpose seting out for Trenton about the 30th Octo.[1] It is necessary you should be informed of this, that if you think proper to appoint some person in my stead to receive the Taxes here, there will be time for the appointment to arrive before I leave the State; If I should not have the honor of hearing from you on the subject before my departure, I shall leave that business during my absence which I suppose will not exceed six weeks with my Brother Joseph Whipple in whom I can place implicit Confidence. As I shall be so near Philadelphia I intend doing myself the honor of waiting on you there before I return.

MS: LbC, Whipple Letterbook, John Langdon Papers, PHi.

1. Whipple was the receiver of Continental taxes for New Hampshire. For a discussion of the long-standing dispute between Pennsylvania and Connecticut over the Wyoming Valley, see the editorial note in Boyd, ed., *Jefferson Papers*, VI, 474–487.

From the Quartermaster General (Timothy Pickering)

Camp Verplanks Point [New York] Sepr. 29. 1782

Mr. Ogden has very importunately applied for the second payment due on his contract for camp kettles.[1] I have no way, consistent with the numerous engagements I have been obliged to make, of satisfying his demand, but by a draught on you, and that (to comport with the representation of his necessities) payable at sight, for 566⁶⁄₉₀ dollars. Such a draught I have this day remitted to Mr. Ogden. Had he complied with his engagements, this sum would have been long since due: but I am sorry to say that in the performance he has very essentially failed. When he entered into the contract, he told Mr. Forman (who acted in my behalf) that he could make 200 per week, and if there were a great demand double that number. The demand was in fact very great, and Mr. Ogden was again and again informed of it—he was told often of the extreme suffering of the army for want of the kettles. The Soldiers were in reality obliged to broil their meat on the coals, or wait to boil the pot in succession from morning to evening. Yet these representations did not appear to quicken Mr. Ogden; and instead of delivering the first five hundred in three weeks and the second five hundred and[2] the three weeks next following, his kettles have been received at the army, in small parcels, at the late periods mentioned in the inclosed note.[3] The kettles too are deficient in quality; and many that would have been rejected, have been received for the like reason that the troops have often accepted bad provisions from the contractors—to save themselves from starving. To prevent the very defect of which I complain, I mentioned to Mr. Ogden that the kettles should when complete have a certain weight, which would have insured a proper thickness to the sheets of iron: but he waved this, and said that the kettles should be *good*. Mr. Ogden's kettles weigh about two pounds each—those procured by Colonel Miles in Philadelphia about three pounds and a half, are strong—and will last,—the former will yield to the slightest stroke, and be soon burnt thro'.

For all these reasons, I confess, I felt in no great haste to make this second payment, at least not until Mr. Ogden had compleated two hundred on the score of the third payment, which is not to be made till three months after the delivery of the whole fifteen hundred kettles. It seems that he has now finished *thirteen* hundred: I have therefore to request that the second payment may be made, agreeably to the draught before mentioned.

Had you been a *stranger* to Mr. Ogden, I would not have troubled you with this detail. Should you now deem it unnecessary, or impertinent, I shall beg your pardon. Mr. Ogden will tell you that his hands fell sick: But he knew where to engage as many more as he wanted, in one weeks time; only it would have occasioned a *small expence,* which he placed in competition with the *good of the service,* the *convenience,* and the *health* of the *army.*

MS: LbC, WDC, DNA.
    1. See the Quartermaster General to RM, June 6, 1782 (second letter), and notes.
    2. This word, an ampersand in manuscript, may have inadvertently been included by a slip of the pen.
    3. Enclosure not found.

Diary: September 30, 1782

Mr Geary Clerk to Wm. Duer Esqr. and Co. called respecting money and notes to be paid them on account of the Contract. I agreed that he might draw on me for the Sum due to People here and that I will furnish notes as requested.

Mr. Whiteside applied for payment due to him for Goods sold to the Quar[ter] Mr. General for public use referred him to Colo. Miles.

Mr Perry from Fort Pitt brought a Letter of recommendation from Genl. Irwin.[1] He wants to Contract for that Post. I informed him what has passed on that Subject with Colo. Blaine. I advised him to wait that Gentlemans return.[2]

Mr. R. Sands for Money and Notes. I agreed to supply him to Morrow.

Capt. Jno. Green called to Settle his Accounts directed him to Mr. Milligan.[3]

The Honble. Mr Atlee called to Consult respecting the memorial on the New Jersey representation and I gave my Sentiments fully.[4]

The Honble. Mr. Jackson called to Shew me letters from Boston respecting Capt Samuel Nicholson representing his Case as hard and the Treatment he received from the Court of Enquiry and their Conduct as Improper. I assured Mr. Jackson of my desire to render impartial Justice.[5]

I sent a Note received from Capt. Turner to Mr. Milligan the Comptroller as it respects his Department and desired Mr. Milligan to give Capt. Turner a proper, peremptory and final Answer on the Subject of his Accounts.[6]

Mr. Carter brought Letters from Mr Wadsworth respecting the Contract. I also received one from General Cornell and upon considering the Contents I am of Opinion that we must wait farther intelligence before any thing can be done.[7]

His Excellency the Minister of France came to Consult me respecting the Cost of building Ships &c. I gave him some Opinions and promised to procure Estimates for him.[8] I also laid before him the tenor of some part of my Plans and advices to Doctor Franklin and requested that he will write in Support thereof which he promised to do.[9]

Issued a Warrant on Mr Swanwick in favor Sands, Livingston & Co. £49.7.0.

Wrote a Letter to James Warren Esqr.

Wrote a Letter to James Milligan.

Wrote a Letter to Danl. St Thos. Jenifer.

1. See William Irvine to RM, September 12. The bearer, John Perry, had been appointed commissioner of purchases for Westmoreland County by the Supreme Executive Council in 1780, but was removed from office the following year on account of irregularities. *Colonial Records of Pennsylvania*, XII, 465, 648, 653–654.

2. See Diary, September 21, October 3, 7, 8, and RM to Irvine, October 3 and 7.

3. See RM to the Comptroller of the Treasury, September 30.

4. Samuel John Atlee was a Pennsylvania delegate to Congress. For the New Jersey memorial, see RM's report to Congress of September 27, and notes.

5. The letters brought by Jonathan Jackson, a Massachusetts delegate to Congress, have not been found. RM's disapproval of the court's proceedings is dated October 17.

6. The note received from George Turner has not been found. On his accounts, see Diary, March 21, 1782, and notes.

7. None of the letters mentioned have been found. Jeremiah Wadsworth and his partner John Carter, contractors for the French army, were in the process of negotiating a new contract for West Point and the Moving Army with Ezekiel Cornell, the recently appointed inspector of contracts for the main army.

8. See Diary, October 1 and 2; and RM to La Luzerne, October 4, which enclosed an estimate.

9. See RM to Benjamin Franklin, September 27 (two letters) and September 30; RM also wrote a private letter to Franklin on September 28.

In a letter to French Foreign Minister Comte de Vergennes of October 6, La Luzerne merely reported that, although he had not given the Financier the slightest hope of success in obtaining any additional loans from France, he had promised to inform the ministry of RM's financial embarrassments, which he affirmed surpassed all credibility. Moreover, in dispatches to Vergennes written on September 5, 10, and 28, La Luzerne had been even less supportive of RM's efforts to secure further loans. Although praising RM's financial management, and indicating the necessity for some further French subsidies should the war continue, La Luzerne stressed that the French court should not expect to be repaid. Americans reluctant to pay taxes to support the war were hardly likely to tax themselves to repay old debts once the danger was past. Furthermore, La Luzerne noted, the United States would require peacetime loans as well, for which they would seek French backing. RM had already queried him whether the king would be willing to grant a peacetime loan of 20 million livres. Characterizing as ridiculous RM's argument that such a loan, by preserving American credit, would be the most effective way of facilitating American repayment of earlier loans from France, La Luzerne declared that he saw no advantage to the French in rendering themselves the "cashiers" of the Americans, or even in allowing them any hope of it. (For the long-term impact of this remark, see John Jay to Gouverneur Morris, July 17, and to RM, July 20, 1783.) That La Luzerne's views reflected those of the French ministry is indicated by Vergennes's letter to him of

October 14, written before the receipt of these dispatches, praising the ambassador for holding firm on the question of subsidies. In light of the king's past generosity to the Americans, Vergennes did not doubt Louis XVI would make further efforts to save the United States, if the war continued, but the king wanted to keep his options open and saw no reason for supporting the Americans once peace arrived. La Luzerne was therefore to inform Congress, if asked, that he did not know the monarch's intentions regarding subsidies, but he was to make it clear to RM that the French were astonished at the demands being made upon them while the Americans refused to pay taxes and that it seemed infinitely more natural for the Americans to tax themselves rather than to dun the French for the funds needed for their own self-defense. La Luzerne followed his instructions and continued to refuse to make any commitments regarding further French aid. News of the French decision to grant one last subsidy of six million livres, less than a third of the amount requested, did not arrive until March 1783. See La Luzerne to Vergennes, September 5, 10, 28, and October 6, and Vergennes to La Luzerne, October 14, 1782, Correspondance politique, Etats-Unis, XXII, 188–195, 215–220, 281–293, 355–359, 368–373, AMAE; also Franklin to RM, December 14 and 23, 1782, RM to La Luzerne, January 13, 1783, and La Luzerne to RM, January 18 and March 15, 1783.

To Benjamin Franklin

Office of Finance 30th September 1782

Sir,

I have received and already acknowledged your Letters of the 9th January, two of the 28th January, those of the 30th January, 4th March, 9th March, and 30th March. The Acknowledgement of the three last was by mine of the first of July. I am now to acknowledge yours of the eighth of April and twenty fifth of June. I have written to you since the Ninth of March[1] (which you acknowledge the Receipt of in yours of the twenty fifth of June) on the twenty second and twenty third of March, on the seventeenth of April, on the seventeenth, and twice on the eighteenth and twenty third of May, also on the twenty ninth of May, twenty sixth of June, first and fifth of July.[2]

It is in some Respects fortunate that our Stores were not shipped, because, as you observe, they might have been taken;[3] but I hope they are now on the Way, for if they are to lie in France at a heavy expence of Storage &c while we suffer for the Want, it will be even worse than if they were taken. You will find by the Letters which are to go with this, that Mr. Barclay is prohibited from making any more Purchases on Account of the United States.[4] I confess that I disapprove of those he has made: for the Purchase[5] of unnecessary Things, *because they are cheap,* appears to be a very great Extravagance. We want Money as much as any Thing else, and the World must form a strange Idea of our Management, if, while we are begging to borrow, we leave vast Magazines of Cloathing to rot at Brest, and purchase others to be shipped from Holland. I have said Nothing on this Subject to Mr. Barclay, because the Thing, having been done, could not be undone, and because the pointed Resolutions of Congress on the Subject will prevent any more such Operations. What I have now said however will, I hope, lead you to urge on him the Necessity of making immediate Shipments of all the Stores in Europe. A Merchant does not sustain the total Loss of his Goods by their Detention, but the Public do. The Service of the Year must be accomplished within the Year by such Means as the Year affords. The Detention of our Goods has obliged me to purchase Cloathing and other Articles at a great Expence, while those very Things were lying about at different Places in Europe. I am sure that any Demand made for Money on our Part must appear extraordinary, while we shew so great Negligence of the Property we possess. The Funds therefore, which were obtained for the Year 1781, are not only rendered useless during that Year, but so far pernicious, as that the Disposition of them will naturally influence a Diminution of the Grants made for the Year 1782.

You mention in yours of the twenty fifth of June, that you would send enclosed the Account of the Replacing of the Fayette's Cargo, if it could be copied in Season. As it did not arrive, I shall expect it by the next Opportunity.

I have received Mr. Grand's Accounts which are not stated in the Manner I wish; and in Consequence I have written to him by this Opportunity to alter them.[6] I have desired him to give your Account Credit for every Livre received previous to the current Year, including therein the Loan of 10,000,000$^\#$ in Holland, tho a Part of it may not have been received until this Year. I have desired him to debit your Account for every Expenditure made by your Order, which will include all your Acceptances of Bills &c, and of Course Mr De Beaumarchais' Bills, if they shall have been paid. Finally, I have desired him to carry the Balance of your Account to mine, in which he is to credit all Monies received for the current Year: for Instance the six Millions (and the other six, if they are obtained) together with such Monies as may come to his Hands from the Loan opened for the United States by Messrs. Willink Staphorst &c.

I did expect to have had some kind of Adjustment made by this Time of Captain Gillon's Affair, but Congress referred much of it to a Committee with whom it has long slept; but I have informed Mr. Gillon that I must have a Settlement, and at present I wait a little for the Determination of Congress.[7]

You mention to me that the Interest on the 10,000,000$^\#$ Dutch Loan is payable at Paris annually on the fifth of November at four per Cent.[8] I must request you to send me the particular Details on this Subject, such as who it is payable to, and by whom, that I may make proper Arrangements for a punctual Performance, so as not to incur unnecessary Expence. I presume that the first Year's Interest may be discharged before this reaches you; but at any Rate I enclose a Letter to Mr. Grand,[9] to prevent any ill Consequences which might arise from a Deficiency of Payment.

I informed you in mine of the first of July, that Congress had resolved to appoint a Commissioner to settle the public Accounts in Europe: This is not done, but they have reconsidered and committed the Resolution.[10] Where the Thing will end I do not know. I think however that eventually they must send over some Person for the Purpose.

The Appearances of Peace have been materially disserviceable to us here, and general Cautions on the Subject from Europe, and the most pointed Applications from the public Officers, will not prevent that Lethargy which the very Name of Peace extends thro' all the States. I hope Measures will be taken by our public Ministers in Europe to prevent the People from falling into the Snares which the Enemy has laid. Undue Security in Opinion is generally very hurtfull in Effect; and I dread the Consequences of it here if the War is to be carried on, which is not improbable. I am, Sir, Your most obedient and humble Servant,[11]

Robt Morris

His Excellency Benjamin Franklin Esquire

ENDORSED: Office of Finance/Sept. 30. 1782/Various Subjects
MSS: LS, Franklin Papers, PPAmP; LS marked "Duplicate," Franklin Papers, CtY; LS marked "4th," Ferdinand J. Dreer Collection, PHi; Ofcl LbC, DLC; extracts in the writing of Arthur Lee, Records of Boundary and Claims Commissions and Arbitrations, RG 76, DNA.

1. RM's letter of March 9, 1782, has not been found.
2. The Lee extracts comprise the next three paragraphs.
3. The reference is to the goods obtained to replace those lost on the *Lafayette*. See Franklin to RM, June 25, 1782.
4. See RM to Franklin, and to Thomas Barclay, both September 25.
5. To this word Arthur Lee keyed a note he wrote at the bottom of one page of his extracts as follows:

"Grand the Banker credits himself June 12th. 1782

By Ths. Barclay paid his 7 Bills dated Amsterdam 25 Feby. per order Ingraham and Broomfield.	£36000	
Do. April 13 paid his Bill order Ingr: and Bromfield	7500	
Ths. Barclay Bills from Amsterdam for Goods Shippd	30667	
Do. Do Do order Ingraham and Broomfield	17745	
Do Do Do	9429	101,331."

The figures actually total 101,341.
6. See RM to Ferdinand Grand, September 28.
7. For the investigation of the Gillon affair, see Diary, September 19, and notes.
8. The reference is to the French-guaranteed Dutch loan of 1781. See Franklin to RM, June 25, 1782.
9. Dated September 30.
10. The reference is to the resolution of May 28, 1782, which Congress recommitted on July 29. See RM to John Morin Scott, August 15, and notes.
11. This letter was entrusted to Captain Joshua Barney of the *General Washington*. See RM to Barney, October 7 (first letter).

To Ferdinand Grand

Office of Finance 30 Septem. 1782[1]

Sir,

His Excellency Mr. Franklin informs me that the Interest of 10,000,000₶ borrowed in Holland for the United States is payable on the fifth of November next.[2] Should it not have been provided for before this reaches you I am to request that you pay it, for which this Letter is to be your Authority. I am Sir your most obedient and humble Servant

RM

ms: Ofcl LbC, DLC.
    1. Grand was banker to the United States in Paris. This letter to him was sent by Captain Joshua Barney of the *General Washington*. See RM to Barney, October 7 (first letter).
    2. See the preceding letter.

To Daniel of St. Thomas Jenifer

Office of Finance 30th Septem 1782[1]

Sir,

Captain Greene has brought me the twenty Thousand dollars mentioned in your Letter of the twentieth Instant.[2] The Bill on Mr. Swanwick will form a proper Payment to Mr. Harwood the Receiver. I hope he may have applied and received it with such other Monies as may be in the Treasury before this Day in Order that Maryland may have Credit for the Payments she has made in Publication of October.[3]

I observe that in your Letter of the sixth you mention that altho I have not received Money immediately from the Maryland Treasury yet very considerable Sums have been advanced on continental Account by that State since the first of January last to wit £45,497.19.2 Specie $\frac{Cr.}{816.2.17}$ Flour, 105,500 lb Tobacco and 76,162 Rations. Now Sir altho these Sums may and I suppose have been advanced yet you must be sensible that your Observation does not apply because those Advances altho made within the current year can by no Means be considered as a Part of the Quota of this Year. No Articles can be admitted in Deduction from the Amount of that Quota but Payments in Cash to the Receiver. I have authorized no other Payments nor can I pass any other Expenditure. Congress may if they please but I perswade myself that they will not because if every State is permitted to spend the Money raised within it as it pleases there is no longer any Need of such an Institution as Congress. With perfect

Esteem and Respect I have the Honor to be Sir Your Excellency's most obedient and humble Servant

RM

MS: Ofcl LbC, DLC.
1. Jenifer was Maryland's intendant of the revenue.
2. See Diary, September 24.
3. For the receivers' monthly publication of tax receipts, see notes to RM to William Whipple, June 4, 1782.

To the Comptroller of the Treasury
(James Milligan)

Office of Finance 30. Septem: 1782

On the 23d. August last I directed Capt. John Green to proceed to Head Quarters where his Excellency [General] Washington would furnish him with a Flag to go into New York on publick Business. And on the 18th. Instant I directed him to go to Annapolis in Order to receive and bring on with him a sum of public Money—both of which Journeys he has performed, and he will deliver you the Accounts of his Expences on these two Journeys which you will please to have Examined and forward your Certificate to this Office.

MS: Ofcl LbC, DLC.

To James Warren

Office of Finance 30 Septem: 1782

I have received your Favor dated at Boston on the ninth Instant.[1] The Letter you mention was intended for Doctr. Joseph Warren late Director of the Hospital,[2] to whom I request you will Cause it to be delivered. Its coming into your Hands, I suppose must have been owing to a Mistake in the Address.

MS: Ofcl LbC, DLC.
1. Letter not found. Warren was a merchant of Plymouth, Massachusetts, and a former commissioner of the Navy Board of the Eastern Department.
2. The text is in error; the reference almost certainly is to RM's letter to Dr. John Warren of August 13. Dr. Joseph Warren was his deceased brother.

Diary: October 1, 1782

This Morning I sent for Mr. Benjm. Eyre, Mr Joshua Humphreys and Mr. Thomas Penrose eminent Ship Wrights and requested the Favor of them to make an Estimate of the Cost of a 74 Gun Ship and of an 80 Gun Ship in order to transmit the same to the Court of France thro the Minister. Mr. Humphreys and Mr Penrose came but Mr. Eyre was out of Town. The two Gentlemen very readily agreed to form the Estimates &c.[1]

Mr. Bache[2] applied on behalf of a young Gentleman lately arrived from France to have him made a mid Ship Man on Board the Ship

Genl. Washington Capt Barney, but I decline all thoughts of encreasing the number of naval Officers untill the Number of Ships are also encreased.

Upon the application of Mr Sands I agreed to pay him eight hundred Dollars in Specie and 5,000 in Notes for the Use of the Contractors for the moving Army.

This Day I sent for Mr Geo Eddy and obtained a Letter of Credit from him upon Eddy Sykes & Co. in New York in favor of Monsr Barbé at the request of Monsr De Marbois being on behalf of his Excelly. the Chevalier De La Luzerne who proposes sending the said Monsr. Barbé into New York with a Flag &c.[3]

Capt S. Nicholson respecting his Trial but I have not had sufficient time to read the Proceedings.[4]

The Honble. Mr. Hemsly and Mr. T. Smith a Committee of Congress called on me respecting Mr Eddison when I related to them his Conduct and informed them that he has received £150 of the public Money.[5]

Mr. Lewis R Morris[6] applied for a Passage for an Italian Gentleman in the Ship Genl. Washington. I referred him to Capt. Barney.

Capt. Barney applied for Liberty to hire a Pilot for the Voyage. I agreed provided he gets him at Notes Wages &c &c.

Wrote a Letter to Benjm. Harwood Esqr.

Issued a Warrant on Mr Swanwick in favor Samuel Wheeler £83.0.0.

1. The estimate was enclosed in RM to Chevalier de La Luzerne, October 4. Benjamin G. Eyre, Joshua Humphreys (1751–1838), and Thomas Penrose (1734–1815) were prominent Philadelphia shipbuilders, all previously known to RM well before his work on the Marine Committee involved him in the naval ship construction program begun by Congress in 1775. In 1774 Penrose had built a ship owned by Thomas Willing, RM, Thomas Morris (RM's half brother), and Penrose himself. Of the three consultants mentioned in the Diary of this date, however, Humphreys was the most outstanding; he would later furnish superlative designs for frigates constructed for the United States navy after 1794 and build the first of these, the *United States*, which was launched in 1797. On Eyre, see *PMHB*, V (1881), 476, XXVI (1902), 344, LXIII (1939), 110. On Humphreys, see *DAB;* Fowler, *Rebels Under Sail*, 193–195; and for the influence of the *South Carolina* on his designs, notes to RM to the President of Congress, July 30. On Penrose, see William Penrose Hallowell, comp., *Record of a Branch of the Hallowell Family Including the Longstreth, Penrose, and Norwood Branches* (Philadelphia, 1893), 150–155; and *PMHB*, XXXIX (1915), 193, LXIII (1939), 104–105.

2. Probably Richard Bache, Benjamin Franklin's son-in-law and the former Postmaster General.

3. The reference is probably to Pierre François Barbé, younger brother of François Barbé-Marbois, secretary to the French legation and consul general in Philadelphia. The mission was to provide assistance for 120 Spanish prisoners in New York, obtain lists of Frenchmen who had died there, and repurchase the personal effects of Comte de La Touche-Tréville captured aboard the *Aigle*. The British declined to let Barbé within the lines, but offered to let an agent at New York carry out the business. Beginning in 1783 the younger Barbé served in the French consular service, holding appointments in Rhode Island, Maryland, Philadelphia, and New York. See E. Wilson Lyon, *The Man Who Sold Louisiana: The Career of François Barbé-Marbois* (Norman, Okla., 1942), 34; Abraham P. Nasatir and Gary E. Monell, *French Consuls*

in the United States: A Calendar of Their Correspondence in the Archives Nationales (Washington, 1967), 566; and letters of October 2 and 12, 1782, between La Luzerne and Sir Guy Carleton in *Report on American Manuscripts in the Royal Institution*, III, 148, 165.

4. RM's determination on the proceedings of the court of inquiry is dated October 17.

5. The congressmen were William Hemsley (1736/1737–1812) of Maryland, a planter, former state senator, and delegate to Congress, 1782–1783; and Thomas Smith (1745–1809), a Scots-born lawyer from Pennsylvania who served in the state assembly, 1776–1780, and Congress, 1780–1782. They were members of the committee of the week. On Hemsley, see Edward C. Papenfuse *et al.*, *A Biographical Directory of the Maryland Legislature, 1635–1789* (Baltimore, 1979), I, 432–434. On Smith, see *Biog. Dir. Cong.*; and Burnett, ed., *Letters*, V, lxii, VI, 1. On the committee of the week and Edison's case, see *JCC*, XXIII, 629, 640; and notes to Diary, June 28, 1782.

6. Morris was an undersecretary to Secretary for Foreign Affairs Robert R. Livingston.

To the President of Congress
(John Hanson)

[Marine Office, October 1, 1782]

The Agent of Marine has the Honor to present his Complements to His Excellency the President of Congress and begs leave to acquaint him that at the request of the Minister of France he has postponed the sailing of the Packet Washington 'till the End of this week,[1] and the more readily, from being informed, that several of the Enemys Ships are now in the Bay.[2]

Theusday Morning
October 1. 1782

ADDRESSED: His Excellency/The President of Congress ENDORSED: 94/Card from Agent of Marine/October 1st. 1782 postponing/the sailing of the packet Wash/ington MSS: D, PCC, DNA.

1. The delay followed by one day Chevalier de La Luzerne's promise to write letters in support of RM's request for French aid. See Diary, September 30.

2. For the British infestation of the American coast at this time, see the headnote to RM's State of American Commerce and Plan for Protecting It, May 10, 1782, and notes.

To Benjamin Franklin

Office of Finance 1st October 1782

Sir,

In my Letter of the twenty seventh of September last, I express my Wish "that the Court of Spain should give Orders for the Shipment of a Million of Dollars at the Havanna free of Duties, and *to be convoyed by one or more Ships of the Line* to an American Port &c."[1] Upon farther Reflection I am induced to believe that the Court of Spain will not readily go into the whole of this Arrangement; for altho they may and probably will agree to so much of it as will procure them an Equivalent in France for the Million Dollars to be shipped from the Havanna, yet there are Reasons to doubt whether they will convoy the Washington hither. I wish you therefore (should you meet with Difficulties in that Quarter) to apply to the Court for such Convoy. I wish it may consist of a Ship of the Line, because none but Frigates will cruize on this Coast during the Winter, and therefore One Ship of the Line will afford more Protection than two or three Frigates. However this will depend entirely on the Convenience or Inconvenience which may attend the Business.[2] I shall communicate both this Letter and that of the twenty seventh to the Chevalier de la Luzurne,[3] on whose Representations I rely much, as well for procuring the Aid asked for, as for accomplishing the necessary Arrangements after it is procured. I am, Sir, Your most obedient and humble Servant[4]

Robt Morris

His Excellency Benjamin Franklin Esqr

ENDORSED: Office of Finance/Oct 1. 1782
MSS: LS, Franklin Papers, PPAmP; LS marked "Triplicate," NSyU; LS marked "4," Sol Feinstone Collection, PPAmP; Ofcl LbC, DLC.
    1. The passage is from RM's second letter to Franklin of September 27. The emphasis was added in this letter.
    2. The convoy for the *General Washington* was ultimately unnecessary; see notes to RM to Le Couteulx and Company, September 24.
    3. See RM to La Luzerne, October 2.
    4. This letter was sent by Captain Joshua Barney of the *General Washington*. See RM to Barney, October 7 (first letter).

From the Governor of Maryland (Thomas Sim Lee)

Annapolis
In Council 1 Octor 1782

Sir

We have furnished the Troops under the Command of Majr Lansdale[1] with a quantity of shoes, without which they could not March to Phila.—and nothing but a ⟨desire⟩ determination to adhere to your Regulations, and a full confidence that they would be furnished with Blankets at Phila. prevented us from supplying them with that article also.[2] But we are so desirous that the Troops should not go into the Field at this season without Blankets, that we have requested our Delegates in Congress to procure them ⟨at the expence⟩ on the Credit of the State, in case you cannot furnish them.[3]

Honble Mr. Morris

ENDORSED: 1 Oct. 1782/Honble Robert Morris/1273/Entered
MS: ADft, Executive Papers, MdAA.

1. Major Thomas Lansdale of the 3d Maryland Regiment. Heitman, *Register*.
2. Following this sentence the governor began to write "But if they cannot," then "But we are so desi[rous?]," and finally "But if," crossing out each false start in succession.
3. See the Maryland Council to the Maryland Delegates in Congress, September 30, 1782, *Maryland Archives*, XLVIII, 272. For subsequent correspondence on this matter, see RM's reply of October 8, and the Governor of Maryland to RM, October 25.

Walter Livingston to Gouverneur Morris

Fishkill [New York] Octr. 1st. 1782[1]

Sir

Mr. Morris will be informed by General Cornell that the Contractors for the Moving Army and West Point will continue their exertions and supply the Army till the 15th Instant and if Mr. Cornell will furnish 1,000 or 1,200 bb: of Flour they will feed the army till the last of the month with the whole Ration Whisky excepted[2] in full expectation that Mr. Morris will supply them with Bills. If Mr Morris intends continuing to furnish the army by Contract during the next Campaign[3] some of the Gentlemen at present engaged viz Mr. Duer and Mr. Parker with myself will undertake the executive part, provided you will engage with some of your monied friends to embark with us and supply the necessary cash.[4] I would rather that Whiskey did not compose part of the Ration.[5] Those who undertake the Executive part will engage to deliver[6] the Ration at a certain fixed price to be agreed on between the Parties[7] and the remainder shall be divided[8] among the Concern[9] in such proportions as shall be thought proper. The Gentlemen who advance the money will by this proposal reduce their profits to a certain sum which will enable them to calculate and ascertain[10] whether it will answer their purpose. This method I think would relieve Mr. Morris and the army be furnish[ed] cheaper than by the states supplying specific articles.

If this mode is adopted, it will be necessary that the agreement be made immediately, for in my opinion not less than 3,000 bb: of Beef must be cured next month, its not only the cheapest but best month in the year to salt Beef. It will take some time to procure such a number of casks and such a quantity of salt.[11] If Mr. Morris will allow a generous price such as will satisfy the monied Gentlemen I wish to hear from you immediately[12] and one of the Parties (Mr. Duer) will wait on Mr. Morris and the Gentlemen to be concerned and close the agreement.[13] You may depend on it there is not a day to be lost. If any Persons will supply the Army at 10d. per Ration receiving the payments we do, I cannot object to their furnishing them, but if an additional price is given I think we ought to have the offer till[14] our contract expires for the Army can be supplied much cheaper in the Months of Novr. and Decemr. than in the Months of May and June.

If this proposal does not take place I wish it to remain a Secret.

MSS: LbC in Livingston's hand, Walter Livingston Letterbooks, Robert R. Livingston Papers, NHi; ADft, Robert R. Livingston Papers, NHi.

1. Livingston was a principal of Sands, Livingston and Company, the contractor for West Point and the Moving Army; the firm was currently negotiating with Ezekiel Cornell, the recently appointed inspector of contracts for the main army, to define the terms under which it would continue to supply the army. Cornell's letter to RM of October 5 would suggest indirectly that this letter to Gouverneur Morris, RM's assistant, was occasioned by Livingston's belief that the existing contract was about to be vacated and that Livingston wrote it in full knowledge that the Superintendent was negotiating with John Carter of the firm of Wadsworth and Carter. The letter, Livingston told William Duer (see note 4 below), was written "in such a manner as cannot offend his delicacy." Livingston also "sent a Message to [Jeremiah] Wadsworth," possibly on the same subject. See Livingston to Duer, October 2, 1782, Duer Papers, NHi; see notes to Comfort Sands, Walter Livingston, William Duer, and Daniel Parker to RM, September 11, for a discussion of the dissolution of the West Point and Moving Army contract.

The recipient's copy of this letter has not been found. A comparison of the two extant autograph texts suggests that Livingston, after revising his draft, copied it with a few additional changes into his letterbook. Presumably, therefore, the LbC most closely corresponds to the text Gouverneur Morris received and is accordingly printed here.

2. Livingston had interlined the remainder of the sentence in the ADft.

3. In the ADft Livingston had substituted this word for "year."

4. William Duer and Daniel Parker, besides being partners in the Northern Department contract, had been assigned shares in the Moving Army contract by Walter Livingston. See notes to RM's Contract for the Moving Army, April 6, 1782.

5. Livingston had interlined this sentence in the ADft, striking out the word "Spirits" in favor of "Whiskey" and crossing out the remaining words "[which?] would make the Price appear less [one or two illegible words]."

6. In the ADft Livingston had substituted this word for the word "supply."

7. Livingston had interlined the preceding seven words in the ADft.

8. Here in the ADft Livingston had written, then crossed out, the word "equally."

9. Livingston had interlined the remainder of the sentence in the ADft.

10. Here in the ADft Livingston had written "calculate (their profits) and (know) ascertain."

11. Here in the ADft Livingston had written the following sentences which, though not fully marked by him for omission, are not in the LbC. "The latter I believe might be procured from New York (this Article) it is excepted from the prohibited Articles in our Law. (I wish to hear from you on that Subject.)"

12. In the ADft Livingston substituted this word for "by express."

13. In the ADft Livingston had originally written this and the following sentence as one. From this point the words continued as follows: "immediately (that) for you may depend on it that there is not a day to be lost."

14. Here in the ADft Livingston had first written, then lined out, "the end of."

To Ferdinand Grand

Office of Finance 1. October 1782[1]

Since my last Letter to you of the tenth of August advising of my having drawn on you in favor of different Persons as specified in the List then enclosed No. 251 to 298 inclusive making forty eight Setts and amounting to $239,742.13.4.^{\text{Livrs. S D}}$ also of my having drawn on Messrs. Fizeau Grand and Co. of Amsterdam four Setts of Bills of Exchange No. 1 a 4 amounting to $9,929.10.^{\text{Livrs. S}}$

I have further drawn on you in favor of sundry Persons as mentioned in the enclosed List[2] No. 299 to 361 inclusive making sixty three Setts and amounting to $779,702.2.6^{\text{Livres S D}}$ which as well as my former Bills, you will be pleased to honor and punctually Pay on Account of the United States of North America.

MS: Ofcl LbC, DLC.
1. Grand was banker to the United States in Paris. This letter was sent by Captain Joshua Barney of the *General Washington*. See RM to Barney, October 7 (first letter).
2. Enclosure not found.

To Benjamin Harwood

Office of Finance 1st. October 1782

I have received your Favors dated at Annapolis on the twenty first and twenty fifth of last Month, with your Bond mentioned in the latter.[1] I am pleased that you have accepted the Office of Receiver, and desire you will apply to the Treasurer for such Monies, Notes &c as have been paid on Account of the Quota of the State, and make Publication of your Receipts agreeable to the Instructions which have been delivered to you.[2]

MSS: LS, Morris-Harwood Papers, MdHi; Ofcl LbC, DLC.
1. Harwood's letters and bond as receiver of Continental taxes for Maryland have not been found. RM had offered him the appointment in a letter of September 13.
2. Directions for the publication of tax receipts were contained in RM's instructions to the receivers of February 12, 1782. For a discussion, see notes to RM to William Whipple, June 4, 1782.

Diary: October 2, 1782

Mr. Carter called with Letters from Mr Cornell &c and we are still of opinion that the Business of the Contract must be finished at Camp.[1]

Honble. Doctor Witherspoon called again for my Opinion respecting the Hireing of british Soldiers to Work. I am against it, as a measure that will operate against our Views in regard to the Hessians.[2]

This Morning Mr Benjm. Eyre called in Consequence of my Note to him,[3] when I explained my desire of an Estimate of the Cost of building Ships of the Line here. Messrs. Penrose and Humphreys sent me an Estimate; Mr Eyre took it, to join those Gentlemen in Consultation after which it is to be returned to me.[4]

Capt. Jno. Nicholson of the navy called to pay his respects to the Agent of Marine.

Mr Oliver Pollock to Urge on his affair.

This Day Jesse Brown the Express rider returned and brought but little remittance.

Wrote a Letter to his Excellency the Minister of France.

Wrote a Letter to Wm Duer Esqr.

Wrote a Letter to Messrs. Otis and Henley.

1. The letters from Ezekiel Cornell have not been found; for their dates, see RM to Cornell, October 3.
2. On this subject, see Diary, May 1, 1782, and notes.
3. Note not found.
4. See Diary, October 4; and for the estimate as sent, see RM to Chevalier de La Luzerne, October 4.

To William Duer

Office of Finance 2d October 1782

Sir,

I have now before me your several Letters of the sixth, fourteenth, nineteenth and twenty first of September.[1] The Confidence you reposed in my Resources was well founded, and had I been able to employ the Means submitted to my Disposal neither you nor Others would have had Reason to complain.[2] These Means were however locked up by a total Stoppage of mercantile Business on the Appearances of Peace exhibited by Sir Guy Carleton shortly after his Arrival:[3] Appearances which are not yet entirely dissipated, and which operate with powerful Influence against my Department in many different Ways. Against an Event so unforeseen, and against the Negligence of the States so unaccountable, it was not in human Prudence to provide. I am therefore to acknowledge that you have had some Reason to complain, tho that would not have been the Case if you had received the eight Thousand Dollars which would I thought have been transmitted by General Washington, and in which I experienced a new Disappointment.[4] But under the present Circumstances I think the Accounts between us may be stated thus, up to the first of the present Month: to wit

Due from you the contracted Advance within six Months from the 1st April	5,333³⁰⁄₉₀
Sent you by Mr. Hale Specie	5,000
Assumed to pay Mr. Holker for you on Mr. Geary's Drafts	2,000
	12,333³⁰⁄₉₀
Sent you by Mr. Stewart in Notes	10,000
by Mr. Hale ditto	2,000
	24,333³⁰⁄₉₀
Deduct: Supposed to be due on the first of October as by your Letter of the fourteenth of September	22,538⁴⁵⁄₉₀
Balance in advance to you	1,794⁷⁵⁄₉₀
Add now sent you in Notes	6,000
Total Advance 1st October	7,794⁷⁵⁄₉₀

The above mentioned Sum of Six Thousand Dollars will be delivered to the Bearer hereof Mr. John Dewandlaer,[5] and then (if the

Notes be considered as Cash) I shall be about a Month in Advance. But you insist that these Notes be not considered as Payment to you until they come into me by Taxes or Otherwise.[6] This I cannot consent to, for it would be very useless to attempt a Paper Credit which would answer no valuable Purpose to the Public. Whenever they produce to you Money or the Value of Money they must be considered as a payment of Money; and if they purchase Supplies as Money at a Cash Price, then surely they are a Payment of Money the Moment they are deliver'd to your Agent. If for Instance, Colonel Hamilton should when your Messenger returns have three Thousand Dollars in Hand, and the People are willing to receive [the] other three Thousand Dollars for their Produce in Notes, surely the six Thousand are not only as effectual a payment as if it had been made in Silver, but more useful, because it can be transported with greater Rapidity, less Expence and more Security. Waving however these Observations, it will be admitted that if by the End of the Month of November all your Paper is converted into Silver, you will not then be in Advance more than the One Month stipulated for in the Contract. I am pleased however to perceive from the whole of your Letters that you are determined to persevere in the Execution of this Business. I am fully sensible of your Difficulties, and you may depend on my Exertions to give you every Releif in my Power. I am, Sir, Your most obedient and humble Servant

Robt Morris

William Duer Esquire
Contractor for the Northern Posts

ENDORSED: Letter from the Honble. Robt./Morris to Wm. Duer Esqr./Dated 2d Octr. 1782
MSS: LS, Duer Papers, NHi; Ofcl LbC, DLC.
    1. Duer was the contractor for the posts north of Poughkeepsie in New York. Of the letters acknowledged, only that of September 6 has been found.
    2. For RM's difficulties in paying the contractors, see Comfort Sands, Walter Livingston, William Duer, and Daniel Parker to RM, September 11, and notes.
    3. For references to Carleton's peace overtures, see notes to the Secretary of Congress to RM, May 7, and to Diary, June 18, 1782. Other reasons given by RM for his inability to sell bills of exchange were French competition and British commerce raiding. See the headnote to RM's State of American Commerce and Plan for Protecting It, May 10, 1782, and notes.
    4. See RM to Duer, August 29, and notes.
    5. See Diary, October 3.
    6. See Duer to RM, September 6.

To Chevalier de La Luzerne

Office of Finance 2d. Octobr. 1782

Sir,
    I have the Honor to enclose, for your Excellency's Perusal, the Copies of Letters from this Office to Mr. Franklin, of the twenty

seventh of last Month, and the first Instant. I am to entreat Sir that you will represent to your Court the Necessity of the Application which Congress have directed their Minister to make, for a Loan of four Million Dollars.[1] The Resolutions on this Subject have, I suppose, been communicated to you by the Secretary of Foreign Affairs. I have also to request, that you will facilitate the Arrangements proposed in my Letters already mentioned, the Advantages of which are so well known to you that I shall not dwell on them. With real Esteem and Respect I have the Honor to be your Excellency's most Obedient and humble Servant

Robt Morris

His Excellency The Minister of France

MSS: LS, Correspondance politique, supplément, Etats-Unis, AMAE; Ofcl LbC, DLC.
1. See RM to Franklin, September 27 (first letter). For La Luzerne's response, see notes to Diary, September 30.

From George Washington

Head Quarters [Verplancks Point, New York] Octr. 2nd. 1782
Dear Sir

Tho' it is not my wish or design to wound you with fruitless complaints, of which I know you are not the cause, and for the consequences of which you cannot be responsible, yet I have judged it expedient you should be made acquainted with the actual temper and disposition of the Army, a sketch of which is given without diminution or exageration (to the best of my knowledge) in the enclosed Copy of a Letter to the Secry. at War.[1] I confess it seems to me, not only an act of policy but of justice, instead of irritating the Minds of our Officers and Men, to soothe and accomodate them in all their reasonable wishes and expectations, so far as the circumstances will admit. I am sensible you coincide entirely in the same sentiment.

In the ⟨Cloathing⟩ Store Ship, which has lately arrived from Amsterdam,[2] I am informed (tho' not thro' a proper channel) there was a considerable quantity of Linnen and Hose for Officers. These or any other Articles proper for them I should think it would be expedient to have forwarded and delivered upon account of their pay. I have written by this conveyance to the Clothier Genl on the subject; and pressed him to use the utmost exertions to send on the Cloathing, particularly the Soldiers shirts—respecting which I had previously given him my sentiments. That Letter, he has probably communicated to you,[3] for the purpose of obtaining the means of transportation &c. I have the honor to be &c.[4]

The Honble Robt Morris Esqr
Superintendt Finance

ENDORSED: To/The Honble. R Morris Esqr./2d. Octr. 1782
MSS: Dft in the writing of David Humphreys, Washington Papers, DLC; Varick transcript, Washington Papers, DLC.

1. Washington's letter to Benjamin Lincoln, dated October 2, 1782, describing "the dark side of our affairs" and "Without disguize or palliation" advising "candidly of the discontents which, at this moment, prevail universally throughout the army," passionately reiterated his complaint that the army received "bare rations" and remained unpaid while civilian government officials regularly received their salaries (see Washington to RM, June 16, 1782, and notes). He also called attention to delayed promotions and other grievances, "particularly the leaving the compensation for their services, in a loose equivocal state, without ascertaining their claims upon the public, or making provision for the future payment of them" (presumably a reference to half pay), and warned that "the patience and long sufferance of this Army are almost exhausted, and that there never was so great a spirit of Discontent as at this instant: While in the field, I think it may be kept from breaking out into Acts of Outrage, but when we retire into Winter Quarters (unless the Storm is previously dissipated) I cannot be at ease, respecting the consequences. It is high time for a Peace." Lincoln enclosed the letter to Congress in a communication of October 14 in which he declared that "unless a payment can be made to the Army prior to the first of January, the most disagreeable consequences may be expected." Lincoln also requested permission to confer with Washington at headquarters; Congress committed the letters and granted him leave on October 15 (*JCC*, XXIII, 657n.). After conferring with RM and the congressional committee considering the letters, Lincoln departed for camp on October 16, possibly carrying his reply to Washington of October 14 (marked "private") in which he argued that money for half pay would only be appropriated if Congress asked the states to provide for their respective officers, that the officers needed to make their wishes known to Congress in this matter, and that in his opinion the army should look to the states rather than Congress for half pay (Washington Papers, DLC). See Lincoln to the President of Congress, October 14, 1782, PCC, no. 149, II, 53–56; Washington's letter to Lincoln of October 2 and 7, 1782, Fitzpatrick, ed., *Writings of Washington*, XXV, 226–229n., 239–241; James Madison to Edmund Randolph, October 29, 1782, Hutchinson and Rutland, eds., *Madison Papers*, V, 225, 227n.; Tench Tilghman to RM, October 5, Diary, October 16, and RM to Nathanael Greene, October 17. Concerning the issues of half-pay pensions and current pay, see respectively, notes to Diary, July 3, 1782; and RM's Report to Congress on the Representation of the New Jersey Legislature, September 27, and notes.

2. The *Heer Adams*. See RM to the President of Congress, September 13, and notes.

3. See Washington to John Moylan, September 25, 1782, Fitzpatrick, ed., *Writings of Washington*, XXV, 207–208. There is no indication among RM's papers that Moylan had communicated the letter to the Superintendent. Washington reiterated his request in a letter to Moylan of October 7; see *ibid.*, 242.

4. RM replied to this letter on October 15 and 16; see also his reaction as recorded in the Diary, October 16.

To Otis and Henley

Office of Finance 2d. Octor. 1782

I have received your Favor dated at Boston on the seventh of last Month.[1] The Goods mentioned in the Invoice which was therein inclosed, you will dispose of agreable to the Directions of Mr. John Moylan the Clothier General who will write what may be necessary on the Subject.

MS: Ofcl LbC, DLC.

1. Letter and enclosed invoice not found. Samuel Allyne Otis and David Henley were merchants who had previously served as clothing agents for the Board of War and were soon to be engaged by the Clothier General. See RM to Otis and Henley, October 23.

Diary: October 3, 1782

Mr. Carter called to Converse respecting the Contracts but no Determination was taken.

Mr. Jesse Brown for the Warrants to discharge him of his remittances.

Mr. Vaughan and Mr. Jacob Morris to Consult relative to Genl Lee's Funeral.[1]

Capt. Saml. Nicholson called respecting the Court of Inquiry which has been held on his Conduct the last Cruize in the Dean Frigate. He complains bitterly of the Proceedings of that Court, Charges them with Partiality and a predetermination to bring him to a Court martial. I assured him of my Determination to render impartial Justice to every one if in my power and that I will give his Affairs a cool deliberate Consideration before I determine any Point.[2]

Mr. John Perry respecting the Fort Pitt Contract. I persuaded him to wait Colo. Blaines return and he concludes to stay until Monday.

Mr. Alexr Robertson wrote me a note proposing to take Bills of Exchange in discharge of Mr Pierces Notes[3] to which I very readily agreed.

Mr. Jno. De Wandleer employed in Mr. Duers Affairs applied for a Passport which I gave and sent by him a remittance in notes.[4]

This Day I had Invited His Excellency the Prest. and the Honble. Congress, His Excellency the Minister of France, Monsr. Marbois and Monsr Oster, Consul and Vice Consul of France, Monsr Rendon President [i.e. Resident] of Spain, The Honble Secry of Foreign Affairs, Secy at War, Secy of Congress &c who with the Baron Viominel dined with me to celebrate the Acknowlegement of american Independance by the United Provinces of the Low Countries which was done with great Festivity, suitable Toasts being Drank for the Occasion &c.[5]

Wrote a Letter to Heze. Merrill Esqr.	Ebenezer Hazard Esqr
Wrote a Letter to Ezel. Cornell.	Commissr. for settling
Wrote a Letter to Brigd. Genl.	Accounts
Irwin [Irvine].	James Lovell.
Wrote a Letter to Wm C. Houston.	James Milligan.[6]
Wrote a Letter to Wm Denning.	Geo. Olney.
Wrote a Letter to Wm Imlay.	Report on the representa-
Wrote a Letter to Colo. Pickering.	tion of Chs. Young
Wrote a Letter to John Hopkins.	and Bartles Shee.
Wrote a Letter to Saml. Patterson.	
Wrote a Letter to Wm Denning.	

1. Major General Charles Lee had died on the evening of October 2 at Philadelphia, where he had come to complete the sale of his Prato Rio estate to John

Vaughan. Major Jacob Morris of New York, Lee's warm friend and former aide-de-camp, shared in Lee's bequest of the estate. In defense of his memory Morris published the record of Lee's court-martial in 1823. See Alden, *Charles Lee*, 128, 238, 296–300, 301, 302; Heitman, *Register;* RM and Jacob Morris to Edmund Randolph, October 7, and for RM's assessment of Lee's career, Diary, October 4.

2. See RM's determination on the court's proceedings under October 17.

3. Note not found.

4. See RM to Duer, October 2. The passport issued by RM has not been found.

5. See Notice for the *Gazette de France*, October 3, and notes. Secretary for Foreign Affairs Robert R. Livingston was absent, Congress on September 16 having approved his request for a leave of absence to visit New York for a few weeks. He left Philadelphia by September 20 and returned by October 29 (see PCC, no. 79, II, 283–286, 321, 367, no. 185, III, 40, no. 186, p. 53).

For RM's previous comments about the recognition of the United States by the United Provinces on April 19, 1782, see RM to the President of Congress, July 29, and notes, and to John Adams, September 25 and 27.

6. The two letters of this date to Comptroller of the Treasury James Milligan were written by James McCall, RM's clerk in the Office of Finance.

Circular to the Commissioners of Accounts for the Departments

Circular   Office of Finance 3. Octor. 1782
Sir,

In the Course of the Business committed to your Care[1] a doubt will naturally enough arise how far Payments to Deputies in a Department shall discharge the Principal. I think it proper therefore to give you my Sentiments. When of two Officers appointed by Congress the one is from the Nature of his Office to receive Money from the other in such Case the Payment on public Account and for the Purposes of such Office must finally discharge the Party paying. In all other Cases the Advances made should be carried (in the first Instance) to the Credit of the Person who made them and be charged to the Receiver. But in any Case where there shall have been a Default the Amount thereof must be recharged to the immediate Superior of the Defaulter; And if it be still unaccounted for and unpaid by him then it must be recharged to his immediate Superior and so on until it finally stand as a Charge against some Person appointed by Congress and then in the last Resort, Congress (who are alone competent to it) will determine upon a Consideration of all Circumstances whether the Principal shall be held to pay the United States or whether he shall be finally discharged. I am Sir Your most obedient Servant

RM

MSS: Ofcl LbC, DLC; copy, PCC, no. 137, II, 83, DNA; copy, PCC, no. 137, III, 13, DNA; copy, PCC, no. 5, II, 789, DNA.

1. For the recipients of and background to this letter, see notes to RM's letter to the commissioners of accounts for the departments of September 19. The texts in

PCC, no. 137, were enclosed respectively in RM to Thomas Barclay, December 5, 1782, and to the President of Congress, August 26, 1783.

Report to Congress on the Representation of Charles Young and Bertles Shee

[Marine Office, October 3, 1782]

The Agent of Marine to whom was referred the Representation of Charles Young and Bertles Shee,[1] begs Leave to report

That the Matters and Things in the said Representation contained, being related to, and connected with, the general Law of Nations and the particular Treaty with his most Christian Majesty, As well the Enquiry into the State of Facts as the proper Proceedings thereon when ascertained, appear to be peculiarly within the Department of foreign Affairs.

He therefore submits the following Resolution:

That the Representation of Charles Young and Bertles Shee be referred to the Secretary of foreign Affairs ⟨to take Order⟩.[2]

Robt Morris

ENDORSED: 77/Report of Agent of Marine/on Representation of/Cha Young and Bertles Shee/Passed Oct 7. 1782
MSS: DS, PCC, DNA; AM LbC, MdAN; copy, PCC, no. 167, DNA.

1. On September 30 Young and Shee, Philadelphia merchants and part owners of and agents for the privateer *Letitia*, had represented to Congress that their ship, while at anchor in May near Basseterre, on the French-held island of St. Christopher in the West Indies, had captured a passing British vessel with a valuable cargo. Claiming that it was protected by the terms of the capitulation agreement under which the island was taken from the British in February, the French harbor master at Basseterre seized the prize; nevertheless, the French themselves sold it without securing condemnation in the island's admiralty court. Arguing that the seizure violated international law and the French alliance, and conceiving themselves "entitled to *National* protection and support against *National* Insults," Young and Shee requested Congress to take "Active, ennergetic and efficient mediation" to recover the prize as "Protectors of the Rights and Guardians of the honour of the American Flag, Commerce and People." Congress referred the petition to RM as Agent of Marine on September 30. RM's undated report, registered in the Diary of October 3 and accordingly printed here, was read in Congress on October 7 and adopted with one minor alteration (see note 2 below). The Secretary for Foreign Affairs referred the issue to Chevalier de La Luzerne, the French minister to the United States, who transmitted the matter to the governor of St. Christopher, but the final disposition of the case has not been determined. See Young and Shee's petition and related documents in PCC, no. 167, pp. 161–171; and Wharton, ed., *Rev. Dipl. Corr.*, V, 838, 867–868.

2. The words in angle brackets were erased while the letter was before Congress and do not appear in the PCC copy.

To William Irvine

Office of Finance 3d October 1782[1]

Sir

Your Favor dated at Fort Pitt on the 12th of last Month has been delivered by Mr. Perry. Colo. Blaine having Assumed the Contract for supplying the Troops at Fort Pitt until the first of January next I have proposed to Mr Perry to Join him in it expecting from his Influence and Credit beneficial effects. I am Sir with Esteem your most obedient Servant

Robt Morris

Brigadr. Genl. Irvine

MSS: LS, Irvine Papers, PHi; Ofcl LbC, DLC.
   1. Brigadier General Irvine was the commander at Fort Pitt.

To James Lovell

Office of Finance 3 October 1782

Sir,

I have now before me your several Letters of the sixth, ninth, eleventh, sixteenth and nineteenth of September.[1] That of the sixth encloses [a] Copy of one written on the nineteenth of June which as you rightly Conjecture I had not before received. The Affair of the Hospital at Boston I had already referred (before the Receipt of your Letter) to the entire Discretion of General Lincoln. I am very sorry that you find any difficulty in discharging my Drafts upon you and more so that any Gentlemen should experience Disappointments on that Account particularly Mr. Russel whose Exertions on this Occasion certainly merit a better Reward. I shall desist from drawing on you until I know you are in a better Situation and have sent by this Conveyance an hundred thousand Livres by the Sales of which you will I hope be considerably relieved.[2] I should not have drawn on you the little which I have done but pressed by my Necessities on one Hand and encouraged by the Assurances I had received that the State of Massachusetts would by the Plentifulness make up for the tardiness of her Supplies I was induced to do it from not knowing what else to do. I find (from all whom I converse with) that the Capital defect in the Eastern States is that they do not provide properly for a speedy Collection of the Taxes. Every Day's Experience convinces me that until some capital Alterations take Place in our whole System we shall neither be a great, a happy nor an united People but the Prejudices which are opposed to such Alterations are so strong that we must as yet only wish for better Prospects. One small amendment proposed is yet adopted only by New Jersey namely that the Receiver have power to call on the Collectors. I expect this little Circumstance will have good Consequences.[3]

The Remittances by Brown you will find have been properly carried to Account. I am glad that you stopped White for I dare say he must have travelled very slowly as he is but just returned. I am Sir your most obedient Servant

RM

MS: Ofcl LbC, DLC.
1. Letters not found. Lovell was the receiver of Continental taxes for Massachusetts.
2. See RM to Lovell, October 5.
3. See the New Jersey act cited in notes to William Churchill Houston to RM, June 15 and August 10, 1782. It should be added here that the act empowered the receiver to sue the county collectors for nonpayment of taxes.

To the Postmaster General
(Ebenezer Hazard)

Office of Finance 3. October 1782

Sir,

In a Letter which I have received from George Olney Esqr. dated at Providence on the ninth of last Month[1] is the following Paragraph. Viz: "Since mine of the 29 July Mr. Carter the Postmaster in this Town, informed me that the mail from Philadelphia is detained at Fish Kill and Hartford two or three days each, to afford the Printers an Opportunity of inserting into their respective Papers the Southern and Western Intelligence to be brought along by the Post the same Week. This unnecessary detention encreases the Credit of those News papers; but it lessens in a much greater Degree the Value of the Post Office: for no Man will now send his Letters by the Post, if he has the Prospect of a private Opportunity a week later, knowing they will get to hand by the latter sooner than by the former Conveyance. I thought this information necessary, lest a Conduct so reprehensible, should not be known by the Post Master General." I have no Doubt but you will make the proper use of this Information. I am Sir your most obedient and humble Servant

RM

MS: Ofcl LbC, DLC.
1. This letter and the one of July 29 mentioned below have not been found.

To the Quartermaster General
(Timothy Pickering)

Office of Finance 3rd October 1782

Sir

I have received your Letter dated at Verplanks Point on the 29th of last Month. Mr. Ogden ought in every particular to fulfil the Terms of his Contract, in the forming of which I would suppose you was careful that the Interests of the United States were properly attended to. I am Sir Your most obedient and humble Servant

Robt Morris

Colo. Timothy Pickering
Quarter Master General

ENDORSED: Robert Morris Esqr./S. of F. Octor. 3d. 1782/Mr. Ogden ought to fulfill/the terms of his Contract, in/framing which, presumes I/attended to the interests of/the United States
MSS: LS, Manuscript File, WDC, DNA; Ofcl LbC, DLC.

To the Governor of Rhode Island
(William Greene)

Marine Office 3d October 1782

Sir,

Your Letter of the twenty fifth of August last to the Delegates of Rhode Island covering a Resolution of your General Assembly has been referred to me. It gives me very particular Pleasure that the Transmission of the anonymous Letter written to the President of Congress, has produced the honorable Testimonial in favor of Messrs. Clarke and Nightingale.[1] This is the Effect which my own good Opinion of those Gentlemen led me to expect from it. I am persuaded your Excellency will think with me that when a Charge is made to Congress against Persons of respectable Character, in Justice to the Parties complained of, an Opportunity should be afforded them to obviate the Malignity of their Enemies. With perfect Respect I have the Honor to be Sir Your Excellency's most obedient and Humble Servant

Robt Morris

His Excellency The Governor of Rhode Island

MSS: LS, R-Ar; AM LbC, MdAN.
1. The anonymous letter charging John Innis Clark and Joseph Nightingale (1748–1797), merchants of Providence, with complicity in importing British goods by way of Ostend and the West Indies had been transmitted in RM's circular to the governors of Massachusetts, Rhode Island, and Connecticut of June 27, 1782, where it is printed. The texts of the August 25 letter and the enclosed resolution referred to RM as Agent of Marine by Congress on September 9 have not been found. The resolution, noting that a "strict inquiry" had been made into the charge, concluded that it "does not appear to be founded on the least degree of evidence" and was "wholly groundless." See John R. Bartlett, ed., *Records of the Colony of Rhode Island and Providence Plantations in New England* (Providence, 1856–1865), IX, 595; on Clark and Nightingale, with whom RM had formerly done business as chairman of the Secret Committee of Trade in 1776 and 1777, see Showman, ed., *Greene Papers*, I, 204n.; and East, *Business Enterprise*, 71, 72, 78–79, 182.

To Marquis de Vaudreuil

Marine Office 3 Octo: 1782

Sir,

I had the honor to receive your Excellency's Favor of the twentieth of September.[1] It gives me infinite Pleasure to be informed of the good Conduct of an American Officer from so high an Authority. Be perswaded Sir that your Recommendation will always Command my respectful Attention. Whenever my Sovereign shall determine on a Promotion in the marine it will be an agreable Duty in me to present Mr. Douville to them in the most favorable Terms. With perfect Esteem and Respect I have the honor to be Sir your most obedient and humble Servant

RM

MS: AM LbC, MdAN.
1. Louis Philippe de Rigaud, Marquis de Vaudreuil, was the commander of the French fleet at Boston. His letter has not been found, but evidently sang the praises of Pierre Douville (d. 1794). Apparently a Frenchman or French Canadian who had established himself as a merchant and ship captain at Providence, Rhode Island, by the beginning of the war, Douville later served as a lieutenant in the Continental navy on the *Queen of France* and was captured when that ship was sunk during the fall of Charleston in 1780. After his exchange, Douville served with the French fleet that same year at the behest of Comte de La Touche-Tréville and remained with the French navy after the war. See the references to him in *The Heath Papers* (Massachusetts Historical Society, *Collections*, 5th ser., IV, 7th ser., IV–V [Boston, 1878, 1904–1905]), III, 75, 78; Clark and Morgan, eds., *Naval Documents*, II, 57, 214, 1032–1033, V, 396–397, VI, 650; André Lasseray, *Les Français sous les treize étoiles (1775–1783)* (Paris, 1935), I, 186–187; Hedges, *The Browns: Colonial Years*, 219–220; and RM to Douville, October 25.

Notice for the *Gazette de France*

De Philadelphie, le 3 Octobre 1782[1]

Le Congrès ayant reçu des nouvelles authentiques de l'admission de l'honorable John Adams, en qualité de Ministre plénipotentiaire des États-unis auprès des États-généraux, il a été recommandé aux Assemblées des différens États d'informer les peuples de cet évènement, afin qu'ils considèrent les Sujets des Provinces-unies comme amis, et les traitent en toute occasion comme une Nation avec laquelle ils doivent être incessamment unis par une alliance[2] qui, si l'on en juge par celle qu'ils ont contractée avec la France, contribuera à la prospérité des deux États.

Le peuple a marqué sa joie de cet évènement et les Ministres du Congrès se sont également empressés à donner des témoignages de la leur. En l'absence du sieur Livingston, Ministre des Affaires étrangères,[3] le sieur Morris, Surintendant des finances, a donné un repas à tout le Congrès, au Ministre de Sa Majesté Très-Chrétienne et à tous les autres Étrangers de distinction résidens à Philadelphie par ordre de leurs Souverains. D'autres personnes dans les emplois publics, et plusieurs particuliers, se proposent de manifester la joie que cette union cause à tous les Américains et à leurs amis.

[TRANSLATION]

Philadelphia 3 October 1782[1]

Congress having received authentic intelligence of the admission of the Honorable John Adams, in the capacity of Minister Plenipo-

tentiary of the United States to the States General, it has been recommended to the Assemblies of the different States to inform the
people of this event, so that they may consider the subjects of the
United Provinces as friends, and treat them on every occasion as a
nation with whom they will be united in the immediate future by an
alliance[2] which, if one judges it by the one that they have contracted
with France, will contribute to the prosperity of the two States.

The people have demonstrated their joy at this event and the
ministers of Congress have equally hastened to give testimony of
theirs. In the absence of Mr. Livingston, Minister of Foreign
Affairs,[3] Mr. Morris, Superintendent of Finances, gave a dinner to
the whole Congress, the Minister of His Most Christian Majesty and
all the other eminent foreigners residing in Philadelphia by order of
their sovereigns. Other persons in the public employ, and many
private individuals, intend to make manifest the joy that this union
brings to all Americans and their friends.

PRINTED: *Gazette de France,* December 3, 1782. MS: D, Correspondance politique,
Etats-Unis, AMAE.
    1. This document almost certainly originated in the Office of Finance. Chevalier
de La Luzerne enclosed a French text entitled "Bulletin pour la Gazette de france"
(now in AMAE) in his dispatch to Comte de Vergennes of October 6, 1782, noting
that he had been asked by RM to insert it in the gazettes of France or Holland.
Received in France on November 26, it appeared with minor alterations in the *Gazette
de France* on December 3, 1782. See Correspondance politique, Etats-Unis, XXII, 359,
AMAE; and Diary, October 3, and notes. On the *Gazette,* the official newspaper of the
French government since 1762, see Eugène Hatin, *Bibliographie historique et critique de
la presse périodique française* (Paris, 1866), 3–12.
    The transcription and translation of this document were prepared by Mary A.
Gallagher, assistant editor, and Robert W. Hartle, Professor of Romance Languages,
Queens College of the City University of New York.
    2. The AMAE text reads "les Liens d'une alliance."
    3. The AMAE text omits "Ministre des Affaires étrangères." For Livingston's ab-
sence, see notes to Diary, October 3.

From George Washington

Head Quarters [Verplancks Point, New York] 3d. October 1782
Dear Sir
I have been honored with three of your letters bearing date the
19th. and one the 25th. of Septembr.[1] Inclosed you have Colo. Varricks receipt for 800 dollars.

General Cornell is at present at Fishkill at a meeting with the
Contractors. You may be assured he shall have all my countenance
and assistance in the execution of his business. I hope he will be able
to make it unnecessary for me to address a circular letter to the
States.[2]

The Commissioners did but meet and break up. The dis-similarity
of their powers was a bar to business. I have, agreeable to the in-

structions of Congress, informed Sir Guy Carleton that it will be impossible for us to go on with the subsistence of prisoners with out an immediate compensation, or a proper security for the payment of what we advance.[3]

The Commissioners have returned me Eight and one quarter dbb loons,[4] five Moydores, four half Johannes, twenty one English Guineas and Five french Guineas, which I shall apply to the use of my Family and account for. The remainder of what was delivered to me by Mr. Mullins was expended by the Commissioners and is to be charged to that account. I have the honor to be &c.

Honble. Mr. Morris

ENDORSED: 3d. October 1782/to/Honble. Mr. Morris
MSS: Dft in the writing of Tench Tilghman, Washington Papers, DLC; Varick transcript, Washington Papers, DLC.
    1. Here Tilghman first wrote then crossed out the following sentence: "Colo. Varicks receipt shall be provided to you as soon as he transmits it to me." On this matter, see Washington to RM, September 11.
    2. For Cornell's negotiations with the contractors, see his letter to RM of October 5. Regarding the proposed circular letter, see Washington to RM, September 22, and notes.
    3. See Washington to Carleton, October 2, 1782, Fitzpatrick, ed., *Writings of Washington*, XXV, 231–232. The reference is to the recent conference held at Tappan, New York, for negotiating outstanding issues pertaining to prisoners; see Washington to RM, September 2, and notes.
    4. "Doubleloons" in the Varick transcript.

To Ezekiel Cornell

Office of Finance 3. October 1782
    I have received your favors dated on the twenty seventh and twenty eighth of last Month.[1] I have no doubt but salutary Effects will be derived from your Attention to the Public Business Committed to your Care and I shall therefore rely with Confidence on your Efforts.

P.S. Your letter of the 26 is just come to hand.

MS: Ofcl LbC, DLC.
    1. These letters and the one acknowledged in the postscript have not been found. Cornell was the inspector of contracts for the main army.

To William Denning

Office of Finance 3. October 1782
    Your favor dated at Bethlemen [Bethlehem] on the twenty ninth of last Month with its Enclosure has been received. The latter I immediately transmitted to Congress.[1] I hope your health with that of your Family will be speedily restored.

MS: Ofcl LbC, DLC.
    1. Denning was the commissioner for settling the accounts of the Quartermaster Department. His letter and enclosure have not been found, but the enclosure very likely consisted of a memorial of Joseph Frost requesting compensation for livestock that had died in Continental service and Denning's report on it. Congress had re-

ferred the memorial to Denning on September 12; on October 4 it assigned the papers to the Superintendent for referral to the commissioner for settling Connecticut's accounts with the Union.

To William Denning

Office of Finance 3. Octo: 1782

I have received your Favor of the twenty sixth of August last which I am now to acknowlege. The several Books, Papers and Instructions will I trust be speedily transmitted and in the last you will find a Provision for the Case mentioned in your Letter.[1]

MS: Ofcl LbC, DLC.
1. Denning's letter has not been found. For the materials sent to him, see RM to the Commissioners of Accounts for the Departments, September 19, and documents cited in the notes thereto.

To John Hopkins, Jr.

Office of Finance 3 Octor. 1782

I have been favored with your Letter dated at Richmond on the seventeeth Ultimo. The Bills of Exchange agreable to the List you sent enclosed have been received[1] and the proper Discharge sent to you by Mr Hillegas the Treasurer per the last Post.

MS: Ofcl LbC, DLC.
1. The letter and enclosure received from Hopkins, the Continental loan officer of Virginia, have not been found, but were undoubtedly sent in response to RM's September 9 circular to the loan officers.

To William Churchill Houston

Office of Finance 3rd October 1782[1]

I have to acknowledge the receipt of your Favors dated at Trenton on the 21st and 28th of last Month with their respective Enclosures. I hope and believe your Receipts will soon be encreased, knowing that your Endeavours for that Purpose will not be wanting.

MSS: LS, Houston Collection, NjP; Ofcl LbC, DLC.
1. Houston was the receiver of Continental taxes for New Jersey. According to his endorsement, Houston received this letter on October 8.

To William Imlay

Office of Finance 3 October 1782

I have received your favors dated on the twenty first and twenty fourth of last Month, with Bills of Exchange agreable to the List contained in the Latter.[1] Mr. Jesse Brown carries to you the proper Discharge for those Bills.

P.S. 51 Setts of 12 Dollars each should have been *21 Setts of 12 Dollars* each. The latter makes the Amount carried out on your List.

MS: Ofcl LbC, DLC.
1. The letters and enclosure received from Imlay, the Continental loan officer of Connecticut, have not been found. The September 24 letter probably was written in response to RM's circular to the loan officers of September 9.

To Hezekiah Merrill

Office of Finance 3. October 1782

I have received your Favor dated at Hartford on the twenty fourth of last Month, with Notes and Bills of Exchange agreable to the List that was enclosed,[1] for which the proper Discharge is forwarded to you by Mr. Jesse Brown.

MS: Ofcl LbC, DLC.

1. Letter and enclosure not found. Merrill was the receiver of Continental taxes for Connecticut.

To George Olney

Office of Finance 3. October 1782

I have received your several Favors dated at Providence on the ninth, sixteenth and seventeenth of last Month.[1] I have furnished the Post Master General with an Extract from that of the ninth, respecting the detention of the Post,[2] and have no doubt but Measures will be taken to prevent unnecessary Delay in future.

Mr. Brown has delivered the Notes &ca. agreeable to your List dated the seventeenth and carries to you the proper Discharge for them.

MS: Ofcl LbC, DLC.

1. The letters, and the enclosed list mentioned below, have not been found. Olney was the receiver of Continental taxes for Rhode Island.
2. See RM to the Postmaster General, October 3.

To Samuel Patterson

Office of Finance 3. October 1782

I have received your Letter dated on the twenty first of last Month.[1] You will be so kind as to send all the public Bills of Exchange that are in your Possession and if any particular Evils arise from the general Regulation, the Remedy must be sought for by special Application.

I hope a proper Person for Commissioner to settle the Accounts will soon be found and he shall be immediately nominated.

MS: Ofcl LbC, DLC.

1. The letter from Patterson, the Continental loan officer of Delaware, has not been found. It was apparently written in reply to RM's circular to the loan officers of September 9.

James McCall to the Comptroller of the Treasury (James Milligan)

Office of Finance 3d. October 1782

Enclosed is Major Jelles Fondas Account with the United States, Colo. Hay's Agreement with him and other Papers respecting the same, His Petition to Congress and their Resolve of the 6th. September 1781, which Mr Morris desired I would transmit to you.[1]

MS: Ofcl LbC, DLC.

1. On August 19, 1782, Congress had directed the Superintendent "to take order" on a petition from Jellis Fonda "praying payment for provisions furnished the Onei-

das and Tuscaroras, for which actions are commenced against him." For the individuals and documents mentioned in the present letter from RM's secretary, see RM to Philip Schuyler, November 16, 1781, and notes, and February 21, 1782, and notes.

James McCall to the Comptroller of the Treasury (James Milligan)

Office of Finance 3. Octo: 1782

Mr. Morris requested of me to send you Mr. Nicholas Whites Account against the United States, also the Secretary at War's remarks on it, with a Certificate of yours in his favor. All which is enclosed for your farther Consideration.[1]

MS: Ofcl LbC, DLC.
1. None of the enclosures have been found.

Diary: October 4, 1782

This morning Mr. G. Morris and myself attended the Funeral of the late Major General Charles Lee who formerly rendered considerable Services to America, but who by an excentricity of Character had been latterly led into a Conduct unworthy of his Talents and Abilities and by means whereof he had lost the Esteem even of those who wished to be his Friends. He was buried with the Honors of War and the Funeral attended by his Excelly. the President of Congress, many members of Congress and other respectable Characters.[1]

John Jacob Faesch Esqr. applied for money due to him on Genl. Lincolns Contract for Shot and Shells, on which I agreed to pay him 4,000 Dollars in Notes.

Mr. T. Penrose, Mr. Joshua Humphreys and Mr. Benjm. Eyre brought me their Estimate of the Cost of building Ships of the Line &c. in consequence of which a Letter was written of this Date to His Excellency the Minister of France &c.

Capt. Danl. Brodhead desiring some conversation with me on the Subject of his Dismission from this Office,[2] came this Day agreeable to Appointment when after hearing him, I assured him that I have no resentments on Account of the Indiscretion that occasioned his Separation from the Office, that I consider the Thing as proceeding from meer want of thought, and that it is only for Example Sake that I do not agree to reinstate him. This young Gentleman has behaved on this Occasion with great Delicacy, shewn strong and proper Sensibilities, and I wish to serve him when Opportunity Offers.

Colo. Jno. Patton requested an Order for Hessian Soldiers on Account of the Debt due from the Board of War for Shot and Shells. I gave an Order that his note shall be received for them as Cash.

Messrs. Mease and Caldwell proposed Terms for Bills of Exchange for themselves and Mr. Jno. Barclay which I accepted and signed the Bills.[3]

Wrote a Letter to his Excellency the Minister of France.

Wrote a Letter to James Milligan Esqr.

Issued a Warrant on Mr Swanwick in favor John Moylan	£54. 2.1
Issued a Warrant on Mr Swanwick in favor the Bank	53.14.5

1. See Diary, October 3, and notes.
2. See Diary, May 29, 1782.
3. See RM to James Lovell, October 5.

Report to Congress on the Memorial of Samuel Nicholas

[Marine Office, October 4, 1782]

The Agent of Marine to whom was referred the memorial of Samuel Nicholas[1] begs Leave to report.

That the Officers of the marine appear to be entitled to the same measure of Justice, as to the Depreciation of their Pay with those in the Land Service.[2]

That the referring such officers to the several States with a Promise on the Part of the United States that the monies which may be paid by such State, shall be carried to Account of the particular State, is only a different mode of Payment, with this disadvantage, that it tends to keep up Ideas of Disunion which cannot be useful.

That it appears therefore to be most proper, that all such accounts should be settled in like manner with others and the Ballances put upon Interest at six per Cent to be funded on such Revenues as may be provided for liquidating the public debts. All of which is humbly submitted.[3]

Robt Morris
Marine Office 4th. Octbr. 1782[4]

ENDORSED: N8/Report of the Agent of Marine/on a memorial of/Saml Nicholas/Delivered Oct 7. 1782/Read/Novr. 18. 1782/Referred to Mr Duane/Mr Madison/Mr Clark
MSS: DS, PCC, DNA; AM LbC, MdAN.

1. Nicholas was a major in the Continental marines; his memorial has not been found. See Diary, September 23, for his recent application to RM.

2. With this report RM committed himself to supporting the payment of depreciation to marine officers on the same principles as for army officers, seeking to add this obligation to the national debt payable by Congress and to be funded by Continental revenues, rather than assigned to the various states for payment. Depreciation pay for army officers had been established on April 10, 1780, when Congress had authorized the states to make up back and current pay owed to their soldiers in Continental service and to compensate them for losses incurred in receiving depreciated currency (for RM's effort to reverse this policy, see notes to RM to Daniel of St. Thomas

Jenifer, March 12, 1782). Congress subsequently provided, on July 11, 1780, that payment of future marine pay and subsistence "be hereafter considered as and paid in specie or other money equivalent," with Continental currency valued at $40 to $1 of specie. Although Congress on March 16, 1781, resolved that "all debts now due from the United States, which have been liquidated in specie value, and all debts which have been or shall be made payable in specie, or other money equivalent," were to be paid either in specie or its equivalent according to the current rate of exchange, the act evidently was not intended to extend to marine creditors, for Congress on June 12, 1781, provided that "balances now due" and sums for future "wages, subsistence or bounty" were to be paid to naval personnel in specie or money equivalent according to the current rate of exchange at the time of payment. The result was that Congress left marine personnel uncompensated for depreciation before July 11, 1780, and applied the official 40 for 1 rate rather than the current market value for the period between July 11, 1780 and June 12, 1781. See Joseph Pennell to RM, September 16, 1783.

3. Congress on November 18 referred this report to a committee composed of James Duane of New York, James Madison of Virginia, and Abraham Clark of New Jersey. Two days later the committee also was assigned a report of Secretary at War Benjamin Lincoln on the memorial of John Hall which had recommended that Pennsylvania pay Hall for depreciation of pay as an overseer of armorers "and charge the same to the United States." In its report of November 21, the committee proposed that Congress grant to deranged officers of the artillery, cavalry, and infantry, marine officers, mustermasters general and their deputies, and commissaries and artificers of the department of military stores, depreciation pay in the same manner as given officers of the line by the act of April 10, 1780, and that their accounts be settled and the balances placed on interest at 6 percent.

Congress assigned the report for consideration on November 26, but on January 14, 1783, referred it to the grand committee which had been appointed on the preceding January 6 to consider the claims of the army. After considerable debate on the grand committee's report, Congress resolved on January 25, 1783, that the states were to be responsible for the settlement of accounts with their respective lines of the Continental army up to August 1, 1780, while RM was directed to take "such measures as shall appear to him most proper for effecting the settlement from that period." No specific mention was made of marine officers or those not members of state lines. RM then placed the task of settling army accounts, including claims for depreciation, in the hands of Paymaster General John Pierce (see Madison's Notes on Debates, January 24 and 25, 1783, Hutchinson and Rutland, eds., *Madison Papers*, VI, 121–122, 127n.–128n., 129; and RM to the Paymaster General, March 15, 1783). The cases of those not covered under state lines was partly resolved on February 27, 1783, when Congress, responding to the grand committee's report on the memorial of John Hall, voted that "all those for the settlement of whose accounts no special provision hath heretofore been made, either by references to the states, or by the appointment of commissioners for states or departments, or otherwise, do settle their accounts at the treasury in the usual manner," and that any balances due to them prior to January 1, 1782, be placed at 6 percent interest in common with other debts due from the United States. Although specific mention of pay and depreciation was deleted from the report, such accounts were probably intended to be included.

Congress provided for the settlement of marine depreciation accounts on April 21, 1783, when it approved RM's recommendation of April 19, that such accounts be referred to the commissioner soon to be appointed to settle the accounts of the Marine Department. Later in the month the officers of the navy petitioned Congress for pay and depreciation for the period prior to July 11, 1780. On May 16, 1783, Congress referred their memorial to a committee which reported on August 19 in favor of allowing depreciation to all naval personnel in actual service on or after April 10, 1780, for all periods when they were entitled to pay, but Congress took no action on the subject until 1787. Although RM, in conformity with Nationalist goals, had therefore augmented the Continental debt and prevented the referral of additional payments to the states, he had not yet succeeded in obtaining payment of depreciation to marine personnel before July 11, 1780. For the question as it recurred when the settlement of Marine Department accounts got underway, see Joseph Pennell to RM, September 16, RM to Pennell, September 18, and to the President of Congress, September 20, 1783, and to Pennell, May 24, 1784.

4. The AM LbC is undated. The following notes, probably written by James Duane, appear on the endorsement page of the DS: "Makes this Act [retrospective?]/Not the fault of the/officers./The Right of the [*illegible*]/Is it the Intention."

To Chevalier de La Luzerne

Office of Finance 4. Octor. 1782

Sir,

In Compliance with your Request I have consulted our best Ship wrights as to the Cost of different vessels.[1] They have estimated them by the Tonnage and therefore I must explain what I mean by a Ton, and to do this it is necessary to shew the Manner of determining how many Tons a Vessel measures which Measure is what is meant by the Term *Carpenters* Tonnage. Supposing the Keel of the Ship to be on a horizontal Line and the Timbers all put together, before she is planked up then a Right Line thro the extremest width of the Ship is what is called the length of Beam. The Length of Keel is found as follows: a perpendicular Line from the fore Part of the Top of the Stem Post (or foremost Timber) upon the Continuation of a Line drawn along the lower Part of the Keel. The length is then measured from the forepart of the Stern Post to the Point where the Perpendicular intersects the Base and from that is deducted three fifths of the Length of Beam. The Remainder is what is called the Length of Keel. To discover the Number of Tons the Number of Feet english Measure in the Length of Beam is multiplied by one half of itself and the Product is again multiplied by the Number of such Feet in the length of the Keel, that Product is divided by ninety five and the quotient is the Number of Tons. Thus Suppose the Length of Beam to be twenty feet and that a Line drawn from the fore Part of the Stern Post along the Bottom of the Keel until it intersects a perpendicular Line let fall from the forepart of the Top of the Stem should be sixty five feet then from sixty five deduct three fifths of twenty (or twelve) the Remainder being forty three is the Length of Keel Then multiply twenty by half of itself (or ten) and multiply the Product (two hundred) by forty three and divide that Product (eight thousand six hundred) by ninety five the quotient will be Something more than ninety and of Consequence such a Vessel would be considered as measuring ninety Tons. According to this Mode of Measurement they consider a Ship of ninety Guns as being two thousand Tons which they estimate at twenty Pounds or forty eight Crowns[2] per Ton such Ship therefore would Cost forty thousand Pounds or ninety six thousand Crowns. They consider a Ship of eighty Guns as measuring eighteen hundred and fifty Tons which they estimate at nineteen Pound per Ton, such Ship therefore would cost thirty five thousand one hundred and fifty Pounds or eighty four thousand three hundred and sixty Crowns. They consider a seventy four Gun ship as measuring seventeen hundred Tons which they estimate at sixteen Pounds per Ton such Ship therefore would cost twenty seven thousand two hundred Pounds, or sixty five thousand two hundred and eighty Crowns. Lastly they consider a Frigate of thirty two Guns as measuring seven hundred Tons— which they estimate at ten Pounds per Ton, such Frigate therefore would cost sixteen thousand eight hundred Crowns.[3] These Estimates are made also upon a Supposition that the Building were to take Place in a Time of full Peace and the white Oak Timber to be used. If they were built of the Live Oak and red Cedar which must be brought from the southern States it would be an Addition of thirty shillings per Ton to the Price with this advantage that it never Rots. But this Timber cannot be got during the war. Further it must be observed that during the war there would be an Advance of two thirds to the Price. However to make it all more clear I have enclosed an Estimate shewing the different Prices which for the sake of Round numbers may perhaps be stated thus, for a ninety Gun Ship 1,000,000#, for an eighty Gun ship 800,000# and for a seventy four Gun Ship 600,000#. You will observe Sir that this Calculation is made as you expressed on what the Ship would Cost when launched exclusive of Rigging, Guns, Stores &c. &ca. &ca. I confess I think it is so high that if the Experiment were made it could be done for less Money.[4] I am Sir with Esteem and Respect your most obedient Servant

RM

[ENCLOSURE]

Estimate

In Time of Peace Ships built of white Oak

1st. Rate 90 Guns supposed to measure	2000 Tons at £20	is £40,000 or 576,000#
2d Rate 80 Guns supposed to measure	1850 Tons at £19	is £35,150 or 506,160
3d. Rate 74 Guns supposed to measure	1700 Tons at £16	is £27,200 or 391,680

In Time of Peace Ships built of Live Oak and red Cedar

1st.	2000 Tons at £21.10	is £43,000 or 619,200#
2d.	1850 Tons " £20.10	" £37,925 " 546,120
3d.	1700 Tons " £17.10	" £29,750 " 428,400

In Time of War Ships built of White Oak—Advance of ⅔ on Peace price

1st.	950,000#
2d.	843,600
3d.	652,800.

The Masts will cost twenty Shillings per Ton on the Tonnage of the Ship.

MSS: Ofcl LbC, DLC; partial French translation, Correspondance politique, Etats-Unis, AMAE.
1. See Diary, September 30, October 1, 2, and 4. For a discussion of early American shipbuilding with general reference to the concerns of the present letter, see

Joseph A. Goldenberg, *Shipbuilding in Colonial America* (Charlottesville, Va., 1976), 3–5, 15–16, 77–95.

2. The figures here are expressed in Pennsylvania pounds and French crowns respectively. The round numbers cited at the end of the letter are expressed in livres. The enclosed estimate is calculated in Pennsylvania pounds with the totals converted to livres.

3. The partial French translation begins with the next sentence and continues to the end of the estimates. See the following note.

4. La Luzerne forwarded an extract of this document (see the preceding note) to Comte de Vergennes, the French foreign minister, in a dispatch of October 1, with the suggestion, inspired by the recent gift of the *America* to France (see John Paul Jones to Gouverneur Morris, September 2, and notes), that one or two ships might be partially constructed in Boston while the French fleet wintered there after the approaching campaign in the West Indies. The equipment and crews of decayed or damaged French vessels could then be transferred to the new vessels, thus completing their outfitting at relatively low cost. In this way American manpower and raw materials would reinforce French efforts at naval construction. On December 20, 1782, Vergennes replied that the signing of the preliminary peace treaty rendered such a plan unnecessary, but advised La Luzerne to encourage the production of naval timber in various states for the French market. See La Luzerne to Vergennes, October 1, and Vergennes to La Luzerne, December 20, 1782, Correspondance politique, Etats-Unis, XXII, 318–321, 576–580. For other efforts to promote naval construction in America, see Francisco Rendón to Josef de Gálvez, April 20, 1782, and notes, printed in Appendix I to volume IV of this series, and RM to the President of Congress, July 30, and notes. See also Paul W. Bamford, "France and the American Market in Naval Timber and Masts, 1776–1786," *Journal of Economic History*, XII (1952), 21–34.

To the Comptroller of the Treasury (James Milligan)

Office of Finance 4 Octo. 1782

On the eighth of September last I employed Mr. William Blake to go to Richmond in Virginia with public Dispatches from this Office. He returned here on the twenty first of the same Month and now waits upon you with his account of the Expence attending said Journey which you will please to have examined and forward your Certificate.

MS: Ofcl LbC, DLC.

From Abraham Yates, Jr.

Albany [New York] the 4th October 1782

Inclosed I do myself the pleasure to transmit you A Return for the Month of Septr. and also A Bill of Exchange of 18 dolls which remained in my Office on the receipt of your favor of 9th Instant.[1]

MS: Dft, Yates Papers, NN.
1. The return from Yates, the Continental loan officer of New York, has not been found. The letter of September 9 was RM's circular to the loan officers.

Diary: October 5, 1782

Mr. Carter called for Letters and to take Leave the Affair of the Contract being left to Mr Cornell and Mr Wadsworth.[1]

Commo. Gillon applied respecting the enlisting of Hessians. I had not then seen the Act of Congress but afterwards got it and then fixed Monday Morning to do the Business.[2]

Charles Thompson Esqr. for money. I signed the Warrant for his Department but told him there is not money enough. He is to call only as necessity shall impel thereto.

Genl. Lincoln wrote also for Money[3] the Accounts of the civil List being settled I desired Mr. Swanwick to pay the Generals note in the Bank in part of his Warrant.

His Excelly. Willm Moore Esqr. called with a Letter from the Council to Genl Irwin ordering him to pay the money sent up for the Expedition now laid aside to Mr. Hoofnagle the Contractor but I desired that Letter to be altered and that Genl. Irwin may be requested to hold the Money at my Order.[4]

Wrote a Letter to James Lovell Esqr.

Wrote a Letter to Alexr. Hamilton Esq.

Wrote a Letter to the Governors of the States.

Wrote a Letter to the Receivers.

Wrote a Letter to James Lovell Esqr.[5]

1. See Ezekiel Cornell to RM, October 5, and notes.
2. The act of Congress is not recorded in the *Journals*. See Diary, October 7, and notes.
3. Letter not found.
4. The letter was revised in accordance with RM's wishes and sent out to Brigadier General William Irvine, the commander at Fort Pitt, under date of October 5. The £1,500 specie had been sent to Irvine by President William Moore of the Supreme Executive Council of Pennsylvania on September 18. See *Pennsylvania Archives*, 1st ser., IX, 635, 648; *Colonial Records of Pennsylvania*, XIII, 372; RM to Irvine, October 7, and on the intended expedition, Diary, September 7, and notes.
5. Only one letter of this date to Lovell has been found.

Circular to the Governors of the States

Circular   Office of Finance 5th. October 1782[1]
Sir,

I do myself the Honor to enclose to your Excellency the Copy of an Act of the first Instant.[2] You must permit me Sir to call the particular Attention of your State to this important Act. I shall not attempt to add any thing to it because it appears to me that Congress have said all which can be necessary. Neither shall I on this Occasion attempt to display the extraordinary Merit and Sufferings of our Army because I will not suppose any Persons in the United States to be ignorant of what is so generally acknowleged. Besides it is not my present Business to ask for our Officers and Soldiers any *Reward* but meerly the Means to do them *Justice*. Your Excellency will I hope excuse however this one Observation that their exemplary Patience under the Detention of their Dues gives them a double Title to what Congress now ask for these their faithful Servants. With perfect Respect I have the Honor to be Sir your most obedient and humble Servant

Robt Morris

His Excellency The Governor of New Hampshire[3]

ENDORSED: Office of Finance 5 Octo. 82/inclosing an Act of Congress/of the first Instant
MSS: LS, Robert Morris Papers, DLC; LS, to the Governor of Massachusetts, M-Ar; LS, to the Governor of Connecticut, Jonathan Trumbull Papers, Ct; LS, to the President of Delaware, Executive Papers, De-Ar; LS, to the Governor of Virginia, Continental Congress Papers, Vi; Ofcl LbC, DLC; LbC, Letterbook of Governor Alexander Martin of North Carolina, 1782–1785, Nc-Ar; copy, William Churchill Houston Collection, NjP; copy, Morris-Harwood Papers, MdHi; copy, Robert Morris Papers, CSmH; copy, George Washington Papers, DLC.
    1. The endorsement on the LS sent to Connecticut indicates that it was received on October 19. RM enclosed copies of this letter in his circular to the receivers of Continental taxes and his letter to Generals Greene and Washington of this date.
    2. For the resolutions of Congress of October 1, see notes to RM's Report to Congress on the Representation of the New Jersey Legislature, September 27.
    3. This line is in Gouverneur Morris's hand.

Circular to the Receivers of Continental Taxes

(Circular)   Office of Finance 5th October 1782
Sir,

I enclose you the Copy of an Act of the first Instant with the Copy of my circular Letter to the Governors enclosing it.[1] You will consider this Act as an additional Evidence of the firm Determination of our Sovereign to persevere in those Systems which they have adopted. I recommend this Act to your serious and vigilant Attention in all its Parts. It is a mighty fashionable Thing to declaim on the Virtue and Sufferings of the Army, and it is a very common Thing for these very Declaimers to evade by One Artifice or an Other the Payment of those Taxes which alone can remove every Source of Complaint. Now, Sir, it is a Matter of perfect Indifference by what Subterfuge this Evasion is effected, whether by voting against Taxes, or, what is more usual, agreeing to them in the first Instance, but taking Care in the Second to provide us no competent Means to compel a Collection; which cunning Device leaves the Army at last as a Kind of Pensionary upon the voluntary Contributions of good Whigs, and suffers those of a different Complection to skulk and skreen themselves entirely from the Weight and Inconvenience. I am far from desiring to involve in general and indiscriminate Censure all the Advocates for wrong Measures. I know that much of it may be attributed to an Ignorance which exists both from the Want of proper Means and Materials of Instruction, and from the Defect of Experience. But the Evil exists, and you must labor assiduously for the Remedy. I am, Sir, Your most obedient Servant[2]

Robt Morris

To the several Receivers for the different States

ENDORSED: Robt Morris/5. Octr. 1782/with an Act of Congress 1. Oct 1782.
MSS: LS, to Benjamin Harwood of Maryland, Morris-Harwood Papers, MdHi; LS, to William Churchill Houston of New Jersey, Houston Collection, NjP; Ofcl LbC, DLC; copy, Robert Morris Papers, CSmH; copy, George Washington Papers, DLC.
    1. See the preceding letter and notes.
    2. According to his endorsement, Houston received the letter on October 9. A copy of this circular was enclosed in RM's letter of October 5 to Generals Washington and Greene.

To Benjamin Franklin

Office of Finance 5th. October 1782

Sir

I have the Pleasure to enclose you the Copy of an Act of Congress of the ninth of September last.[1] I shall make no Comments on this Act which as it relieves you from farther Trouble and Anxiety on the Subject it relates to will I am sure be agreable. I am Sir Your Excellency's most obedient and humble Servant[2]

Robt Morris

His Excellency Doctor Franklin

ENDORSED: Office of Finance/Oct. 5. 1782
MSS: LS, Franklin Papers, PPAmP; Ofcl LbC, DLC.
    1. The act was no doubt that which ended the practice of paying interest on loan office certificates by drawing bills of exchange on France. See RM's Circular to the Continental Loan Officers, September 9, and notes.
    2. This letter was sent by Captain Joshua Barney of the *General Washington*. See RM to Barney, October 7 (first letter).

To Nathanael Greene and George Washington

Office of Finance 5th. October 1782

Sir

I do myself the Honor to enclose with an Act of Congress of the first Instant my two circular Letters of this date, one to the several Governors and the other to the Receivers. I think it my Duty to communicate to you this Act that you may have an Opportunity at every convenient Season to shew the Military Servants of the Country that their Sovereign is attentive to their just Claims. I have added Copies of my Letters that you may apprize any such Officers of Influence and Discretion as may be about to pass from your army to the Legislatures of the whole of what has passed on this Subject, so that the Views and Efforts of all the public Servants being directed to the same Object may produce the desired Success. I am Sir Your most obedient and humble Servant

Robt Morris

The Honorable Major General Greene

ENDORSED: From Mr. Robt. Morris/Octr. 5th 1782.
MSS: LS, Robert Morris Papers, CSmH; LS, to Washington, Washington Papers, DLC; Ofcl LbC, marked "Circular," DLC.

To Alexander Hamilton

Office of Finance 5th. October 1782[1]

Sir,

I have now before me your Letters of the fourteenth and twenty first of the last Month. I am sorry to find that you are less sanguine in your pecuniary Expectations than the Governor appears to be,[2] for I have always found that the worst forebodings on this Subject are the truest. You will find at the Bottom of this Letter a List of all those which I have hitherto received from you.[3] I think they have all been already acknowledged, but lest they should not you will see in One Moment by the List whether any have miscarried.

I am not suprized to find that the Contractors apply with their Paper in the first Instance to the Receivers and Collectors: This I expected, because much of that Paper is not fit for other Purposes. Some of it however which is payable to the Bearer is calculated for Circulation, which you observe is not so general as otherwise it might have been; by Reason of the Largeness of the Sums expressed in the Notes. Mr. Duer's Letters contain the same Sentiment.[4]

In issuing this Paper one principal View was to facilitate the Payment of Taxes by obviating the too general (tho unjust) Complaint of the Want of a circulating Medium. In substituting Paper to Specie the first Obstacle to be encountered was the total Diffidence which had arisen from the late Profusion of it. Had a considerable Quantity been thrown into the Hands of that Class of the People whose Ideas on the Subject of Money are more the Offspring of Habit than of Reason, it must have depreciated. That this Apprehension was just is clear from this Fact, that the Paper I first issued, and the Bank Paper which came out after it, did[5] depreciate from ten to fifteen per Cent in the Eastern States not withstanding all the Precautions which were used. If I had not taken immediate Measures to create a Demand for it on the Spot, and to stop Issues to that Quarter it's Credit would have been totally lost for a Time, and not easily restored; besides that the Quantities which were pouring in from thence, would have done Mischief here. Confidence is a Plant of very slow Growth, and our political Situation is not too favorable to it. I am therefore very unwilling to hazard the Germ of a Credit which will in its great Maturity become very useful. If my Notes circulate only among mercantile People, I do not regret it, but rather wish that the Circulation may for the present be confined to them and to the wealthier Members of other Professions. It is Nothing but the greater Convenience which will induce People to prefer any Kind of Paper to the precious Metals, and this Convenience is principally felt in large Sums. Whenever the Shop Keepers in general discover that my Paper will answer as a Remittance to the principal Ports, and will be readily exchanged by the Receivers, they will as readily exchange it for other People. When the People in general find that the Shop Keepers receive it freely, they will begin to look after it, and not before; For you must know that whatever fine plausible Speeches may be made on this Subject, the Farmers will not give full Credit to Money merely because it will pay Taxes, for that is an Object they are not very violently devoted to; but that Money which goes freely at the Store and the Tavern, will be sought after as greedily as those Things which the Store and the Tavern contain. Still, however, your Objection remains good, that the Traffickings in which the greater Part of the Community engage do not require Sums so large as Twenty Dollars. This I shall readily acknowledge; but you will observe that there is infinitely less Danger that large Notes which go only thro the Hands of intelligent People, will be counterfeited than small ones, which come to the Possession of illiterate Men. When public Credit is firmly established, the little Shocks it receives from the Counterfeitors of Paper Money do not lead to material Consequences; but in the present ticklish State of Things there is just Ground of Apprehension. Besides this, the Value of Paper will depend much upon the Interchanges of it for Specie, and these will not take place when there is a Circulation of small Paper. Lastly, I have to observe, that until more Reliance can be placed on the Revenues required, I dare not issue any very considerable Amount of this Paper, lest I should be run upon for more than I could answer, and as the Circulation of what I dare issue by increasing the general Mass, enables People (so far as it goes) more easily to get hold of other Money, it consequently produces in its Degree that Object of facilitating Taxation which I had in View. I am, Sir, Your most obedient and humble Servant

Robt Morris

Alexander Hamilton Esquire
Receiver for New York

ENDORSED: Superintendent of Finance/5 Octr. 1782
MSS: LS, Hamilton Papers, DLC; Ofcl LbC, DLC; transcript, Francis Baylies Papers, DLC.

1. Hamilton was the receiver of Continental taxes for New York.
2. See the postscript to RM to Hamilton, September 14, and notes.
3. The list has not been found.
4. William Duer's letters on this subject have not been found. RM's recent letter to him of October 2 did not take up the problem, but similar complaints were discussed in the Quartermaster General to RM, September 19, and RM to Ralph Pomeroy, September 25.
5. Here the editors have deleted the word "not." The word is not in the Ofcl LbC.

From Ezekiel Cornell

Verplanks Point [New York] October 5th 1782

Dear Sir,

I have detained the Express a long Time, but I assure you that as soon as I could write you with any Degree of Certainty I embraced the earliest Moment to dispatch him.[1] I have experienced more uneasy Hours in transacting this Business than in any I ever undertook before. I found the Officers in general very Reasonable in their conversation, but they one and all feel themselves exceedingly distressed for Want of Money, and have Complaints that have Weight in them, many of which I hope and believe will be remedied as soon as the new Contract takes place. Every Method will be taken to make the Contract so plain and explicit as to prevent any Mistakes or uneasiness: Those Complaints that arise from other Causes I shall do myself the honor to state to you, but more particularly to the Secretary at War. But in One Word I am clearly of Opinion that if the Army should be reduced to the Situation for only two Days that they have experienced in not receiving their Subsistence that the Consequences would be more fatal than any Thing that has hitherto taken place.

On the 30th. Ultimo I met the Contractors agreable to a previous Appointment that I had made. I gave them a Letter of which the enclosed paper No 1 is a Copy.[2] They say that your Non-performance has been the sole cause of their Failure, and they pressed me hard to promise them a speedy Advance of Money. I mention these Circumstances as they tend in some Measure to explain some Parts of my Letter to them. I was also apprehensive that they would take Advantage of our Situation and stop the Supplies immediately, as they had got Information of the Proposals made to Mr Carter[3] before my Arrival in Camp. I therefore thought that prudence dictated to treat them gently:[4] And the Tenor of your private Letter of the 23d Ultimo was such as did not admit of my urging them to continue their Supplies. On the first Instant I received their answer, a Copy of which is enclosed No 2. I then immediately repaired to Camp, and communicated the whole Proceeding to His Excellency the Commander in Chief, and after mature Consideration we were both decided in Opinion that there was no Alternative but that of agreeing with Colo. Wadsworth on the best Terms we could, at the same Time we were sensible it must be on his own, as he knew our situation. I immediately set about this Business but Colonel Wadsworth has been so engaged with the French Army on Account of Mr Carter's Absence,[5] that Nothing could be agreed upon untill last Evening—when he engaged to furnish the moving Army and the Garrison at West Point at thirteen Ninetieths of a Dollar per Ration from the 16th Instant unto the last Day of December next both days included. Payments to be made at the following Periods. For the Supplies furnished for the Half Month of October on the 1st Day of February; for the Month [of] November on the first Day of March, and for the Month of December on the second day of April next. As there is many Difficulties that now exist respecting the Issuing Provisions and some other Matters, it was thought proper that all those Difficulties should be settled by a Board of Officers, which cannot meet until Tomorrow;[6] and altho Nothing that will be done by the Board is to effect the Price of the Ration, yet it may be necessary to make some Alteration in the Contract when it comes to be made out, which will be done as soon as possible, agreable to your Direction, and sent forward.[7] I hope what is now about to take place will give entire Satisfaction to the Army respecting their Subsistence, which appears to me to be absolutely necessary, until they can receive some Part of their Pay at least.[8] The price to be given is high, but it is the best that I could do in our present Situation, and I hope it will meet your Approbation. The Contractors have created Difficulties among themselves by dividing their Contract. The Beef Contractors demand Damages of the Others; they say that they sunk £2000 by the high Price that they gave for Beef in the first Part of their supplying, and that they have not yet made themselves whole: To settle this Matter I endeavoured to prevail with Colonel Wadsworth to take the Beef of them; he will not agree to do it unless I will promise to pay 4/ lawfull Money per C.[9] This I did not think myself authorized to do. The Contractors expect that the Public will pay all Damages, as they say the Failure was on their Part. If you should think it best that Colonel Wadsworth take the Beef on the Terms proposed, I should be happy to be informed as soon as possible.[10] I should have been more particular on this Subject, but Colonel Tilman informs me that he has wrote you by this Conveyance on the same Subject.[11]

It appears to me that the Contractors have crouded your Notes too hard: They have lodged them in the Hands of the Collectors on every Part of the Country where Money is collecting for Taxes which disgusts those who have taken them for Supplies, and has I apprehend hurt their Credit, and if the Practice is pursued I think it will tend to depreciate them. All this tends to confirm me (if it were possible) in Opinion that you was perfectly right in not agreeing to the Request of the Contractors.

My whole Attention has been hitherto turned to the great Object. I have not examined into any Complaints tho I have heard many. I have done myself the Honor to enclose to you a Letter from Mr Stevens complaining of Mr Sands.[12] I expect there will be Difficulty in settling any Thing with this Gentleman. The Commander in Chief informs me that Arbitrators had been appointed by his Orders for several Months to settle some Disputes, but Mr Sands will not attend, and in a Word the Commander in Chief has no Confidence in him.[13] I have many other Things that I want to mention; but this Letter is too long already. I have the Honor to be Your most obedient Servant

(Signed) Ezek: Cornell

The Hon'ble Robt. Morris Esquire

P.S. Since Writing to Day Colonel Wadsworth has been with me, and seems desirous of having the Affair of the Beef settled, and says that he will endeavour to settle the Matter with the Contractors in the most easy Manner he can, if you should approve of the Measure, but whether he has the public Interest or his own most in View I cannot undertake to say. I could wish this Matter to be settled; if it is not I fear it will have some evil Tendencies. Mr Edwards is gone Home. Mr Phelps I have not seen; he was gone to Boston before I arrived. I expect them both in Camp in a few Days.[14]

E.C.

ENDORSED: *Number five*/Copy of a /Letter from/Ezekiel Cornell/to Super: of Fin./5 Octr. 1782.
MSS: Copy, PCC, DNA; copy, Benjamin Franklin Papers, PPAmP.

1. Cornell, the recently appointed inspector of contracts for the main army, was at Washington's headquarters conducting negotiations with Sands, Livingston and Company and with Jeremiah Wadsworth of Wadsworth and Carter to determine the future of the combined West Point and Moving Army contract (for the background, see Comfort Sands, Walter Livingston, William Duer, and Daniel Parker to RM, September 11, and notes). This letter reached RM on the evening of October 9.

2. Enclosures nos. 1 and 2 were Cornell·to the Contractors for the Moving Army, September 30, and Comfort Sands and Walter Livingston to Cornell, October 1, 1782. The texts received by RM have not been found, but copies kept by Walter Livingston have been printed as enclosures to Walter Livingston, William Duer, and Daniel Parker to RM, October 9.

3. For RM's discussions with John Carter about a replacement contract for West Point and the Moving Army, see Diary, September 18, 23, 30, and October 2 and 3.

4. PPAmP copy: "genteely."

5. Wadsworth and Carter were supply agents for the French army.

6. See Tench Tilghman to RM, October 5, and notes.

7. The contract as concluded is dated October 12.

8. For the status of the continuing question of army pay, see RM's Circular to the Governors of the States, October 5, and notes.

9. That is, per hundredweight.

10. Oliver Phelps and Timothy Edwards, two of the contractors of record for the Moving Army, had relinquished their shares in exchange for a subcontract to supply all the beef needed under the contract (see Diary, May 13, and notes, and June 14, 1782). The beef subcontractors were themselves bound by contracts with others to purchase large supplies of beef through the end of the year and threatened to sue the

Moving Army contractors unless the meat was purchased at the original contract prices. Wadsworth and Carter, who were to take over the West Point and Moving Army contract on October 15, refused to purchase it at the specified price, which had been set well above the current market price in order to compensate for high beef prices earlier in the year and to compensate Phelps and Edwards for relinquishing their share of the profits of the original Moving Army contract. Although Cornell, Wadsworth, and Tench Tilghman all advised RM to avoid legal entanglements by allowing Wadsworth and Carter an additional 4 shillings per hundredweight of meat purchased from the subcontractors, the Financier refused, referring to the arrangement as a form of "hush money." He agreed to render compensation for damages arising from government actions, but asserted that this guarantee did not apply to private agreements among the contractors themselves. The protracted legal disputes which ensued were not resolved until 1834. See Sands, Livingston and Company to RM, September 25 and October 8, Walter Livingston to Gouverneur Morris, October 1, Tilghman to RM, and Wadsworth to RM, both October 5, Walter Livingston, William Duer, and Daniel Parker to RM, October 9, and enclosures, RM to the contractors for West Point and the Moving Army, to Cornell, to Tilghman, and to Wadsworth, all October 10, Livingston to RM, December 14, and RM to Livingston, December 24, 1782; also Charles Stewart to Livingston, November 12 and December 13, 1782, Stewart Papers, MH.

11. See Tench Tilghman to RM, October 5, and notes.

12. Nathaniel Stevens, deputy commissary general of issues at Fishkill, had been assigned the task of delivering various public provisions and stores to Comfort Sands and Company, the West Point contractor, early in 1782 when the Commissary Department was in the process of disbandment after the contract system went into operation. On September 17 RM instructed Charles Stewart, formerly commissary general of issues and now issuing contractor for West Point and the Moving Army, to submit a return of the stores delivered to Sands. Although Stewart believed that a return had been previously made, he was unwilling "that any Returns or papers in our power to furnish should delay a Settlement between Mr. Morris and the Contractors," and in his capacity as commissary general sent Stevens a copy of RM's letter, requesting him "to make One Return of the whole Stores delivered . . . that I may fully answer Mr. Morris letter." The letter from Stevens which Cornell enclosed here has not been found, but very likely concerned this unresolved problem. RM referred the matter to Cornell in a letter of October 10; according to Stevens, Sands was uncooperative and refused to submit the issue to arbitration. The problem was still outstanding early in 1783. See Stewart to Stevens, September 26, and Stevens to Stewart, November 16, 1782, Stewart Papers, NCooHi; and RM to Stevens, March 3, and to the Comptroller of the Treasury, March 26, 1783.

13. For Washington's conflicts with Comfort Sands, see Washington to RM, May 17–25, 1782, and notes.

14. The PCC text of this letter from Cornell was enclosed in RM to the President of Congress, October 21, 1782; the PPAmP copy was enclosed in RM to Franklin, January 11, 1783.

From Alexander Hamilton

[Albany, New York, October 5, 1782]

In my last[1] I informed you that the Committee appointed by the Legislature on the subject of taxation were together. In spite of my efforts, they have parted without doing any thing decisive. They have indeed agreed upon several matters and those of importance but they have not reduced them to the form of a report, which in fact leaves every thing afloat to be governed by the impressions of the moment when the legislature meet.

The points agreed upon are these—that there shall be an actual valuation of land and a tax of so much in the pound. The great diversity in the qualities of land would not suffer them to listen to an estimated valuation [or][2] to a tax by the quantity agreeable to the idea in your late report to Congress.[3] That there shall be also a tariff of all personal property to be [also] taxed at so much in the pound— that there shall be a specific tax on carriages, clocks, watches and other similar articles of luxury—that money at usury shall be taxed at a fixed rate in the pound excluding that which is loand to the public—that houses in all towns shall be taxed at a certain proportion of the annual rent—that there shall be a poll tax on all single men from fifteen upwards and that the Collection of the taxes should be advertised to the lowest bidder at a fixed rate per Cent bearing all subordinate expenses.

Among other things which were rejected I pressed hard for an excise on distilled liquors; but all that could be carried on these articles was a license on taverns.

The Committee were pretty generally of opinion that the system of funding for payment of old debts and for procuring further credit was wise and indispensable but a majority thought it would be unwise in one state to contribute in this way alone.

Nothing was decided on the[4] quantum of taxes which the state was [able] to pay; those who went furthest [did][5] not exceed 7000£ of which fifty for the use of the United States.

I send you My Cash Account,[6] which is for what has been received in this County. We have not heard from the others. I &c.

Albany Octr. 5. 1782

ENDORSED: To Robert Morris/Octr. 5. 1782
MSS: ADft, Hamilton Papers, DLC; transcript, Francis Baylies Papers, DLC.
    1. Dated September 28. Hamilton was the receiver of Continental taxes for New York.
    2. The editors have conjectured this and the other bracketed words below with guidance from the Baylies transcript and the text as printed in Syrett and Cooke, eds., *Hamilton Papers*, III, 181.
    3. The reference is to RM to the President of Congress, July 29, where the Superintendent argued for a uniform land tax by acreage rather than value.
    4. The manuscript is torn here, with the possibility that a word was obliterated.
    5. Syrett and Cooke conjecture this word as "would."
    6. Cash account not found.

From William Churchill Houston

Trenton [New Jersey] 5 Octr. 1782

Sir

My Return of last Week[1] missed the Post, by his Passing several Hours earlier than his usual Time. It went the next Day by a private Hand, Dr. Harris of Cape May, who promised to deliver it. Hope it has been received. It amounted to 5240 Dollars.

The Legislature of this State has been sitting for some Time past in this Town and rose yesterday. I had the Honour to inform you of their Assembling in mine of the 21 ultimo. Their only Act which has ⟨come to my Knowledge and which interferes⟩ any Relation to the Subject of Finance, as far as I know, is one which appropriates such Sum of Money as may be necessary to give a Month's Pay to the Troops of the State in the federal Army, provided the same exceed not £3400 Pounds, the same to be payable out of the Arrears of the former Taxes.[2] As this Act passed the Day they rose, I have not seen it. I am sorry for the Necessity of it; and in Sentiment against the Principle. I never knew these partial, separate Grants of Clothing, Money or other necessaries produce any Good, but the contrary; and if they do not carry Confusion into the publick Accounts, My Idea of their Consequences in that Respect is wrong. I believe indeed that the Soldiery ought to have some Money, and that the Necessity is great; it is said to be indispensible.[3]

WCH

1782 Dr   The Receipt of Continental Taxes in the State of New-Jersey
from 28 Septr to 5 Octr inclusive
To Cash received from the State Treasurer six Hundred and
fifty-four Dollars and seventy-four ninetieths   Dlls 654⁷⁴⁄₉₀

ENDORSED: Letter to Robt Morris Eqr/Superintendent &c/5 Octr. 1782/return 654⁷⁴⁄₉₀
MSS: ADftS with ADftS return on verso, Houston Collection, NjP; extract, PCC, DNA.
1. See Houston to RM, September 28. Houston was the receiver of Continental taxes for New Jersey.
2. For the background, see RM's Report to Congress on the Representation of the New Jersey Legislature, September 27, and notes; see also Houston to RM, October 12.
3. The PCC extract, also dated Trenton, October 5, 1782, was enclosed in RM to the President of Congress, October 7. Evidently copied from the text of Houston's letter received by RM, it differs significantly from the ADftS and, except for the dateline, is given here in its entirety: "The Legislature of this State has been sitting here for some Time past, and rose this Day. I had the Honor to advise you of their assembling in mine of the 21st Ultimo. Their principal Act which has any Relation to Finance, and which only passed to day, so that I have not yet seen it, is the appropriation of such a Sum of Money, out of the arrears of the former Taxes, as may be sufficient to give a Months pay to the Troops of the State in the fedral Army, provided the same exceed not £3400. I am sorry for the necessity of this act and in Sentiment against its Principle; though I am told almost every State to the Eastward has done the like I never knew these partial, separate Grants of Cloathing, Money or other necessaries produce any Good, but the contrary: and if they do not carry Confusion into the public accounts my Idea of their Operation in that respect is wrong. I believe indeed the necessity of the Soldiery for a little Money is great and perhaps not unalarming; it is thought to be indispensible."

From Arthur Lee

Philadelphia 5th. October 1782

Sir

My Nephew Ludwell Lee[1] will have the Honor of presenting you this. He is exceedingly pressed for money to Pay his entrance with a

Lawyer with whom he means to study; I shall therefore be very much obliged to you, if you can supply him with 200 £ on my Account. As this hardly amounts to the interest of what is due to me from the Public, and the occasion is very urgent, it not being in our Power to obtain the money necessary in any other way, I hope that what I request will not meet with any Obstacle.[2] I have the Honor to be Sir with great esteem Your Most Obedient humble Servant

(signed) A. Lee

MS: Copy, PCC, DNA.

1. Ludwell Lee (1760–1836) was the second son of Richard Henry Lee. His education was often supervised and financed by his uncles William and Arthur Lee. In March 1783 Ludwell reentered the College of William and Mary (from which he had resigned to enlist in the army) and studied law under George Wythe. Cazenove Gardner Lee, Jr., *Lee Chronicles: Studies of the Early Generations of the Lees of Virginia* (New York, 1957), 280–281; Edmund Jennings Lee, *Lee of Virginia, 1642–1892: Biographical and Genealogical Sketches of the Descendants of Colonel Richard Lee* (Philadelphia, 1895), 323–327.

2. Arthur Lee, a Virginia delegate to Congress and a persistently vocal critic of RM and his policies, had addressed a memorial to Congress on July 12, 1782, complaining that he alone of the former ministers to foreign courts had not yet been paid his salary and expenses as commissioner in Europe while "Agents and Factors, who had profits on large sums of public monies advanced to them" had received considerable payments out of monies borrowed in France. He viewed "his standing thus the sole object of neglect" as "a mark of the displeasure of Congress," which he was "far from conceiving he has deserved." Lee therefore requested payment of his salary on the same basis as the other foreign ministers in accordance with Congress's resolution of August 6, 1781 (see Lee's memorial in PCC, no. 41, V, 281–284; on the payments to foreign ministers and the settlement of his accounts, see Silas Deane to RM, September 10, 1781, and notes). The committee to which his memorial had been referred recommended on July 18 that the Superintendent draw a bill on Benjamin Franklin for the balance and interest due on Lee's salary and expenses and that the certificate of debt previously given Lee be cancelled. Congress sent the report of RM on July 19 to take order. Since Lee's claim was the only one of its type RM expected to receive, he indicated his intention to comply until he learned that Lee had received payment of his salary in loan office certificates payable in one year, with interest, under an order of the Board of Treasury of August 10, 1781. Perhaps fearing criticism for favoring a member of Congress over other holders of loan office certificates who were already incensed by the suspension of interest payments in bills of exchange on September 9 (see Charles Thomson's Notes of Debates, July 25, 1782, Burnett, ed., *Letters*, VI, 393–394; and the headnote to RM to the President of Congress, July 29), RM declined to pay Lee without an express order from Congress. To Lee's contention that he was the only foreign minister paid in certificates rather than cash and that Congress had intended to remove him from the mass of certificate holders by its resolution of July 19, RM responded with a report to Congress of November 14, in which the present letter was enclosed, recommending that Lee be paid but proposing a specific resolution authorizing him to exchange Lee's loan office certificates for the equivalent in bills of exchange on France. RM's report was read and approved in Congress on November 18, but not before Lee and the Superintendent clashed personally over the issue. See the Register of the Treasury to RM, October 7, and RM to Lee, both October 9, Lee to RM, November 2, and RM to Lee, November 18 and 26, and Diary, October 7, November 22, 27, and December 11, 1782; Sumner, *Financier*, II, 52–54; Hutchinson and Rutland, eds. *Madison Papers*, VI, 119–120, 126n. For Lee's current opposition to RM's policies, see, for example, notes to RM to Benjamin Franklin, September 28; for RM's involvement in the payment of Lee's brother William, see RM's Report to Congress on a Letter from William Lee, June 6, 1782, and notes.

From Tench Tilghman

Head Quarters [Verplancks Point, New York] 5th October 1782[1]
My dear Sir,

I am happy to find that matters are so far advanced as to have
little doubt but Colo. Wadsworth will take up the Contracts.[2] He will
make good terms for himself but he will execute in such a Manner
that I am confident he will give entire Satisfaction. Before I knew
that you and Mr Carter had been in Treaty, I told the General that
the Plan which is now in Agitation, that of an advanced price upon a
long Credit, was the only one which you possibly under present
Circumstances of the Public can engage in and I am pleased to find
that you have been of the same opinion. It would have been better to
have given the double of what Mr Wadsworth asks, than to have
dropped the System of Contracts. There may possibly be a Clamor
among People who may be disappointed, but you will be supported
by all honest and good Men, who pay a due attention to the Situation of public Affairs.

There will be some matter of difficulty between Mr Sands and the
under Contractor for Beef. Wadsworth has proposed to Gen Cornell
a mode of settling that, which he refers to you.[3] I think you had best
close with it, for the following reasons. It will take away from Sands
all ground of Complaint against you, and will probably put a stop to
a suit which the under Contractors for Beef will certainly bring
against him, if the Cattle which they have been providing are left
upon their Hands. If they bring suits against Sands, he will institute
Suits against you, and involve you in trouble, and it will give him a
handle to stop paying off the due Bills to the Army. Now, if matters
can be amicably adjusted Sands will take the Balance due from the
public to him in such payments as you can conveniently make him,
and he will continue paying off his due Bills.

At a meeting we had last Night I found Mr Wadsworth wished to
know precisely what mode of Issuing, and what Quantities of the
different Species of a Ration would give perfect Satisfaction.[4] I proposed the following Mode: to take the opinion of a judicious Officer
and one of influence from each Line. In this I had two Views one
really for the sake of Information the other to interest as many as I
could in supporting the Contract after it should be formed.[5] The
Gentlemen we have pitched upon are General Knox for the Artillery, Colo. Barber for New Jersey, Colo. Cortlandt for New York,
Colo. Swift for Connecticut, Colo. Olney for Rhode Island, Colo.
Henry Jackson for Massachusetts.[6] These Gentlemen their respective
Lines have perfect Confidence in, and they are Men of Sense and of

much cool deliberation, in short they have not from long military habits, forgot they are Citizens.

Thus I hope we have provided for the future Subsistence of the Army. Now my good Sir, permit me to recommend every possible exertion to give two or three Months pay upon going into Quarters. To the Officers it will be the most acceptable thing upon Earth, for they are really in a distressed Situation for want of it. Two Months pay to the Soldiery cloathed and fed as they ⟨will be,⟩[7] will be sufficient. Their Pay Master might be directed to give out a quarter of a Dollar per Week to the Privates and a half a Dollar to the Non Commissioned, that would serve them to amuse themselves, and that is all the Use that a well fed and well cloathed Soldier has for Money. I am aware of your embarrassments, and therefore only recommend to you what would make this Army the most contented of any in the World. They have as I mentioned in my last some few grievances which it is not with you to redress. I wish the Secretary at War could find time to make a short visit to the Army. I think we could concert measures with him that would do away several disagreeable Matters.[8]

ENDORSED: Number six/Extract from a Letter of/Colo. Tench Tilghman/to/The Superint. of Finance/5 Octr. 1782
MSS: Extract, PCC, DNA; extract, Benjamin Franklin Papers, PPAmP.

1. Lieutenant Colonel Tilghman was George Washington's aide-de-camp. The PCC extract from his letter printed here was enclosed in RM to the President of Congress, October 21, 1782, the briefer PPAmP extract in RM to Benjamin Franklin, January 11, 1783.

2. See the headnote to RM's contract with Wadsworth and Carter of October 12.

3. See Ezekiel Cornell to RM, October 5, and notes, for RM's involvement in the dispute between the Moving Army contractors and the beef subcontractors.

4. For previous problems with the mode of issuing rations, see Washington to RM, May 17–25, 1782, and notes.

5. The PPAmP extract begins with the next sentence and concludes at the end of the extract printed here.

6. Major General Henry Knox, Colonel Philip Van Cortlandt, and Lieutenant Colonel Jeremiah Olney have been previously identified. The other participants were Lieutenant Colonel Francis Barber (d. 1783) of the 1st New Jersey Regiment; Colonel Heman Swift of the 2d Connecticut Regiment; and Colonel Henry Jackson (1747–1809) of the 9th Massachusetts Regiment. Heitman, *Register;* and Boatner, *Encyclopedia of the American Revolution,* 547–548, 1085.

7. These words are not excised in the PPAmP extract.

8. See notes to Washington to RM, October 2.

From Jeremiah Wadsworth

Crompond [New York] Oct. 5th 1782

Dear sir,

Genl. Cornell writes you by this Express, how far we have advanced in the Contract.[1] The proposition he makes respecting the Bee[f] Contract with Phelps & Co. appears to me to be the probable means of saving you the trouble of an Arbitration with the Contractors. If you agree to it, I will do all in my power to reduce their price; and from a conversation I have had with their agent since I left General Cornell I am persuaded they had rather Secure part of their money by a compromise with me and discharge their other Contractors than risk a Suit to recover the whole. Genl Cornell writes you "the price is great." I do not believe you will think so, when every Circumstance is considered; and if you do, saying so will do you or the Continent no good, and may injure us. I am certain, that if I had asked more, the present Situation of the Army would have justified Genl. Cornell in giving it, and I had no doubt I could have obtained more of him when I asked that.

Colo Tilghmans Letter[2] to you will give you an Idea of the feelings of the Army, and their want of Pay. I assure you that every Man of them with whom I have conversed believes you have done more, much more than you was bound to do as a public Man; and nothing but real Distress will bring them to do or say anything that is disagreeable to you. I believe there has been some pains taken here as well as at Phila. to prejudice you; but it will finally do you no real injury: on the contrary the evil intended you will recoil on the Heads of your Enemies.

As Mr Carter will be on the way from Phila. I dont write him, but I hope he has taken some Measures with you to secure some Money to begin with, as all ours is in paper.[3] Whoever undertakes after the last of Decr. should be taking Measures now; especially for the salted Provisions. You will have other offers than W[adsworth] and Crs. and I doubt not on lower Terms than we can propose. If you can spare the time to write us, I wish to have your oppinion of the prices of Flour, Salted Pork &c. at Phila. in the month of Novr.—and as you have been so conversant in Contracts, ours being made, your advice, as to the execution, will be usefull and gratefully acknowledged.

I beg you will present my Compliments to Mr G. Morris. I will thank him for any Information he will give us. I am Dear sir your very humble Servant

J Wadsworth

Robt Morris Esqr

Copy

MS: LbC, Wadsworth and Carter Letterbook 3, CtHi.

1. See Ezekiel Cornell to RM, October 5, and notes. Wadsworth and John Carter were agents for supplying the French army. The firm was now negotiating a new contract for supplying West Point and the Moving Army, Wadsworth with Cornell in New York and Carter with RM in Philadelphia. For a discussion, see the headnote to the contract, dated October 12.

2. See the preceding letter.

3. For the dimensions of this problem, see notes to Diary, August 20.

To James Lovell

Office of Finance 5. Octo. 1782[1]

This serves to advise that I have this day drawn on you two Drafts. One in favor of Messrs. Mease and Caldwell or Order at twenty days sight for one thousand three hundred and thirty three Dollars $^{30}/_{90}$ and the other in favor of Mr. George Latimer or Order at the same Sight for five hundred Dollars. This Money I expect you will be enabled to pay out of the sales of Bills of Exchange which I have lately sent you.[2]

MS: Ofcl LbC, DLC.
1. Lovell was the receiver of Continental taxes for Massachusetts.
2. See RM to Lovell, October 3.

To Matthew Ridley

Philadelphia October 6th.1782[1]

My Dear Sir,

You will find enclosed herewith a Copy of what I wrote you the 8th July, since when your several letters of the 1st and 24th April, 22 June, 8th 11th and 13th July have reached me some of the originals and some Copies.[2] We lament here that you did not send the several Articles intended for Mrs. Morris and for the House by the Alliance Captain Barry, because she got safe and we are alarmed lest these same things were onboard L'Aigle Captain La Touche which is now in the hands of the Enemy, but we cannot learn any certainty that our things were or were not onboard.[3] Your letters say they are to come with the Marquies De la Fayette and this give[s] hopes that they may still be safe. After reading my letter of the 8th July, you will readily conclude that none of those which I have received from you are calculated to quiet my anxiety on account of my Sons, the loss of time at their Age can never be retrieved and I begin to apprehend that they may forever lament my determination to Educate them in Europe. When you found Geneva was not the proper place to fix them at, A proper place should have been sought and determined on immediately, Lausanne is said by many People to have as good or better Schools than Geneva, thither then they should have gone instantly, in short any place where their time would have been employed in the pursuit of proper branches of Education, was better than loosing it at Passy or Paris, forgive me my Dear Sir if my anxiety on this Subject should draw forth expressions that imply blame on your Conduct, were you in my place and I in yours, you would find it impossible to restrain yourself and Remember also that by accepting the charge you stand responsible untill you have acquitted yourself of it. I have not a Doubt of your determination to Execute all that you undertook but I fear you are not Sufficiently impressed with the importance of *Time* it is in every Stage of

life the most valuable part of our Inheritance if the days of youth
are mispent those of manhood pay the penalty. I will not say more
because I think your determinations must be taken and executed
before this letter can possibly reach you. These Boys must have a
finished Education and I shall not repine at any expence that is
proper and necessary to the attainment of it. I shall very soon place
some more Money with their Banker but you will always Remember
that they are only to be cloathed and Supplied with money just
Sufficient to put them on a Footing with the general Run of Boys at
the same Schools.

Your letter of the 24th April is only a Copy the original never
reached me consequently Bobs letter on your Illness, has not appeared, poor Fellows they write and indite but badly, their letters
however are very acceptable to us and we console ourselves with the
hope of amendment and improvement. Mrs. Morris puts great dependance on your attention to these Boys, She has your promises,
believes in them, and will exact a rigid performance, so see what
trouble you have brought on yourself by the offers which a Friendly
disposition prompted you to make.[4] I thank you for the Political
information contained in your letters. Peace seemed for a while to be
forceing herself suddenly upon us, and altho the prospect is not now
so strong and clear as it was yet it seems to me impossible that the
war can Continue much longer, The expence of the Belligerent
Powers in Europe must be immense, particularly to Great Britain,
and that People seem already tired of their Burthens, for my part I
wish most sincerely and ardently for Peace that I may get rid of a
most Troublesome Office and spend the Remainder of my Days
with more ease and in less hurry than those which are past. But was
I to confine myself to the Language of a Patriot, I should[5] speak in
another manner and tell you that a continuance of the War is Necessary untill our Confederation is more strongly knit, untill a Sense of[6]
the Obligations to Support it shall be more generally diffused
amongst all Ranks of American Citizens, untill we shall acquire[7] the
Habit of paying Taxes (The means we possess already) and untill the
Several Governments have derived from Experience and action that
Vigour and self Confidence which is necessary to ensure the safety
and promote the happiness of the People. The expence of the War,
as now conducted is not very heavy to this Country and the payment
of our Public Debt will hardly be felt by those that come after us, as
this Country has abundant Resources as yet untouched. In this View
of things Peace may not[8] be really so desireable as at first View[9] one
would think, and perhaps you may be surprized when I tell you that
in this City, The prospect of Peace has given more general discontent than any thing that has happened of a long time, particularly
amongst the mercantile part[10] of the Community, I have been much
surprized at it, but so is the Fact, however, again I repeat my wishes

for a speedy and Honorable Peace, it is Idle for Great Britain to think of wheedling us into a Seperate or disgracefull Peace—No man in this Country seriously thinks of such a Thing even the disaffected are convinced of the Impracticability of it. For my own part I will sooner Sacrifice all my prospects of ease and enjoyment throughout the whole course of my Life than consent to close the Contest by any Act derogatory to the Integrity, Honor and Glory of a Young and rising Nation. Your Friend Gouverneur and myself are great Slaves, our confinement is constant, our attention unceasing and my Anxiety great, but our Spirits carry us through and with some degree of Reputation, altho there are Enemies hanging on our Skirts constantly on the look out, and ready to run us down if they can get the least foot hold. If the strictest Integrity and an ardent desire to pursue and promote the true Interest of our Country, with close application to execute what we have undertaken, can secure us against the Envious, and Malicious, we shall have nothing to fear. If not, we will at least have nothing to reproach ourselves with.[11]

Holker is full of Schemes, I cannot pass much time with him nor enter into his Plans and Views, he will write every thing you wish on those Subjects and I shall ever be glad to promote his and your Views as far as in my Power. I had the Pleasure of seeing Mr. Pringle lately and like him much. I shall not have time to make use of Cypher therefore must refrain from the mention of some things that relate to Characters on your side the Atlantic, it is not however very material. Mrs. Morris desire[s] her most affectionate and Friendly Wishes for your Health and happiness may be presented to you and by you on her behalf[12] to Mrs Ridley, Miss Livingston the same, She poor Girl has been Ill this Nine Weeks but is mending. I am my Dear Friend, Yours most truely

Robt Morris

Mathew Ridley Esqr.

ENDORSED: Robert Morris/Philadelphia Octob 6 1782/Received Novem 5 1782/Answered Novem 20 1782.
MSS: LS, Ridley Papers, MHi; L[S], incomplete, Ridley Papers, MHi; extract, Jared Sparks Papers, MH.
1. Ridley, who had gone to Europe late in 1781 as Maryland state agent, was acting as guardian for RM's two eldest sons, Robert, Jr., and Thomas Morris (see RM to Ridley, October 14, 1781, and notes). The text printed here, carried by Captain Joshua Barney of the General Washington, was received by Ridley on November 5 and later endorsed by him under the dateline as having been answered on November 20 (see his reply of that date). Commas are frequently used in place of periods in this text, and the editors have in a few instances substituted the latter to break up extended passages. Minor variations in the incomplete L[S], which continues for approximately two-thirds of the letter (see note 10 below), have not been noted. In addition to the Sparks extract, a fourth text, no doubt an ADftS, has long since disappeared from the autograph market and has not been found. A portion of this text, described as an "A. L. S. with initials," was printed in Stan. V. Henkels' catalogue

no. 1183 (January 16, 1917), lot 70. This "Original rough draft" was again offered for sale by the Anderson Galleries on February 1–2, 1927, lot 37. For notes jotted down by RM in preparation for this letter, see the following document.

2. The letter of April 1 has not been found. The letters of July 8 and 11 are printed as postscripts to the June 22 letter. RM did not acknowledge and possibly did not receive Ridley's May 7 addendum to the April 24 letter. See the following document.

3. See RM to Vicomte de Noailles, September 25.

4. The Sparks extract begins with the next sentence.

5. This word is interlined in RM's hand. In the incomplete L[S] the word "might" is interlined in an unidentified hand.

6. The preceding three words are interlined in RM's hand. The phrase is not found in the incomplete L[S].

7. In the incomplete L[S]: "shall have acquired."

8. This word is interlined in RM's hand.

9. The preceding 13 words are omitted from the incomplete L[S].

10. Here the extant portion of the incomplete L[S] ends.

11. Save for the complimentary close, signature, and inside address, the Sparks extract ends here.

12. The preceding three words are interlined in RM's hand.

Memorandum of Letters from Matthew Ridley

[Philadelphia, on or before October 6, 1782][1]

1st April	Things for Mrs Morris, not sent per Barry—will per de Touche
	Boys Well—Geneva—Lauzanne
	purchase of Goods per Doctr Franklin not made
	Letters to Holker junr
24th April	Copy only. Original not received
	Bobs letter on his Illness not come to hand
22d June	Negotiating Continued
	Must make Peace at last
	Dutch no Seperate Peace
	Continuance of War usefull to them
	Marqs De Fayetts detention will delay Mrs Morris's things
	Boys, Geneva &c
	Bob Montgomery
	Count Vergennes Dictating &c
	Chevr. Luzerne and Secy
July 8	respecting Treaty of Peace
July 11th	English Ministers
July 13th	Geneva—Ministers of England

MS: AD, Robert Morris Papers, NN.

1. RM jotted these notes for the preceding reply to Ridley on the reverse side of a small sheet containing the July 11 postscript to Ridley's letter of June 22. That letter and another of July 13 did not reach RM until September (see notes to the July 13 letter for the arrival of the *Heer Adams* and *Sukey;* on the latter, see also RM to Thomas Barclay, September 23). Of the letters recorded in the memorandum, only that of April 1 has not been found; RM, however, did not acknowledge Ridley's May 7 addendum to the April 24 letter. The communication of July 8 was also a postscript to the June 22 letter.

Diary: October 7, 1782

Capt. Ths. Truxen and Mr Randal his Partner[1] Called on me this Morning and informed that they are Creditors of Monsr C. P. Ra-

guet a french Merchant who had been sometime Settled and transacting considerable Business in this City, that he owes them £5,000
and they were informed by himself that he owed to the Supert. of
Finance about £2,900 on Account of Bills of Exchange bought of the
Broker,[2] that they were well informed he owed large Sums to many
People and that his Effects are so scattered over the World as to
convince them it is time to secure their Debt in the best manner they
can. They therefore Propose to purchase a new Ship which he has
lately Launched as he agrees to let them have her at first Cost; they
propose that I should join in this Purchase and hold concern to the
Account of the Debt. I informed them that Don Francisco Rendon
had mentioned this very thing to me on Friday last, that the said Mr
Rendon is a Creditor to Monsr. Raguet to the Amount of 5,000
Dolls. and that I had determined to make this purchase so as to
include Mr. Rendon that however I would join them in it, provided
Mr. Rendon was included. This they agreed to and went to finish
the Bargain with Monsr. Raguet.[3]

Mr. John Perry Called and informed me that Colo. Blaine is returned. I sent for the Latter who adheres to his bargain, says he will
enter into the Contract for Fort Pitt and give Security for Performance, but that he cannot join Mr Perry having before agreed to
join a Mr Wilson who is to execute the Business.[4]

Mr. Francis Hopkinson applied for payment of a Certificate of
pay due to him as one of the late navy Board. I promised to
Consider of it.

Como. Gillon called respecting the Hessian Soldiers which he
wants to enlist on Board his Ship. I told him that altho my Sentiments on that Subject differ from Genl. Lincoln's, yet I am unwilling
to give an Opposition that may cause any Delay to his Cruise but that
I am of the Opinion he or the State of Carolina ought to enter into a
positive Security for the eighty Dollars per head which the Hessians
are to pay for their Liberation. He refused to give such Security but
will agree to pay the same from Prize money agreeable to Genl.
Lincoln's report.[5] I again reminded Commodore Gillon that my
Duty as an Officer calls upon me to seek Justice from him to the
United States for breech of his Contract with Colo. Laurens &c. and
desired him to be prepared for a Suit which Duty and not inclination
obliges me to Commence.[6]

I sent for Mr Rendon and informed him of the Steps taken with
Monsr. Raguet which he very much approves.

Mr. Jos. Hilborn[7] being possessed of Genl. Green's Drafts on me
Called for the Money which I am not able to pay at present but
promised payment as fast as money came in, or Bills of Exchange
now. He departed and soon after sent for the Bills of Exchange.

Capt. Saml. Nicholson called and Urged for my Opinion on the proceedings of the Court of Enquiry which I am not ready to give.[8] He then pressed for money. I ordered 100 Dolls. for the present.

Mr. Andw. Doz for money. I promised the payment of his last Certificate very speedily.

Colo. Seth Warner for money due him for former Services.[9] I recommended his getting his Accounts Settled, but assured him no money can now be paid thereon.

Mr. Mordecai Sheftal called respecting his Memorial to Congress referred to me a few Days since.[10] I read the same and shewed him that the Commissioner of the Commissaries Department can alone settle his Accounts and that if Settled no Money can now be paid thereon.

After sending repeatedly for the Clothier Genl. the Deputy Clothier[11] came. I delivered to him the List of Articles wanted for the Albany Indians as reported by the Secretary at War[12] [and] desired he would enquire if those Articles can be had at what Price and on what Credit.

Monsr. Du Tretre and Monsr. La Forest paid their Visit (to take leave) and I gave them a Letter to Capt. Barney authorizing him to take them Passengers to France agreeable to the request of the Minister of France.[13]

Como. Hazelwood for Money, granted 1,000 Dollars.

Honble. Mr. Holker applied by Letter for money on Account of the Cloathing,[14] and I ordered a payment in Bills of Exchange equal to £1550 Currency.[15]

This Night we compleated our Letters and dispatched Capt. Barney in the Washington Packett for France.[16]

Wrote a Letter to his Excellency the Presdt. of Congress.

Wrote a Letter to Danl. St. Thomas Jenifer Esqr.

Wrote a Letter to Genl. Irwine.

Issued a Warrant on Mr Swanwick in favor Jos. Pennell £37.10.0.

1. Thomas Truxtun, a prominent privateer captain and owner, was a partner in Thomas Randall and Company. A New York City sea captain and merchant, Randall (ca. 1723–1797), withdrew to Elizabeth, New Jersey, in 1776 where he sent out privateers commissioned by the New York Provincial Congress. He subsequently moved to Philadelphia and after the war returned to New York and became a stockholder of the Bank of New York. See Eugene S. Ferguson, *Truxtun of the Constellation: The Life of Commodore Thomas Truxtun, U.S. Navy, 1755–1822* (Baltimore, 1956), 48, 50; John Austin Stevens, Jr., ed., *Colonial Records of the New York Chamber of Commerce, 1769–1784* (New York, 1867), II, 157–158; and East, *Business Enterprise*, 191, 328.

2. Haym Salomon.

3. For the background to this entry, see Diary, September 2, and notes.

4. See Diary, September 30, and notes.

5. Lincoln's report has not been found. See RM to Gillon, and to the Secretary at War, both October 8.

6. See Diary, September 19, and notes.

7. Joseph Hilbourn (1732–1802), apparently a Quaker merchant, who had been treasurer of the Pennsylvania Hospital from 1773 to 1780. See Labaree and Willcox, eds., *Franklin Papers*, XX, 450n., 451.

8. RM's determination is printed under date of October 17.

9. Formerly commander of an additional or separate Continental regiment, Warner (1743/1744–1784) retired when the unit was disbanded on January 1, 1781. *DAB;* Heitman, *Register;* and Fred Anderson Berg, *Encyclopedia of Continental Army Units: Battalions, Regiments and Independent Corps* (Harrisburg, Pa., 1972), 134–135.

10. Sheftall's memorial has not been found, but was described by a congressional committee as "setting forth that the loss of several of his official papers when he was made prisoner at Savannah makes it impossible for him to settle his accounts in the regular method and praying relief and also that a sum of money may be paid to him." Congress referred it to RM on October 4. Concerning Sheftall's claims, see John L. Clarkson to Sheftall, February 1, 1782, and notes.

11. Jacob S. Howell.

12. The report of Benjamin Lincoln and "an Estimate of Cloathing necessary for the Oneida and other Tribes of Indians reported by the Commissioners for Indian Affairs Northern Department" have not been found. Congress had referred them to RM on September 24. See also *JCC,* XXIII, 524–525.

13. See Diary, September 9, and RM to Joshua Barney, October 7 (second letter). Antoine René Charles Mathurin de La Forest, a member of the French legation at Philadelphia, was carrying Chevalier de La Luzerne's dispatches to Vergennes (see Benjamin Franklin to RM, December 14, 1782). The other passenger, Captain Du Tertre, had been wounded while serving with the French forces at Yorktown; the editors have been unable to determine whether he was Joseph Jacob Du Tertre, a Frenchman who came to the United States by way of Santo Domingo during the winter of 1778–1779. See Amblard Marie Raymond Amédée, Vicomte de Noailles, *Marins et soldats français en Amérique pendant la Guerre de l'indépendance des Etats-Unis* (1778–1783) (Paris, 1903), 240; and PCC, no. 41, VII, 33–48.

14. John Holker's letter has not been found. On the clothing, see RM's agreement with him of November 2, 1781.

15. A copy of RM's warrant on Michael Hillegas, the Treasurer of the United States, dated October 7, 1782, with a copy of Peter Marmie's receipt to John Swanwick, is in the Holker Papers, MiU-C.

16. The letters are listed in notes to RM to Barney, October 7 (first letter).

To Joshua Barney

Marine Office 7 October 1782[1]

Sir,

With this you will receive sundry Letters which you will make up in such Manner that in Case of Capture they may be sunk before you strike your Colours. I hope however that you may meet a happier Fate. You will make the first Port which you can arrive at in Europe. France will be better than any other Port. The various Letters which may be directed to private Individuals you will put in the Post office but the public Letters you will yourself take Charge of and proceed with all possible Expedition to Paris where you will deliver them. Enclosed are Letters of Introduction.[2] Any necessary Expences for the Ship will be defrayed by Mr Barclay the american Consul to whom you will apply for that Purpose. If you arrive at L'Orient you will probably find him there. You will take Mr. Franklins Orders after you get to France for your Departure and Destination. He may perhaps direct you to call at some Port in the West Indies in which Case he will give you ample Instructions.

As your safe and speedy arrival is of great Importance you will take Care not to Chace any Vessel but to avoid as much as possible every Thing which can either delay or endanger you.

I hope your Expenditures in Europe may be moderate for we can ill afford any which are unnecessary and I trust your Continuance there will be but short. You will shew this Letter to Mr Franklin when you see him and he will probably be able in some short Time to determine your future Movements. Should you return to America I think it will be safest as the Enemy are now about to evacuate Charlestown and it will be in mid Winter when you arrive that you should fall in to the Southward and run up the Coast into the Chesapeak but of this you will determine according to your own Discretion and be directed by Circumstances as they arise.[3] I am Sir your most obedient and humble Servant

RM

MS: AM LbC, MdAN.

1. Lieutenant Barney was captain of the *General Washington,* a ship purchased during the summer by RM for Continental use as a packet to Europe. For the background to these instructions and Barney's role in bringing back money from France, see notes to RM to Le Couteulx and Company, September 24; see also Diary, October 7, and RM's second letter of this date to Barney.

2. Among the "private" letters carried by Barney were RM to Vicomte to Noailles, September 25, and the September 27 letter to Marquis de Lafayette mentioned in the notes thereto, RM to Matthew Ridley, October 6, and Gouverneur Morris to Ridley, October 7. The "public Letters" from the Office of Finance borne by Barney, the most important of which related to the proposed loan from France for 1783 and RM's plan for importing specie from Havana, were RM to Le Couteulx and Company, September 24 and 27, to Jacques, Louis and Laurent Le Couteulx and Company, September 24, to the Willinks, van Staphorsts, and de la Lande and Fynje, September 24 (two letters) and September 28 (two letters), to Thomas Barclay, September 23 and 25, to Ferdinand Grand, September 24, 25, 28, 30, and October 1 and 7, to John Adams, September 25, 27, and October 7, to John Jay, October 7, to Benjamin Franklin, September 25, 27 (two letters), September 28 and 30, and October 1, 5, and 7, and RM's letter to Franklin, Adams, and Jay, September 25. For Barney's letters of introduction, see RM to Franklin, Jay, Lafayette, Adams, and William Carmichael, October 7.

Barney also carried official dispatches from Secretary for Foreign Affairs Robert R. Livingston to Franklin, Adams, Henry Laurens, and C. W. F. Dumas. See their acknowledgments of letters received in Wharton, ed., *Rev. Dipl. Corr.,* V, 854, VI, 5, 110, 138; for the significance of their arrival, see Richard Oswald's reports from Paris to Thomas Townshend, British Secretary of State for the Colonies, in Morris, ed., *John Jay: Winning of the Peace,* 407, 412, 418, 421. Copies of Thomas Paine's *Letter Addressed to the Abbe Raynal* also went by Barney (see notes to Paine to RM, September 6). For the dispatches sent on the *General Washington* by Chevalier de La Luzerne, the French minister at Philadelphia, see Franklin to RM, December 14, 1782.

3. The *General Washington* reached Lorient on October 30 or 31 after a swift voyage of 22 or 23 days; Barney arrived in Paris with the dispatches from RM and Livingston on November 5. Departing Lorient on January 17 bearing the preliminary articles of the peace treaty, 600,000 livres in specie advanced from the French loan of 1783, and a British passport, the *General Washington* arrived at Philadelphia on March 12, 1783. See Powers, "Decline and Extinction of American Naval Power," 131–133; [Thomas Barclay] to Franklin, [January 1783], Hays, comp., *Calendar of Franklin Papers,* IV, 90; notes to Matthew Ridley to Gouverneur Morris, October 10, 1782; and Diary, March 12, 1783.

To Benjamin Franklin

Office of Finance 7th. October 1782

Sir

Captain Barney having been detained until this Day and it being probable that he will not arrive in Europe so early as I expected I am very doubtful whether it would be proper to send him to the Havanna but think it would be better he should return immediately hither because it is likely that the Negotiation I proposed will consume more time than he can spare.[1] His Ship is small but she sails remarkably well and will therefore give us a good Chance of being well informed of the Situation of our Affairs. If there is likely to be any Delay or Difficulty in the Havanna Plan it will be best that you endeavor to obtain the Shipment of a considerable Sum in Europe on Board some of the King's frigates. At any Rate, we must have Money and I think you may venture fifty thousand Crowns by this Vessel.[2] You will see that Capt. Barney is put under your Directions and is to wait your Instructions but I must at the same time inform you that Congress have directed his Ship to be purchased and sent to France among other Things for the Purpose of obtaining a better Communication with their Servants and more frequent and accurate Intelligence from Europe.[3] You will see therefore the Propriety of dispatching her as speedily as possible and I think we may probably fall upon Ways and Means to afford you frequent Opportunities of writing with a great Chance of Security. I am Sir your most obedient and humble Servant[4]

Robt Morris

His Excellency Benjamin Franklin Esqr.

ENDORSED: Office of Finance/Oct. 7. 1782
MSS: LS, Franklin Papers, PPAmP; LS marked "3d.," PPIn; Ofcl LbC, DLC.

1. See RM to Franklin, October 1.
2. In his ship, the *General Washington*, returning under a flag guaranteeing safe passage, Barney brought back 600,000 livres, more than the 50,000 crowns (300,000 livres) requested. For the "Havanna Plan," see notes to RM to Le Couteulx and Company, September 24.
3. See Diary, August 26, and notes.
4. This letter to Franklin was carried by Captain Barney. See the preceding letter.

To Benjamin Franklin

(By C[ipher] No 4)   Office of Finance 7th October 1782

Dear Sir

In a Letter of the second Instant which I have just now received from the Head Quarters of the American Army is the following Paragraph:[1] "In short, my dear Sir, the Want of Money gives rise to so many complaints and uneaseinesses, that with out a portion of it, I fear this infection will spread from Officer to soldier. It is most vexatious to see the parade of the states upon every occasion; They declare in the most pompous manner that they will never make peace but upon their own terms,[2] and yet call upon them for the support of the war, and you may as well call upon the dead. If they persist in their present accursed system, I do not see but they must accept Peace upon any terms." I am Sir your most obedient Servant[3]

Robt Morris

His Excellency Benjm. Franklin Esqr.

PS. I would have sent the whole Letter from which this is extracted but I have not time to put it in Cypher.

ENDORSED: Office of Finance/Oct. 7. 1782/Letter from Head Quarters/decyphered
MSS: LS, part in cipher with interlinear decipherment, Franklin Papers, PPAmP; Dft in the writing of Gouverneur Morris, Franklin Papers, CtY; deciphered copy, Correspondance politique, Etats-Unis, AMAE; LS marked "Triplicate," part in cipher, Sol Feinstone Collection, PPAmP; LS marked "4th," part in cipher, NSyU; Ofcl LbC, part in cipher, DLC.

1. The complete text of the October 2 letter has not been found. Guided by usage in the CtY and AMAE texts, the editors have supplied quotation marks for the extract, which is written in a cipher previously employed in RM's encoded letters to Franklin. The decipherment reproduced here was written interlinearly on the manuscript by an unidentified amanuensis of Franklin's. The misleading parenthetical notation at the top of the letter was probably written in the same hand; for an explanation, see notes to RM to Franklin, September 28.

2. On the state declarations regarding conditions for peace and support of the French alliance, see notes to the Secretary of Congress to RM, May 7, 1782; and Gouverneur Morris to John Jay, August 6.

3. This letter to Franklin was carried by Captain Joshua Barney of the *General Washington* (see RM's first letter to Barney of this date). The AMAE text was sent by Franklin to Vergennes. See notes to RM to Franklin, September 27 (first letter).

From George Washington

Head Quarters [Verplancks Point, New York]. 7th Octo. 1782
Sir

Applications are making to me from the States individually, respecting the Exchanges of marine prisoners, which are in their respective possession.

As I consider myself to have no Agency in this Matter, and must expect to be constantly teized in this Business, unless it is put into a more Systematical Train than at present, I must beg that you will be so good, as to relieve me in this instance, by sending on some person from you, or authorizing some one here, who may under your Instructions have the general Superintendence and direction of these proposed Exchanges.[1] I am &c.

GW

Hono Robert Morris Esqr

MSS: Dft in the writing of Jonathan Trumbull, Jr., Washington Papers, DLC; Varick transcript, Washington Papers, DLC.

1. On the exchange of marine prisoners and RM's appointment of George Turner as commissary for marine prisoners on October 15, see notes to Diary, June 18, 1782.

From William Whipple

Portsmouth [New Hampshire] 7th Octor 1782

Sir

I am Honoured with Your Letters of the 12th of last month[1] with the inclosures also one of the 17th. I have been f[l]attered with the Expectation of receiving some money in the Course of last month, but my disappointment lays me under the disagreeable necessity of informing you that I have not yet received a Shilling. I have the Honor of being &c

Honble Robt Morris Esqr

MS: LbC, Whipple Letterbook, John Langdon Papers, PHi.

1. This was RM's Circular to the Receivers of Continental Taxes. Whipple was the receiver for New Hampshire.

To John Adams

Philada. Octr. 7th. 1782[1]

Some of my Friends and yours have requested a letter of Introduction for Mr Robert Gilmore of Baltimore, a Gentleman whom they assure me will be found deserving of every service you can render or Notice you may find convenient to take of him. Mr Gilmore is not personally known to me neither am I fond of giving Letters of Recommendation, but it is not always in our power to Refuse and the Gentlemen who apply for this Merit my utmost attention. I shall thank you for the favours Mr Gilmore may experience at your hands and remain Your Excellencys Most obedient and humble servant

MS: Copy signed by and in the writing of RM, Robert Morris Papers, NN.

1. This private letter, addressed to Adams at the Hague, was carried by Captain Joshua Barney of the *General Washington* (see RM's first letter to Barney of October 7) and delivered to Adams at Paris. See Adams to RM, November 6.

To Joshua Barney

Marine Office 7 Octo: 1782

This Letter will be delivered to you by M: du Tertré a Captain in the Service of his most Christian Majesty and Mr. de La Forest Secretary of Commerce. These are the Gentlemen whom I formerly spoke to you of and who are recommended to me by the Minister of France to go in your Ship to Europe. I recommend them to your Attention being perswaded that you will Endeavor to render their Passage as agreable as you can.[1]

MS: AM LbC, MdAN.

1. Lieutenant Barney was captain of the *General Washington*. See the first letter of this date to him.

To the President of Congress
(John Hanson)

Marine Office October 7th 1782

I hope Your Excellency and Congress will excuse me for troubling them with the Extract of a Letter I have received from Captain Jones.[1] I cannot resist the desire of laying Sentiments which do him so much Honor before my Sovereign who I am well perswaded will always feel a disposition to do justice to so meritorious an officer.

MSS: LS, PCC, DNA; AM LbC, MdAN.

1. Jones's letter is dated September 22. The endorsement on this covering letter from RM indicates that it was read in Congress on October 9.

To the President of Congress
(John Hanson)

Office of Finance 7th October 1782

I think it my Duty to enclose for the Inspection of Congress the Extract of a Letter just now received from William C. Houston Esqr. Receiver of Taxes for New Jersey dated on the fifth Instant.[1]

MSS: LS, PCC, DNA; Ofcl LbC, DLC.

1. According to its endorsement, this letter and its enclosure were read in Congress on October 9.

To Benjamin Franklin, John Jay,
Marquis de Lafayette, John Adams, and
William Carmichael

Marine Office 7th. October 1782[1]

This Letter will be delivered to you by Joshua Barney Esqr. a Lieutenant in the Navy of the United States and now commanding the Packet Ship Washington. This young Gentleman is an Active, gallant Officer, who has already behaved very well on many Occasions, and I recommend him to your particular Notice and Attention from the Conviction that this Conduct will do Honor to those by whom he is patronized and introduced.

MSS: LS, to Franklin, Franklin Papers, PPAmP; LS, to Jay, Jay Papers, NNC; LS, to Adams, Adams Papers, MHi; AM LbC, MdAN.

1. The addressees are given in the AM LbC. All but Carmichael, the American chargé d'affaires in Spain, were in France when Barney arrived.

To Ferdinand Grand

Office of Finance 7. Octo: 1782[1]

Since my Letter to you of the first Instant which comes by this Opportunity I have further drawn on you twenty eight Setts of Bills of Exchange amounting to one hundred and eighty four thousand, nine hundred and forty Livres Tournois in favor of different Persons as mentioned in the enclosed List[2] which as well as my former Bills you will be pleased to Honor and punctually Pay on Account of the United States of North America.

P.S. Should I have Occasion to make any further Drafts on you before the departure of Capt. Barney must beg you will honor them, tho perhaps I may not have Time to forward a Letter of Advice.

MS: Ofcl LbC, DLC.
1. Grand was banker to the United States in Paris. This letter to him was carried by Captain Joshua Barney of the *General Washington*. See RM's first letter to Barney of this date.
2. Enclosure not found.

To William Irvine

Office of Finance 7. Octo: 1782

I do myself the honor to enclose a Letter from his Excelly. the President and Supreme Executive Council of this State to you,[1] whereby you will perceive they have assigned the Money sent by Mr. Carnaghan [Carnahan] to be held to my Order. Colo. Ephm. Blaine having undertaken to supply your Garrison I shall very soon transmit you a Copy of the Contract and Directions for the Application of these four thousand Dollars in the mean while you will hold them Subject to my future Orders.

MS: Ofcl LbC, DLC.
1. Brigadier General William Irvine was the commanding officer at Fort Pitt. For the enclosed letter, see Diary, October 5, and notes.

To John Jay

Office of Finance 7. Octo: 1782[1]

I have to acknowledge the Receipt of your Letter of the twenty eighth of April to the Contents of which I shall pay the proper Attention. I am so much engaged that I cannot write to you particularly the State of Things here and must therefore refer you to Doctor Franklin. I enclose in a Number of Packets the News Papers of this City for about three Months past which will perhaps be both of Use and Amusement to you.

MS: Ofcl LbC, DLC.
1. The American minister to Spain, Jay was currently serving as a peace commissioner in Paris. This letter was carried by Captain Joshua Barney of the *General Washington*. See RM to Barney, October 7 (first letter).

To Daniel of St. Thomas Jenifer

Philadelphia 7. Octo: 1782[1]

I have already informed our mutual Friend Thomas Stone Esqr. that the Appointment of the Collectors of 5 per Cent Impost remains in Congress and that I apprehend your Delegates will be called upon to Nominate. It will always afford me pleasure to render Service to Gentlemen of such worthy Character as Colo. Stone.

MS: Ofcl LbC, DLC.
1. Jenifer was Maryland's intendant of the revenue. On the subject of this letter, see the Draft Ordinance for the Five Percent Impost, printed as Appendix I to this volume.

Robert Morris and Jacob Morris to Edmund Randolph

Philada. October 7th. 1782[1]

The late Major Genl. Charles Lee ⟨being?⟩ having come to this City in order to perfect the Sale of His Estate in Berkley County Virginia was suddenly seized with a Fever and died last Week. He had entered into a Contract with a Mr. John Vaughan for the Sale of Estate but the Conveyance is not actually made. It is said Genl. Lee made a Will at Frederick Town in Maryland and deposited the same with some of his Friends in that State. We have sent an Express to find out the Person who has it in possession in order that it may be opened and his Executors known. In the mean time it is said here that there are Persons who have intentions to administer. We therefore Request that you will enter a Caveat and stop all proceedings untill Genl Lee's Will shall be found or rather untill we shall be ⟨perfectly⟩ satisfied. One of us, Mr. Robert Morris, has at various times advanced Monies for Genl. Lee and is the largest Creditor of the Deceased, the other Mr Jacob Morris was the Genls Aid in days of service in the american Army, enjoyed his Confidence and appears now on behalf of the Family and Heirs of Genl Lee, besides that he has conducted and advanced the monies for his Funeral. These Circumstances will We apprehend justify you in entering a caveat on our behalf as they also entitle us to see that his affairs fall into proper hands and we depend that no Administration will be granted in your state but with our Consent. We have the Honor to be with great Respect, Sir Your Obedient humble Servants

MS: Dft in RM's hand, Robert Morris Papers, NN.
1. This unsigned, private letter to Randolph, the attorney general of Virginia, was addressed to him at Richmond. The authors have been supplied by the editors on the basis of internal evidence. On Jacob Morris and the background to this letter, see Diary, October 3, and notes.

Gouverneur Morris to Matthew Ridley

Phila: 7 Octr. 1782[1]

I write a few Words to assure you of my Remembrance and Esteem. I am in the Midst of so many other Things that if you would see me you would I am sure be led to think there was a Value even in the little which I can write. I dare not touch on Politics because I have not time to write you fully, half Information is worse than none. Always remember me and believe me yours

P.S. I will write to you fully at my first Leisure. My Watch is not arrived.

MS: ALS, Ridley Papers, MHi.
1. This letter was one of several private communications carried by Captain Joshua Barney of the *General Washington* (see RM's first letter to him of this date and notes). The endorsement indicates that Ridley received it on November 5 and replied on November 20, 1782.

From Samuel Hodgdon

Philadelphia Octo 7th 1782

The Month being expired since the Gunsmiths received the first payment on their accounts in Notes drawn at sixty days sight, they Unitedly apply for the second payment. You will recollect you desired me to inform them they should receive their full dues in those drafts within three Months in Monthly payments—agreeable to which is the present application. The sum due as at the first payment is six hundred and fifty dollars, for which when notified I will do my self the honour to wait on you.[1]

MS: LbC, WDC, DNA.
1. See Diary, October 9. Hodgdon was the commissary general of military stores.

From the Register of the Treasury (Joseph Nourse)

[Philadelphia] Registers Office 7th October 1782[1]

The United States in Congress Assembled, by their Act of the   [2] August 1781 on a Report of the Board of Treasury having ordered the whole Amount of the Honble Arthur Lee's Expenditures in Europe for Cloathing Shipped on public Account, his ordinary and extraordinary Expences and his Salary as foreign Minister to his Credit, On the 20th August last with the concurrence of the Comptroller, I closed the Accounts of Mr Lee's Transactions in the Treasury Books.

When I had the honor of laying an Estimate of the home public Debt before you on the 16th July 1782[3] (his Accounts not being then entered) I grounded the Ballance of 7,150$^{51}\!/\!_{90}$ Dollars on a State of his Account of Salary made by the late Auditors, not recurring to an Order of the late Board of the 10th August 1781 on Thomas Smith Esqr. Loan Officer of the State of Pennsylvania, for payment of the whole Amount of Salary in Loan Office Certificates of Specie Value[4] for 9,950 Dollars $^{55}\!/\!_{90}$ payable in one Year with Interest from the Day of Issuing. The Act of Congress allowing the whole Amount of Money received in Europe to his Credit, on his honorary Declaration, that the same had been paid on public Account occasioned the difference. As I have charged the general Account open in the public Book of "Salaries and Expences allowed to foreign Ministers and Agents" All Mr Lee's Accounts are finally closed, his demand now resting on the public Security of the Specie Loan Office Certificates to the amount of nine thousand nine hundred and fifty Dollars, fifty five ninetieths of a Dollar.

Permit me to apologize for the oversight, which has occasioned my troubling you with this Letter being with the greatest respect Sir your most obedient and most humble Servant
(Copy)

MS: Copy, PCC, DNA.
1. This letter was enclosure no. 3 in RM to the President of Congress, November 14, 1782. For a discussion, see notes to Arthur Lee to RM, October 5.
2. Space left blank in manuscript. The act was that of August 6, 1781.
3. This estimate is printed as the enclosure to RM to the President of Congress, July 29.
4. On these specie certificates, see notes to RM's Circular to the Continental Loan Officers, October 13, 1781.

Diary: October 8, 1782

This Day I dispatched Mr Jesse Browne Express for the Eastern States.

Mr. Geo Eddy Called respecting the Tobacco bought by Mr Clarke, from whom I have not received Advice by this Post.

Mr Jno. Perry Called respecting Fort Pitt Contract. I informed him what had passed with Mr Blaine on that Subject and delivered him my Letters for Genl. Irwin.[1]

Sundry Persons for Money but I was much employed with Dispatches for the Post Office &c.

| Wrote a Letter to Como. Gillon and the Secy at War. | His Excelly the Govr. of Maryland. |
| Wrote a Letter to Benjm. Harwood Esqr. | His Excelly the Govr of Virginia. |

1. For the letters, see RM to William Irvine, October 7, and notes.

To Alexander Gillon

Office of Finance 8. Octo: 1782[1]

Sir

The Reference to take Order which Congress have been pleased to make to the Secretary of War and myself of his Report of the third Instant on a Motion for permitting you to enlist fifty German Prisoners subjects the Decision on that Subject to our Discretion and consequently renders us responsible.[2] I conferred on the Subject with the Secretary Yesterday and he declared to me his Opinion that his Report ought to be carried into Effect. It was my opinion and I declared it to you that some responsible Persons should engage for the Payment of the Liberation Money at a precise Period to be fixed for the Purpose. I in Consequence proposed it to you which you declined.[3] I have every Disposition to promote the Views of South Carolina and to facilitate the Departure of the Ship (tho I must remark that there is Nothing in the Report from whence it can be collected that the State is at all interested) but I do not think this Matter is put upon a proper footing. If it is to be considered as a meer personal Application from you there can be no Reason why you should have a Preference over any other Citizen of the United States and Consequently no good Reason can be assigned for refusing to accept of similar Terms from any other Citizen. And the Terms appear to me to be Nothing more than to receive the Liberation Money when the Party liberated shall have earned it except that there is in your Case an Addition of Risque without any adequate Compensation. As a Bargain therefore with an Individual it is not such as ought in my Opinion to be made.

But if this Matter is to be considered as on an Application from the State of South Carolina for aid in manning a Frigate to cruize against the common Enemy then I think it is equally improper for any Thing to be stipulated in Compensation by the United States. The People should be considered in the same Point of View as if they enlisted in the federal Army. Their Services should secure their Freedom and the Prize Money which is in Lieu of Wages should be their own Property.[4]

The enclosed Letter to General Lincoln[5] contains my Sentiments on the Subject. If he continues of his Opinion I will not impede the Progress of the Business in this Stage tho I confess to you candidly that I would not have agreed to it in it's present Form had it originally been submitted to me. I am Sir your most obedient Servant

RM

mss: Ofcl LbC, DLC; copy, Benjamin Lincoln Papers, MHi.

1. Commodore Gillon of the South Carolina navy was commander of the state frigate *South Carolina,* which was refitting at Philadelphia.

2. The act of Congress is not recorded in the *Journals.* For a discussion of the antecedents, see notes to Diary, May 1, 1782.

3. See Diary, October 7. Concerning the "Liberation Money," see the July 11, 1782, instructions of RM and Secretary at War Benjamin Lincoln.

4. For the 52 Germans enlisted on the *South Carolina* and retaken when the British captured the ship, see their original depositions in the Lossberg Papers, Marburg Preussisches Staatsarchiv, Militaria O.W.S. 1268 (photostats: DLC no. CXXXIX, box 2426, fols. 140–155); English translations in the Guy Carleton Papers, PRO, are briefly calendared in *Report on American Manuscripts in the Royal Institution,* III, 314–315. For these references the editors are indebted to Lion G. Miles of West Stockbridge, Massachusetts.

5. Dated October 8.

To Benjamin Harwood

Office of Finance 8th October 1782

Sir

I have been favored with your Letter dated at Annapolis on the first Instant with its Enclosure.[1] I agree that you shall receive the Notes of Mr. Pierce the Paymaster General[2] on account of the Taxes payable by your State on the same Terms as Bank Notes or those Signed by me. I am Sir Your most obedient Servant

Robt Morris

Benjamin Harwood Esqr.
Receiver for Maryland

endorsed: Robt. Morris/8th. Octr. 1782
mss: LS, Morris-Harwood Papers, MdHi; Ofcl LbC, DLC.

1. Harwood had just assumed office as receiver of Continental taxes for Maryland. His letter and enclosure have not been found, but the latter may have been his first account of tax receipts, dated September 30 and totalling $23,240, as listed in PCC, no. 137, III, 377.

2. On Pierce's promissory notes, see RM to Washington, January 26, 1782 (second letter), and notes.

To the Governor of Maryland
(Thomas Sim Lee)

Office of Finance 8. Octo: 1782

Sir,

I had the Honor to receive your Excellency's favor of the first Instant Yesterday afternoon. On the arrival of the Troops you mention the Secretary at War will doubtless make Application for every necessary they may stand in Need of and you may rely on my Disposition to obtain them for which no Efforts shall be omitted. If the Troops could have proceeded without Shoes they could have been furnished by the Cloathier General who obtains very good ones on Contract at from eight and four to eight and six per Pair. Would but the several States comply fully and punctually with the Requisitions of Congress you may rely on it that every Corps in our Army would be amply provided with every Thing which they could rightfully ask for. This would spare to your Excellency and to every other Gentleman charged with public Administration many anxious Cares and many painful Emotions. With perfect Esteem and Respect I have the Honor to be your Excellency's most obedient Servant

RM

MS: Ofcl LbC, DLC.

To the Governor of Virginia
(Benjamin Harrison)

Office of Finance 8. Octo: 1782

Sir,

I had the honor to receive your Excellency's Letter of the twenty third of September yesterday afternoon. The Business it relates to is very important and will command my Attention. I could wish to have received it some Days sooner as I yesterday made up my Dispatches to go by a Packet to France. I will write to your Excellency fully by the next Opportunity but in the Interim I pray you to be assured of my Disposition to comply with your Wishes and to the utmost of my Abilities to forward the Interest and promote the Convenience of the State over which you preside.

RM

MS: Ofcl LbC, DLC.

To the Secretary at War
(Benjamin Lincoln)

Office of Finance 8th October 1782

Sir,

I do myself the Honor to enclose the Copy of my Letter to Mr Gillon[1] in this which he will deliver to you. I need add Nothing to what I have said. If you think with me I will freely join you in a Letter to Congress: If not, let me know your Determination, and I will have a proper Obligation drawn for Mr. Gillon and Mr. Stanley to execute. I assure you that Nothing would induce me to go into this Measure but the Respect I have for your Opinion, and my Idea that it was the Intention of Congress it should be adopted. I am, Sir, With Esteem and Respect your most obedient and humble Servant

Robt Morris

Honorable Secretary at War

ENDORSED: R. Morris/8th Octr: 1782
MSS: LS, Stark-Morris Papers, Frank Streeter Collection, NhIIi; Ofcl LbC, DLC.
  1. Dated October 8.

From Sands, Livingston and Company

Fishkill [New York] October 8th, 1782[1]

Sir:

Mr. R. Sands informs us, that you have advanced him 1,000 dollars in specie, and of the 20,000 in your notes, requested in ours of the 25th ultimo you have given him 5,000,[2] and that you did not choose to make any greater advances till you heard from Gen. Cornell. By this time we presume you have, and that he has informed you, in consequence of your instructions to him, that he refused giving us any assurances of indemnification at the close of the contract, or make any advances of money under three months.[3] This is so directly contrary to all your former promises, that we are at a loss to account for it. As honest men we have performed our part of the contract, and had we been punctually paid, we could have gone through it with ease, and made a very great saving, both to ourselves and the public. You have refused to give that assurance of indemnification we were justly entitled to, and have given the contract to others at 3d. per ration more than you gave us;[4] had you offered us the one-half of what you give them more, we would have continued through the year. When we found your inability to pay us specie, we calculated to take as many of your notes as we could put off; this relieved us some; and when we requested the last 20,000 dollars, it was not a third of the sum due us in specie, and we did not expect to be disappointed in them.

We some time past drew a bill on Mr. R. Sands, for 1,500 dollars, in favor of Mr. Duer, which is discounted at the bank, and will be due in a few days, which we request you will advance him in specie to that amount, in season to prevent its being protested.

Our accounts are now making out, and you shall, in a few days, have a state of the whole, when the contractors will all, personally, wait on you, and they expect that justice done them, they are so justly entitled to. We are, with great respect, Sir, Your most obedient servant,

Sands, Livingston, & Co.

The Honorable Robert Morris, Esq.

PRINTED: U.S., Congress, Senate Document 62, February 25, 1820, pp. 26–27.
1. A manuscript text of this letter from Sands, Livingston and Company, the contractors for West Point and the Moving Army, has not been found. The editors wish to thank Robert C. Gramberg of Hickory Hills, Illinois, for calling their attention to the text reproduced here; the letter was also published in *American State Papers*, Class 9, Claims, I, 717. RM received it on October 14 (see Diary of that date). For the context, see Comfort Sands, Walter Livingston, William Duer, and Daniel Parker to RM, September 11, and notes.
2. See Diary, October 1.
3. See Ezekiel Cornell to the Contractors for West Point and the Moving Army, September 30, 1782, enclosed in Cornell to RM, October 5.
4. The reference is to RM's West Point and Moving Army contract with Jeremiah Wadsworth and John Carter of October 12.

Henry Knox to Gouverneur Morris

West Point [New York] 8th October 1782[1]

You were perfectly right in your conjectures[2] my dear ⟨Sir⟩ friend that the British commissioners would not be able to meet us with equal powers. I cannot conceive how any persons should think that Sir Guy Carelton [Carleton] could have such powers ready prepared. ⟨The persons⟩ General Heath and myself, on our side and Lieut Genl Campbell, and Mr Elliot on the part of ⟨Sir Guy⟩ the Enemy are the Commissioners. Our old friend Dalrymple occasioned such a [racket?] in New York that these Gentlemen came out under ⟨such⟩ [*illegible word*] of caution, which occasioned [much reserve?] unlike our former meeting.

Genl Campbell, altho [well bred?] is the reverse of Genl Dalrymple in social intercourse, his [taciturnity?] is as great as the [*illegible word*].

I have to apologize to you for not replying to your favor sooner, But I have had much private affliction, in the loss of a fine Child, and the excessive sickness of Mrs Knox and the rest of my family. I hope this together with the public business I have been engaged in which has generally deprived me of the opportunity of the post, will be a sufficient excuse.

I beg you to present Mrs Knox and my Compliments to Mrs and Mr Morris, and believe me to be with great sincerity your very humble Servant

Knox

Gouverneur Morris Esqr

MS: ADftS, Knox Papers, MHi.
    1. A portion of this text is badly faded, making some passages and important excisions illegible. The editors have conjectured excisions in this letter only when they could be reconstructed with any degree of certainty.
    2. See Gouverneur Morris to Knox, September 13, and notes.

Diary: October 9, 1782

Doctr. Chevett applied to me for Leave to go into the City of New York to secure £400 &c. due to him. I answered that I have no Authority to Grant Passports of that Kind and recommended him to apply to Genl. Potter as Vice President and the Supreme Executive Council of Pennsylvania.[1]

Capt Blewer respecting Debts due to him from the late Pennsylvania Bank.[2] I promised to pay him and take those Debts to my own Account.

Mr. Ludwell Lee applied for £200 which the Honble Arthur Lee desired me to pay in part of the Debt due to the Latter by the United States.[3] I shewed to Mr. Lee a Letter which I had received from Mr. Nourse Register of the Treasury[4] whereby it appears that Mr Lee has received Loan Office Certificates for his Debt which changes the Nature of his Claim and puts him on the same footing with other Persons holding Loan Office Certificates. See my Letter to the Honble. Arthur Lee Esqr. of this Date.

Mr. Oliver Pollock called this morning and requests me to report on his Case. I had advised him to go first to Virginia and Settle his Accounts with that State but he prefers finishing here first and I agreed to comply with his request.[5]

Mr. Hartley of Carolina alledged that Genl Green had given him a Credit for 100 Guineas but on recurring to the Letter[6] it appeared a mistake.

Mr. Simmons and Mr Comegys for their pay as Clerks under Mr Milligan. I desired they may not teaze me on that Score as the Money will be provided fast as possible.

I sent for Colo. Bayard and agreed with him to send a Quantity of the public Goods to his Auction and intended to agree respecting the Commission but he informed me it is fixed by law at 2½ per Cent.[7]

Mr. Robt. Tuckniss applies for money for Hay delivered to Colo. Miles for public Use. I told him it will soon be paid.

Jno. Pierce Esqr Paymaster General applies for money for several Purposes in such Terms of necessity that I signed a Warrant for 1000 Dollars to pay for Office rent, Wood, Subsistence of Officers and a trifle on Account of his own Pay.

Saml. Hodgdon Esqr. for notes to pay Gun Smiths &c.[8] I also signed a Warrant for his Department.

Mr. Jno. Gartley for money on Account of his Pay. I referred him to Colo Charles Stewart who employed him.

Mr. Jno. Bendon offers his Service as a Commr. to settle Accounts. I agreed to enquire into his Character and then give him an answer.[9]

Mr Reuben Haines applies for money for Mr. Pierces Notes &c which I promised.

Colo. Humpton applies for money to pay for enlisting Germans &c. I gave Genl Lincoln my opinion upon this Application of the Colo. that we had better keep money to feed the Soldiers we have than pay it away to enlist more when there is not any apparent use for them.[10]

Henry Hill Esqr. called to inform me that he will pay £1,000 in about twelve Days.

Henry Dering for money on account of his Contract.

Wrote a Letter to the Honble. Mr Holker.

Wrote a Letter to Mr Jos: Watson.

Wrote a Letter to Geo. Olney Esqr.

Wrote a Letter to Wm. Whipple.

Wrote a Letter to Nathl. Appleton.

Wrote a Letter to His Excelly the Prsdt. of Congress.

Wrote a Letter to Wm. C. Houston Esqr.

Wrote a Letter to Hezk. Merrill.

Wrote a Letter to the Honble. Arthur Lee Esqr.

1. Dr. Abraham Chovet (1704–1790) was an English-born surgeon and anatomist who had come to Philadelphia before the war and whose "Anatomical Museum" housed his collection of wax models. According to Marquis de Chastellux, who met him in 1780, Chovet was "a real eccentric: his chief characteristic is contrary-mindedness; when the English were at Philadelphia he was a Whig, and since they left he has become a Tory; he is always sighing after Europe, without ever making up his mind to return there, and declaims incessantly against the Americans, while remaining among them. His reason for coming to the continent [from the West Indies] was to recover his health, so that he would be able to cross the seas; this was at about the time that the war broke out, and, since that time, he imagines he is not at liberty to leave, though nobody prevents him from going." Chovet's application for a pass to and from New York was read and rejected by the Supreme Executive Council on October 18. DAB; Chastellux, Travels, I, 146, 311n.–312n.; and Colonial Records of Pennsylvania, XIII, 398.

2. On the Bank of Pennsylvania, see notes to RM's Plan for a National Bank, with Observations, May 17, 1781.

3. On this claim, see Arthur Lee to RM, October 5, and notes.

4. Dated October 7.

5. See RM to James Duane, October 11, and notes.

6. Letter not identified.

7. John Bubenheim Bayard was the state-appointed auctioneer for the city of Philadelphia. See *Colonial Records of Pennsylvania*, XII, 525; and the act of April 13, 1782, establishing the current commission rates for public auctions in Mitchell and Flanders, eds., *Statutes of Pennsylvania*, X, 469.

8. See Hodgdon to RM, October 7.

9. The caller was Joseph Bindon, whom RM subsequently appointed commissioner to settle the accounts of the Clothing Department. See RM to the President of Congress, October 11.

10. Colonel Richard Humpton was recruiting for the Pennsylvania line. On the enlistment of German prisoners, see notes to Diary, May 1, 1782; and for RM's change of mind on Humpton's application, Diary, October 11 and 14.

To Nathaniel Appleton

Office of Finance 9 Octo: 1782

Sir,

I have received your Favor dated at Boston on the twenty fifth of last Month.[1] It was not in the Contemplation of Congress to issue Bills for Payment of Interest due for any Term less than one Year. No more Bills can be sent you for the Payment of Interest[2] but if particular Evils have arisen from the general Regulation the Remedy must be sought for by special Application. I am Sir your most obedient and humble Servant

RM

MS: Ofcl LbC, DLC.

1. Letter not found. Appleton was the Continental loan officer of Massachusetts.

2. On September 9 Congress had stopped the payment of interest on loan office certificates in bills of exchange on France. See notes to RM's Report to Congress on the Continental Loan Offices, June 13, 1782.

To the President of Congress (John Hanson)

Office of Finance 9th October 1782

Sir,

His Excellency the Governor of Virginia, in a Letter of the twenty third of September, has proposed to me that sundry Articles of Cloathing now in France belonging to the State of Virginia, should be taken for the Use of the United States. These are Part of those Articles which were furnished by the Court for that State on Credit. Congress will be pleased to recollect that the Court were desirous of charging the Amount of all these Articles to the United States. How that Matter has been finally adjusted I do not know, but I should suppose it would be best to comply with the Governor's Proposition, as it will be a great Convenience to the State, and not injurious to the

Union. If this Matter had not been already brought before Congress, I would not now trouble them with it; but as it is I could wish their Instruction to take Order before I proceed.[1] The Copy of the List sent by the Governor is enclosed. With perfect Respect I have the Honor to be Sir Your Excellency's most obedient and humble Servant[2]

Robt Morris

His Excellency The President of Congress

[ENCLOSURE][3]

[Richmond, Virginia, September 24, 1782]
Extract from the Invoice of Necessaries wanted for the Defence of the State of Virginia delivered to his Excellency the Chevalier de la Luzerne Minister of France the 17 Day of Feby. 1782

6,000 Suits of Cloth Cloaths for Soldiers
36,000 English Yards of coarse Linnen for Soldiers Shirts
100 lbs of Thread to make it up
6,000 Soldiers Hats larger in the Crown than generally
    made in France
12,000 Pair of Soldiers coarse yarn Stockings
6,000 Blankets
6,000 Pair of strong Shoes

Copy
Wm Hay C[ommercial] A[gent]
Richmond Sepr 24th 1782
Copy
Office of Finance 9 Octr.

ENDORSED: 98/Letter 9 Oct. 1782/Superint. Finance/[Read?] 10./Referred to Mr Ramsay/Mr Osgood/Mr Gilman/relative to goods in F[rance] belonging/to Virga. which the govt wishes/the cont[inent] to take and pay for
MSS: LS, PCC, DNA; Ofcl LbC, DLC; copy, Continental Congress Papers, Vi.
1. For Congress's response, see notes to RM to the Governor of Virginia, April 27, 1782.
2. A copy of this letter was enclosed in RM to the Governor of Virginia, October 23.
3. MSS: Copy in Gouverneur Morris's writing, PCC, DNA; copy, Ferdinand J. Dreer Collection, PHi; copy, Benjamin Franklin Papers, PPAmP; copy, Franklin Papers, CtY. The extract was also enclosed in letters to Thomas Barclay and Franklin of October 27.

To William Churchill Houston

Office of Finance 9th October 1782[1]
Sir,
I have received your Favor dated on the 5th Instant with the Enclosure. I cannot but regret the Determination of your Legislature in making the Appropriation you mention, as it is a Deviation from that System which has been conceived to be the best calculated

for promoting the public Interests. My Letter to you of the 5th enclosed an Act of Congress of the first Instant, to which I beg Leave to refer, and remain, Sir, Your obedient Servant

Robt Morris

William C. Houston Esquire
Receiver for New Jersey

ENDORSED: Letter Honorable Robert Morris/Financier Octr. 9 1782/Answered
MSS: LS, Houston Collection, NjP; Ofcl LbC, DLC.
   1. Houston was the receiver of Continental taxes for New Jersey.

To John Paul Jones

Marine Office 9. Octo: 1782[1]

Sir,

I have received your Letter of the twenty second of last Month, the Sentiments contained in it will always reflect the highest honor upon your Character they have made so strong an Impression upon my Mind that I immediately transmitted an Extract of your Letter to Congress.[2] I doubt not but they will view it in the same Manner which I have done. I am Sir with very sincere Esteem, your most obedient and humble Servant

RM

MSS: AM LbC, MdAN; copy from "Extrait du Journal des mes Campagnes," Jones Papers, DLC.
   1. Captain Jones was in Portsmouth, New Hampshire, overseeing the completion of the America, a 74-gun ship which Congress on September 3 had voted to present to France.
   2. See RM to the President of Congress, October 7 (first letter).

To Arthur Lee

Philadelphia 9. Octo: 1782[1]

Sir,

Upon the Receipt of your Letter of the fifth Instant by Mr. Ludwill Lee, being engaged in making up Dispatches for Europe I appointed him a meeting on this Day[2] and in the mean Time (according to Custom) sent to the Treasury for a State of your Account. I have now the honor to enclose a Copy of the Register's Letter to me on that Subject.[3] The Circumstances there mentioned I was not apprized of before; but you will see that it is not in my Power to make you any Payment without a special Resolution of Congress for the Purpose, until Funds are provided for paying other Loan Office Certificates which are become due. I should have informed you of this when you spoke first to me but as there was a Balance returned as appearing to be due to you on the Treasury Books in the Estimate of the public Debt[4] I did not then conceive it to be (as it is) involved in the general Mass of Loan Office Certificates. I am Sir your most obedient Servant

RM

MSS: Ofcl LbC, DLC; copy, PCC, DNA.

1. A Virginia delegate to Congress, Lee had been granted a leave of absence by Congress on October 4; he left Philadelphia on October 6 and arrived in Richmond on October 31 (see James Madison to Edmund Randolph, October 8, 1782, Hutchinson and Rutland, ed., *Madison Papers,* V, 187–188, 190n.). For the context of this letter, see notes to Lee to RM, October 5. The PCC text was enclosed in RM to the President of Congress, November 14, 1782.

2. See Diary, October 9.

3. See the Register of the Treasury to RM, October 7.

4. The estimate is printed as the enclosure to RM to the President of Congress, July 29.

To James Lovell

Office of Finance 9 Octo: 1782

Sir,

I am favored with your Letter dated on the twenty sixth of last Month with the Enclosure.[1] The smallness of your Receipts is Matter of much Regret, and affords just Cause to complain of the Remissness of the State in paying its quota. I hope you will make the proper Representation and assure them that unless the most Solid reliance can be placed on the Supplies it is not only impossible to conduct the public Business with Oeconomy,[2] but that it will soon become impracticable to conduct it at all.[3] I am Sir your most obedient Servant[4]

RM

MSS: Ofcl LbC, DLC; copy in Lovell's hand, M-Ar.

1. Lovell was the receiver of Continental taxes for Massachusetts. His letter and enclosure have not been found, but the latter probably was his return no. 9 of September 25 for $1,703.25, his smallest return of taxes to date. See PCC, no. 137, III, 349.

2. Lovell underlined the preceding two words in the M-Ar copy.

3. Lovell underlined the preceding two words in the M-Ar copy.

4. The M-Ar text was enclosed in Lovell's letter to the Speaker of the Massachusetts House of Representatives of November 8, 1782 (Massachusetts Archives, CCXXXVIII, 255–256), outlining "a few plain Facts, of a Nature, in my Opinion, to allarm and call into the fullest immediate Exertion the Patriotism of every Member. Under that Opinion, any formal Reasonings by me would appear to be an Insult to their Understandings.

"The Facts are, That Ten Twelfths of the current Year elapsed when my Receipts did not amount to one Half of one Twelfth of the Quota required by Congress for defraying the Expences of it; That the Superintendant of Finance having in a most extraordinary Manner advanced with his œconomical Contracts to the Month of October was then obliged to submit to the Penalty of two pence per Ration to the old Contractors, and to give three pence higher to new ones for the last Quarter of this Year, so that the States, in Consequence of the Deficiency of Taxes, are losing five

Pence per Ration; a Sum equal to one Half of the former Contract: That my published Monthly Returns are in a gradual Decrease, to the further Ruin of the Credit of the United States, and raising a Difficulty of finding Contractors for a new Year on Terms of *any* Œconomy." Lovell concluded with a plea that the members of the House "will individually exert throughout the Counties, in their Recess, to promote the Speedy Collection of the whole Balance due upon the Requisitions for this Year." Following Lovell's appeal, the General Court on November 12 ordered the state treasurer to call upon the collectors to pay the first half of the Continental tax previously levied "without further delay, it being absolutely necessary for the public safety," and to issue executions against those collectors who had not paid the first half thereof by January 1 and the second half by February 1, 1783. See *Acts and Laws of Massachusetts, 1782–1783*, p. 354; notes to RM to Lovell, May 14, 1782, for Massachusetts' compliance with the requisition for 1782; and notes to Comfort Sands, Walter Livingston, William Duer, and Daniel Parker to RM, September 11, for RM's problems with the contractors.

To William Whipple

Office of Finance 9. Octo: 1782

Sir,

I have been favored with your Letter dated at Portsmouth 23d. August (suppose it should have been Sepr.).[1] I have endeavored to Aid you in disposing of the Beef you mention but have not succeeded. The Gentlemen who purchase for the french Army made Objections to the quality having seen some of it that had been purchased by the Contractors for our Army. As it had been received for Taxes, I was not without my Fears on that particular, it being not unreasonable to suppose that those who are to pay in that Manner will be more attentive to private than public Interests. I am Sir your most obedient Servant

RM

MS: Ofcl LbC, DLC.
1. The letter was written on September 23. Whipple was the receiver of Continental taxes for New Hampshire.

From John Carter

Hon. R. Morris Esq.　　　　　　　Crompond [New York] Oct. 9. 1782
Dear Sir

I arrived here on Monday morning and found Wadsworth had fixed with Gen Cornell that we should take up the Contract and begin our Issues on the 16th. Instant and I have read the Copy of J[eremiah] W[adsworth's] Letter to you.[1] I have sent Chaloner your Note due the 4th. Novr. for Twelve Thousand five Hundred Pounds; this agreeable to your agreement with us is to be paid the day it becomes due, in case we accepted the Contract[2] and I find since I came here notwithstanding the Supplies the french have received, the Debts they owe to the civil Departments of the Army and other Demands on them are so very great that they will not be able to pay us the Money they owe us other ways than in Bills of Exchange.[3] This makes it absolutely necessary to urge you by every consideration not to disappoint us in this payment as other ways we shall be distressed, and it will hurt both you and us if the Army should suffer as they have raised their Expectations of being well supplied to the highest pitch. And as the French Army will move in five Days[4] we shall be seperated from the American Army and cannot be present to obviate any difficulties that may arrise our only dependance therefore will be on the Friends [i.e., Funds?] we leave in the hands of our agents to procure the necessary Supplies. This gives us the fullest confidence you will not disappoint us.

As we shall be at a considerable distance, if you advertise for a new Contract and the period is short, it will be necessary to send the advertisement to Genl Cornell to forward to us immediatly that we may Send you our proposals in Time.[5]

Genl Schuylers elder son who is going to Phila. with my little Daughter[6] will have the honor to deliver you this Letter. I beg the favor of you to have the Goodness to take him by the hand and give him your Countinance. He is a raw youth, unacquainted with the world and unused to Company. His Father as well as myself will be particularly obliged for all favors &c

J. Carter

MS: LbC, Wadsworth and Carter Letterbook 3, CtHi.

1. Wadsworth and Carter had agreed to take over the combined West Point and Moving Army contract for the remainder of 1782. Ezekiel Cornell, whom RM had authorized to negotiate the terms of the new contract, acquainted the Superintendent with the terms in a letter of October 5; Wadsworth's letter on the subject was also dated October 5. Carter had recently left Philadelphia after conferring with RM. See Diary, October 5.

2. On RM's debts to John Chaloner, Wadsworth and Carter's Philadelphia agent, see Diary, August 20, and notes.

3. On the financial arrangements between Wadsworth and Carter and the French army, see the headnote and notes to RM's Contract with Jeremiah Wadsworth and John Carter, October 12. On the long awaited arrival of specie from France aboard the frigates *Aigle* and *Gloire*, see Diary, September 16, and notes. This event lessened Wadsworth and Carter's need to raise cash for the French through the sale of bills of exchange, but the firm continued to be paid as suppliers for the French army in bills of exchange rather than in specie. See John Chaloner to Wadsworth, September 16, Wadsworth to John Trumbull, September 21, and Carter to Wadsworth, September 25, 29, October 2, and November 25, 1782, Wadsworth Papers, CtHi.

4. For the movements of the French army, see notes to the Quartermaster General to RM, September 19.

5. See the Advertisement for Contracts for 1783, October 10.

6. Carter (John B. Church) married Philip Schuyler's eldest daughter, Angelica, in 1777; their daughter was Catherine. Schuyler's eldest son was John Bradstreet Schuyler (1765–1795). See Syrett and Cooke, eds., *Hamilton Papers*, III, 508; and Don R. Gerlach, *Philip Schuyler and the American Revolution in New York, 1733–1777* (Lincoln, Nebr., 1964), 314.

From Nathanael Greene

Head Quarters Ashley Hill [South Carolina]
Octr. 9th. 1782[1]

Dear Sir

Since my letter of the 1st. Ultimo I have made at George Town a considerable purchase of rum and some stores for the hospital.[2] The rum was offered at so reasonable a price that I thought it best to buy as much as will supply this army untill Decr. next. In payment for these stores I have taken the liberty to draw on you in favour of Messrs. Edwards and Lushington for 1200 dolls payable the 1st. of Novr. next, and for 8024 Dollars payable the 1st. of Decr. next, also a bill in favour of Majr. Forsyth for 690 Dollars payable the 1st. Decr. next. I hope these will be the only drafts I shall be obliged to make 'till December unless it is for a small sum for the Hospital.

Every preparation is making for the evacuation of C[harles] Town which event I hope will take place during this month.[3] I have the honor to be &c.

N. Greene

R Morris Esqr.

MS: DftS, Greene Papers, CSmH.
1. This draft letter from Major General Greene, commander of the southern army, is in the writing of Ichabod Burnet, Greene's aide.
2. Here the words "at George Town" are crossed out.
3. The evacuation was not completed until December 14, 1782.

From Alexander Hamilton

[Albany, New York, October 9, 1782]

Sir

I wrote you a hasty letter by the last post[1] which arrived late and set out very soon after its arrival.

Since that I have received two thousand dollars all in your bills on Mr. Swanwick in favour of Messrs. Sands & Co. One half the sum is in bills payable in February next exchanged by them for specie with one of the County treasurers. I am sensible there is an inconvenience in this in different ways; but it appears by your letter of the 19th. of July[2] that you mean to have those bills received upon the same footing with your and the bank-notes, without regard to the time they have to run. I have however induced the treasurer to write in a manner that I hope will discourage like exchanges in future, without giving any unfavourable impression. Besides the inconvenience from this practice which I mentioned in a former letter, there is another which I am persuaded will result. People will get into a way of discounting your bills and notes with the treasurers and collectors to the injury of their Credit.

Probably you are apprised of a fact which however I think it my duty to mention; it is that the bank notes pass pretty currently as Cash with a manifest preference to your Notes.

I have not yet received the other papers relative to the account of supplies I have sent you.

I hope to be able to enclose you a copy of the address of the public creditors in this town to the rest of that denomination in this state.[3] It inculcates the ideas, which ought to prevail.

I have not yet heard of your Messenger, Mr. Brown. I presume his circuit is regulated by your occasional direction. I have the honor to be &c

Albany Octr. 9. 1782

ENDORSED: to R Morris Esqr./October 9, 1782
MSS: ADft, Hamilton Papers, DLC; transcript, Francis Baylies Papers, DLC.
  1. Dated October 5.
  2. RM's circular to the receivers.
  3. See notes to Hamilton to RM, September 28.

From Walter Livingston, William Duer, and Daniel Parker

Manor Livingston [New York] Octr. 9th. 1782[1]

Sir,

We do ourselves the Honor of transmitting Copies of the Correspondence which has passed betwixt the Contractors of the moving Army, and General Cornell relative to the Objects mentioned in our company letter of the 11th. Sepr.[2] We observe with Astonishment and Regret that General Cornell is prohibited from giving any assurance of an Indemnification for the loss we have and may sustain from a non Performance of your Engagements or hopes of a considerable payment in money for the Prosecution of the Contract.[3] Your Instructions to Genl. Cornell as to the first point are so contrary to what we conceive we had a right to Expect, not only from our contract, but from the Declarations, which Mr. Richardson Sands informed us you was pleased to make in a late personal conference with him on the subject of the company letter of the 11th. Ultimo[4] that we should have supposed Genl. Cornell conceived his Powers of a more limited nature than they really were, if he had not favored us with a perusal of your Instructions. We shall not take upon us, Sir, to determine how far it is for the Public Interest or Honor, to avoid giving us the assurance we have requested. Our claim to Indemnification[5] in case of failure stands upon the broad Basis of Equity and cannot be shook by the communication which General Cornell has made, though we should continue to execute our part of the Contract, so far as the means put in our power will admit of. We lament with Genl. Cornell that Events which no Human Prudence could foresee should have prevented you from Executing your Engagements with that punctuality we expected and we are fully convinced of the goodness of your intention, but as these circumstances could not have justified a non Performance of the covenants on our Part, we can never admit them to operate so far as to preclude any Indemnification for the losses which we may prove we have sustained by the Failure on yours.

You will observe by the letter from the Beef Contractors,[6] that whatever may be your determination with respect to ourselves, they conceive us personally liable to them for every failure we shall make in performing our Engagements, and that they will continue, whether we pay them or not to furnish Beef, so long as we will receive it. When an answer was wrote to Genl. Cornells letter of the 30th Sepr. the Contractors indulged some expectation that Messrs. Phelps & Co. might be induced to recede in some degree from the Engagements we have entered into. But as this is not the case it has become essential for our own Security to take every Measure, which the Contract will authorise to prevent our becoming Victims to the Confidence we have placed in the Engagements we have entered into.

We therefore embrace the Earliest opportunity of informing you that whatever may be the determination of Messrs Sands,[7] or the other Gentlemen concerned in the Contract we on our part will continue to Supply by Contract the moving army, in as adequate a manner as the means placed in our Power will admit of during the Term of the Contract.

With respect to the Article of Beef it shall be regularly furnished, whether we are paid regularly agreably to Contract, or not.

The Articles of Flour and Liquor can hardly at this time be commanded at a Credit, even at any Price; but we will make every exertion in our power to procure all we can on the most reasonable Terms possible on credit, in case we are not furnished in Season with the monies due the Contract to purchase at a Cash price.

It becomes our duty however to inform you that very little dependence can be placed in procuring a Supply of Liquor and flour at this Period in any degree adequate to the Consumption of the army. We have therefore to request that you will immediately give directions to the Person who agreably to the Terms of our Contract is to purchase in case of failure of Supply from the Contractors, to procure and deliver to our Commissary at Kings Ferry four thousand Barrels of good common Flour, and fifteen thousand gallons of

Whiskey for which he is directed to give the proper receipts. No time must be lost in sending in this supply, as it will be impossible to transport it from Philadel: after the 20th. of Novr.

We have not received any official information whether General Cornell is the Person vested with this power; but from a Presumption that he is, we have transmitted him this letter for his perusal and requested him to forward it by Express and have given him timely Notice of the failure likely to happen that measure[s] may be taken for preventing the want of the Articles we have mentioned.[8]

We think it necessary to observe[9] that we propose this Supply of Flour and Whiskey to be sent on, upon this Condition only, that the whole amount due on our accounts is not immediately paid in Specie agreably to our contract; if it should be, there will be only occasion for half the quantity of Flour and Liquor we have mentioned, for though the delay in former payments renders it necessary that measure[s] should be immediately taken by the Public for supplying the quantity of Flour and Whiskey last mentioned, even though the whole balance due should be now paid in Specie; we are ready to perform[10] every covenant we have entered into in the Contract, provided the stipulations you have entered into are complied with on your part.

In the company letter of the 11th. Sepr. it was proposed in order to render the payments as easy as possible that only one half of the monthly payments should be made in specie, provided the other stipulations proposed in that letter were acceded to. But, as it has not been judged advisable to give the Assurance we requested, this Proposition (which was conditional on the Part of the Contractors) we shall conceive ourselves totally freed from in case we take upon us the future execution of the contract. Whatever covenants we have entered into shall be as strictly performed as the means put in our power will admit of, and we shall expect in future Regular monthly payments for the whole Rations issued, in Gold and Silver coin agreably to our contract. We are reduced to the painful and disagreeable necessity of coming to the determination, from the extraordinary communication made us by General Cornell. We on our parts have never entertained the most distant Idea of deriving greater Profits in consequence of your Embarrassments than that we originally had a right to expect. All our aim was to be placed on an equal footing. But as Genl. Cornells letter (whatever may be the Intention) has a tendency to bring about a Surrender of the Contract in a manner ruinous to our Interests and prejudicial to our characters, we must build our hopes of indemnification upon the Contract itself, and trust for the justification of our conduct, to the claims we have, and to the equitable propositions we have made; If any set of Gentlemen are willing to take the Contract for the moving army on the Terms first agreed upon (namely 10d. per ration) under the circumstances mentioned in Genl. Cornells letter, we on our part shall have no objection to their doing it, and will give up every farthing which may have been made by it from the begining to this day, provided they will place themselves in the Predicament we stand in with the Beef contractors; But we have still that Confidence in yours and the Publics Honor, as not to entertain an Idea, that it is your wish we should be made a Sacrifice in this Business, in order to pave the way for a Contract to others on terms which it has not been thought advisable to accede to with us.

It is far, Sir, from our wish by continuing this contract to throw any obstacle in the way of other arrangements which may be in contemplation for the supply of the army. We aim only at securing ourselves from Ruin and this it is our duty to prevent. Should it be your wish that the contract should be given up, declare it as such, and give us an explicit assurance that we shall be placed on the same footing[11] as we were before the Contract commenced, and we will chearfully renounce it. Any Prospects of Profit we may have entertained, or compensation for the Trouble we have taken in Supporting your measures we are willing to give up, and we trust no more can in reason be expected.

If the ruin of a few Individuals could restore Vigor to the operations of our Governments, or Contribute to the Subsistence of the army, a Spirit of Patriotism might induce us to make a greater Sacrifice than what we propose; but since this is not the case, we flatter ourselves the Public opinion will be Satisfied with the offer we now make.[12] We are Sir with great Respect and Esteem, Your Obedient Humble Servants[13]

Walter Livingston
William Duer ⎱   By their Attorney
Daniel Parker ⎰   Walter Livingston

The Honle. Robert Morris Esqr.
Superintendant of Finance
Philadelphia

[ENCLOSURES]

Ezekiel Cornell to Walter Livingston

Ver Planks Point [New York] Sepr. 27. 1782

Sir

The Tennor of your letter of the 11th. Instant to the Superintendant of Finance is such as has induced him to send me to camp with powers to do what may appear expedient respecting the contracts and Supplying the army. That I may execute my commission with propriety, it is necessary that I should see the Contractors together. I intend being at Fish Kill at the house of Mr. Comfort Sands on Monday next at 12 OClock at which time and place I request that you will be so kind as to meet me. I beg you will not fail. In the mean time permit me to Subscribe myself your most obedient and very Humble Servant.

Ezekl. Cornell

Walter Livingston Esqr.
at the Manor

Walter Livingston to Ezekiel Cornell

M[anor] L[ivingston] Sepr. 29. 1782

Sir

I was favored with your letter of the 27 Instant this moment desiring me to attend as one of the Contractors at the Fish Kill tomorrow morning. The notice is so short and my health so much impared as to render a compliance almost impossible. I will be at Fish Kill on Tuesday morning ⟨to meet you⟩ and must request it as a favor that you will tarry ⟨at that place⟩ till I can have the pleasure of seeing you.

Ezekiel Cornell to the Contractors for the Moving Army

Fish Kill Sept. 30. 1782

Gentlemen

My appointment and Instructions are such as makes it necessary that I should at all times know the quantity of Supplies you have on hand and your future prospects. But when I consider the Tenor of your letter to the Superintendant of Finance dated the 11th. Instant it appears indispensably at this time. And least it should be expected that I agree in behalf of Mr. Morris to make the indemnification requested in said letter, I take this early opportunity to inform you gentlemen that I can give no assurances of that kind neither can I flatter you that Mr. Morris will speedily be able to make you any considerable advances of money, at the same time I am confidant that it is not his wish to take any undue advantage, and if you suffer any inconveniencies on account of any non performance on his part it ought to be imputed to some Events that have taken place, that no human Prudence could forsee and not Design. Being thus convinced of his just Intentions it would be highly criminal in me to endeavour to act a contrary part. Therefore I have nothing further to request of you than that you will immediately and explicitly inform me how long you can Supply the moving army, the garrison of West Point and its Dependencies under present circumstances, and that you will consider the distress that must take place in the Army if the Supplies should immediately fail. I flatter myself that they will not, for I am confident you have the Good of the common cause too much at heart. I cannot close this letter without pressing you to give me a Speedy answer.

(Signed) Ezekl Cornell
Inspector for the Main Army and its Dependencies

To the Contractors for the
Moving Army and its Dependencies

Comfort Sands and Walter Livingston to Ezekiel Cornell

Fish-Kill Octobr. 1. 1782

Sir

We were favored with your letter this day dated yesterday.

When we wrote to Mr. Morris on the 11 Ultimo to which you refer we informed him of our Situation and that unless he would make good his Engagements in part or Indemnify us at the close of the Contract we could continue the Supplies no longer than to this day, of which you declare you can give us no Assurances nor a promise of payment agreable to the proposal made him.

When we wrote that letter to Mr. Morris, it was upon mature consideration determined that it was impossible in our Situation to furnish a regular Supply which we wished to inform him of. We did not intend to take any advantage of his distress, we only asked a Compensation for Damages that we might Sustain on account of his engagements not being complied with, requesting him to give us only one half of the Specie he by Contract was to furnish which you say you cannot promise to do. In this Situation and from a regard to the Common Cause and a wish not to let the Army want till some better method is taken for Supplying it, we have determined to exert ourselves in furnishing the two most essential articles Beef and Bread till the 15th. Instant. Whiskey we cannot Supply, nor even pay for, that article must be excepted.

The Gentlemen who by contract are to Supply the moving army with Beef have engaged to continue furnishing us till that time and if we think proper will to the end of the Month. The quantity of Flour laying at Trenton and Morristown, (if money can be advanced to transport it to the River) will Serve the army till the 15th. For the remainder of the month you must furnish that article.

Should Mr. Morris send on Notes as he has been requested the

Beef Contractors for West Point will doubtless furnish that Article to the end of the month. If notes cannot be obtained Beef for that Post must also be provided for by you.

Signed Comfort Sands
Walter Livingston

Walter Livingston and Comfort Sands to Oliver Phelps and Company

Fish Kill Octr. 2d. 1782

Gentlemen

We enclose you a Copy of a letter from General Cornell Intendant for the main army &c. On perusal of it you will readily see the distressed situation we are in and consequently the future uncertainty that will attend payments from the United States. Our own feelings are much wound'd and yours will doubtless be, when you know that all our endeavors to fulfil our engagements with punctuallity are rendered abortive by the Public failure. We give you the earliest notice in our power of the prospects before us and hope you will not involve yourselves farther than you can avoid, we shall do every thing in the power of Honestmen to save you and ourselves. Our confidence in the Honor of the Financier seems to be our greatest Security. By General Cornells letter he demands to know how long the Supplies can be kept up under the present circumstances which we have engaged to do till the 15 Instant and probably to the end of the month provided he can furnish the remainder of the Flour, which should he agree to we will give you notice. As to the Salted provisions we suppose it needless to procure any more, as we have no prospects of geting the money for it.

(signed) Comfort Sands
Walter Livingston

Timothy Edwards, William Bacon, and Daniel Penfield to Sands, Livingston and Company

Fishkill Octr. 2d. 1782

Gentlemen

To yours of this day enclosing a Copy of General Cornells letter of the 30th. Ultimo we have attended. You may be assured that our feelings of almost every discription are not less wounded than yours by this information. Relying on Faith both Public and Private which hath been pledged to us, we have involved ourselves by Contracts with Messrs. Trumbull and House, with Messrs. Fellows and Noble for large Supplies to the end of this year. From these and others of less amount we cannot expect to extricate ourselves at small expence. We ever have been and still are prepared to fulfil our part of the contract with Messrs. Sands Livingston & Co. In confidence of your ability as well as Honor and integrity, we expect to be indemnified in every latch on your part which hath or may take place. Should you neglect to pay us agreable to Stipulation, we shall nevertheless furnish Beef according to contract as long as you will receive of us. We have on this River about three hundred barrels of Salted Provisions, 400 more are probably purchased on Connecticut River. We shall forbear purchasing such provisions when we receive your desisive instructions therein. We are Gentlemen, for Oliver Phelps & Co.

Tim: Edwards, Wm. Bacon
Daniel Penfield

MS: LbC and enclosures in Livingston's hand, Walter Livingston Letterbooks, Robert R. Livingston Papers, NHi.

1. Livingston, Duer, and Parker were partners with Comfort Sands and Company and others in Sands, Livingston and Company, holder of the combined West Point and Moving Army contract (for Ezekiel Cornell's role in renegotiating the contract, see Cornell to RM, October 5, and notes). This letter was previously published, evidently from one or more manuscript sources no longer available, in U.S., Congress, Senate Document 62, February 25, 1820, pp. 27–30, and in *American State Papers*, Class 9, Claims, I, 717–718. The most significant variations have been indicated in notes 9–12 below.

2. The probable enclosures are printed at the end of the letter. The only doubtful one, Livingston and Sands to Phelps and Company of October 2, has been included to complete the record. The company letter is Comfort Sands, Walter Livingston, William Duer, and Daniel Parker to RM, September 11.

3. See RM to Cornell, September 20.

4. Meetings with Richardson Sands took place on September 18 and 30, but no record of the conversation appears in RM's Diary for those dates.

5. On the issue of indemnification for damages, see Cornell to RM, October 5, and notes.

6. See the last enclosure printed below.

7. See note 9 below.

8. See Walter Livingston, William Duer, and Daniel Parker to Cornell, October 9, *American State Papers*, Class 9, Claims, I, 718.

9. The preceding two words were omitted in the previously published texts cited in note 1 above.

10. The words "in future" appear here in both previously published texts.

11. The words "in point of interest" are added here in both previously published texts.

12. The preceding three words are omitted from the previously published texts.

13. In a letter of October 9 to Comfort Sands at Fishkill (Walter Livingston Letterbooks, Robert R. Livingston Papers, NHi), Livingston enclosed the present letter to RM and another to Cornell of the same date (see the preceding note), which he and Duer "after mature deliberation" had written for themselves and Parker. "If you, your Brother and Mr. Stewart agree with us in Sentiment we wish you would Signify it, and Subscribe the letter[s] if not and you should decline executing the Contract beyond the last day of October we request that you would be pleased to forward the letters without a moments delay to General Cornell and Signify to us Your dissent."

To John Holker

Office of Finance 9. Octo: 1782

I have received your Favor of the fourth Instant.[1] In Answer I have to inform you that I shall comply with the Proposition contained in it and am in Consequence to request that you would send me a List of the Bills you wish to have the Sum due to you divided into calculating the Exchange at fifteen ninetieths of a Dollar per Livre.

MS: Ofcl LbC, DLC.

1. Holker was a French merchant and business associate from whom RM had purchased clothing for the Continental army. His letter has not been found, but see Diary, October 11.

To Hezekiah Merrill

Office of Finance 9. Octo: 1782

Your Favor dated at Hartford on the thirtieth of last Month has been received,[1] with the remaining Parts of the Notes therein mentioned.

MS: Ofcl LbC, DLC.

1. The letter from Merrill, receiver of Continental taxes for Connecticut, has not been found.

To George Olney

Office of Finance 9. Octo: 1782

I have received your favor dated on the twenty third of last Month with the enclosures.[1] It is not necessary to cut the Bills you mention. Your Indorsement on them to Michael Hillegas Esqr. continental Treasurer will equally answer the Purposes of Security against fraudulent Applications for Payment and duplicate Lists will sufficiently provide against the Accidents of Conveyance.

MS: Ofcl LbC, DLC.

1. The letter and enclosures from Olney, receiver of Continental taxes for Rhode Island, have not been found, but one of the enclosures was probably Olney's return no. 13 for £807.3 (see the list in PCC, no. 137, III, 353). For the bills of exchange mentioned in the present reply, see RM's Circular to the Receivers of Continental Taxes, July 19, 1782, and notes.

To Joseph Watson

Office of Finance 9. Octo: 1782

I have just now received your Letter of the eighth[1] and wish I could return such Answer as you desire; but that is not in my Power. As to any Debt which may be due to you by the Continent it must rest on the same Footing with other public Debts. If in the Transaction you mention your Conduct has been perfectly upright, and such I dare say it has been, it is highly probable that your Creditor would consent to your Release upon assigning to him a Part of your Demand against the United States. But this is a private Arrangement in which I can take no Part.

MS: Ofcl LbC, DLC.

1. The letter, which has not been found, was probably from Joseph Watson (1729–1805), a Bucks County, Pennsylvania, Quaker who had served in the assembly from 1767 to 1771 and on the county committee of safety in 1774. See Labaree and Willcox, eds., *Franklin Papers*, XVII, 256n.

Diary: October 10, 1782

Mr Henry Dering called again for Money.

Mr Edwd. Fox brought Letters recommending him for a Commissioner to settle accounts in Consequence of which I agreed to recommend him to Congress.[1]

I sent for Major George Turner and offered him the Appointment of Commissary of Naval Prisoners. He desired to know the Heads of his Business, the Duties of the Station and time to Consider of it to which I assented.[2]

Dispatched Mr Llyod [Lloyd] the Express to Camp with Letters respecting the Contract.[3]

Wrote a Letter to the Contractors   Jeremiah Wadsworth Esqr.
for West Point.

Wrote a Letter to Ezekl.   Colo. Tench Tilghman
Cornell Esqr.

Wrote Advertizement respecting Proposals of Contracts.

Wrote a letter to his Excelly the Prest of Congress.

1. See RM to the President of Congress, October 10. The letters of recommendation have not been found.

2. Turner accepted; RM commissioned him on October 15. See notes to Diary, June 18, 1782.

3. See the first four letters listed below in this Diary.

Advertisement for Contracts for 1783

Office of Finance, October 10, 1782[1]

PUBLIC NOTICE is hereby given to all persons who may incline to contract for the supply of rations, that the seven following contracts will be entered into for the year 1783.

A contract for all rations which may be issuable by the United States.

1st,   Within the four Eastern States,
2d,   Within the States of New-York and New-Jersey,
3d,   Within the State of Pennsylvania,
4th,   Within the States of Delaware and Maryland,
5th,   Within the State of Virginia,
6th,   Within the State of North-Carolina,
7th,   Within the States of South-Carolina and Georgia.

Proposals for these contracts will be received as follows:

For the first, by James Lovell, Esq; at Boston, until the 1st day of December.[2] For the second and third, at this office, until the 10th day of November.[3] For the fourth at this office;[4] for the fifth, by George Webb, Esq; at Richmond;[5] and for the sixth and seventh, by Major-General Greene, until the first day of December.[6]

The rations are to consist of one pound of bread or one pound of flour, one pound of beef or three quarters of a pound of pork, and one gill of rum to each ration; one quart of salt, one quart of vinegar, two pounds of soap, and one pound of candles to every hundred rations. The Contractors are to issue the rations, and upon large issues, three per cent. is to be added to the flesh, to compensate for the wastage in distribution.

The payments are to be made as follow[s]:

The accounts of the issues for the month of January, are to be made out by the Contractors, and transmitted, as soon as conveniently may be, after the close of the month, to the treasury for settlement, and the amount which shall be certified by the Comptroller to be due, shall be paid on the first Tuesday in May. The issues for the month of February shall, in like manner, be paid for on the first Tuesday in June: And in like manner for the other months, so that the issues in December 1783, will be paid on the 1st Tuesday of April, 1784.[7]

And for the prevention of disputes, in cases where the ration or any part thereof shall be increased or diminished, the proposals are to contain the prices of the several component parts of the ration, and the Contractors shall be bound to furnish to the several officers the said component parts at such prices so specified, whether the same be drawn for by such officers proportionately or disproportionately, provided that they shall not be bound to issue in the whole to any officer, beyond the amount of the subsistence money allowed by Congress to such officer; and in like manner they shall be bound to issue to the soldiers such articles of the ration at the said prices as the commanding officer for the time being shall order and direct: And to the prisoners, such as the person for the purpose authorised by the Secretary at War, shall order and direct.

SOURCE: Printed D, Morris-Harwood Papers, MdHi.

1. RM enclosed this advertisement in his October 15 circular to the receivers of Continental taxes and his October 17 letter to Nathanael Greene. The text reproduced here, that received by Benjamin Harwood, the receiver for Maryland, is apparently a clipping from the first newspaper publication in the *Pennsylvania Packet* of October 12. It was republished in the issues of October 17 and 31, November 9, 10, and December 7 and 14, as well as in the Philadelphia *Freeman's Journal* of October 16, 23, and November 6, 1782, and in various newspapers in the states. It should be noted that for the first time the contracts were grouped by states rather than by specific posts or military departments. For this and other differences, compare the advertisements for the 1782 contracts under the dates of October 22 and December 5 and 12, 1781. For stipulations proposed for the contracts by Washington, see his letter to RM of October 31. The plan for issuing rations under the 1783 contracts, prepared by RM and Benjamin Lincoln, is dated November 20, 1782.

2. On the contract for the New England states negotiated by James Lovell, receiver of Continental taxes for Massachusetts, see RM to Lovell, December 17, 1782.

3. For the bidding on the contracts for New York, New Jersey, and Pennsylvania, see Diary, November 11, 12, and 13, 1782. The New York–New Jersey contract is dated November 29; the Pennsylvania contracts are dated December 18, 1782.

4. For the bidding on the contract for Delaware and Maryland, see Diary, November 29, 30, December 2 and 9, 1782; the contract is dated December 10, 1782.

5. On the contract for Virginia negotiated by George Webb, receiver of Continental taxes for Virginia, see RM to Webb, November 19, 1782.

6. The contract for North Carolina, South Carolina, and Georgia is dated February 15, 1783; for the negotiations, see RM to Nathanael Greene, October 17, and Greene to RM, December 3, 1782.

7. The three-month credit RM required for these contracts was identical to the terms accepted by Wadsworth and Carter in the renegotiated West Point and Moving Army contract in exchange for a one-third increase in the price of rations. This requirement limited the number of bidders and increased the prices for the major 1783 contracts. RM also found it necessary to make various concessions to enable the contractors to raise money needed to finance their contracts. See, for example, Diary, November 14 and 25, December 7, 1782, and March 20, 1783, Nathanael Greene to RM, December 3, and RM to Lovell, December 17, 1782.

To the President of Congress (John Hanson)

Office of Finance 10th October 1782

Sir

Mr. Edward Fox an Inhabitant of this City, and formerly Secretary to the Board of Treasury, has been recommended to me as a Person well acquainted with the Nature and extent of Accounts, and one whose Attention, exactitude and Integrity may be relied on. From the Conversations I have had with this Gentleman I am induced to believe that he is well qualified to undertake the Settlement of one of the principal Departments. I therefore do myself the Honor to report his Name to Congress as the Commissioner for settling the Accounts of the Hospital Department. Should Congress disapprove of this Appointment I hope to be favored with their Orders.[1] I am Sir Your Excellency's most obedient and humble Servant

Robt Morris

His Excellency The President of Congress

ENDORSED: 100/Letter 10 Oct 1782/Supi Finance/Edward Fox appointed/to settle the hospital Accounts
MSS: LS, PCC, DNA; Ofcl LbC, DLC.

1. Congress did not disapprove the nomination when the letter was read on October 11. For the background to Fox's appointment, see notes to RM to the President of Congress, February 18; James McCall to Fox, September 25, and Diary, September 17, 25, 26, and October 10, 1782.

To the Contractors for West Point and the Moving Army

Office of Finance 10. Octo: 1782

Gentlemen[1]

Mr. Cornell, in a Letter of the fifth Instant which I received last Evening, informs me that he has agreed for the Supply both of West

Point and the moving Army, after the fifteenth Instant until which Time you had agreed to continue your Supplies under your Contracts. He has also enclosed me the Copy of your Letter of the first Instant upon that Subject.[2] I confess to you Gentlemen, that these Events give me Pain. In forming the Contracts I did expect that Money would have been saved to the Public, Contentment produced to the Army, Ease to me, and Honor to yourselves. I did hope too that you would have found a pecuniary Advantage adequate to your Labors. It is unnecessary to investigate the Causes which have led to the present disagreable Situation, because they will come more properly into Contemplation at a future Period.

In your Letter of the eleventh of September, you asked of me certain Stipulations which I could not consent to. The object of a Contract is, to *substitute a certain to an uncertain Expence.* Had I agreed to your Propositions this Object would have been lost. No *Distress* therefore should have induced my Consent: Nothing but *absolute Necessity.* I again repeat Gentlemen, that I am sorry Things have taken the Turn which they have done. But I will not vent a Reproach, on the contrary I will (from a Regard to Justice) do that *now,* which the Duty of my Station[3] prohibited *then.* I will *join* you in every proper Measure to obtain ample Compensation for any Damages you may have sustained, by a Failure in Performance of that Part of the Contract, which imposes Obligations upon the Public. To entitle yourselves to such Compensation, it will be incumbent on you to shew *the Failure* and the Damage which *necessarily* followed from it. A complete Settlement of Accounts will be a Step previously necessary, and the Amount of the Ballance, will be a Point of important Evidence. You will observe that you stand charged with the Sum Total of Paper received; you will therefore (I suppose) find it prudent to return all which you have not disposed of. I mention this Circumstance that I may at the same Time assure you of my Readiness to receive the whole, or any Part, and to deduct it from the Payments made; so that (whatever may be the Mode of ascertaining whether the Public should compensate any Damages sustained, and what should be that Compensation) you may be in Capacity to shew clearly your Claims, and have the fairer Chance of obtaining Justice. It is however my Duty to observe that no Notice can be taken of your private and subordinate Agreements with each other.[4] I have the Honor to be with perfect Respect Gentlemen Yours &ca.[5]

RM

MSS: Ofcl LbC, DLC; copy, PCC, DNA; copy, Benjamin Franklin Papers, PPAmP.
1. Sands, Livingston and Company, consisting principally of Comfort Sands and Company, Walter Livingston, William Duer, and Daniel Parker, held the combined contract for West Point and the Moving Army. For the contractors of record and other interested parties and the internal arrangements among the contractors men-

tioned by RM at the close of the letter, including the troublesome beef subcontract held by Oliver Phelps and Timothy Edwards, see notes to Diary, May 13, 1782. For the collapse of the combined contract, see notes to Comfort Sands, Walter Livingston, William Duer, and Daniel Parker to RM, September 11.

2. The contractors' letter is printed as an enclosure to Walter Livingston, William Duer, and Daniel Parker to RM, October 9.

3. "Situation" in PPAmP text.

4. Sands, Livingston and Company replied to RM on October 21.

5. The PCC text was enclosed in RM to the President of Congress, October 21, 1782, the PPAmP text in RM to Benjamin Franklin, January 11, 1783. Another copy, not found, was enclosed in RM to Ezekiel Cornell, October 10.

To Ezekiel Cornell

Office of Finance 10. Octo: 1782[1]

Sir,

I received your Letter of the fifth last Evening. The Proposition of allowing sixty ninetieths of a Dollar per hundred Weight on Beef to be furnished by some of the Contractors is utterly inadmissible. I have written to the Contractors this Day "that no Notice can be taken of their private and subordinate Agreements with each other." I enclose for your Perusal a Copy of the whole Letter. I will not subject them to the Necessity of Law suits for obtaining Justice; such Artifice is beneath the Dignity of Government. But I will not give three fifths (or if the fifth Quarter of Beef is included three fourths) of a ninetieth on every Ration meerly to silence Clamors which may perhaps have no just Foundation.

I have read the Copy of the Letter from Nathaniel Stevens and I authorize and desire you to cause that Dispute[2] and all others of the Kind to be finally settled according to Equity and good Conscience. I am Sir Your most obedient and humble Servant

RM

MSS: Ofcl LbC, DLC; copy, PCC, DNA; copy, Benjamin Franklin Papers, PPAmP.

1. Cornell was the inspector of contracts for the main army. The PCC text of this letter was enclosed in RM to the President of Congress, October 21, 1782, the PPAmP text in RM to Benjamin Franklin, January 11, 1783.

2. The letter has not been found. On the dispute, see notes to Cornell to RM, October 5.

To Tench Tilghman

Office of Finance 10. Octo. 1782[1]

Dear Sir,

I have received your Letter of the fifth for which I am very much obliged to you. I cannot now answer it so fully as I could wish. General Cornell will shew you my Letter to him,[2] by which you will see that I decline the Proposition of the Beef Contractors. As to the due Bills I am inclined to think it would be best to have a Return made of the Amount regimentally because by this Means we should better see what real Expenditure of Money had been made by the Contractors. I wish you would think of this and give me your Sentiments on the Subject. I much approve of and am much obliged by your Plan for settling the future Issues. The Price which Messrs. Wadsworth and Carter obtain[3] is sufficient to enable them to supply most unexceptionably and therefore I hope the Officers will take good Care both of themselves and of the Troops. God knows it is my wish to afford them every accomodation. I labor hard to procure the Pay but what can be expected from a Person in my Situation pressed on all Hands by Demands and unsupported by those who can alone releive. However Perseverance has done a great Deal hitherto and will I trust do more.

I am extremely pleased to find that my Sentiments on what was necessary to be done so entirely coincide with yours. Indeed the Necessity was but too apparent and yet I shall not be surprized if I meet with Blame for doing the only good Thing possible in one of the worst of all possible Situations. Those my good Friend who wish to hunt down the Financier can be at Times either all alive or quite indifferent to the Feelings of the Army just as it may best suit the Purposes of the Chace. For my own Part I am not much concerned about the Opinions of such Men while I have in my favor the Voice of the wise and the good added to the fair Testimony of an approving Conscience. Believe me I pray very sincerely your most obedient and humble Servant

RM

MS: Ofcl LbC, DLC.
1. Lieutenant Colonel Tilghman was an aide to George Washington.
2. See the preceding document.
3. See the contract with Wadsworth and Carter of October 12.

To Jeremiah Wadsworth

Office of Finance 10 October 1782

Sir,

I have received your Letter of the fifth Instant. I shall give you my Sentiments of the Contract when I see it and will take Occasion to render you the Information you request:[1] I write this meerly to inform you that I have written to General Cornell on the Subject of the four Shillings lawful Per hundred required by the Beef Contractors which you and Tilghman both seem to consider as a Kind of hush Money.[2] I will not agree to it be the Consequences what they may. I am Sir your most obedient and humble Servant

RM

MS: Ofcl LbC, DLC.

1. Wadsworth, a Connecticut merchant and business partner of John Carter, had negotiated a new contract for West Point and the Moving Army with Ezekiel Cornell, the inspector of contracts for the main army. The contract, dated October 12, was effective October 16.

2. See Cornell to RM, and Tench Tilghman to RM, both October 5, and the preceding three letters of this date.

Matthew Ridley to Gouverneur Morris

Paris Le 10 Octobre 1782[1]

My Dear Sir,

With real pleasure I received your two Letters dated the 10 June and 6 August Last.[2] The first I received Just on my return from Visiting the Mynhers the end of August. My long stay in Holland threw so many affairs on my hands upon my return that I have been greatly occupied ever since and has indeed occasioned some Delay in Answering my Friends Letters. I am fully Sensible of your Kindness and Friendship towards me and can assure you I often look forward with a kind of rapture to the time that will once more unite me with those I love.

E'er this I hope you have received the watch. It is my desire to have pleased you in the choice.

I can with great content of mind inform you my Boys are well; and without any partiality or flattery I think them as fine children as ever I knew. Bobs application for a boy of his age is really astonishing. Tom is not so steady but possess[es] an acutness and talents that make me flatter myself he will become a shining character. His application is not to be complained of tho' not equal to Bob's; but as he has a Spirit of emulation I think when the Boyish Period is a Little passed he will not need Spurring. I have hitherto kept them in the Same pension where I placed them on first coming here. The Situation of Geneva would not admit of carrying them there and except Colmar which I think too much of a military Establishment; there have hitherto been almost insuperable Objections to placing them anywhere else. I can however assure you they have lost no time, French, Dancing, Cyphering and writing. I am Sorry however to Say I do not think the advantages to be acquired in Education in Europe will by any means repay the anxieties of Parents in parting with them or the not having a proper Person properly attatch'd to them. These children are very near my Heart. I have been consulting Mr Jay about them. I write Mr Morris by this occasion on the Subject,[3] and I beg to refer you to him as I have no doubt he will communicate with you.

The Virginia parties give me pain.[4] I think with you there is more of Personality than Plan in what they ⟨say⟩ do. Such men are however bad members of Society and tho' the Plan be not to Serve our Enemies they have on every occasion endeavoured to profit of Such Conduct. If ever I was to adopt an Ostracism or other such regulation it should be for People of the above description. Instead of the People a Committee of the Coolest old Fellows should analyze the Public complaint of one Citizen against another and if there was found to be any Personality in the accusation he should be banish'd. Men of personality and Talents are there most dangerous I know in a Community. Things the most Venial if done by the man disliked are ever viewed through the magnifying End of the Spy Glass: for those esteem'd their Friends the end of the Glass is changed even for the Grossest. Thus in one Instance the Public may be deprived of a Valuable Servant and in the other be Saddled with a knave.

Festina Lente is Said to be a good maxim[5] and Litteraly it certainly is so but it is very difficult to define because it is Success only which proves the right application. The Dutch have had a great deal of the lente this war but as to the Festina I am afraid they will miss it. My opinion is that a virtuous Body of People will Surmount any difficulties. When they cease to be Virtuous I care very little what becomes of them. A large circle put in motion will continue its action longer than a smaller one with even the same force but unless assisted it must Stop. So it is with Governments, the Largest are the longest in crumbling to pieces; And without Virtue in the Individuals of it to continue the force nothing can ultimately [alter?][6] it's fate.

That America will become a maritime Power is to me as clear as the Sun in his Meridian Splendor. It is however my Friend one of the advantages of America which has often employed my moments of Serious Reflection. To establish the marine in such manner as that the whole may partake of the advantages and power resulting from it is where I apprehend the greatest difficulty. Nothing can counter balance natural advantages but are united with Industry in the greatest degree; with Suitable Rewards for encouraging a Spirit of Enterprize and activity. Local Situations may some times compell a People to follow a particular profession. Where the Local advantages are wanting, the Subject must be led on with a gentle hand, Caress'd and Sooth'd by Rewards, or otherways, untill the profession becomes so woven in the Constitution of the Government, and the habits of the Individuals that nothing but the Anihilation of both can root it out.

The Capture of Colo. Livingston was an unfortunate affair. Carmichael in a Letter to me[7] regrets much the loss of all his Letter[s] by that opportunity. He Says he has written to all his Friends. He now stays in Spain I believe some what in quality of chargé d'affaires. Mr Jay and Madame have been here Some time. They with their little girl are in Good health. That is to say the two former as well as usual. Their constitutions are delicate. Mr. Jay from close application complains now and then. I have the happiness of being with them frequently. The firmness of Mr. Jay in the Commission he is Charged with[8] does him the greatest honor. Our country owes him much; and I flatter myself she will not be insensible of it. Such Sound honest patriots are not the production of every Soil.

I observe what you Say about Peace: But taisez vous. A good Peace my Friend will do us no harm. In answer to all thy Metaphors I will cite my Almanack: "War begets poverty, Poverty Peace, Peace makes Riches flow, war ne'er Doth cease." The end of war is Peace: but the worst of all Wars are perhaps those carried on in ones own Country. Property is uncertain; Enjoyments precarious; the cords of society broken a Sunder. "Let us Eat Drink and Sleep for tomorrow we Die" is in the mouth of every one. In short morals become corrupt, often from necessity and poor humanity Stands Shivering like extreme old age in a cold frosty Morning. Peace cures all these, and though luxury (which is certainly an evil) is introduced, yet it is to this luxury we owe all the finest feelings. Would you be without them? Indeed, Indeed my Friend you would not. There is this observation to be made, that whilst the People remain virtuous they will chuse virtuous Representatives. That Period passed a revolution becomes necessary. It is like "dying to be born again." There is generally a time with all governments that these events ought to happen and when that time is, I pity the people if it does not for depend upon it they will become Slaves.

I know not how you will relish my doctrines. But as the French say I am not "opiniatre" I always like to hear the opinions of others.

In the news of political way I have but very little to give you. The affair of Gibraltar has thrown a little damp in the ardor of the Spaniards. Howe is out with a Fleet of 34 or 36 sails destined to Gibraltar, the Combined fleet is said to be waiting for him with 52 at agesires [Algeciras]. All are impatient to know the event some pretend to foretell it. They say that Howe will throw in whatever he desires to assist the fortress with and make the best of his way back again; and that the combined fleet will go to Cadiz, That both will keep themselves very snug this winter and that perhaps next summer there will be nothing for them to do.[9]

The Dutch have made a very poor campaign of it. Their parties are so opposite and violent that it is almost impossible they can do anything well. There is a Country now which requires a Revolution.

The King of Prussia keeps himself pretty quiet. The Emperor continues reforming and some say he carries it too far an old friend like an old Fashioned musket is laid aside.

The Count du Nord[10] with the Countess are I believe at Vienna where for fear they should interrupt the Mother with Count Orlow it is said they will stay some time.

Being informed that there is an opportunity to send this Letter immediately I am obliged to break off to beg you will remember me kindly and respectfully to everyone. If I dared I would Desire you to salute La: Kitty for me. She has not a Friend who esteems her ⟨so much⟩ more than I do.

MS: LbC, Ridley Papers, MHi.

1. The following notes were written in the margin of this letter: "The first by the Danaide frigate Saild from Rochefort [*three lines left blank*]. The Second by the Packet G1 Washington Capt Barney Sailed from L'orient Janry 17. 1783. Arrived March the 12th at Philadelphia." Neither of these texts have been found, but Gouverneur Morris evidently received the first one, for he replied on January 1, 1783. For Ridley's activities in Europe as an agent of Maryland, guardian of RM's two eldest sons, and onlooker in the peace negotiations in Paris, see notes to RM to Ridley, October 14, 1781; and Herbert E. Klingelhofer, ed., "Matthew Ridley's Diary During the Peace Negotiations of 1782," *WMQ*, 3d ser., XX (1963), 95–133.

2. The letter of June 10 has not been found.

3. See Ridley to RM, October 12.

4. In his June 10 letter Gouverneur Morris had evidently commented on the opposition to Office of Finance policies among some prominent Virginians. On this subject, see RM to Benjamin Franklin, September 28, and notes.

5. See Gouverneur Morris to John Jay, August 6, and notes.

6. Editors' conjecture for an estimated one word inadvertently omitted by the copyist.

7. William Carmichael's letter to Ridley has not been found. On the capture of Henry Brockholst Livingston, see Gouverneur Morris to Jay, May 21, 1782, and notes.

8. On this point, see Jay to Gouverneur Morris, October 13, and notes.

9. British Admiral Lord Richard Howe succeeded in relieving Gibraltar from Spanish siege later in October. See Morris, *Peacemakers*, 342; and Piers Mackesy, *The War for America, 1775–1783* (Cambridge, Mass., 1964), 479–484.

10. The Count de Nord was Paul (1754–1801), son of Catherine the Great and Peter III of Russia, who succeeded his mother as czar in 1796 and reigned until his death by assassination; Count Grigori Grigorievich Orlov (1734–1783) was the former favorite of Catherine the Great. *Webster's Biographical Dictionary* (Springfield, Mass., 1972), 1154, 1126.

Wallace, Johnson, and Muir to John Swanwick

Nantes 10th October 1782[1]

We have now before us Copies of yours of the 25 March and 27 June also original of the 9 August[2] the contents of all which we have most attentively observed. It fills us with pleasure to find you approve our management of the Nonsuch and trust that she will turn out a profitable Vessell to us especially shou'd she arrive here again safe with a Cargo of good Tobacco. We thank you for informing us of the safe arrival of the Favorite at Baltimore, we wish we could hand you the safe arrival of her here in turn but we now esteem her a missing ship. We attend to the appointment Mr. Morris has made of you for the management of His private concerns and have now the pleasure of congratulating you on it, this mark of that great Man's good opinion of and confidence in you is the greatest proof of your merit, whatever matters of his that remains in our management we shall with much pleasure hereafter correspond with you for and we have now to inform you that we have [made?][3] him a Shipment of Goods amounting to $_{444}$£$_{3.8}$ by the

Brig Speedwell Capt. Samuel Mansfield who will sail in a few days for Baltimore by her we shall address you and hand you Invoice and Bill of lading and so soon as our present hurry is a little over we will make up the Nonsuch's Account of last Voyage and ship you whatever more shall be coming to Mr. Morris at the same time give you every satisfaction in our powers. We are glad to find that the Goods we sent for Mr. Jay has reach'd you in safety we are also thankful to you for your care of them, we have since heard from Mr. Jay, that those sent for Miss Kitty was such as fitted. Refering you to what we purpose writing you by the Speedwell we are with sincere esteem and regard, Sir your very Humble Servants

Maryland Tobacco 90 a 100$^{\#}$

Virginia . . . 100 a 118 per Ct

ms: LbC, Wallace, Johnson, and Muir Letterbook, NN.

1. This letter is addressed to Swanwick as "Attorney to the Honorle. Robt. Morris Esqr. Philadelphia"; according to a note in the margin of the letterbook, it was sent "per Congress Capn Geddes." Wallace, Johnson, and Muir was a mercantile firm of Annapolis and Nantes specializing in the tobacco trade; Joshua Johnson was the firm's representative at Nantes.

2. Letters not found.

3. Editors' conjecture for an estimated one word inadvertently omitted by the copyist.

Diary: October 11, 1782

The Honble. Secry at War took the Papers of the Court of Enquiry on the Conduct of Capt. Samuel Nicholson and very kindly gave me his Opinion on the informality of those proceedings.[1]

Mr. Henry Dering for Money which I granted in Cash and Notes.

Oliver Pollock Esqr. respecting his affairs on which see my Letter to James Duane Esqr.

Colo Humpton for Money for enlisting Germans. I desired a return of all that are enlisted and promised the payment.

Majr Geo: Turner informed me of his Intention to accept the Appointment of Commissary of Prisoners. I desired him to answer my Letter in Writing.[2]

The Honble. Mr. Holker desired Bills of Exchange for the Balance due to him for Cloathing and I directed the same to be made out.[3] After which I set out for the Country to return on Monday Morning.

Wrote a Letter to the Honble. Mr Duane.

Wrote a Letter to his Excelly the President of Congress.

Wrote a Letter to Majr Geo Turner.

Wrote a Letter to Saml Miles Esqr.

Wrote a Letter to Jos. Nourse.

1. RM's determination on the proceedings is dated October 17.

2. Turner's letter of acceptance has not been found. RM commissioned him on October 15.

3. See RM to John Holker, October 9.

To the President of Congress
(John Hanson)

Office of Finance 11th October 1782

Sir

Mr. Joseph Bindon who was formerly a Merchant in Canada has offered his Service as Commissioner for settling the Accounts of one of the public Departments. I have been well informed of this Gentlemans character for Integrity and Abilities, and also of his strong attachment to the Cause of America. I therefore do myself the Honor to report his Name to Congress as the Commissioner for settling the accounts of the Cloathing Department. Should Congress disapprove of this appointment I hope to be favored with their Orders.[1] With perfect Respect I have the Honor to be Sir Your Excellency's most obedient and humble Servant

Robt Morris

His Excellency The President of Congress

ENDORSED: 99./Letter Oct 11. 1782/Read 14./Joseph Bindon/a Comr. for settling Accounts/of the Cloathing department
MSS: LS, PCC, DNA; Ofcl LbC, DLC.
1. Congress offered no objections, and Bindon took the oath of office on October 26, 1782 (see PCC, no. 195, p. 313). For this and other appointments of commissioners of accounts for the departments, see RM to the President of Congress, February 18, 1782, and notes.

To James Duane

Office of Finance 11 October 1782[1]

Sir

I received the enclosed Letter from Mr. Pollock to the President of Congress[2] in a Letter from the Honorable Mr Clarke which is as follows. "Septr 22nd. 1782 Sir, You have enclosed for Perusal a Letter from Mr. Pollock. The Committee to whom the same is referred desire you will as soon as possible give them such a State of the Matters therein mentioned as your Means of Information may enable you to do."[3] Understanding that you are the Chairman of that Committee, I have taken the Liberty to address this Letter to you. I have carefully perused Mr. Pollocks Letter above mentioned and collected such Evidence relating to the Transaction as my Time and Means would permit. The Enclosure marked No. 1 contains the Copies of Letters from the Secret and Commercial Committee to Mr. Pollock. That marked No. 2 contains Copies of Letters from Mr. Pollock, and that marked No. 3 contains the Copies of Letters relating to him by Don Galvez and Don Miro.[4] In addition to what is contained in all these Documents I have frequently been informed by Persons from that Quarter of the World of Mr Pollocks good Conduct. I am myself therefore fully persuaded that Oliver Pollock Esqr. late Commercial Agent of the United States at New Orleans having manifested great Zeal, Integrity and Abilities during his Residence at that Place is entitled to the most favorable notice and attention. I doubt not that the Committee will on a full Examination find sufficient Reason to present him in the most favorable Manner to Congress.

With Respect to the State of his accounts I find that on the sixth Day of February 1781 the Treasury were directed to pass to his Credit thirty seven thousand, eight hundred and thirty six Dollars Specie bearing Interest at six per Cent and on the seventh of November 1781 a further Sum of twenty one thousand, four hundred and nineteen Dollars Specie bearing Interest at six per Cent from the sixth of February 1781 so that there appears to be due to Mr. Pollock fifty nine thousand two hundred and fifty five Dollars. But I am prohibited by the Act of the seventh of November from paying any Part of this until advice is received from Don Galvez of the Sums by him advanced to Mr. Pollock for the Service of the United States and what Measures have been taken by Mr. Pollock for reimbursing those Sums. This together with an Order of the same date to report a Letter to Don Galvez was in Consequence of a Letter from James Seagrove of the Seventeenth of September 1781 and one from Don Galvez of the twenty second of July 1780. A Copy of these Letters and of that which I reported (and which being approved of by Congress was transmitted) is contained in the Paper Number four.[5]

I have good reason to be convinced that my Letter to Don Galvez[6] was received but no answer to it has yet reached me. I shall forward however more Copies at convenient Opportunities and endeavour to obtain a Decission on the Points contained in it. I think it highly probable that many Articles of Mr. Pollocks Account against the State of Virginia will on a final Adjustment be found justly chargeable to the United States and therefore I think that as well from the Want of an Answer from Governor Galvez as from that Circumstance his Accounts with the United States must be left open until those with the State of Virginia are closed.

You will observe Sir among the Papers which I have had the Honor already to enumerate an application from Don Miro to enable Mr. Pollock to do Justice to sundry Subjects of his Catholic Majesty. It is unnecessary to observe to Gentlemen so conversant in public Business as the Committee that the Injury sustained by the

United States from a non Payment of what is due to Foreigners greatly exceeds the Value of the Sums due. And as to the Advance made by Governor Galvez as he declares that and many Circumstances concur to shew that it was without the Order or even Privity of his Court the Difference will not be very material whether it is due by Mr. Pollock or by his Country.

There appear to me Sir three good Reasons for recommending Mr. Pollock to the State of Virginia, and for requesting that State to adjust his Accounts; First because as has been already observed his faithful Services merit the favorable Notice of his Masters. Secondly because the final Settlement of his Account with the Union will depend upon the Settlement with that State And Thirdly because a Settlement with both is necessary to relieve our public Credit abroad, and do the Justice which is called for by Don Miro. I say nothing on this Occasion of those Principles of Justice and Gratitude which will always I am sure have their proper Influence.[7] I am Sir with perfect Esteem and Respect Your most obedient Servant

Robt Morris

The Honorable Mr. Duane
Chairman of a Committee of Congress

ENDORSED: Report of Supintt. of/Finance to the Committee on/Mr Pollock's memorial
MSS: LS, PCC, DNA; Ofcl LbC, DLC; copy, Executive Communications, 1782, Vi.

1. Duane, a member of Congress from New York, was chairman of a committee of Congress that included Abraham Clark of New Jersey and Hugh Williamson of North Carolina, to whom Congress had referred a letter of September 18, 1782, from Oliver Pollock (see note 2 below). Clark apparently was the original chairman, but was currently absent from Congress. See Burnett, ed., *Letters*, VI, xlviii.

2. Oliver Pollock, the former commercial agent at New Orleans for the United States and Virginia, had been endeavoring to have his accounts settled, but the efforts of his agents John Henderson and Daniel Clark had failed to secure payment from either source. Threatened with arrest unless his creditors were paid, Pollock resolved to come to the United States. In accordance with Spanish law, he left another person, Thomas Paterson, "hostage" for his return and payment of his debts. Traveling via Havana, where he arrived in May 1782, Pollock reportedly helped secure the release of ships of the American mercantile fleet long kept in port by a Spanish embargo. Their safe arrival in the Delaware in May and June brought much-needed specie into American hands (see Diary, May 28, June 11, 18, 1782).

Landing at Wilmington in one of the ships of the Havana fleet, Pollock traveled first to Richmond to settle his accounts with Virginia. Governor Benjamin Harrison, having developed suspicions about the fraudulent use of bills of exchange in payment of supplies for the western campaigns of George Rogers Clark, wanted Pollock to settle his claims through the special commission the state had appointed for liquidating western accounts (see notes to Diary, September 27). Pollock, however, objected to such a long and dangerous trek westward to deal with a commission totally unfamiliar with his transactions. Since the assembly was not then in session, he journeyed to Philadelphia in August to seek payment on his Continental accounts.

After conferring with RM, Pollock addressed a letter to the president of Congress on September 18, recounting at length his activities on behalf of the American cause as United States agent at New Orleans and requesting reimbursement for funds expended on Continental account. The letter was read on September 23 and referred to the committee mentioned in the preceding note; it is printed in James, *Oliver Pollock*, 347–355, from the text in PCC, no. 50, pp. 1–13.

3. No other text of Clark's letter has been found.

4. Enclosure no. 1, consisting of letters dated June 12, 1777, to July 19, 1779, is in PCC, no. 50, pp. 29–49. Enclosure no. 2, comprising letters from Pollock to Congress with enclosures and related materials dated October 10, 1776, to May 3, 1782, is in PCC, no. 50, pp. 51–158. Enclosure no. 3, containing a letter from Bernardo de Gálvez to President Samuel Huntington of Congress, July 30, 1781, and one from Esteban Rodríguez Miró to the President of Congress, May 4, 1782, is in PCC, no. 50, pp. 159–168. A list of documents relating to Pollock's claims sent to RM by Secretary of Congress Charles Thomson on October 11, 1782, which enumerated many of those enclosed in the present letter, is filed in the Miscellaneous Papers of the Continental Congress, 1774–1789, RG 360, DNA. On Miró (ca. 1744–1795), formerly an aide to Gálvez, who became acting commandant and governor of Louisiana upon Gálvez's departure early in 1782, see Hutchinson and Rutland, eds., *Madison Papers*, III, 346n.; and Burson, *Don Esteban Miró*.

5. Enclosure no. 4 is in PCC, no. 50, pp. 169–180; for the documents contained therein, see RM's Report to Congress of a Letter to Bernardo de Gálvez, November 21, 1781, and notes.

6. Dated November 23, 1781.

7. Following RM's suggestion, Duane and Williamson reported on October 22 that Pollock's Continental accounts were so intertwined with his Virginia claims that their settlement had to be deferred until those with Virginia were liquidated. Citing Pollock's apparent "zeal and industry" on behalf of the United States to the extent of having "advanced large sums out of his private fortune," the committee acknowledged "that public faith, justice and humanity require that the sundry accounts should be liquidated and the balances paid, or at least security given for payment of the same, whenever the state of our public funds shall render it practicable." Congress adopted the report, recommending that Virginia settle its accounts with Pollock "with as much despatch as may be practicable." RM enclosed it in his letter to the governor of Virginia of October 29, and Pollock set out for Richmond after obtaining money from RM to finance his journey.

Although the Virginia legislature reached a settlement of Pollock's accounts in December 1782, and committed itself to payment by installments, it was unable to make the initial payment, and in June 1783, after items in his claim were challenged, it suspended all further payment to Pollock. Moreover, the legislature had in December postponed issuing certificates to Pollock for sums due on protested bills of exchange it had authorized Pollock to draw in 1779 on the now bankrupt firm of Penet D'Acosta Frères and Company until Pollock gave security satisfactory to Virginia's congressional delegates against further demands on the state by the holders of the bills. Under the procedure agreed upon by Pollock and the Virginia delegates, the holders of the bills were required to forward them to Francisco Rendón, the unofficial Spanish resident in Philadelphia, to be recovered with damages and placed at 6 percent interest until paid by the Virginia treasury. This arrangement was unacceptable to the holders of the bills and the Louisiana government; Pollock's creditors brought suit against him, causing his arrest for debt in Havana in 1784. See *Journal of the House of Delegates of the Commonwealth of Virginia; Begun and Held in the Town of Richmond. In the County of Henrico. . . .* (Richmond, 1828) [October 1782 session], 83–84, [May 1783 session], 83–85; the correspondence in McIlwaine, ed., *Official Letters*, III, 260–261, 320–322, 461; also James, *Oliver Pollock*, 241–242, 269–279, 299–301; Hutchinson and Rutland, eds., *Madison Papers*, VII, 8–12; Kinnaird, ed., *Spain in the Mississippi Valley*, pt. 2, pp. 10, 68–69, 76, 77–78, 87–88, 91–92; and Diary, October 28, 29, 30, November 1, and RM to Daniel Clark, December 31, 1782. For action on Pollock's Continental accounts upon his return to Philadelphia in January 1783, see notes to Diary, September 10, 1781, and documents cited there; and Diary, January 31, February 10, 21, March 1, 17, 29, April 1, 3, 12, May 1, 17, 29, April 1, 3, 12, May 1, 5, 10, 14, August 21, 1783, and RM to Bernardo de Gálvez, May 16, and to Daniel Clark, May 30, 1783.

James McCall to Samuel Miles

Office of Finance 11. Octo: 1782

Sir,

Your letter of Yesterday's date[1] respecting a Balance due Paul Huber has been received by Mr. Morris and in Answer thereto he has desired me to inform you that he never has given any Encouragement to partial or seperate Payments nor never will, and in future desires that all Applications for Money for your Department may come from yourself. I am Sir your most obedient and humble Servant

J. McCall secy to RM

MS: Ofcl LbC, DLC.
    1. Letter not found. Miles was the deputy quartermaster general for Pennsylvania.

To George Turner

Office of Finance 11. Octo: 1782

Sir,

The enclosed Act of Congress of the twenty fourth of July will inform you in some Degree of the Duties of the Office of Commissary of naval Prisoners.[1] You will perceive that this alone will not find you sufficient Employment for your whole Time. When I cast my Eyes upon you for a Commissary of naval Prisoners I had it in View that as soon as you should have obtained all those Accounts and Informations which may be necessary to make you compleatly Master of that particular Business you should occasionally employ those Talents which I conceive you to be possessed of in other Matters of a public Nature. What these may be Time and Circumstances must determine as they arise but as you will certainly (should you accept this Office) be desirous of doing as much of the Public Business as your Time will admit of so it is my desire to give you the Opportunity. One general Principle with me both for myself and others is that all those who receive Salaries from the public Treasury should devote their whole Time to the public Service. I take this Occasion Sir to repeat that I have made you a tender of this Office from the good Character given of you by others and from my own Conviction of your Abilities. How far it may consist with your Views and Pursuits you alone can determine. With Respect I am Sir your most obedient and humble Servant

RM

MS: Ofcl LbC, DLC.
    1. The act of July 24, 1782, vested RM as Agent of Marine with the power of negotiating the exchange of marine prisoners and authorized him to appoint a com-

missary of marine prisoners who was to be subject to his orders. Turner's salary was set at $1,200 per annum, including any pay or allowances as a Continental army officer. See George Washington to RM, October 7, Diary, October 10 and 11, and on the exchange of marine prisoners, notes to Diary, June 18 and August 13, 1782.

James McCall to the Register of the Treasury (Joseph Nourse)

Office of Finance 11. Octo: 1782

Mr. Morris desired I would transmit you a Sheet of Certificates for two hundred Dollars each—blank Names, Dates and Numbers received this Morning from Francis Hopkinson Esqr. late Treasurer of Loans, being a surplus Sheet and which you are to Charge to Michael Hillegas Esqr. Continental Treasurer taking his Receipt for the same.

MS: Ofcl LbC, DLC.

Contract with Jeremiah Wadsworth and John Carter

This contract with Wadsworth and Carter, contractors for the French army, was for supplying West Point and the Moving Army from October 16 to December 31, 1782.[1] It was designed both to remedy Morris's financial inability to fulfill the terms of the combined West Point and Moving Army contract held by Sands, Livingston and Company[2] and to alleviate the conflicts between the contractors and the army over the mode of issuing rations.[3]

Wadsworth and Carter had previously considered involvement in the Moving Army contract, but had decided it was not worth their while.[4] However, with the French army now moving northward under conditional orders for the West Indies,[5] the partners apparently reconsidered. On September 18, the day after Morris had received the ultimatum contained in the existing contractors' letter of September 11, Carter informed the Financier of the firm's intention to bid for the 1783 contract.[6]

By that time the affairs of Morris and Wadsworth and Carter had become increasingly intertwined. In May the Superintendent had borrowed money from the firm which he still had not completely repaid.[7] The French, their specie supply in America running low, increasingly were resorting to the use of bills of exchange on France to finance their operations. Under an arrangement made with the French army in June 1782, Wadsworth and Carter had agreed to advance cash in exchange for a monopoly on the sale of French army bills.[8] This left the Financier as their only important competitor in the sale of bills on France, and John Chaloner, the firm's agent in Philadelphia, began to cooperate with him to maintain the exchange rate on bills. As the French army moved north, Wadsworth and Carter's agents (and speculators hoping to sell to them) had also begun to compete with American contractors in the purchase of supplies, to the detriment of both. Combining French and American purchasing into the hands of one firm would alleviate the competition and relieve Morris of the necessity of selling bills at low rates to raise money to pay the contractors.

Under these favorable circumstances it was now more attractive for

Wadsworth and Carter to assume the 1782 contract. The firm's financial commitments to the French, however, left it unable to supply the requisite credit unless Morris repaid the sums owed and otherwise aided Wadsworth and Carter in raising cash.[9] Even after the Superintendent promised Carter he would repay all his debts to them as they fell due if they would assume the contract, Wadsworth and Carter were still not anxious to do so because it would interfere with other business plans and would "come too suddenly for the State of their Funds."[10] Although the Financier left the actual negotiation of the new contract, should it prove necessary, to Wadsworth and Ezekiel Cornell, inspector of contracts for the main army, at army headquarters in New York, he also continued discussions with Carter in Philadelphia.

The turning point came on September 23 when the mails brought the Superintendent a meager weekly return of revenues from the states. Unless the army could be provisioned "at a long Credit," Morris wrote Cornell later that day, he would have to order the current contractors to stop issuing and advise Washington to begin military impressment of supplies; the Financier therefore urged Cornell to make the best possible agreement with Wadsworth under Washington's "Inspection." Cornell and Washington quickly agreed that there was no alternative but to contract with Wadsworth even though "it must be on his own [terms], as he knew our situation." The parties reached an understanding on October 4 when Wadsworth agreed to supply West Point and the Moving Army until the end of the year at $^{13}\!/_{90}$ of a dollar per ration (one-third higher than the previous price) and give three months' credit. Tench Tilghman, Washington's aide, wrote approvingly to Morris of the contract on October 5, noting that Wadsworth would indeed "make good terms for himself" but would execute the contract so as to give "entire Satisfaction." Contractual details relating to the long-disputed questions on the mode of issuing provisions were to be added to the agreement after consultation with a board of officers, a procedure adopted in part, Tilghman explained, "to interest as many as I could in supporting the Contract after it should be formed." Although reserving judgment until he saw the contract, Morris hoped the officers, in light of the high price given, would "take good Care both of themselves and of the Troops." The Superintendent, however, rejected the suggestion, endorsed by Cornell, Wadsworth, and Tilghman, that a premium be paid to the beef subcontractors for the Moving Army for beef purchased from them by Wadsworth, thereby inviting litigation from Sands, Livingston and Company against the United States that was to extend into the next century.[11] After reminding Morris of his promise to pay the sums owed the firm, Carter signed the final contract for himself and Wadsworth at camp on October 12. Receiving the contract on the 21st, the Superintendent that day wrote a full explanation to Congress and a pointed letter to the states citing the new, more expensive, agreement as the inevitable result of their procrastination in levying and collecting Continental taxes.

A comparison with the Moving Army contract of April 6, 1782, indicates that the Wadsworth and Carter agreement, by embodying many of the reforms in issuing procedures previously adopted in August, accorded the officers most of the points they had demanded in their disputes with Comfort Sands. The language of the new contract also shows that Cornell had succeeded in his intention of making the contract "so plain and explicit as to prevent any mistakes or uneasiness." Unambiguous phrases relative to the quality of components were added: all were required to be of "good" grade, with "merchantable" flour, beef, salt, and hard soap, "full proof" whiskey, and "well saved" pork specifically designated. Issues were to be made in as many drafts as there were companies, rather than by regiment, and provision was made for those who could not draw with their own regiments. Officers could draw any number of rations not exceeding the number allowed to them, with the accounts to be closed at the end of each month, and could substitute West India rum for whiskey rations. A 3 percent allowance on meat to make up for wastage in cutting was provided to all drawers. The exemption of the contractors' property from seizure in the event of nonperformance was qualified to permit seizure "only by the express Orders of General Washington, and him only in Cases wherein the Army is not regularly supplied by the Contractors or the Provision is condemned by the Inspector." Other clauses facilitated the settlement of the contractors' accounts and otherwise made palatable to them the concessions awarded to the officers. These changes largely eliminated the bones of contention between the contractors and the army. Wadsworth and Carter did not personally administer the contract, traveling instead to New England with the French army, but their agents (including Charles Stewart, who stayed on as issuing commissary with a small share in the new contract) executed it efficiently. Few complaints emanated from the army about provisioning under the new contract. Save for minor differences with the contractors over the settlement of accounts,[12] it required little more of the Superintendent's time and attention.

Although the new contract satisfied the army, gave Morris needed flexibility in the sale of bills of exchange, and eased the pressure on his own notes, as the time for payment approached with the new year, the Financier was no better able to pay than before. Consequently, in January he accepted Wadsworth and Carter's offer to receive bills of exchange on France to the estimated value of the rations issued under the contract in return for giving Morris their notes payable at the times stipulated for his payments under the contract.[13] On the specified dates the Superintendent would pay over the notes to Wadsworth and Carter, thus cancelling them. Because Morris's French bills were drawn at 100 days' sight, the actual payment would not take place in Europe until after the last due date for payment on the contract. Lending risk to the transaction was the fact that Morris did not know at the time he gave the bills to Wadsworth and Carter whether there would be any funds available in Europe to pay them. Wadsworth and Carter's anxiety over the fate of the payment was partially relieved by a steady flow of information from Gouverneur Morris and Alexander Hamilton, and with the return of Captain Joshua Barney from France in March 1783 with news of the French loan for 1783, the Superintendent was able to assure Carter that the bills would be paid therefrom.[14] The entire cost of the contract was thus borne by French rather than domestic resources.

As Tilghman had predicted, the contract proved very profitable for Wadsworth and Carter. Carter estimated that it would clear about £12,000 not including the substantial profits realized on the French bills.[15] Arthur Lee, a persistent adversary of Morris, later criticized the arrangement, alleging that the contractors had been overpaid and that the January transaction wiped out the three months' credit that was supposed to justify the higher price of the agreement.[16] Congress, however, had not challenged the contract,[17] and Morris considered the mode of payment agreed to by Wadsworth and Carter in January "a good Bargain for the Public."[18] Whatever its shortcomings, the Superintendent regarded the contract as a necessary but temporary expedient until the contracts for 1783 could be negotiated at lower prices. As such, it effectively served as a bridge between the early contracts of 1781 and 1782 and the contracts of 1783, which embodied a new system of issues prepared by Morris and Secretary at War Benjamin Lincoln.[19]

[Headquarters, Verplancks Point, New York, October 12, 1782]

Articles of Agreement made and Concluded this twelfth day of October in the year of our Lord one thousand seven hundred and eighty two Between Robert Morris Esqr: Superintendant of the Finances of the United States of America duly Authorized and appointed by the Honorable United States of America in Congress Assembled in behalf of the United States of the One Part and Jeremiah Wadsworth of the State of Connecticut and John Carter of the State of New York of the other Part. Whereas the Honorable Congress did on the Tenth day of October [i.e., July] in the year of our Lord One thousand seven hundred and Eighty One Resolve that the Superintendant of Finance be and is hereby Authorized either by himself or such Person or Persons as he shall from time to time appoint for the Purpose to Procure on Contract all necessary supplies for the use of the Army or Armies of the United States and also for the Navy, Artificers and Prisoners of War and also the Transportation thereof and all Contracts or agreements heretofore made or which shall be hereafter made by him or Persons under his Authority for the purposes aforesaid are hereby declared to be binding on the United States.

Now therefore the said Jeremiah Wadsworth and John Carter for themselves, their Heirs, Executors and Administrators do jointly and severally Covenant, Contract and agree to and with the said Robert Morris in behalf of the United States, that they the said Jeremiah Wadsworth and John Carter shall and will furnish to all the Troops of the Moving or Main Army in the service of the United States Eastward of the Delaware River and the Post or Garrison of West Point and such other subordinate Posts as shall from time to time be dependant thereon or subject to the order of the Commanding officer of the said Post or Garrison of West Point such number of Rations of Provisions each Ration to Consist of one Pound of Good Merchantable Bread made of Good Wheat Flour or one Pound of Merchantable Flour at the option of the Contractors. One Pound of Good Merchantable Beef or three Quarters of a Pound of salt Pork of good Quality and well saved. One Gill of good Whiskey that is full proof also one Quart of good Merchantable Imported or three pints Home made Salt to every hundred Rations of fresh Meat Issued, and twelve pounds of good Merchantable Hard Soap and three pounds of good Candles to seven hundred Rations as shall from time to time be demanded for the use of the Troops and Artificers in the service of the United States and Prisoners of war from the sixteenth day of October until the last day of December next Inclusive. The number of Rations to be Assertained weekly or at such other Periods as shall be settled by the Secretary at War or the Person or Persons Authorized by him for that purpose. Whereof timely notice shall be given to the said Contractors and the said Secretary at War shall by himself or the Person or Persons appointed for the purpose from time to time settle and duly Inform the said Contractors or some of them of the vouchers or orders on which the said Rations are to be supplyed and delivered which said Vouchers or orders and the proper Receipts thereon are hereby declared to be conclusive, authority for and Evidence of the delivery of all Rations thereon specified and the said Contractors do hereby Covenant, Promise, Contract and agree to deliver and Issue the said Rations in such Proportions, numbers and quantities as follows, to General Officers for themselves and families to draw Provisions and Stores on their own Returns or those of their Aid de Camps to any number of Rations they may think proper not exceeding the number allowed them, their accounts with the Contractors to be closed at the end of each Month. The Officers of Regiments to draw as many Rations as they are entitled to if they please, and each Commissioned and Staff Officer shall draw one Gill of good West India Rum per Day full proof in lieu of which the Contractor shall stop One Gill of Whiskey per day from all Officers that draw the said West India Rum, but to draw together on the usual days of Issue. Three per Cent to be allowed on all Meat Issued in order to make the weight hold out, the same allowance to Extend to Soldiers and every Person entitled to Draw. Regiments and Corps to be served in as many draughts as they have Companies, and the Contractors to have an allowance of two per Cent on all the Meat they shall Issue as a Compensation for the increase of Draughts. When in the Course of service on Detachment, Officers cannot draw Provisions with their Regiments the Returns where they do Draw shall specify their Rank and the Corps to which they Respectively belong. They shall also Issue to Guards, marching Parties, to all[20] Artificers and those employed in the Quarter Master General and Commissary General of Military Stores Departments, to such Person or Persons in those Departments as shall be appointed to receive the same by the Heads of such Departments respectively so that the Issue be made to as few Persons as the good of the service will permit. All Issues made in the Hospital

Department shall be to the stuart of the Hospital upon the orders of the Director General or senior officer and the Contractors do hereby Covenant and agree that in Case any Dispute shall arise respecting the Quantity or Quality of Provision to be Issued that the same shall be determined by the Inspector who now is or may hereafter be appointed by the Superintendant of Finances, and his Determination shall be conclusive as well upon the United States as the Contractors and all the Articles of the Rations declared by him to be of bad Quality and Unfit to be Issued as Rations or parts thereof shall be rejected by the United States and the said Contractors shall be obliged to replace the same with good Merchantable Articles. And in Case the said Contractors do not immediately on demand made by the said Inspector replace the Articles so rejected with good Merchantable and sufficient articles then the said Inspector shall direct a Quantity of good Merchantable Provisions and Stores equal to the number of Rations so rejected to be purchased and Issued and the Price given for such Provisions and Stores and all Costs attending the same shall be reducted by the Superintendent of Finance or the Person or Persons authorized to settle and adjust the said Contractors Accounts out of the first Money that is due from the United States by Virtue of this agreement to the said Contractors, and it is further agreed that it shall be in the Power of the Secretary of War or the Person by him Authorized to Diminish the Rations so as to take only such certain parts thereof as shall seem expedient. And the value of any parts not Issued as fixed in the Component Parts of a Ration herein shall be deducted on settlement of the said Contractors Accounts, and also that the said Secretary at War may direct that Rum or Whiskey in particular Cases be not Issued but Vegetable[s] or other articles of equal Value shall be furnished in Lieu thereof if to be had, the Value thereof to be determined by the said Inspector. And whereas parts of Rations may be Issued by order of the Secretary at War and Difficulties might arise, if the price of the Component Parts of a Ration were not previously settled it is hereby further agreed that the value of the Different parts of a Ration shall be as follows and shall be Estimated and allowed in the settlement of accounts, to wit, for one pound of Beef or three quarters of a Pound of Pork five and one Quarter ninetieths, for one pound of Bread or Flour four ninetieths, for one Gill of Whiskey two and one Quarter ninetieths, for Salt, Soap and Candles, one and one half ninetieths of a Dollar, and the said Robert Morris as Superintendant of Finance doth hereby Covenant, promise and Engage in Pursuance of the authority from the United States in Congress Assembled as before recited to and with the said Contractors their Heirs, Executors and Administrators, that he the said Robert Morris will well and truly pay or cause to be paid out of the Monies of the United States to the said Contractors, their Heirs, Executors, and Administrators or any Person or Persons Authorized by them to receive the same the sum of thirteen ninetieths of a Dollar per Ration, either in Silver or in Gold Coin equivalent for each and every Ration delivered agreeable to the terms of this Contract and at the rates above specified for any parts of a Ration delivered and issued as aforesaid and that he will on account of this agreement pay to the said Contractors on the first day of February next all such sum and sums of Money as shall be found due for Rations Issued in this present Month of October on settlement of the Contractors accounts. And on the first day of March next all such sum or sums of Money as shall be found due on settlement as aforesaid for the Rations Issued in the Month of November, and on the second Day of April, all such sum and Sums as shall be found due on Settlement of Accounts for the Rations Issued for the Month of December. That in Case any of the Magazines the Property of the Contractors Established or disposed at Posts or Places directed or ordered by the Secretary at War or the Commander in Chief shall be distroyed by the Event of War, the same shall be paid for by the United States and the Value thereof shall be determined by the said Inspector, and a Certificate from him shall entitle the Contractors to receive from the United States the amount thereof, and the said Robert Morris does hereby agree that the said Contractors shall have the Use of all Public Stores which have heretofore been Occupied by the Commissaries and also of the Public Scales and Weights all of which shall be appraised and an Inventory of them taken and the Contractors charged for them but on their being delivered up and returned in the same good order Ware and Tare excepted the amount of such appraisment shall pass to their Credit.

Necessary Guards are to be supplied for the security of Cattle and Stores on an application to the Commander in Chief or the Commanding General, of the Number he is to be the sole Judge. The Contractors all and every of them are to pass within the American Camps or Lines Conforming to the Police of the Army unmolested and not be liable to arrest or Detention and also all Persons in this[21] employ first obtaining proper passports from the Commander in Chief or Commanding General for that purpose. The Property of the Contractors shall not be liable to be taken for the Army only by the Express orders of General Washington, and him only in Cases wherein the Army is not regularly supplied by the Contractors or the Provision is condemned by the Inspector.

That in Case any Magazines are by order of the Commander in Chief laid up in any of the Eastern States any part of the Army should remove therein, and Rations be Issued to them the Expence of Transporting the Flour to such Magazines or places of Issue, over and above what it would cost to Transport it to the Post in the State of New York or Jersey from which the Troops may remove to the Eastern States, is to be borne by the United States or such an addition to the price of the Rations to be allowed as may be agreed between the Contractors and the Superintendant of Finance, or such Person as he may appoint for that purpose. That the Contractor shall as requested by the Commanding General make Return to him of the State of the Magazines and Answer as far as in their Power such Questions as he shall ask relating to their Expectations of future supplies. All stores shall be Issued and at such place or places within the limits Aforesaid as shall be ordered by the Commander in Chief or the Commanding General for the time being, and the said Contractors do hereby agree to get all Provisions Transported from the Magazines to such places as the Commander in Chief shall direct, and will follow his Orders Respecting the Transportation thereof, either by purchasing or hiring Teams for the purpose, the amount whereof shall from time to time be paid to the Contractors with an allowance for their services of two and an half per Cent on the amount. And the said Contractors do also agree to furnish the several Hospitals such Quantities of the following Articles as may be required by the Persons duly authorized to grant proper Vouchers in Conformity to the orders and rules that now are or hereafter may be prescribed by the Secretary at War—Viz—West India Rum at the rate of six pence half penny per Gill, Madeira wine nine pence per Gill, Port wine six pence per Gill, Muscovado Sugar sixteen pence per Pound, Coffee two shillings and two pence per Pound, Bohea Tea fourteen shillings per pound, Indian Meal two pence per pint, Vinegar two Shillings per Gallon, Hard Soap one and eight pence per Pound, Candles one shilling and ten pence per Pound Pennsylvania Currency. It is also further agreed that the Contractors give the Superintendant of Finance the same Credit for the Monies that shall be due for the above mentioned Hospital Stores as is given for Money due for Rations under this Contract and Receive their Pay for the same at the same Periods that they receive their Pay for the Rations furnished.[22]

(Signed) John Carter for   Sealed and Delivered in the Presence of
Jeremiah Wadsworth   (Sign'd) Jeremiah Olney ⎫
      and Self   Peter Colt   ⎬ Witnesses
                                                          ⎭

MSS: Copy, Benjamin Franklin Papers, PPAmP; copy, PCC, DNA.

1. This note is based on a study of the Wadsworth Papers at CtHi and the Charles Stewart Papers at NCooHi and MH; Wadsworth to Nathanael Greene, October 17 and December 12, 1782, CtHWa, on deposit CtHi; and John D. R. Platt, "Jeremiah Wadsworth: Federalist Entrepreneur" (Ph.D. diss., Columbia University, 1955), 29–36. In addition to the references to the Wadsworth and Carter contract in RM's papers cited below, see Diary, September 30, October 2, 3, 5, 23, 1782, and January

15 and April 14, 1783, RM to Cornell, September 20, 1782, to Ferdinand Grand, January 2, 1783, and to Franklin, January 3, 1783.

2. See the headnote to Comfort Sands, Walter Livingston, William Duer, and Daniel Parker to RM, September 11, and notes.

3. See notes to George Washington to RM, May 17–25, 1782.

4. See Wadsworth and Carter to Charles Stewart, March 5, 1782, Stewart Papers, MH; and Carter to Wadsworth, and to Stewart, both June 24, 1782, Wadsworth and Carter Letterbook 3, CtHi.

5. See notes to the Quartermaster General to RM, September 19.

6. See Diary, September 18, and RM to the President of Congress, October 21.

7. See Diary, August 20, and notes.

8. See Carter to John Chaloner, June 5, and to Wadsworth, June 10, 1782, Wadsworth and Carter Letterbook 3, CtHi; and Carter to Wadsworth, June 5, and Wadsworth to Carter, June 30, 1782, Wadsworth Correspondence, CtHi.

9. See Wadsworth to RM, October 5, and Carter to RM, October 9.

10. See RM to the President of Congress, October 21; and Carter to Wadsworth, September 23, 25, and October 2, 1782, Wadsworth Correspondence, CtHi.

11. See Cornell to RM, and Wadsworth to RM, both October 5, and RM to Cornell, to Tilghman, and to Wadsworth, all October 10.

12. See Diary, December 16, 1782.

13. See Diary, January 2 and 3, 1783.

14. See Carter to Wadsworth, March 12, 19, April 2, and June 4, 1783, Wadsworth Correspondence, CtHi; and notes to RM to Le Couteulx and Company, September 24, 1782. Ironically, the French court, pressed for funds, cast the firm's affairs into disarray by suspending payment for one year on its navy and army bills, which the partners held or had endorsed to nearly 1 million livres. See Platt, "Wadsworth," 35–36.

15. See Carter to Wadsworth, April 2, 1783, Wadsworth Correspondence, CtHi.

16. See Arthur Lee's post-1784 memoranda, Lee Papers, VIII, 7, MH.

17. See notes to RM to the President of Congress, October 21.

18. See Diary, January 3, 1783.

19. See RM and Benjamin Lincoln's Plan for Issuing Provisions under Contracts, November 20, and RM to the President of Congress, November 22, 1782. To RM's distress, the Rhode Island Assembly rewarded Ezekiel Cornell's key role in negotiating the contract by censuring his acceptance of Continental office while a member of Congress. See RM to Cornell, November 29, 1782.

20. The word "Officers" is crossed out here in the PCC text.

21. The PCC text gives this word as "their."

22. The PCC copy, which lacks the signatories' names, was enclosed in RM to the President of Congress, October 21; the PPAmP copy in RM to Benjamin Franklin, January 11, 1783.

From William Churchill Houston

Trenton [New Jersey] 12 Octr. 1782

Sir

I am honoured with your Letters of the 3 and 5 instant and the Enclosures. The Act of Congress and your Letter to the Executives are seasonable;[1] and will, I hope, induce the Legislature of this State to avoid, in future, every ⟨Interference with the general System⟩ Thing contrary to the proposed Plan. The late vote of three Thousand four Hundred Pounds to our Quota of the Army[2] was a Measure which they very reluctantly adopted; and they declared they looked upon themselves as forced into it by the Measures which other States, particularly the Eastern including New-York, had taken before them. Every one must be convinced that Perplexity and Embarrassment cannot but attend the Administration of the publick Finances, as long as the general System is jostled by such partial and irregular Interferences.

The Sum abovementioned being charged upon the Arrears of former Taxes, my Prospects, at least for some Time, are confined to the Tax which became payable the first instant[3] and I am now writing to every Collectour to leave no Means untried for expediting the Collection.

The Legislature now electing meet at this Place the 22 instant and will probably sit near two months.

Yesterday I remitted to Mr Hillegas 7484⁷⁴⁄₉₀ Dollars in Bills on Mr Swanwick, for which the Warrant and Receipt will be returned.

WCH

1782 Dr   The Receipt of Continental Taxes in the State of New Jersey,
             from 5 Octr. to 12 inclusive
          To Cash from the State-Treasurer six Hundred Dollars   Dlls 600

ENDORSED: Copy Letter Robert Mor/ris Esqr Superintendent/&c/12 Octr. 1782/Return 600 Dollars
MS: ADftS with subjoined ADftS return, Houston Collection, NjP.
    1. The references are to an act of Congress of October 1, 1782, and RM's Circular to the Governors of the States, October 5. Both were enclosed in RM's circular to the receivers of Continental taxes, October 5. Houston was the receiver for New Jersey.
    2. See Houston to RM, October 5, and notes.
    3. See Houston to RM, June 15, 1782, and notes.

From Matthew Ridley

Robert Morris Esqr.   Paris October the 12th. 1782[1]
Dear Sir

I am just informed that Orders are given for a Frigate to sail for America, I therefore hasten to inform you I have received your two esteemed Favors of July 4th: and 8th:. I pass over every other Subject just now to entertain you on that which interests us both first. I mean the Children.

Your Letter of the 8th. has given me much uneasiness because I perceive you have some. I can assure you the part I have taken about the Children I should have done had they been my own. The promise I made you was to watch over them and not think my Duty towards them sufficiently discharged by the mere protecting during the Voyage and then placing them on their Arrival in a distant Academy. From every inquiry I could make, the one where I placed them appeared to me to be the best—The Master sufficiently capable to instruct children of their Age and the most likely of any by a personal attention to them to forward them in the French. I have not been deceived. As they advanced in French I had their Studies increased. They now learn Latin, French, writing, cyphering and Dancing; and I do not believe that in either they have lost the least time. As to their Manners I do not find the cause of complaint you have heard of—Go where they will I see no Children who behave better. I am sensible Notwithstanding this it is not a school to keep them at; nor did I ever intend it. I have been some time looking out for another and have been consulting Mr Jay about it. There is one I have seen and if Mr Jay approves I shall place them there. I have wrote you my Objections to Colmar; and have given you hints about Geneva. I find hardly any Body who approves the latter. With respect to the opinion of the Person you mention,[2] I have never yet been able to get it. The Answers I have always had has been—"Why you know but," "I do not know" "It is hard to say" &ca &ca. When I mentioned to you about Masters coming to them I only thought of it as the last resource. You cannot conceive my Dear Sir the difficulty of finding good Seminaries of Learning in this Country that is to say Europe. The want of them is the general complaint and where they are to be found in this Country we labour under difficulties in the Article of Religion. Some will absolutely a conformity and will take no Scholars without. This I can not submit to and have always made a Condition to the contrary. In short I do not think the Advantages to be gained by an European Education by any means equal to the anxiety of Parting with Children, the heavey additional expences and the many accidents they are exposed to from neglect of their Morals and Persons. In this Country, at Geneva, at Colmar, a Child acquires the French Language; but it happens very often at the expence of his Own. As to the Classics there is no Country where they can be better taught than in America. The first principles of the French are also to be acquired. Once well founded in those, One years education here at a proper Age will compleat them. By living in a strange Country, strange Habits and Customs are acquired, the Affections are much weakend towards the Connections left behind and sometimes the simplicity of home, ceases to please on the return to it. I have weighd all the circumstances since being here with the Children and find we have been deceived. I am therefore of opinion the best way will be to place them in the best Pension I can near at hand, Have them pushed as much forward as possible in their Studies for a year or two and during that time either by a change of circumstances or alteration of times we shall be able to do something else with them. I mean to try to get them an English Master both for their writing and reading.

Rest assured my Dear Sir that the charge I have undertaken shall be religiously executed. I feel as a Parent I feel as a Friend. I beg you not to pay attention to what people may be saying about this or that Pension. Few who have been here have had the real opportunity of forming a competent Judgement of any one. They take up Opinions from hearsay and too often retail them as their Own. I am happy that Mr Jay is here I shall consult with him in whatever I do about them; and wherever they are placed you may be assured my care of and attention to them will not cease while I have the power to exert either.

Inclosed you have Letters from the Boys. Be pleased to tell Mrs. Morris I have rec'd her kind Letter of the 21st. May:[3] and will write her and Miss Livingston shortly. Pray remember me respectfully to both and to all our Friends my best wishes ever attend you and I am respectfully Dear Sir Your much Obliged humble Servant

Matt: Ridley

MSS: ALS, Robert Morris Papers, NN; LbC, Ridley Papers, MHi.

1. Ridley, an American merchant in Paris serving as an agent for Maryland, was also supervising the European education of RM's two eldest sons, Robert, Jr., and Thomas. The following notes were written in the margin of the LbC: "The first by the Danaide Frigate Sailed From Rochefort [*one line left blank*] arrived Decembr. 9th in the Delaware. The Second by the Paket Gl. Washington Capn Barney Sailed from L'orient January 17. 1783. Arrived at Philadelphia March the 12th." RM replied to Ridley on January 4, 1783 (see Ridley to RM, March 24, 1783), but the letter has not been found.

2. Probably Benjamin Franklin.

3. The letters of Mary White Morris and the Morris boys have not been found.

From John Jay

Paris 13 Octr 1782[1]

My dear Sir

Wherever[2] and however occupied, I remember my Friends, and always find my own Satisfaction promoted, when I have Reason to think that I am conducing to their's. This has led me to make your Sons the Subject of this Letter. It is an interesting one to you, and therefore not indifferent to me.

On my arrival here I found them plac'd in a Pension at Passey. My Nephew and Daughter were ill with a hooping-Cough, and lest your sons should catch it, we denied ourselves the pleasure of having them with us, 'till after that obstacle had ceased. I have frequently seen them at Doctr. Franklin's as well as at my own House. They had promised to dine with us every Wednesday but Mr. Ridley prolong'd it to every other Wednesday. They are fine Boys and appear to possess a full share of natural Talents. I am told that they have made a Progress in French proportionate to the Time they have been learning it. Of this I am not an adequate Judge myself, and therefore must depend on the Judgment of others. The Pension at which they are has been so far well enough, but I think with Mr. Ridley that a better is to be wish'd for, and to be sought. He is at present making the necessary Inquiries, and I have every Reason to believe that the Trust you have reposed in him will be conscienciously and faithfully executed.

Mr. Ridley finds it difficult to decide on the Expediency of carrying them to Geneva, and from what I have heard, I think he has Reason to entertain Doubts on that Head; as I have no materials to judge from, but the Report of others, and those perhaps not altogether well founded, it is difficult for me to form[3] a decided opinion on the Subject. I can only say that I have heard more against than for it.

My opinion may perhaps seem singular and the more so as it cannot properly be explain'd in the Compass of a letter,[4] but I think the youth of every *free* civilized[5] Country should, if possible,[6] be educated in it; and not permitted to travel out of it,[7] 'till age has made them so cool and firm, as to retain their National and moral Impressions. Connections founded at School and College have much influence,[8] and are to be watched[9] even at that Period—If judiciously formed, they will often endure[10] and be advantageous thro' Life. American Youth may possibly form proper and perhaps useful[11] Friendships in European Semenaries, but I think not so *probably* as among[12] their Fellow Citizens with whom they are to grow up, whom it will be useful for them to know, and be early known to, and with whom they are to be engaged in the business[13] of active Life; and under the Eye and Direction of Parents, whose Advice, Authority and Example[14] are frequently[15] of more worth than the Lessons[16] of hireling[17] Professors, particularly[18] on the subjects of Religion,[19] Morality, Virtue and Prudence.

The fine and some of the Useful Arts, may doubtless[20] be better acquired in Europe than in America, and so may the living European Languages; but when I consider that a competent Knowledge even of these may be gained in our Country, and that almost all of the more[21] Substantial and truly Valuable Acquirements may in my opinion[22] with more facility and ⟨Constancy⟩ Certainty[23] be attained there than here, I do not hesitate to prefer an American Education.

I fear that the Ideas which my Countrymen in general conceive of Europe are in many Respects[24] rather too high.[25] If we should ever meet again you shall know my Sentiments very fully on this Head.

But your Sons are here and what is to be done? Mr. Ridley is about doing what I think with him is the best thing that can at present[26] be done Vizt. to put them in one of the best Pensions that can be found,[27] and to give them the advantage of such extra Tutors as may be requisite.[28]

Perhaps further Information may place Geneva in a more favorable Light. You shall have frequent[29] Letters from me on this Subject, and while I remain here, you may be assured of my constant Attention to these promising Boys. [Be] pleased to present our

Complements and best Wishes to Mrs Morris. I am dear Sir with sincere Esteem and Regard your affectionate Friend and Servant

John Jay

The Honble Robt. Morris Esqr.

ADDRESSED: The Hon'ble/Robt. Morris Esqr/Philadelphia ENDORSED: Paris 13 Octr. 1782/John Jay Esqr./respecting my Sons
MSS: LS, Robert Morris Papers, DLC; ADft, Jay Papers, NNC.

1. Jay, the American minister to Spain, was an American commissioner at the Paris peace negotiations. Except for the dateline and signature, the text of the LS is in the writing of his wife, Sarah Livingston Jay. Jay's heavily emended ADft is printed with some excisions restored in Morris, ed., *John Jay: Winning of the Peace*, 473–474. The most significant legible revisions and interlineations in that text have been noted below. RM replied to this letter on January 3, 1783.

2. Jay began the ADft with the word "Amidst," but then struck it out.

3. In the ADft Jay substituted the passage "as I have . . . me to form" for some two lines that he lined through which can only be partially reconstructed as follows: "so much so that I dare not [*several illegible words*] for the late Revolution there may [*remainder illegible*]." On the recent developments in Geneva, see notes to RM to Matthew Ridley, October 14, 1781; and Ridley to RM, February 16, 1782.

4. In the ADft Jay originally wrote: "My Ideas of education may perhaps be singular—They cannot be fully explained in the Compass of a letter."

5. Jay interlined this word in the ADft.

6. Jay interlined the preceding two words in the ADft.

7. Jay interlined the preceding two words in the ADft.

8. In the ADft Jay substituted the foregoing three words for "are important."

9. Jay interlined the preceding five words in the ADft, but had inserted them after "even at that Period."

10. In the ADft Jay substituted "endure" for "last."

11. Jay interlined the preceding four words in the ADft.

12. Here in the ADft Jay ultimately settled on the foregoing two words in place of "within our Country [nor?] among those with many [*illegible word*]."

13. In the ADft Jay substituted this word for "affairs."

14. In the ADft Jay wrote the words "Advice ⟨and⟩ Authority [*interlined:*] and ⟨sometimes⟩ Example," which were followed by approximately one line of text which he heavily excised and which cannot be adequately reconstructed.

15. Jay interlined this word in the ADft.

16. Jay interlined the preceding three words in the ADft, ultimately substituting "Lessons" for "Instructions."

17. Jay substituted this word in the ADft for a word that he heavily lined out.

18. Jay interlined this word in the ADft.

19. Jay interlined this word in the ADft.

20. Jay interlined this word in the ADft.

21. In the ADft Jay substituted the preceding five words for "Religion, Morality."

22. Jay interlined the preceding three words in the ADft.

23. In the ADft Jay interlined the words "and Certainty."

24. Jay interlined the preceding three words in the ADft.

25. Jay substituted this word in the ADft for a passage of several words which he lined out too heavily for the editors to reconstruct.

26. Jay interlined the preceding two words in the ADft.

27. In the ADft Jay substituted the remainder of this paragraph for an illegible passage of nearly one line which he heavily lined through.

28. Here in the ADft Jay heavily deleted some six lines which he evidently had been in the process of revising. The editors have tentatively reconstructed the passage as follows: "Conformity to the ⟨*illegible word*⟩ matter[s?] of Religion is indispensible for admission into a ⟨one of the⟩ university here, ⟨and?⟩ but as that would be assuming the [part *or* garb?] of External Conformity without ⟨would?⟩ in my opinion be only proper [in Cases] of [Mental?] Conformity. It is otherwise so like Hypocrasy that I am persuaded you would not chuse that your Sons should be educated in a university on those Terms."

29. In the ADft Jay substituted this word for "further."

John Jay to Gouverneur Morris

Paris 13 Octr. 1782

Dear Morris

I have received your festina lente Letter,[1] but wish it had been, at least partly, in Cypher; you need not be informed of my Reasons for this wish, as by this Time you must know that Seals are, on this Side of the water, rather matters of Decoration, than of use. It gave me nevertheless great Pleasure to recieve that Letter, it being the first from you that had reached me the Lord knows when, except indeed a few Lines covering your Correspondence with a Don.[2] I find you are industrious, and of Consequence useful—so much the better for yourself, for the public, and for our friend Morris, whom I consider as the Pillar of american Credit.

The King of Great Britain by Letters patent under the Great Seal, has authorized Mr Oswald to treat with the Commissioners of the United States of America.[3] His first Commission litterally pursued the enabling act, and the authority it gave him was expressed in the very Terms of that Act vizt. to treat with the Colonies, and with any or either of them, and any part of them, and with any Description of Men in them, and with any Person whatsoever, of and concerning Peace &ca.[4]

Had I not violated the Instructions of Congress their Dignity would have been in the Dust for the french Minister even took Pains not only to perswade us to treat under that Commission but to prevent the second, by telling Fitzherbert that the first was sufficient. I told the Minister that we neither could nor would treat with any nation in the World on any other than an equal footing.[5]

We may, and we may not have a peace this Winter. Act as if the War would certainly continue, keep proper Garrisons in your strong posts, and preserve[6] your army sufficiently numerous, and well appointed until every Idea of Hostility and Surprize shall have compleatly[7] vanished.

I could write you a volume, but my Health admits only of short Intervals of application.

Present my best Wishes to Mr and Mrs. Morris, Mr and Mrs Meredith, and such other of our Friends as may ask how we do. I am dear Morris, very much Yours[8]

John Jay

The Hon'ble G. Morris Esqr

MSS: ALS, Gouverneur Morris Papers, NNC; ADftS, Jay Papers, NNC.

1. Dated August 6.
2. In the ADftS Jay initially wrote "with Don F," but then amended the passage to its final form. The reference is to Gouverneur Morris's correspondence with Francisco Rendón, on which see Gouverneur Morris to Jay, March 10, 1782, and notes.

3. Jay underscored the preceding four words in the ADftS.

4. As Jay noted here, Richard Oswald's first commission of July 25, 1782, written in accordance with the Enabling Act passed by Parliament on June 17, 1782, to authorize George III to conclude a peace or truce with "certain colonies in North America," was carefully worded so as not to recognize the independence or sovereignty of the United States government (see Wharton, ed., *Rev. Dipl. Corr.*, V, 613–614). The proposed commission arrived in Paris on August 6, but on Jay's insistence, the American ministers refused to negotiate with the British on the basis of any commission which did not treat them as representatives of an independent, sovereign state. At Oswald's request, Jay himself drafted the alterations he desired in the commission on September 9 and furnished them to Oswald. The changes were sanctioned by a resolution of the British cabinet on September 19 and a new commission of September 21 was issued to Oswald authorizing him to treat with the "Commissioners or Persons vested with equal powers, by and on the part of the Thirteen United States." Although this formulation was not quite an explicit recognition of American independence, it was generally taken as such in Europe. For Jay's role in formulating Oswald's second commission, see Morris, ed., *John Jay: Winning of the Peace*, 285–286, 347–362; and in general, Morris, *Peacemakers*, 280, 296–297, 301–319, 335–340. On Oswald (1705–1784), a Scots-born London merchant who had been the earl of Shelburne's emissary during the early negotiations with Franklin in Paris and who was sympathetically disposed to the Americans, see *DNB*; and Morris, *Peacemakers*, 261, 453.

5. Jay wrote this paragraph in Office of Finance Cipher no. 1; it is decoded interlinearly in Gouverneur Morris's writing. The paragraph is also enciphered in the ADftS. On the cipher, see RM to Jay, July 7, 1781, and notes.

Although congressional instructions of June 15, 1781, drafted under the influence of Chevalier de La Luzerne, the French minister to the United States, required that the commissioners for negotiating peace place themselves entirely under the advice and control of the French ministry (except for the question of independence), both Jay and Gouverneur Morris, among others, strongly opposed this policy. After his arrival in Paris, Jay entered into a dispute with the French foreign minister, Comte de Vergennes, who sought to induce the American diplomats to treat with Oswald under his first commission. Vergennes was then negotiating with Alleyne Fitzherbert (1753–1839), formerly British minister to Brussels, who had replaced Thomas Grenville in negotiations with the French. As Jay here informed Gouverneur Morris, he had advised Vergennes that he would not negotiate with any diplomat who did not acknowledge the independence of the United States.

Jay had also persuaded Franklin, contrary to the congressional instructions, not to communicate information about their negotiations to the French ministry until after the draft of the preliminary treaty was completed and conditionally signed. Jay's draft of a provisional treaty, submitted to Oswald on October 5, was dispatched to Britain on October 8. However, on October 24 Oswald informed Jay that the provisional treaty was not acceptable to the British ministry. Formal talks resumed on October 30, with John Adams by then having joined Jay and Franklin. The resulting provisional treaty was signed on November 30 without the prior knowledge or advice of the French ministry. In deference to the Franco-American alliance, under which neither party was to conclude a truce or peace with Great Britain without the formal consent of the other, the provisional treaty was not to go into effect until preliminaries of peace had also been ratified between Great Britain and France. Franklin adroitly countered French displeasure by asking Vergennes whether he would permit his court's anger at the Americans' "indiscretion" to give the British the satisfaction of having driven a wedge between France and the United States. Vergennes tactfully chose not to quarrel openly with the Americans and even agreed to make the first payment of the French loan for 1783, which was dispatched on the ship that carried the provisional treaty to Philadelphia (see notes to RM to Le Couteulx and Company, September 24). Once the Anglo-French preliminaries were signed on January 20, 1783, the Anglo-American preliminaries also went into effect; Anglo-Spanish preliminaries were concluded at the same time, and on February 4 the British proclaimed the general cessation of hostilities. Congress received the text of the provisional treaty on March 13 and proclaimed the end of hostilities on April 11. Although criticizing the commissioners for not consulting France, Congress ratified the provisional treaty on April 15, 1783. The definitive treaties of peace were signed in Paris on September 3, 1783, and ratified by Congress on January 14, 1784. See Morris, *Peacemakers,* 245–246, 307–385 *passim;* on Fitzherbert, see *DNB.*

6. In the ADftS Jay substituted this word for "do not suffer."

7. Jay interlined this word in the ADftS.

8. Gouverneur Morris replied to Jay on January 1, 1783; RM registered his approval of Jay's diplomacy in a letter to Jay of January 3, 1783. For Gouverneur Morris's long-standing opposition to the "Servility" of the congressional peace instructions, see his letter to Jay of June 17, 1781, in Morris, ed., *John Jay: Winning of the Peace,* 86–87.

Diary: October 14, 1782

This Morning returned from an Excursion into the Country and was soon Called on by many Persons amongst which the following. Mr. McFarlane pressing much to have money for the Balance due Jelles Fonda instead of a Certificate; I told him it is impossible to pay him money on this Score and after much importunity he departed.[1]

Mr. R. Sands brought me a Letter from Sands Livingston & Co. by which I find they blame my Proceedings with respect to them.[2] I told him of my fixed resolution to assist them in procuring Justice &c.

Jno. Pierce Esqr. respecting several Points in his Business.

The Honble. Mr. Jackson respecting Doctor Franklin's Letters which Mr. G. Morris examined in Order to give him the needful information.[3]

Mr. Holker for his Bills which are not quite ready.[4]

Mr Jenkins asks a Bill on Rhode Island for one of Daniel Clark's now due.[5]

Mr. Edwd Williams for money for the Hospital Department.

Colo. Humpton for money but did not bring the return of German recruits and therefore I did not pay him.

Monsr. Savary respecting Loan Office Certificates. I told him Congress have called for money from the States to pay the Interest and advised him to memorialize Congress respecting some Paper money.

Honble. Secy. at War brought me the papers of the Court of Enquiry with his Opinions &c.[6]

Colo Miles for Money and Notes granted some of each.

Majr. Geo. Turner called but being much engaged I desired him to call in the morning.

Mr. T. Edwards One of the Contractors after some Conversation respecting the Contracts desired him to call to Morrow at 11 OClock.

1. See James McCall to the Comptroller of the Treasury, October 3 (first letter), and notes.

2. The letter is dated October 8.

3. Jonathan Jackson, a Massachusetts delegate to Congress, was a member of a congressional committee investigating Alexander Gillon's affairs in Europe. See Diary, September 19, and notes.

4. Holker received payment of $26,666⁶⁰⁄₉₀ from John Swanwick in the form of RM's warrant on Michael Hillegas, Treasurer of the United States. Copies of the warrant and Holker's receipt, both dated October 15, 1782, are in the Holker Papers, MiU-C.

5. See RM to George Olney, October 15, and to Daniel Clark, October 22 (first letter).

6. A written statement of Lincoln's opinions has not been found. RM's determination on the proceedings of the court of inquiry on Samuel Nicholson is dated October 17.

To John Barry

Marine Office 14. Octo: 1782[1]

Sir

I am acquainted by Mr. John Brown that you have intimated your Intention of calling in at the Island of Martinico therefore I send this Letter in Expectation of your being there; and on receiving it you are to proceed with all convenient speed to Havannah where my further Orders will meet you.[2] I am Sir your most obedient Servant

RM

MS: AM LbC, MdAN.

1. Captain John Barry commanded the Continental frigate *Alliance,* which arrived at Lorient, France, on October 17 after a cruise exceeding two months. See Barry to RM, October 18.

2. RM's "further Orders" to Barry are dated November 23. The present orders were enclosed in RM to Joseph Diant, October 14. Barry received them after reaching Martinique on January 8, 1783; he arrived at Havana on January 31 (see Clark, *Gallant John Barry,* 288–293). For the context of the orders to Barry and the role of John Brown of Pennsylvania, RM's assistant in the Marine Office, in bringing specie from Havana, see notes to RM to Le Couteulx and Company, September 24.

Circular of the Comptroller of the Treasury to the Heads of Staff Departments

[Philadelphia] Comptrollers Office October 14th 1782

Sir

(Circular)[1]   I am directed by the Superintendant of Finance to call upon all those who have received Public monies unaccounted for, to render their Accounts for Settlement. By the Act of Congress of the 27th. February last, the Accounts in your department up to the last day of December 1781, inclusive are directed to be settled by the Commissioner appointed for that purpose.[2] But Mr. Morris being anxious to have all Accounts that have accrued since the commencement of his Administration settled at the Treasury,[3] it will be necessary to make out the Accounts from that time, or rather from the date of the first Warrant granted by him for the use of your department, in Certain periods up till the end of the year 1781, and from thence in Quarterly periods, which rule must be punctually attended to at the end of each Quarter in time to come.

As it is no less essential that the Articles purchased or received should be accounted for, than the Money, you will therefore render your Accounts of the receipts and issues of them, in the same manner and for the same periods. A speedy Compliance with this necessary requisition is expected. I am Sir Your Most Obedient Humble Servant.

Jas. Milligan
Comptr. of the Treasy.

Timothy Pickering Esqr.
Q[uarter] Mr. General

ENDORSED: James Milligan/October 14th. 1782/Treasury Office/Accounts of disbursements since/Mr. Morris's administration/in 1781 to be made up from the/first warranted [sic] received from/him in that Year. After that/Year to be made out quarterly/accompanied with an Account/of the Articles purchased or received
MS: LS, WDC, DNA.
1. Other recipients of this letter probably included Ephraim Blaine and Charles Stewart (the former commissaries general of purchases and issues), John Moylan (clothier general), and John Cochran (director general of military hospitals).
2. See the Comptroller's instructions of this date to the commissioners of accounts for the departments.
3. See notes to Diary, June 12, 1782.

Instructions of the Comptroller of the Treasury to the Commissioners of Accounts for the States

[Philadelphia] Comptrollers Office October 14th 1782[1]

Sir
Circular   The United States in Congress assembled, by their Act of the 20th February 1782 for appointing Commissioners to adjust, and finally to Settle all Accounts between the United States, and each particular State, having amongst other matters therein mentioned, thought proper to direct in the Words following "That the said Commissioners, in the various branches of duty herein directed shall, in such matters of form, as regard meerly the Stating of his Accounts, proceed agreeable to Rules to be prescribed to him by the Comptroller of the Treasury." And the Superintendant of Finance having acquainted me that you have been duly appointed the Commissioner to Settle the Accounts between the United States and the State of   [2]

It becomes my duty to frame such Instructions, and Regulations as I conceive to be necessary for your Government in Stating the Accounts.

A Strict attention to them will, not only, be absolutely necessary, to enable the Register, upon a final Completion of the Accounts, to enter them in the Books at the Treasury, with a proper degree of accuracy; But I am fully convinced, from my own experience, that you will find it of the greatest Utility in the course of your duty, to adhere strictly to a regular System in these matters on all occasions.

1st. You will receive, herewith, a Sett of Books, in which are to be recorded, in a fair and regular manner, all Accounts and Settlements by you made.

These Books are ruled with double Setts of Money Columns; in the first of which will be inserted the Nominal Sum in Dollars, and Ninetieths parts of a dollar, and in the Second, the Specie Value of each Sum according to the dates, in Dollars and Ninetieths parts likewise.

When Accounts are liquidated in Specie, and without any referrence to, or connection with Nominal Money, the Specie Columns only will be used. Between the two Setts of Money Columns, is introduced a Single Column for the rate of Exchange or Depreciation. It is found absolutely necessary to keep all Books, and Accounts at the Treasury, in Dollars, that being the Currency most generally known throughout the Union.

2nd You will receive, herewith, an Account Numbered 1, which is taken from the Treasury Books, and, so far as it goes, is a running Account Current between the United States, and the State of .[3] This Account may be entered in the Books, charging the State Dr. to the U States for the Debit side of it, inserting in detail every particular Sum, Date, and purpose mentioned; and charging the United States Dr. to the Individual State for the Credit Side of it, likewise in detail. You have also herewith an Account of Taxes required by Congress in the old Emission No. 2. An Account of Old Emissions required to sink the same No 3. An Account of Specific Supplies required No. 4. An Account of Specie or New Emission and of Specie for the support of our Prisoners with the Enemy, required by the Acts thereon mentioned No 5.[4] All which, it will be proper to have entered in your books as already mentioned, taking care to raise an Account for each of them; being so opened in the Treasury Books. The Commissioner General of Military Stores, the Quarter Master General, and other Public officers, who may have furnished the State of [5] with Stores in their respective Departments, will be directed to transmit you Accounts of the same in order that you may charge them to the State in your Books.[6]

3rdly You will endeavour, as far as possible, to get the State, or Individuals in it, to render all Accounts to you for Settlement, under proper and distinct Heads; where it is found impracticable to have them rendered in this manner, it will be necessary that you arrange them so, upon examination under a final adjustment, enter them under these General Heads in the Books. Those that at present occur to me are the following Viz

PROVISION, delivered to the Commissaries &ca specifying to whom: Exclusive of those required by Congress, as Specific Supplies, which must be carried to their proper Account.

FORAGE, and other Articles furnished in the Quarter Masters or Forage Masters Department, specifying to whom delivered: Exclusive of those required by Congress in Specific Supplies, which must be carried to their proper Account.

ARMS, Ammunition, and Ordnance Stores, Specifying to whom delivered and for what purpose.

TRANSPORTATION, by Land or Water with particulars.

CLOATHING for the Army .... ditto[7]

DEPRECIATION on Pay of the Army &ca. expressing the Names and Ranks with the Corps &ca. to which each Individual belonged, to whom the State have assumed paying such Depreciation.

PAY &CA of the Militia, expressing the times and places of Service and by whose order called out.

BUILDING, and repairing Fortifications, expressing where and by whose Orders.

BUILDING BARRACKS or Disbursements in that department, distinguishing between those for our own Troops, and those for Prisoners of War.

RECRUITING the Army, expressing the Corps, and other particulars.

EXPENCES in laying obstructions in Rivers, Bays &ca expressing where, and by whose order &ca.

BUILDING Armed vessels, with every particular.

DISBURSEMENTS in the Hospital Department

DITTO   for Indian Affairs

DITTO   for Prisoners of War, with every particular and Voucher

CERTIFICATES given by Quarter Masters for Articles furnished, or Service performed Specifying the Persons Names by whom, and to whom granted, and the Articles or Services.

CERTIFICATES given by Commissaries of Provisions in the same manner as for the Quarter Masters department.

There may be some other charges that cannot, with propriety be arranged under any one of these Heads; if there are, you may open an Account of Contingent Expences, and carry them into that; taking care to insert every particular in the Entries. It is probable you may not have occasion to make use of all the above enumerated heads, as the Expences that would come under some of them, may not have accrued in your State, or may not be admitted as proper charges against the Union; and it is likewise probable that some

Certificates like the two indented specimens illustrated here were issued by Continental procurement officers for goods and services sold to or impressed by the army. Although early certificates were drawn by hand, by 1778 printed forms were being used. The Commissary and Quartermaster Departments issued the largest quantities. Like Continental currency issues, the certificates originally drew no interest and their face value eroded as the currency to which they were tied depreciated. On August 23, 1780, Congress ordered that as of September 15 new certificates were to bear 6 percent interest until paid and be stated in specie values. Although Congress assumed responsibility for paying the certificate debt at its actual value, most of the certificates were taken up by the states, especially in the South, which received credit for them on old requisitions. Morris gave his views on the certificate debt in letters to the president of Congress of August 28 and November 5, 1781. The mechanics of liquidating the certificates are addressed in the instructions to the commissioners of accounts for the states printed under October 14, 1782. For a detailed discussion of the certificate debt, see Ferguson, Power of the Purse, *59–68, 181–186.*

Although issued immediately after the new regulations were to take effect, the certificate of September 16, 1780, pictured here, is more representative of the type of non-interest-bearing certificate issued in 1778 and 1779 (see Showman, ed., Greene Papers, *II, 324–325n.). It was issued by Peter Kinnan, quartermaster in Bergen County, New Jersey, during the main army's encampment in that area, almost certainly for forage seized under impressment warrants signed by General Washington. Under the act of August 23, only certificates signed by the quartermaster or commissary generals were to be considered valid, but this proved impractical at the time because Timothy Pickering, the newly appointed quartermaster general, was not yet at army headquarters, and certificates for forage had to be issued almost daily. Washington therefore authorized continuation of the old system until Pickering's arrival (see Fitzpatrick, ed.,* Writings of Washington, *XX, 5, 51–52, 54–56, 62–63). For examples of certificates signed by Pickering that were modeled on the regulations of August 23, 1780, see William G. Anderson,* The Price of Liberty: The Public Debt of the American Revolution *(Charlottesville, Va., 1983), 93–94 (US 122–123). The certificate issued by Kinnan was printed in Philadelphia by Francis Bailey. Written on the back are the notations "No. 251" and "Anna Basset for 405 Dolls 2/6." The certificate is reproduced here courtesy of R. M. Smythe & Co., Inc., New York.*

The certificate of August 20, 1781, expressed in Virginia currency, suggests that some modifications were probably made in the issuing regulations but were not recorded in the Journals *of Congress. Issued for goods sold to the army in August 1781 just prior to the Yorktown campaign, it is signed, not by the quartermaster general, but by Richard Claiborne, deputy quartermaster general for Virginia, and countersigned by the issuer, James Hendricks, assistant deputy quartermaster general at Alexandria. For reasons that are not apparent, the certificate bears a statement of 5 percent interest rather than the 6 percent prescribed by Congress. It is reproduced courtesy of the American Antiquarian Society, Worcester, Massachusetts.*

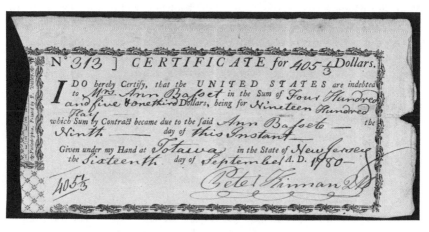

Quartermaster certificate dated September 16, 1780. 8" × 3⅞"

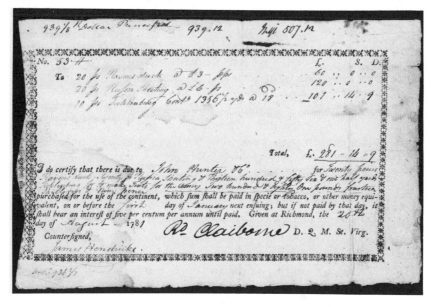

Quartermaster certificate dated August 20, 1781. 8⅖" × 5½"

Heads proper to be used, may have escaped me, in either case you will add, or leave out, as you find Circumstances may require. All these Accounts will be finally closed in your Books by the General Account Current.

4thly. You will likewise receive a Book, in which are to be registered all the Articles purchased or received in the Department of the Commissaries General of Purchases and Issues, the Quarter Masters General, and Tonnage Masters, the Commissary General of Military Stores, the General Hospital, the Clothier General and in short any other Persons who have purchased or received public Stores, and have not accounted for the delivery or Issues of them.

This Book is large enough to admit a considerable number of Columns on one side or Folio; and must be ruled, as you find the Nature of the respective Accounts may require. The first Column on the left hand will shew the dates of the Purchases or Receipts of the Articles: The Second, the Numbers of the Accounts or Vouchers from which they are Collected; the third, the Persons Names of whom purchased, or received; the fourth the Names of the Persons who received them, and are accountable to the Principal; and the Succeeding Columns will contain the Numbers and Quantities of the Articles so purchased or received.[8] In this Book an Account must be opened with the Principal of each Department for the Time being, and with every Person who is properly accountable for Articles purchased by or delivered to him, in which they must be charged, respectively with all such Articles, and for which they are to account with the Commissioners appointed, or to be appointed to adjust the Accounts of those Departments respectively. And in order to enable those Commissioners to call the Principals of Departments and others to Account, it will be necessary that you transmit to them respectively from time to time, and with as much expedition as possible, fair and regular Accounts, made out in the form mentioned, of all Articles whatever to be accounted for in the Departments for which such Commissioners are respectively appointed.[9]

In some of the Departments, more especially the Quarter Master Generals, the Articles may be too numerous to be inserted in Columns in a Folio, or Sheet, and as pasting Sheet to Sheet, is found to be very unweildly and tiresome to the Eye in examining, I suggest for your Consideration the Expediency of throwing them into certain Classes, and allotting a Folio sheet to each Class under these general heads or descriptions Vizt. Horse Waggons; and all kinds of Horse furniture, or the Materials they are made of to form one Class; Tents, and all kinds of Camp Equipage, a Second; Artificers, and Intrenching Tools, a third; Materials for Building Boats, Store houses &ca. a fourth; Forage a fifth; Barracks Expences a Sixth &ca.

This I apprehend may obviate the difficulties arising from a great Number of Articles, and consequently of Columns.

I find it of Considerable use to have all papers folded as near one Size, and form, as possible; and neatly filed with necessary endorsements. The advantages arising from this kind of regularity, and the official appearance it gives them, render this matter not unworthy your attention. I am Sir your most obedient and Humble Servant

Signed   James Milligan

Approved
Signed Robt Morris

MSS: Copy, PCC, DNA; incomplete copy dated April 1, 1783, in the writing of William Barber, commissioner for New York, Philip Schuyler Papers, NN; incomplete copy dated April 1, 1783, Abraham Yates, Jr., Papers, NN.

1. These instructions and the queries and answers that accompanied them (see the following document) had been in the process of formulation under RM's supervision since July, with assistance to Milligan provided by Daniel De Saussure and Lewis Pintard, commissioners for Maryland and New Jersey respectively (see Diary, July 18, and notes, August 30, and September 20, 1782). Their final formulation evidently was not completed until October 14; Milligan delivered them to the Office of Finance the following day (see Diary, October 15). It remains unclear whether early versions of these instructions were given to previously confirmed commissioners (see RM to the Commissioners of Accounts for the States, September 7, and notes), but the earliest date of extant copies is that of the final text printed here, which was enclosed in RM to the President of Congress, August 26, 1783. The instructions were issued seriatim under various dates as additional commissioners were appointed, but some later texts evidently omitted bookkeeping details. See notes 6, 8, 9 below; and RM to the Comptroller of the Treasury, April 1 (two letters), and to Zephaniah Turner, August 4, 1783.

2. Space left blank in manuscript. The words "New York" are inserted in the NN texts here and below at note 3.

3. Space left blank in manuscript.

4. The enclosed accounts nos. 1–5 have not been found. For explanations of nominal money, old and new emission money, specific supply requisitions, and the specie tax for the support of prisoners, see notes to John Morin Scott to RM, May 30, 1781; and the Secretary of Congress to RM, June 29, 1781, and notes.

5. Space left blank in manuscript.

6. The foregoing sentence is omitted from the NN texts.

7. Suspension points thus in manuscript.

8. The paragraph to this point is omitted from both NN texts.

9. Except for the signatories' names and subjoined dateline, the NN texts end with this paragraph.

Queries and Answers on the Settlement of State Accounts with the United States

[Philadelphia, ca. October 14, 1782][1]

These Queries, having been proposed by Lewis Pintard Esqr. Commissioner for liquidating the Accounts in the State of New Jersey, and Daniel Desaussure Esqr. Commissioner in the State of Maryland, have been considered, and the following Answers annexed to them.

In settling the Accounts between a state and the United States, it will be necessary that the Commissioners be previously informed on the following Heads Vizt

1st. Is the whole, or any part of the Expence to be Allowed for fortifications for the Defence of the state or any Particular Place within such State?

2nd. [Is] The whole, or any part, of the Expence for the Militia to be allowed, either when invaded, or in danger of any Invasion by the common Enemy, or for suppression of disaffected subjects rising into a state of Rebellion against the State; or when employed against the Indians?

3rd In what Proportion are the States to be allowed for Clothing the continental Troops raised by each state?

4th. Are all Camp, and Military Stores of every Denomination to be charged to the United States, whether made use of by the Regulars, or the Militia? In this Department, it is presumed, there will be great Quantities of Arms and Ammunition expended by the Militia, which cannot be accounted for?

5th. Are Individual states to be allowed the Disbursements for Gallies, or other armed Vessels, not ordered out by Congress?

6th. Are they to be allowed the Charge for Obstructions Sunk, or Intended to be sunk, in order to prevent the Enemy's Vessels going up to the Cities of the United States?

Answer to No 1. 2. 3. 4. 5. 6. In all these Matters the Commissioner will be regulated by the Resolutions of Congress, according to their true Intent and Meaning. When Charges are authorized by the existing Resolves, they must be Passed: and where they ought not to be admitted they must be rejected. In doubtful Cases Application must be made to the Superintendant of Finance, who will state a general Question to Congress, and receive their Answer without communicating the Name of the State.

7th. Are all Disbursements for Presents to Indians to be admitted as a Charge against the Union?

8th. If a state hath settled and paid Accounts which shall be admitted to be a charge against the Union, and it appears to the Commissioner that a considerable overcharge was made in any Part thereof, shall he deduct so much as he shall judge to be overcharged?

9th. Is it not the Intention of Congress that the Accounts Current between the United States and each State be closed the 31st day of December in every year since the Commencement of the War; and to which End, the Accounts for each Department are to be liquidated accordingly?

10th Shall the Charges made for Expresses to or from Congress or within the State, be admitted in the Account?

11th Shall the states be allowed the Charges for Maintainance of Prisoners of War?

12th Shall Payments made to Continental Officers, either for Recruiting, or other services be allowed, or even where it does not appear for what services he received the same?

7th. No Charges for Presents or Treaties with Indians will be admitted; Unless authorized by Congress.

8th All such Accounts, with their Vouchers must be examined, and all improper, as well as overcharges deducted, and the Commissioner must endeavor, by every means, to detect all frauds and discover all Errors.

9th. The Instructions of the Superintendant of Finance on this subject, of the 7th September 1782[2] contain an Answer.

10th. This will depend on the particular Circumstances; of which the Commissioner will Judge.

11th. All Charges for Maintenance &c. of Prisoners of War, must be supported by such sufficient Vouchers as will authorize a Charge against the Enemy, if not they must be rejected.

12th The Commissioner will be directed by the Resolutions of Congress, whether Charges for Money advanced to Continental Officers for the Recruiting or other Services are to be admitted: But no Charges must be allowed, without Proving the appropriation or actual Expenditure of the Money for the uses mentioned in the Accounts.

13th. Whether Certificates given to Individuals are to be taken as they stand, new ones given of their amount, or whether they are to be reexamined and new Prices affixed to the Articles when they have been over, or under, charged?

13th. Certificates given by Quarter Masters or Commissaries to Individuals, must be reexamined, the Articles shewn, and their Value determined; that the Receiver of them may be charged, and made Accountable to the Commissioners appointed for the respective Departments. See Resolutions of Congress of the 23d of August 1780 relating to them, which must be strictly attended to.

14th. What mode is to be pursued to affix the Prices of Articles furnished and services performed in each state if they are not pointed out in the Instructions: whether it would not be proper for the Commissioners to be directed to apply to the Chief Justice and other Judges of the different Counties to fix the same; as it would be improper for him to take upon himself a Matter of so much Consequence.

14th. The Commissioners are appointed and impowered to make final Settlements, according to Equity, and good Conscience, without applying to other Judges, unless it be for necessary Information.

15th. When an Account or Certificate is brought in by an Individual, is he to be allowed Interest thereon to the Time of Liquidation?

15th The Time when the Money became due is to be ascertained in the new Certificates to be given to the Claimants by the Commissioners.

16th. Are the different Commissioners to correspond with each other, in order to give such Information as may be useful in their Respective Departments: If they are, should not all Letters to and from them, respecting the Business of their Office, be free of Postage?

16th. The Commissioners must correspond with one another when necessary; and keep an Account of Postage: No Franks can be allowed.

17th By what Scale of Depreciation are Accounts to be settled after the 18th day of March

17th. It is expected there will be few or no Accounts with the States after this Period: But if

1780 being the Time the Continental Table of Depreciation Ends?

there are they must be valued by the Scale of the individual state; unless Congress shall otherwise direct, in which case the Commissioners will be furnished with their Act. With Individuals no other scale is necessary than Equity, and good Conscience.

ENDORSED: Queries proposed, with Answers/Annexed, to be observed by all/the Commissioners for Adjusting/the Accounts between the United/States and Individual States.
MSS: Copy, PCC, DNA; copy, Abraham Yates, Jr., Papers, NN.

1. This document was intended as a supplement to the instructions contained in the preceding document. An initial formulation was delivered to RM on July 18, 1782. The answers evidently were drafted by Comptroller of the Treasury James Milligan and emended by the Financier. The final text printed here was enclosed in RM to the President of Congress, August 26, 1783; copies were sent to the commissioners of accounts for the states as they were appointed. The endorsement on the NN text gives the date of "7 Sep 1782." For the background, see Diary, July 18, and notes, and RM to the Commissioners of Accounts for the States, September 7, 1782, and notes.

2. The words "delivered to you" are inserted here in the NN text.

Instructions of the Comptroller of the Treasury to the Commissioners of Accounts for the Departments

[Philadelphia] Comptrollers Office October 14th 1782[1]

Sir

Circular   The Superintendant of Finance having acquainted me that pursuant to an Act of the United States in Congress Assembled of the 27th. of February last, you have been duly appointed the Commissioner for adjusting and finally Settling the Accounts in the Department of the   [2] And having directed me to prepare such Instructions for you, as I judged might be necessary, I have accordingly framed the following for your regulation and Government.

A Strict attention to the modes pointed out, is absolutely necessary to enable the Register finally to enter the Accounts with accuracy in the Treasury Books. And I flatter myself, it will be of great Utility to you in the course of your duty, as without method, it would be impossible to accomplish the end proposed.

1st You will receive herewith a Sett of Books, in which are to be recorded in a fair and regular manner, all Accounts and Settlements by you made.

These Books are ruled with double Setts of Money Columns, in the first of which will be inserted the Nominal Sum in Dollars and

Ninetieth parts of a Dollar, and in the Second, the Specie Value of each Sum according to the Dates of receiving and paying in Dollars and Ninetieth parts likewise. When Accounts are liquidated in Specie Value and without any referrence to, or Connection with Nominal Money, the Specie Column only will be used. Between the two Setts of Money Columns is introduced a Single one for the rate of Exchange or Depreciation.

2ndly   You will herewith receive Accounts taken from the Treasury Books, of the Monies charged to the Principal for the time being, or others in the Department of the   .[3] These Accounts you will enter in your Books, charging the Persons respectively Accountable, with the Monies advanced, with every date and particular in detail. It is probable the Department may be chargeable with other Monies they may have received of Individual States or Public officers, who have not yet rendered their Accounts at the Treasury. Should any such hereafter appear, they will be transmitted to you to be entered; and should you obtain certain knowledge of any other advances with which they are Chargeable, you will likewise enter them.

3rdly   The several Principals of the Department are to render to you fair and regular Accounts of the Expenditures of all Monies they are respectively accountable for, shewing the Nature of the Services performed, and the Quantity and Quality of the Article purchased or received, also the Persons of whom received and by whom performed. Such regulation as Congress have directed respecting the mode of keeping and rendering these Accounts must be attended to. Some of the Deputies or Assistants, may have been so far detached from, or little connected with the Principal as to render a Separate Settlement with them proper and necessary.

The particular circumstances attending such, will enable you to Judge of the propriety of departing from the General rule of holding the Principal only Accountable. In Examining all Accounts you will employ your utmost care in Judging of the propriety of Charges, and the Authenticity and Validity of all Vouchers rendered in Support of them, rejecting such as are not sufficiently supported, and curtailing such as may be overcharged. It will be your particular duty to discover and rectify errors, and to endeavour to detect all frauds and embezlements of every kind.

4thly   The Cash being accounted for to your Satisfaction, and the Accounts fairly and regularly Stated, you will enter to the Credit of the Accountant in your Books all the Expenditures or charges admitted, Taking care to Specify in such Entries, the nature of the Services performed and the Quantities, Qualities and prices of all Articles purchased.

5thly   The next thing necessary to be done, is to Account for the Stores or Articles purchased, or in any manner received, this is no less essential than Accounting for the Cash. For this purpose they must render you fair and regular Accounts of all the Articles purchased or received, which you will enter in a Book herewith delivered you, charging the Persons respectively Accountable with them and Specifying the Quantities and Qualities, this you will Check by their Account of Expenditures, Returns and other documents. The Commissioners for adjusting the Accounts between the United States and each Individual, are instructed to transmit to you regular Accounts from time to time, of such Articles as may come to their knowledge, and ought to be accounted for in the Department of the   .[4] These you will likewise Charge to the Persons respectively Accountable unless already charged to them from their own Accounts. It is probable you will often find that one Officer may have purchased or received large Quantities of Stores and forwarded or delivered them to another, in such cases, you will naturally charge the receiver and Credit the deliverer.

This Book (which may be called a Store Book) is large enough to admit a considerable number of Columns on one side or folio, and must be ruled as you find the nature of the Account may require. The first Column on the left hand will shew the dates of the purchases or receipts of the Articles, the Second the Number of Accounts or Vouchers from which they are collected, the third the Persons Names of whom Purchased or received, the fourth the Names of the Persons who received them, and the succeeding Columns will contain the Number, Quantities and Qualities of Such Articles. If the Articles are too Numerous to be inserted in one page or folio, you may divide them into Classes, taking in as many Articles in each, as a Page or folio will conveniently contain, and allotting to each Class as many pages or folios as may be necessary.

6thly   The Accountant will also render you an Account of the Issues or deliveries of the Articles which must be supported by proper Vouchers, shewing by whose order, to whom, and for what uses such issues or deliveries were made, with proper receipts for the same. In all cases where los[s]es are accompanied by the Retreat of our Army, or Capture and destruction of Stores by the Enemy, are alledged, you will require the Strongest, most Authentic and most particular proofs possible to be obtained, of such los[s]es, Captures or destruction, before you admit them to the Credit of the Accountants.

7thly   The Stores or Articles being accounted for to your Satisfaction, and the Accounts fairly and regularly Stated, you will enter to the Credit of the Accountant in your Store Books, all the Issues, deliveries &ca properly proven and admitted, in as particular a manner as possible. Having then compleated the Settlement, you will then make out a fair and particular State of the Cash Account, and also a State of the Account of Stores, shewing the balance due on each if any to or from the United States as the case may be, which you will transmit to the Superintendant of Finance; that he may take further order thereon. To this may be added a Report to him, containing your observations on the whole of the Accounts and Settlements. I find it of considerable use to have all Papers folded as near one Size and form as possible, and neatly filed with necessary Indorsements; the advantages arising from this kind of regularity and the official appearance it gives them, render this matter not unworthy of your attention. I am Sir your Most obedient Humble Servant

Signed   James Milligan

ENDORSED: Copy of General/Instructions from the/Comptroller of the Treasury/to the Commissioners for/Adjusting the Accounts/in the Staff departments
MS: Copy, PCC, DNA.

1. As with Milligan's instructions of this date to the commissioners of accounts for the states, it seems likely that these instructions had been in preparation under RM's supervision for some time. Earlier drafts may have been sent to previously appointed commissioners (see Diary, August 2, and RM's circular to the commissioners for the departments of September 19), but the final version, represented by the text printed here (which RM enclosed in his letter to the president of Congress of August 26, 1783), was very likely delivered to the Superintendent by Milligan on October 15 (see Diary of that date) and issued seriatim as appointments were made.
2. Space left blank in manuscript.
3. Space left blank in manuscript.
4. Space left blank in manuscript.

From Benjamin Franklin

[Passy, October 14, 1782][1]

The three millions you mention previous to 1778 were two of them given and the third was an Advance on a Contract with the Farmers General of tobacco.

MS: Extract in the writing of Arthur Lee, Records of Boundary and Claim Commissions and Arbitrations, RG 76, DNA.

1. The complete text of this letter has not been found, but Franklin was apparently providing a further response to RM's letter of July 1 (see Franklin to RM, September 26, and notes). Franklin's letter was read in Congress on December 27 (PCC, no. 185, III, 50); RM acknowledged it in his reply to Franklin of January 13, 1783. Subjoined to the extract printed here was a paragraph which Lee copied imperfectly from the contract for the 6-million-livre loan for 1783 dated February 21, 1783, and signed by Franklin and Comte de Vergennes four days later. The paragraph, which comprises the words "In the third class are comprehended . . . of the said thirteen United States," is printed in JCC, XXV, 776. Franklin forwarded the contract to RM in a letter of March 7, 1783; RM enclosed it in his letter to Congress of June 22, 1783.

From Matthew Ridley

Robert Morris Esqr.   Paris October the 14th: 1782
Dear Sir

I have already wrote you per this Conveyance under date of the 12 Current; the unexpected delay in setting out of the Gentleman who goes by the Frigate give me the opportunity of addressing you again.

The Anniversary of the 4th: July cannot fail to enliven the Hearts of every American who has been personally interested in securing American Liberty. That you should feel more so than most others is not in the least surprizing. You undertook one of the most difficult tasks to assure success in the Struggle, and contrary to the expectations of many Friends and the wishes of all Ennemies you have succeeded. I am not one of those who rejoices the least on the occasion. On the 4th. of July I was in Holland, where we had an Elegant Entertainment given by Dutch patriots, well wishers to the Liberties of Mankind; And who are not without Hopes the Wisdom of America may extend herself over great part of Europe. I was witness to a Scene there that few would believe. A Band of Music was provided and the Ceremony was fixed that on naming the Favorite Toasts every one should drink a Bumper, The Company give three Cheers and the Band of Music strike up. After a variety of Toasts, and to all which the Ceremony was gone through, The statholder was given. Not a drop to cool the parch'd Lip, not a whisper of applause, or a single Note to celebrate the Honors of the chiefs! So public a mark of disapprobation I never heard of—there were about 80 Persons at Supper.

That you wish to return to your private Station I readily believe—I always foretold you would. For the comfort of your Friends it is much to be desired. For the Interest and Credit of America I think otherwise. I however hope whenever the favorable period arrives that you can resign public applause for Domestic Tranquillity you will not neglect it. In saying so there is a little selfishness at Bottom also. I expect to return: and I know I never shall have so much of your Company in one station as my Vanity, and your partiality towards me, give me Reason to expect in the other.

I am still without Mrs. Ridley but expecting every post a summons to meet her at Calais. This post has been open sometime past. I will not tell you all I have suffered from my separation. "One hours Bliss repays whole years of Pain."

I communicated to Messrs Le Couteulx what you said on their Accounts.[1] They were not a little pleased, and live in Hopes.

With respect to the Children I have written you as fully as the present Moment would admit. They are now by my side. I brought them home to write Letters that you Might have the latest accounts possible from them. Inclosed you have two Letters and two for my good Friend G Morris.[2]

For News, Politics &ca I refer you to other Channels.

I hope eir this Mrs. Morris has received all the Things I ordered for her. If the Carpet is equal to the design I chose I think it must please. Having been made at a place some distance from Paris I had not an opportunity of seeing it before sent away.

The boys are getting a fine Doll for their Sister Hetty. It will be sent with some Things for Mrs. Powell.

I hope eir this you and Mrs. Morris and Miss Kitty Livingston, if with you, are well settled in Market street. I envy you the Social Circle and would willingly this Winter change my Beechen Sapling for your Hickory Billett. But I live in Hopes—Hope! the best Kedge Anchor that ever a seaman warp'd up a Winding River with.

May you and yours enjoy many Succeeding Anniversarys of the 4th. July and if so permitted may I long be one of the Guests at the Festival. Accept the sincere wishes of a warm Heart and believe me respectfully Dear Sir Your much obliged and humble Servant

Matt: Ridley

ENDORSED: Paris 12th and 14th Octr. 1782/Mathew Ridley Eqr.
MS: ALS, Robert Morris Papers, NN.
  1. See RM to Ridley, July 8, 1782.
  2. Letters not found.

From George Washington

Head Quarters [Verplancks Point, New York] 14th. October 1782
Sir

I have been honored with yours of the 5th. covering Copy of the Resolve of the 1st. and of your circular letters to the Executives of the States and your Receivers.[1] I am in hopes they will have ⟨a proper⟩ the desired effect, and I shall take every proper opportunity of making the use of them which you request. I have the honor to be with real Esteem Sir your most obedient Servant

Honble. Mr. Morris

ENDORSED: 14th: October 1782/to/Honble. Mr. Morris
MSS: Dft in the writing of Tench Tilghman, Washington Papers, DLC; Varick transcript, Washington Papers, DLC.
  1. The circulars are dated October 5. For the act of Congress, see notes to RM's Report to Congress on the Representation of the New Jersey Legislature, September 27.

To Joseph Diant

Marine Office 14. Octo: 1782[1]

Should Captain John Barry in the Frigate Alliance arrive at your Island I request the favor of you to deliver to him the enclosed Letter.

MS: AM LbC, MdAN.
  1. Diant was a merchant of St. Pierre, Martinique, who conducted American business there in a private capacity (see RM's second letter to John Barry of July 12 and his report to Congress of June 21, 1782). The enclosure was RM to Barry, October 14.

Diary: October 15, 1782

The Honble. Mr Osgood called respecting the Letter from his Excelly. Benjm. Harrison Esqr. Govr. of Virginia desiring that the United States should take to their Account certain Articles of Cloathing bought by the Court of France for the State of Virginia.[1] I gave my Opinion in favor of the Governors request.

Saml Hodgdon Esqr. made Application on behalf of Coleman[2] and others Iron Masters for liberty to agree with German Prisoners to the Amount of their respective Claims on the War Office[3] to which I agreed as those Claims are founded on Special Agreements and promises of Payment at the War Office and the Shot and Shells were used at the Seige of York Town therefore I signed a Paper declaring that Colemans notes to the Amount of 6,000 Dollars shall be received as Cash for the Liberation of German Prisoners.

The Honble. Mr Wharton called to see some of Doctr Franklins Letters which were produced to him.[4]

Mr. Timy. Edwards for Money or Notes on Account of the Contract. I agreed to supply notes to the Amount of 22,000 Dollars on Account of Sands Livingston & Co. Contractors.

Colo Miles applies still for money for various Purposes.

Colo. Nichols for the Balance due on his Contract.[5]

Mr. Milligan the Comptroller this Day brought the Instructions for the Commissioners of Accounts[6] and had a Conference on various Subjects.

Mr. R. Sands for money and notes on Account of the Contract in which I promised him Assistance.

Capt. Truxen and Mr. Randal applied respecting Raguets Ship.[7] I desired her Papers and Time to Consider until to Morrow.

Wrote a Letter to Hezki Merrill Esqr.

Wrote a Letter to His Excelly Genl Washington.

Wrote a Letter to Geo. Olney Esqr.

Issued a Warrant on Mr Swanwick in favor of Samuel Miles	£ 101.12.2
Issued a Warrant on Mr Swanwick in favor John Moylan	3750. 0.0
Issued a Warrant on Mr Swanwick in favor the Bank	20.12.6

1. Samuel Osgood of Massachusetts was a member of the congressional committee considering RM's letter to the president of Congress of October 9, relative to Governor Benjamin Harrison's letter of September 23.

2. Robert Coleman (1748–1825), an Irish-born ironmaster who operated Elizabeth Furnace in Lancaster County, has been called "the most enterprising and successful iron-master in Pennsylvania." He later served as a member of the General Assembly in 1783–1784, a delegate to the Pennsylvania convention to ratify the Federal Consti-

tution of 1787, a member of the Pennsylvania Constitutional Convention of 1789–1790, an associate judge for Lancaster County, and a presidential elector in 1792 and 1796. See William H. Egle, "The Federal Constitution of 1787: Sketches of the Members of the Pennsylvania Convention," *PMHB*, XI (1887), 71–72; and Joseph Livingston Delafield, "Notes on the Life and Work of Robert Coleman," *PMHB*, XXXVI (1912), 226–230.

3. On September 24 Hodgdon had transmitted to RM a letter he had received from the Philadelphia ironmaster John Patton, evidently requesting that debts owed by the United States to various ironmasters for munitions be partially repaid by allowing them the services of German prisoners of war as indentured servants (for the background, see the Instructions of RM and Benjamin Lincoln on the Liberation of German Prisoners, July 11, 1782, and notes). After RM consented to this proposal on September 25, various ironmasters presented applications for German prisoners. See Diary, July 5, 6, September 25, October 4, and November 9, Hodgdon to RM, October 30 and November 7, 1782, January 25 and April 14, 1783, and January 16, 1784; and Hodgdon to Coleman, October 17, 1782, and Hodgdon's Circular to the Ironmasters, January 27, 1783, WDC, no. 92, pp. 264, 299.

4. Samuel Wharton, a delegate to Congress from Delaware, was a member of a committee appointed to consider RM's letter to Congress of May 24, 1782. See notes to that document.

5. Francis Nichols, in partnership with Moses Rawlings, held the contract for Frederick, Maryland, and Winchester, Virginia.

6. The instructions, both to the commissioners of accounts for the states and for the departments, are printed under the date of October 14.

7. See Diary, September 2, and notes.

To John Langdon

Marine Office 15 October 1782

Sir,

I have received your Letter of the twenty first of the last Month,[1] and in answer to your Questions respecting the Ship America I have to observe that I can have no Doubt but it was the Intention of Congress that the Hull of that Ship should be completely finished and delivered in the Water, therefore the Joiners Work, Smiths, Pumpmakers, Painters, Carvers Work &ca. being clearly within that design are to be done at the Expence of the United States.

As the State of Massachusetts have passed an Act for the collecting the other half of their Taxes[2] I have strong hopes that Mr. Lovell will soon be able to take up all the Notes which are to to be paid by him and when that is the Case, I shall immediately send you a further Remittance. I am Sir your most obedient and humble Servant

RM

MS: AM LbC, MdAN.

1. Letter not found. Langdon was supervising the completion of the *America* at Portsmouth, New Hampshire. Congress had recently offered the vessel to France. See notes to John Paul Jones to Gouverneur Morris, September 2.

2. RM refers to "An Act for Apportioning and Assessing a Tax of Two Hundred Thousand Pounds." The decision to pass the act was made on September 24, but was later reconsidered. Although final passage of the act was not recorded in the legislative records of the General Court, the act was published separately under the date of 1782 (see Charles Evans, Clifford K. Shipton, and Roger P. Bristol, comps., *American Bibliography: A Chronological Dictionary of All Books, Pamphlets and Periodical Publications*

Printed in the United States of America from . . . 1639 . . . to . . . 1820 [Chicago and Worcester, Mass., 1903–1959], VI, 173, no. 17597). It called for half the tax to be paid on March 1, 1783, and the remainder on June 1, 1783. The act was reprinted in *Acts and Laws of Massachusetts,* 1782–1783, pp. 153–174, where it was incorrectly assigned the date of March 22, 1783, one the editors mistakenly accepted in the notes to RM to James Lovell, May 14, 1782.

To Hezekiah Merrill

Office of Finance 15. Octo: 1782[1]

Sir,

Mr. Edwards one of the Contractors has represented to me that you declared you could not exchange my Notes or Bills of Exchange before they became due (if this be so) you must have misapprehended my Views which are, that all the Notes be exchanged as they are presented without regard to the Time of Payment mentioned therein. That time was inserted to prevent the Paper from becoming payable here too soon but not to prevent the Payment of it in or for Taxes.[2] I am sir your most obedient Servant

RM

MS: Ofcl LbC, DLC.

1. Merrill was the receiver of Continental taxes for Connecticut.

2. On the timed Morris's notes and bills of exchange referred to here and the pressure the contractors placed on them, see RM's Circular to the Receivers of Continental Taxes, August 29, and notes, and documents cited there.

To Thomas Russell

Marine Office 15 October 1782

Sir,

I am favored with your Letters of the 11th and 16 of the last Month.[1] I am much obliged by your Information respecting the seventy four Gun ship which is on the Stocks at Boston and very much so by your Offer of advances; but I think it will be better to dispose of that Vessel and the valuable Bed of Timber which she lies on, if it can be done on good Terms.[2] I beg to be favored with your Sentiments on the Subject. I am sorry that I cannot gratify your Wishes respecting Captain Smith[3] as it is not in my Power to give him a Commission. All I can do at this Time is to have his name entered in the Office as having applied for a Lieutenancy that he may be promoted when the Service shall require it and that I have done. I agree with you in Opinion of the Necessity of having a Marshall of the Admiralty at your Port but that Business depends on Matters to which I am not competent as a Law of the state will be necessary to regulate the Admiralty Jurisdiction of your State. Were the Appointment of such an Officer in me your Recommendation should be properly attended to.

I enclose the Copy of a Memorial sent by the Count de Vergennes to Dr. Franklin respecting the Capture of a Danish Vessel which I request you will inquire after and transmit as full and authentic Documents of the Circumstances of the capture and Condemnation as can be obtained.[4] I have received the Proceedings of the Court of Enquiry on Captain Nicholson and shall in due Season forward to you my Determination.[5] I am Sir your most obedient and humble Servant

RM

MS: Ofcl LbC, DLC.

1. Letters not found. Russell was the deputy agent of marine for New England stationed at Boston.

2. The reference is probably to the 74-gun ship which Congress had authorized for construction in Massachusetts by a resolution of November 20, 1776. According to one authority, the vessel "was framed but then abandoned and left to rot." Fowler, *Rebels Under Sail*, 216–217.

3. Samuel Smith. See RM to Russell, August 8.

4. For the memorial of Otto Blome, the Danish minister at Paris, concerning the *Providence* or *Providentia* and the transmittal letters of Vergennes and Franklin, see Wharton, ed., *Rev. Dipl. Corr.*, V, 321, 512; for future references, see RM to Thomas Russell, November 26, 1782, and February 17, 1783, and to the Secretary for Foreign Affairs, February 15, 1783. For an earlier complaint, see RM to the Secretary for Foreign Affairs, June 6, 1782 (second letter), and notes.

5. RM's disapproval of the proceedings, dated October 17, was enclosed in RM to Russell, October 19.

To George Washington

Office of Finance 15th.[–16] October 1782

Sir

I have received your Letters of the second, third and seventh Instant. There is no Man in America more heartily disposed than I am to remove from the Army and from all others who have Claims on the Public every just Ground of Complaint. But with the Means in my Power, how is it possible? I have been obliged to submit to cancelling one Contract and forming another at one third advance on the former Price, for the want of a meer Trifle compared with what we had a Right to expect. I am in advance on Credit to an Amount which you can scarcely form an Idea of altho I have declined every Expenditure not indispensible. That Part of the late arrival of Cloathing which is unfit for Soldiers Use is now selling to pay off Debts contracted by the Cloathing Department during my Administration. Among these Debts are twelve thousand Dollars for needle Work done by People in extreme Indigence.[1] The Cloathing which arrived fit for the Officers wear was inadequate to the Purpose of Cloathing them all. The Division must have created Confusion and raised Disputes. If this had not been the Case still it would have been liable to the Inconveniencies attending partial Payments and we should have been justly Reproached for having broken repeated Promises that no such Payments should take Place. Congress have done all in their Power to procure Money for the Army. My own Efforts I shall not dwell upon. If money is obtained that will produce Satisfaction. I am sure that Nothing else will. My Credit has already been on the Brink of Ruin. If that goes all is gone, but if it can be preserved there will in the last necessity be some Chance of making advances on Credit to the Army as well as to others. Thus Sir you will see that I look forwards as far as my distressed Situation will admit; but after all if the states cannot be prevailed on to make greater Exertions it is difficult to foresee where the Thing is to terminate.

I have this Day commissioned Major Turner as Marine Commissary of Prisoners, and I trust he will soon be in Capacity to prevent your Excellency from any further trouble on that Subject. I am Sir with sincere Respect and Esteem Your most obedient and humble Servant

Robt Morris

His Excellency General Washington

16 October[2]

I have received yours of the fourteenth for which be pleased to accept my Acknowlegements.   RM

ENDORSED: Philadelphia 15th Octo 1782/from/Hono Robert Morris/Mjr Turner appointed Comry of/marine prisoners
MSS: LS, Washington Papers, DLC; Ofcl LbC, DLC.
    1. Regarding these workers, see RM to Washington, September 25, and notes.
    2. This postscript is written on the verso of the LS.

Circular to the Receivers of Continental Taxes

(Circular)[1]   Office of Finance 15th October 1782
    On perusing the Advertisement enclosed herewith[2] you will see the Propriety of it's having a general Circulation throughout the United States: I therefore request you will cause it to be published in the several News Papers that are printed in your State.

MSS: LS, to William Churchill Houston of New Jersey, Houston Collection, NjP; LS, to William Whipple of New Hampshire, Miscellaneous Papers, MHi; LS, to Benjamin Harwood of Maryland, Morris-Harwood Papers, MdHi; Ofcl LbC, DLC.
    1. The text addressed to the receiver for Maryland was inadvertently addressed to Thomas Harwood, the Continental loan officer and brother of the receiver.
    2. See the Advertisement for Contracts for 1783, October 10.

To George Olney

Office of Finance 15. October 1782[1]

Mr. Jeremiah F. Jenkins having presented me a Sett of Exchange drawn by Daniel Clarke Esqr. dated at Richmond Virginia the fifteenth of July last in his Favor and being desirous of receiving the Money in your State I have this Day drawn on John Swanwick Esqr. of this City in favor of said Mr. Jenkins at sixty Days sight for two thousand three hundred and thirty three Dollars and one third of a Dollar (the Amount of the above Bill) which I must request you will take up as soon as you possibly can.

MS: Ofcl LbC, DLC.
1. Olney was the receiver of Continental taxes for Rhode Island. On the transaction mentioned in this letter, see Diary, October 14, and notes.

Commission to George Turner

[Marine Office, October 15, 1782]
By Virtue of the Powers and Authorities in me vested by an Act of the United States in Congress assembled of the twenty fourth of July 1782, I do hereby constitute and appoint you George Turner Esqr. to be the Commissary for Marine Prisoners giving and granting to you all and singular the Rights, Privileges, Authorities and Emoluments to the said office of Commissary of Prisoners belonging or in any wise appertaining.

Given under my Hand and Seal in the Marine Office of the United States this fifteenth day of October in the Year of our Lord 1782.

MS: AM LbC, MdAN.

From the Secretary at War
(Benjamin Lincoln)

Trentown [Trenton, New Jersey] Oct 15 1782
Please to pay Abraham Hunt Esqr. One hundred and sixty dollars for Value received of him and you will oblige your obedient Servant

MS: ALS, Lincoln Papers, MHi.

The Secretary at War (Benjamin Lincoln)
to John Swanwick

War Office Octr: 15th: 1782
Please to pay unto Joseph Carleton on his order the Sum of one Hundred sixty six dollars and two thirds of a Dollar, on account of the Warrants in my favour remaining in your Hands.[1]

MS: LS, Lincoln Papers, MHi.
1. The body of the letter is in Carleton's writing; on verso is Carleton's receipt dated October 22, 1782. Swanwick was the cashier of the Office of Finance.

Diary: October 16, 1782

Jos. Nourse Esqr. called for information as to the manner of opening some Accounts in the public Books on which I gave him my Opinion.

The Honble. Secy at War called to advise on several matters which were adjusted and then I went with him to the War Office to meet a Committee of Congress consisting of the Honble. Mr Bland, Carrol and Osgood to whom was referred the Letter of the Secy at War and of Genl Washington relative to the Pay of the Army.[1] After some Conversation I remarked that Congress had Called on the States in November last for 8,000,000 of Dollars in which was included the Estimates for pay of the Army, that by their Act of the first Instant[2] they had required a full and speedy compliance with that Call, declaring that the Pay of the Army for the Year 1782 depends upon their Compliance and as we have not Funds in Europe at Command Congress can do nothing more than to direct the attention and Expectations of the Army to the several Legislatures who alone are Competent to their releif, But that in the mean while I would not only urge the States to Compliance by all possible Means but also take immediate Measures for bringing such Funds as we may have in Europe speedily to Aid in the intended Payments to the Army. The Committee agreed to report accordingly.[3]

Sundry Persons applied to me relative to the Exchange of Prisoners &c. Referred them all to Majr Turner.

Mr. Howell Deputy Clothier Genl. applied for Cloathing for the Maryland Recruits. I agreed to his purchasing Blankets &c.

Sundry Persons apply for Money &c.

Wrote a Letter to William Whipple Esqr.

Wrote a Letter to Alexander Hamilton.

Wrote a Letter to His Excellency Genl Washington.

Wrote a Letter to James Lovell Esqr.

Wrote a Letter to Geo Olney Esqr.

Wrote a Letter to William C: Houston.

1. For the letters, see notes to George Washington to RM, October 2.

2. See notes to RM's Report to Congress on the Representation of the New Jersey Legislature, September 27.

3. The committee reported accordingly on October 16. See RM to Washington October 16, and notes.

To Alexander Hamilton

Office of Finance 16 Octo: 1782

Sir,

I am indebted for two of your Favors, one of which is without date,[1] the other of the fifth Instant enclosing the Account of your Receipts to that Time. I am sorry the Propositions I made did not suit Colo. Malcolm and Mr. Lawrence. I am pleased that you approve the Plans for restoring public Credit and wish they had been adopted, as I conceive the substituting a mere temporary Expedient is dangerous. I am happy to find that the public Creditors are organizing themselves, their Numbers and Influence joined to the Justness of their Cause must prevail if they persevere. The Proceedings of the Committee on Taxation are just what are to be expected on such Occasions.

The Establishment of solid Systems require Time and Industry and the Bulk of Mankind are so attached to their particular Interests, that they are seldom perswaded to extend their Efforts in favor of general Regulations, until Experience convinces them of their Necessity. I hope the People of America will feel that Conviction before it be too late, and remain Sir, your most obedient and humble Servant

RM

ms: Ofcl LbC, DLC.

1. The letter is printed under September 28. Hamilton was the receiver of Continental taxes for New York.

To George Washington

Office of Finance 16 Octr 1782[1]

Sir

I have, for some time past, anticipated the reflections[2] which you have made, on the situation of the army.[3] I know that some money is necessary, and my efforts to obtain it, both at home and abroad, have been unceasing. I am now about to purchase a vessel, and send a person on board of her to the Havanna, for the purpose of vending bills of exchange to the amount of half a million dollars. I have issued orders to the Alliance frigate, to go thither in quest of it[4] and taken the proper measures for payment of the bills in Europe. This plan was adopted, from a conviction that a considerable sum would be wanted about the close of the year, and my experience that bills could not be sold to the amount.[5] Your letters confirm me in my ideas of its propriety.[6] If I suceed, a part of the money shall be applied as pay. If the plan should fail, the army will not be the only persons who will have reason to lament the failure. This matter I mention to you sir, in confidence, as well[7] because I will not raise hopes which may prove abortive,[8] as because it is necessary the profoundest secrecy should be observed lest the enemy should prevent the execution of it. You observe in your letter, that a Peace is necessary; but if I were to hazard an opinion on the subj[e]ct, it would be, that war is more likely than Peace to produce funds for the public debts, increase of authority to congress,[9] and vigor to the administration as well of the union as of its component parts. These things all appear necessary to our future prosperity, safety, and happines[s].[10] Believe me I pray you with sincere Esteem your most obedient and humble Servant

Robt Morris

His Excellency Genl. Washington

ENDORSED: The Honble Rob. Morris/16th Octr. 82
MSS: LS, part in cipher, Washington Papers, DLC; Ofcl LbC, part in cipher, DLC; Dft in the writing of Gouverneur Morris, Robert Morris Papers, CSmH; deciphered copy in the writing of Tench Tilghman, Washington Papers, DLC.
1. Except for RM's signature and the dateline, salutation, complimentary close, and the inside address in the writing of Gouverneur Morris, the LS presented here is enciphered in Gouverneur Morris's hand. The editors have deciphered it by using the key to the code previously sent to Washington (see notes to RM to Washington, August 22, 1781). The texts in the Washington Papers indicate that Washington received the letter, though no reply has been found.
2. This word is singular in the deciphered copy.
3. For his latest comments on the army's plight, see Washington to RM, October 2, and notes.
4. The remainder of the sentence is interlined in the Dft.
5. For the mission of John Brown to Havana on the *Duc de Lauzun,* and the role of the *Alliance,* see notes to RM to Le Couteulx and Company, September 24.
6. The preceding two sentences are inserted in the margin of the Dft; the last 12 words in the first sentence are interlined.
7. The preceding two words are interlined in the Dft.
8. The remainder of the sentence is interlined in the Dft.
9. In the Dft Gouverneur Morris originally wrote the remainder of the sentence as "and Vigor to the Administration of the Union and of its component Parts." He then revised it to its final formulation.
10. For other views on peace held by RM and Gouverneur Morris, see Gouverneur Morris to John Jay, August 6, and notes. For Washington's views, see Ver Steeg, *Morris,* 247n.–248n.

From Ephraim Blaine

Philada. 16th. Octr. 1782

Sir

Inclosed you have an Estimate the quantity of provisions which is Absolutely necessary to deposit in the Garrison of Fort Pitt and its dependancies before Christmass, and the sum of money those provisions will cost.[1] My credit and the person concearned with me will help a little, but money and as large a sum as you can spare will be wanted immediately. My princaple supplies must go from this side the mountains, as the people in that Country except a small settlement upon the Monongahala have been drove from their Habitations by the savages.

Your furnishing me with the means will enable me to lay in a proper supply, keep the troops from complaining, this I am sure will give you satisfaction, and I shall give you no further trouble untill next Summer. I have the honor to be with much Respect sir your Most Obedient and Most Humble Servant,

Eph. Blaine

The Honble. Mr. Morris

ENDORSED: a Copy of a Letter/wrote Mr. Morris/16th. Octr 1782
MS: Copy, Blaine Papers, Peter Force Collection, DLC.
1. Estimate not found. Blaine, the former commissary general of purchases, had agreed to assume the recently expired contract for Fort Pitt for the remainder of

1782, evidently in collaboration with William Wilson. See Diary, September 21, and notes, and October 7.

To William Churchill Houston

Office of Finance 16th October 1782

I have received your Favor, dated at Trenton on the 12th Instant, with the Enclosures.[1] A Warrant has been issued on you for seven thousand four hundred and eighty four $^{74}\!/_{90}$ths Dollars in Favor of Mr Hillegas, the Treasurer, which I suppose he has forwarded with the proper Receipt endorsed thereon.

MS: LS, Houston Collection, NjP; Ofcl LbC, DLC.
1. "Enclosure" in Ofcl LbC. Houston was the receiver of Continental taxes for New Jersey.

To James Lovell

Office of Finance 16 Octo: 1782

I have received your favors dated at Boston on the second and ninth Instant with the Enclosures.[1] As Mr. Dugan paid his Money to the public Service I agree to your allowing him the half per Cent you mention; it being Just, that he should be repaid the full amount of his Advances.

MS: Ofcl LbC, DLC.
1. Letters and enclosures not found. Lovell was the receiver of Continental taxes for Massachusetts.

To George Olney

Office of Finance 16. Octo: 1782

I have received your favor dated at Providence on the 30th. of last Month with its Enclosure.[1] A Commissioner is appointed to settle the Accounts of the Quarter Masters department and yours will come in of Course, but the Payment of it is impracticable. All that can be done will be to place the Balance on Interest; for the Payment whereof Revennues are yet to be granted by the several States and it is to be lamented that Rhode Island has not followed the Example of her Sisters in regard to the Impost on Importations &ca.

MS: Ofcl LbC, DLC.
1. The letter and enclosure from Olney, the receiver of Continental taxes for Rhode Island, have not been found, but evidently concerned his outstanding claim on the Quartermaster Department. See notes to RM to Olney, May 14, 1782.

To William Whipple

Office of Finance 16th October 1782[1]

I am favored with your Letter dated at Portsmouth on the twenty eighth of last Month. I have no Objection to your deputing your Brother to transact the Business of Receiver during your Absence, and shall be very glad to see you at this Place.

MSS: LS, Robert Morris Papers, NN; Ofcl LbC, DLC.
1. Whipple was the receiver of Continental taxes for New Hampshire.

John Swanwick to Gouverneur Morris

Philada Octr. 16th. 1782[1]

Enclosed you have a State of your Account with me—the Balance of which shall in a day or two be at your Credit in the Bank.

I have transmitted my Accounts for the last Quarter to the Treasury and Copies of them to the Super Intendant of Finance. Should it fall in your way to Notice them, I hope they will by their extent and the Fatigue they have Required Confirm me in your good Opinion which I exceedingly Value, and hope to Possess.

The little Patrimony I had a Right to expect, I have lost in the Conflicts of the day and many Gratifications Suitable to my Age and Education, have I been obliged to sacrifice to a Spirit of Unremitted Industry, but at these things I shall never Repine—if I have the Esteem and Friendship of Worthy Men to Oppose to them. It shall be my constant endeavour to Merit yours by an Imitation of your own Zeal and Industry in the Publick service. I am with much Esteem Sir Your obedient humble servant.

[ENCLOSURE]

G. Morris Esqr.		Pha. Octr. 16. 1782
To Cash paid his Subscription to Dancing assembly & Ball		£ 6.15.
	Postage	2. 4
	Do.	2. 4
	Do.	13. 7
	Do.	3.11
To Cash paid himself		163. 2. 6
Do.		225.
	his Cold Spring Club	6.
	Postage	14. 8
	Do.	4.
To 3 pr. thread Hose for your Servant		15.
		403.13. 4
Cr. Balance due G. Morris Esqr.		153. 4. 2
		£556.17. 6
By Cash Received on a Warrant in your favor on the Treasurer		£325.12. 6
By Do. of Mr. McCall		231. 5.
		£556.17. 6

Pha. Octr. 16. 1782
Errors Excepted
J Swanwick

MS: ALS, Gouverneur Morris Papers, NNC.

1. Swanwick was RM's cashier in the Office of Finance; he also was handling RM's private business affairs at this time. Gouverneur Morris was RM's assistant in the Office of Finance.

Diary: October 17, 1782

This Day Mr Thomas Randal came to me respecting the new Ship bought of Monsr Raguet and after a good deal of Conversation I offered to take his and Partners Interest in that Ship for which I proposed to give him a Spanish Dollar in France for a Spanish Dollar here. This he refused and instead thereof proposed to take Bills for the amount of 7/ for 5 Livres to which after some Consideration I agreed. I then sent for Mr Rendon and proposed taking his Concern on the same terms as Mr Randals to which he agreed.[1]

I sent for James Mullins who had returned last Week from his Attendance on the Commissions for settling a general Cartel[2] and was proceeding to reprimand Mr Mullins for not calling here in due Season but found that he had got a hurt in the Course of his Journey that disabled him from Walking. I desired that he should settle his Accounts immediately with Mr. Milligan, and as Charles Stewart Esqr. late Commissy. Genl. of Issues had endorsed a Receipt on the back of a Blank Warrant for 185 Dollars I had it filled up for that Sum in favor of said Commissary General.

Lewis R. Morris Esqr. brought for my Inspection the Dispatches received last Night from Jno. Adams Esquire.[3]

Mr. Fitzsimmons[4] called respecting some regulations proposed at the Bank.

I sent for Capt Angus[5] informed him that I have bought the Ship he now Commands but that I cannot continue him in the Command as he has not a Continental Commission. He behaved perfectly well and thought my reasons good.

I sent for Capt. John Green who is the only Continental Capt of the navy now here as I beleive and from a Conviction of his Capacity and Merits &c. I gave him the Command of this new Ship.[6]

His Excellency the Minister of France for news.[7]

Wrote a Letter to Jona. Burrell Esqr.

Wrote a Letter to Govrs. Rhode Island and Georgia.

Colo. Carrington

His Excellency the Governor of North Carolina

General Greene

His Excelly the Governor of South Carolina

Mr Daniel Clarke

George Abbot Hall Esqr.

George Webb Esqr.

Issued a Warrant on Mr Swanwick in favor John Moylan £144.5.9.

1. See Diary, September 2, and notes, for the antecedents.
2. See notes to Diary, June 18, 1782.
3. The dispatches included John Adams's letter to Secretary for Foreign Affairs Robert R. Livingston of August 18, 1782, from the Hague, which among other things advised that 1.3 or 1.4 million guilders of the Dutch loan would be ready for payment to the order of Congress upon receipt of congressional ratification of the contract. See Wharton, ed., *Rev. Dipl. Corr.*, V, 665; Hutchinson and Rutland, eds., *Madison Papers*, V, 207n., for the identification of the other papers; and Diary, September 11, and notes.

4. Thomas Fitzsimons, a director of the Bank of North America.

5. Probably John Angus (b. ca. 1750), a Philadelphia privateer captain. See the description of him in PCC, no. 196, V, 95; also Maclay, *History of American Privateers*, 116, 134; and the first paragraph of this Diary.

6. For Green's mission on the new ship, the *Duc de Lauzun*, see notes to RM to Le Couteulx and Company, September 24.

7. La Luzerne's request was no doubt inspired by the arrival of dispatches from Europe. See text at note 3 above.

To Edward Carrington

Office of Finance 17. Octo. 1782

Sir,

I have received your Letter of the first of September.[1] I entirely approve of your Conduct in the several Matters you have mentioned to me and pray you will accept my Thanks for the attention you have shown to the Business committed to your Care and for your Regard to the public Interests. The Contract of Mr James[2] is in a Train which is I beleive satisfactory to him and you may rely that when I begin to feel Revennue from Virginia I shall readily apply it for your Releif and in Discharge of your Engagements. I have perused the Correspondence with Govr. Martin and think you was perfectly right not to receive Articles of Supply at the enormous Rates calculated in the Resolutions of Congress.[3] These were made on the new Paper which was to have been issued at the Destruction of the old[4] and considering the rapid Depreciation which attended whatever was issued the Prices were not exorbitant: but such are not to be admitted in Discharge of a Requisition for solid Coin. I enclose you the Copy of my Letter to Governor Martin on this Subject.[5] With perfect Esteem and Respect I have the Honor to be Sir your most obedient Servant

RM

MS: Ofcl LbC, DLC.

1. Letter not found. Carrington was the deputy quartermaster general for the southern army.

2. For supplying the post at Cumberland Old Court House, Virginia. See notes to RM to Carrington, June 6, 1782.

3. See RM to the Governor of North Carolina, October 17, and notes.

4. The "new Paper" refers to the new emission money authorized by the act of Congress of March 18, 1780. See notes to John Morin Scott to RM, May 30, 1781.

5. Dated October 17.

To Nathanael Greene

Office of Finance 17. Octo: 1782[1]

Dear Sir

I have received your Letter of the first of September for which I pray you to accept my Acknowlegements. Amid the many Distresses and Cares which await every Step of my Administration it is a great Releif and Consolation to have met with the Support of those who command (and what is more who worthily command) the Armies of the United States. I have felt my dear Sir your Efforts to support my Measures and I know that they have been useful. I wish it were in my Power to give to you and to your brave Army that full Releif which their Conduct, their Sufferings and above all their Patience have merited. I had intended to have supplied their Subsistence and the little Contracts in Virginia[2] from the quota of that State as the Money there collected would have been nearest the Spot where it was to be applied but I need not tell you how deficient that State has been. The Consequence is that I must endeavor to supply the Deficiency from other Sources which I am now doing but in the precarious State of Things at present there is no Reliance to be placed on any Measure. I suppose however that the Evacuation of Carolina will enable you to move Northward with a considerable Part of your Army. These will I hope meet the Releif intended. I shall direct a State of the whole to be made out by the Paymaster General and do whatever may lie in my Power but as to Pay my inviolable Determination is that the whole Army shall equally share whatever is disposed of in that way.

I will confer with the Minister of War after his Return from the Army to which he went this Morning[3] upon the Propriety of continuing or discontinuing the Purchase of Horses in Maryland and give Directions accordingly.

The Disposition of the State of North Carolina to pay in Specifics is far from being peculiar to that State. Attempts of the same Kind have been made by others and they have invariably been opposed and shall be. There is however, a Distinction to be taken. You recollect that Congress called for large quotas of Specifics. I am perfectly perswaded that no State has fully obeyed that Call but many and indeed almost all aver that they have overpaid. The last Requisitions have been for Money and if I had not by the Publications[4] prevented such Assertions it would not be surprizing that they should be repeated even as to the money Quotas. Now if the State of North Carolina are desirous of paying in Specifics on the Requisitions for Specifics I shall not have the least Objection, but on the Requisitions for the Service of the current Year I will receive Money alone. I make this Distinction in such clear and peremptory Terms to avoid all further Cavils on the Subject. I see that it has been already drawn into some Length and must therefore be finally terminated. Besides under the present Appearances there can be little Doubt but that Specifics in North Carolina will be almost as useless as if they were in Otaheite.[5] A Copy of my Letter to Governor Martin on this Subject[6] shall be enclosed to you.

With Respect to the Settlement of an Account of contingent Expences in the Southern Department I must inform you that I cannot appoint a Commissioner. I am indeed empowered to nominate a Commissioner for settling the Accounts of the Quarter Masters, Commissaries, Cloathiers, Marine and Medical Departments. These Accounts are to be settled up to the End of the Year 1781. Other Accounts are to be settled at the Treasury here. The Contingent Expences are either those of the several Departments or those of the Army at large such as secret Service, Guides, Expences of Officers going on extra Duty and the like. The former of these Contingencies must be settled under their proper Heads at the Treasury, the latter are to be paid by special warrants of the General out of the military Chest. Those Warrants form the Vouchers for the Paymaster and ought regularly to Specify the Service for which as well as the Person in whose favor they are drawn with other Circumstances unless where particular Reasons render such Specification improper. Where it takes Place it supports the Propriety of the Vouchers, where it is omitted the Transaction is to be supported by the Confidence necessarily reposed by every wise Sovereign in the great Military Servants. I know perfectly well that the Modes of doing Business which have hitherto prevailed do not entirely accord with these Ideas but those loose Modes must be amended.

I have spoken to the Paymaster General on the Subject of Mr. Clay's Accounts and I find that he is appointed by Congress so that his Accounts are not to be settled with the Paymaster General but at the Treasury Office here. He ought therefore to repair hither for that Purpose and I rather think it might be well to accept his Resignation that he may have Leizure to attend to the arranging his Accounts and Vouchers.

You will find enclosed an Advertisement for Contracts[7] in which I have taken the Liberty to direct the Proposals for those of North and South Carolina and Georgia to be made to you. I did this because it was possible you might be on the Spot until that Period but if you find the Business at all inconvenient I will be glad that you in the Republications of the Advertizement point out some other Person. If Colo. Carrington is in that Quarter he will, I dare say, undertake it. I will in due Season send forward the Form of a Contract, the Modes of Issues and other proper Materials for the Information of yourself or of such other Person as you may direct to take the Management of it.[8]

You have in several of your Letters made very just Observations on the Business of my Department and such as convince me you have turned your Attention to it. I have therefore taken the Liberty to enclose to you the Copy of a Letter to Congress on the Subject of a Mint, of one on the establishing public Credit by funding our

Debts and of a third on the Estimates for the ensuing Year.[9] I also enclose the Duplicate of my Letters of the 11th. September and 5th. October.

As there is a Report that the Enemy got several Letters intended for you and if so it is possible that some or other of those may be among the Number. I pray you to beleive me with very sincere Esteem your most obedient Servant[10]

RM

MSS: Ofcl LbC, DLC; extract of the sixth paragraph in the writing of Samuel Lyons, PCC, no. 155, II, 651, DNA; copy of extract, PCC, no. 172, II, 164, DNA.

1. Major General Greene was the commander of the southern army.

2. In addition to the Cumberland Old Court House contract held by Richard James, the Virginia contracts in 1782 included a provision, forage, and timber contract held by John Callaway for the post at New London, a subsistence contract for Armand's Corps at Staunton with "Whoever will Sell," one for supplies to "passing Troops and Waggons" at the post of Peytonsburg for which no contractor is listed, and Quartermaster Department contracts with James Hunter and James Callaway. See the undated "State of Contracts and Engagements made by Lieut Colonel Carrington, in consequence of Powers given by Mr Morris, and General Lincoln," signed by Edward Carrington and endorsed "State of Contracts on which Sums will be due in Octo 82 and Jan. 83," in Manuscript File, no. 28293, WDC, DNA.

3. See notes to George Washington to RM, October 2.

4. A reference to the monthly publications of tax receipts in local newspapers by the receivers of Continental taxes. See notes to RM to William Whipple, June 4, 1782.

5. The former name of Tahiti.

6. Dated October 17.

7. Dated October 10.

8. The Lyons extract of this paragraph was prepared in the Office of Finance on August 23, 1783, and addressed to Comptroller of the Treasury James Milligan.

9. The letters, all to the president of Congress, are dated January 15 (first letter) and July 29 and 30, 1782.

10. Greene replied to RM on December 3, 1782.

To the Governor of North Carolina (Alexander Martin)

Office of Finance 17. Octo: 1782

Sir,

Since the Receipt of your Excellency's Favor of the twentieth of August last I have received Copies of a Correspondence between yourself and Colo. Carrington on the Subject of specific Supplies.[1] The Disposition which you have expressed (in your Letter to me and which indeed breathes thro your whole Correspondence) to promote those Plans of Regularity and Oeconomy which Congress have adopted command my sincere Acknowlegements.

I perceive that there is a Difference of Opinion between the Officers of the Continent and your State on the Receiving specific Supplies—which I attribute principally to some misunderstanding of the Matter. The Specific Supplies called for by Congress in their several Resolutions on that Subject are undoubtedly receivable (and ought above eighteen Months ago to have been received) on the Requisitions which were made at the Rates for that Purpose mentioned.[2] Such as it may now Suit any State to deliver on these Requisitions, ought in like Manner to be carried to Account. But it is very clear that they cannot be received on Account of the subsequent Money Requisitions. The several Quotas of the eight Millions asked for last Year to supply the current Expenditures of the Year 1782 must be paid in Cash or what is equivalent to it in my Notes or Bank Notes. I cannot consent to receive any Thing else. It is by this Means alone that Occonomy can be established, Order restored and Confusion that Parent of Fraud (too apt to introduce itself into public Accounts) banished and destroyed.

I incline to think that as Congress have determined to have all Accounts settled and liquidated to the End of 1781, Your State would rather choose to attend only to the Money Requisition and leave the further Delivery of Specifics to a Liquidation in the old Accounts but if not there can be no Doubt but the Specifics will be received and in such Case I will give the Gentleman whom I shall appoint as Receiver of Taxes in your State Instructions how to dispose of them but I must again repeat Sir that I will not accept one Particle of them in Abatement of the State quota for the Year 1782.

Before I close this Letter I must take the Liberty to mention a Matter which suggests itself from one of your Excellency's Letters to Colo. Carrington. You tell him that you will continue the Prohibition against sending certain Things out of the State in Order that he may purchase for the United States on better Terms. Now Sir while I feel it my Duty to require Justice for the United States it is equally my Duty to take Care that equal Justice be done to the several States individually considered, as well as to the Individuals which compose them. I am therefore to request that all such Restrictions be taken off. They sower the People's Minds, destroy the Spirit of Industry, impair by a rapid as well as a certain Progress the public wealth of the State and producing a Dearth of the Things embargoed eventually enhance the Prices far more than they could have been encreased by any other Mode Whereas perfect Freedom makes the People easy, happy, rich and able to pay Taxes and the Taxes when paid can be expended amid a Plenty of Products and consequently be expended to advantage. I say a Plenty of Products because I know that Liberty to dispose of them to the greatest Advantage will encourage Men to raise them and produce a Plenty. Your Excellency will I hope excuse Reflections which arise from an ardent Desire to promote the general Welfare and Happiness of all the Inhabitants of the United States. I have the Honor to be &c[3]

RM

MSS: Ofcl LbC, DLC; LbC, Letterbook of Alexander Martin, 1782–1785, Nc-Ar.

1. The correspondence between Governor Martin and Edward Carrington, which had been sent to RM by the latter, has not been found but probably included Martin's letters to Carrington of July 14 and August 9, 1782 (on the July 14 letter, see notes to the Governor of North Carolina to RM, June 22, 1782). In the August 9 letter, citing the depressed condition of trade, Martin declared that the state could pay its quota of the requisition only in specific supplies and expected them to be received at prices established under Congress's specific supply requisition of November 4, 1780. In the event Carrington refused to accept the supplies on these terms, the governor offered various alternatives for converting them to cash. Martin also advised that he had prohibited cattle from being sold out of state so that the southern army could be supplied. See Saunders and Clark, eds., *State Records of North Carolina*, XVI, 699–701; and RM to Edward Carrington, October 17.

2. Dollar values assigned to specific supplies received from the states in fulfillment of their quotas were included in the requisitions of Congress of February 25 and November 4, 1780. The earlier specific supply requisition of December 11, 1779, had not provided a dollar valuation, although a supplementary act of December 14, 1779, required the states to furnish articles at "equitable prices," the supplies to be credited "at equal prices for articles of the same kind and quality, and for others in due proportion."

3. Copies of this letter were enclosed in the preceding letters to Edward Carrington and Nathanael Greene.

To the Governors of Rhode Island and Georgia

Office of Finance 17th October 1782

Sir,

I do myself the Honor to enclose to your Excellency the Copy of an Act of the United States of the 10th Instant,[1] to which I am to pray your Attention. It gives me the most sensible Concern to find that the very important Business of funding the public Debts hangs suspended by the Delay of the States mentioned in the Resolution. The State of Georgia has been so recently delivered from Invasion, that the Neglect there can only be imputed to the distracted State of the Country, but I hope before this Letter shall have reached your Excellency both Rhode Island and Georgia will have complied. I would wish to say Nothing on this Subject, but I feel myself irresistibly impelled to observe that the public Creditors are numerous, meritorious and important. It is a Body composed of the most zealous Whigs in America. It contains those who have supplied and those who have composed our Armies under the most trying Circumstances. The Revenues asked for, are to repay the Monies advanced for our Freedom, and the Blood which has been shed in our Cause: And if it were necessary that Pity should come in Aid of Gratitude and Justice, I might observe that the Widows and Orphans of those who have spent their All and lost their Lives in Defence of America, are reduced to the extremest Want by withholding their just Dues. But I will not dwell any longer on these painful Reflections, but meerly repeat my Hope that every Ground of Complaint may speedily be removed.[2] With perfect Respect I have the Honor to be Sir your Excellency's most obedient and humble Servant

Robt Morris

His Excellency the Governor of Rhode Island[3]
and
His Excellency the Governor of Georgia

MSS: LS, to the Governor of Rhode Island, R-Ar; Ofcl LbC, marked "Circular," DLC; Sparks transcript, MH.

1. Acting on a report of the grand committee appointed on July 22, 1782, to consider ways of supporting the public credit, Congress on October 10 called upon Rhode Island and Georgia for "an immediate definitive answer" as to whether they would ratify the 5 percent impost. For the response of the Rhode Island delegates to Congress's demand, see Jonathan Arnold and David Howell to Governor William Greene of Rhode Island, October 15, 1782, Staples, *Rhode Island in the Continental Congress*, 394–398. For another appeal, see RM to the Governor of Rhode Island, October 24.

2. For Georgia's failure to take any action, see notes to RM to the Governors of South Carolina and Georgia, December 6, 1781; on Rhode Island's rejection, see notes to RM to the Governor of Rhode Island, August 2.

3. The remaining words are in Gouverneur Morris's writing. Rhode Island evidently did not answer this letter; Georgia, however, may have acknowledged it. See RM to the Governor of Georgia, January 22, 1783.

To George Webb

Office of Finance 17. Octo: 1782

Sir,

I have received your Favor dated at Richmond on the fifth Instant.[1] Mr. Clarke was in Virginia for the particular Purpose of purchasing Tobacco and as the Notes furnished him to pay for it are to be received by you on Account of the Continental Taxes,[2] some Degree of Perplexity would be introduced in the Accounts by sending such Notes to you to purchase with, who was afterwards to receive them back on public Account, exclusive of which I could not know that you were acquainted with the Tobacco Business.

My Confidence is such, that I shall be glad to engage your Assistance in the Transaction of any Business that may be Advantageous to yourself and beneficial to the Public. I am Sir your most obedient Servant

RM

MS: Ofcl LbC, DLC.

1. Webb was the receiver of Continental taxes for Virginia. His letter has not been found, but probably queried why RM had not asked him to purchase tobacco in the state.

2. See RM to Daniel Clark, September 23, and notes.

Determination on the Court of Inquiry on Samuel Nicholson

[Marine Office, October 17, 1782]

The Agent of Marine having perused and considered the Proceedings of a Court of Enquiry on certain Charges exhibited against Samuel Nicholson Esqr. Captain in the Navy of the United States disapproves of those Proceedings.[1]

Courts of Enquiry are appointed for the Purpose of examining whether the Charges made are cognizable by a Court Martial and whether it is probable that they can be supported, before such Court. In Order that the Public may not unnecessarily be exposed to the Expence of a Court martial, nor a good officer prevented from serving his Country.

From the Nature of a Court of Enquiry it follows that their Examinations should be private because otherwise Prejudices may be imbibed by Spectators for [or] against the accused, the subsequent Decissions may be influenced by those Prejudices or at least the Reputation of the Party in the intermediate Time may be much affected. It follows in like Manner that the Examinations should only be in support of the Charges because if they be intirely unsupported all contrary Evidence is unnecessary and if they be supported it is improper because the Trial is to be made by a Court martial and only the Accusation by the Court of Enquiry.

The Officer who is brought before a Court of Enquiry (if it be publickly held) must frequently be obliged either to enter into a Defence or suffer his Reputation to be impaired. The former involves an Expence which is unnecessary because the Decision cannot be final and the latter is what no good Officer can possibly submit to.

It appears on the present Occasion that the Court was held openly and publickly, that Witnesses were examined on both Sides and that it sat near a Month which could not have happened if it had been conducted privately and no Witnesses examined but those in Support of the Charges.

It appears also that the Party accused went into a cross Examination of Witnesses and a formal Defence of his Conduct all which was unnecessary.

And it appears that the Accuser was permitted to make many Observations on the Testimony in Support of the Charges which was both unnecessary and improper.

Sending forward the Minutes and Evidence was also unnecessary because the Object was (or at least ought to have been) only to examine into the Charges and not to try the Party; but the Observations transmitted by the Court on their Proceedings are improper because if they were to Answer any Purpose it must be to prejudice the Mind of him who is finally to decide.

The Proceedings on this Occasion have been drawn into very great Length and both time and money have been spent unnecessarily and improperly. The Court appear to have entirely mistaken the Business to which they were appointed which was to *enquire into the Conduct of Samuel Nicholson Esqr. Captain of the continental frigate Deane on certain Charges exhibited against him.* Instead of which they have acted as a Court martial appointed to try him on such Charges and have accordingly declared that the Court *After due and mature Consideration of each distinct Charge and of all the Evidence produced as well on the Part of the Prosecution as defence are of Opinion that each of the Charges is fully Supported and that he is guilty of the whole.*

For these Irregularities the Proceedings of the Court must be considered as void and altho the Witnesses appear to have been on Oath yet as the Judge Advocate who certifies the Depositions was not on Oath the whole can only be taken as meer Allegation. The cross Examinations of the Witnesses and the Testimony adduced by the accused as well as the various Observations which have been made by the Court and by the Parties must be totally rejected.

What will then remain to be considered are the Allegations against Capt Nicholson and in this Point of View it appears necessary both for the honor of the Officer if he be innocent and for the public Justice of the Country if he be Guilty that he be tried by a Court Martial on the following Charges.

1st. For Tyranny and Oppression injurious to the Service in that he on the ninth day of March 1782, appointed Samuel Smith Esqr. a private Gentleman to be a Lieutenant on Board the Ship Deane commanded by him and in Consequence of such Appointment during the subsequent Cruize took from Lieutenant Knies his rightful Command on Board that Ship.

2d. For waste of public Property and Provisions in ordering two pounds of Beef to each Man per day during his late Cruize.

3d. For dishonorable and ungentlemanlike Behaviour in violating his Promise made to Prisoners taken during his last Cruize.

4. For neglect of Duty in Leaving his Ship at a single Anchor in an open Road (at his Return from his last Cruize) exposed to the Danger of the Sea and of Enemies with a Number of Prisoners on Board and without a competent Number of Officers for her Security.

Given at the Marine Office of the United States the seventeenth of October 1782.

RM

ms: AM LbC, MdAN.

1. The proceedings on Nicholson, formerly captain of the Continental frigate *Deane* (renamed the *Hague*), have not been found. Disputes between Nicholson and some of his officers had produced a welter of charges and countercharges. On June 26 RM as Agent of Marine had issued a warrant for the court-martial of Lieutenant Arthur Dillaway on complaints brought by Nicholson and simultaneously ordered that a court of inquiry into Nicholson's conduct be convened to consider charges preferred by Lieutenant Michael Knies, whom Nicholson was alleged to have "damned . . . for a Bugger and told him he would heave him Over Board." Following receipt of a letter from Nicholson of July 24 containing accusations against Knies, RM on August 14 ordered the latter tried by court-martial. In the ensuing proceedings (held at Boston) Dillaway and Knies were acquited while Nicholson was found guilty. Although RM here disallowed the judgment against Nicholson on the grounds that the procedures of the court of inquiry were grossly improper, a decision he made after studying the opinions of Secretary at War Benjamin Lincoln, he ordered that Nicholson be court-martialed on various charges. RM enclosed the determination along with the court-martial warrant of October 18 in a letter to Thomas Russell of October 19, but the trial was not held until September 1783. No firsthand evidence has been found, but a board composed of Captains John Green, Thomas Read, and Silas Talbot apparently exonerated Nicholson of all charges. See Powers, "Decline and Extinction of American Naval Power," 117–123, 205–212, and Powers, "Robert Morris and the Courts-Martial of Captains Samuel Nicholson and John Manley of the Continental Navy," *Military Affairs*, XLIV (1980), 13–17; also Knies to RM, June 5 and 9, and RM to Russell, August 8, 1782. The quotation is from the fragmentary transcript of the proceedings of the Knies court-martial, Knies Collection, DN.

From the Quartermaster General (Timothy Pickering)

Camp Verplanks Point [New York] Octor. 17. 82

Sir,

Last Spring I applied to you for the means of paying the owners of the oxteams employed with the army during the last campaign.[1] Those hired in Connecticut have been paid by the aids given by that state to my deputy there. You at the same time supplied Colo. Neilson with your notes, to pay the hire of the horse teams raised by him in Jersey for the same service. Those of Massachusetts alone remain unprovided for. The case of the owners of those oxteams is singularly unfortunate. Besides obtaining nothing for their whole summers work, a great proportion of their teams perished in Virginia; for which too they have not yet received the smallest compensation. Colonel Hatch my deputy at Boston, has applied to the General Court for assistance, but they have declined yielding it, lest the same should not be allowed them in the current taxes. An Extract of Colo. Hatch's letter on this subject, and the copy of an extract he inclosed, of a letter of the Secretary at War, I beg leave to lay before you.[2] If any means of doing justice to the sufferers can be applied, I shall be happy.

In my letter of the 20th: of Feby. last[3] I inclosed an estimate of the pay that would become due to the conductors, waggoners and artificers for the service of the present campaign. The time for discharging most of them is near at hand. I have not the means of paying them agreeably to the contracts made with them. Could money be furnished previous to their being discharged, it would be best: but this I do not expect. A little money to carry them home, and efficient orders payable by the receivers of taxes in the several States, within reasonable periods, would make them tolerably easy. In part to compensate them for their services, I have thought of selling the public oxen at their value, to such of the Conductors and Teamsters as should be willing to receive them, and horses to the waggoners. For I am satisfied, it will be for the public interest to sell both, altho' we should be obliged to purchase in the spring. Excepting perhaps eighty or a hundred of the best horses for the artillery to answer any contingent services in the course of the winter.

You will oblige me, sir, by favouring me with your sentiments and expectations relative to the objects of this letter as early as you can.[4] I have the honor to be &c.

Tim: Pickering QMG

MS: LbC, WDC, DNA.

1. Although RM agreed to send notes to pay for the ox teams used in the 1782 campaign, payment for the hire of teams and drivers employed in the Yorktown campaign remained at issue until 1784. RM authorized payment for horses hired in New Jersey from money derived from the French loan of 1781 and by issuing a warrant on the Continental loan officer for New Jersey for new emission money. However, Pickering had long relied on the states for payment of teams hired in New England, and with his funds for 1781 exhausted, RM wanted this practice continued for debts contracted before the official start of his administration in 1782. Ralph Pomeroy, the deputy quartermaster general for Connecticut, made arrangements to furnish teamsters in that state with pay-table notes, state-issued certificates which were receivable in taxes (see Hints on Tax Notes from the Quartermaster General, July 24). But similar accommodations could not be made for the £16,152 lawful money due in Massachusetts because the assembly demanded that the state receive credit on the specie requisition for 1782. This RM refused to sanction, despite the distress of the conductors who had in many cases lost their oxen in the southern campaign and were now in danger of being jailed for debt. Nor would the Financier make payment in his own notes falling due at distant dates in the future. His position was that the tax revenues of 1782 could not be applied to debts which had not been contracted by him or during his effective administration; their status was similar to other old claims, with their accompanying injustices, and they could only be merged with the public debt which he proposed to fund with federal taxes. Early in 1784 the conductors asked Massachusetts to make payment from the state treasury and charge the sum to the United States; the state in turn addressed its delegates in Congress, proposing that payment could be made only if Massachusetts were permitted to deduct the amount from the "State's quota of the Continental tax, now coming into the treasury." RM renewed his objections to appropriations from the requisition of 1782 for past debts, and Congress on June 1, 1784, mindful of his impending departure from office, ordered the Superintendent instead to draw on Massachusetts for payment of the ox team debt and authorized Massachusetts to charge the amount, with interest from the date of payment, "as part of the state's quota which may be made for the year 1785." See Pickering's "An estimate of the hire of ox teams raised by Colo. Hatch deputy quarter master in his district, viz. in Massachusetts and Rhode Island, and which served with the main army in 1781," totaling $40,000, dated Philadelphia, April 6,

1782, and notated as having been "presented to Mr. Morris," WDC, no. 103, p. 83; Quartermaster General to RM, February 5, June 20, August 16, 28, and October 1, 1783, RM to the Quartermaster General, September 2, 1783, Diary, March 27, 1783, and April 16, 1784, Thomas Jefferson to RM, April 9, and RM to Jefferson, April 29, 1784; Pickering to Jabez Hatch, January 7, October 9, and December 15, 1782, and March 6, 1783, to Benjamin Lincoln, March 10 and April 8, 1783, to Hatch, June 20 and September 3 and 29, 1783, and to Tristram Dalton, Speaker of the Massachusetts House of Representatives, January 23, 1784, WDC, no. 84, pp. 8–9, 194–195, no. 86, pp. 8–9, 73, 80–81, 143–145, 246, no. 87, pp. 20, 37–38, 82, 93, 108–109, 253; Jefferson to Pickering, April 9, and Pickering to Jefferson, April 26, 1784, Boyd, ed., *Jefferson Papers*, VII, 92, 125–129; Order of Massachusetts General Court authorizing letter from Governor John Hancock to the Massachusetts Delegates in Congress, February 18, 1784, *Acts and Laws of Massachusetts, 1782–1783,* pp. 837–838; and the Massachusetts Delegates to the Massachusetts Assembly, June 4, 1784, Burnett, ed., *Letters,* VII, 542.

2. The first of the missing extracts may have been from Jabez Hatch's letter to Pickering of September 25, 1782 (see the complete text of the letter in the Manuscript File, no. 23435, WDC, DNA). Pickering had recently promised to seek money from RM for the ox team debt. See Pickering to Hatch, October 9, 1782, WDC, no. 84, pp. 194–195.

3. The reference is probably to Pickering's second letter of February 19, 1782.

4. See RM to the Quartermaster General, October 22 (second letter), the endorsement to which establishes that RM in fact addressed only the second paragraph of the present letter.

To Jonathan Burrall

Office of Finance 17. Octo: 1782

I am to request that you would examine the enclosed Memorial and let me have your Sentiments upon it.[1]

MS: Ofcl LbC, DLC.

1. For the memorial, see the notes to Burrall's reply of October 21.

To Daniel Clark

Office of Finance 17. Octo: 1782

I have received your Letter dated at Richmond on the fourth Instant.[1] I do not mean that your Purchases of Tobacco from the State should be confined to particular Kinds; any that has passed the Inspection will answer at a Price proportioned to the quality being always careful not to give too much.

MS: Ofcl LbC, DLC.

1. Letter not found. Clark was RM's agent for purchasing tobacco in Virginia. On his purchases from the state, see RM to Clark, September 23, and notes.

To George Abbott Hall

Office of Finance 17. Octo. 1782

I have received yours of the first of September.[1] Enclosed you have Duplicates of my Letters of the eleventh of September.[2]

MS: Ofcl LbC, DLC.

1. Letter not found. Hall was the receiver of Continental taxes for South Carolina.

2. There is only one letter to Hall of September 11; the other duplicate was probably of RM to Nathanael Greene of that date.

To Thomas Randall and Company

Marine Office 17. Octo: 1782

Be pleased to deliver the new Ship with all her materials, Stores &ca. as bought of Monsr. Raguet into the Care of Capt John Greene who is to command her. I shall perfect the Papers necessary to fulfill the Agreement made between you and Gentleman your obedient humble Servant[1]

MS: AM LbC, MdAN.

1. This letter was delivered to Captain John Green on October 18 (see Diary of that date). For the antecedents regarding the *Duc de Lauzun*, see Diary, October 17.

To the Governor of South Carolina
(John Mathews)

Office of Finance 17. Octo: 1782

I write this short Note meerly to acknowlege the Receipt of your Excellency's Letter of the twenty fifth of August[1] and to assure you of the Respect with which I have the honor to be Sir your most obedient Servant

MS: Ofcl LbC, DLC.

1. Letter not found.

Diary: October 18, 1782

William Bingham Esqr. brought me the proposed bye Laws of the Bank for Consideration.[1]

Capt. Jno. Green came to give me an Account of the new Ship. I gave him a Letter to Messrs. Randal and Co. for the Delivery of her[2] and Instructions on several Points.

Mr. Lyon applied for a Masters Birth referred him to Capt Greene.

Capt Saml Nicholson, told him his Affairs would be soon finished.[3]

Colo Nichols for Money and finished with him.

Honble. Mr Boudinot to search Letters and Papers relative to Doc. Franklin.[4]

Honble. Mr L'Hommedieu to recommend Capt Greenwell[5] to command the Hazen [i.e., Hague], told him she is at Sea under command of Capt Manly.

Mr. Jno. Sansum respecting his Accounts he wants more money allowed than I agreed for therefore advised him to apply to Congress.

I sent for Mr. Thos. Fitzsimmons and proposed to him to fit the new Ship and Load her for 2½ per Cent Commission to which he agreed.

Mr. Edwd. Williams for money for the Hospital which he represents as in the utmost Distress.

Mr Jacob Zoll wanted to have Germans for Quarter Masters Certificates bu[t] this I declined as every Body cannot have pay in the same Way.[6]

Wrote a Letter to James Milligan Esqr.

Issued a Warrant on Mr Swanwick in favor Jos:
Pennell   £34.17.11

Issued a Warrant on Mr Swanwick in favor the
Bank   10. 6. 3

1. Bingham was a director of the Bank of North America.
2. The letter is dated October 17.
3. See RM's Determination on the Proceedings of the Court of Inquiry on Samuel Nicholson, October 17, and notes.
4. Elias Boudinot was a member of Congress from New Jersey. The antecedents of this entry have not been identified.
5. Ezra L'Hommedieu was a member of Congress from New York. His nominee was probably Thomas Grenell (variant spellings include Grennel, Grennell, Greenhill, Grenale, Grinnell), who had been commissioned captain of the *Montgomery* in 1776 but later switched to the *Congress*. Both Continental frigates, being built in New York, were burned before they were completed in order to prevent their capture by the British in 1777. Grenell also served as a commissioner for erecting fortifications on the Hudson River. See *JCC*, V, 444, VI, 861, 873; Clark and Morgan, eds., *Naval Documents*, II, 32, 895, 938, 972, 1108, 1325, V, 549, 568, VI, 274, 928, 1201; and *Dict. Amer. Naval Ships*, II, 163, IV, 428.
6. On the use of German prisoners of war as indentured servants, see notes to Diary, May 1, 1782.

To the President of Delaware
(John Dickinson)

Philadelphia October 18th 1782[1]

Sir

The Conduct of Mr. Luke Shields as Pilot onboard His Most Christian Majesties Frigate L'Aigle lately lost near Cape Henlopen was such as to Merit the approbation of the Compte La Touch and the other Officers onboard that Ship, in so much that they have recommended him to His Excellency The Chevr. De La Luzerne, and such other Persons, as they have thought might be instrumental in procuring His Pardon from the State over which Your Excellency Presides; I believe it is unfortunate for him that Compte La Touche is not permitted to come out of New York, as he most Probably would, in compliance with the Promises he made Mr Shields, have interested himself Warmly in his favor. Mr. Shields Reminds me that before he joined the Enemy, his Distress for want of Employment and for want of means to support his Family induced him to make frequent applications for permission to go to Sea, which was refused on account of his knowledge of Delaware River and Bay. I can also from personal knowledge say that previous to the War Mr Shields supported the Character of a Sober, orderly, Honest Man and a Good Pilot in which Capacity he may, if permitted, become again an

Usefull Citizen. With great Respect and Esteem, I have the Honor to be Your Excellency's Most Obedient and humble Servant

Robt Morris

His Excellency The Governor of Delaware State

MS: LS, Delaware State Papers, DLC.

1. As RM notes in this private letter, Luke Shields (or Shield), a former Delaware River pilot from Lewes, Delaware, had entered British service earlier in the war. Shields had been aboard the *Raccoon*, out of New York City, when it was captured by the *Aigle* under the command of Comte de La Touche-Tréville. He thereupon aided the French vessel as it attempted to enter Delaware Bay on its way to Philadelphia. The frigate, however, was wrecked (see Diary, September 16, and notes) and Comte de La Touche was captured. Having aided the French, Shields feared imprisonment by the British if he were exchanged and sent back to New York City. When he returned to Delaware instead, he was threatened with punishment for high treason and subsequently was arrested.

President Dickinson presented this letter from RM, together with another from La Luzerne of October 14, to the Delaware legislature on October 30. The following year, after another appeal by La Luzerne, a committee of assembly recommended that Shields be pardoned and that a committee be appointed to prepare and bring in a bill for that purpose. As late as the June session efforts to obtain a legislative pardon were unsuccessful; since assembly records for the next 12 months are missing, the editors have been unable to determine how the case was ultimately resolved. See *Delaware Archives* (Wilmington, 1911–1916), II, 940–942; *Minutes of the Council of the Delaware State, from 1776 to 1792,* Historical Society of Delaware, *Papers,* VI (1887), 750–752; and *Votes and Proceedings of the House of Assembly of the Delaware State* (Wilmington, 1783), 92, 93, 95.

Circular of the Comptroller of the Treasury to the Commissioners of Accounts

[Philadelphia] Comptrollers Office, October 18th. 1782[1]

Sir

(Circular)   In addition to the Books and Stationary mentioned in the General Instructions to you,[2] I now send you by direction of the Superintendant of Finance   [3] Sheets of Paper intended for Certificates to be issued for debts due by the United States to Individual Claimants upon Accounts by you Liquidated.[4]

This paper has been purposely made, with a good deal of care, and at considerable expence, each Sheet will make Six Certificates, each Certificate having in Water letters "US National debt" in one line, and underneath that line, some one letter of the Alphabet in Capital. I say some one letter, because there are a Number made use of with a View to operate as a check in case of Counterfeits, and as a further precaution, it will be necessary that you attend Strictly to the following directions on issuing them, Vizt. You will open a Book properly ruled for the purpose of Recording all such Certificates by you issued. The first Column on the left hand will shew the Number of the Certificate, which is to be inscribed by you on it in a fair and conspicuous manner, beginning at Number one. In the second you

Final settlement certificates were issued for balances due creditors of the United States by the commissioners of accounts for the states, for the staff departments, and for the army appointed by Morris to settle the Revolutionary war debt. The certificates drew 6 percent interest and stated in dollars the specie value of debts originally stated in either currency or specie values. They were ultimately taken up under Alexander Hamilton's funding program of 1790 and in other settlements authorized by the United States Congress up to 1822.

Of the certificates issued by the commissioners of accounts for the states, an undetermined number issued by Edward Chinn, including the one illustrated here, departed from the text as prescribed by Morris in his letter to Jonathan Burrall of August 19, 1782, and used the term "Dollars in Specie." No specimens issued by the commissioners of accounts for the departments have been found. An example of the notes issued by the commissioner of army accounts is described below. For a discussion of the commissioners' work, see Morris's letters to the commissioners of September 7 and 19, 1782, and notes, and the detailed instructions to the commissioners printed under October 14, 1782. Regarding the certificates and their watermarks, in addition to the letter to Burrall cited above, see the Circular of the Comptroller of the Treasury to the Commissioners of Accounts, October 18, 1782. The certificate illustrated here is watermarked "U S NATIONAL DEBT" with the letter "C" underneath. Cancelled with a punch, it was liquidated during the settlement of 1818. The certificate is filed in Account 37503 of the 1818 settlement, Miscellaneous Treasury Accounts, First Auditor of the Treasury Department, Segregated Series, Records of the United States General Accounting Office, RG 217, National Archives, Washington, D.C. Courtesy of the National Archives and Records Service.

Final settlement certificate issued by Edward Chinn, commissioner of accounts for Rhode Island, August 19, 1784. 7¾" × 4"

Final settlement certificates of this kind were given to creditors in the Continental army during the settlement of the army debt and drew 6 percent interest. Issued for arrearages of pay and subsistence, forage, recruiting expenses, and other charges, Pierce's notes represented the largest segment of the consolidated Federal debt (for a discussion, see notes to Morris's letter to the commissioners of accounts for the departments of September 19, 1782). Morris gave detailed instructions to Pierce in a letter of March 15, 1783. Most of the more than 95,000 certificates he and his deputies issued are listed with numbers, recipients, and amounts in the appendix to the Seventeenth Report of the National Society of the Daughters of the American Revolution . . . *(Washington, 1915), printed as 63d Congress, 3d session, Senate Document 988 (February 19, 1915), pp. 149–712. The certificate shown here, watermarked "*NATIONAL DEBT,*" was liquidated and cancelled with a punch during the 1818 settlement. It is filed in Account 37380, Miscellaneous Treasury Accounts, First Auditor of the Treasury Department, Segregated Series, Records of the United States General Accounting Office, RG 217, National Archives, Washington, D.C. Courtesy of the National Archives and Records Service.*

No. 52.697 — State of N[ew] H[ampshire] March 1, 1784

ON the final Settlement of an Account between the United States and Samuel Barker ———— there appeared to be due to him —— the Sum of Fortyseven 79 ——————————— Dollars : I do therefore cer-tify, that the said Sum is payable with Interest at fix per Cent, from the Fourth —— Day of November —— 1783 —— to the said Samuel Barker —— or Bearer.

Jno. P[ierce]

W. I. T[...]M.

Final settlement certificate issued by John Pierce, commissioner of army accounts, March 1, 1784. 6⁹⁄₁₆″ × 3¹¹⁄₁₆″

will carefully and correctly insert the Water Capital on the Certificate issued, which you will see under the Words "National debt" as before mentioned, the third the date of the Certificate or day of Issuing, the fourth the persons Name to whom the debt is due, the fifth the time when it became due, from which time the Interest is to Commence. And the sixth Column will contain the Amount of the debt in Dollars and Ninetieth parts of a Dollar. In order to elucidate my meaning still more clearly I enclose you a form of a Page of this Book, as I have described it.[5] This Book will not only serve as a check in case of Counterfeits but it will also assist you in rendering an Account of this Paper now sent, which it is expected you will do, with as much exactness as if it were Cash or Bills of Exchange. The receipts which it will be necessary to take of the Claimants for the Certificates when issued as a barr against a second demand, will serve as Vouchers for the paper used, which will be corroborated by their Accounts Liquidated, which must be carefully and neatly filed, with the same Number endorsed on them as may be inserted in the Certificates by you issued for them respectively; and should any of the paper be defaced or Spoiled in making out the Certificates, you will carefully preserve all such, as Vouchers for itself on Settlement.

It is probable you may not have occasion for all the quantity now sent, in this case you will of course return the remainder, and if you should have occasion for more, you will apply for it in Writing specifying how much. You will please to sign duplicate receipts for the paper, and transmit them to me by different and early opportunities. I am Sir your Most obedient Humble Servant.

John Pierce Esquire
PayMaster General

ENDORSED: From Mr. Milligan r[eceive]d July 14, 1783
MS: Copy, Manuscript File, WDC, DNA.

1. This circular very likely was sent to the commissioners of accounts for the states and the departments; however, the only text found by the editors is that received by John Pierce, whom RM appointed commissioner to settle army accounts by letter of March 15, 1783.

2. The instructions of Comptroller of the Treasury James Milligan to the commissioners of accounts for the states and the departments are printed under October 14.

3. Space left blank in manuscript.

4. These certificates, known as "final settlement certificates," were issued by the commissioners of accounts and formed one part of the liquidated national debt. To avoid counterfeiting, RM at the outset discarded his original intention of using "printed Blanks" and instructed the commissioners to draw the certificates wholly by hand. In the letter printed here, special paper was made available to the commissioners to further inhibit counterfeiting. The Superintendent later changed his mind, however, and ordered preprinted certificates, although it is not clear when the commissioners first began to use them. For the text of the certificates and a discussion, see RM to Jonathan Burrall, August 19, and notes; for references to the printing of the certificates, see RM to Lewis Pintard, January 10, Joseph Pennell to Mark Willcox, January 16, Diary, January 24, 25, February 8, 14, 19, 22, March 10, 21, and July 8, 1783.

5. Enclosure not found.

From John Barry

Extract of a Letter from Captain John Barry dated L'Orient Octobr. 18th. 1782

Sir

I have the Pleasure to inform you of my Proceedings since I sailed from New London which I hope will meet your Approbation.[1] A few hours after I sailed . .[2] a Brigantine and sent her in there, proceeded as fast as possible off Bermudas. In my way I took a Schooner from that place for Hallifax. After cruizing off there for twelve or fifteen Days I retook a Sloop from New London and sent her for Cape Francois, finding the Prizes I had taken of little Value either to myself or Country and in all likleyhoods should be obliged to return into Port soon for want of Men, was Determined to alter my Cruizing Ground. I therefore thought it best to Run off the Banks of Newfoundland. On my way there I fell in with a Whaling Brigantine with a Pass from Admiral Digby. I Man'd her and sent her for Boston. A few days after off the Banks of Newfoundland I took a Brigantine from Jamaica bound to London loaded with sugar and Rum and sent her for Boston, by this Vessel I found the Jamaica Fleet were to the Eastward of us. I then carried a press of Sail for four Days, the fifth Day I took two Ships that had parted from the Fleet, after Manning them and fresh Gale Westwardly I thought best to order them for France. A day or two after I took a Snow and a Ship belonging to the same Fleet, being short of Water and a number of Prisoners on Board, the Westwardly winds still blowing fresh and in expectation of falling in with some more of them I thought it best to proceed for France with a determined View to get those I had already taken, in safe and after Landing the Prisoners to put out Immediately, but meeting with blowing Weather and a high Sea I lost the Rails of the Head and was in great Danger of loosing the Head, which accident Obliged me to put in here where I arrived Yesterday with the Above four Prizes. After repairing the Damages and getting what the Ship may want I shall put to Sea on a Cruize. I have likewise to Inform you that the Ramillies Admiral Graves's Ship Foundered but all the Crew were saved several of which were on Board the Prizes I took, we have likewise an Account that another ship of the Line was Lost and the Crew saved. The Merchant Ships suffered very much, there are a few Vessels of the same fleet in here, taken by American Cruizers belonging to Salem. There are about Twelve hundred Hhds. Sugar and Four hundred Hhds. Rum in the four Prizes besides some Coffee and Logwood. I have the Honor to be with Proper Respect Sir Your Most Obedient humble Servant

Signed   John Barry

The Honble Robt. Morris

ms: Extract, PCC, DNA.
1. Barry, commander of the Continental frigate *Alliance*, had sailed from New London on August 4. RM received Barry's report on December 12 and enclosed the extract printed here in a letter to the president of Congress the following day. For a more detailed secondary account of Barry's cruise, see Clark, *Gallant John Barry*, 271–276.
2. Suspension points thus in manuscript.

From George Washington

Head Quarters [Verplancks Point, New York]. 18th Octo 1782
Sir

I take the Liberty to inclose to your Care a Letter for the Chevalr de La Luzerne on the Subject of Expence, which at his Request, I have incurred for the purpose of ⟨procuring and⟩ forwarding Intelligence of the Movements of the Enemy at N York, to the Marquis de Vaudrieul.[1]

If our Circumstances would admit,[2] I should be very glad that this Expence should be defrayed by the United States; it is infinitely short of the Debt which Gratitude imposes on us. I submit therefore to your Judgment, whether to deliver the inclosed—or to send forward the Money from your own Funds, agreable to the Monthly Estimate sent[3] to the Minister.[4]

The Chain of Expresses was instituted about the middle of August, and will probably be continued 'till the sailing of the french fleet from Boston.[5] I am &c

Superintendant of Finance

ENDORSED: Head Quarters 18th Octo 1782/to/Superintend of Finance/Expences of Chain of Expresses/to Boston
mss: Dft in the writing of Jonathan Trumbull, Jr., Washington Papers, DLC; Varick transcript, Washington Papers, DLC.
1. Washington's letter to La Luzerne, the French minister at Philadelphia, dated October 18 (Fitzpatrick, ed., *Writings of Washington*, XXV, 275–276), enclosed an "Estimate of Expences" for the expresses to Vaudreuil, commander of the French fleet at Boston, which has not been found, and added: "It has been communicated to me from the Q Master General, who was instructed by me to institute the Chain of Expresses; and at the same Time it is intimated to me, that he shall be obliged, in a short Time to call on me for Money to defray the Expence."
2. Before Trumbull emended the Dft, the preceding phrase had been written thus: "If the Circumstances of our Finances would admit."
3. This word is interlined. Above it is interlined the word "inclosed," but that word does not appear in the Varick transcript.
4. RM forwarded the enclosed letter to La Luzerne, who promised payment. Washington advised the French minister on November 6 that "The Treasurer of the French Army has remitted 537 dollars to our Quarter Master General according to your direction." See the translation of La Luzerne to Washington, October 25, 1782, Washington Papers, DLC; and Fitzpatrick, ed., *Writings of Washington*, XXV, 320.
5. The French fleet sailed from Boston for the West Indies on December 24.

Warrant Appointing a Court-Martial for the
Trial of Samuel Nicholson

Marine Office, October 18, 1782. This document, entitled "Order for a Court of Enquiry on Capt. Samuel Nicholson and an Order for a Court Martial for his Trial," is addressed "To John Barry, Thomas Read, John Paul Jones, James Josiah, John Green and Silas Talbot Esqrs. Captains in the Navy of the United States of America," who were to sit "for the Trial of Capt Samuel Nicholson on the several Charges hereunto annexed."[1] The text is otherwise identical to RM's Warrant Appointing a Court-Martial for the Trial of Arthur Dillaway, June 26, 1782.

MS: AM LbC, MdAN.
    1. For the charges, see RM's Determination on the Proceedings of the Court of Inquiry on Nicholson, October 17. This warrant was enclosed in RM to Thomas Russell, October 19.

James McCall to the Comptroller of the
Treasury (James Milligan)

Office of Finance 18. Octo. 1782[1]
Enclosed you have Copy of a Letter from his Excellency Genl. Washington of the third Instant, by which you will perceive the Appropriation of the five hundred Dollars which was sent for the Use of the Commissrs. and be able to have the proper Charges made to the Persons for whom the same was expended.

MS: Ofcl LbC, DLC.
    1. McCall was RM's secretary in the Office of Finance.

Diary: October 19, 1782

Jona. Burrall Esqr called for a Conference on the Nature and extent of his Powers and Duties as Commissioner for Settling the Accounts of the Commissary's Department on which Mr Morris and myself gave him our Opinions fully and delivered also the written Instructions to him.[1]

Capt. Saml Nicholson applied to know my Determination with respect to the Proceedings of the Court of Enquiry held upon him and what farther was to be done. I informed him that the Business is finished so far as depends on me and that I shall transmit to Mr Thos. Russell at Boston the necessary Papers who will communicate the same to all Persons concerned.[2] Captn. Nicholson observed that his Character is injured and his Honor wounded by those Proceedings of the Court of Enquiry and was exceedingly anxious to know my Determinations but as I judged it most proper to have them first known in Boston, I did not Satisfy him in this Point.

Mr Gridley of Boston[3] applied for Payment of a Bill drawn by Capt Saml Chew of the Continental Brigantine Resistance[4] on the late Admiralty Board and as I think the preservation of public Credit abroad essential to the true Interest of this Country I ordered that it shall be paid.

Mr. Jno. Sansum pressing for the Settlement of his Accounts he was put in a way to accomplish the Same.

Doctr. Tillotson agreed to accept the Appointment of Receiver of Continental Taxes for the State of New York.

Oliver Pollock Esqr. soliciting the finishing his affairs.

His Excellency the Minister[5] to inform me of an Opportunity from Boston to France.

Mr Thos. Fitzsimmons to Consult respecting the Outfit of the new Ship.[6]

1. See the Instructions of the Comptroller of the Treasury to the Commissioners for Settling the Accounts of the Departments, October 14, and notes.
2. See RM to Thomas Russell, October 19, and notes.
3. Probably Samuel Gridley (ca. 1734–1800), who solicited from RM a tentative nomination as commissioner of accounts for New Hampshire. For reasons that have not been ascertained, James Lovell, the receiver of Continental taxes for Massachusetts, suppressed the appointment with RM's approval. For the little data obtained on Gridley, see Michael Hillegas to Nathaniel Appleton, October 21, 1782, General Correspondence, box 1, Records of the Comptroller General, RG 4, PHarH; *Columbian Centinel* (Boston), January 11, 1800; RM to the President of New Hampshire, November 5, and to Lovell, November 6 and December 17, 1782.
4. Samuel Chew (ca. 1750–1778), a Virginia-born mariner of New London, Connecticut, was commissioned a captain in the Continental navy and appointed to command the *Resistance* in June 1777. Killed in action in an engagement with a British privateer in the West Indies on March 4, 1778, Chew was one of only three naval captains who lost their lives in the Continental service. See *Dict. Amer. Naval Ships*, I, 100; Charles Oscar Paullin, ed., *Out-Letters of the Continental Marine Committee and Board of Admiralty, August, 1776–September, 1780* (New York, 1914), I, 138–141, 232, 241; and Paullin, *Navy of the American Revolution*, 165.
5. Chevalier de La Luzerne, the French minister to the United States.
6. The *Duc de Lauzun*.

To Thomas Russell

Marine Office 19. October 1782[1]

Sir,

You will find enclosed my Determination on the Court of Enquiry on Captain Samuel Nicholson the Proceedings of which I have disapproved.[2] And also a Warrant for instituting a Court Martial for the Trial of Capt. Samuel Nicholson on certain Charges which are annexed to it.[3]

Should the Frigate Hague return to your Port or any other in the Eastern States then you will please to Summon the Officers who are to compose that Court to repair to the Place where the Frigate Arrives and if any of them are in this Quarter and it is necessary, I shall order them to attend.

Inclosed is my Determination on the Proceedings of the Court martial for the Trial of Lieutenant Michael Knies confirming his Acquittance which please to Communicate to whom it may Concern.[4] I am Sir your most obedient and humble Servant

RM

MS: AM LbC, MdAN.
1. Russell was the deputy agent of marine for New England stationed at Boston.
2. The determination is dated October 17.
3. The warrant is dated October 18.
4. The determination is dated October 19. Russell had already communicated the court's verdict to Knies in a letter of September 17 (Knies Collection, DN). "I am so sure of this decree being confirm'd by the Honbl Mr Morris—as you are wanted in your line of duty on board the Frigate Hague—you are now reinstated; it is my desire you will take your place Accordingly."

Determination on the Court-Martial of Michael Knies

[Marine Office, October 19, 1782]
Determination on the Trial of Lieut. Knies
The Agent of Marine having read and duly considered the Proceedings of a Court Martial for the Trial of Lieut. Knies begun and held at the House of John Marston in the Town of Boston on the thirteenth day of September in the Year of our Lord one thousand seven hundred and eighty two Does hereby approve and confirm the Acquittal of Lieut. Knies.[1]
Given at the Marine Office this nineteenth day of October 1782.

MS: AM LbC, MdAN.
1. A fragment of the proceedings of the Knies court-martial is in the Knies Papers, DN. See notes to RM's Determination on the Court of Inquiry on Samuel Nicholson, October 17.

From Samuel Hodgdon

[Philadelphia] Ordnance Office 19th Octo 1782
The inclosed letter was handed the Secretary at War a few minutes before he set out for Camp.[1] As a part of it is on business which comes under your immediate notice he directed it to [be] laid before you, in obedience to which I do my self the honour to inclose it.

MS: LbC, WDC, DNA.
1. The letter has not been identified. Hodgdon was the commissary general of military stores.

From William Churchill Houston

Trenton [New Jersey] 19 Octr. 1782
I am favoured with your Letters of 9th., 15th and 16th instant.[1] One Copy of the advertisement of 10th. I sent to the Printer in this Place, and shall forward the other to the Printer at Chatham. ⟨Mr Collins proposed⟩ They will propose charging for inserting and continuing it, but ⟨have⟩ Mr Collins has agreed ⟨to be⟩ and probably the other will also, to be determined by the Custom in Philadelphia in such Cases.[2] Be so obliging as to inform us what that is.

My Prospects respecting Money are faint and unpromising; and am afraid that my Returns, at least for some Time, will scarcely deserve the name.

MS: ADft, Houston Collection, NjP.
1. The letter of October 15 was a circular to the receivers of Continental taxes enclosing a copy of the advertisement for the 1783 contracts. Houston was the receiver for New Jersey.
2. Houston interlined the preceding three words.

Diary: October 21, 1782

Colo. Miller of York Town one of the Contractors for that Post applies for money on the Account of Contract.

Mr Grier for Money on account of the Clothier Genl. to whom I referred him.

Colo. Humpton applied on account of Forage for the Officers on Duty. I promised to speak to Colo. Miles, at the same time assuring him that I have not money to pay for Forage.

Capt Lyon applies for a Birth on board the New Ship referred him to Capt. Green.[1]

The Honble. Ralph Izzard Esqr brought me a Bundle of Papers relative to the Affairs of Commodore Gillon, requested me to read them, and he thinks I shall not find Cause to institute a Suit against him.[2]

Capt Saml Nicholson Requested me to inform him of my Determination on his affairs respecting which he is extremely anxious and I thought it best to gratify him by reading the Papers which I did.[3]

Lieut. Liston[4] applied for Subsistence money, referred him to the Pay Master General.

Jno. Hazelwood Esqr. for money on Account of the Contract.

Mr. Randal applies to have the Business respecting Monsr Raguet Ship compleated.

Mr. Lloyd Express Rider respecting his Accounts.

Mr. Burrall Commissioner on Commissaries Department desired a Conference respecting the memorial of Issuing Commissaries on which he had much Conversation.[5]

Doctor Tillotson applied for some money in part of his Account which was refused. He signified his Intention to accept the Appointment of receiver of Taxes for the State of New York.

Several Persons applied for Money on various Occasions.

Wrote a Letter to the Governors of the Several States.

Wrote a Letter to the Governor of Rhode Island.

Wrote a Letter to His Excellency the President of Congress.

Wrote a Letter to Edward Fox Esqr.

Issued a Warrant on Mr Swanwick in favor Jos:
Pennell   £ 79.0.0

Issued a Warrant on Mr Swanwick in favor John
Moylan   101.2.2

1. On Captain John Green and the *Duc de Lauzun,* see Diary, October 17, and notes.

2. Izard was a congressman from South Carolina. On the investigation into the affairs of Alexander Gillon, see notes to Diary, September 19.

3. See RM's Determination on the Court of Inquiry on Nicholson, October 17, and notes, and his Warrant Appointing a Court-Martial for the Trial of Nicholson, October 18.

4. Thomas Liston, 1st lieutenant of the South Carolina Artillery. Taken prisoner at Charleston in May 1780 and exchanged in June 1781, he served until the end of the war. Heitman, *Register.*

5. See Jonathan Burrall to RM, October 21, and notes.

Circular to the Governors of the States

Circular   Office of Finance 21st. October. 1782
Sir

I have on many Occasions warned the States of the Consequences which must follow from delays in supplying the Public Treasury. The Expence which attends such delays has frequently been mentioned and Instances daily occur to shew how much the public Burthens are encreased by the Want of a timely Provision. To cite them all would be endless but there is one of no inconsiderable Magnitude which I think it proper to state for your Consideration. I had contracted on the Part of the United States for the Supply of Rations to the main Army at ten Pence Pennsylvania Currency and to the Garrison at West Point for nine Pence half Penny and had agreed to pay at the Commencement of each Month for the Issues of the preceeding Month. These beneficial Contracts have been dissolved by my Inability to make punctual Payments which rendered the Contractors incapable of performing their Engagements.[1] After many Efforts on my Part to supply the Want of Cash and on their Part to substitute private Credit and Promises in the Place of ready Money they found it impracticable to proceed farther on the moderate Terms stated in the Contract. Some of them told me so and asked (what any Persons in their Situation naturally would have asked) *the Promise of Indemnification for any damages they might sustain.* And a Promise to pay at the End of each Month one half the Amount of Issues for the preceeding Month in Coin; and three Times the remaining half in Bills or Notes receivable in Taxes. They offered if I would agree to these Propositions to go on and supply the Army but declared that if I would not they could no longer perform their Engagements.

From this Moment I was obliged to consider the Contract as dissolved; because the Dissolution of it appeared to be inevitable. I had already by entering into the Contract promised on the Part of the

Public a Payment of the whole Money due for the monthly Issues. A new Promise of the half would have given no additional Security and therefore I considered that Stipulation as a Request that I should on my private and personal Honor assure them the public funds would enable me to make such Payment. But of this I had no good Prospect. The greater Part of what little came in from Taxes was the same Kind of Paper with that which they asked for being what I had long before Issued for other Services. If indeed I could have trusted the Assurances made *to me,* I might have given the Assurances required by *them.* But Experience had taught me Caution. And the Event has shewn that if I had made the Promise I should now have been chargeable with falsehood.

I think the Contractors were prudent in requiring a *Promise of Indemnification.* Their Situation made it necessary. But it was a Promise which I could not make for altho I had Reason to confide in their Integrity and would have done it in my private Capacity yet as a public Officer I could not. For there would have been no longer any Certainty of the Extent to which their Expenditures might have been carried after it should have become a Matter of Indifference to their private Interest what Price[2] should be given for Supplies.

Thus Sir I found myself reduced to the Alternative of making a new Agreement for Subsistance of the Army and Garrison or of leaving them to subsist themselves by military Collection. The latter was to be avoided if possible for it would have been the most expensive Mode of obtaining Supplies not to mention other Consequences. The former therefore was to be adopted and I accordingly gave Instructions to Mr. Cornell the Inspector of the Contracts to consult with the Commander in Chief and take the necessary Arrangements.[3] It could not be expected that a Contract dictated by Necessity could be made on oeconomical Terms and the Inability to perform old Engagements would necessarily influence the Rate of new Ones. Besides this it was indispensibly necessary to obtain a longer Credit because otherwise the Burthen would have been shifted not removed, and the Evil must have returned with equal Speed and greater Magnitude. Under such unfavorable Circumstances it was necessary to pay for Credit in Order to obtain it. A new Contract is made[4] and the Rations issued now are to be paid for three Months hence at the Rate of thirteen Pence Pennsylvania Currency per Ration[5] which is an Advance of about one third upon the former Price. The Public therefore will pay for this Advance of Monies equal to feeding the Army at the Rate of thirty three and one third per Cent for three Months or to make the Matter more simple they must pay for feeding them three Months as much as would have fed them four Months. Besides this the public Credit sustains material Injury and damages will be expected by the former Contractors.

If Sir it should be supposed that this is the only Instance of Loss sustained from the low State of the Treasury it is a great Mistake. The Attempt to establish oeconomical Systems is vain unless we can support them by Punctuality. Congress have placed me in a Situation where I am exposed in the first Instance to Claims and demands but these must come home to the several Legislatures and eventually to their Constituents. My Situation therefore makes it a duty to expostulate freely on the Circumstances of my Department. I am not to learn that free Representations will sometimes give Offence and I know that those will always be most offended who are most in fault but I shall make no Appologies for what I have to say. It is necessary that the Truth should be known to the People. To our Enemies it is known already and has been for a long Time. They hold up to Contempt and Derision the Contrast between Resolutions to carry on the War at every Expence[6] and Receipts of Nothing in some States and very little in all of them put together. Those who court public favour at the Expence of public Good are very apt to inveigh against Taxes and to flatter the indolent and avaricious with the Idea that War can be carried on without Labor or Money. But it is Time for the People to distinguish between their Flatterers and their Friends. Sooner or later the current Expence must be paid and that Payment must come from the Purses of Individuals. If it were made in Season it would be lighter by one half than it is. Congress have called for a certain Sum and that Sum punctually paid would have answered the Purpose but they cannot be responsible for the Consequences of delay. The Expence will necessarily in such Case exceed their Calculations and of Course further Sums must be required.

There are certain Arguments Sir which ought not to be used if it is possible to avoid them but which every one invested with public Authority should suggest to his own Mind for the Government of his own Conduct. How long is a Nation who will do nothing for itself to rely on the Aid of others? In a War waged by one Country to obtain Revenue from another what is to be expected in Case of Conquest? How long will one Part of a Community bear the Burthens of the whole? How long will an Army undergo Want in the Midst of Plenty? How long will they endure Misery without Complaint, Injustice without Reproach, and Wrongs without Redress? These are Questions which cannot be solved by arithmetical Calculation. The moral Causes which may procrastinate or precipitate Events are hidden from mortal View. But it is within the Bounds of human knowledge to determine that all earthly Things have some Limits which it is imprudent to exceed, others which it is dangerous to exceed, and some which can never be exceeded. It is possible that we are near the Close of this War, and perhaps we are only in the

Middle of it. But if the War should continue we have to blame ourselves; for were those Resources called forth into Action which we really possess the foreign Enemies would soon lose all Hope and abandon their Enterprize. The greatest Injury therefore which we sustain is not from foreign but from domestic Enemies: from those who impede the necessary Exertions.

I have mentioned one among many Instances to show the Consequence of withholding the public Revenue and I take the Liberty to observe that it would be more manly to declare at once for unlimited Submission to british Tyranny than to make specious Declarations against it and yet take the direct Road to bring it about by opposing the Measures necessary for our Defence. That open Declaration will doubtless be restrained by the Fear of general Resentment;[7] but the other Conduct is so much the more dangerous as it is calculated to close Peoples Eyes while they approach the Precipice that they may be thrown down with greater Ease and more absolute Certainty.

I trust that your Excellency and every other real friend to our Country will urge forwards that speedy and effectual Collection of Taxes which can alone give Vigor and Stability to all our Measures. And I risk nothing when I assert that the public Service shall be performed (if the proper Revenues be obtained) at less than half of what would otherwise be expended. I am Sir with perfect Respect your Excellency's most obedient and humble Servant

Robt Morris

His Excellency The Governor of Connecticutt[8]
Examined

ENDORSED: 21 Octr 1782 Honble Robt Morris/de Collection of Taxes &c received 12th Novr. seq
MSS: LS, to the Governor of Connecticut, Jonathan Trumbull Papers, Ct; LS, to the President of New Hampshire, Meshech Weare Papers, Nh-Ar; LS, to the Governor of Rhode Island, R-Ar; LS, to the Governor of New Jersey, Ferdinand J. Dreer Collection, PHi; LS, to the President of Delaware, Executive Papers, De-Ar; LS, to the Governor of Virginia, Continental Congress Papers, Vi; Ofcl LbC, DLC; copy, PCC, DNA; copy, Benjamin Franklin Papers, PPAmP; LbC, Letterbook of Governor Alexander Martin of North Carolina, 1782–1785, Nc-Ar; Force transcript, to the President of New Hampshire, DLC.

1. On the dissolution of the combined West Point and Moving Army contract held by Sands, Livingston and Company, see the headnote to Comfort Sands, Walter Livingston, William Duer, and Daniel Parker to RM, September 11, and notes.
2. "Prices" in all other texts.
3. See RM to Ezekiel Cornell, September 20.
4. RM's contract with Jeremiah Wadsworth and John Carter is dated October 12.
5. The remainder of the sentence is omitted from the PPAmP text.
6. Probably a reference to the resolutions discussed in RM to Daniel of St. Thomas Jenifer, June 12, 1782, and notes.
7. In the DNA copy "open Declaration" and "general Resentment" are underlined.
8. In this and all other LS texts the addressee's name is in Gouverneur Morris's hand. The DNA text was enclosed in RM to the President of Congress, October 21, the PPAmP text in RM to Benjamin Franklin, January 11, 1783.

To the President of Congress
(John Hanson)

Office of Finance 21st October: 1782

Sir

The Negligence of the several States, in supplying the Public Treasury, has at length brought on one Evil which I had long apprehended, and attempted (in Vain) to guard against. Congress will recollect that I had contracted for the Supplies of the Garrison of West Point at Nine Pence half Penny, and to the moving Army at ten Pence, Pennsylvania Currency per Ration. The Vicinity of the Army to West Point, induced the two Companies of Contractors to join themselves together, and thus they presented for Payment a monthly Account of from forty five to sixty Thousand dollars. I found myself incapable to supply the Monies required. The Expectations I formed from the Taxes proved extremely falacious, and the Reliance I made on a Sale of Bills failed with the Failure of a Demand for them, which was utterly unexpected, and arose from the Appearances of Peace.[1] It is unnecessary to go into a Detail of the Expedients which I have been driven to; it is sufficient to say, that they proved unequal to the Object. Among other Things, I drew Bills in Anticipation of the Taxes, but those Taxes came in so slowly that they were of little Use. The Bills were drawn by me on Mr. Swanwick. The Receivers were directed to receive them as Cash (in Payment of Taxes) and remit them to the Treasury.[2] When they came to the Treasury, Mr. Swanwick took them up, with the Receipts given to him for so much Money by those who originally received the Bills, and thus Time was gained for about Six Weeks or two Months, and sometimes longer. It is not necessary to observe, what is known to every Body, that altho Contrivances may be used to procrastinate a Payment, it must at Length come from some Quarter or other. I exhausted all the Expedients I could devise, but at last I became in Arrears.

In Consequence of this, four of the Contractors joined in a Letter to me of the eleventh of September, of which the enclosed Paper Number one is a Copy. In this Letter those Parts which commanded my particular Attention were first, the Demand of two Promises, one that they should be indemnified for all Damages sustained from the public Inability to perform their Engagements and the other that I should, on producing the monthly Accounts, immediately pay one half the Amount in Specie, and three Times as much more in the Notes above described. And secondly; the Declaration that unless those Assurances were given by the first day of October, the Supplies must cease. I had no Prospect of being able to make this Payment and therefore that Matter was out of the Question; but even if I could have complied, the previous Assurance of Indemnification was what I would not give.

I had on the tenth Day of September appointed Ezekiel Cornell Esqr. in Pursuance of the Act of the seventh of May last to be Inspector for the main Army;[3] and therefore on the twentieth of September I enclosed a Copy of the Letter above mentioned in that of which the Paper Number two is a Copy.[4]

Altho the Letter of the eleventh of September was the first Express Declaration of the kind made by the Contractors; yet I had long had Reason to be convinced, that if the Supplies of Cash from the Treasury should be for any considerable Time suspended, they would be unable to perform their Stipulations: and it was very clear, that the Public could have no Right (under such Circumstances) to exact them. When I found, therefore, that I might be obliged to suspend the Payments, it became necessary to look at and provide for the Consequences. I enclose in the Paper Number three my Communications on that Subject to the General.[5]

It happened, that Messrs: Wadsworth and Carter (during their Passage thro this City from Virginia) mentioned their Intention of bidding at the Contracts I should offer for the Year 1783 if they could accomplish certain previous Arrangements. In the Course of the Conversation, the several Disputes which had arisen in the Execution of the existing Contracts were mentioned, and the Inconveniences of a Stipulation for monthly Payments were naturally connected with some of those Disputes. In discussing the Advantages of longer Credit, those Gentlemen informed me that they intended to offer a Credit of three Months. I then took Occasion to suggest the Possibility, that the Animosities between the Army and some of the Contractors might lead to a dissolution of the Contract, and asked if they would take it up. They declared that in the last Necessity they would, but that (as it would materially interfere with other Views, and come too suddenly for the State of their Funds) they wished to avoid it.

It was partly in Consequence of this Conversation that I wrote to Mr. Cornell the Letter of which Number four is a Copy.[6] I was influenced in some Degree, by the Desire to obviate complaints which existed in the Army, and which (however trivial in themselves) yet when combined with the Want of Pay and other Circumstances, were not to be neglected. The Generals Want of Confidence in Mr. Sands (one of the Contractors) was an additional Reason.[7] But the Letter itself contains that which decided my Conduct. And it was with very great Regret that I found myself impelled to such a Decission. With the Means of Payment, I could and would have compelled and facilitated such Performance of the Contract as to remove the Uneasiness of the Army from that Quarter. But without those

Means, it was impossible. Besides, to have vacated the Contract, from the default or Misconduct of the Contractors, would have involved no Loss of Credit. I saw too that any new Contract must be more expensive, and yet not to have made any would have encreased the Mischief. These evil Consequences were not the less sensible, from a Consideration that the Moment had arrived when it was necessary to advertise for the new Contracts: And they affected me still more when I reflected, that the Loss of our Credit (slender as it is) might have some Influence on the Negotiations for Peace. In a Word Sir, I felt the Situation I was in, and the Determination I was driven to, as the most distressing of an Administration which, from the first Moment of my Acceptance, has not been without Care and Anxiety. I was reduced to a Choice of Difficulties, and I had no Time to look for the Means of extricating myself. I should indeed, have directed Mr. Cornell to apply to the Contractors for a longer Credit, but to this there were many Objections. I shall mention however only this one, that they had on various Occasions taken Pains to convince me, and did convince me, that they had not Funds by any Means sufficient for the Purpose.

Number five contains the Copy of Mr. Cornells Letter to me of the fifth of October with its Enclosures; and Number six is an Extract of Colo: Tilghman's Letter of the same date which is referred to in that of Mr. Cornell. My Answer to the former (of the tenth) is contained in Number seven. On the same day I wrote to the Contractors a Letter of which Number eight is a Copy. And this Morning I received the Contract executed by Mr. Carter for himself and Mr. Wadsworth[8] of which the Paper Number nine is a Copy. From this it will appear that the principal Differences between the former and the present Agreements are that the Price of a Ration is advanced to thir[teen][9] Pence, and Credit given to the Public for three Months. If it be as[ked whether this] be a good Bargain, I answer at once that it is not. But I believe it to [be the best which] could be made. In a Situation where only bad Things can be done, [to adopt the least] pernicious is all which can be expected. I have however, made Use of [this Occasion to] write a very pointed Letter to the several States.[10] I enclose a Copy in the Paper Number ten, for the Perusal of Congress, as it contains some Observations on the Business which are not repeated in this Letter.

I have taken the Liberty to trouble your Excellency with this detail, that the United States (being fully informed) may give any Directions they shall think proper.[11] I am Sir, With perfect Respect and Esteem your Excellency's most obedient and humble Servant

Robt Morris

His Excellency the President of Congress

ENDORSED: 101/Letter 21 Oct 1782/Superintendt finance/Read. 24. 1782/The difficulties in which he has been/involved by the neglect of the states in supplying/the public Treasury. The dissolution of/the Contract for supplying the army/at 10d per ration. New Contract entered/into at 13d. His letter to the states
MSS: LS, PCC, DNA; Ofcl LbC, DLC; copy, Benjamin Franklin Papers, PPAmP.

1. On this point, see the headnote to RM's State of American Commerce and Plan for Protecting It, May 10, 1782, and notes.

2. See RM's Circular to the Receivers of Continental Taxes, July 19, 1782, and notes.

3. RM's commission to Cornell, however, is dated September 19.

4. The contractors' letter was enclosed in RM to Cornell, September 20.

5. RM's letters to Washington of August 29 (first letter), 30, and September 9 (second letter).

6. The letter is dated September 23.

7. See, for example, Washington to RM, June 16, 1782.

8. Dated October 12.

9. The LS is torn away here and below. The bracketed material has been supplied from the Ofcl LbC.

10. Dated October 21.

11. This letter was read in Congress on October 24, but no further action was taken. The PPAmP copy was enclosed in RM to Benjamin Franklin, January 11, 1783.

From Jonathan Burrall

Philadelphia October 21st 1782

Sir,

Agreeably to your directions I have considered the enclosed Memorial signed by a number of Gentlemen late in the department of the Commissary General of Issues, and beg leave to Report.[1]

That, previous to the settlement of any Accounts of Provisions *Issued* it is necessary to settle all Accounts of Provisions *purchased* as the charges against the Issuing department for provisions received, cannot be obtained untill this is done.

That this will take up much time, as they are of great Magnitude (few having been settled since the commencement of the war) and are dispersed throughout all the States.

That the *whole* of the Issuing Accounts from the begining of the War are unsettled; and I leave you to form an Idea of the time necessary to examine those Accounts and Vouchers which have employed some hundreds of Persons for Six years, and of course the time which some of them must wait before their Issuing Accounts can be settled by me. And it must be acknowledged a great hardship upon such of them as have discharged their duty faithfully (and some such I hope there are) to be kept from a settlement for their services, and from obtaining any acknowledgement or security for the Money due them till their Issuing Accounts are all examined, which probably many of them may never live to see.

I am sensible that the Public good ought to be the first consideration and that it is not probable they will pay as much attention to the settlement of their Issuing Accounts after having obtained such securities as they would before, altho' the Bonds which they gave for the faithfull performance of their trust, will still lay against them; therefore I have stated the facts and submit it to the determination of Congress how far this consideration ought to operate against their Claim.

There are several other Matters in some measure connected with this, which I conceive ought to be determined by Congress, I therefore beg leave to state them and request their direction.

1st. I conclude that those Issuing Commissaries, who were in actual service the 10th. April 1780 (upon a general principle adopted in consequence of a Resolution of Congress of that date)[2] are entitled to the amount of their Pay in Specie deducting therefrom such sums of Continental Money as they have received on Account, at the Value it was when they received it: it therefore becomes necessary to determine what their pay in Specie is Per Month. And find that on the 16th of June 1777 Congress fixed the Pay of a Deputy Commissary General of Issues at 75 Dollars per Month, and an Assistant at 40, and the 2d. July and 7th. August following they raised the former to 100 and the latter to 60 Dollars per Month. Depreciation by the Scale adopted for Loan Office Certificates, does not commence untill the first of September though an Actual depreciation had commenced long before.[3] The question is, which stating of their pay is to be considered as Specie?[4] The great number of Persons employed in the department makes this of some importance.

2d Whether in the settlement of Accounts I am to make use of the above mentioned Scale of depreciation for ascertaining the value of any balances which may be due in Continental Money to or from the United States, or the scale established by the Laws of the State in which the business was transacted?

3d. Where Money of the new emission[5] has been paid in part for articles contracted for by the Commissary General or on account of Liquors, Provisions &c. Seized for the Use of [the] Army or on Account of pay to the Issuing department, what rule is to be adopted for ascertaining its' value, or is it to be considered as Specie?[6] I am Sir very respectfully your most obedient and very humble Servant

> (Sign'd) Jonth. Burrell Comr.
> for Settling Comy. Dept.
> Copy

The Honble. Robert Morris

ENDORSED: Mr. Burrell/Commissr for Setling/Accounts/Report and Quere/21 Oct. 1782
MS: Copy, PCC, DNA.
1. The enclosed memorial to Congress, dated at Verplancks Point, New York, September 27, 1782, and signed by Nathaniel Stevens and 22 other former commis-

saries in the now defunct department of the commissary general of issues (PCC, no. 42, IV, 62–65), was read in Congress on October 9 and referred to RM on October 15 "so far as relates to settlement of accounts and pay." On October 17 the Financier sent it for comment to Burrall, the commissioner for settling the accounts of the Commissary Department. The memorial stated that the commissaries had received virtually none of the clothing that they were entitled to draw, and that between September 1777 and the disbandment of the department early in 1782, they had received no more than the value of three months' pay. Consequently, on their dismissal, they were left "without Money, Decent Clothing, or the means of procuring the necessaries of life, for ourselves, or Families." They therefore asked to be put on a par with officers in the line of the army and the other staff departments, by having their claims for depreciation and pay referred to their respective states for payment or acknowledged as a loan with interest. The commissaries apparently hoped to receive interest-bearing certificates for the sums claimed (see James Gray to Charles Stewart, n.d., Stewart Papers, NCooHi) which would give them sufficient credit to return to their former civilian occupations. To offset objections against making payments to them before their accounts were settled, they offered to increase the amount of their performance bonds above $5,000 if that sum was not deemed sufficient to cover what they might be found to owe upon final settlement of their accounts.

2. The resolution of Congress of April 10, 1780, provided for compensation to the army for depreciated pay. It applied only to troops "as were engaged during the war, or for three years, and are now in service, or shall hereafter engage during the war." For a discussion of the act in terms of state responsibility for the army debt, see notes to RM to the Quartermaster General, September 6, 1781, and to RM to Daniel of St. Thomas Jenifer, March 12, 1782, and notes.

3. For the scale of depreciation adopted by Congress on June 28, 1780, see notes to RM to the President of Congress, August 28, 1781.

4. That is, whether the raises given after June 16, 1777, were to be considered merely an accommodation to the actual depreciation of money received as pay.

5. On new emission money, see notes to John Morin Scott to RM, May 30, 1781.

6. RM submitted this letter to Congress on October 23. His report was read on October 24 and referred to a committee composed of George Clymer of Pennsylvania, Eliphalet Dyer of Connecticut, and James Duane of New York (see Dairy, October 30, for Clymer's call at the Office of Finance). The report of this committee, which has not been found, was on November 12 referred to a committee consisting of Duane, James Madison of Virginia, and Abraham Clark of New Jersey, whose report, delivered on November 21, concluded that it was "inexpedient" to decide on the first report at this time. Congress on January 14, 1783, referred the Duane committee's report to the grand committee on army pay and accounts; on the grand committee's recommendation, Congress assigned the report to a smaller committee on March 6. Although that committee was renewed on April 28, 1783 (PCC, no. 186, p. 67; and JCC, XXIII, 748n.) no action appears to have been taken at this time, and Burrall continued his policy of settling the accounts of the purchasing commissaries before those of the issuing commissaries. For the issue as raised anew in 1783, and largely settled by a resolution of Congress of April 15, 1784, see Diary, October 3 and 31, Burrall to RM, November 4, RM's report to Congress of November 5, 1783, James Gamble to RM, April 30, and Diary, May 1 and 3, 1784.

From Sands, Livingston and Company

Manor Livingston [New York], Oct. 21, 1782[1]

Sir:

We had the honor of receiving your letter of the 10th of October, in which you acquaint us that you had received information from General Cornell, on the 5th instant, that he had agreed for the supply, both of West Point and the moving army, after the 15th instant. Our feelings, Sir, as well as our interest, are deeply affected by the manner in which the contract for the moving army has been precipitately wrested out of our hands by the contract which General Cornell has entered into with Messrs. Wadsworth and Carter.[2]

We never can consider an answer to the question put to us by General Cornell,[3] as a voluntary surrender of the contract on our part: on the contrary, we protest against General Cornell's act in the most explicit manner, and hold ourselves entitled to a reparation of all damages which we may sustain in consequence of it.

You will observe, Sir, by our letter of the 9th, which General Cornell has no doubt transmitted to you, that we were far from wishing, by a continuance of the contract, to impede any arrangements which might be in contemplation for the supply of the army, and which the exigencies of affairs might render necessary. Our only aim and wish was to secure ourselves from ruin, and to be treated with that candor and delicacy which we conceive ourselves entitled to, not only from our private characters, but from the nature of our public deportment.

If a sacrifice of our interest was to be made on public considerations, we wished to have the merit of it; but as General Cornell's conduct has put this out of our power, we consider the overtures made to you in our letter of the 9th October, as altogether void; and shall, therefore, lose no time, in making a final settlement of our accounts. When this is effected, we are ready to join in a submission of our claims to three arbitrators: the one to be chosen by yourself and the parties interested in the contract, and after this choice is made, the other two to be appointed by the parties respectively.[4]

We are extremely concerned that you should have conceived yourself restrained, by the duty of your office, from giving us that assurance of indemnification which we requested in our letter of the 11th September; and you will forgive us in observing, that the reason assigned has not that weight with us, which, at first view, it may appear entitled to.

It is true, the object of a contract is to substitute a certain for an uncertain expence, and that the object would have been lost by an indemnification to be ascertained at a future period.

But we submit it to your consideration, whether it was not in your power to obviate these objections, by proposing an addition of price in consideration of a greater extent of credit, than was fixed in the contract; in the same manner as has been offered to Messrs. Wadsworth and Carter—the latter mode would have been more agreeable to us, and we are persuaded a very considerable saving would have been made to the public: as we could not know the motives you could have for not giving these assurances which we conceived ourselves equitably entitled to, or that general Cornell was vested with a power of increasing the price of the ration in consideration of a longer credit, it was not possible that this proposition could come from us.[5]

If general Cornell had informed us what he could do, as well as what he could not do, this turn of affairs, which gives so much pain, would never have happened.

You will permit us to observe, that some other reasons, not assigned, but which may be the subject of future consideration, might have led to the measure of depriving us of our contract.

It is not our province to decide, under present circumstances, whether a misunderstanding which unhappily prevailed between the army and the acting contractor, was well or ill founded.[6] We always understood that this gentleman enjoyed your highest confidence; but we can assure you, that, on the least intimation from you, the parties concerned would have made such an arrangement in the executive part, as the good of the service and the circumstances of affairs might render requisite.

You observe in your letter that you will not vent reproach. Though we are not conscious of having merited it, (and therefore cannot apply this term to ourselves,) there is an ambiguity in the expression, which, in an official letter, under present circumstances, may lead those under whose perusal it may come, to apply it to ourselves; we therefore wish, (if you mean it in this sense,) that you would be candid enough to inform us, and that you would mention the points at which your reproach is levelled. We shall be ready to submit every part of our conduct to a candid and dispassionate discussion. We confess ourselves anxious for an explanation of this expression, because unwearied pains are taken to vent the grossest falsehoods against the former concern; with what view we shall not pretend to say. Certain we are, that such bare attempts to prejudice the public opinion, can never meet with your approbation; because they are inconsistent with your personal character and conduct. It is necessary, however, these rumors should be discountenanced, or we shall be reduced to the necessity of entering into a public discussion of matters; and from the present state of politics and of the disposition of the people, we are sensible this would not promote the common interest.

So far we have been obliged to observe, in our own justification, though the respect we have for your personal and official character restrains us from placing general Cornell's transaction in the point of view it must appear to well informed and dispassionate judges.

We would not wish to add to that distress which you declare you feel from the late events which have taken place; and if we have made use of any expressions which give you uneasiness, we entreat you not to impute it to a want of sensibility for the embarrassments of your department, or of personal respect, but to the peculiarity of our situation; which has rendered it hardly possible to say less than we have, without sacrificing what we owe to our own reputations. Notwithstanding the mode of conducting the late transaction appears to us at present somewhat mysterious, we have such confidence in your sense of justice, and personal honor, and will do every thing in our power to bring our claims to a speedy and amicable issue. We are, with great respect, Your most obedient humble servants,

Sands, Livingston, & Co.

The hon. Robert Morris, Esq.

PRINTED: U.S., Congress, Senate Document 62, February 25, 1820, pp. 32–34.

1. The editors have not found a manuscript text of this letter from Sands, Livingston and Company, the former contractors for West Point and the Moving Army. The editors are grateful to Robert C. Gramberg of Hickory Hills, Illinois, for supplying a copy of the text printed here. The letter was also published in *American State Papers*, Class 9, Claims, I, 719.

2. The contract with Wadsworth and Carter is dated October 12 and went into effect on October 16. For the dissolution of the West Point and Moving Army contract held by Sands, Livingston and Company, see notes to Comfort Sands, Walter Livingston, William Duer, and Daniel Parker to RM, September 11.

3. For the question and the answer, see Ezekiel Cornell to the Contractors for the Moving Army, September 30, and Comfort Sands and Walter Livingston to Cornell, October 1, letters which were first enclosed in Cornell to RM, October 5, but which are printed as enclosures to Walter Livingston, William Duer, and Daniel Parker to RM, October 9.

4. For the arbitration of the contractors' claims against the United States, see notes to Cornell to RM, October 5.

5. For the Superintendent's explanation that Sands, Livingston and Company lacked sufficient capital for advances on the contract, see RM to the President of Congress, October 21.

6. The reference is to disputes between the army and Comfort Sands. See George Washington to RM, May 17, and notes, and June 16, 1782.

James McCall to Edward Fox

Office of Finance 21. Octo: 1782

Enclosed herewith you have your Commission as Commissioner for settling the Accounts of the Hospital Department.

Mr. Morris desires you will take the Oath of Office before the President of Congress and have it Recorded.[1]

MS: Ofcl LbC, DLC.

1. Fox's oath, dated October 24, 1782, is in PCC, no. 195, p. 312. His commission has not been found. McCall was RM's secretary in the Office of Finance.

To the Governor of Rhode Island
(William Greene)

Office of Finance, October 21, 1782. This letter nominating Edward Chinn as commissioner for settling Rhode Island's accounts with the United States is identical in substance to RM's letter to the governor of Maryland of May 7, 1782. Chinn is described herein as follows: "This Gentleman is a Citizen of the State of New York, and was lately a Commissioner of the extra Chamber of Accounts."

MSS: LS, R-Ar; Ofcl LbC, DLC.

Diary: October 22, 1782

Mr Ths. Fitzsimmons applied for Money to fit and Load the new Ship,[1] and to know whether she is to be fitted on the Principles of a Merchant Letter of marque Ship, to which I answer in the Affirmative and promised him Money.

Capt Nicholson[2] again applies for money and says he cannot go back to Boston without one hundred Dollars more.

Mr Eddy applied for my Assistance to get money from New York in which I declined meddling.

Mr Francis Hopkinson Communicated to me a curious plan for measuring a Ships way at Sea instead of the Log commonly Used.[3]

Como. Gillon respecting the Hessians and Mr Randal to finish his Business.[4]

Various Applications for Money &c.

Wrote a Letter T. Pickering Esqr.

Wrote a Letter Daniel Clarke.

Wrote a Letter Benjm. Harwood.

Wrote a Letter Daniel Clarke.

Wrote a Letter His Excellency the Prest of Congress.

Issued a Warrant on Mr Swanwick in favor the Contractors for York and Carlisle £375.0.0.

1. The *Duc de Lauzun.*
2. Samuel Nicholson, who was returning to Boston to face a court-martial.
3. Hopkinson read a paper on this plan to the American Philosophical Society on July 11, 1783, and subsequently published it under the title of "Description of a Machine for Measuring a Ship's Way through the Sea." See George Everett Hastings, *The Life and Works of Francis Hopkinson* (Chicago, 1926), 360 and n.
4. See, respectively, Diary, October 7 and 17.

To Daniel Clark

Office of Finance 22. Octo: 1782

Sir,

I received yours of the eleventh Instant by Yesterday's Post.[1] Having found some Inconveniences from the Acceptance of Bills I gave general Orders to Mr. Swanwick not [to] accept of any but upon the Presentation to note the Time they would fall due.[2] The Bill you mention to have been sold to Mr. Jenkins is paid[3] and that in Favor of Fox and Dorsey is not paid only because it suits the Holder to wait for his Money.

The Orders I gave you with Respect to the public Tobacco[4] were purely on public Account and it is with me a most inviolable Rule never to connect my private Affairs with those of the Public.[5] I am Sir your most obedient Servant

RM

MS: Ofcl LbC, DLC.

1. Letter not found. Clark was RM's agent for purchasing tobacco in Virginia.

2. On these bills of exchange, see RM's Circular to the Receivers of Continental Taxes, July 19, 1782, and notes.

3. See RM to George Olney, October 15, and notes.

4. See RM to Clark, September 23, and notes.

5. RM had not observed such a rule earlier in his public career, having in fact combined purchasing for public and private account in tobacco and other commodities while member and chairman of the Secret and Commercial Committees of Congress (1775–1778). His practices had aroused much criticism, especially during the Deane-Lee affair, and had contributed to controversies regarding the settlement of Secret and Commercial Committee accounts (see notes to RM to Thomas Mumford, April 8, 1782; and volume I of this series, xxiv–xxv). Although RM had placed his private business in other hands by the beginning of 1782, accusations that the Financier was conducting business for private as well as public account continued to come up during his term of office. See for example, in connection with the sale of surplus flour at Fort Pitt, Diary, August 20, and notes. For RM's earlier career in Congress, see Ferguson, *Power of the Purse*, 70–94, 102–105; Nuxoll, "Congress and the Munitions Merchants," 51–57, 68–73, 146–156, 195–209; and Ferguson and Nuxoll, "Investigation of Government Corruption During the American Revolution," *Congressional Studies*, VIII, no. 2 [1981], 18–22. For the conduct of RM's private business while Superintendent of Finance, see Ver Steeg, *Morris*, 187–191; also the headnote to RM to a Committee of Congress, March 26, 1781.

To the Quartermaster General (Timothy Pickering)

Office of Finance 22nd October 1782

Sir

I received your Letter of the eighth Instant.[1] I sincerely wish to relieve so worthy an Officer as Colo. Neilson but I can by no means consent to the Issue of any[2] Paper Money. The Mischiefs of such a measure are beyond Computation. I am Sir Your Most Obedient Servant.

Robt Morris

Colo Pickering
Quarter Master General

ENDORSED: Honble Robert Morris Esqr./S.F/October 22nd. 1782/Wishes to releive Col. Neilson,/but cannot consent to issues/of Paper money from the State/Treasury (of Jersey) on continental Ac/count.

MSS: LS, Manuscript File, WDC, DNA; Ofcl LbC, DLC.

1. Pickering's letter of October 8 has not been found, but evidently relayed the request of John Neilson, the deputy quartermaster general for New Jersey, for use of paper money in the hands of the Continental loan officer of New Jersey. See Pickering to Neilson, November 5, 1782 (in which a copy of the present letter was enclosed), WDC, no. 85, p. 237, DNA.

2. This word is omitted from the Ofcl LbC.

To the Quartermaster General
(Timothy Pickering)

Office of Finance 22 October 1782

Sir

The Post brought me yours of the seventeenth Instant. I will send you Notes to Pay off the Ox Teams you mention as soon as you let me know the Amount and the Sums which will be convenient to draw them in.[1] As to your Oxen I certainly think with you that it will be good Occonomy to sell them but I think you should consult the Commander in Chief because it is possible that he may want them if it be only to Move the Army into their Winter Cantonments. I am Sir Your most Obedient and humble Servant.

Robt Morris

Timothy Pickering Esqr.
Quarter Master General

ENDORSED: Robert Morris Esqr. S.F/Octr. 22. 1782./Will furnish notes to pay for teams./N.B. The different demands in/my letter to which this is an/answer, were confounded together/and mistaken by Mr. M. See my/letter of Octr. 17.
MSS: LS, Manuscript File, WDC, DNA; Ofcl LbC, DLC.
1. As the endorsement above suggests, RM refers only to the oxen mentioned in the second paragraph of Pickering's October 17 letter. Pickering replied on November 5.

To Daniel Clark

Philada. 22. Octo: 1782

I have received your Letter of the eighteenth of September last,[1] and I gave a Copy of it to the Minister of War who was on his Way to Head Quarters. How far your wishes can be complied with must depend on the general Arrangements.

MS: Ofcl LbC, DLC.
1. Letter not found.

James McCall to the President of Congress
(John Hanson)

Office of Finance 22. Octo: 1782[1]

I am directed by Mr Morris to inform your Excellency of an Express going as far as Georgia (and which will set off at ten OClock tomorrow Morning) to the End that if any Gentlemen in Congress wish to write by the same, that their Letters be sent to this Office before that Time and Care shall be taken to forward them.

MS: Ofcl LbC, DLC.
1. McCall was RM's secretary in the Office of Finance.

To Benjamin Harwood

Office of Finance 22d. October 1782[1]

I write this short Note meerly to inform you that I have received no Letters by the two last Posts. I suppose this is to be attributed to your having had nothing material to write but I wish to hear from you regularly if you should only tell me that you have received Nothing.

MSS: LS, Morris-Harwood Papers, MdHi; Ofcl LbC, DLC.
 1. Harwood was the receiver of Continental taxes for Maryland.

Diary: October 23, 1782

Willm. Bingham Esqr. applied for a farther payment in Bills of Exchange on account of the Debt due to him on the public Books.[1]

Jos. Borden Esqr. Loan Officer brought a monthly Return and came to enquire whether the Bills he had Issued before my Counter Orders reached him would be paid.[2] I declined giving him Satisfaction on that Point as I disapprove what he has done.

Como Gillon Respecting the Hessians he has engaged. I desired to have a return of their Names &c. and that he would have a proper Bond made out for my Inspection and Approbation.[3] I then repeated my Intention of requiring Satisfaction for his breach of the Contract made with Colo. Laurens.[4]

Jno. Chaloner Esqr. applied for money due to Messrs. Wadsworth and Carter on Acceptances.[5]

Monsr. Savery[6] applied for my Report to Congress on his Memorial and after a long investigation of his Case I advised him to apply to the State of Massachusetts for the Justice due to his Employers by that State, which he agreed to do and desired me not to Report to Congress until I shall hear farther from him.

Mr Edwd. Williams on behalf of Doctor Thos. Bond junr. represents the Hospital Affairs to be so deplorable that I ventured to sign a Warrant for 4,000 Dollars of which 1,000 Dollars to be paid in Cash and 3,000 in Notes.

Honble. Mr. Blount called to recommend Mr Caswell of No. Carolina[7] as a proper Person to be appointed Commissioner for settling the Accounts of that State and I should have been happy to appoint him, but being a Citizen of the Said State he is not eligible to the Office. Mr Blount held a long Conversation on the Affairs of that State during which I gave him my Sentiments and every information he desired.

Colo. Miles for Money. I desired him to buy Wood and promised to pay for it.

Sundry other Persons for money &c.

Wrote a Letter to John Moylan Esqr.

Wrote a Letter to Geo: Olney.
Wrote a Letter to Abram Yates.
Wrote a Letter to Wm. C. Houston.
Wrote a Letter to His Excellency the Prest. of Congress.
Wrote a Letter to Abram Yates Junr.
Wrote a Letter to Messrs. Otis and Henley.
Wrote a Letter to Wm. Whipple.
Wrote a Letter to Alexr. Hamilton.
Wrote a Letter to the several Governors.
Wrote a Letter to the Govr. of Virginia.

Issued a Warrant on Mr Swanwick in favor Hazelwood and Blackiston	£300. 0. 0
Issued three Warrants on Mr Swanwick in favor Jos. Pennell	271.14. 6
Issued three Warrants on Mr Swanwick in favor Sam Hodgdon	202.19.10

1. On the settlement of William Bingham's accounts as American agent at Martinique, see James Lovell to RM, July 5, 1781, and notes; on payment to him in bills of exchange, see notes to Diary, August 20.
2. Borden's return as Continental loan officer of New Jersey has not been found. For RM's "Counter Orders," see his Circular to the Continental Loan Officers, September 9; see also Diary, September 11.
3. See RM to Alexander Gillon, October 8, and notes.
4. See Diary, September 19, and notes.
5. See notes to Diary, August 20.
6. Jean Savary de Valcoulon was representing Penet and Company in its settlement of accounts with the Continental and state governments. His memorial (see Diary, October 14) has not been found; it is not mentioned in the *Journals*.
7. William Blount (1749–1800) was a member of Congress from North Carolina in 1782–1783 and 1786–1787 (*DAB*). His nominee was Richard Caswell, state comptroller and former governor of North Carolina, whose name RM had offered for receiver of Continental taxes in a letter of April 26, 1782, to the governor of North Carolina.

Circular to the Governors of the States

(Circular)   Office of Finance 23d October 1782
Sir,

I do myself the Honor to transmit the Copies of two Acts of Congress of the sixteenth and eighteenth Instant.[1] I hope these Acts will meet that early Attention which is due to their Importance. With perfect Respect and Esteem I have the Honor to be Sir Your Excellency's most obedient and humble Servant

Robt Morris

His Excellency The Governor of Connecticutt[2]

ENDORSED: 23d. Octo 1782/Office of Finance/enclosing Resolves of Congress/16 and 18th instant/received 12 Novr 1782

MSS: LS, to the Governor of Connecticut, Jonathan Trumbull Papers, Ct; LS, to the President of Delaware, Executive Papers, De-Ar; LS, to the Governor of Virginia, Continental Congress Papers, Vi; Ofcl LbC, DLC; LbC, Letterbook of Governor Alexander Martin of North Carolina, 1782–1785, Nc-Ar.

1. The act of Congress of October 16 estimated the service of the year 1783 at $6 million and requisitioned the states for $2 million; that of October 18 assigned the quotas for each state. See RM to the President of Congress, July 30, and notes.

2. The addressee's name in all the LS texts is written in Gouverneur Morris's hand.

To Alexander Hamilton

Office of Finance 23rd. October 1782

Sir

I have received your favors of the 9th. and 12th. Instant with the account of your Receipts to the latter Date.[1]

As the purposes for which Mr Brown[2] is employed will not admit of his passing through Albany, I shall consider of some arrangement for making Remittances from thence; of which you shall be seasonably Informed. Your Letter for General Green shall be forwarded.[3] I shall soon have Occasion to write you Respecting the appointment of Doctor Tillotson and his acceptance which I am prevented, by much business, from doing by this Post.[4] I am Sir Your most Obedient and humble Servant[5]

Robt Morris

Alexander Hamilton Esqr.
Receiver for the State of New York

ENDORSED: From the Superintendant/of Finance/October 23d. 1782/Answered November 2d. 1782
MSS: LS, Hamilton Papers, DLC; Ofcl LbC, DLC; transcript, Francis Baylies Papers, DLC.

1. Hamilton was the receiver of Continental taxes for New York. His letter of October 12 and accompanying account of tax receipts have not been found. Up to October 9 he had received $2,709%o. See PCC, no. 137, III, 361.

2. Jesse Brown, express rider to the states east of the Hudson River. See RM's circular to the receivers for those states of May 15, 1782.

3. The letter, dated October 12, is in Syrett and Cooke, eds., Hamilton Papers, III, 183–184.

4. No such letter has been found. For Tillotson's succession as receiver, see notes to RM to Hamilton, August 28.

5. Hamilton's reply of November 2 has not been found.

To William Churchill Houston

Office of Finance 23d October 1782[1]

Sir

I have received your Favor dated at Trenton on the 19th Instant. The Advertisement being on a Subject in which the Public are interested, the Printers ought to insert it in their Papers as an Article of

Intelligence for the general Information of their Customers. If one Paper contains it and another does not it is easy to see which will have the Preference as yet no Demands have been made on me for this Service. I have the Honor to be Sir your most obedient and humble Servant

Robt Morris

W. C. Houston Esqr.
Receiver for New Jersey

ENDORSED: Robert Morris Esqr 23/Octr. 1782 Received 24
MSS: LS, Houston Collection, NjP; Ofcl LbC, DLC.
1. Houston was the receiver of Continental taxes for New Jersey. The advertisement discussed in this letter is dated October 10.

To George Olney

Office of Finance 23. Octo: 1782

Sir,

I have received your Favor dated at Providence on the seventh Instant.[1] No decision has yet been made respecting the Certificates you mention.[2] I wish to accomodate the State as far as it can be done consistent with the general Arrangements, and this will be accomplished eventually, by charging the United States in Account with so much money as the Certificates amount to, which being passed at the Treasury, the Balance will be paid in Notes, and these can be paid to the Receiver.

By this mode the Amount will be secured without violating the general System; but lest a Precedent should be established which in its Application might Produce public Inconveniences I think it best not to do any Thing in that Matter yet. I have the honor to be Sir your most obedient Servant

RM

MS: Ofcl LbC, DLC.
1. Letter not found. Olney was the receiver of Continental taxes for Rhode Island.
2. The reference is probably to clothing certificates which Rhode Island wished RM to accept in payment on the specie requisition for 1782. See RM to Olney, June 23, 1782, and notes, and March 31, May 6, and June 22, 1783.

To the Governor of Virginia (Benjamin Harrison)

Office of Finance 23d. Octbr. 1782

Sir,

On Receipt of your Excellency's Letter of the twenty third of last Month I wrote to Congress on the subject of it a Letter[1] of which a

Copy is enclosed together with a Copy of their order of yesterday by which the matter is referred to my Discretionary Disposition.[2] In Consequence thereof I have now the Honor to inform your Excellency that I agree to your Proposal and will in Consequence Direct Mr. Barclay to ship out the goods on account of the United States.[3] I cannot at present advise you to any particular mode by which the Arms you mention can be brought out safely but I would rather suggest to your Consideration whether in the present state of military operations it might not be as well to omit the Importation of Arms which would be a great Risque of so much Property and probably they would be useless after their arrival. I do not by this mean that it will not be highly proper to have in the important State over which you preside every proper means of Defence but only that it may be prudent to avoid the Expenditure and the Risque under present Circumstances.[4]

However if I can devise any means for the safe Transportation of them I will give due notice of it to Mr. Barclay who will be possessed of your orders and either use or omit the Occasion as you may have directed. With great Respect I have the Honor to be Sir, your Excellency's most obedient and humble Servant

Robt Morris

His Excellency The Govr. of Virginia

ADDRESSED: On public Service/His Excellency The Governor of Virginia/R Morris/ Richmond ENDORSED: Ro Morris to the/Govr of Virginia/Oct 23d. 1782/Enclosing Mr Morris letter of/the 9th to Congress and the reso/lution of that body thereon.
MSS: LS, Continental Congress Papers, Vi; Ofcl LbC, DLC.
    1. Dated October 9.
    2. See notes to RM to the Governor of Virginia, April 27, 1782.
    3. See RM to Thomas Barclay, and to Benjamin Franklin, both October 27.
    4. In his reply of November 16, however, Harrison requested RM's assistance in having the arms shipped immediately.

To William Whipple

Office of Finance 23d. Octobr. 1782

Sir

Your favor dated at Portsmouth on the 7th. Instant has been received. I am sorry to hear that you have not yet received any Money on Account of the Taxes for your State. Surely they will soon enable you to write differently. I am Sir Your Obedient Servant

Robt Morris

William Whipple Esqr
Receiver for New Hampshire

ENDORSED: Office of Finance Octo. 23. 1782
MSS: LS, Sturgis Family Papers, MH; Ofcl LbC, DLC.

James McCall to the Clothier General
(John Moylan)

Office of Finance 23. Octo: 1782

By Desire of the Honble. Superintendant of Finance I enclose you sundry Papers received from Messrs. Otis and Henley of Boston.[1] You are requested (after Copying such as you may have Occasion for) to return them to this Office.

MS: Ofcl LbC, DLC.

1. McCall was RM's secretary in the Office of Finance. The papers, which had been enclosed in a letter from Samuel Allyne Otis and David Henley to RM of October 10, have not been found. See RM to Otis and Henley, October 23.

To the President of Congress
(John Hanson)

Office of Finance 23d October 1782

The enclosed Memorial of the late Issuing Commissaries was transmitted by me to the Commissioner for setling the Accounts of that Department.

I have now the Honor to transmit your Excellency the Copy of this Letter (of the twenty first) on that Subject.[1]

MSS: LS, PCC, DNA; Ofcl LbC, DLC.

1. For a discussion of the memorial of the former issuing commissaries and Congress's response to it, see Jonathan Burrall to RM, October 21, and notes.

To Otis and Henley

Office of Finance 23d. Octo. 1782

I have received your Favor dated at Boston on the tenth Instant with the Enclosures.[1] You mention thirty two Bales of Cloathing being received per the Ship Apollo which I suppose to be a Mistake: Twenty two being the Number of Bales specified in the Invoice. This Letter will be forwarded by the Clothier General who informs me that he means to engage your Assistance in the Business of his Department.

I doubt not but your Conduct in transacting the public Business will be such as will entitle you to the Approbation of all who wish well to the public Interests.

MS: Ofcl LbC, DLC.

1. The letter and enclosures received from the firm of Samuel Alleyne Otis and David Henley have not been found.

To Abraham Yates, Jr.

Office of Finance 23d October 1782

I have received your Favor dated at Albany on the 4th Instant, with its Enclosures.[1] And you will in Return receive from the Treasurer of the United States a Discharge for the Bill of Exchange therein mentioned.

MSS: LS, Yates Papers, NN; Ofcl LbC, DLC.

1. Yates was the Continental loan officer of New York. According to the endorsement on the LS, he received the letter on November 1.

James McCall to Abraham Yates, Jr.

Office of Finance Octr. 23d. 1782[1]

I have the Honor to enclose you the Treasurers Receipt for the Bill of Exchange for Eighteen dollars forwarded by you to this Office.

MSS: LS, Yates Papers, NN; Ofcl LbC, DLC.
1. According to the endorsement on the LS, Yates received this letter from McCall, RM's secretary in the Office of Finance, on November 1.

Gouverneur Morris to Matthew Ridley

Philadelphia 23 Octr. 1782[1]

I have heard of but not from you since the political Letter you wrote on the Change of british ministers.[2] I wish you would write me often not only because it would be useful to me but because it might become so to you. Your Conjectures have proved tolerably just which is a good Encouragement for continuing the Business of Conjecture. If I had any thing new to write you I would do it but really there is as little of this as you can easily conceive. I presume you are perfectly domesticated chez Madame Jay and therefore I do not know how I can put into better Hands the assurances of my Love and Esteem. Accept them for yourself and always beleive me yours

MS: ALS, Ridley Papers, MHi.
1. Notes on the face of this letter indicate that it was received on December 9, acknowledged on December 14, 1782, and answered on March 24, 1783. The date of receipt is written in an unidentified hand; the others are in Ridley's hand. An endorsement in the unidentified hand on the verso imparts the same information, except the acknowledgment is given as December 18, probably an error since the only extant text of the letter of acknowledgment, from Ridley's letterbook, is dated December 14.
2. Dated April 20, 1782.

Diary: October 24, 1782

Jos. Borden Esqr. applied this morning to have his Accounts as Loan Officer for the State of New Jersey returned to him in Order to have them settled by the Commissioner.[1] This I refused, alledging that the Accounts are Papers of Record in the Treasury Office and must not go out again.

The Honble. James Duane Esqr. called to give some Advice respecting a Letter which he and a Committee of Congress to which he is Chairman wishes may be written to Rhode Island stating the necessity of Granting revenue and grounding that necessity on their non payment of Taxes.[2]

Lieut. Dowler brought a Bill of 1,000 Dollars from Colo. Pickering to exchange for money which I declined, alledging that I had given it to Colo Pickering to save me from such Calls and not to expose me more pointedly to them.

The Honble. Messrs. David Howell and Doctr. John Arnold[3] Delegates of Rhode Island called for Advice and information on some public Matters. Doctr. Arnold delivered me a Letter from Geo. Olney Esqr.[4] to which see my Answer this Date. I delivered to Doctor Arnold the Letter and Certificate that was enclosed.

I sent for Thos Paine Esqr. and recommended that he should Address the Public in terms to induce the payment of Taxes, to establish better modes of Taxation &c.[5]

Sundry other Applications on various Matters unneccessary to relate.

Wrote a Letter to Wm. Denning Esqr.

Wrote a Letter to Geo. Olney.

Wrote a Letter to his Excellency the Govr of Rhode Island.

Issued a Warrant on Mr Swanwick in favor of Thos. Fitzsimmons £202.19.10.

1. The commissioner for settling New Jersey's accounts with the United States was Lewis Pintard. The commissioners had been authorized to settle loan office accounts in their respective states. See notes to RM's report to Congress of June 13, 1782.

2. Duane, a delegate from New York, was chairman of several committees dealing with financial matters, including one appointed on July 22 "to enquire into the obstacles which have retarded a compliance with the requisition of Congress of the 3d of Feby 1781 and to report the proper means of obtaining the full effect of the said requisition." There is no record of a report by this committee. See PCC, no. 186, pp. 44, 56, 57, 58. RM's letter to the governor of Rhode Island is dated October 24.

3. Jonathan Arnold (1741–1793), a Providence physician and former surgeon and administrator in the Continental Hospital Department, had arrived in Philadelphia on October 5 and taken his seat in Congress on October 10. He continued to serve until July 1783 or later. *DAB; Biog. Dir. Cong.;* and Burnett, ed., *Letters,* VI, li, VII, lxxiv.

4. George Olney's letter of September 13 has not been found.

5. From this recommendation came Paine's six essays in support of the ratification of the impost in Rhode Island under the pseudonym "A Friend to Rhode-Island and the Union" (see Paine to RM, November 20, 1782). On Paine's relationship to the Office of Finance, see RM's Memorandum on Paine, printed at the end of February 1782, and notes.

To George Olney

Office of Finance 24. Octo: 1782

Sir,

In answer to your Letter of the thirteenth of last Month[1] I have to inform you that there is no Money at my Command which can be applied to the Payment of old Debts due from the Public. I expect a Commissioner will soon be appointed, who will be invested with proper Powers to settle all the Accounts of the marine, of which due Notice will be given in the several states. Mrs. Harrison's Accounts will come in Course of Settlement and when finally adjusted a Certificate of the Balance will be given to her; but to pay it will be impracticable; all that can be done will be to place it on Interest, nor can even the Interest be paid until the States shall have granted Revenue for that Purpose. I have no doubt but the Picture you have exhibited of Mrs. Harrison's Situation is faithfully drawn; my feelings are constantly Pained by narratives of similar Distress from public Creditors, and it is greatly to be lamented that Rhode Island should contribute to the Continuance of that Distress by delaying to follow the Example of her Sister States respecting the Impost on Importations &ca. But I hope the Time is at Hand when your Legislature will perceive the Necessity, Propriety and Justice of establishing permanent Revenues for paying the Interest of the Public Debts. I am Sir your most obedient and Humble Servant

RM

 MS: Ofcl LbC, DLC.
1. Olney was the receiver of Continental taxes for Rhode Island. His letter has not been found; for its delivery, see Diary, October 24.

To the Governor of Rhode Island (William Greene)

Office of Finance 24th October 1782

Sir,

My circular Letter of the twenty third Instant contains the Estimates and Requisitions for the Service of the Year 1783.[1] I must take the Liberty to make a few Observations on them which apply particularly to the State of Rhode Island.[2] In the Letters to Congress of the twenty ninth and thirtieth July last, Copies of which were transmitted in my circular Letter of the twelfth of September, I have so fully expressed my Sentiments on the Subject of Credit and Loans, that I shall not repeat them. Your Excellency will perceive that in the Act of the sixteenth Instant, altho the Estimates amount to six Millions, yet only two are required, and that farther Requisitions are suspended until the Result of Measures for obtaining Loans shall be known. It is unnecessary to mention that Congress have directed an Attempt to borrow four Millions.[3]

The Propriety of this Step will be self evident when the Fate of their Requisitions for the present Year is considered. The Sums brought in from the several States being regularly published in the Gazettes will spare me the Pain of repeating them. I say the Pain, because every such Repetition will have in some Degree the Air of Reproach. It must be remembered that the Duration of the War does not depend upon Congress. This is an invaded Country. Invaded for the Purpose of Conquest. And between Opposition and Submission there is no middle Line. The Idea of a Submission is and ever ought to be rejected with Disdain. Opposition therefore becomes a Matter of Necessity; and that Opposition involves Expence.

There is then a certain Degree of Expence which cannot be avoided; and this must be provided for. The Estimates being formed under the Idea of Money in Hand to pay for Services required, they are stated as low as possible. It appears therefore that the six Millions mentioned in the Estimates must be had. It appears from the Experiments already made that the People are either unwilling or unable to pay the whole in Taxes: And whether Want of Power or Inclination be the true Cause is immaterial to the present Enquiry; for the Fact is clear. Now there are but four Modes of obtaining the Supplies. Either they must be given to us, or lent to us, or raised in Taxes, or taken by Force. As to the first, we can place no Dependence on it; and as to the last, it is neither the most constitutional, the most oeconomical nor the most pleasing Way. Necessity may justify it; but it will be very difficult to justify the Necessity. The Supplies therefore must be obtained by Loans or Taxes, so that if they cannot be obtained by Loans, Taxation is the only Resource; and in that Case there is no Medium between legal Taxation and military Collection: For if we will not submit to Great Britain we must carry on the War, and if we carry on the War we must obtain the Means, and if we cannot get the Means abroad we must provide them at Home, and if we do not provide them by Law they must be taken by Force.

The Inattention of the States to the Requisitions of the United States leaves Congress no Choice between Loans and military Collections. Whether they can obtain Loans must depend upon other People. They cannot obtain Loans without Credit, and they cannot have Credit without funds. They cannot get Funds without the Concurrence of the States. They must ask that Concurrence before they can obtain it; and they must determine on the Funds before they can ask. The making yearly Requisitions of Quotas to pay the Interest of public Debts will not do. It is in itself a futile Measure; but if it were the best Thing in the World, yet if those who are to lend do not think so, there is an End of the Matter. Now the Fact is that no Body will lend upon the Promise of such Requisitions. And truly the Compliances made with those for carrying on the War give very little Encouragement. It follows then that Congress *must* ask for particular Funds. They have asked for one, and it is not complied with by two States out of thirteen.[4] Shall Congress then adhere to this Demand, or shall they change their Application? If they should change it could they expect that there would not then be one or two opposing States? To Answer this Question let it be enquired what Objects of Taxation can be devised to which Exceptions cannot be made. Surely there is none. Let it be enquired next whether there is any Object so unexceptionable as that which they have fixed upon. The Answer is no. It follows then that in changing the Application there would be less Prospect of Success than at present. Congress then must adhere to their Requisition, and if that Fund be not granted we cannot expect Loans. But it is demonstrated by Experience that we cannot get sufficient Taxes. We certainly cannot get Rid of the War, and therefore the People must have their Property taken by Force. The Necessity will justify this, But as I said before who will justify the Necessity? Surely the Authors of it should think of that in Season.

Will it be a sufficient Justification to say that the Demand of Congress is *unconstitutional?* If a Thing be neither wrong nor forbidden it must be admissible.[5] Such a Requesion is no where forbidden; and therefore it is admissible if it be not wrong. Now it cannot be wrong to do that which One is obliged to do, be the Act what it may: And Congress are obliged to make such Requisitions. But further it must be admitted that they are not contrary to the moral Law. Supposing then, for Argument's Sake, that the Thing asked for would, if granted, be Contrary to the Confederation. If so, the Grant would alter the Confederation. But the Grant is not to take Effect without general Consent. The Confederation was formed by general Consent, and by general Consent it may be altered. The Requisition therefore, if complied with, will by that very Compliance become constitutional.

But it may perhaps be suggested that the five per Cent Impost will not be sufficient for the Object in View. This must be acknowledged; but what Inference is to be drawn from thence? Not that Congress should ask for more. Under the Circumstances in which they are placed it is difficult to ascertain what Line of Conduct is to be pursued. If they ask further Revenues it may be said that there is Weakness in framing new Demands before old Ones are complied with. Every Fund will meet with some Opposition, and every Opposition encourages new Opponents. The Evil presses hard. Public Credit is at the last Gasp, or rather it is expired. Not only are we to expect a formidable Clamor from the abused and injured Creditors, but there is really very little Hope of obtaining foreign Loans: For how can it be expected that a Republic without Funds should persuade Foreigners to lend their Money, while it's own Citizens who have already lent theirs can neither obtain the Interest nor any solid Security either for Interest or Principal.

This, Sir, is an Object of great Magnitude, and one which directly or indirectly concerns every Inhabitant of the United States. The critical Situation we stand in has rendered it necessary for Congress to demand a decided Answer. No Time is to be lost, for if the Revenues cannot be obtained the public Creditors must be told so in plain Terms. The Efforts to borrow farther Sums must cease of Course, and then the whole Weight of the War must fall on the People in one Mode or the other. It is a very serious Question whether the little Applause which Individuals may gain by specious Declamations and Publications should over balance every Consideration of national Safety. This serious and important Question your Legislature is now by the Representative of all America most solemnly called on to decide. I am Sir With perfect Respect your Excellency's most obedient and humble Servant[6]

Robt Morris

His Excellency The Governor of Rhode Island

MSS: LS, R-Ar; Ofcl LbC, DLC.
1. For commentary by the Rhode Island delegates on the resolutions enclosed in RM's October 23 letter, see Jonathan Arnold and David Howell to Governor Greene, October 19, 1782, Staples, *Rhode Island in the Continental Congress*, 398–399.
2. See Diary, October 24, and notes, for the antecedents to this letter. For arguments counter to those expressed here, see Arnold and Howell to Governor Greene, October 15, 1782, Staples, *Rhode Island in the Continental Congress*, 394–398.
3. On the loan of $4 million called for by acts of September 14 and 23, 1782, see notes to RM to the President of Congress, July 30.
4. The impost of February 3, 1781, had not been ratified by Rhode Island and Georgia. RM had appealed to these states in a letter of October 17.
5. On the Nationalists' argument for implied powers, see Nathanael Greene to RM, August 18, 1781, and notes.
6. This letter evidently went unanswered. For Rhode Island's rejection of the impost, see notes to RM to the Governor of Rhode Island, August 2.

To William Denning

Office of Finance 24. Octo: 1782
Your Letter dated on the seventh Instant has been received and submitted to the Comptroller of the Treasury who will do what is necessary respecting the Subject of it.[1]
Mr. Chinn is recommended to the State of Rhode Island for Commissioner to settle the Accounts between that and the United States.[2] I have no Doubt but he will be acceptable. And when their acquiescence is signified to me by the Government of that State I shall write to him on the Subject.

MS: Ofcl LbC, DLC.
1. Denning was the commissioner of accounts for the Quartermaster Department. His letter has not been found.
2. See RM to the Governor of Rhode Island, October 21.

Diary: October 25, 1782

Messrs. William Harris and Wm. Nichols called to consult respecting the Contracts now Advertized for. I gave them every encouragement to bid at them.[1]

Mr. Patton[2] applies for Money to buy Wood. Refer him to Colo. Miles.

Majr Franks applies for a repayment of   [3] Livres Tournois charged to his Account in the Settlement Credited Doctr Franklin who has drawn upon him for the same. I desired that he might bring me a Certificate from the Comptroller of his being charged with said Sum.

Colo. Patton and Colo. Gurney brought the Accounts of the Ship Genl. Washington and wanted Money.[4] The last I refused for the present, but took the Accounts to be examined.

Sent for William Nourse[5] to give Directions respecting the making out the Accounts of the public Expenditures.

Lieut Dowler applies for Money for the Quarter Master General.

1. The contracts were announced in RM's advertisement of October 10. On the bid offered by Harris and Nichols, see Diary, November 11, 1782.
2. Robert Patton, messenger and doorkeeper of Congress.
3. Space left blank in manuscript.
4. See Diary, September 1, and notes.
5. The reference most likely is to Joseph Nourse, the Register of the Treasury (for his brother William, see notes to Diary, August 23). Concerning the accounts mentioned in this entry, see notes to Diary, June 12, 1782.

To Le Couteulx and Company

Office of Finance 25 Octo: 1782[1]

Gentlemen

Since my Letter of the twenty fourth of September last enclosing one for Messrs. Le Couteulx at Cadiz of same Date (in which I detailed a Plan for introducing Monies to this Country from the Havanna) I have appointed Mr. John Brown to draw Bills of Exchange upon the House of Messrs. Le Couteulx at Cadiz. Of this I have given them Notice by the enclosed Letter of this Date which I am to request that you will (after Perusal) seal and forward. I am Gentlemen, your most obedient and humble Servant

RM

MSS: Ofcl LbC, DLC; copy, PCC, DNA.
1. Le Couteulx and Company was a Parisian banking firm. For their role and that of John Brown in the Financier's plan to import specie from Havanna, see notes to RM to Le Couteulx and Company, September 24. The recipient's copy of the present letter may have been carried by Captain Charles Wells (see RM's Instructions to Wells, October 25); the PCC copy was enclosed in RM to Theodorick Bland, Jr., April 16, 1783 (first letter).

Instructions to Charles Wells

Office of Finance 25. Octo: 1782[1]

Mr. Wells will receive with this two Packetts of Letters, which in Case of Capture he will take Care to have sunk.[2] Should he arrive at any Port where Mr. Barclay is he will deliver both the Packets to him, otherwise he will send them. For that which is directed to Mr. Franklin he will procure a special Messenger in whom he can confide. Mr. Franklin will pay the Expence of the Express.

RM

MS: Ofcl LbC, DLC.

1. Wells, a Baltimore mariner, was captain and part owner of the *Nonsuch*, in which RM and Peter Whiteside also held a share. Built at Nantes under the direction of Joshua Johnson, the *Nonsuch* had been launched in 1781 and had recently returned with a profitable cargo under the direction of Wallace, Johnson, and Muir of Annapolis and Nantes. Papenfuse, *In Pursuit of Profit*, 112, 175; Hays, comp., *Calendar of Franklin Papers*, III, 432; Wallace, Johnson, and Muir to RM, May 15, and to John Swanwick, October 10, 1782.

2. The packets probably contained RM's letters to Thomas Barclay and Benjamin Franklin of October 27 and accompanying enclosures as well as RM's October 25 letters to Ferdinand Grand and the Paris and Cadiz offices of Le Couteulx and Company. Franklin acknowledged the October 27 letter in his reply of December 14, 1782.

From the Governor of Connecticut
(Jonathan Trumbull)

Hartford Octr. 25th 1782[1]

Sir,

The general Assembly of this State, which met here the 9th. of the present month, are now about to rise, expecting soon to be convened again. They have had under consideration the necessity of further grants of mony to the United States, both for the current expences of the year and providing for the interest of the domestick debt, and also the State of the taxes that have been heretofore granted.[2] Of those, tho' granted seasonably, and for sums adaquate to the purposes[3] for which they were intended, it appears that but partial payments have been made, which has induced the necessity of adopting further measures to invigorate their collection. Those measures are adopted,[4] and the Assembly have judged it most expedient and for the general good, to give them time to operate, unimbarrassed by further requisitions, until their next meeting. By which time it is expected they will have had a salutary affect and prepared the way for further grants, which the Financier may be assured it is the disposition of this State to make to the utmost of its ability, as the common safety shall require, and as may be necessary fully to support him in his views and arrangments. The Legislature of this State, and its citizens in general manifest an unabated ardour for persevering in the common defense, notwithstanding the present condition of its resources which may be more impaired than that of (several) most others, especially owing to the destruction of several of its most valuable towns, the continued defence of an extensive sea Coast and the repeated requisitions that have been made upon it by congress of mony and services more than is conceived to have been its just proportion.

The Honble. Robert Morris Esqr.

[*On verso:*]
Genl Assembly, Hartford Octr. 1782

The within Draft, for a Letter, &c being read, is approved, and ordered to be transmitted to the lower House

Test George Wyllys Secrety

Concurred in the lower house

Test S. M. Mitchell Clerk

ENDORSED: Draft of a Letter/to Mr. Morris
MSS: Dft in the writing of Oliver Ellsworth, Jonathan Trumbull Papers, Ct; copy, Connecticut General Assembly Papers, CtHi.

1. The Dft can be confidently ascribed to Oliver Ellsworth, state attorney and a member of the Connecticut Council, on the basis of a careful comparison with other texts in Ellsworth's hand generously provided to the editors by Wilda Van Dusen of The Papers of Jonathan Trumbull at Ct. Whether through his own or a copyist's error, RM in his reply of November 5 acknowledged the text received over Trumbull's signature as one of October 24, but there can be little doubt that only one letter was sent. Although Ellsworth was a delegate to Congress, he was not in attendance at this time (Burnett, ed., *Letters*, VI, xliii). The CtHi copy is endorsed "Assemblys Letter/to R. Morris/October 1782."

2. For Connecticut's previous levies in compliance with Congress's specie requisition for 1782, see notes to RM to Hezekiah Merrill, May 14, 1782.

3. This word is singular in the CtHi copy.

4. For the legislature's efforts to "invigorate" the collection of taxes in Connecticut, see Hoadly and Labaree, eds., *Public Records of Connecticut*, IV, 273, 290.

From Horatio Gates

Camp [Verplancks Point, New York] 25th: Octr: 1782

Dear Morris

I am well, and as happy as an Old Soldier can be, in a Tent the latter End of October;[1] we move in a day to Winter Quarters,[2] where I hope to get warm for once, since I arrived in Camp—upon talking with The General, I have sent for Mrs. Gates to keep me from Freezing this Winter, at, or somewhere in the Neighbourhood of New Windsor; Mrs. Washington is, I understand, upon the road. All is Secret, and uncertain in regard to The Enemy, Sir Guy[3] is so Damn'd Close, that he must be doing something He is ashamed of; for everything offensive on his part, is at an End, and things must Strangely Alter, before the power of G. Britain can revive—I verily think that is departed, never to rise again in this Hemisphere. You will help my poor Woman on her way, for I fear she will want *it'*, my respectfull Compliments to Mrs. Morris, I hope your little folks are recoverd, may ever Future Blessing be yours, and those you Love. I am your much obliged Humble Servant

Horatio Gates

P.S. Compliments to Peters,[4] and all Friends!
Honble: Robert Morris Esq.

ADDRESSED: To/The Honble:/Robert Morris Esq;/Superintendant of Finance/Philadelphia   ENDORSED: Camp 25 Octr. 1782/Genl Gates
MS: ALS, Simon Gratz Collection, PHi.

1. Major General Gates had rejoined the Continental army earlier in the month.

2. The Continental army moved to its winter cantonment at Newburgh on October 26 and 28. See Douglas Southall Freeman *et al.*, *George Washington: A Biography* (New York, 1948–1957), V, 426.

3. Sir Guy Carleton, commander in chief of the British army in America with headquarters at New York City.

4. Richard Peters, formerly of the Board of War.

From the Governor of Maryland
(Thomas Sim Lee)

In Col. [Council] Anns. [Annapolis] 25 Octr. 1782

Sir,

Without having the smallest desire of advancing any money for the Army on Account of the United States, we frequently find ourselves under the necessity of doing it, to our no small mortification.[1]

Some Months before the recruits raised in the State the present year received marching orders, an officer was sent to Phila. for the express purpose of procuring Clothing for them, yet when they were about to march they wanted several very essential articles, without which indeed, they could not proceed, particularly Shoes. We were reduced to the alternative of furnishing them, or letting the Troops remain in the State, we chose the former, as the lesser Evil.[2] ⟨It is expected that there will be⟩ There are now about 70 more recruits ⟨to March in three weeks⟩ ⟨collected at this place⟩ in the State ⟨they will be⟩ who are almost naked, and unless Clothing can be sent to this place or the head of Elk for them, we shall be obliged to supply ⟨them with⟩ such things as ⟨they⟩ cannot ⟨March without⟩ be done without. We mention this to shew you, that however essential it ⟨may be⟩ is that the regulations adopted by Congress be strictly adhered to, yet from the nature of things, they must be broke through in some instances, unless some other mode than we know of, for supplying Troops at a distance, be adopted at Phila. We have written to the Secy at War,[3] on the subject of the Clothing wanted.

Permit us to inform you, that the Legisture of Maryland, meets the 4th. of next Month. ⟨The earlier therefore⟩

ENDORSED: 25th Oct. 1782/Robr. Morris Eq/1291/Entered

MSS: ADft, Executive Papers, MdAA; LbC, Council Letterbook, MdAA.

1. Governor Lee refers to the state's desire to comply with the act of Congress of October 1 which RM had enclosed to the governors in a circular of October 5. See RM's Report to Congress on the Representation of the New Jersey Legislature, September 27, and notes.

2. See the Governor of Maryland to RM, October 1.

3. The letter to Benjamin Lincoln, dated October 25, is in *Maryland Archives*, XLVIII, 292–293.

To Pierre Douville

Marine Office 25 October 1782

I have received your Favor of the thirtieth of September which has been long on the Way.[1] There is to be a Commissioner appointed for settling all the marine Accounts up to the last day of the Year 1781. Your Demands will naturally fall within the Purvieu of his Authority.

MS: AM LbC, MdAN.

1. Douville's letter has not been found, but evidently related to claims against the United States derived from his earlier service in the Continental navy. See notes to Marquis de Vaudreuil to RM, October 3.

To Ferdinand Grand

Office of Finance 25. Octo: 1782[1]

My last Letter to you was of the seventh Instant per the Ship Washington Captain Barney enclosing a List of Bills of Exchange drawn on you No. 362 to 389 inclusive making twenty eight Setts and amounting to one hundred and eighty four thousand nine hundred and forty Livres Tournois.

Herewith you will receive a further List of Bills of Exchange drawn on you No. 390 to 429 inclusive[2]—making forty Setts and amounting to four hundred and five thousand five hundred and ten Livres eight Sous Tournois. These as well as my former Bills you will be pleased to Honor and punctually pay on Account of the United States of North America.

MS: Ofcl LbC, DLC.

1. Grand was banker to the United States at Paris.
2. Enclosure not found.

To Joseph Kendall

Marine Office 25. October 1782[1]

Sir

I have received your Letter dated at Boston on the tenth Instant annexed to a Copy of one dated on the 12. of September last the original whereof has not been received. My Opinion as to your Claim against Captain Barry for Services rendered on Board the Frigate Alliance is the same as when I wrote you having had no Evidence before me which should induce an Alteration in it. If Mr. Lovell said any Thing which might place the Matter in a different Light from that in which it appeared by your Letter of the first of April it must have been in Consequence of some Conversation which I do not recollect, and therefore cannot now, give any Direction or Opinion different from what is contained in my Letter to you of the 10th. of April last. I have no Objection to your going to France if it suits you and enclose a Leave of Absence[2] which you may use but you will recollect that no Officer of the Navy is entitled to pay from the United States when not in actual Service. The Proposition for exchanging your Warrant is what is is not in my Power to comply with.

MS: AM LbC, MdAN.

1. Kendall was a former surgeon on the *Alliance*. None of the letters RM received from him have been found. For the antecedents to this letter, see RM to Kendall, April 10, 1782, and notes.
2. Enclosure not found.

To Jacques, Louis and Laurent Le Couteulx and Company

Office of Finance 25. Octo: 1782[1]

Since writing to you on the twenty fourth of September I have proceeded in Execution of the Plan therein mentioned to appoint Mr. John Brown for the Purpose of drawing the Bills therein mentioned upon you. His Signature is enclosed and he shall be instructed to send by various Opportunities exact Lists of such Bills as he may draw enclosed in proper Letters of Advice. I expect they will be duly honored.

MSS: Ofcl LbC, DLC; copy, PCC, DNA.
1. The addressee was the Cadiz branch of Le Couteulx and Company of Paris. The recipient's copy was enclosed in a letter of this date to the Paris firm; the PCC text was enclosed in RM to Theodorick Bland, Jr., April 16, 1783 (first letter).

From Daniel De Saussure

Extract of a Letter from D. De Saussure Dated at Annapolis the 25th October 1782.[1]

Soon after my arrival here, I applied to the Intendant, for this States Accounts against the United States he informed me none were made out; a few Days after, I wrote to his Excellency the Governor, and informed him I was ready and Requested that he would be pleased to give the necessary orders.[2] Copy of my Letter (I have been told) was sent to the Intendant,[3] notwithstanding he has not yet order'd the Accounts to be made out.

MS: Extract, Maryland State Papers, Red Books, MdAA.
1. De Saussure was the commissioner for settling the accounts of Maryland with the United States. This extract was enclosed in RM's Circular to the Governor and Intendant of Maryland, November 30, 1782.
2. De Saussure's letter to Governor Thomas Sim Lee of August 20, 1782 (*Calendar of Maryland State Papers*, no. 3, The Brown Books, p. 117), advised that all charges had to be supported by vouchers, that doubtful cases would be referred to RM, and that "if the first years' account can be delivd me, I shall be doing something."
3. See the Maryland Council to Daniel of St. Thomas Jenifer, the state intendant of the revenue, August 21, 1782, *Maryland Archives*, XLVIII, 239.

Diary: October 26, 1782

Mr. Fitzsimmons Called this morning and had a long Conference respecting the Ship Duke De Lauzern, respecting the Bank &c.[1]

Mr. Nourse respecting the Public accounts and I was all this Day employed on the Accounts &c.[2]

Issued a Warrant on Mr Swanwick in favor the Bank £21.0.9.

1. Thomas Fitzsimons, a Philadelphia merchant and a director of the Bank of North America, was outfitting the newly acquired *Duc de Lauzun*.
2. See Diary, October 25, and notes.

From Alexander Hamilton

[Albany, New York, October 26, 1782]

Sir

I am honored with your letters of the 5th., 15th and 16th instant.[1]

The detail you have been pleased to enter into in that of the 5th. exhibits very cogent reasons for confining yourself to pretty large denominations of notes. Some of them had occurred to me; others had not; but I thought it my Duty to state to you the operations which that circumstance had, as in the midst of the variety and extent of the objects, which occupy your attention you may not have so good opportunities of se[cing][2] the effect of your plans in detail. While I acknowlege that your observations have corrected my ideas upon the subject and showed me that there would be danger in generally lessening the denominations of the [paper iss]ued I should be uncandid not to add that it still appears to me, there would be a preponderance of advantages in having a *part* of a smaller amount. I shall not trouble you at present with any further reasons for this opinion.

I have immediately on the receipt of your [letter] taken measures for the publication of your adver[tisement] in the newspapers of this state.

You will perceive by the inclosed account, that since my last, I have received five and twenty hundred dollars.[3] This was procured in part of the loan I mentioned to you.[4] It was chiefly paid to me in specie and I have exchanged it with Colo. Pickering and Mr. Duer for your notes; the latter had twelve hundred dollars. Taxes coll[ect] slowly, but I must shortly receive two or three hundred pounds more, of which Mr. Duer will have the principal benefit, as it appears by your letter to him,[5] that you hoped he might receive three thousand Dollars from me.

As I may shortly set out for Philadelphia I wish to surrender to Mr. Tillot[son] as soon as you think proper the office in which he is to succeed.[6] I have the honor to be with sincere respect and esteem Sir Your Most Obedient Servent

Alx Hamilton

Albany October 26 1782

ENDORSED: To the Superintendant of Finance/October 26. 1782
MSS: Copy, Hamilton Papers, DLC; transcript, Francis Baylies Papers, DLC.

1. The letter of October 15 was a circular to the receivers of Continental taxes enclosing RM's advertisement of October 10 for the 1783 contracts. Hamilton was the receiver for New York.

2. In supplying the bracketed words here and below the editors have been guided by Syrett and Cooke, eds., *Hamilton Papers*, III, 190–191.

3. Hamilton's last letter, of October 12, has not been found (see RM to Hamilton, October 23, and notes). The enclosed account has not been found but is listed in PCC, no. 137, III, 361; for his receipt to the state treasurer, see Syrett and Cooke, eds., *Hamilton Papers*, III, 191n.

4. On the loan, which was evidently discussed in one of Hamilton's missing letters to RM, see notes to Hamilton to RM, July 22.

5. See RM to William Duer, October 2.

6. The New York legislature had appointed Hamilton a delegate to Congress on

June 22; his commission was issued October 25. Hamilton surrendered the receivership to Thomas Tillotson on November 10, but did not take his seat in Congress until November 25. See notes to RM to Hamilton, August 28.

From William Churchill Houston

Trenton [New Jersey] 26 Octr. 1782[1]

Sir

Though I have not received any Money during the past week, yet I have Reason to believe the Collection of the Taxes is in some Progress. I have given the Collectours Directions to receive Bank Notes and your Bills drawn on Mr Swanwick in Payments, and when they have Specie in Hand to ⟨buy them⟩ exchange it for them, which will, I hope forward the publick Service essentially. My most earnest Exhortations to the Collectours are not wanting, and I have some Reason to believe they will ⟨have⟩ ⟨not be without their⟩ not be wholly unsuccessful.

I have often intended to take the Liberty of mentioning to you a Point of Economy which might produce some Saving; but have been informed the Reform was under the Consideration of Congress. It is in the ⟨Arrangement of the⟩ Quarter-Master-General's Department, which I take it for granted is continued under the System of 15 July 1780.[2] Since the Supply of the Army was put upon Contract the Deputy-Quarter-Masters in each State, with their Subordinates must have very little to do; yet I have understood they are continued on the expensive appointments allowed them under that arrangement. ⟨I well⟩ If I rightly recollect that these Salaries and Wages were fixed not without Respect to Paper Currency and Depreciation; and are now greatly disproportionate to the Duties which remain. Indeed it should seem that many Parts of that Arrangement might be altogether discontinued under the present Modes and Circumstances of carrying on the publick Business.[3]

Our Legislature is now sitting, having entered on Business a few Days ago. I am &c.

Robt. Morris Esqr

ENDORSED: Letter to Robert Morris/Esqr Superintendant &c/26 Octr 1782/no return
MS: ADft, Houston Collection, NjP.

1. Houston was the receiver of Continental taxes for New Jersey.
2. See *JCC*, XVII, 615–635; the system was adopted when Houston was a delegate from New Jersey. For the reduction of the Quartermaster Department voted by Congress on October 23 and 29, 1782, see notes to Diary, April 27, 1782; for earlier cuts imposed, see the Quartermaster General to RM, February 19, 1782, and notes.
3. That RM did not allude to this paragraph in his reply of October 29 suggests that Houston may have omitted it in the recipient's copy.

To Thomas Barclay

Office of Finance 27. Octo: 1782

Sir,

I do myself the Honor to enclose the Copy of an Extract from the Invoice of Goods which the State of Virginia made Application for to the Court of France thro their Minister here.[1] I have agreed to take these Things on Account of the United States and therefore you will be pleased to have them shipped in such Manner as you may find most convenient and safe. I am Sir your most obedient and humble Servant[2]

RM

MS: Ofcl LbC, DLC.

1. The extract is printed as the enclosure to RM to the President of Congress, October 9. Barclay was the American consul general in France.

2. The missive was sent by the same conveyances as the following letter to Benjamin Franklin.

To Benjamin Franklin

1st.[1]   Office of Finance 27th October 1782

Sir

I do myself the Honor to enclose the Copy of a Paper transmitted to me by the Governor of Virginia.[2] The Cloathing there mentioned is a Part of those Supplies for the State of Virginia which the Court of France have charged to the United States. You will recollect the Discussions on this Subject.[3] It is with a sincere Desire to remove every disagreeable Trace of them that I have agreed to a Proposition made me by the Governor of Virginia in his Letter dated in Council Chamber the twenty third of September last of which the following is an Extract.

"The Regulations you have entered into for Cloathing the continental Army will render useless to the State a quantity of Necessaries now in France furnished by his most Christian Majesty, as the Terms we have them on (which I have before transmitted to you) are such as will make the Payment easy to the United States we shall be obliged to you to take them off our Hands, and take the Debt so far as they go on the States. You have a Copy of the Invoice inclosed by which you will see that they will be useful and necessary for the Army which will I hope induce you to oblige the State." The Enclosure referred to is that above mentioned.

I make no Doubt that the Court will chuse to consider the whole of these Supplies as advanced on the Credit of the United States, and therefore there is so much the less Objection to taking a Part of the Goods. As for the Remainder I think it better for Congress to adjust the Matter with Virginia than to plague the Kings Ministers with altercations about it. I am Sir Your most obedient and humble Servant

Robt Morris

His Excellency Benjamin Franklin Esquire

ENDORSED: Office of Finance/Oct. 27. 1782/Proposition from Virgi/nia, to take Cloathing
MSS: LS, Ferdinand J. Dreer Collection, PHi; LS, Franklin Papers, PPAmP; LS marked "2d.," Franklin Papers, CtY; Ofcl LbC, DLC.
1. This dispatch probably was carried by Captain Charles Wells of the *Nonsuch;* the triplicate may have gone by the French fleet at Boston. See RM's Instructions to Wells, October 25, and Diary, October 28.
2. RM refers to the enclosure transmitted in his letter to the president of Congress of October 9.
3. The reference is to the exchange of letters between RM and Chevalier de La Luzerne, the French minister at Philadelphia, on November 24 and 26, 1781. RM had enclosed them in his first letter to Franklin of November 27, 1781.

From William Whipple

Portsmouth [New Hampshire] Octor 27th 1782[1]

Sir

Your Circular Letter of the 5th Instant with its inclosures I had the Honor of receiving the 25th: I have long seen the evils you mention and have endeavor'd to prevent the effects of them, but I fear they never will be cured till the Idea of raising a revenue on specific articles is entirely erradicated. That is a principal Cause of the backwardness here, and will have that effect till the measure is changed, of which, I am sorry to say there is no immediate prospect. A considerable Quantity of Beef has been sent to the Army from this State and more going the whole proceeds of which I have the promise of, but I cannot ascertain the Amount.

I shall set out for Trenton the 30th instant and shall leave the Business in the hands of Mr: Joseph Whipple[2] as I informed you the 28th: Sepr: unless you should order otherwise. I hope to have the pleasure of waiting on you in Philadelphia some time in Novr:. I have the Honor to be with the Greatest Respect Sir &c

W.W.

Honble Robt: Morris Esq

MS: LbC, Whipple Letterbook, John Langdon Papers, PHi.
1. Whipple was receiver of Continental taxes for New Hampshire.
2. Joseph Whipple (1738–1816), brother of William Whipple, was a Portsmouth merchant and owner of a large plantation in Dartmouth, New Hampshire, who served in the state legislature in 1776–1778 and 1782–1783. Appointed collector of

customs for the port of Portsmouth in 1789, he served until 1798 when he was removed for anti-Federalist political activity. As an outspoken Republican, he was reappointed in 1801 after the election of Thomas Jefferson, and served until his death. See Levi W. Dodge, "Colonel Joseph Whipple and His Dartmouth Plantation," *The Granite Monthly,* XV (1893), 20–31. The editors wish to thank William Copely, Associate Librarian, NhHi, for supplying this source.

George Plater to Gouverneur Morris

[Sotterley near Leonardtown, Maryland, October 27, 1782]

Dear Morris

On my Return home the other Day from the western Part of our State, where I had been on Business, and which has been the Reason why you have not heard from me lately, your agreable Favors of 25th last and 2d of the present Month were put into my Hands,[1] for which be pleased to accept my sincere Thanks. Your Observation that the States have not done their Duty with respect to the War, so as to have brought about a speedier Peace, is very just, but whether they can be persuaded to do more I doubt. Trade and an Expectation of Peace, without taking the proper Steps to procure it, seem to have pervaded the Hearts of allmost all Men. However if we cannot have Matters as we cou'd wish, we must put up with them as they are. [Our fretting?], my Friend, will answer no good Purpose. People will follow the Dictates of their wild Imaginations tho' the Apostle Paul was here preaching against them. I do not believe there is more Virtue in America than elsewhere, if so much—but this is a theme that neither you nor I like to dwell on, therefore for the present I will pass it over. Mrs. P intended to write under Cover of this, but she has heard that a Sloop and Barge are in the River and a Ship at the Mouth, which has a little discomposed her, and no Wonder. Our best Wishes ever await you, and I am Yours most sincerely

Geo: Plater

Sotterley, Oct. 27th 1782

ADDRESSED: Honble Mr. Gouverneur Morris/Philadelphia   ENDORSED: 27 Octr. 1782/ Mr. Plater
MS: ALS, Gouverneur Morris Papers, NNC.
1. Gouverneur Morris's letters have not been found. Plater, a former delegate to Congress, was president of the Maryland Senate.

Diary: October 28, 1782

Geo. Gray Esquire applied for an Order in favor of Curtis Grub Esqr. to liberate Hessians by which I signed to the Amount of the Debt due to him.[1]

Mr. Jno. McAllister wrote and applied Personally for information respecting Contracts.[2]

Colo. Miles applied to know if I would Order the Sale of the public Plantation at french Creek[3] but as a magazine of Powder is there I choose to Consult Genl. Lincoln on the Subject before any Determination is taken.

Lieut Dowler Applies again for money for Colo. Pickering.

Honble. Mr Holker applies for Money on Account Wm. Duer & Co.;[4] ordered Mr Swanwick to pay it.

Oliver Pollock Esqr. for Letters to Virginia and for Money.[5]

Honble. Doctor Witherspoon to Consult relative to Rhode Island not passing the Impost.[6]

Lewis R. Morris to take leave and for Dispatches to Camp: NB. Sent by him the Triplicate Dispatches for France.[7]

Honble. Mr Osgood respecting the Clothier General's Department. I advised that Congress do not meddle with it at present as I think it will be unecessary.[8]

Jno. Pierce Esqr Paymaster General returned from Camp and informs me of many Complaints amongst the Officers of the Army. I beleive money (if we had enough to pay them) would remove all Complaints.[9]

Mr. Geo. Eddy for News from Mr Clarke[10] but I had no Letters from that Gentleman last Post. Mr Eddy gave me his note at 60 Days for 5,000 Dollars; delivered it to Mr Swanwick to be Discounted.

Wrote a Letter to Alexr. Hamilton Esqr.

Wrote a Letter to his Excellency the Govr. of Connecticut.

Wrote a Letter to Geo. Webb Esqr.

Wrote a Letter to Geo: Olney.

Issued a Warrant on Mr Swanwick in favor Samuel Miles £58.7.4.

1. See Diary, July 5, 1782, and notes.

2. Undoubtedly with reference to RM's advertisement of October 10 for the 1783 contracts.

3. See notes to Mathias Slough to RM, August 30, 1781.

4. John Holker was a partner in William Duer and Company, holder of the Northern Department contract.

5. See RM to the Governor of Virginia, October 29.

6. John Witherspoon of New Jersey was a member of the grand committee of Congress considering ways of supporting the public credit; he appears to have played a role in drafting a report of the committee, adopted by Congress on October 10, calling upon Rhode Island for a categorical answer with regard to the ratification of the impost. See *JCC*, XXII, 407–408, XXIII, 642–643n.; and RM to the Governors of Rhode Island and Georgia, October 17, and notes.

7. Lewis R. Morris of New York, Gouverneur Morris's nephew, was an undersecretary in the Department of Foreign Affairs. The dispatches he carried—very likely those identified in notes to RM's instructions to Charles Wells of October 25—were probably sent via a chain of expresses established between Continental army headquarters and the French fleet at Boston. See George Washington to RM, October 18, and notes.

8. Samuel Osgood of Massachusetts was chairman of a committee of Congress considering ways of reducing expenditures in various departments. The committee, which had been referred a missing letter from Clothier General John Moylan of April

10, 1782, reported to Congress on November 18 that the Superintendent was taking measures to abolish the Clothing Department, whereupon Congress discharged the committee from that assignment and referred Moylan's letter and the question of continuing the department to RM for report. The Superintendent did not make a special report on the subject, but he took up questions relating to clothing in letters to Congress of September 18 and October 10, 1783, proposing in the latter that clothing be supplied by contract rather than by a Clothing Department. For the Osgood committee, which had formerly been chaired by Ezekiel Cornell, who left Congress in September to take up duties as inspector of contracts, see notes to Diary, April 27, and to RM to the President of Congress, July 30, 1782.

9. Regarding complaints of the army at this time, see George Washington to RM, October 2, and notes.

10. Daniel Clark, RM's agent for purchasing tobacco in Virginia.

To Alexander Hamilton

Office of Finance 28th October 1782

Sir,

I have received your Favor dated at Albany on the 19th Instant with the Enclosures.[1] What you say of your Prospect with Respect to the Receipt of Money for Taxes, is as you may easily suppose very unpleasing. I hope it will soon assume a different Appearance. Unless Something more be done by the States, many very dangerous as well as disagreable Consequences are to be apprehended. With Sincere Esteem I am Sir Your most obedient Servant

Robt Morris

Alexander Hamilton Esquire
Receiver for the State of New York

ENDORSED: 28 Oct 1782/Robert Morris
MSS: LS, Hamilton Papers, DLC; Ofcl LbC, DLC; transcript, Francis Baylies Papers, DLC.

1. Letter and enclosures not found.

To George Webb

Office of Finance 28 Octo: 1782

Sir,

I have been favored with your Letter dated at Richmond on the eighteenth Instant.[1] And am happy to find that you approve of the Principles and Reasoning contained in my Letter to Congress of the twenty ninth day of July.[2] My own perfect Conviction of the Solidity of the Principles I attempted there to establish gives me an earnest Desire to see correspondent Measures carried into Execution.

As the Negligence of Rhode Island in delaying to grant the Impost required some time ago has prevented Congress from making farther Requisitions your Legislature will not be I imagine in a Situation to make any particular Exertion for the support of public Credit farther than by squaring their Impost Law exactly to the Requisition on which it was founded.[3] It might also be well to pledge the Faith of the State in general Terms that they will grant the necessary Revenues when required. And if in addition to this your Delegates in Congress were Instructed to urge Requisitions for the Purpose it might have a good Effect, both by accelerating the Progress of the Business and removing Obstructions.

As the generality of Mankind are much more influenced by Objects which from the Vicinity of their Situation are likely to affect their Feelings, than by those of equal or greater Magnitude when more remote, Good Arguments might be drawn from the great Amount of Debts due the People of Virginia for Articles taken from them for support of the War. The Consideration also that a Land Tax must chiefly affect great Landholders may have its Influence over the democratic Interest of your Commonwealth. How far this is the Case you will be able to judge from what passes during the Session. Funding the Public Debts is certainly an Object equally prompted by Justice and Policy. The Probability that the War may continue yet a long Time and at a heavy Expence is (among the many others) a very solid Reason why the Establishment of public Credit should be most industriously pursued; for until that be effected we cannot be truly Independent either in War or Peace. I am Sir your most obedient and humble Servant

RM

MS: Ofcl LbC, DLC.

1. Letter not found. Webb was the receiver of Continental taxes for Virginia.

2. The letter had called for the establishment of domestic public credit and had renewed RM's earlier request for land, poll, and excise taxes to pay the interest on the public debt. RM had enclosed it in his circular to the receivers of September 12.

3. On Virginia's act, which the state suspended in January 1782, see the headnote to RM's Circular to the Governors of Massachusetts, Rhode Island, New York, Delaware, Maryland, and North Carolina, July 27, 1781, and notes, and RM to the President of Congress, February 11, 1782, and notes. Virginia ultimately repealed its act of ratification in December 1782. See Main, *Antifederalists,* 74 and n., 92–93.

To the Governor of Connecticut
(Jonathan Trumbull)

Office of Finance 28th. Octobr. 1782[1]

The Letter which your Excellency did me the Honor to write on the 19th Instant has been received.[2] I have the Pleasure to inform you that I expect Mr. Smith will soon enter on the business for which he has been appointed; his Instructions and other matters relative thereto being already expedited from this office.[3] They will I trust be speedily received by him in which Case he can immediately begin the Business entrusted to him.

MSS: LS, Trumbull Papers, Ct; Ofcl LbC, DLC.

1. The endorsement on this letter indicates that it was received on November 12.

2. Governor Trumbull's letter has not been found but evidently inquired as to when Melancton Smith, the commissioner for settling Connecticut's accounts with the United States, would begin work. See Diary, September 19, and notes.

3. See Instructions of the Comptroller of the Treasury to the Commissioners of Accounts for the States, October 14, and notes.

To George Olney

Office of Finance 28. Octo: 1782

I am favored with your Letter dated at Providence on the fourteenth Instant.[1] I hope your Receipts will be so increased as to enable you to make a considerable Remittance by Mr Brown on his return hither.

MS: Ofcl LbC, DLC.

1. Letter not found. Olney was the receiver of Continental taxes for Rhode Island.

Diary: October 29, 1782

The Honble. Mr. Hemsley[1] called to offer me Money for a Draft that will pass in payment to the Treasury of Maryland to which I assented.

Oliver Pollock Esqr. applies very pressingly for Money on Account of his Claims alledging that he cannot go to Virginia to procure the Settlement of his Accounts with that State so as to enable a final Settlement with the United States unless I pay him a small part of his Demand.[2]

Jno. Pierce Esqr. applies for Money for himself and the Subsistence of various Officers &c.

Mr. Jno. McAllister for an Answer to his Enquiries respecting the Contracts which I gave to his Satisfaction.

Colo. Gurney and Colo. Patton for Money on Account of the Ship Washington &c.

Monsr. Savery applies frequently for the Bills drawn by Penet Da Costa & Co. which were delivered up to me on Settlement of the Accounts. I finally desired Mr. Pennell[3] to inform him that those Bills are Vouchers to the Account Settled and cannot be given up.

Mr. T. Fitzsimmons called on the Business of the Ship Duke De Lauzun and afterwards proposed to purchase 20,000 Livres Tournois in Bills to pay 1600 Dollars down and the Remainder in a short Time.

Robt. L. Hooper Esqr.[4] applied respecting Interest due him on Loan Office Certificates. I desired him to state the matter to me in Writing.

Mr. James Johnston brought a List of Germans going with Commodore Gillon and the Draft of a Bond for their Liberation Money, which not being properly drawn we agreed to Draft one in this Office.[5]

Wrote a Letter to Willm. Churchill Houston Esqr.
Wrote a Letter to his Excellency the Governor of Virginia.

1. William Hemsley, a member of Congress from Maryland.
2. For the background, see RM to James Duane, October 11, and notes.
3. Joseph Pennell, who was settling the accounts of the Secret and Commercial Committees of Congress.
4. Almost certainly Robert Lettis Hooper, Jr. (1730–1797), of Pennsylvania and New Jersey, son of Robert Lettis Hooper II (1708–1785) of New Jersey. Surveyor, landowner, merchant, proprietor of ironworks in Ringwood, New Jersey, and a former deputy quartermaster general, Hooper had subscribed £5,000 to the Bank of Pennsylvania in 1780 and chaired a meeting held in Trenton in July 1782 to tighten restrictions against illicit trade with the British in New York. He was vice-president of the New Jersey Council, 1785–1788. See Charles Henry Hart, "Colonel Robert Lettis Hooper, Deputy Quartermaster General of the Continental Army and Vice President of New Jersey," *PMHB*, XXXVI (1912), 60–91.
5. Neither the list nor the bonds have been found. For the background, see RM to Alexander Gillon, October 8, and notes.

To William Churchill Houston

Office of Finance 29th. Octobr. 1782

Sir,

I have received your Favor of the twenty Sixth Instant. Enclosed you have the Extract of a Letter which was written to Mr. Olney the Receiver of Rhode Island on the first of June last. If you can carry into Execution the views expressed in that Letter I shall be very glad. It is my Wish to obviate the fraudulent Practices which prevail in the Collection of Taxes. The exact List of weekly Receipts might be filed with the Clerk of each County Weekly. Transcripts of them might be furnished to you by every convenient opportunity. Your Publications of Receipts from the Collector[1] would stimulate Curiosity and besides that, when Persons of Influence in the Counties have paid it would be well to hint to them an Enquiry why others have not paid. If it should appear that Persons who have paid are not on the List the Collector should be punished. If otherwise the Enquiries and Clamors of those who have paid would stimulate and aid the Collectors in doing their Duty. Such Men of Influence as do not pay might on the other Hand be urged by the apprehension of loosing that Influence from the Report of their non Payment. Public opinion is always an useful Reinforcement to the operation of Laws. It goes farther. Thus in the Case before us altho in the first Moment men will not consent to very severe Laws for enforcing a Collection or if such Laws were passed would very reluctantly consent to the Execution of them yet when a part of the Community have paid punctually they feel a Degree of Resentment existed against the negligent and unwilling. Those half Tories who want to be considered as Whigs will not suffer the Public to know that they do not pay Taxes and in a very little time they feel that very Payment interesting them to make others pay. Thus the Cords of Government get wound up by Degrees to their proper Tone. And what is of infinite Importance Morals and Laws march with an equal Pace towards the same object of public Utility. I am Sir, your most obedient and humble Servant

Robt Morris

Wm. Churchill Houston Esqr.
Receiver for New Jersey
Trenton

ENDORSED: 29 Octr. 1782 Answered
MSS: LS, Houston Collection, NjP; Ofcl LbC, DLC.
1. This proposal and the suggestions contained in RM's June 1 letter to George Olney went beyond the monthly publication of receipts RM required of the receivers of Continental taxes. See notes to RM to William Whipple, June 4, 1782.

To the Governor of Virginia (Benjamin Harrison)

Office of Finance 29. Octo. 1782

Sir,

It becomes my Duty to transmit to your Excellency the enclosed Copy of an Act of the twenty second Instant, and to pray that the Settlement of Mr. Pollocks Accounts with your State may be facilitated in Order that those with the United States may be adjusted.[1] The Act is couched in such favorable Terms that it might be unnecessary to say any Thing personally relating to that Gentleman. But the many Reasons I have to entertain the most favorable Opinion of him would convert my Silence into Injustice. I feel it my Duty to assure your Excellency that a variety of Evidence has concurred to convince me that Mr. Polluck with much Abilities to serve his Country has joined unwearied Industry to disinterested Zeal. I must add also that he has been essentially useful in those Moments when our extreme Distress gave double Value to every Office of Friendship. With perfect Respect I have the honor to be Sir your Excellency's most obedient and humble Servant

RM

MSS: Ofcl LbC, DLC; copy, Executive Communications, Vi; copy, Miscellaneous Papers of the Continental Congress, 1774–1789 (Microcopy 332, roll 9, f. 317), RG 360, DNA; copy, Miscellaneous Letters (Letters Received), January–March 1791, Records of the Department of State, RG 59, DNA; copy, filed with petitions of Oliver Pollock, Committee on Claims, Records of the United States House of Representatives, RG 233, DNA.
1. On the act of Congress of October 22 and the settlement of Oliver Pollock's accounts as former commercial agent at New Orleans, see RM to James Duane, October 11, and notes. Despite RM's previous private letter of January 15, 1782, to Governor Harrison on behalf of Pollock, suspicions about him prevailed in Virginia. See Diary, September 27, and notes.

Robert Morris and Jacob Morris to
Edmund Randolph

Philada. Octr 29th. 1782[1]

We are honoured with the receipt of your Letter of the 18th[2] and are much obliged by the alacrity with which You agree to comply with our request respecting Genl. Lees affairs. We have seen since the date of our former letter to you, the Copy of a Will said to have been made by him at Fredk Town on his way up here, by which he appointed Alexr White Esqr. and   his Executors.[3] As this Will must be proved and we have no exception to those Gentlemen it will not be necessary to give you farther trouble on the matter. You will be kind enough to draw upon us for any expence or charge you think proper to make on this occasion and the bill shall be punctually paid by Sir Your most Obedient and humble Servants

MS: Dft in RM's writing, Robert Morris Papers, NN.
1. This unsigned letter to Randolph, the attorney general of Virginia, was addressed to him at Richmond. For the authors, see their earlier letter to Randolph of October 7.
2. Letter not found.
3. The foregoing space was left blank in manuscript; the other executor was Charles Minn Thurston. See Charles Lee's will as printed in *Lee Papers*, IV, 29–33.

The Secretary at War (Benjamin Lincoln)
to John Swanwick

War Office Oct. 29. 1782

Please to pay unto Cæsar Lloyd the Sum of fifty Dollars on account of the Warrant in my favour remaining in your hands.[1]

MS: LS, Lincoln Papers, MHi.
1. Lloyd's receipt of October 30, signed with his mark and witnessed by James Cottringer, appears on the verso of the manuscript. Swanwick was RM's cashier in the Office of Finance.

Diary: October 30, 1782

Jno. Pierce Esqr. with Letters and Applications for Money.

Mr. James Johnston applying on Como Gillons business. I gave him back his Papers and Draft of a Bond.[1]

Henry Hill Esqr. called this Day and told me he will pay 5,000 Dollars on Account of Bills of Exchange altho he has not yet received the Funds that ought to be applied to that Use.[2]

Honble. Mr. Clymer called respecting the Application of the Issuing Commissaries.[3] I furnished him with a return of their Numbers.

His Excelly. the Minister of France[4] called partly for news and on some little matters of Business.

Oliver Pollock Esquire for money.

Colo. Ephm. Blaine called respecting the Advertizements for new Contracts[5] on which I gave him the best Advice in my Power and he promised to continue the needful Supplies to the Garrison of Fort Pitt until the new Contract is made.

Honble. Secretary at War being returned from Camp did me the Honor to Call and we had a long Conference respecting the Complaints of the Army &c.[6]

Issued a Warrant on Mr Swanwick in favor John Pierce £75.0.0.

1. See Diary, October 29.
2. See Diary, April 17, 1782, and notes.
3. George Clymer of Pennsylvania was chairman of a committee considering RM's letter to the President of Congress of October 23 and the enclosed memorial of the issuing commissaries.
4. Chevalier de La Luzerne.
5. Dated October 10.
6. See notes to George Washington to RM, October 2.

John de Neufville and Company to John Swanwick

[Amsterdam] 30 Oct 1782[1]

We are honoured lately by the Honble. Robert Morris Esqr. letter of the 25 of March Last, and with your esteemed of the 27 June.[2] The charge said gentleman has taken on himself by the important office he now is in we are sensible leaves him no time for corresponding on subjects that are foreign to it. Thus we shall not intrude on a time so much more precious to his country than his friends. May he receive from it the reward his great abilities merit, tho' should it fail him we are persuaded he will have those which an honest man most values the aprobation of his own heart Ever attending the consciousness of having done ones duty. We beg you will present him our best respects and assure him that we entertain a proper Sence of his friendly expressions towards us and be pleased to accept our Sincere thanks for your very polite letters assuring you that we shall be happy for opportunities of testifying our sentiments to both. We can impart no news but what you will already have been inform'd of with respect to the state of politicks in Europe. Those of this Country seem to take a turn as the influence of the court declines which is now low indeed tho' not so much as we hope shortly to see it, different opinions will be probably entertain'd of it in America, than the erroneous ones that have been formed of it. May every measure adopted be for the advantage of both republicks. 'Tis the sincere wish of allies who are with the greatest esteem and regard

MS: LbC, John de Neufville Papers, NHi.
1. De Neufville and Company was a Dutch firm and mercantile correspondent of RM's. Marginal notes in the company's letterbook indicate that this letter was sent by the *Hero*.
2. Neither letter has been found. RM had probably advised that he had placed most of his private business in the hands of John Swanwick.

From Samuel Hodgdon

[Philadelphia] Ordnance Office 30 Octr 1782

Messrs: Udree & Co. having applied for like indulgence with other Iron Masters relative to German Prisoners I take the liberty to inclose their accounts agreeable to your direction in similar cases.[1] If convenient should be glad to have the necessary document to day as Mr. Udree waits in town untill it is obtain'd.

MS: LbC, WDC, DNA.

1. The enclosed accounts have not been found. For the background, see Diary, October 15, and notes. Hodgdon was the commissary general of military stores.

Diary: October 31, 1782

Oliver Pollock Esqr. applied for money but I had this Day engaged in settling the public Accounts for 1781 in Order to lay it before Congess[1] and gave Orders not to be interrupted unless absolutely necessary, therefore Mr Pollock was desired to wait until to Morrow.

Mr. Fitzsimmons, Mr. Bingham and Mr Nesbit brought a State of the Bank and desired a Conference respecting the Election of new Directors which took up some time.[2]

1. See, on these accounts, notes to Diary, June 12, 1782.
2. The document brought by these three directors of the Bank of North America has not been found. On the election, see Diary, November 4, 1782.

From George Washington

Head Quarters [Newburgh, New York] 31st October 1782

Dear Sir

As the Contracts for the ensuing Year will shortly be made,[1] I take the liberty of suggesting several matters which appear to me necessary either to be inserted in the Body of the Contracts themselves, or to be provided for by special stipulations with the Contractors.

Under the former arrangement, If the Contractors made an offer of provisions which should be deemed entirely bad or not of so good a quality as they ought to be, there was a right of rejection, and of purchase in the neighbourhood of the Army. The following inconvenience will ever attend this mode. ⟨If⟩ Tho' the provision should be found ⟨absolutely bad it must⟩ of inferior Quality yet rather than let the troops go without, it will be received and Vouchers passed for it, as good, for the Inspector will find it impossible to purchase, at a moments warning, the supplies of one or two days. And the Contractor, if he is a designing Man, (and such we have had to deal with)[2] will find it to his advantage to keep on hand Articles of inferior price and Quality[3] finding he can get them off at full price. This I conceive may be remedied in the following Manner. The Inspector, upon Complaint, to be the Judge of Quality. If he finds the provision not unwholesome, he may order it to be issued, but at under price, the deficiency either to be made up by giving a due Bill for it, or an addition in some other Article. This would make it the interest of the Contractor to keep a supply of good and wholesome Articles.

In the Contract for Garrisons a certain quantity of salt provision is specified, but in that for the moving Army, it is optional in the Contractor to furnish it or not. There are many ocassions upon which salt provisions are most essentially necessary. An opportunity of striking a post might present itself, if a Body of Men could march suddenly with three or four days provision. Salt Meat will only answer the purpose in warm weather; and in the course of the War, many advantages have been lost, merely for want of this Article. I would therefore wish that the Contractors might be obligated to keep a Magazine of at least 200 Barrels of Salt Meat in the Vicinity of the moving Army—as much more as they please.

Hard Bread is another Article often wanted for the purposes before enumerated. An agreement for a certain quantity of that would be found advantageous. As the Contractors will have Ovens in the Vicinity of the Army, The necessary[4] Quantity might from time to time be demanded by the Commander in Chief or Commanding Genl. not more at a time than 150 or 200 Barrels.

Were we always certain of having Men of honor and of liberal principles in the Contracts there would not be so much need[5] of the foregoing and many other guards. But we have experienced so many inconveniencies from a Man of contrary conduct that too much care cannot be taken in future. I have the honor to be &c

P.S. In ascertaining the prices of the component parts of a Ration care should be taken that a less value is not put upon the smaller species than they can be really purchased for, otherwise the Contractor will find it his interest to give the troops due Bills for these Articles—instead of the Articles themselves—which would be a greivance—and a heavy one. I wish a particular attention might be paid to the Article of Vinegar.

Honble. Robt: Morris Esqr.

ENDORSED: 31st: October 1782/to/Honble. Mr. Morris/subject of new Contracts.
MSS: Dft in the writing of Tench Tilghman, Washington Papers, DLC; Varick transcript, Washington Papers, DLC.
    1. See RM's Advertisement for Contracts for 1783, October 10.
    2. The reference is to Comfort Sands.
    3. Tilghman interlined the remaining words in this sentence.
    4. Tilghman interlined this word.
    5. Tilghman had initially written "there would be no need," then revised the phrase.

APPENDICES
INDEX

APPENDIX I

Draft Ordinance for the Impost of 1781

The draft ordinance printed here almost certainly was the one which Thomas McKean, a Delaware delegate to Congress and chief justice of Pennsylvania, left with the Financier on July 25.[1] Congress on February 3, 1781, had requested the states to vest it with the power to levy a 5 percent duty on imports and prizes and prize goods to be applied to the discharge of the principal and interest of Continental debts incurred during the war. Four days later, taking military operations in the southern states into account, Congress voted to collect the duties "so soon as all the states, whose legislatures shall and may assemble," consented to the grant, and to carry the revenues "to the general credit of all the states" which ratified in the first legislative session held after the receipt of the February 3 act.[2]

Upon receiving notification of New Hampshire's ratification, the fourth state to comply, Congress on April 23 appointed a committee to draft an ordinance for collecting the impost "so soon as acts have been passed by the legislatures of the states" in accordance with the February 3 and 7 resolutions. The committee originally consisted of James Duane of New York, George Clymer of Pennsylvania, and Thomas Bee of South Carolina, but McKean replaced Duane on June 13, 1781. In letters of July 2 and 25, 1781, Morris urged Congress to proceed with preparation of the ordinance. Congress referred the latter letter, and added James Madison, to the committee on July 25[3] but no further committee action was recorded in the Journals for over ten months, evidently because all the states with assembled legislatures had not yet ratified.

With the arrival of Connecticut's act of ratification on June 14, 1782, however, Congress reconstituted the committee with a membership of McKean, Madison, and John Lowell of Massachusetts and directed it to confer with the Financier.[4] No record of its meeting with Morris has been found, but it can be reasonably conjectured that by July 15, when the Maryland act of ratification reached Congress, leaving the impost pending only in Rhode Island and Georgia,[5] the committee was already at work on the draft ordinance printed here. The Superintendent evidently returned the draft ordinance to the McKean committee, for it is now filed among the papers of the Continental Congress. Copies of the committee's report of the ordinance were later forwarded to Massachusetts and Rhode Island,[6] but no record of its submission to Congress is recorded in the *Journals* or other records of Congress.

The enforcement provisions of the draft ordinance vested extensive powers in Congress. Perhaps the most important was the power to appoint collectors.[7] Although Congress had eliminated from its impost resolution any formal claim to the appointment of collectors,[8] congressional appointment appears to have been already largely established in principle since nine states had vested the authority in the United States.[9] This proposal, however, had not fared well in New

England. Massachusetts had provided that "Officers for collecting the [impost] shall be chosen by the Senate and House of Representatives, in the same Manner as the Constitution directs all Civil Officers shall be chosen," but authorized the collectors to turn over the revenues to "such Person or Persons, he or they to be Inhabitants of this Common-wealth, as the United States in Congress assembled may hereafter from Time to Time appoint." The Massachusetts act did permit Congress to fill a vacancy if the state legislature failed to appoint a collector within fifteen days after it received notice of the vacancy.[10] While Connecticut had vested appointment in Congress, its ratification provided for state removal of collectors guilty of misconduct.[11] Rhode Island's insistence on state-appointed collectors was one of the reasons why it rejected the impost.[12]

Other enforcement provisions were also bound to evoke fears of centralized authority. The draft ordinance countenanced warrantless searches by collectors, qualifying their extent only by stipulating that for the search of "any mansion or dwelling house" a collector was required to obtain a warrant upon probable cause from "a Justice of the Supreme court of Judicature or of a Justice of the peace, within the State." Not only did the ordinance provide severe penalties for forcible obstruction, but it left collectors wide latitude as to the site of court prosecutions. Persons physically interfering with collectors could be fined and punished upon conviction "in any court having cogni-zance of criminal offences and in any court within the United States," and penalties could be recovered "in any court of record within any of these United States."[13] According to the historian William Gordon, a copy of the draft ordinance circulating in Boston early in 1783 "ex-cited the resentments of all who h[ad see]n it. One of the Senate, upon hearing that section wherein is the power of the collectors to break open houses, shops, etc., and the punishments to be inflicted on those who opposed them, cried out immediately *that was drawn up surely by an Englishman;* and one of the Council said *we may as well go under Great Britain again at once.* The ordinance has all the evils in it, that we have been exclaiming so bitterly against; and had it been composed by an artful enemy to the impost with a view of damning it, he could not have done it more effectually. Several of our General Court have had a sight of it, and say they now perceive the *cloven foot,* and Congress will be watched more narrowly than ever. The ordinance could not have taken place here, for the Act of this State granting the Impost, made an express exception to all regulations contrary to the consti-tution."[14] David Howell afterward reported that "The States are now generally astonished that they should ever have been led into such an error as to give Congress the vast and uncontrolable powers contained in this ordinance."[15]

Failing to secure ratification of the impost of 1781, Congress in-cluded a new impost proposal in the funding plan it adopted on April 18, 1783. In concession to objections previously raised in the states, Congress restricted the grant to 25 years, confined it to the discharge of the principal and interest of debts contracted by the Confederation during the war, and lodged the appointment of collectors in the states.[16] This impost, like the earlier one, failed to secure unanimous ratification by the states, and no enforcement bill was either reported or passed by the Confederation Congress.[17]

[Philadelphia, July 1782?][18]
In the seventh year of Independence Annoque Domini 1782.

An Ordinance for raising a revenue for the use of the United States of America, on goods, wares and merchandize, of foreign growth and manufacture, imported from foreign parts.

Whereas in pursuance of a recommendatory Resolve of Congress, bearing date the third day of February in the year of our Lord one thousand seven hundred eighty and one, the confederate States of New-Hampshire, Massachusetts, Rhode-Island and Providence Plantations, Connecticut, New-York, New-Jersey, Pennsylvania, Delaware, Maryland, Virginia, North-Carolina, South-Carolina and Georgia, have severally granted to the United States of America in Congress assembled a duty or impost ⟨of⟩ not exceeding five per centum ad valorem, at the time and place of importation, upon all goods, wares and merchandize of foreign growth and manufacture, which may be imported into any of the said States from any foreign port, island or plantation, except arms, ammunition, cloathing and other articles imported on account of the United States, or any of them; and except wool-cards and cotton-cards, and wire for making them, and also except salt during the war: And also a like duty of five per centum on all prizes and prize-goods condemned in any court of Admiralty within the same.

And Whereas ⟨the several states aforesaid have enacted, that the said duty or impost shall be laid and collected in such manner and form; and under such pains, penalties and regulations; and by such officers as Congress shall from time to time make, order, direct and appoint, subject to certain limitations, promises and restrictions in the Acts of the several legislatures of the said States respecting the same contained.⟩ it is necessary that regulations should be made for the effectual levying and collecting the said duties.

⟨And Whereas it is indispensibly necessary, that Congress should have a permanent fund for discharging the debts, which have been or may be contracted, on the faith of the United States, for supporting the present just and necessary war; and it will conduce to the general interest, that the commercial regulations throughout these confederated States be uniform and consistent.⟩

Sec. 1.   Be It Therefore Ordained, and it is hereby ordained by the United States of America in Congress assembled, as by the authority of the same, that there shall be levied, collected and paid for the use of these United States, a duty or impost of five per Centum ad valorem at the time and place of importation, upon all goods, wares and merchandize of foreign growth and manufacture, which may be imported into any of these States from any port, island or plantation not within the said United States,[19] from and after the   day of   [20] next; except arms, ammunition, clothing and other articles imported on account of the United States, or any of them; and except wool-cards and cotton-cards, and wire for making them; and also except common[21] salt during the present war: and also a like duty of five per centum on all prizes and prize-goods condemned in the court of Admiralty of any of these States as lawful prize.

2.   And Be it further Ordained that the said duties shall be payable in gold
Quere.   or silver, and that a gold half Johannes of Portugal[22] weighing nine penny weight, and a spanish milled silver dollar, weighing seventeen penny weight and six grains, may and shall be received by the Officers appointed to collect the said duties, the former at the rate of   and the latter at the rate of   [23] and all other gold and silver coin at the like rates and proportions.

3.   And Be It Further Ordained that all ships or vessels arriving from parts beyond the seas except ships or vessels of war or privateers[24] into any port or place where goods are usually unloaded in any of the said States,[25] shall come directly into the same (unless apparently hindered by contrary winds, draught of water, or other just cause of impediment, to be allowed by the Collector of the duties, or one of his deputies for such port;)[26] and the Master or principal navigator ⟨thereof⟩ (for that voyage) of such ship or vessel shall, within three days after such arrival repair to the office of the said Collector, and then and there make a just and true entry upon oath, or ⟨affirmation⟩ (if conscientiously scrupulous of taking an oath) upon affirmation, of the burthen, contents and lading of such ship or vessel, with the particular marks, numbers, qualities and contents of every parcel of goods, wares and merchandize therein laden, to the best of his knowledge; also where and in what port she took in her lading, of what country built, how manned, who was master during the voyage, the na[mes] and abodes of the owners thereof; and shall also produce such documents as are usually furnished in such place of lading, to masters of vessels sailing from thence with goods, wares and merchandize; under the penalty of ⟨five hundred pounds⟩ Fifteen hundred dollars.

4.   And Be It Further Ordained, that no Captain, Master, Purser nor any other person or persons taking charge of any ship or vessel of war or privateer, (whether the same ship or vessel shall have commission from, or belong to the United States or any of them or shall belong to or have commission from any foreign Prince or State) wherein any goods, wares or merchandize shall have been laden, or brought from Ports beyond the seas, shall unload or put on board any lighter, boat or bottom, or lay on land, or suffer to be discharged or put into any lighter, boat or bottom, or to be laid on land out of any ship or vessel as aforesaid, any goods, wares, or merchandize whatsoever, before such Captain, Master, Purser or other person taking charge of the ship or merchants goods for that voyage; ⟨shall have exhibited a true Manifest in writing?⟩ shall have signified and declared in writing, under his or their hands, to the Collector of the port where he arriveth, the name of every merchant or lader of any goods or merchandize on board the said ship or vessel, together with the number and marks, and the quantity and quality of every parcel of goods and merchandize, to the best of his knowledge; and shall have answered upon his oath or affirmation to such questions touching such goods and merchandize as shall be publicly administered to him by the said Collector or his Deputy; and[27] the said ships or vessels shall be liable to all rules and searches which merchant ships are subject unto (victualling bills and entering excepted) upon pain to forfeit ⟨five⟩ fifteen hundred ⟨pounds⟩ dollars; and upon refusal or neglect to make such entry within three days after arrival as aforesaid, the said Collector, or any of his Deputies, shall and may freely enter and go on board ⟨such⟩ all and every such ship or vessel of war or privateer, and bring from thence on shore into the Custom-House belonging to the port where such ship shall be, all goods, wares and merchandize liable to the duties imposed by this Ordinance which shall be found on board any such ship or vessel as aforesaid.

5.   And Be It Further Ordained, that the value and price of all goods, wares and merchandize liable to the duty hereby imposed (except prizes and prize-goods)[28] shall be ascertained, either by the original invoices thereof, a sale at public auction by inch of candle,[29] or by oath or affirmation of the merchant or owner, or his, her or their factor, consignee or agent, in case of

the merchants or owners absence, to be administered by the Collector or his deputy, or in his presence; or by all or any of the said ways,[30] as to the said officer shall seem best. And the better to prevent frauds, and that all persons may be on an equal foot in trade, the said Collector or any of his deputies may open, view and examine such goods and merchandize, paying duty ad valorem, and compare the same with the value and price thereof so sworn to or affirmed; and if upon such view and examination, it shall appear, that such goods or merchandize are not valued by such oath or affirmation, according to the true value and price thereof, agreeable to the true intent and meaning here shall then and in such case, the importer and proprieter shall, on demand made in writing, by the Collector, or his deputy, of the port where such goods or merchandize are entered, deliver, or cause to be delivered, all such goods or merchandize into the public ware-house at the port of importation, for the use and benefit of the United States; and upon such delivery, the Collector of such port or his deputy shall, out of any public[31] money in his hands, pay to such importer or proprietor the value of such goods and merchandize so sworn to or affirmed as aforesaid, together with an addition of ten pounds per centum to such value, taking a receipt for the same from such importer or proprietor, in full satisfaction for the said goods, as if they had been regularly sold: and the said Collector or his deputy shall cause the said goods, wares or merchandize to be fairly and publicly sold for the best advantage, and out of the produce thereof, the money so paid, or advanced as aforesaid, shall be repaid to such Collector or his deputy, and replaced to the public money in his hands; and the nett produce or overplus (if any) after deducting the charges of warehousing, sale &c. is to be accounted for by the said Collector to the United States by the title of "goods ⟨under⟩ imported, under-valued." And in case any such importer or proprietor shall refuse or neglect to deliver the goods or merchandize so sworn to or affirmed, after demand made and offer of the value or price[32] as aforesaid, to the Collector or his deputy, then and in such case the said Collector may seize the same, or sue for and recover the possession thereof, either in his own name, or the name of "The United States of America," by action of replevin or otherwise, together with double costs.

6) And Be It Further Ordained,[33] that the value and price of all prizes and prize-goods shall be ascertained by the ⟨account and⟩ oath of the Marshal of the Admiralty of the nett amount of the same at public auction, exclusive of all costs and charges; and that the Marshals of the Admiralty courts in these States respectively shall exhibit the accounts of sales[34] and ⟨shall⟩ pay the ⟨said⟩ duty on ⟨said sums⟩ said nett amount to the Collector of the State in which the prize or prize-goods were condemned, within one month after sale thereof; and that the Bonds or Recognizances by them given for the faithful discharge of their said office shall be a security for their compliance with the directions of this Ordinance.

6. 7).[35] And Be It Further Ordained, that the said Collector or his deputy shall, upon due entry of any goods, wares and merchandize imported as aforesaid, and upon payment of ⟨or securing⟩ the duties thereon, or securing the same[36] by a sufficient[37] bond or obligation, payable within thirty days after the date thereof, to the said United States, and not otherwise, grant a permit for the landing thereof. And if the captain, master or purser of any ship or other vessel, importing goods as aforesaid, shall not, upon making the entry or delivering the manifest of his cargo to the Collector or his deputy as aforesaid, pay, or secure in manner herein before directed, the duties pay-

able thereon, then every particular importer, his factor or agent, may pay or secure in manner aforesaid the duties on his own property, and shall be thereupon intitled to a permit for the landing of the same.

8.   And Be It Further Ordained, that if any goods, wares or merchandize, ⟨imported into⟩ liable to the aforesaid duty shall remain in any ship or vessel after ten days, to be reckoned from the day of the arrival of such ship or vessel into port, without the said duty being paid or secured to be paid as aforesaid, it shall and may be lawful for the Captain, Master or Purser of the same, and he is hereby required under the penalty of three[38] hundred ⟨pounds⟩ dollars to deliver such goods or merchandize ⟨for which the said⟩ to the Collector or his deputy to be warehoused or otherwise secured and kept at the charge and risque of the owner thereof; and such delivery shall exonerate the said Captain, Master or Purser[39] from any action or demand for the same: And the said Collector shall keep all goods, wares and merchandize so delivered to him, other than perishable goods, for and during the term of three months; after which, being first appraised, they may be sold at public auction, by the said Collector, and the money thence arising after the said duty and all charges shall be deducted, shall be safely kept by him for the use of the owner.

9.   And Be It Further Ordained, that if ⟨any⟩ the captain, master or purser of any ship or vessel, or any other person or persons, shall unload or discharge from or[40] out of ⟨any such ship⟩ the same, coming in and arriving from foreign parts, any goods, wares or merchandize (except the wearing apparel, and beds, with the furnature thereof, belonging to him, or to passengers or mariners on board, and not for sale ⟨only excepted⟩ with an intent to land the same, before entry and without having obtained a warrant or permit for so doing; or if any person or persons whatsoever shall be aiding and assisting in unshipping,[41] landing, or in conveying on shore or housing any goods, wares or merchandize, ⟨liable to⟩ whereof the said duty is unpaid or not secured to be paid as aforesaid, and without such warrants or permit, every such person so offending shall forfeit and pay the sum of three hundred ⟨pounds⟩ dollars; and the goods, wares and merchandize so landed or unshipped, and likewise the boats, hoys, vessels, horses and carriages employed in removing them, shall be forfeited.

10.   And Be It Further Ordained that all goods, wares and merchandize liable to the said duty, found concealed on board[42] any ship or vessel, after the captain, master or purser has made his report at the Custom-house, and not mentioned in such report, shall be forfeited; and the said captain, master, purser, or person having charge of the vessel, if any ways, consenting or privy to the concealment, shall likewise[43] forfeit the value of the ⟨goods⟩ same.

[11][44]   And Be It Further Ordained, that the ⟨person or persons who shall be appointed for managing the customs of these United States, and the Collectors and⟩ Collectors of the Customs, their Deputies and Assistants, shall have full power and authority by virtue of this Ordinance to go and enter on board any ship or vessel, as well ships of war as merchant ships, and from thence to bring on shore all goods, wares and merchandize whatsoever, for which the said duty was not paid or secured in manner aforesaid, within ten days after the first entry of the ship, to be put and remain in a public warehouse, until duty thereupon be fully satisfied, unless the said officers shall see just cause to allow a longer time; and the said Officers and their deputies may freely stay and remain on board until all the goods are delivered and discharged out of the ⟨said⟩ ships or vessels: And if any master,

purser, or other person taking in any ship or vessel, or other person whatsoever, shall suffer any bale, truss, pack, cask, trunk or other package to be opened on board the ⟨said⟩ ship or vessel, and the goods therein to be imbezzled, carried away, or put into any other form or package, after the ship comes into the port of her discharge in such case the said master, purser or other person, shall forfeit the sum of three hundred[45] ⟨pounds⟩ dollars. And the said ⟨person or persons, who shall be appointed for managing the customs, and the⟩ Collectors, their Deputies and Assistants are hereby authorized and enabled, in the day time, to enter into any house, shop, cellar, warehouse or other place whatsoever, not only within their own particular port, but within any other port or place within these United States, where they shall suspect any dutiable goods to be concealed and[46] there to make diligent search, and in case of resistance to break open any door, trunk, chest, case, pack, truss, or any other package or parcel whatsoever, for any goods, wares or merchandize whereof the said duty has not been duly paid; and the same to seize to the use of the United States and to put and secure in a warehouse in the port next to the place of seizure and generally to do all other acts and things necessary for the effectual securing the said duties, and the goods, wares and merchandizes forfeited for non-payment thereof, or otherwise. Provided always, that no search of any mansion or dwelling house shall be made in manner aforesaid, untill due cause of suspicion has been shown to the satisfaction of a Justice of the Supreme court of Judicature or of a Justice of the peace, ⟨of⟩ within the State, where such search is desired, and ⟨a⟩ his Warrant obtained for that purpose.

1[2].   *And Be It Further Ordained,* that if any Officer of the Customs appointed in pursuance of this Ordinance, ⟨being⟩ shall be forcibly hindered, ⟨affronted, abused,⟩ wounded, beaten or abused, either on board any ship or vessel, or upon the land or water in the due execution of his office, by any person or persons whatsoever, every such offender and all others who shall act in their assistance, shall upon conviction in any court ⟨of⟩ having cognizance of criminal offences and ⟨with⟩ in any court within the United States,[47] be fined at the discretion of the said court, and be sent on board some vessel of war, there to ⟨do duty without⟩ remain for any term not exceeding seven years; and if they shall desert the service before the expiration of the term they shall be ⟨confined in close prison and liable to⟩ punished for desertion according to the constitution and laws of the Navy.

1[3].   *And be it further ordained,* that the several fines, penalties and forfeitures, which shall or may be incurred for any offence against this Ordinance, not otherwise hereby disposed of,[48] may be sued for and recovered in any court of record within any of these United States, by action of debt, indictment, information, bill or plaint, wherein no essoin,[49] protection or wager of law, or more than one imparlance[50] shall be allowed; and shall be divided the one third part thereof to ⟨the use of⟩ the United States ⟨of America⟩, another third part thereof to ⟨the use of?⟩ the President or Governor of the State, for the time being, where the recovery or conviction, shall be had and the remaining third part to ⟨the use⟩ him, her or them, who shall prosecute or[51] sue for the same. And ⟨if⟩ upon every[52] suit or information to be brought as aforesaid for goods ⟨seized⟩ as forfeited, ⟨if the property thereof be claimed⟩ the ⟨proof of entry and payment of the duty⟩ onus probandi[53] shall be upon the owner or claimer thereof; and no claim for the same shall be received or admitted before security be given for the costs of suit.

1[4]   *And be it further ordained,* that all officers belonging to the Admiralty, captains and commanders of ships of war, and privateers, and also all other officers, ministers and citizens whatsoever, whom it may concern, shall be aiding and assisting to all and every the officers of the customs and their respective deputies, in the due execution of all and every act, and acts, thing and things in and by this present ordinance required and enjoined; and all such, who shall be aiding and assisting unto them in the due execution thereof, or in bringing offenders against the same to justice, shall be defended and saved harmless by virtue hereof, and be ranked among the friends of their country.

1[5]   And be it further ordained, that there shall be an officer appointed and commissioned by the United States of America in Congress assembled, ⟨who⟩ for each of the confederate States, who shall be called the Collector of the customs, and shall be an Inhabitant and Citizen of the State for which he shall be appointed, and whose duty shall be to carry this Ordinance into execution, and to appoint a sufficient number of deputies ⟨within the State for which he shall be appointed⟩ for whom he shall be responsible. Which said Collectors, their deputies, clerks and servants, who shall have any office or place ⟨or office⟩ in or about the customs, shall before they enter upon the execution of their said Office or Place severally[54] take the *oaths directed to be taken by the civil officers of Congress, by an Act passed the third day of February in the year one thousand seven hundred seventy and eight.* And the said Collector shall also enter into duplicate[55] obligations to the United States of America, in such a penalty as the President or Governor of the State for which he shall be appointed shall think proper, with two sufficient sureties at the least[56] to be approved of by such President or Governor; conditioned for the true and faithful execution and discharge of the said trust and employment: one of which obligations shall be filed in the office of the Secretary of Congress, and the other with the Secretary of the said State.

1[6]   *And be it further ordained*, that the said Collectors shall severally keep fair, distinct and true accounts of all monies by them received by virtue of this Ordinance, and of all their proceedings in the premises, in Books to be by them provided for that purpose, and shall once in every three months render their said Accounts to the Treasurer of the United States, on their corporal oaths to be before the Chief Magistrate or one of the Judges of the Supreme or superior court of Judicature of the State for which they are severally appointed; and also pay the monies by them then respectively received to the said Treasurer, or on the Warrants of the President of Congress or the Superintendent of Finance for the time being. And the said Collectors shall, at all times when required, submit their Books and Papers to the inspection of the Supreme Executive Power of the said States respectively, and of every Delegate in Congress. And the said Collectors for their reward in carrying this Ordinance into execution shall have and receive as follows, to wit, the Collectors of Massachusetts, Rhode-Island, New-York, Pennsylvania, South-Carolina at the rate of,   per centum, and the Collectors of the other States respectively at the rate of   [57] per centum on the amount of the whole of the monies by them severally received and paid, and two shillings and six pence from the party executing any bond, for every such bond; and no other allowance or ⟨perquisites⟩ recompence whatsoever.

1[7].   *And be it further ordained*, that if any of the said Collectors shall ⟨neglect⟩ refuse or neglect to pay the several sums of money by them received by virtue of this Ordinance into the Treasury of the United States by quarterly payments, upon the days to be appointed by the Treasurer for the payment thereof, or within forty days after; or to discharge any Warrant signed by the President of Congress of the Superintendent of Finance within three days after the same shall be presented, if he had received money sufficient for the purpose at the time (over and above[58] the aforesaid allowance to him for collecting the same ⟨is deducted⟩ then such Collector shall for every such offence of himself or his deputies forfeit the sum of four hundred ⟨pounds⟩ dollars to him or them that shall sue for the same,[59] in any court of record, by action of debt, bill, plaint or information, wherein no Essoin, Protection or Wager of law, nor more than one imparlance is to be allowed. And if any such Collector shall knowingly or wilfully, through favor or malice, under-rate or over-rate, the value or price of any goods, wares or merchandize liable to the duty imposed by this Ordinance, or omit to charge any person or persons liable to the same, or shall be guilty of any corrupt or illegal practices in the execution of his office, he shall for every such offence as aforesaid forfeit the sum of ⟨one⟩ hundred ⟨pounds⟩ dollars to him or them that shall sue for the same in manner aforesaid, and be dismissed from said employment.

1[8].   *And be it further ordained,* that upon any actions, suits or informations, that shall be commenced or brought concerning the duty aforesaid or any forfeiture incurred by virtue of this ordinance, there shall not be any party Jury, but such only as are lawful citizens of the State where the trial shall be had.

1[9].   *And be it further ordained,*[60] that no Collector of the customs, deputy Collector, nor any of their Clerks or Servants, having any office or place in or about the customs, shall either in his own name, or in the name or names of any other person or persons whatsoever, nor in partnership with any other, trade as a merchant for himself, nor as a factor or agent, in any goods, wares or merchandize, nor keep a victualling house, or house of public entertainment, during ⟨their⟩ his continuance in the said trust or employment under the penalty of ⟨five hundred pounds⟩ one thousand dollars, to him, her, or them, that shall sue for the same in any court of record, by action of debt, bill, plaint or information wherein no essoin, protection or wager of law, nor any more than one imparlance shall be allowed.

2[0].   *And be it further ordained,* that the net sum of money raised and received by virtue of this Ordinance shall be applied, in the first place, to pay and discharge the interest due and to become due on Loan-Office and other Certificates given for monies lent to or due from the United States of America; and in case the same shall be more than sufficient to answer and pay the said Interest, then the said surplus shall be issued and paid for discharging the principal sums so loaned or due[61] as far as the same shall annually extend; and be applied to no other use or purpose whatsoever.

2[1].   *And it is hereby further ordained,* that if any action or suit shall be commenced against the said Collectors, or any of them, or against any other person or persons for any thing done in pursuance of this ordinance, or by virtue of their office, in every such case, the action or suit shall be brought within six months next after the fact committed, and not afterwards; and shall be laid and brought in the county wherein the cause of action shall arise, and not elsewhere: And the defendant or defendants in such action or suits may plead the general issue and give this ⟨Act⟩ Ordinance and the special matter in evidence at any trial to be had thereupon; and that the same was done in pursuance of and by ⟨virtue of⟩ the authority of this Ordinance; and if the same shall appear to have been so done, or if any such action or suit shall be brought after the time before limited for bringing the same, or shall be brought in any other county or place, then the jury shall find for the defendant or defendants; or if the Plaintiff or Plaintiffs shall become nonsuited, or suffer a discontinuance of his, her or their action or

actions, or if a verdict shall pass against the Plaintiff or Plaintiffs, or judgment shall be given against him, her or them on demurrer, or otherwise,
then such defendant or defendants shall have treble costs to him or them
awarded against such Plaintiff or Plaintiffs.

2[2].   Provided Always, *and be it further ordained,* that this Ordinance and every
clause, matter and thing therein contained, shall ⟨continue⟩ commence and
be in force from and after the   day of   [62] next; and shall so continue
until the whole of the principal and interest of the debts already contracted,
or which may be contracted on the faith of the United States for ⟨the⟩
supporting the present war shall be fully and finally discharged, and no
longer.

ENDORSED: Draft of an Ordinance/for raising a revenue for/the use of the United
States/On all goods, wares and merchan/dize of foreign growth and/manufacture
imported/from foreign parts./1782.
MSS: Dft in the writing of Thomas McKean, PCC, no. 59, III, 317–330, DNA; copy,
PCC, no. 49, pp. 581–592, DNA; transcript, Charles Thomson Papers, DLC.
    1. See Diary of that date. In volume I, 401n., the editors mistakenly conjectured
the ordinance to have been composed in December 1782.
    2. See the headnote to RM's Circular to the Governors of Massachusetts, Rhode
Island, New York, Delaware, Maryland, and North Carolina, July 27, 1781, and notes.
    3. By this date seven states had ratified the impost.
    4. See PCC, no. 186, p. 35; and the Connecticut Delegates to Governor Jonathan
Trumbull, June 17, 1782, Burnett, ed., *Letters,* VI, 372 and n.
    5. See notes to RM's Circular to the Governors of Massachusetts, Rhode Island,
and Maryland, January 3, 1782. It should be noted that Virginia had suspended its
ratification; see notes to RM to the President of Congress, February 11, 1782.
    6. See below at notes 14–15.
    7. See section 15 below.
    8. See *JCC,* XIX, 112. McKean, however, reported on the day of passage that
Congress "are to levy and collect [the duty] in such manner as by experience from
time to time shall be found most beneficial, or tend least to the discouragement of
trade." He also noted that Congress had "the exclusive collection and appropriation
of it." McKean to Thomas Collins, speaker of the Delaware Council, February 3,
1781, Burnett, ed., *Letters,* V, 557.
    9. For citations to the state acts of ratification, see the documents cited in notes 2
and 5 above; and notes to RM to Benjamin Franklin, November 27, 1781 (first letter).
RM presumed the right of appointment to be in Congress (see his letters to Nathaniel
Appleton, May 28, and Samuel Holden Parsons, June 5, and Diary, August 13, 1782).
After learning that the impost proposed in 1783 vested the appointment of collectors
in the states, he presented arguments in support of congressional appointment in a
letter to the president of Congress of March 8, 1783.
    10. *Acts and Laws of Massachusetts,* 1780–1781, pp. 591, 590.
    11. Hoadly and Labaree, eds., *Public Records of Connecticut,* III, 314–316.
    12. See Objections to the Impost in Rhode Island from David Howell, printed
under July 31. New Hampshire's act of ratification did not address the question of
collection.
    13. See sections 11–14 below. The quotations that follow are from sections 12–13.
The question of the site of prosecutions was raised by David Howell even before he
had seen the draft ordinance. See the document cited in the preceding note.
    14. Gordon to Horatio Gates, February 26, 1783, "Letters of the Reverend William
Gordon, Historian of the American Revolution, 1770–1799," Massachusetts Historical
Society, *Proceedings,* LXIII (1930), 487.
    15. Howell to Jabez Bowen, deputy governor of Rhode Island, April 12, 1784,
Burnett, ed., *Letters,* VII, 492.
    16. See Ferguson, *Power of the Purse,* 166; and Joseph L. Davis, *Sectionalism in
American Politics, 1774–1787* (Madison, Wis., 1977), 48. For RM's opposition to the

terms of the impost of 1783 and the funding requisition of which it was a part, see his letters to the president of Congress of March 8 and May 1 and 3, 1783.

17. The first Federal tax on imports was enacted under the United States Constitution on July 4, 1789; the enforcement act was passed on July 31, 1789. See *The Public Statutes at Large of the United States of America . . .*, 2d ed. (Boston, 1848), I, 24–27, 29–49.

18. The editors have noted many of the interlineations and restored the most significant legible excisions of the McKean Dft printed here. They have also renumbered the sections beginning with number 11. See note 44 below.

19. McKean interlined the preceding 12 words.

20. Spaces left blank in manuscript.

21. McKean interlined this word.

22. McKean interlined the preceding two words.

23. Spaces left blank in manuscript. Although Congress on January 7, 1782, had directed the Superintendent to prepare a table of rates at which foreign coins would be received by the United States Treasury, RM did not submit his report until December 12, 1782. See the headnote to RM to the President of Congress, January 15, 1782 (first letter).

24. McKean substituted the preceding eight words for a passage which he lined through heavily and which is now illegible.

25. McKean interlined the preceding six words.

26. McKean interlined the preceding three words.

27. McKean interlined the next five words.

28. McKean interlined the words in parentheses.

29. An auctioneering procedure whereby a pin was placed in a burning candle an inch from the top, with bidding permitted until the pin fell out. See Ralph Cassady, Jr., *Auctions and Auctioneering* (Berkeley, Calif., 1967), 31–32, 75.

30. McKean interlined the remainder of the sentence.

31. McKean interlined this word.

32. McKean interlined the preceding seven words.

33. McKean drafted this section on a separate sheet of paper and inserted it at the end of section 5. He renumbered the next section without cancelling the original enumeration. See note 35.

34. McKean interlined the preceding six words.

35. Thus in manuscript. See notes 33 above and 44 below.

36. McKean interlined the preceding four words.

37. McKean interlined this word.

38. McKean appears to have originally written "one" before reworking it into "three."

39. McKean interlined the preceding five words.

40. McKean interlined the preceding two words.

41. McKean interlined this word.

42. McKean interlined this word.

43. McKean interlined this word.

44. McKean inadvertently left this section unnumbered in manuscript, assigned number 11 to the next section, and continued consecutively to number 21. The editors have renumbered those sections to conform to the clean copy in PCC, no. 49.

45. McKean appears to have originally written "one" before reworking it into "three."

46. McKean interlined the preceding 11 words.

47. McKean interlined the preceding eight words.

48. McKean interlined the preceding five words.

49. Excuse, exemption, or delay; specifically, the "allegation of an excuse for non-appearance in court at the appointed time." *OED.*

50. "An extension of time to put in a response in pleading a case, on the (real or fictitious) ground of a desire to negotiate for an amicable settlement; a continuance of the case to another day; a petition for, or leave granted for, such delay." *OED.*

51. McKean interlined the words "recovery or" and "prosecute or."

52. McKean interlined this word.

53. The burden of proof. *OED*.

54. McKean interlined this word.

55. McKean interlined this word. He had originally written "an obligation" before reworking the phrase.

56. McKean interlined the preceding two words.

57. Spaces left blank in manuscript.

58. McKean interlined the preceding three words.

59. In the DNA copy "in the manner aforesaid" is written here.

60. McKean wrote this section after section 20 and keyed it for insertion here.

61. McKean interlined these two words.

62. Spaces left blank in manuscript.

APPENDIX II

Remonstrance and Petition to Congress from Blair McClenachan, Charles Pettit, John Ewing, and Benjamin Rush

[Philadelphia, July 8, 1782][1]

To the honorable The Delegates of the United States of North America, in Congress assembled,

The Remonstrance and Petition of the Proprietors of Loan Office Certificates in the City and Neighbourhood of Philadelphia, by their Committee, chosen and instructed for that Purpose at a general Meeting of the said Proprietors,

Humbly Shew,

That your Petitioners; who claim the Merit of being among the earliest Promoters of the glorious Revolution in America, were also among the foremost to testify their Zeal in supporting the Measures of Congress, as well by contributing their Substance, as by yielding their personal Services.

When our Independency was so recently declared as that it was yet unacknowledged, and in a great measure unpatronized by any other Nation; When the military Power of the Enemy was in its greatest Vigor, and they were able to carry it, almost without control, to whatever Point it was directed, and our Governments, yet newly formed, had scarcely become sufficiently organized for Legislation; When many, who are now coming forward to enjoy the Benefits and share in the Honors of the Revolution, were either opposed to the glorious Undertaking, or shrinking from the Toils and Dangers of the Conflict; At such a Time, and under such Circumstances did your Petitioners, confiding in the plighted Faith and Solemn Assurances of Congress, cheerfully contribute their Property in Loans to the United States; and so great was the Ardor to comply with the Requisitions of Congress that many have committed the whole of their Substance into their Hands: Among these are to be found The Widow, the Orphan, the Aged, and the Infirm, whose only Hope to Screen them from the most wretched Poverty, depends on the Payment of the stipulated Interest. How great and how affecting must be their Distress on being informed that the Payment of that Interest in the Mode hitherto practised is suddenly to cease, and that no Fund is yet appropriated to supply its Place.[2]

On the gradual Diminution of an Income, the Prudent may find some Mitigation of the Misfortune in the gradual accomodation of Circumstances to the change; but to fall suddenly from a situation of Ease and Comfort to the Depths of extreme Poverty, must give a Poignancy to Distress, which can only be heightened by the mortifying Reflection that they have been deluded by a mistaken Confidence, and that the Evil arises from an undue Proportion of the Public Burden unjustly heaped upon them.

These Observations are more peculiarly applicable to the early Loans, the Interest of which has heretofore been paid in Bills of Exchange. But Your Petitioners are no less concerned respecting the Loans of a later Date, on which but little Interest has been paid for two years past, and for the last year none at all. And though it may be supposed that the Feelings of Humanity may be less affected by the Delay of the Interest on these, than of that on the others, the calls of Justice are nevertheless equally clear and strong in their favor.

Your Petitioners apprehend it cannot be necessary to offer Proofs that the Lenders of Money to the Public are generally, if not altogether, among the most decided friends and the warmest Supporters of the Revolution. When Supplies have been wanted and the public Agents had not Money to purchase them, they have been the People who chiefly furnished them: When Loans of Money have been demanded *They only* have contributed to relieve the Public Wants. Many of them have so much of their Capital in the Hands of the Public that their remaining Stock is too small to admit of their carrying on Business on an equal Footing with their Neighbours; and they have the Mortification to find that while others, enjoying the full Benefit of their Property, can easily pay the Taxes assessed on them out of Part of their Profits, the holders of Loan Certificates are deprived of even common Interest for their Money, and obliged to pay at least equal Taxes besides, by which their Contributions to the Public Service are most unequally and in many Instances oppressively accumulated. The Partiality in these Cases is so flagrantly unjust that Your Petitioners cannot but hope it will meet with due Attention and speedy Redress.

But besides these Evils, so great in themselves, Your Petitioners conceive it necessary to urge the Apprehension of another still greater. The mere Suspension of the Payment of Interest for a year or two, though it would be injurious to all and distressing to many, would not, provided there was a certainty of punctuality afterwards, occasion so great an Injury as is now apprehended. But from the Delay of the Interest on some, the threatened Suspension of that on the others, and the want of established Funds appropriated to these Payments, the Capital Sum is already depreciated; and unless some speedy and effectual Measures are taken to revive that Confidence in the Justice and Integrity of the Public, on which alone any Degree of Public Credit can be founded, a much greater Degree of Depreciation will take Place, and the honest Lenders of the Money, who have risked their *all* on the Public Faith will become a Prey to Speculators. Necessity will oblige them to sell at whatever Price they can get, however small, those Certificates which are at once the Vouchers of their Attachment to a cause which has purchased Freedom and Opulence for others, and the sad Remembrancers of the Property they once had, and which the calls of Nature or of Decency compel them to part with for a Trifle.

These are Considerations which respect the Interests of Individuals. But the Number of these Individuals is too great, and their Merit as Patriots too conspicuous to be undeserving of Attention. Were it possible that the Feelings of Humanity and the Calls of Justice could cease to operate in their Favor, the Dictates of Policy alone would be sufficient to induce Attention to their Claims and the most strenuous Exertions to redress their Grievances.

The Experience of other Nations ought to have warned us of the Danger of abandoning the strong Hold of Public Credit, and relying on concurrent Taxes alone for carrying on an extensive War. The utmost Stretch of Taxation on such Occasions can never keep Pace with the Demands, especially in the peculiar Circumstances of a young and growing Country whose strength is yet so far short of Maturity. The Necessity of anticipating, by public Loans, such Revenues as the Country can afford, is therefore the more conspicuous. But it is not to be expected that such Loans can be obtained either from our own Citizens or from Foreigners, without the Establishment of solid and permanent Funds for the regular Payment of the Interest, and for the Repayment of the Interest [i.e., principal] at a future Time. If the[3]

Resources of the United States were duly arranged, Your Petitioners feel a confidence that a Part of them, turned to these Purposes, would be abundantly sufficient to afford a Foundation on which the Public Credit might be revived and the Means obtained of supporting the Army and defraying all the other necessary Expences of the War, as well as of relieving the Public Creditors, and rendering that Burden light and easy, by a more equal Distribution, which, resting chiefly on a Part of the Community only, is found to be oppressive.

Your Petitioners feel a conscious Pride in having been thus far Instrumental in contending for the Freedom of America and the Rights of Mankind; and, whatever may be the Will of Providence as to their tasteing the Fruits of it in Peace, they are desirous that succeeding Generations should enjoy the Benefit. Their Ardor is not abated, and they are willing to contribute their Proportion, in common with their Fellow Citizens, even to the last Shilling if it should be necessary, to secure Peace, Liberty, and Independence to the United States. A fair and equal Distribution of the Public Burden is all they ask, and the Justice of their Claim is so evident, that they hope they shall not be disappointed. They confide in the strong Assurances of Congress, and the Faith of the United States solemnly and repeatedly pledged in their several Resolutions on the Subject of the Public Loans, that the Interest will be punctually paid.

Your Petitioners hope to be excused in adopting the Language of Congress in the Close of their Circular Letter of the 13th. of September 1779,[3] on an Occasion to which it is so peculiarly applicable. "Humanity as well as Justice makes this Demand upon you, the Complaints of ruined Widows, and the Cries of Fatherless Children, whose whole support has been placed in your Hands and melted away, have doubtless reached you. Take Care that they ascend no higher." "Let it never be said that America had no sooner become Independant than She became Insolvent, or that her infant Glories and growing Fame were obscured and tarnished by broken Contracts and violated Faith, in the very Hour when all the Nations of the Earth were admiring and almost adoring the Splendor of her Rising."

Your Petitioners therefore earnestly pray that Congress will be pleased to direct the Payment of the Interest on the Debts due from the United States, and more especially that on Loan Office Certificates; and that they will establish effectual and permanent Funds for the continuance of such Payments until the Principal shall be fairly discharged.

Philadelphia   Blair McClenachan
July 8th. 1782   Chas. Pettit
                                                     John Ewing
                                                     Benjn: Rush

ENDORSED: No. 31./Remonstrance and Petition/of Blair McClenaghan and/others in behalf of the/public creditors and parti/cularly the holders of loan Office Cer/tificates, for the payment/of Interest/July 8. 1782/Read and referred to the Superintendt. of finance/to report.
MS: DS, PCC, DNA.

1. This petition was referred to RM for report on July 8 (see Diary, July 9, 1782, and notes). For the report, and a discussion of its antecedents and consequences, see the headnote to RM to the President of Congress, July 29. The petition was printed in the postscript to the *Pennsylvania Packet* of September 5, 1782.

2. See RM's Report to Congress on the Continental Loan Offices, June 13, 1782, and notes.

3. The preceding 10 words, not including the editorial interpolation, are interlined.

4. See *JCC*, XV, 1051–1062.

INDEX

Page references to the notes identifying persons are italicized and immediately follow the names of the persons identified.

THE PAPERS OF ROBERT MORRIS
has been set by photocomposition in Baskerville, a transitional typeface
first cut in the eighteenth century and in use during Morris's lifetime.